D0203204

Crisis Intervention Strategies
Eighth Edition

Richard K. James
University of Memphis

Burl E. Gilliland
Professor Emeritus, University of Memphis

CENGAGE
Learning®

Australia • Brazil • Mexico • Singapore • United Kingdom • United States

CENGAGE Learning®

Crisis Intervention Strategies, Eighth Edition
Richard K. James, Burl E. Gilliland

Product Director: Jon David Hague

Product Manager: Julie Martinez

Content Developer: Elizabeth Momb

Product Assistant: Stephen Lagos

Marketing Manager: Margaux Cameron

Content Project Manager: Rita Jaramillo

Art Director: Vernon Boes

Manufacturing Planner: Judy Inouye

Production Service: MPS Limited, Lynn Lustberg

Text and Cover Designer: Cheryl Carrington

Cover Image: Teradat Santivivut/Getty Images

Compositor: MPS Limited

© 2017, 2013, Cengage Learning

ALL RIGHTS RESERVED. No part of this work covered by the copyright herein may be reproduced or distributed in any form or by any means, except as permitted by U.S. copyright law, without the prior written permission of the copyright owner.

For product information and technology assistance, contact us at
Cengage Learning Customer & Sales Support, 1-800-354-9706.

For permission to use material from this text or product,
submit all requests online at **www.cengage.com/permissions.**
Further permissions questions can be e-mailed to
permissionrequest@cengage.com.

Library of Congress Control Number: 2015913300

Student Edition:
ISBN: 978-1-305-27147-0

Loose-leaf Edition:
ISBN: 978-1-305-86637-9

Cengage Learning
20 Channel Center Street
Boston, MA 02210
USA

Cengage Learning is a leading provider of customized learning solutions with employees residing in nearly 40 different countries and sales in more than 125 countries around the world. Find your local representative at **www.cengage.com**.

Cengage Learning products are represented in Canada by Nelson Education, Ltd.

To learn more about Cengage Learning Solutions, visit **www.cengage.com**.

Purchase any of our products at your local college store or at our preferred online store **www.cengagebrain.com**.

Printed in the United States of America
Print Number: 01   Print Year: 2016

In the spring of 2015, I was honored by my undergraduate and master's degree alma mater, Eastern Illinois University, with a lifetime achievement award. In my acceptance speech, I spoke to the writing, research, and service paths that led to that award. But I also spoke to something much more important than those "things" I did. Indeed, it is what I believe has been my greatest achievement in 50 years of doing counseling and teaching and is best represented by two people who attended that ceremony. I would like to introduce them to you now and say why this book is dedicated to them.

First is Steve Allen, Ed.S., who was an intern of mine in 1973–74 in the Title III ESEA Intensive Care Unit innovative education program for socially and emotionally maladjusted children in Mattoon, Illinois. Of the roughly hundred interns I have supervised, Steve was the best. Steve went on to become a world class K–12 school counselor in rural east-central Newman, Illinois. He garnered enough well deserved honors and recognition over the course of his career to also be recognized by Eastern Illinois University as a lifetime achievement recipient for the work he has done in innovative teaching, counseling, and educational practices.

The second person is Kay Dorner, Ph.D., who was a junior high school student I counseled in Mattoon, Illinois, in 1968. Kay has had a distinguished career as a psychologist in private practice and as an administrator in high schools in California and Oregon. Among her noteworthy achievements has been the principalship of a Bill and Melinda Gates small school grant to establish Technology High School in Rohnert Park, California. She is presently working as a school psychologist in Central Point, Oregon.

But those are not the reasons this eighth edition is dedicated to these two outstanding therapists and educators. The real reason is that both of these individuals have fought through many of the crises' snares and traps in this book that could have easily defeated them. Put in life's furnace and fired, they came out tempered steel. Many in their place would have turned to cinders and burned up. Neither Steve nor Kay did and, in fact, they grew stronger from the adversity they have faced.

I am honored and humbled that both of these fine people believe that I have had some influence on their lives by counseling and teaching them. Both of them have felt indebted to me, but it is really I who am indebted to them for what they have become and I have become with them. They have repaid the debt they felt they owned me for that counseling and teaching back in the 1960s and 1970s over and over with the many lives they have touched and changed for the better. They are my legacy and best epitaph. They have, indeed, paid it forward.

My fervent hope for any of you neophytes starting out in this business is that you can also manifest the sterling character, strength, compassion, skills, resiliency, and empathy that these two professional human services workers possess and continue to pay forward in 2015. If this book helps you in some way to do that, then I have done my job.

Dick James
Professor of Counselor Education
University of Memphis

Brief Contents

Contents

2 Handling Specific Crises: Going Into the Trenches

143

Chemical dependency

3 On the Home Front: Crisis in the Human Services Workplace 481

No Man's Land: Facing Disaster

Preface

Rationale for the Book
The Primacy of Crisis Intervention

The Chinese characters embedded in the front of the book and the beginning of each chapter symbolize both "danger" and "opportunity!" That is the essence of *crisis*—the human dilemma that is common to all cultures. We believe that practically all counseling is initiated as crisis intervention. As much as the helping professions would prefer otherwise, people tend either to avoid presenting their problems to a helper until those problems have grown to crisis proportions, or become ensconced in situational dilemmas that wind up in unforeseen crises. Our ideal objective, as human services workers, is to establish primary prevention programs so effective that crisis intervention will seldom be needed. However, it appears that people will not be as quick to adopt preventive measures for their psychological health as for their physical health.

The Case for an Applied Viewpoint

The materials and techniques we promote in this book come from two sources: first, the authors' own experiences in teaching and counseling in crisis situations; second, interviews with people who are currently in the trenches, successfully performing counseling and crisis intervention. We have obtained input from many different individuals in the helping professions, whose daily and nightly work is dealing directly with human dilemmas, and related their views to the best of current theory and practice from the professional literature. Through many hours of dialogue, these experts have provided the most contemporary strategies and techniques in use in their particular fields. They have also reviewed the content on each crisis category and have provided much helpful commentary and critique of the ecology and etiology, tactics and procedures, terminology, and developmental stages of the specific crises with which they work. Therefore, what you read in the case-handling strategies comes directly from the horse's mouth.

Where controversies exist in regard to treatment modalities this text attempts to present as many perspectives as possible. Dr. Gilliland has been dead for 13 years, so if you encounter problems with the tactics and techniques presented in the current edition, the fault is undoubtedly in Dr. James's rendition of the current research and therapeutic modalities.

The authors have endeavored to incorporate, synthesize, and integrate the case-handling strategies of these resource people in a comprehensive, fluid, and dynamic way that will provide crisis workers with a basic set of tenets about effective crisis intervention. This book is not about long-term therapy or theory. Neither is it a volume dealing with crisis from only one theoretical perspective, such as a psychoanalytic approach or a behavioral system. The book incorporates a wide diversity of therapeutic modalities and reflects our eclectic and integrated approach to crisis intervention.

Specific crises demand specific interventions that span the whole continuum of therapeutic strategies. The strategies present in this book shouldn't be construed as the only ones available for a particular crisis. They are presented as "best bets" based on what current research and practice indicate to be appropriate and applicable. Yet these strategies may not be appropriate for all practitioners with all clients in all situations.

Good crisis intervention, as well as good therapy of any other kind, is a serious professional activity that calls for creativity and the ability to adapt to changing conditions of the therapeutic moment. To that extent, crisis intervention at times is more art than science and is not always prescriptive. Therefore, we would caution you that there are no clear-cut prescriptions or simple cause-and-effect answers in this book.

The Case for an Experiential Viewpoint

The fact that no single theory or strategy applies to every crisis situation is particularly problematic to those who are looking for simple, concrete answers to resolve the client problems they will face. If you are just beginning your career in the human services, we hope that while reading and trying out activities in this book you will suspend your judgment for a while and be open to the experience as you read about crisis workers attempting to implement theory into practice.

Moral Dilemmas. Another issue that permeates many of the topics covered in this book is the emotions they generate and the beliefs about what is morally "right" and what is morally "wrong" that pervades them. People have been willing to go to prison or die because of the strong beliefs they held about many of these topics. Where such moral issues and beliefs abound, we have attempted to deal with them in as even-handed a manner as possible. This book is not about the morality of the issues covered, but rather about what seems to work best for the people who are experiencing the dilemma. We ask you to read the book with that view in mind, and for at least a while, suspend your moral view of the situation or problem as you read about crisis workers attempting to grapple with these heart- and gut-wrenching problems.

Finally, because of a virtually unlimited supply of different crises situations, we have had to make tough decisions about what kinds of problems to illustrate in the most *generic and comprehensive way possible* so as to reach the broadest possible audience. We understand and empathize very deeply with readers who may have suffered terrible crises that are not mentioned in this book and are puzzled, chagrined, and angry that we have not given space and time to the particular crisis that they have suffered through. For that we apologize. The space available means that we simply cannot include all situations. However, what we the authors would like you to do rather than rail at our callous treatment in ignoring your particular dilemma, is to imagine how the strategies and techniques you are reading about might apply to the particular crisis you have experienced. Hopefully, what we say about those crises may help you come to understand the dynamics of your own a bit better.

Basic Relationship Skills. The listening and responding skills described in Chapter 3 are critical to everything else the worker does in crisis intervention. Yet on cursory inspection these techniques and concepts may seem at best simplistic and at worst inane. They do not appear to fix anything because they are not "fixing" skills. What they do is give the crisis worker a firm basis of operation to explore clearly the dilemma the client is facing. Basic listening and responding skills are the prerequisites for all other therapeutic modalities.

Our experience has shown us over and over that students and trainees who scoff at and dismiss these basic relationship skills are the ones who invariably have the most trouble meeting the experiential requirements of our courses and workshop training sessions. We feel very strongly about this particular point and thus ask you to read Chapter 3 with an open mind. Much the same can be said about Chapter 4, The Tools of the Trade. Students and veterans who operate out of a client-centered mode may find what we are proposing pretty close to heresy because a lot of these tools are directive and judgmental as to the action to be taken, particularly when client safety is concerned. Again we ask you to suspend judgment and give these tools a good tryout in this new venture.

Role Play. If this volume is used as a structured learning experience, the case studies in each chapter are a valuable resource for experiential learning. So are the exercises your instructor will give you as well as the videos. It is essential that you observe effective crisis intervention models at work and then follow up by actually practicing and enacting the procedures you have observed. Intensive and extensive role play is an excellent skill builder. A critical component of training is not just talking about problems but practicing the skills of handling them as well. Talking about a problem is fine, but attempting to handle a live situation enables the trainee to get involved in the business of calming, defusing, managing, controlling, and motivating clients. Role play is one of the best ways of practicing what is preached, and it prepares human services workers for developing creative ways to deal with the variety of contingencies they may face. Role play gives human services workers the chance to find out what works and doesn't work for them in the safety of a training situation and affords their fellow students and trainees an opportunity to give them valuable feedback.

A major problem in role playing is the perception of standing up in a class or workshop and risking making a complete fool of oneself. We want to assure you that in our classes and training sessions we don't expect perfection. If our students and trainees were perfect at crisis intervention, they wouldn't be taking instruction from us in the first place! Therefore, put your inhibitions on the shelf for a while and become engaged in the role plays as if the situations were real, live, and happening right now. Further, be willing and able to accept critical comments from your peers, supervisors, or instructors. Your ego may be bruised a bit in the process, but that's far better than waiting until you are confronted with an out-of-control client before you think about what you are going to do. Over and over, our students report that this component of instruction was the most profitable to them and was also the most fun!

Give the exercises that go with each chapter your best effort, process them with fellow students or trainees, and see what fits best with your own feelings, thoughts, and behaviors. Many times our students and trainees attempt to imitate us. Although it is gratifying to see students or trainees attempting to be "Dr. J.," it is generally an exercise in futility for them. What they need to do is view us critically as we model the procedures and then incorporate their own style and personhood into the procedures. We would urge you to do the same.

Some of these chapters are REALLY long. We didn't put all that "stuff" in there to beat you to death with verbiage. We did it because the field of crisis keeps expanding rapidly as does the knowledge base. Therefore you need to know "the stuff" to do your job effectively. If you just watch the PowerPoint presentations, you might get enough knowledge to pass your instructor's tests. However, you won't know enough though to help your client or yourself when you get in a tight spot. So read, read, read.

Finally, if you are never, ever going to be a crisis interventionist, but a "consumer," this book still can be very useful. Sad to say, but just through living, you are going to encounter a lot of crises in this book that are going to afflict you, your loved ones, your friends, your workplace and the ecosystem in which you live. To that end, this book can give you the basic knowledge to deal with the crisis or know when it's time to get help.

Organization of the Book
Part One, Basic Training

Part 1 of the book introduces the basic concepts of crisis intervention as well as telephone and online crisis counseling. It comprises Chapters 1 through 6.

Chapter 1, Approaching Crisis Intervention. Chapter 1 contains the historical background, basic definitions, and the theoretical and conceptual information needed for understanding applied crisis intervention.

Chapter 2, Culturally Effective Helping in Crisis. Chapter 2 is concerned with how crisis and culture interact. Dealing effectively with people from diverse backgrounds who are undergoing a crisis or have survived a disaster mandates an understanding and sensitivity to multicultural issues. What are called "social locations" for both worker and client play a major role in crisis intervention work. A new derivation of those social locations, called SAFETY locations, has been formulated to specifically deal with a person in crisis.

Chapter 3, The Intervention and Assessment Models. Chapter 3 introduces the task model for crisis intervention as well as the triage assessment system for rapidly assessing the severity of the crisis in a multidimensional way in real time.

Chapter 4, The Tools of the Trade. Chapter 4 introduces the basic communication techniques and skills applied to crisis intervention. It also details the strategies used to attack various kinds of problems that hinder individuals as they attempt to resolve the crisis and details how crisis workers operate on the directive–nondirective action continuum.

Chapter 5, Crisis Case Handling. Chapter 5 is an overview of how crises are handled. Long-term therapy is compared with crisis intervention. Different venues where crisis intervention operates are explored to give an overview of the general tactics and strategies that are used.

Chapter 6, Telephone and Online Crisis Counseling. The majority of crisis intervention is still done on the telephone by trained volunteers. However, with the advent of the Internet and social media, more and more crisis intervention is being done online. Chapter 6 explores the issues and techniques that are involved in these two mediums of crisis communication.

Part 2, Handling Specific Crises: Going into the Trenches

Part 2 (Chapters 7 through 13) addresses a variety of important types of crises. For each chapter in Part 2 the background and dynamics of the particular crisis type are detailed to provide a basic grasp of the driving forces behind the dilemma. Although some theory is present to highlight the therapeutic modalities used, comprehensive theoretical systems are beyond the scope of this book. For sources of that information, turn to the reference section at the end of each chapter.

In Part 2 we provide scripts from real interventions, highlighted by explanations why the crisis workers did what they did. Throughout this section techniques and cases are used to support live tryout, experiencing, and processing of the cases and issues in each chapter.

Chapter 7, Posttraumatic Stress Disorder. Chapter 7, Posttraumatic Stress Disorder (PTSD), is the linchpin chapter of this section. Many of the following chapters will have problems that may be the precursors of PTSD, or alternatively, represent the manifestation of it. This chapter examines both adults and children who have suffered traumatic experiences and are in crisis because of them.

Chapter 8, Crisis of Lethality. Chapter 8 focuses on strategies that crisis workers need in working with people who are manifesting lethal behavior. Suicidal and homicidal ideation flows through many other problems that assail people the human services worker is likely to confront and is a consideration for all providers of crisis intervention services both in regard to the safety of those clients and keeping the interventionists safe.

Chapter 9, Sexual Assault. Chapter 9 addresses another societal crisis that practical every human services worker will eventually encounter—clients who have either experienced or been affected by sexual assault. Sexually assaulted clientele are a special population because of the negative moral and social connotations associated with the dehumanizing acts perpetrated on them. This chapter is in three parts. First, it details crisis intervention techniques in the immediate aftermath of sexual assault on adults. Second, the chapter examines the long-term traumatic wake adult survivors of sexual abuse experienced in childhood. Third, the chapter details intervention techniques with children who have suffered sexual abuse and the family systems they live in.

Chapter 10, Partner Violence. Chapter 10 deals with a crisis that many people in a domestic relationship face: being treated violently by their partners. This chapter provides strategies to help people who are suffering abuse in *any kind of domestic relationship*. The chapter also deals with emerging treatment techniques for the batterers themselves.

Chapter 11, Family Crisis Intervention. Chapter 11 is a new chapter that deals with the whole family as they seek to navigate the family system through a crisis. This chapter also introduces spiritual and religious components in the intervention process and the part they play in it.

Chapter 12, Personal loss: Bereavement and Grief. Chapter 12 presents a type of crisis that every person will sooner or later face: personal loss. Even though the phenomenon of loss has been with us as long as the human species has existed, many people in our contemporary culture are poorly prepared and ill-equipped to deal with it. This chapter examines a variety of loss models and looks at different types of losses. This chapter also provides models and strategies for coping with unresolved or complicated grief.

Chapter 13, Crises in Schools. Schools have become a focal point for the violence perpetrated by gangs and disenfranchised and socially isolated children and adolescents. This chapter will examine crises as it impacts schools from preschool through higher education. It will examine what crisis workers need to do in assessing, screening, and working with the potentially violent individual student who is estranged from the social mainstream of the school. It will also deal with what the crisis worker needs to know in dealing with suicide, a problem that has become endemic in youth. This chapter will detail how and what goes into making up a crisis response team for a school building and system and how and what they respond to when a crisis occurs.

Part 3, On the Homefront: Crisis in the Human Services Workplace

Part 3 (Chapters 14 through 16) concentrates on the problems of crisis workers themselves and their employing institutions.

Chapter 14, Violent Behavior in Institutions. Chapter 14 tackles the little publicized, and badly neglected, type of crisis that workers in many institutions face daily: violent behavior within the walls of the institution. Regardless of the organizational settings where they are employed, workers will find in this chapter useful concepts and practical strategies that they and the institution can put to immediate use with agitated and potentially assaultive clients.

Chapter 15, Legal and Ethical Issues on Crisis of Trauma. Legal and professional ethical standards for the practice of psychotherapy have been in existence for over 50 years. Those laws and standards were intended for in-house, stabile, therapeutic settings. With the advent, growth, and maturation of crisis intervention services, these laws and standards are not always amenable to crisis situations. Another complicating factor in the ethical dilemmas that abound in crisis situations are the moral and political dilemmas that often go hand in hand with them. Those two issues are rarely mentioned in standard legal and ethical texts, but they almost always exist in some degree and form in crisis.

Chapter 16, Human Services Workers in Crisis: Burnout, Vicarious Traumatization, and Compassion Fatigue. Chapter 16 is about you and all human services workers who are in the helping professions. No worker is immune to stress, burnout, and the crises that go with human services work. This fact is particularly true in crisis work. This chapter should prove invaluable information for any worker anywhere whose work environment is frenetic and filled with crisis intervention or whose personality tends to generate compulsive behavior, perfectionism, or other stressors that may lead to burnout.

Part 4, No Man's Land: Facing Disaster

Part 4 focuses on an ecosystem view of crisis and crisis intervention in large-scale disasters.

Chapter 17, Disaster Response. Chapter 17 explores the theoretical basis and operating paradigm for large-scale disasters through an ecosystemic viewpoint. It details a family as they experience a natural disaster and how they interact with a variety of crisis workers, and the services the workers provide for the family as they move through postdisaster events over a course of a year. Finally, the chapter highlights the personal impact of large-scale disasters and the experiences of crisis workers who were involved with them at the scene of the disaster.

Online Chapters

Chapters 18 and 19 are available through MindTap; see the section below for more information.

Online Chapter 18, Chemical Dependency: The Crisis of Addiction. Addiction to substances is one of the most pressing issues of our time. Because chemical addiction is such a pervasive scourge in our society, no human services worker in the public arena can escape dealing with its effects. Crises of codependency and the long-term effects of substance abuse that create crises in the lives of adult children of addicts are also examined in this chapter.

Online Chapter 19, Crisis/Hostage Negotiation. This chapter presents another issue that human services workers pay little attention to, until it happens to them. The taking of hostages has become well publicized through terrorism and other acts violence. However, many hostage takings occur within the confines of human services work settings. This chapter provides basic crisis negotiation strategies and survival techniques that may enable a human services worker to contain and survive a hostage situation.

In summary, we have not been as concerned with intellectualizing, philosophizing, or using theoretical interpretations as with simply focusing on practical matters of how to respond in crisis situations as a way of giving you an understanding of some of the general types of crises you will face and the basic skills you will need to do something about them.

Supplementary Materials

This text is accompanied by several supporting products for both instructors and students.

MindTap

MindTap for *Crisis Intervention Strategies*, 8th ed., engages and empowers students to produce their best work—consistently. By seamlessly integrating course material with videos, activities, apps, and much more, MindTap creates a unique learning path that fosters increased comprehension and efficiency.

For students:
- MindTap delivers real-world relevance with activities and assignments that help students build critical thinking and analytic skills that will transfer to other courses and their professional lives.
- MindTap helps students stay organized and efficient with a single destination that reflects what's important to the instructor, along with the tools students need to master the content.
- MindTap empowers and motivates students with information that shows where they stand at all times—both individually and compared to the highest performers in class.

Additionally, for instructors, MindTap allows you to:
- Control what content students see and when they see it with a learning path that can be used as is or matched to your syllabus exactly.
- Create a unique learning path of relevant readings and multimedia and activities that move students up the learning taxonomy from

basic knowledge and comprehension to analysis, application, and critical thinking.

- Integrate your own content into the MindTap Reader using your own documents or pulling from sources like RSS feeds, YouTube videos, websites, Googledocs, and more.
- Use powerful analytics and reports that provide a snapshot of class progress, time in course, engagement, and completion.

Online Instructor's Manual

The Instructor's Manual (IM) contains a variety of resources to aid instructors in preparing and presenting text material in a manner that meets their personal preferences and course needs. It presents chapter-by-chapter suggestions and resources to enhance and facilitate learning.

Online Test Bank

For assessment support, the updated test bank includes true/false, multiple-choice, matching, short answer, and essay questions for each chapter.

Cengage Learning Testing Powered by Cognero

Cognero is a flexible, online system that allows you to author, edit, and manage test bank content as well as create multiple test versions in an instant. You can deliver tests from your school's learning management system, your classroom, or wherever you want.

Online PowerPoint

These vibrant Microsoft® PowerPoint® lecture slides for each chapter assist you with your lecture by providing concept coverage using images, figures, and tables directly from the textbook.

Acknowledgments

In writing a book that covers so many diverse areas of the human condition, it would be extremely presumptuous of us to rely solely on our own expertise and theories of truth, beauty, and goodness to propose crisis intervention techniques as the one true path of enlightenment to dealing with crises. We decided that the only realistic way to present the most current, reliable, and practical techniques to crisis intervention would be to go straight to the people who do this work day in and day out. They are not "big names," but rather people who go methodically about the business of crisis intervention daily in their respective venues. They work in such diverse occupational roles as ministers, police officers, psychologists, social workers, psychiatrists, nurses, marriage and family counselors, correction counselors, and school counselors. They work in every kind of agency and institution that deals with people and their dilemmas. They range geographically from across the United States to across the world. They are an encyclopedia of practical knowledge, and we are deeply in their debt for the help, advice, time, interviews, and critique they have given us. This book would not be possible without their assistance and we thank them one and all.

We would also like to thank the students in our crisis intervention classes at the University of Memphis. If you watch the videos that accompany this text, you are going to meet some of them up close and personal—both as crisis interventionists and wild and crazy clients! You will see that they are not perfect as rookies, but they are pretty darn good. They had fun doing the videos and hope you will have as much fun practicing these skills as they did. Thus, we want you to know we appreciate you deeply and have stood in awe and admiration in regard to how many of you have gone on to excel in this field.

Finally, we extend our grateful appreciation to the following professionals who have served as our editors and other gophers: Julie Martinez, Product Manager; Elizabeth Momb, Content Developer; Mary Noel, Content Development Manager; Stephen Lagos, Product Assistant; Vernon Boes, Sr., Art Director; and Rita Jaramillo, Sr. Content Project Manager. They practiced their own crisis intervention skills when we have become oppositionally defiant to written comments and suggestions.

Basic Training
Crisis Intervention Theory and Application

Part 1 introduces you to the fundamental concepts, theories, strategies, and skills needed to understand and conduct effective crisis intervention. Chapter 1 presents a brief historical overview of the field and introduces the conceptual dimensions of crisis work. Chapter 2 deals with the ecosystemic and multicultural considerations involved in providing crisis intervention. Chapter 3 serves as a key to the application of assessment and intervention strategies in crisis intervention. Chapter 4 describes the basic skills and techniques crisis interventionists use. Chapter 5 explains the major components of effective case management in crisis intervention. Chapter 6 discusses two of the main ways that crisis intervention is delivered—by telephone and Internet.

Approaching Crisis Intervention

1

LEARNING OBJECTIVES

After studying this chapter, you should be able to:

1. Understand the origins and evolution of the practice of crisis intervention.
2. Learn the basic definitions of individual crisis.
3. Differentiate between the concepts of individual crisis, systemic crisis, transcrisis, and metastasizing crisis.
4. Know the different types of theories of crisis intervention.
5. Understand the different applied crisis intervention action models.
6. Know the specific action steps of psychological first aid.
7. Assess yourself against traits and attributes common to competent crisis interventionists.

A Brief History of Crisis Intervention

We open the eighth edition of this book with **LO1** a brief history of crisis intervention. While crisis itself has probably been in existence ever since Eve ate the apple in the Garden of Eden, formal crisis theory, research, and intervention comprise one of the newest fields in psychotherapy. Probably most laypersons would think of formal crisis intervention as historically having to do with large-scale disasters, such as hurricanes or 9/11, and most typically performed by government agencies like the Federal Emergency Management Agency (FEMA) in the United States or by charitable organizations like the Red Cross. While the Red Cross and the Salvation Army have been involved in disaster relief for approximately the past century, FEMA has been in existence only for about 35 years, and until quite recently none of these organizations has had much to say or do about crisis intervention from a mental health perspective. Like Topsy in Harriet Beecher Stowe's classic, *Uncle Tom's Cabin,* "it just sorta growed." Understanding just how much it has "growed" in such a short time will help you understand why there's still a lot we don't know. But what we do know in 2015 is light-years ahead of what we knew when the first edition of this book appeared in 1987. If you could find a first edition in your library, it would look very little like this book does now.

The First Crisis Line. Suicide prevention is probably the longest running intervention program in which individual crisis is addressed from a mental health standpoint. The first identifiable crisis phone line was established in 1906 by the National Save-a-Life League (Bloom, 1984). Dr. Edwin Shneidman's (2001) landmark research into the causes of suicide, which started in the 1950s, has spanned six decades. Suicide has achieved such importance that it has become an "ology" and has a national association devoted to its study.

Cocoanut Grove Nightclub Fire. However, most people who study the field would probably say the benchmark for crisis intervention was the Cocoanut Grove nightclub fire in 1942, in which more than 400 people perished. Dr. Erich Lindemann (1944), who treated many of the survivors, found that they seemed to have common emotional responses and a need for psychological assistance and support. Out of Lindemann's work came the first notions of what may be called "normal" grief reactions to a disaster. Dr. Gerald Caplan (1961) was also involved in working with the Cocoanut Grove survivors. Sometimes referred to as the father of crisis intervention, his experiences led to some of the first attempts to explain what a crisis is and to build a theory of crisis. However, not until the

1960s did the first attempts occur to provide a structure for what would become crisis intervention.

The Community Mental Health Act of 1963. This federal act completely changed the way mental health services were delivered in the United States by mandating the development of community centers to deal with the mentally ill in the United States, who, prior to that act were generally housed in large state "insane asylums." As the large state insane asylums were closed down and replaced by community mental health centers, one of the primary mandates of those centers was to provide emergency services and crisis intervention 24/7. While the community mental health concept was laudable, the idealistic notion that patients would be docile, medication compliant, and fully functional proved to be problematic and those problems would end up in homeless shelters and prisons.

The New Asylums—Prisons. Although the statistics are dated (James & Glaze, 2006), they are probably conservatively representative of where the mental health problems of the United States currently reside. In 2006 more than one million two hundred thousand inmates in federal and state prisons and local jails could be identified as having a diagnosable mental illness. James and Glaze's (2006) grim statistical analysis of incarcerates portrays a sad legacy of the Community Mental Health Act and what this country has done about it. Three quarters of prisoners with mental illness also suffer from co-occurring substance abuse disorders. They are three times more likely to have been sexually or physically abused in their past than their fellow inmates. Women with mental illness make up an even higher proportion of incarcerates (approximately 70 %) than do men (approximately 56%). Prison is also not a safe place if you are mentally ill. Incarcerates with mental illness are twice as likely to be injured in fights as compared to fellow inmates who are not mentally ill. Finally, they also do not stay out of jail. Nearly 25% of those inmates with mental illness have served three or more prior incarcerations. In summary, if you were to go looking to find a fertile field to do crisis intervention with the mentally ill, you would need look no further than your local jail.

How could this happen with such good intentions of the Community Mental Health Act? One of the overarching tenets of crisis intervention that flows through every theoretical model is the concept of support. When familial supports either wear down and out or were never there in the first place, when no medical professional is there to monitor medication, when mental health clinics are underfunded and overwhelmed with clients, and when little vocational opportunities or rehabilitation counselors are available, persons who are mentally ill become the "crazy" panhandler you are bothered by when you are on the streets of a big city. As a result of this evolution in mental health care (or the lack of it), it should not be surprising that a great deal of crisis intervention is now done on the streets and in the homes of local communities. What might surprise you is that a lot of it is being done by police officers.

Birth of the Police Crisis Intervention Team. Indeed, one of the major, serendipitous outcomes of the return of mentally ill to the community has been the birth of the police Crisis Intervention Team. Faced with continuous interactions with the mentally ill who were off their medication, many confrontations with the police ended violently with the mentally ill consumer forcibly being taken into custody. That interaction often resulted in the consumer or police officer being injured or being killed. These continuous confrontations culminated in the city of Memphis in 1987 with a man suffering a severe schizophrenic episode being shot to death by the police. The resulting hue and cry from the citizens of our city resulted in a radical shift in police thinking and the establishment of the first **police Crisis Intervention Team** specifically trained to de-escalate and defuse people who are mentally ill and demonstrating dangerous behavior to themselves or others (James & Crews, 2009).

Word about what we were doing in Memphis soon spread, and other law enforcement jurisdictions that were grappling with the same problems across the country began asking for help in training their officers. What started out as a small group of mental health professionals, government officials, and police officers attempting to deal with a critical local political problem has now spread across over 2,400 jurisdictions in the United States, Canada, Australia, Europe, and Africa and is now considered a "best practices" model for police departments (Watson & Fulambarker, 2012), which we will thoroughly explore in Chapter 5, Crisis Case Handling.

International Movement. The United States has not been alone in its endeavors to organize large-scale crisis intervention operations. Internationally, the

United Nations Inter-Agency Standing Committee (IASC, 2007) has published guidelines for mental health provision in emergency situations. Europe has established the **European Network of Traumatic Stress** to develop evidence-based responses to large-scale disasters and provide assistance to those parts of the European Union that suffer from a lack of psychological resources. The **International Federation of Red Cross and Red Crescent Societies** has entered into the psychosocial facet of disaster relief by helping individuals and communities heal the psychological wounds and rebuild social structures after an emergency or a critical event. Its mission is to change people into active survivors rather than passive victims (International Federation of Red Cross and Red Crescent Societies, 2014). Most notably, the Australians have been in the vanguard of dealing with the mental health issues of large-scale disasters particularly through the research and writing of Beverley Raphael (Raphael, 1977, 1986; Raphael & Wilson, 2000).

Grassroots Movements

To really understand the evolution of crisis intervention, though, is to understand that several social movements have been critical to its development, and these did not start fully formed as "crisis intervention" groups by any means. Three of the major movements that helped shape crisis intervention into an emerging specialty were Alcoholics Anonymous (AA), Vietnam veterans, and the women's movement of the 1970s. Although their commissioned intentions and objectives had little to do with the advancement of crisis intervention as a clinical specialty, they had a lot to do with people who were desperate for help and weren't getting any. These groups all started as grassroots movements.

The need for crisis intervention services remains unrecognized by the public and by existing institutions until a critical mass of victims comes together to exert enough legal, political, or economic pressure to cause the particular crisis category, malady, or social problem to become formalized. Until that time, it remains informal, nonprofessional, and unsubsidized. The problem is responded to or handled mainly through ad hoc, informal means by former victims, current victims, friends, or significant others who are affected by the problem. The free storefront clinics for Vietnam veterans that grew out of a refusal of the Veterans Administration to handle their problems and the attempt by Mothers Against Drunk Driving (MADD) to deal with the crisis of drunk driving in

the face of resistant state legislatures are excellent examples of grassroots responses to unmet needs.

Initiators of crisis intervention services are generally concerned with one particular crisis category that personally affects them in some way. Typically, the crisis gets far enough out of hand to cause noticeable problems before remedial responses are initiated. At first, the initiators are mavericks who are starting a victims' revolt. The revolt is against an entrenched status quo or power structure that shows little awareness of or responsiveness to the problem. The victims' revolt somehow manages to get a fledgling crisis agency started despite the benign neglect and reluctance of mainstream society. In the 1970s, Vietnam veterans' efforts to get posttraumatic stress disorder (PTSD) categorized as a mental disease and get financial support for research and treatment are a classic example of this revolt. So are the efforts of the National Organization for Women and other women's groups in the 1970s to raise the curtain on domestic violence and child abuse in the United States and to get state legislatures to deal with them as criminal acts.

The fledgling crisis agency is initially funded by private donations, as with the many telephone call-in lines for victims of domestic violence that were started at local YWCAs in the 1970s. The services are often provided by volunteers who are loosely organized. The crisis agency gains access to public funding only after the agency has attained validation and some recognition by a substantial portion of the power structure. If, after a time, the crisis agency does not attain credibility sufficient to garner substantial private support or a modicum of public support, the agency begins to falter and eventually folds and ceases to operate.

It is this grassroots influence that often captures the attention of the media, impels people to join as volunteers, and causes a greater number of clients and victims to seek the services of the agency. Initially, community leaders may deny that the crisis exists, minimize its seriousness, or express doubt that it represents a recurring problem. But when the crisis persists, they finally come to realize that someone must become proactive—someone must exert the leadership, energy, time, resources, and resolve to confront the crisis. Thus the formation of an agency is sanctioned or even encouraged. If the fledgling agency born from the need to contain the crisis succeeds and is publicly recognized as fulfilling a need, the quest to expand and mature begins.

As mainstream institutions, such as governmental structures, become aware of the problem and as volunteer centers reach the saturation point at which needs are obviously going unmet, some governmental or institutional funding is provided. Pressure politics, public relations, and public image building affect the course and growth of an organization and the problem it seeks to solve. For example, the plight of the Vietnam veterans suffering from PTSD was largely ignored until the problem spilled over from the streets into the seats of power and authority—from personal crisis to politics. When the PTSD problem began to affect members of Congress, the power of the federal government and the resources of the Veterans Administration were brought to bear not only to create a network of veterans centers throughout the country, but also to slash bureaucratic red tape to ensure that services for Vietnam veterans were taken to the streets where PTSD sufferers were living rather than requiring veterans to report to regular VA hospitals.

The activism of those veterans in the 1970s can be seen today in the comprehensive frontline treatment and exit programs of the armed services and the extensive use of veterans outreach centers across the United States. Satellite outreach centers throughout the country have now been established by the VA to make it substantially easier for veterans of the Middle Eastern conflicts to access services that would otherwise require them to travel to mainstream VA hospitals.

The Importance of Volunteerism

Contrary to the popular misconception that paid veteran crisis workers descend on a large-scale disaster like smoke jumpers into a forest fire, most crisis intervention in the United States is done by volunteers. Volunteer workers perform all kinds of services in most crisis agencies—from menial chores to answering the phone to frontline crisis intervention with clients. Volunteerism is often the key to getting the fledgling crisis agency rolling. The use of trained volunteers as crisis workers has been a recognized component of many crisis centers and agencies for years (Clark & McKiernan, 1981; Roberts, 1991, p. 29; Slaikeu & Leff-Simon, 1990, p. 321). Probably the greatest number of frontline volunteers are used in staffing 24-hour suicide hotlines in major cities. Such hotlines require an enormous number of crisis workers because the crisis service never ceases—it must be provided 7 days a week, 52 weeks a year. Roberts (1991, p. 29) reported that more than three quarters of all crisis centers in the United States indicate that they rely on volunteer crisis workers and

that such volunteers outnumber professional staff by more than 6 to 1. Typically, as the numbers and needs of the clientele increase, the agency reaches the point where compassion and volunteerism alone cannot handle all of the complex personal, social, economic, public relations, psychological, and political problems that assail it.

The Need for Institutionalism

As crisis agencies become well known and as their clientele are drawn from a wider segment of the community (to the point that the work cannot be handled by the communication system of grapevine, word of mouth, notepad, e-mail, and Twitter), the agency sees that if it is to continue to grow and serve its clients, it must institutionalize. The seeds of bureaucracy are thus born.

To manage all of its vital functions, the agency must centralize and formalize most aspects of its operation. It takes on a formal board of directors, establishes rigorous auditing and record-keeping functions, and requires more money, paid staff, and staff support. As crisis agencies become crisis organizations, they gain more power, prestige, and notoriety. They tend to attract the attention of the human services professions because they offer fertile fields for funded research, placement of practicum and internship students, and employment of graduates. Crisis agencies sometimes attain eminent success, to the point that it becomes a vested interest of the human services professions to formalize the competencies of the personnel of such successful agencies through certification, licensure, and accreditation. The progression from the humble origins of Alcoholics Anonymous as a support group formed by fellow alcoholics in the 1930s to the current classification of alcoholism as a disease, the proliferation of thousands of treatment centers around the world, huge government funding for research and prevention, university courses on the subject, and the state licensure or certification of substance abuse counselors provides an outstanding example of the evolution from self-help by a group of recovering alcoholics in crisis to the full institutionalization of the crisis of drug abuse.

As a specialty evolves, it develops its own empirical base, professional research, and writings. For example, for crisis intervention we have publications such as *Crisis Intervention, Journal of Interpersonal Violence, Victimology, Violence and Victims, Journal of Family Violence, Death Studies, Journal of Traumatic Stress, Suicide and Life Threatening Behavior, Child Abuse and*

Neglect, Journal of Child Sexual Abuse, Aggression and Violent Behavior, and *Violence Against Women.* The amount of data and information in the field has expanded so much that the *Encyclopedia of Psychological Trauma* (Reyes, Elhai, & Ford, 2008) includes 720 large pages covering everything from A (Abuse, child physical) to W (Workplace violence).

Specialty areas may also attain a distinct level of recognition by building a base of national or regional affiliates, as with various topic- or malady-centered hotlines, chat rooms, and websites; AA chapters; spouse abuse centers; and victim assistance programs. Local, state, regional, and national conferences are organized to provide for exchange of ideas and problem-solving strategies. These conferences range from specialty areas that bring together some of the greatest research minds in the field—such as the First Annual Conference on Trauma, Loss, and Dissociation in 1995—to "in the trenches" conferences such as the Crisis Intervention Team International (CITI) convention which provides practical, hands-on programs for crisis intervention police officers who deal with the mentally ill.

The emergence of hundreds of crisis-oriented organizations in the 1970s, 1980s, and 1990s (Maurer & Sheets, 1999) and the realization of the role that immediate intervention plays in alleviating traumatic stress (Mitchell & Everly, 1995) attest to the dramatic transformation and professional acceptance of crisis intervention from a psychological backwater field to a pervasive specialty. Probably the best testament to the center stage on which crisis intervention is now playing is the birth in 2006 of the American Psychological Association's newest division, Division 56, Trauma Psychology, along with the provision of counseling (Council for Accreditation of Counseling & Educationally Related Programs, 2009) and school psychology (National Association of School Psychologists, 2010) professional accreditation standards for training graduates in crisis intervention. One of the major players in the field of trauma, Christine Courtois (Courtois & Gold, 2009), has eloquently stated the critical need for inclusion of psychological trauma training in all helping service curricula. Thus, like lots of other concepts in mental health that evolve and continue to grow to meet increased demands for crisis services, it is incumbent that beginners in the mental health field understand the processes and evidence-based practices associated with crisis intervention (Cutler, Yeager, & Nunley, 2013) that this book is about.

The Media and the Societal Impetus for Crisis Intervention

Why, from the 1970s to the present, has the crisis intervention movement experienced such extraordinary growth? Probably no single factor alone can explain why. In the United States, the bombing of the Murrah Federal Building in Oklahoma City, 9/11, the mega natural disaster of Hurricane Katrina, mass shootings at Virginia Tech, Northern Illinois University, Columbine High School, Sandy Hook elementary school, and a variety of public massacres have all given rise to the demand for crisis intervention. Yet such natural and human-made disasters have been with us since the city of Pompeii was buried by Mt. Vesuvius and Rome was sacked and burned. What has changed public perception to the extent that the acronym PTSD—which in the first edition of this book was a brand new term that lots of psychologists were unfamiliar with or didn't believe was a valid diagnostic—is now common parlance?

The media's role in creating awareness of crises and crisis intervention has probably generated the most profound change in public consciousness of what it means to be in crisis after a large-scale disaster. When Matthew Brady's pictures of the windrows of dead from the American Civil War battle of Antietam were put on display in New York in 1863, this first use of photographic media changed forever how people would perceive wars and the psychological trauma that invariably comes with them. Public perception of war as glorious changed forever as its horror and carnage were brought to the American doorstep by Brady's harrowing pictures. Since that time, the ability of the media has advanced from the still-life daguerreotypes of Brady to real-time sound and video of New Orleans citizens sitting on top of flooded buildings, of Baghdad residents running from a car bombing, of the jumpers from the Twin Towers. It is unclear exactly what impact such real-time media has on the public, but clearly it does have an impact and changes our perception of the world as ever smaller, more interconnected, and certainly more dangerous, unsafe, and crisis prone (Marshall et al., 2007).

There are valid reasons for the widespread acceptance of crisis intervention as a therapeutic specialty. People in general have become more positive in their acceptance of outreach strategies following a crisis and are more knowledgeable about its psychological ramifications such as PTSD. There is less "blaming the victim" as somehow psychologically inadequate. Probably most important from a pragmatic point of view, it is cost effective (Roberts, 1991). People in human services and political leadership positions have discovered that when they either ignore crisis situations or leave solutions entirely to the experts who have little political clout, lasting solutions elude them, and the leaders themselves are blamed and held publicly responsible. Reactive responding has not worked very well. Leaders have discovered that endemic crises will not easily go away, that reaction or no action may result in problems' metastasizing out of control. In a sense, then, political expediency has dictated not only the widespread acceptance of effective crisis intervention strategies but also that crisis intervention become proactive, preventive, and integrated on the local, national, and international levels. One need go no further than the aftermath of Hurricane Katrina to understand the full impact of what this paragraph is about.

The Case Against Too Much "Helping"

With the rise of postintervention psychological assistance in the last 20 years, an interesting phenomenon has started to emerge. "Do-gooder" individuals and paternalistic bureaucracies appear on the scene and want to "straighten" things out and "help" people. Van den Eynde and Veno (1999) report the case of an Australian community that literally had to kick government "help" out of town after the discovery of a case of long-term mass pedophilia in their midst. Even though the community clearly had the situation under control, the government authorities kept insisting they did not. What they had to do to get the government out of their town is interesting reading indeed.

In a worst-case scenario, crass commercialization, pseudoscience, vicarious thrills, and outright fraud mark the traumatic wake of a crisis (Echterling & Wylie, 1999; Gist, Lubin, & Redburn, 1999; Gist, Woodall, & Magenheimer, 1999; Lohr et al., 1999). Gist, Lubin, and Redburn (1999) have coined the term "trauma tourism" to describe the burgeoning industry in postintervention psychological trauma replete with trade shows, trade publications, talk shows, and charitable giving and bus tours of trauma areas. Indeed, such tours have become so acrimonious in New Orleans that tour companies have been fined by city officials for bus tours through the devastated ninth ward of that city (Brown, 2012).

The assumption is that disaster invariably leads to psychopathology, and psychopathology sells. If people are seen as incapable of caring for themselves and are traumatized and in a panic state after a disaster, it follows that they must be somehow infirm and unequal to the task and need assistance. A paternalistic government is then tasked with taking care of them. This view may be even more true with "noble savages," transients, indigenous people, or other marginalized and disenfranchised groups who are seen as socially or technically unsophisticated and in need of benevolent and well-intentioned guidance and protection (Gist, Lubin, & Redburn, 1999; Kaniasty & Norris, 1999; Ober et al., 2000). On the other hand, such groups of disenfranchised and dislocated persons, particularly if they are migrants or undocumented aliens, may be given short shrift from the authorities and may be persecuted if they come to the attention of bureaucracies that are dealing with a crisis (Brown, 2009, pp. 215–226). It is with good reason that activists in the counseling field have proposed that "Social Justice" is the new benchmark against which therapy should be measured (Ratts & Pedersen, 2014), and that is particularly true in the aftermath of disasters.

However, the fact is that in most instances victims of disaster do not panic. They organize themselves in a collective manner and go about the business of helping one another and restoring equilibrium (Kaniasty & Norris, 1999). Called the "altruistic or therapeutic community," the typical immediate collective response to a disaster is characterized by the disappearance of community conflicts, heightened internal solidarity, charity, sharing, communal public works, and a positive "can-do" attitude (Barton, 1969; Giel, 1990). So, as of 2015, crisis intervention has emerged from a psychological backwater 30 years ago when we started writing the first edition of this book to a veritable tidal wave of interest, although at times controversial and full of heated debate, and that includes defining exactly what a crisis is.

Definitions of Crisis

LO2

This book is mainly about doing crisis intervention with individuals and the microsystems such as families and workplaces. To a lesser extent, it is also about macrosystems in crisis and how the crisis interventionist functions within those systems, whether in institutions such as hospitals, schools, and mental health centers or as service providers after large-scale disasters. To that end we start this book in a pretty boring way by giving you not only a history lesson but also a long list of definitions of crisis as it applies to both individuals and systems. We apologize for that, but we do this because we want you to understand that this business is still so new that a definition of an individual or a system in crisis is by no means fixed or absolute. As a matter of fact, as you are going to find throughout this book, there is a whole lot about crisis and crisis intervention that is not fixed or absolute! Consider, then, the following definitions of individuals in crisis.

Individual Crisis Definitions

1. People are in a state of crisis when they face an obstacle to important life goals—an obstacle that is, for a time, insurmountable by the use of customary methods of problem solving. A period of disorganization ensues, a period of upset, during which many abortive attempts at solution are made (Caplan, 1961, p. 18).
2. A crisis arises from a traumatic event that is unpredictable and uncontrollable. There is an inability to influence it by one's actions. The nature of the event changes values and priorities, and indeed changes everything (Sarri, 2005, pp. 19–24).
3. Crisis is a crisis because the individual knows no response to deal with a situation (Carkhuff & Berenson, 1977, p. 165).
4. Crisis is a personal difficulty or situation that immobilizes people and prevents them from consciously controlling their lives (Belkin, 1984, p. 424).
5. Crisis is a state of disorganization in which people face frustration of important life goals or profound disruption of their life cycles and methods of coping with stressors. The term *crisis* usually refers to a person's feelings of fear, shock, and distress *about* the disruption, not to the disruption itself (Brammer, 1985, p. 94).
6. Crisis is a temporary breakdown of coping. Expectations are violated and waves of emotion such as anger, anxiety, guilt, and grief surface. Old problems and earlier losses may surface. The event's intensity, duration, and suddenness may affect the severity of response to the crisis (Poland & McCormick, 1999, p. 6).
7. Crisis is a loss of psychological equilibrium or a state of emotional instability that includes elements of depression and anxiety which is caused by an external event with which individuals are unable to cope with at their usual level of ability (Kleespies, 2009, p. 15).
8. Crisis in a clinical context refers to an acute emotional upset arising from situational, developmental, or sociocultural sources, and results in a temporary inability to cope by means of one's usual problem-solving devices (Hoff, Hallisey, & Hoff, 2009, p. 4).
9. A crisis may be a catastrophic event or a series of life stresses that build rapidly and accumulate such that the person's homeostatic balance is disturbed and creates a vulnerable state, which, if not resolved, avoided, or redefined will cause self-righting devices to no longer be effective and plunge the person into psychological disequilibrium (Golan, 1978, p. 8).

It should immediately become clear that the term *crisis* has different meanings to different people and is used to describe a variety of incidents, settings, situations, and the adaptations, albeit less than adequate, that people attempt to make in response to them. To summarize these definitions, for an individual, **crisis** is the perception or experiencing of an event or situation as an intolerable difficulty that exceeds the person's current resources and coping mechanisms. Unless the person obtains relief, the crisis has the potential to cause severe affective, behavioral, and cognitive malfunctioning up to the point of instigating injurious or lethal behavior to oneself or others. At that point the crisis becomes a behavioral emergency (Kleespies, 2009).

Behavioral Emergencies

A **behavioral emergency** occurs when a crisis escalates to the point that the situation requires immediate intervention to avoid injury or death to oneself or others or the person is in imminent risk of serious injury or death by another. Direct or intentional behavioral emergencies fall into the general categories of engaging in self-injurious behavior, perpetrating violent interpersonal behavior, and being a victim of violence as opposed to a behavioral crisis which may not necessarily be potentially lethal (Kleespies, 2009, p. 13; Kleepies, 2014, pp. 11–12). Suicides/homicides resulting from broken romances provide a classic example of these categories.

We believe that **indirect and noncommissioned behavioral emergencies** can also occur. Indirect behavioral emergencies occur when people make bad decisions and wind up placing themselves in potentially lethal situations. Indirect and noncommissioned behavioral emergencies are crises that happen with no directed purpose or intentionality to do something harmful to oneself or others. Drunk driving, boating, snow skiing, swimming, and project construction may all turn into behavioral emergencies that have the potential for injurious or lethal behavior and call for intervention. A parent who, after receiving a phone call informing her that her child has been seriously injured in a school bus accident, becomes hysterical, leaves her newborn at home with a pot of cooking oil boiling on the stove, and drives 90 miles an hour to the hospital is creating a behavioral emergency to put it mildly. Persons with borderline personality disorder are the archetype of people whose unstable lifestyles continuously set them up to fly into crisis after crisis and oftentimes move quickly into behavioral emergencies by impulsively deciding to commit suicide or committing **parasuicide** (accidentally doing something or going into a situation a reasonable person wouldn't and getting himself or herself killed).

More often than we would like to imagine, crisis interventionists will deal with people whose behavior has escalated to the point that they can be considered to be behavioral emergencies. For that reason, when you first make the acquaintance of the Triage Assessment Form in Chapter 3 you will note that scores of 10 (maximum) on the form's scales all have lethal feeling, behaving, and thinking as part of their assessment anchors.

Systemic Crisis Definitions

"Individual crisis" is really something of an **LO3** oxymoron, because as most crises unfold, they rarely remain confined to one person. They ripple out and affect numerous other people who interact with the person in crisis. To think that the crisis created by a date rape or an alcoholic mother affects only the young woman who was assaulted or the housewife who drinks is to have a very wrong notion indeed about what a crisis is and what you may have to do and with whom you may work. Therefore, when we consider a definition of crisis, we are bound to look at how that crisis affects the system within which the individual operates. For most individuals the first ripple effect of a crisis will be with the family system. Although you will meet numerous family members as they are affected by various kinds of crisis in this book, we have developed a new chapter that looks more closely at the family system itself as it is impacted as opposed to the individual originally targeted by the crisis.

Systemic crises may come in many forms. They may be economically based, perhaps affecting only the families of a small produce chain that goes bankrupt when the refrigeration in their warehouse fails or as large as a worldwide recession that throws millions of people out of work. They may be natural disasters, as small as a tornado tearing up a small Kansas farming community or as large as a pandemic flu epidemic that kills millions. They may be human-made, ranging from a structural failure that causes a building to collapse to wars that kill and displace millions of people. They may be psychologically based, ranging from fear of a school bully to an entire nation rendered paranoid by the terrorist attacks of 9/11. As you will see in the last chapter of this book, large-scale disasters that become systemic crises most generally fit the public perception of what crisis intervention is about. Indeed, the role of crisis interventionists as mental health service providers in that setting is becoming larger and larger. Consider, then, the following definitions of a system in crisis, in which the term *system* ranges across families, churches, businesses, neighborhoods, communities, large cities, geographical flood plains, and nations:

1. A crisis that threatens the organization is unexpected, demands a rapid response in a short time frame, and threatens its basic values (Hermann, 1963, p. 63).
2. Communities in crisis have several characteristics in common with individuals. Within the group there is an atmosphere of tension and fear. Rumors run rampant. Normal functioning is at a standstill, schools and businesses are closed, and health and emergency resources may be in short supply (Hoff, Hallisey, & Hoff, 2009, p. 209).
3. Communities in crisis go through chronological stages following a disaster that are known as the impact, heroic/rescue, honeymoon, disillusionment, and reconstruction/recovery phase. Each phase has identifiable characteristics and sequential timelines, and depending on how the various systems in the community react, may move forward positively or not (Roberts, 2005, p. 205).
4. A systemic crisis is a negative event or outcome, which includes the element of surprise, disruption of operations, and is a threat to the property, financial and physical resources, well-being of individuals within the system, and the reputation of the system to provide for the well-being of its constituency (Zdziarski, Dunkel, & Rollo, 2007, p. 6).

To sum up what we believe generally defines a **systemic crisis**: When a traumatic event occurs such that people, institutions, communities, and ecologies are overwhelmed and response systems are unable to effectively contain and control the event in regard to both physical and psychological reactions to it, the crisis has become systemic. The size of the system may range from a family, to a mental health clinic, to a nation, but the main identifying factor is that the system is in disequilibrium and previous response systems and coping mechanisms no longer work. If adequate intervention doesn't occur, the potential exists for irreparable damage or termination of the system. Sandwiched between individual and systemic crises is another type of crisis with which the interventionist is likely to be faced, which we have called a "*metastasizing* crisis."

Metastasizing Crisis

A **metastasizing crisis** occurs when a small, isolated incident is not contained and begins to spread. The analogy to the spread of cancer is apt because what may start out as a focal and localized problem that could have been easily cured with early, preemptive intervention is not diagnosed or remedied, but is allowed to grow through benign neglect and suddenly becomes endemic within the system. At that point it is anything but easy to excise or remedy. A school system's neglect in dealing with isolated cases of bullying can soon lead to a culture of bullying that moves out of the classroom and into cyberspace to pervade and wreak havoc on students' lives 24 hours a day. Predispositioning both personnel and resources can go a long way toward what is called *primary* intervention, which seeks to proactively handle problems before they metastasize and get out of control. From that standpoint many crisis interventionists are also engaged in **primary prevention**, stopping a problem before it starts, as well as **secondary intervention**, minimizing the harmful effects that have already occurred (Caplan, 1964).

Characteristics of Crisis

The following discussion of characteristics of crisis represents an expanded definition of what *crisis* means.

Presence of Both Danger and Opportunity. Crisis is a *danger* because it can overwhelm the individual to the extent that serious pathology, including homicide and suicide, may result. Crisis is also an *opportunity* because the pain it induces impels the person to seek help (Aguilera & Messick, 1982, p. 1). If the individual

takes advantage of the opportunity, the intervention can help plant the seeds of self-growth and self-realization (Brammer, 1985, p. 95). People can react in any one of three ways to crisis. Under ideal circumstances, many individuals can cope effectively with crisis by themselves and develop strength from the experience. They change and grow in a positive manner and come out of the crisis both stronger and more compassionate (Danish, 1977).

Others appear to survive the crisis but effectively block the hurtful affect from awareness, only to have it haunt them in innumerable ways throughout the rest of their lives. Yet others break down psychologically at the onset of the crisis and clearly demonstrate that they are incapable of going any further with their lives unless given immediate and intensive assistance (Rapoport, 1967).

Seeds of Growth and Change. In the disequilibrium that accompanies crisis, anxiety is always present, and its discomfort provides an impetus for change (Janosik, 1984, p. 39). Often anxiety must reach the boiling point before the person is ready to admit the problem is out of control. One need look no further than the substance abuser for affirmation of this assertion. By waiting too long, for example, the substance abuser may become so entrenched that he or she may need a therapeutic jackhammer to break the addiction down into manageable pieces. Even here, however, a threshold point for change may be reached, albeit in last-ditch desperation, when the abuser finally surrenders to the fact that something must be done.

No Panaceas or Quick Fixes. People in crisis are generally amenable to help through a variety of forms of intervention, some of which are described as *brief therapy* (Cormier & Hackney, 1987, p. 240). For problems of long duration, however, quick fixes are rarely available. Many problems of clients in severe crisis stem from the fact that the clients sought quick fixes in the first place, usually through a pill. Such a "fix" may dampen the dreadful responses but doesn't change the instigating stimulus, so the crisis deepens.

The Necessity of Choice. Life is a process of interrelated crises and challenges that we confront or not, deciding to live or not (Carkhuff & Berenson, 1977, p. 173). In the realm of crisis, *not to choose is a choice,* and this choice usually turns out to be negative and destructive. *Choosing to do something* at least contains the seeds of growth and allows a person the chance to set goals and formulate a plan to begin to overcome the dilemma.

Universality and Idiosyncrasy. Disequilibrium or disorganization accompanies every crisis, whether universal or idiosyncratic (Janosik, 1984, p. 13). Crisis is universal because no one is immune to breakdown, given the right constellation of circumstances. It is idiosyncratic because what one person may successfully overcome, another may not, even though the circumstances are virtually the same. It is foolhardy to maintain a belief that one is immune to psychic assaults, that one can handle any crisis in a stable, poised, and masterful fashion. Thousands of "tough" veterans of the Vietnam, Afghanistan, and two Gulf Wars suffering from posttraumatic stress disorder (PTSD), who have turnstiled through VA hospitals, veterans' centers, and other medical facilities, are convincing proof that when a crisis boils over, disorganization, disequilibrium, disorientation, and fragmentation of an individual's coping mechanisms can occur no matter how conditioned against psychological trauma the person may be.

Resiliency. Yet the National Comorbidity Survey found that while their nationally representative sample had better than a 50% prevalence of traumatic events for both men and women, only about 5% of men and 10% of women contracted PTSD (Kessler et al., 1995). One of the key jobs of the crisis interventionist is finding the right combination of support systems and coping mechanisms, and forming them into action plans that will tap the reservoir of resiliency that most people have to move them through and beyond the crisis.

Perception. As paradoxical as it may seem, the precipitating event is not the major cause of the crisis. It is the *perception* of the event that plays a huge role in a crisis. How individuals interpret events has a great deal to do with how amenable the crisis will be to resolution (Callahan, 2009, p. 21). As the old adage states, "One man's fruit may be another man's poison." It is no accident that the Cognitive scale in the Triage Assessment Form that you will encounter in Chapter 3 is the most complex of the three scales. How people appraise precipitating events and what the interventionist can do to reframe and temper catastrophic interpretations of the event will have a great deal to do with how well and how quickly the crisis is alleviated.

Complicated Symptomology. Crisis is *not* simple; it is complex and difficult to understand, and it defies cause-and-effect description (Brammer, 1985, p. 91; Kliman, 1978, p. xxi). The symptoms that overlie precipitating crisis events become tangled webs that crisscross all environments of an individual. When an event reaches a flash point, there may be so many compounding problems that crisis workers must intervene directly in a variety of areas. Furthermore, the environment of people in crisis strongly affects the ease or difficulty with which the crisis can be handled. Families, individuals, partners, institutions, and employees may all directly affect problem resolution and a return to stability. When large numbers of people are affected at the same time by a crisis, the entire ecological system of a neighborhood, community, geographical region, or country may need intervention. A stark but global example of such a nationwide ecological crisis occurred in the United States in the immediate aftermath of the September 11, 2001, terrorist attacks (Bass & Yep, 2002; Pyszczynski, Solomon, & Greenberg, 2003).

Transcrisis States

Crises have typically been seen as time limited, usually persisting a maximum of 6 to 8 weeks, at the end of which the subjective discomfort diminishes (Janosik, 1984, p. 9). That view is now changing, and the effects of the original crisis may extend a good bit beyond that time frame (Callahan, 1998; Salzer & Bickman, 1999). Indeed, the impact of a crisis may last a lifetime (van der Kolk & McFarlane, 1996). What occurs during the immediate aftermath of the crisis event determines whether or not the crisis will become a disease reservoir that will be transformed into a chronic and long-term state. Although the original crisis event may be submerged below awareness, and the individual may believe the problem has been resolved, the appearance of new stressors may bring the individual to the crisis state again. This emotional roller coaster may occur frequently and for extended periods of time, ranging from months to years. An adult who has unresolved anger toward a dead parent and transfers that anger to other authority figures, such as supervisors or employers, is in a **transcrisis state**.

The adult may have apparently attained functional and normal mental health. However, this appearance is gained at the cost of warding off and repressing the "unfinished business" of making peace with the lost parent. Later, during the stress related to getting along with another authority figure, the person blames that authority figure and has no conscious awareness that the unfinished repressed material (submerged as a transcrisis state) is at the root of the problem. Although the person with the transcrisis state may come to identify the problem as poor relationship skills and enter counseling to improve those skills, this action is also a symptom of the psychological roller-coaster ride that started with the unfinished business. The relationship skills may be temporarily improved, but the source of the transcrisis state may not have been recognized or expunged. It has merely subsided, and a temporary state of equilibrium has been achieved, but the original trauma will usually reemerge and instigate a new crisis the moment new stressors are introduced. Dynamically, this pattern is defensive repression. Therapeutically, this transcrisis state calls for crisis intervention techniques.

Transcrisis Differentiated From Posttraumatic Stress Disorder

People familiar with posttraumatic stress disorder (PTSD) may ask, "So how is a transcrisis state different from PTSD?" First, PTSD is an identifiable anxiety disorder (American Psychiatric Association, 2013) caused by an extremely traumatic event, and very specific criteria must be present for a diagnosis of PTSD to be made. Although a person who is suffering from PTSD may be in a transcrisis state, not all people who are in a transcrisis state suffer from PTSD. Indeed, it would probably be more appropriate to look at all the different kinds of anxiety and personality disorders found in the fifth edition of the *Diagnostic and Statistical Manual of Mental Disorders* (DSM-5; American Psychiatric Association, 2013) as representative of transcrisis states because of the chronic kinds of thinking, feeling, and acting that keep these individuals constantly in psychological hot, if not boiling, water.

But it is not just persons with anxiety and personality disorders who may be in a transcrisis state. A broad range of people, from so-called normal individuals who are constantly fired from jobs because of their uncontrollable tempers to those with psychoses who quit taking their medicine because it has unpleasant side effects, are also representative of individuals in transcrisis states. Armsworth and Holaday (1993), in their review of affective, behavioral, cognitive, and physiological-somatic effects of trauma, identified a number of factors that, although not found in PTSD descriptors, would probably be inherent in many

transcrisis states. The key differentiating element of a transcrisis state is that, whether it is due to trauma, personality traits, substance abuse, psychosis, or chronic environmental stressors, the state is residual and recurrent and always present to some degree. Although people in a transcrisis state are generally capable of functioning at some minimal level, they are always at risk, and any single small added stressor may tip the balance and send them into crisis. Therefore, when we assess individuals in crisis, our focus is not only on the current clinical/diagnostic state of the individual, but also, and as importantly, on the repetitious cycle of problems and the historical precursors that may have caused the crisis to arise. A medical analogy would be the person suffering from a chronic sinus condition who continually takes nasal decongestant and so can function, although at a less than optimum level. However, if the person is exposed to a virus, the sinus condition may progress to an infection and eventually pneumonia.

Being aware that someone is operating in a transcrisis state also gives us important information regarding the kind and degree of therapeutic intervention to provide, in both the short and the long term. We probably would deal far differently with the salesperson who just turned 45, lost her job with a company she had been with for 20 years, has been unemployed for 6 months, and is now clinically depressed and suicidal, than we would with the salesperson who just turned 45, lost her job for the 20th time, has been unemployed for 6 months, and is now clinically depressed and suicidal. Although immediate intervention in regard to the suicidal ideation of both women might be very similar, our view as to what caused the depression, how we would treat it, and what transcrisis issues we might expect would be very different.

Transcrisis Points

Transcrisis points occur frequently in transcrisis states within the therapeutic intervention. These points are generally marked by the client's coming to grips with new developmental stages or other dimensions of the problem. Transcrisis points do not occur in regular, predictable, linear progression. For example, an abused spouse may go through transcrisis point after transcrisis point talking to a crisis worker over the telephone before making a decision to leave the battering relationship, often calling crisis workers a dozen times in the course of a few days. The abused spouse may then make a decision to leave the battering relationship and go to a spouse abuse shelter, only to find that the necessity of making a geographic move or finding a job instigates a crisis almost as potent as the battering.

Human services workers who practice long-term therapy are often shocked, confused, and overwhelmed by the sudden disequilibrium their clients experience. Handling these transcrisis points can be the equivalent of standing in the middle of a Los Angeles freeway and attempting to stop traffic. Behaviorally, such clients may vacillate from a placid to an agitated state so fast that the worker puts out one brush fire only to be confronted by yet another. It is at these transcrisis points that standard therapeutic strategies and techniques are suspended and the therapist must operate in a crisis intervention mode.

Transcrisis points can be seen as benchmarks that are crucial to progressive stages of positive therapeutic growth. These points are characterized by approach-avoidance behavior in seeking help, taking risks, and initiating action steps toward forward movement. Encountering these transcrisis points, a person will experience the same kind of disorganization, disequilibrium, and fragmentation that surrounded the original crisis event. Leaping one hurdle does not necessarily mean that the entire crisis is successfully overcome. Survivors of a catastrophe may expunge the event from memory and then be faced with repairing gaping wounds in personal relationships that have been torn apart by their long-term pathological behavior. People who have spinal cord injuries may be successfully rehabilitated physically, but may retreat into substance addiction or become depressed and/or suicidal as they attempt to begin a new lifestyle from a wheelchair.

Therefore, it is not only the initial crisis with which the worker must contend but also each transcrisis point, as it occurs, if clients are not to slip back into the pathology that assailed them in the first place. Transcrisis points should not be confused with the jumps and starts that go with working through typical adjustment problems. Although these points may be forecast with some degree of reliability by workers who are expert in the particular field, their onset is sudden, dramatic, and extremely potent. In that regard, these psychological aftershocks can be just as damaging as the initial tremor and may require extraordinary effort on the part of the human services worker to help the client regain control. This book is also concerned with these transcrisis states and points; the cases portrayed represent both components.

Theories of Crisis and Crisis Intervention

LO4

No single theory or school of thought encompasses every view of human crisis or all the models or systems of crisis intervention. We present here a brief overview of theories relevant both to crisis (as a phenomenon) and to crisis intervention (as an intentional helping response). Janosik (1984) conceptualizes crisis theory on three different levels: basic crisis theory, expanded crisis theory, and applied crisis theory. The newly emerging ecosystem theory has been expanded into a comprehensive chapter (Chapter 17) in this text.

Basic Crisis Intervention Theory

The research, writings, and teachings of Erich Lindemann (1944, 1956) gave professionals and paraprofessionals a new understanding of crisis. Lindemann helped caregivers promote crisis intervention for many sufferers of loss who had no specific pathological diagnosis but who were exhibiting symptoms that appeared pathological. Lindemann's basic crisis theory and work made a substantive contribution to the understanding of behavior in clients whose grief crises were precipitated by loss. He helped professionals and paraprofessionals recognize that behavioral responses to crises associated with grief are normal, temporary, and amenable to alleviation through short-term intervention techniques. These "normal" grief behaviors include (1) preoccupation with the lost one, (2) identification with the lost one, (3) expressions of guilt and hostility, (4) some disorganization in daily routine, and (5) some evidence of somatic complaints (Janosik, 1984, p. 11). Lindemann negated the prevailing perception that clients manifesting crisis responses should necessarily be treated as abnormal or pathological.

Whereas Lindemann focused mainly on immediate resolution of grief after loss, Caplan (1964) expanded Lindemann's constructs to the total field of traumatic events. Caplan viewed crisis as a state resulting from impediments to life goals that cannot be overcome through customary behaviors. These impediments can arise from both developmental and situational events. Both Lindemann and Caplan dealt with crisis intervention following psychological trauma using an equilibrium/disequilibrium paradigm. The stages in Lindemann's paradigm are (1) disturbed equilibrium, (2) brief therapy or grief work, (3) client's working through the problem or grief, and (4) restoration of equilibrium (Janosik, 1984, pp. 10–12). Caplan linked Lindemann's concepts and stages to all developmental and situational events and extended crisis intervention to eliminating the affective, behavioral, and cognitive distortions that precipitated the psychological trauma in the first place.

Differentiating Basic Crisis Theory From Brief Therapy. The work of both Lindemann and Caplan gave impetus to the use of crisis intervention strategies in counseling and brief therapy with people manifesting universal human reactions to traumatic events. Whereas **brief therapy theory** typically attempts to remediate more or less ongoing emotional problems, **basic crisis theory**, following the lead of Lindemann and Caplan, focuses on helping people in crisis recognize and correct temporary affective, behavioral, and cognitive distortions brought on by traumatic events. Although brief or solution-focused therapy may be the equivalent of crisis intervention (in that it seeks to restore the person to a state of homeostasis or equilibrium), not all brief or solution-focused therapy is related to crisis intervention.

Perhaps the following example will clarify the difference between the two. A student fails one algebra test and concludes that he or she can never pass algebra, therefore cannot become an engineer (as the parents are perceived to expect/demand). The student progresses to a feeling of helplessness, then to hopelessness, and then contemplates suicide. Here, crisis intervention that focuses on suicide prevention is clearly indicated. Another student fails one algebra test and, feeling uncomfortable, disappointed, and confused, makes an appointment to see the school counselor. Here, the modality becomes a typical brief or solution-focused therapy situation wherein the emphasis is on how to improve study habits and test-taking skills.

Differentiating between brief or solution-focused therapy and crisis intervention depends on how intensely the client views the problem as intolerable or on how much emotional disequilibrium the client experiences. Severe emotional disequilibrium over the event may escalate the person into crisis and the therapist into a crisis intervention modality.

Expanded Crisis Theory

Expanded crisis theory was developed because basic theory, which depended on a psychoanalytic approach alone, did not adequately address the social, environmental, and situational factors that make an event a crisis. As crisis theory and intervention have expanded, it has become clear that an approach that identifies predisposing factors as the main or only causal agent falls short of the mark. A prime example of this restrictive view was the erroneous diagnosis, by practitioners who first encountered PTSD victims, that pathology preceding the crisis event was the real cause of the trauma. While preceding factors can certainly create a fertile field for PTSD and other psychopathology, it has become apparent that given the right combination of developmental, sociological, psychological, environmental, and situational determinants, anyone can fall victim to transient pathological symptoms. Therefore, expanded crisis theory draws not only from psychoanalytic theory but also from general systems, ecosystems, adaptational, interpersonal, chaos, and developmental theory. The following are synopses of these major theoretical components of an expanded view.

Psychoanalytic Theory. Psychoanalytic theory (Fine, 1973), applied to expanded crisis theory, is based on the view that the disequilibrium that accompanies a person's crisis can be understood through gaining access to the individual's unconscious thoughts and past emotional experiences. Psychoanalytic theory presupposes that some early childhood fixation is the primary explanation of why an event becomes a crisis. This theory may be used to help clients develop insight into the dynamics and causes of their behavior as the crisis situation acts on them.

We have come almost completely full circle in our view of this approach. First thought to be the only valid way to view pathology resulting from trauma, then dismissed as patently false and an excuse for the government not to meet the medical needs of veterans suffering from PTSD, currently treatment approaches see predisposing factors as one of the many factors that can contribute to PTSD and other psychopathologies.

Systems Theory. Systems theory (Haley, 1973, 1976; Hardy, 1997) is based not so much on what happens within an individual in crisis as on the interrelationships and interdependence among people and between people and events. Belkin (1984) adds that this theory "refers to an emotional system, a system of communications, and a system of need fulfillment and request" in which all members within an intergenerational relationship bring something to bear on the others, and each derives something from the others (pp. 350–351). Indeed, Slaikeu (1990, p. 6) defines crisis as "a helping process aimed at assisting a person or a *family* so that the probability of debilitating effects is minimized and the probability of growth is maximized."

Systems theory represents a turning away from traditional approaches, which focus only on what is going on within the client. A standard systems approach to crisis may be thought of in interpersonal terms. Systems theory is contextual in that it suggests that we look at the environment within which the person lives and the dynamic interactions the person has within that environment, which can provide information into the predisposing factors, onset, length, intensity, and resolution (Slaikeu, 1990, p. 34). Normally the "environment" in basic systems theory can be thought of as the extended family unit, the neighborhood, school, job, social clubs, fraternal or civic organizations, beauty parlors, bars, church, and so on.

Ecosystems Theory. Ecosystems theory (Bronfenbrenner, 1995) broadens out the base of the system and looks at crisis in relation to the environmental context within which it occurs (James, Cogdal, & Gilliland, 2003; Myer & Moore, 2006). Systemic interactions may occur from the microsystem (family and community) out to the macrosystem (nation) or vice versa. There is great value in looking at crises in their total social and environmental settings—not simply as one individual being affected in a linear progression of cause-and-effect events (Hardy, 1997; James & Gilliland, 2003, pp. 336–368). Cook (2012, pp. 6–7) proposes that an ecological counseling perspective operates with three fundamental propositions: First, while behavior is personal (the individual) it also contextual (the physical environment and the culture within which the individual operates); second, behavior is interactional in the sense that individuals influence and are influenced by the environments within which they function; third, individuals attempt to control and make sense of what environments they are engaging that ranges from their romantic choices, their career preferences, the churches they decide to attend, or their recreational decisions to collect stamps as opposed to climbing mountains. Thus people continuously attempt to make meaning of the multiple contexts in the environment so they can operate effectively, and that is no small chore. These three propositions take on added importance during a crisis because all the previous meaning making and

sense of how one *has* operated effectively in a familiar environment may go flying out the window in a crisis environment where chaos calls for a whole new set of tactics and strategies.

The fundamental concept of ecosystems theory is analogous to "ecological systems in which all elements are interrelated, and in which change at any level of those interrelated parts will lead to alteration of the total system" (Cormier & Hackney, 1987, p. 217). Passage of time, proximity to the epicenter of the crisis, and what develops over time and the environment all contribute to the ultimate resolution of the crisis. Ecosystems theory comes into play most typically when large-scale disasters occur and affect very large **macrosystems (the total culture in which people live)**. The expanding role of communication systems and their ability or inability to link systems is a critical ingredient that will be explored in Chapter 17, Disaster Response.

Adaptational Theory. Adaptational theory, as we use the term, depicts a person's crisis as being sustained through maladaptive behaviors, negative thoughts, and destructive defense mechanisms. Adaptational crisis theory is based on the premise that the person's crisis will recede when these maladaptive coping behaviors are changed to adaptive behaviors.

Breaking the chain of maladjusted functioning means changing to adaptive behavior, promoting positive thoughts, and constructing defense mechanisms that will help the person overcome the immobility created by the crisis and move to a positive mode of functioning. As maladaptive behaviors are learned, so may adaptive behaviors be learned. Aided by the interventionist, the client may learn to replace old, debilitating behaviors with new, self-enhancing ones. Such new behaviors may be applied directly to the context of the crisis and ultimately result in either success or reinforcement for the client in overcoming the crisis (Cormier & Cormier, 1985, p. 148). People who have learned ineffective coping skills and continue to use them even though they continually wind up in psychological hot water best manifest this approach. Changing ingrained and entrenched behaviors and thoughts that create transcrisis invariably means changing adaptive mechanisms and coping skills—not an easy job!

Interpersonal Theory. Interpersonal theory (Rogers, 1977) is built on many of the dimensions Cormier and Hackney (1987) describe as enhancing personal self-esteem: openness, trust, sharing, safety, unconditional positive regard, accurate empathy, and genuineness (pp. 35–64). The essence of interpersonal theory is that people cannot sustain a personal state of crisis for very long if they believe in themselves and in others and have confidence that they can become self-actualized and overcome the crisis. When people confer their locus of self-evaluation on others, they become dependent on others for validation of their being (Raskin & Rogers, 1995). Therefore, as long as a person maintains an external locus of control, the crisis will persist.

The outcome goal in interpersonal theory is returning the power of self-evaluation to the person. Doing so enables the person once again to control his or her own destiny and regain the ability to take whatever action is needed to cope with the crisis situation. In terms of crisis intervention, interpersonal theory is reflected in the initial tasks of Predispositioning, Problem Exploration, and Providing Support in our overall crisis intervention model to be introduced in Chapter 3.

Chaos Theory. Why is a meteorologist (Lorenz, 1993) who thinks a butterfly cruising along in a jungle path in the Amazon capable of starting a hurricane in the Atlantic getting a reference in a crisis intervention book? Furthermore, what in the world do words like *fractals, bifurcations, intermittences, folded towel diffeomorphisms,* and *smooth noodle maps* have to do with crisis? These are all concepts that seek to capture the structural complexity underlying chaos theory, and Edward Lorenz in his attempts to better predict weather patterns is seen as its founder. The primary reason we include chaos theory is, as you may well imagine, that in most crises there is a lot of chaos! But lo and behold, it turns out that chaos isn't random and that it has all kinds of ramifications for a range of other occupations, including crisis interventionists. Early conceptualizations of chaos theory by scientists in the fields of meteorology, mathematics, and physics viewed the theory as applying to systems or events that appeared random but, on closer inspection, revealed an underlying order (Gleick, 2008). Paradoxically, what happens in chaotic systems appears to be random and unpredictable so that there is no possibility of determining what future outcomes will be, but in fact there is (Lorenz, 1993, p. 9).

Chaos theory is really sort of a theory of evolution when applied to human functioning such as crisis intervention. It is evolutionary in that it is essentially an open-ended, ever-changing, "self-organizing" system whereby a new system may emerge out of the crisis (Butz, 1995, 1997; Chamberlain, 1993, 1994). A chaotic (crisis) situation—which Postrel (1998, p. xv) calls "emergent complex messiness"—evolves into a "self-organizing" mode whenever a critical mass of people come to perceive that they have no way to identify patterns or preplan options to solve the dilemma at hand. Because the chaotic situation falls outside of known alternative solutions, both physicists and human services workers necessarily resort to spontaneous, trial-and-error experimentation to try to cope with the crisis. The "messiness" of the crisis lies not in disorder but in an order that is unknown, unpredictable, and spontaneous, an ever-shifting pattern driven by millions of uncoordinated, independent factors that necessitate experimentation, yet may finally result in a global clarification of the crisis. Such experimentation may lead to false starts, temporary failure, dead ends, spontaneous innovation, creativity, improvisation, brainstorming, cooperative enterprise, and other "evolutionary" attempts to make sense of and cope with the crisis (Gleick, 2008, pp. 33–42). Indeed, chaos theory has many parallels with another emerging field called evolutionary psychology which, as you can also well imagine, is not without its controversial aspects (Confer et al., 2010).

The crisis intervention attempts in the wake of British Petroleum's Deep Horizon well blowout provide a vivid example of chaos theory at work—in both a positive and a negative sense. So it is not just the "messiness" of an utterly new phenomenon like the blowout of the deep well in the Gulf of Mexico and attempts to look at and fix the disaster at one fixed point such as the wellhead. While that point is critical, it is also reductionistic in terms of chaos theory and doesn't look at the total gestalt, or "big picture," of the economic, ecological, and psychological costs of the crisis. All the tangled threads and points on the fabric of the crisis don't portray the underlying and interlocking patterns that provide information about the big picture and the potential ramifications of these dynamic systems on one another and on the total system after the crisis erupts.

Okay, so you didn't sign up for a course in higher mathematics or physics, which is where chaos's roots are, and the foregoing paragraphs are making your hair hurt! But a basic understanding of this exotic and esoteric theory should give you two important pieces of information. First, big crises call for a lot of different people working from a lot of different perspectives in a well-coordinated manner who can connect the myriad dots in a chaotic situation, see the underlying patterns, make sense of them, and change to meet changing conditions as new eddies and vortexes swirl out of the crisis. Myer and his associates have attempted to demonstrate what this theory looks and acts like when combined with ecosystemic theory after a disaster on a college campus (Myer, James, & Moulton, 2011).

Second, transcrises come close to manifesting chaos theory at work. Lots of times transcrises don't make sense and don't appear to have any discernable pattern, but much like the theoretical mathematician, just because you don't have an equation to solve the problem doesn't mean that one doesn't exist. There is an underlying pattern, and that's why all professional crisis interventionists use the right side of their brain a lot because dealing with crisis calls for a lot of creative thinking. No other writers at present are discussing chaos theory as it applies to crisis intervention, but our guess is that they will as we attempt to unravel and understand the genetics that make up this field.

Developmental Theory.

Because many crises have their bases in developmental stages that humans pass through, developmental theory must play a part in crisis intervention. Developmental stage theorists such as Erikson (1963), Levinson (1986), Levinson and Levinson (1996), and Blocher (2000) clearly believe that movement through various developmental life stages is critical. Developmental tasks that are not met and accomplished during particular life stages tend to pile up and cause problems. As individual needs and wants butt heads with the demands and expectations of society, and the individual fails to move on to the next life stage, the potential for crisis arises. Neglected, abused, and bullied children; alienated and isolated adolescent drug abusers; people who lack education or lack vocational satisfaction or success; or those exposed to domestic violence, divorce, suicide, homicide, and a host of other problems may be unable to meet life stages effectively. When an external, environmental, or situational crisis feeds into preexisting developmental crises, intrapersonal and interpersonal problems may reach the breaking point.

Applied Crisis Theory

Brammer (1985, pp. 94–95) characterizes applied crisis theory as encompassing three domains: (1) normal *developmental crises,* (2) *situational crises,* and (3) *existential crises.* Given the ecosystem theory perspective, we have added a fourth domain, (4) *ecosystemic crises.*

Developmental Crises.

Developmental crises are events in the normal flow of human growth and evolution whereby a dramatic change or shift occurs that produces abnormal responses. For example, developmental crises may occur in response to the birth of a child, graduation from college, midlife career change, retirement, or even the aging process. Developmental crises are considered normal; however, all persons and all developmental crises are unique and must be assessed and handled in unique ways.

Situational Crises.

A situational crisis emerges with the occurrence of uncommon and extraordinary events that an individual has no way of forecasting or controlling. Situational crises may follow such events as terrorist attacks, automobile accidents, kidnappings, rapes, job loss, or sudden illness and death. The key to differentiating a situational crisis from other crises is that a situational crisis is random, sudden, shocking, intense, and often catastrophic.

Existential Crises.

An existential crisis includes the inner conflicts and anxieties that accompany important human issues of purpose, responsibility, independence, freedom, and commitment. An existential crisis might accompany the realization, at age 40, that one will never make a significant and distinct impact on a particular profession or organization; remorse, at age 50, that one chose never to marry or leave one's parents' home, never made a separate life, and now has lost forever the possibility of being a fully happy and worthwhile person; or a pervasive and persistent feeling, at age 60, that one's life is meaningless—that there is a void that can never be filled in a meaningful way.

Ecosystemic Crises.

Ecosystemic crises typically occur when some *natural* or *human-caused* disaster overtakes a person or a (large or small) group of people who find themselves, through no fault or action of their own, inundated in the aftermath of an event that may adversely affect virtually every member of the environment in which they live. Such crises may be the result of natural phenomena such as hurricanes, floods, tsunamis, earthquakes, volcanic eruptions, tornadoes, blizzards, mudslides, drought, famine, and forest or grassland/brush fires. Other instances of ecosystemic crises may be *biologically derived,* such as a disease epidemic like ebola, or the effects of a huge oil spill; *politically based,* as in war, a refugee crisis associated with war, or ethnic cleansing; or *severe economic depression,* such as the Great Depression of the early 20th century.

Crisis Intervention Models

Three basic crisis intervention models discussed by both Leitner (1974) and Belkin (1984) are the *equilibrium model,* the *cognitive model,* and the *psychosocial transition model.* These three generic models provide the groundwork for many different crisis intervention strategies and methodologies. Two new models that target ecological factors that contribute to crisis are the *developmental-ecological model* (Collins & Collins, 2005) and the *contextual-ecological model* (Myer & Moore, 2006). Two field-based practice models are *psychological first aid* (Raphael, 1977; U.S. Department of Veterans Affairs, 2011), which is used in the immediate aftermath of disasters and terrorist attacks, and Roberts' (2005) ACT model, which is more generic but primarily trauma based.

The Equilibrium Model

The equilibrium model is really an equilibrium/disequilibrium model. People in crisis are in a state of psychological or emotional disequilibrium in which their usual coping mechanisms and problem-solving methods fail to meet their needs. The goal of the equilibrium model is to help people recover a state of precrisis equilibrium (Caplan, 1961). The equilibrium model seems most appropriate for early intervention, when the person is out of control, disoriented, and unable to make appropriate choices. Until the person has regained some coping abilities, the main focus is on stabilizing the individual. Up to the time the person has reacquired some definite measure of stability, little else can or should be done. For example, it does little good to dig into the underlying factors that cause suicidal ideation until the person can be stabilized to the point of agreeing that life is worth living for at least another week. This is probably the purest model of crisis intervention and is most likely to be used at the onset of the crisis (Caplan, 1961; Leitner, 1974; Lindemann, 1944).

The Cognitive Model

The cognitive model of crisis intervention is based on the premise that crises are rooted in faulty thinking about the events or situations that surround the crisis—not in the events themselves or the facts about the events or situations (Ellis, 1962). The goal of this model is to help people become aware of and change their views and beliefs about the crisis events or situations. The basic tenet of the cognitive model is that people can gain control of crises in their lives by changing their thinking, especially by recognizing and disputing the irrational and self-defeating parts of their cognitions, and by retaining and focusing on the rational and self-enhancing elements of their thinking.

The messages that people in crisis send themselves become very negative and twisted, in contrast to the reality of the situation. Dilemmas that are constant and grinding wear people out, pushing their internal state of perception more and more toward negative self-talk until their cognitive sets are so negative that no amount of preaching can convince them that anything positive will ever come from the situation. Their behavior soon follows this negative self-talk and begets a self-fulfilling prophecy that the situation is hopeless. At this juncture, crisis intervention becomes a job of rewiring the individual's thoughts to more positive feedback loops by practicing and rehearsing new self-statements about the situation until the old, negative, debilitating ones are expunged. The cognitive model seems most appropriate after the client has been stabilized and returned to an approximate state of precrisis equilibrium. Basic components of this approach are found in the rational-emotive work of Ellis (1982), the cognitive-behavioral approach of Meichenbaum (1977), and the cognitive system of Beck (1976).

The Psychosocial Transition Model

The psychosocial transition model assumes that people are products of their genes plus the learning they have absorbed from their particular social environments. Because people are continuously changing, developing, and growing, and their social environments and social influences (Dorn, 1986) are continuously evolving, crises may be related to internal or external (psychological, social, or environmental) difficulties. The goal of crisis intervention is to collaborate with clients in assessing the internal and external difficulties contributing to the crisis and then help them choose workable alternatives to their current behaviors, attitudes, and use of environmental resources. Clients may need to incorporate adequate internal coping mechanisms, social supports, and environmental resources in order to gain autonomous (noncrisis) control over their lives.

The psychosocial model does not perceive crisis as simply an internal state of affairs that resides totally within the individual. It reaches outside the individual and asks what systems need to be changed. Peers, family, occupation, religion, and the community are but a few of the external dimensions that promote or hinder psychological adaptiveness. With certain kinds of crisis problems, few lasting gains will be made unless the social systems that affect the individual are also changed, or the individual comes to terms with and understands the dynamics of those systems and how they affect adaptation to the crisis. Like the cognitive model, the psychosocial transition model seems to be most appropriate after the client has been stabilized. Theorists who have contributed to the psychosocial transition model include Adler (Ansbacher & Ansbacher, 1956), Erikson (1963), and Minuchin (1974).

The Developmental–Ecological Model

Collins and Collins (2005) have developed a developmental-ecological model of crisis intervention that integrates developmental stages and issues with the environment within which the individual operates. In this model, the crisis worker needs to assess both the individual and the environment as well as the interrelationship between the two and then factor in the developmental stage within which the person is operating. Any situational crisis must always be considered in relationship to the stage of development the person is in, and the potency of the crisis may depend on how well there has been stage mastery of the tasks affected by the crisis.

The Contextual–Ecological Model

Myer and Moore (2006) have developed an ecological model that focuses on contextual elements of the crisis. Their first premise is that contextual elements may be seen as layered. These layers are dependent on two elements: proximity to the crisis by physical distance, and reactions that are moderated by perception and the meaning attributed to the event.

The second premise of this model is that reciprocal impact occurs between the individual and systems affected by the event. Understanding the reciprocal effect of the crisis involves recognition of two elements: the interaction among the primary and secondary relationships, and the degree of change triggered by the event. Primary relationships are those in which no intervening component (other individuals or systems) interacts with or mediates the connection. An example of a primary relationship would be between an employee and a company. If an accident occurred and the company immediately took a number of steps to support employees and assure them that safety measures had been increased so that such an accident would be unlikely to happen again, the employees might feel secure, safe, and satisfied with the company's efforts. A secondary relationship is mediated by at least one other individual or system. For example, if the employee's family members were so terrified for the safety of their loved one that no amount of assurances would satisfy them, then the primary relationship between the employee and the company would be affected.

The third premise is that time directly influences the impact of a crisis. The two major time elements are the amount of time that has passed and special occasions such as anniversaries and holidays following the event.

Myer and Moore (2006) propose a formula for gauging the impact of the crisis on the individual or system. The formula can be summarized as a function of proximity to the event, reaction to the event, relationship to the event, and amount of change caused by the event, which is then divided by the amount of time that has passed. What is critical in this formula is understanding that no single component can be considered separately. Close proximity alone may not have as much bearing on the impact of the crisis as the degree of change resulting from it. While this highly theoretical model as of yet has no empirical basis, nor does it yet have a great deal of utility for intervention, it poses questions and generates premises that can help us understand the impact of the crisis as it interacts between and within a variety of systems and individuals.

Psychological First Aid

Slaikeu (1990, p. 6) breaks crisis intervention **LO6** into two parts: First-order intervention, or **psychological first aid**, seeks to address the immediate crisis situation and provide immediate relief, possibly to a wide range of individuals. Second-order intervention, or **crisis therapy**, seeks to resolve the crisis and is generally provided by trained, licensed human services professionals. In this book, most of what would be seen as psychological first aid and initial crisis therapy is what we define as crisis intervention. To attend to the mental health needs of survivors of large-scale disasters, public health personnel are now being taught to use empirically grounded, best practice techniques called psychological first aid that are designed to provide immediate, palliative mental health assistance to survivors (Parker, Barnett, Everly, & Links, 2006).

The National Institute of Mental Health (2002) defines psychological first aid as establishing the safety of the client, reducing stress-related symptoms, providing rest and physical recuperation, and linking clients to critical resources and social support systems. Raphael (1977) first coined the term *psychological first aid* in her discussion of crisis work with an Australian railway disaster. She described a variety of activities that provided caring support, empathic responding, concrete information and assistance, and reuniting of survivors with social support systems. Paramount in psychological first aid is attending to Maslow's needs hierarchy and taking care of survival needs first. Many counselors, social workers, and psychologists helped meet basic support needs of food, shelter, clothing, and other survival needs during the aftermath of Hurricane Katrina before they ever did any "counseling."

Controversy has arisen over who should get care, what kind of care should be provided, how it should be delivered, by whom, and under what circumstances immediately after a traumatic event—especially after a mass disaster. Much of this controversy has arisen in regard to critical incident stress debriefing (Mitchell & Everly, 1995) and the notion that everybody exposed to a traumatic event needs to talk about it as quickly after the event as possible to stave off PTSD. A huge controversy has erupted over this treatment approach (to be discussed in Chapter 17), to the point that the prevailing approach for immediate disaster intervention is now psychological first aid that is nonintrusive and does not promote discussion of the traumatic event (Young, 2006). The notion is that not all people will need psychological help and the initial paratraumatic symptoms that most people manifest will self-eradicate in a short period of time (National Institute of Mental Health, 2002).

The National Center for PTSD (U.S. Department of Veterans Affairs, 2011) has published a field manual, *Psychological First Aid: Field Operations Guide*, that offers an evidence-informed modular approach for assisting people in the immediate aftermath of disaster and terrorism, to reduce initial distress and to foster short- and long-term adaptive functioning. The manual states that it is for use by first responders, incident command systems, primary and emergency health care providers, school crisis response teams, faith-based organizations, disaster relief organizations, Community Emergency Response Teams, Medical Reserve Corps, and the Citizens Corps in diverse settings. This approach to psychological first aid includes eight core actions (U.S. Department of Veterans Affairs, 2011, p. 18):

1. **Contact and Engagement**
   Goal: To respond to contacts initiated by survivors, or to initiate contacts in a nonintrusive, compassionate, and helpful manner.

2. **Safety and Comfort**
   Goal: To enhance immediate and ongoing safety, and provide physical and emotional comfort.

3. **Stabilization** (if needed)
   Goal: To calm and orient emotionally overwhelmed or disoriented survivors.

4. **Information Gathering: Current Needs and Concerns**
   Goal: To identify immediate needs and concerns, gather additional information, and tailor psychological first aid interventions.

5. **Practical Assistance**
   Goal: To offer practical help to survivors in addressing immediate needs and concerns.

6. **Connection with Social Supports**
   Goal: To help establish brief or ongoing contacts with primary support persons and other sources of support, including family members, friends, and community helping resources.

7. **Information on Coping**
   Goal: To provide information about stress reactions and coping to reduce distress and promote adaptive functioning.

8. **Linkage with Collaborative Services**
   Goal: To link survivors with available services needed at the time or in the future.

Psychological first aid provides the bare-bones basics of crisis intervention. It is designed to be palliative. It is not designed to cure or fix anything, but rather to provide nonintrusive physical and psychological support. Social workers would be very comfortable with this model because a great deal of it resembles social work services. If we consider the first four tasks (Predispositioning, Problem Definition, Providing Support, Safety) of the model of crisis intervention you will meet in Chapter 3 as being close to what is meant by psychological first aid, then psychological first aid is clearly necessary. Whether it is also *sufficient* in providing immediate crisis intervention services is another matter. Certainly not all people need immediate psychological assistance, nor should they have it forced on them, but the high adrenal moments of a lot of crisis intervention make us believe that something more than psychological first aid is needed to defuse emotional volatility, de-escalate life-threatening behavior, and reframe and cool the insane, irrational, hot cognitions that typify many crisis situations.

The ACT Model

The ACT model proposed by Roberts (2005) is an acronym:

Assessment of the presenting problem, including emergency psychiatric and other medical needs and trauma assessment

Connecting clients to support systems

Traumatic reactions and posttraumatic stress disorders

The model has seven generally linear stages: crisis assessment, establishing rapport, identifying major problems, dealing with feelings, generating and exploring alternatives, developing plans, and providing follow-up (pp. 104–106). This model has been designed to deal with the onset of a traumatic event and, probably even more appropriately, with what Kleespies (2009) calls behavioral emergencies.

Playbook/Game Plan Model

As you will see in detail in this book, specially trained police officers called Crisis Intervention Team (CIT) officers are playing a larger and larger role as first line responders to the mentally ill and other emotional distraught individuals who come to the attention of law enforcement. Major Sam Cochran (retired former co-ordinator of the Memphis Police Department CIT) has developed a crisis intervention model based on coaching, which has a great deal of face validity given that most police officers have engaged in some kind of team sport so a playbook/game plan makes perfect sense and there is ready acceptance in trying to learn it. It is specifically tailored to diffuse and de-escalate angry, distraught, out-of-control potentially lethal individuals that are in the middle of a crisis and who come to police attention through 911 "mental illness" calls (Kirchberg, James, Cochran, & Dupont, 2013). It trains first line responders through a game plan strategy that teaches them how to assess individuals' verbal and nonverbal behavior and develop a game plan that uses a combination of verbal de-escalation techniques (plays) to defuse individuals who may be manifesting lethal behavior toward themselves or others. We will visit some of these "plays" in Chapter 4, The Tools of the Trade.

Eclectic/Integrated Crisis Intervention Theory

In current psychotherapeutic theory the term "eclectic" has taken on a somewhat negative connotation as a sort of "anything goes, try and see if it works" approach and has generally been replaced with the term "integrated", which critics of "eclecticism" believe implies a more purposeful and planful treatment methodology. As far as we're concerned, it's a "rose" by any name so call it what you will; we believe it's a best bet on how to go about doing the business of crisis intervention. Eclectic/integrated crisis intervention involves intentionally and systematically selecting and integrating valid concepts and strategies from all available approaches to helping clients. Eclecticism/integrated theory is thus a hybrid of all available approaches. It operates from a task orientation, as opposed to concepts. Its major tasks (James & Gilliland, 2003, p. 374; Lazarus, 1989; Thorne, 1973, p. 451) are (1) to identify valid elements in all therapeutic systems and integrate them into an internally consistent whole that does justice to the behavioral data to be explained; (2) to consider all pertinent theories, methods, and standards for evaluating and manipulating clinical data according to the most advanced knowledge of time and place; and (3) to identify with no specific theory, keep an open mind, and continuously experiment with those formulations and strategies that produce successful results. This theoretical approach would find favor with current multicultural and social justice approaches to counseling because the workers enter into the relationship with no preconceived notion of the "right" therapeutic approach, but rather allows the social and cultural factors that contribute to the client's problems to unfold before making a decision on what the "best bet" approach to take might be (Ratts & Pedersen, 2014, p. 7).

Throughout this book, you will find an eclectic/integrated approach to the interventions presented. Much of what happens will depend on the situation with which we find ourselves. "Situation" may be defined as including the type of crisis, the physical and ecological setting in which it occurs, individual characteristics, cultural background, and significant others who may be directly or indirectly involved. Probably more important than all the factors that affect clients are the knowledge, strength, and skills that interventionists bring to the crisis and meld these into the client's world.

The eclectic/integrated approach fuses two pervasive themes: (1) all people and all crises are unique and distinctive, and (2) all people and all crises are similar. We do not see these themes as mutually exclusive. All people and all crises are similar in that there are global elements to specific crisis types. The dynamics of bereavement are generic and provide us with general guidelines for intervention. However, treating individual cases of bereavement is anything but generic. How a family perceives the impact of the death of a member depends on a number of factors: the deceased member's place in the family, what each member of the family does in response to the death, and how the changed family system now operates. Treatment of surviving family members who have lost a child after rearing five others, as opposed to those who have lost their only child, born late in the parents' life, who had become the focus of existence for the couple, may call for far different intervention strategies even if bereavement is the generic issue.

An eclectic/integrated approach does not mean taking a therapeutic shotgun and aimlessly blasting away at the crisis. Using an eclectic approach means not being bound by and locked into any one theoretical approach in a dogmatic fashion. Rather, it means being well versed in a number of approaches and theories and being able to assess the client's needs so that appropriate techniques can be planned and fitted to them. Many human services workers avow an eclectic/integrated approach but actually use the word to rationalize not being able to do anything very well. Being a true eclectic/integrated interventionist means doing lots of hard work, reading, studying, experiencing, and being supervised and critiqued by other professionals. It also means taking risks and being willing to abandon an approach that on first inspection might seem reasonable and proper but, once entered, proves fruitless for the particular situation.

Eclectic/integrated therapy performed well is equal parts skill and intuition. Paying attention to your feelings as much as to your cognition about the situation is crucial. Changing to a more effective intervention is often based on nothing more scientific than a feeling that something is amiss. Although having a "gut" feeling is little justification, in the scientific sense, for doing something, it can nevertheless be a sound basis for action. There is no known formula for deciding when to move from a nondirective to a highly directive stance with a client in crisis; nor is there an equation that tells a therapist that mental imagery may be more effective than confrontation as an intervention technique. An eclectic approach done well is the zenith of the performing art of crisis intervention.

Characteristics of Effective Crisis Workers

LO7

Almost everyone can be taught the techniques in this book and with practice can employ them with some degree of skill. However, the crisis worker who can take intervention to the performing art level is more than the sum of techniques read about and skills mastered. A master of this art is going to have not only technical skill and theoretical knowledge but also a good deal of the following characteristics.

Life Experiences

The worker handles a crisis or not to the extent that he or she is a whole person or not (Carkhuff & Berenson, 1977, pp. 162–163). A whole person has a rich and varied background of life experiences. These life experiences serve as a resource for emotional maturity that, combined with training, enables workers to be stable, consistent, and well integrated not only within the crisis situation but also in their daily lives. However, life experiences alone are not sufficient to qualify one to be a crisis worker and can be debilitating if they continue to influence the worker in negative ways.

This issue is central to crisis intervention because many people who work as volunteers, support personnel, and professionals are products of their own crisis environments. They have chosen to work with people experiencing the same kind of crisis they themselves have suffered, and they use their experiential background as a resource in working with others. For example, recovering addicts may work in alcohol and drug units, battered women work in spouse abuse centers, and PTSD victims counsel in veterans' centers. These professionals have had firsthand experience with the trauma their clients have experienced. Does this background give them an edge over other workers who have not suffered the same pain?

The answer is a qualified yes—qualified in that the person who carries emotional baggage into the helping relationship may be even less effective than the person who has had few if any life experiences. One sees examples of emotional carryover into the intervention process in the proselytizing recovering alcoholic who vilifies others to assuage his own insecurities and fears about "falling off the wagon" and in the child abuse worker, herself a former victim of sexual abuse, who castigates mothers for their failure to confront abusing fathers.

Such human services workers may have tremendous difficulties because they mingle many of their own problems with those of their clients. The workers alternate among feeling states characterized by sympathy, anger, disappointment, and cynicism, which are detrimental both to themselves and to their clients. We do not believe crisis workers must have "lived in the crisis" to be able to understand and deal with it effectively. We do believe that interventionists who have successfully overcome some of life's problems and have put those problems into perspective will have assets of maturity, optimism, tenacity, and tough-mindedness that will help them marshal their psychological resources to assist their clients.

You should also be cautioned that on-the-job training in this business is a very arduous way to win one's spurs, particularly for a worker who has led a sheltered, constricted life and decides through misguided idealism to become a Florence Nightingale and fix the problems of the world. This rose-colored view does little for clients in general and may do considerable harm to workers as their good intentions pave the road to **burnout**. We hasten to add that chronological age has very little to do with having or not having self-enhancing life experiences and a broader, more resilient viewpoint. We know people ranging in age from 21 to 65 who are emotional adolescents. When threatened by face-to-face encounters with the real world, they may be characterized by rigidity, insularity, and insecurity. The ideal crisis worker is one who has experienced life, has learned and grown from those experiences, and supports those experiences in his or her work by thorough training, knowledge, and supervision. This individual constantly seeks to integrate all these aspects into his or her therapeutic intervention in particular and into living in general.

Personal Characteristics

Poise. The nature of crisis intervention is that the worker is often confronted with shocking and threatening material from clients who are completely out of control. Probably the most significant help the interventionist can provide at this juncture is to remain calm, poised, and in control (Belkin, 1984, p. 427). Creating a stable and rational atmosphere provides a model for the client that is conducive to restoring equilibrium to the situation. Effective crisis workers are as steady and well-anchored psychologically as the Rock of Gibraltar. This does not mean that effective crisis workers are made of stone and are not frightened, tense, anxious, and at times unsure

of themselves. However, in the very act of making self-disclosing owning statements of his or her own frailties and shortcomings, the worker models the assuredness, transparency, and congruency that are prized professional assets in any professional human service worker (Carkhuff, 1987; Rogers, 1961).

Creativity and Flexibility. Creativity and flexibility are major assets to those confronted with perplexing and seemingly unsolvable problems (Aguilera & Messick, 1982, p. 24). In our courses and training workshops, students and trainees often have difficulty conducting role plays with peers because they have no formula for getting the "right" answer. Although practice in tough role-play situations builds confidence, how creative individuals are in difficult situations depends in large measure on how well they have nurtured their own creativity over the course of their lives by taking risks and practicing divergent thinking.

Energy and Resiliency. Functioning in the unknown areas that are characteristic of crisis intervention requires energy, organization, direction, and systematic action (Carkhuff & Berenson, 1977, p. 194). Professional training can provide organizational guidelines and principles for systematic acting. What it cannot do is provide the energy requisite to perform this work. A crisis worker must also be resilient. By its very nature crisis work has many "downs" when, no matter how capable, no matter how committed, no matter what was tried or done, "success" was not achieved. Crisis workers must have "bounce back" potential. They take care of themselves physically and psychologically and make wise use of their available energy.

Quick Mental Reflexes. Crisis work differs from typical therapeutic intervention in that time is a critical factor. Crisis intervention requires more activity and directiveness than ordinary therapeutic endeavors usually do. Time to reflect and mull over problems is a rare commodity in crisis intervention. The worker must have fast mental reflexes to deal with the constantly emerging and changing issues that occur in the crisis. The worker who cannot think fast and accurately is going to find this business very frustrating indeed.

Assertiveness. One of the major problems that interventionists who have been trained in formal professional programs experience in attempting to apply the skills in this book is their reticence at times to be proactive, assertive, and directive. These therapeutic stances run counter to what has been hammered into them with regard to not being judgmental, not breeding client dependence, not imposing their values on the client, being accepting, and unconditionally positively regarding their clients as human beings of worth. While we believe wholeheartedly in those dictums, and employ them whenever possible, crisis intervention has different rules.

Many clients who are in crisis do not talk or act nicely. For that reason you need to be able to assertively set limits to behavior, both in regard to maintaining your own integrity and keeping the client stabilized so that intervention can occur. Clients are likely to have exhausted their repertory of coping skills and drained their psychological resources to the point that their ability to take action, think constructively, or control feelings is gone. At such times crisis interventionists cannot be passive. You are the expert on the scene, you have the fund of knowledge needed, and you need to employ your skills, knowledge, and abilities in as clear and directive manner as you possibly can. The nine intentional helping strategies described in Chapter 4 are predominately interventionist driven and have little passivity or reactivity. Much like competitive athletics, if you are going to do this well, you need to get your game face on and get actively involved.

Other Attributes.   Crisis workers have found the following attributes to be of utmost importance to themselves and their clients: tenacity, the ability to delay gratification, courage, optimism, a reality orientation, calmness under duress, objectivity, a strong and positive self-concept, and abiding faith that human beings are strong, resilient, and capable of overcoming seemingly insurmountable odds. They also have a spiritual sense in that they know when to seek nourishment from that spiritual source and when to let that higher power take over for them (Hardiman & Simmonds, 2013; Naz, Suri, & Parveen, 2012). Poll yourself: Do you have these attributes? We also want

you to understand that admission into the inner circle of the profession is not reserved solely for a few supermen and superwomen. Most interventionists we know, certainly including ourselves, are at times perplexed, frustrated, angry, afraid, threatened, incompetent, foolish, vain, troubled, and otherwise unequal to the task. We allow ourselves and our students and trainees at least one mistake per day and go on from there. We would very much like you to remember that cognitive billboard, "You get one free," and place it squarely in the forefront of your mind. Few readers of a book ever look at the dedication. We'd like you to do that now and meet the two people to which the eighth edition of this book is dedicated. They represent the very best of what one aspires to be in this business, and you could do far worse than model your career after these two consummate professionals.

Rewards

Standing up to the intense heat of the crisis situation to help people through seemingly unsolvable problems is some of the most gratifying and positively reinforcing work you can do in the psychotherapy business. The intense personal rewards that accrue to crisis workers lead us to believe that this work would be high on Glasser's (1976) list of positive addicting behaviors.

Now consider for a moment yourself as a client. Everyone is at times subject to the whims of a randomly cruel universe, and the kinds of crises that are dealt with in this book are apt to be visited on us all. Understanding how to navigate through these constellations of problems is a valuable resource. How well we live depends on our ability to handle the problems that confront us when we least expect them. As you read through the material, you may find yourself "living into" some of these problems and asking yourself, "I wonder how I'd fare if I were a client?" We believe that this too is a worthwhile perspective if you can look beyond the dilemmas to the coping techniques and bank them for future reference and use.

SUMMARY

Historically, crisis intervention has developed and evolved in about the last 60 years. Its origins have typically been in grassroots organizations, groups of people who came together to solve a specific crisis

that was assailing them. Through both natural and human-made crises and the influence of the media, crisis intervention has moved from a backwater psychological specialty into the mainstream of helping skills.

Our composite definition of *individual crisis*, derived from the sources given at the beginning of this chapter, is *a perception or experiencing of an event or situation as an intolerable difficulty that exceeds the person's current resources and coping mechanisms. Unless the person obtains relief, the crisis has the potential to cause severe affective, behavioral, and cognitive malfunctioning up to the point of instigating injurious or lethal behavior to oneself or others.* Because systems play an equally important part in the business of crisis intervention, we define *systemic crisis* as follows: *When a traumatic event occurs such that people, institutions, communities, and ecologies are overwhelmed and response systems are unable to effectively contain and control the event in regard to both physical and psychological reactions to it, the crisis has become systemic.* These general definitions are enhanced by considering several important principles and characteristics of crisis:

1. Crisis embodies both danger and opportunity for the person experiencing the crisis.
2. Crisis is usually time limited but may develop into a series of recurring transcrisis points.
3. Crisis is often complex and difficult to resolve.
4. The life experiences of crisis and other human services workers may greatly enhance their effectiveness in crisis intervention.
5. Crisis contains the seeds of growth and impetus for change.
6. Panaceas or quick fixes may not be applicable to many crisis situations.
7. Crisis confronts people with choices.
8. Emotional disequilibrium and disorganization accompany crisis.
9. The resolution of crisis and the personhood of crisis workers interrelate.

Understanding transcrisis states and transcrisis points helps in understanding many crises. Clients experiencing crises rooted in their transcrisis states or transcrisis points show recurring trauma-like symptoms derived from earlier traumatic events. Transcrisis states and points have parallels with and differences from PTSD.

Basic crisis theory views crisis as situational or developmental rather than pathological in nature. *Expanded crisis theory* adds to and enhances basic theory by incorporating and adapting components from psychoanalytic, general systems, ecosystems, adaptational, interpersonal, chaos, and developmental theory.

Five fundamental crisis intervention models are equilibrium, cognitive, psychosocial transition, developmental-ecological, and contextual-ecological. The *equilibrium model*, probably the most widely known model of the five, defines equilibrium as an emotional state in which the person is stable, in control, or psychologically mobile. It defines disequilibrium as an emotional state that accompanies instability, loss of control, and psychological immobility. The *cognitive model* views the crisis state as resulting from faulty thinking and belief about life's dilemmas and traumas. The *psychosocial transition model* assumes that people are products of both hereditary endowment and environmental learning and that crisis may be caused by psychological, social, or environmental factors. The *developmental-ecological model* considers developmental stages in relation to the ecological system within which the individual develops. A *contextual-ecological model* looks at layers, relationships, and time when it examines a crisis. The *psychological first aid* and *ACT* models are both practice-based field models that deal with disasters and trauma-related crises. The *playbook/game plan* model is targeted toward police officers and other first line responders who deal with potentially lethal, out-of-control clients. An eclectic/integrated theoretical position incorporates and integrates all valid concepts of crisis intervention.

Effective crisis workers share a number of positive personal characteristics. They maintain poise, quick wittedness, creativity, tenacity, assertiveness, and resiliency, among a host of other attributes, while confronting the difficult issues of clients in crisis.

Visit CengageBrain.com for a variety of study tools and useful resources such as video examples, case studies, interactive exercises, flashcards, and quizzes.

Culturally Effective Helping in Crisis

2

Multicultural Perspectives in Crisis Intervention

Laura Brown is the past president of Division 56, **LO1** Trauma Psychology; she is a diplomate (recognized as knowing a lot and contributing a lot) in clinical psychology, has received numerous awards, and has authored what we believe is the best book on cultural competence when it comes to doing trauma therapy, *Cultural Competence in Trauma Therapy: Beyond the Flashback* (2008). So we can pretty much assume she knows what she's talking about when she says, "After three decades of working intentionally with trauma I can say with utter certainty that I know that I have no idea of how any particular person will have experienced and made sense, or not, of her or his traumatic experiences" (p. 16). Therefore, as you read this chapter, understand that one of the best minds in this field is confessing to her ignorance when it comes to ferreting out all the ways that culture affects her clients. The message is that we're a long way from knowing all we need to know to effectively weave multiculturalism into crisis intervention. However, we do know more than we did in the last edition of this book, and the way research is moving (Bernal & Rodriguez, 2012; Brown, 2008, 2009; D'Andrea & Heckman, 2008; Ponterotto & Mallinckrodt, 2007; Ratts & Pedersen, 2014; Ridley & Shaw-Ridley, 2011; Worthington & Dillon, 2011; Worthington, Sott-McNett, & Moreno, 2007), we're going to know more and more. So please understand that this chapter isn't a GPS for multicultural competency in crisis intervention that will precisely target your destination, but more like a compass that will point you in the right general direction.

In the United States in the 21st century we live in a pluralistic culture (Sue & Sue, 2013), and the same

LEARNING OBJECTIVES

After studying this chapter, you should be able to:

1. Understand the importance of multiculturalism as it pertains to crisis intervention.
2. Identify attributes that crisis workers who intervene with clients in the multicultural world in which they work will need.
3. Know the unintended cultural biases that may exist in crisis workers.
4. Understand the difference between a universal and a focus view of culture.
5. Understand the difference between individual/collectivist and high/low-context cultures.
6. Understand the difference between an emic and etic view of multiculturalism.
7. Understand and use the SAFETY model as it applies to cultural social locations and crisis intervention.
8. Understand how ecology and multiculturalism are interrelated.
9. Understand the current issues of multiculturalism as it is applied to crisis and crisis intervention.
10. Identify culturally effective helping attributes.
11. Understand the part language barriers play in providing crisis intervention.
12. Understand the role of religion and spirituality as it applies to crisis intervention.
13. Understand that there are variances in how support systems are utilized in multicultural systems.
14. Understand the importance of occupational boundaries as cultural barriers.
15. Understand the importance of geography as a cultural barrier.
16. Become aware of the dilemma between acting quickly in crisis situations where safety is a concern and respecting cultural beliefs that implies nonintervention.

could be said for practically every country in the world. So just what is this abstract and amorphous thing called "culture"? And how does it become "multi"? Furthermore, what makes it important in the crisis business? Bernal and Rodriguez (2012, p. 4) propose that **culture** is an intergenerationally transmitted system of meaning shared by a group of people and may have both concrete objects such as buildings and art and subjective components such as social norms, and beliefs that define it as separate and distinct from other cultures.

Adler (1997) defines **culture** as "that complex whole which includes knowledge, beliefs, arts, laws, morals, customs and capabilities acquired by a person as a member of society. It is a way of life of a group of people, the configuration of all the more or less stereotyped patterns of learned behavior which are handed down from one generation to the next through the means of language and imitation" (p. 14). Members of a given culture hold all of the foregoing to be pretty much self-evident truths to live by, as a way of making order and sense out of their lives. Thus, they are generally able to live with one another in an overall peaceful, profitable way with some sense of control over their lives and the community within which they reside. The "multi" part comes into play when we start to mix up people from different cultural communities with different assumptions about all those variables Adler is talking about. As it was originally formulated in the counseling field, **multiculturalism** refers to race, ethnicity, and culture and has focused on four racial-ethnic minority groups (Asian, Black/African, Latino/Hispanic, and Native American). The term **diversity** refers to dimensions of personal identity and individual differences (Arredondo & Glauner, 1992). These two terms are the foundation on which counselor cultural competency based training has been built (Arredondo & Archiniega, 2001). However, as we move into the 21st century global community, that training model may be limited in preparing human service workers to effectively meet the needs of more diverse societies (Tomlinson-Clarke, 2013). Cross national boundary interaction through streamlined technological connectedness has resulted in the globalization of the counseling profession (Tomlinson-Clark, 2013), and that is particularly true of the crisis intervention business. One need look no further than the Crisis Intervention Team International convention to see law enforcement and human service workers from around the world grappling with the role of the police in dealing with the mentally ill.

Therefore, understanding and being able to be culturally competent in the heat of a crisis event is critical because few clients will be mirror cultural images of the interventionist. Thus, culturally competent human service workers should be aware of their personal beliefs, values, biases, and attitudes; have an awareness of and knowledge of the world view of culturally diverse individuals and groups; and have the ability to employ culturally appropriate intervention skills and strategies with a diverse clientele (Sue & Sue, 2013).

The role that culture plays in crisis intervention has to do with what Savicki (2002) has termed uncertainty avoidance—and, as you will see in this book, attempting to avoid uncertainty and get back in control of a situation gets a lot of playing time. **Uncertainty avoidance** has to do with the degree to which cultures feel threatened by uncertainty and ambiguous situations, so rules, procedures, rituals, and laws may be formulated to buffer uncertainties of individual judgment (Savicki, 2002, p. 27). What this means in crisis intervention is that a crisis worker who ventures into a different culture had better be aware that the residents of that culture are basing their ability to get though the crisis on their own set of cultural survival standards, and those don't necessarily square up with the worker's.

Core Multicultural Attributes

Kiselica (1998, p. 6) identifies four attributes **LO2** that are widely accepted as necessary for crisis workers and other mental health workers who intervene with clients in the multicultural world in which we work: (1) self-knowledge, particularly an awareness of one's own cultural biases; (2) knowledge about the status and cultures of different groups; (3) skills to effect culturally appropriate interventions—including a readiness to use alternative strategies that better match the cultures of crisis clients than do traditional strategies; and (4) actual experience in counseling and crisis intervention with culturally different clients.

Sue (1992, p. 12; 1999a, 1999b) reminds us that failure to understand clients' worldviews may lead human services workers to make erroneous interpretations, judgments, and conclusions that result in doing serious harm to clients, especially those who are culturally different. A vast majority of the world's population lives by non-Western perspectives, and a lot of those perspectives are making their way to the United States through immigration. Despite the fact that the world is culturally pluralistic, many of our books, professional teachings, research findings, and implicit theories and assumptions in the field of counseling and crisis intervention are specific to North American and European cultures. Such theories and assumptions are usually so ingrained in our thinking that they are taken for granted and seldom challenged even by our most broad-minded leaders and professionals (Pedersen, 1998; Ponterotto & Pedersen, 1993; Ridley, 1995).

As an example, critics of "culture-blind" crisis interventionists propose that their reductionistic and outmoded logical positivism (based solely on observable scientific facts and their relationship to each other and natural laws of nature) has no place in dealing with widespread violence and social upheaval in large, ethnically different populations caught in long-term wars, rebellions, or other social disasters. They further believe that Western traumatologists adopt a naive view that trauma leads in linear fashion to PTSD in all people in all cultures. Social constructivists in particular rail at this normative view of trauma. They believe it may be much more appropriate to look at trauma, and the crisis intervention that follows it, in much broader social terms, such as safety, grief, injustice, and faith, as opposed to distinct clinical categories of PTSD and depression (Silove, 2000).

There is also a great deal of debate on the validity of any measures that are used to assess the various aspects of crisis that are dealt with in this book, because cultural bias and cultural artifacts can skew results to make clients look very different from what they actually are and lead to erroneous treatment decisions (Brown, 2008; Cokley, 2007). Further, the biggest mental health assessment measure of all, the *Diagnostic and Statistical Manual* of the American Psychiatric Association (2000), has come under fire (Brown, 2008; Zalaquett et al., 2008) for its limited inclusion of social and cultural factors in the diagnoses of mental disorders. The newest version, the DSM-5 (American Psychiatric Association, 2013), has faired no better with Ratts and Pedersen (2014) severely castigating it by proposing that when helping professionals take it as dogma without taking cultural or systemic factors into consideration, they are letting a small, self-interested medical profession dictate to the rest of the counseling profession what is normal and abnormal, which is both careless and dangerous for clients (p. 6). These critics believe that the normative, disease-based, medical model of the DSM, which emphasizes client deficits, top-down expert-professional-to-client relationships, medication as a major form of treatment, and universal interpretation for persons from

various cultures, flies in the face of a counseling view of idiosyncratic behavior and often leads to ethnocentric and grossly inaccurate diagnoses (Zalaquett et al., 2008).

Ivey (1987) and Arredondo (1999) emphasize that counseling and therapy should begin with counselors' awareness of their own assumptions, values, and biases regarding racial, cultural, and group differences before considering individual variations on those themes. Ivey (1987) states that "only by placing multicultural counseling at the core of counseling curricula can we as counselors truly serve and be with those whom we would help" (p. 169). That statement is probably exponentially true for crisis workers. Specifically in regard to crisis, Brown (2009, p. 167) believes that more than any other form of distress, persons who have suffered complex trauma do so in relation to their psychosocial cultural context, and to deny the social identities they bring out of that culture is a pretty effective way to stop intervention before it starts.

Culturally Biased Assumptions

Unintentional and unexamined cultural and [LO3] racial assumptions can impair functioning of counselors (Arredondo, 1999; Ober et al., 2000; Ridley, 1995; Thompson & Neville, 1999). That statement holds doubly true for crisis workers given the cross-cultural circumstances within which they often operate—particularly in large-scale disaster relief. The following culturally biased assumptions taken from Pedersen (1987) and Martin-Baro' (1996) are ones that crisis workers would do well to remember:

1. People all share a common measure of "normal" behavior (the presumption that problems, emotional responses, behaviors, and perceptions of crises are more or less universal across social, cultural, economic, or political backgrounds, and theories and concepts can be modified to fit all groups).
2. The definition of problems can be limited by academic discipline boundaries (the presumption that the identity of the crisis worker is separate from the identity of the theologian, medical doctor, sociologist, anthropologist, attorney, or representative from some other discipline, and these have little applicability to methods of therapeutic intervention).
3. Western culture depends on abstract words (the presumption of crisis workers and counselors

in the United States that others will understand these abstractions in the same way as workers intend them).

4. Formal counseling is more important than natural support systems surrounding a client (the presumption that clients will be better-off with the support offered by professionals over the support of family, peers, and other support groups).

5. Everyone depends on linear thinking (the presumption that each cause has an effect, and each effect is tied to a cause—to explain how the world works—and that everything can be measured and described in terms of good or bad, appropriate or inappropriate, and/or other common dichotomies, and there are no gray areas).

6. Individuals need to fit into the system (the presumption that the system does not need to change to fit the individual).

7. The client's past (history) has little relevance to contemporary events (the presumption that crises are mostly related to here-and-now situations, and that crisis workers should pay little attention to the client's background).

8. The belief that knowledge should be based on logic, facts, and empirical evidence alone (the presumption that society operates much like the laws of physics and qualitative measures such as community attitude should be rejected).

9. The belief that all humans seek pleasure and happiness over pain and sorrow and these negative emotions should be avoided or sublimated (the presumption that human growth can never occur through suffering that is a natural aspect of all human development).

10. Independence is valuable and dependencies are undesirable (the presumption of Western individualism that people should not be dependent on others or allow others to be dependent on them).

11. Individuals are the basic building blocks of all societies (the presumption that crisis intervention is directed primarily toward the individual rather than units of individuals or groups such as the family, organizations, political groups, or society).

12. Psychological homostatsis and balance must be maintained so people sail through life on an even keel (the presumption that disequilibrium, change, and crisis are always bad and cannot have seeds of growth in negative life events).

13. Human services workers already know all their assumptions (the presumption that if workers were prone toward reacting in closed, biased, and culturally encapsulated ways that promote domination by an elitist group, they would be aware of it).

All the foregoing assumptions are flawed and untenable in a pluralistic world. Cormier and Hackney (1987) warn that human services workers who do not understand their own cultural biases and the cultural differences and values of others may misinterpret the behaviors and attitudes of clients from other cultures. Such workers may incorrectly label some client behavior as resistant and uncooperative. They may expect to see certain client behaviors (such as self-disclosure) that are contrary to the basic values of some cultural groups (pp. 256–258). Specifically in the field of crisis intervention, there has been criticism of the Western-based trauma model and particularly the elevation of PTSD as a pathological entity that has been coined in self-serving ways by victims' groups, politicians, and profiteering lawyers and therapists when there is little empirical evidence to support such an assumption (Silove, 2000; Summerfield, 1999).

Universal Versus Focused Views

There are both universal and focused views on   **LO4**
multicultural counseling. A **universal view** considers not only racial and ethnic minorities, but other minority or special populations as well. A **focused view** looks at multicultural counseling in relation to "visible and racial ethnic minorities" (Sue, Arredondo, & McDavis, 1992). We agree with Brown (2008, p. 12) that using racial designation, ethnic label, or any one characteristic, trait, preference, or other category to identify people may have little or nothing to do with the crises they are encountering and is probably a pretty poor unimodal cultural lens through which to view a person who has been traumatized. To view culture from such a narrow perspective is, we believe, asking for a lot of trouble in crisis intervention.

Working on the Individualist/Collectivist–High/Low-Context Continuum

From a multicultural perspective, we may   **LO5**
generally look at communication along an individualist/collectivist continuum. **Individualism** is a worldview that centralizes the personal—personal goals, personal uniqueness, and personal control—and peripheralizes the social group or social context within which the individual operates. **Collectivism** is based on the assumption that groups bind and mutually obligate individuals, that the personal

is simply a component of the larger social group or context and subordinate to it (Oyserman, Coon, & Kemmelmeier, 2002). These concepts are important because they tend to dictate how the client sees himself or herself in relation to self-concept, sense of well-being, emotional control, and relational and attributional styles (Williams, 2003), which are all critical components in how crisis intervention strategies are formulated and applied to traumatized individuals. For instance, a person who lives in a collectivist culture—and they certainly do exist in the United States—who suffers a traumatic event that may be construed as shameful may have that extrapolate out to all members of the family, with family often defined as extending a good deal beyond a biological basis (Brown, 2009, p. 161).

In a meta-analysis of 170 studies on the individualist/collectivist worldview, Oyserman, Coon, and Kemmelmeier (2002) found that individualism centers on one's self-concept rather than one's family life, as opposed to collectivism, in which the opposite is true. In regard to "sense of well-being," individualists see well-being as related to a sense of personal control; collectivists do not. Even more important in terms of crisis intervention, individualism proponents tend to see the event in terms of their own personal preferences, whereas collectivist proponents interpret the event in relation to what they believe the expectations of others might be. A rather startling discovery contradicts the accepted belief that people who are collectivist consider the group, and particularly the family, as taking precedence and obligation over individual well-being. They found essentially no difference between individualists and collectivists regarding "sense of family obligation." When a dilemma was presented, collectivists responded by identifying themselves as part of a cooperative group, whereas individualists considered themselves to be individuals participating as part of a team effort.

Finally, Osyerman and associates (2002) discovered that communication and conflict resolution styles were found to vary in relation to individualism and collectivism. Individualism consistently predicted goal-oriented, low-context, direct communication; collectivism opted for indirect, high-context communication. In confrontational situations, individualists adhered to a confrontational and arbitrational approach; collectivists preferred an accommodation and negotiation approach.

But how do people in a collective society operate under stress and traumatic conditions? The Heppners and their associates (2006) conducted research in establishing a collectivist coping styles inventory that attempts to discern how stressful and traumatic events are handled from an Asian perspective. Indeed, the 3,000 Taiwanese college students in the study endorsed coping strategies very different from those of their Western counterparts. Their acceptance, fatalism, efficacy, and interpersonal harmony strategies when faced with stressful events are unlike any other factors endorsed on traditional coping strategy inventories in the Western world. Family support and religious and spiritual resources are also different from their Western counterparts. Filial piety and elder support are important, and advice is generally sought within the sanctity of the family.

The Chinese kanji characters of crisis and opportunity that appear on the cover of this book are evident in the Taiwanese students' approach to coping with crisis. The Confucian and Buddhist philosophies that one endures suffering, looks for positive meaning, and exercises control and restraint predominate in their responses. Finally, their avoidance and emotional detachment from the stressful event and private emotional outlets are also different. Whereas in the United States we might expect an outpouring of emotion and immediate public support and grief following a traumatic event (Halpern & Tramontin, 2007, p. 98), the results from this study suggest that these students seek outside help as a last resort, and when they do, it is most often in a confidential and anonymous manner. Their coping strategies revolved around avoiding shame and seeking help in safe, anonymous ways. The Heppners and their associates (2006) suggest that these students might go to a mental health professional who was unknown to them or their families or go into a chat room on the Internet to discuss their problems. The point is that, at least for these Taiwanese students, when under stress or traumatized, they might seek mental health help very differently than would their American counterparts.

High/Low-Context Approaches. To put the foregoing analysis in operational terms useful to the crisis worker, the individualist/collectivist continuum uses what Hall (1976) calls a high/low-context approach. In low-context cultures, one's self-image and worth are defined in personal, individual terms. In high-context cultures, one's self-worth and esteem are tied to the group. In low-context cultures, information is generally transmitted explicitly and concretely through language; in high-context cultures, information is transmitted in the physical context of the interaction or internalized in the person. In high-context cultures, facial expressions, gestures, and tone of voice are as important as the meaning of words that are said. Thus, in high-context cultures, the individual will expect the other person to know what the problem is so that he or she does not have to be specific and become embarrassed and lose face by talking directly about the issue. This communication style can be very problematic to a crisis worker who operates from a low-context style in which specific and concrete information is sought to determine what is needed to take care of the problem.

From the high-context client's standpoint, the low-context worker's attempt to gather specific information about the client's personal and social status in relationship to the crisis may be seen as intrusive, rude, and offensive. A high-context culture uses stories, proverbs, fables, metaphors, similes, and analogies to make a point (Augsburger, 1992). Thus, a high-context crisis worker might be very delicate, ambiguous, sensitive, and somewhat circumlocutory in discussing personal and social issues related to the crisis. In trying to help a low-context client, a crisis worker using such a communication style might be viewed as not being remotely aware of what the frustrated client's needs are.

As a result, one of the major problems in crisis intervention with culturally different people lies in both sending and receiving communications that are understandable, clearly communicating what we are attempting to do while not exacerbating an already potentially volatile situation. While it is impossible to know the nuances of every culture and the subtleties of the client's native language, one of our rules of the road in crisis intervention in which cultural differences are an issue is that there are these two broad camps, and we need to find out which one the individual is operating in and act accordingly.

Crisis worker: (*speaking to an East African male, a recent immigrant, who has been injured in a train wreck and doesn't know what has happened to his family*) I understand you are from Somalia. I don't know a lot about your country or customs, so please let me know if what I am saying doesn't agree with what you think is right and I'll do my best to explain why that is so here in the U.S. and how we might be able to still fit your cultural background as we try to find out about your family and get you the medical help you need.

We also need to clearly own that we may be culturally ignorant and thus appear to be insensitive to the crisis client's needs. Such admissions early on go a long way in letting the client clarify what his or her needs are. Those owning statements are true whether we are dealing with survivors of an east Kentucky coal mine explosion, war refugees in Liberia, or survivors and their families from the 9/11 attacks.

High/Low–Uncertainty Avoidance Approaches. High- and low-context cultures get a lot of space in professional human service publications. What doesn't, and is particularly appropriate to crisis intervention, is understanding whether the culture one is entering is operating on high or low uncertainty avoidance principles (Savicki, 2002, p. 27). High uncertainty avoidance cultures develop a broad range of rules and regulations and procedures to cover a multitude of contingencies. In other words, if you are entering that high uncertainty avoidance culture, you had better understand they have a playbook of what is right and proper that will rival that of a playbook from the National Football League (if you are not a football fan, those books are huge and enormously complicated). If you don't understand and operate within it, you'll wind up butting your head against a very large cultural wall. On the other hand, if you are entering a low uncertainty avoidance culture you may well be frustrated by a "Relax! Be happy! We're all alive! We have food and water! Hurricanes come and go! We'll rebuild tomorrow!" view. That sort of a "chill out" worldview can sabotage the herculean efforts of highly motivated disaster workers who are operating on short time frames and deadlines, leaving them embittered and burned out from the experience.

Meet the Super Multicultural Crisis Worker. Here's an abridged definition of what Sue and Sue (2013, p. 46) believe a competent multicultural human services worker should be. They should be able to use therapeutic modalities consistent with the life experiences and cultural values of their clients. They should include individual, group, and universal dimensions of the person. They should achieve a balance between individualism and collectivism in assessing, diagnosing, and treating their clients. That's a whole lot of "shoulds" and sounds like a human services worker straight out of Marvel comics superheroes. As of yet, we have not discovered that superworker, so how can a human services worker at least get close to what Sue and Sue are proposing. We believe workers can come closest to that high standard when they operate from what cultural anthropologists call an *emic* model (Kottak, 2006) and what Brown (2008) calls *social location* when applied to people in trauma.

Emic Versus Etic Models of Multiculturalism

An **emic** model encompasses the smorgas- **LO6** bord of components that make up individuals from their subjective view of who they are, not just what their individual parts are, but more the total gestalt of how they come together, while an **etic** model describes traits and factors common to all within the group that can be objectively identified by outside observers (Friedman & Schustack, 2010; Kottak, 2006). While both are important in obtaining what cultural and contextual factors are operating in the crisis, when face to face for the first time with a person in crisis, finding the parts of the individual that make up the total Gestalt of the crisis and fitting those to the worker are of critical importance. Why is this so?

There is a great deal of research that more than anything else, the strength of the therapeutic alliance or working relationship that is created between the worker and the client will determine how effective the outcome of therapy will be (Bernecker, Levy, & Elison, 2014; Falkenstrom, Granstrom, & Holmqvist, 2013, 2014; Kivlighan, Mamarosh, & Hilsenroth, 2014), and that may be particularly so with individuals suffering psychotic behaviors (Owens, Haddock, & Berry, 2013). One of the critical training components of the Memphis CIT training program is how the CIT officer makes initial contact with a consumer because those first few moments of contact have profound ramifications on the building of a working bond between the officer and the consumer and the ultimate positive resolution of the crisis (Kirchberg, 2014).

So please meet the emic model of Dr. Dick James, 70-something, grandfather who is mostly happy about being above ground still, but worries about his grandson, husband who thinks he's been married longer than he's been alive sometimes, hard of hearing from too many years in construction working his way through school and gets yelled at for not wearing his hearing aid enough, fisherman and hunter who pals around with one of his daughters doing those activities, white guy who grew up in a university town but had blue-collar parents, now has digestive trouble eating pizza and drinking beer, trains police officers to deal with the emotionally disturbed and severely agitated mentally ill, played baseball and ran track in an integrated high

school in the 1960s that he loved so has had some life-long friends who are both white and black, has been a school counselor in a blue-collar Midwestern town, a Presbyterian who goes pretty regularly to church but has been a Baptist and a Methodist and has a lot of friends who are Catholic and Jewish, writes books like this one instead of the great American novel he thought he would when he was an English major at Eastern Illinois University, has a sense of humor that leaks out and sometimes gets him in trouble and likes to send jokes over the Internet and make people laugh, and had his first real crisis when he got shot in the chest at age 21 while with a girl who he would have probably married . . . if he hadn't gotten shot, and so on.

These are what Laura Brown (2008, p. 24) calls **social locations,** the individual identifiers that go far beyond, race, sex, and skin tone that make us the specific and unique individuals that reside in a cultural group. Both she and we believe they are important from a multicultural standpoint when you are doing this work. So if you compare all that to just Dr. James old dude, or Dr. James professor, or Dr. James white guy, or any other unitary, focused etic view of Dr. James, you surely aren't getting the view you got a couple of sentences ago and our guess would be you might not respond in quite the same way if you were doing crisis intervention with him. Thus, we take a universal /emic rather than a focused/etic view in crisis intervention. Therefore, when we speak of cultural diversity, we are speaking in the broadest possible terms in regard to all factors that somehow make clients "different" from the interventionist. Hopefully, the following analogies illuminate what is meant by a universal/emic view.

Your worldview, if you are a New York City social worker and you have spent your entire life in the city and are now trying to help a Midwestern farmer who has just lost everything in a flood, is going to be as different from his worldview as ours would be from Pakistani survivors of an earthquake we were attempting to help. Or how about your first encounter (assuming you are heterosexual) with a gay man who has just discovered he is HIV positive from his longtime, supposedly faithful partner? Or consider a staunchly devout Baptist woman who believes divorce is a sin but who is being severely beaten by her preacher husband. Does that mean you will be ineffective and should not go to Keokuk, Iowa, or we should not go to Karachi, Pakistan? Never work with gay men or Baptist women? Certainly not! What it does mean is that "multiculturalism" does not necessarily stand out in large neon lights saying "I am from Ethiopia or Nepal, and I am different from you" or "I have red, black, yellow, or green (there may be some of those aliens from Area 51 in Roswell, New Mexico, reading this, and we don't want to leave them out) skin." In a statement that absolutely captures the essence of what is meant by a universal view, Halpern and Tramontin (2007) quote New York regional mental health officials: "In the large and diverse state of New York, when you know one county in the state you know one county" (p. 316). So how in the world do you do this business if there is that much diversity, not just in the world, but in one state?

Laura Brown (2008, p. 12) has used Hays's **ADDRESSING model** (2001, 2008) as one of the bases for her book on multiculturalism and trauma. The ADDRESSING acronym encompasses Age, acquired and Developmental Disabilities, Religion, Ethnicity, Social class, Sexual orientation, Indigenous heritage, National origin, and Gender. D'Andrea & Daniels (2005) have developed a comparable model called **RESPECTFUL** (Religious/spiritual, Economic class, Sexual identity, Psychological development, Ethnic/racial identity, Chronological age, Trauma and threats to well-being, Family, Unique physical issues, and Language and location of residence). From our own experience we would add geographic locale, living area (urban, suburban, rural), occupation, education, and marital or partner status. We believe these variables are major components that start to capture the essence of how the crisis interventionist needs to think about clients and work with the multiple identities that intersect with the crisis.

However, Brown is about the business of doing trauma therapy, and while crisis may certainly occur in the delivery of trauma therapy, it isn't the same as doing crisis intervention with an out-of-control suicidal/homicidal client who has just been dumped by the love of his life and is now standing on the guardrail of the I-40 Hernado De Soto bridge over the Mississippi river. We believe that when such a crisis occurs, a more specific model to operationalize social locations is warranted.

The SAFETY Model. To that end Kristi `LO7` Nobbman of the University of Memphis Counseling Department Crisis Research team has developed a further iteration of social locations that we believe applies more specifically to the work of crisis intervention. Kristi has developed the **SAFETY model** (Stability, Affect, Friction, Environment, Temperament, and Yearning) (Nobbman et al., 2014). The SAFETY acronym is not happenstance. Safety is the overriding task for everyone involved in a crisis. Please understand that

the SAFETY model is newly hatched, and we are still "fiddling" with it. Indeed, we certainly invite you to fiddle along with us as you read about it.

In terms of the SAFETY model here is a short definition of the acronym:

Stability: Stability refers to consistency, logic, and strength of purpose in terms of thinking and behaving. Getting stability in the crisis is the primary goal.

Affect: Affect is observed emotions, both verbal and nonverbal. Intent is to move the client from agitated and blunted locations to calm and tranquil ones.

Friction: Friction is identified by the triggers that escalate the situation, whether they are intrapersonal, interpersonal, or systemic. Finding Friction locations and easing them is critical to stability.

Environment: Environment refers to the physical and/or personal setting, as well as the social aspects of what/who is involved. Changing the environment by physically moving locations or removing individuals or other noxious stimuli that may agitate the individual are often critical.

Temperament: Temperament is how I and the consumer generally act based on all our cultural experiences and knowledge. Additionally, for the crisis worker, temperament is the specific cultural set of the mental health world and experience handling crises in that milieu.

Yearning: Yearning refers to what drives the client into crises and his or her attempt to alleviate it. It may be physical, psychological, social, and/or spiritual desire/longing. Most often the yearning locations of clients are to ease frustrated attempts to obtain something ranging from drugs, a lost love, to getting rid of the coffin worms eating their brains out.

Compounding the issue even more is the fact that you, the interventionist, are bringing all these social locations into the equation too. Consider Figure 2.1 and how the social locations of Dr. James fit (or not) with Leron, an individual you will meet in Chapter 3, who is having a really bad day. Dr. James will do a quick assessment of Leron's affective, behavioral, and cognitive functioning and immediately start identifying his social locations, which he believes may affect his intervention with Leron. By owning who he is, he is attempting to engage the client, the first task of the crisis intervention model you will meet in Chapter 3. Besides

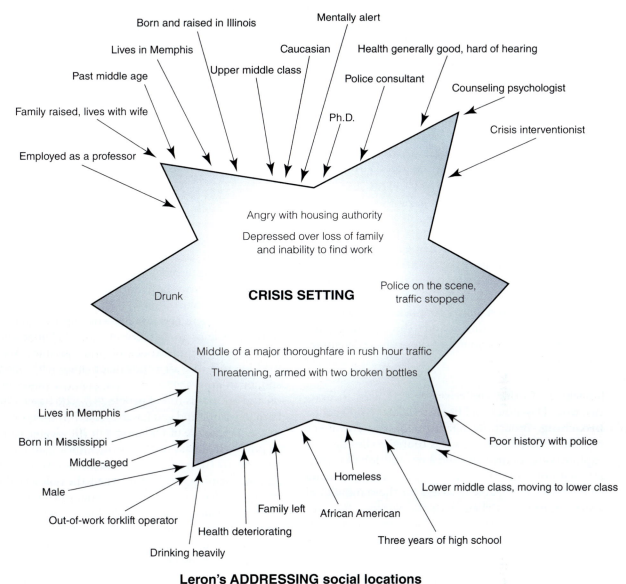

FIGURE 2.1   ADDRESSING Social Locations: Dr. James and Leron

dealing with the very obvious social locations that differ between crisis workers and their clients, you need to be aware of *all* the baggage you carry into this particular environment that may hinder your efforts. Thus, Dr. James's social location of hearing impairment may not be visible, but on a noisy street it can be problematic to say the least if he misinterprets what he hears and is too proud not to mention this fact early on to a client who may see him as a whole lot of other things that are not helpful if he can't respond clearly and correctly.

So he needs to be very aware of his own **friction** and the **environment locations** in the SAFETY model.

Likewise, he needs to be sensitive to the fact that one of Leron's present social locations is intoxication and it may be more the whiskey than the man doing the talking in regard to his **temperament location**. So while our crisis interventionist may or may not have trouble because of his skin color, perceived social class difference based on his clothes and the way he talks, and the fact that he is a police consultant, he needs to be cognizant that those factors may indeed be operating and may exacerbate the friction Leon is already feeling toward authority figures, the government, and the MAN. Thus, for the master practitioners of crisis intervention, it is critical to their success that they are sophisticated enough to know when social locations they inhabit may become the major dynamic they are dealing with (Brown, 2009, p. 40) and what they need to do about it.

It is of more than passing interest that in workshops we have conducted with three different groups of counselors (Nobbman, Skirius, & James, 2014), counselor educators (James, Myer, Skirius, & Nobbman 2013), and CIT police officers (James, Kirchberg, Nobbman, & Skirius, 2013) that involved identifying their social locations with videos of persons in crisis, the CIT officers were able to name more of their social locations than either the counselors or counselor educators. Why do you suppose that is so? We believe it has a good deal to do with CIT officer training and their experience and ability to quickly assess the social locations of consumers, and to broach the gap between their own locations and those of the consumer and bond with them.

Broaching. To that end crisis workers need to practice what Day-Vines and her associates (2007) called **broaching.** Broaching refers to the crisis worker's consistent display of openness to invite the client to explore issues of diversity and a recognition that race, ethnicity, or some universal trait may be contributing to the crisis. Being able to assess for those individual social locations, fit them with the worker's and rapidly tap into the client's social locations is critical in establishing an empathic working alliance.

Leron: What the hell you doin' out here you honkie, cracker? 'Lessen you from Channel Five I ain't got nuthin' fo' you. I wants the whole world to know about them Nazis down at the housin' 'thority what done kicked me out fo' no good reason.

Dr. James: I realize that I'm a white guy who isn't homeless and furthermore that I have a police T-shirt on that says I work for the man. I understand that may affect your ability to trust me that I can help you out, but the T-shirt also says CIT which means I am a person who trains police officers to deal with folks who have problems that frustrate them and cause them to take actions they normally wouldn't do unless they felt they had no other options, and that seems to be about where you are right now. So if you

have questions about who I am, I'll be glad to answer them. By the way, one of the "Who I ams" is that I'm a little hard of hearing and it's noisy out here so I'd appreciate it if you could speak up a bit so I am sure I get everything you are saying. So I wonder if you might not trust me enough to tell me what got you out here in the middle of one of the busiest streets in Memphis to get the attention you seem to need.

While making a number of owning statements to let Leon know what his social locations are both professionally and physically, our sweat-drenched doctor immediately attempts to find what Leon is *yearning* for and what the *friction* he is currently suffering is critical enough to put his life at risk by standing in one of the busiest streets in Memphis at rush hour.

To make things even more problematic, it isn't just "culture" that factors into this increasingly complex picture but the "ecology" you are working in as well. By "ecology" we mean the living environment in which the intervention occurs. It is 98 degrees Fahrenheit out on that street where Leron is. Do you suppose that adds to the problem? Your intervention will change and be influenced by a number of ecological variables. Are you working in a nice air-conditioned office with one person, or in an evacuation center with the power going on and off that is full of people 24/7 who haven't had a bath in a while and you haven't either? Are you working in the panhandle of Oklahoma in 100-degree weather in July with a blast furnace wind blowing all the time and you are from Minnesota? Or perhaps you are from an Iowa farming community where the tallest building is a grain elevator and you find yourself on Michigan Avenue in Chicago buried in the canyon of skyscrapers. So it isn't just culture by itself, it is also the ecological landscape you are operating in that is going to affect how and what you do.

Awareness of Both Ecology and Multicultural Competencies

Figure 2.2 is a diagram of the effects of ecol- **LO8** ogy/culture on client–worker interactions. Notice that the "crisis" triangle has a component at each corner: the crisis worker, the client, and their ecological/cultural determinants. The two-way arrows connecting the three corners indicate the mutual and dynamic interaction that constantly occurs among all the possible ecological/cultural factors that affect both crisis worker and client: family, race, religion, locale, physical ability, sex, economic class, vocation, physical needs, social affiliations, and so on.

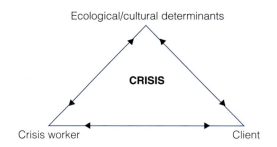

FIGURE 2.2   The Dynamic Effect of Ecology/Culture on Client–Crisis Worker Interactions

The triangle itself represents the environment in which you are working and the ecological background and cultural attitudes, beliefs, and heritages you and the client bring into that setting. Thus, for a therapy to be ecologically valid, it needs to correlate with clients' ethnocultural and linguistic experiences that they bring into therapy and the cultural structure of the therapy provided for them (Rodriguez & Bernal, 2012). For this to happen, Rodriguez and Bernal (p. 25) propose that a complex constellation of language, persons, metaphors, content, concepts, goals , methods, and context need to be in place. Now add attempting to try to carry all these out in a crisis, and you may begin to understand how daunting ecologically/culturally valid crisis intervention can be.

Two examples illustrate this interaction well. The relationship of age to PTSD is an outstanding example of the effect of cultural context. Norris and Alegria (2006) report that among three samples of disaster survivors, manifesting PTSD occurred at higher rates in younger Mexicans, middle-age Americans, and older Poles. Clearly, there was no one consistent effect of disaster by age. Rather, the cultural context of the country and the variation in historical social roles that are dictated in those countries would seem to have a great deal of influence on how the crisis will unfold when age is a factor.

Ghafoori and Hierholzer (2010) studied personality disorders (PDs) among black, white, and Hispanic combat veterans who were diagnosed with PTSD. They sought to examine whether there were differences among the three groups on Cluster A PD (odd or eccentric behavior, including paranoid, schizoid, and schizotypal disorders), Cluster B PD (dramatic or erratic behavior, including histrionic, narcissistic, antisocial, and borderline disorders), and Cluster C (anxious or inhibited behaviors, including avoidant, dependent, and obsessive-compulsive disorders).

Based on previous literature reviews, the researchers hypothesized that blacks would have more Cluster A symptoms, blacks and Hispanics would have an increased likelihood of manifesting Cluster B symptoms, and the association between race, ethnicity, and PD symptoms would not be fully explained by combat exposure, PTSD, or the potential confounding variables of age, education, and income. What they found was in sharp contrast to what they had hypothesized. Their outcomes indicated that Hispanic veterans were significantly more likely to have personality disorders that fit under Category A compared to the other two groups. They also found that those veterans who had Cluster A symptoms were one and a half times more likely to have PTSD. Finally, they found that greater level of combat exposure was likely to manifest in Cluster C symptoms for all groups.

So if you are in the PTSD treatment business with combat veterans, it ought to become apparent that the interaction between environment and ethnicity will have some profound effects on what these clients bring into the therapeutic setting, and is certainly going to dictate that your treatment plan is most likely going to be different given the different clusters of PDs with which you are faced.

Locus of Control.   When the crisis worker is factored into the equation, then intervention becomes even more complex. Internal versus external locus of control is a particularly aggravating problem that may bedevil crisis workers. Most crisis workers have a high internal locus of control and believe that through personal effort, one can start to regain psychological homeostasis and equilibrium (Atkinson, Morten, & Sue, 1998). Understand, then, that no therapy is done in a sterile vacuum, free from the multiple effects of the ecological/cultural background. That statement is even truer in the highly charged emotional context of crisis intervention.

The wise crisis interventionist understands this complexity and, when faced with an out-of-control client whose ecological context and background may be extremely different from his or her own, goes slowly and carefully. The wise worker is highly sensitive to and asks questions about the person's preferred mode of receiving assistance. As an example, Weisaeth (2000) reports on deciding *not* to do critical incident stress debriefing (CISD) with a U.N. peacekeeping battalion of Fiji Islanders who were doing duty in South Lebanon. After an artillery attack that left many dead and wounded civilians they had been sheltering in their compound, the Fijis worked through their stress by using a very intense and emotional group ceremonial ritual that involved a mildly intoxicating drink called *kawa*. Weisaeth wisely decided to drop any attempt at a standard CISD because it was apparent the Fijis had their own quite adequate way of dealing with the trauma. Any attempt to shoehorn CISD into the Fiji cultural tradition might have caused a great deal of resistance and done more harm than good.

A recurrent comment we are confronted with in our classes comes from an apparent belief that "to counsel one, you gotta be one!" We believe that this stance is neither true nor workable. Particularly in crisis intervention, we seldom have the freedom to choose which clients we will get or take, and we generally do not have the luxury of making referrals simply because the client's ecological /cultural background does not fit nicely into our own. What we can do and must do is be acutely sensitive to the emerging needs of the individual, and in Carl Rogers's terms (Raskin & Rogers, 1995), prize that person in regard to his or her distinctive individuality in the context of the crisis situation. Above all else, research on the outcomes of therapy tells us that establishing a relationship built on trust and credibility is far and away the most important condition for a successful outcome of any kind of therapeutic endeavor (Capuzzi & Gross, 1995, pp. 12–25).

Shortcomings of a Multiculturalist Approach to Crisis Intervention

First and foremost, there is a lot of contro-   **LO9**   versy over what the terms *ethnicity, race, ethnic and racial identity,* and *culture,* as definable and measurable constructs, actually mean (Cokley, 2007). That's problematic for multiculturalism in general and multicultural counseling in particular in trying to serve an increasingly culturally diverse society (Trimble, 2007), because if we can't define those words, then explaining what multicultural counseling is and how we go about doing it is really going to be difficult (Ponterotto & Mallinckrodt, 2007).

The multicultural approaches to crisis intervention described here do not have universal support among helping professionals. Those professionals are definitely not opposed to the concepts or the consideration of the various forms of diversity that are encountered in the helping and mental health services; nor are we. However, several serious questions must be posed about the current multiculturalist view of counseling. Those questions particularly apply to crisis intervention.

Perhaps the most prevalent alleged shortcoming is the flawed assumption on the part of many "multiculturalists" that the current theories of counseling, psychotherapy, and crisis intervention are inherently biased and oppressive (Weinrach & Thomas, 1998; Wubbolding, 2003). Another critique asserts that many of the current "cultural competency" practices are themselves too exclusive (Weinrach, 2003). Still another alleged shortcoming of the current multiculturalist approach is that much of the pertinent literature on multicultural competencies has not been subjected to peer review or empirical research (Brandsma, 2003; Sullivan & Cottone, 2010). A pretty sophisticated study by Owen and his associates (2011) that had clients rate therapist multicultural competencies along with the outcome of therapy found that multicultural competency didn't account for very much of therapy success, although their study has certainly been taken to task by other multicultural researchers (Ridley & Shaw-Ridley, 2011; Worthington & Dillon, 2011). As such, critics of the current multicultural movement believe that they are merely the unfounded views of those disaffected with the current theories and practices of mental health, and their complaints are expected to be accepted on faith with no evidence to back up their claims. Trimble (2007) puts the issue straight forward when he states that if we can't define these concepts clearly and concretely we have no business trying to measure them.

As a very vivid example, there has been a major assumption that certain Asian and Latino cultures have a much more collectivist view than Americans or Western Europeans in regard to how issues and problems are handled. The belief has long been held that Americans and Western Europeans are much more individualistic in their worldview. In a very large meta-analysis of this worldview hypothesis, Oyserman, Coon, and Kemmelmeier (2002) found that Indonesians were not significantly different from European Americans, Australians, and Germans in regard to individualism, and that European Americans were lower in individualism than people from more than half the countries in Latin America. A truly startling finding was that Americans were significantly higher in collectivism than the Japanese and no different in collectivism than Koreans. Oyserman and his associates' meta-analysis of 170 multicultural studies raises critical questions about the blind acceptance and division of cultures into collectivist and individualist camps.

Kim, Liang, and Li (2003) found that Asian American counselees responded more positively to European American counselors than to Asian American counselors. In attempting to unravel this puzzling outcome, the researchers found that European Americans displayed more positive animation (smiling, postural shifts), which seemed to lead to more positive attribution to the counseling by the Asian American clients, as opposed to less positive ratings for the Asian American counselors, who were more passive and unemotional. This finding brings into question whether being passive, noncommittal, and seemingly uninvolved is indeed the best approach to take with a client who is Asian—or at least one who is Asian American.

Shectman, Hiradin, and Zina (2003) examined the notion of group self-disclosure in Israeli Jewish, Muslim, and Druze adolescents. They hypothesized that because of the standard view that Muslims come from a collectivist culture and the Druze come from a very tightly knit rural collectivist culture far removed from the cultural mainstream, both groups would be far less likely than Jewish adolescents to self-disclose in group counseling. What they unexpectedly found was that while, true to form, the Druze adolescents self-disclosed little, the Muslim adolescents self-disclosed a great deal more than the Jewish adolescents. They hypothesized that these results may be due to the biculturation of Muslim youth, who may have a much greater need for an avenue to self-disclose than their Jewish counterparts. The behavior of the adolescents in this study does not operate along a linear pattern of the stereotypical notion of how ethnic groups self-disclose. It appears that if there is a moderately strong bicultural identity, participants may take advantage of the communication possibilities they are offered.

What these studies indicate is that to arbitrarily organize worldview differences—and therefore counseling approaches—along racial, ethnic, and nationality lines is indeed questionable and is likely to cause the very stereotyping of individuals that multiculturalism rails against (Cohen, 2009). Parallel to this criticism, questions arise as to how and to what extent validated cross-cultural studies are conducted to provide a solid research base for such competencies (Wubbolding, 2003), particularly when small samples of undergraduate foreign students are used as the basis to extrapolate questionable interpretations to entire ethnic populations (Oyserman, Coon, & Kemmelmier, 2002). Oyserman and his associates'

(2002) meta-analysis confronted multicultural counseling with a number of uncomfortable facts. One in particular was debunking the notion that the individualist–collectivist construct is a valid means of understanding how cultures operate. That notion is a sacred cow to many multiculturalists and assumed to be self-evident. While there are certainly general differences *between* ethnic, racial, and national groups, and we see the individualist–collectivist concept as a nice theoretical model, we would argue that the differences *within* groups are just as critical.

Because this book is used in a number of countries (for example, there is a Chinese translation), it is worth mentioning that multiculturalists in the United States seem to be unaware or unwilling to state how the multicultural competencies apply to those working in contexts outside the United States (Johannes, 2003), and very few studies are looking at cross comparisons of cultures. Perhaps even more problematic is that little research has been done on determining how effective counselors are in putting their learning to work in the real world of conceptualizing client concerns and formulating effective treatment plans that factor in culture (Worthington, Soth-McNett, & Moreno, 2007).

In the new millennium therapy business, evidence-based therapies (EBTs) have become the gold standard for treatment. In other words if there is not hard research evidence that a therapy works, then it shouldn't be used. However, as Bernal and Rodriguez (2012, p. 12) report, the National Institutes of Health's 1994 (NIH,1994) mandate on inclusion of minority populations in testing EBTs has seen little progress in regard to their inclusion in EBT studies nor has any guidance been offered on how to adapt EBTs to minorities. We bring these issues up because we are a long way from knowing what we need to know about multiculturalism and how it operates in crisis intervention. Thus, you should be a very discerning consumer of what proponents of a multicultural counseling view extol as ultimate truth and beauty when they are arbitrarily generalized to all therapeutic situations and settings.

Culturally Effective Helping During a Crisis

The plain and simple truth is that we don't **LO10** know a lot about how culture, crises, and crisis intervention interact (Brown, 2008, pp. 256–257). Very little research has been done in the area. Certain cultures don't even have words for trauma (Silove, 1998)! However, we do know that deeply held cultural beliefs and previously learned ways of dealing with the world rapidly surface when individuals are placed in a crisis situation (Dass-Brailsford, 2008). When a traumatic event occurs, there is a high probability that people will revert to their long-held cultural beliefs no matter where they live and work at the moment (Brown, 2009, p. 154).

There is a good deal of evidence that minorities in the United States use mental health services a great deal less than European Americans do (Breux & Ryujin, 1999; Chen & Mak, 2008; Sue, 1977). That underutilization becomes very problematic when a disaster strikes, because research indicates that ethnic minorities tend to suffer more in a disaster than the majority group (Norris & Alegria, 2006).

Certainly much human-made crisis revolves around lack of cultural understanding and conflicts between cultures. Eidelson and Eidelson (2003) have documented how distorted beliefs may produce excessive death, suffering, and displacement as a result of conflicts among and between groups regarding ethnicity, nationality, religion, or other social identities and issues. These researchers focused on five core belief domains that propel both individuals and groups to make dangerous assumptions about people who are different from themselves. The domains are identified as revolving around assumptions regarding superiority, injustice, vulnerability, distrust, and helplessness. Deeply entrenched patterns for understanding, perceiving, and interpreting events appear to govern and produce emotions and behaviors that may ultimately lead to conflicts and problematic and destructive crises. Distorted and dysfunctional beliefs appear to be at the core of many of the problems that crisis interventionists and other helping professionals face.

An example of such a distortion is the widespread belief among New Orleans African Americans that levees were blown up to save white residential districts from Hurricane Katrina's floodwaters. There is, in fact, a historical precedence for blowing up New Orleans levees to save parts of the city. The fact that it did not happen in Katrina's case makes little difference to those people who lost everything but the shirts on their backs. How do you think you would be received if you attempted to do crisis intervention with these individuals—particularly if you were white, and more particularly if you told them you didn't believe that the levees were intentionally blown up? Do you give up before you start? Not hardly!

Past history and experience may play a pivotal role in how recipients of service perceive crisis intervention. Mexican American families whose homes had been damaged in the 1989 Northern California Loma Prieta earthquake refused to go to mass shelters in schools and auditoriums. They continued to live in tents and also refused to go back to their damaged homes. The same was true after the 1995 Northridge earthquake near Los Angeles, even after authorities assured the Mexican Americans that it would be safe. The reason for their refusal was that aftershocks from the 1985 earthquake in Mexico City had killed and injured many people who had gone to such shelters or had returned to damaged homes. It finally took bicultural, bilingual "assurance teams" of crisis workers to convince the recent immigrants in California to go to shelters or return to their homes (Myers & Wee, 2005, pp. 59–60).

Positive Aspects of an Effective Multicultural Counselor

Sue (1992) states that multicultural helping is enhanced when the human services worker "uses methods and strategies and defines goals consistent with the life experiences and culture values of the client" (p. 13). Belkin (1984) points out that cross-cultural counseling need not be a negative experience; that it may effectively resolve client problems as well as provide a unique learning experience for both client and helper; and that the main "barrier to effective cross-cultural counseling is the traditional counseling role itself, which is not applicable to many cross-cultural interactions" (p. 527). Belkin further states that the principal cross-cultural impediments are (1) language differences, (2) class-bound values, and (3) culture-bound values (p. 534). Belkin concludes that perhaps the most positive discovery and/or belief of the effective cross-cultural counselor is that humans everywhere are more alike than they are different (p. 543).

Cormier and Hackney (1987) cite several strategies that culturally effective helpers use. For instance, such helpers (1) examine and understand the world from the client's viewpoint, (2) search for alternative roles that may be more appealing and adaptive to clients from different backgrounds, and (3) help clients from other cultures make contact with and elicit help from indigenous support systems (p. 259). Cormier and Hackney also specify that to be culturally effective, helpers should not (1) impose their values and expectations on clients from different backgrounds, (2) stereotype or label clients, client behaviors, or cultures, and (3) try to force unimodal counseling approaches upon clients (pp. 258–259).

As an example of such unimodal expectations, Sue (1992) notes that traditional helpers may tend to emphasize the need for clients to verbalize their emotions. He points out that some clients (such as traditional Japanese) may have been taught as children not to speak until addressed; that many cultures highly value restraint in expressing strong feelings; and that patterns of communication, contrary to ours in the United States, may "tend to be vertical, flowing from those of higher prestige and status to those of lower prestige and status" (p. 12). The unenlightened worker seeking to help such a client may perceive the client to be inarticulate, unintelligent, lacking in spontaneity, or repressed (p. 13).

School crisis worker: (*speaking softly to a recently immigrated Japanese family whose son has just been severely injured in a high school football game and is going to be out of school for an extended period*) I would like to be helpful to your family in this difficult time for you, not knowing how well your son will recover from his injuries and what that means as far as his academic work and chances of going on to college are. I have had experience in dealing with these kinds of issues with a number of students and their parents and could certainly act as your advocate if you would like someone from the school to do that. It is what I do, and it would be my pleasure and honor to do it for you if you so desire. I'll leave my business card and you may call me at any time.

At the other end of the continuum, Dass-Brailsford (2008) notes that African American culture, particularly in the South, uses physical contact to establish connections, so hugging, ritual handshakes, demonstrative grieving, and joyful exclamations all have healing and bonding power.

School crisis worker: (*speaking animatedly and emphatically to an African American family whose son has just been severely injured in a high school football game and is going to be out of school for an extended period*) (Gives mother a heartfelt embrace and then shakes father's hand and grasps his forearm.) I hate this for you and Rashad. It is a terrible blow, not knowing how this will affect his football career and chances for college. You must be really scared and anxious to know how this will all play out. If you would let me be the point man on this with the school, I'd appreciate the opportunity to help you. I've done this with a lot of kids. I know Rashad

and can get things coordinated with his teachers and see that the college applications go out like they're supposed to. I'll get on that tomorrow, or if you want to think on it I'll wait for your call, but understand you and Rashad are important to this school and we'll be with you. You are part of the Arlington High School family and that's how it is.

If the parents of our football player happen to be Hispanic, and the parents don't speak English and you took French in high school, you are going to need a translator you can trust who has the cultural background to know exactly how to put your words in tone, decibel level, gestures, body language, and directed to mom, dad, or both so that you convey your intent as closely as possible (Zalaquett, Carrion, & Exum, 2010). That means you are going to have to do a little planning ahead if you are counseling individuals who don't speak the language that most people in your country do.

So now you are thinking, "This is impossible. I can't begin to know the words and the culture of everyone I meet, so I'm bound to screw up." Not so! If you pay attention to Cormier and Hackney's points a few paragraphs back, you are going to be pretty much on course. The major themes in both of the foregoing examples are that the worker demonstrates empathy, caring, and positive regard while searching for a role that is compatible with the client's worldview, and offers to act as advocate without injecting his or her own values or conditions into the situation. While at times we do make mistakes in entering into clients' cultural worlds, there are very few clients who do not respond positively when these general facilitative conditions are in operation.

When in Rome, Italy . . . or Georgia

Understanding the cultural milieu in which he or she operates is of critical importance to the crisis worker who performs fieldwork or outreach services. The crisis interventionist's notion of what kind of help is needed and what is or is not appropriate help is a manifestation of his or her own cultural and societal upbringing, education, and views (Kaniasty & Norris, 1999). Cultural differences are particularly problematic when the worker is transported to and works on the "turf" of the client and has little time to become attuned to the cultural and ecological framework within which the client operates. We are not simply talking about "foreigners," either. Within the United States, residents of Jackson, Tennessee, made homeless by an F4 tornado; survivors of those killed in the Oklahoma City federal building bombing; American Indian families whose children were killed in the school shooting at Red Lake, Minnesota; or transient street people in dire need of social, medical, and mental health services may have views about what constitutes helpful intervention that are very different from the crisis worker's. Such individuals may take umbrage at the crisis worker's attempts to intrude into their world (Hopper, Johnston, & Brinkhoff, 1988). It is absolutely incumbent upon workers to be aware of these cultural subtleties, because victims and survivors will be (Golec, 1983).

Language Barriers

Although it may be difficult enough to work **LO11** with people in crisis from the same generic cultural background and who speak the native language as a first language, the manifestation and communication of first-generation Americans' or immigrants' personal problems may be very different from what the crisis worker is used to handling. As a result, assessment and intervention become more complex and difficult. Confidentiality issues are also problematic because translators or children of parents who do not speak English have to act as interpreters. People in the United States with "green cards" or student visas run the risk of having information about their mental health status given to government agencies, which may then make negative evaluations about their immigration status. This issue is further compounded by language problems that make communicating clients' needs and crisis workers' offers of services subject to misinterpretation. Particularly for foreign students, having to leave school because of "mental problems" may cause tremendous loss of face in their families and in their home countries. If not handled sensitively, the worker's attempts to provide help may exacerbate rather than mollify the crisis (Oropeza et al., 1991).

If the crisis worker is not fluent in the native language, how can information be conveyed? While not the ideal, a good translator is critical to this endeavor, as opposed to using a family member as translator—particularly since the children, who because of their schooling know more English than their parents do, would probably serve as family translators. The need to discuss intimate details and preserve family roles makes it paramount that third-party translators be available (DeWolfe, 2000).

Crisis worker: (*speaking through a translator to a Pakistani family who lost all their belongings in a house fire and whose only members who are fluent in English are their children*) Please tell Mr. and Mrs. Maqsood that I apologize for not speaking Urdu. I can either speak through you or through their children, and I would like to know which they might prefer.

Religion and Spirituality

Religion and spirituality are so loaded with **LO12** emotionality that many human services workers regard it as an exposed electrical wire, not to be touched on pain of death for fear they will be seen as either proselytizing for their religion or insensitive to other spiritual beliefs. However, to deny or act as if religion, faith, and spirituality are not part of any crisis is to neglect a large part of a crisis response for most people. Exclusive of pastoral counseling, it is interesting that little space is given to the effects that religion has in the counseling business (Schlosser et al., 2010). Yet for most people trauma is the ultimate challenge to meaning making, and for most people, that meaning making is attached to some kind of faith (Brown, 2009, p. 228).

Perilla, Norris, and Lavizzo (2002) found that after Hurricane Andrew, besides being exposed to more of Andrew's wrath because of their poor economic state, Latinos and non-Hispanic blacks showed **differential vulnerability** to traumatic effects compared to whites. That is, they were more traumatized than whites, and at least part of this difference related to their fatalistic view that they had little control over the situation. They believed that whatever God willed would happen. Crisis workers who face such fatalism do themselves and their clients no service when they attempt to persuade clients to change their worldview from an external to an internal locus. In fact, the crisis workers would do far better to use the religious and spiritual beliefs that minorities have to guide their intervention (Myers & Wee, 2005, pp. 60–61).

There is a reason that the triage assessment system you will encounter in Chapter 3 has a spiritual/moral component. Religious and spiritual beliefs play a huge role in the outcome of a crisis as people attempt to make sense of events that seemingly make no sense at all. Faith plays a large part in how people try to come to terms with a randomly cruel universe that crashes down on the notion of a supreme being that runs a just and moral world. As Bingham (2010) states for African Americans, "What is difficult to understand is that the church is far more than family" (p. 22), and if you are not attuned to the importance of their church and faith for many African Americans (Grills, 2004), numerous other ethnic minorities (Taylor, Chatters, & Levin, 2004) and for that matter many Southern whites, you are probably going to have trouble helping them through the crisis.

It should not be surprising that recent immigrants who have seemingly adapted to the culture of their new country rapidly revert to old and customary ways of behaving in a crisis (Augsburger, 1992), just as the Caribbean and Latin American clients of Shelby and Tredinnick (1995) did after Hurricane Andrew struck south Florida. Shelby and Tredinnick spent considerable space reporting on the cultural differences they encountered doing disaster relief work in the aftermath of Hurricane Andrew. The large Caribbean and Latin American populations they dealt with had punitive religious interpretations of the disaster and punitive child-rearing practices, particularly under stress, that differed greatly from what the crisis workers believed to be ethically and morally right. The workers had to be very sensitive in not challenging these deeply held beliefs. In short, while it may appear to you to be voodoo, if it is bringing solace and respite, crisis workers need to put their own beliefs on the shelf and encourage spiritual coping behaviors that help people heal (Dass-Brailsford, 2008).

So just what do you do when you are confronted with spiritual issues? What the workers did with Andrew survivors was allow them to process feelings of guilt and responsibility in line with their religious interpretation of the event, without passing any judgments on the merit of those beliefs. Furthermore, educating parents with ethnically different views of child rearing about the ways children generically respond after a trauma, along with the normal developmental issues they face, may indeed be a tall order given the brevity of crisis intervention. Such interventions, although needed, may be something the crisis worker wishes to consider very carefully.

To offload this tricky issue by merely suggesting that persons consult with their minister, priest, rabbi, or imam is to abdicate your responsibility as the crisis worker. Further, while you may certainly seek advice and counsel from a religious leader of a particular person's faith, that by no means guarantees that you will be congruent with that particular individual's sense of meaning making. There is also no way in the world you can become an expert in all the religions and practices of people in crisis that you will encounter. What we believe is that you can do what Schlosser and his associates (2010) propose and what has worked for us by making an owning statement that directly addresses the issue.

Crisis worker: (*working with a client whose family members have just been killed and injured in a landslide*) You have not mentioned your faith or religious

affiliation. When I have been involved in similar situations with people who have lost loved ones, for many people faith is an important part of how they deal with such terrible tragedies. Even though one's faith is a deeply personal matter, and I may know very little about your religious faith, I am wondering if you would like to talk about that with me, or perhaps I can find a leader of your faith with whom you can talk if you would prefer that. One way or the other, I want you to know that I am going to be here with you to help you work your way through this difficult time.

After that, you generally need to practice the listening and responding skills you will encounter in Chapter 4. For people who are in a transcrisis state due to a loss of faith and have unresolved grief, we will have more to say about spirituality and faith in Chapter 12, Personal Loss: Bereavement and Grief.

Support Systems

As you will soon see, providing support is **LO13** so critical that we designate it as a separate task in our crisis intervention model (Chapter 3). Social supports—family, friends, peers, and professionals when no other supports are there or those former social support systems have been abandoned—are critical because they work (Taylor, 2007)! However, how people in crisis utilize social support systems is not always linear or direct. Shelby and Tredinnick (1995) found that African American and Hispanic populations tended to rely on extended support systems much more heavily than did European Americans. Dass-Railsford (2008) had a number of conversations with social service authorities, convincing them that children whose biological parents were missing post-Katrina were not abandoned but in the care of other competent adults who would care for them and keep them safe. For some cultures, "family" means a lot more than the residents in the house at 708 S. Grove Street. Therefore, the workers' efforts needed to focus more on systemic approaches that dealt with extended family networks rather than individuals.

As helpful as social support may be, for some people the cultural prohibitions against opening oneself up to receive social support may be like going from the frying pan into the fire. In their research on Asians and Asian Americans, Kim, Sherman, and Taylor (2008) found that the college students they studied were far more hesitant than their European American counterparts to seek any support systems because their inability to handle the crisis would bring shame not only on themselves but on their families as well. One reason for this reluctance, they suggest, may be that the very act of seeking support would require the students to self-disclose personal issues, which would put even more stress on them. Reframing such support in more culturally acceptable terms may be one way of allowing individuals to receive help. Organista and Munoz (1996) suggest using manuals and homework assignments, much like a teacher and a classroom assignment, to avoid the stigma of being seen by a mental health worker and receiving psychotherapy.

Crisis worker: (*dealing with a female Asian college student who is thousands of miles from home and who has been sexually assaulted and is largely noncommittal or oblique in her response to the assault*) Li Mai, suffering and enduring what you have is hard for any woman. It is very difficult to speak of such personal violations for almost every woman I have encountered who has undergone what you have. It is very common to not want to talk about a sexual assault because of all the negative emotions that go with it—particularly the guilt for thinking you were not cautious enough or the shame if it becomes known. However, I also know there are some things that you need to know about and could use some help with. You might wish to think of me more as a teacher who can give you important information which you can then use as you see fit. Or perhaps a coach who can help you make adjustments, just like a soccer player or a figure skater so that they are able to perform better. I hope you will think about what I have said and perhaps frame this incident in that manner and see me as that teacher or coach.

The shame of self-disclosure about a perceived moral or personal failing is not to be taken lightly. One of the hallmarks of domestic violence is the embarrassment and shame if word gets out that the person is being physically abused. Certainly no Jewish women are ever beaten by their spouses because that does not happen in the Jewish religion/culture. Whoa! Unless the city of Memphis has a different Jewish population than most other places in the world, the domestic violence reports that flow into our Family Trouble Center would indicate otherwise. However, such myths have a powerful social influence and pressure people not to seek support (Zimberhoff & Brown, 2006). Myth busting is part and parcel of a lot of the crises in this book, and providing education is a primary task of the worker.

Crisis worker: I want you to be aware that there's a notion that Jewish women do not get beaten by their husbands. Or at the very least good Jewish wives and mothers don't get beaten. Yet the fact is that we have many, many reports that in Memphis, Tennessee, Jewish women do get beaten, and I don't think there are that many bad Jewish wives and mothers around, so I want you to understand that is a myth and you are not the only Jewish wife who has been beaten. In fact, I would like you to come to a group of women in a support group who are coming out of the kind of battering relationship you have been in. It may interest you to know that there are three women in the group I am thinking of that are in fact Jewish.

Occupation as a Cultural Barrier

The ecological model in Chapter 1 may also **LO14** be applied to the "culture" of particular occupations. It is interesting that most multiculturalists, with the exception of Laura Brown (2008, p. 25), give little or no acknowledgment to occupation as a major social location. An occupation is inextricably tied to most of our lives and is how we identify ourselves. Go to a party, meet a stranger, and after some initial pleasantries, we'll bet that somewhere in there will be a "So what do you do?" or "Where do you work?" question.

The occupational agriculture of Chandler Mountain, Alabama, is far different from the financial culture of Wall Street, New York. We believe that to not take occupation into consideration as a defining part of one's culture and ecosystem is to be absolutely oblivious to a major contributing factor in how one lives. Police work is an excellent example. Police officers might be thought of as psychologically at risk due solely to the high stress and potentially lethal situations they face. However, that is far from true.

Any crisis worker who proceeded to deal with a police officer based on the erroneous notion that high stress caused by exposure to lethal situations was the sole factor contributing to a crisis would be very mistaken. Police officers constitute a distinct occupational culture and closed ecosystem because of their authority roles, their segregation from the rest of society, their irregular work schedules, the reactive nature of their job, the constant exposure to the negative side of life, the constant emotional control they must maintain, and the definitive manner in which they must judge right and wrong (Winter & Battle, 2007).

A major issue that bedevils law enforcement officers is their married life. They have one of the highest divorce rates of any occupation. They do not usually talk about their jobs or their feelings because they sense their spouses are uncomfortable hearing about such matters. Their job stress occurs because of "burst stress." That is, they may go from a long period of tedium and boredom to an immediate high-adrenaline moment. Over the long run, that psychological roller-coaster ride is extremely stressful. Furthermore, because law enforcement officers see the failure of the mental health system every day in the United States, they are likely to have a very jaundiced view of the mental health profession as a whole (Hayes, 1999).

It is not to seek thrills that trainers of the Memphis Police Department Crisis Intervention Team (CIT) ride patrol shifts with CIT officers. Although those rides provide us with valuable on-the-scene experience, they also help us appreciate the ecosystem within which the officer operates. The alliance with CIT officers that emerges from riding the Saturday night shifts with them helps break down occupational barriers and establish our own "bona fides" as being "culturally aware" of what the officers are going through. No amount of reading or expertise that we know of compensates for lack of knowledge and sensitization to this cultural milieu.

Geographic Locale as a Cultural Barrier

Lenihan and Kirk (1999) have developed a **LO15** rural, community-level crisis intervention plan for very small towns and rural areas that lack the typical crisis infrastructure and support systems available to even medium-sized communities. Many small communities and isolated rural areas are assailed by crises, yet these crises are not large enough to call for federal responses. However, the state emergency management agency may send crisis workers from neighboring counties and state agencies to assist the target community. Or the community itself may request volunteer help from universities, charities, civic groups, and local governments in close proximity. People in these areas may be very suspicious of outsiders, even those from neighboring communities, attempting to "tell them what to do." Yet collective fear, rumor, parochialism, and inaccessibility to services can keep the community traumatized and immobile without such help. Lenihan and Kirk propose that intervention strategies must absolutely address the cultural issues that will exist between outside service providers and recipients of service before any meaningful work can be done. They advocate an immediate assessment of the traumatic event's effect not only on individuals, but on the culture as well. In a sense, they are "triaging" the whole

community. They propose that no outside crisis response team can do an adequate job if it does not first seek out, identify, and consult with a broad cross section of community leaders about how and with whom crisis intervention should proceed.

Particularly important is ascertaining what the community's belief systems are and if there are subcultures within the system that may have different responses from those of the community at large (Chemtob, 2000). Any crisis response must be integrated into the community leadership and organizations such as social clubs, churches, civic groups, and fraternal organizations. Providing sensitive consultation for community leaders without "ramming it down their throats" is imperative. The same is true of using basic listening skills in hearing what the community has to say, instead of a bull-in-a-china-shop, officious, expert, "we know what's best for you" approach (van den Eynde & Veno, 1999).

Evaluating and finding the natural leaders of the community and teaming up with them are important in forming workable alliances and providing the citizens an anchor of familiarity, security, and control at the scene. Any action plans should be developed cooperatively and should be concrete, doable, and manageable, considering the available community financial and human resources (Lenihan & Kirk, 1999). In short, outside interventionists in such communities do best when they function as guides and helpers who operate along a continuum of directive to nondirective intervention. That is, the interventionist should be only as directive as the degree to which the client (the community) is immobilized.

The Dilemma of Local Consultation

A real dilemma occurs in consulting and working with the local authorities. On the one hand, they know best the infrastructure and needs of the community. Involving community representatives and leaders as intermediaries and consultants can give workers much easier access to the population and can provide helpful tips in regard to local taboos or cultural artifacts that can interfere with service delivery (Chemtob, 2000).

On the other hand, because outside workers are not invested in the local infrastructure and are not enculturated, they may blithely go about their business and in the process attempt to redress a variety of long-held social injustices and practices (Golec, 1983). The wise crisis worker who goes into a different geographical area needs to understand that this dilemma *always* exists, whether the location is Kabul, Afghanistan, or Collettsville, North Carolina. We are *absolutely not* proposing that crisis workers go about the business of changing and redressing all the perceived evils and shortcomings they may run into. However, as with Shelby and Tredinnick's (1995) report on the cultural reactions of their clients to a disaster, we are not so sure that one should stand passively by while victims project their frustrations by beating their children. What we do urge is that crisis workers *absolutely* need to be aware of this dilemma.

So should crisis workers leave well enough alone? Certainly the ability of a community to take care of itself is paramount. Members of the community understand the political, religious, and cultural roots and infrastructure far better than outsiders. Yet when a disaster strikes, and the community's resources are exceeded, there is a good deal of research that indicates such altruism does not extend to the poor, the elderly, the less educated, and ethnic minorities. Such groups may be disenfranchised and denied a part in the "democracy of a common disaster" (Kaniasty & Norris, 1995). Although the elderly, in particular, may be seen as needing assistance with physical complaints or illness, such attention does not necessarily extend to dealing with property damage or keeping a roof over their heads, food on the table, and medicine in their cabinets (Kaniasty & Norris, 1997; Kaniasty, Norris, & Murrell, 1990).

Kilijanek and Drabek (1979) coined the term "pattern of neglect" in regard to the lack of aid received by the elderly in their study of a Kansas tornado's devastation of Topeka. The "squeaking wheel gets the grease" is probably even more true in the wake of a disaster. **YAVIS clients**—those Young, Attractive, Verbal, Intelligent, and Socially well-connected clients from higher socioeconomic backgrounds—get better service because they have the power, influence, technical savvy, and verbal articulation to get help. People whose social locations differ from those of YAVIS clients tend to do less well and are not knowledgeable enough, not verbal enough, not able enough, not young enough, not technologically sophisticated enough, and not assertive enough to get the help they need (Brown, 2009). Crisis interventionists need to be acutely aware of this pattern and take pains to ensure that all individuals who seek and desire assistance in the traumatic wake of a disaster obtain it.

The Necessity of Acting

When we are in the heat of the moment in a **LO16** crisis, observing the "niceties" of another culture that tends to deal obliquely and subtly with problems may not be in the best safety interests of those clients.

The foregoing statement is made very conditionally. That is, whenever possible we want to take as much time as we can to understand the client's issues and perceptions, and that holds true of the collective populace as well. Certainly, being sensitive to the clients' cultural and ecological background is part of a patient and thorough problem exploration.

We further believe that one of the worst therapeutic errors a worker can make is to attempt to "hurry" the process. Crisis intervention should never be hurried. Although it may seem paradoxical, the fastest way to resolve a crisis is to take your time to understand what is going on. Still and all, if we have a client who is "running amok" (a Filipino cultural term for going absolutely, violently crazy), his cognitive processes are going to be seriously impaired, his behavior is going to be threatening, and his emotions will be out of control. What that means in the reality of the situation is acting rapidly and in a very concrete manner to assure his and others' safety. Finally, helping anybody, no matter how culturally different, is complex in a crisis. So take your time.

Many culturally diverse families have years of coping with crisis and are extremely resilient. If a person from a different cultural background is a recent immigrant, these successes may be minimized in the immigrant's new country or territory and seen as irrelevant or inconsequential. They are not! The astute crisis worker will attempt to recognize and marshal these past successes to the current dilemma. Normalizing the crisis experience is particularly important for the culturally diverse who may already be isolated socially and believe no one else is having similar responses. Empowerment, particularly for the culturally diverse, is the watchword in crisis intervention (Congress, 2000).

There is a delicate balance between helping and interfering. This is a constant bipolar dilemma for both recipients and providers of service after a disaster. On the one hand, the recipient appreciates the help, good intentions, and sincere concern. On the other hand, those same providers may be met with confusion, skepticism, and perceived psychological threat by the same recipients (Wortman & Lehman, 1985). Our experience has been that this bipolar dilemma can occur not only on the same day but in the same hour!

Training

The American Red Cross training for mental health disaster relief certification has course work in diversity training and cross-cultural differences. The National Institute of Mental Health (2002) report and recommendations for dealing with the traumatic wake of mass violence cautioned practitioners that disaster mental health training needs to incorporate cross-cultural training, because variations in understanding the meaning of thoughts, behaviors, and feelings by ethnically different persons can influence the validity of assessments, treatment protocols, and general interaction with survivor populations. Whether the crisis worker is going to Kobe, Japan, or Long Beach, Mississippi, understanding that it is culturally alien turf is critical to crisis work. The U.S. Department of Health and Human Services' *Developing Cultural Competence in Disaster Mental Health Programs: Guiding Principles and Recommendations* (2003) contains a variety of helpful suggestions for working with people in a large-scale disaster.

Where It Stands Now . . . Sorta

Multiculturalism has evolved through stages of raising consciousness levels. At present, the criticisms leveled in the past about treatment modalities that are biased toward ethnocentric European American populations seem unfounded or questionable at best. What does seem reasonable and shows some success is **cultural adaptation** that modifies evidence-based treatments to accommodate the cultural beliefs, attitudes, and behaviors of the cultural group to whom

one is providing services (Whaley & Davis, 2007). To that end—and this is certainly easier said than done in the field of crisis where chaos theory tends to run rampant when service delivery is most critical—carefully controlled studies need to occur that measure both traditional therapeutic approaches against well-described cultural adaptations of those therapies and cultural specific practices that look nothing like our current intervention models. Moreover, there need to be more ethnic minorities involved in those studies (Atkinson, Bui, & Mori, 2001)—in itself a tall order since, as previously stated, minorities are not overly keen on using mental health services. Rodriguez and Bernal (2012) have compiled and reported on a variety of models that are attempting to culturally adapt evidence-based treatments. It will be interesting to see which, if any of these models emerge as valid and if they have transferability to crisis intervention. It would also be very interesting to see what effect client–interventionist congruency, in terms of Brown's (2008) social locations hypotheses, has on treatment. To this point we have been unable to find any research that asks the most essential question arising from this chapter: "How sensitive was the interventionist in regard to your social locations, and was it helpful when she was?"

SUMMARY

While not a great deal is yet known about exactly how ecological/cultural determinants interact with crisis, it is clear that they do. This interaction has significant implications for crisis interventionists as they work with people from different cultural backgrounds. One of the major differences interventionists need to recognize is the different methods of communication and allegiances between individualist/collectivist–high/low-context systems. Social locations, the many facets that make up each person's life, are as important "within" culture/ethnicity variables as the "between" variables that differentiate one group from another. This chapter espouses a more universal/emic as opposed to a focused etic view in defining multiculturalism and cautions the reader to be a discerning consumer in regard to what prevailing multicultural views may hold for the practice of crisis intervention. We have generated a new SAFETY social

locations model that we believe seems to fit the specific environment of a crisis setting.

Particularly important to crisis interventionists is disabusing themselves of tunnel vision perspectives, assumptions, and unconscious biases they may have about people from different cultures. If you want to get a really good multicultural cross section of how people around the world deal with trauma, then read Ani Kalayjian and Eugene Dominique's (2010) two volumes on *Mass Trauma and Emotional Healing Around the World: Rituals and Practices for Resilience and Meaning Making.*

Visit CengageBrain.com for a variety of study tools and useful resources such as video examples, case studies, interactive exercises, flashcards, and quizzes.

3

The Intervention and Assessment Models

LEARNING OBJECTIVES

After studying this chapter, you should be able to:

1. Understand the concepts of equilibrium/ disequilbrium and mobility/immobility as they apply to stabilizing an individual in crisis.
2. Understand how the hybrid model of crisis intervention is used, what its component parts are, and how they are applied.
3. Understand and use the Triage Assessment System and its affective, behavioral, and cognitive components in doing real-time assessment of an individual in crisis.
4. Understand the role that psychobiology plays in assessing crisis.
5. Understand the role that the duration of time, the degree of emotional stamina, the developmental stage of the client, and the ecosystem contribute to the crisis.

Introduction

The purpose of this chapter is to present an **LO1** applied crisis intervention model that describes in detail the major tasks involved in dealing with a crisis. The Triage Assessment System is introduced as a rapid but systematic technique for the crisis worker to use to adjudicate the severity of a client's presenting crisis situation and gain some sense of direction in helping the client cope with the dilemma. Finally, this chapter shares some ideas on using referrals and gives some suggestions regarding counseling difficult clients. This chapter and Chapter 4, The Tools of the Trade, are a prerequisite for succeeding chapters, and we urge you to consider this foundation material carefully.

The model of crisis intervention you are about to encounter emphasizes an immediacy mode of actively, assertively, intentionally, and continuously assessing, listening, and acting to systematically help the client regain as much precrisis equilibrium, mobility, and autonomy as possible. Two of those terms, **equilibrium** and **mobility**, and their antonyms, **disequilibrium** and **immobility**, are commonly used by crisis workers to identify client states of being and coping. Because we will be using these terms often, we would like to first provide their dictionary definitions and then give a common analogy, so their meaning becomes thoroughly understood.

Equilibrium. A state of mental or emotional stability, balance, or poise in the organism.

Disequilibrium. Lack or destruction of emotional stability, balance, or poise in the organism.

Mobility. A state of physical being in which the person can autonomously change or cope in response to different moods, feelings, emotions, needs, conditions, influences; being flexible or adaptable to the physical and social world.

Immobility. A state of physical being in which the person is not immediately capable of autonomously changing or coping in response to different moods, feelings, emotions, needs, conditions, influences; inability to adapt to the immediate physical and social world.

A healthy person is in a state of approximate psychological and behavioral equilibrium, like a motorist driving, with some starts and stops, down the road of life—for both the short and the long haul. The person may hit some potholes but does not break any axles. Aside from needing to give the car an occasional tune-up, the person remains more or less equal to the task of making the drive. In contrast, the person in crisis, whether it be acute or chronic, is experiencing serious difficulty in steering and successfully navigating life's highway. The individual is at least temporarily out of control, unable to command personal resources or those of others in order to stay on safe psychological pavement.

A healthy person is capable of negotiating hills, curves, ice, fog, stray animals, wrecks, and most other obstacles that impede progress. No matter what roadblocks may appear, such a person adapts to changing conditions, applying brakes, putting on fog lights, and estimating passing time. This person may have fender benders from time to time but avoids head-on collisions. The person in a dysfunctional state of equilibrium and mobility has failed to pass inspection. Careening down hills and around dangerous curves, knowing the brakes have failed, the person is frozen with panic and despair and has little hope of handling the perilous situation. The result is that the person has become a victim of the situation, has forgotten all about emergency brakes, downshifting, or even easing the car into guardrails. He or she flies headlong into catastrophe and watches transfixed as it happens. The analogy of equilibrium and mobility applies to most crisis situations. Thus, it becomes every crisis worker's job to figuratively get the client back into the driver's seat of the psychological vehicle. As we shall see, sometimes this means the client must temporarily leave the driving to us, sometimes it means sitting alongside the client and pointing out the rules of the road, and sometimes it means just pretty much going along for the ride!

All of that being said, the crisis worker will meet a number of individuals who were not poster children for psychological equilibrium before the crisis. Many people who were displaced by Hurricane Katrina, for example, were physically and psychologically fragile before the hurricane. We will have more to say about such people, who are more typically in a state of transcrisis, in Chapter 5, Crisis Case Handling.

A Hybrid Model of Crisis Intervention

There are numerous models for crisis intervention (Aguilera, 1998; Kanel, 1999; Kleespies, 2009; Lester, 2002; Roberts, 2005; Slaikeu, 1990). All of these models depict crisis intervention in some linear, stage, or stepwise fashion. Indeed, through 25 years of publishing this book we did much the same, with the admonition that changing conditions might well mean that the interventionist would have to recycle and move back to earlier steps. We no longer believe

LO2

that a stage or purely step model captures the way crisis intervention works, and here's why.

The problem that we have struggled with as we try to teach students like you about crisis intervention is that at times crisis is anything but linear. A lot of the times crisis intervention absolutely epitomizes chaos theory—with starts, stops, do-overs, and U-turns. At times doing crisis work is a lot like being a smoke jumper, controlling a psychological brush fire on this side of the mountain only to be faced with a new one on the other side of the valley. Fighting those psychological fires according to a neat, progressive, linear plan is easily said but not so easily done. Therefore, we have combined our former linear model with a systems model we helped develop (Myer, James, & Moulton, 2011), resulting in what could more appropriately be called a hybrid model for individual crisis intervention that is generally linear in its progression but can also be seen in terms of tasks that need to be accomplished. While certainly some of these tasks would usually be done in the beginning, middle, or end of a crisis, changing conditions may mean you have to accomplish some task you would normally do later, first. Or indeed, a task you thought was already accomplished comes apart and has to be done over not once, but multiple times.

A further problem with a strict linear model is that each step should be discrete, following from step one to step two and so on, with particular techniques to employ in each of those steps. In crisis intervention, issues suddenly erupt that defy discrete, stepwise techniques. Focus on getting a commitment from a person to do something, which would normally come at the end of a crisis session, may need to happen immediately if that person is standing out in the middle of a busy intersection at rush hour! Likewise, gaining that commitment to get out of the street may call for assertion techniques that are anything but what we might normally do when making initial contact with a client. Consider the following analogy.

Picture yourself as a linesperson on the cross arm of a power pole, hard hat on, heavy insulated clothing, leather over insulated gloves, dug in with your climbing spikes, attempting to repair a high-voltage (crisis) transmission line in North Dakota in January with the wind blowing sleet in your face at 20 miles an hour. On your utility belt are a variety of tools. You know the steps required to get the transformer hooked back up and the sequential manner in which you will employ the tools on your belt to get the job done. The problem is, Mother Nature is not happy and the wind picks up and a coupling breaks loose or a new fuse you just put in blows and you have to start all over again! If you can picture this analogy in your mind's eye, you are well on the way to understanding how crisis intervention works. As we describe the model, we will give you some examples of when you have to change tools to meet the changing conditions up on that pole.

The model you are about to examine is the hub around which the crisis intervention strategies in this book revolve, and the tasks/steps are designed to operate as an integrated problem-solving process (Myer, Lewis, & James, 2013). It is not complex, but rather is designed to be simple to implement, easy to use, and adaptable to just about any crisis we can think of you would likely encounter.

Task 1. Predispositioning/Engaging/Initiating Contact

Predispostioning may be seen as first and foremost getting ready to do something. It is usually the first step in a crisis model: placing oneself, or something, in a position to be of use in some future occurrence. Typically, systems such as the armed forces and government agencies such as FEMA use **predispositioning** to get supplies, equipment, and personnel ready to meet some future emergency. Indeed, in Chapter 17, Disaster Response, you will see predispositioning in operation on a very large scale. In the counseling literature, predisposition was originally studied by Prochaska, DiClemente, and Norcross (1992) in regard to what motivated people who were suffering from addiction to decide to change. Since their seminal work, the concept of predisposing clients to get them ready for counseling has become widespread.

In crisis intervention, predisposition is somewhat different. It means predisposing individuals to be receptive to our intervention when, in many instances, they may not be at all enthused about our presence or be so out-of-control that they are only vaguely aware of us. Therefore, predisposition has a lot to do with the attitudinal set and predisposition of how the crisis worker enters the situation. A number of clients the crisis worker will meet do not act, talk, look, or even smell nice! The ability to convey empathy and be authentic as to who and what you are doing without pretense is critical (Kleespies & Richmond, 2009).

Particularly with a first contact, predispositioning the client as to what to expect is critical. Along with letting the client know what is going to occur, it is important to make contact in such a way that the client can see the interventionist as an immediate ally and support, and not another in a long line of people,

representative of bureaucracies and institutional authorities, who have been anything but helpful in resolving their problems. One of the most critical initiating components of crisis intervention is how the worker introduces himself or herself to a client who has never met the crisis interventionist—which is a fairly common occurrence in this business. It is not just to fill time that our practicum training with aspiring crisis intervention team police officers now devotes an initial session specifically to how the officer introduces himself or herself to a recipient of services (Memphis Police Department, 2010). Our primary objectives in predisposing an individual to accept crisis intervention are twofold: (1) to establish a psychological connection and create a line of communication and (2) to clarify intentions with regard as to what is going to happen.

Establishing Psychological Connection. First and foremost, you need to introduce yourself in a way that is nonthreatening, helpful, and assumes a problem-solving as opposed to an adversarial approach.

Leron: (*standing in the middle of a main city street in five o'clock rush hour traffic waving two broken whiskey bottles*) The God damned house authority. NO place to live. Kicked me out, the rotten bastards. Everybody needs to know them for the crooks they are.

CIT officer: (*slowly approaching the subject from a distance with hands visible, empty, and open*) Man! You really are angry with them to make this kind of statement out in the middle of Union Avenue during rush hour. My name's Scott Lewis, a CIT officer with the Memphis Police Department. I didn't catch your name. Mind telling me?

One of the most important elements in making **first contact** is getting the client's name and introducing yourself in a nonthreatening manner. Note that Scott approaches the subject slowly, not only because he is armed with two whiskey bottles (which has to do with another task that is pretty important here, providing for the client's safety and your own), and responds to his current affective and behavioral state of being. Before he ever asks a question about why this has happened, he immediately states his name and asks for the client's. Also note that his full name, not his rank or the police department, comes first.

Another advantage with the approach used by Scott is that he allows Leron to maintain some control over the situation. The housing authority has already taken his home and barred him from his belongings. Imagine if Scott rolled onto the scene and immediately began demanding Leron to get out of the street and put down the whiskey bottles. Scott would likely get the response "screw you, cop." Scott would be seen as just another authority figure who doesn't listen. By establishing a problem-solving, helpful connection, Scott allows Leron to maintain momentary control of the situation. By reflecting Leron's anger, the crisis worker immediately attempts to convey empathic understanding of the extreme measures the client has taken in attempting to problem-solve.

Clarifying Intentions.   Clarifying intentions means informing the client about what the crisis intervention process is and what the client can expect to happen. For many clients who are in crisis, this will be their first contact with a crisis interventionist, and they will have little if any idea of what is going to happen or how it is going to happen. Leron most likely has had experiences with the police that lead him to believe that nothing positive is going to happen with Officer Lewis. Thus, the CIT officer needs to quickly apprise him of what will happen.

CIT officer: Okay I can see right off you clearly have some issues with the housing authority. Right now I am going to listen very closely to what got you out here. I may ask you some questions so I get a clearer notion of the problem. We've got some time and I am going to take the time to hear you out. I'll also probably kinda sum up what you're saying so I'm sure I heard you right. So I wonder if we could move this over underneath that shade tree cause it's hot and not very safe out here.

Leron: (*weaving unsteadily and sweating profusely*) No! As soon as I do that, those other cops will bum rush me. Long as I'm out here they got to pay attention and that News 5 chopper stays up there. Lost my job through no fault of my own and now kicked out.

CIT officer: Okay. I hear what you're saying about keeping the evil stuff the housing authority has done to you in the public's eye. However, sooner or later we're going to need to get out of the street. I'd like that to be sooner since it is 98 degrees out here and my guess is you're getting thirsty and would like to get it settled and get out of the sun. Nobody's going to bum rush you. It's between you and me right now. That's the way I'd like to keep it.

Officer Lewis uses basic listening and responding statements that own what is going to happen in the next few minutes. He also states the immediate end goal of the crisis resolution for him as "getting out of the middle of the street." He clearly states his intention to listen, get the client's perspective, and do no harm to him while this is going on. While the client's end goal may be completely different—bringing the housing authority to justice in some manner—the interventionist states from the outset in pretty clear terms what he is going to do. In clear, concise statements, the interventionist creates a line of communication by using open-ended questions, reflection of feelings, and owning statements (all of which you will learn about in the next chapter) that reinforce and encourage the client to tell his story. The major intentional strategy here is allowing the client to cathart but also keeping the client in real time and not allowing the interaction to degenerate into all the perceiving injustices ever perpetrated on him.

This introduction "stuff" may sound pretty simplistic, but in the heat of the moment it is surprising how that can go by the wayside. It may also seem like a "once and done" deal, but even for a client who has known the interventionist for a long time and is currently out of touch with reality, anchoring the client by stating who the interventionist is, clarifying intentions, and stating what needs to happen is a critical ingredient for a successful intervention.

Task 2. Problem Exploration: Defining the Crisis

A major initial task in crisis intervention is to define and understand the problem from the client's point of view. This is particularly difficult in the middle of a chaotic situation where there are complex biopsychosocial contributors interacting with one another (Kleespies & Richmond, 2009). Unless the worker perceives the crisis situation as the client perceives it, all the intervention strategies and procedures the helper might use may miss the mark and be of no value to the client. Intervention sessions begin with crisis workers practicing what are called the **core listening skills**: empathy, genuineness, and acceptance or positive regard (Cormier & Cormier, 1991, pp. 21–39).

Problem definition of a crisis does not mean going on a psychological archaeological dig to dredge up and sift every artifact of the client's past. Defining the crisis does mean attempting to identify the precipitating event across the affective, behavioral, and cognitive components of the crisis. This task serves two purposes. First, the interventionist sees the crisis from the client's perspective. Second, defining the crisis gives the interventionist information on the immediate conditions, parties, and issues that led to eruption of the problem into a crisis.

CIT officer: I understand that the housing authority screwed you over somehow. So tell me what got you so mad and frustrated you needed to get everybody's attention.

As Leron angrily expounds on the housing authority's injustices toward people and himself, Officer Lewis uses an expansion strategy to broaden the client's view of the problem without letting the problem escalate. He restates the client's complaint and follows with an open lead.

Inevitably other issues will surface as the interventionist attempts to define the crisis. In the case of Leron, Officer Lewis may suspect that Leron is dependent on alcohol, given the fact that he has two empty whiskey bottles in his hands and is having trouble keeping his balance. He also is now aware that Leron has recently been laid off from his job. While these issues need attention, at the moment the interventionist needs to remain focused on the crisis—getting Leron out of the street and assisting him to access the resources needed to address the eviction from his apartment. The other issues should be placed on the back burner and may well be discussed after the crisis has been resolved.

CIT officer: So they lost your application for delayed payment while you wait for unemployment to kick in, then said you hadn't filed and kicked you out. I understand how that could make you so mad. So how about putting those bottles down and stepping over to that shade tree. I see you're sweating pretty hard out here in the hot sun and bet you could use some water. I just happen to have some bottles in my lunch cooler. I've got a couple of ideas about how to get you out of this predicament.

Task 3. Providing Support

The third task in crisis intervention emphasizes communicating to the client that the worker is a person who cares about the client. Workers cannot assume that a client experiences feeling valued, prized, or cared for. In many crisis situations, the exact opposite will be true. The support step provides an opportunity for the worker to assure the client that "here is one person who really cares about you." We believe that providing support occurs in three ways.

Psychological Support. First and most immediate is providing psychological and physical support. Deep,

empathic responding using reflection of feelings and owning statements about the client's present condition serves as a bonding agent that says emphatically, "I am with you right here." In Task 3, the person providing the support is the crisis worker. This means that workers must be able to accept, in an unconditional and positive way, all their clients, whether the clients can reciprocate or not. The worker who can truly provide support for clients in crisis is able to accept and value the person no one else is willing to accept. While Officer Lewis is attempting to get Leron out of the street, he also offers genuine support and help in getting the client out of his predicament with the housing authority.

Logistical Support. In a more general sense, support may be not only emotional but also instrumental and informational (Cohen, 2004). At times the client may not have money, food, clothing, or shelter. Little psychological support will be desired or progress made until the basic necessities of living and surviving are met. Physical support means giving clients concrete assistance to help weather the crisis. This support comes in many forms, ranging from providing pamphlets to arranging transportation of clients to organizations that have the resources needed to help them to simply giving them a drink of water.

CIT officer: I can't imagine what it's like not to have a job or a roof over your head. Where's your family in all this?

Leron: Tormeda and the kids done went to her momma's in Arkansas. Nothin' to eat and no place to live ceptin' the street. Momma took her back cause I ain't no account and cain't feed 'em or put a roof over dere heads.

CIT officer: The words "terrifying" and "hopeless" come to mind. I can see why this might come down to the only solution you can think of. I really do want to help you out with this and get you back on your feet, and I do maybe have an idea or two about how to do that. But I don't want to see you arrested and if we don't move this out of the middle of the street so I can share some of my ideas with you, nothing will happen except you going to jail. So you have a choice. What's your wish? Help getting this resolved or jail?

Leron: Jail don't sound good . . . been there, done that.

CIT officer: I hear that. I don't want to see you in jail either, so come on over here and let's look at some options.

Leron: (*walks slowly over to the curb and sets the bottles down*) Okay, I be done. I be givin' you a shot at dis. I guess I be needin' some hep.

In this exchange, Officer Lewis forms a bond with Leron. Officer Lewis does not judge Leron, instead he encourages him to stay out of jail. This encouragement helps Leron regain a belief that the situation is not as dire as it seems and maybe with help a solution can be found. Encouragement is a critical component in crisis intervention because, for most clients, what they are going through is anything but encouraging. Catching clients' even feeble attempts to problem-solve gives them a chance to regain some hope, validates that they still have capabilities, and starts reframing thinking toward a proactive, problem-solving mode (Courtois & Ford, 2009, pp. 86–87).

Social Support. Third, providing support means activating clients' primary support system: family, friends, coworkers, church members, and so forth. For many people in crisis, this primary support system may be absent (a car accident 600 miles from home), fed up with their behavior (lying and stealing from them to subsidize an addiction), or unequal to the task of providing support as a result of the crisis (symptoms of posttraumatic stress disorder). Conversely, clients may feel too embarrassed or guilty to ask for help from their immediate support system such as Sunday school members (loss of job and inability to contribute to their church financially). At such times, the interventionist is not only the initial point of contact and immediate psychological and physical anchor, but also the "expert" who provides information, guidance, and primary support in the first minutes and hours after the initiating event (Aguilera, 1998; Cohen, 2004).

Informational Support. At other times, clients do not have adequate information to make good decisions. The need for informational support is particularly critical in the next step, examining alternatives. One of the best techniques a crisis interventionist can be in command of is the ability to provide information on where, how, who, and what resources clients can access to get out of the predicament they are in. That is particularly true of people who after a disaster are trying to access the basic necessities of living (Ruzek, 2006).

Default Task: Safety

Safety is a default task that is *always* operational. Safety is a primary consideration throughout crisis intervention for a variety of reasons that are both physically

and psychologically based. The task of assessing and ensuring the client's and others' safety is always part of the process, whether it is overtly stated or not. When we speak of safety, we are concerned about the physical safety not only of the client but also of those who may interact with him or her and, just as important, about keeping ourselves safe. Whether by commission or omission, clients often put themselves in hazardous situations as a result of their affective, behavioral, and cognitive reactions to the crisis. Leron's attempt to publicize his plight clearly puts him, the general public, and the officer at risk. While Leron's crisis is with the housing authority, the immediate crisis of Leron in the middle of a main street with two broken whiskey bottles in his hands is a safety issue. Nothing is more paramount in a crisis than ensuring safety.

We have personally known three human services workers who have been killed at the hands of clients in crisis. One of your authors could very easily have been added to that list early in his career when he talked a violent juvenile into handing over a gun pointed a foot from his face. He didn't think the weapon would work. After the youth was taken into custody, blanks were loaded in the gun and it fired very well, to the shock of a shaken 24-year-old junior high school counselor who thought he was immortal! There are no dead heroes in this business, only dead interventionists. We will have a great deal more to say on the subject of the interventionist's safety in Chapter 14, Violent Behavior in Institutions.

Generally, when we think about safety in a crisis, we assume that someone is engaging in lethal behavior toward self or others. But limiting the task of ensuring safety to issues of life and death overlooks many clients whose safety is in jeopardy. The fact is that in much crisis intervention people do not intend to cause harm to themselves or others but engage in activities that have a high potential for that to happen. You can extend the task of ensuring safety to include meeting the daily needs of clients such as finding shelter and food.

CIT officer: Leron, I want to keep you safe, man, and the middle of Union Avenue at rush hour is anything but that. I can get you some help not only as far as the housing authority is concerned but also in regard to getting some food in your belly and a roof over your head, but that has to start happening over in my squad car. Otherwise the TAC team will come and take you in to custody and none of that will happen. When did you eat last?

Leron: Don't remember . . . yesterday maybe . . . no, a couple of days ago I think. Got some stuff out of the back of one of them restaurants on Beale Street.

Officer Lewis is working to protect Leron from inadvertently being injured. Food and the offer of shelter are used to entice Leron off the street. This offer makes a clear point that all crisis interventionists need to heed: If a person's basic physical needs are not being met, it is unlikely that the crisis will diminish until those needs are met.

Safety also includes assuring clients that they are psychologically safe. As we shall see in Chapter 9, Sexual Assault, many clients who have been subject to vicious assaults by sexual perpetrators have suffered secondary victimization, being revictimized by authority figures, government bureaucracies, religious entities, social service agencies, and, yes, incompetent therapists (Ochberg, 1988). Making it safe for a client in crisis to trust the interventionist comes before everything else and is a critical part of creating the trust and bond necessary to move forward (Courtois & Ford, 2009). Safety is a default task that is merged and subsumed in all the other tasks in the model, from predispositioning to follow-up.

Tasks 1, 2, 3, and the safety task involve a lot of listening activities, although they are not necessarily passive or devoid of action, particularly when safety issues are involved. Taken together, these four steps most nearly represent what has become known in the field as *psychological first aid* (see Chapter 1).

Task 4. Examining Alternatives

Examining alternatives addresses an area that both clients and workers in crisis intervention often neglect—exploring a wide array of appropriate choices available to the client. In their immobile state, clients often do not adequately examine their best options. Some clients in crisis actually believe there are no options. Clients may develop tunnel vision and become stuck in an endless merry-go-round of attempting to engage in the same futile behavior.

Alternatives can be viewed from three perspectives: (1) **Situational supports** are people known to the client in the present or past who might care about what happens to the client. (2) **Coping mechanisms** are actions, behaviors, or environmental resources the client might use to help get through the present crisis. (3) **Positive and constructive thinking patterns** on the part of the client are ways of reframing that might substantially alter the client's view of the problem and lessen the client's level of stress and anxiety. The effective crisis worker may think about an infinite number of alternatives pertaining to the client's crisis but discuss only a few of them with the client. Clients experiencing crisis do not need a lot of choices; they need appropriate choices that are realistic for their situation. Some of these coping skills may be already present in the client but under the stress of the crisis may be forgotten or dismissed as ineffective because they were used "back when" or "back there" and are no longer workable in the here and now.

Leron: Used to have money in ma pocket. Had me a car 'n' a house 'n' food on de table. Fok lift op . . . e . . . ray . . . tore and damn good. Could figger stuff out. Fo'man on ma crew. Lotsa ideas 'bout movin' on up, din da compnee go bust. No mo'! Ain't got no job, no skills, no family, no nuthin' ceptin' damn housin' a-tho-it-tee.

CIT officer: Leron, it sounds like right now you're out there all alone against this big monster called MHA. I've got an idea. Okay, so your application for rent reduction got lost in the bureaucracy when you got laid off and they made it sound like it was your fault and blamed you for not submitting it when in fact you did. Your gripes to them haven't gotten you anywhere, and now you want everybody to know that they are trying to weasel out of their mistake. I've got one idea that might help, and that's the pro bono law advocacy student association of the Memphis University Law School. They take on stuff like this. I can take you down there and introduce you to somebody I know there, but I've got another concern. I wonder when was the last time you had something to eat and a place to lay your head down where you felt safe, could get some sleep and get some energy back?

By offering to physically transport Leron to the law school, Officer Lewis indicates that he is involved with Leron beyond his being a nuisance to get off the street. He also makes a hunch about Leron's physical condition, and that hunch segues into one of the most important tasks of crisis intervention, which is safety.

Examining alternatives is literally a "right here, right now" activity. Rapidly changing conditions may mean discarding old options that worked a half hour ago for completely new ones. One of the hallmarks of a world-class crisis worker is the ability to be resilient and rapidly brainstorm new ideas and implement them in a hurry.

CIT officer: (*noticing Leron's unsteady gate*) Leron, how much have you had to drink today?

Leron: 'Bout most of them two bottles.

CIT officer: I can understand why you'd need all that liquid courage to do this. Okay! Maybe we need to think about getting you sober before you talk to anybody down there. What about me taking you out to the Bartlett Salvation Army halfway house, getting some food in your stomach, cleaned up, some sleep so you got it all together and can talk real straight to the folks at the advocacy center.

Task 5. Planning in Order to Reestablish Control

A hallmark of people in crisis is the feeling of the loss of control. Chaos reigns and every effort to manage the situation has failed. Reestablishing control means helping clients create a plan to guide them in the resolution of the crisis. Such a plan needs to consider what options are available to the client and what choices need to be made in regard to those options. One of the primary strategies in planning to reestablish control is mobilizing the client.

The fifth step in crisis intervention, making plans, flows logically and directly from Task 4 alternatives. Much of the material throughout this book focuses either directly or indirectly on the crisis worker's involvement with clients in planning action steps that have a good chance of restoring the client's emotional, behavioral, and cognitive equilibrium. A plan should (1) identify additional persons, groups, and other referral resources that can be contacted for immediate support, and (2) provide coping mechanisms—something concrete and positive for the client to do now, definite action steps that the client can own and comprehend. The plan should focus on systematic problem solving for the client and be realistic in terms of the client's coping ability.

While it may be that crisis workers have to be very directive at times, as much as possible it is important that planning be done in collaboration with clients so that clients feel a sense of ownership of the plan. At the very least, explaining thoroughly what is about to occur and gaining client acquiescence is extremely important. The critical element in developing a plan is that clients do not feel robbed of their power, independence, and self-respect. The central issues in planning are clients' *control* and *autonomy*. The reasons for clients to carry out plans are to restore their sense of control and to ensure that they do not become dependent on support persons such as the worker. It should be emphasized that planning is not what clients are going to do for the rest of their lives. Planning is about

getting through the short term and getting some semblance of equilibrium and stability restored. Most plans in crisis intervention are measured in minutes, hours, and days, not weeks, months, or years.

CIT officer: I can't give you much more time. I gave you a choice. Those alternatives are to do something about the issue rather than going to jail. What do you want to do? I need for you to put those bottles down and walk over here and get in the car. Are you willing to do that and get some help for your problem and some food in your stomach?

Leron: (hesitates and shrugs; puts bottles down and walks over to the car) Okay . . . maybe you can get me some help.

(*Next afternoon at the legal aid office.*)

Legal aid worker: Mr. Brown, I believe we can exert some leverage on the housing authority and can make a case for you. This will take at least a couple of weeks, though, and I understand you have nowhere to stay.

(*Officer Lewis before dropping Leron off at the Salvation Army has made a promise to pick him up and take him to the legal aid office.*)

Officer Lewis: Leron, have you thought perhaps you might go over to Arkansas?

Leron: Man, I don't want to be beholden to my mother-in-law. She don't care much for me no how.

Officer Lewis: Well, you don't have a job, so you could go back out to the Salvation Army new halfway house. You'd qualify to get in it based on being out of work and the fact that your use of alcohol helped get you into that predicament.

Leron: Man, I ain't no charity case.

Officer Lewis: I hear that and understand you got your pride, but what about using their job counseling program out there to help you get back to work? I mean it's not like you're going there forever, and you'd be right there if anything comes in. They'd also do some job counseling.

Leron: Well, when you put it that way, could be okay.

Many times in crisis the alternatives are not what the client wants but what is necessary. When Officer Lewis reframes the stay at the Salvation Army as not charity but a way of getting Leron back to work, it becomes much more palatable and makes the alternative a much more positive and desirable one. Being able to reframe the alternative is empowering and one of the key ingredients in getting clients involved and energizing them to move forward.

Psychoeducation. At the time of the first edition of this book in 1987, there was not a great deal of information about many of the maladies in this book. Thus, interventionists didn't have a lot of information to give clients about the psychological course of the aftermath of a crisis. However, in the intervening 28 years, a tremendous amount of reliable and valid information has been discovered about the course of the crises discussed in this book. Giving clients this information, called *psychoeducation,* can be of tremendous benefit in helping them understand what is going on with them psychologically.

Psychoeducation means providing information to victims and survivors about what is happening and is probably going to happen to them psychologically in the aftermath of a traumatic event. Psychoeducation has become an extremely important treatment component in helping people in crisis get control back in their lives, not only in preemptive work such as educating people about suicide, domestic violence, and sexual assault, but also in understanding what happens in the traumatic wake of a crisis such as the terrifying flashbacks and nightmares of PTSD (Briere & Scott, 2006; Courtois, Ford, & Cloitre, 2009; Kleespies, 2009). Psychoeducation is a task in and of itself. However, for the present we have put it under planning because of the critical part it plays in helping to mobilize the client. Psychoeducation means providing clients with information about their condition, what they can expect in the way of affective, behavioral, and cognitive dimensions of it, and how they can develop coping skills to alleviate it.

We would not expect a first grader to have much knowledge or many psychological resources to deal with bullying, so we would be pretty directive in providing the child with information and strategies to deal with it. Likewise, for a person who knew nothing about how to deal with housing bureaucracies, options to get out of an unemployment line, and the common depressive symptoms that might exacerbate those problems into a full-blown crisis, the crisis worker's best treatment option is to start providing information and instructing the client about what needs to be done and how to take care of oneself psychologically while doing it.

Rehabilitation counselor: (*at Salvation Army Treatment Center a week later*) Leron, we have a lot of information that I believe will help you as far as getting employable is concerned. We also found out that you are most likely clinically depressed. That's important information because it goes a lot toward answering why you have been in such a rut, unable to do much about your problems, and why you wound up in the middle of the street a frustrated and angry man. We're going to set you up with an appointment to get some medication for that and also to get some counseling. I am going to give you a lot of information on why we think this is a good plan, so if you have any questions, stop me and I'll try and answer them.

Task 6. Obtaining Commitment

The sixth task, obtaining commitment, flows directly from Task 5, and the issues of control and autonomy apply equally to the process of obtaining an appropriate commitment. It may seem like overkill to devote a specific task/step to commitment as opposed to just making it a part of planning. However, getting a specific commitment from a client in crisis to do something differently than what has not been working is a big deal. The commitment step is clear, concise, and behaviorally specific. As a result, it is clear to the client what he or she is going to do and what the worker will do.

CIT officer: So tell me what we're going to do.

Leron: We gonna get out to the Salvation Armee and get me sobered up, din two' morro you gonna come git me 'n' tak me dow to legal aid 'bout 4:30, if'n I git in de polelesse car now and don't be givin' you no mo' trouble.

If the planning step is done effectively, the commitment step is apt to be easy. Many times the commitment step is brief and simple, consisting of asking the client to verbally summarize the plan. Sometimes a handshake may be used to seal the commitment. In some incidents where lethality is involved, the commitment may be written down and signed by both parties. The objective is to enable the client to commit to taking one or more definite, positive, intentional action steps designed to move that person toward restoring precrisis equilibrium. The worker is careful to obtain an honest, direct, and appropriate commitment from the client before terminating the crisis intervention session. No commitment should be imposed by the worker. Commitments should be free, voluntary, and believed to be doable. The core listening skills are as important to the commitment step as they are to the problem definition or any other step. Any hesitation on the part of the client to commit to the plan of action should be reflected and queried by the worker. A worker-imposed plan or commitment will not work.

Task 7. Follow-up

When we speak of follow-up in crisis, we are not talking about days, weeks, or months. Long-term follow-up after a disaster is a special condition we will deal with in Chapter 17, Disaster Response. We are generally speaking of following up in a time frame of minutes, hours, and days. Follow-up in crisis intervention has to do with keeping track of clients' success in maintaining precrisis equilibrium, not whether they are maintaining long-term goals or changing deep-seated personality traits.

CIT officer: (*stopping by Salvation Army halfway house the next day*) Leron, glad to see you. You look lots better today. Clean and sober. I checked with the coordinator and they have you set up for some vocational evaluation. While I'm not your social worker, I did stop by the U of M law students' pro bono advocacy service and they are willing to look into your problem with MHA. I think you can get a voucher here to get a bus down there. You've got my card, let me know if I can do anything for you.

Short-term follow-up is also important as a reinforcing event that tells clients you are still in this with them. Engaging in follow-up is extremely important when clients have little other social support system.

The model of crisis intervention we have been describing in some detail is summarized briefly in Figure 3.1.

ASSESSMENT

Overarching and continuous throughout the crisis:
Evaluating the client's present situational crisis in terms of the client's coping ability, mobility, support systems needed, physical resources required, and degree of threat to self and others. Making judgments as to type and kind of action needed, based on the crisis worker's action continuum.

TASKS

Overarching default task: Ensuring safety. Continuous assessment of how safe the client, others in the environment, and the worker are throughout the crisis. Putting in place and implementing procedures that will ensure the safety of *all* those involved in the crisis, including the crisis worker.

1. **Predispositioning/engaging/initiating contact.** Making initial positive contact with the client. Setting the stage for what the worker is going to do, what the client can expect from the worker, and how the worker will operate throughout the crisis.

2. **Exploring the problem.** Defining the problem as it currently manifests itself across the affective, behavioral, and cognitive domains of the individual. Exploring the intrapersonal, interpersonal, and systemic effects of the crisis as it operates in the current environment within which the person operates.

3. **Providing support.** Determining what kinds of support systems have worked in the past, what support systems are currently available, and what support systems will be needed. More

specifically, determining how much the worker will need to function as the main support system during the crisis and indicating to clients how that will happen.

4. **Examining alternatives.** Considering immediate short-term options to de-escalate the crisis and defuse the situation. Examining the choices the client currently has available in a realistic and time-efficient manner; includes finding situational supports, installing coping mechanisms, and reframing thinking to be more positive and solution focused to generate achievable short-term goals.

5. **Making plans.** Generating a short-term plan from the alternatives that are positive and doable, and translating into immediate action steps the client can comprehend, own, and implement.

6. **Obtaining commitment.** Obtaining a verbal or written commitment to a plan that can be comprehended, owned, and put in operation by the client.

7. **Follow-up.** Immediate, short-term follow-up by the worker to ensure that the plan is working and that the client and others are safe.

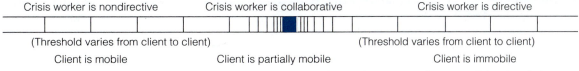

Crisis Worker's Action Continuum

Crisis worker is nondirective	Crisis worker is collaborative	Crisis worker is directive
(Threshold varies from client to client)		(Threshold varies from client to client)
Client is mobile	Client is partially mobile	Client is immobile

The crisis worker's level of action/involvement may be anywhere on the continuum according to a valid and realistic assessment of the client's level of mobility/immobility.

FIGURE 3.1 Model of Triage Assessment Form for Crisis Intervention

CIP-Solutions, June, 2009

Assessment in Crisis Intervention

Assessment is a pervasive strategy throughout **LO3** crisis intervention. This action-oriented, situation-based assessment is the basis for systematically applying our task model. Thus, the entire task process is carried out under an umbrella of assessment by the crisis worker. Because many of the assessments in crisis situations occur spontaneously, subjectively, and interactively in the heat of the moment, we are not dealing here with formal techniques such as DSM-5 diagnostic criteria or assessment instruments that are typically used in ongoing clinical evaluations. Kleespies and Richmond (2009) have a laundry list of mental status exam questions that cover everything from orientation/memory to visual/spatial organization. While these may be extremely useful in a set-piece intake assessment session at a hospital, lots of times there is neither the time nor the setting to engage in even a verbal comprehensive mental status examination.

Assessment is critically important because it enables the worker to determine (1) the severity of the crisis; (2) the client's current emotional, behavioral, and cognitive status—the client's level of mobility or immobility in these three areas; (3) the alternatives, coping mechanisms, support systems, and other resources available to the client; (4) the client's level of lethality (danger to self and others); (5) and how well the worker is doing in de-escalating and defusing the situation and returning the client to a state of equilibrium and mobility.

Assessing the Severity of Crisis

It is important for the crisis worker to evaluate the crisis severity as quickly as possible during the initial contact with the client. Crisis workers generally do not have time to perform complete diagnostic workups or obtain in-depth client histories. Therefore, a rapid assessment procedure, such as the Triage Assessment System (Myer, 2001; Myer et al., 1991, 1992) and its assessment siblings—the Triage Assessment Checklist for Law Enforcement (TACKLE; James, Myer, & Moore, 2006), the Triage Assessment System for Students in Learning Environments (TASSLE; Myer et al., 2007), and the Triage Assessment Form: Family Therapy (Myer, 2015)—are recommended as a quick and efficient way of obtaining information relevant to the specific crisis situation. These triage systems enable the worker to gauge the severity of the client's current functioning across affective, behavioral, and cognitive domains. The degree of severity of the crisis may affect the client's mobility, which in turn gives the worker a basis for judging how directive to be. The length of time the client has been in the present crisis will determine how much time the worker has in which to safely defuse the crisis.

The ABCs of Assessing in Crisis Intervention

Crisis is time limited; that is, most acute crises persist only a matter of days or weeks (the exception being large-scale disaster events) before some change—for better or worse—occurs. The severity of the crisis is assessed from the client's subjective viewpoint and from the worker's objective viewpoint. Objective assessment is based on an appraisal of the client's functioning in three areas that may be referred to as the ABCs of assessment: *affective* (feeling or emotional tone), *behavioral* (action or psychomotor activity), and *cognitive* (thinking patterns).

Affective State. Abnormal or impaired affect is often the first sign that the client is in a state of disequilibrium. The client may be overemotional and out of control or severely withdrawn and detached. Often the worker can assist the client to regain control and mobility by helping the client express feelings in appropriate and realistic ways. Some questions the worker may address are: Do the client's affective responses indicate that the client is denying the situation or attempting to avoid involvement in it? Is the emotional response normal or congruent with the situational crisis? To what extent, if any, is the client's emotional state driven, exacerbated, or otherwise influenced by other people? Do people typically show this kind of affect in situations such as this?

Behavioral Functioning. The crisis worker focuses much attention on *doing, acting out, taking active steps, behaving,* or any number of other psychomotor activities. In crisis intervention, the quickest (and often the best) way to get the client to become mobile is to facilitate positive actions that the client can take at once. People who cope with crisis successfully and later evaluate their experiences favorably report that the most helpful alternative during a crisis is to engage in some concrete and immediate activity. However, it is important for the worker to remember that it may be very difficult for immobilized people to take independent and autonomous action even though that is what they need to do most.

These are appropriate questions that the worker might ask to get the client to take constructive action: "In cases like this in the past, what actions did you take that helped you get back in control? What would you have to do now to get back on top of the situation? Is there anyone who, if you contacted them right now, would be supportive to you in this crisis?" The fundamental problem in immobility is loss of control. Once the client becomes involved in doing something concrete, which is a step in a positive direction, an element of control is restored, a degree of mobility is provided, and the climate for forward movement is established.

Cognitive State. The worker's assessment of the client's thinking patterns may provide answers to several important questions: How realistic and consistent is the client's thinking about the crisis? To what extent, if any, does the client appear to be rationalizing, exaggerating, or believing part-truths or rumors to exacerbate the crisis? How long has the client been engaged in crisis thinking? How open does the client seem to be toward changing beliefs about the crisis situation and reframing it in more positive terms of cooler, more rational thoughts, or is the client engaged in a downward spiral of catastrophic thinking with no hope of ameliorating the crisis?

The Triage Assessment System

Because rapid and adequate assessment of a client in crisis is one of the most critical components of intervention (Hersh, 1985), assessment has a preeminent place in the crisis intervention model, as an overarching and ongoing process. Constant and rapid assessment of the client's state of equilibrium dictates what the interventionist will do in the next seconds and minutes as the crisis unfolds (Aguilera, 1998). Unhappily, many assessment devices that can give the human services worker an adequate perspective on the client's problem are unwieldy and time consuming, and require that the client be enough in control to complete the assessment process or be physically present while undergoing evaluation. Although we might gain a great deal of helpful information with an extensive intake form, a background interview, or an in-depth personality test, events often occur so quickly that these are unaffordable and unrealistic luxuries.

What the interventionist needs in a crisis situation is a fast, efficient way of obtaining a real-time estimate of what is occurring with a client. Such a tool should also be simple enough that a worker who may have only rudimentary assessment skills can use the device in a reliable and valid manner. It should enable the assessment to be performed rapidly by a broad cross-section of crisis workers who have had little if any training in standardized testing or assessment procedures. What you are about to encounter (see Figure 3.2) is a composite of several forms of the Triage Assessment Form (TAF), which we believe admirably fits the foregoing criteria.

The Triage Assessment Form

Variations of the general TAF have been tested with police officer trainees, veteran crisis intervention team police officers who deal with the mentally ill, school counselors, community agency workers, secretaries, undergraduates, agency and crisis line supervisors, volunteer crisis line counselors, university professors, residence hall staff, and counselors-in-training (Blancett, 2008; Conte, 2005; Logan, Myer, & James, 2006; Myer, 2001; Myer et al., 1991, 1992; Pazar, 2005; Slagel, 2009; Watters, 1997). Before training, none of the groups had any familiarity with the TAF.

Ratings of these groups were compared with expert triage ratings on a variety of different crisis scenarios (Minimal Impairment, Moderate Impairment, and Severe Impairment). These researchers found that police officer trainees tended to overrate and label the Moderate Impairment scenario as Severe Impairment (probably because they were very sensitive to not underrating the severity for fear of criticism or making a mistake that could cause a fatality). Veteran crisis intervention team police officers' ratings almost replicated the expert ratings (Logan, Myer, & James, 2006; Pazar, 2005). The most problematic area of the scale appears to be the Moderate Impairment range (Watters, 1997). Veteran mental health workers either underrated or overrated Moderate Impairment scenarios. When queried, those veteran mental health workers who gave lower ratings than the experts indicated that they had seen, heard, and handled far more problematic behavior and felt Moderate was too high a rating. Conversely, other veteran mental health workers interpreted subtle responses in the Moderate scenarios to imply greater threat than what was being portrayed, and thus gave higher ratings than the experts. Overall, the ratings of all the other groups, such as the school counselors and volunteers, were deemed reliable and comparable with the ratings of the experts. All groups were congruent with the Minimal Impairment and Severe Impairment range (Blancett, 2008;

Client Name: _____ Time/Date: _____

Crisis Worker: _____ Contact Type: _____ Phone: _____ Office: _____

Field

Crisis Event:

_____

_____

_____

Disposition:

_____

_____

_____

Observations (Check as many that apply)

___ off medication*

___ medication not effective***

___ hallucinating*** (___smells___ sights___sounds___touch)

___ bizarre behavior/appearance

___ poor hygiene

___ absurd, illogical speech ***

___ paranoid/suspicious thoughts ***

___ flashbacks, loss of reality contact

___ intoxicated/drugged*

___ under the influence of mood altering substance

___ other (explain)

___ oppositional defiant to verbal suggestions

___ coercion/intimidation

___ aggressive gestures *

___ reckless behavior

___ self injurious behavior

___ physically violent *

___ verbal threats to self or others

___ suicidal/homicidal thinking/verbalizing

___ suicidal/homicidal gestures/behaviors *

___ suicidal/homicidal plan clear *

___ uncooperative

___ flat affect

___ impulsivity

___ hysterical

___ confusion

___ unable to follow simple directions

___ unable to control emotions

___ cannot recall personal information (phone, address)

___ situation perceived as unreal (spectator)

___ nonresponsive ***

Notes:

_____

_____

*** psychiatric evaluation recommended* * hold for law enforcement officers or EMTs

FIGURE 3.2 Triage Assessment Form for Crisis Intervention.

SOURCE: Compiled from Triage Assessment Form (TAF), Triage Assessment System for Students in Learning Environments (TASSLE), Triage Assessment Checklist for Law Enforcement (TACKLE). Crisis Intervention & Preventions Solutions Inc. Pittsburgh, PA.

Digital Download Download at CengageBrain.com

SEVERITY SCALES
Check those that apply

	1 No Impairment	2/3 Minimal Impairment	4/5 Low Impairment	6/7 Moderate Impairment	8/9 Marked Impairment	10 Severe Impairment
A F F E C T I V E	❍ Stable mood, control of feelings.	❍ Affect elevated but generally appropriate.	❍ Evidence of negative feelings pronounced and increasingly inappropriate.	❍ Feelings are primarily negative and are exaggerated or increasingly diminished.	❍ Feelings are negative and highly volatile or may be nonexistent.	❍ Feelings are extremely pronounced to being devoid of feeling.
	❍ Feelings are appropriate.	❍ Brief periods of slightly elevated negative mood.	❍ Duration of feeling intensity longer than situation warrants.	❍ Efforts to control emotions are not always successful.	❍ Extremely limited control of emotions.	❍ No ability to control feelings regardless of potential danger to self or others.
	❍ Emotions are under control.	❍ Emotions are substantially under control.	❍ Emotions are controlled but focused on crisis event.	❍ Emotions not under control but remain focused on crisis.	❍ Emotions start to generalize from crisis event to other people and situations.	❍ Emotions of the crisis are generalized to other people and situations.
	❍ Responses to questions/ requests are calm and composed.	❍ Responses to questions/ requests are emotional but composed.	❍ Responses to questions/ requests vary from rapid and agitated to slow and subdued.	❍ Responses to questions/ requests are emotionally volatile or beginning to shut down.	❍ Responses to questions/ requests noncompliant due to interference of emotions.	❍ Cannot respond to questions/requests because of interference of emotions.
B E H A V I O R S	❍ Behaviors are socially appropriate.	❍ Behaviors mostly effective, outbursts if present are inconsequential.	❍ Behaviors are somewhat ineffective, yet not dangerous.	❍ Behaviors are maladaptive but not immediately destructive.	❍ Behaviors are likely to intensify crisis situation.	❍ Behaviors are totally ineffective and accelerate the crisis.
	❍ Daily functioning unimpeded.	❍ Can perform tasks needed for daily functioning with minimal effort.	❍ Performing tasks needed for daily living minimally compromised.	❍ Performance of tasks needed for daily living is noticeably compromised.	❍ Ability to perform tasks needed for daily functioning seriously impaired.	❍ Unable to perform even simple tasks needed for daily functioning.
	❍ Threat or danger nonexistent.	❍ Behavior demonstrates frustration, but is nonthreatening.	❍ Behaviors minimal threat to self or others.	❍ Behavior is a potential threat to self or others.	❍ Impulsivity has the potential to be harmful to self or others.	❍ Behaviors are highly destructive possibly to cause injury/ death to self or others.
	❍ Behavior is stable and non-offensive.	❍ Behaviors mostly stable and non-offensive.	❍ Behavior becoming unstable and offensive.	❍ Upon request, behaviors can be controlled with effort.	❍ Behaviors are very difficult to control even with repeated requests.	❍ Behavior is out of control and nonresponsive to requests.

FIGURE 3.2 (continued)

Digital Download Download at CengageBrain.com

SEVERITY SCALES (continued)

	1 No Impairment	2/3 Minimal Impairment	4/5 Low Impairment	6/7 Moderate Impairment	8/9 Marked Impairment	10 Severe Impairment
C O G N I T V E	○ Decisions are considerate of others.	○ Decisions may not be considerate of others.	○ Decisions are inconsiderate of others.	○ Decisions are offensive and antagonistic of others.	○ Decisions have the potential to be harmful to self or others.	○ Decisions are a clear and present danger to self and others.
	○ Decisions are logical and reasonable.	○ Decisions becoming indecisive but only with respect to crisis.	○ Decisions becoming illogical, unreasonable, and generalized beyond crisis.	○ Decisions about crisis beginning to interfere with general functioning.	○ Decisions are illogical, have little basis in reality, and general functioning is compromised.	○ Decision making frenetic or frozen and not based in reality and shuts down general functioning.
	○ Perception of crisis event substantially matches reality.	○ Thinking influenced by crisis, but under control.	○ Thinking focused on crisis but not all consuming.	○ Thoughts are limited to crisis situation and are becoming all consuming.	○ Thoughts about crisis have become pervasive.	○ Thoughts are chaotic and completely controlled by crisis.
	○ Able to carry on reasonable dialog and understand and acknowledge views of others.	○ Able to carry on reasonable dialog, understand and acknowledge views of others.	○ Ability to carry on reasonable dialog restricted and problems in understanding and acknowledging views of others.	○ Responses to questions and requests are restricted or inappropriate and denies understanding views of others.	○ Defiant to requests and questions and/or inappropriate with and antagonistic of others.	○ Requests and questions are believed as threat and responded to aggressively.
	○ Problem solving intact.	○ Problem solving minimally compromised	○ Problem solving limited.	○ Problem solving blocked.	○ Problem solving ability absent.	○ Problem solving not observable with no ability to concentrate.

CRISIS EVENT

Identify and describe briefly the crisis situation: _____
_____
_____

AFFECTIVE DOMAIN

Identify and describe briefly the affect that is present.

(If more than one affect is experienced, rate with #1 being primary, #2 secondary, #3 tertiary.)

ANGER/HOSTILITY: _____
_____
_____
_____

ANXIETY/FEAR: _____
_____
_____
_____

FIGURE 3.2 (continued)

Digital Download Download at CengageBrain.com

CRISIS EVENT (continued)

SADNESS/MELANCHOLY: _____
_____
_____
_____

FRUSTRATION: _____
_____
_____
_____

BEHAVIORAL DOMAIN
Identify and describe briefly which behavior is currently being used.
(If more than one behavior is utilized, rate with #1 being primary, #2 secondary, #3 tertiary.)
APPROACH: _____
_____
_____

AVOIDANCE: _____
_____
_____

IMMOBILITY: _____
_____
_____

COGNITIVE DOMAIN
Identify if a transgression, threat, or loss has occurred in the following areas and describe briefly.
(If more than one cognitive response occurs, rate with #1 being primary, #2 secondary, #3 tertiary.)
PHYSICAL (food, water, safety, shelter, etc.): _____
_____
_____

Transgression_____ Threat_____ Loss_____
PSYCHOLOGICAL (self-concept, sense of emotional well-being, ego integrity, self-identity, etc.): _____
_____
_____

Transgression_____ Threat_____ Loss_____
SOCIAL RELATIONSHIPS (positive interaction and support, family, friends, coworkers, church, clubs, etc.): _____
_____
_____

Transgression_____ Threat_____ Loss_____
MORAL/SPIRITUAL (personal integrity, values, belief system, spiritual reconciliation): _____
_____
_____

FIGURE 3.2   (continued)

Digital Download   Download at CengageBrain.com

CRISIS EVENT *(continued)*

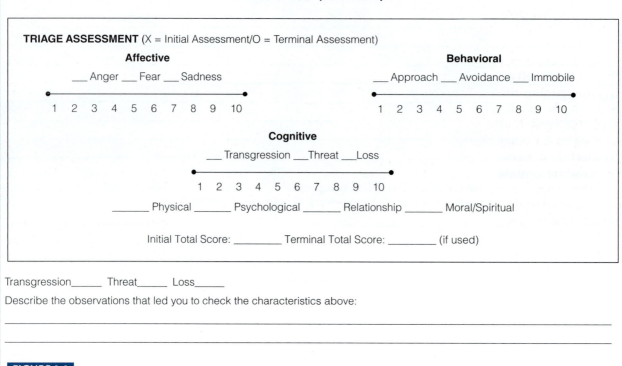

TRIAGE ASSESSMENT (X = Initial Assessment/O = Terminal Assessment)

Affective

___ Anger ___ Fear ___ Sadness

1 2 3 4 5 6 7 8 9 10

Behavioral

___ Approach ___ Avoidance ___ Immobile

1 2 3 4 5 6 7 8 9 10

Cognitive

___ Transgression ___ Threat ___ Loss

1 2 3 4 5 6 7 8 9 10

_____ Physical _____ Psychological _____ Relationship _____ Moral/Spiritual

Initial Total Score: _____ Terminal Total Score: _____ (if used)

Transgression_____ Threat_____ Loss_____

Describe the observations that led you to check the characteristics above:

_____

_____

FIGURE 3.2

Digital Download Download at CengageBrain.com

Logan, Myer, & James, 2006; Pazar, 2005; Watters, 1997). What the research seems to imply is that the scales should be taken at face value, and the less interpretation made of what the affect, behavior, and cognition implies, the more congruent ratings will be. In other words, trying to read too much or too little into what is being observed appears to invalidate the instrument when clients are operating in the moderately impaired range.

Although simple to use, the TAF is also elegant in that it cuts across affective, behavioral, and cognitive domains, or dimensions, of the client; compartmentalizes each dimension as to its typical response mode; and assigns numeric values to these modes that allow the worker to determine the client's current level of functioning. These three severity scales represent mechanisms for operationally assigning numeric values to the crisis worker's action continuum in Figure 3.2. The numeric ratings provide an efficient and tangible guide to both the degree and the kind of intervention the worker needs to make in most crisis situations. Perhaps more important, they not only tell the worker how the client is doing, but also tell the worker how he or she is doing in

attempting to de-escalate, defuse, and help the client regain control. The rationale and examples for each of the scales are discussed on the following pages. Because the original TAF scales were not parallel across numerical ratings with different numbers of anchors, workers reported having difficulty with assessment. As a result, Myer (2014) has developed a more efficient parallel set of ratings for each dimension.

The Affective Severity Scale. No crisis situation that we know of has positive emotions attached to it. Crow (1977) metaphorically names the usual emotional qualities found in a crisis as yellow (anxiety), red (anger), and black (depression). To those we would add orange (our students chose this color) for frustration, which invariably occurs as clients attempt to meet needs. These needs range all across Maslow's needs hierarchy, from inability to get food, water, and shelter (Hurricane Katrina) to interpersonal issues (attempts to regain boyfriend/girlfriend) to intrapersonal issues (get rid of the schizophrenic voices) to spiritual concerns (God can't let this happen). Frustration of needs is often the precursor of other negative emotions, thoughts, and behaviors that plunge the client further into crisis. Even more problematic, some very famous psychologists have investigated the relationship between frustration and aggression and found that aggression is always a consequence of frustration (Dollard et al., 1939, p. 1). That outcome particularly does not bode well when the client is in crisis.

Undergirding these typical emotions may lie a constellation of other negative emotions such as shame, betrayal, humiliation, inadequacy, and horror (Collins & Collins, 2005, pp. 25–26). Clients may manifest these emotions both verbally and nonverbally, and the astute crisis worker needs to be highly aware of incongruencies between what the client is saying, how the client is saying it (voice tone, inflection, and decibel level), and what the client's body language says.

Invariably, these negative emotions appear singularly or in combination with each other when a crisis is present. In their model, Myer and associates (1992) have replaced the term *depression*, because of its diagnostic implications, with *sadness/melancholy*. When any of these core negative emotions becomes all-pervasive such that the client is consumed by them, the potential for these emotions to motivate destructive behavior becomes extremely high.

The Behavioral Severity Scale. While a client in crisis is more or less behaviorally immobile, immobility can take three different forms. Crow (1977) proposes that behavior in a crisis approaches, avoids, or is paralyzed in the client's attempts to act. Although Crow's proposal may seem contradictory, it is not. A client may seem highly motivated but be acting maladaptively toward a specific target or acting in a random, non-goal-directed manner with no specific target discernible. Alternatively, the client may attempt to flee the noxious event by the fastest means possible, even though the immediate threat to the client's well-being is gone. Whereas in many instances taking stock of the situation before acting is an excellent plan, clients transfixed in the face of immediate danger need to flee or fight. Although a great deal of energy may be expended and the client may look focused, once the crisis goes beyond the client's capacity to cope in a meaningful and purposeful manner, we would say that the client is immobilized, stuck in the particular approach, avoidance, or static behavior in a continuous loop no matter how proactive he or she may seem to be. At the severe impairment end of the continuum, maladaptive behavior often takes on a lethal aspect in regard to either the client or others.

The Cognitive Severity Scale. Ellis has written at length about the part that thinking plays in emotions and behavior (Ellis, 1971; Ellis & Abrahms, 1978; Ellis & Grieger, 1977; Ellis & Harper, 1975). In a crisis situation, the client's cognitive processes typically perceive the event in terms of transgression, threat, loss, or any combination of the three. These "hot" cognitions, as Dryden (1984) calls them, can take on catastrophic dimensions at the extreme end of the continuum.

Such highly focused irrational thinking can cause the client to obsess on the crisis to the extent that little, if any, logical thinking can occur within or beyond the boundaries of the crisis event. The event itself consumes all of the client's psychic energy as the client attempts to integrate it into his or her belief system. The client may generate maladaptive cognitions about intrapersonal, interpersonal, or environmental stimuli. Transgression, threat, or loss may be perceived in relation to physical needs such as food, shelter, and safety; psychological needs such as self-concept, emotional stability, and identity; relationship needs such as family, friends, coworkers, and community support; and moral and spiritual needs such as integrity and values.

To differentiate between transgression, threat, and loss, think of these dimensions in terms of time. *Transgression* is the cognition that something bad is happening in the present moment, *threat* is the cognition that something bad will occur, and *loss* is the cognition that something bad has occurred. When cognitions of the crisis move to the severe impairment end of the continuum, the perception of the event may be so extreme as to put the client or others at physical risk. Sometimes the client's thinking moves from "It's a pain in the neck that this is happening, but I'll get over it" to "It's absolutely intolerable, I will not stand for this, and I'll never get over it." This kind of shift, from cool to hot cognitions (Dryden, 1984), is setting the client up to make some bad decisions. Such decisions most probably will result in even worse behavioral consequences for the client and others.

Certainly the innate intellectual capacity of clients has much to do with how they respond cognitively to a crisis and how the crisis worker should respond to them. Given the same crisis, a client with borderline intelligence may perseverate on the need to obtain basic nurturance while an intellectually gifted person might brood on the existential issue of whether God had a hand in the crisis.

There are four basic areas of cognitive functioning that are likely to become involved in a crisis: physical, psychological, social relationships, and moral/spiritual beliefs. These look a lot like Maslow's needs hierarchy, and in some ways they are and some ways they aren't. In a disaster, as you will see in Chapter 17, people are pretty much concerned with getting food in their bellies and a roof over their heads first and worrying about other things second. On the other hand, it is not uncommon for all of these dimensions to come into play at once. Physical: "I am hungry, cold, and don't know how much longer I can stand it on top of this roof." Psychological: "I screwed up by not listening and preparing for the hurricane." Social: "Where is my family? Have they survived?" Moral/Spiritual: "How could God have done this to us?"

Some of you who are reading this book may take issue with the moral/spiritual component if you are agnostic, atheist, or just think the supreme being is currently on vacation in an alternate universe. But whatever your spiritual persuasion and whether you believe deities are named the Great Spirit, Allah, God, Vishnu, a large Douglas fir tree, your personal fitness trainer, guru, or preacher, or Charlie Brown's Great Pumpkin, we believe as others do that spirituality is a key component in the crisis business. We like Pargament and Sweeney's definition (2011) of spirit in their work developing the spiritual fitness component of the new U.S. Army's Comprehensive Soldier Fitness Program (see Chapter 7, Posttraumatic Stress Disorder). They define *spirit* as "the essential core of the individual, the deepest part of the self, and one's involving human essence" and *spirituality* as "the continuous journey people take to discover and realize their essential selves." Pargament (2007) adds that it is looking for the *sacred* in one's life. If you think that people who are in crisis don't get down to the core of their being and at times try like crazy to figure out what is sacred, morally right, and how their spirit and spirituality tie into this business, and that this is not really worthy of your consideration, you would be dead wrong.

Comparison With Precrisis Functioning. Although it may not always be possible, the worker should seek to assess the client's precrisis functioning with the TAF as a guide to determine how effectively the client functioned prior to the event. Comparing precrisis ratings with current ratings lets the worker gauge the degree of deviation from the client's typical affective, behavioral, and cognitive operating levels. The worker can then tell how atypical the client's functioning is, whether there has been a radical shift in that functioning, and whether that functioning is transitory or

chronic. For example, a very different approach would be used to counsel someone with chronic schizophrenia suffering auditory hallucinations compared to an individual experiencing similar hallucinations from a prescription drug. Such an assessment can be made in one or two questions without having to ferret out a great deal of background information.

Rating Clients. In rating clients on the TAF, we move from high to low. This backward rating process may seem confusing at first glance, but the idea is that we rule out more severe impairment first. So if we were rating affect, we would first look at whether the client fits any of the descriptors under Severe Impairment. If not, we would then consider the descriptors under Marked Impairment. If we were able to check off at least two of those descriptors, the client would receive a rating of 9. If we could identify fewer than two of the descriptors, the client would receive an 8. We would repeat this rating process across all three dimensions to obtain a total rating. Based on the total rating, which will range from 3 to 30, we generally group clients into three categories. A 3–10 rating means minimal impairment; these clients are generally self-directing and able to function effectively on their own. A rating of 11–19 means that clients are more impaired; they may have difficulty functioning on their own and need help and direction. This midscore range is the most problematic as far as disposition of clients is concerned. Low teen scores (11–15) call for at least some guidance and directiveness from the worker to get the client on course as opposed to a single-digit score where the client can be pretty much self-directed with minimal guidance and information. High teen scores (16–19) are indicative of clients who are losing more and more control of their ability to function effectively and call for a good deal more than passive and palliative responses from the worker so that they do not escalate into 20 territory. Clarity in setting boundaries and finding specific and continuous support systems for the immediate future is generally called for when scores fall into this range. Clients with a total score of 20 or above are moving deeper into harm's way; they are likely to need a great deal of direction and a secure and safe environment so they do not escalate into the lethal range. Scores in the high 20s almost always mean that some degree of lethality is involved, whether it is premeditated or clients are simply so out of control that they cannot stay out of harm's way.

Rating clients on the triage scale also means rating the crisis worker! How is this so? If the worker is effective in stabilizing a client, the triage scale score should go down. If it does not, then the worker probably needs to shift gears and try another approach. While the TAF is not absolutely precise and is not intended to be, it does give a good numerical anchor that the crisis worker can use in making judgments about client disposition and the effectiveness of the intervention. Our students very quickly become skillful at making these ratings on sample cases, and so will you.

One rating issue that constantly arises is the question, "What do you mean by severe? Shouldn't a mother who just got news that her son was badly injured in a school bus accident be pretty hysterical and out of control?" That is certainly true. However, what puts the mother into a crisis category and allows us to rate her as "severely impaired" on the TAF is twofold. First, even though the feelings, thoughts, and behaviors may seem reasonable responses given the horrific situation, what kind of potential trouble does that get the mother into? Are her feelings, thoughts, and actions liable to exacerbate the situation further? Second, it is not just the intensity but also the duration of the feelings, thoughts, and actions. We might reasonably expect an initial response that is highly volatile, but if after 4 hours that same degree of emotional energy were still present, it would be obvious that the client is out of control, in crisis, and in need of assistance.

Alternate Forms of the TAF

The TAF has been modified for use with police departments (Logan, Myer, & James, 2006), higher education/student affairs personnel (Armitage et al., 2007), and disaster relief workers (James, Blancett, & Addy, 2007), and is currently being adapted to families (Myer, 2015) based on the increased interaction with and need to provide services or actions for mentally ill and emotionally disturbed individuals in each of these venues. All these alternate forms of the TAF have been developed because of the expanding needs of a variety of workers who do not have a mental health background yet who come in contact with emotionally disturbed individuals for whom they are expected to render service of some kind. All of the following variations of the TAF have been modified for ease and simplicity of use and have or are undergoing field testing.

TACKLE. The Triage Assessment Checklist for Law Enforcement (TACKLE; James, Davis, & Myer, 2014;

James, Myer, & Moore, 2006) was developed in cooperation with a focus group of police officers and mental health workers from the Montgomery County, Maryland, police department. It is used by police officers to make on-the-scene assessments of how they are doing in defusing and de-escalating emotionally out-of-control recipients of service, to provide the officers with concrete behavioral assessments for placing recipients of service under legal confinement for psychiatric evaluation and/or commitment, and to provide behavioral assessments in legal proceedings to back up actions taken against recipients of service (see Chapter 14, Violent Behavior in Institutions).

The second section of the TAF form is titled "Observations" (see Figure 3.3). This section is divided into three columns listing some of the behaviors that may be seen with an individual in crisis. Several of the items have been identified as critical for either getting clients support or removing them to a place of safety. A general guideline is the more items you check, the more likely a person will either need support or should be removed. Most often checking numerous items means the individual's rating on the severity scales will also be high. High scores on the severity scales generally mean an increased need for support services and an increased potential for hospitalization.

The first column addresses psychological problems. Check appropriate descriptors in this section based on your observations and questioning of individuals. You may not be able to gather all this information because clients may be uncooperative or simply unable to respond to questions. A good source for some of this information is other people who may know the client. Asking them about the individual may give you the information needed to check the appropriate descriptors in this column. The second column focuses on clients that are dangerous to themselves or others. They may be only threatening harm or actually making suicidal or homicidal gestures. If they are simply threatening harm, you will need to make a judgment as to whether the person is an immediate danger to self or others. Simply making threats to harm oneself or others does not automatically mean the student needs support services or removal. A standard guideline is if a person has a plan formulated and if the means to carry out the plan are available, that person is a threat and needs to be monitored in a safe place by qualified mental health workers until the threat has abated.

The third column relates to the severity scales most directly. Listed in this column are feelings, behaviors, and thoughts persons may experience when in a crisis. These correspond to characteristics on the severity scales. Generally, you can complete this section based on your observations and experience with students. Four of the descriptors have been identified as being critical: (1) hysterical, (2) confusion, (3) unable to follow simple directions, and (4) nonresponsive. Individuals who fit these descriptors are vulnerable, mentally fragile, and unable to care for themselves.

In summary, the TAF and its derivative alternate forms provide multiple three-dimensional combinations of the domains of assessment regarding the degree of impairment the crisis is causing, target specific areas of functioning, and let the crisis worker evaluate the client quickly and then construct specific interventions aimed directly at areas of greatest immediate concern.

Psychobiological Assessment

Although psychobiological assessment for **LO4** psychopathology is beyond the scope of this book and most crisis situations, in terms of both immediacy of assessment and the assessment skills required of most human services workers, there is clear evidence that neurotransmitters, the receptors they land on and physical changes in brain structures play an exceedingly important role in the affective, behavioral, and cognitive functioning of individuals both during a crisis and, for some, long after a crisis (Briere & Scott, 2006; Elharrar, Warhaftig, Issier, Szainberg, Dikshtein et al., 2013; Lanius, Frewen, Nazarov, &

McKinnnon, 2014; Nicholson, Bryant, & Felmingham, 2013; Strawn & Geracioti, 2008; van der Kolk, 1996a; Vermetten & Landius, 2012; Yehuda, 2006; Yehuda & LeDoux, 2007).

It is becoming pretty clear that the limbic system in the brain plays a part in "catching" and "carrying" PTSD. It also appears possible that the gene pool you jumped out of may have something to do with how susceptible you are to anxiety disorders, because there is substantive evidence that a lesser volume of certain limbic system components makes people more susceptible to PTSD (Gilbertson et al., 2002; Glat et al., 2013; Skelton et al., 2012). The good news is that certain drug therapies and psychotherapies can potentially increase the volume and change neurotransmitter conductivity that goes with symptomatic improvement in PTSD, depression, and other anxiety disorders (Chapman, 2014; Felmingham et al., 2007; Klavir, Genud-Gabai, & Paz, 2012; Lippy & Kelzenberg, 2012; Niv, 2013; Pietrzak et al., 2014; Tomko, 2012; Vermetten et al., 2003).

For at least three reasons, human psychobiology can be an important consideration in crisis intervention. First, evidence exists that when people are involved in traumatic events, dramatic changes occur in the discharge of neurotransmitters, such as endorphins, and in the central and peripheral sympathetic nervous systems and the hypothalamic-pituitary-adrenocortical axis (Bailey, Cordell, Sobin, & Neumeister, 2013). These two systems regulate one another. When PTSD enters the picture, the balance of these two systems is not maintained and the responses

---

Observations (Check all that apply)

___ off medication*	___ aggressive gestures	___ hysterical*
___ hallucinating† (___smells ___sights ___sounds ___touch)	___ physically violent†	___ confusion*
	___ verbal threats to self or others	___ unable to follow simple directions*
___ bizarre behavior/appearance	___ suicidal/homicidal thinking/ verbalizing*	___ unable to control emotions
___ poor hygiene		___ cannot recall personal information* (phone, address)
___ absurd, illogical, nonsensical speech	___ suicidal/homicidal gestures/ behaviors†	___ situation perceived as unreal* (spectator)
___ paranoid/suspicious thoughts	___ suicidal/homicidal plan clear†	___ nonresponsive*
___ flashbacks, loss of reality contact*	___ uncooperative	
___ intoxicated/drugged*	___ reckless behavior	
___ possible developmental disability	___ impulsivity	

*Support services recommended.
†Protective custody recommended.

FIGURE 3.3 Triage Assessment System for Students in Learning Environments (TASSLE): Observational Checklist.
SOURCE: Myer et al., 2007.

Digital Download Download at CengageBrain.com

of both systems are affected (Raison & Miller, 2003). These neurological changes may become residual and long-term and have subtle and degrading effects on emotions, acting, and thinking (Antunes-Alves & Comeau, 2014; Bovin, Ratchford, & Marx, 2014; Burgess-Watson, Hoffman, & Wilson, 1988; Scaer, 2014; van der Kolk, 1996b). Client education about the psychobiological effects of trauma is important in letting clients know they are not going "nuts" and that the urges of their bodies to spring into physical action even though the original stressor is long past have a neurological basis (Halpern & Tramontin, 2007, p. 83).

Second, research indicates that abnormal changes in neurotransmitters such as dopamine, norepinephrine, and serotonin are involved in mental disorders that range from schizophrenia (Crow & Johnstone, 1987) to depression (Healy, 1987) and affective and anxiety disorders in general (Petrik, Lagace, & Eisch, 2012). Psychotropic drugs are routinely used for a host of mental disorders to counteract such neurological changes. A common problem faced by human services workers and police officers is the deranged or violent client who has gone off medication because of its unpleasant side effects or an inability to remember when to take it (Ammar & Burdin, 1991; Miller, 2006). Individuals with psychosis who have gone off their medication and taken their reactivated psychosis out onto the streets are legion and are the bane of crisis intervention team police officers.

Third, both legal and illegal drugs have a major effect on mental health. Although the way illegal drugs change brain chemistry and behavior has gained wide attention, legal drugs may promote adverse psychological side effects in just as dramatic a manner. In particular, combinations of nonpsychotropic drugs are routinely given to combat several degenerative diseases in the elderly. At times, these drugs may have interactive effects that generate unanticipated psychological disturbances. One has to read no further than the consumer trade books on prescribed drugs to obtain a rather frightening understanding of the psychological side effects prescription drugs can cause.

Therefore, the human services worker should attempt to assess prior trauma, psychopathology, and use, misuse, or abuse of legal and illegal drugs in an effort to determine whether they correlate with the current problem. "Talking" therapies do little good when neurobiological substrates are involved. If the human services worker has reason to suspect any of the foregoing problems, an immediate referral should be made for a neurological/drug evaluation. Officer Lewis's question about how much Leron had been drinking is almost a default question in regard to use or misuse of both prescription and nonprescription medications.

The following questions are practically mandatory during initial exploration activities with a person in crisis and should be asked in a nonaccusatory way.

Crisis worker: Lots of times people have a reaction to medication or changes in medication. Are you on any medication right now? Is it for emotional problems? Have you stopped taking it? Are you on any medications for other physical problems? Have you stopped taking or changed medications? Did you have any alcoholic beverages with your medication? Has there been any way you feel like you have changed or felt different since you went on or changed or went off a medication?

Assessing the Client's Current Emotional Functioning

Four major factors in assessing the client's **LO5** emotional stability are (1) the duration of the crisis, (2) the degree of emotional stamina or coping at the client's disposal at the moment, (3) the ecosystem within which the client resides, and (4) the developmental stage of the client.

The duration factor concerns the time frame of the crisis. Is it a onetime crisis? Is it recurring? Has it been plaguing the client for a long time? A onetime crisis of relatively short duration is called *acute* or *situational*. A long-term pattern of recurring crisis is labeled *chronic, long-term,* or *transcrisis*.

The degree factor concerns the client's current reservoir of emotional coping stamina. During normal periods of the client's life the coping reservoir is relatively full, but during crisis the client's reservoir is relatively empty. Assessing the degree factor, then, involves the crisis worker's determining how much emotional coping strength is left in the client's reservoir. Has the client run out of gas, or can the client make it over a small hill?

The ecosystem is a very large extraneous variable that can dramatically influence client coping (Collins & Collins, 2005; Halpern & Tramontin, 2007; James, Cogdal, & Gilliland, 2003; Myer & Moore, 2006). Geographic region and accessibility, communication systems, language, cultural mores, religious beliefs, economic status, and social micro- and macrosystem interactions are only some of the ecosystemic variables that may have subtle or profound effects on a client's emotional coping ability. No individual's crisis can be taken out of the ecosystemic context in which it occurs, and to believe it can be somehow treated separately without considering that context is to make a grave intervention error.

Developmental stages (Collins & Collins, 2005) certainly play a part in the client's emotional functioning during a crisis. Merely transitioning from life stage to life stage has its own potential for crises (Blocher, 2000; Erikson, 1963). Understanding the developmental tasks of different life stages, which may frame a client's view of a crisis and how the client responds to it, is critical for crisis workers. Further compounding the issue, developmental tasks are sometimes not accomplished at a particular life stage, and developmental crises occur (Levinson, 1986). It does not take much imagination to foresee that adding a situational crisis may have a tremendous impact on a "stuck-in-stage" individual's emotional coping skills.

The Client's Current Acute or Chronic State. In assessing the crisis client's emotional functioning, it is important that the crisis worker determine whether the client is a normal person who is in a *onetime* situational crisis or a person with a *chronic,* crisis-oriented life history. The onetime crisis is assessed and treated quite differently from the chronic crisis. The onetime crisis client usually requires direct intervention to facilitate getting over the specific event or situation that precipitated the crisis. Having reached a state of precrisis equilibrium, the client can usually draw on normal coping mechanisms and support people and manage independently.

The chronic crisis client usually requires a greater length of time in counseling. That individual typically needs the help of a crisis worker in examining available coping mechanisms, finding support people, rediscovering strategies that worked during previous crises, generating new coping strategies, and gaining affirmation and encouragement from the worker and others as sources of strength by which to move beyond the present crisis. The chronic case frequently requires referral for long-term professional help.

The Client's Reservoir of Emotional Strength. The client who lacks emotional strength needs more direct responses from the crisis worker than the client who retains a good deal of emotional strength. A feeling of hopelessness or helplessness is a clue to a low reservoir of emotional strength. In some cases, the assessment can be enhanced by asking open-ended questions for the specific purpose of measuring that reservoir. Typically, if the reservoir is low, the client will have a distorted view of the past and present and will not be able to envision a future. Such questions can reveal the degree of emotional stamina remaining: "Picture yourself after the current crisis has been solved. Tell me what you're seeing and how you're feeling. How do you wish you were feeling? How were you feeling about this before the crisis got so bad? Where do you see yourself headed with this problem?" In general, the lower the reservoir of emotional strength, the less the client can get hold of the future. The client with an empty reservoir might respond with a blank stare or by saying something like "There are no choices" or "No, I can't see anything. The future is blank. I can see no future." The worker's assessment of the client's current degree of emotional strength will have definite implications for the strategies and level of action the worker will employ during the remainder of the counseling.

Strategies for Assessing Emotional Status. The crisis worker who assesses the client's total emotional status may look at a wide array of social locations (Brown, 2008) that affect both the duration (chronic versus acute) and the degree (reservoir of strength) of emotional stability. Some factors to be considered are the client's age, educational level, family situation, marital status, vocational maturity and job stability, financial stability and obligations, drug and/or alcohol use, legal history (arrests, convictions, probations), social background, level of intelligence, lifestyle, religious orientation, ability to sustain close personal relationships, tolerance for ambiguity, physical health, medical history, and past history of dealing with crises. A candid look at such factors helps the crisis worker decide whether the client will require quick referral (for medical treatment or examination), brief counseling, long-term therapy, or referral to a specific agency.

Ordinarily, no one factor alone can be used to conclude that the client's reservoir of emotional coping ability is empty. However, some patterns can often be pieced together to form a general picture. A person in middle age who has experienced many disappointments related to undereducation and subsequent underemployment would be viewed differently from a young person who has experienced a first career disappointment. A person who has experienced many serious medical problems and hospital stays would feel different from a person who is having a first encounter with a medical problem. The foregoing example is a *facilitative* affective assessment of the individual. By "facilitative assessment," we mean that data gleaned about the client are used as a part of the ongoing helping process, not simply filed away or kept in the worker's head.

Assessing Alternatives, Coping Mechanisms, and Support Systems

Throughout the helping process, the crisis worker keeps in mind and builds a repertoire of options, evaluating their appropriateness for the client. In assessing alternatives available to the client, the worker must first consider the client's viewpoint, mobility, and capability of taking advantage of the alternatives. The worker's own objective view of available alternatives is an additional dimension.

Alternatives include a repository of appropriate referral resources available to the client. Even though the client may be looking for only one or two concrete action steps or options, the worker brainstorms, in collaboration with the client, to develop a list of possibilities that can be evaluated. Most will be discarded before the client can own and commit to a definite course of action. The worker ponders questions such as: What actions or choices does the client have now that would restore the person to a precrisis state

of autonomy? What realistic actions (coping mechanisms) can the client take? What institutional, social, vocational, or personal (people) strengths or support systems are available? (Note that "support systems" refers to people!) Who would care about and be open to assisting the client? What are the financial, social, vocational, and personal impediments to client progress?

Assessing for Suicide/Homicide Potential

Not every crisis involves the client's contemplating suicide or homicide. However, in dealing with crisis clients, workers must always explore the possibility of harm to self or others, because destructive behavior takes many forms and wears many masks. Crisis workers need to be both wary of and competent in their appraisal of potential suicidal and homicidal clients. What may appear to the crisis worker as the main problem may camouflage the real issue: the intent of the client to take his or her life, or someone else's life. Contrary to popular belief, most suicidal and homicidal clients emit definite clues and believe they are calling out for help or signaling warnings. However, even the client's closest friends may ignore those clues and do nothing about them. For that reason, every crisis problem should be assessed as to its potential for suicide and homicide. The most important aspect of suicidal/homicidal evaluation is the crisis evaluator's realization that suicide and homicide are always possible in all types of clients.

SUMMARY

The hybrid model in this chapter has to do with tasks to be accomplished during a crisis that do not always move in a stepwise linear progression. Overarching all tasks is safety—not only for the client, but for others and the worker as well. Making initial contact in a crisis is not always easy. That's why we have designated predispositioning, engaging, and initiating contact as a new primary task that is critical in laying the groundwork for the intervention to follow. Problem exploration includes affective, behavioral, and cognitive dimensions of the current crisis; it involves finding out what got the immediate crisis going and generally does not delve into all the past issues of the client. Providing support means finding what human resources are available to help the client and what role

the crisis worker will play in either finding or being part of the support system. Examining alternatives and options, making plans, obtaining commitments, and following up are neither extensive nor long-term. They are target-specific attempts to find short-term solutions to restore precrisis equilibrium.

A major difference between crisis intervention and other human services endeavors, such as counseling, social work, and psychotherapy, is that the crisis worker generally does not have time to gather or analyze all the background and other assessment data that might normally be available under less stressful conditions. A key component of a highly functioning crisis worker is the ability to take the data available and make some meaningful sense out of it. This may be somewhat unsettling to those human services workers who are accustomed to having complete social and psychological workups available to them before they proceed with intervention. However, the ability to quickly evaluate the degree of client disequilibrium and immobility—and to be flexible enough to change your evaluation as changing conditions warrant—is a priority skill that students should seek to cultivate. That's why you have been introduced to the hybrid task model and the Triage Assessment Form.

From onset to resolution of the crisis, assessment is a central, continuous process. The crisis worker must not assume that because the crisis appears on the surface to have been resolved, assessment is no longer needed. The balance sheet of assessing the client's crisis in terms of severity, current emotional status, alternatives, situational supports, coping mechanisms, resources, and level of lethality is never complete until the client has achieved his or her precrisis level of mobility, equilibrium, and autonomy. Only then are the psychological debts of the client reconciled. The resumption of precrisis equilibrium does not imply that the client needs no developmental or long-term therapy or medical treatment. It does mean that the crisis worker's job is done, and the acute phase of the crisis is over.

Visit CengageBrain.com for a variety of study tools and useful resources such as video examples, case studies, interactive exercises, flashcards, and quizzes.

The Tools of the Trade

LEARNING OBJECTIVES

After studying this chapter, you should be able to:

1. Understand and employ the use of open-ended leads in responding to people in crisis.
2. Understand and employ the use of closed-ended questions in responding to people in crisis.
3. Understand and employ the use of restatement and summary clarification in responding to people in crisis.
4. Understand and employ the use of owning statements in responding to people in crisis.
5. Become aware of the concept and techniques of facilitative listening.
6. Understand and employ the nine basic strategies of crisis intervention.
7. Understand the basic facilitative conditions of empathy, genuineness, and acceptance to promote human growth and how they are used with a person in crisis.
8. Understand how these tools of the trade move out into and are employed in the field.
9. Determine levels of acting on the directive, collaborative, nondirective action continuum.
10. Understand and employ action strategies to mobilize individuals in crisis.

Introduction

Accurate and well-honed listening skills are necessary and indeed sometimes sufficient skills that all therapists, but particularly crisis interventionists, must have. For that reason, listening skills are a major component of the crisis intervention model. Our preferred conceptual model for effective listening comes from person-centered counseling (Egan, 1982, 1990; Rogers, 1977). Those skills will be familiar to even neophyte human services workers. However, using them effectively in the heat of a crisis may become daunting. That said, there are a variety of other basic verbal techniques you will meet in this chapter with which many human services workers will probably not be familiar. Many of these verbal sets are much more directive, action oriented, judgmental, and may take some getting used to by veteran workers when first tried out.

Listening in Crisis Intervention

Open-Ended Questions

Often workers are frustrated by a client's lack **LO1** of response and enthusiasm. Workers may make statements such as "All my clients ever do is grunt or shake their heads indicating yes or no." We can do something about getting fuller, more meaningful responses if we ask questions that are not dead ends. **Open-ended questions** usually start with *what* or *how* or ask for more clarification or details. Open-ended questions encourage clients to respond with full statements and at deeper levels of meaning. Remember that open-ended questions are used to elicit from clients something about their feelings, thoughts, and behaviors and are particularly helpful in the Problem Exploration phase of intervention in the Task model. Here are some guidelines for forming open-ended questions.

1. *Request description:* "Please tell me . . . ," "Tell me about . . . ," "Show me . . . ," "In what ways does . . . ?"
2. *Focus on plans:* "What will you do . . . ?" "How will you make it happen?" "How will that help you to . . . ?"
3. *Expansion:* "Tell me more," "Could you give me some more details?" "How about expanding on that a bit," "So then what happened?"

4. *Assessment:* "How is that different from before?" "What are you doing about that?" "When that happened, how did you handle it?" "Who might you get to help you?"
5. *Stay away from "why" questions:* Beginners in the crisis intervention business invariably are intrigued and puzzled by the odd and bizarre things people in crisis think, feel, and do. As a result, beginners feel compelled to find out why a person thinks, feels, or does those "really crazy" things. It is our contention that "why" questions are generally poor choices for obtaining more information. Even though they may provide the client with an opening to talk more, they also make the client defend his or her actions. Notice the response of Jake, the husband of Rita, whom you will meet later in this chapter, as the crisis worker queries him about the reasons for his behavior.

CW: Why do you continue to beat your wife?

Jake: Hey! If she'd be a little more affectionate, I wouldn't have to beat her up! It's her fault!

As this example demonstrates, what generally happens is that clients become defensive and attempt to intellectualize about the problem or externalize it to somebody or something else without taking responsibility for or ownership of the problem.

Closed-Ended Questions

Closed-ended questions seek specific, con- **LO2** crete information from the client. They are designed to elicit specific behavioral data and yes or no responses. Closed questions usually begin with verbs such as *do, did, does, can, have, had, will, are, is,* and *was.* Contrary to what typically occurs in long-term therapy, closed-ended questions are often used early on in crisis intervention to obtain specific information that will help the crisis worker make a fast assessment of what is occurring. In most counseling programs, closed-ended questions are a "no-no!" because they indeed tend to close off interaction rather than facilitate dialogue. Thus, using closed questions is problematic for many graduate students whose instructors have harped at them, "Keep it open!" Whereas in long-term therapy the formulation of a plan of attack on the problem might be weeks or months in the making, crisis intervention often calls for instigating plans of action immediately. Closed-ended questions are particularly suited to obtaining commitments to take action. They are also highly appropriate in regard to safety

issues. We don't mince words about safety issues, and we are not interested in circuitous responses. "Are you going to kill yourself?" may seem insensitive, coarse, and callous. It is not! We'll have a great deal more to say about this issue in Chapter 8, Crises of Lethality.

Here are some guidelines for forming closed-ended questions.

1. *Request specific information:* "When was the first time this happened?" "Where are you going to go?" "Are you thinking of hurting her?" "Have you gone back there?" "Does this mean you are going to kill yourself?"
2. *Obtain a commitment:* "Are you willing to make an appointment to . . . ?" "Will you confront him about this?" "Do you agree to . . . ?" "When will you do this?"
3. *Increasing focus:* "Do you understand what I am saying?" "Can you do this for me now?" "Are you on track with me?"
4. *Avoid negative interrogatives:* A negative interrogative is a closed question often used as a subtle way to coerce the listener into agreeing with the speaker. *Don't, doesn't, isn't, aren't,* and *wouldn't* all tend to seek or imply agreement. The negative interrogative statement "Don't you believe that's true?" really is a camouflaged exclamatory statement saying, "I believe that's true, and if you have an ounce of sense you'll agree with me!"

CW: Don't you think it'd be a good idea if you stay away from Rita?

Such statements generally have little place in a crisis interventionist's repertoire of verbal skills. A far better way of asking for compliance is with an assertive owning statement.

CW: Jake, I understand how difficult it is for you, but for the sake of both you and Rita, I'd really like you to continue to build on last week's success by agreeing to the "stay away from her" contract again this week.

Restatement and Summary Clarification

Restatement and summary clarification are **LO3** critical ingredients in crisis intervention. Clients in crisis may have difficulty expressing themselves because of their disjointed thought processes or the chaos that is going on around them in the environment. By restating what the client is saying in the crisis worker's own words, the crisis worker can gain agreement from the client on what the client is attempting to say, feel, think, and do. Further, good **restatement** is particularly important in crisis because it tells the client that "Somebody is listening to me!" Restatement generally has to do with the content of the crisis event rather than the underlying feelings and thoughts about it. A sort of a default way of looking at this technique is using a famous line coined by Sgt. Joe Friday in the TV series *Dragnet*, "All we want are the facts," and then giving those facts back in your own words. Restatement can also serve as an effective break point for a client who is freewheeling in an ideational flight of emotions or thoughts.

CW: Time out a second, Jake. You've put a lot out here and my memory banks are getting pretty full. Let me summarize what you've said, and let's see if we are on the same track.

Restatement sounds simple. It is simple if the crisis worker focuses totally on the client's world. Restatement is not simple if the crisis worker is distracted by environmental stimuli or becomes preoccupied with his or her own thoughts, questions, evaluations, agenda, biases, or stereotypes about what the client is saying. So be wary! There are usually lots of environmental stimuli in a crisis, and it is easy to become distracted. Finally, **summary clarification** ribbon-wraps the dialogue. That is, it packages the preceding dialogue and lets both client and crisis worker know they are on the same wavelength. Particularly at the commitment stage intervention, the crisis worker or, better yet, clients may be asked to summarize what the plan is and how they are going to go about doing it.

CW: I want you to summarize what the game plan is, then, when the urge starts to overtake you to go see Rita.

Jake: OK, so I do this thought-stopping thing when the urge to give her a call or cruise by her house starts going off in my head. I don't go to my favorite bar because that just adds to it. Instead I go to the driving range and start hitting golf balls or go get on my game machine and kill aliens. When I get settled down, I write down all my thoughts and feelings and bring them into you next session. As a last resort, I call the crisis line.

Owning Feelings

Owning means communicating possession: "That's mine." Often in conversation we avoid specific

LO4

issues by "disowning" statements with phrases such as "They say . . . ," "I heard the other day that you . . . ," "It's not right for you to . . . ," and "Don't you think you ought to . . . ?" Whether intentional or not, such verbal manipulation functions to avoid ownership of responsibility for what's being said or to avoid awareness of one's own thoughts and feelings concerning an issue.

Using owning or "I" statements is probably more important in crisis intervention than in other kinds of therapy because of the directive stance the crisis worker often has to take with clients who are immobile and in disequilibrium. It is further important in creating a direct bond between client and worker, particularly when a behavioral emergency is occurring and the worker wants the undivided attention of a wildly out-of-control client. Therefore, we illustrate a number of different types of owning statements the crisis worker may find useful for particular problems that occur during intervention. Although used more often in crisis intervention than in normal therapeutic settings, owning statements should nonetheless be employed sparingly, because the crisis worker's main job is to focus on the client and not on himself or herself. Given that admonition, when working with clients in crisis, it is very important to own your feelings, thoughts, and behaviors because many clients are using you as a model. So if you imply "We think this way" (meaning I and the director of the clinic, the school principal, the chief of police, the population of North America, the world, or God), then the client does not have much of a chance against that awesome cast and is liable to become dependently compliant or defensively hostile as in the following example.

CW: (*authoritatively*) You know that the Family Trouble Center is a branch of the police department, and we can have you arrested, don't you?

Jake: (*defiantly*) Yeah, well, so what? I might as well be in jail anyway.

Collaborative Owning Statements. Early on in crisis intervention the use of "we" is generally not advised because it implies not only the interventionist's thoughts but a host of others' as well. The only parties we are concerned about are the person in crisis and the interventionist. Everybody else can get put on the bench and stay out of the game, at least for the time being. That being said, at some point "we" are going to strike a deal and make movement toward a short-term goal if at all possible. A critical component in eliciting cooperation and compliance from people who are sometimes less than cooperative is to build here-and-now relationships that emphasize a collaborative approach that says "you" are not alone, but "we" are in this together, using what Weiner and Mehrabian (1968) term **Relational markers.** Relational markers shorten the psychological distance between the client and the worker through the use of such words as "this," "these," "we," "our," "here," and "now" as opposed to "that," "those," "mine," "there," and "then." Notice the difference between the two words "this" and "that" in the crisis worker's response to Jake's statement that it is really hard to change.

CW: Jake, I know it is tough, but *this* (*right now, right here*) is something we can work out. While I can't do much about *that* (*past time, out there*) stalking behavior, we can start on *this* (*right now, right here*) self-monitoring anger management model.

Using this language sets the stage for examining alternatives, making plans, undertaking commitments, and engaging in safer behavior. It distances the stalking and jealous behavior and brings the new concept up close and personal. It also acknowledges Jake's attempts and desire to change and how tough it is to do that all alone, but indicates that now help has arrived. The crisis worker's response hooks "we" together with "this" thing right here in front of us, as opposed to "you" and "that" thing way out there that is much harder to get a handle on.

Disowned Statements. Many of us chronically disown many human qualities that indicate we are less than perfect! Beginning crisis workers are particularly vulnerable to this fallacy because they do not want to be seen as inadequate, insecure, or otherwise unequal to the task. Small wonder that clients learn to distrust or become dependent on such all-knowing, well-integrated individuals. Let us take, for example, my feeling of confusion.

If I pretend I understand when in fact I am confused, the client who is listening to me is going to be doubly confused. Being willing to own my confusion or frustration and attempt to eliminate it is a trust-reinforcing event for two reasons: (1) both client and worker can reduce the need to pretend or fake understanding of one another and begin to see more clearly where communications are getting crossed, and (2) the client can begin to become actively involved with the worker in an attempt to work together.

CW: Right now I don't know what to think. You say you love her, yet your actions do everything to drive her away.

Jake: I know 'cause it confused me too! Well, it's like I want her to love me, and then I get jealous and paranoid, and like a switch gets flipped, and then I lose it. It frustrates me. I'm my own worst enemy, and I hate myself for it.

Conveying Understanding. Clients in crisis often feel that no one understands what they are going through. The **"I understand"** statement is an owning statement that clearly conveys to the client that you do understand that what is happening right now is causing the client distress. This does not mean that you understand what the client is going through, because you don't. I cannot understand what it is like to have prostate or breast cancer. I can understand the fear and anxiety that the client is presently demonstrating and acknowledge that. The "I understand" statement may have to be combined with what is commonly called a "broken CD" (repeated) response because the individual may be so agitated or out of touch with reality that he or she does not hear what is being said the first time.

CW: OK, Jake, I do understand it's frustrating when she gives you the cold shoulder, and all the ways you try to win her affection don't work.

Jake: (*pounding his fist on the table and yelling*) Every damn thing I do anymore is wrong!

CW: I understand right now that it's so frustrating the only thing that seems to work is lashing out at her physically.

Value Judgments. At times the crisis worker has to make judgment calls about the client's behavior, particularly when the client is in danger of doing something hurtful to himself or herself or to others. Owning statements speak specifically to the worker's judgment about the situation and what he or she will do about it.

Jake: (*making threatening gestures and with a trembling voice*) I…I…just caaann't taaake much more…of this. I'll huuurt her … huuurt her real bad.

CW: (*making a judgment*) The way you say that really concerns me. I believe that would not be in your best interests and wouldn't get you what you want, which is back with Rita. I'd have to call the police to see that you are both kept safe.

However, using owning statements does *not* generally mean making value judgments about the client's character, because such judgments are putdowns and do nothing to change behavior.

CW: (*sarcastically*) Yeah, you're a really big man to have to punch your wife out because you aren't as smart as she is. That really shows me a lot. I think maybe a stint out on the county work farm might take some of that energy out of you.

Positive Reinforcement. To be genuine in crisis work is to say what we feel at times. When a client has done well and we're happy and feel good about it, we say so. However, such positively reinforcing statements should always be used in regard to a behavior, as opposed to some personal characteristic.

Positive reinforcement is used a great deal in crisis intervention to gain compliance. Many times taking mini-steps to get a client to calm down or stop engaging in a dangerous behavior is tied to positive reinforcement.

CW: (*Jake is standing up and pounding his fist on the table, swearing.*) I need for you to take a deep breath and let it out gently. (*With difficulty, Jake complies.*) Great! That shows me you can get control of your emotions.

We often use positive reinforcement to successively approximate a client toward a larger goal we are seeking to achieve.

CW: Good! You were able to take a deep breath. Now could you cue yourself that every time you start pounding your fist, you will take at least three deep breaths, lower your arms, and allow yourself to relax and picture that tranquil lake scene? Just do that now. Excellent, I see you starting to relax. Can you feel the tension draining out? Terrific! Just continue to do that and feel the difference. See how great that feels and how you have gained mastery over your emotions? It shows me you have the guts to handle your emotions.

Crisis interventionists use positive reinforcement a lot to *successively approximate* (use small steps to move toward an ultimate goal) in diffusing out-of-control clients.

CW: Jake, I know this is about the last place you'd like to be, and I think it took a lot of guts to come in here and admit to me you've got some problems. You've had a lot of tough steps to take but you've made progress and I think are ready to take the next one to watch for ALL the cues you have learned and combine them into the new improved "Serendity Now Jake" (*both laugh*).

However, the use of positive reinforcement is also a double-edged sword. Many times in crisis intervention, reinforcing a client for a behavior may breed dependency or be seen as anything but reinforcing by the client. So be careful about what behavior gets reinforced. That is particularly true of clients with borderline personality disorder who may constantly try to solicit positive comments from the worker to feed their need for approval and acceptance.

Jake: (*sneeringly*) Guts my ass! If it weren't for the cops, I sure as hell wouldn't be in this stink hole with a jerk like you doing this crap.

CW: (*owning feelings*) I'm sorry you feel that way, but I meant what I said.

Personal Integrity and Limit Setting. When a client starts to browbeat, control, or otherwise put us on the hot seat, it does little good to try to hide our anger, disappointment, or hurt feelings. Furthermore, it is important to set clear limits with clients who are starting to get out of control or are trying to manipulate the crisis worker.

Jake: (*sneeringly*) What do you know? You're nothing but a snot-nosed girl! I don't have to take this crap!

CW: (*calmly, owning feelings and setting limits*) I don't appreciate the demeaning comments, the language, or your attitude toward me. I'd like an apology, and I'd also like you to be civil. If you can't, I'll assume you'd rather explain your problems to your probation officer, and we'll terminate the session.

Assertion Statements. Finally, because crisis intervention often calls for the crisis worker to take control of the situation, requests for compliance in the form of owning statements are often very directive, short, and point specific. These owning statements, also known as **assertion statements,** clearly and specifically ask for a specific action from the client.

CW: I want you to commit to me and yourself that you'll stay away from her for the next week. I want you to sign this contract that you'll do that for your own safety and hers as well.

Jake: (*wistfully wringing his hands*) I dunno, that's a long time. I really miss her right now.

CW: I understand it's hard, particularly when you'd like to do something, but I need for you to sign this paper, so I can be sure you're committed to doing this.

Facilitative Listening

In summary, listening is the first imperative LO5 in crisis intervention. When the word *listening* is used, the term is being applied broadly to several important behavioral and communications skills discussed in this chapter. To function in a facilitative way, workers must give full attention to the client by:

1. Focusing their total mental power on the client's world.
2. Attending to the client's verbal and nonverbal messages (what the client does not say is sometimes more important than what is actually spoken).
3. Picking up on the client's current readiness to enter into emotional and/or physical contact with others, especially with the worker.
4. Emitting attending behavior by both verbal and nonverbal actions, thereby strengthening the relationship and predisposing the client to trust the crisis intervention process.

One important aspect of listening is for the worker to make initial owning statements that express exactly what he or she is going to do. These **predispositioning** statements are extremely important in crisis intervention because many times the client is making contact with the worker for the first time and has no idea what is going to happen or what the worker may do in a threatening, chaotic environment.

CW: Rita, I can see you're really hurting. To fully understand what's going on and what needs to be done, I'm going to focus as hard as I can on what you're saying and how you're saying it. As well as listening to what you say, I'm going to be listening for those things that aren't said, because they may have some bearing on your problems too. So if I seem to be really concentrating on you, it's because I want to fully comprehend in as helpful and objective a way as possible what the situation is and your readiness to do something about it.

The second important aspect of listening is to respond in ways that let the client know that the crisis worker is accurately hearing both the facts and the emotional state from which the client's message comes. Here we are searching for both the affective and content dimensions of the problem. The crisis worker combines the dilemma and feelings by using restatement and reflection.

CW: As you lay the problem out—the abuse by your husband, the job pressures, the wonderful yet guilt-ridden times with Sam—I get the feeling of an emotional juggling act with everything from bowling pins to hand axes being juggled and now a burning baton has just been tossed into the mix. Now you're just sitting paralyzed wishing you'd never taken the job, wondering how you can get out, wanting answers, but having so many problems that you don't even know the right questions to ask.

The third facet of facilitative listening is facilitative responding. It provides positive impetus for clients to gain a clearer understanding of their feelings, inner motives, and choices. Facilitative responses enable clients to feel hopeful and to sense an inclination to begin to move forward, toward resolution and away from the central core of the crisis. Clients begin to be able to view the crisis from a standpoint of more reality or rationality, which immediately gives them a sense of control. Here the crisis worker targets an action.

CW: So, given all the things you are juggling, which ones do you want to throw out and which ones do you want to keep juggling? You've given me all kinds of information about how well you've handled the business up to this crisis point. Look back on how you handled that particular piece of juggling. What worked then that might work now? Using that as an example, can we sort each one of these out and get the act cleaned up and just say that particular ball isn't important right now and throw it out for at least awhile?

The fourth dimension of facilitative listening involves helping clients understand the full impact of the crisis situation. Such an understanding allows clients to become more like objective, external observers of the crisis and to refocus on it in rational ways rather than remaining stuck in their own internal frame of reference and emotional bias.

Rita: I feel like the whole world is caving in on me. I wonder if I'll ever be able to get out from under all the mess I'm in now.

CW: You're sounding emotionally frozen by what is happening. I'm wondering what would happen if we could step back for a moment and look at it as if we were third-party observers to your situation—as if you were someone else in a soap opera. What would you say to that person?

Rita: Well . . . (*moment of thought*) . . . I'd say she's not the first or only one to experience lots of trouble—that things may look horrible now, but that eventually things get worked out—especially if she's lucky and can bear up long enough.

CW: Then looking at it from outside yourself does give you an additional view.

Helping clients refocus is not a solution in itself. It is an extension of the art of listening that may facilitate forward movement when clients are emotionally stuck.

These four aspects of listening don't operate in a fragmented or mechanical way. Such listening requires skill, practice, an emotionally secure listener, and both physical and emotional stamina on the part of the listener. The following dialogue gives a brief but comprehensive demonstration of how facilitative listening is combined in its many dimensions. The client now is Jean, Rita's daughter. Don't be perplexed at the shift in clients. One person in crisis may well also put a significant other into a crisis situation as you will see when you meet the Smith family in Chapter 11, Family Crisis Intervention. In this instance, Rita's problems have boiled over into her 13-year-old daughter's life.

Jean: I feel put down and ignored by my mother. Every time anything is mentioned about Sam—that's her secret boyfriend—she gets mad and leaves the room. Everything has changed. It's like I'm no longer important to her. I don't know what's happening or what to do.

CW: You're feeling hurt and disappointed, and you're also bewildered by her responses to you.

Jean: (*crying and very upset*) I . . . I feel like I no longer count. I'm feeling like I'm in the way. Like I'm suddenly no good. . . . I feel like now I'm the problem.

CW: You're blaming yourself even though you're trying to understand what has happened and what you should do.

Jean: (*crying is slowing down*) By Sunday night I felt like killing myself. I planned to do it that night. I was feeling abandoned, alone, and hopeless. I just wanted to find some way to end the hurting. I didn't think I could go on another day. I felt like I was no longer her daughter—like she had either disowned me or had been living a lie. I don't know if I can go on.

CW: Even though you were feeling you were at the brink of death, you somehow managed to pull out of it. What did you do, and what are you doing now to keep from killing yourself?

Jean: (*not crying—pondering the crisis worker's last response*) Well, Marlene and her parents came by. I spent the night with them. That really helped. It was lucky for me that they came by and invited me. They were so kind and understanding. I had a bad night. Worrying about all that stuff. But they, especially Marlene, helped me so much.

CW: Let's see if you can tell me what you have learned from that experience that can help you the next time you feel like killing yourself.

Jean: (*pause, as if studying the crisis worker's response*) To get away . . . with someone who cares and understands.

CW: Tell me someone you can contact whenever you feel hopeless and lonely and suicidal so that next time you won't have to depend on luck.

Jean: Well, I'd call Marlene again . . . or my uncle and aunt. They'd be quick to invite me over . . . and there are several friends at school I could call. (*Dialogue continues.*)

This segment of dialogue contains several of the elements of listening that have been described. It contains accurate reflective listening, open-ended questions, and attention to the client's safety (without asking closed questions, giving advice, or encroaching on the client's prerogatives and autonomy). Also, the crisis worker keeps the focus right on the central core of the client's current concerns, paving the way for the client's forward movement from the immediate crisis toward safer and more adjustive actions. The worker's selective responses are geared toward enabling the client to become aware of and pursue immediate short-term goals. The worker does not digress into external events, past events, the mother, the secret boyfriend, gathering background information, or conducting long-term therapy.

Basic Strategies of Crisis Intervention

Myer and James (2005) have formulated nine **LO6** strategies used in crisis intervention. The basic core listening and responding skills already discussed are the foundation of these strategies. There is no formula for using these strategies. They may be used singly or in combination. Their use depends a great deal on the crisis context, the triage level of the client, and on what task of the crisis intervention model the interventionist is working. Here are the nine strategies.

Creating Awareness. The crisis worker attempts to bring to conscious awareness warded off, denied, shunted, and repressed feelings, thoughts, and behaviors that freeze clients' ability to act in response to the crisis. **Creating awareness** is particularly important for Task 2, Problem Exploration.

CW: It would be easier to just put it out of your mind, but I wonder what shoving it back will get you? You came here, so I'm pretty sure you want to get this out in the open and get some resolution. What would all this mess look like if it were sitting out there on the table?

Allowing Catharsis. **Catharsis** means simply letting clients talk, cry, swear, berate, rant, rave, mourn, or do anything else that allows them to ventilate feelings and thoughts; it may be one of the most therapeutic strategies the crisis worker can employ. To do this, the crisis worker needs to provide a safe and accepting environment that says, "It's OK to say and feel these things." By so doing the crisis worker clearly says he or she can accept those feelings and thoughts no matter how bad they may seem to be. A word of caution here! Allowing angry feelings to continue to build and escalate may not be the wisest course of action. This strategy is most often used with people who *can't* get in touch with their feelings and thoughts, as opposed to those whose feelings are already volcanic. This strategy is most likely to be used for Task 2, Problem Exploration, and Task 3, Providing Support.

CW: It's tough to talk about it. After all, it is an affair you are having. Perhaps you think I'll pass moral judgment on you for that. I won't! What I would most like you to do is to open up those push-pull feelings. Tell me more about being scared and angry at the same time.

Providing Support. Often the crisis worker is the *sole* support available to the client. As such, the crisis worker attempts to validate that the clients' responses are as reasonable as can be expected given the situation. Many times clients believe they must be going crazy, but they need to understand that they are not "crazy" and that most people would act in about

the same way given the kind, type, and duration of the crisis. Oftentimes in crisis, in an attempt to calm clients, workers state that it is "normal" to have such and such reactions. Nothing could be further from the truth. There is nothing "normal" at all about stress reactions associated with a sexual assault. Such attempts are at best placating and at worst discounting of the client. A far better description, we believe, is the word "common." Clients need to understand that while there is nothing "normal" about their feeling, acting, and thinking in a crisis situation, it is certainly "common" to most people. This kind of affirmation is particularly critical to clients who feel they have no support system available to them. That being said, the crisis worker *never* supports clients' injurious or lethal feelings, thoughts, or actions toward themselves or others.

Providing support is particularly useful when the client is attempting to move into action. In standard therapy, supervisors often express a great deal of concern about breeding dependence on the therapist. It should be clearly understood that when we are dealing with clients in crisis they may well need to be dependent on us for a short while. That doesn't mean we are going to adopt clients and take them home with us! It does mean that when the client is drained of emotional, cognitive, or behavioral resources, we are supportive, and we provide a shoulder to lean on.

Rita: I don't know which way to turn, what to do. This is not me! I am so confused and so alone. My God! How did I ever get in this awful mess?

CW: Right now you may feel that way, but I am in this with you, and I am going to stay in it until we get some control and direction back for you.

Rita: I don't know how there can ever be any control. (*Starts sobbing.*)

CW: We are going to get some control, and I am going to stay with you until that happens.

Promoting Expansion. The crisis worker engages in **expansion** activities to open up clients' tunnel vision of the crisis. Oftentimes clients are so wrapped up in the crisis and are continuously engaging in self-defeating thoughts and behaviors that they are unable to see other perceptions and possibilities. Increasing expansion helps clients step back, reframe the problem, and gain new perspectives. This strategy is primarily used to help clients resolve stuck cognitive reactions. By confronting clients' narrow and restrictive views, crisis workers help clients consider other perspectives. This strategy is particularly effective with clients who are not able to recognize environmental cues that may help them to perceive alternate meanings of events and possible solutions to them.

CW: This may be distasteful, but I want you to think about this. You know one possibility would be to get a restraining order. That is pretty common in most domestic violence situations, but it is used in other instances too.

Emphasizing Focus. Conversely, at times the problem is that clients are too expansive and need to **focus** their freewheeling, out-of-control flights of ideation about the crisis that have little basis in reality. The crisis worker attempts to partition, compartmentalize, and downsize clients' all-encompassing, catastrophic interpretations and perceptions of the crisis event to more specific, realistic, manageable components and options. This strategy has utility across all tasks of the crisis intervention model.

CW: Given this huge mess, what is the one thing you need to do right now to get some relief? What could you focus on that would tell you immediately that some pressure was off rather than trying to take care of everything and everybody?

Providing Guidance. The term *guidance* has come to have somewhat of a negative connotation in the field of counseling because it implies that clients are incapable of helping themselves. However, many times clients in crisis do need **guidance** and direction. They don't have the knowledge or resources available to make good decisions. Thus, the crisis worker provides information, referral, and direction in regard to clients' obtaining assistance from specific external resources and support systems. For example, one of the handiest tools that crisis workers have is a directory of all the social services available in their catchment area. This strategy is used almost exclusively to respond to clients' behavioral reactions.

Rita: I have no idea how to go about getting a restraining order.

CW: Up until now you would have had no reason to. However, the staff at the Family Trouble Center can do that for you and would be glad to help you do it. I can give you that number if you want.

Promoting Mobilization. The crisis worker attempts both to activate and marshal clients' internal resources and to find and use external support systems to help generate coping skills and problem-solving abilities so they become **mobilized** and do not remain stuck in the crisis situation.

CW: There is a support group of women I know of that meets regularly at St. Michael's Catholic church. They all struggle with some of the same relationship issues that you are having. Hearing and interacting with them might give you some new ideas on how to go about solving this knotty problem. You have some good ideas and are pretty geared up to act on them, but it might not hurt to get their perspectives.

Implementing Order. The crisis worker provides **order** and methodically helps clients classify and categorize problems so as to prioritize and sequentially attack the crisis in a logical and linear manner. Too often clients see the crisis as a mountainous tidal wave washing over them when what they need to do is grab a metaphorical life jacket and float along until it dissipates or build a small dike and let it rush by them. These actions, while apparent to an outside observer, are oftentimes blind to the client in the maelstrom of a crisis.

CW: It seems overwhelming, but let's put it into pieces you can manage. Break it down. If this were your business instead of your love life, how would you parcel the problem out, and what order of priorities would you give to each part? What's the first thing you would do? While it might not make it perfect, what would it take to make this situation more tolerable?

Providing Protection. Providing **protection** is paramount in crisis intervention, so important that it is its own overarching task in our model. The crisis worker safeguards clients from engaging in harmful, destructive, detrimental, and unsafe feelings, behaviors, and thoughts that may be psychologically or physically injurious or lethal to themselves or others.

CW: I want to make the clearest personal statement I can to you Rita. I really fear for your safety. I would not confront Jake alone after work at the garage. I understand you don't want a big scene in front of other people, but to do that alone with nobody around seems to me a really dangerous thing to do.

When these nine strategies are used with the basic verbal crisis intervention skills in this chapter, they form the backbone of crisis intervention techniques. By using them with the Triage Assessment Form, crisis interventionists should have a comprehensive real-time assessment of how they are doing as they move the client through the model.

Climate of Client Growth

According to Rogers (1977), the most effective **LO7** helper is one who can provide three necessary and sufficient conditions for client growth. These conditions he named *empathy, genuineness,* and *acceptance* (pp. 9–12). These therapeutic conditions are particularly critical to doing effective crisis intervention. To create a climate of **empathy** means that the crisis worker accurately senses the inner feelings and meanings the client is experiencing and directly communicates to the client that the worker understands how it feels to be the client. The condition of **genuineness** (also called *realness, transparency,* or *congruency*) means that the worker is being completely open in the relationship: nothing is hidden, there are no facades, and there are no professional fronts. If the worker is clearly open and willing to be fully himself or herself in the relationship, the client is encouraged to reciprocate. The term **acceptance** (also referred to as *caring* or *prizing*) means that the crisis worker feels an unconditional positive regard for the client. It is an attitude of accepting and caring for the client without the client's necessarily reciprocating. The condition of acceptance is provided for no other reason than that the client is a human being in need. If these conditions of empathy, genuineness, and acceptance can be provided for the client, then the probability that the client will experience positive emotional movement is increased.

Communicating Empathy

In describing the use of empathy to help clients, we will focus on five important techniques: (1) attending, (2) verbally communicating empathic understanding, (3) reflecting feelings, (4) nonverbally communicating empathic understanding, and (5) silence as a way of communicating empathic understanding (Cormier & Cormier, 1991; Gilliland & James, 1998, pp. 116–118). First, however, it is necessary to differentiate empathy from sympathy and distancing.

Sympathy. Beginners in the field confuse empathy with sympathy. Sympathy is fine at the right time and conveys support, but it means essentially taking on the person's problems and feelings rather than attempting to experience and convey what the person is feeling. Mostly we think of sympathy as a sad feeling with tears attached to it. It can just as well be righteous indignation and anger. Particularly when we are attempting to do exploration with a client in crisis, we will do better to put sympathy on the shelf for a while.

CW: You poor thing. That's terrible! Nobody should be allowed to get away with that kind of behavior. How about I call the police right now!

The behavior, indeed, may be terrible, but the crisis worker will do better to make a deep, reflective response that captures the client's feeling.

CW: You seem really torn—kicking yourself for being a fool, but still wanting and hoping the relationship to be something and go somewhere. It sounds like you know it is over, but you don't quite know what to do yet.

Distancing. At times, crisis workers may be so overwhelmed and frightened by what they are confronted with that they seek to distance themselves from the overwhelming affect by engaging in what we call "funeral home counseling." Here are a few examples of what people say when they have no idea what to say but feel they need to say something. These attempts to be palliative are generally not helpful and can, in fact, hinder intervention. Lots of times these statements are centered on a religious/spiritual theme: "It's God's will." "God works in mysterious ways." "Heaven wouldn't be heaven if it were only filled with old people." "He/she's in a better place." Another way of distancing is by rationalizing, discounting, and minimizing: "Well, you still have your health." "It could have been worse." "Don't feel guilty about it." "Try to get your mind off it." "Just try and relax a little." "It's tough, but you need to calm down." These statements probably say more about the *worker's* crisis state than they do about the client's. A far better way, when aspiring crisis workers don't know what to say, is to say nothing or to own the feeling of what they are experiencing. At times, owning our own inability to find words to convey the depth of feeling is probably one of the best ways to indicate that you do feel for the client.

CW: (*reaches out and touches Rita's arm and says nothing for a few moments*) I wish I had something to say that would take this pain and confusion away and make this all right, but right now I just don't.

Attending. The first step in communicating empathy has little to do with words and a lot to do with looking, acting, and being attentive. The foregoing crisis worker response is much more about attending than saying or doing. In most initial counseling and therapy sessions, the client enters with some anxiety related to the therapy itself in addition to the stress brought on by the crisis. In crisis situations, such anxiety is increased exponentially. Shame, guilt, rage, and sorrow are but a few of the feelings that may be manifested. Such feelings may be blatant and rampant or subtle and disguised. Whatever shape or form such feelings take, the inattentive crisis worker can miss the message the client is attempting to convey. Worse, an inattentive attitude implies lack of interest on the part of the worker and does little to establish a trusting relationship.

Mehrabian (1971) reports that 55% of emotional output and communication occurs through face and body while 38% comes from voice tone and only 7% from words used. Whether these percentages of overwhelming nonverbal communication are precise or not, one thing is for sure in the crisis business, the effective worker focuses fully on the client, both in facial expression and in body posture. By nodding, keeping eye contact, smiling, showing appropriate seriousness of expression, leaning forward, keeping an open stance, and sitting or standing close to the client without invading the client's space, the crisis worker conveys a sense of involvement, concern, commitment, and trust. Vocal tone, diction, pitch, modulation, and smoothness of delivery also tell clients a great deal about the attentiveness of the crisis worker. By attending closely to the client's verbal and nonverbal responses, the crisis worker can quickly tell whether he or she is establishing an empathic relationship or exacerbating the client's feelings of distrust, fear, and uncertainty about becoming involved in the relationship.

Attentiveness, then, is both an attitude and a skill. It is an attitude in that the worker focuses fully on the client right here and now. In such moments the crisis worker's own concerns are put on hold. It is a skill in that conveying attending takes practice. It is just as inappropriate for the crisis worker to look too concerned and be in too close proximity as it is to lean back with arms folded and legs crossed, giving a cold stare. Here is an example of an appropriate blend of both verbal and nonverbal skill in attending to a client empathically.

Rita: (*Enters room, sits down in far corner, warily looks about the room, crosses her legs and fidgets with her purse, and avoids direct eye contact, manifesting the appearance of a distraught woman who is barely holding together.*)

CW: (*rises behind desk, and observing the behavior and physical appearance of the client, moves to a chair a comfortable distance and a slight angle from Rita's, sits down, leans forward in an open stance, and with an appearance of concern and inquisitiveness looks directly at Rita*) I'd like to be of help. Where would you like to start?

The crisis worker sees the apprehension in the client and immediately becomes proactive. The crisis worker moves close to the client but does not sit directly in front of her in what could be construed as a confronting stance. The worker inclines forward to focus attention—eyes, ears, brain, and whole body—onto the client's world. The whole posture of the crisis worker is congruent with the verbal message of offering immediate acceptance and willingness to help. In summary, effective attending is unobtrusive, natural, and without pretense. It is a necessary condition for empathic listening.

Verbally Communicating Empathic Understanding. When you can accurately hear and understand the core emotional feelings inside the client and accurately and caringly communicate that understanding to the client, you are demonstrating effective listening. The deeper your level of listening (understanding), the more helpful you will be to your clients. For instance, reflecting a client's message at the interchangeable level is helpful.

Rita: I'm thinking about just walking in and telling Jake I want a divorce—regardless of what Sam is ready to do. I don't think I can go on much longer. My ulcer is beginning to act up, I'm an emotional wreck, and everyone is expecting more of me than I can give.

CW: You sound like you are feeling a sense of urgency because it's adversely affecting your physical and emotional well-being.

A deeper level of listening and communicating empathic understanding to Rita might be expressed thus:

CW: Rita, your sense of urgency is getting to the point where you seem about ready to take a big risk with both Jake and Sam. I sense that your physical and emotional stresses have about reached their limits, and you're realizing that no one else is going to act to give you relief—that you are the one who is going to have to decide and act.

The second response is more helpful because it confirms to Rita a deeper understanding than the first response. Both responses are helpful because they are accurate, and neither adds to nor detracts from the client's verbal, nonverbal, or emotional messages. Whereas the first response is considered minimally helpful, the second response is more facilitative because it lets the client know the worker heard a deeper personal meaning (risk) and a personal ownership of possible action. A word of caution to the worker, however: Beware of reading into the client's statements more than the client is saying, and take care to keep your response as brief as possible.

Reflection of Feelings. Reflection of feelings is a powerful tool to get at shunted or denied affect. In standard therapy, we constantly hammer at uncovering affect because of client resistance to dealing with threatening and warded off feelings. However, in crisis intervention the desire to uncover feeling is not always the therapeutic best bet. A client who is scoring an 8, 9, or 10 on the Affective Scale of the Triage Assessment Form probably does not need to have a crisis worker attempt to elicit even more feelings. It is not the job of the crisis worker to tell the client what he or she is feeling. The following dialogue moves from a reflection to a judgment and tells the client how she feels.

CW: You are bitter and resentful about being in this dead-end marriage. You can't figure a way out.

Rather, what the crisis worker should do is make an educated guess using conditional statements that allows the client to accept or reject the worker's guess.

CW: It *seems* that you are pretty bitter and resentful about this dead-end marriage and are frustrated that you can't figure a way out.

Effective communication of empathic understanding to the client means focusing on the client's expressed affective and cognitive messages. The worker deals *directly* with the client's concerns and does not veer off into talking *about* the client's concerns or some tangential person or event. That distinction is important.

Rita: I'm afraid Jake might attack me even worse if I tell him I want a divorce.

CW: He did beat you pretty badly. Sam would probably go bananas at that. Your husband Jake has such a violent temper. (*talking about the situation and tangentially focusing on Jake*)

CW: You're feeling some reservations about telling Jake because you really don't want to be beaten up again. (*dealing with Rita's current feelings and concerns*)

The latter response is preferred because it stays on target with Rita's feelings and concerns in the here and now and because it avoids getting off onto Jake, Sam, or any other third party or issue.

The central issue in empathic understanding is to hone in on the client's current core of feelings and concerns and communicate to the client (in the worker's own words) the gist of what the client is experiencing.

Nonverbal Communication. Empathic understanding means accurately picking up and reflecting more than verbal messages. It involves accurately sensing and reflecting all the unspoken cues, messages, and behaviors the client emits. Nonverbal messages may be transmitted in many ways. The worker should carefully observe body posture, body movement, gestures, grimaces, vocal pitch, movement of eyes, movement of arms and legs, and other body indicators. Clients may transmit emotions such as anger, fear, puzzlement, doubt, rejection, emotional stress, and hopelessness by different body messages without using the words that go with those feelings. Crisis workers should be keenly aware of whether nonverbal messages are consistent with the client's verbal messages. "Keenly aware" means that you are always monitoring body language for signs of aggression—particularly toward you! While this may sound like harping, throughout this book we will continuously be talking about safety—both the client's and yours. In fact, Chapter 14, Violent Behavior in Institutions, is specifically designed to keep you out of the hospital or mortuary. Thus, a part of empathic understanding is the communication of such inconsistency to the client who may not be consciously aware of the difference. For example:

CW: (*observing the way Rita's face lights up whenever she speaks or thinks about Sam*) Rita, I notice you are talking about all the trouble it is for you to keep seeing Sam on the sly. But your body tells me that those are the moments you live for—that right now your only ecstasy is when you're with Sam.

The crisis worker's main concern with nonverbal communication also involves the worker's own body messages. All the dynamics of the client's body language apply to the worker as well. Your nonverbal messages must be consistent with your verbal messages. It would not be empathic or helpful if your words were saying to the client, "I understand precisely what you're feeling and desiring," but your body was saying, "I don't care," or "I'm bored," or "My mind isn't fully focused on what you're saying." Your voice, facial expression, posture—even the office arrangement and environment—must say to the client: "I'm fully tuned in to your world while you're with me. I want to give my total mental and emotional energy to understanding your concerns while you're here. I will not be distracted." If your body can communicate such messages so that they are unmistakably understood by the client, then you will have effectively communicated empathy to the client nonverbally, and you will stand a better chance of being helpful.

Silence. Silence is golden. Beginning crisis workers often feel compelled to initiate talk to fill any void or lapse in the dialogue because they believe they would not be doing their job otherwise. Nothing could be further from the truth. Clients need time to think. To throw out a barrage of questions or engage in a monologue says more about the crisis worker's insecurity in the situation than it does about resolving the crisis. Silence gives the client thinking time—and the crisis worker too.

Indeed, at such times, verbiage from the crisis worker may be intrusive and even unwelcome. Remaining silent but attending closely to the client can convey deep, empathic understanding. Nonverbally, the message comes across: "I understand your struggle trying to put those feelings into words, and it's OK. I know it's tough, but I believe you can handle it. However, I'm right here if you need me."

Rita: The last beating . . . I was so ashamed, yet I couldn't seem to do anything except go back to him.

CW: It hurts you not only to get beaten but also that others might find out—which seems even worse. As a result, you don't see any alternatives.

Rita: (*thinks hard, eyes focused into the distance for more than a minute*) Yes and no! I see alternatives, but I guess until now I haven't had the guts to do anything. I rationalized that something must be wrong with me or that the situation would get better, but it hasn't for five years. It has gotten worse.

CW: (*silence; looks at Rita for some 30 seconds while collecting thoughts*) A couple of things strike me about what you said. First, you've decided to quit blaming yourself. Second, by the fact that you're here now, you've chosen at least one alternative to that five-year merry-go-round of abuse.

In this scene, silence is allowed to work for both the client and the worker. The client needs time to work through her response to the worker, and she is unconditionally allowed to do this. The same is true of the crisis worker. The client's comment is synthesized and processed for its full meaning. By reacting immediately, the crisis worker might make less than a potent response. Taking time to digest both the content and the affect of the client enables the worker to formulate a response that is more likely to be on target and helpful.

Taking Time. Cochran (2014) proposes that we have "time." At the point that a crisis erupts, clients often have tapped out their human supports, people are tired of them, and don't want to waste any further time with them. It is critical that you are not hurried and that you take your time and the client gets a clear sense that you are taking time to carefully understand what's going on.

CW: I know things are hectic, but I want to take time to understand your side of it as it played out today. We have plenty of time, so I'm going to sit down and listen. Start where ever you'd like because we do have time.

Communicating Genuineness

Contrary to the thinking of most beginning human services workers, as evidenced by their behavior, being fully oneself and not some pseudotherapist or mimic of a particular therapist one has heard or seen is an absolutely necessary condition, particularly in crisis intervention. Rogers (1969, p. 228) puts it in clear, simple, and succinct terms:

> When I can accept the fact that I have many deficiencies, many faults, make a lot of mistakes, am often ignorant where I should be knowledgeable, often prejudiced when I should be open-minded, often have feelings which are not justified by the circumstances, then I can be much more real.

Rogers's statement means putting on no false fronts but rather being oneself in the relationship and communicating what "oneself" is to the client. In short, it is being honest.

The advice to be honest is not simply a platitude. To be honest is to be congruent; it means that the crisis worker's awareness of self, feelings, and experience is freely and unconditionally available and communicable, when appropriate, during intervention in a crisis. Egan (1975, 1982, 1986, 1990) has listed essential components of genuineness that would serve the beginning crisis worker well.

1. *Being role free.* The crisis worker is genuine in life as well as in the therapeutic relationship and is congruent in both experiencing and communicating feelings (Egan, 1975, p. 91).
2. *Being spontaneous.* The crisis worker communicates freely, with tact and without constantly gauging what to say, and behaves freely, without being impulsive or inhibited, rule bound or technique bound. Worker behavior is based on a feeling of self-confidence (p. 92).
3. *Being nondefensive.* Crisis workers who behave nondefensively have an excellent understanding of their strengths and weaknesses. Thus, they can be open to negative, even hostile, client expressions without feeling attacked or defensive. The crisis worker who is genuine understands such negative expressions as saying more about the client than the worker and tries to facilitate exploration of such comments rather than defend against them (pp. 92–93).
4. *Being consistent.* People who are genuine have few discrepancies between what they think, feel, and say and their actual behavior. Crisis workers who are consistent do not think one thing and tell a client another or engage in behavior that is contrary to their values (pp. 93–94).
5. *Being a sharer of self.* When it is appropriate to the situation, people who are genuine engage in self-disclosure, allowing others to know them through open verbal and nonverbal expression of their feelings (p. 94).

The following dialogue between the crisis worker and Rita demonstrates comprehensively the points both Rogers and Egan make.

Rita: Just what the hell gives? Here I am going crazy, and you put it back on my shoulders. You're supposed to help get me out of this mess!

CW: I can see that you're really mad at me because I don't behave the way you think I ought to.

Rita: Well, how can you be such a caring person if you let me hang out there, pushing me to take such risky chances? I could lose everything.

CW: You see me as being a real hypocrite because I'm pushing you to take some action rather than sympathizing with you.

Rita: God knows I could use some . . . and when you act so callously (*cries*) . . . you're like every other damn man!

CW: What would I be doing if I were acting in the most helpful way I possibly could, in your opinion, right now?

Rita: Well, I know you can't solve this for me, but I'd sure as hell like for you to point the way or help me solve this.

CW: So, what you're really wanting is to be able to solve this dilemma on your own, and what you're wanting from me is to help you find your own inner choices that are best for you. What I want to do is to help you find those choices. Let's look at your current options right now.

The dialogue aptly depicts the crisis worker owning feelings, using "I" statements, and focusing on the client's emergent concerns rather than allowing the focus to shift to tangential matters or defensive responses by the worker. Such statements allow the crisis worker to retain integrity, squarely face client hostility without becoming hostile in turn, and model a safe and trusting atmosphere in which clients see that it is all right for them to demonstrate angry feelings and still be accepted by the crisis worker. At the same time, the crisis worker stands by and is consistent with a therapeutic approach without being intimidated by or defensive with the client. The crisis worker above all has the self-confidence and congruence to make such statements in a way that is facilitative for the client.

Communicating Acceptance

The crisis worker who interacts with complete acceptance of clients exudes an unconditional positive regard for clients that transcends clients' personal qualities, beliefs, problems, situations, or crises. The worker is able to prize, care for, and fully accept clients even if they are doing things, saying things, and experiencing situations that are contrary to the worker's personal beliefs and values. The worker is able to put aside personal needs, values, and desires and does not require clients to make specific responses as a condition of full acceptance. That is not easily done with clients in crisis. There is a preferred client acronym in therapy named YAVIS for the young, attractive, verbal, intelligent, and sociable therapist dream client. In most crises situations the YAVIS client is not going to magically appear. By the time many clients in crisis get to the worker, they don't act, talk, look, or even smell good. Thus, acceptance is easily said and less easy to manifest.

Rita: (*disheveled, clothes look slept in, under arm deodorant has failed, make-up in sad repair*) I hate to bother you with all my problems. I know you're married and have never been divorced. You must think I'm a terribly screwed-up mess. I look a mess and probably smell like it too. I was so scared I didn't go home, sent Jean to her aunt's, and slept in my truck at the state park.

CW: I hear your concern, and I want you to know that what has happened to you, or even how you look and what you choose to do have nothing to do with my regard for you. What I'm really hoping we can do is to help you arrive at those choices that will best help you get through this crisis and successfully get back in total control of your life.

Rita: I appreciate that very much. But sometimes I wonder whether my running around with Sam doesn't strike you as unwise and immature. Like some barfly, or gutter slut with no morals.

CW: I hope I'm not giving off negative vibes to give you that impression, because your personal preferences have nothing to do with my caring for you. It seems like you really have a concern about my feelings about how you should act.

Rita: Not really. It's just something inside me—that if I were you, I'd be wondering.

CW: So, a source of concern inside you is whether I may evaluate you negatively. What I want you to know is that my esteem for you is not based on what you do.

Even when clients persist in projecting onto the crisis worker negative evaluations or notions such as those expressed by Rita, the worker doesn't have to buy into such notions. If the worker can truly feel an unconditional positive regard for the client, there will be no need for denial, defensiveness, or diversion from the reality of the worker's true feelings. If the worker demonstrates caring and prizing of the client, regardless of the client's situation or status, the client will be more likely to accept and prize himself or herself. That is the essence of acceptance in crisis intervention.

In the Field

The foregoing scenarios all occur in an office **LO8** where there is time to think, formulate responses, and make thoughtful comments, all with knowledge about the client's history. As such, it is more crisis therapy for a client in a transcrisis state and at a transcrisis point. What happens, when the worker is in the field, has little knowledge about clients or their problems, and the crisis is escalating by the minute? Above anything else in this situation, the crisis worker's initiating techniques are critical to bonding with an out-of-control client who is unknown to the responder (Kirchberg, James, Dupont, & Cochran, 2014). While Major Sam Cochran, retired, has formulated the following coaching plan and plays specifically for CIT officers (Cochran, 2014), these four plays can be used by any crisis worker in the field. These are simple, initial steps in creating trust and quick bonds that are critical to de-escalation. Interestingly enough, in the heat of the moment when we are training mental health workers or police officers, they sometimes *forget to use them!*

1. Introduce yourself in a way that says, "I am here for you and I am no threat." CW: "Hi, I'm Dick James, I'm part of the mobile crisis team. I can see you are really frustrated. I'd like to help if I can."
2. Obtain the person's name and personalize it if possible. CW: "It must be pretty serious for you to have run everybody out of the house, got a can of gas, and are considering blowing the house apart. I am sorry I didn't get your name. Could you tell me your name please?"
3. Express what you are seeing across affective, behavioral, and cognitive dimensions and use "I" statements to do it. CW: "So first off you are really angry and frustrated that your boss wouldn't listen to your plan to save money and blew you off. As a result, it was the last straw and you kicked everybody out of the shop and now won't let anybody back in. Seems like you're thinking this will finally get his attention."
4. Summarize the information you have obtained and feed it back so both parties are on the same page. CW: "Is that about right what I said? Let me know if there is something I missed because I want to be sure we are clear between each other."

Safety in the Field. Setting limits is part of safety procedure and that involves determining the degree of threat a person is feeling and how they intend to protect themselves from it (Cochran, 2014). It is not uncommon to meet people in crisis in the field who are armed with some kind of a weapon that they are not displaying. They are armed not necessarily to hurt someone else, but rather are trying to protect themselves. Therefore, if the person is acting in a defensive manner and your triage rating on them is high, assume a person may have a weapon, and ask to see it.

CW: Lots of times people in your situation have good reason to believe someone might hurt them and so have a weapon of some kind. If you do, I'd like you to just lay it down beside you. I want to help you out, but I need to feel safe too.

If the person is noncompliant or seems not to hear, back off and get law enforcement help.

Assessing for Medical Problems in the Field. Many of the people the crisis worker will meet in the field have medical problems that are contributory to the crisis. Finding medical staff who have worked with clients is often critical in de-escalating a crisis by getting clients to their medical support system. Many of the clients are well known as repeaters by police officers, EMTs, and 911 operators. Getting them to medical staff and facilities that know them and are their care providers is a first priority. After making initial contact with clients, potential medical issues, both physical and psychological, need to be checked out.

CW: You look a bit pale and fatigued to me. Have you been having some medical problems lately?

If the person doesn't acknowledge any medical issues, don't just dismiss the issue. Query them in regard to any medical staff they have seen.

CW: So OK no major medical problems then. What about the small ones? Have you seen any doctors, nurse practitioners, chiropractors, or counselors lately for the day-to-day stuff?

Drugs in the Field. Next to weapons, gathering information on drug use and misuse for both illegal and prescription drugs is critical in planning action steps (James, 2014). It does little good to attempt to de-escalate a person who has misused drugs or, as frequently is the case in mental illness, has stopped taking psychotropic medication, and the illness has resurfaced. It is also not uncommon, particularly in geriatric clients who are taking a variety of drugs, for

bad drug interactions to occur when a new drug is introduced into the client's regimen.

CW: (*suspected mental illness*) You said you are smelling bad things. Have you been taking any medicine for those bad smells? When was the last time you took it?

CW: (*suspected bad drug interaction*) Mrs. Smith, your children tell me you have really been down in the dumps the last few days since you last visited the doctor. What did the doctor tell you and did he change your medication at all?

Support in the Field. Finding what human support systems are available, what have ceased to exist, and what the client has done to access these systems, if any, are primary to any intervention plan and the disposition of where the client is physically going to go.

CW: Is there anyone now available to give you some support? By "anyone" I mean family, friends, ministers, human service workers, boss, coworkers.

Meeting Basic Needs in the Field. If basic needs of food, water, clothing, medical, and shelter are not being met, then little resolution to the crisis will occur, or, at the very least, helping the client get some of these needs met will go a long way toward gaining trust and compliance.

CW: I wonder when the last time it was you had a decent meal. So I wonder if getting something in your stomach wouldn't at least start to feel like you had some control back.

Using Cochran's (2014) basic plays and immediately checking out safety, drug use, support systems, and basic needs are typically the precursors of any other techniques used when you are in the field and it is your first meeting with the client.

Acting in Crisis Intervention

As shown in Figure 4.1, the crisis worker's **LO9** level of action and involvement in the client's world, based on a valid and realistic assessment of the client's level of mobility/immobility, may be anywhere on a continuum ranging from nondirective through collaborative to directive. The appropriateness of alternative coping mechanisms hinges on the client's degree of mobility. Thus, assessment of client mobility is a key concept governing the degree of the crisis worker's involvement. One of the first things

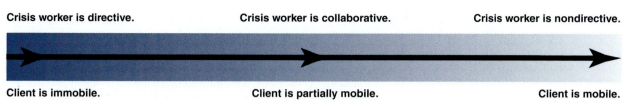

Crisis worker is directive.   **Crisis worker is collaborative.**   **Crisis worker is nondirective.**

Client is immobile.   **Client is partially mobile.**   **Client is mobile.**

From the initiating crisis event to resolution, counseling should move from left to right on the directive–nondirective worker continuum as the client moves from immobile to mobile.

Darker shading indicates a more directed approach to counseling when the client is assessed as immobile.

Lighter shading indicates the crisis worker becoming more nondirective and the client becoming more mobile.

FIGURE 4.1   The Directive–Nondirective Action Continuum

the worker must determine is what event precipitated the crisis. What brought on the disequilibrium? The answer may not be very clear in the client's complex and rambling story. So the worker may have to ask, early in the interview, "What *one event* brought you to seek counseling today?" When you discover the major precipitating event that took away the client's autonomous coping ability, it will likely signal your primary focus with the client.

Directive Intervention

Because the gold standard for standard beginning training in long-term psychotherapy has been to learn the practice of person-centered or nondirective therapy we find that our students have difficulty transiting into an active, assertive, directive stance as they start to practice crisis intervention. Yet Allen, Wilson, and Armstrong (2014) report that when clinicians received training in trauma-focused cognitive-behavioral therapy their beliefs changed toward the utility of structured/directive approach to treatment. Directive intervention is *not* about passing moral judgments or general character appraisal on an individual. **Directive intervention** is about providing specific information and guidance clients need to make decisions, setting limits on behaviors that range from inappropriate to lethal, and apprising them of consequences of their affective, cognitive, and behavioral responses to the crisis based on the interventionist's expert clinical judgment and the self-same lack thereof in the client. The directive approach is necessary when the client is assessed as being too immobile to cope with the current crisis. A triage score in the high teens or twenties typically calls for a good deal of directiveness from the worker. The crisis worker is the principal definer of the problem, searcher for alternatives, and developer of an adequate plan, and

instructs, leads, or guides the client in the action. Directive counseling is an "I" approach. This is an example of a worker-directed statement: "I want you to try something right now. I want you to draw a deep breath, and while you are doing it, I want you to just focus on your breathing. Don't let any other thoughts enter your mind. Just relax and notice how your tensions begin to subside." By using a very directive stance, the worker takes temporary control, authority, and responsibility for the situation.

Rita: I don't know which way to turn. My whole world has caved in. I don't know what I'll do tonight. It's all so hopeless. I'm scared to even think about tonight. (*Rita appears stunned and in a state of panic.*) I don't know what to do.

CW: I don't want you to go home in the state you're in now. I'm going to call Domestic Abuse Services, and if they have room for you at their shelter, I want you to consider spending at least one night there. Keep Jean at your sister's house for the time being. Domestic Abuse Services has offices and a counseling service at one location and a shelter at a different address, which is unlisted. I don't want you to worry. We have a van that can take you to the shelter. In the morning you can leave the shelter and go talk with the Domestic Abuse Services counselors, or you can come back and talk with me; but right now my main concern is that you are safe for today and tonight.

There are many kinds of immobile clients: (1) clients who need immediate hospitalization because of chemical use or organic dysfunction, (2) clients who are suffering from such severe depression that they cannot function, (3) clients who are experiencing a severe psychotic episode, (4) clients who are suffering from severe shock, bereavement, or loss, (5) clients whose anxiety level is temporarily so high that they cannot function until the anxiety subsides, (6) clients who, for any reason, are out of touch with reality, and (7) clients who are currently a danger to themselves or others. Immobile clients are more apt to be suicidal or homicidal than are clients who are ready to respond to collaborative or to nondirective counseling. Or, because of their inability to function effectively, they are more likely to engage in activities that put themselves or others at risk for serious injury. The worker must be able to make a fairly accurate and objective assessment of the client's level of mobility.

However, if the worker makes an error of judgment (believing a client to be immobile when in fact he or she is not), no harm is usually done because the client may simply respond by refusing to accept the worker's direction. In most cases of this sort, the worker can then shift into a collaborative mode and continue the helping session. Many times a worker will begin in a directive mode and then shift into a collaborative mode during the session. For example, with a highly anxious client the worker may begin by directing the client in relaxation exercises, which may lower the client's anxiety level to the point where the worker can make a natural shift into a collaborative mode to continue the counseling.

Collaborative Counseling

The collaborative approach enables the crisis worker to forge a real partnership with the client in evaluating the problem, generating acceptable alternatives, and implementing realistic action steps. When the triage assessment indicates that the client cannot function successfully in a nondirective mode but has enough mobility to be a partner in the crisis intervention process, the worker is collaborative to that degree. When a client has a triage score that is in the high single digits to middle teens, the crisis worker can typically operate in a collaborative mode. Many crisis interventions operate in this mode. Collaborative counseling is a "we" approach, in contrast to the "I" approach of directive counseling and the "you" approach of nondirective counseling. Consider some typical worker statements in the collaborative mode: "What 'they' are going to do sounds overpowering as you say it, but we haven't really considered what 'we' can do if we come up with a plan." "You've come up with a lot of good ideas, but you sound a little confused about which one to act on. Could we put our heads together and make a priority list of alternatives?" The collaborative client is a full partner in identifying the precipitating problem, examining realistic alternatives, planning action steps, and making a commitment to carrying out a realistic plan. The collaborative client is not as self-reliant and autonomous as the fully mobile client, but does have enough ego strength and mobility to participate in resolving the problem. The worker is needed to serve as a temporary catalyst, consultant, facilitator, and support person. Here is an example of a collaborative response to a client.

Rita: I've thought about going to my mother's or going to the battered women's shelter or even calling my school counselor friend for a place to stay tonight.

CW: Let's examine these three choices, and maybe some others available to you that I know of, and we'll see which one will best meet your requirements.

Nondirective Counseling

The nondirective approach is desirable whenever clients are able to initiate and carry out their own action steps. While the crisis worker will want to be as nondirective as possible and give the client as much control as the client can handle, in the initial stage of a crisis the worker is seldom nondirective because of the high level of ratings on the Triage Assessment Form (see Chapter 3). With the "you" approach of nondirective counseling, the worker uses a great amount of active listening and many open-ended questions to help clients clarify what they really want to do and examine what outcomes various choices might produce. These are some possible questions: "What do you wish to have happen?" "What will occur if you choose to do that?" "What people are available now who could and would assist you in this?" "Picture yourself doing that—vividly see yourself choosing that route. Now, how does that image fit with what you're really trying to accomplish?" "What activities did you do in the past that helped you in situations similar to this?" The worker does not manage, manipulate, prescribe, dominate, or control. It is the client who owns the problem, the coping mechanisms, the plan, the action, the commitment, and the outcomes.

The worker is a support person who may listen, encourage, reflect, reinforce, self-disclose, and suggest. Nondirective counseling assists clients in mobilizing what already is inside them—the capacity, ability, and coping strength to solve their own problems in ways that are pretty well known to them already but that are temporarily out of reach. Here is an example of a nondirective response.

Rita: This is it. I've had the last beating I'm going to take from that jerk! I'm simply going to get myself out of this hell!

CW: You've made a decision to choose a different life for yourself, and you've decided that you are the one who is going to start it.

Action Strategies for Crisis Workers

A number of action strategies and considera **LO10** tions may enhance the worker's effectiveness in dealing with clients in crisis. However, before committing to doing anything with the client, consider the following "rules of the road."

Recognize Individual Differences. View and respond to each client and each crisis situation as unique. If you really believe you are multiculturally sensitive, this is the essence of an emic multicultural view where both your and the client's social locations will play a big part in what will happen. Even for experienced workers, staying attuned to the uniqueness of each person is difficult. Under the pressures of time and exhaustion, and misled by overconfidence in their own expertise, workers find it all too easy to lump problems and clients together and provide pat answers and solutions. Treating clients generically is likely to cost the worker and the client a great deal more in the long run than it saves in time and effort in the short run. Stereotyping, labeling, and taking for granted any aspect of crisis intervention are definite pitfalls.

Assess Yourself. Ongoing self-analysis on the part of the worker is mandatory. At all times, workers must be fully and realistically aware of their own values, limitations, physical and emotional status, and personal readiness to deal objectively with the client and the crisis at hand. Crisis workers need to run continuous perceptual checks to ascertain if they have gotten in over their heads. (See Chapter 16 for a thorough description of the phenomenon called "burnout.") If for any reason the worker is not ready for or capable of dealing with the crisis or the client, the worker must immediately make an appropriate referral.

Show Regard for Client Safety. The worker's style, choices, and strategies must reflect a continuous consideration of the client's physical and psychological safety as well as the safety of others involved. The safety consideration includes the safety of the worker as well as the ethical, legal, and professional requirements mandated in counseling practice. The greatest intervention strategies and tactics are absolutely useless if clients leave the crisis worker and go out and harm themselves or others.

The golden rule is "When in doubt about client safety, get help." If you aren't sure what to do, consult with another crisis worker. Consultation does not mean you are inadequate. What it does mean is that you are a professional practitioner who is seeking a second opinion to validate your own, or you realize that this problem is not an area of your expertise so you are conferring with a person who does have the expertise. Thus, concern for a client's safety may mean appropriate referral interventions, including immediate hospitalization. You need to understand that when you do this, clients may be extremely angry at you; they may say you are unethical, have violated their trust and confidentiality, and even threaten to sue you for unprofessionalism. As hurtful and anxiety provoking as that may be, we will see in Chapter 15, Crisis Intervention: Legal and Ethical Issues, that such actions are not only ethical but legally mandated.

Provide Client Support. The crisis worker should be available as a support person during the crisis period. Clients may need assistance in developing a list of possible support people, but if no appropriate support person emerges in the examination of alternatives, the worker can serve as a primary support person until the present crisis is over. A warm, empathic, and assertive counseling strategy should be used with clients who are extremely lonely and devoid of supports. For example:

CW: I want you to know that I am very concerned about your safety during this stressful time, and that I'm available to help. I want you to keep this card with you until you're through this crisis, and call me if you feel yourself sliding back into that hopeless feeling again. If you call either of these numbers and don't get an answer or get a busy signal, keep trying until you get me. You *must* make contact with *me*. I will be very disturbed if you are in a seriously threatening situation again without letting me become involved with you. I really want to impress on you my genuine concern for you and the importance of making an agreement or contract to call me whenever your safety is threatened. Will you give me that assurance?

Define the Problem Clearly. Many clients have complicated and multiple problems. Make sure that each problem is clearly and accurately defined from a practical, problem-solving point of view. Many clients define the crisis as someone else's problem or as some external event or situation that has happened. Attempting to solve the crisis of some third party (who isn't present) is counterproductive. Pinpoint the client's own problem with the event or situation, and keep the focus on the client's central core of concern. Also, attempt to distill multiple problems down into an immediate, workable problem and to concentrate on that problem first. We cannot overemphasize the tenacity with which the worker must avoid being drawn off on tangents by some highly emotional or defensive clients with difficult problems.

Consider these exchanges with Rita's husband, Jake.

Jake: You don't seem to like me much.

CW: Right now, that's not the issue of importance. What I'm trying to do is help you identify the main source of your problem.

Another example:

Jake: Haven't you ever hit your wife too?

CW: No, but that's not what we're working on now. I'm trying to help us figure out a way for you to avoid fighting with her when you first get home each evening.

In both instances, the worker stays focused on the client and does not get caught up on side issues such as worker competency, beliefs, and attitudes. Now the worker is ready to work on Task 4, Examining Alternatives.

Consider Alternatives. In most problem situations, the alternatives are infinite. But crisis clients (and sometimes workers) have a limited view of the many options available. By using simple open-ended questions and open-ended leads, the worker usually can elicit a surprising number of choices from the client of which he or she was previously unaware. Then add your own list of possible alternatives to the client's list. For example, "I get the feeling that it might help if you could get in contact with a counselor at the Credit Counseling Bureau. How would you feel about our adding that to our list?" Examining, analyzing, and listing alternatives to consider should be as collaborative as possible. The best alternatives are ones that the client truly *owns*. Take care to avoid imposing your alternatives on the client if at all possible.

The alternatives on the list should be workable and realistic. They should represent the right amount of action for the client to undertake now—not too much, not too little. The client will generally express ownership of an option by words such as "I would really like to call him today." Worker-imposed options are usually signaled by the worker's words, such as "*You need to* go to his office and do that right away." Beware of the latter! An important part of the quest for appropriate alternatives is to explore with the client what options have worked before in situations like the present one. Often the client can come up with the best choices, derived from coping mechanisms that have worked well in the past. But the stresses created by the immediate crisis may keep clients from identifying the most obvious and appropriate alternatives for them. Here the crisis worker facilitates the client's examination of alternatives.

CW: Rita, you say you're feeling frightened and trapped right now, and you don't know where to turn. But it sounds like you'd take a step in a positive direction if you could get some of your old zip back. What are some actions you took or some people you sought out in previous situations when you felt frightened or stuck?

Rita: Oh, I don't know that I've been in a mess quite this bad before.

CW: Well, that may be true. But what steps have you taken or what persons have you contacted before in a mess like this, even if it wasn't this bad?

Rita: Hmm . . . Well, a time or two I did go talk to Mr. Jackson, one of my auto mechanics instructors when I was at the Area Vo-Tech School. He's very understanding and helpful. He always seemed to understand me and believe in me.

CW: How would you feel about reestablishing contact with him whenever you're down again?

Plan Action Steps. After developing a short, doable list of alternatives, the worker needs to move on to making plans. In crisis intervention the worker endeavors to assist the client to develop a short-term plan that will help the client get through the immediate crisis as well as make the transition to long-term coping. The plan should include the client's internal coping mechanisms as well as sources of help in the environment. The coping mechanisms are usually brought to bear on some concrete, positive, constructive action that clients can take to regain better control of their lives. Actions that initially involve some physical movement are preferred. The plan should be realistic in terms of the client's current emotional readiness and environmental supports. It may involve collaboration with the worker until the client can function independently. The effective crisis worker is sensitive to the client's need to function autonomously as soon as feasible.

Rita: Right now I'd like to just be free of the whole mess for a few days . . . just get off this dizzy merry-go-round long enough to collect my thoughts.

CW: It sounds to me like you really mean that. Let's see if together we can examine some options that might get you the freedom and breathing space you need to pull the pieces back together.

Rita: I can't really let go. Too many people are depending on me. That's just wishful thinking. But it would be wonderful to get some relief.

CW: Even though you don't see any way to get it, what you're wanting is some space for yourself right now—away from work, kids, Jake, Sam, and the whole dilemma.

Rita: The only way that would happen is for my doctor to order it—to prescribe it, medically.

CW: How realistic is that? How would that help you?

Rita: It would call a halt to some of the pressures. The treadmill would have to stop, at least temporarily. Yes, I guess that kind of medical reason wouldn't be so bad.

CW: Sounds like consulting your doctor and laying at least part of your cards on the table might be one step toward getting medical help in carving out some breathing space for yourself.

Rita: I think so. Yeah, that's it! That's one thing I could do.

CW: Let's together map out a possible action plan—for contacting your doctor and requesting assistance in temporarily letting go. Let's look at *when* you want to contact your doctor, *what* you're going to say, and *how* you're going to say it—to make sure you get the results you must have right now.

The crisis worker is attempting to work collaboratively with Rita and to facilitate Rita's real ownership of her plan. The worker also implies a view of Rita as competent and responsible.

Use the Client's Coping Strengths. In crisis intervention it is important not to overlook the client's own strengths and coping mechanisms. Often the crisis events temporarily immobilize the individual's usual strengths and coping strategies. If they can be identified, explored, and reinstated, they may make an enormous contribution toward restoring the client's equilibrium and reassuring the client. For example, one woman had previously relieved stress by playing her piano. She told the worker that she was no longer able to play the piano because her piano had been repossessed. The crisis worker was able to explore with her several possible places where she could avail herself of a piano in times of stress.

Use Referral Resources. An integral aspect of crisis intervention is the use of referral resources. A ready list of names and phone numbers of contact people is a necessity. It is also important for the crisis worker to develop skill in making referrals as well as in working with a wide variety of referral agencies. Many clients need to be referred early to sources of help regarding financial matters, legal assistance, long-term individual therapy, family therapy, substance abuse, severe depression, or other personal matters. Here are suggestions we have found to be useful in working with a variety of agencies. Generally, we find that a breakdown in communication with agencies follows our having overlooked a few obvious and simple cautions. So do as we say, not as we sometimes do!

1. Keep a handy, up-to-date list of frequently used agencies. Keep up with personnel changes.
2. In communities that publish a directory of human services, have available the most recent edition.
3. Cultivate a working relationship with key people in agencies you use frequently. Get on community boards, join organizations, and become integrated into the provider system.
4. Identify yourself, your agency, and your purpose when telephoning. Know secretaries and receptionists by name, and use their names when you call. Treat them with dignity, respect, and equality, and thank them for helping you.
5. Follow up on referrals you make—within 24 hours if at all possible.
6. Don't assume that all clients have the skill to get the services they need. Be prepared to assist clients who may be unable to help themselves avoid runaround and bureaucratic red tape.
7. Whenever necessary, without engendering dependency, go with clients to the referral agencies to assist and to ensure that effective communication takes place.

8. Write thank-you messages (with copies to their bosses) to persons who are particularly helpful to you and your clients.

9. Don't criticize fellow professionals or the agencies they represent, and don't gossip about either workers or agencies.

10. Keep accurate records of referral activities, so you have a paper trail.

11. Know frequently used agencies' hours, basic services, mode of operation, limitations, and, if possible, policies such as insurance and sliding scale fees.

12. Be aware of any agency services the client is already using, so services don't get duplicated.

13. Use courtesy and good human relations skills when dealing with agency personnel. Put yourself in their shoes, and treat them as you would like to be treated.

14. Avoid expecting perfection of other agencies. Give agencies feedback on how they did, and obtain feedback from them.

15. Be aware of sensory impairment in clients, especially in older adults, and make those impairments known in referrals.

16. If the agency has an orientation session, seek to attend and to participate in it.

17. Practice honesty in communicating to referral agencies regarding the status or needs of clients. (Honest and ethical portrayal of the client's needs will build credibility with other agencies.)

18. Don't be afraid to use the Internet or geographically distance agencies that you have checked out as legitimate. It can bring a wealth of agencies and people to your electronic doorstep, and they may have the resources that you locally don't have.

Develop and Use Networks. Closely allied with referral is a function called networking (Haywood & Leuthe, 1980). Networking, for crisis workers, is having and using personal contacts within a variety of agencies that directly affect our ability to serve clients effectively and efficiently. Although each person in your network is a referral resource, it is the relationship you have with that individual that defines it as a network. Effective crisis workers can't sit behind a desk and wait for assistance to come to them. They must get out into the community and get to know personally the key individuals who can provide the kinds of services their clients require. A personal relationship based on understanding and trust between the worker and vital network people is invaluable in helping the worker cut through bureaucratic red tape, expedite emergency assistance, and personalize many services that might otherwise not be available to clients.

As crisis workers, we do not operate alone in the world. We are interdependent. Networking permits us to spread the responsibilities among other helping professionals. We mean "helping professionals" in the broadest possible context: lawyers, judges, parole officers, ministers, school counselors, federal, state, and local human services workers, directors and key people in crisis agencies, prison staff, business and civic leaders, medical doctors, dentists, police, and political leaders may play important roles in the networking process. The development and use of effective networking are indispensable functions of the successful worker.

Get a Commitment. A vital part of crisis intervention is getting a short-term commitment from the client to follow through on the action or actions planned. The crisis worker should ask the client to summarize verbally the steps to be taken. This verbal summary helps the worker understand the client's perception of both the plan and the commitment, and gives the worker an opportunity to clear up any distortions. It also provides the worker an opportunity to establish a follow-up checkpoint with the client. The commitment step can serve as a motivational reminder to the client and also encourage and predispose the client to believe that the action steps will succeed. Without a definite and positive commitment on the part of the client, the best of plans may fall short of the objectives that have been worked out by the worker and the client.

CW: So, Rita, it seems to me that what you've decided to do is to reinitiate some kind of meaningful contact with Mr. Jackson. So that we're both very clear on what you've committed yourself to doing, would you please summarize how and when you're going to proceed?

Rita: I'm going straight to my office today and phone him at school. I'll either talk to him or leave a message for him to call me. As soon as I talk to him, I'll set up a definite day and time to meet with him.

CW: And when you've set up . . .

Rita: Oh, yes! And when I've set up my appointment with him, I'm going to phone you and let you know how it went.

CW: Good. And in the meantime, you have my number on the card if you need me—especially if the safety of either you or your children becomes jeopardized.

Rita: That's right, and I'll call if I lose my nerve with Sam. I've got to get some space for myself there—at least some temporary space.

Experienced crisis workers are generally able to sense how far and how fast the client is able to act.

Usually the client is encouraged to commit to as much action as feasible. If we cannot get her or him to make a giant leap forward, we'll accept one small step in a positive direction. The main idea is to facilitate some commitment that will result in movement of the client in a constructive direction.

SUMMARY

Crisis intervention from a practitioner's standpoint incorporates a number of fundamental counseling skills that are specifically tailored to crisis intervention. Listening is fundamental to all successful counseling, including crisis intervention, and includes such techniques as restatement, reflection, owning statements, and open- and closed-ended questions. Essential components of effective listening and communication include effective attending, empathy, genuineness, and acceptance. Action skills range across nondirective, collaborative, and directive worker strategies. These strategies may include helping the client focus or expand awareness, providing guidance and information, allowing cathartic release of emotions, providing support and protection, and mobilizing the client to action. As opposed to doing crisis therapy with a client whom the worker has a working history, field work

often means meeting a client for the first time. Thus, basic introduction and attending skills along with an assessment of client weapon and drug use, availability of support systems and whether basic food, water, shelter, clothing, and medical needs are being met are critical to de-escalation and stabilization. Finally, the worker is not an island unto himself or herself. Building human services provider resources and establishing working relationships with them is critical to any crisis work.

Visit CengageBrain.com for a variety of study tools and useful resources such as video examples, case studies, interactive exercises, flashcards, and quizzes.

Crisis Case Handling

Handling Crisis Cases Versus Long–Term Cases

To understand crisis case handling, we need to **LO1** distinguish between what crisis interventionists and long-term therapists do, the principles that underlie the two modes, their objectives, client functioning, and assessment procedures. On first glance, typical models for long-term therapy do not look radically different from a crisis intervention model. Our own long-term, eight-step systematic counseling model (James & Gilliland, 2003, pp. 376–381) incorporates predisposition, exploration, examining alternatives, planning courses of action, and obtaining client commitment in much the same operational format as crisis intervention.

What is radically different is that in long-term therapy, defining problems, identifying alternatives, and planning are much broader in scope, more methodological, and rely on continuous feedback loops to check effectiveness of intervention. A typical counseling session with a long-term client reviews progress since the previous session, collaboratively refines the plan of action if needed, processes the content of the session and the client's feelings about it, and then proposes a new homework assignment to be tried out before the next meeting. Crisis intervention models do not operate with such liberal time dimensions or problem scopes. In crisis intervention, exploring the problems, identifying alternatives, planning, and committing to a plan are all much more compressed in time and scope. What in long-term therapy may occur in a rather leisurely fashion over a period of weekly sessions, in crisis intervention may occur in a half-hour to 2 hours.

LEARNING OBJECTIVES

After studying this chapter, you should be able to:

1. Know the difference between handling long-term therapy and crisis intervention.
2. Understand how a walk-in mental health facility handles crises.
3. Understand what a police Crisis Intervention Team is, how it is trained, and what it does.
4. Understand what "suicide by cop" means.
5. Know the generic types of transcrisis in long-term therapy.
6. Identify and understand persons with borderline personality disorder.
7. Know the rules of the road for counseling difficult clients.

Whereas in long-term therapy a great deal of background exploration may provide the therapist a panoramic view of client dynamics, the crisis worker's exploration typically is narrow, starting and stopping with the specific presenting crisis. The long-term therapist's view of alternatives and planning a course of action commonly incorporate psychoeducational processes that seek to change residual, repressive, and chronic client modes of thinking, feeling, and acting. In contrast, the crisis worker seeks to quickly determine previous coping skills and environmental resources available to the client and use them in the present situation as a stopgap measure to gain time and provide a modicum of stability in an out-of-control situation. While crisis workers use psychoeducational techniques a great deal, they typically do so to solve immediate short-term problems that evolve from the crisis itself by providing specific information about what is going on with the client, such as PTSD symptoms, or specific information on how to access resources, such as getting help from FEMA for a housing loan after a tornado.

Whereas the long-term therapist would view comprehensive personality change as a necessary part of the therapeutic plan, the crisis worker endeavors to change personality only to the degree necessary for restoring precrisis functioning. A long-term therapist would look toward an evidence-based methodological manipulation of treatment variables, assess those variables on a variety of dimensions, and process the outcomes with the client. A crisis worker often uses a "best guess" based on previous experience with what does and does not work with a particular problem. Protocols for treatment in long-term therapy are typically evidence based and involve many tryouts as the protocol is fine-tuned to the individual's particular needs. Crisis intervention is a good deal more creative. Although it also operates from evidence-based techniques, it adapts and changes quickly as conditions warrant. Paradoxically, it is fairly rigid in that it employs set procedures for moving the client from an immobile to a mobilized state.

Finally, assessment and feedback of outcome measures in long-term therapy typically involve a great deal of processing between client and therapist as to the efficacy of treatment. If treatment outcomes are not as expected, a feedback loop is integrated into the model that will allow a return to any of the previous steps. Feedback and assessment in crisis intervention typically occur on a here-and-now basis, with emphasis on what changes have occurred in the previous minutes and what the client will do in the next few hours.

It should be clearly understood that in long-term therapy when a transcrisis state or point emerges, the therapist now becomes a crisis worker, and all the principles of crisis intervention are applied as crisis therapy until the client is stabilized. Beginning therapists are often blindsided by such transcrisis events and paralyzed as they try to get back to "normal" operating mode when "normal" went flying out the window and there is small chance of getting it back until the crisis is contained. Such events may particularly occur when therapy has been successful, the client is to be terminated, the client is frightened to death at the prospect of going out to face the world alone, and quickly deteriorates to the shock and chagrin of the therapist.

There are many approaches to long-term therapy. Although Thorne's (1968, pp. 11–13) approach is almost fifty years old, it is a classic representation of one of the most comprehensive and integrated systems to be found. To provide a clear delineation

between crisis intervention and long-term therapy, we have compared our model of crisis intervention with Thorne's *principles, objectives, client functioning,* and *assessment* of case handling. Tables 5.1, 5.2, 5.3, and 5.4 summarize the contrasts.

Case Handling at Walk–In Crisis Facilities

Types of Presenting Crises

Clients who present themselves for crisis coun- **LO2** seling at walk-in facilities generally fall within one of three categories: those who are experiencing (1) chronic mental illness, (2) acute interpersonal problems in their social environment, or (3) a combination of the two. Most clients who avail themselves of community mental health clinics suffer from financial problems that prohibit them from seeking private therapy.

Chronic Crisis. Since the enactment of the federal Community Mental Health Act of 1963, the major responsibility for treatment of the mentally ill has fallen on community mental health centers. Although in theory the act was designed to deinstitutionalize patients and return those who are able to functional living, in fact the act has placed many people in chronic crisis.

In addition, increased drug abuse, a rise in crime, fragmentation of families, and a host of other societal ills have caused a tremendous upsurge in the need for mental health services. Originally focused on reintegrating long-term hospital patients into the community, mental health centers have tended to assign chronic cases a less-than-priority status. The unspoken reason is that these clients are extremely frustrating to mental health providers because they show little progress and are a constant financial and emotional drain on the resources of the agencies that come in contact with them. Many community mental health centers have de-emphasized this role and moved more toward dealing with developmental problems of "normal," more highly functioning people (Slaikeu, 1990, p. 284). Perhaps more ominously, funding cutbacks have forced community mental health centers to look more closely at a client's ability to pay as a precondition for treatment, which means that people who may most need service may be relegated to a waiting list. Furthermore, because of legal ramifications and funding problems, severely disturbed people who are committed to state hospitals typically have very brief stays and are turnstiled back onto the streets.

TABLE 5.1   Principles Compared Between Long-Term Therapy and Crisis Intervention

Long-Term Therapy Mode	Crisis Case-Handling Mode
1. *Diagnosis:* Complete diagnostic evaluation with observation; background of social, educational, and work history; intellectual, personality, and malady specific psychological testing.	1. *Diagnosis:* Rapid triage crisis assessment face-to-face.
2. *Treatment:* Focus on basic underlying causes; on the whole person with continuous individual and group work over an extended time.	2. *Treatment:* Solution-Focus on the immediate traumatized/crisis component of the person to stabilize and restore psychological equilibrium.
3. *Plan:* Personalized comprehensive prescription directed toward fulfilling long-term needs across work, academic, and social environments.	3. *Plan:* Individual problem-specific prescription focused on immediate needs to alleviate the crisis symptoms in the current environment.
4. *Methods:* Knowledge and use of a variety of techniques to systematically effect a wide array of short-term, intermediate-term, and long-term therapeutic gains.	4. *Methods:* Knowledge of time-limited brief therapy techniques used for immediate control and containment of the crisis/trauma.
5. *Evaluation of results:* Systematic behavioral validation of therapeutic outcomes in terms of the client's total functioning through testing, long-term observation, and supportive reports from significant others in work and social environments.	5. *Evaluation of results:* Target crisis- specific behavioral validation by client's return to precrisis level of equilibrium through observation of client actions.

TABLE 5.2   Objectives Compared Between Long-Term Therapy and Crisis Intervention

Long-Term Therapy Mode (Listed in No Particular Order, But Global in Scope)	Crisis Case-Handling Mode (Listed in Linear Order with a Crisis-Specific Focus)
1. *Prevent problems:* More basic than cure. Use preventive procedures whenever possible. Explore comprehensive future needs based on current assessment of intra- and interpersonal skills and social, vocational, and financial resources.	1. *Ensure client safety:* Always assess client lethality and provide for the physical and psychological safety of the client and significant others.
2. *Correct etiological factors:* Involves comprehensive evidence-based treatment of broad-based psychological and environmental factors in both the past and present.	2. *Predisposition.* Facilitate conditions for client–worker bonding. Reduce threat level.
3. *Provide systematic support:* Comprehensive measures directed toward improvement of the state of psychological and physical health and well-being of the individual. Across social and work environments.	3. *Define problem:* Clarify in concrete terms the issues that precipitated the crisis.
4. *Facilitate growth:* Treatment should ideally facilitate rather than interfere with natural environmental and developmental processes.	4. *Provide support:* Establish conditions, by either the crisis worker or significant others, whereby the client feels secure and free of threat or abandonment as the current crisis is resolved.
5. *Reeducate:* Treatment seeks to reeducate and teach new models of adjustment for lifelong coping.	5. *Examine alternatives:* Provide options for alleviating the immediate situational threat in relation to the crisis.
6. *Express and clarify emotional attitudes:* Major emphasis is on methods of securing emotional release and expression in a permissive and accepting environment.	6. *Develop a plan:* Formulate a stepwise procedure using client coping skills, crisis worker expertise, and systemic measures to energize the client to take immediate action.
7. *Resolve conflict and inconsistencies:* Therapy aims to help the client achieve insight and understanding into the causation and dynamic roots of the behavior and change.	7. *Obtain commitment:* Obtain agreement as to specific time, duration, and number of activities required to stabilize the client and/or crisis situation.
8. *Accept reality:* Help the client to accept what cannot be changed. Move forward into new realities and discard problematic histories.	8. *Follow-up.* Short-term follow-up to determine if crisis intervention strategies continue to work.
9. *Reorganize attitudes:* Move the person toward exhibiting a more positive view of life and more effective social integration.	
10. *Maximize intellectual resources:* Improve the functions of sensing, perceiving, remembering, communicating, thinking, behavior management, and self-control.	

TABLE 5.3	Client Functioning Compared Between Long-Term Therapy and Crisis Intervention
Long-Term Therapy Mode	**Crisis Case-Handling Mode**
1. Client shows sufficient *affect*; manifests some basis for experiencing and understanding his or her emotional state.	1. *Affectively*, the client is impaired to the extent that there is little understanding of his or her emotional state.
2. Client shows some ability to *cognitively* understand the connection between behavior and consequences—between what is rational and irrational.	2. *Cognitively*, the client shows inability to think linearly and logically and formulate strategies to alleviate the crisis. Irrationality is the norm.
3. There is some modicum of *behavioral* control.	3. *Behaviorally*, the client is out of control and may pose a danger to self or others.

TABLE 5.4	Assessment Compared Between Long-Term Therapy and Crisis Intervention
Long-Term Therapy Mode	**Crisis Case-Handling Mode**
1. *Intake data:* Client is stable enough to provide in-depth background regarding the problem. Lengthy intake form may contain details of the client's total history: family, medical history, drug use, education, therapy background, social history. Comprehensive personality and intellectual tests may be given.	1. *Intake data:* Client may not be able to fill out an intake form because of instability or time constraints; a verbal and/or visual evaluation of current maladaptive state may be the only data available.
2. *Safety:* Client safety is not the primary focus unless there are clues pointing toward imminent danger to self or others.	2. *Safety:* Crisis worker's first concern is client's and others' safety; determining whether client is suicidal, homicidal, or otherwise a danger or threat to someone by intentional or unintentional acts.
3. *Time:* The therapist has time to procure a variety of assessment data to confirm or contraindicate the hypothesized problem. Total case diagnosis and workups are gathered before the treatment plan is developed. Personality assessment indexes are generally gathered to compare client functioning against norm groups on standard pathology measures.	3. *Time:* Crisis worker has no time for administering formal instruments. Worker must rely on immediate verbal and nonverbal cues emitted by the client to make assessment of degree of pathology.
4. *Reality testing:* The therapist assumes the client is in touch with reality unless assessment data or other clues indicate otherwise.	4. *Reality testing:* Using simple questioning procedures, the crisis worker must determine whether the person is in touch with reality and how effectively the person is functioning in real time.
5. *Referrals:* Referral resources have implications for long-term development. Examples of referrals might be to family services, mental health centers, vocational/educational assistance, and job placement services.	5. *Referrals:* Referral resources have implications of immediacy in terms of getting the client to safety and some degree of stability. Examples of referrals might be to the police, hospital emergency room, psychiatric or medical evaluation, or immediate support people.
6. *Consultation:* Consultants and other backup resources are available as needed. Collaboration is normally initiated after consultation with the client and/or the therapist's supervisor.	6. *Consultation:* Professional consultants who are trained in the diagnosis of pathology may be on call for backup purposes. Police and mobile crisis teams are sometimes available. Most likely the worker is on his or her own.
7. *Drug use:* The therapist relies on data from the intake material and on information developed in the normal course of the therapy to ascertain the level and type of prescription medication or illicit drug or alcohol use.	7. *Drug use:* The crisis worker relies on verbal and visual responses to ascertain the level and type of prescription medication or illicit drug or alcohol use.
8. *Disposition:* Client typically starts and finishes with the same therapist over a course of months. May occasionally be referred to adjunctive therapeutic specialization during the course of therapy. Clients come and go voluntarily and return to home environment.	8. *Disposition:* Client typically starts and stops with the same worker over a course of hours or days. May be referred permanently to long-term treatment with a therapeutic specialization once stabilized. Client may be involuntarily committed, arrested and jailed, or released back to supervised care of custodians, guardians, or significant others.

The result is that a host of chronically mentally ill people who are poorly functioning, impoverished, homeless, victims or perpetrators of crime, and without support systems of any kind are left to fend for themselves. These people often have multiple problems besides a primary diagnosis of psychopathology. They may be noncompliant with treatment, disregard their medication, abuse alcohol and drugs, have other severe physical problems, and be victimized financially, physically, and psychologically by others (Bender, 1986; Nurius, 1984; Pope, 1991). It is easy to see why such people often wind up in crisis when understaffed and underfunded mental health clinics (Roberts, 1991, p. 31) and other social services agencies cannot care for them. The chronically mentally ill are often on a first-name basis with local police and personnel in emergency rooms, mental health clinics, and social services agencies.

Social/Environmental Crises. People with chronic mental health issues are not the only people who avail themselves of, or are brought to, walk-in facilities. Runaways, addicts, the battered, physically disabled, crime victims, survivors of violent events, the sexually abused, the terminally ill, veterans, the unemployed, and relatives of the chronically physically and mentally ill are some of the many participants in a drama of social crisis that is played out every day and night in mental health clinics, emergency rooms, student counseling centers, social services agencies, and police stations across the country. Many precipitating events may be unexpected and sudden and may have an impact far beyond the individual on families and communities, leaving these systems disorganized and out of control. Crises that are generated in the social environment are some of the most potent for mental health workers because of their ramifications across systems and the heightened emotionality and immediacy that accompany them for both clientele and workers.

Combination of Types. The foregoing crisis types rarely occur as discrete categories. Overlapping among types and problems that face crisis workers is the rule rather than the exception. Attempting to stabilize someone with chronic schizophrenia without providing food and shelter, treating a trauma survivor without first working on a drug addiction, or considering vocational exploration without handling the depression of a middle-aged executive who has just lost her job is a waste of valuable time. Handling multiple crises with the same client is the rule rather than the exception.

Case Handling at a Community Mental Health Clinic

We have chosen Midtown Mental Health Clinic in our hometown of Memphis, Tennessee, as a generic representation of how clients are taken care of who walk into or are brought to a community mental health facility. This clinic's catchment area includes a number of housing projects, the downtown area, the University of Tennessee medical facility, the city hospital, the Memphis Veterans Administration Hospital, the Memphis Mental Health Institute (a state psychiatric hospital), the county jail, several halfway shelters for drug addicts and homeless people, and a variety of other social services agencies. Furthermore, its catchment area has the highest crime rate and incidence of domestic violence in the city, a high percentage of school dropouts, and some of the most impoverished areas of the city.

Entry. Clients may come to the mental health clinic on their own, be brought by relatives or social services agencies, or be taken into custody by the police. At the moment of entry, disposition of the case begins. A person in crisis who walks in or is brought to Midtown may range across the triage scale from mildly to severely disturbed. If the person is severely disturbed, a senior clinician is summoned. An attempt is made to remove the client to an isolated office to reduce environmental stimuli and calm the client so that an assessment can proceed. The clinician tries to obtain a case history. If this is not possible, the clinician makes a visual and verbal assessment in regard to information-processing problems, tangential thinking, hallucinations, disassociation, threats to self or others, or severe drug abuse. If any of these symptoms is present, then a psychiatrist is called to evaluate the client and decide whether hospitalization is warranted.

Commitment. If the client is so mentally fragmented as to be clearly out of touch with reality or deemed an imminent danger to self or others, he or she is committed to an inpatient mental health facility. The person is asked to voluntarily commit to hospitalization. If he or she is unwilling to do so, a physician may write an involuntary commitment order. An officer of the Crisis Intervention Team, a special unit of the Memphis Police Department trained to deal with the mentally ill, is then called to transport the patient. Under no circumstances do mental health workers become involved in transportation, because of safety concerns and the possibility of stigmatizing themselves as punitive agents in the patients' eyes. If patients are financially able, they may be transported to a private psychiatric facility. If they are indigent, they are taken to the city hospital psychiatric emergency unit for evaluation and subsequent placement at the Memphis Mental Health Institute state hospital.

Intake Interview. If the individual is coherent enough to provide verbal and written information, an intake interview is started. Following closely the crisis intervention model in Chapter 3, the intake worker first attempts to assess for client safety, define the problem, and apprise the client of his or her rights. In a patient and methodical manner, the intake worker goes through a standard intake interview sheet. Through open-ended questions and active listening, the worker tries to obtain as comprehensive a picture of the client as possible. The worker also attempts to determine the precipitating problem that brought the client to the clinic. The intake worker must be nonjudgmental, empathic, and caring and must also obtain concrete and specific information from a client who may not be able or willing to reciprocate.

Two critical components are always appraised in this initial assessment: degree of client lethality and drug use. It is a given that crisis situations either involve or have the possibility of acting-out behavior. Therefore, the intake worker evaluates clients in relation to their plans or intent to do harm to themselves or others. Because of the widespread use of prescription and illicit drugs, the worker checks to determine if drugs are involved in the presenting problem. Thus, intake workers need to have a copy of and familiarity with the *Physician's Desk Reference (PDR) or computer access to prescription drugs.* The intake worker must also have a working knowledge of the side effects of "street drugs" because of the high incidence of their use in the Midtown area.

Disposition. After the intake has been completed, the worker constructs and writes a proposed diagnosis and treatment recommendations. The intake worker discusses the treatment recommendations and possible services with the client. It is then the client's decision to accept or reject services. If services are accepted, the intake worker introduces the client to the therapist who will most likely be in charge of the case. A full clinical team meeting is held to confirm or alter the initial diagnosis and treatment recommendations. At that time a primary therapist is designated and assumes responsibility for the case.

Anchoring. On their initial visit, clients are never left alone. From their intake interview to disposition to a primary therapist, workers help clients feel that a personal interest is being taken in them and their problems. The worker takes and hands over the client to the therapist who will be in charge of the case. The therapist gives the client a verbal orientation about what is going to occur. The idea behind this methodical orientation is to demystify the world of mental health, familiarize clients with what their treatment will be, and provide them with a **psychological anchor** in the form of a real person who will act as their advocate, support, and contact person. Quickly establishing rapport with the primary therapist is helpful in forestalling future crisis and is extremely important to unstable clients, given the threatening implications of entering a mental health facility, possible loss of freedom, and the bureaucratic maze of the mental health system. It is also designed to immediately empower clients and make them feel they have taken a step in the right direction. In many instances, a compeer volunteer is assigned to the client. **Compeers** are trained volunteers who act as support and socializing agents for clients who do not have friends or relatives to assist and encourage them.

Short-Term Disposition. Many crises relate to the basic physical necessities of living. If that's the case, the intake worker makes short-term provisions for food, clothing, shelter, and other necessities while setting in motion the wheels of other social services agencies to provide long-term subsistence services. If clients are unable to care for themselves, the Tennessee Department of Family Services is appointed as a conservator to handle their money and look after their basic needs. Thus it is very important that the intake worker and other staff thoroughly understand and can access the local social services network.

Long-Term Disposition. An interdisciplinary team reviews and evaluates the intake worker's diagnosis and recommendations. If the team considers it necessary, a psychiatrist and a pharmacist conduct a psychiatric or pharmacological evaluation of the client. If a psychological evaluation is required, a psychologist evaluates the person on standardized personality and intellectual measures. Depending on the client's needs, people from various specialty units join the team. Once the team is complete, it formulates objectives and goals, and an evidence-based therapeutic plan is put into operation. The team reviews this plan on a regular basis and changes it if necessary.

Twenty-Four-Hour Service. Midtown operates 24 hours a day. After regular working hours, telephone relays are linked into the crisis hotline. Telephone workers there evaluate the call and make a decision on who should handle it. That may be a mobile crisis team or, in the city of Memphis, the Memphis Police Department Crisis Intervention Team, which we will examine at length later in this chapter.

Mobile Crisis Teams. MCTs have become an integral part of emergency psychiatric services (Ng, 2006). Mobile crisis teams (MCTs) operate for two distinct reasons. For certain clients, particularly geriatric or physically disabled clients, it may be necessary to make home visits to provide services. In other cases, when a client is out of control and unwilling or unable to go to the clinic, crisis workers go wherever the client is.

The Community Mental Health Act of 1963 mandated that those clinics receiving federal funds must provide 24-hour emergency service. The mobile crisis team has been one answer to that mandate. With the advent of the police department's Crisis Intervention Team, this need has diminished a good deal in Memphis. However, in many other cities these mobile teams are on call and often follow up either along with or after local police departments have contained the situation.

Typically a hotline or 911 mental disturbance call will ask for assistance. Either a police car with a mental health worker riding along will go to the scene, or mental health workers will follow up after police. These teams are typically equipped with sophisticated communication and information retrieval systems that can call up client mental health files or criminal records. In some instances, psychiatric nurses may be members of these teams and can administer psychotropic medication in consultation with psychiatrists (Ligon, 2000).

Depending on state statutes, either the police or licensed mental health workers in these mobile units have the power to take clients into protective custody and transport them to a hospital rather than to jail. There are three problems associated with this approach. First, most such units operate in urban areas; many rural counties in the United States have little provision for such emergency services, in regard to either staff or a mental health facility to transport a client to or the ability to administer on-site crisis intervention (Aron et al., 2009; Bain, 2011; Rouse, 1998; Rural Assistance Center, 2011). Second, no local police jurisdiction is going to transport someone 100 miles if it takes that police officer out of service for any length of time. The bottom line is that the mentally ill wind up in the place most convenient to put them—and that is usually jail, the very last place they need to be. Finally, although it has been purposed that MCTs are cost efficient and can reduce hospitalization (Bengelsdorf, Church, & Kaye, 1993), there is little current research on their ability to do "on the scene" emergency psychiatric services.

Police and Crisis Intervention

It may seem odd to many of you reading this section that we are going to spend a lot of time talking about police officers and crisis intervention since crisis workers generally fall into counseling, social work, psychology, nursing, and other medical and social service professions. So why cops? A fat lot they know about empathic responding to people in crisis, right? Just look at Ferguson, Missouri, New York City, and a host of other places where cops allegedly hurt and kill people for no good reason. We'd like you to now meet a different kind of cop from what you have been exposed to in the media.

Changing Role of the Police

The role of the police is rapidly changing and expanding. In most communities, police departments are being tasked with more and more responsibilities in addition to traditional law enforcement. Increasingly, crisis work with the mentally ill and emotionally disturbed is one of those responsibilities. It is commonly thought that patrol officers concern themselves mainly with **instrumental crimes** such as theft, robbery, and assault. The fact is that police officers deal with a multitude of **expressive** kinds of crime, in which individuals pose a serious threat to themselves or others because of their own anger, fear, vulnerability, depression, or lack of emotional control. Even though police departments do not relish investing much of their time away from providing for public safety and enforcing the law, they have found themselves more and more in a modality of law enforcement/crisis intervention (Borum, 2000; Miller, 2006; Saunders, 2010).

Police and the Mentally Ill/ Mentally Disturbed

The problem has been ongoing and increasing **LO3** since the advent of the Community Mental Health Act of 1963 and the changes it brought in releasing many mentally ill persons back into the community.

That change meant that the first institutional authority likely to have interaction with that mental ill person would not be a mental health professional but a police officer (Lamb, Weinberger, & DeCuir, 2002; Watson & Fulambarker, 2012). As a result, sadly, for many mentally ill individuals release into the "community" has actually meant release to jail as a holding facility. Survey research has revealed that among incarcerates, approximately 15% of men and 30% of women meet the criteria for a mental health disorder (Steadman, Osher, Robbins, Case, & Samuels, 2009). Latest figures estimate there are over 350,000 inmates with mental illness (OMI) in 2012 (Treatment Advocacy Center, 2014) because essentially there is no other place to house them and their first contact is the police officers who put them there. Gillig and associates (1990) studied a sample of 309 police officers in Cincinnati and Hamilton County, Ohio, and found that during a 1-month period, almost 60% of the officers had responded to at least one call in which a presumably mentally ill person had to be confronted. Almost half of the officers had responded to more than one such call during the 1-month period.

This dilemma puts a heavy responsibility on the shoulders of law enforcement officers, and although many dislike spending their time on crises of a social service nature, they are accepting encounters with the mentally ill as an appropriate aspect of modern police work and are more empathic to their illness (Bahora et al., 2008; Watson et al., 2010; Watson & Fulambarker, 2012). They are also requesting more information, training, and collaboration with mental health and crisis intervention agencies (Compton et al., 2006). The foregoing has highlighted a need to develop training models that include police crisis intervention training with the mentally ill (Compton et al., 2006; Erstling, 2006; Gillig et al., 1990; Luckett & Slaikeu, 1990; Vermette, Pinals, & Applebaum, 2005).

Because of that ongoing need, the Memphis Police Department developed the **Crisis Intervention Team** (CIT; James, 1994; James & Crews, 2014). CIT was developed specifically to train patrol officers to deal with the mentally ill and emotionally disturbed. The authors of this book were fortunate enough to be involved in that initial, innovative endeavor, which started in Memphis in 1987. Little did we realize at the time that this program, with its humble beginnings attempting to resolve a local problem, would catch fire nationally. Today, the program has come to be known as the Memphis Model for police crisis intervention with the mentally ill. In 2005 the first national

convention for Crisis Intervention Team police officers was held in Columbus, Ohio. More than 1,000 police personnel came to that program from all over the country. It is with a good deal of pride that your authors had a hand in training many of those officers who came to Memphis from such diverse jurisdictions as Anchorage, Alaska; Ft. Lauderdale, Florida; Montgomery County, Maryland; Hutchinson, Kansas; Canada, Sweden, and Australia. Currently, in over 2,400 jurisdictions across the United States, law enforcement jurisdictions are establishing CITs, and thousands of police officers are being trained along the lines of what you are about to read in the next few paragraphs (Addy & James, 2005; CIT International, 2014).

The Crisis Intervention Team (CIT) Program

Because budget constraints, economic factors, and social problems have generated enormous numbers of homeless people, dumped-onto-the-streets mental patients who formerly would have been hospitalized as inpatients, many more mentally disturbed people now come into contact with the general public than ever before. Consequently, the Memphis city government, the mental health community, and the police department realized that incidents of police involvement with the mentally ill had resulted in the mentally ill themselves being vulnerable to serious harm and the increased possibility of police officers, untrained in dealing with the mentally ill, getting seriously injured or even killed. Why can't mental health workers take care of the enormous numbers of emotionally out-of-control people on the streets? Because it is a physical and fiscal impossibility to put enough mental health workers onto the streets to monitor and serve the needs of these out-of-control people and to do so in accordance with the "least restrictive environment" movement in a democratic society.

Spearheaded by the local affiliate of the Alliance for the Mentally Ill, the Memphis Police Department, the mental health community, the city government, and the counselor education and social work departments of two local universities formed a unique and creative alliance for the purpose of developing and implementing proactive and preventive methods of containing emotionally explosive situations in the streets that frequently lead to violence. Because the police were the first and often the only responsible officials on the scene of an out-of-control situation, calling in outside consultants proved unworkable. Therefore, the unique and cohesive alliance of several important community groups determined that highly trained and motivated police officers were the logical personnel to form a frontline defense against the crisis of dangerously expressive, out-of-control persons in the streets. This massive alliance effort resulted in the CIT program's becoming an example of how a successful program can work to accomplish the objectives of public safety and welfare, economic feasibility, and police accountability (James & Crews, 2014).

The Concept. To comprehend what a difficult and delicate task it has been to bring to fruition a successful and workable CIT program, one must understand how the alliance network functions. If your community does not have such a program, and you think it would be a good idea to get one started, read the following very carefully. The problem of the mentally ill, particularly the homeless mentally ill, is endemic and pervades all jurisdictions that attempt to establish CIT programs. Major Sam Cochran, who was the longtime coordinator of the Memphis CIT program and has been instrumental in helping disseminate the Memphis Model all over the country, puts it very well when he says, "It is not just a program to train police officers to deal with the mentally ill. It is a concept that brings all kinds of interest groups together in a network, and if that concept is not nourished, the program will fail."

The network behind the Memphis CIT program consists of the Memphis city government and the Memphis Police Department (hereafter just referred to as the police); the Alliance for the Mentally Ill; five of the six local community mental health centers; the emergency room components of public hospitals; academic educators from the Department of Counseling, Educational Psychology and Research at the University of Memphis and the School of Social Work at the University of Tennessee; the YWCA Abused Women's Services; the Sexual Assault Resource Center; and several private practice psychologists (hereafter referred to as the mental health community). The power, force, and success of the alliance derive from the process and fundamental working relationship that the police and mental health community have used to both form and maintain the CIT program. The alliance was formed because both the police and the mental health community realized that the problem of crisis in the streets was too severe for either to handle alone and that working together would make life much easier and safer for both as well as provide improved and safer service for clients and the community (James & Crews, 2014).

The alliance conducted a great many collaborative, systematic, and democratic meetings over a period of several months to hammer out a workable CIT blueprint. As a result of these meetings, key individuals from all segments of both police and the mental health community developed effective working relationships with one another and learned a great deal about each other's problems, competencies, rules, and boundaries.

Police were brought into mental health facilities for orientation into the world of mental health. Mental health personnel were brought into the police academy and accompanied police on patrols to learn about the problems, procedures, competencies, roles, and boundaries that law enforcement officers face in their everyday work. Then formal training was developed to ensure that not only the CIT officer selectees but also all supervisory-level police personnel understood the problems, objectives, and operational procedures of the CIT program (James, 1994, p. 187; James & Crews, 2014). The development and training phases provided some essential attitudinal and professional understanding between the police and the mental health community. As a result, CIT officers and their superiors know precisely what training and consultation resources the mental health community can provide. And the mental health professionals know what competencies and resources the police in general and the CIT officers in particular have to offer.

This model is not just about training cops, but developing collaborative efforts among police, the mental health community, and consumer advocates to provide first response mental health help to acutely ill individuals (Kasick & Bowling, 2013). Concomitantly, all sides develop mutual respect, understanding, trust, and cooperation. A CIT officer intervening with a distraught mental patient will likely listen empathically to the patient's feelings and concerns, be familiar with the mental health services available (will possibly know the patient's caseworker personally), and will, within the boundaries of professional ethics, communicate to the patient an understanding of the short-term needs of that person as well as a desire to provide for the immediate safety and referral requirements to contain and stabilize the patient's current crisis. The mental health center caseworker will also understand and have confidence in the CIT officer's ability to be a stabilizing and safe influence on the patient and will, if needed, likely call on the CIT officer for emergency assistance with a particular client. The mental health caseworker may collaborate with the CIT officer in obtaining anecdotal information needed to enhance the patient's treatment plan and prevent the recurrence of that particular patient's crisis in the streets (James, 1994, p. 191). All of the foregoing happens with consumer advocates such as the local Alliance for the Mentally Ill playing a critical advisory role in the process.

Based on the trust and confidence built through the powerful and cohesive alliance just described, the police department opted to select experienced police patrol officers to receive training and then serve in the dual role of police officers and Crisis Intervention Team specialists. Volunteers for the program had to have good records as officers, pass personality tests for maturity and mental stability, and be recommended, interviewed, screened, and selected to receive CIT training. The police department committed itself to putting trained CIT officers on duty in every precinct in the city, 24 hours every day. All upper-echelon supervisory officers received formal orientation about the role and function of CIT officers so that whenever any call involving a suspected mentally disturbed person anywhere in the city is received, the CIT officer is the designated responsible law enforcement official at the scene—regardless of rank—and all other officers at the scene serve as backups to the CIT officer who handles the case (James, 1994, p. 194; James & Crews, 2014).

CIT Training Using Mental Health Experts and Providers. An integral part of the CIT program is the special preservice training provided for the officers. The importance of effective training by competent, committed, motivated professionals cannot be overemphasized. We also insist that they ride with experienced CIT officers on a Friday or Saturday evening shift prior to the scheduled training of each new group of CIT officers. As Erstling (2006) states, spending 8 hours in a patrol car together goes a long way toward learning to trust and understand one another.

The following topics are covered in the 40 hours of CIT training:

1. Cultural awareness of the mentally ill
2. Substance abuse and co-occurring disorders
3. Developmental disabilities
4. Treatment strategies and mental health resources
5. Patient rights, civil commitment, and legal aspects of crisis intervention
6. Suicide intervention

7. Using the mobile crisis team and community resources
8. Psychotropic medications and their side effects
9. Verbal defusing and de-escalating techniques
10. Borderline and other personality disorders
11. Family and consumer perspectives
12. Fishbowl discussion on-site with mentally ill patients on patient perceptions of the police

While most of these training components are in a lecture-discussion format, two are not. These two components are considered absolutely critical in the training of police officers who do crisis intervention with the mentally ill. They are verbal de-escalation and defusing, and the client fishbowl.

De-escalation and Defusing Techniques. Verbal de-escalation and defusing techniques are taught throughout the weeklong training. These skills are considered so critical that four different trainers are used for 12 hours of training. Basic introductory techniques are taught first. How do you introduce yourself? What is the nonverbal message you convey by your body posture and language? What voice tone do you use? These skills are taught on the second day of training.

Next come basic exploratory skills and establishing a relationship. Skills taught include (1) how and when to use open-ended and closed-ended questions, (2) what owning statements are and why they are important, (3) how to keep clients secure without cornering them (see Chapter 14, Violent Behavior in Institutions), (4) officer and client safety, (5) crowd control, (6) when and when not to use reflection of feelings or thinking, and (7) a summary recapping techniques and restatement for client and officer understanding and communication. These skills are taught on the third day of training.

The training is also greatly enhanced if it can skillfully integrate the conceptual with the experiential. Realistic role play, video technology, playback, and discussion are essential. On the fourth day, 4 hours of training are devoted to role plays of actual police–client encounters. Veteran CIT officers role-play clients. These officers bring many valuable firsthand experiences into the learning environment that heighten interest, enhance motivation, and provide realism (James, 1994, p. 187). Trainees are divided into teams of four, and each member of the team is given 4 minutes onstage to attempt to defuse and de-escalate the client. The rest of the trainees (there are usually about 24–30) watch all of the teams perform and hear their critiques. The idea is that by watching others perform, trainees learn from the others' successes and failures. Scenarios range from clients with senile dementia to schizophrenics to diabetic psychosis to enraged jilted lovers. The role players escalate or de-escalate their violent behavior depending on how and what trainees do. Each team segment is videotaped, and after all four trainees have performed the videotape is played back, during which veteran CIT officers comment honestly and objectively on both positive and negative aspects of trainees' performance.

On the fifth day of training, complex CIT scenarios are demonstrated. All of the verbal skills used in preceding sessions are integrated to deal with very difficult clients. Such difficult scenarios as suicidal and severely psychotic clients are demonstrated, and then intervention techniques are broken down and analyzed as to appropriate and inappropriate responses. At the end of the week, trainees are in possession of the basic skills necessary to intervene with the mentally ill. Like most beginners, the new CIT officers are a little unsure of themselves. However, one of our most rewarding experiences in this business has been seeing these officers come back to aid in training, having developed some of the most outstanding crisis intervention skills we have seen in the 40-plus years we have been doing this work.

Fishbowls With Clients. Fishbowl discussions are unique and powerful sessions for CIT trainees. During this component of the training, trainees are brought into a mental health facility to meet in a discussion group circle with selected mental health patients. A mental health professional, who also serves as an instructor in the CIT training program, sits in the center of the circle with the patients surrounded by the CIT trainees. The professional engages in interviews and dialogues with the mental health patients, in the "fishbowl," so to speak. CIT trainees observe and hear what the mental patients have to say about their own personal needs and about their prior interactions, experiences, and perceptions of the police. After the fishbowl interview and dialogue, trainees who had been observing the professional–patient dialogue have an opportunity to ask questions and interact directly with the patients. The fishbowl discussion has been described by CIT trainees as profoundly motivational and an essential part of their learning, orientation, and training.

The Success of CIT. In more than two decades since its start in Memphis, CIT has grown exponentially, with training centers now located throughout the country and thousands of police officers trained in its protocols (Saunders, 2010). It is noteworthy that the CIT concept is now international, with its own newsletter and convention. *The Team News*, the newsletter of CIT International, is available at http://www.citinternational.org. CIT programs can now be found across the United States, Canada, Australia, and Sweden. But is there any evidence it really works?

In its first 16 months of operation in 1987–1988, Memphis CIT officers responded to 5,831 mental disturbance calls and transported 3,424 cases to mental health facilities without any patient fatalities. Both calls and transports have increased significantly over the 20-plus years the program has been in operation. This increase in "mental disturbance" service calls happens in other jurisdictions as well (Kisely et al., 2010; Teller et al., 2006) and is most likely attributable to increased awareness by the public of the CIT program. That increased awareness is particularly true of relatives and others responsible for the care and well-being of the mentally ill. Publication and support by the National Alliance on Mental Illness (2011) for CIT officers has led to the belief that caregivers' loved ones will be handled in a sensitive manner and not be killed or injured by the police.

Along with increased calls, there appears to be a reduction in the use of force, more diversion from jail to hospitals (Compton et al., 2014b; Lamb, Weinberger, & Gross, 2004; Ritter et al., 2011; Skeem & Bibeau, 2008), decreases in time spent on each call, and increased cooperation between mental health service providers and police (Kisely et al., 2010). In a comprehensive review of research outcomes, Compton and associates (2008) found that there was indeed a reduction in the use of force by CIT officers, more sensitivity toward the mentally ill with commensurate diversion instead of arrest, fewer officer injuries, and reduced hostage team callouts. In Memphis it is noteworthy that only two fatalities have occurred to a recipient of service by CIT officers during the more than 20 years the Memphis Police Department CIT has been in operation, and in both of those cases police officers were found to be justified in killing the person.

Suicide by Cop. Indeed, it is extremely significant that the death toll is so low when CIT officers make the scene. A fairly common phenomenon called "suicide by cop" has been well established. In essence,

LO4

people who do not quite have the courage to kill themselves engage in some activity that gains the attention of the police. Once the police arrive, they engage the police in a threatening manner and succeed in getting themselves shot. In short, the cops complete the suicide (Lindsay & Lester, 2004). We will speak to this phenomena more in Chapter 8, Crisis of Lethality. Police are highly aware of this dangerous phenomenon and are also very interested in learning how to handle it (Lindsay & Lester, 2004; Vermette, Pinals, & Applebaum, 2005). Indeed, the research suggests that tighter bonds and coordination between police and mental health providers such as occurs in CIT programs can reduce this phenomenon (Dewey, Allwood, Fava, Arias, Pinizzotto, & Schlesinger, 2013). At least in Memphis we believe the ability of the police to avoid helping complete this suicidal act and to reduce other mortalities is directly attributable to CIT training. Although no figures exist to determine how many persons have been injured while being taken into protective custody during the 20-plus years CIT has been in operation, statistics indicate that injuries to officers have been reduced significantly. Furthermore, barricade situations have also been reduced significantly. The advent of the CIT program has almost put the Memphis Police Department hostage negotiation team out of business because CIT officers arriving on the scene are often able to defuse and control the situation before the hostage team arrives (James, 1994, pp. 189–190).

Why is this so? A number of studies (Bonfine, Ritter, & Munetz, 2014; Compton et.al., 2006, 2014a; Ellis, 2014) have examined a number of variables of CIT officers immediately before and after undergoing CIT training. After training, those officers demonstrated much-improved attitudes, more support for treatment, more knowledge, less social distancing, more confidence in dealing with the mentally ill, and less stigmatization of them. In summary, besides their increased skill at defusing and de-escalating the violent mentally ill and emotionally disturbed, CIT police officers have become some of the most caring and concerned crisis workers the mentally ill have.

Transcrisis Handling in Long–Term Therapy

Clients in long-term therapy are not immune **LO5** from crisis. Therapy tends to move in developmental stages with psychological troughs, crests, and plateaus. Even though clients have success in meeting therapeutic goals, each new stage brings with it what are seen in many instances to be even more formidable obstacles. The beginning therapist who has seen a client make excellent progress is often in for a rude awakening when the client's progress comes completely undone and behavior regresses to pretherapeutic functioning—or worse!

Anxiety Reactions

A puzzling aspect of therapy occurs when clients are highly successful in achieving tremendously difficult goals and then are completely undone by a task that to the objective observer does not seem all that difficult. Although it seems cognitively irrational, the fear of failure to achieve this minor goal becomes a self-fulfilling prophecy. The client fears that others will see through her or his sham of competence and irrationally thinks that any real progress is a delusion. At such times, clients engage in various types of flight behavior. Severe anxiety is one way of escaping the threatening situation. Consider Melanie's present dilemma. Melanie has escaped from an alcoholic marriage and subsequently completed 2 years of secretarial science at a community college, but she has fallen apart when faced with an interview for a job she desperately wants.

Melanie: (*extremely anxious and agitated, calling her therapist at 1 A.M.*) I hated to call you, but I'm so scared. I've thrown up twice, and I've got the shakes. This hasn't happened since I walked out on Bill over 3 years ago. God, I can't get a grip, and I need to do my best tomorrow. I know I'll just blow it. I can't think straight, and I can't remember a thing about interviewing. Everything's just running together.

The therapist puts Melanie at a 5 on the triage scale for cognitive and behavioral threat and a 6 for affective anxiety/fear. If the therapist does not help diminish the anxiety, the potential is that Melanie may move upward to 8–9 on these scales by the time she goes for her job interview.

TH: Just do this for a minute, Melanie. Take a deep breath, and let it out slo-o-owly. That's right! Now take another! OK, again. (*Continues in a patient, calm voice for about 2 minutes, taking Melanie through a brief deep-breathing exercise to calm her anxiety attack.*)

After the deep-breathing exercise, when Melanie has regained some semblance of control, the therapist paces with her through the role play they had conducted the previous session, has her write down her blunders and strong points, discusses those with her, determines that her attack is receding, and assesses her as now being between a 2 and a 3 on the subscales. A quick review of the client's other successes reinforces and further buttresses the positive change in current functioning.

TH: Now notice the change in your voice. I'll bet you've also calmed down to where you aren't shaking. Did you notice how much more you're in control now? Remember what you're there for. Although a lot depends on this for you, you've also done even bigger, more threatening and scary things in your life like getting the hell out of that malignant marriage. Remember! You've become very good in secretarial science. They need you as much or more than you need them. I want you to put that up as a big signboard in your head, in Day-Glo pink: THEY NEED YOU JUST AS MUCH AS YOU NEED THEM!

By role-playing the scene, the therapist puts Melanie back on familiar ground and puts the problem back into context—getting a job as opposed to having a free-floating anxiety attack. By marshaling the client's resources and very specifically and objectively reminding her of what her strengths are, the therapist concretizes the vague dread she feels at having to face the interview. The therapist's exhortation about who needs whom is not placating here. It is realistic. Melanie's ego needs to be reminded of these facts so that she will have a positive mental set toward both her personhood and her skills as she enters the interview. Finally, the therapist offers her the opportunity to have a safety net.

TH: Melanie, I think you're ready to get some sleep and go knock their socks off tomorrow. However, if you wake up tomorrow morning and really have some questions or think you need to role-play that interview once more, give me a call. I've got some free time before your interview, and we can go over it once more. Now go to bed, get some sleep, and dream about that Day-Glo pink billboard.

By leaving her with a positive injunction and making time for her the next day, the therapist continues to provide a support system and a security net for Melanie.

Regression

The risk of taking the next step in therapeutic development may become too overwhelming even though clients have been highly successful in attaining prior goals. When clients are overwhelmed, they may regress in their behavior, retreating to maladaptive but familiar ways of behaving, feeling, and thinking (Stewart, 2012).

Melanie: (*somewhat embarrassed and mumbling in a childlike voice*) I know what you're going to say, but I was thinking I really couldn't cut this, and Bill made that offer even after I got him arrested that he still loved me and was getting help, and I know he doesn't drink much anymore.

TH: (*interpreting the dynamics*) What you're really saying is the prospect of that interview is scaring the hell out of you, and it's so scary that you'd give up 3 years of hard work and sacrifice to go back to a really lousy, not to mention dangerous, way of living, when you're about to get the gold ring. I'm wondering why you've decided to sabotage yourself now.

By interpreting the dependency needs of the client, the therapist welds regressive thinking to the current threat of becoming independent as manifested in the job interview. Although the client's behavior and affect are not blatant, she is moving insidiously higher on the triage cognitive loss subscale. Left alone, that negative self-talk could convince the client to give up her new self-identity and go back to the long-dead and dangerous marriage.

Melanie: Oh, I just knew you'd say that, but I'm not sure I can do this. I mean a big outfit like United Techtronic.

TH: (*in a cool, clear, no-nonsense, but not condemning, voice*) Big or small, United Techtronic is not the question. The question is, Are you going to choose to blow this before you even see if you can cut it? That's one way of never finding out if you're good enough. You can make that choice, although you've now been making a different one for 3 years. I'd hope you wouldn't do that—I believe you are good enough—but then, it's your choice.

This reality-based approach directly confronts the client with the underlying and unwarranted irrational decision she is about to make and vividly points out how she is trying to delude herself into buying back into a dependent status and revictimizing herself.

Problems of Termination

When clients have met their goals for therapy, are fully functioning, and are ready to get back to the business of living their own lives, they may suddenly produce terrible problems that only their therapist can solve. Whatever these problems are, it is an excellent bet that they have been told that it's time to terminate, or they have figured out that termination is about to happen. At such times it is a common occurrence for dependency issues to arise. These problems generally can be resolved by successively approximating the client to termination. For example, instead of every week, the therapist schedules the client every 2 weeks, then once a month, and then for a 6-month follow-up. The other option is to clearly discuss the possibility that this issue will arise.

TH: Melanie, I think it's time we discussed your spreading your wings and flying away from here. You landed that job and . . .

Melanie: (*interrupts*) But I couldn't have done that without you. You give me the courage to try those things. You've been so wonderful. I just couldn't have done any of this without you. And there's still the problem with the kids and . . .

TH: (*gently interrupting*) I appreciate those compliments. They mean a lot to me. Yet although we've worked together on those things, it's been you who's done it, not I. What I want to talk about with you now is some of those fears and really being on your own, like what you just said. That's pretty normal to have those feelings; lots of people do. Sort of like when you left home the first time. I want you to know I'll be here if you need me, but I want you also to know that I think it's time for you to be on your own. I'd like to discuss this with you in today's session.

Crisis in the Therapy Session

One of the scariest times for a therapist occurs when a technique has done its job exceedingly well, and the client gains insight or release from a deeply buried traumatic experience—and then completely loses control. This unexpected turn of events can unsettle the most experienced therapist. As this wellspring of affect emerges, it may go far beyond cathartic insight and leave the client in a severe state of disequilibrium.

At this point it is absolutely mandatory to stay in control of the situation and take a firm and directive stance, no matter how frightening the client's actions or how personally repulsive the uncovered material may be. Our own admonition to students is, "You may feel physically sick, start to break out in a sweat, and wish to be anyplace else but in that room. After the session is over, you can have a world-class anxiety attack if you wish—you

probably deserve it—but right now you are the therapist, and you are going to stick with the client." By demonstrating cool levelheadedness to the client, the therapist is modeling behavior that the client can emulate.

TH: I'm just wondering if the reason you ever got into that abusive marriage is that sometimes your father might have abused your mother, and that's what was modeled as the way a marriage ought to be.

Melanie: (*recoils in a shocked state*) He never did have intercourse with me.

TH: (*taken aback*) I'm not quite sure what you said— "intercourse"?

Melanie: (*breaking down and sobbing*) For 12 years that bastard would mess with me and my sister, and Momma knew. She knew and wouldn't do anything about it. (*completely breaks down*) I . . . God . . . he beat us if we didn't do . . . he'd make us masturbate him . . . oh Lord . . . how could he . . . I've kept this secret . . . I can't handle this. I should have done something . . . killed him . . . (*uncontrolled and wracked sobbing and shaking*).

TH: (*recomposing herself and gently touching Melanie's arm and quietly talking in a consoling and affirming voice*) I am truly sorry for uncovering that old wound, but you *can* handle it. You've finally got it out. You lived with that hell as a child and another hell as an adult. You are a survivor.

Psychotic Breaks

Staying calm and cool is even more important when a person is having a psychotic break with reality. No matter how delusional or dissociative the client becomes, the central thesis is that the client can maintain contact with reality and take constructive action.

Manuel: (*walks into the therapist's office unannounced and unknown*) I need help, and they recommend you. But no telephones, they listen to me through the telephone. (*Picks up the telephone in a threatening manner.*)

TH: (*in a slow, even voice*) I need for you to put that telephone down before we go any further. I will help you, but I want you to put the telephone back on the stand. We've never had the pleasure of meeting. What is your name?

Manuel: It's Manuel. (*hesitates*) I'm just coming apart. They won't leave me alone.

TH: I understand that, but I need you to put the phone down and keep it together, so you can tell me who's after you. Go ahead and sit down and tell me what's bothering you.

Manuel: It's my supervisor. He wants to fire me and catch me stealing, so he listens in on my phone conversations. He's in league with Satan, and he's probably in this room. I can smell the brimstone. (*Starts to become agitated and mumble about Hell.*)

TH: (*calmly but in an assertive voice*) OK! You're having trouble with your supervisor. Now we're getting somewhere. That's good, but stay with me, I personally guarantee Satan is not here. I want to know about your supervisor and how long this has been going on. I also want to get you to a safe place where nobody can hurt you, but to do that I need your help, and I need you to stay in contact, so I can help you.

Manuel: OK. (*Sits down and starts to talk about his supervisor.*)

The therapist immediately seeks to establish contact by obtaining the client's name, while at the same time establishing ground rules for conduct in the therapist's office. When the young man starts to dissociate and talk incoherently, the therapist directively seeks to keep Manuel in contact with reality by focusing discussion on his grievance with his supervisor. While he validates the client's fear, the only acknowledgment he gives to evil spirits is his concern for the client's safety. The therapist reinforces the client for staying in contact with him and repeats his request to put the telephone down. Because psychotic clients may have difficulty hearing others because of the intrusive hallucinations assailing them, the therapist slowly and clearly repeats his requests for compliance. By staying in control, the therapist turns a potentially violent situation with an unknown client into a satisfactory resolution.

People With Borderline Personality Disorder

Most clients try to manipulate their therapists **LO6** during the course of therapy for a variety of reasons. These reasons may range from avoiding engagement in new behaviors to testing the therapist's credibility. Clients with personality disorders are the ultimate test of the therapist's ability to handle manipulative behavior, and can create severe crises for themselves and the therapist if not dealt with in very specific ways (Kocmur & Zavasnik, 1993). In 1938, Adolph Stern, an American psychotherapist, described a group of clients who did not respond well to treatment and in fact generally got worse. He labeled them as a "borderline group" that lay somewhere between neurosis and psychosis (Stern, 1938). While that notion is no longer deemed valid (Paris, 2008, p. 3), no one has yet come up with a better way to describe clients who have some of the most intractable, stubborn character pathology imaginable and has been named borderline personality disorder (BPD). Current estimates are that about 2.7% of the adult population in the United States are candidates for a BPD diagnoses and also are likely to have co-occurring mood, anxiety, and substance abuse disorders (Tomko, Trull, Wood, & Sher, 2014).

Personality implies stable and enduring patterns of thinking, feeling, and acting across time and situation (Reyes, Elhai, & Ford, 2008). The borderline personality is the antithesis of that construct, and this particular disorder of personality is a handmaiden to many of the crises in this book—particularly if the traumatic event occurred during childhood (Zanarini, 2000). Indeed, a whole field of therapy called **mentalization** (Bateman & Fognagy, 2006; Kvarstein et al., 2015) has developed that specifically targets trauma in childhood and lack of attachment to significant positive parenting figures as a major precursor to "getting" BPD.

Probably the best way to describe this disorder is through the title of Kreisman and Straus's (2010) classic book for people attempting to live and deal with borderline personalities: *I Hate You—Don't Leave Me*. There is good reason for this ambivalence. Indeed, there is a good deal of evidence that many individuals with borderline personality disorder have had a rogues' gallery of childhood horrors of physical and sexual abuse and long-term parental neglect (Allen, 2001; Brown, 2009; Herman, Perry, & van der Kolk, 1989; Sroufe et al., 2005; Stalker & Davies, 1995). The rate of childhood sexual assault has been estimated to be a staggering 75% in people with borderline personality disorder (Battle et al., 2004). As a result, they are likely candidates for what many practitioners and researchers refer to as "complex PTSD" (Briere & Scott, 2006; Courtois & Ford, 2009), a concept we will examine in Chapter 7, Posttraumatic Stress Disorder, and Chapter 9, Sexual Assault. So while they are tough customers and can be extremely trying, there are some pretty good reasons that persons with borderline diagnoses act the way they do and are the hallmark of the client who is in transcrisis. Because of these early experiences with trusted others who could not be trusted, the borderline personality has serious attachment problems that can rapidly surface in therapy. There is evidence that these individuals also harbor a deep sense of betrayal (Kaehler & Freyd, 2009). As you can readily see, there is good reason for this mistrust, sense of betrayal, and thus the constant vigilance, testing of the relationship, and paranoia that mark therapy with these individuals.

All-pro, all-star, and all-world therapists have trouble dealing with these individuals, so why in the world are we exposing you rookies to them? First of all, they provide a good example of how manipulative clients can work you over and lead you into being a case example in our chapter on burnout. More important perhaps, they are clients you will run into that manifest many of the crises in this book. Among other maladies, they abuse drugs, become violent, are suicidal, are sexually promiscuous, practice self-mutilation, get raped, have PTSD, and on and on, so here is a snapshot of a client who can blindside you if you are not careful. The saying goes that "You haven't won your spurs as a therapist until you have dealt with a person with BPD."

The borderline personality type in therapy is an open Pandora's box of crises, in terms of the presenting problems and issues that occur in therapy, as graphically described by numerous researchers, therapists, and family members (Bagge et al., 2004; Beck & Freeman, 1990; Belling, Bozzatello, De Grandi, & Bogetto, 2014; Borschmann et al., 2013; Borschmann & Moran, 2011; Brockian, 2002; Chatham, 1989; Drapeau & Perry, 2004; Fonagy, Luyten, & Strathearn, 2011; Freidel, 2004; Jimenez, 2013; Kreisman & Straus, 2004; Kroger, Roepke, & Kliem, 2014; Lachkar, 2011; Lawrence, Allen, & Chanen, 2011; Leichsenring et al., 2011; Paris, 2008; Sansone, Chu, & Wiederman, 2011; Wirth-Cauchon, 2001; Zeigler-Hill & Abraham, 2006) and summarized below.

Presenting Problems. People with borderline personality disorder have problems like no other client has. They include the following in therapy:

1. A wide variety of presenting problems that may shift from day to day and week to week
2. Unusual combinations of symptoms ranging across a wide array of neurotic to subpsychotic behaviors
3. Continuous self-destructive and self-punitive behavior ranging from self-mutilation to suicide attempts
4. Impulsive and poorly planned behavior that shifts through infantile, narcissistic, or antisocial behavior

5. Intense emotional reactions out of all proportion to the situation
6. Confusion regarding goals, priorities, feelings, sexual orientation, and so on
7. A constant feeling of emptiness with chronic free-floating anxiety
8. Unstable low self-esteem and high and unstable negative affect
9. Poor academic, work, and social adjustment
10. Extreme approach and avoidance behavior to social relationships
11. Chronic suicidal and/or homicidal ideation
12. Paranoid ideation
13. Depersonalization and hallucinations
14. Drug abuse including alcohol
15. Sexual promiscuity and sexual victimization
16. High dropout rate from therapy and poor therapeutic alliance

Therapeutic Relationship. People with borderline personality disorder do everything in their power to turn the therapeutic relationship upside down. They have:

1. Frequent crises such as suicide threats, abuse of drugs, sexual acting out, financial irresponsibility, and problems with the law.
2. Extreme or frequent misinterpretations of the therapist's statements, intentions, or feelings with strong transference issues that can illicit even stronger countertransference issues in the therapist.
3. Unusually strong, negative, acting-out reactions to changes in appointment time, room changes, vacations, fees, or termination in therapy.
4. Low tolerance for direct eye contact, physical contact, or close proximity in therapy.
5. Unusually strong ambivalence on issues.
6. Fear of and resistance to change with inability or resistance to carry out therapeutic assignments.
7. Frequent phone calls to, spying on, and demands for special attention and treatment from the therapist.
8. Inordinate hypersensitivity to significant others including the therapist.

People with borderline personality disorder vacillate between autonomy and dependence, view the world in black-and-white terms, are ever vigilant for perceived danger, have chronic tension and anxiety, are guarded in their interpersonal relationships, and are uncomfortable with emotions (Beck & Freeman, 1990, pp. 186–187; Lachkar, 2011; Linehand, 1993; Paris, 2008). Because of these personality traits, they are apt to continuously test the therapeutic relationship to affirm that the therapist, like everybody else, is untrustworthy and not capable of living up to their expectations, while at the same time they desperately crave attention, love, and respect (Brockian, 2002; Freidel, 2004; Kreisman & Straus, 2004; Lachkar, 2011; Linehand, 1993; McHenry, 1994; Paris, 2008; Yeomans, 1993). Do you start to get the picture of why they can become psychological albatrosses around therapists' necks?

When dealing with someone with borderline personality disorder, it is important to set clear limits, structure specific therapeutic goals, provide empathic support, validate the client's actions as understandable, model a safe environment, caringly confront manipulative and maladaptive behavior, and rigorously stick with these guiding principles (Briere & Scott, 2006; Chatham, 1989; Kreisman & Straus, 2004; Lachkar, 2011; Linehand, 1993; Paris, 2008). This is easier said than done because of the dramatic kinds of problems and emotions that these people display. The following dialogue with Tommy, a college student, depicts such problematic behavior.

Tommy: (*calling the therapist at 2 A.M.*) I can't take this any longer. Nobody cares about me. I think I'm going crazy again—all these weird voices keep coming into my mind. It'd just be easier if I got a gun and blew myself away.

TH: I can understand the belief that nobody cares about you, considering how you were put in foster care as a kid and how that uncaring attitude of others seems to follow you wherever you go. If that's the case that those abandonment fears are driving you to this point, then I'm concerned enough about your welfare to call 911 and get the police there immediately to take you to the hospital. (*Wise in the ways of people with borderline personality disorder, the therapist immediately confronts Tommy's statement while validating his fears.*) If things are that serious, a phone conversation won't get the job done.

Tommy: Well, I didn't say I was going to kill myself right now! You always jump to conclusions. I just couldn't sleep or study because of all these voices, and I really need to talk about them.

TH: I'm willing to talk for 15 minutes, but if I don't see you calmed down and functional by that time, I'll feel warranted in calling 911.

Setting limits and monitoring client safety is critical (Kreisman & Straus, 2004; Paris, 2008). By voicing legitimate concerns about the client's safety and setting

a specific time limit on the conversation, the therapist reaffirms therapeutic control and does not become engaged in a rambling dialogue. The latter would serve nothing other than to reinforce maladaptive client behavior and cause a sleepless therapist to be angry and irritable the next day! No special considerations other than those normally given to any other clients should be given to those with borderline personality disorder.

Tommy: But Dr. James, I really need to change the appointment and see you tomorrow. I've got this research presentation, and my group's meeting during our appointment time. Can't you move somebody else around?

TH: I have an appointment with another client at that time, Tommy. As I told you, to reschedule I need to know 48 hours in advance. It wouldn't be fair to him anymore than it would be fair to you if I did that to your regular time.

Tommy: (*sarcastically*) You just really don't give a damn about me, do you?

TH: The fact is, I do give a damn, and that's why I'm not going to cave in and change the appointment time. We're not talking about rejection here; we're talking about a reasonable policy that I use on everybody. I know lots of times it would be easy for you to believe I'm blowing you off. At times you certainly aren't the easiest client to deal with, but I knew that going in, and I committed to see this through with you. I'll expect you at our regular Thursday time.

The therapist owns both his positive and his negative feelings about the client and directly interprets and confronts the client's underlying fear of rejection (Chatham, 1989). Finally, by reminding the client of his regular appointment, the therapist targets behavior rather than affect. Focusing on behavior is far less problematic than dealing with relational issues, either inside or outside therapy, because of the client's low tolerance for intimacy (Beck & Freeman, 1990; Drapeau & Perry, 2004; Freidel, 2004).

Treatment noncompliance is par for the course with clients with borderline personality disorder.

TH: So how did your assignment go in thought stopping and not arbitrarily categorizing women as saints or prostitutes?

Tommy: Well, I was real busy this week. Besides which, you didn't really make that thought stopping stuff very clear. And then the rubber band reminder on my wrist broke.

TH: (*frustrated, voice raised, and becoming agitated*) This is the sixth week I've gone through this with you. You continuously put women in those one-up or one-down positions. Yet you continuously complain that no females are interested in you. How do you ever expect to have an equitable relationship unless you change your thinking?

Tommy: (*flushed and shouting*) Oh yeah? You're so perfect? I'll bet your supervisor would like to know the way you verbally harass your clients. Screw you! Who needs therapy or bitches, anyway? They're all sluts anyway. (*Storms out of the room and slams the door.*)

Maintaining professional detachment and keeping one's cool are critical and difficult (Kreisman & Straus, 2004). The therapist's frustration may turn to anger if the therapist ascribes malicious intentions to the client's nonperformance, particularly when trying to change the client's black-and-white thinking. Overt frustration often results in reciprocal acting out by the client. The client's passive noncompliance is a balancing act between fear of change and fear of offending the therapist through outright refusal to comply with therapeutic requests. When noncompliance is consistently the normative response, the therapist needs to step back from the situation, seek outside consultation, confront these issues openly, and acknowledge freely the client's right to refuse an assignment rather than doggedly proceeding (Beck & Freeman, 1990).

TH: Tommy, I feel really frustrated right now. We've been going at this one assignment for six sessions. Maybe I'm the problem—pushing too fast. On the other hand, I feel you maybe don't want to make me disappointed, so you go through the motions. You've always got the right to say no to an assignment, and we can certainly discuss the pros and cons of that. What do you want to do about this assignment?

A favorite ploy of people with borderline personality disorder and other dependent types of clients is to externalize and project their problems onto others. They then attempt to get the therapist to intercede for them by acting as an intermediary or otherwise "fixing" the problem.

Tommy: If you could just write my econ professor a note telling him I'm under your care. I've only missed five classes, and he's threatening to flunk me.

TH: School and therapy are separate, and I won't get into that.

Tommy: (*whining and pleading*) But you know how bad off I've been.

TH: If you are sick enough to miss class, perhaps you should consider an academic withdrawal for medical reasons.

Tommy: Well, I'm not that bad off that I need to quit school.

TH: How has getting others to make excuses for you helped in the past?

In refusing to be used by the client, the therapist avoids a pitfall that would invariably lead to more dependent behavior and the continuation of cyclical, self-reinforcing, dependent, and manipulative behavior. Finally, the watchword with people with borderline personality disorders and other clients who consciously or unconsciously seek to manipulate the therapist is: Remain calm throughout therapy, and do not respond to each new crisis as an emergency. The key question therapists must ask themselves is, "Who's doing the majority of work here?" If the answer is, "Not the client!" then there is a good chance the therapist is being manipulated.

Counseling Difficult Clients

Crisis workers must be prepared to deal with **LO7** many different types of clients, some of whom are "difficult." To assist in coping with such clients, here are some examples of appropriate ground rules as well as suggestions for confronting difficult clients.

Ground Rules for Counseling Difficult Clients

Workers who must deal with difficult clients regularly may wish to print a set of ground rules to place in the hands of clients at the initial session or before the first meeting. The following rules may be used with individuals, couples, or groups:

1. We start on time and quit on time. If couples are involved, both parties must be present; we will not meet unless both parties are present.
2. There will be no physical violence or threats of violence.
3. Everyone speaks for himself or herself.
4. Everyone has a chance to be fully heard.
5. We deal mainly with the here and now; we try to steer clear of getting bogged down in the past and in blaming others.
6. Everyone faces all the issues brought up—nobody gets up and leaves just because the topic is

uncomfortable, and everyone stays for the entire session.

7. Everyone gets an opportunity to define the current problems, suggest realistic solutions, and make at least one commitment to do something positive. At least one positive action step is desired from each person present.

8. Limits to graphic descriptions, abusive language, and swearing and cursing need to be clear as to what will and will not be tolerated.

9. Everyone belongs, because he or she is a human being and because he or she is here.

10. The crisis worker will not take sides.

11. There will be no retribution, retaliation, or grudges over what is said in the session. Whatever is said in the session belongs and stays in the session.

12. The time we spend together is for working on the concerns of the person or people in the group—not for playing games, making personal points, diversion, ulterior purposes, or carrying tales or gossip outside the session.

13. When we know things are a certain way, we will not pretend they are another way—we will confront and deal with each other as honestly and objectively as we possibly can.

14. We will not ignore the nonverbal or body messages that are emitted—we will deal with them openly if they occur.

15. If words or messages need to be expressed to clear the air, we will say them either directly or with role playing—we will not put them off until later.

16. We will not expect each other to be perfect.

17. Being drunk or otherwise drug intoxicated is not acceptable in therapy. We do not work with "wet" clients.

18. In the event the ground rules are broken, the consequences will be discussed by the persons involved immediately with the crisis worker. People who comply with the rules will not be denied services because one person disobeys the rules.

The crisis worker may go over the ground rules, in person or over the phone, before the first session. If this is not possible, a brief orientation that includes the ground rules is advisable at the start of the first meeting.

Confronting Difficult Clients

In dealing with difficult clients, the worker may have to *confront* such behavior directly. We must be able and ready to use confrontation, assertion, and directive tactics, such as saying, "I will not permit you to violate our ground rules by attacking her that way." There is a possibility that a client may be so difficult that the session may have to be terminated. (This should happen very, very infrequently.) In such a rare case, the worker would openly admit, "We're getting nowhere, so let's adjourn and see if we can figure out a way to try again." Consultation with a professional colleague for suggestions would be one of the first steps the therapist would take after such an adjournment.

Confidentiality in Case Handling

One benchmark of crisis is the dramatic onset of potentially violent behavior. Although we deal extensively with the control and containment of such behavior in Chapter 14, a particular admonition to the crisis interventionist is appropriate here in discussing case handling. That admonition involves the issues of confidentiality and privileged communication, and the legal and moral dilemmas that swirl within many crisis settings will be discussed in Chapter 15, Ethical and Legal Issues for Crisis Intervention.

SUMMARY

Case handling in crisis intervention differs from long-term therapy. Although crisis intervention deals with many of the same components as long-term therapy, crisis work can be differentiated by its emphasis on expediency and efficiency in attempting to stabilize maladaptive client functioning, as opposed to fundamental restructuring of the client's personality. Case handling in crisis intervention emphasizes concern for client safety, brevity in assessment, rapid intervention, compressed treatment time, and termination or referral once equilibrium has been restored. Case handling in crisis intervention can occur both at walk-in facilities and in long-term therapy settings.

Since the Community Mental Health Act of 1963, the major responsibility for treating the mentally ill has fallen on community mental health centers. Such centers, along with a wide variety of other community social services agencies, are on the front lines in dealing with crises of chronic mental illness, severe developmental problems, and social and environmental issues that afflict individuals. Because of the wide variety of clientele seeking services, walk-in facilities must have close linkages with other social services agencies, the legal system, and both short-term and long-term mental health facilities. Mental health workers who staff such facilities must have a broad background in dealing with a wide variety of psychological problems and be ready and able to deal with whatever crisis walks in the door.

Because of the consequences of the Community Mental Health Act of 1963, police departments have assumed greater and greater responsibility for initial contact and disposition of the mentally ill. Creation of the Memphis Model of the Crisis Intervention Team (CIT) has resulted in the development and use of regular patrol officers to defuse and de-escalate the mentally ill and other emotionally violent clients. Variations of this model are now in use throughout the United States.

Clients in long-term therapy may also experience crises as they move through the therapeutic process. These crises may be instigated by situational events in the client's environment; by attempts to engage in new, more adaptive behaviors; or by past traumatic material that is uncovered in the therapy session. When such crises occur, therapy may degenerate to the point that clients undergo severe traumatic stress and revert to pretherapeutic functioning levels. At these points in therapy, long-term work must be suspended, and the therapist must concentrate on the emergent crisis until the client has achieved success in overcoming the current stumbling block. The borderline personality disorder is probably the archetype of difficult and crisis-prone clients with which the therapist will work in long-term therapy.

Visit CengageBrain.com for a variety of study tools and useful resources such as video examples, case studies, interactive exercises, flashcards, and quizzes.

Telephone and Online Crisis Counseling

6

LEARNING OBJECTIVES

After reading this chapter, you should be able to:

1. Understand why crisis lines are popular and effective.
2. Know the steps handling different types of clients at crisis line centers.
3. Know that no one is perfect in doing crisis line intervention and mistakes are repairable.
4. Learn how crisis line interventions handle difficult callers.
5. Learn how to deal with a severely disturbed caller.
6. Know the administrative rules for handling difficult callers.
7. Know the different types of hotlines and their use.
8. Understand the role of the Internet in providing crisis intervention.
9. Understand why texting in crisis intervention is important.
10. Understand the role of virtual reality in providing transcrisis intervention.

Introduction

By far and away the vast majority of crisis counseling is now handled by telephone. Most probably the person on the other end of that telephone is a volunteer who does *not* hold a degree in social work, psychiatric nursing, counseling, or psychology. As we move further into the 21st century, the Internet is playing a larger and larger part in real-time crisis counseling as is the smartphone with its app and texting ability. Whether the service provider on the Internet will be a professional with credentials, a well-meaning volunteer with no training, a charlatan out to steal your money or your daughter, or a computer programmed to do crisis intervention is an interesting question (Hsiung, 2002; Gross & Anthony, 2003; James & Gilliland, 2003, pp. 417–428).

This chapter is mainly about the large, current venue of telephone use in crisis counseling, but clearly online crisis counseling has arrived, and it is growing at such a staggering rate that books specifically targeted to e-therapy protocol and use are now being written (Adlington, 2009; Anthony & Nagel, 2010; Jones & Stokes, 2009), and an International Society for Mental Health Online has come into existence (https://www.ismho.org/home.asp). The final section of this chapter will deal briefly with what is the new, cutting edge of psychotherapy, virtual reality therapy (Gaggiolli, 2014; Stevens, 2014; Wiederhold & Wiederhold, 2005). Here is a quote from the noted physicist Max Planck: "A new scientific truth does not triumph by convincing its opponents and making them see the light, but rather because its opponents eventually die, and a new generation grows up that is familiar with it" (as cited in T. S. Kuhn, 1962). What do you think of it? You might want to think carefully about Planck's quote, because these new technologies are going about the business of how the whole notion of therapy is carried out. The problem is that little is still being done in professional programs to train therapists on how to use these new technologies and still focus on face-to-face encounters, and as a result don't believe that therapeutic alliances can be built with computer-based technology (Lopez, 2014). Amichai-Hamburger and associates (2014) propose a model for using online therapy with the therapist at the center of the technology. So the question becomes one of, "Will you be at the center of this new technology or will we be waiting to go to your funeral?"

Case Handling on Telephone Crisis Lines

The telephone has long played an integral role `LO1` in crisis work. The old Bell Telephone advertisement "Reach out and touch someone!" is a slogan that is particularly appropriate to crisis counseling. Slaikeu (1990, pp. 105–141) refers to emergency telephone help as "first-order intervention" or "psychological first aid." Indeed, the telephone is the most prevalent medium for the initial contact in most crisis service delivery. There are several reasons for the popularity of the telephone in solving psychological problems.

Convenience. Convenience is paramount (Leffert, 2003; Reese, Conoley, & Brossart, 2006). Particularly cell phones have become such an easy way of communicating that calling for psychological assistance is a natural extension of "taking care of business." The tremendous upsurge in the use of cell phones allows a person to call a crisis line from anywhere, including the site of the crisis as it is happening in real time. Further, with the new "smart" phones, not only can clients avail themselves of a crisis hotline or their therapist, they can also access a variety of self-help groups in chat rooms, computer-assisted therapy, and psychoeducational materials (Boschen, 2009; Gross & Anthony, 2003; Preziosa et al., 2009). As in the case of battering, most crises do not occur during normal business hours. When help is needed in a crisis, it is needed immediately, and mobile phones make 24/7 assistance even more available.

Client Anonymity. Guilt, embarrassment, shame, self-blame, and other debilitating emotions make face-to-face encounters with strangers very difficult, particularly in the immediate aftermath of a traumatic event. Opening oneself to another is an act of vulnerability. The ability to hide one's identity may facilitate greater openness and freedom from inhibition (Reese, Conoley, & Brossart, 2006). This is particularly true of adolescents (Christogiorgos et al., 2010; Tolmach, 1985), those who are socially isolated or psychologically desperate, and the relatively stable person who has a one-shot crisis (Lester & Brockopp, 1973, pp. 86–87). Telephone counselors understand that clients have such feelings and are generally not concerned about identifying a client unless a life-threatening emergency is involved. Conversations are usually on a first-name-only basis for both the worker and the client. Thus, a victim of date rape may call a rape hotline and freely discuss her emotions without having to muster the courage to face what may be perceived as a judgmental human services worker.

Control. A great deal of fear, anxiety, and uncertainty occur when a client's life is ruptured by a crisis (Lester & Brockopp, 1973, pp. 81–82). The concept of secondary victimization by institutions (Ochberg, 1988) is well known to victims of a crisis who have sought assistance from a social agency and then been victimized by its bureaucratic callousness. Going for help may be positively humiliating. In telephone counseling, the client decides when and if assistance is to be sought. At any time during a dialogue on a crisis line, the client may terminate the conversation without fear of recrimination. Finally, looks don't matter in phone counseling. Anybody who is self-conscious about how they look finds the phone a wonderful way to obtain counseling (Wark, 1982).

Immediacy of Access. Crisis intervention can occur any place a telephone, or for that matter a computer, is available (Masi & Freedman, 2001). Most institutions and clinics and many private practitioners use pagers. At our own university, a harried residence hall supervisor who is trying to deal with a distraught, suicidal student who is suffering from severe homesickness and academic failure can call campus police. The police will page a member of the staff of the student counseling center who is the after-hours "beeper keeper." The psychologist immediately responds to the request for assistance by checking with the residence hall supervisor on the current mental status of the student and will then come to the residence hall, talk to the student over the phone, or request additional help from the police to transport the student to the city crisis stabilization unit. In case of an imminent threat such as a tornado or the presence of a potential assailant on campus, text and computer messages can go out to all the students and university staff.

Cost Effectiveness. Crisis lines are inexpensive—for both the client and the community (Masi & Freedman, 2001). Clients who cannot pay for private therapy or afford transportation can usually avail themselves of a phone. Most community agency hotlines are staffed by volunteers and are paid for out of United Way or other charitable funds. Reese, Conoley, and Brossert's (2006) study of telephone counseling strongly implies that, for people of limited financial means, face-to-face counseling where money is a factor is not an option as opposed to a free community crisis line.

Therapeutic Effectiveness. Volunteers who staff crisis lines have probably been the single most important discovery in the history of suicide intervention (Dublin, 1969). Volunteers have few pretensions about their "professional role" and are often seen by callers as having more credibility than a paid professional because they "do it out of the goodness of their hearts." Although the idea of obtaining counseling from a volunteer may seem no better or worse than talking to a bartender or hairdresser, and when they receive little training they are probably worse (Derkx et al., 2009), volunteers typically go through a good deal of training in initial point-of-contact mental health counseling. Phipps, Byme, and Deane (2007) found that volunteers who went through training specifically designed to deal with trauma showed significant gain in knowledge and skills from pre- to posttraining. Mishara and his associates (2005) found that less than 0.3% of 2,611 calls they monitored at 14 participating call-in centers were found to be blatantly unacceptable in helper responses and could possibly put the lives of the callers at risk. Gould (2007) and her associates found a significant decrease in suicidal ideation in the course of crisis line calls and continuing decreases in caller hopelessness and psychological pain in follow-ups with suicidal callers.

While there is still a good deal of contempt by professionals for crisis hotlines, research indicates that they are probably as good as other types of face-to-face counseling and are particularly attractive to young people, old people, and people who do not have financial access to professional therapists (Bryant & Harvey, 2000; Day & Schneider, 2002; Evans et al., 1986; Fukkink & Hermanns, 2009; Lester & Brockopp, 1973, p. 86; Reese, Conoley, & Brossart, 2002, 2006; Rohland et al., 2000).

Access to Support Systems. One of the major reasons people call hotlines is for social support (Watson, McDonald, & Pierce, 2006). Many people who are lonely, anxious, or isolated by physical illness are in need of support (Burgess et al., 2008). Whether you are a shut-in, shy, ugly, recently divorced, widowed, abused, addicted, or you have leprosy, panic attacks, bad thoughts, or any of the issues of problem callers you are about to meet in this chapter, the need for social support and an empathic ear and voice is the common thread that runs through most crisis lines.

Beyond the support of the line itself are the telephone and online support systems to which you can be referred or gain access on your own.

Support groups make extensive use of telephone networks (Lester & Brockopp, 1973). From A (Alcoholics Anonymous) to Z (Zen) support groups, telephone support networks provide constant links to group members between organized meetings. A Google search conducted on February 23, 2015, identified 371 million sites for support groups. The bottom line is that if you can't find a support group out there somewhere for your problem, you are probably an alien escapee from Roswell's Area 51 and this book isn't going to be a lot of help to you.

Avoidance of Dependency Issues. A user of telephone crisis lines can't become dependent on a particular human services worker who may not always be readily available. Standard practice in most crisis lines discourages workers from forming lasting relationships with clients so that dependency issues do not arise (Lester, 2002).

Worker Anonymity. The fact that workers are anonymous has as many benefits as client anonymity. The absence of body language, facial expressions, and a visual image allows clients to project whatever idealized view they may conjure up of the therapist. By facilitating the development of transference, within limits, the client can make positive changes. The point here is that not only can clients make of the therapist what they will, they can make of them what they need (Lester & Brockopp, 1973, p. 85; Williams & Douds, 2002, pp. 60–61).

Availability of Others for Consultation. Crisis lines are seldom staffed by one person. When someone encounters a difficult client, other staff at the agency are available for consultation. Furthermore, at least one phone line is reserved for calling support agencies when emergency services are needed.

Availability of an Array of Services. A vast array of information, guidance, and social services is quickly available via telephone linkages. The specialized services of different agencies and the expertise they offer can provide on-the-spot guidance for emotionally volatile situations. Many an angry mother or father has received "5-minute parenting sessions" from the staff of a metropolitan "parenting line," thus short-circuiting potential child abuse. Any crisis hotline should have readily available a list of phone numbers of specialized agencies to which they can refer callers. The LINC, or Library and Information Network for the Community, is available in most large metropolitan areas and is standard reference for most telephone crisis lines.

Service to Large and Isolated Geographic Areas and Populations.
Many rural areas that have no after-hours mental health facilities or staff are tied in to toll-free crisis lines that cover huge geographic areas. These crisis lines in turn are tied in to emergency service staff such as police, paramedics, and hospital emergency rooms that serve those rural areas and can respond to a crisis line call for assistance that may be 150 miles away. Certainly populations that are homebound, such as the elderly, physically disabled, or agoraphobic, have a lifeline they would not otherwise have (Lester & Brockopp, 1973, p. 82; Williams & Douds, 2002, pp. 59–60).

Telephone Counseling Strategies

Conducting crisis intervention over the telephone is a double-edged sword. Although phone counseling offers the advantages just listed, for generating responses the crisis worker is entirely dependent on the content, voice tone, pitch, speed, and emotional content of the client. Telephone counseling, and Internet counseling for that matter, isn't for everyone, and that includes both clients and interventionists (Eckardt, 2011). For many human services workers, it is unsettling to deal with ambiguous client responses and not be able to link body language to verbal content. Furthermore, the worker depends entirely on his or her own verbal ability to stabilize the client and has little physical control over the situation. It takes only one experience of having a suicidal client hang up on a worker to understand how frustrating and emotionally draining crisis intervention over the telephone can be. Consequently, a great deal of care and effort needs to be taken in responding to clients. The following section outlines some effective telephone counseling strategies.

Making Psychological Contact

First, psychological contact needs to be made, and this endeavor takes precedence over anything else the phone worker does. Psychological contact means that the worker attempts to establish as quickly as possible

a nonjudgmental, caring, accepting, and empathic relationship with the client that will give the worker credibility and elicit the client's trust. Therefore, *provide support* becomes the first order of business. It is safe to assume that people who use crisis lines have exhausted or are separated from their support systems. If the client feels no trust in the relationship and hangs up the phone, the crisis worker cannot make an astute dynamic analysis, synthesize material, diagnose the problem, and prescribe a solution! In establishing psychological contact on the phone, providing support is a first priority and is highly integrated with defining the problem through active listening and responding skills.

CW: (*Two A.M. on Monday morning. Phone rings.*) Metro crisis line. This is Chris. Can I help you?

Telephone caller (TC): (*Silence with soft muffled sobs.*)

CW: (*Waits patiently.*) I understand it's pretty hard to talk sometimes, especially when things seem so overwhelming, but if you could, just take a deep breath and then let it out. I wonder if you could just do that?

TC: (*Takes a deep breath and exhales. Sobs less frequently.*)

CW: (*in a soft, modulated, soothing tone*) That's good! Just do that a few more times. Just relax. I'll stay right on the line until you feel like talking. We've got plenty of time. I'd like to know your name when you feel ready?

The phone worker must be able to react in a calm and collected manner. Thus, the worker's voice must be well modulated, steady, low keyed, with an adequate decibel level but not high pitched. Neither should the content of the worker's response be deprecating, cynical, cajoling, or demeaning. Although the foregoing criteria may seem obvious, few people realize how their voice sounds or are aware of what happens to their voice level and pitch when they are caught up in a rapidly escalating and evolving emotional event. Furthermore, when the person on the other end of the line is acting out, angry, intoxicated, or otherwise demanding of the worker to "fix things right now," the worker needs a great deal of self-discipline and emotional security to refrain from becoming caustic, judgmental, and demanding.

While crisis line counseling is on first name basis only, making initial contact means getting a name out to the caller and attempting to get one back. As simple as this sounds, in the heat of the initial moments of a call, neophyte workers forget to do this.

Chris the veteran does not and patiently queries the caller for her name.

Defining the Problem

Once psychological contact is established, the worker attempts to define the problem by gaining an understanding of the events that led to the crisis and by assessing the client's coping mechanisms. Open-ended questions on the *what, how, when, where, who* continuum usually let the worker get a clear picture of the event itself. However, in assessing the coping mechanisms of the client over the phone, it may be hard to get a clear picture of the client's affect. Thus it behooves the worker to become more sensitive to the underlying emotional content and to try to reflect the implied feeling content more than might be required in a face-to-face encounter. Reflecting feelings is a tough job for most beginning mental health workers and is even more difficult on the phone. Yet the worker absolutely must try to reflect feelings, because there is no way to visually assess the client.

One real plus of phone counseling is that the beginning crisis worker can have supportive aids readily at hand without detracting from the counseling session. One useful tactic is to have a reference list of feeling words that cover the gamut of emotions. A second tactic is to have at hand a list of standard questions the counselor can check off to be sure that all areas typically pertinent to the problem are covered. A third tactic is to keep handy a notepad on which the worker can jot down the salient aspects of the events and coping mechanisms the client has used and make a rapid assessment on the triage scale.

TC: (*timorously*) O . . . O . . . O . . . K. I just don't know where to start, it's just an avalanche. I've got no place to turn, so I thought this was my only chance, so I called.

CW: I'm glad you did call. Sounds like right now you're really overwhelmed, so perhaps you could just take it from where you felt like things fell apart and tell me about that. And I want you to take your time. Take plenty of time, and tell me what's going on. We've got all the time in the world, and I'm here to listen until you say everything you need to and we get a real clear picture of what's going on and what needs to happen.

TC: It's Cicily.

The client goes on to explain she has just moved to town from out of state in an attempt to reconcile with her estranged husband. The husband indicated that he wanted nothing more to do with the marriage and was filing for divorce. She indicates that she was pretty much in denial about the failed marriage and had taken a last chance on getting it back together. The denial has now been given a rude reality check. The job that was supposedly waiting for her has also fallen through. She is currently at a friend's house, with her 4-year-old son, with less than $200 and a car on its last wheels. She has no relatives or support system besides her friend from college days.

The crisis worker, Chris, listens intently to the client's story. He interrupts only to clarify and summarize what's going on with the client. Chris deeply reflects the feelings of aloneness, hopelessness, and helplessness that wash over her. The crisis worker allows the client to grieve and ventilate over her failed marriage. When the client's emotional behavior starts to escalate, the crisis worker uses calming techniques such as asking the client to take a deep breath or reinforces the concept that they have plenty of time to work through this problem. As Chris listens to her, he is rapidly jotting notes down and making an assessment on the triage scale. Her predominant emotion is anxiety, which is free-floating into all areas of her life. She is having a lot of difficulty controlling her emotions.

Her score on the Affective Severity scale is 7. She indicates that she has been essentially frozen in time for the last 4 days after her meeting with her estranged husband. Her friend has been taking care of her son while Cicily either has sat paralyzed staring aimlessly at TV or has been hysterically sobbing in bed. Finally, at the urging of her friend, she called the crisis line. Her score on the Behavioral Severity scale is 7 because clearly her daily functioning is impaired. She is immobilized and frozen. As she relates her problems, her thinking seems fairly linear, and she is able to put her story together logically. However, she has been perseverating on the crisis to the exclusion of anything else. There is a lot of wishing and hoping for things to get better and that somehow her husband will have a change of heart. She is filled with self-doubt and cannot make a decision about what to do. Her score on the Cognitive Severity scale is 8.

Overall her triage scale score is 22. This woman is clearly in crisis and may need more help than the crisis line can provide over the phone. Chris's immediate concern is with a statement Cicily made that "this was my only chance."

Ensuring Safety and Providing Support

During problem definition, the phone worker must be very specific in determining the client's lethality level. If the worker detects the potential for physical injury, then closed-ended questions that obtain information specific to the safety of the client should be asked, not only without hesitation but also with empathic understanding that clearly depicts the worker's overriding concern for and valuing of the client. These questions typically start with *do, have,* and *are,* and in phone dialogues they should be put directly and assertively to the client. (For example, one might ask, "Do you have the pills there with you now?" Or "Are you alone, or is someone there who might help you before you do it?") The phone counselor should check what support systems are available to ensure the client's safety. For many phone clients, there will be no support system—the phone counselor is the immediate and sole support system.

CW: I can really hear the hurt and fright in your voice. It's scary being all alone, seeming to have nobody to lean on. I'm concerned about your saying this was your "last chance." Do you mean by that you're thinking of suicide?

TC: (*somewhat emphatically*) I had, but I just couldn't bear to see that bastard and his new girlfriend get custody of Jimmy.

CW: OK. That's good! I needed to check that out. Now you said you were staying with an old college friend, and she asked you to call. Is that where you are now?

TC: Yes, but I hate putting her out like this. But I don't have any other place to go. (*Starts sobbing heavily again.*)

CW: But she's OK with you staying there?

TC: Yesssss. But I hate being a burden on her.

CW: But that's what friends are for. Would you do the same for her if things were reversed?

TC: Well, sure, no question.

CW: So for the time being you've got a roof over your head, something to eat, and are safe?

TC: Yes, I guess so, but I don't know how long this can go on.

CW: What we're going to do is see if we can get some stuff done that will allow you to get back on your own. OK? Are you willing to do that? (*Cicily acknowledges she'll try.*) Good! Although I can't get

your husband back, and I know that really left you feeling hopeless and all alone, I can find out about the job problem and perhaps see if we can't do something about that. So let's start with that if it's OK with you. We've got a number of referral sources here that might be able to match your skills, education, and abilities with a job. Would you be willing to tell me a little bit about yourself in that area—education, employment background, desired kind of work? I could pass that on to some of our referral sources and see what we could do. (*Chris listens while Cicily goes through her background, education, and other pieces of pertinent information, reinforcing her for staying on task, mobilizing her thoughts, and keeping her terrifying emotions in control.*)

Looking at Alternatives and Making Plans

Creating alternatives and formulating a plan are integral to one another in any crisis situation but are even more closely tied together in phone counseling. To alleviate the immediate situational threat, the phone counselor needs to jointly explore alternatives that are simple and clear-cut. Without the benefit of an eyewitness view or an in-depth background of the client, the worker needs to be cautious about proposing alternatives that may be difficult to carry out because of logistical or tactical problems of which the worker is unaware. Alternatives need to be explored in a slow, stepwise manner with checks by the worker that the client can do the physical and psychological work necessary to complete the task. Role play, verbal rehearsal, and having the client recapitulate objectives are vital ingredients of a functional plan. No plan should be accepted until the client can reassure the worker that he or she thoroughly understands the plan and has the means and ability to put it into action.

CW: OK! I've got that information. I'll pass it along to the day shift, and they'll pass it along to the JOBS Council and a couple of employment agencies that work with us. I want you to call back to our number tomorrow about 1 P.M. and we'll have some information for you. Can you do that?

TC: Well yes, I can do that. (*Cicily has calmed down and is only occasionally sniffling and lamenting her outcast state. Her triage scale score has moved down to about 15. Chris now approaches other areas of her crisis.*)

CW: I wonder what you did when you got into predicaments beforehand? Maybe there was nothing quite like this, but I'm guessing there were other times when you were overwhelmed.

TC: Well, nothing like this, but I did take care of my mother before she died, kept a job with a printing company, and worked on my degree. Sometimes that was pretty overwhelming.

CW: So what did you do to take care of being overwhelmed?

TC: I'd make a list and set down my goals of what I was going to do and what I had to do. Like Alcoholics Anonymous, one day at a time, you know. It worked pretty well, but I just have got so many things now, I don't know if I can get it all lined out.

CW: But that worked before, and I understand there are lots of things going on like never before, but if it worked then, how's about giving it a try now? (*Chris immediately seizes on her past coping technique and attempts to put it to work. He acknowledges her belief that this is indeed different than before and doesn't discount the fact that it may be tough. He methodically helps her develop a game plan for tomorrow, not the rest of her life.*) So we've got day care for Jimmy taken care of, and you don't really need the car for a while, you can get a bus or streetcar and go anywhere you need to. Even though you've only got 200 bucks cash, you could cash in that $3,000 worth of U.S. savings bonds your mother gave to Jimmy if you had to, until you got back on your feet. You could then repurchase them, so you won't feel like you're robbing your son of his inheritance. So you've written those things down that you can do tomorrow, right? So we're just managing this, like you say, one day at a time, not worrying much beyond that and doing what can be done. Do you feel like we're making progress?

TC: I guess I do. I can do those things.

Obtaining Commitment

Commitment to a plan of action generated over the phone should be simple, specific, and time limited. If at all possible, the worker should try to obtain the client's phone number and call the client back at a preset time to check on the plan or, if the agency accepts walk-in clients, the worker should try to have the person schedule an appointment as soon as possible. If the worker is linking with other agencies, then a phone call should be made to the referral agent to check whether the client has completed the

task. Although it is preferable to have the client take the initiative in contacting other agencies so that dependence on the worker is not created, conditions may block the client from doing so. In that case, the worker should have no hesitation in offering to make the call.

CW: So there are three things you're going to do tomorrow. First you're going to call the day care number I gave you and get Jimmy in there. Second, you're going to go to the bank and open an account and cash in the bonds. Third, you're going to call back here at 1 P.M. and ask for the information on the job hunt. Those places I told you about will probably want you to come down, so you'll call them and make an appointment. Will you call back tomorrow night and ask for me? I come on at 11 P.M. I know this has been a pretty upsetting deal, so could you kinda repeat that to me and write down that stuff?

TC: Yes. I've got it. (*Cicily repeats to Chris the steps he has outlined.*) And I'll call back. Thanks a lot. You're a real lifesaver.

CW: You're welcome. Now get a good night's sleep. It's a fresh day tomorrow, and you'll get through it fine with that attitude. (*Chris judges Cicily now to be at a total triage rating of about 8. Affectively she is in control of her emotions. She is thinking clearly enough to help establish a plan in a collaborative manner with the crisis worker and has committed to act on it the next day. Chris judges her to be mobilized enough that he can let her go off the line and reinforces her for getting back into equlibrium.*)

The call has taken more than an hour and a half, but in that time a woman who is in a severe developmental and situational crisis has been able to grieve away some of the lost relationship with her husband, work through her terror of being all alone and jobless in a strange city, and start to make specific plans on how she'll get out of the dilemma. She still has many issues and a long road ahead of her, but she has returned to being a functional human again. By any criterion of therapy, the crisis worker has done a good night's work!

Errors and Fallacies

For most of our students who volunteer **LO3** for crisis line duty, to say that they are scared pea green on their first shift is putting it mildly! Lamb (1973, 2002) has listed a number of irrational ideas that beginners indoctrinate themselves with as they start their careers as phone counselors. We list them here as a way to depropagandize and calm those of you who are about to start on this grand adventure.

First, you are not omnipotent! You are not there to be the instant expert. Your thoughts of "if only I were a psychiatrist, licensed social worker, counseling supercomputer, I could help this person" are doomed to failure. Nobody is an expert on everything that comes into a crisis line. There is no specific piece of information, if found, that will magically transform the caller into a paragon of good mental health.

Second, talking about "it," whatever "it" is, from suicide to getting a hair replacement, will not make "it" happen, and you will not be the instigator of causing "it" to happen. Callers are resilient and need somebody to talk honestly and openly about "it." Particularly in regard to suicide, tiptoeing around the topic generally indicates to the client that "it" is indeed scaring the daylights out of you too! If you can get an inkling of what "it" is, bring it out into the light of day, specify "it," and talk about "it."

Third, if you feel at times you are being manipulated, you probably are, and that is okay too—within limits. Understand that the caller's need to manipulate you is serving a purpose. As long as that purpose results in restoring the caller to psychological equilibrium without harming anyone, you are doing what you need to do. On the other hand, you are not a doormat to be walked over.

Fourth, all callers are not loving human beings, and you do not have to be Mother Teresa, loving and caring and sharing to all. Many people call exactly because they are *not* loving human beings! They are often overbearing, boring, nasty, insulting, hateful, and a pain in the neck! Having made that assessment, you now know why the caller is facing rejection from others and can directly speak to how his or her actions affect you and reflect on how those actions must be problematic when dealing with others.

By the same token, some callers like to gripe about the incompetence of other agencies, therapists, and significant others who have failed miserably to help them and have made their lives worse. They may be right. Agencies, therapists, and significant others are composed of human beings who get tired of being manipulated and taken advantage of. Questioning your credentials is really more of a question of "Can I really trust you? Can you understand what I am feeling?" Defending yourself and your credentials is pointless. Dr. James, licensed psychologist, licensed

professional counselor, National Certified School Counselor, licensed English teacher, licensed school administrator, licensed real estate agent (retired), licensed fisherman, and world-renowned author of crisis textbooks can't! So why should you think you can? Don't get caught up in defending yourself, but rather turn the question back on the caller: "I don't think that is really what you are concerned about, but maybe you are wondering whether you can trust me. Why not run it by me, and let's see?"

Finally, there is the delusion of fixed alternatives. The beginner believes either "If I can't think of it, there must be no answer" or "If that's all I can think of, it must be the only answer." Or, alternatively, "I'll call a consultant. Surely he or she will know." None of these is correct. When you fall under this delusion, crisis intervention is stopped dead in its tracks. Crisis intervention is one part inspiration and nine parts perspiration. You muddle through this together. Solutions are created, not found. Further, you need to understand that you can't palm this caller off on another agency just because the problem is a tough one and you are at a loss as to what to do. Calling the police department Crisis Intervention Team may be appropriate, or it may not. You need to know what other agencies can or cannot do. If you don't know, find out before you embarrass yourself.

What in the world can you do then? You can be yourself. You got into this because you thought you have some pretty good human qualities. You undoubtedly do, so use them. You are there to listen. Few beginners ever believe this, but sometimes, a lot of times in fact, listening is more than enough. You can help the caller come up with alternatives and solutions, or suggest some resources to pursue. You won't know *all* the resources available, but as time goes on you will learn more. You will also learn your own limits and can be honest in owning when you are tired, confused, lacking in knowledge, or downright irritated with the hateful way the caller is acting. You are a pretty good human being doing your best under some trying circumstances. That's it! End of omnipotence!

Regular, Severely Disturbed, and Abusive Callers

LO4

The foregoing dialogue is a textbook example of how things ought to go in telephone crisis line work. The problem is that the real world seldom functions in such neat and tidy ways. Many callers use the crisis line for reasons other than its intended use. When this happens, the overriding questions telephone workers must pose to themselves are: What is the person getting out of using the crisis line at this time, and is it helpful to the person? How is this person's use of the crisis line at this time affecting its operation (McCaskie, Ward, & Rasor, 1990)? Crisis lines should not cater to a caller's every whim, fantasy, deviant behavior, or self-indulgence.

Chronic callers can be a plague to crisis lines and devour time and energy of staff, which legitimate callers may desperately need (Peterson & Schoeller, 1991; Spittal et al., 2015). Chronic callers can also be very frustrating to telephone workers because they do not improve (McCaskie, Ward, & Rasor, 1990). These callers can pose a serious morale problem for the volunteers and staff who receive such calls, particularly when the calls become sexually explicit and the deviant fantasies of callers are directed at the crisis worker (Brockopp & Lester, 2002; Knudson, 1991; Tuttle, 1991).

A counterpoint to this negative view is the approach of the staff at the Lawrence, Kansas, Headquarters Crisis Center, who believe that "chronic" is a negative term and implies that these callers will never improve (Epstein & Carter, 1991). All behavior is purposive. If seen in that light, no matter how aberrant or weird the content of the call, it is important to remember that those who regularly use the crisis line do so for a reason—it helps them make it through the day. For these clients, it becomes part of their lifestyle and method of coping. Indeed, Spittal and associates' (2015) research on Australia's largest crisis line found that undergirding these regular callers were legitimate problems that ranged across suicidality, mental health issues, crime, child protection, and domestic violence issues all predicted being a frequent caller. Bassilios and her associates (2015) found from a large national representative survey of Australians that they had a poor clinical profile with increased risk of suicide. Repeat calls were associated with anxiety disorders, receipt of mental health care from general practitioners, and social disadvantage.

Middleton and associates (2014) reviewed research into frequent caller problems and how they were handled by a large sample of call-in centers. The composite solutions they found for responding to frequent callers included: limiting the number and duration of calls allowed, assigning a specific counselor to the calls, implementing face-to-face contact with a mental health or human services agency, initiating contact with the caller instead of waiting for callers to contact the service, providing short-term anxiety and depression treatment by telephone, and creating a specific management plan for each frequent caller.

Therefore, although the term *chronic* is often used in telephone crisis work, we believe it to be somewhat pejorative and agree with the staff at the Headquarters Crisis Center that "regular" better captures the essence of this clientele. If the caller's dynamics are reframed as lonely, isolated, and reaching out, then the response may be very different from one of mere aggravation (Brockopp & Lester, 2002). By setting limits of 10 to 20 minutes for **regular callers**, workers acknowledge their needs but also do not become controlled by the regular callers (Lester, 2002).

Understanding the Regular Caller's Agenda

Helping people in crisis is different from being nice to them. The agenda of regular callers places the crisis worker in a dilemma. Although the worker may feel ethically bound to respond to the caller, and the agency's protocol dictates that all calls must be taken, that does not mean that workers need to suffer the abuse and invective leveled at them by such callers. A very real difference exists between what callers may want and what they may need, and helping a caller is generally predicated much more on needs than on wants. Often what these regulars want is a reaffirmation that their problems are unsolvable. Thus they become dependent on the telephone worker to sustain their problem. The worker therefore needs to recognize such patterns and not support them when this blocks progress (McCaskie, Ward, & Rasor, 1990). Telephone workers do themselves and their callers a service when they show that they are not willing to be manipulated or abused and that they value their own needs as highly as they value those of the caller. Generally, if a telephone worker spends more than 15 to 20 minutes with a caller, the client's crisis becomes the worker's crisis (Knudson, 1991).

Given the foregoing admonition, the telephone worker needs to remember that the sameness of the material and the dependency these clients demonstrate day in and day out make it easy to forecast their repetitive behavior and treat them as bothersome, inept, boring, and unimportant clients. Many of these are "Yes, but . . ." callers. Although they seem highly receptive to the suggestions and plans that crisis workers make with them, in the end they find all kinds of excuses and explanations to not follow through on what they promised to do—which makes them extremely exasperating (Waters & Finn, 1995, p. 269). Regular callers may tend to be placed in a stereotypical catchall category because they represent an aggravation to the crisis line. However, the reasons these people call are diverse. Identifying specific types is at least as important as identifying the specific caller (Peterson & Schoeller, 1991). To this end, McCaskie, Ward, and Rasor (1990) have constructed brief descriptions of some of the more typical personality disorders of regular callers, their outward behavior, inner dynamics, and strategies for counseling them.

Paranoid. People with paranoia are guarded, secretive, and can be pathologically jealous. They live in logic-tight compartments, and it is difficult if not impossible to shake their persecutory beliefs. They see themselves as victims and expect deceit and trickery from everyone. The counseling focus is to stress their safety needs.

Schizoid. Those with schizophrenia have extremely restricted emotional expression and experience. They have few social relationships and feel anxious, shy, and self-conscious in social settings. They are guarded, tactless, and often alienate others. The counseling focus is to build a good sense of self-esteem through acceptance, optimism, and support.

Schizotypal. People with schizotypal behavior have feelings of inadequacy and insecurity. They have strange ideas, behaviors, and appearances. The focus of counseling is to give them reality checks and to promote self-awareness and more socially acceptable behavior in a slow-paced, supportive manner.

Narcissistic. Narcissists are grandiose, extremely self-centered, and believe they have unique problems that others cannot possibly comprehend. They see themselves as victimized by others and always need to be right. The focus of counseling is to get them to see how their behavior is seen and felt by others, while not engaging in a "no-win" debate or argument with them.

Histrionic. People with histrionic personality disorder move from crisis to crisis. They have shallow depth of character and are extremely ego-involved. They crave excitement and become quickly bored with routine and mundane tasks and events. They may behave in self-destructive ways and can be demanding and manipulative. The focus of counseling is to stress their ability to survive using resources that have been helpful to them in the past.

Obsessive–Compulsive. Those with obsessive-compulsive disorder are preoccupied by and fixate on tasks. They expend and waste vast amounts of time and energy on these endeavors. They often do not hear counselors because of futile attempts to obtain self-control over their obsessions. The focus of counseling is to establish the ability to trust others and the use of thought stopping and behavior modification to diminish obsessive thinking and compulsive behavior.

Bipolar (Manic Depressive). The extreme mood swings of these callers range from "superman/superwoman" ideation when in a manic phase to "born loser" ideation in a depressive stage. If they feel thwarted in their grand plans, they may become very aggressive to those who would stop them. At the other end of the continuum, their depressive "doom, despair, and agony on me" outlook puts them at risk for suicidal behavior. Slowing down and pacing these callers in the manic phase is difficult but needs to be done to put a psychological governor on their runaway behavior. Confrontation about their grandiose plans only alienates them. In the depressive stage, suicide intervention is a primary priority.

Dependent. People with dependent personality disorder have trouble making decisions and seek to have others do so—often inappropriately. Feelings of worthlessness, insecurity, and fear of abandonment predominate. They are particularly prone to become involved and stay in self-destructive relationships. The focus of counseling is to reinforce strengths and act as a support for their concerns without becoming critical of them or accepting responsibility for their lives.

Self–Defeating. Those with self-defeating behavior choose people and situations that lead to disappointment, failure, and mistreatment by others. They reject attempts to help them and make sure that such attempts will not succeed. The focus of counseling is stressing talents and the behavioral consequences of sabotaging themselves.

Avoidant. People with avoidant personality disorder are loners who have little ability to establish or maintain social relationships. Their fear of rejection paralyzes their attempts to risk involvement in social relationships. The focus of counseling is encouragement of successive approximations to meaningful relationships through social skills and assertion training.

Passive–Aggressive. Those with passive-aggressive behavior cannot risk rejection by displaying anger in an overt manner. Rather, they engage in covert attempts to manipulate others and believe that control is more important than self-improvement. The focus of counseling is to promote more open, assertive behavior.

Borderline. Borderline personality disorder is so named because such people are chameleon-like and at any given time may resemble any of the foregoing mental disorders. Also, they are always on the "borderline" of being functional and dysfunctional. One of the most problematic of callers, they are dealt with at length in Chapter 5.

Handling the Severely Disturbed Caller

"The behavior of the severely disturbed is **LO5** primitive, disorganized, disoriented, and disabling. These people are likely to elicit discomfort, anxiety, and outright fear in the observer. These are strange people. These are different people. These are people we lock away in mental institutions, pumping them full of strong drugs that turn the mania into docileness" (Greenwald, 1985b). This stereotypical public view of the mentally disturbed, quoted in the University of Illinois at Chicago's Counseling Center hotline training manual, introduces hotline workers to the mentally disturbed. These are many of the people who call crisis hotlines. On the neophyte phone counselor's first meeting with the disorganized and disjunctive thought processes of the mentally disturbed, all the training the crisis worker has ever received is likely to fall by the wayside.

These callers represent a cornucopia of mental illnesses. They may be delusional and hallucinatory; be unable to remotely test what they are doing, believing, or thinking against reality; be emotionally volcanic or conversely demonstrate the emotionality of a stone; lack insight or judgment about their problems and be unable to relate any linear or logical history of these problems; be so suspicious in their paranoid ideation that they believe even the phone worker is out to get them; be manipulative, resistant,

and openly hostile and noncompliant to the simplest requests; not have the slightest idea of appropriate interpersonal boundaries with significant others or the crisis worker; demonstrate obsessive behavior and compulsive thoughts that they continually harp on to the exclusion of any effective functioning; have no meaningful interpersonal relationships with the possible exception of crisis line workers; impulsively place themselves in problematic and dangerous situations over and over; and present themselves in childlike or even infantile ways (Grunsted, Cisneros, & Belen, 1991). Whether these behaviors are biochemically or psychologically based makes little difference. These people are so distanced from our own reality and so threatening that the beginning phone counselor's immediate reaction is to get off the line! However, if the worker pictures the disturbed client as a person whose developmental processes have gone terribly awry, then the call may take on structure and sense and become less intimidating. No matter how bizarre the call may be, these primary axioms apply to the caller's behavior (Greenwald, 1985a, p. 1):

1. Behavior is always purposeful and serves motives that may be either conscious or unconscious.
2. Behavior is comprehensible and has meaning even though the language used may not.
3. Behavior is characteristic and consistent with personality even though it is exaggerated.
4. Behavior is used to keep a person safe and free of anxiety.

The following rules for dealing with disturbed callers are abstracted from a number of crisis hotlines (Epstein & Carter, 1991; Greenwald, 1985a, 1985b; Knudson, 1991; Lester & Brockopp, 1973; Tuttle, 1991).

Slow Emotions Down. Although disturbed callers have many feelings that have been submerged from awareness, it is not the best strategy to attempt to uncover these feelings. The caller is being besieged by too many feelings and needs to find a way to get them in control. Focusing on here-and-now issues that are concrete and reality oriented is the preferred mode of operation. Do not elicit more feelings with open-ended questions such as "Can you tell me more about that?" Instead, use calming interventions that force the person to order thinking in small, realistic bits of detail.

CW: I understand how scary those thoughts are that keep creeping into your mind and the "things" you think are in the room. What I want you to do right now is look around the room and tell me what is there. Then tell me what happened to start this thinking.

The idea is to slow emotions down. Although the worker may acknowledge the feelings, they are not the focus of attention. By breaking up freewheeling ideation into discrete, manageable pieces, the telephone worker gives the caller a sense of regaining control. The worker may also bring the caller back to reality from a flashback by asking the client what he or she is doing.

CW: You say you're in that alley and he's assaulting you. Were you smoking a cigarette then? I know you just lit a cigarette a minute ago. I want you to slowly inhale, smell that smoke, and tell me where you are. Now blow the smoke out and see where it goes around the room.

Refuse to Share Hallucinations and Delusions.
If a caller is hallucinating or delusional, the telephone worker should never side with the psychotic ideation.

Caller: Do you see, hear, smell, feel those things?

CW: No! I'm sorry, I don't. I understand right now you do, and that's terrifying, but what I want to do is get you some help. So stay with me. What is your address so we can get some support for you?

Little if any good ever comes of participating in such thinking, and as the delusion increases, it becomes difficult to extricate oneself from it. Yet grandiose thinking, no matter how bizarre, should not be denied.

CW: (*inappropriate and sarcastic*) Come on, now. The CIA isn't really listening to an auto mechanic by electronic eavesdropping. Certainly they've got better things to do than that. Why do you believe that?

CW: (*appropriate and empathic*) It's pretty clear that you really believe the CIA is listening to you. When did this start?

The worker affirms the paranoid delusion is real without agreeing to its veracity. By asking a *when* question, the worker can start eliciting information that will allow assessment of the scope and extent of the paranoia. A *why* question is never appropriate because of the defensive reaction it may elicit in any caller, especially a paranoid.

Determine Medication Usage.
If at all possible, the worker should elicit information as to use of any medication, amount and time of dosage, and particularly, stopping medication without consulting the attending physician. Changing, forgetting, or disregarding medication is one of the most common reasons that people become actively psychotic (Ammar & Burdin, 1991). Furthermore, having this information will give the worker a better idea of the type of mental disturbance the caller is being treated for. Regardless of the reasons or excuses clients give for not taking medicine, the worker should endeavor to get them to their prescribing physician so medication can be adjusted or reinstituted.

CW: Lemuel, I want you to call up your doctor as soon as we get off the phone. I understand that the medicine gives you a bad taste in your mouth and makes you feel queasy. However, your doctor needs to know that, and you need to let her know you're not on your meds.

Becoming familiar with the major tranquilizers, antidepressants, and antipsychotic drugs is important for this work (Pope, 1991). However, given all the different kinds of drugs and their numerous generic and trade names, keeping track of them all is extremely difficult. The *Physician's Desk Reference (PDR)* provides information on what these drugs do, how much is generally given, and what the side effects are. No crisis line office should be without a current edition.

Keep Expectations Realistic.
The telephone worker should keep expectations realistic. The caller did not become disturbed overnight. No crisis worker is going to change chronic psychotic behavior during one phone call. The crisis worker is buying time for the caller in a period of high anxiety and attempting to restore a minimum amount of control and contact with reality. If the caller is trying to "milk" the worker through an interminable conversation, confronting the problem in a direct manner will generally determine whether the caller is lonely or is in need of immediate assistance.

CW: It seems as if this can't be solved, and you say you can't wait until tomorrow to go to the clinic. I'm concerned enough that I think we ought to make arrangements to transport you to the hospital right now.

Maintain Professional Distance.
Calls from severely disturbed individuals may evoke all kinds of

threatening feelings in phone workers, leaving them feeling inadequate, confused, and in crisis themselves! Maintaining professional distance when exceedingly painful and tragic stories are related is difficult for even the most experienced phone worker. When these feelings begin to emerge, it is of utmost importance for workers to make owning statements about their own feelings and get supervision immediately. Passing the line to another worker in no way indicates inadequacy.

CW: Frankly, I'm a bit confused as to what to do. I've done everything I know, and I'm tapped out. I'd like to connect you with Irma, who may have some other ideas, while I talk to our director.

As confused and disoriented as disturbed callers may be, they seem to have a sixth sense about sensitive areas in others. **Countertransference** (the attributing to clients of the therapist's own problems) is not uncommon, and disturbed callers can sometimes unearth the worker's own hidden agendas and insecurities. A worker's strong reactions, either positive or negative, to these callers should alert the hotline worker that processing and feedback with a coworker or supervisor are needed.

Caller: (*paranoid*) I know who you are, when you work on the hotline, and where you live.

CW: (*inappropriately responding to the threat in a shaky voice*) What have I ever done to you? I'm trying to help you, and you get bent out of shape. I've got a good mind to hang this phone up right now or even call the police. We can trace these calls, you know!

CW: (*appropriately responding to the implication in a clear, firm, but empathic voice*) Jacques, those things are not important to what's going on with you right now. What is important is making you feel safe enough to go back to your apartment tonight and go to the doctor in the morning. I understand why you might get upset over my suggesting you see the doctor, but I also want you to clearly understand it's your safety I'm concerned about. So what's making you angry with me?

By deflecting the caller's paranoia and refocusing the dialogue back on the client's issues, the telephone worker directively forces the caller, in an empathic manner, to respond to his own emotional state.

Avoid Placating. Placating and sympathizing do little to bolster the caller's confidence or to help move the client toward action.

Caller: (*depressed*) I'm just not any good to anybody, much less myself.

CW: (*inappropriately sympathetic*) From all you've told me, you've had a really rocky road. Nobody should have to suffer what you have, but things can only look up.

Rather, by empathically responding and exploring past feelings and coping skills when life was better, the telephone worker not only acknowledges the dilemma but also focuses on the client's strengths.

CW: You do sound pretty hopeless right now, but I wonder how you were feeling when things weren't this way, and what you were doing then that you aren't doing now.

Assess Lethality. Many clients who call crisis lines have active suicidal or homicidal ideation. It may seem puzzling that such people would call a crisis line when they seem so bent on harming themselves or others. Regular callers in particular should be assessed for suicidal or homicidal ideation because they are very prone to underscore the critical nature of their problems and "prove" their need for help by threatening lethal behavior (Brockopp, 2002a). What all suicidal callers are doing is trying to put distance between their thoughts and the actions that might result from those lethal thoughts. As much as the callers may avow intentions of lethality, they are still in enough control of themselves to attempt to place a buffer (the telephone worker) between thinking and acting (McCaskie, Ward, & Rasor, 1990).

Caller: If I can't have him, she sure as hell won't. I'll kill them both, and you, the police, or nobody else can stop me.

CW: Yet you called here, for which I'm glad. Something is holding you back, and I'd like to know what that something is.

Caller: Well, I'm a Christian, but their sins go beyond redemption.

CW: So as a Christian, you probably think the commandment "Thou shalt not kill" is pretty important. What you're saying is you're about to commit sin, just as they did. How will that help you, and how will it look in the eyes of God?

Although it may be construed that the telephone worker is manipulating the spiritual philosophy of the caller to achieve an end, the major goal of the crisis worker is to disrupt the irrational chain of thinking that is propelling the client toward violence. In that regard, when dealing with the disturbed caller, the overriding thesis is "Save the body before the mind" (Grunsted, Cisneros, & Belen, 1991). Crisis intervention over the telephone with those who are severely disturbed is clearly not meant to be curative. It is a stopgap measure designed to be palliative enough to keep action in abeyance until help arrives.

Although no crisis line staff members that we know of would ever instruct their workers to give out their full names or home phone numbers, at times callers can be very seductive in their attempts to extract personal information from crisis line workers. Rookies on the crisis line may be very taken with the heartbreaking stories they hear or feel very gratified by the strokes that dependent callers can give them. Under no circumstances should a crisis line worker ever give out his or her full name or other personal information, nor should the worker ever agree to meet the caller for social or professional reasons. The crisis line's credibility is built on anonymity, and that works both ways. In addition, serious ethical problems may arise when that anonymity is breached. Finally, crisis line workers who do not observe the foregoing run the risk of putting themselves in physical harm's way.

Given all that we have said about severely disturbed callers, our admonition is still to treat these clients not as types, but as individuals with their own idiosyncratic problems. However, those who are severely disturbed are not the only regular or problem callers.

Other Problem Callers

Telephone crisis workers must sometimes deal with covert callers, pranksters, silent callers, manipulators, sexually explicit callers, or even callers presenting legitimate sexual problems. It must be remembered and accepted that every call is an attempt by the caller to fulfill some need or purpose. Following are several types of problem callers and suggestions that should help workers understand and cope with such callers.

Rappers. Some callers may just wish to "rap," or talk. The question becomes whether time should be spent listening to someone who only wants to talk, with no seemingly pressing issues. However, if "lonely" is tacked onto the description of the person, this may change the telephone worker's perception of the problem. It may also be that the caller is having trouble bringing issues into the open and is testing the waters to get enough courage to jump in. By allowing

some leeway in approaching issues, but at the same time gently confronting the caller's loneliness, the worker sets reasonable limits on the conversation and still provides a supportive forum (McCaskie, Ward, & Rasor, 1990).

Covert Callers. Callers who ask for help for another individual may actually be asking for help for themselves. As a result, always assume that the call is about the caller, but never attempt to prove the call is about someone else (Brockopp, 1973a, p. 164; Brockopp, 2002a, pp. 171–175). Other callers may act surprised, "Oh, I thought this was a recording." The response is to affirm that it is not. "No it isn't. I am Joe, and this is the crisis line. How can I help you this evening?" Yet others may make humorous jests as a test. "You must be really crazy to work there. I'll bet there are some real nuts who call up." The response to these calls is to avoid the "test" and respond empathically by saying, "I wonder if you're concerned that calls are handled seriously here?" These are most likely ways that timid and embarrassed callers have of checking out the crisis line to see what the opening response is and whether it is safe to talk. Intellectual types, on the other hand, tend to be know-it-alls who probably do have more expertise than volunteers. On their own intellectual ground they always "win." In actuality, these callers are often very insecure and unsure of themselves under their self-assured exterior. The key to dealing with intellectualizers is to immediately let them defeat you. "You're right. I am a volunteer here, and I don't know as much as you do about bipolar disorder. What I do know is you sound pretty concerned about it and seem to be looking for some help." Other callers may call and be silent or say they have the wrong number. Particularly at a suicide center, there are no wrong numbers. "May I help you?" or "What number were you calling?" are default responses to "wrong numbers."

Pranksters or Nuisance Callers. Teenagers who are bored at an overnight party may call the line just to bedevil the workers. If the prank call is treated seriously, they will probably hang up and not call back. If they are hung up on, they will continue to call (Brockopp, 1973b; Waters & Finn, 1995, p. 270). Many calls may appear to be of a nuisance nature. However, any person making a nuisance call should be considered to have a problem. Therefore, it is important that calls not be arbitrarily seen as pranks. The crisis line must answer all calls in a straightforward, no-nonsense manner. The crisis line must clearly convey that they are not playing games with people but that callers will be listened to honestly and responded to directly no matter what the purpose (Brockopp, 1973b, pp. 206–210). By so doing, the crisis line builds the perception in the community that the line is serious about what they do (Brockopp, 2002a, pp. 187–190). The teenager who is a prankster one night may be the suicidal teenager another night.

CW: Is it a prank or a dare you're playing or maybe something else that you really do need to talk about?

CW: I do wonder if there is something you might like to talk about. If you do, feel free to call back.

Silent Callers. One of the most frustrating of callers is the person who is silent. Silent callers are ambivalent. Either through embarrassment or hurt they are reticent, or from previous negative experiences they fear rejection and are just plain unable to muster the courage to talk. The worker must overcome his or her initial reaction to hang up, demonstrate acceptance, and attempt to remove any impediment that may keep the person from communicating (Brockopp, 2002b). For the silent caller, an appropriate response would be, "I'll be here when you feel you can talk."

CW: Sometimes it is really difficult to say what you need. Maybe it hurts so much you can't find words. Maybe you are not sure you can trust me. Whatever the reason you feel unable to talk, I am going to wait a little bit before I take another call. Even if you can't talk now, understand that this line is open for you when you need to talk.

If there is still no response, after a minute or so you could say, "I guess it is difficult to talk about this right now. I'll stay on the line for another minute, and then I'll have to go to another call. Call back when you feel ready to talk."

Manipulators. A variety of callers achieve their unmet needs by playing games with telephone workers. Typical manipulative games include questioning the worker's ability, role reversal in which the worker is tricked into sharing details of his or her personal life, and harassment. Redirecting the manipulative ploy and focusing on the unmet needs of manipulators force them to look at the reasons for their manipulative behavior (Brockopp, 2002a, p. 174; Waters & Finn, 1995, p. 269).

CW: You certainly know a great deal more about that subject than I do. How does it feel to be in control like that?

CW: When you question my integrity or try to get me to share intimate details, I wonder if you realize that is trying to meet some of your own needs for control. I wonder if you have considered what those needs to control and manipulate others are getting you.

Sexually Explicit Callers. "Call 1-900-LUST. Cindy's lonely and wants to talk to you!" The proliferation of these ads on late-night television, the Internet, and in porn magazines is a sad testimony to the existence of tens of thousands of men whose sexual insecurities, aberrance, and deviance make "sex talk" a multibillion-dollar business. An even sadder testimony is given by those individuals who use crisis lines for the same purpose. It should not be too amazing that Wark's (1984) interviews with a number of sexually explicit callers found them to be characterized by low self-esteem, feelings of isolation, lack of trust, a sense of being sexually unfulfilled, and little insight into their behavior. The primary purpose of the sexually explicit caller is to masturbate while talking to a female.

The sexually explicit caller is a particular millstone hung on the crisis line because many female volunteers become angry, embarrassed, and afraid and resign out of frustration with frequent sex calls (Baird, Bossett, & Smith, 1994; Brockopp & Lester, 2002, pp. 133–135; Fenelon, 1990). Brockopp and Lester (2002, p. 136) propose staying on the line and tolerating the behavior while attempting to build a more trusting relationship without condoning the behavior itself. That is a very idealistic way of treating the problem, and in the opinion of your authors is a great way to lose a lot of volunteers in a hurry! We will take a stand here and state that the crisis line is just not the place for that behavior to occur. Switching the caller to a same-sex worker and reframing the call in a context suggesting that the caller needs help put a severe damper on such calls.

Callers With Legitimate Sexual Problems. However, many people who have serious sexual or sexually related problems call crisis lines because of the anonymity allowed to frankly discuss their most private issues. These calls may embarrass workers who are not psychologically prepared for such intimate details, feel shocked at what they hear because of the criminal or exploitative nature, or do not have the technical expertise to handle them. Telephone workers must have education in dealing with sexual concerns and training in legal and ethical knowledge about what to do if the caller is a danger to a third party (Horton, 1995, p. 292). The very nature of calls dealing with sexual matters places crisis workers in a potentially value-laden, belief-centered moral and religious arena in which the worker's own opinions come into play. Although in most instances the major role of the worker is to *not* let his or her opinions hold sway and influence clients, avoiding these hot areas may also mean denying the caller much-needed information (Horton, 1995, p. 307). Providing options and information about "responsible" sex is a viable approach, although it should be understood that a very fine line runs between the worker's own biases and providing balanced information and must be monitored carefully.

Even though the preceding types of callers are striving to fulfill their needs, they often pose problems for telephone workers. Following are some techniques to help prepare crisis workers to deal with this sometimes difficult clientele.

Handling the Problem Callers

Pose Open-Ended Questions. Appropriate use of open-ended questions can help defuse the problems generated by frustrated callers (Epstein & Carter, 1991).

TC: You people don't know anything. Everything you've told me is a bunch of crap.

CW: What did you expect to gain from this call, then?

TC: Just to tell you what I think of your lousy service.

CW: If you were me, what would you be doing or saying right now?

These questions refocus the problem back to the caller and force movement toward problem solving rather than keeping the worker subjected to condemnatory statements.

Set Time Limits. When it is apparent that attempts to refocus the problem to the caller are futile, then a time limit should be set (Knudson, 1991).

TC: You ought to be congratulating me on getting my act together, no thanks to you.

CW: I'm glad you've done something positive since you last called. Now we can talk about your

current situation for 5 minutes. Then I'll have to take another call.

Terminate Abuse. When the caller's behavior escalates to what the worker perceives as abusiveness, the call should be terminated in a clear and firm manner (McCaskie, Ward, & Rasor, 1990).

TC: You bitch! Don't you dare hang up this goddamned phone!

CW: (*assertively*) I'm sorry, but that is language we do not tolerate, so I'm going to another caller now. When you can talk appropriately, feel free to call back.

Switch Workers. Particularly with a sexually explicit caller, switching the call to another worker, preferably a male, takes the stimulus thrill out of the situation and makes it very difficult for the caller to bring masturbation to orgasm, which is usually the end goal of such a call (Knudson, 1991).

TC: I'd love to cover you with honey and lick you all over.

CW (female): (*calmly and coolly*) Given your specific problem, I'm going to switch you to Ralph. *(Signals to Ralph.)*

CW (Ralph): (*assertively*) I understand you have a problem. How can I help you?

If a male is not available, the call should be shifted to a supervisor and terminated. The caller should be told that the worker will hang up and that action should be taken immediately (McCaskie, Ward, & Rasor, 1990).

CW (supervisor): (*authoritatively and firmly*) We are *not* here to answer demeaning remarks while you masturbate. You need to know that our calls are taped, and obscene calls and using this service to masturbate are illegal. I am going to hang up. You may call back when you are ready to discuss this problem.

To bait a telephone worker and hold her on the line, sexually explicit callers often externalize their fantasies by reporting some hypothetical significant other's problem in florid detail. When the first hint of this ploy occurs, the worker should interpret the behavior as the caller's own and make the switch (Knudson, 1991).

TC: I'm really worried about my uncle and his 10-year-old daughter. She's a little doll, and he's always giving her these massages in her bedroom and I . . .

CW: (*Interrupts.*) That's out of my area of expertise; please hold the line and let me switch you to our child abuse expert, Ralph.

Use Covert Modeling. Covert modeling or conditioning (Cautela, 1976; Kazdin, 1975) has been used by Baird, Bossett, and Smith (1994) to extinguish repeated calls, particularly by sexually explicit clients. In covert modeling, the client is asked to use mental imagery to picture either reinforcing or extinguishing a particular behavior. The following worker response is abridged from their technique.

CW: As you're talking, I'm wondering if you recognize your real problem and want help with it. I know this would be pretty difficult to give up. But sometime soon, I'm not sure exactly when, as you reach for the phone you'll think to call a therapist instead. And this notion that you'll call a therapist and get help will get stronger every day as you think of it. You'll also start to feel better as you realize the crisis line isn't fulfilling your needs as therapy will. I'm going to hang up now and let you think about getting help with your real problem.

By suggesting that the need to call the therapist will grow, the worker plants the seed for anxiety about the caller's present behavior to grow along with the need to change. Both negative and positive reinforcers are used in the image: the need to seek help and the good feeling that will come from doing so. The worker also speaks of seeking help for the "real problem." This unspecified problem allows the worker to respond emphatically without accusing the caller of terrible, deviant behavior but still clearly states that the caller needs help. The worker does not continue in a dialogue with the client but instead hangs up to let the seed start to grow.

Formulate Administrative Rules. Administra **LO6** tively, crisis lines need to set specific rules to extinguish abusive behavior by doing the following (Knudson, 1991; McCaskie, Ward, & Rasor, 1990; Middleton, Gunn, Bassilios, & Pirkis, 2014):

1. Limiting the number and duration of calls from any single caller
2. Limiting the topics that will be discussed
3. Requiring that only specific workers versed in handling abusive callers take such calls

4. Using speaker phones for on-the-spot consultation
5. Requiring the caller to establish a face-to-face relationship with an outside worker and allow communication between the therapist and crisis line personnel
6. Allowing the staff to prohibit calls for a day, a week, or more, if physical threats are made
7. Service initiating contact with the caller instead of waiting for caller contact and coordinating short-term treatment programs for anxiety and depression by telephone
8. Creating a specific management plan for each caller

The Headquarters Crisis Center of Lawrence, Kansas, uses a tracking log for regular callers that lists their name, phone number, address, style of interaction, major and tangential issues, effective and ineffective response modes, their physician/therapist, medications, support groups, and lethality levels. The log is kept current and available to staff, saving them a great deal of time and energy. This center also has an internal messages notebook labeled "Client Concerns." It contains information about regular callers that workers can quickly read to become updated on the caller's circumstances. It is an effective method to keep staff current and can be used to offer feedback and suggestions to clients (Epstein & Carter, 1991). Staff should be brought together on a regular basis to discuss these callers, plan strategy for them, make suggestions, and voice personal concerns (McCaskie, Ward, & Rasor, 1990). Finally, supervisors need to be acutely aware of the impact that such callers can have on personnel. Crisis center administrators should be ready, willing, and able to process debilitating emotions that such calls often evoke in workers in a caring, empathic, and supportive manner through regularly planned supervision and emergency debriefing sessions when necessary. Crisis intervention over the telephone is tough, grueling work, particularly when clients such as the foregoing emerge. Crisis calls are frequently onetime events with very little opportunity for positive feedback. Particularly because crisis lines are run chiefly by volunteers, they need to be aware that not everyone can be helped (Waters & Finn, 1995, p. 271).

Hotlines

As noted in Chapter 1, the first telephone cri- **LO7** sis hotline was established in 1906 by the National Save-a-Life League to prevent suicide (Bloom, 1984). Indeed, the growing suicide prevention movement in the 1950s adopted the telephone as the primary mode of treatment because of its immediacy (Lester & Brockopp, 1973, p. 5), and over the course of time has been the most often used method of suicide intervention (Lester, 2001; Mishara et al., 2005; National Suicide Prevention Lifeline, 2011; SAMSHA, 2014; Seely, 1997a, 1997b; Slaikeu & Leff-Simon, 1990) with dedicated suicide hotlines in many countries, states, provinces, and cities.

Indeed, in the United States, because of the increase in veterans' suicides a suicide hotline 1-800-TALK was established in 2007 to meet the unique needs of veterans (King et al., 2014; Tull, 2013). Most veterans' calls can be generally categorized as mental health issues, suicidal ideation, and substance abuse issues. Research indicates that all age ranges of veterans avail themselves of the hotline, but for very different reasons. The middle age and older veterans called with issues that were based in loneliness while younger veterans focused on mental health issues (King et al., 2014). Britton and his associates (2013) examined incoming calls for 1 week (October 1–7, 2010, N = 665 calls) found that the veterans hotline was highly effective in 84% of the calls received with 25% being resolved on the phone and 59% referrals to a local health care provider. Probably more impressive was the finding that callers identified as high risk for suicide had greater odds of ending in referral than not. Even more importantly those favorable odds were found on the weekends when essentially few if any other mental health resources were readily available.

It is with good reason there are telephones with direct hotlines to crisis intervention call centers placed on bridges and one of the most notorious jump sites, the San Francisco Golden Gate Bridge (Jacobs, 2010). Since its start in 2005, the National Suicide Prevention life line has fielded over 6 million calls (SAMSHA, 2014).

However, suicidal individuals are not the only callers. The tremendous growth of "hotlines" and "warmlines" in number, types of assistance, kinds of problems handled, and geographical coverage attests to the fact that people in crisis avail themselves of telephones to solve a wide variety of personal problems. These services may range from generic crisis hotlines to a variety of specialized services such as local "warmlines" for latchkey children to the National Centers for Disease Control AIDS Hotline. Generic crisis phone lines are typically open 24 hours a day, 365 days a year, whereas more specialized services may operate during regular business hours. People who are lonely, have panic attacks, gamble and drink to excess, abuse relationships, grieve, are depressed, suffer psychotic breaks, or experience a whole smorgasbord of crises that could qualify for Ripley's "Believe It or Not" call crisis lines. There is indeed a specific helpline for current and former NFL players, coaches, team league staff, and their family members who may be in crisis (NFL lifeline, 2012).

Time-Limited Hotlines. A time-limited hotline is one that is put into operation for a specified period of time; it is typically used to deal with a specific problem or to engage a special client population, such as immediately before a potential disaster or after a disaster. It may provide brief supportive therapy or serve as an information or referral source.

A particular use of such a hotline was in the wake of 9/11. The New York City Missing Persons Hotline was created to develop a database of missing persons and provide crisis counseling and information services. Counselors were given updated daily resource lists to provide information on everything from practical issues about returning to apartments to air toxicity levels. Lists of hospital admissions were compiled to cross-check against missing persons lists, enabling workers to call back to relatives inquiring about missing persons. However, the primary purpose of the hotline was to help grieving, scared, anxious people work through the trauma. To that end, workers used what would generally be the first four tasks of the model presented in Chapter 3 to provide psychological first aid to the callers.

Continuous National Hotlines. Specialized, toll-free, national hotlines deal with specific topics, such as troubled youth. Although brief supportive therapy may occur on such hotlines, generally the major purpose is to provide information about the geographic location nearest the caller where help can be obtained. These lines are heavily used and cut across all geographic areas, cultural groups, and socioeconomic classes. The national runaway hotline (1-800-RUNAWAY) not only spends time talking to runaways about their problems, but also encourages them to get off the streets and into the nearest runaway shelter (National Runaway Safeline, 2015). The national domestic violence hotline (1-800-SAFE) is available to any victim of domestic abuse in the United States (National Domestic Violence Hotline, 2015). These are a few of the national call centers that specialize in every kind of imaginable human dilemma.

Local Crisis Hotlines. Local crisis hotlines typically handle all kinds of calls, ranging from suicidal ideation to lost cats (some calls are not as life threatening as others). They are staffed by volunteers from the local community, are listed in the yellow pages, and provide telephone crisis intervention services for a specific geographic locale or a specific population, such as a university student body.

The Internet's Growing Role in Crisis Intervention

Suppose you are a cost-conscious student [LO8] and found a cheap first edition of this book from 1988, you now would be finished reading this chapter because what follows didn't exist then. Hard to imagine for all of you 20-somethings because the Internet has always been a part of who you are and what you do to communicate with others. Winston Churchill said, "Take change by the hand, because if you don't it will take you by the throat!" Since the advent of the Internet and websites, there has never been any doubt that there would be counseling services on the "net." However, the computer is not only a communication device; it can also function as a simulation device (Wolf, 2003). Both of these applications have great potential for psychotherapy and crisis intervention. So far, however, most professional therapists do not use computer-assisted counseling or provide online therapy. Various reasons are given, including ethical concerns, commitment to humanistic values that conflict with technology, cost, and the absence of training (Hertlein, Blumer, & Mihaloliakos, 2015; Lawlor-Savage & Prentice, 2014). Yet, if one reads current writing on the use of technology in counseling (Adlington, 2009; Anthony & Nagel, 2010; Cicila, Georgia, & Doss, 2014; Jones & Stokes, 2009; Rose 2014; Parikh & Huniewicz, 2015), it should be patently clear that the Internet and various forms of electronic communication have become and will become more important in the delivery of psychotherapy and particularly crisis intervention.

Although therapists have been slow to adopt this mode of intervention, most consumers have not been—particularly young consumers who are not at all intimidated by the Internet (Calam et al., 2000) and see it as an integral part of their lives. Why is this so? Haim Weinberg (2014) has written a very interesting book called *The Paradox of Internet Groups: Alone in the Presence of Virtual Others*. This book explores the multiple paradoxes of being involved in Internet groups. Weinberg states that on the one hand people in their bedrooms are far removed and detached and untouched by what is going on in the group, but on the other they are involved, invested, and perhaps even enmeshed in the group. So does one really care about people thousands of miles away or is it merely curiosity? While these paradoxes exist, they allow users a great deal of freedom to say when they want to be involved and feel an integral and contributing member to the World Wide Web, but still decide how much they wish to self-disclose, keep self-boundaries, and preserve their own individuality. Thus, while face-to-face encounters with others are usually either/or in nature, online connections with others can be "both," and that is what makes the social medium of the Internet group so attractive according to Weinberg.

Palfrey and Gasser (2009) identify anyone born after 1980 as a "digital native." Digital natives have access to digital technology networks, use them, and have never known any other way of life—as opposed to "digital settlers," who use digital technology but still rely heavily on analog forms of communication (which would characterize the authors of this book). So about how many natives and settlers are out there, and are they restless? In 2010, 8 out of 10 Americans used the Internet to find out health information about themselves and 9 out of those 10 worried so much about it they kept digging down until they found out what was TRULY wrong with them and have helped coin a new phobia called **cyberchondria** (Moyer, 2012).

So people are worried about their health and by the appearance of how many hits and chat rooms there are that are devoted to mental health they number in the many millions (Number of "cyberchondriacs," 2005). Right now on June 1, 2015, at 5:15 P.M. CST on Healthful Chat's website there are 241 people chatting about anxiety, bipolar, body dysmorphic, depression, eating, gender identity, OCD and PTSD disorders (Healthful Chat, 2015). People log into chat rooms for support groups by the millions to discuss mental health issues, and chat rooms are only one part of what has come to be known as "behavioral telehealth."

Behavioral Telehealth

Behavioral telehealth is the use of telecommunication and information technology to provide access to behavioral health assessment, intervention, consultation, supervision, education, and information across distance (Nickelson, 1998); it can include e-mail, chat rooms, blogging, apps, websites, games, and Internet video teleconferencing (Dowling & Rickwood, 2014; Novotney, 2014). In some shape or form, all of the foregoing are already being done (Anthony & Nagel, 2010; Deleon, Crimmins, & Wolf, 2003; Ho et al., 2014; Kass et al., 2014; Jones & Stokes, 2009; Marsac et al., 2015; Misurell et al., 2014; Novotney, 2014). Crisis intervention on the web can operate in an asynchronous (time-delayed, such as e-mail, blogging, and websites) or a synchronous (real-time, such as chat rooms, videoconferencing, Skype, and instant messaging) format. The relevant questions, then, are "How can we ethically and effectively do crisis intervention on the Internet?" and "What crisis intervention services can be ethically and effectively provided on the Internet?" (Ruiz & Lipford-Sanders, 1999, p. 12).

Websites that provide opportunities for net "surfers" to seek emergency help or advice, counseling, or psychological help continue to grow exponentially. Befrienders International is a component of the Samaritans in Cheltenham, England. This group provides an excellent example of a website that offers help to suicidal individuals and other people in crisis. This group has been in the business of helping people for more than 40 years via letter, telephone, and in-person visits. E-mail sent to the Samaritans remains anonymous if the sender desires. Responses are asynchronous but trained volunteers read and reply to e-mail once a day, every day of the year. There are 20 centers around the world, and a trained volunteer with the universal counselor name "Jo" reads all e-mails and answers them within 24 hours (Hurtig, Bulitt, & Kates, 2011; Wilson & Lester, 2002). Their address is jo@samaritans.org. However, many telephone hotlines are also Internet capable and are synchronous. For example, the National Runaway switchboard operates a synchronous live chat room that can be reached at www.1800runaway.org/.

The Appeal of Online Counseling

Clearly, the Internet, websites, e-mail, and other technological, wireless, and online electronic advances are much like the telephone in having the potential to provide a great deal of help to people who are geographically or psychologically isolated from specialized crisis services; are suffering physical or mental disabilities that do not permit them to travel to those services; are shy and do not want to meet face to face; need anonymity; have time management problems; are unavailable during normal working hours; or find it convenient, cost effective, or simply natural to their way of life (Anthony & Nagel, 2010, p. 35; Harris-Bowlsby, 2000; James & Gilliland, 2003, pp. 416–433; Jones & Stokes, 2009, pp. 2–5).

Feedback. When it comes to direct therapeutic intervention, not all aspects of online conversation may be seen as better than face to face, but there are many aspects of it that are. In crisis intervention, continuous and immediate feedback is critical, and synchronous Internet applications can serve this function well. Once the client has regained emotional equilibrium, the therapist can use asynchronous e-mail to check on how well the client is maintaining homeostasis. Feedback several times an hour, day, or week lets the client know the interventionist is present, listening, and thinking about the client. Clients can initiate contact when they feel the greatest need. Regular and frequent e-mail reports require the client to constantly monitor and report behavior, which is critical in crisis intervention (Castelnuovo et al., 2003). However, as the interventionist, would you really want to sit at your computer all day long, doing instant messaging, or perhaps text message on your cell phone while eating in a restaurant? Of course, if you could turn your counseling computer on and let "HAL" do the counseling, you would have ample free time (James & Gilliland, 2003, pp. 420–428).

Disinhibition. A phenomenon that Suler (2004) named the **disinhibition effect** has appeared in e-therapy. What this effect means is that people tend to open up earlier with more distressing issues then they would normally do in an F2F (net acronym for face-to-face) therapy session. It is not clear why this effect happens, but it may be due to the absence of visual cues that might be perceived as judgmental or merely not having to look the therapist in the eye and tell him or her about the seamier side of one's life. The depersonalization and distance involved seem to make it safer to share intimate information. This appears particularly true for males, who may be reticent to come for face-to-face counseling or even telephone counseling but will use e-mail at least as much as women (Wilson & Lester, 2002).

Whether this phenomenon changes with the increased use of Skype, where there is synchronous F2F, is another interesting e-therapy question. There is also some evidence that there is greater depth of emotional processing when people have to read something as opposed to listening (Hiltz, 1992). There may also be greater depth to cognitive processing, and that includes both client and worker. Certainly it takes a great deal more time and thought to compose a written response; a cursory "hmmmm" probably won't be satisfactory (Wilson & Lester, 2002).

Problems of Online Counseling

Along with this potential, and even some unique advantages over traditional and telephone interventions, some major areas of concern cloud this new electronic horizon. As the flat worlders said to sailors who they thought were going over the edge of the world, "Be wary, there be demons and dragons out there!" While it is one thing to chat casually with another person half a world away, it is quite another to have people providing therapy or interventions about whose credentials you know nothing more than what they tell you. The reverse may also be true for clients who may not be who they say they are. At their most malevolent, clients could attempt to infect the crisis interventionists' computers with viruses or other "malware" that could compromise their files (Maheu, 2001, 2003).

Confidentiality. One of the major issues of therapy on the net is confidentiality. Excellent encryption programs are used by ethical therapists to keep information confidential. However, there is no such guarantee if you are working out of a cybercafe. Even though websites may guarantee anonymity, once a message goes out, there is no absolute guarantee that it cannot be pulled out of the ether by people or agencies you might not be too thrilled to have read your thoughts and pictures. An e-mail message is less like a letter and more like a postcard (Barnett & Scheetz, 2003). So! Do you really want to talk about your sexual inadequacies on a postcard? Additionally, the possibility of violating client confidentiality and the Health Insurance Portability and Accountability Act (HIPAA), which carries severe penalties for doing so, are real concerns for practicing mental health professionals (Fisher & Fried, 2003).

It may also be argued that online therapy is problematic because of identity verification in emergency situations involving homicide, suicide, or other life-threatening events. In most telephone crisis intervention, there is usually some way to access emergency help for the individual. But if the client is in Vilnius, Lithuania, and the crisis interventionist is in Brisbane, Australia, this may be more difficult. Sandra DeJong's book (2014) *Blogs and Tweets, Texting and Friending: Social Media and Online Professionalism in Health Care* is a must read if you are going to venture into online therapy .

Charlatans. Sad to say, the field is ripe for electronic snake oil salespeople and nefarious individuals who may have somewhat less character and goodness in their hearts than Florence Nightingale. In his review of Internet sites that purport to provide "crisis counseling," Myer (1999) reported that not only are some of the fees exorbitantly high, but based on the questionable claims of their promotional advertisements, people who choose some of these services might be putting themselves at risk for even more traumatization through secondary victimization at the hands of some very incompetent or outright charlatan "service providers." Clearly, although this venue holds much promise, it is a "buyer beware" situation. A cursory review of 1,980,000 hits returned by a search for "crisis intervention therapy" in June 2011 leads us to believe things haven't changed a lot since Myer's study.

Licensing and Insurance. There are other demons that abound in the legal world of the Internet. Do you need to carry professional indemnity insurance even if you are a volunteer at a crisis line (Jones & Stokes, 2009, pp. 141–142)? What happens when you do therapy across state lines or countries? Do you need a license in that state or country, and what can happen if somebody commits suicide or homicide on your watch? Do you know how to be sure your data are encrypted? Do you know how to password protect your files? Do you know how to download files safely, how to keep the downloads secure, how to back them up, and how and where they are stored? Are you familiar with the Online Therapy Institute's Ethical Framework for the Use of Technology in Mental Health (Nagel & Anthony, 2011b) and, for disaster responders, an ethical framework for the use of technology in disasters (Nagel & Anthony 2011a), or other professional ethical standards in your country for the use of technology? If you don't, you have no business doing business on the net.

Learning the Language. If you are going to operate in this world, you not only need to be technologically competent and savvy about the Internet, you also need to know the language. There are now "netizens" among us! **Netizens** are people who spend a great deal of time in online communities. They operate in what is generally called Web 2.0, which is a way of using the web to develop cultural communities and social networking sites (Anthony & Nagel, 2010, p. 9). These individuals and sites are replete with their own language and **netiquette** (civil and appropriate rules of discourse when operating on the net, particularly in synchronous time with other netizens). Anthony and Nagel (2010, pp. 5–6) contend that real life and online life are not separate but more and more blended, to the point that for millions of people virtual life and real life are one and the same! For many of these netizens, the virtual world they surf through *is* the real world, so it is not hard to see how they would perceive the Internet as the most viable way to access crisis intervention services.

Netiquette

As yet, there is no "Miss Manners" to rule on netiquette. However, Jenicus (2013) has compiled a list of websites that cover netiquette in regard to general rules, e-mails, listservs, business, Twitter, and netiquette for kids. Following are some basic netiquette rules you need to observe if you are working on the net (Anthony & Nagel, 2010; Jones & Stokes, 2009).

1. A typo or two, particularly in synchronous time, is okay. Sloppy writing with lots of typos and grammar problems is not and indicates you don't care much about your client.
2. Emoticons can be helpful in conveying an emotion. They also can be too cute! Check with your client before you use them.
3. Lots of tweeters who use the net have their own expansive set of acronyms. You need to be clear about what those are; don't hesitate to ask if you don't know an abbreviation.
4. Keep your text neutral by using a simple black font; 12-point Times, for example, is easy to read and even bland. Other fonts and colors can get pretty exotic. Your clients can give you a lot of information through what they use.
5. You know what you mean when you write something. But as people read words (a novel is a good example), they attribute their own meaning and subsequent emotional response. So be careful as you construct your responses.
6. Stay cool! Use standard counseling skill responses to do exploratory work. Let the client talk. Brevity in written responses is a good thing.
7. Keep flame wars (intentionally written inflammatory remarks or misinterpreted ones) under control. If you make a mistake, discretely and quickly apologize for it. If you are running a group online, they need to know the limits and that they will be called on their inappropriate behavior.

Congruent with overall netiquette are some basic ways of enhancing text to make it more conversational and add emphasis (Anthony & Nagel, 2010, pp. 51–55). On the negative side, conflict seems to occur more in online than in face-to-face intervention, so it appears that communications need to be constantly clarified so they do not get muddled (Mallen, Day, & Green, 2003). Even when emoticons (keyboard symbols rotated 90 degrees clockwise to look like facial expressions), such as :) and :(, or emotional bracketing or altered text formats (different type sizes and fonts for emphasis) are used, it may be very difficult to tell when and to what degree emotions are being displayed.

Predispositioning

Because of the nature of online counseling and the great possibility that in a text-only situation miscommunication can occur (Adlington, 2009, pp. 158–159), predispostioning is critical—setting the tone as an empathic, genuine, caring, unconditionally positive regarding intervener on first contact (Jones & Stokes, 2009, p. 17). It is also important to get across to the client how crisis intervention takes place on the Internet, and how that is different from typical Internet exchanges, tweets, and chat room dialogue.

E-mailer online to crisis center: **I'm Featherlite. I've got a problem at home. I'm a 16 year old girl and I need some help with it. I've never done this before. I'm thinking about running away because I can't take much more of my parents climbing my frame because of my boyfriend. So where do we go from here? Can u help?**

Dr. J: (*synchronous online in real time*) Featherlite, I'm glad you e-mailed us. Call me Dr. J. Pleased to make your acquaintance, Featherlite. Interesting online name. I am curious. Are you as light as a feather?

While it may seem tangential, the interventionist seeks to establish psychological contact by querying her Internet name.

Featherlite: **Pretty much I guess. Especially when I dance. I'm on the modern dance team at my high school. Anyways that what Dad used to say when I was a little kid and he'd pick me up on his shoulders and it kinda stuck. Right now I'd like to pick him up and drop him off the Hernando De Soto Bridge.**

Dr. J: Okay. I'd like to read what you have to say. Note I said "read" so that is a bit different from listening. There are some different rules of the road here and I'd like to go over them with you so things don't get messed up. First, we can't see each other so a lot of what passes for nonverbal communication won't happen. Also I can't catch the tone of your voice nor you mine. We might use emoticons to convey an expression, and I use things like brackets and boldface and some other ways of attempting to make clear what I am hearing and asking so there are some ways of using the computer to get meanings across, but there's still room to misread stuff and I don't want that to happen. I'm not going to worry too much about misspells and grammar, although I might ask you to clarify something if I don't understand it and you can do the same with me. I want us to be really clear on what's going on so I won't try to read your mind and misinterpret the issues. So please don't be offended if I ask for clarification, okay? Even though we are working in real time, I may take some time to think about what you are saying. I'll let you know that by using some dots . . . so that you know I haven't stopped and there is more to come. If you like you can do the same. This is a crisis Internet center so it is not long-term therapy. My whole purpose is to get you back on level ground so you can make some good, realistic short-term decisions about your problem and act on it. If you think you need more extensive help down the line we can discuss that. I'll be asking you a lot of questions to get the problem real clear in my mind. I'll probably restate what you say so we are both in agreement on what's going on. To do that I may cut out your words and paste them back into my response in boldface. I'll take some guesses at what you are feeling and thinking. If I am wrong, just tell me so and I'll try again. So this is a no fault deal okay? Now, Featherlite, if you would, think a moment . . . and then tell me the one main thing that caused you to write in tonight. I do see you are pretty **put out with your dad** right now. You said **"it"** and that **"you'd**

never done this before." Can you tell me what "it" means and what it is that you haven't done?

This opening statement is designed to give the e-mailer an idea of how online counseling works and to get an idea of what the initiating problem is and the subtext underlying the initial query (Jones & Stokes, 2009, pp. 14–16). This rather long introduction gives the client at least a thumbnail sketch of how the interventionist will operate. A lot of owning statements are used to convey who and what the interventionist is and what he will and will not do. Not engaging in this preliminary discussion is likely to put the intervention in peril from the start, particularly with a client who has never engaged in crisis intervention let alone done so over the Internet. The interventionist's focus is on the immediate precipitating factors that got her to go online.

Featherlite: **Well "it" is like my parents y'know. They 4bid me to see my boyfriend, Arley, who is out of high school. They don't like him because they think he is like 2 old for me and they think he does dope and wants me to do it 2 y'know. We really got in it tonight. I'm down at the city library and just serched u up so I haven't done this crisisline thing ever before. I also haven't run way from home, but Arley says we can go to Kentucky and gt married there without my p's consent. I don't want to gt married right now. I want to finish h.s., but I love Arley and don't know how I can go home. I kinda slapped my mom and then my dad really slapped me and I took off.**

Dr. J: SO YOU'VE BEEN FIGHTING WITH YOUR P'S BECAUSE THEY THINK YOUR BOYFRIEND IS SUPPLYING YOU WITH DOPE AND YOU'RE SO IN LOVE WITH HIM YOU CAN'T SEE ALL THE FAULTS THEY SEE. RIGHT?

Featherlite: **Why are you SHOUTING. You sound like my father. Always critical. YOU THINK I M CRAZY TOO! Am I that bad? Maybe I will run off with him.**

Dr. J: Oops $#%$#%%! I accidentally hit the caps lock. Sorry. Not shouting, just old arthritic fingers LOL [laugh out loud]. No I don't think you're crazy. The "right" was just asking if I was on the money not whether you are right or wrong about your feelings.

While lots of shorthand and acronyms get used by clients, the interventionist needs to be careful in this regard. The word *right* in the above example can have many implications. Is our well-intentioned interventionist just seeking acknowledgment, or is he implying somebody is "right," and if so, is it Featherlite, her parents, or somebody else? So it might be a bit better if he were to make things clearer by saying "Am I right?"

Adlington (2009, pp. 8–40) uses a variety of text formats to build rapport with clients. Bracketing and boldfacing serve to indicate that the interventionist is listening closely and thinking about what has been said (pp. 13–14). Adding dots conveys some time spent pondering the issue and that the writer is going to continue with the thought.

Dr. J: Man! That really struck me about comparing me to your dad. Let me think on that a moment. . . .

As in F2F it is easy, perhaps even easier, to get lost in all the verbiage and as a result come back to the client with a whole flock of issues that get the client lost trying to determine which ones are important. A better way is to think of the core issue you want to cover and, as Adlington suggests, direct one central issue back to the client in boldface.

Dr. J: Featherlite, I get the sense this is more than me just sounding like your dad and being critical of your love life that's making you think of running away with Arley. Could you think a bit and tell me some of the long-term issues between you and your parents? I am guessing there may be a bit more than a boyfriend. Although right now **I do understand that the major issue is your wanting to be with Arley and your folks against it and that's what we will work on right now.**

Using the client's own font is one possible way of clearly restating what is being said in the client's own words.

Dr. J: So it seems right now you are so sensitive to your parents constant **criticism** that my goof up puts you on edge and **I sound like your dad.**

It should also be of interest as to what type of font the client uses (Adlington, 2009, p. 15). Would you respond differently if Featherlite were using **𝕭𝖗𝖆𝖌𝖌𝖆𝖉𝖔𝖈𝖎𝖔**, 𝕱𝖊𝖙𝖙𝖊 𝕱𝖗𝖆𝖐𝖙𝖚𝖗, or *𝓔𝓭𝔀𝓪𝓻𝓭𝓲𝓪𝓷 𝓢𝓬𝓻𝓲𝓹𝓽* rather than Comic Sans MS? Or, for that matter, if the e-mail came with certain words in color (Adlington, 2009, p. 17)? Do you suppose it would make a difference in your interpretation if anger came back in red, purple, blue, or green?

Featherlite: **I am so mad [crimson]. They're just jealous [green] because they were never in love like I am with Arley.**

Dr. J: OK. I see the feelings. I have a series of questions to ask. They'll come one at a time. First, do you feel safe to go home tonight?

Featherlite: **I don't know. The library closes at 11. I don't want to be on the streets then.**

Dr. J: Do you have a friend or relative's house you could go to?

Featherlite: **Maybe my aunt. Although my p's woud be mad if I went there. Mom doesn't get along with her sister well. Arley would come and take me to his apartment if I called him. He gets off at 11.**

Dr. J: You are probably not going to like my response, but right now that might not be your best option. I can get you on the line to Runaway. They would get transportation there, then contact your Ps. That is escalating the situation some because there would have to be a meeting between them and you and your parents and social services would be involved. Right now it is important for you to stay safe. We can continue e-mailing and set some longer term plans up, but I want to see you under cover tonight.

Featherlite: **U R probably right. I guess I could call my aunt.**

Dr. J: Please do that and then either call into the crisis line phone number or e-mail me back . . . say 10 minutes. OK?

Featherlite: **OK. I appreciate u. Pretty kul for an old ((((((gy)))))) ! ! ! [The parens denote hugs.]**

While this online dialogue is representative of what most crisis interveners would do in any format, there are some notable exceptions. First and foremost, triaging Featherlite is difficult because it is hard to put numbers to her affect or cognition without seeing her facial expressions and hearing her voice. The intervener has to make a best guess based on what he actually knows. Therefore, the default approach is to make best-guess ratings that are generally high. The fact this is a 16-year-old girl about to be on the streets of Memphis alone at night gets her a 9 on the behavioral scale and dictates most of the worker's actions in getting her to a safe place. Second, until practice makes the intervener unconsciously competent with the technology, he will have to be very cognizant of operating and conversing in this new system. Invariably, then, some focus is taken away from the client to deal with system conversance, as is demonstrated by Dr. J's poor fine motor coordination in hitting the caps lock key.

Texting

It may come to pass, and very quickly, that crisis interventionists will need to be better using their thumbs instead of their mouths because texting is becoming the preferred mode of communication with the coming generation (Ling, Bertel, & Sundsøy, 2012; Zhao, Qiu, & Xie, 2012). The Pew Research Center (2011) reports that cell ownership and text messaging are nearly universal among American 18–24 year olds—95% own a cell phone and 97% of these cell owners use text messaging—and this group sends or receives an average of 109.5 messages every day. One quarter of 18–24 year old text messaging users report sending or receiving more than 100 texts per day. Just over 1 in 10 say that they send or receive more than 200 messages on an average day—that equals 6,000 or more messages per month, and the open rate approaches 100%. That research indicates a very powerful and efficient communication system in operation, and note that research is more than 5 years old as you read about it!

Why texting? Survey results indicate that young adults use it because of promptness, convenience, and the ability to be more honest (Crosswhite, Rice, & Asay, 2014). Jacey Eckart (2014), a writer for Military. com Spouse makes this point about her own son as she writes on texting as a preferred technique in suicide intervention. "During conflict, my son seemed to need the space and distance that texting could provide in order to get his point across. The sooner he felt 'heard' via text, the sooner he started talking again." When Nancy Lublin, a therapist in New York, started texting teenagers to solicit help with her social advocacy organization, she was amazed that numerous return texts were about their own problems of bullying, depression, and abuse (2012). These texts were numerous enough and alarming enough that Lublin has started a text hotline, Text "START" to 741-741. This textline has trained volunteers, supervisors for high-risk texts, and backup and referral ability to other online crisis centers (crisis textline, 2015). Indeed, it seems to increase participation in help-seeking

behavior among young people. Evans, Davidson, and Sicafuse's (2013) study found that publicizing a crisis line's ability to accept text messages increased youth help-seeking behaviors.

However, it is not just teenagers that textlines are focusing on. The Veterans Administration has, along with it telephone, e-mail, and chat room services, established a textline, Text to 838255 to Get Help NOW (U.S. Department of Veterans Affairs, 2014). Texting is also becoming part of police training to deal with crises. Law enforcement officers are increasingly being called upon to defuse violent, unpredictable situations through the typed word and CIT officers are doing exactly that (Thompson, 2014). It should thus become pretty clear that, if you are going to be in this business, you need to start doing thumb exercises.

Virtual Reality

Many computer programs available today perform assessment and self-help psychoeducational and therapeutic functions that are seen as effective and reliable (Christensen et al., 2014; Egan et al., 2014; van Ballegooijen et al., 2014; Twomey et al., 2014). The other great potential use of computer technology in cybercounseling is in simulation and interactive **virtual reality** (Wiederhold & Wiederhold, 2005). Virtual reality (VR) can be defined as a set of computer technologies that when combined provide an interface to a computer-generated world (Wiederhold &Wiederhold, 2005, p. 5). A wide variety of computer programs are being tested for use with panic attacks, phobias, anxiety, depression, obsessive-compulsive disorder, addictions, PTSD, sexual dysfunction, eating disorders, obesity, physical rehabilitation, interpersonal skills deficits, and schizophrenic hallucinations.

Many of these programs are designed as games. Called "serious games," they are designed to reduce negative or promote positive behavior change rather than be played solely for leisure. These games are used to treat a wide variety of maladaptive behaviors (McCann et al., 2014; Swirsky, Carfagno, Milligan, & Raiff, 2014; Quero et al., 2014; Yin et al., 2014). They are reported to have a high level of acceptance by clients, and outcomes are comparable with those obtained in working with face-to-face therapists (Castro et al., 2014; Golomb et al., 2011; Li, Theng, & Foo, 2014; Moritz et al., 2014; Park et al., 2015; Reger et al., 2011; Tortella-Feliu et al., 2011; Wuang et al., 2011).

Probably the most intriguing of these approaches is the creation of virtual reality environments in which clients can be exposed to a variety of situations through a computer simulation of reality (Glantz, Rizzo, & Graap, 2003; Riva, 2003). Second Life is a virtual reality community that manifests such adjunctive computer therapy successfully (DeAngelis, 2009; Sutano et al., 2011). Clients can choose their avatar, set up housekeeping, and with assistance and assignments from their cybertherapist, try out new behaviors and see how they work. It does not take a great stretch of the imagination to see how these programs could be used to relax, calm, and defuse crisis clients who are geographically distant from immediate help. Anything you can do in real life you can do in Second Life (Robbins & Bell, 2008), which makes it an excellent medium to safely try out new skills and behaviors.

Need for Training

This brief dialogue is meant to give you a snapshot of how crisis intervention works in real time on the net. It is not meant to make you a net-competent crisis interventionist. Also, reading this brief section in a book is not going to make you a cyber crisis interventionist. Crisis workers engaging in this work and employing supportive computer programs need to have training beyond standard computer skills to deal with the inevitable technical problems and computer glitches. Understanding how the new medium integrates traditional and cybercounseling is critical (Anthony & Nagel, 2010, pp. 127–141). Further, cultural diversity and linguistic differences make understanding "multiculturalism" as it applies to crisis intervention paramount on the net (Anthony & Nagel, 2010, p. 63).

The worker also needs to be comfortable in the medium. Writing counseling responses using instant messaging or in chat rooms is altogether different from saying them over the telephone or in a face-to-face dialogue. Recognizing when clients are in trouble by their e-mail message content is very different from doing a visual assessment of clients face to face. Knowing how to obtain backup, use referral services, and contact emergency services over vast geographic distances is paramount. Even more important is getting supervision while doing the foregoing (Anthony & Nagel, 2010, pp. 127–141). Finally, the worker needs to educate clients about what cybercounseling can and cannot do for them and gain their informed consent (Castelnuovo et al., 2003; Maheu, 2003; Ragusea & VandeCreek, 2003).

Legal, Ethical, and Moral Issues of Telephone and Internet Counseling

The bottom line is that there is still much to be done in the way of research and protocol development in behavioral telehealth and cybercounseling. Certainly, any crisis worker or agency moving into this venue needs to know professional ethical standards and state and federal regulations and laws. The technological advances of caller identification, call blocking, and call tracing pose some complex legal and ethical dilemmas for the telephone hotline. Given the ability to screen and identify calls, is it right to deny services to problem clients? Furthermore, given the expectation and the safety callers feel due to the anonymity of call-in services, using these technologies could easily put confidentiality on a collision course with duty to warn. Could other agencies demand the logs of such hotlines when involved in legal proceedings? Would the hotline workers be held civilly or criminally liable for their actions, given knowledge of whom they were working with and what they might have said?

Because most telephone hotline workers are volunteers, they receive minimal training, and the agencies they work for are not bound by state or federal supervision or legislation (Seely, 1997a, 1997b). These issues further compound the problems of how to ethically use these new technologies. There are no clear answers to these dilemmas at present, but they are issues that need to be addressed at every level of government and most certainly within the agencies that provide such services. It clearly behooves social services agencies and schools to develop policies and procedures for e-mail and texting and determine what role they will play in therapy (Dejong, 2014; Dejong & Gorrindo, 2014; Moon, 2014).

With all of these forewarnings, crisis interventionists have one clear ethical responsibility, particularly if that interventionist happens to work in a room that has "School Counselor" on the door: Being knowledgeable about digital technologies is a nonnegotiable ethical responsibility because that's the land your natives inhabit.

Does It Work?

A number of inexpensive commercial products that are soon to be released will undoubtedly foster need and demand for virtual reality and serious games that target psychological problems (Turner & Casey, 2014). The bottom line for any therapeutic endeavor is how well it works. Doing rigorous controlled-outcome studies is difficult, to say the least, in this anonymous world of electronics. Determining level of expertise and skillful intervention is equally problematic given that the vast number of crisis workers are volunteers. However, a number of studies have been done that sampled users of phone and electronic intervention services (Beebe, Smith, & Phillips, 2014; Chiang, 2012; Dalgin, Maline, & Driscol, 2011; Evans et al., 1986; Farrer et al., 2014; Gonzales et al., 2014; Mishara et al., 2005; Padach, 1984; Reese, Conoley, & Brossart, 2002, 2006; Rhee et al., 2005; Swirsky et al., 2014; Tolmach, 1985; Wuang et al., 2011; Wark, 1984). Overall, they consistently rated electronic crisis intervention as helpful, there was a reduction in presenting issues, and a number stated they preferred it to face-to-face counseling. The question remains: Does telephone and Internet counseling work? The

answer to that, whether it is done by volunteers working crisis lines or professionals working with their own clientele, is pretty much "Yes."

It appears to be particularly true when we look at a sampling of personal issues where crises are almost always present. Controlled studies and meta-analyses that range across suicide (Rhee et al., 2005), anxiety (Diemer, Muhlberger, Pauli, & Zwanzger, 2014; Nordstrom et al., 2014), cancer (Marcus et al., 2010), depression (Mohr et al., 2008), gambling (Shandley & Moore, 2008), agoraphobia (Castro et al., 2014), stress (Gaggioli et al., 2014), HIV+ (Cook et al., 2009), schizophrenia (Moritz et al., 2014), and incapacitating and debilitating physical disabilities (Dorstyn, Mathias, & Denson, 2011), to name but a few, all indicate generally positive outcomes across a wide range of personality dimensions, coping mechanisms, and positive behavioral adaption and change. Telehealth intervention can even help you get off the couch, exercise, eat your veggies, and get your daily dose of fiber (Eakin et al., 2007)!

SUMMARY

Telephone counseling and cybercounseling account for most crisis intervention work done in the world. Typically, local crisis lines field all kinds and varieties of calls while national hotlines field special, problem-specific issues such as runaways. Special crisis lines that are time limited may be set up immediately after major disasters. These services are staffed mainly by volunteers, who are generally seen as effective helpers by the people who call them. However, there are problem callers who can bedevil crisis lines. Some callers may use crisis lines for their own sexual gratification. Others may constantly call and tie up phone lines because of their loneliness.

Cyber crisis counseling will undoubtedly play a larger part in the future of crisis intervention. Many questions about its use and the ethical safeguards that need to be part of it remain unanswered. However, professional associations such as the American Counseling Association, the National Board for Certified

Counselors, and the recently formed International Society for Mental Health Online are working hard on many of the birthing pains of this new baby.

Overall, the use of telephone and online services are seen as beneficial by consumers because they are fast, convenient, accessible, cheap, anonymous, and helpful, and there is evidence from empirical studies that supports consumer opinion about the efficacy of using these multiple electronic resources during a crisis event.

Visit CengageBrain.com for a variety of study tools and useful resources such as video examples, case studies, interactive exercises, flashcards, and quizzes.

Handling Specific Crises
Going Into the Trenches

Part 2 focuses on applying intervention strategies to several of the currently most prevalent types of crises in the human experience. The purpose of Part 2 is to provide crisis workers with information about the background, dynamics, and intervention methodologies needed to effectively help individuals or groups in various kinds of crises.

Part 2 contains a wide array of crisis case illustrations to enhance descriptions of not only the usual and accepted intervention practices for various types of crises, but also many innovative and cutting-edge strategies for intervention. Indeed, some of these strategies are controversial, but they have gained enough treatment notoriety and preliminary research to be included. Part 2 examines posttraumatic stress disorder (PTSD), suicide, sexual assault, domestic violence, personal loss, crises in schools, and families in crises. Three central themes pervade these chapters:

1. Some crises are *time limited* and some are *transcrisis*, in that the person in crisis may progressively experience severe problems, either deal with or suppress them, and then experience and exhibit repeated responses and symptoms of the same crisis over a period of many years.

2. No one set of theories, assumptions, strategies, or procedures is appropriate for intervening in all crisis situations; rather, a systematic and integrative approach is recommended and demonstrated as the preferred mode of helping in a broad assortment of crisis problems and settings. The techniques employed in these chapters are "best bets" for the particular kind of client in the particular environment. They are, however, not the only "bets." They are meant to give you a variety of approaches and situations that will start to help you form your own "Gestalt" of an effective crisis worker.

3. Crisis intervention is hallmarked by elastic, fluid situations that change in seconds and minutes and may move from a very benign to a volatile situation in that time. Many of the case illustrations model such dynamics to give you a flavor of what the crisis worker must do to respond quickly and effectively.

143

Posttraumatic Stress Disorder

Introduction

Part II's discussion of the more common types of crises that you, as a mental health worker or consumer of mental health care, are likely to encounter opens with **posttraumatic stress disorder (PTSD).** The reason for beginning here is that many other crises reviewed in this book may be rooted in PTSD. For example, suicide (Chu, 1999; Kramer et al., 1994) and substance abuse (Ouimette, Read, & Brown, 2005; Read, Bollinger, & Sharansky, 2003) may be the end products of attempting to cope with trauma. In contrast, rape, sexual abuse, battering, loss, physical violence, hostage situations, and large-scale natural and human-made disasters may precipitate the disorder (Ackerman et al., 1998; Bigot & Ferrand, 1998; Darves-Bornoz et al., 1998; Davis et al., 2003; Elklit & Brink, 2004; King et al., 2003; Lang et al., 2004; Melhem et al., 2004; North, 2004; Pivar & Field, 2004). Going one-on-one with PTSD is tough enough, but to make matters worse, lots of times PTSD turns into a gang war with a host of other comorbid (occurring along with it) problems that make it even harder to deal with as individuals bounce in and out of transcrisis (Masino & Norman, 2015). Finally, PTSD-like symptoms may appear in the very people who attempt to alleviate the mental and physical suffering of people in crisis (Figley, 2002; Halpern & Tramontin, 2007; Pearlman & Saakvitne, 1995) and have become known as compassion fatigue (Figley, 2002) and vicarious traumatization (Pearlman & Saakvitne, 1995).

We know this is a long chapter and you might need to take a nap or a snack break to get through it. Try as we might to prune it down, we felt that "all this stuff" was critical to giving you the background for understanding not only what PTSD is about, but

LEARNING OBJECTIVES

After studying this chapter, you should be able to:

1. Know the history and evolution of PTSD into a classified psychological diagnostic.
2. Understand the difference between peritraumatic, acute traumatic, posttraumatic, and complex PTSD terminology and the traumatic states they represent.
3. Know the current diagnostic PTSD criteria for adults.
4. Understand the basic neurophysiology of PTSD.
5. Know and understand the incidence of different trauma types and their effect on PTSD.
6. Recognize and understand maladaptive coping patterns of PTSD.
7. Understand the current state of affairs in providing therapy and support to the armed forces.
8. Know and understand the different types of assessments used in diagnosis and treatment of PTSD.
9. Understand the different phases of recovery in PTSD.
10. Understand how to initiate intervention.
11. Know the risks of treatment for PTSD.
12. Know and understand the use of different types of adult treatment protocols for PTSD.
13. Understand the role of psychotropic medication in the treatment of PTSD.
14. Know how trauma-focused therapy is operationalized throughout the recovery phases of PTSD.
15. Understand the part group therapy plays in PTSD and how it operates.
16. Understand how EMDR therapy is used to treat PTSD.
17. Know the diagnostic criteria for PTSD in children.
18. Understand the importance of support systems for children in combating PTSD.

19. Know and understand differences between Type I and Type II (complex) trauma in children.
20. Know and understand differential treatment methods for PTSD in children.
21. Understand that there is potential for hope and growth after trauma.

what occurs in treating the other crisis and transcrisis topics in this book. What we knew about PTSD in the first edition of this book in 1987 and what we know about it now—particularly the neurobiology and just how complex that is in manifesting the various traumatic responses that occur in humans—is like the difference between writing with a goose quill, inkwell, and papyrus scroll and word processing with an Apple Thunderbolt, OSX Lion operating system, and high-speed printer/scanner/fax. So bear with us! If you nail this chapter down, the other chapters will make a whole lot more sense as to how "all this stuff" goes together. In summary, PTSD has moved from the psychological backwaters of the Vietnam War to now being so central to treatment issues in mental health that there is the National Center for PTSD (http://www.ptsd.va.gov) and the National Child Traumatic Stress Network (NCTSN) www.nctsn.org.

Background

Psychic trauma is a process initiated **LO1** **LO2** by an event that confronts an individual with an acute, overwhelming threat (Freud, 1917/1963). When the event occurs, the inner agency of the mind loses its ability to control the disorganizing effects of the experience, and disequilibrium occurs. The trauma tears up the individual's psychological anchors, which are fixed in a secure sense of what has been in the past and what should be in the present (Erikson, 1968). When a traumatic event occurs that represents nothing like the person's experience of past events, and the individual's mind is unable to effectively answer basic questions of how and why it occurred and what it means, a crisis ensues. The traumatic wake of a crisis event typically includes immediate and vivid reexperiencing, hyperarousal, and avoidance reactions, which are all common to PTSD. The event propels the individual into a traumatic state that lasts as long as the mind needs to reorganize, classify, and make sense of

the traumatic event. Then, and only then, does psychic equilibrium return (Furst, 1978).

The typical kinds of responses that occur immediately after the crisis may give rise to what are called **peritraumatic** (around, or like, trauma) symptoms. These are common responses as the mind attempts to reorganize itself and cope with a horrific event. For many people, these responses will slowly disappear after a few days. Most people are amazingly resilient in the aftermath of a traumatic crisis and quickly return to mental and physical homeostasis, but if the symptoms continue for a minimum of 2 days and a maximum of 4 weeks and occur within 1 month of the traumatic event, then those time frames will meet the criteria of **acute stress disorder** (**ASD**) (American Psychiatric Association, 2013). Acute stress disorder diagnostic criteria are similar to the criteria for PTSD, which you will soon meet, except that the diagnosis can only be given in the first month after a traumatic event. ASD is somewhat different than PTSD because **dissociative symptoms** such as memory loss, a sense of detachment from the world, belief that things and people are unreal, a blurred sense of identity, and a general disconnect from reality are present (International Society for the Study of Trauma and Dissociation, 2015). As we will see, it is important to tackle ASD symptoms immediately and head on, because they tend to be valid predictors for "catching" PTSD. Percentage rates for ASD vary a great deal depending on trauma type from vehicle accidents that range in the teens, to victims of robbery in the twenties, and to rape which skyrockets to the nineties (Gibson, 2015).

If the person can effectively integrate the trauma into conscious awareness and organize it as a part of the past (as unpleasant as the event may be), then homeostasis returns, the problem is coped with, and the individual continues to travel life's rocky road. If the event is not effectively integrated and is submerged from awareness, then the probability is high that the initiating stressor will continue to assail the person and become chronic PTSD. It may also disappear from conscious awareness and reemerge in a variety of symptomatic forms months or years after the event. When such crisis events are caused by the reemergence of the original unresolved stressor, they fall into the category of delayed PTSD (American Psychiatric Association, 2013).

PTSD is a newborn compared with the other crises we will examine, at least in regard to achieving official designation. In 1980, PTSD found its way into the third edition of the American Psychiatric Association's (1980) *Diagnostic and Statistical Manual of Mental Disorders* (DSM-III) as a classifiable and valid mental disorder. However, the antecedents of what has been designated as PTSD first came to the attention of the medical establishment in the late 19th and early 20th centuries.

Two events serve as benchmarks in the history of PTSD. First, with the advent of rail transportation and subsequent train wrecks, physicians and early psychiatrists began to encounter in accident survivors trauma with no identifiable physical basis. Railway accident survivors of this type became so numerous that a medical term, **railway spine**, became an accepted diagnosis. In psychological parlance, the synonymous term **compensation neurosis** came into use for invalidism suffered and compensated by insurers as a result of such accidents (Trimble, 1985, pp. 7–10).

Concomitantly, Sigmund Freud formulated the concept of **hysterical neurosis** to describe trauma cases of young Victorian women with whom he was working. He documented symptoms of warded-off ideas, denial, repression, emotional avoidance, compulsive repetition of trauma-related behavior, and recurrent attacks of trauma-related emotional sensations (Breuer & Freud, 1895/1955). However, what Freud found and reported on the pervasive childhood sexual abuse of these women as the traumatic root of their hysteria was anathema to a puritanical Victorian society, and he was forced to disavow and then reject his findings (Herman, 1997, pp. 13–17).

Second, the advent of modern warfare in World Wars I and II, with powerful artillery and aerial bombardment, generated terms such as **shell shock** and **combat fatigue** to explain the condition of traumatized soldiers who had no apparent physical wounds. As early as the American Civil War, soldiers were diagnosed with **neurasathenia**, a state of mental and physical exhaustion. This malady was also termed "**soldier's heart**" because of the belief that nerves at the base of the heart were somehow affected by combat. The term **nostalgia**, a 19th-century military term coined by physicians for combat soldiers with extreme homesickness, would be seen as combat-induced PTSD in current terms. The thought was that soldiers became nostalgic for home and thus started to manifest a variety of physical symptoms that would relieve them from combat and allow them to go home (Kinzie & Goetz, 1996). Various hypotheses such as the foregoing were proposed to account for

such strange maladies (Trimble, 1985, p. 8), but Freud (1919/1959) believed that the term **war neurosis** more aptly characterized what was an emotional disorder that had nothing to do with the prevailing medical notion of neurology-based shell shock, the idea that concussion from the massive shelling common in World War I injured the brain's neurological systems. The U.S. Medical Service Corps came to recognize combat fatigue (being on the front line too long) in World War II and the Korean War as a treatable psychological disturbance. The treatment approach was that combat fatigue was invariably acute and that treatment was best conducted as quickly and as close to the battle lines as possible. The idea was to facilitate a quick return to active duty. The prevailing thought was that time heals all wounds and that little concern needed to be given to long-term effects of traumatic stress. Such has not been the case (Archibald et al., 1962). Indeed, a notable proponent of establishing the Vietnam Veterans Centers, Arthur Blank, ruefully commented that when he was an army psychiatrist in Vietnam, he believed there would be no long-term difficulties for veterans (MacPherson, 1984, p. 237).

Although PTSD can and does occur in response to the entire range of natural and human-made catastrophes, it was the Vietnam War that clearly brought PTSD to the awareness of both the human services professions and the public. Through a combination of events and circumstances unparalleled in the military history of the United States, veterans who returned from that conflict began to develop a variety of mental health problems that had little basis for analysis and treatment in the prevailing psychological literature. This combination of events and circumstances had insidious and long-term consequences that were not readily apparent either to the individuals affected or to human services professionals who attempted to treat them. Misdiagnosed, mistreated, and misunderstood, military service personnel became known to a variety of social services agencies that included the police, mental health facilities, and unemployment offices (MacPherson, 1984, pp. 207–330, 651–690).

As the war continued to grind on, more and more veterans started having psychological problems. Rebuffed by the Veterans Administration, these veterans formed self-help groups to try to come to terms with their psychological issues. These "rap" groups rapidly coalesced and became a political force that pushed the federal government to come to grips with their problems. One major result of their lobbying efforts was the establishment of the Vietnam Veterans Centers, where alienated veterans could seek help for a variety of readjustment problems. An informal network of mental health professionals became interested in the veterans and started to classify their symptoms and compare them to the work Kardiner (1941) had done on war neurosis. Their review of clinical records led them to generate 27 of the most common symptoms of the Vietnam veterans' "traumatic neurosis" (van der Kolk, Weisaeth, & van der Hart, 1996, p. 61). Interestingly, many of the physical or somatic complaints resemble those of a large retrospective archival study on the medical records of American Civil War Union veterans (Pizarro, Silver, & Prause, 2006)!

At the same time, researchers in the growing women's movement were looking at psychological problems after domestic violence, rape, and child abuse. What they were finding in the individuals who had suffered from these civilian assaults closely paralleled the problems that Vietnam veterans were experiencing. Their research rediscovered what Freud had found 80 years before and had dismissed: that victims of physical and sexual assault suffered long-term effects of the psychological trauma (Herman, 1997, p. 32). These different research avenues culminated in combining the "Vietnam veterans syndrome," the "rape trauma syndrome," the "abused child syndrome," and the "battered woman syndrome" into one diagnostic category—posttraumatic stress disorder—in the third edition of the American Psychiatric Association's *Diagnostic and Statistical Manual* in 1980 (van der Kolk, Weisaeth, & van der Hart, 1996, p. 61).

Although the Vietnam War may be no more to you than a reference in a high school history book, the wall memorial in Washington, DC, or your "crazy old Uncle Harold" who continues to wear combat fatigues and a headband with a ponytail, the war's effects are a crucial history lesson in mental health provision (or the lack thereof) that any aspiring mental health worker should learn. For that reason, the psychological lessons learned from the Vietnam War continue to play a major role in the discussion of PTSD in the eighth edition of this book. It should be clearly understood that, even 50 years after the fact, the events that caused the trauma in many of these approximately 1 million veterans who suffered and suffer from PTSD are as alive for them today as they were then (Price, 2011). What is perhaps even more ominous in regard to the Vietnam veterans is their "graying." Mounting evidence indicates that World War II and Korean War veterans have manifested delayed onset or worsening of posttraumatic complaints as they have grown older.

Aging, with its subsequent loss of social supports through death, increased health problems, declining physical and mental capabilities, and economic hardship, appears to put older veterans at increased risk (Aarts & Op den Velde, 1996, pp. 359–374; Hamilton & Workman, 1998). Thus, it would appear that as this population ages, the mental health professions are a long way from being done with the legacy of Vietnam.

Perhaps even more ominous, the current wars in Iraq and Afghanistan have eerily similar parallels to Vietnam. There are no front lines, the enemy fades into the population, everyone in the theater of operations is essentially in combat. As a result, vigilance must be constant, 24/7, throughout one's entire rotation. Degree of combat exposure has been found to be one of the major predictors of PTSD (Miller et al., 2008; Smith et al., 2008), and anybody that goes into the "sandboxes" as they now called can expect just that.

There are two major differences in these conflicts. So far there is general public support for the troops, whereas in Vietnam there was not. A support group is critical in any crisis, and this is particularly true of troops in an increasingly unpopular war. Lack of support and outright hatred of returning troops was a major contributing factor for PTSD in Vietnam veterans. However, while the armed forces in the current conflicts are all volunteers and not 18-year-old draftees, there are a tremendous number of reserve units in combat action, and there are also huge differences in the number of women involved in direct combat action. The question then becomes what the use of reservists and women in combat portends for the onset of PTSD. Preliminary results regarding mental health problems in veterans returning from Iraq and Afghanistan have ranged from 19% to 44% of the samples examined (Hoge, Auchterlonie, & Milliken, 2006; Lapierre, Schweigler, & LaBauve, 2007).

Dynamics of PTSD
Diagnostic Categorization

PTSD is a complex and diagnostically trou- **LO3** blesome disorder. To be identified as having PTSD, a person must meet the following conditions and symptoms as specified in the *Diagnostic and Statistical Manual-5* (American Psychiatric Association, 2013). In the new DSM-5, a subcategory for children under 6 years of age has also been formulated. The following criteria are specific to adults, adolescents, and children older than 6. Examples have been provided to illuminate the specific criteria.

First, the person must have been exposed to a trauma in which he or she was confronted with an event that involved actual or threatened death or serious injury or actual or threatened sexual violence. Then the person must meet the following criteria for a diagnosis of PTSD.

Criterion A. That exposure must include *one* of the following stressors:

1. Direct exposure to the experience.
2. Or witnessing its occurrence.
3. Indirectly by learning that a significant other was exposed to a trauma that involved actual or threatened death either by a violent or accidental event.
4. Repeated or extreme exposure to aversive details of the event most usually through professional duties associated with it such as EMTs working accidents where dead and mangled bodies are present or therapists working child abuse cases. Vicarious exposure of nonprofessionals through watching or listening to electronic media does *not* meet this criteria. Examples include but are certainly not limited to military combat, physical or sexual assault, kidnapping, being held hostage, severe vehicle accidents, earthquakes and tornadoes, being a refugee from a war zone, concentration camp detention, and life-threatening injuries or illness.

Criterion B. The traumatic event is reexperienced through at least *one* of the following intrusive symptoms:

1. Recurrent, involuntary, and intrusive memories. These occur despite efforts or admonitions to "forget it and move on." In children intrusion may occur through repetitive play.
2. Traumatic nightmares. Typically they regularly occur and are terrifying enough that alcohol or other mind altering substances are used to dampen their onset and diminish their effect. In children nightmares occur which may have no apparent relation to the traumatic event.
3. Dissociative reactions or flashbacks to the traumatic event which may range from brief, momentary episodes, to complete loss of consciousness. These flashback episodes, including those that occur on awakening or when intoxicated, may include all types of sensory hallucinations or

illusions which cause the individual to dissociate from the present reality and act or feel as if the event were recurring. Children may dissociate through play by reenacting the event.
4. Intense or prolonged distress after being exposed to stimuli that spark reminders of the traumatic event; such as anxiety/panic attacks, excessive and obsessive worry and concern.
5. Marked physiological responses upon exposure to traumatic stimuli. An example such as a person who was in a tornado starting to shake violently at every approaching storm.

Criterion C. The person engages in persistent and purposeful effort to avoid distressing stimuli that are reminiscent of the event through *one* of the following methods:

1. Trauma-related thoughts or feelings; such as impeding thoughts of doom or feelings of hopelessness.
2. External reminders of the events such as people, objects, situations, activities, conversations that trigger negative memoires.

Criterion D. The person experiences negative alteration in cognitions and mood after the experience in at least *two* of the following ways:

1. Excluding head injury drugs or alcohol abuse, the person cannot remember key features of the traumatic event. Memory of the event is foggy, distorted, repressed, or jumbled as to sequence, place, persons, or time.
2. There are persistent and often distorted negative beliefs about oneself or the world such as "I am a bad person" and "the world is a terrible and dangerous place."
3. There is persistent and distorted blame for oneself or others for causing the traumatic event.
4. The person experiences persistent trauma-related negative emotions such as fear, horror, anger, sadness, guilt, shame.
5. Markedly diminished interested in pretraumatic activities that include hobbies, recreations, work, avocations, organizations, and other pastimes.
6. The individual feels alienated from others and is estranged or detached from significant others.
7. Affect of the person is constricted such that he or she has persistent inability to experience positive emotions.

Criterion D includes many of the symptoms that were included in the DSM-IV-R (American Psychiatric Association, 2000) criteria under "Numbing" (Marx & Gutner, 2015). We believe that exclusion deserves an editorial comment with all due respect to the developers of the current criteria. One of the classic signs of an individual who has PTSD are the emotional "numbing" effects it leaves. We believe that the current descriptors really don't do service to this hallmark symptom and is something that neophyte interventionists needs to be aware of and look for when assessing for PTSD.

Criterion E. The individual has trauma-related alterations in arousal and reactivity that began or became worse after the traumatic event. At least two of the following criteria are required.

1. Irritable or aggressive behavior; such as picking a fight for no apparent reason.
2. Self-destructive or reckless behavior; such as legal but highly dangerous behavior like free hand rock climbing up 90 degree cliffs or illegal behavior such baiting the police while driving recklessly.
3. Hypervigilance; which may result in overprotective behavior of significant others or extreme paranoia about objectives that were previously associated with threat such as being extremely restrictive of children's recreational activities or swerving to avoid a dead animal carcass along the highway that when in the service was previously known to be a place to conceal explosives in wartime.
4. Exaggerated startle response; examples of noises previously associated with threat such as engine backfires, carpenter nail guns, news helicopters, or sudden movements of other persons such as children sneaking up on parents or partners/bedmates jostling.
5. Problems in concentration; where previously tasks could be accomplished with ease are now difficult to do so, or train of thought is lost while attempting to do them.
6. Sleep disturbance, not only due to nightmares but to any nighttime uncommon noises, movements of others.

Criterion F. The duration of the foregoing symptoms persist more than 1 month.

Criterion G. There are significant symptoms of any of the foregoing criteria that cause enough related distress or ability such that the individual is unable to function either socially or occupationally. Examples are divorce and alienation from family, inability to keep and hold jobs, and starting and dropping out of educational programs.

Criterion H. The disturbance is not due to medication, substance use, or other illnesses.

Additionally, the person may be specified as having PTSD along with dissociative symptoms if they report either:

1. **Depersonalization** as if the person is watching herself from a grandstand or seeing herself as in a movie such that it can't really be happening to her.
2. **Derealization** as if this is unreal and can't be happening, or the images become distorted and blurred and are hard to sort out and make sense of them.

At times, full criterion onset may be delayed for at least 6 months or more, although onset of some of the symptoms may occur immediately. It should become clear that because of the multiple, specific criteria for a diagnosis of PTSD, not everybody who undergoes a traumatic event automatically "catches" PTSD. Also, it should be apparent from the foregoing criteria that what the crisis interventionist is going to be dealing with are the transcrisis symptoms that exist in the foregoing criteria and arise unbidden into the individual's life. As stated previously in Chapter 1, while PTSD invariably involves multiple transcrisis events and situations, transcrisis does not always involve PTSD, such as in the case of domestic violence, alcohol abuse, or school bullying.

Complex PTSD

If "catching" PTSD isn't bad enough, the dramatic personality changes that may occur with long-term, intensive trauma have led many respected researchers and practitioners to call for a diagnostic category of **complex PTSD** or "disorders of extreme stress not otherwise specified" (DESNOS) (Briere & Scott, 2006; Courtois & Ford, 2009; Herman, 1997, p. 121; Mooren & Stöfsel, 2015; van der Kolk, 1996b, pp. 202–204). The term refers to a broad range of symptoms resulting from exposure to a prolonged or repeated severely traumatizing event. The lobbying effort for this diagnostic category has so far fallen short of achieving official recognition, but the three cardinal symptoms are **somatization** (physical problems, associated pain, and functional limitations), **dissociation** (division of the personality into one component that attempts to function in the everyday world and another that regresses and is fixed in the trauma), and **affect dysregulation** (alterations in impulse control, attention and consciousness, self-perception, perception of perpetrators, relationships to significant others, and systems of meaning) (Courtois, Ford, & Cloitre, 2009, pp. 85–86), all of which go beyond the diagnostic criteria of "simple" PTSD.

The DESNOS classification opens a Pandora's box of psychological evils that include the inability to regulate feelings, suicidal and other self-destructive behaviors, impulsive and dangerous risk-taking behaviors, anger management problems, amnesia and dissociation from reality, somatic complaints that take a variety of physical forms, chronic character changes that range from consuming guilt to permanent ineffectiveness in coping with life, adopting distorted and idealized views of perpetrators of the trauma, an inability to trust others, a tendency to victimize or be revictimized, and despair and hopelessness that previously held beliefs about a "fair and just" world are no longer valid. Typical inhabitants of a DESNOS world are persons with long-term exposure to combat service, adult survivors of chronic childhood sexual and physical abuse, and concentration camp survivors. Whether simple or complex, it should be readily apparent that PTSD is an extremely serious condition with all kinds of associated problems and comorbid mental illness (Masino & Norman, 2015) and that the DSM-5 criteria do not begin to depict all the consequences and effects of the disorder that assail the individual and ripple out to significant others in the individual's life.

Conflicting Diagnoses

Given the wide variety of maladaptive behaviors that characterize the disorder, it is not uncommon for those who suffer from PTSD to have companion diagnoses of anxiety, depressive, organic mental, and substance use disorders (American Psychiatric Association, 2000, p. 427). In fact, it is probably more common to have **comorbidity** (the presence of two diagnosable disorders such as major depression and substance abuse) (Marx & Gutner, 2015). Further, because of presenting symptoms, PTSD may be confused with adjustment, paranoid, somatic, and personality disorders (Herman, 1997, pp. 116–117; Zanarini et al., 1998; Zlotnick et al., 1999).

One of the hallmarks of PTSD is that it is often comorbid—particularly with alcohol abuse (Najavits,

2012; Ouimette & Read, 2014). That is, the person will have another preliminary mental illness diagnosed in the course of treatment. There are few "pure" cases, and few symptoms are unique to the disorder (Atkinson, Sparr, & Sheff, 1984; Masino & Norman, 2015). Thus, *no matter what the diagnosis, assessment in crisis intervention should always attempt to determine if there has been exposure to prior trauma,* particularly when the crisis seems to have occurred spontaneously, with no clear, immediate, precipitating stimulus.

The Question of Preexisting Psychopathology

For a variety of political and social reasons, society does not perceive (and has not perceived) being a victim of war, domestic violence, or other types of human cruelty as the equivalent of being mentally ill. Vietnam veterans who early on sought help from Veterans Administration (VA) hospitals were misdiagnosed or thought to have some preexisting psychopathology or character disorder. As a result, they were revictimized by a bureaucratic and rigidly conservative mental health system that added psychic insult to psychic injury (Ochberg, 1988, p. 4). Victims of domestic violence fared no better and were often seen to have a "masochistic" personality that subconsciously enjoyed physical assaults (Herman, 1997, p. 117). Such revictimization and discounting by supposedly "caring" professionals exacerbate the trauma survivor's problems exponentially.

There is evidence of a heritable component to the transmission of PTSD (Glatt et al., 2013; Skelton et al., 2012) and to one's ability to be resilient to its assaults (Southwick & Watson, 2015). Undoubtedly some people, because of a previous psychiatric history, are more predisposed to breaking down under stress than are others (Norris et al., 2002; Ullman & Siegel, 1994). Furthermore, the number and magnitude of the trauma will predict higher potential for PTSD (Norris et al., 2002; Shalev, 1996, p. 86). Exposure to multiple rapes, being held in a concentration camp, extended child abuse, the loss of loved ones, or prolonged frontline combat typically puts the individual at far greater risk for PTSD than a onetime physical assault by a parent or an auto accident in which no one was killed. Additionally, lack of education, community support, chronic child abuse, low economic status, increased number in family, gender (females are seen as at greater risk), age (younger age at time of event), marital status (not married), and lack of family support systems have all been seen as contributing factors for developing PTSD (Jovanovic et al., 2004; Myers & Wee, 2005; Norris et al., 2002; Southwick & Watson, 2015; Suar & Khuntia, 2004; Wilson, Friedman, & Lindy, 2001).

However, no absolute factors guarantee that one person as opposed to another will develop PTSD. Brewin (2005) found that although there are a number of risk factors for PTSD, their effect sizes tend to be small and vary according to the nature of the trauma. Given the right conditions, it appears *anyone can be a candidate*. The collapse of a concrete walkway in a crowded hotel gives us a prime example of how one event may suddenly produce PTSD symptoms. Biographical data gathered following the Kansas City Hyatt Regency skywalk disaster revealed that few survivors had character disorders before the event. Yet 6 months after the event, many were suffering from a variety of presenting symptoms (Wilkinson, 1983). White (1989) found the same result in a study of burn victims suffering PTSD symptoms. The overwhelming majority of these individuals had no previous psychiatric history.

Probably the best summing statement about who will and who will not manifest PTSD was made by Grinker and Spiegel (1945) in their study of World War II veterans. They concluded that no matter how strong, normal, or stable a person might be, if the stress were sufficient to cross that particular individual's threshold, a "war neurosis" would develop. It should also be clearly understood that PTSD is not culture bound. While there are variations on the theme cross-culturally, there is a great deal of evidence that PTSD is a cross-cultural phenomenon common to all people (Brewin, 2003; Marsella et al., 1996). In summary, susceptibility and ability to be resilient to PTSD is a function of several factors: genetic predisposition, ecological factors, constitution, personality makeup, previous life experiences, state of mind, cultural artifacts, phase of maturational development at onset, spiritual beliefs, social support system before and after the trauma, and content and intensity of the event (Brewin, 2003, 2005; DeVries, 1996; Furst, 1967; Green & Berlin, 1987; Halpern & Tramontin, 2007; Kaniasty & Norris, 1999; Norris et al., 2002; Shalev, 1996; Southwick & Watson, 2015; Wilson, Friedman, & Lindy, 2001).

Neurophysiological Responses

In the last 20 years a tremendous number of psychobiological studies have conclusively demonstrated that trauma affects the individual in a variety of physical ways. Researchers

have discovered that neurotransmitters, hormones, cortical areas of the brain, and the nervous system play a large role in PTSD (Daniels et al., 2013; Herringa et al., 2013; Lanius, Bluhm, & Frewen, 2013; Lu et al., 2013; Macdonald, Franz, & Vasterling, 2012; Rothschild, 2000; Schore, 2013; Tyrka et al., 2013; van der Kolk, 1996a; Vasterling & Brewin, 2005). Putting this complex neurobiological puzzle together has tremendous ramifications about what kinds of drug therapies might be used in its treatment.

When a person is exposed to severe stress, neurotransmitters, neuromodulators, hormones, endogenous opioids, and specific cortical functions designed to deal with the emergency are activated (Grinker & Speigel, 1945; Santa Ana et al., 2006; Selye, 1976; Siegel, 1995; van der Kolk, 1996a, pp. 215–234; Vermetten & Bremner, 2002). Although cessation of the traumatic event may remove the person from danger and no longer require the body's system to function on an emergency basis, if the stress is prolonged, the nervous system may continue to function in an elevated and energized state as if the emergency were still continuing (Burgess-Watson, Hoffman, & Wilson, 1988; van der Kolk, 1996a, pp. 214–234).

Furthermore, there is evidence that intense and continuous stress can cause permanent physical changes in the brain (Copeland, 2000; Daniels et al., 2013; Malizia & Nutt, 2000; McDonald, Franz, & Vasterling, 2012; Vermetten & Bremner, 2002). These changed physiological states are important because they not only cause individuals extreme physical and psychological duress long after the traumatic event but also help explain why people do not "get over" PTSD.

In their study and review of the neuroanatomical correlates of the effects of stress on memory, Bremner and associates (1995, 1997) and Gurvitz, Shenton, and Pittman (1995) found in combat veterans significant decreases in the hippocampal area of the brain where explicit memory encoding, memory consolidation, and organization take place, as did Stein and associates (1994) in women who had experienced severe child sexual abuse. Whether the smaller hippocampus is a causal factor for PTSD or PTSD causes the hippocampus to become smaller is not known. However, Astur and associates' (2006) study of identified PTSD experimental subjects versus non-PTSD controls supports these findings of decreased hippocampal activity.

A great deal of psychophysiological assessment evidence indicates that stimulus presentation to PTSD sufferers of sights, sounds, and smells associated with the long-past traumatic event will immediately send the neuroendocrine system into overdrive and cause physiological responses such as increased heart rate, blood pressure, and triglyceride and cholesterol levels, along with decreased blood flow to the skin and gastrointestinal and renal areas. These psychophysiological responses are not evinced in control subjects who are presented with the same stimuli (Lating & Everly, 1995).

Affective-State-Dependent Retention

There is now very clear evidence that physiological changes occur in the presence of trauma (Briere & Scott, 2006; Friedman, 2015) and are exacerbated when the trauma becomes ongoing and complex (Ford, 2009). Changed physiological functioning due to traumatic stimuli is important as a building block in Bower's (1981) hypothesis of *affective-state-dependent retention*. Bower has proposed that because the traumatic event was stored in memory under completely different physiological (increased heart rate, higher adrenal output) and psychological (extreme fright, shock) circumstances, different mood states markedly interfere with recollecting specific cues of the event. Karl, Malta, and Maercker's (2006) meta-analysis supports the hypothesis that changes in memory processing accompany PTSD. Therefore, the important elements of the memory that need exposure in order to reduce anxiety are not accessible in the unaroused state (Keane et al., 1985, p. 266) and can be remembered only when that approximate state of arousal is reintroduced by cues in the environment (Keane, 1976). Indeed, there is evidence that release of neuromodulators such as norepinephrine when an individual is in a stressful situation leads to pathological response to recall of previous traumatic events for which the individual has no previous memory (Bremner et al., 1995).

To the contrary, the classic dissociative, numbing response and "forgetting" of the traumatic event may be caused by excessive endogenous opioids secreted during prolonged stress (van der Kolk, 1996a, p. 227). Thus the notion that a victim of PTSD can "just forget" or adopt a "better, more positive attitude" does little to effect change in the individual (Keane et al., 1985, p. 266). This proposal has important implications for treatment, particularly with respect to returning the person to as close an approximation of the event as possible. These neurological issues are even more ominously true for children.

Children and Neuropathology

There is a high likelihood for children who experience traumatic events in early childhood to develop neuropathology (Lewis, 2005; Lu et al., 2013; Tryka et al., 2013). If the trauma occurs during early developmental stages, there is a dramatic shift in the brain's functioning from an inquisitive, exploring, learning mode to a reactive, defensive, surviving mode. When the stress response survival systems of the child's brain are operating in overdrive, the learning systems take a back seat. As a result, a wide array of normal developmental activities are placed on hold, with potentially catastrophic consequences across social and educational environments. In plain language, operating systems in the child's brain get damaged.

Damage occurs in three areas: emotional dysregulation, which may be characterized by emotional emptiness or constant distress; dissociation, which manifests as mental disorientation and confusion; and hyperarousal, which physically drains the body to the point of exhaustion. The potential for these devastating outcomes to occur is particularly enhanced if the trauma comes at the hands of a caregiver who is supposed to be nourishing the learning brain of the child rather than activating the survival system (Ford, 2009). You will meet some of the characteristics of these neurological train wrecks later in this chapter and in Chapter 9, Sexual Assault. The foregoing paragraphs should give you a fair idea of why treating childhood PTSD and survivors of extended childhood trauma is so difficult and why transcrisis states are so common with these individuals.

Incidence, Impact, and Trauma Type

Incidence

If PTSD has been with us for so long, what made it finally surface with such profound impact? Epidemiological studies indicate that the total U.S. population will experience a lifetime rate of 56% and 7.8% can be expected to develop PTSD with women twice as likely (10.4%) as men (5%) (American Psychiatric Association, 2000, p. 466; Kessler et al., 2005, Perkonnig et al., 2000). So, in the common course of events, the chances of "catching" PTSD are fairly small. The average "catch it" rate for PTSD appears to be about 20% after a trauma is experienced (Norris et al., 2002). However, when studies target particular at-risk groups such as adolescents and young adults, people in hazardous occupations, sexual assault victims, severe burn cases, psychiatric cases, and refugees, the incidence of PTSD in these populations is much greater (McFarlane & de Girolamo, 1996, pp. 129–154). The classic at-risk example is the Vietnam veteran. The numbers of returning Vietnam veterans who were having some kind of personality disorder far exceeded what statistics would predict. It is estimated that 26% , or 960,000 Vietnam veterans, have had episodes of PTSD (Kukla et al., 1990). This massive number of veterans in severe psychological trouble was simply too large to ignore.

Residual Impact

People's basic assumptions about their belief in the world as a meaningful and comprehensible place, their own personal invulnerability, and their view of themselves in a positive light account to a great extent for their individual manifestations of PTSD (Figley, 1985b, pp. 401–402; Kaniasty & Norris, 1999). Even in the most well-integrated people, who have excellent coping abilities, good rational and cognitive behavior patterns, and positive social support systems, residual effects of traumatizing events may linger. An outstanding example of such residual effects is the experience of a retired Marine captain who had seen extensive field duty as a combat infantryman in Vietnam in 1968. The anecdote he relates typifies the residual effects in an individual who is psychologically well integrated, is securely employed in a professional job, has a tightly knit, extended family support system, and on the whole enjoys life and has a positive outlook on it.

Chris: I had just gotten home from work late one summer evening. The kids had decided to camp out in the woods down by the creek. A thunderstorm was rolling in and I decided I'd better go down and check on them to see if they were packed in for the night. It had started to rain pretty heavily, and there was a lot of thunder and lightning. I pulled on a poncho and got a flashlight, crossed the road, and went into the woods. I don't suppose it was 200 yards to where the kids were camped. Now, I'd grown up running those woods, so I knew it like the back of my hand.

However, once I got into the woods things kinda went haywire. I immediately thought, "Get off the trail, or you'll get the whole platoon zapped." I slipped off the path and became a part of the scenery. Every sense in my body went up to full alert. I was back in Nam again operating with my platoon,

and I was on a natural, adrenaline high. Time and place kinda went into suspended animation, and I eased through the woods, kinda like standing off and watching myself do this, knowing it was me, but yet not me too. The last thing I remember before walking into the clearing where the kids had their tent set up was that we could have ambushed the hell out of that place. I don't harp and brood on Nam, put it behind me after I got out of the Corps, but that night sure put me in a different place than central Indiana, July 1984. I just couldn't believe that would ever happen. It's a bit unnerving.

Importance of Trauma Type

Catastrophes, when viewed by the public, tend to fall into one category: bad. However, one of the interesting phenomena around PTSD is that there is a marked distinction between natural and human-made catastrophes. Acts of God create far fewer instances of PTSD than do human-made ones. As an example, the volcanic eruption of Mount St. Helen's incident rate of PTSD was a very low 3% to 4% (Shore, Tatum, & Vollmer, 1986).

Human-made acts of trauma create even more instances of PTSD when the trauma directly affects the social support system of the family. Holocaust survivors, hostages, rape victims, children of murdered parents, and victims of incest are all strong potential candidates for PTSD. Survivors of both uncommissioned human-made disasters such as the breaking of the Buffalo Creek dam and commissioned trauma such as the Chowchilla bus kidnapping carry high potential for PTSD. (The Buffalo Creek disaster occurred in 1972 when a coal company retainer dam broke during a series of heavy rainstorms; the resulting flood wiped out the residents of the Buffalo Creek valley in West Virginia. The bus kidnapping occurred in 1976 when a Chowchilla, California, school bus carrying elementary and secondary school children was hijacked at gunpoint. The children were taken from the bus and forced into a truck buried underground; eventually they were able to tunnel out.) The distinction between the two types of human-caused traumatic events is that one is a "sin of omission" and the other is a "sin of commission." While the human acts of omission such as oil tank car derailments and explosions in towns can certainly cause PTSD, the school shootings such as Sandy Hook elementary school and Columbine High School are potentially far more toxic because they are unpredictable, trust within the community is broken, and people are in shock and disbelief that such a heinous and nonsensical act can happen in their peaceful community (Jurgersen, Dailey, Uhernik, & Smith, 2013).

What makes these events so particularly terrible is that they seem to be tragedies that should not have happened, responsibility for them can be readily assigned, and they clearly violate accepted standards of moral conduct (Figley, 1985a, pp. 400–401). As a result, there exists in any human-made catastrophe the likelihood of more severe posttraumatic psychological problems as compared to natural disasters. The problem is that the line between the two is becoming less clear. More and more people look at technology as a means of controlling nature. Thus, for example, Mother Nature makes the rain, but the Army Corps of Engineers builds dikes and opens floodgates (Kaniasty & Norris, 1999), and when things go wrong individuals (and lawyers) start looking for culprits.

Vietnam: The Archetype

In a comparative analysis of PTSD among various trauma survivor groups, Wilson, Smith, and Johnson (1985) isolated 10 variables that were hypothesized as predisposing to PTSD: degree of life threat; degree of bereavement; speed of onset; duration of the trauma; degree of displacement in home continuity; potential for recurrence; degree of exposure to death, dying, and destruction; degree of moral conflict inherent in the situation; role of the person in the trauma; and the proportion of the community affected. They compared these variables in a variety of trauma survivor groups: Vietnam combat veterans as well as victims of rape, auto accident, armed robbery, natural disasters, divorce, life-threatening illness of a loved one, family trauma, death of a significant other, multiple traumas, and a control group.

Veterans were significantly affected in 7 of the 10 dimensions, with rape victims a distant second in terms of number of predisposing variables present. When the data were transformed to fit precise PTSD criteria, all trauma groups were significantly different from the control group (pp. 142–172). In plain words, the data suggest that one could not experience a catastrophic event more likely to produce "complex" PTSD than Vietnam—with one exception. With the advent of women in combat, if sexual assault and combat are combined, such as has occurred in Iraq and Afghanistan, then either women or men who have been in combat and have also been sexually assaulted are one-and-a-half more times likely to be diagnosed with a mental health condition than those who have not been assaulted (Munsey, 2009).

Why did Vietnam mark the birth of what was to become PTSD? Although any war could be construed to produce many PTSD symptoms, the rules of war changed in Vietnam. First, the average age of the soldier in Vietnam was 19.2, compared with 26.0 in World War II (Brende & Parson, 1985, p. 19). A psychologically immature 19-year-old soldier was not mentally prepared for the psychic trauma that awaited him in Vietnam (MacPherson, 1984, pp. 62–63).

Hypervigilance. In Vietnam, there was no front line and no relief from constant vigilance. A 365-day combat tour was exactly that. In comparison to World War II troops, who might be in acute combat situations for a few days or weeks and then be pulled off the line, Vietnam "grunts" spent extended periods of time in the field, and even when they were in a base camp, they had to be alert for rocket attacks and combat assaults on their position. Hypervigilance became an ironclad rule of survival.

Listen to Billie Mac, a composite character of many combat veterans Dr. James has interviewed. Following is his writing as part of a **narrative therapy exposure** component (Mørkved et al., 2014; Mott et al., 2015) of cognitive processing therapy (Resick & Schnicke, 1993; Resick, Monson, & Chard, 2008; Resick, Monson, & Gutner, 2007). Narrative therapy is designed to encourage recall through writing(Mott et al., 2015) and get individuals unstuck (Monson & Shnaider, 2014) from the endless cycle of attempts to avoid the trauma yet continuously perseverate on it. The purpose in his written narrative is twofold.

First, the primary goal of trauma-focused therapy (TFT) is to help survivors thoroughly examine and unpackage traumatic memories so they can reappraise and reframe those events for healthier living. While TFT will work on here-and-now trauma-related problems the survivor is confronting, initial therapy focuses on the historical feeling, behaviors, cognitions, and context that are hypothesized to play a central role in the onset of PTSD (Monson & Shnaider, 2014).

Second is the concept of **meaning making**. Meaning making is both *global* and *situational* (Steger & Park, 2012, pp. 172–174). A global meaning system is the composite set of beliefs, goals, and sense of purpose that we operationalize to live our lives. This global meaning system then goes smoothly about its business of assigning good, bad, and neutral meanings to specific situations encountered on the road of life. However, what happens when an extraordinary situation lands in the middle of our nice, safe, justice-for-all, fair-play world and shatters it to the point that our global meaning system overloads and blows a psychological fuse? When this chasm in meaning occurs, loss of control, predictability, or ability to comprehend the world as one once knew it as a reasonable, predictable one goes in the dumpster, and in our attempts to control the emotional and cognitive dysregulation that occurs, PTSD emerges as a major player in our now modified and distorted global belief system.

Meaning making is the attempt to restore the original global meaning system and not let it be driven by the one traumatic event that changed it. Meaning making calls for reviewing and reframing the traumatic event in such a way that an acceptable appraisal of the event can be made. The bottom line is that the event itself can never be undone, but both the negative self and global appraisals of it can (Steger & Park, 2012, pp. 174–175). Billie Mac's tortured narrative is one component of a comprehensive therapeutic endeavor to bring meaning back into his life.

Narrative Exposure Through Journaling. For PTSD clients, speaking of what has happened to them is extremely difficult. Journaling is an excellent method of opening up affect and allowing nonverbal catharsis to occur. By engaging in written narrative exposure, putting down their thoughts in their own words and then hearing them, individuals place the terrible memories at a safe enough psychological distance that they and the human services worker can analyze them (Cienfuegos & Monelli, 1983).

Journal writing gives the human services worker a catalyst for encouraging the kind of free association necessary to open the crystallized defenses of the individual who might otherwise never explore the traumatic event (Progoff, 1975). One of the veterans who formed the basis of our composite combat therapy group character, Billie Mac, writes a description of one of those endless nights when no sleep will come or, worse, when the terror comes with sleep as the introduction to the group.

*Where Did B.M. Go?**
What happened to B.M.—the boy from Mississippi—happy-go-lucky, not a care in the world, who loved life, sports, the sunshine, the rain . . . and everything in the used-to-be-beautiful world. Everyone told B.M., "Go to school. Play sports. Go to college." But B.M. decided to do for his country. B.M. wanted to go to war and fight to win . . . to serve his country . . . to make everyone proud of him. B.M. went to war. B.M. killed, massacred, mutilated, burnt, hated—a hate that was like a drunk hate—tore his own heart out a little at a time, time after time.

B.M. fought and survived a war that 127 warriors that went with B.M. didn't.

B.M. looked at everyone around him and wondered why the people hated him.

Why they were scared of him . . . why they feared the warrior from Vietnam who went to a fight they were scared to fight.

B.M. wanted to love . . . to be loved. It seemed like the world was completely different from him and didn't have the same ideals about life and love.

B.M. became a drunk. He drank to forget the war, the brave warriors who had given their lives in Vietnam, to forget the people that he was living around. To these people B.M. was a cold-blooded murdering S.O.B.—a baby-killing M.F.

B.M. had been taught all his life, "Thou shalt not kill, love thine enemy." B.M. lost his morals. B.M. killed his enemies. B.M. cut the heads and ears off some of his enemies. B.M. lost his soul. B.M. is lost to God and can't be forgiven. People can say, "Ask God to forgive you, B.M." But B.M. can't forgive himself and can't ask for forgiveness. B.M. has accepted that feeling like someone took his heart out and stomped it into the ground. There is not a day in his life that he doesn't feel hurt or hurt the ones he loves.

B.M. just wants to be loved . . . to love himself again; to get rid of that hard feeling deep down inside of his heart. B.M. wants to have peace of mind. Is it too much for him to ask, to seek, to search for? Is death what it will take for B.M. to finally find peace within himself?

Why can't B.M. get out of all these depressing moods he stays in . . . and cries about nothing when he is driving down the road.

Sometimes B.M. thinks he is a crazy S.O.B. Maybe the people are right. Why can't B.M. keep a job? Because B.M. was a fuck-up after he got back from Vietnam.

---

* Used with permission.

His vengeance and his screwed-up attitude keep him in trouble. B.M. would get so much on his mind and B.M. would keep putting it back inside. The more he put it back, the worse his depression would get until it would erupt in a rage of vengeance, which would always wind up hurting himself or the people he loved.

Even the government deceived B.M. They told B.M., "Don't worry, B.M. You go and fight this war for your country and if anything happens we will take care of you." B.M.'s response to this is, "Fine! I will do all I can for my government and my country." But give me my heart and soul back. Make me sleep at night. Make me quit crying. Take this depression away. Help me find a job and help me feel alive again. Give me back what you took from me. B.M. is what you took and I want myself back.

I wish I could give back the lives I have taken from the world, but I know that I can't. I would if I could, and I am the one that will have to live with that in my heart throughout eternity.

B.M. vividly and dramatically illustrates the anguish of PTSD in his writing—anguish from both an intrapersonal and interpersonal standpoint, of guilt he feels within himself for his moral transgressions and rage at the transgressions visited on him by an impersonal government and an uncaring society; anguish over what he was and is and how he is now attempting to resolve and reintegrate these two vastly different people that were and are B.M. Billie Mac continuously uses his initials, pointing over and over to himself, but in the third person. Only in the last paragraph does his plea change clearly to subjective, first-person owning statements. Even these statements are couched in terms of magical thinking—wish fulfillment. The use of Billie Mac's initials as an identifier of what he really perceives himself to be is not happenstance. The initials "B.M." also stand for "bowel movement." Indeed, Billie Mac's self-assessment is that he is mostly worthless "shit" to himself and others. This is typical of the kind of self-condemnation that an individual who is both victim and victimizer experiences.

This excruciating piece of writing is an initiating step in the long process that moves from self-condemnation to what Lifton (1973) calls **animated guilt**. Animated guilt enables the individual to start taking responsibility for past actions and start to experience new degrees of personal liberation. This rather dramatic example of journal writing was done

voluntarily, but when clients in a crisis situation will not talk about their experiences, sometimes suggesting that they write down their feelings can be a way of breaking the impasse (James & Gilliland, 2003). Keeping a journal not only can be an extremely effective way of dealing with unbidden feelings and thoughts as they surface, but also can provide the worker and the client with an assessment of how therapy is progressing (Pearsons, 1965). Journaling goes beyond standard CPT written work of writing down daily monitoring of events, thoughts, and emotions of which one must be trauma related (Monson & Shnaider, 2014, p. 70). For anyone like Billie Mac who suffers survivor's guilt or victim/victimizer status, journaling may be a particularly effective way to ventilate feelings that the person might otherwise be unable to talk about with the worker but now can because it is on paper and psychologically distanced. Billie Mac's journaling is a very good personal analysis of what went badly wrong in Vietnam.

Billie Mac: I was 18 when the plane set down at Da Nang. The crew chief told us to hit the ground running because Da Nang was under a rocket attack. I was scared stiff. Well, Da Nang was heaven, rockets and all, to what later happened. It got a lot, lot worse than that.

Lack of Goals. No territory was ever "won," so there was no concrete feeling of accomplishment. Combat troops felt betrayed by U.S. politics over a war for which there were no fixed goals for winning and a command structure that was waging a war of attrition, with "body counts" being the primary way of judging whether a mission was successful (Lifton, 1974; MacPherson, 1984, p. 58).

Billie Mac: We swept that one village at least a half dozen times. Sometimes we'd dig in and dare the NVA to hit us, and they did. We lost a half dozen guys in that pesthole. For what? For nothin'. We gave it up, and they moved right back in.

Victim/Victimizer. It further compounded the virulent psychological milieu of Vietnam that veterans, unlike most individuals who suffer from PTSD, played two roles—victim and victimizer. Because both enemies and allies were Vietnamese, a soldier could not distinguish friend from foe, nor could vigilance be relaxed around women or children because of their potential lethality. Also, because the enemy was Asian and had extremely different cultural values from Americans, it was relatively simple to dehumanize killing or maiming them, particularly when troops saw such things done to their comrades. The nasty way guerrilla war is fought brought out brutality on both sides (Lifton, 1974). Shifts of role from victim to aggressor could occur in seconds (Brende & Parson, 1985, p. 96).

Billie Mac: I couldn't imagine killing a kid or woman. That was true until our medic tried to take care of a kid covered with blood. We all thought he was wounded. When John went over to the dink, he opened up his arms and had a grenade. Blew him and the medic away. Kill them after that? You bet!

Bonding, Debriefing, and Guilt. The way the armed services filled units had much to do with lack of a support system within the service itself. Personnel replacements were parceled piecemeal into units, which is a bad idea if you are trying to avoid PTSD. Current research indicates that unit cohesion is a critical buffer against PTSD (Armistead-Jehle et al., 2011). Although this method put rookies with veterans, it was not the best way to bond a unit together. The rotation system also took its psychological toll. Each person did a 365-day tour. The stress of being "short" caused men to become very self-preservative and immobilized. Units as a whole were never moved out of combat, and a man who entered combat singly returned singly without benefit of debriefing time. The war was essentially fought in patrol and platoon actions. It was a loner's war, and the soldier who fought alone went home alone (MacPherson, 1984, pp. 64–65). A man might be sweating out an ambush in the jungle one day, and two days later be sitting on his front porch back home.

It is no great surprise that returning soldiers who had no transition period from Vietnam to the United States were viewed as "different" and "changed" by their relatives (Brende & Parson, 1985, pp. 48–49). Such rapid transitions out of life-threatening situations left many with survivor's guilt (Spiegel, 1981). They were glad to be out of Vietnam, but felt guilty of betrayal for leaving comrades behind; or they took responsibility when they were away from their units and friends were hurt or killed (MacPherson, 1984, p. 237).

Billie Mac: It was inside of a week from jungle to home. My folks thought it was pretty weird because I put my fatigues on and slept in the woods.

I just couldn't take being confined in that house. I kept thinking about the guy who took my place as squad leader, Johnson. I knew he was gonna get somebody wasted. I needed to be there, but I sure didn't want to be. I immediately got drunk and stayed that way for a long time.

Civilian Adjustment. The rapid change from intense alertness in order to preserve one's life to trying to readjust to a humdrum society made many question where the "real world" was. Furthermore, the returnee's basic belief system would be quickly jarred when, on his arrival home, he was greeted with insensitivity and hostility for having risked his life for his country (Brende & Parson, 1985, p. 72). Veterans quickly found that for all the ability they had shown in making command decisions of life-or-death importance and the authority they had exercised over expensive equipment in Vietnam, the onus of having been there relegated them to civilian jobs far below their capabilities (MacPherson, 1984, p. 65).

Billie Mac: Any job I could get stunk. They were all menial, and they acted like they were doing me a favor. Hell! I'd made a lot bigger and smarter decisions than anybody I ever had as a boss.

Substance Abuse. The ease with which soldiers could obtain alcohol and drugs to numb themselves and escape mentally from the reality of Vietnam had severe consequences, both in addiction on return and in the public's growing misconception that veterans were all "drug-crazed baby killers," to be shunned as erratic and undependable (Brende & Parson, 1985, p. 72; MacPherson, 1984, pp. 64–65, 221–222). Substance abuse is a major comorbid player in PTSD (Ouimette & Read, 2014) and alcohol is a major self-medication used in attempting to get rid of the mind demons that lurk in the hellish dream worlds of those individuals who have PTSD as their bedmates.

Billie Mac: Yeah, I drank. Yeah, I shot kids. I drank mainly to try to forget about shooting kids. Anybody who hadn't been there could never understand. I drink now to get some sleep and keep the damned nightmares at bay. I drink after I get fired from a job, I drink when I have fights with the ole lady. I drink when the cops are chasing me at 100 miles an hour. Sounds like I need to be in AA rather than this combat group.

Attitude. The time period during which a vet served in Vietnam seems to be highly correlated with PTSD. Historically the war can be divided into trimesters. Anyone serving in Vietnam during the last two trimesters, from the time of the Tet offensive in 1968 to the U.S. withdrawal in 1973, would have, from a psychological standpoint, a much greater reason to question the purpose of being there than those who had served early on. The prevailing attitude of "Nobody can win, so just concentrate on surviving" cynicism was in direct opposition to the "Save a democracy from the perils of communism" idealism of the first trimester (Laufer, Yager, & Grey-Wouters, 1981).

Antiwar Sentiment. The impact of the antiwar sentiment that veterans met on their return home cannot be minimized. It is unique to the Vietnam War and found its focal point in returnees. Veterans were spurned immediately on their arrival in the United States, suffered prejudice on college campuses as they came back to school, were left out of jobs because of antiwar sentiments, and were disenfranchised from government programs through meager GI Bill benefits and government disavowal of physical problems associated with exposure to the chemical defoliant Agent Orange. Perhaps worst of all were the comparisons their fathers made—men who had fought the "honorable" fight of World War II and could not understand the problems their sons suffered in a war that was not black-and-white but a dirty shade of gray (MacPherson, 1984, pp. 54–58). It is interesting to note that Vietnam combat veterans diagnosed with PTSD whose fathers were also combat veterans are likely to have more severe problems than those Vietnam veterans whose fathers had not seen combat (Rosenheck & Fontana, 1998).

Billie Mac: I tried to talk to my old man about it. He'd been in World War II on Okinawa. Hell, he might as well have been in the Revolutionary War for all he could understand about Nam. He finally got so mad that he told me I was nuts and no damn good. He didn't mean that, but I'll never forget it.

All these factors came together in a sort of witch's brew for veterans trying to make meaning out of a situation that was life-threatening and generally considered pointless (Williams, 1983). Emotional support and reintegration with society and family are major tasks for veterans (Whealin, Decarvalho, & Vega, 2008), and strong social support is a major

antagonist to PTSD (Southwick & Watson, 2015). To survive such a hostile lack of both societal and familial support called for imposing psychological defense mechanisms that made a fertile breeding ground for PTSD. When these psychological defense mechanisms go awry, symptoms are typically seen in the three major PTSD diagnostic categories of intrusive thoughts, avoidance, and increased nervous system arousal.

Intrusive–Repetitive Ideation

Intrusive-repetitive thoughts become so problematic for the individual that these thoughts begin to dominate existence. Intrusive thoughts generally take the form of visual images that are sparked by sights, sounds, smells, or tactile reminders that bring the repressed images to awareness (Donaldson & Gardner, 1985, pp. 371–372).

Billie Mac: That day at the village when Al got it keeps coming back. I don't go fishing in the bayou anymore. It smells and looks like Nam, and every time I'd go I'd start thinking about that village, and I'd get the shakes.

Over time, triggers for intrusive thoughts may become associated with subtle and more generalized stimuli that are seemingly irrelevant to the trauma (van der Kolk & McFarlane, 1996, p. 10). These thoughts occur not only in conscious contact with reality but also in the form of flashbacks and nightmares.

Billie Mac: The reason that got me to the vets center is real simple. I was having these awful nightmares about being in a firefight while on a long-range reconnaissance patrol near Laos. The next thing I know, I'm dug into a bunker watching an enemy truck convoy's headlights come down the Ho Chi Minh Trail with my rifle aimed at them. The only problem was that it was on the banks of the Wolf River in Memphis, Tennessee, and it was headlights on I-40. It was also not 1970 but 1988. I knew if I didn't get help I was going to kill somebody.

Denial/Numbing

Accompanying emotions of guilt, sadness, anger, and rage occur as the thoughts continue to intrude into awareness. To keep these disturbing thoughts out of awareness, the individual may resort to self-medication in the form of alcohol or drugs.

Self-medication may temporarily relieve depressive, hostile, anxious, and fearful mood states (Horowitz & Solomon, 1975), but what usually occurs is a vicious cycle that alternates between being anesthetized to reality by the narcotic and experiencing elevated intrusion of the trauma with every return to sobriety. The ultimate outcome is increased dependence on the addictive substance as a method of keeping the intrusive thoughts submerged (LaCoursiere, Bodfrey, & Ruby, 1980).

Billie Mac: The drinkin' is no damn good. I know that, but try going without sleep for a week and knowing every time you nod off, that horrible nightmare's gonna come. Then it starts popping up in the daytime and you drink more to keep it pushed back.

As people attempt to cope with catastrophes, they become passive (immobile and paralyzed) or active (able to cope with the situation). Individual reactions fall into three major groupings: momentary freezing, flight reaction, and denial/numbing. In the prolonged stress of a combat situation, denial/numbing is the most common response and allows the soldier to cope and live with the experience in three ways: by believing he is invulnerable to harm, by becoming fatalistic, or by taking matters into his own hands and becoming extremely aggressive. Any of these proactive stances allows the individual to get through the trauma and cope with it without losing complete control (Figley, 1985a, pp. 406–408). Typically, survivors of trauma will let down these defense barriers and will have acute stress disorders immediately after the trauma, but will recover. For those who do not, continued emotional numbing and repression can have severe consequences.

Billie Mac: Looking back on it, I can't believe how callous I have become. SOP [standard operating procedure] was "It don't mean nothin', screw it, drive on." This would be right after a B-40 round had blown your buddy's brains all over you. You had to put it behind you to survive. A guy fell off the construction site I was working on last fall and splattered himself all over the pavement. I sat on a steel beam about 30 feet above the guy and just kept eating my lunch. No big deal!

Submerging emotions out of conscious awareness does not mean that they are summarily discarded. The price is that emotional numbing left in place and not relieved can generalize to other aspects of one's life and result in later psychological difficulties (Wilkinson, 1983). Shunted into the unconscious for a long time, trigger events in the form of everyday stressors can pile up and cause emotional blowouts when the individual is least prepared for them (Figley, 1985a, p. 408).

Increased Nervous Symptom Arousal

Autonomic hyperarousal in people with PTSD causes them to be nondiscriminating to stimuli that may hold no threat to them at all. Acoustic startle response is a cardinal feature of the trauma response (van der Kolk, 1996a, p. 221).

Billie Mac: I can't stand the sound of a chopper. Every time I hear one, I want to run. I get the feeling that every time I hear the 5 o'clock traffic chopper, it's gonna circle in, pick me up, and take me to a hot LZ [landing zone]. One came over the building I was working on. I didn't hear it at first. When I did hear it, I jumped and fell 10 feet and broke my arm.

In the same vein, **hypervigilance**, being on constant guard for threats when there is no immediate threat, is constantly with the person and causes concentration and attention problems. As these problems distort information processing, the resulting inability to decode messages from the central nervous system causes the person to react to the environment in either exaggerated or inhibited ways (van der Kolk & McFarlane, 1996, pp. 14–15).

Billie Mac: This may sound kinda weird, but I don't ever sit with my back to a door. Matter of fact, I really don't like sitting anywhere where my back might be to somebody else! I get real jumpy.

Dissociation

Dissociation symptoms are so potent that the DSM-5 (American Psychiatric Association, 2013) lists them as a special category of PTSD. Dissociation at the moment of trauma is perhaps the most important long-term predictive variable for PTSD and is invariably connected to "complex" PTSD (Herman, 1997, pp. 118–129; Marmar et al., 1991). Dissociation can range from numbing or lack of emotional responsiveness to the event to derealization ("this is not real; it isn't happening; it's a bad dream") or depersonalization ("I'm out of my body and looking at this from a grandstand") to complete amnesia of the event.

Dissociation splits off the memory from conscious awareness, but that does not mean the noxious stimulus event is extinguished. To the contrary, dissociation can be a last-resort adaptive way of coping with the trauma while it is going on, but the lack of integration of the traumatic event seems to be a leading cause of PTSD. If dissociation continues, it can severely interfere with daily living and breed disconnectedness and isolation (van der Kolk, 1996b, p. 286). At its penultimate, dissociation can become dissociative identity disorder (formerly known as multiple personality disorder).

Billie Mac: It's like a lot of times I'm looking at me doing something sorta through a video camera, maybe. Like I'm smaller than real life, and I sorta know it's me, but it's not like I'm really there. The first time I did that was when we were in that village and my buddy Al got it.

What the person needs most is to bring these thoughts and behaviors into conscious awareness and come to grips with them, so they can be resolved. Yet, rather than confronting the intrusive and threatening material, the person is more likely to deny its existence and use a variety of avoidance responses to escape from the situation (Horowitz et al., 1980). This issue is particularly problematic in therapy and is why those who suffer from PTSD may be particularly resistant and noncompliant to approaches that reexpose them to the feared trauma (Bernstein, 1986).

Social Supports

Natural disasters leave so few emotional scars because such disasters often strike intact social support systems simultaneously (Figley, 1988). In natural disasters that affect the whole community, everyone becomes a survivor. As we shall see in Chapter 17, Disaster Response, community support is critical to the individual's returning to a sense of normalcy after a major traumatic event (Halpern & Tramontin, 2007; Harvey, Tummala-Narra, & Hamm, 2012; Zinner & Williams, 1999). For Billy Mac and his fellow Vietnam veterans that community support was severely lacking. Family members help each other through the horror of the disaster, and there is no blaming the individual (Figley, 1985a, p. 409; Kaniasty & Norris, 1999). One of the keystones for bridging the gap between traumatic events and a return to adequate and wholesome functioning is a strong support system that is most generally based within the family (Monson & Shnaider, 2014, pp. 102–103; Southwick &

Watson, 2015, p. 24). But when the trauma is intrafamilial and takes the form of child and spouse abuse, those who are most traumatized are most generally the ones who are denied the most social support within the family and that becomes a major progenitor for PTSD (Courtois & Ford, 2009; Saxe, Ellis, & Kaplow, 2007). Those who should provide the most comfort are the ones who are inflicting the most pain (Figley, 1985a, p. 411).

Further exacerbating family relationships is the ingrained tendency in trauma victims to "not feel." Whereas the individual would like to be able to demonstrate feelings of caring and love, experience has taught him or her that exposure of feelings is foolhardy because it invariably makes one vulnerable to further pain. These concepts strike at the very heart of what sustains family life—trust. The response of family members is to feel misunderstood, unloved, fearful, and angry. The response is reciprocal and plunges all members deeper into a vortex of family discordance.

From a family system perspective, if children, parents, or spouses attempt to regulate the continuing warfare in which the individual is engaging, they will be worn down and out by the effort. The individual may also become so dependent on the stabilizing person (usually the spouse) that the individual's needs breed resentment in anyone else who demands time and effort (usually children). The outcome of this spiral is what the individual may fear most from the support system—rejection. Feelings of guilt, numbing, anger, and loss plague the individual, and the spiral continues ever downward into more inappropriate behavior patterns and ultimate disintegration of the family.

Family members who cannot deal with the trauma may paradoxically turn on the victim. Sadly, this is too often the occurrence in the case of mothers who deny their spouses' abuse of the children, finally are confronted with the issue by children and family services, and then blame the children for the trouble they have caused! The same is true for rape victims who, if children, may have parents who are psychologically unable to provide support for them and indeed revictimize them for having done something that led to the assault in the first place. If adults, rape victims may have a spouse who is unable to respond in supportive ways or who blames the victim for "promiscuous or seductive" behavior that invited the rape or claims the victim "didn't resist enough" (Notman & Nadelson, 1976).

In attempting to deal with a family member who has suffered a traumatic experience, other members may experience the stress to the degree that they become "infected" by it (Figley, 1988). Indeed, if other family members have inadequate coping skills, their own problems may escalate to crisis proportions as the individual's reactions to the trauma create stress within the family. Or, if other members of the family have a hidden agenda of keeping the family in pathological homeostasis, they may engage in enabling the individual's disorder, much as an alcoholic's family may sabotage attempts at recovery. In summary, it should be clear that treating trauma victims also means treating the family (Tarrier & Humphreys, 2003).

Maladaptive Patterns Characteristic of PTSD

Summed dynamically, PTSD involves five **LO6** common patterns: death imprint, survivor's guilt, desensitization, estrangement, and emotional enmeshment.

Death Imprint. The traumatic experience provides a clear vision of one's own death in concrete biological terms (Ochberg, 1988, p. 12). Particularly in young individuals, the sense of invulnerability is vanquished and is replaced by rage and anger at one's newfound mortality (Lifton, 1975). For veterans in particular, there is a continuing identity with death. The normal boundary between living and dying is suspended. It is not unusual for veterans to describe themselves as already dead. The only way they have of testing the boundary between life and death is to seek sensation, even if it means danger and physical pain (Brende & Parson, 1985, p. 100). The remodeled criterion E of the DSM-5 (American Psychiatric Association, 2013) makes pointed reference to reckless and dangerous behavior. Combined with rage reactions, sensation-seeking behaviors put individuals squarely on a collision path with law enforcement agencies, employers, and families.

Billie Mac: After every law officer in Mississippi started chasing me, I ditched the car and ran into a woods. They even had bloodhounds after me. I slipped through them like they were a sieve. It was crazy, but for one of the few times since I've been back I really felt alive. I'd done that a hundred times on patrol.

Survivor's Guilt. A second pattern is guilt. Guilt comes in a variety of forms: guilt over surviving when others did not, guilt over not preventing the death of another, guilt over not having somehow been braver under the circumstances, guilt over complaining when others have suffered more, and guilt that the trauma is partly the individual's fault (Frederick, 1980). Most commonly, guilt takes the form of intrusive thoughts such as "I could have done more, and if I had he/she'd still be here," or "If I had just done this or that, it (the trauma) wouldn't have happened." Dynamically, the basis of these thoughts may be relief that the other person was the one to die, or the individual was lucky to get off so lightly (Egendorf, 1975).

Billie Mac: I was the only one in my outfit to get out of the Tet offensive without a scratch. I wonder why. Why me out of all those people? I've screwed my life up since then. Why did I deserve to get out clean when all those other good men didn't? Going to the wall in D.C. last year tore me to pieces. I cried and cried when I saw the names of my buddies up there. Things really got screwed up after that.

For other types of trauma individuals, bereavement is closely allied to survivor's guilt. Facilitating grief includes the expression of affect, reconciliation of the loss of a loved one or a missed part of one's life, the ambivalence of not having shared the same fate as others, and moving on to new and meaningful relationships (Ochberg, 1988, p. 10). Because numbing of affect is a major dynamic response to PTSD, it is extremely difficult for survivors to let loose their emotions and grieve.

Desensitization. A third pattern is desensitizing oneself to totally unacceptable events and then trying to return to a semblance of normalcy in a peaceful world. Feelings of guilt and fear may arise over pleasurable responses to physical violence against others. These feelings may become so acute that the individual conceals firearms for protection against imagined enemies but is simultaneously terrified of the guns and what might happen because of the violence that continuously seethes below the individual's own calm outer appearance. These strong bipolar emotional currents that flow back and forth within the individual lead to hostile, defensive, anxious, depressive, and fearful mood states that find little relief (Horowitz & Solomon, 1975).

Billie Mac: I don't hunt anymore. I hate it. Yet this one guy who was my boss didn't know how close he came to getting killed. I was within one inch of taking him out; I was so hot. It would have been a pleasure; the guy was such an ass.

Estrangement. A fourth pattern is the feeling that any future relationships will be counterfeit, that they mean little or nothing in the great scheme of things. As the person tries to ward off reminders of the experience, severe interpersonal difficulties occur. Because of the vastly different experiences they have undergone, PTSD individuals become estranged from their peers and truncate social relationships with them because "they don't understand"—and indeed "they" do not. Victimization may also be part of estrangement.

From being victimized in the original trauma, to possible secondary victimization by social services, hospitals, and mental health providers, to revictimization by significant others, the survivor is crushed under the weight of dealing with these initial and secondary assaults (Ochberg, 1988). The result is that the person becomes more isolated from social support systems and develops secondary symptoms that range across diagnostic categories of psychopathology (Horowitz & Solomon, 1975).

Billie Mac: I was sitting at my dad's watching TV when Saigon fell. I went nuts and trashed the house. What the hell was it all for? That really cooked it with my old man. I moved out after that and haven't said anything to him since.

Particularly for victims of sexual abuse, estrangement may take the form of negative intimacy. Invasion of one's personal space and being causes feelings of filthiness and degradation that make reestablishing old relationships or engendering new relationships an extremely difficult ordeal (Ochberg, 1988, pp. 12–13).

Emotional Enmeshment. A fifth pattern is a continuous struggle to move forward in a postholocaust existence but with an inability to find any significance in life (Lifton, 1975). Emotional fixation, particularly for veterans, has disastrous effects on family life. Sent to Vietnam as adolescents and exposed to prolonged trauma that the majority of the population will never experience, these individuals cannot bring themselves to engage in equitable relationships with their families and friends, nor can their families begin to understand their aberrant behavior (Brende & Parson, 1985, pp. 116–117). Depression, anger, avoidance, and alcohol abuse are hallmarks of veterans with PTSD, and these show up in mediating family functioning (Evans et al., 2003). It should not be surprising that those angry feelings are reciprocated by family members and create large fractures in a family structure that is already cracked and breaking.

Billie Mac: I can't believe what I've done to my kids. I love them more than anything in the world. At times, I'm the greatest dad in the world, coach the Little League team, take them everywhere. The next minute I'm all over them. I've knocked them around in a rage, and that scares the hell out of me. I'm some kind of Jekyll and Hyde, and my kids are afraid of me. My wife hates my guts for it and said if I didn't shape up *now* she was leaving. My solution to that was to go get drunk. When I came home she was gone with the kids. They and me would be better off if I was dead.

Now that you have read the foregoing descriptors of PTSD and Vietnam War veterans, think about current combat theaters in Iraq and Afghanistan. Do you see any similarities? Do you think there will be Billie Macs (or Jenny Lynns) coming home from Iraq or Afghanistan?

The Traumatic Wake of Iraq and Afghanistan

LO7

At this writing more than 2.5 million military personnel have cycled through these two theaters (Adams, 2013) and more are still going. Most of these personnel have been exposed to the petri dish of death, violence, bloodshed, and destruction in which PTSD grows so well. As in Vietnam, there are no front lines; it's hard to tell friend from foe; vigilance must be maintained 24/7 because a firefight, bombardment, or IED can occur at any moment or any place; no territory is "won"; political goals become cloudy; it is increasingly unclear why we are in those places; and termination dates are ill defined.

Further, there is a clear relationship between duration and intensity of specific types of trauma exposure and the number of symptoms of posttraumatic stress disorder (Baker, Risbrough, & Schork, 2008). In contrast to Vietnam, which was a one-year rotation and back to the "world," many veterans have served two or three tours of duty in the Middle Eastern conflicts, which piles stress not only on them but on their families as well. Many combat units are National Guard or reserve units based in hometowns rather than on military bases. These soldiers are both male and female, and they are older and have families and jobs as opposed to their younger counterparts who come from intact regular army regiments and divisions.

About half of service personnel are married and more than 70% have children. In real numbers that means 1.85 million children have one or both parents in the military, and 900,000 of those children have had one or both parents deployed one or more times since 2001 (Chandra et al., 2008). Those deployments cause all kinds of physical, psychological, personal, social, and academic issues with these children (Barnes, Davis, & Treiber, 2007; Engel, Gallagher, & Lyle, 2010; Flake et al., 2009), and that family stress kicks back to soldiers at the front. Combat stress clinics have found the major precipitating factor in homicide/suicide is a stressful relational event that comes from home via e-mail or telephone (Mental Health Advisory Team V, 2008).

Studies so far indicate the PTSD expectancy rate is somewhere between 11% and 12% for Middle Eastern war veterans in contrast to the estimated 30% of Vietnam veterans (National Center for PTSD, 2014a, 2014b). Even if only 10% of service personnel wind up with PTSD, the medical corps and Veterans Administration can expect another 250,000 cases to land on their doorsteps. Now consider the families of these service personnel. Even more ominous perhaps is the service suicide rate, which has increased enough to get national headlines. The grimness of these figures is reflected in a study by Matthews (2009), who asked seniors at West Point whether they believed they would develop PTSD. Only 22% thought they "would not" or "most likely would not."

The Department of Defense and the Veterans Administration have been very proactive in designing interventions that range from frontline, in-theater crisis intervention with combat troops through Post-Deployment Health Assessment and Reassessment programs that are designed to detect physical and psychological problems of returning active duty soldiers and veterans and immediately start treating them (Brenner, Vanderploeg, & Terro, 2009). There are now manualized protocols for treating both the symptoms of PTSD (Resick, Monson, & Chard, 2008) and readjustment to civilian life and the stressors that come with it (Whealin, DeCarvalho, & Vega, 2008). Evidence-based strategies that are specifically tailored to the military have been put in operation (Adler, Bliese, & Castro, 2011). Further, the Veterans Administration has been extremely proactive in

providing outreach programs to veterans who cannot easily reach a VA hospital. However, this is a reactive stance, and with the high incidence of mental health problems the Army has initiated the Comprehensive Soldier Fitness (CSF) program, which is an integrated, proactive approach to developing psychological resilience in soldiers, family members, and the Army's civilian workforce (Casey, 2011).

The Comprehensive Solider Fitness Program

The CSF program consists of four components. The Global Assessment Tool, which is used online by soldiers, is confidential, and provides feedback on the following psychological dimensions: positive emotions, negative emotions and depression, optimism, flexible thinking, work engagement, problem-focused coping, character strengths of wisdom, courage, humanity, justice, temperance, transcendence, social fitness components of trust and friendship, family fitness, and spiritual fitness. This comprehensive psychological fitness exam also comes with self-help modules for each of these areas that soldiers can access independently (Peterson, Park, & Castro, 2011). However, CSF goes far beyond online self-assessment/help. It is also designed to be delivered face to face.

The Master Resilience Trainer course (Reivich, Seligman, & McBride, 2011) is designed to train sergeants who will then teach soldiers in their units. The course has three components. The first, preparation, includes resilience and mental toughness, identifying character strengths, and strengthening relationships. The second is a sustaining component, which focuses on sustaining resilience across the deployment cycle. The third is an enhancement component that uses a lot of the following sport psychology concepts: mental skills foundations, which involves understanding the nature of performance, the relationship between training and trusting mindsets, and identifying the connection between thoughts, emotions, physiological states, and performance; building confidence, which involves learning effective ways to create energy, optimism, and enthusiasm; attention control, which addresses the concentration demands associated with critical military tasks; energy management, which consists of practical skills used to activate, sustain, and restore optimal levels of energy while minimizing the negative effects of stress; and integrating imagery, which involves ways of creating successful experiences that can enhance aspects of performance. If you start to get the idea of positive psychology at work, you would be right on target.

As we have indicated, support systems are critical in combating PTSD. For the current military, the problem is that while there may be instantaneous communication with family members via cell phone, Skype, Twitter, and other Internet access, they are physically thousands of miles apart with all the stress that brings. The family skills component (Gottman, Gottman, & Atkins, 2011) is designed to educate both service personnel and families on how to alleviate much of this stress. Frontline troops can take relationship enrichment courses along with their families, who are linked via the Internet to access the course materials. Topics include creating and maintaining friendship and intimacy, increasing trust and honesty, managing conflict constructively and gently, de-escalating conflict, practicing cognitive self-soothing, containing cognitive flooding and physical stress responses, soothing and calming one's partner, converting posttraumatic stress to posttraumatic growth through the relationship, building positive relationships and effective discipline with children, and surviving breakups. You don't need a certificate in marriage and family therapy to see that this component of the CFS could be a powerful tool in preventing the critical incidents that according to Mental Health Advisory Team V (2008) turn soldiers' thinking toxic and lethal. In summary, the U.S. Defense Department knows a lot more than it did during the Vietnam War and is now very actively involved in the business of both preventing and alleviating PTSD and its comorbid disorders.

As of 2015, the Army has issued a series of reports on the effectiveness of the CSF programs and has found them to be generally effective in meeting the designed objective of creating more psychological resilience in soldiers (Harms et al., 2013; Lester et al., 2011). However, the program has sustained a great deal of criticism from its inception. Chief among these are the fact that it is a massive research project and has no human protection of its subjects, is ill defined in its problem definition so any results would be global and ill defined as well, it seeks to promulgate religious values, war is bad and since CFS is designed to help soldiers become better warriors it is bad too, its basic premises are bad because it is not based on military personnel but on a civilian population and outcomes on that original format have not been all that positive, and focus should be on primary prevention of PTSD rather than building resistance to it through CSF (Dyckman, 2011; Eidelson, Pilisuk, & Soldz, 2011; Krueger, 2011; Phipps, 2011). Indeed,

critics have railed at the lack of objective review and analysis of CSF and have issued calls for independent reviews of it (Smith, 2013; Steenkamp, Nash, & Litz, 2013). Each of these criticisms has been vigorously counterpointed (Lester, McBride, & Cornum, 2013). So it will be interesting to see how one of the largest psychological experiments ever created will eventually turn out.

Components of Treatment for Adults

Given the constellation of problems that afflict the person with PTSD, treatment is complex, and the human services worker can expect numerous transcrisis events and crisis points to occur during treatment. The treatment of PTSD has three principal components: (1) processing and coming to terms with the horrifying, overwhelming experience; (2) controlling and mastering physiological and biological stress reactions; and (3) reestablishing secure social connections and interpersonal efficacy (van der Kolk, van der Hart, & Burbridge, 2002). For individuals with complex PTSD, treatment priorities are somewhat different and will be dealt with in Chapter 9, Sexual Assault. Before the worker tackles any of these components, however, comprehensive assessment needs to occur. Assessment is particularly important in PTSD because it is camouflaged by so many other symptoms and problems.

Assessment

Assessment of PTSD should consider at least **LO8** three goals: First, are symptoms of PTSD present? Although their presence may seem to be a given, length of time from onset may mean that different symptoms are more pronounced at different times. Second, diagnoses of presenting problems such as drug abuse or a variety of personality disorders may mask PTSD unless care is taken to assess for prior trauma. It is highly probable that people in crisis will present with comorbid problems, and PTSD may not be identified as the undergirding problem unless care is taken in assessing for traumatic incidents. Third, because of contextual differences in terms of physical, temporal, social, and political climate, these variables may have a great deal to do with how the event is interpreted (Newman, Kaloupkek, & Keane, 1996, pp. 242–245).

The following examples indicate just how important contextual variables are in assessment. A Vietnam veteran with PTSD in the 1970s would be perceived as a crazed baby killer as opposed to a Gulf War, Afghanistan, or Iraq veteran in the 2000s, who would be viewed with compassion because of the dramatic change in the political climate and the social view of men and women who fought in these wars. Likewise, domestic violence, which was formerly seen as a private matter between husband and wife, is now viewed as a societal ill to the extent that the label "battered woman syndrome" has been attached to it.

The self-reliant and tightly knit community of Joplin, Missouri, with its extended support system may react to the devastation of a tornado far differently from the way insular and emotionally distant apartment dwellers in New York City react to being forced out of their apartments by the collapse of the World Trade Center towers. Or, even though they are large urban areas on the eastern seaboard and all the events were terrorist initiated, how the cultural and environmental and situational differences of the Boston marathon bombing and Charleston, South Carolina, church shooting (much more population specific, closer and personalized) compares to the twin towers explosions in New York. Thus, in determining the potential to acquire PTSD or manifest it, one should always take into consideration a thorough background assessment that includes gender, race, socioeconomic class, experience, culture, religion, time components, geographic area, number of incidents of prior exposure to trauma, strength of interpersonal relationships, occupational risk, sociopolitical attitudes, and a host of other contextual variables that may have unforeseen impact on the resiliency of the individual to withstand or fall victim to PTSD. In short, just because you go through a traumatic event doesn't mean you automatically get PTSD or are even a "victim" as opposed to a "survivor" (Gist, Lubin, & Redburn, 1999; Kaniasty & Norris, 1999; Kroll, 2003).

Assessment of PTSD falls into two main categories: structured or semistructured interviews and empirically derived measures.

Structured Interview. If time is available, the structured interview probably remains the best diagnostic device for determining whether a person has PTSD. One of the best structured interviews is the Clinician-Administered PTSD Scale (CAPS-1; Blake et al., 1990). It assesses all the symptoms outlined in the DSM-5 as well as eight associated symptoms: guilt over acts committed or omitted, survivor's guilt, homicidality,

disillusionment with authority, feelings of hopelessness, memory impairment, sadness and depression, and feelings of being overwhelmed.

It also examines the impact of symptoms on social and occupational functioning, improvement in PTSD symptoms since a previous CAPS-1 assessment, overall response validity, and overall PTSD severity. Current status for all symptoms is assessed first, and if criteria for PTSD are not met, the questions are asked again for a "worst case," 1-month period since traumatic onset. The items also have a QV code, for question validity, when the interviewer has doubts about the truthfulness of the response. The CAPS-1 pays very careful attention to the assessment of lifetime PTSD. Its major drawback is the length of time required for administration (Newman, Kaloupkek, & Keane, 1996, p. 253).

Self-Reports. Self-reports are useful for their efficiency in time, cost, and ease of administration. Because crisis intervention often allows only the most rudimentary assessment, if time is of the essence, we prefer Figley's (1989, 1990) Traumagram Questionnaire, a graphically represented client self-report. It can be self-constructed on the spot. The questionnaire elicits the number of traumatic events, length of time, circumstances, age of client, persons who may have been involved with the events, and self-reported degrees of stress for all previous traumatic experiences and can be easily incorporated into a standard interview format. Clients are then asked to rate their stress level on a 1 (low) to 5 (high) scale at the time of the event, one year later, and in the present. Clients are then asked to consider each traumatic experience, what helped them cope, and what helped them adjust or not to the aftermath of the traumatic event.

Figley's traumagram is also a useful tool in determining the causes of transcrisis. In the course of therapy, at times clients present with symptoms and problems that seem to have no logical basis in reality. They are clearly in crisis. Their symptoms are causing them all kinds of trouble at school, at home, and at work, yet there appears to be nothing in real time that would be causing the problem. This puzzling dilemma is not uncommon when working with people who have been traumatized and have either dismissed the trauma as ancient history or have submerged it from conscious awareness (Shallcross, 2010). At this point we start looking at two distinct possibilities: delayed onset of PTSD or complicated grieving, which we will exam at length in Chapter 12, Personal Loss: Bereavement and Grief. To ferret out these issues, we have modified Charles Figley's (1989) traumagram protocol in the following way. We ask clients to consider not only stressful events in their life but also losses they have suffered. Clients are urged to consider not only loss to death, but also financial loss, job termination, death of a pet, romantic breakup, divorce, geographic moves, and acute onset of a disabling condition either for oneself or a loved one.

By plotting the number of events across the length of time that they were acutely felt on an *x*-axis, and then plotting the degree of stress on the *y*-axis using a scale of 1 (minimum) to 10 (maximum), the interviewer can quickly gain a graphic representation of the total number, type, and duration of traumas and the degree of stress the client has experienced. It gives the interviewer a good picture of what the client feels are the

relative power of significant events and also gives the interviewer an opportunity to explore the dimensions of each of these events. It also allows the crisis worker to examine one of the "best bet" indicators for delayed PTSD or the inability to resolve a loss—that is, the repeated exposure of the subject to traumatic events. Its major weakness is the subjective bias of the individual, but its strength is that clients may have "aha" experiences as events and losses they had submerged from awareness are brought into the light of day.

Dr. James's traumagram in Figure 7.1 presents a graphic description of his life history of trauma and loss over several decades. Seven events are depicted, as listed below. The intensity or level of stress and the duration of the stress for each event vary considerably. In this traumagram, the darker the area under each graph line, the more stresses that have accumulated during that time.

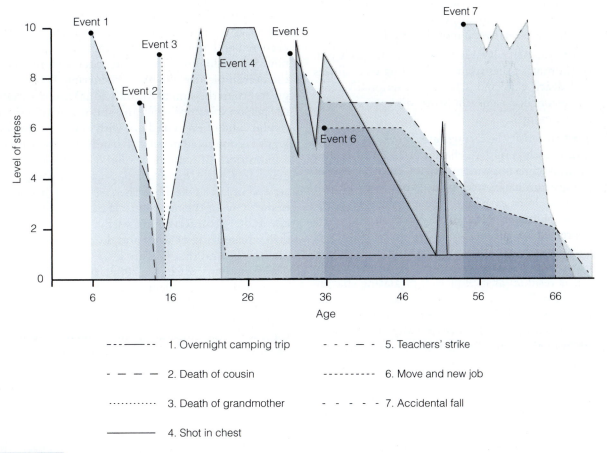

FIGURE 7.1 Traumagram: Dr. James

Event #1. Intensity level is 10+. Client is 6 years old on his first overnight camping trip with a summer camp group. After camp counselor sends boys off to bed with "Old Man Pollywog," the story of a creature who lives in the nearby swamp abducting small boys and carrying them off, the client is somehow locked out of the cabin and forced to sleep on the ground, easy prey for the swamp thing. A terrorizing night that indelibly imprints young Dickie to the point that he does not camp again until he is 23 years of age and canoeing in the Boundary Waters of Quetico Provincial Park in Ontario. The first night out on his canoeing trip Dick has an anxiety attack and is in desperate need of his mommy. Dick becomes desensitized after 14 days in the wilderness, but decides never to camp again if at all possible.

Event #2. Intensity level is 7. Client is 12 years old and is exposed to death for the first time. Traumatic death of 3-year-old cousin due to respiratory paralysis from anesthetic during tonsillectomy. Client is not emotionally close. Onset is acute but quickly resolved over 2-month period.

Event #3. Intensity level is 9. Client is 13 years old. Grandmother dies from cancer. Long-term illness and death expected. Client is emotionally close but reconciled to death. Stress dissipates to zero after 1 month.

Event #4. Intensity level starts at 9, moves to 10+ over a 12-month period. At the age of 21, client is shot in chest while out with girlfriend. Gunshot causes physical problems and what comes to be known 20 years later as PTSD. Client's social relationships plummet. Has anxiety attacks, becomes depressed, socially isolated, and contemplates suicide. After 1 year and 9 months bullet is removed. Client seeks counseling. Intensity drops sharply but is residual at level of 4–5, escalating sharply and acutely for over 3 years in heterosexual relationships until client marries current wife. Intensity level drops to 1 but occasionally spikes during times of severe physical or emotional stress.

Event #5. Intensity level is 9. Client is 32 years old, married father. Caught in the middle of a teachers' strike. Sees nationally validated program he directed disintegrate. Job loss. Complete job change and geographic change of 300 miles. Depression, anxiety attacks, PTSD symptoms resurface. Seeks counseling, makes commitment to job change out of education. Intensity level goes to 7 due to job change and continues for a year and a half, diminishing to level of 2–3 with increasing familiarity in new job in petroleum industry.

Event #6. Intensity level is 6. Client is 34 years old, married, a father. Reenters education with job as university professor. Moves 500 miles. Initial anxiety but mentorship reduces it quickly.

Event #7. Intensity level is 10+. Client is 54, married, father of two. Suffers accidental fall with severe external head trauma and edema while repairing roof on daughter's tree house. Severe pain for approximately 2 months from 300+ stitches and 52 staples in skull to reattach scalp. Self-image issues due to facial scarring. Residual injuries and interventions include plastic surgery on head and herniated C-6 disc operation over following 5 years, with spike levels of 10 and residual levels of 1–3.

(There's more, but this is merely an example and not a soap opera of Dr. James's life.)

After completing the traumagram, we query our clients on their affective, behavioral, and cognitive responses to specific traumas, both at the time they occurred and how those incidents are affecting them now. We are looking not just at specific events but at the overall picture of what is occurring. Is the whole greater than the sum of the individual traumas? Does the person show resiliency and stamina with one particular kind of event and not with another? This dialogue is conducted in a user friendly manner with the admonition, "If some emotions you didn't know were associated with that event pop up, and you get upset and need to take a breather, we'll stop. Just let me know." One of the most critical components of therapy and crisis intervention with a client with PTSD is demonstrating by word and deed that this is a *safe* place to be and that you are a *safe* person to be with (Courtois, Ford, & Cloitre, 2009; Herman, 1992).

As we query our client we are looking for recurrent psychodynamic themes that might give us clues to what is driving current maladaptive behavior. Does the client have continuing anger, regrets, guilt over past experiences? Is there a common affective, behavioral, or cognitive theme running through traumatic events? Do the events seem as potent now as they were then, with the client suddenly flushed and angry as he thinks about a physically abusing father who had the unmitigated gall to go and die on him before he could pay the abuser back? If the client has been fired for insubordinate behavior a number of times, can we trace these incidents back to a primary causal agent?

We are also very interested in how the client reports the events. Recently in class, one of our students was going over her traumagram in a very fluid way with even voice tone and a well-modulated voice level—until she came to event 6, which was about her discovery of a longtime close male friend who lied to her about a sexual assault he perpetrated and was later arrested and convicted of it. Her hesitation, loss of words, and trembling voice clearly indicated that this event was profoundly shocking to her and had caused her to deeply question her ability to gauge and assess people she had come to trust. When the professor reflected on her abrupt change in voice, she was taken aback because she had not recognized how deeply it still affected her. In summary, self-reports can sometimes uncover material that normative, empirical scale tests do not.

Empirically Derived Scales. A large variety of empirically derived PTSD instruments have been generated. Of them, the following seem to have reasonable utility in determining if PTSD is present and are reasonably efficient in terms of time and cost to administer. The Mississippi Scale for Combat Related PTSD (Keane, Caddell, & Taylor, 1988) is widely used and has a number of versions for different client populations. The Impact of Events Scale (Horowitz, Wilner, & Alvarez, 1979) is one of the most widely used instruments for detecting PTSD and has been employed with a variety of trauma-related populations. The scale assesses only the extent of avoidance/numbing rather than the full scope of PTSD symptoms that are covered by the other tests mentioned here. A revised form of the Impact of Events Scale–Revised (IES-R) has added five questions to better capture the DSM criteria for PTSD (Weiss & Marmar, 1997).

The Keane PK scale of the MMPI/MMPI-2 has been formulated for the specific purpose of diagnosing PTSD (Keane, Malloy, & Fairbank, 1984). Because it is embedded in the MMPI/MMPI-2, its score can be compared to the validity scales of the total instrument to determine whether faking or malingering is occurring. Note that some people, such as insurance claimants, malingerers, or incarcerates, may have less than honorable motives in claiming they have PTSD, and their reports may not be valid.

Overview of Assessment. Their responses to questions about social affiliation show a clear distinction between individuals with character disorders and those suffering from PTSD. In general, individuals

with PTSD avoid interpersonal relationships, as opposed to the ingratiating gregariousness of a sociopath. Those with PTSD have few close friends, prefer being alone, and discuss few intimate details of their lives. Unexpected contact with other people or stimuli reminiscent of the traumatic event may make these individuals extremely "jumpy" and "edgy" (Keane et al., 1985, p. 270).

The human services worker should never dismiss a report, no matter how trivial it may seem, of involvement in a catastrophic situation or a major loss (Scurfield, 1985, pp. 238–239). Because individuals with PTSD may be very reluctant to talk about the trauma they have been through, human services workers should try to get background information from relatives, coworkers, and any other people who have personal knowledge of the individual. The personal history is particularly important when substance abuse is involved, because if PTSD is not identified, all the efforts of the worker will not ameliorate the substance abuse problem.

Our own and many, many colleagues' clinical experience with depressed and borderline clients has uncovered many who have suffered sexual abuse as children. Until ruled out, PTSD should be suspected as a causative agent. However, getting at it may prove extremely difficult, particularly given the severe social taboos associated with talking about incestuous and abusive relationships. Therefore, in an initial assessment, even though the interviewer may have a strong hunch that repression of a traumatic event is causing the problem, the causative agent should never be exposed, interpreted, or even guessed at until a high degree of trust has been built (Scurfield, 1985, pp. 238–239).

Finally, assessment in treatment of PTSD must be ongoing and overarching, particularly during the course of therapy. The changes that occur in the client vacillate dramatically—sometimes daily or even hourly. Because of the intrusive nature of much of the therapy, it is common to see upsurges in symptoms and problem behaviors (Flack et al., 2002).

Assessment of Billie Mac. In the case of Billie Mac, a CAPS-1 interview showed little if any evidence of traumatic experience prior to Vietnam besides the death of a grandfather, to whom he was quite close. In Vietnam, he was in major battle after major battle, interspersed with patrols and sweeps. He was the only man out of his original company to walk away physically unscathed after the Tet offensive.

After Vietnam, the traumatic wake continued. Violent episodes with his father, his wife, and his children, scrapes with the law, drunken binges, barroom brawls, prolonged bouts of depression interspersed with manic acting out, alcohol addiction treatment, job loss due to nonperformance, suicidal ideation, plus the standard symptoms of PTSD marked his years since Vietnam with almost continuous crises. There were very few months in the 25 years since his return that he would not rank extremely high on the Triage Assessment Scale. Affectively, he goes far beyond what the situation warrants, with large mood swings that cycle through anger, fear, and sadness. He rarely ranks lower than 6 on the Affective Severity scale, and his average is 7.

In the cognitive domain he has suffered physical, psychological, social, and spiritual transgression, threat, and loss. His problem-solving abilities are characterized by self-doubt, confusion, and excessive rumination on Vietnam and his abortive attempts to reacclimatize to the civilian world. His severity rating is consistently an 8 to 9, in the Marked Impairment range.

Billie Mac's behavior invariably makes the situation worse. He either approaches the situation in a hostile-aggressive manner or avoids it for fear of acting out against others. He is immobilized between these two extremes, and significant others report that they feel he is erratic, unpredictable, and dangerous. A most conservative estimate places him at a minimum of 8 on the Behavioral Severity scale. His total scale score is 24, which places him in the lower range of the Marked Impairment category. Perhaps even more ominously, his individual scale scores frequently hit a 10. As he presents for treatment, he is in serious trouble, and at times of stress his triage rating scale score spikes into the lethal Severe Impairment range. He has suicidal thoughts, and at times his behavior verges on homicidal. His CAPS-1 interview ratings indicate a very high frequency and intensity of PTSD symptoms, and the MMPI-2 PK scale confirms his PTSD surely falls into the more complex variety. If he refuses inpatient treatment, he should have closely supervised outpatient treatment.

Phases of Recovery

Brende and Parson (1985, pp. 185–186) have **LO9** compiled the work of Wilson (1980), Figley (1978), and Horowitz (1976) to construct five phases of recovery in the individual with PTSD. These phases directly parallel treatment approaches, and each has its own crisis stage.

1. *The emergency or outcry phase.* The individual experiences heightened "fight/flight" reactions to the life-threatening situation. This phase lasts as long as the survivor believes the situation to last. Pulse, blood pressure, respiration, and muscle activity are all increased. Concomitant feelings of fear and helplessness predominate. Termination of the event itself is followed by relief and confusion. Questions about why the event happened and what its consequences are dominate the individual's thoughts.
2. *The emotional numbing and denial phase.* The survivor protects psychic well-being by burying the experience in subconscious memory. By avoiding the experience, the individual temporarily reduces anxiety and stress symptoms. Many individuals remain forever at this stage unless they receive professional intervention.
3. *The intrusive-repetitive phase.* The survivor has nightmares, volatile mood swings, intrusive images, and amplified startle responses. Other pathological and antisocial defense mechanisms may be put into place in a futile attempt to rebury the trauma. At this point the delayed stress becomes so overwhelming that the individual is propelled to seek help or becomes so mired in the pathology of the situation that outside intervention is mandated.
4. *The reflective-transition phase.* The survivor develops a larger personal perspective on the traumatic events and becomes positive and constructive, with a forward- rather than backward-looking perspective. The individual comes to grips with the trauma and confronts the problem.
5. *The integration phase.* The survivor successfully integrates the trauma with all other past experiences and restores a sense of continuity to life. The trauma is successfully placed fully in the past.

Neat and orderly progression for the PTSD individual through these stages is the exception rather than the rule. More likely is a precipitating crisis far removed in chronological time from the event itself and then a continuing series of crises that escalate until the individual voluntarily seeks help or is forced to seek it. Once intervention occurs, a cyclic pattern of avoidance, recall, recovery, and more avoidance continues until the core issues that gave birth to PTSD are resolved (Figley, 1985a, pp. 402–404). The human services worker can expect a series of transcrisis events as this process unfolds.

Initiating Intervention. Generally, victims of LO10 trauma refuse early intervention because they either see the event as too difficult to deal with or believe that people of good character ought to be able to cope with such events on their own without outside intervention. These two faulty assumptions get individuals into the delayed part of the disorder, where most of the treatment population will emerge.

Importance of Acceptance

Given the variety of negative and conflicting emotional baggage the individual brings to the session, it is of paramount importance that the human services worker provide an accepting atmosphere so that the individual can start to recount and encounter the trauma. Disclosure of the trauma is difficult for the PTSD client because recounting what has happened may be horrifying and socially unacceptable. Also, open-minded acceptance of the client's story may be extremely difficult for and repugnant to the human services worker; but if therapeutic progress is to be made, nothing less will do (Brende & Parson, 1985, p. 178).

Billie Mac: (*thinking to himself*) If I tell about killing that kid, what will the counselor think? A baby killer, that's what! Yet, it's bugging the hell out of me. (*Slowly tells the counselor about the incident.*)

Human Services Worker (HSW): (*stating personal feelings*) I can see how hard it was for you to talk about that. A part of me wonders how you or anybody could ever kill a child. However, I understand how scared you were, wondering whether he had a grenade, what a moral quandary that put you in, and the guilt and anguish you feel as you recall the incident.

We currently live in an evidence-based world as far as therapy is concerned as you will soon see in this chapter. However, as in most crisis interventions, initiating and forming a bond with Billie Mac is critical and involves the empathic listening, owning statements, and reflection of feeling demonstrated in this opening dialogue (Lindy, 2012).

Therapy with veterans, either individually or in groups, is ideally conducted with veterans as leaders because of the defensiveness and hostility with which most veterans view professionals who have not undergone the experience of combat. The same is true of the firefighters, police officers, and emergency medical technicians (EMTs) you will meet later in the chapter. One could easily extrapolate this notion to group work with other kinds of trauma victims. The problem is that professionals who have also experienced the trauma or the setting within which it occurs are often not readily available. Therefore, the Veterans Center of Memphis published a list of 12 "rules of the road" for establishing the credibility of nonveterans who work therapeutically with veterans (Memphis Vietnam Veterans Center, 1985). These rules should be adapted to any intact group such as police officers, EMTs, nurses, and others whose common bond is more than the incidence of PTSD and where you as the therapist are considered an "outsider" due to your ignorance of their culture whether it be oil well rigging, farming, or emergency medical responders.

1. The client has the experiential knowledge you don't have; you have the clinical and technical knowledge he or she doesn't have. Together you can forge a working alliance.

2. Make your desire to understand come across so that considerable experiential gaps are bridged.

3. Realize that the client wants you to help him or her help you understand. In the process, he or she recreates and reexperiences the sources of the problems, and you, by providing the therapeutic climate, gain an in-depth understanding of the traumatic experience.

4. An opposite-sex therapist serves as a role model—that is, in the case of a male veteran, a woman who can understand and accept the individual for what he is and has done without prejudging him.

5. Clinical experience and expertise are built over time—as your understanding and technical expertise grow, you will be accepted by the individual or the group despite your lack of direct experience.

6. As a nonmember of the "exclusive" group, you can challenge the defense of exclusivity, that one who wasn't there can't understand, thus serving to break through his or her feelings of isolation and "contamination."

7. Your technical naiveté often helps the individual explore and express himself or herself. In his or her effort to help you understand the technical aspects of combat, emergency medical service, or police tactical procedures, he or she uncovers unknown areas of conflict.

8. At the same time, because of your naiveté, you must guard against becoming too involved in problems and memories, thereby "triggering" situational stress that may need immediate attention and treatment.

9. Realize that moral conflicts will probably be raised for you personally as stories unfold; guard against any display of emotional revulsion to a client who describes atrocities. Be nonjudgmental and objective.

10. Guard against overidentification or hero worship, or you will blunt your problem-solving ability.

11. Expect to need controls and to have to clearly enforce them for your sake and the client's—don't try to do therapy with a client who is drunk or "stoned," refuse to be a party to long tirades on the phone, and bar all weapons and mean it.

12. Heed the signs of burnout: thinking or talking too much about your clients to others, finding yourself having client-specific symptoms such as nightmares, and so on. Step back and evaluate whether you may be too immersed in trying to do too much for too many.

These rules are adaptable to any kind of trauma survivors and the people who work with them *and apply particularly to those who work with adult survivors of childhood sexual abuse or children who have suffered chronic physical and/or sexual abuse.*

One further admonition is necessary for any human services worker who would work with trauma survivors. Frick and Bogart (1982) identified one of the stages that veterans go through as "rage at their counselor." This transference stage (attributing to the human services worker qualities and attributes of significant others in the client's life) is important in coming to terms with the traumatic experience. Human services workers may well become the focal point of all the frustration, grief, fear, lost opportunity, confusion, lack of progress, and attempts at reconciliation with society, family, and friends that mark the trauma survivor's attempt to reintegrate into the social mainstream. Human services workers need to deal with such anger by owning their mistakes in being insensitive to issues, accepting and reflecting the individual's anger while at the same time not being defensive, containing impulsive responses after being attacked, owning their own anger, and not becoming discouraged and giving up.

Risks of Treatment

It is also incumbent on the human ser- **LO11** vices worker to state clearly the risks inherent in treatment. It may be hard to make such statements and to propose a poor prognosis, but probably the individual will have pondered many of the same questions. After the initial crisis has passed and the individual is back to a state of at least semiequilibrium, the human services worker should convey clearly the following risks, as outlined by Brende and Parson (1985, pp. 168–174):

1. There may be only partial recovery; there are no magical cures for this tenacious and pernicious problem.

2. Because of the continuing nature of the crisis, either long bouts with hospitals or weekly trips to the therapist are required that will play havoc with keeping a job.

3. As catharsis of the event occurs, and if exposure therapies are used, it is inevitable that the individual gets worse before getting better. Fear of a psychotic breakdown may occur as the individual learns more about the disorder.

4. As the struggle to find oneself goes forward, personality change may put heavy burdens on interpersonal relationships as significant others see a very different person emerge from the therapeutic experience.

5. Psychic pain may become almost intolerable as the individual reexperiences disturbing memories and emotions that, as they are voiced, may cause rejection by friends and professionals alike.

6. Because of the numerous self-constraints placed on volatile emotions, the individual may fear that giving vent to those emotions will lead to uncontrolled anger and result in physical harm to others. Because of the hurt suffered, it will also be very difficult for the individual to give up the idea of revenge on both real and imagined perpetrators of the traumatic event.

7. Because of the compartmentalized and constricted lifestyle that follows the trauma, the individual will safeguard against change and may have extreme difficulty following directions and doing what others may suggest, no matter how reasonable and proper. Giving up such maladaptive self-reliance will put the individual at the mercy of others, a seemingly intolerable situation.

8. A great deal of pain will result from coming to accept the world as it is with all its frailties and injustices. In attempting to gain reentry into such an imperfect world, the individual is in danger of losing patience with it and falling back into the vortex of PTSD.

9. Correlative with accepting the frailties of the world is also the acceptance of one's own set of infirmities; bad memories may return; relationships may not always be excellent; others may obtain better jobs for no legitimate reason.

Acceptance of oneself, including the guilt, sorrow, and regret that go with it, is the sine qua non of getting through PTSD, but it may be an extremely difficult and fearsome task that will call for far more courage than surviving the catastrophe itself.

Multiphasic/Multimodal Treatment

Trauma-Focused Cognitive-Behavioral Therapy. **LO12**

Individual treatment goes hand in hand with group work in PTSD treatment. From crisis stage to crisis stage, a multimodal therapeutic approach is used with heavy reliance on various combinations of trauma-focused behavioral and cognitive-behavioral therapy (Scurfield, 1985, p. 250). What **trauma-focused cognitive-behavioral therapy (TF-CBT)** does is focus directly on the memories, reminders, stimuli, environments, and events of the trauma and its symptoms (Monson & Shnaider, 2014, pp. 4–5). In one form or another, it attempts to roll over the psychological rocks that cover bad memories up and start to reconcile them so they do not stay the PTSD albatrosses forever hung round their victims' necks. It also seeks to rebuild the negative attributions individuals have about themselves and the trauma world that surrounds and suffocates them and replaces it with new, positive statements that breathe life back into them and create a larger, more positive real-time social world.

Evidence-Based TF-CBT.

Several meta-analyses have confirmed that TF-CBTs are the most effective therapies to reduce symptoms (Bisson & Andrews, 2009; Bisson et al., 2007; Bradley et al., 2005; Lenz et al., 2014). Best practices using them have been developed (Forbes et al., 2010) and are now seen as gold standard, first-line treatment modalities by the Veterans Administration (U.S. Department of Veterans Affairs, 2008) and international professional mental health organizations (Australian Center for Posttraumatic Mental Health, 2007; National Institute for Health Care and Excellence, 2005). Indeed, TF-CBT approaches have been the therapeutic modality with the most successful outcome data to date (Bryant et al., 2003; Ehlers et al., 2005; Gradus et al., 2013; Gutner et al., 2013; Jeffreys et al., 2014; Iverson et al., 2015; Reinecke

et al., 2014; Yoshimura et al., 2014; Voelkel et al., 2015; Wachen et al., 2014). TF-CBT evidence-based approaches may be divided into three general treatment categories.

Prolonged Exposure (PE).

There is a great deal of neurological evidence previously mentioned that indicates trauma rewires the brain and creates the pathological defense mechanisms that are characteristic of PTSD. A good deal of failed therapeutic approaches over the years has taught us that unless the client is returned to conditions that closely approximate the traumatic event, no change will occur (no new rewiring or growth occurs in the brain). Thus, following an in-depth explanation of what this procedure is about and what the unpleasant side effects of it may be, the client is returned to the conditions that closely approximate the traumatic event. This occurs either by imaginal exposure by having clients close their eyes and listen while the therapist recreates the scene, or by using computer-generated virtual reality scenarios. Clients may then be given in vivo exposure where they are given gradual, but increasing exposure to the feared and threatening stimuli (Bernardy & Friedman, 2015, p. 104).

To do this, a great deal of specific information is collected in regard to the visual, auditory, tactile, and olfactory sensations that existed in the traumatic event so that the client is flooded with continuously fear-provoking stimuli from the event. This procedure occurs by continuous and prolonged exposure (PE) until the client becomes desensitized to the previously fear-producing stimuli (Stampfl & Lewis, 1967).

Cognitive Processing Therapy (CPT).

CPT was developed by Patricia Resick (Resick & Schnicke, 1993) to treat PTSD in sexual assault victims. CPT conceptualizes PTSD as a disorder of nonrecovery wherein individuals get "stuck" with distorted beliefs about the traumatic event and can't get out of the psychological ruts their distorted beliefs sunk them into. There are three phases to treatment that involve education about the procedure, trauma processing, and learning how to disrupt the flow of negative feedback individuals generate for themselves. Trauma processing occurs through both written and verbal activities designed to bring the trauma out of the dark and into the light. Homework assignments are given to monitor daily thoughts, feeling, and events of which at least one must be trauma related. This procedure is particularly well suited for groups as well as individual sessions. Negative appraisals, attributions, and overgeneralizations about oneself, others, and the world are ferreted out and disputed through work sheets designed to change distorted beliefs into more rational cognitions. Socratic dialogue is used to challenge hot, all-or-none, self-blaming, distorted thinking and create alternative cooler cognitions and more positive self-statements. The overall goal is to create a new narrative about the event that gives the individual hope and a forward-looking positive view of the world and puts the trauma as part of one's history and firmly into the background.

Stress Inoculation. Stress inoculation was originally developed by Donald Meichenbaum (1985) to deal with anxiety, so it certainly fits well with PTSD which is chock full of it. It is a three-phase procedure that starts with a good deal of psycho-education about the procedure and an in-depth exploration of where the major physical, behavioral, affective, and cognitive focal points of the anxiety are located in the individual. In the second phase, specific skill acquisition training is done at the anxiety focal points to inoculate the individual. In the third phase the individual takes the skills learned in therapy and goes out into the real world to test them out and fine-tune them to see how well the inoculation is working.

Telehealth. All of the foregoing TF-CBT techniques can be incorporated into teleheath components with success. As indicated in Chapter 6, telephone and telehealth have many conveniences such as privacy, convenience, and economy, and most importantly they seem to work with PTSD (Frueh et al., 2007; Niles et al., 2012; Tuerk et al., 2010). There are now numerous CBT and PTSD apps online and available for download. Chief among them is *PTSD Coach I*, which is constructed by the U.S. Department of Veterans Affairs, National Center for PTSD (2014). This application provides reliable information on PTSD and treatments that work, tools for screening and tracking symptoms, techniques to help handle stress symptoms, direct support links, and is operational 365-24-7.

Virtual Reality. Virtual reality (VR) has found a great deal of utility in treating anxiety disorders through prolonged exposure (Goncalves et al., 2012; Nelson, 2013). Abbas and Hoyt's (2014) meta-analysis of VR exposure therapy for TF-CBT found strong treatment effects for its use. VR exposure therapy works on emotional processing and emotional dysregulation of PTSD sufferers by presenting multisensory stimuli targeted to the individual's traumatic memory. In so doing, VR activates their fear response and desensitizes them to it (Reger, Rizzo, & Gahm, 2015). A hybrid of imaginal exposure and in vivo exposure, VR therapy typically puts individuals in VR helmets and exposes them to threatening stimuli. An added advantage to this hybrid exposure is that a simulator allows the therapist to increase or decrease exposure of not only sights and sounds, but smells and tactile sensations as well.

Ram and associates (2014) used this procedure with veterans from Iraq and Afghanistan against a control condition where exposure was created by watching a television screen with no other stimuli beside the video on the screen. Their results showed significant improvement in experimental conditions against the visual stimuli only group. As measured by the Clinically Administered PTSD Scale (CAPS), these treatment gains held up over time. McLay and associates (2012) used VR with combat service members with PTSD and found that not only did the group achieve gains that held up on PTSD symptoms, but they also had significant reduction on depression and anxiety measures as well.

Brandt (2014) argues that the design of *Virtual Iraq*, a VR system designed to assist clinicians doing prolonged exposure not only impacts therapeutic practice, but cultural conceptions of therapy as well due to its gamelike quality in destigmatizing therapy among young male "digital generation" soldiers. Because of its success, it is now being upgraded into *Virtual Iraq/Afghanistan* with wider applications into medical corpsman, victims of military sexual assault, and predeployment resiliency training scenarios (Rizzo et al., 2015).

The Rest of the Evidenced-Based TF-CBT Story. While the foregoing approaches generally work well in eradicating the symptoms of PTSD, they are not without controversy. Because they have been extolled as a first-order intervention by the largest single provider of mental health services in the United States, the Veterans Administration recommendation of these as first-line techniques tend to sway the total treatment field toward blanket approval. However, a number of writers have been critical of the now almost unquestioned approval of these therapies (Holt & Beutler, 2014; Holt et al., 2013; Steenkamp & Litz, 2014; Rothschild, 2010; Wheeler, 2014). Chief among their complaints have been the sometimes disastrous push to remember the trauma in vivid detail, which is one of the reasons that drop out of treatment is high. There are also questions about their validity in the real world as opposed to highly structured randomized controlled studies. Further, while TF-CBT approaches work, the question is do they work well and do they have lasting effects. Further, are they reliable? Results seem variable. They work well for some and not so well with others, which is actually not too surprising considering how tough and intractable the disorder is to treatment.

Wheeler (2014) makes a valid argument when she proposed Eye Movement Desensitization and Reprocessing (EMDR) as a valid treatment alternative to TF-CBT. As you will soon read about EMDR, it doesn't involve detailed descriptions of the event, nor does it require extended exposure, nor does it require disputing one's beliefs and doesn't require homework involving any of the foregoing. Indeed, the *VA/DOD Clinical Practice Guideline for the Management of Posttraumatic Stress Disorder* (Department of Veterans Affairs & Department of Defense, 2010) recommends EMDR as a first-order treatment, yet Wheeler notes it is not included in the list of disseminated psychotherapies that are evidence based at the VA.

There are also some tough ethical questions regarding exposure treatment and the individuals who do the treating. These techniques directly target what individuals spend a great deal of psychic energy trying to cover up and submerge from reality. In doing so they are exposing core beliefs and emotions that are likely to be terrifying and if not closely monitored and supervised may put the person in harm's way. As such, these are extremely serious psychotherapeutic techniques and require specific training and supervision in how to use them. Done incorrectly they can do much harm to clients. In our own practice we have seen some clients become extremely agitated when the uncovering process starts, and it has taken every bit of our years of experience and training to stabilize them. We believe that in-depth psychoeducation, clear informed consent on what will happen, and after-session debriefing are critical to client well-being and safety in these protocols.

As a student you need to read thoroughly about these potent techniques, ask questions to yourself and your professor, see it modeled, ask more questions of your professor, observe it being done, then ask questions of your clinical supervisor, and then under close supervision, start to practice it, and then ask more

questions of your supervisor. Rothschild (2010, p. 2) states the case admirably when she says that trauma recovery involves more than remembering the trauma because first and foremost it needs to improve one's quality of life and anything that does that is good for you and anything that doesn't, isn't!

Alternate Approaches. Mindfulness (Rothschild, 2010) and acceptance and commitment therapy (ACT) (Hayes, Strosahl, & Wilson, 1999) also targets avoidance processes of life problems that surround PTSD but in a much more benign fashion without strenuous and intrusive exposure protocols. A core component of ACT that is taking root and growing in many therapeutic endeavors is the concept of **acceptance**, being open and aware of unpleasant emotions, thoughts, and experiences and just letting them be without making attempts to alter their frequency or form (Hayes et al., 1999). At the same time, clients are practicing **mindfulness**, the art of being nonjudgmentally aware of body sensations, feeling, and thoughts as they move in and out of consciousness in the present moment (Rothschild, 2010). Finally, by practicing **defusion**, those previously toxic thoughts have much less power than we give them credit for having. Defusion focuses on decreasing the perceived literality (it is absolutely true and fact) of the avoidance language that debilitates and keeps sufferers of PTSD stuck in maladaptive value systems. The notion is that clients can be taught to detach from being fused with any idea (Engle & Follette, 2012, pp. 362–365) (including the really bad ones that go with PTSD) by practicing acceptance and mindfulness when negative self and world attributions surface, and by continuous practice can come to believe that these are "just thoughts" that don't control one's behavior.

Further, because of the idiosyncratic nature of the course of PTSD, various other techniques that employ psychodynamic (Lindy, 1996, pp. 525–536) and humanistic approaches (Turner, McFarlane, & van der Kolk, 1996, pp. 537–558) may also be appropriate. Contextual (Gold, 2009) and contextual behavior therapy (Follette, Iverson, & Ford, 2009) and eclectic experiential and emotion-focused therapy (Fosha et al., 2009) are newer approaches that specifically target complex traumas. Curran (2013) has published a workbook entitled *101 Trauma-Informed Interventions* that are drawn from tools and techniques from the most effective trauma modalities that are a theoretical smorgasbord. Although this may sound like a shotgun approach that aimlessly blasts away at the problem, such is not the case. The complexity of this malady calls for some of the very best in integrative/eclectic therapy and treatment planning. Further, an important component of any psychotherapeutic approach in the treatment of PTSD is the use of psychotropic medication.

Psychotropic Medication

From what is presently known about the biol- **LO13** ogy of PTSD, drugs that regulate neurotransmitters and neuromodulators ought to be helpful in providing at least some palliative relief from the psychophysiological responses that occur with the disorder. Because so many different psychobiological abnormalities may predominate in various PTSD cases, almost every class of psychotropic medication has been prescribed for PTSD clients (Bernardy & Freidman, 2015; Donnelly, 2003; Fichtner, Podding, & deVito, 2000; Filteau, Leblanc, & Bouchard, 2003; Kreidler, Briscoe, & Beech, 2002; Marmar, Neylan, & Schoenfeld, 2002; Sokolski et al., 2003; F. Taylor, 2003; Zullino, Krenz, & Besson, 2003). There is as yet no fixed pharmaceutical regimen for PTSD. The effects of medications for PTSD seem to be so narrow for individuals and specific groups that they are often not generalizable to other populations (Davidson & van der Kolk, 1996, p. 511).

Van der Kolk and his associates (1994) found that fluoxetine did indeed reduce numbing and arousal responses in a clinical treatment group but *did not* in a group of veterans. Further compounding the problem is that one of the side effects of fluoxetine is that while it may reduce numbing and arousal responses, it can also *increase* startle responses (Davidson & van der Kolk, 1996, p. 512).

Most clinical practice guidelines for drugs now recommend the new anti-depressant, selective serotonin reuptake inhibitors (SSRIs) such as sertraline (Zoloft) and escitalopram (Lunestra), and the serotonin-norepineprine reuptake inhibitors (SNRIs), venlafaxine (Effexor) and duloxetine (Cymbalta) (Bernardy & Friedman, 2015). With the advent of these SNRIs such as Effexor and Cymbalta and SSRIs such as Zoloft and Lunestra that additionally have antianxiety properties, the addictive properties of the benzodiazepines are no longer recommended (Bernardy, Souter, & Friedman, 2015). It appears that these antidepressants alleviate a variety of PTSD symptoms such as irritability, anger, depression, and anxiety along with the intrusion, avoidance, and numbing components of PTSD as well

(Bernardy & Friedman, 2015). If PTSD is in place, and comorbid with other disorders such as schizophrenia, then antipsychotics may be used in conjunction with antidepressants (Jeffreys, 2015). These drugs are seen as generally more effective when they are combined with TF-CBT (Bernardy, Souter, & Friedman, 2015).

Because presenting symptoms can seriously interfere with treatment, careful prescription and monitoring of psychotropic medication are critical in allowing PTSD therapy to proceed successfully. Medication for PTSD symptoms should be given by someone who has a great deal of medical expertise with the problem and not by a general practitioner. That medical practitioner should also carefully coordinate medication and monitoring with whoever is doing the "talking" part of the therapy.

Individual Intervention Stages
Emergency/Outcry

In the first phase of recovery, the emer- **LO14** gency or outcry phase, the major problem is to get the individual stabilized; this means reducing the anxiety and physical responses associated with the trauma (Meadows & Foa, 1999). Meditation, relaxation, hypnosis, and biofeedback may be used (Evans, 2003; Kolb & Mutalipassi, 1982).

In relaxation training and meditation, the human services worker teaches the client how to relax body muscle groups systematically and to focus calmly on mental images that produce psychic relief of body tensions and stress (Benson, 1976; Wolpe, 1958). Individuals learn how to exercise self-control over many of their stresses and anxieties and dampen debilitating physiological responses.

HSW: OK, Billie Mac. Just imagine that you are lying on the beach with that soft, warm sand, the calm breeze blowing gently over you, the gentle lapping of the cool, crystal-clear water, and just easily focus your attention on that scene. Now just notice the difference in your body too. Notice the difference between how your muscles feel when they are tense and relaxed. Starting with your legs, just tense them up, feel how your muscles tighten up. Now relax them, and just feel that tightness drop away. Notice the difference and the really pleasant feelings that occur when your muscles are just hanging loose and flaccid. Continue to picture the scene on the beach as you work your way up your body, alternating between tensing and relaxing your muscles. Notice as you continue to do this how you can change the way your body feels and what you can focus on in your mind's eye.

Relaxation alone is helpful in alleviating current symptoms and enabling the individual to regain a measure of emotional and behavioral control, and it is also a preliminary step in tackling the cluster of problems characteristic of PTSD. Through deep relaxation or hypnosis, the client may be regressed back to an image of the traumatic event. Regressing the client in this manner is necessary to elevate bad memories of the traumatic event, and the intrusive images that accompany them, to conscious awareness (Brom, Kleber, & Defares, 1989; Kingsbury, 1988; Spiegel, 1989).

Extinguishing Intrusive Images

Given the previously discussed neuropsychological foundations of PTSD, Ochberg (1988) has concluded that PTSD should be viewed first in terms of autonomic nervous system (ANS) arousal, and any treatment should take into consideration the physiological aspects of the disorder. Thus a standing hypothesis for PTSD treatment has evolved that proposes a return of the client to the original state of elevated psychophysiological arousal in order to affect current maladaptive response sets (Malloy, Fairbank, & Keane, 1983). Once the individual has learned how to relax, other specific TF-CBT therapeutic strategies such as systematic desensitization, prolonged exposure, flooding, implosion, and Gestalt techniques may be employed to create ANS arousal (Cohen, 2002, 2003; Fairbank & Keane, 1982; Feeny, Hembree, & Zoellner, 2003; Foa et al., 2002; Forbes et al., 2003; Hembree, Rauch, & Foa, 2003; Keane & Kaloupek, 1982; Paunovic, 2002, 2003; Paunovic & Ost, 2001).

The human services worker continues to work slowly through the relaxation exercises and the mental imagery, continuously reinforcing the client for being able to shift to calm, relaxed scenes and away from the intrusive, anxiety-producing images. Practice for the individual in this and the other techniques to be covered in individual therapy is important. We recommend that sessions be audiotaped so that the client can practice the procedures at home on a daily basis.

Numbing/Denial

Reexperiencing. Once the individual has learned how to relax, the second phase of intervention occurs, coincident with the individual's emotional numbing

and denial phase of recovery. This phase is concerned with bringing to conscious awareness the traumatic event and the hidden facts and emotions about it that the individual denies (Brende & Parson, 1985, pp. 191–192). This is an example of prolonged exposure (PE) and the therapist will tape record it so it can be listened to and processed by the client. In a gentle but forceful way, the human services worker guides the individual, in the here and now of the therapeutic moment, to reexperience in the fullest possible detail what occurred in the traumatic experience so that submerged feelings are uncovered and ultimately expunged (Scurfield, 1985, p. 245). While deeply relaxed, the individual is asked to reexperience the terrible events of the trauma, with the injunction that at any time the memories can be switched off and the individual can return to the pleasant image of the beach.

HSW: Now go back to the village and tell me what is happening.

Billie Mac: (*lying down, relaxed, eyes closed*) The point man all of a sudden comes under fire and gets popped. I see him get hit. He's lying in the open across a ditch about 100 meters from the tree line. It's really getting hot, a lot of fire from concealed bunkers. They're using him as bait. This goes on for about 5 minutes, I guess. All of a sudden I decide to go and get him. Me and some other guys just get up and run across the open field to the ditch. We're getting all kinds of fire and out of five of us, only me and Al make it to the ditch without getting dinged. The point man is only about 5 meters from me, but I can't get at him. (*Billie Mac breaks into a sweat with slight tremors.*) I finally spot where the concealed bunker is that's making it so hot for us. I've got a LAW [light antitank weapon], and I get a bead on the bunker and zap it. At about the same time there's an explosion right next to me, a B-40 grenade, I guess, and that's all I remember until I wake up on the medevac chopper. (*Breaks into profuse sweating and major tremors.*)

HSW: All right, just shift out of that scene and back to the beach, and just relax. Notice the cool water, the warm sand, the gentle breeze, and just let your muscles relax. (*Billie Mac noticeably relaxes and, with continued directives from the human services worker, returns to a calm, relaxed state.*)

Although the account of the combat situation is fearsome in its intensity, the human services worker suspects that it alone is not responsible for the traumatic reaction. Billie Mac was in many such situations, but this village is the focal point of his nightmares and intrusive thoughts. The human services worker suspects that there is more here than what Billie Mac is revealing, and seeks to slowly peel away the psychological walls that defend the trauma from awareness. The human services worker believes that the recounting of the combat situation, despite having psychological value as a defense mechanism, is probably not historically accurate. The individual has left out certain traumatic parts of the story, and the human services worker's job becomes one of trying to fill in the gaps (Horowitz, 1976, pp. 117–118). Having built a very strong rapport and mutual trust with the client (Keane et al., 1985, p. 291), the human services worker probes into the situation and actively seeks to interpret and clarify the content of the client's story with respect to its potentially overwhelming effect (Scurfield, 1985, p. 245).

HSW: Go back to the village and the ditch right before you take out the bunker. What do you see?

Billie Mac: I see the point man. He's alive, but bad off.

HSW: What are you thinking?

Billie Mac: I've got to get him, but I can't. The fire's too heavy.

HSW: What do you feel?

Billie Mac: Scared, I um . . . I can't seem to do anything . . . the rounds are really coming . . .

HSW: What's happening around you?

Billie Mac: Al keeps yelling, "Take the bunker out with the LAW!"

HSW: Then what?

Billie Mac: I . . . can't . . . do it . . . it . . . I'm terrified. (*Starts to shake uncontrollably.*)

HSW: Stay right with that, Billie. I'm right here.

Billie Mac: Al grabs the LAW, stands up and fires it and—Oh, my God! Get down! Oh, Jesus, the B-40 got Al. He's gone. His blood's all over me . . . I killed him. It was my job, and I couldn't do it, and I killed Al. (*Breaks into uncontrollable sobbing and shaking.*)

HSW: It's OK! Just erase that scene from your mind and slide back to that warm, quiet beach. Just put yourself out of the firefight and back to that beach and relax, just focusing that soft sand in your mind.

As the individual breaks through the defenses that have let him numb and shield the actual events from awareness, the full force of the reality of the incident floods over him, along with the overwhelming feelings of fear, guilt, remorse, and terror that accompany the event. As these thoughts come into awareness, they give the human services worker a much clearer picture of the how and why of Billie Mac's phase 2 (denial and numbing) and those of phase 3 (intrusive-repetitive thoughts). The human services worker, using tolerable doses of reminiscence about the event, seeks to push forward into full awareness what the true scene at the event was and not what the individual's mind has fantasized it to be.

HSW: Now shift out of the scene at the beach and go back to the village. The B-40 has just gone off and Al is gone. What happens next?

Billie Mac: I can't remember . . . I don't know . . . I passed out.

HSW: (*gently*) Yes, you can. Just think a moment, and picture the scene. It's scary, but you are there now. Go ahead and just let it come and remember. I am here with you and you can get through this.

The worker gently but forcefully urges Billie Mac forward into the core of his trauma and what he fears most. This is a tightwire the worker walks. Coming to grips with the traumatic core is critical if recovery is to occur. Yet pushed too hard, the client may suffer some severe psychological consequences and lose much of the ground he has gained.

Billie Mac: Oh, God! You've got to get the point man now. You've got to go get him. I'm up and running, the fire is terrible, it's only 20 feet to him, but it's like a mile. I'm so damned scared. (*Breath coming in rapid, ragged gasps.*) I've got him and am dragging him back to the ditch. Bullets are kicking up all around me. I'll be cut in two. He weighs a ton. I get to the ditch and roll him and me into it. I turn him over and . . . Oh, Mother of Mary! He's dead. Why, oh why, didn't I get there sooner? I could have saved him. You puke-faced coward. (*Starts uncontrolled sobbing.*)

HSW: (*very calmly*) You are OK. Just shift out of that scene and back to the beach. Just take all the time you need to relax and erase that scene from your mind. Just let the cool breeze blow over you, smell the clean salt air, and enjoy that feeling of being completely relaxed. (*Time passes, and Billie Mac becomes noticeably more relaxed.*) Now I'm going to count up from 1 to 10, and when I reach 10 you'll be fully alert and refreshed.

The human services worker does this and brings Billie Mac back to present time. The worker then processes the events of the imagery session with Billie Mac.

Interpretation. At this point, the worker uses a more psychodynamic approach, actively intervening in the situation by clarifying and interpreting what the client says. By dynamically integrating the there and then of the trauma with the client's maladaptive attempts to cope and atone in the here and now of the therapeutic moment, the therapist hopes that the client can build a comprehensible picture that will make sense of the memory (Lindy, 1996, p. 534). This interpretation is not typical of TF-CBT and may fly in the face of its structured protocols, but we believe that it is important in that it attempts to empathize with and use words that touch the deeper meaning involved in Billie Mac's anguish (Lindy, 2012, pp. 21–23). With Billie Mac fully awake and the recorder going, the HSW interprets the meaning of the event.

HSW: This is my hunch. See what you think of it and feel free to add, subtract, or tell me I'm full of New Orleans canal water. So it's not just that terrible fight at the village, but more what you didn't do. You feel as if you were a coward there, and that cowardice cost the life of your friend. It's almost as if all these years you'd been trying to atone for that in the only way you know how—that is, by doing things that would almost guarantee that you die too. The brushes with the law, the uncontrollable rage that winds up in knockdown, drag-out fights, the DWIs, and the suicide attempt.

Billie Mac: I don't know. (*sobbing*) I feel so terrible about it. How could I have frozen? It would have been better if I had got killed rather than live with this.

HSW: Yet you did act. You went after the man, and you couldn't know whether a minute or two would have saved his life. It seems as if that minute or two of indecision has caused 30 years of terrible retribution that you can never pay off. I'd like to suggest that it has been paid with interest, and now the time has come to pay the balance. Are you willing to do that?

Billie Mac: (*shakily*) I guess . . . although I don't know how much more I can take. This stinking shit just blows up in my face and I can't control it. (*Red in the face, shaking, and yelling*) You bitch! How could you do this! This really hurts!

Lindy (2012, pp. 21–25) believes that Billie Mac's heated response contains two important messages. First is the use of what Lindy calls a **trauma metaphor** for clients. "Stinking shit blows up in my face" is an idiosyncratic way of describing and attempting to give symbolic meaning to his current state of being (p. 22). These are metaphors the worker needs to be keenly aware of because they often carry the dysfunctional meaning making message of the survivor. Second, these metaphors are symbolic transference terms that can either speak to the actual event (rocket blowing up in his face) or the therapy blowing up his **emotional dysregulated defense systems** (constant angry attitude with frequent, severe temper outbursts out of proportion to the situation in terms of intensity and duration).

HSW: I understand how rough you feel this is and how callous and uncaring I must seem at times. Now the "shit blowing up" right now I believe is not the "bad shit" of the rocket in the firefight, but if you can believe it, the "good shit" of blowing the cover off and getting it in the open. Remember! We've made it this far. Trust me and yourself. Together we can pull through this.

Even if the human services worker is right on target with her interpretation, getting Billie Mac to integrate the material and also allowing him to reconcile himself to the event are much more difficult. Breaking through the subconscious defenses of the client is not a one-shot deal, and denial is more often the rule than insight and acceptance. Billie Mac's negative reaction to the worker is typical of the client's transference of his or her ills to the worker as the hurtful affect is brought into awareness. At this point it is the worker's primary task to remain as empathic as possible to what is going on with the client (Lindy, 1996, p. 536).

Reflection and Transition

Although it can be extremely traumatic for the client, the human services worker will encourage the client to experience the full range of emotional responses he or she felt at the time of the event, as well as how he or she tried to make sense of it (Donaldson & Gardner, 1985, p. 370). This marks the fourth phase of the crisis, the reflective transition phase (Brende & Parson, 1985, p. 192). The human services worker will help the client by combining behavioral techniques of flooding and thought stopping. The technique of journaling, or having the client write down thoughts as the therapeutic process unfolds, will help the client process the experience.

Flooding/Prolonged Exposure. Flooding or prolonged exposure is one of the most effective, if controversial, techniques for getting rid of the bad memories of PTSD (Feeny, Hembree, & Zoellner, 2003; Keane et al., 1989; Lyons & Keane, 1989). In flooding and exposure (Stampfl & Lewis, 1967), the fear-evoking stimuli are presented continuously. The rationale is that if the individual is literally flooded with anxiety-provoking stimuli, the client will discover that there is no basis for fear. Continuously flooding the client causes the stimuli that are generating the anxiety to diminish; that is, repeating the response without reinforcement diminishes the tendency to perform that response. As the individual reenacts the trauma, the human services worker puts in the missing pieces of the puzzle and ferrets out all conditioned stimuli buried in memory. The result is that no noxious components of memory are left to recondition debilitating responses (Foa et al., 2002; Forbes et al., 2003; Hembree, Rauch, & Foa, 2003; Keane et al., 1985, p. 265; Paunovic, 2002, 2003; Paunovic & Ost, 2001; S. Taylor, 2003). In Chapter 9, Sexual Assault, an even more complex variation of flooding and prolonged exposure combined with cognitive restructuring and guided imagery to extinguish intrusive images will be presented. This technique is a very serious therapeutic endeavor and should not be undertaken by neophytes until they have received supervised training.

Thought Stopping. Thought stopping is a simple but powerful device that enables the individual, with help from the crisis worker, to change debilitating, intrusive thoughts to self-enhancing ones. The crisis worker initially sets the scene and builds the images until the fear-evoking stimuli are at maximum arousal, and then shouts "Stop!" and replaces them with positive, self- enhancing thoughts (Williams & Long, 1979, p. 285). The crisis worker tells the individual that at the point when the intrusive scene is most terrifying, the human services worker will slam a book sharply on the table and state in a firm voice, "Stop! Shift back to the beach!" The individual will be passive throughout the procedure, with the human services worker setting and enhancing the scene. A recording of the session is made, and the client is given the assignment of listening to the recording and then using the procedure whenever the intrusive images occur.

HSW: Now erase the beach scene, and come back to the village. You're in the ditch. Smell the stench of that ditch; feel death all around you. You can almost see the grim reaper there. You'd like to run away, but there's nowhere to run. Oh, what a fool you were to ever make the dash out here in no-man's-land! Look back and see your squad members shot up, contorted in pain, with the blood and dirt covering them. Peek over the ditch and see the point man. He's in terrible pain, screaming for help, but there's a blizzard of fire coming from the bunker. It's certain death to stick your head above the dike. Feel the conflict. You want to do something, you know you've got to take the bunker out, but you are paralyzed. You can smell the fear in you, sweating out of your pores. Look at Al. He expects you to do something; you're the squad leader, but you can't. Feel Al's stare. Listen to him yelling, "Take the bunker now, man!" Your fingers are glued to the LAW. Feel Al grab the LAW. Watch him as he stands up in that dreadful hail of death and fires the LAW into the bunker, and in the next instant see the explosion and the dirt fly as the B-40 round hits and Al disappears in the flame and smoke. Smell the smoke of cordite and the sheared copper odor of blood. Enhance those images—hear, smell, feel, see, taste that terrible moment. It's all there now as it really was. (*Billie Mac is writhing in the reclining chair.*) NOW STOP! (*Slams book down on desk.*) Shift away.

Billie Mac: (*screaming*) I can't do it!

HSW: (*in a soft but commanding voice*) Yes, you can! Just slide out of that and into that soft, warm sand. Stay with that beach scene. Smell the salt air, the cool breeze, and know that you can do that any time you want. Notice the difference in how your body feels, what goes through your mind. Just enjoy that feeling of knowing you can move into that scene.

This sequence is repeated over and over until the individual is able to switch volitionally from the intrusive image to the relaxing one with ease. The recording can be taken home to diminish the dissociation and permit externalization of the client's inner dialogue about the event and extinguish the fear that goes with it (Tinnin, Bills, & Gantt, 2002).

Integration

The Gestalt technique of reaching into the individual's past and bringing to conscious awareness what Gestalt practitioners call "unfinished business" (Polster & Polster, 1973) is particularly helpful in draining the pustulant affect that infects the event (Cohen, 2002, 2003; Scurfield, 1985, p. 246). For Billie Mac, this technique will take a different twist and will be the last part of the crisis, that of making atonement, penance, and restitution (Horowitz & Solomon, 1975). A Gestalt technique called the "empty chair" will be used.

HSW: The empty chairs in front of you represent various people. Al, the point man, other members of your squad that got hit on that day in the village. I want you to tell them what you felt about what you did. I may move to one of the chairs or have you take their place. Right now I want you to imagine Al in that chair over there. What are you going to say to him?

Billie Mac: I'm . . . so sorry. I froze. I shouldn't have done that. I killed you, and I can't ever forget that.

HSW: (*takes Al's chair*) Hey, man, what about that time at Chu Lai, and the A Shau valley? You didn't freeze then. You saved my bacon then. Remember how I froze? You didn't say squat. You think you're perfect?

Billie Mac: You were my best friend, and I let that happen. (*Sobs.*)

HSW: (*as Al*) You think you got a corner on the market? Everybody was scared. I just did it. You gave me back my life a half dozen times. I'll never forget that. You did well by me, buddy. I got no regrets.

Billie Mac: Jesus, I miss you. I loved you so damn much.

HSW: (*as Al*) Then remember the good times we had. That R & R in Bangkok, when we took the town apart. Those are the parts I remember. I love you too, buddy, but it's time we were done with that village. It's time for you to say good-bye to me. (*The HSW gets up and goes over and takes Billie Mac into his arms and hugs him. Billie Mac weeps, releasing a flood of emotion.*)

For each man in the squad, the scene is replayed. Sometimes Billie Mac takes the role of the other man, and sometimes the crisis worker does. Each piece of unfinished business is slowly and patiently worked through until Billie Mac has reconciled accounts with each person who was there on that terrible day. Clearly, Billie Mac goes through a painful but necessary grieving process that must take place if he is to put the event behind him (Brende & Parson, 1985, p. 105). As Billie Mac makes atonement for that day long past, and the trauma is expunged, the human services worker seeks to pull him to the present time and help him move forward with his life. Intensive intervention slacks off, and the individual may then go through a series of booster sessions on an "as needed" basis, with a minimum of a booster session once a month for 3 to 4 months (Balson & Dempster, 1980). This point marks the fifth, or integration, phase of the crisis.

Group Treatment

There are three types of treatment groups for **LO15** people who have been exposed to trauma. The first type is preventive, short term, and typically used for those suffering acute distress. These are generally known as *debriefing groups* and are composed of members who have just survived a common traumatic experience (Mitchell, 1983). Debriefing for acute traumatic stress is discussed in detail in the last chapter of this book.

The second type of group is a *structured therapy group* that deals in a step-by-step fashion with PTSD symptoms. CPT techniques are well fitted to a group of this type. It typically uses a manualized treatment program, and operates as a closed group with a fixed starting and ending point. Homework assignments are provided and worked on from session to session. Typically groups run about 12 weeks, once a week for 2 hours at a time.

The third type is longer term and is typically composed of class-specific members who have been exposed to the same type of trauma but at different times and under different circumstances. It is generally an *open group* that is continuous with different members entering and leaving the group at different times. Commonly called a **support group**, this group deals with a variety of transcrisis issues that have to do with members' attempts to reintegrate themselves into a useful, functioning role in society and is the focal point of this chapter's discussion of group work with clients who suffer from PTSD.

Support Groups

Rap or support groups were started for veterans in 1970 by Robert Lifton and Chaim Shatan in

New York City. Lifton and Shatan were human services professionals who had become disaffected with the Veterans Administration's constant refusal to acknowledge that many Vietnam veterans were suffering from combat-induced psychological problems. The outcome of this dilemma was that professionals finally came to recognize the success of rap groups and to integrate them into more traditional formats (Walker, 1983).

Emotional attachment and social involvement are basic and important ingredients in armor plating the individual against PTSD. For most of those who suffer from PTSD, social isolation and emotional estrangement are the norm. Thus, group work is helpful because of the shared experience, mutual support, sense of community, reduction of stigma, and restoration of self-pride it fosters. The primary task of any group therapy is to help people regain a sense of safety and of mastery because of the shared sense of having gone through the trauma (van der Kolk, McFarlane, & van der Hart, 1996, p. 433). Further, confrontation by peers is more acceptable than confrontation by professionals because it is reality oriented (Scurfield, 1985, pp. 247–248).

Groups also serve to educate clients. The terrifying nature of PTSD calls for clearly delineating what is happening and why. Answers to clients' questions—such as "What are common PTSD symptoms?" "Why do people use drugs?" "How long will it take to get better?" "Am I crazy?" "What do I do in this situation?" "Will I ever be as I was before this happened?"—help build a cognitive anchor for the individual (Brewi, 1986).

We now switch our client emphasis to the men and women who work in police, fire, emergency, and disaster services and who, because of their repeated exposure to trauma, are excellent candidates for PTSD (Bierens de Haan, 1998; Corneil et al., 1999; Dreisbach, 2003; Epstein, Fullerton, & Ursano, 1998; Horn, 2002; Tucker et al., 1999; Ursano et al., 1999). We will follow one individual in this group as a generic example of emergency service workers who become at risk for PTSD because of their constant exposure to traumatic events.

The Case of Ryan. Ryan Sanchez is a 35-year-old who has been a patrolman with the police department for 9 years. In that time he has received numerous commendations and citations for his work. Approximately 1 month ago he was referred to the police psychologist for a rather dramatic deterioration in job performance. He was caught sleeping on the job, had missed several days of work, and was insubordinate to his field commander when confronted with his inadequate performance at a crime scene. That episode culminated in his being hauled away bodily by other patrol officers after he attempted to punch his field supervisor. He was referred for clinical evaluation by his watch commander. An MMPI-2 administered by the police psychologist indicated a high potential for faking good—presenting a better picture of one's personality than one actually feels about it. The PK scale also indicated a good possibility of PTSD. The police psychologist believed that Ryan's initial interview and his MMPI-2 scores were an attempt by Ryan to present a better picture of his mental health than he was actually experiencing.

The psychologist then conducted a CAPS-1 interview and found a variety of problems that reached into both Ryan's job and family. Prior to Ryan's career with the police department, he served as an emergency medical technician (EMT) for 8 years. He decided to leave EMT work because of its stress, but still wanted to work in an "exciting and meaningful" job. He then joined the police department. He has a college degree in biology and a certificate in emergency medical technology. He has been married for 15 years to Mary, a nurse, and has two daughters, Katrina, 12, and Stacey, 8. He has been separated from his wife for 5 months, is currently living with his parents, and sees his daughters on his off-duty days.

He reports that his wife had become progressively more paranoid over other women, accused him of having affairs with them, constantly checked to see if he had perfume or lipstick marks on him after work, and finally attempted to run down, in a mall parking lot, an off-duty female police officer whom she suspected of having an affair with Ryan. That incident resulted in her temporary arrest, but charges were later dropped after she apologized to the female officer.

Ryan reports that at about this time he started suffering a bad case of "nerves." Specifically, he started to experience flashbacks to a series of traumatic events he had experienced as both an EMT and a police officer. He reports a series of instances as an EMT in which he was powerless to save the lives of terminal auto accident victims, a number of them children or adolescents. He reports having become very protective of his daughters as a result and says he wishes "I could put them in a castle with high walls and a moat around it and keep them locked up so nothing could hurt them." His protective view of his children severely strained his relationship with them, and they do not want to go and visit him because of his anger when they are not under his close supervision. He was also an EMT respondent to a natural disaster 11 years ago when a propane truck overturned and blew up, killing more than 30 people. They were charred and burned so badly that rigor had set in, but were still alive. He was relegated to being the mayor's aide de camp and spent most of his time passing information to the mayor about rescue efforts. He felt completely helpless and out of control and was enraged over his assignment. He very much wanted to be in on the rescue efforts, although he paradoxically reports that it was the most horrific scene he had ever witnessed. He reports having had nightmares about it for a number of months after the event. In the last 6 months those nightmares have returned with increasing frequency. He also reports that within the last 6 months he has become severely agitated to the point of a panic attack whenever he is near a propane truck, and will go out of his way to avoid them as well as bulk plants and tank farms where petroleum products are stored.

One other traumatic event is reported as remarkable. This event involved a missing person report while Ryan was a police officer. He and two detectives met the father of a young woman reported missing, at her abandoned apartment. Because they did not have a search warrant, they could not conduct a thorough search of the apartment. Ryan had a hunch that the woman's body was in the apartment buried under a huge mound of bags in a closet, but he was admonished by the detectives that there was nothing they could do. Because it was below freezing in the apartment, there was no foul odor to indicate the presence of a body. Two weeks later he again met the father at the apartment. The father had come in a rental truck and had begun to haul his daughter's belongings out of the apartment when he noticed a foul odor. On his arrival, Ryan immediately knew the odor was that of a dead body. On entering the apartment, he immediately found the woman under the bags of clothing. He reports an indelible picture of the father sitting in the yellow rental truck with a glazed stare that he cannot get out of his mind. He also reported that his uniform smelled like death and repeated washings would not get rid of it. He finally threw his whole uniform out, but lately he believes that somehow his new uniforms have soaked up the smell from his leather uniform jacket. He has never undergone formal debriefings for any of these traumatic events and said that although they bothered him some at the time they happened, he moved on past them—or so he thought.

He does not use alcohol, and that fact is confirmed by his watch commander. He reports he has been taking "tranquilizers" and "sleeping medication" since his separation from his wife. He also reports that things are so bad both on the job and at home that he has recently contemplated killing himself, but he has not formulated a plan because he doesn't want his daughters to be labeled because their dad "was another nutso who blew his brains out." He admits to the psychologist that he clearly has lost control of his life and wonders if he indeed does not have PTSD or is suffering a "breakdown" of some kind.

Ryan's symptoms fit a clear diagnosis for PTSD. He has recurrent, intrusive thoughts and dreams about the traumatic events and experiences severe psychological distress to external cues of the events. He now avoids stimuli that remind him of at least two of the events. He has increased arousal symptoms, hypervigilance over his daughters' safety, difficulty concentrating on his job, and problems falling asleep. The psychologist's diagnosis is posttraumatic stress disorder, with delayed onset. Although delayed onset is relatively uncommon (McFarlane & Yehuda, 1996, p. 159), it is not uncommon for a domino effect to occur in emergency medical workers where one event triggers other supposedly long-forgotten ones (van der Kolk & McFarlane, 1996, p. 9). As his social support system has given way at home, Ryan has become increasingly at risk, and the precipitating event of his wife's vehicular assault on a fellow police officer and his subsequent separation from his family has activated the traumatic memories.

Ryan is referred to a behavioral health maintenance organization for individual treatment and is also referred to an independent support group that is cosponsored by the police, fire, and emergency workers unions and the city and county governments. The police psychologist also makes a no harm contract with Ryan and contacts the human services worker who will be attending Ryan, to tell the worker about Ryan's suicidal ideation.

Triage Assessment. Affectively, Ryan is experiencing extended periods of intense negative moods that are markedly stronger than the situation warrants. Although he has no clear intent or plan for committing suicide, he is agitated and depressed enough to consider it. At times he perceives his negative mood states as not being very controllable. His affective rating is

7 to 8. Cognitively, Ryan's thinking is generally equal to the task of moving forward in day-to-day living. However, his ability to control intrusive thoughts and images about the traumatic events is limited, and his perception of events, particularly his obsessiveness about his daughters' safety, differs noticeably from the reality of the situation. His cognitive rating is 6 to 7. Behaviorally, Ryan's inability to function at work is noticeably affecting his job performance. His behavioral rating is 6 to 7. Ryan's full-scale triage ranges between 19 and 22. He is in crisis and in need of immediate therapeutic assistance.

Ryan's initial meeting with the human services worker involves carrying forward the no harm contract, obtaining a referral to a psychiatrist to review his medication, explaining what individual therapy will entail, and receiving an invitation to join a support group.

HSW: We've got some men and women that meet on Wednesday night to talk about many of the problems you're trying to deal with now. I think you've got a lot in common with them and believe it might be helpful for you to meet them. They've all been or are in the police, fire, or emergency departments and are trying to come to terms with their experiences there. You don't have to talk if you don't want to; that's up to you. You'll probably feel a lot of different emotions, and some of those aren't going to be too pleasant. However, all of the people you'll meet have been feeling a lot of the same kinds of things even though they may have different kinds of problems that brought them into the center. From that standpoint they all know what you're going through, and while it may get tough, they'll support you and not pass judgment. I'd really like to see you come in. You don't have to, but we know that social support is one of the most important ingredients to getting better, and right now it sounds like you could use some of that.

The group meets for an hour and a half each week. The first item is that individuals are asked to introduce themselves by name and unit. This structured event is not just for the purpose of getting into "war stories"; it serves to move men and women psychologically back in time and place to the starting point of their trauma and to cement the "we-ness" of the group. After introductions, anything on anybody's mind is fair game for conversation. The whole idea is to get you "unstuck" from the rut you're in and get

some ideas on how to start moving forward. This will be in addition to the weekly meetings.

The group is composed of "veterans" who have been through many such sessions and "greenhorns" who are at their first meeting. Command officers are separated from rank-and-file members, so there are no possibilities of recriminations by command staff. Everything said in the group is confidential, and members indicate their willingness to abide by that rule by signing a statement to that effect. The groups are run by independent contractors who are not answerable to the city or county government about personnel decisions or any other matters that could put their clients' jobs at risk. Topics range from problems of day-to-day living to the institutions they work for, issues and questions about PTSD and trauma, replays of how and what they did during traumatic events, family and job issues, and how all these problems affect them.

The leaders of the group are two psychologists who have extensive experience with the police, firefighters, and EMTs. Although they have never served in any of those occupations, they have credibility because of their previous work with these groups, and that is critically important. Distrust and suspicion are strong in the early stage of such groups, and human services workers can be expected to be tested over and over again until they have proved themselves to be congruent and trustworthy (Gressard, 1986).

The leaders are not group therapists in the truest sense of the word. They are more like participatory members who have been endowed with the task of keeping the group within loose guidelines concerning time, monopolizing the group, facilitating support and responses from the other members, and, in a few extreme instances, acting as empathic but firm sergeants-at-arms. As leaders they must be willing to keep a low profile while group members interact. Their leadership role is subtle rather than directive and requires an infinite supply of patience as the group struggles toward resolution of its problems. If therapy in a classical sense of the word is to occur, it happens much later in the game. A clear distinction between the rap/support group and a long-term therapy group is that trauma and the expiation of associated guilt are the main focus, not life adjustment. Life adjustment problems represent another stage in the crisis of this malady and are handled later. The typical support group starts something like this:

HSW: Hi, everybody. We've got some new people here and because they don't know everybody I'd like you all to introduce yourself and your unit. I'm

Theo Ewing, a psychologist. I work with the Crisis Intervention Team in the city police department.

Jane: Jane Shore, patrol officer, Delta shift, West Precinct, city. Age 21. (*Rookie on the force, training officer shot in a liquor store holdup. Robbers got away. Feels responsible, nightmares, startle reactions, hypervigilance, some paranoid ideation about abilities.*)

Leann: Leann Sung, EMT, RN, county hospital. Age 50. (*Twenty years' emergency room and ambulance duty, attendant at multiple disasters, catastrophes. Burned out, suicide attempt after caught stealing amphetamines from ER pharmacy, peptic ulcer, numbing of affect.*)

Alonzo: Alonzo Brown, sheriff's deputy, Able shift, north sector, county. Age 42. (*Shot and killed carjacker after carjacker killed hostage by cutting her throat. First shooting, first violent deaths witnessed, nightmares, intrusive images, high blood pressure, alcohol abuse problem.*)

Lamont: Lamont Evans, paramedic, Life Flight. Age 29. (*Life Flight helicopter crashed and burned. He and other paramedic thrown clear. Everybody else died—including two auto accident victims being lifted to hospital. Survivor's guilt, hypervigilance, startle reactions, nightmares, wife has left, phobic reaction to helicopters since accident.*)

Rachelle: Rachelle Johnson, driver, Engine House 47, county fire department. Age 36. (*Saw wall collapse on two members of her engine company during warehouse fire. Helped pull both dead firefighters from rubble. One was her best friend. Nightmares, survivor's guilt, somatic and general anxiety reactions, eating disorder.*)

Ryan: Ryan Sanchez, patrol officer, Charlie shift, Center Precinct, city. (*Personal data previously given.*)

(*Introductions continue around the group and group welcomes Ryan.*)

HSW: Has anybody got anything that's hot?

Lamont: Well, two things. I haven't had any more helicopters crashing nightmares since last time; I guess that's something. That prolonged exposure stuff has been tough with Dr. Myer, but I think it's starting to work. I got a prescription for Trazadone which is helping me sleep. And the wife said she might come back.

(*General congratulations from the group.*)

Rachelle: Man! That's something. I wish I could get rid of the damn things. None of those drugs are doing any good. I can't eat. I can't sleep. I don't know how much longer I can take it.

Jane: Ditto that! I can't get by it, and it seems to get worse. I really don't like that flooding stuff. I've heard about EMDR being not so rough, but I don't know who does that.

Lamont: (*gently*) We've all been there and know how tough it is; you knew it'd get worse before it got better; we all told y'all that. It's hell. Y'all been talkin' to your counselors? I'll betcha one of our esteemed facilitators can put you onto somebody who does EMDR (*looks at Dr. James*).

Because of the mutual support and resources within the group, lots of suggestions are given about how Rachelle and Jane can grapple with their emotional turmoil. Survivor's guilt is a common thread that runs through emergency, fire, and police personnel. The expectation is that these people are supposed to lay their lives on the line, and when others die or are injured there are always second-guessing and fears of being seen as letting their comrades down. Lamont's comments are therapeutic in that they are accepting and understanding of the guilt both women feel.

Rachelle: Yeah, I been talkin' to her. But it just seems like the more stuff comes up, the worse I feel. Why did they die and not me?

HSW: So it still boils down to the survivor's guilt stuff we've talked about. Lamont, Rachelle, and Jane have all talked about the same issues. (*The group leader takes a few minutes to speak to the typical behavioral dynamics of someone who has survived a trauma when others did not, which is typical of the psychoeducational function that is also a part of support groups.*) Any thoughts?

Jane: I've always wanted to be a cop, and I really thought I'd make a good one, but it's tough being a rookie and a woman at that. I've replayed that robbery a thousand times. I don't know what I could have done differently, and Loren, my training officer, told me I did fine. I'm glad he's gonna be all right, but I still think I screwed up somehow. Maybe I'm paranoid, but I'm not so sure the other cops on my shift trust me. Hell! I'm not so sure I trust myself.

Ryan: Well, I'm new here, so I don't know much, but I heard about that, and it sounded OK to me. What did you think you did wrong?

Jane: Well, that's what's driving me nuts. I don't think I did, but I think the others think I did.

Ryan: Well, if it's because you're a woman, lose that thought. I've got a female for a partner, and she's tops.

HSW: Jane, did you hear what Ryan said?

Jane: Yeah! And thanks. Dr. Myer did give me a phone app that goes with that mindfulness stuff he's also been doin' and that does help some. When I start to feel that negative self-talk overwhelm me, I flip the phone app on. I just let the anxiety come on but then turn it into dandelion seeds and just blow on it and let it float away on the wind and poof! It's gone. (*giggles*) It sounds kinda screwy but it seems to help.

The leader immediately breaks in so that two people get reinforcement—the newer member of the group for talking and Jane, who can use the affirmation from a male officer who is a veteran.

Alonzo: So what's happened to cause the change in you, Lamont?

Lamont: I'm not blaming myself as much. I still feel bad about the others that died, but I'm getting reconciled to it. I'm really lucky to be alive, and I've got to start working on putting my life back together. And I'm finally realizing that engine failure had nothing to do with Lamont. My counselor calls it *reframing,* kinda lookin' at it from a different viewpoint. I mean both of you were doing what you were supposed to be doing when those things went down. You can't ask more than that. I been writin' stuff down too, usin' that trauma workbook. Man I haven't had so much homework since college.

Alonzo: I wish I could "reframe" my problems that easy. I mean this crackhead carjacks this woman, practically cuts her head off in front of me. I've got no clear shot until he drops her, then I shoot him. Then the shoot team gives me a clouded report. Should have acted sooner, should have had more patience. How the hell do you do both of those at once? I did it all by the book. What that's all about? Then I get a wrongful death suit laid on me by both the victim and the murderer's families. It's not enough I feel bad about both of them, but now I'm the culprit. I'll never get rid of that image. And no damn support from the department. So now I'm going to 12-step meetings, comin' here with you fine folks and getting stress inoculation training with my shrink. He's doing this imagining stuff about the homicide and he's making noises about getting me ready to go back to the scene and talk it through or something. Man I've been a cop for 19 years, and if I can make it for

one more year without having a stroke with this sky-high blood pressure, they can all kiss my ass good-bye. Why shouldn't I drink?

Leann: Yeah well, that's what they do, is use you up. Twenty years at county ER. I've seen it all. When I got caught swiping the speed, I'd been on for four straight shifts through four gun assaults and two knifings, three multiple-injury car accidents, and burn cases of five kids in an apartment fire. I was about to collapse. And I've done that over and over for all these years. And you know what, the ER supervisor who caught me said he could forget it if I could take just the one more shift, said he "knew I needed a pick-me-up." When I said no to that SOB, he turned me in. That's the sum total of my life, no family, a speed freak, a burned-out ER nurse with an ulcer, and a system that uses you up and then dumps you. So tell me why suicide doesn't look like a good career option. (*Starts to weep silently.*)

HSW: Are you still contemplating killing yourself, Leann?

In no uncertain terms, the leader immediately checks out Leann's comment. As she is a past attempter, such comments are never seen as offhand statements.

Leann: No, not really. It just makes me so angry that they'd do that. I told them about that jerk, but they still put me on disciplinary sick leave and didn't do a thing to that blackmailing twerp.

HSW: So it's also the system that you feel betrayed by. It's like after all these years of doing your very best, the system turns its back on you. Not only does it make you madder than hell, but at a deeper level it really hurts to think that somehow an institution that you've given most of your life to would not stick up for you when the chips were down or would even try and blackmail you. (*Leann and Alonzo both nod their heads vigorously in agreement.*)

Although it may appear that the support group has dissolved into a gripe session about uncaring bureaucracies, the stresses put on individuals by notoriously understaffed human services institutions and public safety departments add a great deal to the recipe for posttraumatic stress disorder when emergency situations occur (see Chapter 16, Human Services Workers in Crisis: Burnout, Vicarious Traumatization, and Compassion Fatigue). Expressing emotion is a potent weapon in the arsenal of opening feelings, which is critical in dealing with PTSD (Tarrier & Humphreys, 2003). The group leader reflects these feelings and gives the members a chance at catharsis, but also poses a problem-solving question. Lindy (2012) has been very vocal about neglecting the art of listening to these narratives in favor of manualized cookie-cutter, one-size-fits-all PTSD therapy.

HSW: I wonder what you might do about changing some of that institutional behavior?

Rachelle: I know one thing—if it hadn't been for the union's pushing for this kind of support and now the new debriefing program, we wouldn't be here now. There's got to be more safeguards for people who work in the high-stress jobs we do, and the only way I see that happening is through the union's collective membership. I think I'll talk to my rep about some of that stuff.

Alonzo: That's right! At least they can get all the certifiables in one place and keep an eye on us. (*Group laughs.*) I know how much that hurts, Leann, 'cause I feel the same way. But you gotta think of all you've done and all the lives you saved and the people you've helped. I'm pretty cynical right now, like you, but I had a person stop me the other day and thank me for something I did a long time ago, that he said kept him out of jail. I couldn't really even remember the incident it's been so long ago, but he sure did. It made me feel good. How many people out there do you suppose you've been involved with who wouldn't be alive now if you hadn't been there?

Alonzo, who has been vitriolic in ventilating his feelings, switches roles and becomes a support person to Leann. In mutual help groups such as this, such role shifts are common, and the need to become a helper rather than a beneficiary is extremely important (Silverman, 1986). Theo, the leader of the group, recognizes this shift and wisely lets Alonzo carry the dialogue.

Alonzo: Eh, ah, Ryan. What's happening with you, man?

Ryan: (*Details his problems.*) I mean, I like you guys and all, but I don't know that this group stuff will help much. I mean you can't fix my marriage, and all this other crazy PTSD stuff. I guess the shrink will sort that out. I just don't know. Dr. James is gonna set up an EMDR session for me so I could let you know how that goes.

Rachelle: I understand, Ryan, I haven't been here that long myself, but I'll tell you this much— these people understand what I'm going through. Maybe we can't save your marriage, but we can sure be here for you, 'cause these other folks have sure been here for me.

Rachelle's comment encapsulates the essence of why it is called a *support group*. As the group session closes, each member is given the floor to speak on what has occurred for him or her personally during the meeting. No one else is allowed to respond to his or her comments. Summing statements include both reflections about the impact of the discussion on oneself and reinforcing comments to others. Finally, the group rises, joins hands, and has a silent moment of meditation. The emotionally positive high voltage that flows through the locked hands of some very tough men and women is both touching and powerful, and it conveys far better than words the caring and support each man and woman feel for their comrades.

Evidence suggests that individuals who have suffered other types of catastrophic intrusion into their lives can profit from support groups. Donaldson and Gardner (1985) report that incest victims quickly gain an intense sense of relief in coming together with others in mutual support groups. A typical comment is "No one else understands, but I can come out of the closet here." Defining these groups at a deeper level is Foulkes's (1948) comment that participants in such support groups can reinforce each other's normal reactions and break down each other's pathological reactions because they collectively constitute the very norm from which the individuals deviate. As such, members of a veterans' rap group one of the authors has worked with have what one member called very good "crap detectors": "We can smell it immediately when somebody isn't coming clean with us."

The Life Adjustment Group

PTSD may be seen as having a two-generation, or two-phase, treatment approach. In the first generation, treatment focuses on accessing and working through the trauma and its symptoms. Although this will be difficult, the second generation of treatment may be even more so. In the second generation, treatment moves to the client's attempts to readjust to contemporary society, which will generally not be an easy task (Johnson, Feldman, & Southwick, 1994).

As the guilt and horror of the situation are resolved, clients are moved into the life adjustment group, and another crisis ensues. It is not enough to bring to light hidden traumatic experiences. The key is to integrate past experiences, to find meaning and new ways of coping, to make atonement not only for oneself, but also for others, and to find new directions in life (Brende & Parson, 1985, pp. 199–201). The group at this point will diminish and absences will increase. The reason is twofold.

First, threatening material will again be covered. Second, action and behavioral change now become mandatory. Moving from the insight gained about what happened in the past to taking that insight and applying it to the present time is a giant step, and one that is guaranteed to be rife with crisis. What is now called for is to get on with the business of living. At this juncture, intervention will take many forms, depending on what the particular problems are that the individual faces. Such problems range from maintaining sobriety to salvaging careers. However, one thread will usually run through the circumstances of all clients at this stage. That thread is of vital importance and must be rewoven into the fabric of their lives. It is their family. Any comprehensive PTSD treatment program should take into consideration the need to reestablish the basic support system of the family, which is of critical importance in helping the survivor move forward in his or her posttraumatic world. Getting family members to open up and express some of their beliefs that influence the client's negative coping behaviors is scary for both the individual and the family; they may believe that discussing their posttraumatic problems would cause so much trouble that the family would disintegrate even though it may presently be in complete chaos (Tarrier & Humphreys, 2003).

Family Treatment

If the trauma is unresolved and chronic, its residue will eventually become enmeshed in the individual's interpersonal network (Figley, 1988, p. 91). As reluctant as the survivor of trauma may be to seek help, often the family is even more unwilling to participate in the recovery process (Solomon, 1986). Even though family members may be suffering terribly because of the individual's actions toward them and their respondent actions toward the individual and each other, they offer much resistance to changing the status quo, even though they adamantly maintain that change is needed. As strange as it may seem, although

families may be stressed to the limit in adapting to the PTSD individual, they do try to adapt, at times in pathological ways. As the individual changes, the family may be in for a rude awakening and may not be able to make parallel changes. We will see a great deal of what goes on in families in Chapter 11, Family Crisis Intervention.

Therefore, one of the crisis worker's major tasks is assessing the family's willingness to engage in treatment. The family's ability to resolve the crisis is a function of the nature of the event, the family's definition of the event, the resources they can bring to bear on it, the buildup of stressors that led to the event, and the effectiveness of their past and current coping skills (McCubbin et al., 1980).

Treatment objectives are to develop and implement an intervention program to deal with both the stress disorder of the individual and assorted family dysfunctions that were in place prior to the event or that developed after the event. Learning about the disorder, dealing with the boundary distortions of intimacy and separation caused by it, alleviating psychosomatic results of rage and grief, urging recapitulation of the trauma, facilitating resolution of the trauma-inducing family conflicts, clarifying insights and correcting distortions by placing blame and credit more objectively, offering new and more positive and accurate perspectives on the trauma, establishing and maintaining new skills and rules of family communication, and initiating new coping and adapting skills as family dynamics change are some of the many tasks the worker will have to tackle (Figley, 1988, pp. 86–88).

The foregoing list of tasks is a major order and is best dealt with by referral to a therapist who specializes in families and conjoint therapy. However, it is practically a must if the family has any hope of survival as a healthy system. The crisis worker should understand that at an early point in the therapeutic process, the family members need to be apprised of their role in the trauma and urged to become proactive in its solution. Finally, for the PTSD individuals, relearning how to be effective members of their families and society calls for the same kind of courage that propelled them into treatment in the first place. However, this time it may be much more difficult, because they will be working with the people they need the most and probably have hurt the most. If outcomes of the family component of the Comprehensive Soldier Fitness program are good, we see no reason why they could not be adapted to other workers in high-risk, high-stress civilian occupations.

Eye Movement Desensitization and Reprocessing (EMDR)

The Controversy Over EMDR

Eye movement desensitization and reprocessing (EMDR) has, to say the least, been a controversial technique. Now approved by the Veterans Administration hospitals for use (Department of Veterans Affairs & Department of Defense, 2010), the basic technique of EMDR is to have the person picture the traumatic scene in his or her mind or think about the thoughts or feelings associated with the trauma while following the therapist's finger with his or her eyes as it is moved rapidly back and forth in front of the person's face. Newer approaches employ flashing lights that move across the vision field and handheld buzzers that alternate in speed and strength in sending impulses to the client's hands. The procedure is so simplistic and is extolled as so fast and effective in comparison to combinatorial approaches using cognitive behavior and exposure techniques that it has been viewed with skepticism—particularly because PTSD is so intractable that there are as many failures as successes in treating the disorder. However, a number of replicating studies (Jarero & Ureibe, 2012; Lee & Cuijpers, 2013; McGuire, Lee, & Drummond, 2014; Urhausen, 2015) do show significant results for EMDR when compared with other treatment modalities. At present there is no clear scientific explanation of what it does to erase trauma.

However, Bergman (2012) has written extensively on the possible underlying neurobiological mechanisms of EMDR's potential ability to change the functioning of neural circuitry and it appears that neurobiological effects of EMDR operate differently than the CBT techniques of prolonged exposure, cognitive processing therapy, and stress inoculation (Bergman, 2012; Shapiro, 2014). The hypotheses proposed as to why and how it works mainly revolve around dual processing/focus of attention (if you do two things at once you aren't going to be able to pay attention to both nearly as well as one) or distancing (becoming more detached as you try to process the event while keeping some other activity going on (Bradley et al., 2005; Issacs, 2004; Lee, Taylor, & Drummond, 2006).

So, why use EMDR? There are two major reasons. First, it does seem to work with some people, and not

just as a placebo! Your authors have used EMDR with some very cynical, objective, hard-nosed, empirically oriented health service professionals, and they have been absolutely incredulous that the intrusive images have changed and the thoughts and feelings surrounding those traumatic images have diminished. Yet with some clients we have tried it on it doesn't work at all! But if it does work, it has been our experience that it works quickly and dramatically.

Second, it is far less intrusive than the cognitive-behavioral therapies that have prolonged exposure as their core treatment element. Bryant and Harvey (2000) warn that exposure therapy should not be used or used with extreme caution when treating clients with anxiety or panic attacks, psychosis, severe depression or suicide risk, substance abuse, borderline personality, marked dissociation, or marked ongoing stressors—which would include most people who have PTSD! At this point, from our experience using it, we agree with Briere and Scott (2006, p. 146) that EMDR appears to be at least as effective in treatment of simple PTSD as the cognitive-behavioral approaches and a lot less noxious, but may run into problems with more complex PTSD.

From the standpoint of client welfare, convenience, ease of use, and cost in time and money, it is at least worth a try as a first-order treatment. Indeed, it has now been used effectively in treating coal miners (Blore, 2014), acute stress disorder (Buydens, Wilensky, & Hensley, 2014), dementia (Amano & Toichi, 2014), chronic pain (Tesarz et al., 2014), complex PTSD and dissociation (Knipe, 2015), addiction (Abel & O'Brien, 2015), psychosis (deBont, van Minnen, & deJongh, 2013), breast cancer patients with PTSD and depression (Thompson, 2014), massacre aftermath (Jarero & Ureibe, 2012), disaster (Laub & Bar-Sade, 2014), and children (Diehle et al., 2015). Moving beyond the original protocol in this chapter, EMDR developers have been busy fine-tuning EMDR so there are now protocols being developed for various specific stages and types of PTSD (Shapiro & Laub, 2014).

However, be aware! Like a lot of newcomers into the therapy field, it should become apparent EMDR has been used metaphorically to attempt to fix everything from the crack of dawn to a broken heart. It is not a panacea. So understand that like every other technique in this business, it has its limits and nobody knows for sure how or why it works. So should it indeed be used for serious mental illness like depression, obsessive-compulsive disorder, and psychosis

LO16

without a lot of controlled research (Logie, 2014)? Given these precautionary statements, here are the basics of EMDR therapy.

EMDR Therapy

Eye movement desensitization (EMD) was developed by Francine Shapiro (1989a, 1989b) at the Mental Research Institute in Palo Alto, California. Shapiro (1991) later added the "R" to the acronym to indicate a reprocessing of information, along with changing to more positive cognitions and desensitization of the traumatic memory. According to Shapiro (1995, pp. 55–73; Shapiro & Maxfield, 2002), there are eight basic treatment components to EMDR: history taking and treatment planning, preparation, assessment, desensitization, installation, body scan, closure, and reevaluation.

History Taking and Treatment Planning. Initially, clients are evaluated for their ability to handle the high levels of disturbance that may occur with treatment. A comprehensive clinical picture of the client is obtained, and a determination is made of the specific targets to be reprocessed; these targets include past events, current stimuli that trigger symptoms, and positive attitudes and behaviors needed for the future (Shapiro, 1995, p. 68; Shapiro & Maxfield, 2002).

HSW: (to Ryan) It appears that at least three events from your past are predominant: the propane truck, the dead body of the missing girl, and the young woman in the auto accident who died in your arms. It also seems that the reemergence of all these traumatic work events occurred closely after your wife, in a fit of jealous rage, attempted to run down the female officer. The constant theme that emerges from all of these events is that you feel powerless, frustrated, and angry, but were and are paralyzed to do much about these events because of a variety of social and job prohibitions and your own moral stand. It appears that at least three triggers set these flashbacks and anxiety attacks off: propane trucks, yellow rental trucks, and verbal battles with your wife—particularly over custody and safety of your daughters.

Preparation. Preparation for therapy entails explaining to the client what is going to happen, the effects that can be expected, and safety procedures. Shapiro also makes a point of discussing secondary gain issues. That is, if the therapy is successful and the

pathology is reduced, what will the client have to give up (Shapiro, 1995, p. 69)? Although this may seem strange, a veteran may not want to lose his or her disability payments or "wounded warrior" status if the PTSD is eradicated.

Assessment. Shapiro (1989a, 1989b, 1995; Shapiro & Maxfield, 2002) proposes that EMDR treats traumatic memory by requiring that the client maintain awareness in one or more of the following: (1) an image of the memory, (2) a negative self-statement or assessment of the trauma, and (3) the physical anxiety response. Once the memory is identified, the client is asked to choose the image that best fits it along with a negative cognition and the chief physical response that goes with it. Although Shapiro (1989a, 1989b, 1995; Shapiro & Maxfield, 2002) proposes that it is optimal when all three conditions are held at the same time, she maintains that the presence of any one is sufficient for desensitization to occur.

Ryan: (generating images) I'm standing on the freeway overpass looking down on a scene from Dante's *Inferno*. It looks like a war zone. There are burning wrecks everywhere. I can see blackened bodies. Some are still alive. There are paramedics and firemen and other rescue workers all covered with soot. I can smell burned rubber and flesh. I can hear lots of moans and cries for help and shouting. I can feel the heat coming up out of the freeway on my face and arms. Sometimes when I come upon a propane truck, it all comes back like that. That's why I avoid them if at all possible. (generating negative self-statements) I'm powerless. I need to be down there, but I'm not sure I can take it. I've never seen anything like this. I'm a coward. I hate myself for feeling that way. (generating physical anxiety response) My skin feels like it's been sandpapered. Every nerve in my body is on fire. I want to run, down there or away, but do something. I can't stand just watching it all.

Anxiety level is assessed by Wolpe's (1982) Subjective Units of Discomfort (SUDs) scale (0 = no anxiety; 10 = highest anxiety possible). Because negative self-cognitions are also part of the disorder, shifts in the client's cognitive view of the traumatic event are also assessed by a Validity of Cognition (VOC) scale that Shapiro (1989a) developed (1 = the cognition is completely untrue to 7 = the cognition is completely true). Clients are asked to rate themselves on the SUDs and VOC and indicate the physical location of the symptoms (Shapiro, 1989a, 1989b, 1995, p. 70; Shapiro & Maxfield, 2002).

Ryan: The SUDs is way beyond 10. The VOC is 7.

Clients are next asked how they would like to feel and are told to generate a new positive self-statement that reflects the desired feeling (Shapiro, 1989a, 1989b, 1995; Shapiro & Maxfield, 2002).

Ryan: Like I'm in control. I'm not a coward. Not necessarily a hero.

Clients are then asked to judge how true that new statement is (Shapiro, 1989a, 1989b).

Ryan: A generous VOC for that would be 2.

Desensitization. Shapiro (1989b) then gives the client a standard set of instructions designed to diminish performance anxiety and performance demands. She indicates that this step is important because clients may have difficulty accepting the initial changes they feel in themselves. Her instructions are as follows:

> What we will be doing is often a physiology check. I need to know from you exactly what is going on, with as clear feedback as possible. Sometimes things will change and sometimes they won't. I may ask you if the picture changes—sometimes it will and sometimes it won't. I may ask if something else comes up—sometimes it will and sometimes it won't. There are no "supposed to's" in this process. So just give as accurate feedback as you can as to what is happening, without judging whether it should be happening or not. Just let whatever happens, happen. (p. 213)

Clients are then told to generate the scene, the negative statements, and their noxious feelings and visually track the human services worker's finger. The therapist's finger is moved rapidly and rhythmically back and forth, about 1 foot from the client's face, at approximately two back-and-forth movements per second with a sweep of about 12 inches across the client's field of vision. For clients who may have trouble with this approach, Shapiro uses a slightly different format in which the therapist's fingers are to the side of the client's vision field and are alternately moved up and down. The movement is repeated 12 to 24 times for one set. (This is called a *saccade*, which means a sort of pulling or pressing movement.)

After each set of saccades, clients are asked to erase the scene from their minds and take a deep breath. They are then asked to bring up the noxious image again and ascribe a SUDs level to it. If the SUDs level has not changed after two sets of saccades, the client is asked if the picture has changed or if anything new has come into the image. If so, the new image is desensitized before returning to the old image. Periodically, clients are asked to assess the image, cognition, and memory. Their answers are used to determine new insights, perceptions, or alterations.

Ryan: (*after two saccades*) I dunno. It's not as strong now or something. Maybe an 8. It's like it's moving, or I'm moving. I'm not frozen.

HSW: OK. See yourself moving, and put that "I'm not helpless, I'm moving and taking control" billboard under that picture. Can you think of that?

Ryan: Yeah. It's also like I'm frustrated or angry too now.

HSW: That's OK! New images and thoughts come into this. That's normal. We'll work those through too.

The therapist continues to attack the client's image, but this time has him insert the "I'm a coward" billboard into the scene until it too is diminished and changed to a more positive self-statement. The therapist continues eye movements and processes with Ryan until he reports a SUDs level of 1.

Installation. The idea of the installation phase is to install a new, positive cognition of the event. The installation phase starts once the client's SUDs rating has dropped to a 1 or 0. Ryan has changed his image, and the therapist will continue to pursue this until there are no longer additions to the emotional meaning of the image or there is no longer additional positive input.

Ryan: OK! I'm equal to this. I could handle it down there, but my job is up here coordinating things. I'm where I can do my best.

Note that the cognition is not kept in a negative sense, "I'm not a coward," but is put positively and proactively. While the client focuses on the target image and the new positive cognitions, the eye movements are continued until the client can report a VOC for the new positive thoughts at a level of 6 or 7. If the cognition fails to change after two sets of eye movements, there may be a mismatch between the cognition and the image, or vice versa. In each case, both image and cognition must be congruent with one another. If they are not, then one or the other needs to be replaced (Shapiro, 1989a, 1989b, 1995, p. 71).

Body Scan. After the positive cognition has been fully installed, clients are instructed to think of a physical location of anxiety in their body if the SUDs level remains high. They are asked to concentrate on the body sensation while new saccades are given. When the focal point of physical discomfort subsides, clients are asked to return to the original picture of the trauma and the standard EMDR procedure is resumed (Shapiro, 1989a, 1989b). Shapiro believes there is a physical resonance between the body and dysfunctional material. She believes this phase is important because it can uncover new areas of unprocessed or un-thought-of material (Shapiro, 1995, p. 730; Shapiro & Maxfield, 2002).

Ryan: I wish I could jump out of my skin, I'm so anxious. It feels like it's burning from the inside out.

HSW: OK, I want you to focus in on your skin. Feel the burning sensation. (*Starts and finishes another saccade.*)

Ryan: (*after two more saccades*) Huh. It's kinda gone now. That's really weird!

Closure. When no new events or negative cognitions are elicited, the EMDR procedure is terminated. The client is never left in a state of emotional disequilibrium, whether reprocessing for the event is done or not. The client is debriefed and reminded that additional intrusive images that may arise after the session are a positive sign of additional processing. Shapiro (1995, p. 73) also recommends that clients keep a journal of their thoughts, situations, dreams, and other information that may come to mind about the memory. This information can be used to target new images at the next session.

Reevaluation. At each new session an assessment is made of the previous targets. The client is asked to reaccess previous reprocessed targets, and the client's journal is examined for any intrusion of the previously examined material.

Ryan: It's weird. That image of the propane truck explosion is just kinda vague or misty or something. I decided to drive by a bulk plant that I always avoid. It's right on my way to my folks' house. Well, I decided to hell with it, let's see. Usually I'd think I was going to have a panic attack the last couple of months if I went near it. But I drove by it, and it was just a bulk plant. Nothing more! Didn't feel a thing! Fancy that!

In subsequent sessions the therapist may successively move through images of the propane truck, the body in the closet, the father of the murdered girl in the rental truck, and the scenes with Ryan's estranged wife. However, if the target and the triggers are well worked out, generalization of effect can occur and positive benefits accrue in other areas of the client's life (Shapiro, 1989a, 1989b, 1995, p. 74; Shapiro & Maxfield, 2002).

Children and PTSD
Diagnostic Criteria for Children

PTSD is not confined to adults. Children also **LO17** experience PTSD and manifest symptoms that closely parallel those of adults, with the following notable differences.

The 4th edition of the *Diagnostic and Statistical Manual for Mental Disorders* (DSM-IV) did not have specific criteria for diagnosing PTSD in children, and many of DSM-IV PTSD criteria were not age appropriate for children. As a result, it was difficult (if not impossible) to accurately diagnosis PTSD in children. However, the 5th edition of the *Diagnostic and Statistical Manual for Mental Disorders* (DSM-5) now includes specific guidelines for diagnosing PTSD in children under the age of 6.

A. Children under the age 6 have been exposed to an event involving real or threatened death, serious injury, or sexual violence in at least one of the following ways:

1. The child directly experiences the event.
2. The child witnessed the event (this does not include events that were seen on the television, in movies, or some other form of media).
3. The child learned about a traumatic event that happened to a caregiver.

B. The presence of at least one of the following intrusive symptoms that are associated with the traumatic event and began after the event occurred:

1. Recurring, spontaneous, and intrusive upsetting memories of the traumatic event.
2. Recurring and upsetting dreams about the event.
3. Flashbacks or some other dissociative response where the child feels or acts as if the event were happening again.
4. Strong and long-lasting emotional distress after being reminded of the event or after encountering trauma-related cues.
5. Strong physical reactions (e.g., increased heart rate, sweating) to trauma-related reminders.

C. The child exhibits at least one of the following avoidance symptoms or changes in his or her thoughts and mood. These symptoms must begin or worsen after the experience of the traumatic event.

1. Avoidance of or the attempted avoidance of activities, places, or reminders that bring up thoughts about the traumatic event.
2. Avoidance of or the attempted avoidance of people, conversations, or interpersonal situations that serve as reminders of the traumatic event.
3. More frequent negative emotional states, such as fear, shame, or sadness.
4. Increased lack of interest in activities that used to be meaningful or pleasurable.
5. Social withdrawal.
6. Long-standing reduction in the expression of positive emotions.

D. The child experiences at least one of the below changes in his or her arousal or reactivity, and these changes began or worsened after the traumatic event:

1. Increased irritable behavior or angry outbursts. This may include extreme temper tantrums.
2. Hypervigilance.
3. Exaggerated startle response.
4. Difficulties concentrating.
5. Problems with sleeping.

In addition to the above criteria, these symptoms need to have lasted at least 1 month and result in considerable distress or difficulties in relationships or with school behavior. Finally, the symptoms cannot be better attributed to the use of ingestion of a substance or some other medical condition.

In summary, children must experience disorganized or agitated behavior. Children usually do not have a sense they are reliving the past, but rather relive the trauma through repetitive play. Their nightmares of the traumatic event may change to more generalized nightmares of monsters or of rescuing others. A foreshortened future for a child generally involves a belief that they will never reach adulthood. Children may believe they can see into the future and can forecast ominous events. Physical symptoms may appear that include headaches and stomachaches that were not present before the event (American Psychiatric Association, 2000, p. 466).

For a long time prevailing wisdom was that young children were not developmentally mature enough to be affected by trauma and as a result couldn't "catch" PTSD (Bosquet, 2004; Osofsky, 1995). If anything,

their reaction to disasters would be fleeting. However, with growing research in the field we now know that is anything but true (Devoe et al., 2011; Osofsky et al., 2010). Of the 74 million children in the United States, 30% to 50% will experience at least one traumatic event by their 18th birthday and will probably comprise a substantial proportion of the 2.5 billion people who have suffered some kind of disaster in the last decade (Kazdin, 2008). Trauma for children is also homegrown, with about 1 million cases of substantiated child abuse in the United States reported yearly (DeAngelis, 2007).

Of those who experience at least one trauma, somewhere between 3% and 16% of girls and between 1% and 6% of boys will develop PTSD. What type of trauma children experience makes a big difference. Almost 100% of children will get PTSD if they see a parent killed or sexually assaulted. Approximately 90% of sexually abused children will develop PTSD. Around 77% of children who witness a school shooting experience PTSD, and even witnessing neighborhood violence has a "catch" rate of about 35% (National Center for PTSD, 2011).

It shouldn't take a Ph.D. in child psychology to figure out that PTSD and its treatment are different in children by the mere fact of their developmental levels (Saxe, Ellis, & Kapow, 2007). There is now accumulating evidence, including age of onset, duration, sequence, and co-occurrence of trauma events, which is providing the groundwork for a developmental model that builds on these variables and begins to plot the trauma pathways that are created as the child moves from middle childhood to adolescent to young adulthood (Steinberg et al., 2014). Indeed, PTSD manifests itself very differently in children than in adults in terms of symptoms (DeAngelis, 2007; Terr, 1979, 1981, 1983, 1995) and in how it affects the neurodevelopment of children (Saxe, Ellis, & Kaplow, 2007, pp. 23–45; Zilberstein, 2014).

Thus, not only because of their age, but also because of how children attempt to cognitively handle trauma, even though TF-CBT is seen as a treatment of choice (Chard & Gilman, 2014; Jensen et al., 2014), PTSD in children calls for treatment strategies that are very different from those used with adults (Clay, 2010; Cohen, Mannarino, & Deblinger, 2006; Ford & Courtois, 2013; Malchiodi, 2008; Saxe, Ellis, & Kaplow, 2007; Webb, 2007). Reactions to violence and trauma in children vary greatly and are dependent on their temperament, chronological age/developmental stage when the traumatic event occurred, whether support systems were and are nurturing or toxic, what the ecosystem of the community was and is like, and the degree, and duration of the trauma (Fairbank et al., 2014), do not make a one-size-fits-all treatment approach.

To that end, the National Child Traumatic Stress Network (NCTSN) has been formed (Steinberg et al., 2014) to integrate trauma-informed services and evidence- based practices throughout the United States in clinical and community settings. Practitioners can avail themselves of its services at www.nctsn.org. A wide range of training resources may be downloaded at http://learn.nctsn.org, and NCTSN also has an online knowledge bank developed by network centers at http://kb.nctsn.org.

Support Systems

By now you should clearly understand that **LO18** support systems are critical in crisis intervention. Supportive family systems are even more critical for children in their attempts to master a trauma (Cohen, Mannarino, & Deblinger, 2006; Courtois & Ford, 2009; Devoe et al., 2011; Saxe, Ellis, & Kaplow, 2007; Yule, 1998). Family support systems are important in regard to events both external and internal to the family system. Generally in this chapter we are speaking of family support in the context of a traumatic event that occurs external to the family, such as a hurricane or 9/11. We will speak to family support (or lack thereof) when the trauma is generated within the family, as in child abuse, in Chapter 9, Sexual Assault.

Bowlby's (1982) attachment theory is particularly relevant to traumatized children. In many of the traumas children experience, they are separated from their parents, their homes, and even their communities without warning or preparation. It should come as no surprise that such traumatic separation carries with it a smorgasbord of emotional and personality disturbance. Anxiety disorders, physical maladies, depression, panic attacks, rage reactions, and phobic reactions are common comorbid disorders of childhood PTSD. These are magnified even more when families are rent asunder by a traumatic event and support systems literally disappear in front of the child's eyes (Gordon, Farberow, & Maida, 1999; Halpern & Tramontin, 2007; Norris et al., 2002) and are even more profound when the young child perceives a threat to the caregiver (Devoe et al., 2011). The final ingredient in this witch's brew of pathology is the unresolved grieving that accompanies loss of loved ones when children do not yet have the cognitive

ability to understand and resolve their loss (Cohen, Mannarino, & Deblinger, 2006; Gordon, Farberow, & Maida, 1999; Halpern & Tramontin, 2007; Yule, 1998).

Types of Trauma

Childhood trauma is important not only for **LO19** what it does to children, but also for the after effects that carry into adulthood (Morgan et al., 2003). Terr (1995, p. 302) likens childhood trauma to rheumatic fever. Although rheumatic fever is a serious disease of childhood, the damage it causes can later be lethal in adults in a variety of ways. Childhood trauma operates in the same way and can lead to character problems, anxiety disorders, psychotic thinking, dissociation, eating disorders, increased risk of violence by others and by oneself, suicidal ideation and behavior, drug abuse, self-mutilation, and disastrous interpersonal relationships in adulthood (Pynoos, Steinberg, & Goenjian, 1996, pp. 331–352; Terr, 1995).

Terr (1995, p. 303) proposes a division of childhood trauma into two categories: Type I, which is one sudden, distinct traumatic experience; and Type II (analogous to complex PTSD), which is long-standing and comes from repeated traumatic ordeals. Lack of full cognitive and moral development causes distinctive differences in how children react to trauma. It appears that even infants have the capacity to remember traumatic experiences (Courtois & Ford, 2009; Hopkins & King, 1994). Children who suffer from Type I traumas appear to exhibit certain symptoms and signs that differentiate their condition from those that result from more complicated Type II traumas. Type I events are characterized by fully detailed, etched-in memories, omens such as retrospective rumination, cognitive reappraisals, reasons, misperceptions, and mistiming of the event (Terr, 1995, p. 309).

In contrast, Type II traumas result in the psyche's developing defensive and coping strategies to ward off the repeated assaults on its integrity. Massive denial, psychic numbing, repression, dissociation, self-anesthesia, self-hypnosis, identification with the aggressor, and aggression turned against self are prominent. Emotions generated from Type II traumas are an absence of feeling and a sense of rage and/or unremitting sadness. These symptoms may be diagnosed in childhood as conduct disorders, attention -span deficit disorders, depressive disorders, or dissociative disorders (Terr, 1995, pp. 311–312). As these children move into adolescence, they have poor grades, drug abuse, and a constellation of other behaviors that get them in trouble (Pynoos et al., 2014). It should come as no surprise that there is a high correlation with youth in the juvenile justice system and multiple trauma in their background (Dierkhising et al., 2013).

Terr's (1983) in-depth, 4-year follow-up on children who were Type I victims of the Chowchilla, California, bus kidnapping is the benchmark study in childhood PTSD. The victims of this trauma were a group of 26 elementary and high school children who were kidnapped together with their school bus driver, were carried about in vans for 11 hours by their kidnappers, and were buried alive in a truck trailer for 18 hours before they dug their way out—a horrific Type I trauma.

Etched Memories

Terr (1983) found that the children still had specific feelings of traumatic anxiety over the event after 4 years. When asked to speak about it, children generalized their anxiety from the event to statements like "I'm afraid of the feeling of being afraid." Unlike combat veterans, who might boast about harrowing experiences, the children were profoundly embarrassed by their experience, were unwilling to talk about the event, and shied away from any publicity. They generally voiced feelings of being humiliated and mortified when asked about their experience. Although 8 of 15 children had overcome their fear of vehicles such as vans and buses, they still reported occasional panic attacks triggered by unexpected sudden confrontation with stimuli such as seeing a van parked across the street from their house and vaguely wondering if some of the kidnappers' friends had come back for them.

Eighteen of the children were found to employ suppression or conscious avoidance of the trauma. Parents often aided them in this endeavor, although the two children whose parents encouraged them to talk about the experience were still not spared its residual effects. Their typical response was that they hated the feeling of helplessness they experienced and needed to feel in control of the situation. All the children could remember almost every second and minute of the event. However, they were able to remember few, if any, of the emotions or behaviors they experienced during the ordeal. This remarkable retrieval of full, precise verbal memories of almost all Type I traumas indicates that these memories are indelibly etched into the psyche, no matter how the child tries to suppress them, and are carried forward into adulthood (Terr, 1995, p. 309).

Memory etching may also come from vicariously viewing trauma. Saylor and associates (2003) found that children who saw images of death or injury from the attacks of 9/11 reported more PTSD symptoms than children who did not. Interestingly, the Internet had a more profound effect than television or print media. No measurable benefit was reported in seeing positive or heroic images of 9/11.

Developmental Issues

Trauma may have severe repercussions on developmental expectations and acquisition of developmental competencies in children (Ford, 2009; Pynoos, Steinberg, & Goenjian, 1996). When traumatic events impact a child in the middle of a developmental stage or in transition from one to the next, regressive behaviors occur (Gordon, Farberow, & Maida, 1999). Eth and Pynoos (1985, p. 44) believe that continuous intrusion of a traumatic event, evolution of a cognitive style of forgetting, and interference with mental processes because of depressed affect very definitely influence school achievement. Children who experience trauma are likely to have problems with "narrative coherence"—the ability to organize material into a beginning, a middle, and an end. This inability to organize a linear story has direct repercussions on reading, writing, and communicative ability (Pynoos, Steinberg, & Goenjian, 1996, p. 342).

Early childhood PTSD is marked by general personality traits that include mood instability, difficulty delaying gratification, withdrawal from or obsessive attention seeking, attention deficit and task completion problems, and oppositional defiance (Manly et al., 2001). Toddlers specifically demonstrate nonverbal attempts to communicate fears and anxiety: continuous crying, screaming tantrums, excessive clinging, immobility with trembling, frightened expressions, and either running toward the adult or aimless motion. Regression to thumb sucking, bed wetting, loss of bowel and bladder control, a variety of fears, night terrors, sleeping with a light on or an adult present, marked sensitivity to loud noises, speech difficulties, and eating problems may occur (Gordon, Farberow, & Maida, 1999). These symptoms are indicative of the effect survival-threatening stressors can have in rupturing the early attachment bonds that are so critical to development (Ford, 2009, p. 47).

Fears and anxiety continue to predominate in elementary school children, as do the previously mentioned regressive behaviors. School problems also emerge and range from outright refusal to go to school to poor academic performance, fighting, and loss of ability to concentrate (Gordon, Farberow, &

Maida, 1999). Trauma may cause anxious attachment to caretakers and separation anxiety. The child regresses socially, which can result in poor affiliation with peers, social isolation, and avoidance of school. Parents may exacerbate this behavior because of their own unresolved fears of the traumatic event, and may become overprotective of the child. Conversely, memories in which the primary caretaker was either unable or unwilling to provide help and succor during the traumatic event do severe harm to the developmental expectation that the caregiver is capable of providing nurturance and security (Pynoos, Steinberg, & Goenjian, 1996, pp. 340–345). A constellation of behavioral problems may appear, such as depression, panic and anxiety attacks, conduct and impulse control disorders, eating and sleep disorders, and sexual identity issues (Cook et al., 2005).

Adolescents who experience trauma invariably find disruption in their peer relationships and their school life. Peers who were not traumatized may shun them because of their "weird" behavior and not know how to offer support. Any outward physical problems may exacerbate their fragile self-concept and ability to fit into the peer group. Behavioral trouble signs include withdrawal and isolation, antisocial behavior, awareness of their own mortality, suicidal ideation, academic failure, alcohol and drug abuse, sleep disturbance, night terrors, depression, mental confusion, school failure, truancy, problems with the legal system, gang involvement, teen pregnancy, and various physical complaints (Ford et al., 2008; Gordon, Farberow, & Maida, 1999; Halpern & Tramontin, 2007).

Other Responses to Type I Trauma

Sense of a Foreshortened Future. Terr (1983) found that intrusive thoughts did not repeatedly enter the children's conscious thoughts; however, sleep brought very different problems. Whereas a few reported daydreams, more children had nightmares through which ran many repetitive themes of death. The children believed these dreams to be highly predictive of the future and made comments such as "I'm 11 now, but I don't think I'll live very long, maybe 12, 'cause somebody will come along and shoot me." Adolescents in particular are brought face to face with their own vulnerability and, in the case of those who have experienced the murder of a parent, report that they will never marry or have children because they fear history will be repeated (Cohen, Mannarino, & Deblinger, 2006, p. 9; Eth & Pynoos, 1985, p. 48; Terr, 1995, p. 308).

Reenactment. In an attempt to gain mastery over a Type I trauma, children replay the event and develop a reason or purpose for it. Once the reason is found, children often feel intensely guilty about it. "I should have listened to what Mom said and come home right after school!" In Type I traumas the question is, "How could I have avoided that?" as opposed to the question of Type II traumas, "How will I avoid it the next time?" (Terr, 1995, p. 310).

The play of children with PTSD is very distinctive because of its thematic quality, longevity, dangerousness, intensity, contagiousness for siblings, and unconscious linkage to the traumatic event (Maclean, 1977; Terr, 1981). The clearly prevalent dynamic is a continuing reenactment of the children's plight during the trauma (Eth & Pynoos, 1985, p. 42). This thematic play can be characterized as burdened, constricted, and joyless (Wallerstein & Kelly, 1975). Traumatic play is also problematic because it replaces normal developmental play that is a vital component in childhood maturation (Parker & Gottman, 1989). For adolescents, reenactment may take the form of delinquent behavior (Eth & Pynoos, 1985, p. 47), ranging from truancy, sexual activity, and theft to reckless driving, drug abuse, and obtaining weapons (Newman, 1976).

Physical Responses. Approximately half the children in the Chowchilla kidnapping manifested physical problems that could be construed to be related to the trauma of being held prisoner without food, water, or bathroom access (Terr, 1983). In young children suffering from PTSD, regression may occur and previously learned skills such as toilet training may have to be retaught (Bloch, Silber, & Perry, 1956). Sleep disturbances and severe startle responses can cause a variety of educational and social problems in school (Pynoos, Steinberg, & Goenjian, 1996, p. 350).

Displacement. In the Chowchilla survivors, a great deal of displacement of affect occurred, with emotions about the event being shifted to a related time, an associated idea, or another person—particularly the interviewing psychiatrist. Prior to the follow-up interviews, children displayed a variety of displaced behaviors, including the belief by one of the children that the psychiatrist had placed notes posing questions about the kidnapping in her school locker (Terr, 1983).

Transposition. Misperceptions, visual hallucinations, and peculiar time distortions often occur in children who have experienced Type I traumas—as opposed to Type II traumas, in which the perpetrators and events have a long history with the children and are rarely misperceived once the events are brought to awareness (Terr, 1995, p. 311). In the Chowchilla survivors, one of the most profound changes occurred in transposition of events surrounding the trauma. Events that happened after the trauma were remembered as having happened before the trauma (Terr, 1983). Also, there was a general belief that the traumatic events were predictive of what was about to happen to them. Ayalon (1983), in a study of victims of terrorism, found a similar effect in children. Children attempted to resolve their vulnerability and lack of control by saying they should have listened to the omens and "shouldn't have stepped in the bad luck square." In PTSD, such distortions of time become part of the child's developing personality and are attempts to take personal responsibility and even feel guilty for events over which they had no control.

Terr's (1983) study indicates that whereas children behave differently from adults in their attempt to resolve the traumatic event, they are no more flexible or adaptable than adults after a trauma, and it would be erroneous to assume that they "just grow out of the event." Furthermore, these children did not become toughened by their experience, but simply narrowed their sphere of influence in very restrictive ways to control their environment better.

Type II Traumas

Children who have suffered continued physical and sexual abuse and refugee children from war-torn countries are typical victims of Type II traumas. They are poster children for the affective dysregulation that goes with complex PTSD. Massive denial and psychic numbing are primarily associated with Type II traumas. These children avoid talking about themselves, go years without talking about their ordeals, and try to look as normal as they can. If they do tell their stories, they may later deny they did. This aspect is quite different from Type I children, who tell their stories over and over again. Denial may become so complete that Type II children will forget whole spans of their childhood (Terr, 1995, p. 312). Type II children are indifferent to pain, lack empathy, fail to define or acknowledge feelings, and absolutely avoid psychological intimacy. In adulthood, this massive denial cuts across narcissistic, antisocial, borderline, and avoidant personality disorders (Terr, 1995, p. 313). Although self-hypnosis and dissociation in Type II children

may take the form of dissociation identity disorders (formerly known as multiple personality disorder) in adulthood, such children most often develop anesthesia to pain and to sex and emotionally distance themselves in the extreme (Terr, 1995, p. 314). That does not mean the rage at what happened to them is not there. Rage includes anger turned inward against the self and outward toward others and can range from self-mutilation to murder. Reenactments of anger occur so frequently in Type II traumas that habitual patterns of aggression are formed, and the seething anger is probably as debilitating as the chronic numbing. Paradoxically, defenses may be formed, whereby the child becomes completely passive or identifies with the aggressor (Terr, 1995, p. 315).

At times crossover changes from Type I to Type II traumas may occur, as when a single event such as an accident that requires long-term hospitalization and many painful operations turns into a Type II trauma. Children who come out of Type I traumas with permanent physical handicaps, disfigurement, long-term pain, or loss of significant others may be forced into adaptational techniques of Type II traumas but still retain clear and vivid memories of the event. Children who are physically injured or disfigured and suffer psychic trauma tend to perpetually mourn their old selves and may employ regression, denial, guilt, shame, and rage over their disabilities (Terr, 1995, p. 316). When traumatic shock interferes with the normal course of bereavement, unresolved grief continues, and the child becomes a candidate for a major depressive disorder (Terr, 1995, pp. 316–317).

A variety of problems that have to do with how a traumatized child looks, acts, feels, and thinks may promote secondary stressors in his or her social milieu (Pynoos, Steinberg, & Goenjian, 1996, p. 341). Communicable disease, altered physical appearance, social distancing, memory impairment, decreased intellectual functioning, guilt, and shame are a few of the problems that can follow in the wake of a trauma. All these problems may present very different before-and-after pictures of the child and alter perceptions by family, peers, and teachers to the detriment of the child. These negative response patterns are then additive to the initial trauma and present additional psychological burdens to adaptation.

Intervention Strategies

The methods of assessment and therapy used **LO20** with children are different from those used for adults.

Early assessment is critical in determining the potential for trauma (Terr, 1979, 1981, 1983) and should happen as soon as possible after the event (Mowbray, 1988, p. 206). Generally, assessment needs to occur in two complementary areas: trauma-specific issues and generic behavioral issues. While we are interested in isolating specific traumatic events and their effects, focusing on them may miss more general issues of depression or behavior problems.

Interviewing. There is some evidence that allowing children to talk about their experience in an interview format also helps in reducing long-term symptoms of PTSD (Nader, 1997, p. 293). However, parent resistance may be severe, and interviewers should carefully explain to both the parents and the child what the purpose of the interview is and how it is going to be done. Interviewing should involve determining the degree and severity of exposure to trauma and assessing the child's response as it relates to the degree of exposure (Pynoos & Nader, 1988).

Pynoos, Steinberg, and Goenjian (1996, pp. 336–337) suggest that more precise rather than general features of the traumatic experience be elicited, such as hearing unanswered screams for assistance, smelling bad odors, being close to the threat, being trapped, witnessing atrocities, and remembering the degree of brutality and other specific traumatic conditions. Given the targeting of what will probably be very traumatizing material, the crisis worker needs to proceed in as patient, caring, and empathic a way as possible.

Because children's reports may be affected by fear of disclosure, shame, guilt, and other negative attributions, it is also important to get corroboration from parents or other significant adults about the trauma.

Instruments. Because of the need to systematically measure the response of children to trauma, a number of instruments specifically designed for children have been developed. The Trauma Symptom Checklist for Young Children is a caregiver rating for children ages 3–12. It has validity scales and measures a variety of posttraumatic responses plus sexual concerns, anxiety, depression, dissociation, and anger/aggression (Briere, 2005). The Clinician-Administered PTSD Scale for Children (CAPS-C) (Nader et al., 1994) is a comprehensive children's version of the adult CAPS. It measures standard PTSD symptoms plus symptoms of childhood PTSD. It further determines social and scholastic functioning, along with

how well the child is coping with the event. The Diagnostic Interview for Children and Adolescents–Revised (DICA-R; Reich, Shayka, & Taibleson, 1991) is a widely used semistructured interview to assess common psychiatric diagnoses and includes a PTSD subscale. Briere (1996) has also developed a self-report checklist for children, which covers anxiety, depression, anger, posttraumatic stress, sexual concerns, and dissociation. It has an alternate form that leaves out sexual concerns. The Trauma Symptom Inventory (Briere, 1995) is useful for older adolescents who tend to act out their distress. It also has two validity scales that assess under- and overendorsement in rating items. The Child PTSD Symptom Scale has been developed to assess the severity of PTSD in children exposed to trauma (Foa et al., 2001). The Child Behavior Checklist is a widely used scale that has parents, teacher, and youth self-report forms. This test looks at both external issues such as behavior problems and internal issues such as anxiety and depression, as well as how resilient children are at adapting to stressors (Achenbach, 1991). Finally the University of California Los Angeles Reaction Index (Steinberg, Brymer, Decker, & Pynoos, 2004) is particularly noteworthy because it has reliability and validity across age, sex, race/ethnicity, and trauma variety (Steinberg et al., 2013).

Projective Techniques. Because children submerge their affect and parents are loath to deal with the trauma until it causes severe repercussions in their lives, children are rarely brought in for counseling until behavior has reached crisis proportions (Mowbray, 1988, p. 206). Triage assessment at this time may not reveal that trauma is the underlying agent. In that regard, the crisis worker who works with children should have a good knowledge of both projective and question-and-answer personality inventories that will ferret out the trauma. A classic example is the artwork of sexually abused children whose drawings are replete with exaggerated genitalia (Kaufman & Wohl, 1992).

Therapy

Treatment of PTSD directed specifically to children falls into two main categories: cognitive-behavioral therapy and play therapy. EMDR may also be used in combination with or exclusive of cognitive-behavioral or play therapy. Also of critical importance is building a caring and supportive social context (Saxe, Ellis, & Kaplow, 2007), as discussed in Chapter 9, Sexual Assault.

Cognitive–Behavioral Therapy. There is a great deal of support for cognitive-behavioral therapy as the treatment of choice for children (Cohen, Mannarino, & Deblinger, 2006; de Arellano et al., 2014; Herpertz-Dahlmann, Hahn, & Hempt, 2005; Neubauer, Deblinger, & Sieger, 2007; Webb et al., 2014). Although Saigh (1987) has reported success using flooding techniques with school-age children, it should be strongly emphasized that this is a *hazardous* procedure for children and may exacerbate symptoms. A more benign and controlled approach is the use of desensitization procedures that alternate between relaxing the child and presenting scenes of the trauma that are progressively enhanced to their full florid detail. This is a stepwise procedure that makes small approximations toward exposing the child to the total traumatic event. The key to this approach is that the child can be immediately removed from the noxious image and transferred to a safe, calm, tranquil scene.

Any cognitive-behavioral therapy should give the child a sense of empowerment and control. Relaxation techniques, cognitive restructuring, stress inoculation, anger management, desensitization, and any other behavioral or cognitive-behavioral techniques should be paced *at the child's speed*. A good deal of discussion with the child and the caretakers about what is going to occur, how the child has the power and control over what will be included, and providing adequate time for processing, debriefing, and follow-up should all be a part of the therapeutic regimen (Cohen, Mannarino, & Deblinger, 2006; deArellano et al., 2014; Gordon, Farberow, & Maida, 1999).

Play Therapy. Play is the child's work. Being able to play is at the central core of positive child development. However, the ability to do that must invariably have the support of reliable and nontoxic caregiving and parenting for that to occur. When children suffer chronic deprivation, abuse, or neglect with little positive parental support there is no space, time, or permission to engage in curiosity and discovery through positive play (Tuber et al., 2014). When traumatized children play it is not about the joy of social relationships or discovery of new and wonderful things, but rather a reflection of the toxic trauma they have experienced. We believe therefore that play therapy is a primary therapeutic vehicle for removing that toxicity.

Creative arts and play therapy have considerable merit and can be efficacious with PTSD in children (Gordon, Farberow, & Maida, 1999; Johnson, 2000b; Malchiodi, 2008; Webb, 2007). Play therapy generally falls into two distinct categories: directive, which is collaborative and interactive between the child and the interventionist; and nondirective, which is child centered and interventionist passive. However, nondirective play therapy may be ill advised because **restitutive play** (attempting to reenact the trauma through play and somehow resolve it) becomes increasingly destructive and serves only to increase anxieties that are allowed to go ungoverned (Terr, 1979). We believe a safer approach to reenacting the trauma is to involve the interventionist collaboratively using a variety of play therapy techniques (Gordon, Farberow, & Maida, 1999; Landreth, 1987; Malchiodi, 2008) that include artwork (Drucker, 2001; Loumeau-May, 2008), puppets (Carter, 1987; James & Myer, 1987), sand play (Allan & Berry, 1987; Bethel & Oates, 2007; Vinturella & James, 1987; Zarzaur, 2005), dance (Johnson, 2000a), poetry (Gladding, 1987), writing (Brand, 1987), music (Bowman, 1987; Hilliard, 2008), bibliotherapy (Malchiodi & Ginns-Gruenberg, 2008), computer art (Johnson, 1987), storytelling (White, 2005), and drama (Haen, 2008; Irwin, 1987), as well as drawing the traumatic event and telling a story about it (Chapman et al., 2001; Eth & Pynoos, 1985, p. 37; James, 2003; Schreier et al., 2005). Play therapy is also a nonthreatening way to involve parents in the therapeutic intervention with children who have had trauma exposure (Cattanach, 2008; Haen, 2008; Echterling & Stewart, 2008; Steele & Malchiodi, 2008). All these techniques may be controlled and paced by the therapist in consideration of the psychological safety of the child.

The overarching reason for any of the foregoing techniques is to take the global, nebulous, uncontrollable chaos of the crisis event and make it into a concrete, real object that the child can gain a sense of control over. Play therapy would seem efficacious because it enables the therapist to enter the trauma on the child's cognitive terms, reduce the threat of the trauma, establish trust, and determine the child's current means of coping and ways of defending against the trauma (Gumaer, 1984). Play therapy is a safe exposure technique that allows clients (including adults) to integrate their traumatic memories into active consciousness without the fear of reactivating the sensory trauma demons they are so afraid of letting resurface (Steele & Raider, 2001). Furthermore, as thematic trauma-related play subsides and more socially appropriate play reappears, this is an excellent assessment device for determining how well treatment is proceeding. We will examine three very different cases of how play therapy is used with children in Chapter 9, Sexual Assault; Chapter 13, Crises in Schools; and Chapter 17, Disaster Response.

EMDR. EMDR seems to be effective with children in symptom reduction of PTSD (Adúriz Bluthgen, & Knopfler, 2011; Chemtob, Nakashima, & Carlson, 2002; Oras, de Ezpeleta, & Ahmad, 2004; Sharpiro & Laliotis, 2015; Tufnell, 2005). Shapiro (1995, pp. 276–281) indicates a number of special considerations for using EMDR, especially with young children. First, the worker must give special consideration to safety concerns. Although Shapiro does not believe parents should attend the session with the child, she does believe parents should brief the worker with the child present. Then the parent should leave and allow the child to present his or her version. This two-step sequence allows the parents' authority to be transferred to the worker and also gives the child a sense of being special when the worker's attention is focused exclusively on him or her.

For children, average EMDR sessions should be no longer than 45 minutes, with eye movements interspersed with other activities. Because children do not have the cognitive ability to conceptualize SUDs units, more concrete representations of the degree of discomfort need to be devised. Holding a hand close to the floor can represent a "little" hurt, while holding a hand at shoulder height can represent a much "bigger" hurt. Because most children are familiar with the workings of a body thermometer, we have used pictorial representations of a thermometer to let children indicate how much discomfort they are feeling.

Because play is such an integral part of a child's world, eye exercises can be accomplished more easily by drawing puppets on the worker's fingers or using finger puppets to perform the saccades. Creativity in helping the child "bring up the picture" is important, so sound effects such as starting an engine or "blowing up the picture" with a loud explosion can involve the children at their experiential level. Installing new, positive cognitions needs to be simplified. "I'm fine" or "I'm safe" may be highly appropriate because of their simplicity and straightforwardness for young children.

Artwork may also be effective in helping to concretize the memory. Having the child draw the event and then hold the picture in his or her mind while eye exercises are conducted gives the child a concrete way of visualizing the memory. Shapiro (1995) reports that (much as in Gumaer's [1984] method of serial drawing to determine if treatment is effective) when the child is asked to redraw the event after successive eye movements, the intensity of the event as depicted in the drawings is likely to diminish.

Moving Beyond the Trauma

LO21

We understand that reading this long introductory chapter into the trench warfare of typical crisis events has been pretty grim and maybe even depressing. Therefore, we want to finish with what we believe is some light at the end of the tunnel. So don't give up! One way survivors move from the tightly wrapped intrapersonal world of agony they have lived in to a more self-actualized and healthy interpersonal focus is to use their experience to help other victims (Lifton, 1973, pp. 99–133). Listen to two Vietnam veterans, one a volunteer and one a professional in the human services field.

Jim: I'm in the group not because of what happened in Nam. I'm pretty much through that. A year's worth of the VA and some excellent help from other people got me over being nuts. I'm here because I owe those folks and maybe, I'm not sure how, to pay some back for what I got.

George: Why did I become a social worker at the vet center? Because I'd been in Nam, hassled with my own stuff, and thought I knew something about it and could help other people. Frankly, I think I've done about all I can here, and I believe I'm ready to start something else professionally. I'm going back to school and would like to concentrate on working with kids.

For both these men, the ghosts of PTSD have been exorcised. They have integrated all aspects of the traumatic experience, both the positive and the negative. They know pretty clearly who they were before, during, and after the event. They have accepted responsibility for their own actions, as imperfect as those actions may have been at the time, and have made atonement for any guilt they carried (Scurfield, 1985, p. 246). They epitomize the full meaning of the Chinese characters for *crisis* that represent both danger and opportunity. Yet, do these two tough and resilient combat veterans represent what really happens to people with PTSD? Do the Chinese characters really represent what happens to most people, or can they ever climb out of the sump hole of PTSD? Tedeschi and Calhoun (1995) believe so and have formulated the concept of posttraumatic growth to characterize the personal positive changes that can come out of individuals' struggle with trauma.

Their evolving model (Tedeschi & McNally, 2011) has five components: First, trauma survivors need to understand the negative aspects of PTSD, especially one's shaken assumptions about oneself, others, and the future. They should also understand that the physiological and psychological responses are *normal* reactions to traumatic experiences. (We take some exception to the use of the word *normal* as a way of toning down the very nasty responses people have to trauma. To our mind, there is nothing remotely "normal" about it. It is about as abnormal as one can get without becoming psychotic. Therefore, we prefer to use the term *common* to denote that it is anything but pleasant, but is about what almost everybody can expect to happen.) However, challenges to one's core beliefs have been shown to strongly predict posttraumatic growth (Lindstrom et al., 2013).

Second, learning to gain emotional regulation over intrusive thoughts and images allows the sympathetic nervous system to calm down and let people start to engage in effective rumination over the trauma rather than brooding over it. Rumination occurs in two ways. **Autonomic/intrusive rumination** is the initial intrusion of unwanted thoughts that assails an individual after the trauma. **Deliberate rumination** is a process that issues out of a reflective state when a thorough re-examination of the traumatic event causes the individual to reframe his or her view of life and in fact grow from the experience (Su & Chen, 2015).

Third is constructive self-disclosure that does not harp on the trauma or its symptoms but, by telling the story to others, unravels the cognitive and emotional tangles that go with the trauma, forms new relationships and bonds, and reconciles the past with the deceased who may have been part of the original trauma. Calhoun and Tedeschi (1998) believe that social support is a critical component in allowing this process to occur.

Fourth is creating a trauma narrative out of self-disclosure that understands the paradoxes of how loss and gain, gaining control and giving up control, and vulnerability and strength are not mutually exclusive. By doing so, individuals begin to build new structures of their personality that are based on personal strength, enhanced relationships with other, spiritual change, appreciation of life, and zest for new opportunities.

Finally, Tedeschi and McNally (2011) propose that the end point (or the beginning, for that matter) is to see the trauma as a positive, life-transforming experience that involves becoming more charitable to oneself and others, accepting growth from the traumatic event without guilt, understanding that the experience has transformed oneself in ways others may not be able to comprehend, and becoming a person more in tune and empathic with the human condition and the spiritual aspects that go with it.

Studies are finding that people do indeed grow from traumatic experiences and that positive posttraumatic growth does occur and may even be underestimated (Blix et al., 2015; Hefferon, Grealy, & Mutrie, 2009; Lechner & Weaver, 2009; Rosner & Powell, 2006; Smith & Cook, 2004). For those who have PTSD and for those who treat it, that is heartening research.

SUMMARY

Posttraumatic stress disorder (PTSD) has probably been in existence as long as humankind has been rational enough to personalize the disasters that assail us. However, it was the debacle of the Vietnam War that brought PTSD enough publicity to become a classifiable malady. The psychologically virulent milieu that was the Vietnam War became a breeding ground for trauma, which found its way back to the United States in an estimated 960,000 service personnel who have PTSD or related disorders.

PTSD has multiple symptoms and for that reason is often confused with a variety of other disorders. Its basis is maladaptive adjustment to a traumatic event. The disorder is both acute and chronic. In its chronic form it is insidious and may take months or years to appear. Its symptoms include, but are not limited to, anxiety, depression, substance abuse, hypervigilance, eating disorders, intrusive-repetitive thoughts, sleep disturbance, somatic problems, poor social relationships, suicidal ideation, and denial and affective numbing of the traumatic event. Both natural and human-made disasters may be responsible for PTSD, but it is far more likely to occur in individuals who have been exposed to some human-made disaster that should have been prevented and is beyond accepted moral and societal bounds.

Slow to recognize the disorder, human services professionals did little to ameliorate problems returning Vietnam veterans suffered. Self-help groups were started by veterans when they had no other place to turn. Through lobbying efforts by such men, Vietnam Veterans Centers were set up throughout the United States. Along with other mental health professionals who had been grappling with the problems of veterans and other victims of trauma, staffers at the centers began doing research and developing treatment approaches for PTSD. Those research and treatment approaches have spread out to civilian areas of trauma, and much common ground is being found between war-related and civilian-related traumatic events. Recent research on the psychobiological aspects of PTSD is uncovering a great deal of the intricate interplay between traumatic events and the brain's physiological responses to them. Contemporary treatment includes both group and individual intervention that is multimodal and considers psychological, biological, and social bases as equally important. The United States Army is currently putting in place a comprehensive program that attempts to provide psychological fitness to soldiers to inoculate them against PTSD and other emotional disorders that go with combat.

Children are not immune to PTSD, and they do not just "grow out of it." If PTSD has taught the human services one thing, it is that no traumatic experience should ever be dismissed in a cursory manner and that any initial assessment of a crisis client should investigate the possibility of a traumatic event buried somewhere in the client's past. Assessment and intervention are particularly difficult when the traumatic event is of a familial or sexual nature. A great deal of finesse and skill is necessary to uncover and treat such problems because of clients' reluctance to talk about socially taboo subjects or the feeling that a person should have the intestinal fortitude to bear up under the trauma. From what we now know, the latter assumption is patently false; under the right circumstances, anyone can fall victim to PTSD.

There are three books that we think can be helpful to you if you are going to get into or are already in the PTSD business. They are both focused on the military, but could surely be adapted for civilian use, and are as follows: *Clinician's Guide to Treating Stress After War: Education and Coping Interventions for Veterans* (Whealin, DeCarvalho, & Vega, 2008), *The Veterans and Active Duty Military Psychotherapy Treatment Planner* (Moore & Jongsma, 2009), and Curran's (2013) *101 Trauma-Informed Interventions*. These books have lots of useful tips and worksheets that can be adapted for use with most anyone who has PTSD.

Visit CengageBrain.com for a variety of study tools and useful resources such as video examples, case studies, interactive exercises, flashcards, and quizzes.

Crisis of Lethality

8

Background

In crisis work the possibility of dealing with suicidal and/or homicidal clients is always present. Thus, in Chapter 3 the importance of the crisis worker's continuous awareness and assessment of risk level for all clients in crisis was emphasized. In this chapter strategies are presented to help crisis workers strengthen their skills in assessing, counseling for, intervening in, and preventing lethal behavior, with the major emphasis on suicide. While this chapter's focus on lethal behavior is mainly concerned with the intent to harm oneself, others may not be exempt from harm. Sometimes an individual in crisis may be homicidal and target a specific victim or random victims. These homicides are not about the criminal who murders a shopkeeper in a holdup or the wife who kills her husband for insurance or to be able to marry another person; those are **instrumental acts of homicide** that occur for some financial or other concrete gain. Rather, a suicidal/homicidal person in this chapter is one who is engaged in an **expressive act of homicide** designed to reduce psychological pain. Such suicidal/homicidal people are likely to be emotionally distraught, may feel gravely wronged, depressed, helpless, disempowered, and hopeless, and may attempt to solve their own dilemmas through harm to others and then to themselves.

According to Edwin Shneidman, the founder of suicidology, "Currently in the Western world, suicide is a conscious act of self-induced annihilation, best understood as a multidimensional malaise in a needful individual who defines an issue for which the suicide is perceived as the best solution" (Shneidman, 1999a, p. 155) and who falls into a category of intense and unendurable psychological pain that is caused by unfulfilled psychological needs (Shneidman, 2001, p. 203). To Shneidman's definition should be added "or the murder of significant others."

LEARNING OBJECTIVES

After studying this chapter, you should be able to:

1. Understand the scope of suicide.
2. Understand the moral issues surrounding suicide.
3. Know and understand different theories and models of why people commit suicide.
4. Know the common characteristics of people who commit suicide.
5. Know the common characteristics of people who commit suicide/homicide.
6. Know the myths that surround suicide.
7. Know clues and factors that predispose suicide.
8. Know and understand suicide intervention strategies.
9. Know and understand how crisis management for suicide works.
10. Be familiar with the dos and don'ts of suicide case management.
11. Understand what a psychological autopsy is and why it is used.
12. Understand the reasons for postvention after a completed suicide.
13. Understand the crisis worker's own issues after losing a person to suicide.

The Scope of the Suicide Crisis

As with other maladies discussed in this book, suicide has its own mind-numbing statistics. On a worldwide basis, about 1 million people kill themselves each year, or about one every 40 seconds. Worldwide suicide rates have increased about 60% in the last 45 years. Eastern European countries, particularly in the Baltic Sea area, are the leaders along with Hungary (World Health Organization, 2011). In the United States, 30,000 to 35,000 people kill themselves every year (Centers for Disease Control and Prevention, 2008; U.S. Department of Health and

Human Services, 2003), which translates into about 85 people a day. That number is probably very conservative because many suicides are ruled accidental either due to political, religious, and emotional considerations or because medical examiners just can't say for sure (Granello & Granello, 2007, pp. 3–5). Most official reports indicate that the real numbers of suicide attempts as well as injury caused by suicide attempts are grossly underreported. Experts claim that upward of 60,000 Americans die annually by suicide (Ross, 1999). Bottom line the data are a lot more guesstimate than estimate. The National Violent Death Reporting System (NVDRS) is now in place in 18 states. Presently, the large mass of data on violent deaths (homicide or suicide) remains in local, state, and federal jurisdictions. If the NVDRS ever gets fully funded by Congress, it will be able to provide meaningful data that will help in making decisions on how to combat both (Barber et al., 2013).

Depending on where you live, worldwide suicide completions range between 10 and 40 per 100,000. Between 300,000 and 600,000 U.S. citizens a year survive a suicide attempt, and about 19,000 of those survivors are permanently disabled as a result of the attempted suicide (Stone, 1999, p. 1; U.S. Department of Health and Human Services, 2003). Suicide ranges from the 10th to 11th leading cause of death in the United States (National Institute of Mental Health, 2011).

Young people between the ages of 15 and 24 account for the largest increase in suicides during the past 30 years. Men kill themselves at approximately four times the rate for women (Stone, 1999, p. 10). The highest-risk group for many years has been Caucasian men over 35, but the suicide rate among teenagers and young black males has been increasing dramatically since the middle of the 20th century (Fujimura, Weis, & Cochran, 1985; National Institute of Mental Health, 2003). Native Americans kill themselves at a rate about 1.5 times the national average (U.S. Department of Health and Human Services, 2003). Even though the elderly make up roughly 10% of the total population, 25% percent of all suicides occur in the over-65 population, and rates move up exponentially after age 70 (National Institute of Mental Health, 2011; U.S. Department of Health and Human Services, 2003).

The suicide rate among children and adolescents tripled between 1950 and 1985, and suicide is now the second to third (behind accidents but forging ahead, and in hot competition with murder) leading cause of death among children and teens in the United States and has tended to stay that way (Malley, Kush, & Bogo,

1994; National Institute of Mental Health, 2011; U.S. Department of Health and Human Services, 2003). The bottom line is that a person in the United States is less likely to be murdered than to commit suicide! Granello and Granello's (2007, p. 1) analogy is an excellent one. If an airliner crashed every day and 85 people were killed, there would be national outrage, and the government would be forced to do something about it. Yet the same suicide rate evokes little outcry. Why is that so?

In Goldney's (2005) review of suicide prevention, he noted that as far back as 1993 the World Health Organization laid out six steps for worldwide suicide prevention: comprehensive and follow-up treatment of psychiatric patients, gun-possession control, detoxification of domestic gas and car emissions, and tempering the sensationalism of press reports of suicide. It's pretty safe to say that no other chapter in this book has more written about it, more research done about it, more models and theories of why it occurs and what it actually is than suicide. As one example in a veritable tsunami of books that deal with suicide, you can cruise through 744 pages of the American Psychiatric Association's textbook on suicide assessment and management and find out about everything you ever wanted to know and were afraid to ask about it (Simon & Hales, 2012). Yet, as to good odds specific treatments that could prevent suicide, Goldney's survey found no clear research evidence to indicate what treatments might significantly reduce suicide. Ten years hence that hasn't changed much. Why is that so?

The National Action Alliance for Suicide Prevention (NAASP) (2014), whose mission is to advance a national strategy for suicide prevention, has four questions they believe would reduce suicide deaths by 20% in 5 years. Their four basic questions are (Classen et al., 2014):

1. Why do people become suicidal?
2. How can we better detect and predict risk?
3. What interventions, treatments, and services are effective to predict suicidal risk and behavior?
4. What research infrastructure is needed to reduce suicidal behavior?

This chapter describes what is being done to answer those questions.

Suicide and the Moral Dilemma

Shneidman's (1980) quote from *Moby Dick*'s **LO2** opening paragraph, a "damp, drizzly November in my soul," captures the essence of what most suicide is: a dreary, wintry storm of endless life-or-death debate. It is at times low, moaning, and incessant and other times howling and strident in its demands that consciousness must STOP! It is a titanic and reasoned argument that constantly questions and pleads against the continued struggle in the storm of life. It is into this wind-lashed, flat, frozen, forbidding wasteland of the suicide's mind that the crisis interventionist enters. It is neither a simple nor a painless place to be. If you are planning to become a mental health professional, the odds are about 1 in 4 that you will come face to face with a suicide (Granello & Granello, 2007, p. 1).

Of all the crises in this book, it is perhaps the most written about and the most difficult with which to deal. The simple fact is that the worldwide suicide rate hasn't decreased very much in a very long time despite all of the prevention and treatment approaches (Bell, Richardson, & Blount, 2006, p. 227). The background "attempt" statistic perhaps is as important as suicide itself. About 1.0%–2.5% of the world population attempt it and about 6% think about it every year, but very few of these people ever avail themselves of a mental health service provider (Artieda-Urrutia et al., 2014). Why is that so? First of all, for all its sensationalism, the base rate of completion for any given suicide-prone population is low. So it is difficult to ascertain who are the "few needles in a very large haystack" and study and design treatments that will prevent and stop them from committing suicide. The bottom line is that there are many false positives that are predicted by the conventional risk factors associated with suicide (Goldney, 2005). In other words, lots of people think about suicide, some attempt it, and few complete it. Yet those "few" number in the hundreds of thousands when taken worldwide, and the traumatic wake they leave for survivors numbers in the millions (Granello & Granello, 2007, p. 276).

Perhaps even more problematic for good prevention and intervention outcomes, suicidal ideation and behavior raise complex moral, legal, ethical, and philosophical questions for the crisis interventionist (Stone, 1999, pp. 69–75; Wirth, 1999). Colucci (2013) has examined the reasons why culture is of critical importance in understanding why suicide varies across borders, regions, and ethnicities. Their work pretty much substantiates why Chapter 2's Culturally Effective Helping in Crisis is important to know when dealing with suicide.

Now compare your own philosophical view of death to what Everstine (1998, p. 15) has to say about various kinds of deaths: "Death by murder carries no stigma and is seen as a tragedy" (i.e., It is a criminal act and somebody must pay). "Accidental death is fully condoned providing the person didn't do something stupid or careless" (i.e., It is a tragedy—unless they were bungee jumping or sky diving, then it was idiotic). "Death by natural causes and resistance to the end allows grieving without animosity" (i.e., It was a tragedy but he lived a long, good life; or she was too young and heroic to the end). "Less forgivable is natural death by neglect or overindulgence" (i.e., The speeder had it coming; or what did he think drinking would do to his liver?). "The least forgivable death is suicide, for which there is little sympathy and no absolution" (i.e., A sin! A moral flaw! A character deficit! Not up to the task of living).

While in Eastern culture suicide may be seen as a way of removing dishonor, shame, and humiliation from oneself and one's family (Granello & Granello, 2007, p. 17), that has not been so in the Western world. Historically, suicide has been seen as a sin by almost every major religion. It has been seen by civil authority as an abrogation of the citizen's contract to serve the state and for a long time was called "self-murder." Self-murder was often blamed on the instigation of the devil. In the Middle Ages in England, self-murder was an offense against the king and nature, and all of the deceased's lands and goods were forfeit to the crown. Indeed, it was not until 1961 that the common law of felony self-murder was repealed in England. Further, a Christian burial was denied, and suicides were often buried in the middle of a crossroads with a stake driven through the heart (Williams, 1997, p. 12). (The reason for the middle of the crossroads rumored to be that horses and ox carts would stop at a crossroad and animals would relieve themselves there.)

Freud's (1916) view that suicide resulted from mental illness has been a double-edged sword. On one side he gave credence to the idea that the suicide was not a person of weak moral fiber "seized by the devil." Yet for the general public a stigma of mental illness that attached to the suicide and the suicide's family has equally negative social attributions.

Euthanasia. Counterpointed against suicide as an act of the devil has been the notion from the Stoic and Epicurean philosophers that suicide could be the right thing to do given terminal illness, unremitting pain, and/or astronomical financial burdens (Williams, 1997, p. 12). Beginning in the latter half of the 20th century, much attention has been paid to **assisted**

suicide and **euthanasia** in both the literature and the popular media. The two terms are not synonymous. Stone (1999, pp. 76–89) differentiates between the two by pointing out that in assisted suicide someone else provides the means (lethal agent), but the person who is dying administers it. In euthanasia someone else administers it.

We live in a time characterized by what Stone (1999, p. 77) calls "prolonged dying." Prior to the 20th century, people typically died fairly young and fairly quickly at home. They generally died as a result of infectious diseases or injury. Today 70% to 80% of adults will die in an institution, such as a hospital or nursing home, and probably as a result of degenerative diseases such as heart disease, diabetes, stroke, or cancer. Our deaths may be prolonged, painful, and financially draining for ourselves, our families, and society. Do we have a right to refuse medical treatment, to refuse heroic or artificial interventions to keep us alive when there is no hope of getting better or even of survival?

Further, should a therapist intervene when it is clear that a person wishes to die to end suffering? Every facet of these questions must be examined by our society as we confront the changing human conditions and health care problems in this new millennium (Stone, 1999, pp. 76–82). However, in this chapter, the position is that it is the appropriate role of the crisis worker to intervene and attempt to prevent all suicides and homicides that he or she possibly can.

The Dynamics of Suicide

Psychological Theories

Freudian Inward Aggression. In the Freudian **LO3** (1916) psychodynamic view, suicide is triggered by an intrapsychic conflict that emerges when a person experiences great psychological stress. Sometimes such stress emerges either as regression to a more primitive ego state or as inhibition of one's hostility toward other people or toward society so that one's aggressive feelings are turned inward toward the self. Freud called this a melancholic state, and it is what we now call depression. In extreme cases, the melancholy becomes so severe that self-destruction or self-punishment is chosen over urges to lash out at others.

Developmental. Developmental psychology views suicide in terms of life stages. Individuals who do not

successfully navigate life stages become mistrustful, guilt ridden, isolated, and stagnant (Erikson, 1963) until they are unable to cope any longer and may choose suicide as a way out.

Deficiencies. This model is embedded in the mental illness tradition and proposes that there is some mental deficiency in the suicidal individual as opposed to the nonsuicidal person. These mental deficiencies then become risk factors that can lead to suicide (Rogers, 2001a).

Escape. Escapist suicide is one of flight from a situation sensed by the person as intolerable (Baumeister, 1990). This theory has a six-step causal chain. The first step involves the individual's belief that they fall short of their own or others' imposed standards. Second, self-blame occurs for falling short, and heightened state of awareness as to those shortcomings occurs in the third step. Negative affect follows as a fourth step. The result is cognitive disintegration that becomes more narrowly focused on deficits to the exclusion of broader more integrative aspects of self until the only option is suicide. Closely allied to escape theory is the concept of perfectionism where less than perfect behavior becomes less and less tolerable, amplifies hopelessness, psychache, and the risk of suicide (Flett et al., 2014).

Hopelessness. The hopelessness theory (Abramson et al., 2000) posits that some individuals believe that highly desired outcomes will not occur or that highly aversive outcomes will occur and that there is nothing they can do to change the situation. Hopelessness represents a key cognitive vulnerability for suicide risk. The only escape is death. Beck's (Beck et al., 1979) cognitive triad of negative thoughts about self, the world, and the future are at the heart of hopelessness.

Psychache. Psychache is a term coined by the founder of suicidology, Edwin Shneidman (1993). Shneidman's (1987) **cubic model** combines psychache, **perturbation** (how disturbed one is and degree of pain), and **press** (stress increased due to more negative factors piling up); when all three are combined, they create the critical mass necessary to activate a suicide. While it's hard to define behaviorally, it's about the most impactful word Shneidman could have thought up to describe what most people with suicidal ideation are going through. Psychache refers to the hurt, anguish, soreness, and aching pain of the psyche or mind. It may have to do with guilt, shame, fear of growing old, love lost, or any debilitating cognition or affect. Intolerable psychological pain is the one variable that relates to all suicides. Psychache is tied to frustrated, blocked, and thwarted psychological needs. Suicide thus serves to eliminate the tension related to those blocked needs (Shneidman, 2001). As psychache increases perturbation increases as well and the need press to end it all becomes severe.

Sociological Theory

Durkheim's Social Integration. The most important sociological theory about suicide was originally proposed in 1897 by Emile Durkheim and still holds as the top sociological theory more than a century later. In Durkheim's (1897/1951) approach, societal integration (the degree to which people are bound together in social networks) and social regulation (the degree to which the individual's desires and emotions are regulated by societal norms and customs) are major determinants of suicidal behavior. Durkheim identified four types of suicide: egoistic, anomic, altruistic, and fatalistic (pp. 152–176).

Egoistic suicide is related to one's lack of integration or identification with a group. **Anomic suicide** arises from a perceived or real breakdown in the norms of society, such as the financial and economic ruin of the Great Depression. **Altruistic suicide** is related to perceived or real social solidarity, such as the traditional Japanese *hara-kiri* or, to put it in a current context, the suicide attacks by members of Middle Eastern extremist groups. **Fatalistic suicide** occurs when a person sees no way out of an intolerable or oppressive situation, such as being confined in a concentration camp.

Suicide Trajectory Model. This model considers the total constellation of risk factors: biological (substance abuse, being male, genetic predisposition to depression); psychological (low self-concept, hopelessness, borderline personality disorder); cognitive (rigid, dogmatic, irrational, black-and-white, all-or-none thinking); and environmental (access to firearms, high-stress occupations, loss, family, and job stressors). The more these factors are present and pile up, the greater the potential for suicide (Stillion & McDowell, 1996).

Three Element Model. The three elements composing this model are predisposing factors such as drug abuse and mental illness and potentiating factors ranging from family history to romantic and occupational loses to whether one has easy access to weapons. When enough predisposing and potentiating components are mixed together, over time, at some point a critical mass is created and a threshold into suicidal ideation and behavior is crossed (Westefeld et al., 2000).

Interpersonal Theory

According to Van Orden and associates (2010), two interpersonal states, lack of belongingness and the feeling of burdensomeness, are primary motivators in the need to commit suicide. Thwarted belongingness is manifested by loneliness and the absence of positive, reciprocal relationships and burdensomeness is the perception that one is a burden on significant others and they will be better off if the individual is dead (Ribeiro et al., 2013). Joiner and associates (2009) propose that people commit suicide because they can and because they want to kill themselves. This seemingly simplistic, straightforward statement addresses three central components of interpersonal theory. First and foremost, people **acquire suicidal capability** by decreasing their innate fear of death by habituating themselves to the fear and pain of self-injury. Second, they **perceive burdensomeness** to others to the extent that they are so flawed or defective they are beyond repair. They see themselves as such a millstone for themselves, their family, or society that everyone will be better-off as a result of their death. Third, **failed belongingness** means that the person has no attachments or value to any other member of society. The theory proposes that while many people consider committing suicide, and large numbers develop the capability, few actually do so because all three ingredients must be present at once to create the critical mass necessary for the act to occur (pp. 5–7).

This theory proposes that those with past suicide attempts will be habituated to pain more than other people because their past attempts help inure them to the potential for pain that accompanies most suicide attempts. Second, those whose job entails exposure to the pain of others will themselves have higher suicide rates than other people because of vicariously experiencing others' pain and thus habituating themselves to it. Indeed, there is a fair amount of research that supports these two notions (Hill & Pettit, 2014).

Existential–Constructivist Framework

The existentialist side of the framework comes from Yalom's (1980) work on human pathology and involves what he believes are the four corner posts of existence: **death**, which is unavoidable; **existential isolation**, which means that each of us enters existence alone and leaves it alone; **meaninglessness**, our attempt to make sense out of a universe that is beyond knowing; and **freedom**, the absence of external structure, which means that each person is responsible for making choices, taking actions, and enjoying or suffering the consequences of those decisions.

On the other side of the frame, constructivism views death, existential isolation, and meaninglessness as the principal ingredients that provide the motivation for meaning-making activities central to human life (Neimeyer & Mahoney, 1995). As individuals construct their view of self, others, and their relationships, they also construct a worldview where they encounter environmental challenges to which they have to respond. They essentially have three options in response to these challenges. They can retain their original constructions, alter them to build new constructions, or decide that neither response is viable and consider suicide as a final construct. This final construct occurs because trigger events that come from suicide trajectory risk factors (Stillion & McDowell, 1996) combine to form the critical mass that allows the individual to construct a worldview that it is a better choice to no longer view the world at all (Rogers, 2001b). A study of suicide notes' motivational components (Rogers et al., 2007) supports the existential-constructivist model of suicide. The researchers found that suicide notes contained relational, spiritual, somatic, and psychological motivators that are the primary motivational components of the existential-constructivist model.

Other Explanations

Accident. Individuals who have no real intention of killing themselves may do so by pushing their luck too far. These may range from the teenager who decides in a fit of pique to take "a bunch of pills," passes out, and chokes on her own vomit, to the depressed alcoholic with a blood alcohol content of 0.25 who drives his car into a bridge abutment (Everstine, 1998, pp. 20–21).

Biochemical or Neurochemical Malfunction. This theory proposes that dysfunction in the central nervous system is the primary underlying cause of suicidal/homicidal behavior. Suicide, aggression, and depression are closely related (van Praag, 2001). Bongar and Sullivan (2013, p. 31) report that over the last 30 years that research demonstrates neurochemical changes seem to be highly correlated with

attempted and completed suicides. There is evidence that hyperactivity in the neuroendocrine hypothalamic-pituitary-adrenal axis may have a special relationship to suicidal behavior (Stoff & Mann, 1997, pp. 1–2). It is also now becoming apparent that a serotonin metabolite named 5-HIAA is low (Asberg et al., 1986; Leonard, 2005) in those persons who attempt suicide and that the serotonin transporter 5-HTT gene plays a role in family clustering of depression and suicide (Leonard, 2005; Lopes de Lara et al., 2006). While these biological differences may be correlates and not causes of suicide, evidence continues to mount that they do play a definite role (Asberg & Forslund, 2000; Chiles & Strosahl, 1995, p. 13; Lester, 1988, 1995, 2000; Stoff & Mann, 1997; van Praag, 2001).

Chaos. Chaos theory proposes that, paradoxically, unpredictable behavior can occur within predictable systems. Relatively minor environmental events may lead to suicidal behavior or not within the same individual at different points in time (Rogers, 2001a) while major ecosystem events such as financial depressions can do the same.

Dying With Dignity/Rational Suicide. This type of suicide is typified by a person's rationally choosing death in the face of a painful, decimating, and incurable illness, or some other major calamity that has no foreseeable positive outcome for a reasonable person. The person has further considered the impact on others and found the action to be more beneficial than harmful. As a result, the person makes a reasoned decision to end his or her life (Fujimura, Weis, & Cochran, 1985; Stone, 1999, pp. 76–93; Wirth, 1999).

Ecological/Integrative. In seeking to understand suicide, an ecological/integrative theory takes into account that the painful intrapsychic factors within the individual interact with negative interpersonal and societal issues on multiple systemic levels (Leenaars, 1996, 2004; Potter, 2001). Leenaars (2004) proposes that while a person may be highly perturbed and suffer a great deal of psychic pain, lethality must be present for the person to commit suicide. An ecological/integrative theory proposes that both perturbation and lethality, and the resultant contemplation of suicide, can only result from a complex interaction of all these environmental variables with the individual (Potter, 2001).

Interactional. Everstine's (1998) interactional view of suicide is in direct contrast to Freud's and Durkheim's. Everstine proposes that suicide is not fomented by anger turned inward or social isolation, but by an external rage toward another. It is not at all passive toward the significant other, but is highly aggressive and has a "get even" attitude and revenge as its goal. The suicide's hatred and desire to punish is so consuming that the aggrieved's life or a significant other's life is used as a weapon against the hated other person. The hope is that the survivors have the albatross of guilt over the suicide or homicide hung round their own necks forever.

Ludic. Ludic suicides (Baechler, 1979) relate to the desire to experience an ordeal or a way to prove oneself in gamesmanship. Perhaps the ultimate such game of proving oneself is Russian roulette. Any tribal rite of passage in which death may be an outcome could be considered a ludic suicide.

Oblative. Oblative suicides (Baechler, 1979) are those that are sacrificial in nature and seen to transfigure one to a higher, transcendental plane. Buddhist monks who set themselves on fire and the LSD user who "wants to meet God personally" and overdoses on a smorgasbord of drugs fall into this category.

Overlap Model. The overlap model includes lack of social support, a biological propensity to suicide, the presence of psychiatric disorders, personality issues such as impulsivity, hostility, and depression, and a family history of suicide. The more these areas overlap, the greater the potential for suicide (Blumenthal & Kupfer, 1986).

Parasuicide. **Parasuicide** (closely resembling suicide) involves commissioned acts which, although not directly lethal, can habituate persons to the pain necessary to kill themselves by inflicting **hesitation wounds** (the idea that it is extremely difficult to kill yourself and people hesitate in their initial attempts to complete the act are hesitant (Joiner et al., 2009, p. 8). Clients may also engage in self-injurious behavior, such as cutting or burning their bodies to reconnect to reality from a dissociative state. Or they may indirectly set themselves up to harm themselves by abusing alcohol, driving too fast, combining the two, or engaging in other risky, daredevil behaviors (Jobes, 2006, p. 90). Any one of these acts may end up with the person dead, injured, disabled, disfigured, or maimed.

Suicide by Cop. More a method than a theory or model, **suicide by cop** (as described in Chapter 5) occurs when a person gets the police to kill him or her by engaging in a threatening act toward the police or someone else, such as in a hostage situation. It is an **indirect suicide** wherein suicidal persons may not have the courage to kill themselves, or they seek to publicize their deaths through the media by "going out in a blaze of glory." Suicide by cop is now so common that many cases get a coroner's verdict of **suicide by legal intervention** (Lindsay & Lester, 2004; Miller, 2006).

Characteristics of People Who Commit Suicide

What is it about a person's inner dynamics that may make suicide or expressive homicide seem sensible? Shneidman formulated 10 common characteristics present in an individual when the act is accomplished. His characteristics are grouped under six aspects (1985, pp. 121–149; italics added throughout): **LO4**

1. *Situational characteristics:* (1) "The common *stimulus* in suicide is unendurable psychological pain" (p. 124); (2) "The common *stressor* in suicide is frustrated psychological needs" (p. 126).

2. *Motivational characteristics:* (1) "The common *purpose* of suicide is to seek solution" (p. 129); (2) "The common *goal* of suicide is cessation of consciousness" (p. 129).

3. *Affective characteristics:* "The common *emotions* in suicide are hopelessness and helplessness" (p. 131).

4. *Cognitive characteristics:* (1) "The common *cognitive state* in suicide is ambivalence between doing it and wanting to be rescued" (p. 135); (2) "The common *perception* is of constriction such that one's options become very narrowed and the world is seen through tunnel vision so that no alternative thoughts can emerge" (p. 138).

5. *Relational characteristics:* (1) "The common *interpersonal act* in suicide is communication of intention" (letting another person know that one's decision makes sense) (p. 143); (2) "The common *action* in suicide is egression" (the right to exit or go out as one wishes, or the right to autonomously find a way out of one's pain) (p. 144).

6. *Serial characteristic:* "The common *consistency* in suicide is with lifelong coping patterns when deep perturbation, distress, threat, and psychological pain are present" (p. 147).

This list of characteristics points us toward what makes sense to the individual about to embark on suicide. It is not meant to suggest that all suicides are alike. In using the word "common," Shneidman reminds us that suicides, taken together, do reflect similarities. However, he is also careful to note that each suicide is idiosyncratic and that there are no absolutes or universals (1985, pp. 121–122).

Overarching these characteristics and common to all suicides is the individual's sense of perturbation and degree of lethality (Shneidman, 1999a). *Perturbation* is the degree to which the individual is upset. Perturbation in itself does not lead to suicide. Many of us are upset by events, people, and things a great deal of the time, but we get over being upset. However, when perturbation is combined with how oriented the person is toward death, lethality level rises, and the person becomes more prone to suicide or homicide.

Similarities Between Suicide and Homicide

Often the person who is suicidal is also homicidal. Approximately 30% of violent individuals have a history of self-destructive behavior, and 10%–20% of suicidal persons have a history of violent behavior (Plutchik & van Praag, 1990). West's (1966) study of murderers found that about 30% went on to kill themselves after they killed somebody else, and many had long histories of violent behavior and high levels of aggression. That fact is particularly relevant with murder/suicide in elderly couples, domestic violence, infanticide by overwrought parents, and mental illness (Granello & Granello, 2007; Malmquist, 2006; Nock & Marzuk, 2000). The frequency of murder/suicide in American society emphasizes the similarities of motive, sense of hopelessness, opportunity, means, and lethality of method. The 1999 mass murder and suicide witnessed at Columbine High School in Littleton, Colorado, represents a prime example of the parallels of suicide and homicide. However, it should be emphasized that not all suicides or suicidal persons are homicidal. There is a thin line between murder and suicide as an expressive act. According to Everstine (1998, p. 103), suicide is often intended to take the place of homicide and brand the intended victim as the person who is really responsible for the suicide. Given the right circumstances, the choice of homicide or suicide or both may tilt in either or both directions. The major problem is predicting when either will happen because lethal behavior is internally generated and highly idiosyncratic. Thus, it is not easy for an external observer to ascertain or predict when the individual's thoughts cross a threshold to action (Pridmore & Walter, 2013).

Analyzing Suicide/Homicide Notes/Videos

Suicide/homicide notes can provide valuable information, but they do not necessarily provide an open pathway to understanding suicidal/homicidal intention. Contrary to popular opinion, suicide notes are not commonly left. Notes are left in only about 15%–40% of completed suicides (Holmes & Holmes, 2006; Shneidman & Farberow, 1961). Suicide notes typically fall into four categories (Holmes & Holmes, 2006, pp. 82–97; Jacobs, 1967, pp. 67–68). In the first, the writers beg forgiveness, see their problems as not of their own making but nevertheless overwhelming, and indicate they know what they are doing. Many times financial problems predominate in this type of note. The second category involves an incurable physical or mental illness, and the suicide is tired of putting up with the pain. The third type typically deals with love scorned, and the note is directed toward the significant other who has rejected the suicide. Finally, the fourth type is generally a "last will and testament" with instructions and gives little if any reason for the suicide.

Suicide/homicide notes may generally be characterized by their dichotomous (black-and-white) logic, hostility, and self-blame. As Shneidman (1999c) says, "Suicide notes are testimonials to tortuous life journeys that come to wrecked ends" (p. 277). Many suicide notes are rather mundane, using very specific names, details, and instructions if there are survivors. Interestingly, there tends to be less evidence of how one is thinking and much more about how one is feeling. Hate, disgust, fear, loathing, rejection, shame, disgrace, and failure are constant themes. Rock star Kurt Cobain's suicide note is a classic vitriolic, self-loathing statement about why he ended his life (Shea, 2002, pp. 36–37). As one might suspect, considerable space is given to the various meanings of "love" (Shneidman, 1973).

Unfortunately, a universal, psychodynamic breakthrough in regard to understanding suicide has not occurred after a great deal of research into suicide notes. About the only consistent results found have been that note writers lived alone, were more involved in personal conflicts such as divorce, were less often psychiatrically disturbed, and were less likely to be under medical supervision (Callanan & Davis, 2009;

Haines, Williams, & Lester, 2011). Studies examining the degree to which training could improve participants' ability to determine the authenticity of suicide notes have also been conducted. The results indicated that trainees could not accurately discriminate between real and fake notes beyond chance (Bennell, Jones, & Taylor, 2011).

What suicide notes indicate over and over is the idiosyncratic reasons for the suicides and the tunneled, constricted view that there is absolutely no other way out. Paradoxically, while suicide notes are rather barren in themselves, when they are put into context with a detailed life history of the individual they can tell us a great deal about why the individual committed the act (Shneidman, 1999c). An examination of the following suicide/homicide notes graphically illustrates what Shneidman's (1973) research into suicide notes has uncovered.

An Analysis of Seung-hui Cho. In 2007, Seung-hui Cho, a student at Virginia Polytechnic Institute and State University, killed 32 people, wounded 14 more, and then took his own life on the Virginia Tech campus. His "note," in the form of a videotape that he sent to NBC News, certainly gives a description of him that fits well into Shneidman's (1985) typology of the classic suicidal person who crosses through a psychological door into becoming homicidal as well. Here again are Shneidman's characteristics, supported by Cho's videotaped statements, as excerpted from the *Memphis Commercial Appeal*, April 19, 2007 (Apuzzo, 2007):

1. *Situational characteristics* of unendurable pain: "You have vandalized my heart and raped my soul." His needs are frustrated: "You forced me in a corner."
2. *Motivational characteristics* directed toward ending his emotional problems and becoming a martyr for all the weak and disenfranchised: "You thought it was one weak boy you were extinguishing. Thanks to you, I die like Jesus Christ to inspire generations of the weak and defenseless."
3. *Affective characteristics* of hopelessness, helplessness, and abandonment: "You loved to crucify me. You loved inducing cancer in my head, terror in my heart, and ripping my soul all this time."
4. *Cognitive characteristics* indicated in his previous history of psychotic behavior and by his tunnel vision of an unjust world, with logic-tight compartments of being persecuted by the rich: "Your Mercedes wasn't enough, you brats. Golden necklaces weren't enough, you snobs." Such statements mark him as a person with paranoid schizophrenia and extremely dangerous to both himself and others.
5. *Relational characteristics* marked by his communication of intention, stating why his rampage across the campus makes absolute sense: "You had a hundred billion chances, but forced me into a corner and gave me no option."
6. *Serial characteristic* discerned in a long history of difficulty in coping, of being different, and of being bullied (see Chapter 13, Crises in Schools). The intended victims are those "who had everything and spit on my face and shoved trash down my throat."

The continuing and unendurable *psychache* (Shneidman, 1993) Cho felt and verbalized in the foregoing statements propels him toward an *egoistic* (Durkheim, 1897/1951) suicidal/homicidal rampage. His alienation, along with a lack of integration into and identification with the group, is both chronic and acute. His isolation and aloneness, manifest in the videotape, are profound, and he broods over real and imagined injustices he has suffered that caused him "to be humiliated and be impaled upon a cross to bleed to death for your amusement." At some point his egoistic suicidal impulses transgress a psychological line to move into Everstine's (1998) *interactional* model of suicide. As with other mass murderers, Cho's depression and pent-up anger turn inside out in a classic Freudian dynamic example of the suicidal and homicidal person (Freud, 1916). At that point the paranoid rage he feels explodes outward and focuses externally on others who have persecuted him. When that occurs and blame is externalized, Seung-hui Cho becomes a candidate to commit mass murder on that large amorphous mass of his tormentors. Why is this so? To the survivors it makes no sense and is the very essence of *chaos* theory (Rogers, 2001a) at work. To Seung-hui Cho, with malice and coldness aforethought, it makes perfect sense to end his pain and air his narcissistic grievances to the world. Why? His martyrlike rationalization to justify his act is: "If not for me, for my children and my brothers and sisters . . . I did it for them." But finally, the real reason very simply is, "I had to."

Myths About Suicide

There are a good many commonly held myths **LO6** about suicide that the crisis worker should know and take into account when assessing potentially suicidal clients (Bonner, 2001; Duberstein & Witte, 2009; Fujimura, Weis, & Cochran, 1985; Granello & Granello, 2007, pp. 8–11; Kirk, 1993, pp. 1–4; Lester, 1997; McGlothin, 2008; Shneidman, 1999b; Shneidman, Farberow, & Litman, 1976, p. 130; Stack, 2001; Stone, 1999, pp. 51–63; Webb & Griffiths, 1998–1999, p. B42). Some of the myths are as follows:

1. *Discussing suicide will cause the client to move toward doing it.* The opposite is generally true. Discussing it with an empathic person will more likely provide the client with a sense of relief and a desire to buy time to regain control.
2. *Clients who threaten suicide don't do it.* A large percentage of people who kill themselves have previously threatened it or disclosed their intent to others.
3. *Suicide is an irrational act.* Nearly all suicides and suicide attempts make *perfect sense* when viewed from the perspective of the people doing them.
4. *People who commit suicide are insane.* There is evidence of a high degree of association between mental illness and suicide, particularly with chronic depression; schizophrenia; obsessive-compulsive, borderline, schizoid, panic antisocial personality disorder, and panic disorders; and co-occurring substance abuse. However, most suicidal people appear to be normal people who are acutely depressed, lonely, hopeless, helpless, newly aggrieved, shocked, deeply disappointed, jilted, or otherwise overcome by some emotionally charged situation.
5. *Suicide runs in families—it is an inherited tendency.* This may or may not be a myth. Sometimes more than one member of a family does commit suicide. Blood type has been found to be associated with suicide (Lester, 2005). Blood metabolites also appear to play a part in suicide. There is now a great deal of evidence that 5-HIAA, a main serotonin metabolite, is low in people who attempt suicide (Leonard, 2005; Stoff & Mann, 1997) and that the S Tin2 serotonin transporter gene is variant in families that have a history of suicidal behavior (Lopes de Lara et al., 2006). In counterpoint to a purely gene pool theory, self-destructive tendencies may be learned, situational, or linked to depression or other hopeless environmental conditions. The very act of completion in one family member may propel other family members to model that behavior.
6. *Once suicidal, always suicidal.* Many people contemplate suicide at some time during their lives. Most

of them recover from the immediate threat, learn appropriate responses and controls, live long, productive lives free of the threat of self-inflicted harm, and never again consider it.

7. *When a person has attempted suicide and pulls out of it, the danger is over.* Most suicides occur within 3 months following the beginning of "improvement." One danger signal is a period of euphoria following a depressed or suicidal episode, which often means the person has everything settled and planned and is at peace with the idea of committing suicide. About 10% of those who have previously attempted suicide will go on to kill themselves.
8. *A suicidal person who begins to show generosity and share personal possessions is showing signs of renewal and recovery.* Many suicidal people begin to dispose of their most prized possessions once they experience enough upswing in energy to make a definite plan. Such disposal of personal effects is sometimes tantamount to acting out the last will and testament.
9. *Suicide is always an impulsive act.* There are several types of suicide. Some involve impulsive actions; others are very deliberately planned and carried out.
10. *Suicide strikes only the rich.* Suicide is democratic and strikes at all levels of society. A review of the literature over the past 30 years indicates poor people are generally at greater risk.
11. *Suicide happens without warning.* People invariably give many signs and symptoms of their suicidal intentions.
12. *Suicide is a painless way to die.* It often is not, and many suicide attempts that go awry bring terrible suffering in the form of chronic pain and permanent disfigurement.
13. *Few professional people kill themselves.* Physicians, pharmacists, lawyers, and dentists have high rates of suicide, but who keeps track of truck drivers and laborers?
14. *Christmas season is lethal.* December has the lowest suicide rate of any month.
15. *Women don't use guns to kill themselves because of disfigurement.* Women use guns more often than drugs to kill themselves.
16. *More suicides occur during a full moon.* There is no increased number of suicides during a full moon.
17. *Suicidal people rarely seek medical attention.* Research shows that about 75% of people who kill themselves visit a doctor within the month that they kill themselves.

18. *Most elderly people who commit suicide are terminally ill.* While many elderly who attempt suicide may be depressed, they are not terminally ill.

19. *Suicide is limited to the young.* Suicide rates rise with age and reach their highest level among white males in their 70s and 80s.

20. *Suicidal thoughts are relatively rare.* Each year in the United States approximately 8.3 million people (4%) seriously consider suicide. About 1% make a plan, and about half of those carry it out.

Assessment

Suicide Clues

The overarching, cardinal rule for *all* crisis **LO7** workers is this: Workers who deal with *any type* of crisis client should always assess for the presence of clues and risk factors for lethal behavior. Fortunately for the crisis worker, nearly all suicidal/homicidal people reveal some kind of clues or cries for help. According to Shneidman, Farberow, and Litman (1976), no one is 100% suicidal. People with the strongest death wishes are invariably ambivalent, confused, and grasping for life (p. 128). Most suicidal clients, feeling high levels of ambivalence or inner conflict, either emit some clues or hints about their serious trouble or call for help in some way (pp. 429–440). The clues may be verbal, behavioral, situational, or syndromatic.

> *Verbal clues* are spoken or written statements, which may be either direct ("I'm going to do it this time—kill myself") or indirect ("I'm of no use to anyone anymore").
>
> *Behavioral clues* may range from prowling the Internet suicide sites to slashing one's wrist as a "practice run" or suicidal gesture.
>
> *Situational clues* might include concerns over a wide array of conditions such as the death of a spouse, divorce, a painful physical injury or terminal illness, sudden bankruptcy, preoccupation with the anniversary of a loved one's death, or other drastic changes in one's life situation.
>
> *Syndromatic clues* include such constellations of suicidal symptoms as severe depression, loneliness, hopelessness, dependence, and dissatisfaction with life. (Shneidman, Farberow, & Litman, 1976, pp. 431–434)

All of these clues may be considered as cries for help, no matter how subtle or camouflaged they are.

Risk Factors. Let's suppose you fall into some of the foregoing categories and have decided life isn't worth living and you are going to kill yourself. How good a candidate are you to take yourself off this planet? Here are some of the high probability suicide risk categories, so check them off to see how far gone you really are (Bongar & Sullivan, 2013, pp. 41; Cantor, 2000; Cheng & Lee, 2000; Granello & Granello, 2007; Holmes & Holmes, 2006; Joiner et al., 2009; Kerkhof, 2000; Lester, 2001; Lester & Gunn, 2011; Moberg et al., 2014; Roy et al., 2000; World Health Organization, 2011): You are older than 70 or younger than 20 and a male Caucasian. You came out of a troubled home and got in trouble at school for fighting. You still get in trouble for fighting except now it's in bars. You have a history of alcoholism, and you abuse other drugs. You have been diagnosed (choose one or more): (a) schizophrenic, (b) bipolar, (c) borderline, (d) anorexic, or you are just plain (e) depressed. You are single, and you don't have a very good job because you lost a really good job just lately. To make up for that you got drunk, had a hit-and-run accident, were caught, and are now spending your first night in jail. Your spouse has announced he or she is divorcing you, and most of your former friends won't speak to you anymore. This isn't the first time you've tried to kill yourself, and you have thought about it quite a bit since that time. You collect guns and know how to use every one of them and know a nice, quiet wooded area where no one ventures at night. You are now a resident of Lithuania, and have been planning on moving to Russia if you get out of jail or don't kill yourself first. It is 5 days after Christmas, and the only cards you got were from a lawyer foreclosing your house and the Internal Revenue Service who sent you an audit notice. Meanwhile, your rheumatoid arthritis is really bothering you, the only thing that helped was Vioxx, and it is now off the market. You've been to an internist twice in the last 2 months for stomach pains but you didn't mention anything about being depressed and he didn't ask. Sadly and ominously, your mother and your mother's father both committed suicide. To top it all off, you originally come from a European country that has a lot of low notes in its national anthem and you think it's pretty gloomy. If this now sounds like a bad country music song and you fit most of these criteria, do not despair or go step in front of a train (all really good country songs must include a train, so that is the way you are going to kill yourself, but you better not do it in Japan or the train company will make your estate pay for the damages since so many people do just that in Japan).

The ability to predict suicide and who will attempt or commit it is problematic, to say the least. Here's a really good example of the problem. There's a lot of research evidence that indicates people who commit suicide will have seen a medical doctor for a health problem in the 3 months prior to killing themselves (Ahmedani et al., 2014; Cho et al., 2013; De Leo et al., 2013). This variable is so significant that there are efforts underway to make suicide screens as standard as cholesterol screens when you visit your internist or ER (Ahmedani et al., 2014; Horowitz et al., 2012, 2013; Wintersteen & Diamond, 2013) and direct intervention (Ginnis et al., 2015; Wintersteen & Diamond, 2013). So okay, how many of you have been to the doctor in the last 3 months and never thought about killing yourself or someone else? Get the point! While all of the foregoing demographics, personality traits, behaviors, and socioeconomic risk factors can predict incident rates by group and are certainly risk factors, none of them taken singly or collectively predicts very well whether an individual will complete a suicide (Bonner, 2001; Goldney, 2000; Granello & Granello, 2007). So what a crisis interventionist needs is a fast check off when face-to-face on a bridge with a jumper and here it is.

Warning Signs. There are a number of acronym suicide check off lists that will work in catching warning signs. Here is one of the more common ones. The American Association of Suicidology (n.d.) has created a list of suicide warning signs with the mnemonic IS PATH WARM:

I is for ideation
S is for substance abuse
P is for purposelessness
A is for anxiety and agitation
T is for feeling trapped
H is for hopelessness
W is for withdrawal
A is for anger
R is for recklessness
M is for mood fluctuations

Warning signs are different from symptoms. While symptoms can only be described, warning signs are observable. So how many letters do you have to fill before the path to suicide changes from warm to hot? That's a really good question. Maybe only one or maybe all of them depending on your clinical judgment but in regard to due diligence and any future legal problems it's best to have done them as thorough a risk assessment as

you are able to do under the circumstances (Bongar & Sullivan, 2013; Kleespies, 2014). Thus you can say you did a through on-the-ground clinical assessment and, therefore, at that time the individual needed to be taken into protective custody because not only did he or she spell out IPAHWAM, but he or she totaled up A = 8, B = 9, C = 10 for a total TAF of 27, which means a night's rest in a secure facility and a talk with someone before release.

Assessment Instruments

A variety of instruments have been used in an attempt to identify suicidal ideation and behavior (Joiner et al., 2009; Laux, 2003; McGlothin, 2008; Westefeld et al., 2000). They cover personality characteristics, risk factors, and warning signs. The Minnesota Multiphasic Personality Inventory–2 (Hathaway & McKinley, 1989), the Hopelessness Scale (Beck et al., 1974), the Beck Depression Inventory (Beck & Steer, 1987), and the Psychological Pain Assessment Scale (Shneidman, 1999e) are examples of tests that address personality characteristics associated with suicide.

The Interpersonal Needs Questionnaire (Van Orden et al., 2008) assesses the critical interpersonal issues of burdensomeness to others and lack of belongingness. Along with the Painful and Provocative Events Scale (Bender et al., 2011), which is a self-report of how much the client engages in impulsive, dangerous, pathological, and risk-taking activities, these scales significantly predict high scores on the Acquired Capability for Suicide Scale, which indicates how lethal the client is (Van Orden et al., 2008).

A number of other instruments such as SAD PERSONS (Sex, Age, Depressive symptoms, Previous attempts, Ethanol use, Rational thinking loss, Social support lacking, Organized plan, No spouse, Sickness) (Patterson et al., 1983) are designed to assess manifestations of clinical suicide ideation and empirical factors that have been previously identified as being related to risk for suicide attempts. These scales accumulate data on relevant demographics, symptoms of suicidal behavior, stress, resources outside of self, personal and social history, and historical and situational variables currently identified in the suicide literature as significant predictors of suicide attempts. However, these devices alone have had a notoriously poor track record for prediction. Risk assessment is greatly improved when these instruments are backed up by a clinical interview and third-party collateral information (Rogers, 2001a).

Clinical Interview

The American Association of Suicidology (1997); Battle, Battle, and Tolley (1993); Gunn and Lester (2013); Hazell and Lewin (1993); Jobes (2006); Joiner and associates (2009); Kirk (1993, p. 7); Kleespies (2014, pp. 99–100); McGlothin (2008); Patterson and associates (1983); Stone (1999, pp. 57–60); Webb and Griffiths (1998–1999, pp. A44–45); and Won and associates (2013) have identified numerous risk factors and warning signs that may help the crisis worker in assessing suicide potential. While there are all kinds of scoring systems for the wide variety of checklists available today, they are rife with the possibility of yielding false positives or, worse yet, false negatives (Sullivan & Bongar, 2006). Here is where science and art commingle and the interview and diagnostic skill of the interventionist comes into play. Whenever a person manifests four or five of these risk factors, it should be an immediate signal for the crisis worker to treat the person as high risk in terms of suicide potential. The client:

1. Exhibits the presence of suicidal or homicidal impulses and serious intent.
2. Has a family history of suicide, threats of harm, drug abuse, and abuse of others.
3. Has a history of previous attempts.
4. Has formulated a specific plan.
5. Has experienced recent loss of a loved one through death, divorce, or separation.
6. Is part of a family that is destabilized as a result of loss, personal abuse, violence, and/or because the client has been sexually abused.
7. Is preoccupied with the anniversary of a particularly traumatic loss.
8. Is psychotic (and may have discontinued taking prescribed medications).
9. Has a history of drug and/or alcohol abuse.
10. Has had recent physical and/or psychological trauma or history of it as a child.
11. Has a history of unsuccessful medical treatment, chronic pain, or terminal illness.
12. Is living alone and is cut off from contact with others.
13. Is depressed, is recovering from depression, or has recently been hospitalized for depression.
14. Is giving away prized possessions or putting personal affairs in order.
15. Displays radical shifts in characteristic behaviors or moods, such as apathy, withdrawal, isolation, irritability, panic, or anxiety, or changed social, sleeping, eating, study, dress, grooming, or work habits.
16. Is experiencing a pervasive feeling of hopelessness/helplessness.
17. Is preoccupied and troubled by earlier episodes of experienced physical, emotional, or sexual abuse.
18. Exhibits a profound degree of one or more emotions—such as anger, aggression, loneliness, guilt, hostility, grief, or disappointment—that are uncharacteristic of the individual's normal emotional behavior.
19. Faces threatened financial loss.
20. Exhibits ideas of persecution.
21. Has difficulty in dealing with sexual orientation.
22. Has an unplanned pregnancy.
23. Has a history of running away or of incarceration.
24. Manifests ideas and themes of depression, death, and suicide in conversation, written essays, reading selections, artwork, or drawings.
25. Cognitively has black-and-white, all-or-none cognitions, tunnel vision, limited problem-solving ability, difficult self-soothing, and resolving guilt, and is perfectionistic.
26. Is a burden and doesn't feel belongingness, and makes statements or suggestions that he or she would not be missed if gone.
27. Has easy access to firearms, medications, and other fast lethal means.
28. Experiences chronic or acute stressors, and perseverates on them.
29. Has used the Internet or social media to explore suicide methods.
30. Has recently been to a medical doctor in the last 3–6 months for other than an annual physical checkup.

In and of themselves, each of these factors may mean little in regard to suicide. Further, this extensive suicide shopping list of risk factors would make a lot of people suicidal (false positive in statistical terms) who do not have the remotest notion of killing themselves. The crisis worker must realize that assessing suicidal or homicidal risk is no simple matter. Indeed, some risk factors such as previous attempts or having a concrete plan are more lethal than others and must be given more weight or attention. There are no direct "if–then" connections. Suicidal risk factors are much more relevant when identifying groups than individuals (Chiles & Strosahl, 1995, p. 8). Yet as these risk factors pile up, the potential for the individual to engage in a lethal act most certainly increases. Therefore, the clinical interview and how it is structured and handled are critical in making on-target assessments of lethality.

CAMS. The Collaborative Assessment and Management of Suicidality (CAMS) is a risk assessment clinical interview framework developed by Jobes

(2006). Creation of the therapeutic alliance is critical to this framework, so the emphasis is on collaboration. The Suicide Status Form III is used in this interview to measure psychological pain, self-hatred, hopelessness, stress, and the degree of emotional agitation necessary to take action and end the pain. Clients also give themselves an overall risk of suicide and list reasons for living and dying. Clients self-report their status on these dimensions on a scale of 1 to 5. A rating of 5s across the components signals a clear and imminent danger of suicide.

CASE. Chronological Assessment of Suicide Events (CASE) is a risk assessment clinical interview framework developed by Shea (2002) that has two primary assumptions: first, that people rarely kill themselves without engaging in concrete planning and making plans to do so; and second, that clients may not voluntarily come forward with information about their suicidal thoughts without a lot of rapport building on the part of the interviewer.

RFL. The Reasons for Living scale (RFL; Linehan et al., 1983) is a different kind of suicide assessment tool in that it queries a person's reasons for staying alive by posing 48 questions as to why people would *not* kill themselves. It has a six-point Likert scoring system for each question, and the items can be categorized into six factors: survival and coping beliefs, responsibility to family, child-related concerns, fear of suicide, fear of social disapproval, and moral issues.

SRADT. The Suicide Risk Assessment Decision Tree is a risk assessment clinical interview framework (Cukrowicz et al., 2004; Joiner et al., 1999) that moves through a series of yes-or-no questions to come to a decision about how present and pronounced is the person's acquired capability of killing himself or herself. Interviewers query three domains: previous suicidal behavior, current suicidal symptoms, and empirically related variables that would exacerbate (hopelessness, impulsivity) or diminish (engaging with social supports, stopping drug abuse) suicidal behavior. Completing the decision tree involves obtaining information about the aforementioned areas, inputting the data into the decision tree to determine how high the acquired capability of suicide attempt risk level is, and then using the risk level to determine appropriate intervention. Compelling evidence for a high acquired capability would include multiple suicide attempts or three of the following five symptoms: single suicide attempt, aborted attempt, self-injecting

drug use, self-harm practices such as cutting, and frequent exposure to or participation in physical violence (Joiner et al., 2009, pp. 69–70).

Using the Triage Assessment Form in Addressing Lethality

Crisis workers intervening with clients in acute crises should *never* omit an assessment for suicide lethality (McGlothin, 2008; Jobes, 2006; Shea, 2002; Sullivan & Bongar, 2009). The worker must not hesitate to ask questions such as "Are you thinking about killing yourself?" ". . . about killing someone else?" "How?" "When?" "Where?" We absolutely agree with McGlothin (2008, p. 39) that you don't sugarcoat this question for fear of activating suicidal urges in the client or of sounding callous or offensive in broaching such a personal and culturally sensitive topic. Mealy mouthed questions such as "Have you . . . considered hurting yourself," "thought about giving up," "felt overwhelmed/really down/strung out/at the end of your rope," along with qualifiers such as "sorta" or "kinda," are not the same as straight questions about "killing yourself" and imply wholly different interpretations that can cause the worker to completely miss lethal ideation.

Asking *the* question about killing oneself or others does not mean doing so in an abrasive, callous manner. As in CAM and CASE interview formats previously mentioned, collaboration and empathy are key components. Asking *the* question about killing oneself or others is a closed-ended question that seeks a yes-or-no response. However, there are varying degrees of "yesness" that range from "Well, not in a long time!" to "I have the 9mm cleaned and loaded and am going out to the state park this afternoon" (McGlothin, 2008, pp. 38–39). Therefore, if you get a positive answer, you need to fully explore the dimensions and degree of that lethality by assessing across affective, behavioral, and cognitive dimensions. McGlothin's (2008, pp. 36–37) acronym SIMPLE STEPS provides a step-by-step method to assess lethality and get a good read on the client's affective, behavioral, and cognitive representation of the dilemma.

Suicidal/homicidal? Are you thinking of killing yourself/someone else?

Ideation: How likely are you to kill yourself/somebody else in the next 72 hours?

Method: How will you kill yourself/somebody else?

Pain: On a scale of 1 to 10, how much psychological pain are you in at the moment? Is there anything you can think of that would make it go higher?

Loss: Have you suffered a loss recently or a significant loss in the past you are not over?

Earlier attempts: Have you ever tried to kill yourself/somebody else before? What happened? What made it not work?

Substance use: Are you currently drinking alcohol or using drugs? What medications are you taking, and are you taking them as prescribed?

Troubleshooting: How tied up in this are your job, family, and so on? And what might change to stop this? Are you willing not to consider killing yourself/somebody? If a miracle happened and you awakened tomorrow and everything were fine, what would that look like?

Emotions/diagnosis: Have you ever been diagnosed with a physical or psychological illness? How are you feeling right now, and have you ever felt this way before? If so, how often? Have you or are you currently seeing a human service worker of any kind for this problem?

Parental/family history: Has anybody in your family thought about or committed suicide or homicide? Have your parents experienced any emotional problems?

Stressors and life events: What is going on in your life that leads you to think that suicide/homicide is a viable option or solution to your problems?

The triage assessment of the client in acute crisis provides for immediate revision of the worker's estimate of crisis severity based on the client's responses to these important and necessary questions or on rapidly elevated TAF ratings due to a sudden change in client feeling, behaving, or thinking about committing suicide or homicide when previously there was no indication of ideation. A client triage profile that may have looked safe before such answers may look quite different a few moments later. If the client is seriously thinking of killing or harming some specific other person, the worker will need to consider the duty-to-warn implications dictated by law developed in the *Tarasoff* case, described in Chapter 15, Crisis Intervention: Legal and Ethical Issues.

Consider the following example. *Before* the lethality questions, the client's presenting problem to a career counselor is job loss due to a plant closing. The counselor identifies the client's depression and frustration over failure to find a suitable replacement job, but the estimated TAF affect value of 3 or 4, cognition score of 6 or 7, and behavior score of 4 or 5 (total TAF of 13 to 16) yields a "low to moderate" severity summary. Such a total score shows no urgent or immediate concern for the client's severity/lethality status.

Nevertheless, the career counselor senses that something is not quite right. The client's voice reveals a hint of verbal euphoria, while the body language seems to contradict the verbal behavior with a slight hint of hopelessness. The worker further knows that job loss, particularly after a lengthy tenure, and suicide are related (Stack, 2001). As a result of the emerging hints and cues (as an example, the client makes a nonchalant side remark implying that he or she will not be around much longer), the counselor probes directly into the client's inner world by asking, "What does that mean?" "How?" "When?" and "Where?" and then rethinks and reframes the TAF assessment.

After the lethality questions—the client's responses, which reflect obvious stress and depression, are "For me, there is no future, no life left. I am too old to retrain, and nobody wants me anyway! I might as well curl up and die," and the client answers "Yes" to the question "Are you thinking of killing yourself because things look so hopeless?"—a second TAF assessment of 9 or 10 on affect, 8 or 9 on cognition, and 8 or 9 on behavior (total of 25 to 28), amounts to a dramatic escalation and would trigger an intervention strategy of immediate hospitalization to ensure the client's safety.

This example of using the TAF as a rapid assessment tool shows how quickly the emotional tone may change in a crisis intervention case. It clearly demonstrates that whenever a crisis worker begins to suspect a higher level of severity or lethality than at first revealed, the worker should not hesitate to directly ask the question and probe deeply into the emotionally charged world of the client. A similar rapid increase in the worker's assessment of lethality is also applicable in cases of homicidal intent or any other situation involving threats of harm to self or others.

Level of Risk. The last piece of this complex puzzle is level of risk. Joiner and associates (1999) and Bryan and Rudd (2006) have put together risk tables that range from nonexistent to extreme. As individuals move up the scale to extreme these things happen. They get more courage and a sense of competence as they make preparations for and practice run the attempt. They indeed have made unsuccessful attempts before. They have continuous, intense, and enduring ideation, impaired self-control, severe feelings of hopelessness, multiple other symptoms, and no protective factors.

At this point in time the best bet on making determinations about the potential for lethal behavior is Kleepies' (2014, pp. 108–122) **structured professional judgment.** That is, combining what professional crisis workers' experience tells them as they use the foregoing verbal and visual assessments along with a reliable paper-and-pencil test—if time is available to make a decision on potential lethality.

Intervention Strategies

This section contains examples of general **LO8** counseling strategies to use with adults of different ages and different problems. Lethal children will be addressed in Chapter 13, Crises in Schools. Before you even start reading this section, your question might well be: Should one even try, with treatment outcomes so equivocal? While there are no absolutes in suicide treatment, there are some promising approaches (Goldney, 2005; Hawton & Van Heeringen, 2000; Hepp et al., 2004; Jobes, 2006; Joiner et al., 2009; Lester, 2000; Linehan & Schmidt, 1995; Wenzel et al., 2009), and it is these that will be considered. Suicide intervention strategies involve "interrupting a suicide attempt that is imminent or in the process of occurring" (Fujimura, Weis, & Cochran, 1985, p. 612). Crisis intervention with suicidal/homicidal clients generally falls into two broad categories, dealing with perturbations and reducing lethality levels.

The Three I's

The major causes of perturbation have to do with the three I's. The person confronts a situation he or she believes to be **inescapable** (I can't get away from this pain no matter what I do), **intolerable** (I've gone beyond what any human could endure), and **interminable** (If I don't do something about this now, it'll go on forever). The goal of intervention is to change one or more of these I's (Chiles & Strosahl, 1995, p. 74). At the beginning of the interview, the crisis worker must quickly establish a sense of rapport and trust in order to create a working relationship and provide clients with an anchor to life (Michel, 2011). It is also important to begin to reestablish in clients a sense of hope and to diminish their sense of helplessness—to take immediate steps to speak and act on clients' current pain.

The most effective way to do this is to address not the lethality directly but the perturbation the I's are causing. When the perturbation level of the three I's is lowered and some modicum of control and hope is restored in the person's life, lethality will drop below the explosive level. What this means is not just dealing passively with only the intrapersonal issues but actively confronting the interpersonal and environmental issues that afflict and assail the individual (Shneidman, 1999a).

Clients need to be taught to either use existing problem-solving skills or generate new ones so that they can shed the inescapability of unsolvable problems. Clients need to develop self-awareness and self-observation strategies to observe natural fluctuations in pain levels and make associations between doing things a bit differently and feeling better. As a result, they can learn that emotional pain will not be constantly intense and interminable. Clients also need to learn that negative feelings can be tolerated by distancing and distraction skills so that they are seen as a part of life and not something that is overwhelming and interminable (Chiles & Strosahl, 1995, p. 74). Typically, some form of cognitive-behavioral therapy will be used that employs active support for the person; teaches cognitive restructuring, emotional regulation, and learning to balance change and acceptance of how things are and will be; and changes destructive and negative behaviors through psychoeducation and problem solving (Berk et al., 2004; Guthrie et al., 2001; Linehan et al., 2006; Townsend et al., 2001; Wenzel et al., 2009). The following cases demonstrate how a crisis interventionist goes about "dotting the I's."

LeAnn, Age 21. LeAnn was a senior at a large university. During her freshman year at a small liberal arts college, she had experienced an emotional and suicidal breakdown as the anniversary date of her older sister's suicide approached. She had left the small college, returned home, and undergone psychiatric treatment. LeAnn had later enrolled in the university in her hometown, where she lived in a residence hall. She went home frequently but managed to succeed fairly well in her studies and social life. LeAnn was referred to the crisis worker by her mother following a weekend mother–daughter discussion during which LeAnn disclosed some recurring suicidal thoughts. The mother expressed concern that the fifth anniversary of her sister's suicide seemed to be looming in LeAnn's mind and asked the crisis worker to call LeAnn in for a conference. During the first interview with LeAnn, the worker established that LeAnn did not have a specific, highly lethal plan, but that she did have a lot of suicidal ruminations.

LeAnn: I think Mother thinks I'm crazy. Sometimes I wonder if she's right. (*Long pause.*) I don't seem to handle stress very well, and this is my last semester with my senior thesis due. . . . Sometimes I think I am about to lose it. Do you think I may be going crazy?

CW: No, I certainly don't. What I'm hearing is a lot of confusion and unsettled emotion and a lot of pressure. I'm glad you feel comfortable enough to ask me. I'm wondering what's happening in you to bring up the question. Are you thinking of killing yourself?

LeAnn: Well, I've just been sitting in my room by myself, staring at the wall. I can't get anywhere on that stupid thesis. Not sleeping, not eating, not going out. And I've had this strange sensation of both wanting to run and scream, and to just give up. And I've thought about my sister's death constantly. More than at any time since I was a freshman. It's like I'm destined to go the way she went. Sometimes I think I can't stand it any longer. Then I catch myself and wonder if I *am* nuts. My sister killed herself, and her birthday is coming up. I miss her so much.

CW: Okay, I'm going to ask you a bunch of questions and I've got a couple of forms I want you to fill out. Some of the questions may seem a little intrusive but it's a way of determining where we are going to need to go. When we're done, I'll tell you where I think we need to go.

LeAnn's thoughts and responses are enough to activate the worker to conduct a suicidal assessment process. He first gives her the Suicide Status Form III (Jobes, 2006). Her scores for psychological pain are 3. She reports missing her sister, particularly on the anniversary of her death. Her stress is a 4–5, but she mainly sees her stressors as completing her thesis. Her agitation is low, with no sense of need to take any action that would lead to a suicide. She feels a bit hopeless, but again this has more to do with her senior thesis completion and resulting graduation. She indicates no self-hatred and gives it no score at all. She rates her overall risk of suicide as extremely low. Her reasons for living are graduation, her parents, friends, and a chance to go on to graduate school. She has no reasons for dying, other than she might see her sister in heaven. Her wish to live is "very much" and her wish to die is "not at all." Her Interpersonal Needs Questionnaire (Van Orden et al., 2008) indicates she does not feel she is a burden and has a very strong sense of

belonging to her parents and college sorority sisters. Follow-up questions by the worker using McGlothin's (2008) SIMPLE STEPS indicate few if any of the "hot" cognitions that activate suicidal thinking. The worker relays this information to her in a straightforward, collaborative, and empathic manner.

CW: As you can see, your scale scores are really low, all well within a normal range. I believe that more than anything the anniversary of your sister's death and how much you miss her are contributing to the loneliness and isolation you are feeling. I also think you are pretty normal and reacting pretty normally to school. I wonder if we might talk about those a little and help you make some plans to get out of this rut?

Many people who have suicidal ideation believe they are "going crazy." While some people who are psychotic or suffer from personality disorders are suicidal, suicide is not the first step on the road to "going crazy." The crisis worker positively affirms that LeAnn is not going "nuts" and seeks to normalize the crisis. The crisis worker focuses on the underlying emotional content of the loss of her sister and the upcoming anniversary as likely a key element in decreasing the client's perturbation.

The same is true of getting a handle on a huge source that would perturb most any student—the dreaded senior thesis. While her suicidal ideation is not dismissed out of hand, it is put in perspective as one component of her overall response to the loss of her sister and the other normal stressors she is experiencing at school. For many individuals a suicidal crisis may be a onetime occurrence brought on by acute situational events that, once handled, disappears forever.

Deborah, Age 27. Deborah had been in therapy, on and off, for 11 years—since she was 16. Deborah (1) had a history of suicide attempts, some of them serious, some of them gestures; (2) had used a wide variety of drugs in her college years—in fact, she had dropped out of college after 2 years because of drug use and resulting poor academic performance; (3) had a history of episodes of severe depression, loneliness, hopelessness, and helplessness followed by mood swings to euphoric and deep religious activity and commitment; (4) had been hospitalized numerous times for psychiatric care; (5) had experienced a great sense of loss and grief at the divorce of her parents when she was 16; (6) had recently gone into self-imposed isolation and remorse—cutting herself off from friends, family, and coworkers; and (7) was feeling a new sense of meaninglessness related to her career—she had been seeking something that she really chose to do (as opposed to working for her father). Deborah, in tears, was trembling and in a state of acute anxiety and standing on the railing of a Mississippi river bridge preparing to jump.

The crisis worker is a Crisis Intervention Team police officer, described in Chapter 5, Crisis Case Handling. Police and highway patrol officers have stopped all traffic, and people are out of their cars, watching. The scene is tense, and it appears that at any moment Deborah will jump. The officer immediately implements Cochran's game plan model of giving his name (play 1) and getting her name (play 2) in order to establish personal contact. His use of "I" owning statements (play 3) and reflection and summarization (play 4) (Kirchberg et al., 2013) are designed to let her know he is listening and focused in on her alone and hopefully to develop a working bond.

CIT Officer: (*in a clearly audible but confident, soft, caring, and empathic voice*) My name is Mark. Tell me your name.

Deborah: (*hesitantly*) My name . . . is . . . Deborah. What . . . what do you want?

CIT Officer: I want to help you, if I can, Deborah. I can see that you are under some kind of terrible pressure to make you think about jumping off this bridge. I'd like to talk to you and see if there is any way I can be of help to you.

Deborah: I don't know that anybody can help me. (*a little indignantly*) Certainly not a cop! Shrinks haven't helped. How can you?

CIT Officer: Deborah, I'm concerned about your safety and about what's bothering you right now. I'm a cop all right, but I am also a Crisis Intervention Team officer. I deal with all kinds of people in crisis, and that's why they called me. For you to consider jumping, there must be a lot of pain that you can't seem to get relief from. If the shrinks haven't worked, how about giving a cop a chance? What's the harm? We have plenty of time.

The CIT officer immediately seeks to establish rapport with the jumper by establishing a first-name basis of communication. He validates her suicidal actions as a way to relieve emotional pain by matter-of-factly stating what she is doing and seeks to elicit what is causing her to do it. He uses a validation technique from dialectical behavior therapy (DBT;

Linehan, 1997) that sets up what at first might seem the exact opposite of what one would do. He promotes the central "dialectic" in DBT, which is that he accepts the client exactly as she is in the moment, with her suicide attempt as being her best problem-solving attempt available, but also simultaneously pushes the client toward changing the maladaptive behavior patterns that have gotten her onto the bridge (Rizvi, 2011). He further acknowledges who he is and what he is capable of doing, without any false promises. He works very hard to immediately build a trusting, empathic relationship that demonstrates congruence, honesty, and caring (Kirchberg et al., 2013). While it may seem like we are harping on this subject, building a therapeutic alliance (and this most certainly includes this police officer on the bridge with this client) is absolutely critical. Michel and Jobes's (2011) book spends more than 400 pages on this topic, providing clinicians with an arsenal of theoretical techniques on how to build the relationship. Michel (2011) quotes a woman whom he met in a support group of people with depression who had attempted suicide. She had the chainsaw scars around her neck to prove the gruesome way she had attempted to kill herself. He asked why these people had not sought help. She said, "We could only have talked to another person we knew would not be afraid of listening, without judging. In a suicidal crisis we could never have trusted a person who would want to talk us out of it" (pp. 5–6).

More than other types of crisis workers, though, the CIT officer's job is dealing with the imminent lethality of the situation. Safety of a suicidal/homicidal client (Rudd, Joiner, & Rajab, 2001, p. 152) is the overriding priority, along with the safety of the officer (Memphis Police Department, 2011).

CIT Officer: With the wind blowing and all the commotion around here, I'm having a difficult time hearing you. I need for you to come down off that railing and come over here to the curb and sit down so we can talk. You look like you could use a friendly ear to listen, and I'll take the time to do just that.

Deborah: I'm not sure talking will do any good. Just go away, and leave me alone. I don't need you here.

CIT Officer: Deborah, do you remember my name? My name is Mark. Let's take some time to talk. We've got time, plenty of time to just sit down together and talk. You do remember my name, don't you?

The crisis worker makes a point to try to establish a first-name mutual communication with

Deborah. Whenever a person such as Deborah is emotionally overwhelmed and immobile, one effective way to break through that immobility is to *personalize* the interaction. A good way to personalize a relationship with a client in crisis is to establish a first-name communication as early as possible (Memphis Police Department, 2011). He also attempts to slow the emotionally charged situation by repeating that there is time, plenty of time, to find out what is going on. That tells the client that in this moment, he is committed to the relationship, as transitory as it may be. "We have plenty of time" is almost a default phrase for us to slow down the rapid cognitive and affective cycling that is present in many kinds of crisis and to convey a sense of patience, understanding, interest, and thoroughness that usually is missing in crisis clients' relationships (Kirchberg et al., 2013).

Deborah: Your name is Mark. So? How do I know I can trust you, Mark? I don't see how you can make my life any better. I've about had it with this life, with this great big lump of hurt deep inside me that won't go away. I'm really tired of this. Anyway, how do I know you won't just put me in jail or that nuthouse they put me in last time?

CIT Officer: (*in a calm, low-key, confident, reassuring, caring voice tone*) Deborah, what I want to do is to understand what's bothering you, so I can get you some help. What is it that we need to focus on to get you some relief? Right now, all I'm asking you to do for me is just to come over here to the curb, so you and I can take plenty of time to talk, so I can clearly understand just what is upsetting you. I'm certainly *not* here to put you in jail or the nuthouse. What I want to do is to try to find out what part of you is hurting inside so that I can get you to some place to get the help that you deserve. I can see you're carrying such a heavy load to think that the only way of unburdening yourself is jumping off this bridge. I don't want to see you get hurt. So could you at least step off the railing?

Deborah: (*Steps down off the railing and takes a few tentative steps toward the CIT officer.*) It's just so overwhelming and hopeless. Nothing seems to work. Everything I touch turns to crap, school, love life, job, parents. I am tired of it. So tired.

CIT Officer: Okay, thanks for getting off the railing. (*Deborah sits down. Mark slowly moves by her side, sits down, and listens to her story unfold.*) Wow! That *is* a load. No wonder you felt like jumping. It takes

some courage to step away from ending all that pain and taking a chance on talking to me. I really appreciate that. I want to take you to a guy I know. He's not a shrink. He's a former police resource officer who works on the mobile crisis team. First I have to take you to the medical center and get you checked out. Is that okay?

Deborah: Will they give me electroshock treatments? I don't want those.

CIT Officer: No, they'll just evaluate you. Look! I want you to ride down there with me. I'll have to put you in handcuffs for the ride there because that's part of the police procedure. That may mean an all-night stay at the medical center, I don't know. But I think I can get them to do the evaluation and then see about getting you out of there pretty quickly to a place and a guy I know about. While they are doing that, I'll call Pete, the guy I told you about. As soon as you are checked out I'll come back and get you and take you to see Pete—with no handcuffs. You ride up front with me. I think you'd like talking to him. I know sometimes I sure do when I'm in a bind. But let's just sit down here and talk awhile, so I can kinda clue Pete in. Would that be okay?

Deborah: What the heck! I've never had my head shrunk by a cop. It can't get any worse. Okay! (*Talks a bit more about what got her here while the CIT officer listens attentively.*)

In this case, the crisis worker was able, in a few minutes' time, to validate himself to Deborah and gain her trust by focusing in on what is disturbing her and exploring her issues (Leenaars, 1994). Suicidal clients often cannot concentrate, so the crisis worker repeats himself using the broken record technique and continuously seeks to slow things down. He also attempts to get Deborah to a place of safety by asking her to move off the railing. He immediately reinforces her for getting off the bridge and again for being willing to talk with him. He does not make a promise he cannot keep. As an example, he promises her no electric shock treatments. He can do that because that procedure has not been done in years in his jurisdiction.

CIT officers like Mark have a great deal of discretion in what they can do with emotionally disturbed individuals they take into protective custody. While he might be able to get Deborah off the railing by lying to her about not taking her to jail or the "nuthouse," the next time a police officer was asked to deal with Deborah, she would remember the lie and be much more difficult to work with. Deborah complied with the crisis worker's request and was later taken to the emergency room of a public hospital, where she received medical and psychological evaluations.

The case of Deborah provides a brief example of how some simple verbal techniques, delivered with compassion, caring, and genuineness, can make a dramatic difference in the compliance and survival of many clients who are in acute disequilibrium and actively trying to kill themselves. After being checked out, Deborah meets Pete.

CW: I'm Pete, and you must be Deborah. Mark told me about you. I'm glad to meet you. It sounds like you had a heck of a night, and Mark tells me this isn't the first time you've felt so bad you wanted to kill yourself.

Deborah: He's right. I don't know why I didn't just go ahead. I was as close as I've ever been. I think next time that will be it.

CW: I'd like to do something a little different from what you are maybe used to. Instead of doing crisis intervention, I kinda do crisis management here with the Midtown mobile crisis unit. Are you interested in learning how to manage some of this stuff?

Deborah: Man, if I just could. That would be something else.

Crisis Management. Dealing with chronic `LO9` or episodic suicidal behavior is different from one-time suicide attempts. **Crisis management** refers to the act of planning a response to recurring suicidal behavior in *collaboration* with the client (Bongar & Sullivan, 2013, pp. 157–240; Chiles & Strosahl, 1995, pp. 125–147; Jobes, 2006; Kleespies, 2014, pp. 20–24). While we are indeed involved in treatment of a lethal behavior, there is an important distinction between treatment and management. Treatment implies an end point "cure." Management implies an ongoing problem that needs a continuous collaborative effort between the client and the worker until such time as the client decides that lethality really is no longer a viable option (Jobes, 2006, p. 69). While little can be done about static (unchanging) risk factors such as race, age, and chronic mental illness, dynamic factors (modifiable) and risk factors such as hopelessness, alcohol abuse, financial crisis, or acute depression can be managed (Kleespies, 2014, p. 21), and those individuals who are operating at a moderate risk level can

benefit through outpatient management (Bongar & Sullivan, 2013, pp. 157–200).

The goal is to establish a framework that rewards alternatives to suicidal behavior and minimizes the short-term reinforcements that occur when suicidal ideation and behavior start to develop (Rizvi, 2011; Wenzel, Brown, & Beck, 2009, pp. 173–198) and develop a safety plan (Stanley & Brown, 2012). Pete is a member of the mobile crisis team for Midtown Mental Health Unit and a licensed professional counselor. He is a retired police officer and still serves as a resource officer for police officers who are experiencing personal and professional difficulties. He will use a collaborative cognitive-behavioral therapy approach (Brown, Wenzel, & Rudd, 2011; Wenzel, Brown, & Beck, 2009) with Deborah. To do that he will need to determine the central cognitive pathway that leads her to consider suicide. He will need answers to the following questions:

1. What about the client's history generates the suicidal behavior?
2. What precipitated this crisis, and is it different from other trigger events?
3. How does the client think about suicide?
4. What does she feel during the crisis?
5. What is she feeling physically?
6. What active or planned suicidal behaviors have occurred or are occurring? (Rudd, 2004, p. 67)

He is straightforward, honest, empathic, supportive, a bit cynical and worldly wise, with little professional psychobabble, one-upmanship, or discounting in his approach. He represents the potential for a perfect match in bonding for a person who has had very few positive attachment figures or trustworthy support persons in her life (Holmes, 2011). Overall, his goals and strategies closely follow Bongar and Sullivan (2013), Chiles and Strosahl's (1995), Jobes's (2006), Sommers-Flanagan, Sommers-Flanagan, and Lynch's (2001), and Joiner and associates' (2009) management plans for continuing treatment of a suicidal client:

1. Destigmatize the suicidal behavior by using an objective, personal (self), scientific approach through teaching self-monitoring and hypothesis testing of behaviors.
2. Objectify the client's suicidal behavior by using reframing and problem solving, validate the emotional pain, move suicidal behavior off center stage, and calmly discuss past, present, and likely future suicidal behavior.

3. Address the likelihood of recurrent suicide behavior by developing agreements with clients about a behavioral crisis protocol and crisis management plan.
4. Activate problem-solving behavior in the client through teaching problem-solving skills, look for spontaneous problem solving, reinforce and enhance skills, and better understand short- and long-term consequences of behavior.
5. Develop emotional pain tolerance by teaching the distinction between just having and getting rid of a feeling, understand that suicide is an emotional cop-out, differentiate between emotional involvement and suffering, impart a contextual approach to negative thoughts and feelings as opposed to a global, pervasive view of negative emotion, and learn how to distance oneself by accepting that negative emotions are merely a part of living and not catastrophic.
6. Develop specific interpersonal problem-solving skills that promote interaction rather than avoidance and isolation. Get the concept of belonging back into her life and the idea that she has something to contribute to the world rather than being a burden on it.
7. Develop intermediate-term life direction through concrete, positive, initial steps that stress the process of goal striving as opposed to the all-or-none, success-or-failure approach to reaching goals.
8. Stay calm while listening with empathy.
9. Instill hope and confidence while establishing a therapeutic alliance.
10. Establish a crisis management plan for living and a backup plan that can be employed at the first sign that suicidal ideation is emerging.
11. Find out what part the specific minicultural microsystems (family and community) (Hirsch & Cukrowicz, 2014) play in contributing to suicidal ideation and conversely what they can contribute to lethality resistance.
12. Use the ADDRESSING model of Hays (2001, 2008) and the RESPECTFUL model of D'Andrea and Daniels (2005) to understand and incorporate general cultural components along with Nobbman's (Nobbman et al., 2014) specific crisis SAFETY social locations into the suicide management plan (see Chapter 2, Culturally Effective Helping in Crisis, for these acronyms).

CW: Here are some things that I'd like you to think about doing with me. We work together on this, and sometimes other people get involved, but mainly it is you and I. First off, let's just take it as a given that you will probably consider suicide again. That is at present a fact of life. It is not forever, however. What we want to do is take away the reinforcing value of it as a short-term solution and look at the long-term benefits of doing something else. If it happens again, we don't see that as a failure but rather as something to troubleshoot and figure out what we have to do to fine-tune the plan so it is less and less likely to happen. I also want to take a look at when you are having thought disorders and mood symptoms. Those are important to know when they start in, so we can do something about them as opposed to just waiting for them to become a tidal wave of emotions and thought that wash over and drown you. The same is true of booze and drugs. If you are using those, we need to do something about that because they go hand in hand with thinking about killing yourself.

You don't get lectures from me. You choose what it is you want to do about it and I will support you. If you believe AA or other treatment programs are needed, we can work on that. We need to plan activities that substitute for those times when you might drink or get high. We want to think small, specific, and concrete on this plan and just keep it a few days ahead, so it doesn't get too big and cumbersome and hard to do. We want you to see positive, concrete changes in your life and get control back in it. When that happens, suicide behavior won't happen because you won't see the situation as unchangeable. So if I were to ask you if you were to do *something* in the next two days, and you could, would you see that as a sign of progress, and would you be able to tell me exactly what that was and why it was a sign of progress? Those are the things we are looking for in this plan. Things like decreasing social isolation, increasing pleasant and healthful activities, engaging in a work or leisure activity with someone you like. Something that is small to start with, but very concrete. Something you can hang your hat on and say, "See, Pete, that is progress!"

While this is going to be focused on changing behavior and problem solving, we need to remember that suicidal behavior is supported by emotional pain and the feeling that "I can't escape it, and it is intolerable." To that extent we are going to talk about emotions—journal emotions, tape-record emotions—and take them apart and put them back together again. We are going to listen to those emotions and work through them so they don't build up and blow up and become all-encompassing and overwhelming.

Now, if suicidal behavior shows up again, we need to plan for it and be in control. First, I'd like to write down a crisis protocol card, so that you would know exactly what to do. You would be in control of it and not vice versa. On that card we would put the resources you could use and call on, like telephone numbers, e-mail addresses, hours of operation, and so on. We also want to put two or three cues on the card. Things like "Okay, I am starting to feel anxious. I need to take a deep breath and relax, just relax." Or "Whoa! Wait a second. What am I getting into here? If my hands are sweating, that means I need to step back and take a look at this and see what the behavior is getting me." By having these cue cards, lots of times we can spot trouble and stop it before it gets started.

I am going to text you at random to see how you are doing. I may also call you if things get more complex than a text will take care of. This is not going to be "snoopervising." It is going to be concern. The calls won't be long, just brief checkups of 2 to 3 minutes. You can also text to me or call if you want. Just to keep a check on the plan. If things really go to hell in a handcart and you can't get me for some reason, you'll call the local hotline or the national line. So there are no cop-outs or excuses on this plan. You always have backup just like cops call for backup. Backup keeps you safe and alive.

We are also going to talk honestly about when you need to be admitted to a hospital. If that happens, it would be better if you decided to check yourself in for a time-out rather than having me, or somebody like me, involuntarily hospitalize you. I understand that's not real palatable, but it would be you who would be deciding and not somebody else. We are going to do the same thing with medication. What you have been on has not worked very well. I want to look into getting that reevaluated. The whole idea is for you to take more and more control over your decisions. If suicidal behavior should occur, we will see it not as a failure but as an opportunity to troubleshoot what we are doing and change things. The bottom line is that we want to neutralize the reinforcement of suicidal behavior so that it no longer has positive valence, and have other more positive, addicting behaviors and healthful living activities take its place. I will help you manage this, but it is going to be you

who will have more and more say in what is to be done. That is a big, long speech. And it sounds like a lot, but we will take it one day and one step at a time. What do you think?

Deborah: It's kinda scary, but kinda thrilling too. I don't know. I kinda feel good for the first time. Maybe like in some control, but that's scary, I've been out of it so long.

The key component in crisis management is normalizing the situation and showing the client that everything comes down to problem solving in a matter-of-fact way. Suicide behavior will invariably recur in a client like Deborah. To keep her from getting discouraged, we treat suicide as an annoying, inconvenient, but important piece of business that is not catastrophic and does not mean she is an abysmal failure. By focusing on problem solving, developing tolerance to emotional distress, changing disturbing self-images, halting impulsive behaviors, creating anger-management skills, and generating better day-to-day functioning at home and work (Michenbaum, 2005), we start to build resiliency and emotional toughness in the chronic, suicidal client. This is not an easy task, but it is one that can be done and can be successful.

CW: We are going to work out a treatment plan for living, but first thing is I'm gonna give you my business card with phone and text number and e-mail on it. That is for you to call, no ifs, ands, or buts, if things are really starting to go in the toilet. But the important thing is, it is your crisis card and on the back we are going to brainstorm and come up with five activities that when things start to go to hell in a handcart are positive actions that will break that doom-despair thinking and turn off that emotional motor running wild with affective dysregulation, so you don't need to call me but can take control of things yourself. It sounds simplistic but it works. These are positive activities that will require you to get off your rear end and go do something so that you get busy and take your mind off of those inner voices.

Of all the things that don't work in the lethality intervention business, Pete uses a couple of very simple tactics that do work—particularly for those clients who have been hospitalized: follow-up phone calls

(Vaiva et al., 2006), text messaging (Berrouiquet et al., 2014), and crisis coping cards (Jobes, 2006, pp. 80–82). The phone calls and texts provide follow-up support that says you belong and you are not a burden. The protocol card helps clients kick-start their crisis management plan, because lots of times it is difficult for clients to initiate problem-solving skills on their own. A bullet point cue card that is concrete gives them specific real-time instructions on recognizing warning signs and instituting coping skills (Brown, Wenzel, & Rudd, 2011). While there have been online services (Best et al., 2013) and phone apps developed for suicide intervention (Aguirre et al., 2013), they are so new we are not willing to make any recommendations on them as of yet, although it's fairly clear they'll start to play a larger part in prevention.

Simone, Age 36. Simone was the director of a rape crisis center in a large metropolitan area. She had established a reputation as an effective leader, public relations person, fund-raiser, recruiter, and trainer of volunteer workers for the center. She was tireless, dedicated, popular, and widely known as the leader of one of the best organized and most effective crisis agencies in the community.

Now, after 6 years as director of the center, Simone was approaching burnout. She was also experiencing grief and rage over a broken relationship. Simone was astute enough to finally recognize that she was on the verge of some kind of breakdown and was considering suicide or homicide, so she sought counseling at her agency's employee assistance program (EAP) clinic.

CW: So, Simone, from what I can glean from your intake material and from what you just said, I sense that *you* are fully aware of your vulnerability right now, but are keeping up a good front for the troops.

Simone: (*in a clinical, detached fashion*) That's right. And there's no use in my problems interfering with the work at the center. That's the most important thing. Even so, my issues are affecting me, at least. And, right now, I'm really feeling trapped; no good to them or myself either.

CW: What's the most pressing issue in your entrapment?

Simone: (*Starts to tremble and shake with a tremor in her voice.*) Well, par . . . t of the prob . . . lem is at home. I've had the rug pulled out from under me . . . literally. (*Laughs ironically.*) My partner, Rene, my soul mate for over 6 years, has taken off. It happened right under my nose. (*Hits her chest in recrimination.*) So stupid! So blind! I didn't see it! She has managed to leave me high and dry with little money and with all the bills. She took most of our furniture, much of which I bought myself. And she took both our dogs too! That cold-hearted bitch! This all happened just when we were getting ready for our one big fund-raising event of the year at the center and just as we were preparing for the accreditation site team to visit the center in a few weeks.

I'm feeling so hurt, so humiliated, and so betrayed that I am overwhelmed with anger, disappointment, and depression. I have scarcely slept or eaten for over a week. I thought our relationship was for keeps. I feel like killing her if I could get my hands on the cheating rat, but I still care about her so much! I want the miserable creep back! I'd kill that little blonde bitch if I could find out where they took off to. Her too! I'm feeling so worthless and undesirable and tired of this nightmare that sometimes I just wish I'd sleep forever.

CW: What you've just said worries me. Now I'm concerned about your safety. Are you feeling so depressed and angry that you might consider suicide—or homicide for that matter?

Simone: I don't know how I feel anymore. I guess I wouldn't go that far. Suicide, that is. I want her back more than anything. But I've even thought to myself, "If I can't have her, then nobody can." But I know that's not realistic either.

CW: Simone. Does that mean that you might consider doing harm to Rene or even to her new girlfriend? Have you thought about how you might hurt them if you were going to?

Simone: When it came right down to it, I don't think so. But I'd certainly feel like it sometimes. No, I'm just distraught and mad as hell right now. I'm really harmless, I guess. I don't know what I need. Some space, maybe. Another job, maybe. I don't know. Just some relief and love and rest and to get over this crushing pain.

Simone continues her catharsis about her romantic betrayal and the deep hurt it has caused her for another 30 minutes. The crisis worker listens intently for signs that she may have the means, access, and availability of acting on her stress and perturbation. During that time she gradually subsides emotionally and regains a good deal of her cognitive ability, to the point the crisis worker rates her affect as 7, behavior as 5, and cognition as 5, for a full scale score of 17. Her Suicide Status Form III (Jobes, 2006) is in the average to above range, with 3's and 4's and an overall rating of 3.5. Her Interpersonal Needs Questionnaire (Van Orden et al., 2008) indicates some feelings of burdensomeness and a lack of belonging in the middle range "as somewhat true." However, she does give "very true" endorsements of people who care about and support her, which is a major plus. More ominous is her Maslach Burnout Scale (Maslach & Jackson, 1981), which indicates an extremely high score on the Emotional Exhaustion and Depersonalization scale and a low score on the Personal Accomplishment scale, indicating she is well on the road to burnout (see Chapter 16, Human Services Workers in Crisis: Burnout, Vicarious Traumatization, and Compassion Fatigue).

Some safety measures will need to be put in place before she walks out the door.

CW: I believe you, but I need a no-harm contract from you, written down and signed before you leave here today. Can I trust you to do that? I also want to institute a treatment plan. Your scores on the two lethality assessments are not in the lethal range, but they are fairly high. The fact that you have considered lethal action is a warning we need to take seriously. You are a smart professional, but even smart professionals don't always know when they are in burnout and your scores on the burnout scale tell me you are, along with what you self-report.

The case of Simone provides one glimpse of a crisis worker inquiring about both the client's suicidal and homicidal potential. The worker has determined that Simone's possible threat to herself and others is in the low-to-moderate range on all dimensions of the TAF. However, she writes an anti-suicide/homicide contract with the client. There is a good deal of divisiveness in regard to "no harm" contracts (Dorrmann, 2005; Granello & Granello, 2007; Joiner et al., 2009, p. 92; Range, 2005). Chiles and Strosahl (1995, pp. 131–132) have criticized the no-harm contract because it specifies what a person *should not* do instead of *should* do, and they question its utility if a person starts to feel guilty about not abiding by it and terminates therapy as a result. Everstine (1998, p. 101) somewhat cynically believes that at least a no-harm contract is protection against a malpractice suit, which Joiner and his associates emphatically refute (2009, p. 92). To that end, the American Psychiatric Association has stated that no-suicide contracts should not be used with patients who are actively suicidal.

Reasoning for Living Contracts. Undoubtedly, what we are about to say is going to create some controversy with contemporary suicidologists. First of all "no harm" or "antisuicide" contracts signed between worker and client have absolutely no legal bearing or support if you get sued. They absolutely do not substitute for a thorough management and treatment plan (Bongar & Sullivan, 2013, p. 6), and there is little research to support their use as effective suicide deterrents (Range et al., 2002). However, Davis and associates (2002) interviewed psychiatric patients and found they viewed them as beneficial to treatment with the exception of multiple attempters who did not believe antiharm contracts were helpful. Further, the Granellos (2007, p. 239) and Jacobs (1999) believe that most clients view contracts as positive, and that they communicate a sense of caring and help build a strong therapeutic relationship.

While such contracts have no legal bearing and cannot guarantee the client's or anyone else's safety, your authors have found that clients will rarely if ever go back on their word when asked to commit to such a contract if a commitment to treatment statement is put in place with it. The contract is really a tactical move to buy time and create a bond. It gives time a chance to operate and ameliorate the hot cognitions that are driving the client's suicidal ideation. To be as emphatic as we can possibly be, this is only a technique and NOT A LEGAL FAILSAFE. It does not replace or substitute for a fulsome treatment and management plan either legally or ethically.

Following are two very different types of no-harm contracts. The first is the more standard type of contract. The stay-alive, no-harm contract is instituted and negotiated in a realistic manner. It is simple and to the point, with no vagueness or wiggle room (Hipple & Cimbolic, 1979, pp. 67–73).

Simone's Stay-Alive, Do-No-Harm Contract
I will not harm myself or anyone else for the next month while I work on my problems.

I will not attempt to kill myself or kill anyone else without talking to you first. If I cannot reach you, that is not an excuse for abrogating the contract. I will call the suicide hotline and talk to them. I will voluntarily check myself into Mid-south Hospital if all else fails.

Date_____Signature_____
Date_____Witness_____

A different, somewhat controversial contract has been developed by Everstine (1998, p. 118). Everstine believes that most suicidal/homicidal behavior is caused by our anger toward others. Therefore, his contract focuses on the significant other that the anger is directed toward, but more important, it states that the person's life is important to someone else. Everstine proposes that the self-contract be shown to the beneficiary of it, which will make the contract explicit and change the commitment to a shared one (p. 119). Such a contract fits really well with Simone's anger, so we would attempt to turn her anger and hurt into an asset though the contract.

Simone's Self-Contract

1. The person whom I hate most is: That snake who stole Rene from me. I KNOW THAT THIS HATRED COULD COST ME MY LIFE!
2. If I die, other people who will suffer are: All of the rape victims I could serve and the great staff I have built.
3. I have decided to stay alive because of: The work I do and the possibility of finding another fulfilling relationship.
4. I am also going to commit to a treatment plan that will help with not just my personal issues but professional issues as well, because I need to get a handle on these issues so I can get back to the competent and happy Simone I liked a lot before this happened.

Date _____Signature _____
Date _____Witness (Center Staff)_____

Courtois (1991) cautions that antilethality contracts must not be imposed on clients. Rather, such stay-alive contracts must be mutually agreed on by both client and crisis worker. That caution applies also to no-harm homicidal contracts.

Latasha, Age 51. Latasha was an eminent and successful elementary school principal who had devoted her life to children and the teaching profession. She was exceptionally capable, hardworking, conscientious, and efficient. She was also compulsive and a perfectionist in her work and personal habits. At age 51, Latasha faced some life and career decisions that she regarded as catastrophic: (1) She had recently had bypass heart surgery only to discover she had breast cancer, and she could not bear to think about her physician's recommendation to accept early retirement and undergo a mastectomy.

(2) She felt trapped between the two perceived unacceptable choices of continuing to hold the principalship in her debilitating physical condition, or becoming the ex-principal who had been forced into early retirement. (3) She was totally unprepared to alter her whole identity, which had included serving the students, faculty, parents, community, school, and the teaching profession. Latasha had no family. She had never married because she had devoted all her energies and talents to education. She came to her longtime friend and colleague, the Jefferson Elementary School counselor, in desperation.

Latasha: (*in tears*) It is so hopeless. Why me? Why has God forsaken me? I have been a good Christian. A good person. A good teacher. A good principal. What have I done to cause me to come to this? I don't think I can bear it. (*Sobs. Pause.*) It's so unfair. I have no choice. (*Sobs.*)

CW: (*reaches out and touches Latasha's arm*) You're feeling hurt, hopeless, and vulnerable—and you're looking for better answers and choices than you've been able to find so far. Because so far there are none.

Latasha: (*still in tears*) For the first time in my life I have no ideas, no options.

CW: I want you to know that I'm glad you have the courage to discuss it. What scares me is the desperation and danger you're feeling. You're feeling that, right now, there are no acceptable choices. That's a really tunnel vision view that's not like you at all.

Latasha: (*Still in tears. Nonverbal clues show that she is experiencing acute fear, anxiety, and hopelessness, and has almost given up.*) None. None at all. There is no future.

CW: Latasha, it sounds to me like you've considered suicide. I want to know your thinking on this subject.

Latasha: (*still in tears*) Oh God! I've thought about that a lot. Toyed with it a lot. And I'll have to admit that it becomes more appealing all the time. I have these pain pills for the cancer treatment. I could take them all at once.

CW: Do you have a plan on how to do it?

Latasha: I would put on some Brahms, get a large glass of Chablis, rip the phone line out so I wouldn't chicken out. No one would be in the office. It'd be June 9th, the day school is out, about

11 in the evening. Everything would be finished up at school, and everybody would be gone. I work late a lot on Friday so security wouldn't bother me. That would give them time to get another principal. I even made some recommendations I have written down. It would be all settled. Actually, I am feeling a little peace with myself as I talk about it. Strange!

Latasha's plan is highly lethal. She has thought carefully about it. She has the means and the method, and the plan is close to irreversible. Her contemplation that she feels at peace is another highly lethal indication that she has settled her affairs. The fact that her colleague and friend is hearing this makes the decision the school counselor is about to make terribly difficult, but it is one that her training has instilled in her. In such instances, it is critical not to match the client's anxiety level. Moralizing, placating, coercion, lecturing, or other attempts to discount the client will only exacerbate the problem (Chiles & Strosahl, 1995, pp. 113–115). The potential for countertransference to arise in such situations is high. Disregarding cries for help because of their threatening nature, denying the facts because of the personal relationship with the client, feeling a lack of expertise because the person is not an "expert" suicidologist but merely a school counselor, and being lulled into a false sense of security by who the client has been as opposed to the state of being the client is now in are serious dangers, and staying in self-control and not becoming vague and tangential are critical to the process of stopping this suicide situation (Leenaars, 1994, pp. 56–57). The *Tarasoff* ruling has just come into play here, and if the school counselor did not assess for suicide and did not take action, she could be held legally accountable as negligent (Granello & Granello, 2007, pp. 266–268).

CW: (*Very clearly, empathically, and emphatically makes the following declaratory and exclamatory statements.*) What you have just said scares the daylights out of me, Latasha. I cannot and will not let you do that! If you won't go to the superintendent with me right now and tell him you need some help, I will call him myself! If I have to, I will call the school resource police officer to contain you until we can get you to a place of safety. I believe that you have become so constricted you see no options. There are options, and you need to stay alive to find them out! I don't think you would have talked to me if you didn't believe there was

something left and you needed another view. Well, I am giving you that view. So which do you wish to do? Go with me to the superintendent or have me make the call? You could run right out of here and go swallow all those pills, I suppose, but then we would call an ambulance and they would take you out in front of the kids, which I don't think you would see as real uplifting. So you see there are some choices left, and the first one is, "Do we go now, or do I call now?"

There are no ifs, ands, or buts about this scenario, and there is no need or time to do any kind of written assessment. The TAF puts her clearly in the high 20s. The school counselor is ethically and legally bound to take action (Chiles & Strosahl, 1995, pp. 17–35; Granello & Granello, 2007, pp. 266–268; Hipple & Cimbolic, 1979, pp. 94–100; Leenaars, 1994) no matter what the client's protestations about confidentiality, broken friendship, trust, or any other pleas. The school counselor, like any other helping services professional, has a duty to disclose life-threatening behavior. That the client is her boss makes no difference. The counselor also lays a guilt trip on the principal to stop any impulsive attempts by reminding her that it would not be good form or model very good behavior to be hauled off in front of the school in an ambulance or police car. This tactic is one used by Everstine (1998, pp. 113–114) to remind clients that there are many more potential victims than their constricted view of things allows them to see. Latasha's love for the children of her school would be a powerful deterrent to doing anything foolish and precipitous.

While hospitalizing a potential suicide is no guarantee that the person will not kill herself, given the clear intent to do harm to herself, at the very least the crisis worker is removing the principal's immediate access to killing herself (Joiner et al., 2009, pp. 88–89). Whether she goes ahead in the future is another matter, but putting her in the hospital will bring the psychological perturbation she feels into full view of her oncology team who can then step in to deal with that aspect of her cancer.

While professional ethics frown on close friends or professional associates counseling one another, we believe that crisis lethality issues override that ethical standard. In the real world, this example of a close relationship between two colleagues is included here because all too often this is exactly how the discovery of a potential suicide occurs. Close friends should be aware of what they need to do and do it proactively and without guilt (see Chapter 16, the case of burnout in Dr. Jane Lee). If the worker is not sure about what to do, doesn't feel he or she has the necessary expertise, or is too close to the client personally, the watchwords are "refer if possible" and "consult"! There is no instance in a helping professional's life when consultation with a peer is more important than when dealing with lethality (Leenaars, 1994).

Older Adults

The number of older adults across the world is growing rapidly. As baby boomers age, this fact, combined with the high suicide rate in the elderly, means that a lot more service providers for geriatric populations are going to be needed, and those providers are going to need to get into the suicide prevention/intervention business (Erlangsen et al., 2011). Suicide in the elderly is treatable and preventable (LaPierre et al., 2011), yet it is one of the most neglected areas in the entire field of suicidology (Richman, 1994). It is the age of the highest incidence of suicide and, concomitantly, depression, cognitive impairment, isolation, and physical illness (Granello & Granello, 2007, pp. 75–79; Harwood & Jacoby, 2000; Heisel, 2006). Suicide among the elderly is also the most lethal, in that it uses lethal means and is well planned. It is rarely a cry for help or some spontaneous impulsive act (McGlothin, 2008, p. 124). By far and away, it is the male Caucasian in this age group that is at highest risk (Granello & Granello, 2007, p. 79). Research indicates that the percentage of failed attempted suicides decreases with age, and the percentage of completed suicides increases with age (Stone, 1999, pp. 45–50). The same is true for homicide/suicide in the elderly, which occurs at nearly double the rate of young adults. Usually the perpetrator is a male who kills his wife or other intimate and then commits suicide himself (Cohen, 2003).

The worker's assessment brings to the forefront a special consideration for dealing with older people. That assessment should include ego-weakening factors such as chronic and acute physical and mental illness, elder abuse, alcoholism, prolonged stress, failure to respond to medical treatment, and complicated/prolonged grief (for a complete description of this phenomenon see Chapter 12, Personal Loss: Bereavement and Grief). A variety of social factors, such as having fewer friends, living alone, being excluded or living on the periphery of social and family events, and being separated from the family through children leaving, all contribute to the potential for

suicide (McGlothin, 2008, p. 124–126). Psychodynamic factors most often include the stress and strain of various losses, such as the loss of a spouse, friends, work roles, and income. Chalking these risk factors up to "just growing old" is to put the elderly at risk for suicide (Richman, 1994).

Roy, Age 68. Roy had been a farmer all his life. At age 65 he went into semiretirement, turning his land, equipment, buildings, and livestock over to his two sons, who also were career farmers. One year after he began his semiretirement, his wife died. About a year later, he was despondent and could find no purpose in life, even though he was in excellent health and had the good fortune of financial independence. He has been somewhat alienated and estranged from his two sons because of disagreements and arguments over their "newfangled" farming practices that he doesn't always agree with. The foreman of the farm, Juan, came upon Roy standing on a tractor in the hall of the barn. Roy held a rope with a hangman's noose in it, and he was attaching the rope to an overhead crossbeam. Roy, thinking he was completely alone, was surprised at Juan's appearance.

Juan: What on earth are you doing there, man?

Roy: (*Almost falls off the tractor he is so startled.*) Where the hell did you come from? What are you doing here?

Juan: I'll tell you what I'm gonna do right now! I'm taking that rope away from you this minute! You're going to get in my pickup truck this minute. I'm driving you straight to the mental health center. That's where we're going. And I'll tell those boys of yours what you've tried to do too! Don't you know that it'd just kill those boys if you finished what you were planning to do? What the hell did you think you were doing, anyway?

Juan's alert and decisive actions clearly show that one does not have to be a trained human services worker to contain and control a situation in which human life is at risk. The crisis worker at the mental health center knew nothing about Roy's problems, but he recognized that a person of Roy's age, gender, life circumstance, style, and sense of private independence would rarely, if ever, present himself for counseling (Chiles & Strosahl, 1995, p. 240). In assessing Roy's responses, the worker quickly concluded that he definitely exhibited six of the lethality characteristics that Fujimura, Weis, and Cochran (1985) defined as high-risk factors: (1) the plan was definite and readily accessible, (2) the method was irreversible, (3) there was indication of sleep disruption, (4) support people would not be around, (5) rescue would be improbable, and (6) the most valued possessions had been disposed of. Also, the crisis worker knew that among men Roy's age, there are very few suicide gestures or attempts. Older men are more likely to accomplish the act than to merely attempt it (Shneidman, Farberow, & Litman, 1976; Stone, 1999). The crisis worker immediately suspected loss as a factor in Roy's decision to kill himself. Shea (2002, pp. 27–28) proposes that the elderly are subject to a series of losses, and as they suffer these losses, the potential for lethality rises. They include loss of health, mobility, cognitive functioning, ability for self-care, role with family or society, skills, job or job opportunity, means of self-support, home or cherished possessions, and loved ones including pets.

CW: Roy, lots of times men who have had lots of responsibility find that as they age, their ability to take on those responsibilities becomes more difficult. They also may not feel like they mean much to anyone because they don't have much importance or lose their capabilities—that in fact they are becoming a burden. I'm wondering how you feel about what I just said?

Roy: Well, now there's really nothing else to live for. A man's got to have some purpose. I've got nothing to go to—nothing to get up for in the morning. I just don't know what's gonna happen, and I frankly don't give a tinker's damn. My wife's dead. I can't hardly do anything anymore. The boys don't need me to run the farm, and I damn sure don't need no therapy or no shrink.

CW: (Thinking to himself: "Wow! He's not fooling! With all this intake information pointing toward suicide lethality, I don't need any more assessment data right now. I'm remembering his age, his male image, his having disposed of all his property, his wife's death—these are potent indicators—and this morning, an aborted self-hanging! It's a wonder he's even here!") Roy, what happened this morning is scary indeed. I'm setting up a complete medical evaluation for you today. I have called your family doctor. I have also called your sons, who are on their way in here right now. To say that they are very concerned is putting it mildly. I know you probably hate it that I called them, but we need to get some support systems in place and straighten some things out between you and your family.

While older clients will see their family doctors for a variety of physical complaints, they will seldom, if ever, speak about psychological duress or even consider it as a possibility! Conwell and Heisel (2006) found that up to 75% of older adults who committed suicide had been to their family doctor within the previous 30 days. All of Roy's symptoms indicate he has slid, ever so gradually, into being at least demoralized, if not depressed, by life's circumstances. Even though he would appear to have everything to live for, the loss of his wife, when they had grand plans for retirement together, the death of other close friends, and the disintegration of his social network as friends die, go to nursing homes, or move away, all have slowly led Roy to perceive life is no longer worth living.

The benign neglect and estrangement with his sons is another piece of the suicide puzzle that needs to be dealt with. While it might be readily apparent why elderly people would commit suicide if they were physically abused or neglected, more often their adult children are guilty of benign neglect or annoyance at dealing with the foibles and frailties of older people. Grown children have their own lives to lead. They may either believe that their parents have little or no need of them, or become annoyed by their increasing dependence. As a result, they tend to avoid and exclude their parents not only from activities but from decision making.

Social isolation is further compounded by the loss of friends. As a result, one of the key factors in dealing with the elderly is to set up in step-by-step fashion a new set of life supports. Reconnecting with people is paramount. If a person is unable to engage in former leisure or work activities because of a decrease in physical or mental functioning, then new activities that are socially connective and challenging to the client's physical and mental capacity need to be instituted (Richman, 1994).

While at first glance these therapeutic goals may seem a long way from suicide intervention, they are in fact directly related to it! Disengagement (a progressive withdrawal from the wider world), activity (decreased levels of physical, emotional, and cognitive activity), role exit (social usefulness diminishes as work activity ceases), and social exchange (limited ability to engage in new relationships) theories all play a significant part in whether older persons become suicidal (Granello & Granello, 2007, p. 78).

The other compounding problem is medication and neurotransmitter changes. Jacobs (1999) and Wenzel, Brown, and Beck (2009, p. 267) propose that older adults may engage in **chronic suicide** or **passive suicide** when they decide to quit taking their medication because of side effects, cost, or the notion that stopping taking it will hasten death. In many instances, forgetting to take medication, misdosage, polymedication administered by different doctors, and bad drug interactions contribute to depression. For this reason, it is paramount that primary care providers be contacted and physical and mental health issues be coordinated (McGlothin, 2008, p. 125). Combined with the effects of alcohol or illicit drugs, the potential for psychological problems becomes exponentially greater in older adults (Chiles & Strosahl, 1995, p. 243). Added to the foregoing is the mounting suspicion that serotonin levels are affected by aging. Thus, the mere fact of getting old may biologically predispose a person to suicide (Granello & Granello, 2007, p. 79; Harwood & Jacoby, 2000).

One of the primary techniques for bringing elderly clients out of suicidal ideation is to remotivate them to live. Chiles and Strosahl (1995) have developed a Reasons for Living Inventory that may be given to clients; it covers survival and coping skills, responsibility to family, child-related concerns, fear of suicide, fear of social disapproval, and moral objections. While clients may naysay many items, there are invariably some they will agree with. The crisis worker may then use these items to combat the suicidal ideation and reinforce the elderly client's desire to live.

CW: (*Two days after Roy has been medically evaluated for an antidepressant and has had an emotional but positive family session with his two sons.*) So, after talking with your boys and taking the inventory, you have said at least these items would be important: not wanting to be seen as a coward or selfish; my sons might not believe I loved them; I do want to watch my grandchildren grow up; others might think I am weak or selfish; I wouldn't want people to think I didn't have control; I have had a love of life; and there are some experiences I haven't had yet. So those are some reasons for living. I further think that the antidepressant the doctor has prescribed will kick in and you will start to feel like your old self. I want to let you know that there is a group of folks that meet at St. Mark's church that I work with. I understand that might be pretty repulsive to you, but I asked Jim Joyner if he wouldn't mind talking to you about our group. I believe you know him. In the meantime, I'd just like to make sure that if you start to feel down, you know you can call me before we meet next week. I have also done a little investigating

and I believe the agriculture teacher at the high school would be very interested in your expertise in no-till planting, the top-flight soil conservation you are known for, and working with him on the school ag program.

Roy: Hell, I guess it wouldn't kill me to listen to Jim. It's gut wrenching, but I do appreciate what you're trying to do. I particularly appreciate the head-to-head with Leroy and Ronnie. I couldn't have done that myself. I do take a lot of pride in them and the grandkids. I don't know what got into me. Hmm! The ag teacher said that? Hmmmm! Well, maybe.

CW: Roy, I want you to know that I feel good about your progress and, given I have dealt with a lot of people in a situation like yours, the prognosis for you is good. There are a couple of things I want to do, though. First off, we are going to put together a treatment plan. It isn't a forever plan, and I really believe that it's about 4 to 6 weeks' worth of work. That plan is going to involve coordinating your medication with your primary care doctor; some more meetings with your sons that I want our family therapist here at the clinic to do; getting you back socially involved again; and not just letting all that knowledge you have sit out there and ossify on 1300 County Road 1321 East. I also want you to make a contract for living with me. It is essentially a "I won't kill myself while we are working on this" contract. I believe your word is good, so I am willing to talk through it and get a handshake to seal the deal.

CW: Well you've done okay so far, so I don't see why not. You got my word. (*Leans over and shakes hands.*)

We have spoken to the controversial aspects of no-harm contracting. However, we believe as does Jacobs (1999) that when combined with a treatment plan, a no-harm contract is particularly effective with the elderly because they are excellent at keeping their word and adhering to contracts. Getting Roy involved in a support group with a former friend is a key ingredient in getting a social support group of peers in place. Social support is critical and needs to target the peer groups and pleasurable and stimulating activities with which the elderly are involved (Wenzel, Brown, & Beck, 2009, p. 278). The crisis worker is very directive and active in instigating these interventions because most people who are depressed are going to have a very difficult time initially acting on their own.

CW: (*one week later*) You have a couple of what we call "automatic thoughts" linked with some recently developed core beliefs that have helped kick this depression into high gear. Listening to you, they are very different from what you typically have thought and are really typical of the kind of thing that gets a person depressed. For instance, some of your core beliefs are "I am on a downhill slide and there's no upside. I am a burden and I can't stand that." Some of the automatic thoughts are "It's hopeless and I am helpless to do anything about it. I am a weak old man. I might as well give up. They'd be better off without me." I am going to give you a cue card with what we call positive counter injunctions on it. For instance, when you are at home sitting alone at night watching TV and all of a sudden one of those thoughts pops up, I want you to pull this card out and read it. It will say something like "That's not true! I am engaged and I am putting my knowledge back to work. I am not a hopeless piece of used junk. I have reestablished my relationships with my family and am enjoying the hell out of helping raise my grandkids. Yes! I miss Helen, but I know she'd want me involved in rearing our grandkids. I don't have a terminal case of 'I-can't-stand-it-itis.' I have withstood a lot of things in life as tough as this. It's inconvenient, all these aches and pains, but I can move and think and I intend to do so and enjoy myself, which is what Helen would want."

These are the positive automatic thoughts I want you to get habituated to. I also have another little program called a Hope Kit I want you to assemble. It consists of a container that holds mementos that will serve as reminders to live and enjoy life. It is not about getting all caught up and getting maudlin about what was, but what symbolizes you and the good life you have lived. I particularly would recommend some photographs or keepsakes of the good times and good memories. But this is definitely not about living in the past; in fact, you just might have some new mementos you want to put in there—like that Future Farmers of America hat you are wearing that I might guess you stole (*both laugh*) from the ag teacher. I want you to use that as a negative thought stopping device, so if you get down in the dumps you can pull it out and start going through it.

As simplistic as it sounds, the Hope Kit (Wenzel, Brown, & Beck, 2009) is extremely effective because it is a concrete reminder of all the positive aspects of the person's life (Jobes, 2006, p. 83). The positive counter injunctions are typical of cognitive-behavioral approaches to stop catastrophic thinking (Beck et al., 1979). Putting these on a crisis card (Rudd, Joiner, & Rajab, 2001) and placing the Hope Kit in a readily accessible place are easily implemented crisis intervention techniques designed to stop negative cognitions in their tracks.

Roy's situation is not unique to older clients. Roy is fortunate in a sense. He is not faced with debilitating financial or health problems, as many of his peers are. These problems further exacerbate the notion that suicide is a viable option. Finally, a compounding problem is that sometimes the problems the elderly face ripple over to spouses or significant other caretakers, who may also come under lethal threat.

Guidelines for Family, Friends, and Associates

The crisis worker often has to deal with gritty issues that involve family. Getting clients like Roy to come to terms with long-smoldering family issues is not easy. Urging clients to engage in new, resocializing activities is also difficult. However, if they can be done, the quality of life goes up and lethality comes down. Mishara, Houle, and Lavoie (2005) found that direct intervention with families who called into a suicide prevention line resulted in potential suicides' having less suicidal ideation, fewer suicide attempts, and fewer depressive symptoms. Family and friends reported less psychological distress and use of more positive coping mechanisms, and reported that their communication with the suicidal person was more helpful. The family, friends, and associates of the suicidal/homicidal person can do many things to contribute to prevention, especially in the area of correcting the alienated lifestyle that cuts off the at-risk person's connectedness with others. Indeed, there are parent training programs in suicide prevention such as Parents-CARE (Hooven, 2013) that are effective interventions for suicidal adolescents.

Crisis workers can serve an important educational role by helping families, friends, and associates learn about and become attuned to the risk factors, cues, and cries for help that suicidal/homicidal people generally display in some way (Hipple & Cimbolic, 1979, pp. 76–78). The crisis worker who talked with Roy's sons focused on including Roy back in their lives both as grandfather and as a wise consultant whose knowledge and skill of farming can complement their own. Families can and should be an integral part of treatment and should be fully informed about the positive role (along with the limits) they can play (Rudd, Joiner, & Rajab, 2001, p. 105). Perhaps the most important component of family involvement is helping the whole family system become aware of how the suicidal member's feelings and actions influence the family and how they are reciprocally influenced by the family members' feelings (Softas-Nall & Francis, 1998, p. 227). To that end, dealing with past issues and recriminations is out of bounds. At least until the suicidal events are resolved, bringing up old psychological baggage does little good. Emphasis is on the present and future and developing new behavioral contracts for positive change in the total family constellation (McLean & Taylor, 1994).

Family, friends, and associates who attend to the many cues that have been described in this chapter can help the suicidal/homicidal person by genuinely and assertively confronting the lethal issues. For instance, they can watch for the lethal person's preoccupation with an anniversary date of a significant loss, such as the death of a loved one, or the resulting depression that a job loss or academic failure generates and intervene in a directive manner if needed (McLean & Taylor, 1994). Significant others can help the survivors cope with suicide/homicide after it happens. On the other hand, if fractures in the family system are severe, discretion may be the better part of valor. Pushing family members together who have long-standing agendas of anger and recrimination is about the last thing that needs to happen.

When family or other bereaved groups cannot get past the shock of the death and/or exhibit excessive blame or guilt, crisis workers can meet with them and help them deal with their grief (Shneidman, 1975). On a final note, McGlothin (2008, p. 137) believes that all of the family needs to be checked out for suicidal/homicidal ideation because in many families suicide/homicide and violence are operational ways to settle problems.

Some Don'ts and a Few Dos. A number of authors (Bongar & Sullivan, 2013; Hipple, 1985; Jobes, 2006; Kirk, 1993; Kleespies, 2014; Michel, 2011; Neimeyer & Pfeiffer, 1994; Shea, 2002) have identified some don'ts and dos of suicide management that serve to supplement the intervention considerations already listed. Our comments are added to each point **LO10**

in the following list. These don'ts and dos apply to almost anyone you work with who is suicidal. It's a long list and you don't need to memorize it, but you do need to remember where it is and check it out—particularly when you get those big furry moths flapping around in your stomach making you feel really queasy when you have a hot client in front of you.

1. Don't lecture, blame, give advice, judge, or preach to clients. If that had worked, they wouldn't be with you now.
2. Don't criticize clients or their choices or behaviors. Do remember that as "crazy" and "nuts" as it seems, the lethal behavior makes perfect sense to the client.
3. Don't debate the pros and cons of suicide. Philosophy has nothing to do with what is going on in a lethality case.
4. Don't be misled by the client's telling you the crisis is past. Never just take the client's word that things are "settled" and "okay now." Do keep checking!
5. Don't deny the client's suicidal ideas. Ideation leads to action. If a person says he or she has lethal intent, even in a joking or offhand way, check it out.
6. Don't try to challenge for shock effects. This is not "Scared Straight" therapy. Challenges may be acted on to show you the client means business.
7. Don't leave the client isolated, unobserved, and disconnected. Provision needs to be made for keeping the client safe and secure, and that means somebody needs to monitor him or her.
8. Don't diagnose and analyze behavior or confront the client with interpretations during the acute phase. Psychodynamic interpretations involving "why" are unimportant at this point.
9. Don't be passive. Suicides are high on the triage scale. You must become active and directive.
10. Don't overreact. Suicidal/homicidal behavior is scary, but it is behavior that can be handled. Do stay calm and keep your voice well modulated. That's what this book and chapter are about. You don't have to be a superhero to do this stuff. Just keep calm and practice what you have learned!
11. Don't keep the client's suicidal risk a secret (be trapped in the confidentiality issue) or worry about "snitching" on the client. Whether you are a bosom friend or a professional, this is life-threatening behavior. You do need to tell someone in authority who can keep the client safe.

12. Don't get sidetracked on extraneous or external issues or persons. Forget about all the other real and imagined ills and issues. Do deal with the lethality in a straightforward, businesslike manner. The other stuff can and should be acknowledged as important to the person, but that's it.

13. Don't glamorize, martyrize, glorify, heroize, or deify suicidal behavior in others, past or present. If you want somebody to kill himself or herself or copycat a friend or idol, this is an excellent way to have that happen.

14. Don't become defensive or avoid strong feelings. The possibility for transference is great in lethal behavior. While lethal feelings are scary, they are exactly what need to be discussed and uncovered.

15. Don't hide behind pseudoprofessionalism and clinical objectivity as a way of distancing yourself psychologically from painful and scary material. What you are actually trying to do is insulate yourself from the brutal reality of what is going on, and that is not helpful. You must get into the game and build the relationship.

16. Don't fail to identify the precipitating event. Find what specifically caused the client to decide to become lethal. Global reasons are not helpful. Do identify the reason the client got here today, so action plans can be generated to deal with it.

17. Don't terminate the intervention without obtaining some level of positive commitment (you may get sued if you don't). Even if the person later goes ahead and kills himself or herself or somebody else, try as hard as you can to get a commitment from the client to do no harm.

18. Don't forget to follow up (you may get sued if you don't). Do keep track of lethal people until the crisis has passed.

19. Don't forget to document and report (you may get sued if you don't). Do keep good records of your assessment of the client and when and what you did with your recommendations.

20. Don't be so embarrassed or vain that you don't consult (you may get sued if you don't). Substantiation by another professional in a difficult case makes good therapeutic and legal sense.

21. Don't fail to make yourself available and accessible (you may get sued if you don't). If you come in contact with a suicidal/homicidal client, you must stay the course, be available, and have backup support.

22. Do take your time. Don't be hurried. Things may be frantic and frenetic in the immediate environment, but you are the rock in the middle of the maelstrom. You have time!

23. Do watch for countertransference. Shea (2002, p. 122) poses two questions to keep you grounded: "What am I feeling right now?" and "Is there any part of me that doesn't want to hear the truth right now?" Those are caution lights and reality checks on your potential loss of objectivity and treatment goals. Do get supervision.

24. Don't be blackmailed into caving in to client demands. Do set limits and keep them. Clients with borderline personality disorder are especially adept at treatment blackmail. For example, keeping one's guns isn't an option with a highly suicidal client. Refusal to comply with treatment is not an option, nor is maintaining the right to kill oneself during treatment. Refusal to treat this client is not abandonment, but good clinical judgment.

25. Don't fail to take adequate protective measures. If you are working with an outpatient client who owns guns, do get them in safe keeping. You may get sued if you don't. If you are working in an inpatient setting with a suicidal person, follow the institution's protocol to the t crossed and i dotted. The institution may still get sued but you likely won't.

The Psychological Autopsy

Shneidman (1987) developed the psychological autopsy technique for the purpose of compiling detailed postmortem mental histories following suicides or deaths that were equivocal (not sure of cause). Psychological autopsies involve examination of personal demographics such as work, criminal, school, and medical records along with in-depth interviews of friends, relatives, coworkers, and health care professionals to attempt to ascertain the suicide's intent. They also attempt to determine what the trigger events were that might have contributed to the suicide. For instance, normative data from psychological autopsies indicate that an average of 40% of suicides had a medical illness and that HIV/AIDS and cancer are two particular illnesses that increase suicidal risk (Kleepies, Hough, & Romeo, 2009). Psychological autopsies also attempt to determine what, if any, psychopathology was present in completed suicides. For example, it appears that between 30% and 40% of suicides may meet criteria for personality disorders. Psychological autopsies have determined that besides the big five psychiatric diagnoses of major depressive, bipolar, anorexia nervosa, schizophrenia, and borderline personality disorder that are precursors to suicide (Joiner et al., 2009), schizoid and antisocial personality disorder also have strong associations with suicidal behavior (Duberstein & Witte, 2009). The autopsy was initially conceived by Schneidman to help clinicians become more cognizant of the warning signs of suicide in cases where intent, reason, and motivation are muddled and unclear.

The following questions seek to flesh out the psychological profile of the decedent's death—indeed, to determine first and foremost whether it was a suicide (Shneidman, 1999d). These questions are posed in an empathic manner to the survivors: Why did the person do it? How did he or she do it? When? That is, why at that particular time? What is the most probable mode of death? Besides details of the death itself, the autopsy seeks to determine the person's personality and lifestyle, typical patterns of reactions to stress, emotional upsets, and periods of disequilibrium, particularly in the recent past. What role did alcohol and/or drugs play in the person's life? What was the nature of his or her interpersonal relationships? What were the person's fantasies, dreams, thoughts, premonitions, or fears relating to death, accident, or suicide? What changes, if any, occurred in the person's habits, hobbies, eating, sexual relations, and other life routines? Information is garnered regarding the person's lifestyle, such as mood up- or downswings, successes, and plans for the future. Not only can these questions help determine whether the death was a suicide, they can also help determine how staff who may have been involved with the client can better prevent suicides (Shneidman, 1999d).

As with many important discoveries, Shneidman (1971) found a serendipitous function of the psychological autopsy. By being empathic and supportive to the survivors in order to elicit more information, the autopsy was therapeutic for the survivors. Thus, the psychological autopsy (Shneidman, 1987) may not only provide information that helps prevent future suicides, but may also represent a postvention method of helping survivors either gain a better understanding of why it happened or feel less guilt and responsibility for the deceased's demise. Indeed, what the psychological autopsy spawned was a variety of postvention strategies to help survivors of a suicide.

Postvention

Emotional Toll. The "real victim" of suicide is [LO12] said to be not the body in the coffin but the family

and other loved ones (Hansen & Frantz, 1984, p. 36). Osterweis, Solomon, and Green (1984) report that survivors of the death of a loved one by suicide are thought to be more vulnerable to physical and mental health problems than are grievers from other causes of death (p. 87). The average suicide leaves 6 to 10 survivors who experience extreme grief (Mitchell et al., 2004). Shneidman (2001, p. 154) puts it eloquently when he says that the person who commits suicide puts his psychological skeleton in the survivors' emotional closet. If that is true, then in the United States alone, with about 4 million survivors, the closet is chock-full of skeletons.

Survivors are faced with guilt, shock, trauma from body discovery, police interrogation, legal issues, shame, sleep difficulties, concentration problems, denial, family relationship problems, and complicated long-term grief (Granello & Granello, 2007, pp. 281–282). Survivors may also feel double binds of guilt and anger—guilty that they didn't do enough to stop the suicide, and angry that now they are left behind having to raise children alone, struggle with debts, and so on, while the suicide skipped out on his or her responsibilities (Shea, 2002, p. 95).

Survivors of suicidal people generally receive less sympathy and encounter more social isolation, negative cultural messages, and stigmatization than do other bereaved individuals (Moore & Freeman, 1995). Most of us have lost loved ones and been to funerals; we know the routine. Suicide survivors have no such formal guidelines. Survivors frequently sense that they are the objects of gossip and criticism, and they may be right. Bereaved loved ones often blame themselves for the suicide, and more than in any other form of loss, they tend to perceive that they are being neglected by others. Therefore, the loss of a loved one by suicide is doubly stressful (Edelstein, 1984, p. 21; Rando, 1984, p. 150). Grieving loved ones left behind by a suicide may refer to themselves as "victims" because, in addition to the emotional stress of the death itself, the survivors must also deal with burdens such as social stigma, guilt, blame, a search for the cause or meaning, unfinished business, and perceived rejection wrought by the suicide (Rando, 1984, pp. 151–152).

Child Survivors. The potential for children whose parents have committed suicide to suffer severe pathological problems is extremely high (Cain & Fast, 1966; Sethi & Bhargava, 2003). Psychosomatic disorder, learning disabilities, obesity, running away, tics, delinquency, sleepwalking, fire setting, encopresis, along with social adjustment problems, depression, and PTSD symptoms fly out of a Pandora's box of evil outcomes of a parental suicide. Intervention is particularly important in dealing with children coping with a parent's suicide, who may exhibit shame, denial, and concealment and experience ostracism by their peers. If intervention does not occur, these children may experience a host of feelings that lead them to believe they are bound to suffer the same fate as their parent. Feelings of guilt in the child and distortion in communication between adults and children are constant companions. To neglect such children and assume they'll get over it is an extreme therapeutic error. School counselors, school social workers, and school psychologists are particularly critical in understanding what the suicide of a parent may mean to a child and need to be able to intervene with them and their peers. This kind of traumatic event can cause complicated traumatic grief in children and is absolutely within the purview of crisis workers who operate in school buildings (Cohen & Mannarino, 2011; Webb, 2011).

Parent Survivors. Parents whose children commit suicide are also likely to suffer severe psychological repercussions as they attempt to come to terms with their loss. Herzog and Resnik (1967) and Lester (2004) have found that the immediate parental response to a child's suicide tends to be hostility toward others, denial of the suicide, and rationalization of the death as accidental. Guilt and depression soon follow, and the likelihood of severe and continuing dysfunction with the surviving family members grows. Getting both children and parents into support groups and keeping them from becoming more isolated with their negative feelings are critical.

Support Groups. Crisis workers need to be aware of local services that provide such group support. Many organizations, school systems, and communities fail to develop postvention plans for suicide/homicide loss, with the result that survivors have psychological issues that affect those systems (Berkowitz et al., 2011). Baton Rouge, Louisiana, has a model comprehensive program that provides immediate referral for all survivors of suicides from the local coroner. It utilizes an Active Postvention Model that provides trained crisis workers who specialize in the immediate aftermath of a suicide to provide support services to survivors. It provides group support and 24-hour access to services (Campbell, 2011). Communities could not do better than to adopt this model. The

following model is fairly representative of what these support groups look like.

Hatton and Valente (1984) conducted a supportive group therapy experience for parents who sought relief from painful grief after the suicide of a child. They held 10 meetings with parents who felt shame, guilt, self-doubt, confusion, and isolation. The first three meetings were spent sharing and ventilating feelings. Four reactions surfaced. First, there was a prohibition of mourning by the parents' social network. The outside world was seen as hostile and incapable of understanding their grief. Second, former coping mechanisms for dealing with grief were useless. Attempting to share the pain even with spouses was impeded by the fear of burdening or depressing the person even further. Third, extreme isolation was felt both from friends and from family. Fourth, parents developed an identity crisis and questioned their ability to parent and maintain self-control.

The next five meetings were spent doing grief work. Sessions focused on giving support and reassurance, looking at adaptive and maladaptive coping mechanisms, gaining a new perspective on the loss, considering the effect of the suicide on their other children, and dealing with the anger they felt at society and the bureaucratic bumbling of authorities. The last 2 weeks were spent reminiscing about the good times, becoming more future oriented, letting go of anger, and sadness at termination of the group.

Transcrisis Postvention. Resnik (1969) proposes that crisis intervention should occur in three phases. First is **resuscitation**. Within 24 hours, the crisis worker needs to make a supportive visit to assist the survivors in dealing with their initial shock, grief, anger, and most likely self-recrimination, guilt, and blame. This phase may last for several weeks. Survivors should be encouraged to talk about the suicide and experience the full range of feelings associated with it, without feeling ashamed or embarrassed to do so, and tell the story as many times as it needs to be told (Granello & Granello, 2007, p. 283). Phase two involves **resynthesis**. The crisis worker helps the survivors learn new ways of coping with their loss and prevents the development of pathological family responding. Finding a therapist who is experienced with grief work or a self-help group is critical during this time, and this most assuredly holds for children. This second phase may last for several months. The third phase is **renewal**. The crisis worker helps the family reformulate itself in a context of growth and movement beyond the suicide. This process may occur up to a year after the suicide and is usually terminated on the first anniversary of the suicide. What Resnick proposes in these chronological phases is a vivid example of dealing with transcrisis states.

The Case of Leah. Leah Nichols, 54-year-old manager of a branch bank, returned home from work Friday evening and discovered her 24-year-old son, Ronnie, dead from a gunshot wound. Ronnie had left a suicide note where he had apparently killed himself in his bedroom. Leah's husband, a college professor, had been dead (of heart failure) about a year, and she and Ronnie lived in the family home. Ronnie's siblings, Brenda, age 31, Richard, age 27, and Larry, age 22, were married and living in cities scattered about the region. Ronnie was a warm, friendly, loving, and lovable person who had never married or dated much. He was very sensitive and was given to mood swings from deep depression to euphoria. He had expressed suicidal ideation since his primary school years and had been under psychiatric care since his adolescent years. But in recent months he had appeared to be gaining in maturity and had gotten off his medication.

Leah's grief had moved progressively toward becoming complicated (see Chapter 12, Personal Loss: Bereavement and Grief, for a complete description of this problem), but she felt she should set a controlled and circumspect image for the three siblings and other friends and relatives. After being admitted to the emergency room and spending 3 days in the hospital for nervous exhaustion, she was referred to the crisis worker.

The following intervention strategy was provided for Leah during the days and weeks immediately following Ronnie's suicide and represents one component of Resnik's (1969) resynthesis phase. The individual follow-up grief work dealt with many issues that are common in suicide work: denial, guilt, bargaining, and depression. The issue of Leah's martyrdom came out during an individual session approximately 3 weeks after Ronnie's funeral.

Leah: My kids think I'm holding back. They say I'm too stoic, too unaffected, or too aloof. They think my lack of showing emotions is not normal—not healthy.

CW: What do you think?

Leah: I don't know. I guess I believe somebody has to keep the lid on—keep a steady head during all this. I haven't wanted to trouble any of them with my problems. Their daddy's death, then Ronnie's. They've had enough without me dumping my grief on them.

CW: What are you saying, at a deep level, below the surface, right now?

Leah: I guess I am saying I'm hurting like hell. I guess my actions have looked pretty cold and strange to them. I guess I've been trying to protect them—to keep them from hurting.

CW: What will it do for you to keep them from hurting?

Leah: Make me a martyr, I guess. I don't know what else it could be.

CW: I wonder if it could keep you from the hurt and anger you have pushed back?

Leah: (*Starts sobbing.*) I . . . I . . . guess . . . I feel so helpless and always have had that feeling for that poor little boy I could not help despite everything I did. (*Weeps while the crisis worker moves over and holds and comforts her.*)

The crisis worker does not attempt to steer Leah to any particular conclusion. Rather, the questioning strategy—a combination of techniques from reality therapy, rational-emotive behavior therapy, and Gestalt therapy—is used to help Leah gain conscious contact with her own inner world. This crisis intervention technique would be ineffective if the worker were trying to analyze or identify pathology in Leah's behavior. Diagnosing, prescribing a cure, and managing Leah's recovery for her would have also been inappropriate. Leah needs to move forward at her own speed and pace to Resnik's (1969) renewal phase.

The Case of Handley. Adults who have been traumatized by the suicide of a close associate, coworker, or friend can profit as well. A brief example of one type of group intervention/psychological autopsy illustrates this point.

Handley, age 27, killed himself by carbon monoxide poisoning. He had had a chaotic and turbulent life, punctuated by a destabilized family, drug and alcohol addiction, and numerous suicide attempts. Despite all his problems, he was a friendly, energetic, charismatic person who worked in a restaurant supply business. He left behind several friends and coworkers who admired him and were surprised at his suicide, even though some of them were aware of his dilemmas and his occasional suicidal ideations.

Several days after Handley's funeral, his coworkers were still in acute grief. Some were emotionally stuck, asking themselves and each other, "Why?" Some were feeling guilty because they did not pick up on the cues and do something to save Handley. The following description is a modified psychological autopsy/group processing that we have developed to aid coworkers affected by a colleague's suicide. It is a variation of a grief debriefing procedure (Mitchell & Wesner, 2011) that is designed to help people share feelings, thoughts, and behaviors both of the deceased's actions and their own responses.

Handley's modified psychological autopsy was convened by a crisis interventionist who met with the group of bereaved coworkers and led them through the following steps:

1. *Introduction.* The worker made a brief introduction, outlining the purposes and structure of the meeting.
2. *Constructing the "why."* The crisis worker helped the group piece together the cues, clues, and signs (pooled from the knowledge contained within the group) that made Handley's suicide more understandable (from Handley's point of view).
3. *Commemorating the positive traits and accomplishments.* The group made a list of Handley's attributes and achievements that they particularly wanted to highlight and remember.
4. *Saying good-bye.* During the second round, each coworker was given an opportunity to take care of unfinished business with Handley and to verbally say good-bye using the "empty chair" strategy. Some members expressed anger as well as love. This was a very emotional and cathartic experience for everyone.
5. *Turning loose.* The crisis worker summarized the material from the preceding three steps and led the group in brainstorming and making another list, gleaned from Handley's case, to help them learn how to detect and prevent future suicides. Further, it allowed the group to turn loose the idea that they might have been in any way responsible or negligent in Handley's death.
6. *Absolving guilt.* The crisis worker obtained a commitment from a member of the group to edit and distribute the psychological autopsy lists to every member of the group. Last, the crisis worker made a statement that essentially (a) expressed appreciation for the group's participation, (b) assured the members that they were not responsible for Handley's death, and (c) gave the

group permission to end the acute grieving phase and enter the long-term period of grief.

The crisis worker tapped into the power and cohesiveness of the group to provide stability and equilibrium for individual members. A variation of this group technique would be appropriate with a family, a fraternal group, the employees in a workplace, a school group, or a church group (any group dealing with a loss-related crisis).

Comans and associates (2013) report on a community intervention program in Australia, for people who are bereaved and suffering grief from a suicide. Called the Stand By service, they found that through direct bereavement and grief intervention that health outcomes, quality adjusted additional years of life, time off of work, and medical costs were all positively affected by this community service.

Finally where specialized support groups are not available, the Samaritans are available 24/7. The Samaritans originated in England but now operate in the United States and Australia. While specifically focused on suicide and grieving, they are an eclectic crisis line manned by highly trained volunteers (Hurtig, Bullit, & Kates, 2011). People feeling lonely and hopeless are their stock-in-trade (Jordan & McIntosh, 2011). You can reach them by telephone, chat, or text. Just search "Samaritans crisis line" to get one near you.

Losing a Client to Suicide

Crisis intervention does not always work. **LO13** Client incidence of suicide among psychologists, social workers, and counselors ranges from 22% to 33% (Kleespies & Ponce, 2009). Sometimes even the most skilled professionals and crisis workers cannot succeed. We must remember that if people really intend to kill themselves, despite our best efforts to intervene, they can manage to accomplish the task. The following suggestions have been provided to help workers cope with the loss of clients (Farberow, 2001; Sommers-Flanagan, Sommers-Flanagan, & Lynch, 2001).

Guided debriefings by experts are necessary for workers who have lost a client. Having a client commit suicide or homicide is one of the most stressful events that can occur in the experience of a crisis worker. The guilt, recrimination, rumination, and perseveration may lead to constant second-guessing. The "what ifs," "shoulds," "oughts," and "might have beens" all lead to feelings of owning responsibility. If a client commits suicide or homicide, a psychological autopsy, or debriefing (see the section on critical incident stress debriefing in Chapter 17, Disaster Response), and supervision should be mandatory for the worker.

Indeed, the impact of having failed to save a person who was a client, or a victim of the client, can be overwhelming and can cause the crisis worker to experience what is called *vicarious traumatization* (see the section on vicarious traumatization in Chapter 16, Human Services Workers in Crisis: Burnout, Vicarious Traumatization, and Compassion Fatigue). Such cases call for the utmost of professional expertise to provide intentional and intensive debriefing of the traumatized workers. It is absolutely essential that such workers realistically examine (under the guidance of outside consultants) what happened, learn from the event, and absolve themselves from guilt and responsibility for the regrettable loss.

SUMMARY

The phenomenon of suicide is democratic in that it affects every segment of society, and it is everybody's business. Suicide and homicide as expressive problem-solving acts have many similarities and parallels in terms of motive, risk, and assessment of lethality. Suicide is a serious problem that is on the rise among all groups, especially youth, but the highest-risk group is, and has remained for many years, Caucasian males over 65. Researchers find few common denominators in their quest to identify suicide/homicide risk types and to predict and prevent suicide/homicide. The two oldest and most prevalent theories of suicide are Freud's notion that suicidal behavior is rage at others turned inward and Durkheim's concept that suicide is tied closely to social pressures and influences. Other theories that have emerged more recently see the basis or cause of suicide as largely accidental, a method of escape, a pervasive sense of hopelessness, interactional and revenge driven, biochemically induced, chaotic, interpersonal, or completely rational in the face of unendurable pain or suffering.

The dynamics of suicide are important because crisis workers who deal with suicidal clients need to know that there are several different types and characteristics of suicide. There are many reasons why people kill or attempt to kill themselves, and there are differing moral and cultural points of view about suicide among various social, ethnic, and age groups. Among the many myths of suicide are two that are particularly salient in impeding crisis work: (1) discussing suicide will cause a person to think about doing it or to act upon it, and (2) people who threaten suicide don't do it. Crisis workers are advised to directly question clients who display any suicidal or homicidal ideation.

Many risk factors have been identified that serve as danger signals and help to determine levels of lethality.

Some of the highest risks are the presence of serious intent, a history of prior attempts, and evidence of a specific and lethal plan. These risk factors are important criteria for both assessing and acting in the realm of suicide intervention. Workers who are sensitized to the dynamics find that suicidal people often send out subtle but definite clues and/or cries for help.

Intervention strategies show how crisis workers can be appropriately assertive, directive, and forceful. In work with suicidal clients, workers should not be passive. In suicide intervention, workers must consider many environmental and social factors in addition to attending to client safety (for example, age, gender, social status, availability of supports from family and friends, and community attitudes surrounding the person at risk). Counseling around the issue of suicide/homicide also involves facilitating the grief and healing of clients who are survivors, as well as the care and debriefing of crisis workers who experience the loss of clients to suicide or homicide. Finally, the psychological autopsy is a primary way of both learning how to prevent suicides and alleviating the guilt and shame of survivors.

If you or someone you know is in a bind and you or they can't get through on your local hotline and can't get help with feelings of lethality, the national suicide hotline is open 24/7 at 1-800-SUICIDE. Across the world, the Samaritans in England answer e-mails at jo@samaritans.org. To find help in a language other than English, e-mail www.befrienders.org.

Visit CengageBrain.com for a variety of study tools and useful resources such as video examples, case studies, interactive exercises, flashcards, and quizzes.

Sexual Assault

9

LEARNING OBJECTIVES

After studying this chapter, you should be able to:

1. Understand the variability in the wide range of statistics reported for various types of sexual assault.
2. Know the different definitions of rape/sexual assault and understand the reasons for the intensity of the traumatic wake of a sexual assault.
3. Understand the dynamics of rape.
4. Know the myths about rape.
5. Understand the dynamics of date and acquaintance rape.
6. Understand intervention strategies for rape.
7. Understand how secondary victimization is prevented.
8. Understand the variety of responses sexual assault survivors have.
9. Understand posttraumatic sexual assault behavior.
10. Understand how to treat sexual assault survivors who have PTSD.
11. Understand the dynamics of adult survivors of childhood sexual abuse.
12. Understand the "false memories" controversy.
13. Understand treatment strategies for adult survivors with PTSD.
14. Understand the need for support groups for adult survivors of childhood sexual abuse.
15. Understand the dynamics of childhood sexual abuse.
16. Understand the dynamics of family systems in childhood sexual abuse.
17. Understand the phases of child sexual abuse.
18. Understand how intervention strategies with sexually abused children occur.
19. Understand how a child sexual perpetrator is prosecuted.
20. Understand the traumatic aftermath of child sexual abuse and how it is treated.

The Scope of the Problem

Be forewarned: The statistics in this chapter **LO1** are some of the most controversial and error prone reported in this book! Given the emotional volatility and cultural artifacts that undergird sexual assault, after reading this chapter we hope you'll understand why these statistics may be so error prone. The benchmark National Violence Against Women Survey (National Institute of Justice and Centers for Disease Control, 1998) conducted in 1997 in the United States found that 1 in 6 U.S. women and 1 in 33 U.S. men had experienced an attempted or completed rape as a child and/or as an adult, using a definition of rape that includes forced vaginal, oral, and anal sex. By this writing in 2015, those grime figures have decreased . . . some. The *National Intimate Partner and Sexual Violence Survey: 2010 Summary* reported that 1 in 5 women and 1 in 71 men will be raped (Black et al., 2011). Those statistics are probably very conservative, with other studies ranging from 10% to 15% of American men and 15% to 33% of American women (Lew, 2004; Rowan, 2006).

Contrary to popular myth, these acts were not all committed by sexual perverts and deviants lurking in big-city dark alleys and nabbing unsuspecting young schoolgirls as they walked by. Nearly 1 in 10 women has been raped by an intimate partner in her lifetime (Breiding, Chen, & Black, 2014). In 2002, 3 out of 5 sexual assault victims stated that the offender was an intimate, relative, friend, or acquaintance (U.S. Department of Justice, 2003). It should not be surprising, then, that rape, sexual assault, and child sexual abuse demographics tend to mimic domestic violence statistics. In short, it's an odds-on favorite that someone who knows you will be the one who sexually assaults you (Hassan et al., 2015; Miller, Cohen, & Wiersema, 1996). What research is starting to find out in regard to intimate sexual assault is not just the severity and duration of the sexual abuse as the root cause of the trauma but the profound sense of betrayal by someone who should have never, ever done something as anathematic as a caregiver (O'Rinn et al., 2013).

This chapter will deal mainly with adult males as perpetrators and women or children as their victims. However, no one should labor under the delusion that adult males are not raped (and this excludes the stereotypes of prison sex or gay sex) (Davis, 2002; Gartner, 2005; Isley & Gehrenbeck-Shim, 1997; Mezey & King, 1998; Scarce, 1997), nor should you believe that women are not capable of some of the most heinous sexual and physical abuse imaginable upon their own children, whether boys or girls (Allen, 1991; Elliot, 1994; Gartner, 2005; Holmes, Holmes, & Unholz, 1993; Lew, 2004; Rosencrans, 1997; U.S. Department of Justice, 2000). Although the majority of assaults are perpetrated on children and females under age 25, sexual assault survivors have been identified among males and females from every segment of the population—children, adolescents, adults, and older adults (U.S. Department of Justice, 1998). An estimated 10% to 20% of men are sexually assaulted sometime in their lives (U.S. Department of Justice, 2000). Nor does the United States have a corner on either the rape or child abuse markets (Chen, Dunne, & Wang, 2003; Lalor & McElvaney, 2010; Sanday, 1998; Schwartz-Kenney, McCauley, & Epstein, 2001; Tomoko et al., 2002). About 103,000 children are reported as having been sexually abused in the United States out of 903,000 child maltreatment cases. The true figure is estimated to be between 250,000 and 350,000 (U.S. Department of Health and Human Services, 1997), and Finkelhor and his associates (2005) found in their national survey that 1 in 12 children they surveyed had been sexually victimized in the study year alone! Statistics in nations of Asia, Africa, and Latin America are equally grim (Chen, Dunne, & Wang, 2003; Schwartz-Kenney, McCauley, & Epstein, 2001), and in some cases horrifically worse: Children are sold into thralldom as child prostitutes or indentured servants by their poverty-stricken parents (Rowan, 2006).

Underreporting

The vast majority of crime survey reports do not report sexual abuse of children under the age of 12, yet we certainly see many of those children turnstiling through local child protection centers (Benedict, 1985, pp. 186–192; Brownmiller, 1975, p. 175). The literature consistently estimates that 50% to 90% of all rapes or attempted rapes go unreported. Most instances of incest and molestation are never reported. Further, date rapes and even stranger rapes are not reported out of shame, humiliation, guilt, cultural taboos, and the very real fear of secondary victimization at the hands of medical and legal authorities (Cole, 2006; Matsakis, 2003; Weiss, 2010). Beyond the sensationalism of religious cults that practice polygamy with young children (Bottoms et al., 2003) and Catholic priests who sexually abuse young parishioners (McGlone, 2003), it should be very clear that the kinds of sexual assaults this chapter covers are common, are underreported, and the traumatic wake they spread encompasses millions of people.

David Lisek has done seminal research in this area (Lisek & Miller, 2002; Lisek & Roth, 1988). Lisek reports that in 1998 there were 1,687 reported rapes and 526 arrests made in metro Boston. If one multiplies the prevalence number from the National Violence Against Women study (Tjaden & Thoennes, 2000), the true rape incidence for the 1.75 million women living in the Boston metro area was 15,225 rapes. This disparity suggests that only 1 in 9 rapes is actually reported.

Abundant evidence suggests that crises resulting from sexual abuse and rape are more intense and differ in nature, intensity, and extent from other forms of crisis (Burgess & Holmstrom, 1985; Finkelhor, 1979, 1984, 1987; Gartner, 2005; Lew, 2004; Matsakis, 2003; Rowan, 2006; Williams & Holmes, 1981). In fact, the psychological traumatic wake of rape both in childhood and adulthood marks it as probably second only to prolonged combat in potential for PTSD, and many of the transcrisis rape treatment approaches closely parallel those of standard PTSD treatment (Cloitre & Rosenberg, 2006; Frazier et al., 2001).

Defining Rape: The Unique Situation of Sexual Abuse/Rape Survivors

There are many definitions of rape. Some **LO2** are based on legal constructs; some are derived from other sources. Brownmiller (1975) distinguishes between most legal definitions and what she refers to as a woman's definition of rape. She sees the legal definition of rape as "the forcible perpetration of an act of sexual intercourse on the body of a woman not one's wife" (p. 380) as much too narrow and protective of male supremacy. Brownmiller's preferred definition from a woman's perspective is that rape is "a sexual invasion of the body by force, an incursion into the private, personal inner space without consent—in short, an internal assault from one of several avenues and by one of several methods [that] constitutes a deliberate violation of emotional, physical, and rational integrity and is a hostile, degrading act of violence" (p. 376). That definition appears to encompass the whole scope of rape, as well as other forms of sexual abuse/misuse/harassment. For the purposes of this chapter, your authors will use Koss and Achilles' (2008) definition of **rape** as an unwanted act of oral, vaginal, or anal penetration committed though the use of force, threat of force, or when incapacitated; **sexual assault** refers to a broader range of sexual criminal offenses such as sexual battery and sexual coercion up to and including rape (U.S. Department of Education, 2011).

The Dynamics of Rape

The etiology of rape has roots deeply embedded in the psychosocial and cultural fabric of the particular society in which it occurs (Brownmiller, 1975; Donat & D'Emilio, 1998; Eisler, 1987–1995; Ullman, 1996a, 1996b). According to Brownmiller (1975) and Eisler (1987–1995), the cultural mechanism of male dominance constitutes the driving force in rape in all cultures. The psychosocial, cultural, and personal attitudes and responses of both males and females are important dynamics in considering the phenomenon of rape (Benedict, 1985; Williams & Holmes, 1981).

Social/Cultural Factors

Baron and Straus (1989) characterize rape as a social phenomenon and theorize four different causes: gender inequality, pornography, social disorganization, and legitimization of violence. **Gender inequality** refers to the economic, political, and legal status of women in comparison to men. **Pornography** reduces women to sex objects, promotes male dominance, and encourages or condones sexual violence against women. **Social disorganization** erodes social control and constraints and undermines freedom of individual behavior and self-determination. **Legitimization of violence** is the support the culture gives to violence, as portrayed in the mass media (such as television programming), laws permitting corporal punishment in schools, violent sports, military exploits, and video games. **Social norms theory** proposes that male peer aggression and female submission are part of the norm and justification for violent sexual interaction (Dardis et al., 2015).

The notion of male supremacy has its roots deep in our cultural history, which has always equated the property rights of men with access to and control over the bodies of women, children, and others who are perceived as dependents (Brownmiller, 1975). Indeed, Eisler (1987–1995, pp. 153–154) describes rape and sexual assault as one of several threats widely used to ensure the continued domination and control of women. Historically, the crime of rape has been seen not as a crime against the woman but as a crime against her father or her husband (Donat & D'Emilio, 1998).

Brownmiller (1975) and others have documented a part of the history of rape as a psychosocial means by which the victors in wars reward themselves and humiliate their vanquished foes. The wholesale rape and killing of helpless women and children represents the ultimate vulnerability and defeat of a people. It likewise represents the ultimate humiliation and subjugation of a person. Whether it is inflicted on thousands, as reported in war, or on one person, the purpose is quite similar—the use of unrestrained power to force the vanquished into total submission.

Personal and Psychological Factors

Personal and psychological factors unique to men who perpetrate sexual abuse affect both their decision to assault and the way the assault is carried out (Beech, Ward, & Fisher, 2006; Groth & Birnbaum, 1979; Lisek & Miller, 2002; Lisek & Roth, 1988; Williams & Holmes, 1981). The male offender:

1. Acts in a hostile, aggressive, angry, condescending, and domineering manner, and believes he is strong, courageous, and manly even though he often feels weak, anxious, inadequate, threatened, and dependent and believes women are inherently dangerous.
2. Lacks the interpersonal skills to make his point in society and particularly with women.
3. May need to exercise *power* to prove to himself and to the victim that he is powerful, omnipotent, and in total control.
4. May show *sadistic* patterns—the sadistic rapist frequently uses extreme violence and often mutilates or murders the victim in order to attain a feeling of total triumph over the victim.
5. Sees women as primarily sexual objects and has sexual urges that are uncontrollable and all consuming.
6. Holds stereotypical and rigid views of male and female roles with hypermasculine self-views that validate he is a "real man."

7. Harbors chronic feelings of anger, hostility, and fear toward women and seeks to control them by his sexual "conquests."

Feminists, with good historical reason, have attempted to define rape as basically an exercise in power and control. On that basis most rapists have been cast into one of four categories: **anger** (mad at women), **power exploitative** (show they have power over women), **power reassurance** (continuously feel that they are powerful over women), and **sadistic** (take joy in hurting women). McCabe and Wauchope (2005) found evidence to support these typologies in two studies, one of men who had only been charged with sexual assault and the other of men who were convicted, but they also found outliers who did not fit the four categories well. A number of researchers (Lisek & Miller; 2002; Lisek & Roth, 1988; Scully & Marolla, 1998; Sussman & Bordwell, 1981) have interviewed convicted rapists and have vividly demonstrated that each rapist's reasons for assault are individual. For example:

1. Some men use rape to punish or exact revenge because a specific woman has "done them wrong." They see all women collectively as responsible for one woman's supposed transgressions. Some negative precipitating event with an intimate causes them to "take it out" on and "get even" with some woman who is a total stranger to them. It doesn't make any difference who it is as long as it is a female—a generic symbol of their lost power, virility, and masculinity that they desperately want back.

2. Criminals who commit rape in the perpetration of a crime often see rape as an added bonus. It's there for the taking, so why not?

3. For some men, rape is attaining the unattainable woman, the woman they would never otherwise have a chance with. In this instance, sex is the motivating factor.

4. For some men, rape is an impersonal experience and preferred over any demonstrated caring or mutual affection. There is no obligation, and the power, control, and sexual tension release are gratifying.

5. Finally, in its most heinous form, gang rapists see rape as recreation, adventure, and proving they are "macho." These individuals belong to sexually violent subcultures that reflect both the rapist's views of women and the notion that sexual conquest of as many women as possible is a critical measure of manhood. A gang rape is seen as male bonding at its height. While numerous

interviewees stated they regretted their actions and were now sorry for them, the immediate impact on them postrape in regard to what they had done was slight. Ominously, if they felt anything, they generally felt good about what they did.

Yet the vast majority of rapes have to do with the power relationships between men and women (Sussman & Bordwell, 1981, p. 12). Somehow the contemporary sociocultural milieu produces some males who feel such absence of power and control in their lives that they develop a need to "take it" (control). These males come to believe that it is their "right" (p. 5) and proceed to rationalize and justify their behavior, even though they have invaded and taken by force another person's life and body.

Myths About Rape

One of the most difficult obstacles that **LO4** human services workers face in dealing with all forms and aspects of rape and sexual abuse is the abundance of debilitating myths in society (Benedict, 1985; Burt, 1998; Ganas et al., 1999; Matsakis, 2003). For example:

1. *Rape is just rough sex.* The notion that rape equals sex is perhaps the most destructive myth of all. If we believe that rape is sex, then it follows that rape doesn't hurt (physically or psychologically) any more than sex does. We can even believe that the survivor enjoys and is erotically stimulated by its roughness. Rape is violence, torture, and a life-threatening event. It is utterly humiliating, and the joy of "rough sex" has nothing to do with it. However, research indicates that certain types of rapists are aroused by the use of force and violence against victims, and such arousal may be heightened by aggressive resistance of victims (Drieschner & Lange, 1999; Knight, 1999). Social norms theory supports this myth. Dardis and associates (2015) found that college males' *beliefs* about what their peers thought about sexually aggressive behaviors correlated highly with what their *perception* of the average college male's beliefs were, although in actuality they were not correlated with their friends' *actual* beliefs. However, perpetrators of sexual assault were *highly significant* in their belief in *overestimating* friends' involvement in sexually aggressive behavior.

2. *Women "cry rape" to gain revenge.* Ganas and associates (1999) hypothesize that this myth permeates our society because such myths (a) provide comfort for our social structure (people don't

want to believe that rape really occurred), (b) serve to focus the blame for sexual violence on victims rather than perpetrators, and (c) are easier to believe than the reality of knowing that rape can happen to anyone. As such it is one of the most heated and controversial issues in sexual assault. "Revenge" reports are sometimes heard, and at times the cry of "rape" has been used for secondary gain, such as getting back at a jilted lover, blackmail, job security, or covering up an unwanted pregnancy. A 2% rule has been used by the FBI in its training as the percentage of false accusations. Lisek and his associates (2010) found about a 6% false accusation rate in their investigation of rape allegations. Yet according to police reports, rapes are no more likely to be falsely reported than other crimes (Lear, 1972).

3. *Rape is motivated by lust.* Eisler (1995) and Scully and Marolla (1998) believe that the motivation for rape is most likely to be domination, power, anger, revenge, control, frustration, or sadism. Benedict (1985, p. 8) and Eisler (1995, pp. 237–239) report that some men may come to associate sex with violence, thereby viewing women not as human beings but as objects of prey and/or domination and viewing sex as an act of power, control, and triumph. However, one counterpoint view, based on studies of the evolutionary theories of rape by Thornhill and Palmer (2000), suggests that the motives of rapists are primarily sexual, with the exercise of power mostly a means to an end. This idea is supported at least in part by Scully and Marolla (1998), who found that some of the rapists they interviewed saw it as the only way to get sexual access to women who were unwilling or "out of their league."

4. *Rapists are weird, psychotic loners.* No such contention can be supported by the research. Rapists come from every walk of life. People who rape and commit other forms of sexual abuse/misuse have been identified in every stratum of society—from judges to messenger boys, from weaklings to bodybuilders, from vagrants to corporate executives, from husbands and fathers to strangers, from partners, known friends, and relatives to unknown intruders (Benedict, 1985, pp. 9–10; Burt, 1998). The idea that rapists were mentally ill held sway for a long time (Groth, 1971) and was seen by feminists as a particularly odious way of rationalizing the male-dominated societal power and subjugation motives that undergirded and upheld a repressive, patriarchal society. The sheer

number of rapes make it statistically impossible that the typical rapist is "mentally ill," given the small number of psychopathic men in the population (Scully & Marolla, 1998).

5. *Victims or survivors of rape provoked the rape or wanted to be raped, so no harm was done.* By acting sexy, wearing sexy clothes or lots of makeup, being at a bar and "coming on" to a man, walking along a road alone at night, or doing laundry or grocery shopping late, somehow or other a woman does something that clearly says "Come rape me!" The bottom line is that through a series of weak inferences and rationalizations, the rapist is able to condone his sexual assault. The rapist is no longer responsible for the way he acted because the woman, by her actions, brought it on herself (Burt, 1998). Although most rapists deny that they are rapists, rationalize that women provoke or want it, or deny that their sexual assaults are rape, there are virtually no documented cases in which women have lured men into raping them. Ganas and associates (1999) and Sussman and Bordwell (1981) have clearly shown that what the survivor does before the rape has little if anything to do with the rapist's decision to assault.

6. *Only bad women are raped.* This myth is one of the most blatant examples of a "blame the victim" attitude (Brownmiller, 1975). This myth is taken to mean that if the woman has a "bad" reputation, the rape is justified. The stereotypical "damaged goods" notion means that a woman who has said "Yes" once can no longer legitimately say "No." She has lost her value (Burt, 1998). For many, the extension of this myth means that prostitutes are so devalued that they have no worth at all and therefore cannot be raped (Silbert, 1988). Whether the person is a professional hooker or a minister should make no difference. Neither deserves to be assaulted, and both are entitled to equal protection and treatment.

7. *Real rapes happen only in bad parts of town, at night, in abandoned buildings or lonely fields by strangers who have knives or guns and who engage in brutally beating the victims when they resist heroically—even unto death.* That's pretty much rubbish! While there are rapes that happen that way, remember that half or more of the perpetrators are someone who knows the victim. Most rapes do not involve a weapon or sustaining an injury beyond minor bruises or scratches. And most occur in either the victim's home or the assailant's (Burt, 1998).

8. *If the woman doesn't resist, she must have wanted it.* The old stereotypical notion, which has had some coinage in the courts, is that the woman needs to resist unto death or be so physically drained or hurt that she can't resist any longer. Resisting may get a woman killed, particularly if the assailant is armed and is more physically powerful. Furthermore, there are many psychological obstacles in the way of resisting that have to do with the historical power differential wherein women do submit. Ominously, Kassing and Prietio (2003) found that both male and female counselors-in-training thought that male rape victims should fight back. There is no conclusive evidence that fighting back or not fighting back is better for the victim (Matsakis, 2003).

It is not easy or simple to eradicate or even to refute the preceding myths in society at large (Ganas et al., 1999). Feminists argue that it is to the advantage of the entire patriarchal society to believe such myths, and it is certainly to the advantage of the rapists (Burt, 1998).

Myths about rape and sexual assault are not the sole domain of females. Here are some of the more prevalent myths about males and sexual assault (Male Survivor, 2011).

1. *Boys and men can't be willing victims.* Let's suppose that a 350-pound NFL noseguard decides to have his way with you. What do you think will happen? Boys and adult males are often physically weaker than their attackers or are threatened with weapons. Or the perpetrator may have power and control over the victim through position, influence, knowledge, and prestige. There is essentially no difference between males and females in regard to this myth.
2. *Homosexuals are usually the perpetrators of sexual abuse of boys.* Pedophiles are pedophiles whether they sexually abuse boys or girls. They are not gays or lesbians but pedophiles who happen to have different sex and age preferences.
3. *Boys are less traumatized than girls.* While some studies have found boys to be less negatively affected initially, long-term effects are quite damaging, and when the perpetrators are trusted others (which is often the case, as you will read later in this chapter), they become a psychological abattoir for boys.
4. *Boys abused by males will later become homosexual.* How and why adult sexual orientation develops is a complex question. While being sexually assaulted by an adult is almost a guarantee for sexual role confusion, it does not mean one automatically becomes gay as a result (Tremblay, 2013). In fact, with males, our own experience is that a number of those who have been victimized by males become homophobic or overcompensate by attempting to prove their manhood by having sex with as many females as possible. The bottom line is, though, that at present this is only one variable in a multitude of variables that influence sexual orientation.
5. *Vampire/zombie syndrome.* The notion is that once you are bitten you become one. This is an especially dangerous myth because it can stereotype victims as perpetrators when the victims desperately need help rather than punishment, ridicule, isolation, and abandonment. Generally, getting psychological help early on is critical to not become a perpetrator later in life.
6. *If a boy (or girl) experiences sexual arousal or orgasm from abuse, this means he enjoys it.* We are hardwired for sex. Physical stimulation is likely to happen during sex. That does not mean the child wanted the experience, fully participated in it, or "got off" or "wanted it" as many perpetrators try to rationalize.
7. *If the perpetrator is female, the boy just got lucky.* This is a widely held belief and a very, very dangerous stereotype. Some of the most disturbed clients we have seen have been children and adolescent boys abused by females in authority positions and consanguine relationships. The conflict, confusion, rage, and other extremely volatile emotions and thinking they display toward women as adults mark them as threats for harm to females. Above all, these boys should receive treatment immediately after discovery of the assault.

For men these myths have profound effects. One of the major ones is the shame, embarrassment, and guilt they feel that militates against coming forward, and there is still considerable stigma attached to be a male who has been raped (Easton, Saltzmanm, & Willis, 2014). The problem is that, even among "educated" people, these myths have remarkable staying power. Heppner and associates (1995) found that college students believed many myths about rape. That study identified many differences in men's and women's perceptions of rape during and after a session on rape prevention intervention consisting of didactic, video, and question-and-answer discussion. During the intervention, both men's and women's attitudes showed decreased belief in rape myths; at a 2-month follow-up, however, men had regained more of their former beliefs than women had. Research by Varelas and Foley (1998) indicated that both black and white college students who strongly believed rape myths were more tolerant of rapists and less tolerant of victims than those who had weaker beliefs. In addition, women with strong beliefs in the myths were less likely to report sexual assaults or to assist in legal actions against rapists.

Date and Acquaintance Rape

Much of the research reported on date and **LO5** acquaintance rape deals with sexual assaults on college campuses. Little is known about date rape as it applies to high school students, although at this writing there were 4,000 reported incidents of sexual battery and more than 800 reported rapes and attempted rapes (Robers et al., 2010). According to a 2003 U.S. Department of Justice report, rape is the most common violent crime at U.S. universities. The incidence of rape is 35 per 1,000 female college students per year. Women may decline to report rape out of shame, self-reproach for drinking too much, or fear of social isolation from the perpetrators and her friends. Ninety percent of the college women who are raped know their assailants, and most rapes occur in a social situation such as partying or studying together in a dorm room (Cole, 2006).

Because most of you reading this book are sitting in a college classroom, be advised that nearly 20% of your female classmates will be victims of attempted or actual assault, as will about 6% of the men (Krebs et al., 2007). Frazier and her associates (2009) conducted an online survey that examined the incidence of traumatic events among a large and diverse population of college students. When all of the different types of unwanted sexual contact were combined, they ranked second only to unexpected death in frequency of response to trauma, and Fisher and associates (2003) found that more than 90% of sexual assaults were not reported! Indeed, the really interesting fact in all sexual assault reporting is that a great deal of it doesn't get reported at all, so you can assume that any statistic you see is probably a pretty conservative estimate of what is really happening (Kariane et al., 2005; Weiss, 2010).

Mills and Granoff (1992) found that 28% of college women surveyed acknowledged that they had been victims of rape or attempted rape. In a national survey of college men and women, Koss (1998) found that 8.3% of the women felt they had been forced to engage in unwanted sex. Conversely, only 3.4% of the men felt they had forced a partner to engage in unwanted sex. Few told anyone about the encounters, although those reporting attempted rape were more likely to tell someone than were those who had actually been raped. A number of male respondents admitted to committing what is legally defined as rape and admitted to continuing to make sexual advances even when their dates had told them "No!"

One of the bigger myths of rape is: *Date rape isn't really rape.* The girl went out with him, didn't she? He probably spent a good deal of money on her. What if she kissed him back and engaged in heavy petting? Then she turned him off? That's a "prick tease"! She deserved it and probably even wanted it even though she said no. Even if it was a boyfriend of long standing, and whatever else may have happened before the rape in terms of sexual foreplay, and no matter how much money was spent, "No!" is "No!" and no one has the right or justification to rape a date.

Date Rape Risk

Date rape survivors in college have been found to be more likely to have experienced stress, maltreatment, and negative home environment/neglect during childhood than were women who reported no date rape experience (Sanders & Moore, 1999). Date rape participants in the Sanders and Moore study were also more likely to have experienced sexual abuse during childhood. Himelein, Vogel, and Wachowiak (1994) suggest that child sexual abuse is an underlying risk factor for both heightened sexual activity and sexual victimization in dating. Shapiro and Chwarz (1997) further suggest that precocious knowledge of sex, confusion about sexual norms, isolation, and neediness might predispose a young abuse survivor to early and frequent sexual activity, which may in turn increase the risk of dating victimization.

Candy Is Dandy, but Liquor Is Quicker—and More Violent. Alcohol, partying, sex, and college students combining those activities a lot as they become emancipated from parental governance make sexual aggression shockingly high among male college students (Shorey et al., 2015). Indeed barroom groping, kissing, and touching are pervasive and seen as part of the course of partying (Becker & Tinkler, 2015), and alcohol consumption has also been linked to date and acquaintance rape as a risk factor (Cole, 2006;

Norris & Cubbins, 1992). A study by Abbey, McAuslan, and Ross (1998) found that the mutual effects of college men's beliefs and experiences with regard to dating, sexuality, and alcohol consumption increased the likelihood that a male would misperceive a female companion's sexual intentions, and that this *misperception* might lead to sexual assault. Jozkowski and Wiersma (2015) found that in a large sample of students across the United States that alcohol consumption prior to sexual activity was associated with both external consent (verbal and behavioral cues) and internal consent (feelings associated with giving consent). Ominously, childhood sexual abuse increases the risk for alcohol abuse, and that in turn increases the chances of engaging in sexually risky behavior (Walsh, Latzman, & Latzman, 2014).

In contrast, the use of a *date rape drug* (gamma hydroxybutyrate, or GHB) in the commission of a sexual assault constitutes a premeditated and *deliberate* assault (Boyd, 2000). Ullman, Karabatsos, and Koss (1999) found that both victim's and offender's use of alcohol prior to attack was directly associated with more severe victimization of women and that alcohol use played both direct and indirect roles in the outcomes of sexual assaults.

Schwartz and Leggett (1999) found that women who were raped while intoxicated were not less emotionally affected and did not blame themselves any more than women who were raped by force while not intoxicated. It is interesting to note that most of these women did not classify their experiences as rape, although all were victims under criminal law. Norris and Cubbins (1992) found that three-fourths of acquaintance rapes involved drinking and that if both members of a dating couple had been consuming alcohol, the rape was not judged as severely as when only the woman had been drinking. In the latter case, the man was likely to be viewed as taking advantage of a vulnerable woman.

Preventing Date, Acquaintance, and Other Forms of Rape

Mills and Granoff (1992) and Dunn, Vail-Smith, and Knight (1999) suggest that continuing educational and support services (for both men and women) are critically needed to address, in a culturally unbiased manner, the causes and prevention of date and acquaintance rape. Sexual refusal assertiveness and sexual abstinence do reduce chances for sexual assault (Wigderson & Katz, 2015), and learning assertiveness techniques seems to be a key ingredient in any education program for women. Assertiveness skills seem critical and reduced

rape and attempted rapes between experimental and control groups (Senn et al., 2015), less sexual victimization (Rowe et al., 2015) and even where there were no differences in sexual assaults between controls and experimentals, women in the experimental group experienced less self-blame than controls (Gidycz et al., 2015). Educational programs, especially at the secondary school level, have been recommended as preventive measures in reducing date and acquaintance sexual assaults (Page, 1997). Ullman, Karabatsos, and Koss (1999) recommended that rape and alcohol abuse prevention efforts can benefit from incorporating information about alcohol's role in different sexual assault contexts. It seems reasonable that such prevention initiatives should also address strategies to avoid assaults connected with the use of date rape drugs.

Frazier, Valtinson, and Candell (1994) demonstrated that coeducational and interactive rape prevention programs can succeed in the short run. Their preventive interventions, presented to members of fraternities and sororities, showed that participants endorsed significantly fewer rape-supportive attitudes immediately following the interventions than did control group members. But, like Heppner and colleagues' (1995) participants, experimental and control group members no longer differed after 1 month. Indeed, most studies of rape education programs indicate they do not hold up over time (Garrity, 2011; Vladutiu, Martin, & Macy, 2011). Hillenbrand-Gunn and her associates (2010) have taken a different approach to rape education. They conducted a program for high school students that focused on social norms theory (Perkins & Berkowitz, 1986), which is based on what one thinks one's peers do and believe rather than what the peers actually do and believe. Their program was based on a men as allies philosophy and combined it with social norms theory as their theoretical framework. Group psychoeducational/ discussion sessions were administered to both male and female high school students through a variety of formats that challenged sexist, coercive, and abusive behavior that is a precursor to thinking that sexual assault is acceptable. Pre- to postprogram results indicated that attitudes changed in the experimental group and not in the control group. The results of this methodologically sound experiment held at a 4-week follow-up for both males and females suggest that it holds promise as a creative approach focusing on peers, a formidable force for this age group. Clearly, the research indicates that rape prevention programs should be comprehensive and ongoing, rather than programmed as onetime interventions. Rowe, Jouriles, and McDonald (2015) used a MY Voice, MY Choice assertive resistance training program that used a virtual immersion program emphasizing assertiveness skills and found at 3-month follow-up that the adolescent girls reported less sexual victimization than a wait list group. They also found that psychological victimization and psychological distress were reduced for those girls who had greater prior victimization at baseline. Daigneault and her associates (2015) conducted sexual assault awareness workshops for 15- to 17-year-old high school students and were effective in improving general knowledge regarding sexual assault and awareness of resources in the event of experiencing sexual assault. They also found improved attitudes regarding sexual assault along with their ability to recognize sexual assault in a dating context and diminish responses that deny or minimize assault awareness workshops.

Finally, studies by Sawyer, Pinciaro, and Jessell (1998) on the effects of coercion and verbal consent on university students' perception of date rape concluded that, in an act legally defined as rape, male students are generally more prone to deny that a rape occurred unless an assertive or aggressive "No!" is verbalized by the potential victim. The value and effect of profoundly verbalizing "No!" in situations in which women are vulnerable to rape cannot be overestimated.

Perhaps even more disheartening, Kassing and Prietio (2003) found that male counselors-in-training who had no experience working with sexual assault victims were willing to believe myths about male rape victims, and both male and female counselors-in-training believed that the male victim should have resisted more. The conclusion with regard to training therapists is clearly that they need to be disabused of some myths about sexual assault!

Intervention Strategies for Rape and Battery: The Case of Melody

Melody Swanson is a 50-year-old teacher. **LO6** She has been living alone in a small house since the younger of her two children went away to college 2 months ago. Melody was divorced 7 years ago. She had a long weekend off from school and decided to go away to a casino for a minivacation. When she returned home from her trip at 9:30 yesterday evening and emerged from her car in her driveway, she was met by a gunman in his middle 20s.

She dropped a small bag of groceries and some items from her purse as she was abducted at gunpoint and forced into the gunman's car, which was parked on the street. Melody was beaten, driven away to an isolated area several miles from her home, raped, beaten again, robbed, and abandoned, bleeding and bruised, with her clothing in shreds. She was weak and dazed, but managed to find her way to the nearest house in the early hours of the morning, where she called for help. It is now 8:30 A.M. and Melody is at the trauma center of a hospital in a large metropolitan city, where she has just been taken by the police. Melody is experiencing physical and emotional trauma. She personifies a traumatized person. She is in shock, shaking and trembling, has both eyes black, numerous contusions, abrasions, and cuts, and is still in the muddy clothes she was abducted in. She is about to meet what will become a very important person in her life—a crisis worker from the local sexual assault and domestic violence center who specializes in rape cases.

Immediate Aftermath

In most situations the most helpful and appropriate immediate response from a crisis worker is empathy and assurance that the survivor is still alive. Nowhere in crisis intervention is it more important to provide the core facilitative conditions of building trust, displaying unconditional positive regard, using empathic listening and responding, providing concreteness and clarity, and demonstrating patience. The crisis task is predispositioning the client in regard to what she is going to go through, from vaginal examinations to police questioning to the acute stress symptoms that are likely to follow the initial onslaught of emotions she is now experiencing. The worker is going to quickly build what in the psychotherapy trade is called a **working alliance** (a cooperative and trusting working relationship). Melody's rape is a case in point of how this operates in the immediate aftermath of a trauma. Cloitre and her associates (2004) report that building this alliance is as critical as, if not more important than, mastery of any intervention techniques.

The **impact stage** (Matsakis, 2003, pp. 82–90) occurs during the assault and for approximately 2 weeks following it. During this time a kaleidoscope of emotions, thoughts, and behaviors may occur, or conversely the client may be in a state of shock and dissociation, with both physical pain associated with the sexual assault and dissociation, somatic reactions, hypervigilance, nightmares, and startle responses that are symptomatic of the acute stress disorder that often follows. Stability both from a physical and psychological standpoint are critical at this time (Briere & Scott, 2006, pp. 273). It is the crisis worker's job to do a number of things as soon as the client comes into the hospital or the crisis center.

Some sense of control needs to be restored so the client can go through the physical exam and police report. Paramount is restoring a sense of safety and security to a person whose world has just been turned upside down. To do this, the crisis worker must accurately assess the client's state of mobility and equilibrium and gently but also with assuredness and confidence enter into this upside-down world. The worker needs to gather information while walking a therapeutic tightrope between sensitivity and the need to ask specific behavioral closed-ended questions. Maximum sensitivity means using empathic prefacing statements followed by gathering behavioral information on the assault. To ask for information without voicing sincere concern for the person's trauma is not only callous and insensitive, but likely will terminate intervention before it starts (McCart et al., 2009). To that end, it is critical that the crisis worker immediately start the predisposition task of our crisis intervention model. Courtois and Ford (2009) propose the following capstone statement in regard to treating survivors of prolonged complex trauma, but we believe it also fits well here. Your job at this point is to provide relational conditions that encourage the safety of the attachment between the client and the worker (p. 190), and this may be anything but easy for you or the client.

CW: (*talking slowly while she gently picks up Melody's hand in an examining room in the ER*) Hi, Melody, I'm Jolee Mabry. I am a counselor from the Metro Sexual Assault Unit. You have been through a terrible experience, that no one should ever go through, but you survived it. I can't begin to know what it feels like to experience all the feelings and thoughts you are having right now, but I do understand as traumatic as this is you have survived and I am going to be with you while you go through this, if you would like.

Melody: (*looking fearful and struggling for words*) I don't . . . I don't know . . . what to think, do, . . . what will happen? Where is he? Who was he? Why me? Can he get in here? So many things . . . I . . . I am so cold and it feels like my heart is about to pound through my chest. Is this a nightmare? But I know it's real . . . I think. Where . . . am . . . I? I'm so sorry. I . . . I . . . I don't remember your name. Who are you?

CW: (*Picks up a blanket and gently pulls it around Melody.*) I'm Jolee Mabry. I am a nurse and a counselor at the sexual assault center here. You are safe here. You were brought here by the paramedics and the police. You are in the Elvis Presley Trauma Unit. I'm Jolee Mabry, a counselor here in the trauma unit. You were beaten physically by the man who assaulted you and the paramedics brought you here. You were raped and assaulted, that is very real. That's why you are here to get taken care of, and we do a very good job of taking care of people who have been sexually assaulted. That is my job, to take care of you, steer you through this experience and act as your advocate and just take care of things for you. Do you understand what I just said and know where you are?

Melody: Yes. What's going to happen to me? (*Starts to shake.*)

CW: (*Reaches over and slowly strokes the client's arm with her hand and holds her other hand.*) I can't say it will be pleasant, but the medical staff and police officers who deal with sexual assault here know their business. The nurse who will do the rape kit exam is a specially trained Sexual Assault Nurse Examiner (SANE). She will make it as painless as possible. You will be asked by the police to describe what happened, and there will be a number of medical procedures. As I said, I'll be with you every step of the way, and when they are done I'll be with you to make arrangements to see that you stay safe and do what's necessary to get some stability and control back in your life.

Melody: Absolutely, please stay. (*Grabs Jolee's hand and grips it.*) It was horrible—the rape. I don't know how I came out alive and without any broken bones. He intended to kill me. Part of the time I was in a daze. I don't know what came over me. I must have blacked out. He may have thought I was dead. I don't know how long I lay out there alone after he left me. I certainly didn't fight back or protest. Look at me, I am so dirty. (*Recoils in disgust.*)

CW: Melody, I'm so proud of you for the way you handled it. You did whatever it took to stay alive. You saved yourself, and that took courage. Whatever you did, whether it was blacking out or offering no protests, was right, because it preserved your life, and that's the important thing right now. We are going to get those clothes off of you and get you cleaned up, but we need to get some pictures and take some samples first, so hang in there a bit longer.

Melody: I feel so damn stupid. Always watchful and just let my guard down. So damn angry at me. I'd kill that bastard if I had a chance. Shoot his nuts off! Lord! Did I just say that! I don't say things like that, but that scurrilous low life SOB . . . degrading . . . How can I go back to face my students . . . I feel like I'm in a sort of twilight zone. Maybe part of me did die. I'm feeling so alone and vulnerable. It's like this whole damn thing isn't real. It couldn't be happening to me, but I know it is. I know I keep going back to that and all this whirl . . . I don't know if I can hold it together.

There is no universal response to rape. Melody represents a few of the conflicting emotions that rampage through someone who has been sexually violated. Dissociative responses are a common defense mechanism to try to bring some stability back into the survivor's life as a whirlwind of emotions blow through the survivor's mind. The laundry list of responses that follows this dialogue represents a good deal of, but not all of the dirty emotions the client is trying to wash out of her mind. The crisis worker's job is to continuously provide support, safety, and practical assistance. While it may seem to be minimizing and discounting the gravity of the situation to call it **psychological first aid** (National Child Traumatic Stress Network and National Center for PTSD, 2006; National Institute of Mental Health, 2002), that is exactly what the worker is doing. Psychological first aid comprises three primary tasks of our intervention model: predispositioning/bonding, exploration/assessment, and safety. However, how this usually gets done is anything but stepwise. Crisis workers who ply the trade in the field of sexual assault are indeed engaging in a stand-up act where they have to be quick in changing strategies and responses to meet the kaleidoscope of emotions that may range from catatonic-like shock to unbridled rage.

CW: It's really scary, the thought of losing control with all those thoughts and emotions racing around in your head, Melody, but that is common for sexual assault survivors. It may be hard to imagine, but your mind and body are attempting to get order back into what for the past few hours has been complete chaos. It's your mind and body's normal defensive response to a completely abnormal situation. It will pass, and to help move that process along we are going to take this piece by piece, one step at a time, until you get control back.

Melody: I don't know. I guess, but . . . (*Pause, with apprehensive look.*) I'm a teacher, I maintain control, but I just can't seem to get a handle on this . . . (*Starts to break down again with muffled sobs.*) I'm so sorry, I'm such a mess, and can't get a grip.

CW: You don't have to be sorry about anything. You are not a mess. Grief is also part of this. You have lost a lot tonight. (*Sits patiently while Melody holds on and sobs quietly with her arm around her.*)

The crisis worker acknowledges her grief, which is a common response to the many losses the client has suffered (Matsakis, 2003, pp. 111–127). She also starts to slowly give her information about the psychological processes occurring within her as a start to developing coping skills and regaining emotional and cognitive control. It is important to start providing basic psychoeducation to clients who are experiencing extreme psychological stress (McCart et al., 2009). Melody is suffering from what we call **peritraumatic stress symptoms**. Those are traumalike symptoms that almost all persons would suffer given similar circumstances. Whether these symptoms turn into acute traumatic stress disorder, which we discuss in other parts of the book, or turns into PTSD will depend a lot on what happens in the next few hours and days. The worker has to be judicious in how much information on psychological coping mechanisms she gives out to avoid cognitive overload. Indeed, engaging in any formal therapeutic intervention or formal assessment in the next few days is *not* recommended. What is recommended is planning thoroughly for the next few hours and days to keep the client safe, supported, and stabilized. Healing from a rape requires concentration, effort, thought, and time and cannot be rushed (Matsakis, 2003, p. 14).

CW: This whole procedure is going to take about 3 to 4 hours to complete. We want you thoroughly checked out in regard to not only your sexual assault but the physical assault as well. The police will interview you. Lt. Lenise Balay is going to do the interview. She and I work together a lot on these cases, and I trust her completely. She is one of the most empathic police officers I know. She will ask you some pretty pointed questions, but understand she wants to get this just right so we can catch who did this to you. You are also going to get a pelvic exam and a rape kit done. Andrea Little is a SANE nurse who specializes in doing this. It won't be pleasant, but again she is a specialist in this business and will be very thorough and gentle. I'll be with you every step of the way. OK?

This is a brief synopsis of the practical medical and legal information the worker gives the survivor. In rape cases, thoroughly explaining what is going to happen is critical to not secondarily revictimizing the survivor. The sensitivity that needs to be manifested in doing a rape exam is best demonstrated in Bennett's (2015) article on getting a bra drive going for raped women who did not want the embarrassment of going braless by having to turn their bras over for evidence. The Riverside county multidisciplinary Sexual Assault Response Team conducted a very successful bra collection drive so the SANE nurse could replace the survivor's evidence bra. Sexual Assault Response Teams (SARTs) are growing multidisciplinary teams that provide a variety of support and coordination services for sexual assault survivors throughout the country (Moylan, Lindhorst, & Tajima, 2015).

CW: *(after the police lieutenant and SANE nurse are done)* Excellent! Dr. Zanzar has gone over all your tests and has okayed your release. You got through that well. Where would you like to go and who would you like to be there with you, someone you really trust?

Melody: Well, my brother, Tom. I'd want him there with me. He's an ex-Marine. Although I don't know how he'd feel about all this and his stupid sister who he's always yapping at to be more vigilant and careful. God! I just feel so ashamed to let him know this happened. But I don't know if I can go back in my driveway or not. That's ridiculous but it still scares me, just the thought of it . . .

CW: I understand how you could feel that way, and the last thing you want to do is tell him about this. Would you like me to call him and get him down here and talk with him? I have done this before and I think I can help you out with that.

Using Support Systems and Stopping Secondary Victimization. In the immediate aftermath of **LO7** the rape, getting support and safety measures in place is a high priority, as is educating the significant others in the survivor's life to the foregoing dynamics. A critical component is steering the person through the medical and police procedures that can have a high potential for secondary victimization (Howell, 1999; Ochberg, 1988; Pauwels, 2003). Secondary victim crisis intervention may also be necessary if there are persons in the support system who might either become homicidal or turn on the survivor and blame her (Pauwels, 2003). Particularly husbands, fathers, and

boyfriends may need very firm, clear instructions on how they are going to meet the survivor in their first encounter. The difficulty of this initial encounter after the rape cannot be overemphasized. Both from the survivor's and significant others' standpoint, it may be very easy to affix blame as a way of trying to make sense out of what happened. Secondary victimization must not be allowed to occur, so the crisis worker's job will be to educate the significant others on how they can best support the client.

Therefore, it is extremely important that a counselor from a rape crisis or sexual assault unit be contacted immediately, as in the preceding example. A nationwide nursing service called the Sexual Assault Nurse Examiner (SANE) program provides specially trained nurses for first response medical care and crisis intervention. The SANE program provides comprehensive and consistent postrape medical care, such as emergency contraception and sexually transmitted disease prophylaxis, documents forensic evidence accurately, provides expert testimony, promotes psychological recovery, and coordinates multiple service providers to provide comprehensive care for rape survivors (Campbell, Patterson, & Lichty, 2005).

CW: *(Meets brother Tom at the center reception desk.)*

Tom: *(excited, agitated, and loud)* What's this all about? What's going on with my sister? What's she doing at the Rape Crisis Center? Is she in trouble? Did she get raped? WHAT THE HELL IS HAPPENING AND WHERE IS MY SISTER?

CW: Your sister has been beaten and sexually assaulted and . . .

Tom: What the . . . where did it happen ?

CW: In her driveway, about 9:30 last night. She was just coming back from the casino.

Tom: Casino! What the hell was she doing at the casino? Jesus Christ, when I get hold of her . . .

CW: *(Becoming assertive and using a well-modulated but commanding voice, immediately interrupts his ranting.)* I understand that you were in the Marines, so tell me this. Is it the Marine Corps creed if a guy gets wounded to go yell at him and tell him how stupid he has been?

Tom: Well no I . . . um . . . but this is different.

CW: Tell me how so. You took care of your wounded buddies, didn't you? What was your rank anyway?

Tom: Well, uh . . . Master Sergeant. But, uh . . . I don't see what that's got to do with it.

CW: (*well-modulated but clearly assertive*) I'll tell you what, Tom. I didn't get a chance to introduce myself. I am Jolee Mabry, a counselor and nurse with the sexual assault center. I was a nurse in the Gulf War, wore the Eagle, Anchor, and Globe (Marine Corps insignia) myself. First Lieutenant Mabry, USMC retired, at your service. I served in Saudi Arabia and Iraq with mobile surgical units there. If you are as good a marine as I think you are, you retrieved your wounded and did everything possible to keep them alive and safe, did you not? Is that correct, Master Sergeant Swanson?

Tom: (*sort of snaps to attention and in a rather tentative voice*) Yes, ma'am. That is . . . uh . . . affirmative, ma'am.

CW: Good, so you have a wounded sister. You know about PTSD, right? We don't want her going out on a date with that now, do we? What she needs is all the care and support you can give her, don't we now? No blame, no fault finding, don't you agree? No going out hunting the bad guy because your job is taking care of your troop, and your sister is surely that and more, is she not? A lot of care and understanding, compassion and empathy, for the terrible combat experience she has been through, and make no mistake, it is indeed that. So, Master Sergeant Swanson, can you take this mission on, or do I get somebody else?

Tom: Yes, Lieuten . . . uh, er, ma'am. I can certainly do that.

CW: Semper Fi. Now go in there and take care of your sister. Hold her and tell her how much you love her and take her home. Also tell her how brave she was and how smart she was to survive this. You cannot give her too many "way to go's"! Got it? I'll be in touch with both you and her. Here's my card. If you need help, call me. Marines look out for one another. I'll be back with you two after you spend some time together.

Tom: (*sheepishly, wringing his baseball cap in his hands*) I am sorry for my initial behavior, ma'am. I was pretty wound up. I am squared away now. Thank you for straightening me out. I won't mess this up.

Secondary victimization of a rape victim is always close at hand. It is certainly not uncommon for relatives to become angry and blaming of the victim when they are confronted with news of a rape as they seek to get control over what they perceive as an uncontrollable situation. The crisis worker changes her

approach as soon as she detects the brother's negative attitude and becomes very directive with lots of "I" assertion statements to get the brother's attention. She lays something of a guilt trip on him to get his attention and change his cognitive sets about what needs to happen. She uses a technique that we would generally be critical of, but works well here. That is, she uses a number of negative interrogative statements ("Don't you think/agree?") that ask for agreement with her point of view. By doing so, she shifts focus to positive rather than negative support for this wounded survivor.

Although you are probably not a marine nor usually would by chance meet a survivor's brother who was, the crisis worker manifests the best of creative and adaptive thinking to create a bond and reframe this in terms he can understand. Although he is not now an active sergeant, she knows that once a marine always a marine and that's why her responses aren't to "Tom" but "Sergeant Swanson." That's an all-star performance which goes to the heart of the adaptability that great crisis workers have.

CW: (*Reenters the room with Melody and Tom.*) You're going to have a lot of different reactions to this. They are not the same for every person, so don't be alarmed if you have some and not others. We will talk about all of this when things settled down. People have lots of different ways of coping with this. The main thing is for you to feel as safe and secure as you can. I am going to give you a number that is on call 24 hours a day. Do not feel guilty about calling. I am going to be your main contact from the Center, so don't be afraid to call me. I will be doing some checking in with you, if that is OK.

The crisis worker's intuition is right when she guesses that the place of safety and comfort for Melody would be her own home but that the frightening part would be getting past the place in her driveway where she was abducted. The crisis worker is also correct in reassuring Melody for her actions, which brought her out alive. Clients will immediately begin second-guessing themselves as to what they should have done and negative emotions of guilt, shame, and embarrassment will start building (Courtois & Ford, 2009, p. 188; Matsakis, 2003, pp.118–119; Weiss, 2010). The crisis worker dispels this notion by clearly and empathically stating that what she did was just right because it got her through the ordeal and out the other side alive. If she is able, the crisis worker immediately starts education in gentle and small doses. Primary education concerns getting the client through the next 24 hours, which are indeed going to be unreal for her. Her brother is a critical support and will need to be given some primary education about rape dynamics.

An important issue for rape survivors is control. Whatever will allow Melody to bring some control back in her life is important to do and is a major goal for the crisis worker. That may or may not be attempting to remember details of the assault. She may want to take a long, hot shower, or just sleep. Melody has experienced an emotionally draining loss of control to the attacker, and she needs to be reassured that her loss of control is neither total nor permanent. She did what she had to do to survive, and that took courage. It is important to her for others to recognize her and give her credit. There is no wrong way to survive a rape (Howell, 1999)! Nonjudgmentalism and support are critical so that the client immediately starts moving from victim to survivor status (Ganas et al., 1998).

Responses. Women may exhibit a wide variety **LO8** of responses to the rape and the subsequent recovery process (Benedict, 1985; Matsakis, 2003, pp. 81–98; Williams & Holmes, 1981). The female who is assaulted:

1. May respond by exhibiting no emotions—appearing unaffected.
2. May feel humiliated, demeaned, and degraded.
3. May suffer immediate physical and psychological injury as well as long-term trauma.
4. May experience impaired sexual functioning.
5. May blame herself and feel guilty.
6. May experience difficulty relating to and trusting others—especially men.
7. May experience fantasies, daydreams, and nightmares—vividly reliving the assault or additional encounters with the assailant—or may have mental images of scenes of revenge.
8. Will never be the same, even though most survivors, over time, develop ways to recover, cope, and go on with their lives.
9. May be fearful of going to the police or a rape crisis center.
10. May be reluctant to discuss the assault with members of her family, friends, and others because of the risk of rejection and embarrassment.
11. May become severely depressed and suicidal.
12. May be extremely angry and revenge seeking to the point of becoming lethal.

The Following Three Months

Rape has high potential for PTSD, depression, **LO9** suicide, panic attacks, generalized anxiety disorder, social adjustment disorders, sexual dysfunction, eating disorders, dissociation, and more negative worldviews and cognitive distortions. The crisis worker must not let the client regress and retreat into the past. Blaming external factors, self-blaming, and perseverating on why the rape happened are not helpful along with the guilt of "What if-ing?" oneself to death about where one was, what type of clothing one wore, not paying attention to surroundings, and on and on (Frazier et al., 2001; Matsakis, 2003, pp. 81–98; Weiss, 2010).

Follow-up, proactive, and continuous supportive therapy is essential and may include any of the following topics (Ganas et al., 1998, 1999; Howell, 1999; Matsakis, 2003; Pauwels, 2003).

Critical Needs. During the 3 months following a sexual assault, a survivor such as Melody:

1. May need continuing medical consultation, advice, or treatment; she may experience soreness, pain, itching, nausea, sleeplessness, loss of appetite, and other physical and somatic symptoms.
2. May have difficulty resuming work; the added stress of the sexual assault may create too much stress in the workplace.
3. Needs to have people reach out to her, listen to her, and verbally assure her—not shun her or fear continuing to relate to her.
4. Needs the acceptance and support of family and friends.
5. May have difficulty resuming sexual relations and needs understanding without pressure.
6. May exhibit unusual mood swings and emotional outbursts, which others will need to understand and allow.
7. May experience nightmares, flashbacks, phobias, denial, disbelief, and other unusual effects.
8. May go into depression, which may be accompanied by suicidal ideation or acute traumatic stress disorder.

Critical Supports. Support people can be of great help during this phase of recovery. In fact, one of the most important things a crisis counselor can do is getting and coordinating support systems in place. The recovery of survivors of sexual assault is enhanced by the empathic help and understanding of the people close to them. Whether the survivor's support people are family, friends, associates, medical or legal personnel, crisis workers, or long-term therapists, the important ingredients in the helping relationship are acceptance, genuineness, empathy, caring, and nonjudgmental understanding (Baker, 1995; Benedict, 1985; Howell, 1999; Remer & Ferguson, 1995). These support people can help survivors of sexual assault by:

1. Understanding and accepting the survivor's changed moods, tantrums, and so on, and allowing her the freedom to act them out.
2. Supporting and being available—but not intruding—while encouraging her to regain control and to recover her life.
3. Ensuring that she doesn't have to go home alone (without overprotecting her).
4. Realizing that recovery takes a long time and lots of hard work.
5. Allowing her to make her own decisions about reporting the rape and prosecuting the assailant.
6. Leaving it up to her to decide whether she wants to change jobs or place of residence.
7. Responding to her in positive ways, so she does not sense that the support person blames her for "letting it happen" or feels she is not capable of taking care of herself.
8. Allowing her to talk about the assault to whomever she wishes, whenever she wishes, but not disclosing the assault to anyone without her prior consent.
9. Showing empathy, concern, and understanding without dominating her.
10. Recognizing that she will likely suffer from low self-esteem and finding ways to show her that she is genuinely valued and respected.
11. Recognizing that her hurt will not end when the physical scratches and bruises are gone—that her emotional healing will take a long time.
12. Finding ways to help her trust men again—assisting male associates (friends, coworkers, brothers, her father) to show tolerance, understanding, and confidence.
13. Encouraging female coworkers, friends, sisters, and her mother to believe in her and not avoid her or avoid talking with her openly about the rape.
14. Including her children, if she has any, in many of the considerations concerning help toward emotional recovery.
15. Referring her to sexual assault support groups for survivors and family members.

16. Recognizing that her husband, partner, or lover may develop symptoms similar to those of the survivor (nightmares, phobias, rage, guilt, self-blame, self-hate, and such) and may need help similar to that needed by the survivor herself.
17. Encouraging her husband or lover to give her time to recover, free from pressure, before resuming sexual activity and to let her know he or she is still interested in her, still desires her, but that former patterns of sex life will be resumed at the survivor's own pace. It is important for a husband or lover to talk this out openly with her, to clear the air for both parties.

The foregoing is not a grocery list to just be handed to support persons. It is something that the interventionist needs to do as part of a psychoeducation program that lets people know what to expect and works with them as they struggle through what will be a period of transcrisis events and points.

PTSD. As previously indicated, rape ranks second only to combat in the potential for PTSD. Because it is a less noxious approach, your authors would first use EMDR as a therapeutic intervention. It is far less intrusive than the cognitive-behavioral approaches generally recommended. If EMDR didn't work, then we would use a combination of the three recommended cognitive-behavioral treatments (Briere & Scott, 2006; Cloitre & Rosenberg, 2006; Courtois, Ford, & Cloitre, 2009; Foa & Rauch, 2004; Frazier et al., 2001):

1. Exposure treatment, which calls for repeated emotional recounting of the traumatic memory
2. Affect regulation, which focuses on teaching clients skills to reduce painful internal emotional states
3. Cognitive therapy, to replace dysfunctional cognitions with new, more adaptive thoughts

These procedures will be demonstrated shortly in this chapter in the case of Heather, an adult survivor of childhood sexual abuse. Two supplementary therapy issues that are specific to rape need to be mentioned. First, there is the fact of opening up the old wound of the rape. Confronting the rape may be painful, but it is absolutely necessary, and the client needs to clearly understand what is going to happen. However, opening this wound, whether it be the recent rape of Melody or the old ones of Heather's adolescent abuse, needs to be done in a carefully gauged manner. To start exposure therapy means pushing away defenses that are in place to keep the client stabilized, although that stability may be anything but healthy (Courtois, Ford, & Cloitre, 2009). However, because these defense systems are being rent asunder, sexual assault survivors have a tendency to go rather blindly in harm's way. While therapy is occurring, they are almost a sure bet to experience transcrisis points as they form new defensive systems and coping mechanisms. As a result, it is not just the psychological safety but the physical safety of the client's with which the worker needs to be concerned.

Adult Survivors of Childhood Sexual Abuse

There is ample evidence that the sexual abuse **LO11** of children wreaks lasting damage in their lives that continues into adulthood (Briere & Runtz, 1987, 1993; Briere & Scott, 2006; Browne & Finkelhor, 2000; Courtois & Ford, 2009; Kessler & Bieschke, 1999; Lamoureaux et al., 2012; Maschi et al., 2013; Mitchell & Morse, 1998; Rosencrans, 1997). If survivors are left untreated, they may experience recurring episodes of revictimization and exhibit debilitating symptoms (transcrisis points) for many years (Briere & Runtz, 1993; Cloitre & Rosenberg, 2006; Davis, Combs-Lane, & Jackson, 2002; Kessler & Bieschke, 1999; Noll et al., 2003; Van Bruggen, Runtz, & Kadlec, 2006).

Psychological Trauma and Sequelae

Effects on Adult Survivors. Histories of adult survivors of childhood sexual abuse show higher incidence of (1) depression, anxiety, shame, and humiliation (Briere & Conte, 1993; Briere & Runtz, 1988; Browne & Finkelhor, 2000); (2) borderline personality disorder, dissociative disorder, and posttraumatic stress disorder (Briere & Runtz, 1993; McLean & Gallop, 2003; Mitchell & Morse, 1998); (3) social stigmatization, alienation, inhibitions, introversion, and interpersonal hypersensitivity (Browne & Finkelhor, 2000; Lundberg-Love et al., 1992); (4) more contacts with medical doctors for somatic complaints including chronic pain problems, such as fibromyalgia and irritable bowel syndrome, and long-term serious physical health deficits such as pulmonary, heart, and liver disease, unintended pregnancy, and obesity (Hertel & Johnson, 2013; Kendall-Tackett, 2008; Moeller, Bachmann, & Moeller, 1993; Stevenson, 1999); (5) negative self-image (Courtois, 1988; Herman, 1981); (6) poor interpersonal relationships and poor parenting skills (Browne & Finkelhor, 2000); (7) suicide (Ullman &

Brecklin, 2002; Tripodi & Pettus-Davis, 2013); (8) substance abuse (Bender et al., 2015); (9) incarceration in prison (Tripodi & Pettus-Davis, 2013); and (10) probably worst of all sexual revictimization (Waldron et al., 2015; Zlotnik, 2014). Yet these are not all of the evil bumblebees that fly out of the Pandora's box of childhood sexual assault. Hertel and Johnson (2013) found in their examination of over 17,000 respondents to the Adverse Childhood Experiences study, that the higher the number of adverse experiences children suffered the worse the effects became. Those pernicious effects ranged across physical health problems such as obesity, heart and liver disease, sexually transmitted diseases, unintended pregnancies, partner violence, illicit drug use, suicide attempts, and other mental health and emotional issues.

A long list of studies have found that a significant number of female clients (institutionalized, outpatient, psychiatric patients, and clients in clinics) were sexually abused as children (Briere & Runtz, 1987; Hertel & Johnson, 2013; Kessler & Bieschke, 1999; Maschi et al., 2013; Salter, 1995). Adult female survivors consistently demonstrate symptoms similar to those of Vietnam veterans, in addition to compulsive sexual behavior, sadomasochistic sexual fantasy, sexual identity issues, and loss of sexual interest (Briere & Runtz, 1987; Courtois, 1988; Finkelhor, 1979; Herman, 1981; Mitchell & Morse, 1998). And, like combat veterans, child sexual abuse survivors are prone to use alcohol and drugs to submerge bad memories from awareness, as well as to engage in suicidal ideation and attempts (Duncan, 2004; Hien et al., 2009; Rew, 1989; Ullman & Brecklin, 2003).

Male survivors who were abused by adult males fare no better and report essentially the same symptoms, with concomitant sexual orientation ambiguity, mistrust of adult males, homophobia, hypersexuality, poor physical and mental health, lower emotional and social support, reduced activity, and body image disturbances (Choudhary, Coben, & Bossarte, 2010; Gartner, 2005; Lew, 2004; Myers, 1986; Rowan, 2006). Perhaps more important, Monk-Turner and Light's (2010) study of men who had been sexually assaulted and raped found that if actual penetration of a male's body occurred, it was the major variable in *not* seeking treatment.

Revictimization. Many of the foregoing symptoms appear to be even more profound and multiple if women suffered both sexual and physical assault in childhood (Cloitre & Rosenberg, 2006). Early assault is additive, and it appears that the higher the incident rate and the more profound it is, the higher the potential for later problems. If the abuse continues into adolescence, the potential for adult sexual assault also increases (Van Bruggen, Runtz, & Kadlec, 2006). Further, if both sexual and physical abuse occur in childhood and adolescence, the chance for revictimization again increases (Ullman & Brecklin, 2003). Survivors of childhood sexual abuse do not usually experience repetition of their victimization on the conscious level; that is, they do not intentionally precipitate abuse. It may be that revictimization or repetition of the sexual abuse tends to recur through the survivor's reenactment of the physical, sexual, or emotional abuse that was experienced during childhood (Schetky, 1990). Just like their female counterparts, males who were sexually assaulted in childhood are more likely to be assaulted as adults (Aosyed, Long, & Voller, 2011).

Our own feeling from treating such clients is that they have received very few of the typical parental warnings and admonitions that would naturally have been taught to them if they had had a normal childhood. As a result, they tend not to be aware of or reactive to warning signs and cues that would say to most people, "This is not a safe place to be or a safe thing to do or a safe person to be with." They also may respond very much as our combat veterans do by engaging in risky behaviors to achieve adrenaline highs that let them know they are "still alive and kicking." Because of this, the crisis worker needs to provide psychoeducation on warning signs and cues that may stop survivors from blithely going into dangerous settings and engaging with people who will do them harm.

Child Abuse as a Predictor of PTSD.

Child sexual abuse has been shown to predict the development of PTSD in later life (Darves-Bornoz et al., 1998; Kessler & Bieschke, 1999; Pfefferbaum, 1997; Regehr, Cadell, & Jansen, 1999). In a comparison of the prevalence of PTSD and other diagnoses in abused children, Ackerman and associates (1998) studied three groups: sexual abuse (SA) only, physical abuse (PA) only, and both (BOTH). Children in the BOTH group had more diagnoses overall. PTSD was significantly comorbid (disorder or trauma caused by two variables) with most affective disorders. A younger age of onset of SA and coercion to maintain secrecy predicted a higher number of total diagnoses. Also, children had more diagnoses when PA had come from males rather than from females. The research of Darves-Bornoz and

associates (1998) indicated that adding physical assault during the rape of children was predictive of chronic PTSD. However, to suppose that PTSD is the only or major pathological outcome of child sexual abuse is to severely underestimate the negative consequences that accrue. Developmental processes associated with affect regulation and interpersonal relational skills may be severely disrupted and pave the way for future assaults (Cloitre & Rosenberg, 2006).

False Memories

The "false memory" concept, applied to work **LO12** with both adults who were abused as children and perpetrators of abuse, has raised concern and controversy among human services workers (Rubin, 1996). This debate raged in the 1990s, and while it has now subsided you should understand that it still plays a role in criminal defense of accused abusers. The False Memory Syndrome Foundation was created in 1992 by Pamela and Peter Freyd, who had been accused by their daughter of sexual abuse. They propose that false memories occur for three reasons. First is countertransference, in which mental health professionals who have been abused themselves plant the memories to exact revenge and satisfy their own power needs. Second, angry adolescents who are seeking emancipation lash out at their parents by making accusations of sexual abuse. Third is the child who projects her own strong sexual feelings onto the father as his own toward her (Freyd, 1993). The studies of lost and distorted memories of childhood traumas by Bremner (1998) have raised doubts about the degree to which traumatic memories are susceptible to distortion due to misleading and suggestive statements (as may occur during psychotherapy).

The findings also suggest that stress as well as the adult's neuroanatomical conditions can lead to modifications in memory traces. Studies indicate that a significant percentage of women claiming abuse have only foggy memories of the sexual abuse and some have little, if any (Briere & Conte, 1993; Elliot & Briere, 1995; Williams, 1995). Leavitt (2000) confirmed that women who had been sexually abused—both those who had continuous memories and those who had recovered memories of the abuse—produced significantly different Rorschach interpretations compared to those who had not been abused.

Conversely, from their "recovered memory" survey of 154 psychiatrists, Feigon and de Rivera (1998) concluded that the numbers of false accusations of childhood sexual abuse appearing to emerge from the psychotherapy of adults constitute a real problem requiring public acknowledgment as such by the mental health professions. Their study indicates that the specific content of false memories extracted from client interviews depends on the particular interviewer, the way questions are asked, the context in which the interview takes place, and the emotional state of the interviewee. Mitchell and Morse (1998, pp. 67–93) have laid out a clear structure in regard to what kinds of memory systems are involved and how one goes about legitimately retrieving memories. The worker should collect a good psychosocial history and personality assessment but not uncritically accept or confirm suspicions without corroborating evidence. The clinician should avoid leading questions, not endeavor to pull up "repressed" memories, remain neutral, and remember that a particular set of symptoms may not be exclusive to sexual abuse (Courtois, 1999).

Your authors' own experiences indicate that at some unconscious memory level, the sexually abused person almost never forgets at least some of the essential details of the source of the trauma. Knauer (2000, p. xi) supports our own experience, but she works mainly with children who are not as far removed chronologically from the traumatic event. Perhaps more important, we find that when sexual assault survivors are regressed back to the traumatic event, they are not much different from any other kind of PTSD victim in regard to memory, and they start to fill in the blanks in the same ways.

The debate notwithstanding, psychotherapy with and advocacy of survivors should be done by workers who are highly trained and skilled in dealing with the trauma, the repressed and dissociated memory issues, the risks, and the needs of survivors of child sexual abuse. Similarly, professionals who deal with perpetrators' memories should have a thorough understanding of the complex forms of abuser memory and forgetting that are frequently encountered. The discrepancies, emotions, dissociations, memory blackouts, and discomfort with traumatic memories may affect the way both survivors and perpetrators perceive the past abusive events (Rubin, 1996). To that end, anyone who does this work *absolutely must not* bring their own parental or abuse agendas into therapy. We have witnessed such a happening, and it was extremely destructive for clients and the therapist. Clinicians must strive to neither suggest nor suppress reports of remembered or suspected abuse and trauma. Instead, they must practice from a stance of supportive neutrality (Courtois, 2001).

Intervention Strategies for Adult Survivors: The Case of Heather

Heather was sexually abused by her stepfather **LO13** regularly from ages 8 through 15. For 20 years she suppressed most memories and emotions related to the sexual abuse, which had included fondling, digital penetration, and intercourse. She has vivid memories of the physical abuse she suffered at both her stepfather's and her mother's hands. It is somewhat ironic that her stepfather was employed as a psychologist at a major university. Now, at age 35, she has regained her memory of the sexual abuse and is experiencing severe symptoms of delayed rape trauma syndrome.

Her marriage is breaking up; her career is in shambles; her communications and relationship with her three children are adversely affected by her personal turmoil; her rage toward her stepfather and her anger toward her mother have robbed her of her self-respect and her affection toward her parents, who live across the state from her. Her only daughter, the middle child, recently had her eighth birthday, and Heather is deeply obsessed with her daughter's safety. Heather feels a great deal of guilt, shame, remorse, and loss of self-esteem. For several years she has been experiencing some suicidal ideation, and since the recovery of her memory of the sexual abuse, this ideation has seriously intensified.

Interventions with Heather included both individual counseling and support group work, in which she willingly participated. In support group meetings, Heather received the encouragement, validation, and information she needed to absolve herself from guilt, shame, and remorse. She also acquired essential advice from support group members on implementing safety measures she could take to ensure that her 8-year-old daughter would not fall prey to the kinds of sexual abuse she herself had suffered. That advice allayed her fears and concerns about her daughter's vulnerability. Often the affirmation and informational resources obtained in support groups are key elements in the emotional healing, fear reduction, enhancement of self-esteem, and rehabilitation of adult survivors of child sexual abuse. It was certainly so with Heather (Mitchell & Morse, 1998, pp. 231–238).

Assessment

Particularly among older women such as Heather who suffered childhood sexual abuse under severe societal and family strictures of secrecy and denial, the abuse will be disguised and repressed. Often such clients will have been under the care of mental health professionals and been diagnosed with a variety of mental illnesses ranging from schizophrenia to depression to borderline personality.

Presenting problems are typically depression, anxiety, dissociation, and compulsive disorders (Courtois, 1988). Although the client may present as competent, responsible, mature, and otherwise capable, these characteristics are a facade for underlying emotional problems. Affectively, behaviorally, and cognitively, abuse victims may present themselves in a bipolar manner, rigidly adhering to one end or the other of the continuum—"I'm great" or "I'm terrible"—or rapidly oscillating between the two (Courtois, 1988).

Triage assessment of these people can be problematic, to say the least. At one moment they present as affectively calm and controlled, perhaps to the point of rigidity. At the next moment, because of some real or imagined slight, particularly in interpersonal relationships, they may become extremely labile (emotionally unstable) with angry tirades or uncontrolled crying and then offer profuse, guilt-ridden apologies for their behavior. It should come as little surprise that many individuals with a diagnosis of borderline personality disorder have suffered from child sexual abuse.

Cognitively, they may present themselves as competent and perceptive thinkers and then, when faced with a stimulus that causes a flashback or intrusive image, completely dissociate themselves from present reality and respond in a confused, disjointed manner. Behaviorally, such individuals may run the gamut of DSM-5 (American Psychiatric Association, 2013) diagnostic categories—and then appear perfectly appropriate! If there is any key to making an accurate assessment of adult survivors of childhood sexual abuse, it is their consistent inconsistency across triage dimensions. The astute crisis worker who is struggling to make an assessment in which such inconsistency is displayed should consider childhood sexual abuse as a working hypothesis.

A crisis invariably initiates therapy; as in other forms of delayed PTSD, the crisis may seem unrelated to a past traumatic event. During the intake interview, if some of the common symptoms of PTSD are revealed, then childhood sexual abuse should be suspected as a causative agent and further assessment should target it as a possibility. Construction of a traumagram (Figley, 1985) will often provide clues to the origin of the precipitating event. The crisis worker who suspects PTSD in an adult due to childhood sexual abuse should immediately make plans to refer the client for a comprehensive psychiatric assessment after the initiating crisis is contained.

Heather initially presented at a community mental health center with suicidal thoughts and actions. She had overdosed on sleeping pills, was discovered comatose by a girlfriend, and had been taken to the emergency room, where her stomach was pumped. At intake she showed the counselor cuts she had inflicted on herself with a box cutter. She was dissociative and saw herself "out of her body" as she drew the knife up and down her arms. (Note: Cutting on oneself and other types of bloodletting, as opposed to slashing one's wrists, is not a suicide attempt but rather a tension reduction mechanism, or letting the "bad blood" out. Some cutters save their blood and bandages and find comfort in them. Further, the scar can be a symbol of healing. By doing all this, cutters validate in a very physical way the tremendous emotional pain they feel and have a way of seeing that they really are alive [Mitchell & Morse, 1998].) She had also cut off her parakeet's head (a much more ominous suicidal sign of taking out a prized possession), although she was extremely remorseful about its death and could not imagine why she would have done such a terrible thing. She was currently depressed and saw no reason for living.

The counselor rated her overall on the Triage Assessment Form at 27, set up a stay-alive contract with her, and referred her to a psychiatrist for evaluation and medication for depression. After several false starts and stops at counseling, Heather finally admitted the real issue, that she had been abused sexually and physically as a child by her stepfather from age 8 to 15 and that the abuse had been denied by her mother. Both parents had engaged in physical abuse of Heather during the same time period. At 16 she went to live with her father, who was a functional alcoholic. Those arrangements were chaotic, but no further physical or sexual abuse occurred. That lasted until she moved away to college.

She reports that the behavior that got her to the ER and into counseling has been getting progressively worse, and she can no longer keep thoughts of the abuse submerged. She is experiencing severe social estrangement and has very few social relationships—none of which are with males. She wears numerous layers of clothing that hide her female figure, even in very hot weather. She wears no makeup and appears almost unisexual. She is a talented artist and is employed part-time at a graphic design business.

Treatment of Adults

A major component of therapy is to use a posttrau-matic stress treatment model that uses some combina-tion of prolonged exposure and cognitive processing or cognitive restructuring (Cloitre & Rosenberg, 2006; Foa & Rauch, 2004; Nishith, Nixon, & Resick, 2005) along with techniques to deal with the severe affec-tive dysregulation (inability to monitor and control one's emotions) that accompanies this form of trauma (Briere & Scott, 2006, pp. 76–77; Courtois, Ford, & Cloitre, 2009). A meta-analysis by Ehring and asso-ciates (2014) that dealt exclusively with PTSD with child sexual abuse as a causative agent in adult survivors examined standard CBT treatment, trauma-focused CBT treatments, and EMDR. Overall Parcesepe and her associates' (2015) comprehensive review of treat-ment results found that all three interventions—be-havioral, exposure therapy, and EMDR—were more effective in alleviating symtoms than no treatment. However, they did not find significant differences in treatment effectiveness between the three. They found that trauma-focused CBT was the most ef-fective, and treatment including individual sessions faired better than group treatment alone. However, Finkelhor (1987) proposes that the trauma of child-hood sexual abuse goes beyond other causal agents of PTSD because of the unique dynamics of traumatic sexualization, social stigmatization, betrayal of trust by loved ones, and powerlessness of children, so that trust building and affirmation activities are particu-larly critical.

It is interesting to note that virtual reality treat-ment (Como & Bouchard, 2015) and online counsel-ing targeting sexual abuse (Webber & Moors, 2015) are beginning to appear as well (see Chapter 6, Tele-phone and Online Crisis Counseling).

Discovery and Admission

For survivors of childhood sexual abuse, particular problems arise in the therapeutic process that are ab-sent with victims of other traumatic experiences. If the client is otherwise in crisis and childhood sexual abuse is suspected, do not explore incest material im-mediately because of the likelihood of compounding the present crisis through decompensation, regres-sion, or dissociation. Client safety is paramount and should always be a primary or conjoint consider-ation with exploration of the incest (Courtois, 1988, p. 173). At the time the client chooses to own the trauma of incest, the potential for crisis rises expo-nentially. Stige, Traeen, and Rosenvinge (2013) report

that when attempts to self-manage the trauma finally give way, a high level of distress is reported prior to help seeking. Sensitivity in respecting and exploring the individual's process of seeking help when offering trauma treatment to survivors cannot be over empha-sized. This is a huge undertaking that typically has a mountain of stigma attached to it and is positively re-lated to trauma symptom severity (Deitz et al., 2015). The worker needs to be very sensitive to the client's admission, gently encouraging the client to disclose the abuse and directively and positively affirming the client for doing so. Trust here is critical. Not only have these clients learned that adult caretakers are untrustworthy (Elliot, 1994), but it is more than likely that others in the helping professions have victimized them as well (Ochberg, 1988).

Heather: (*apprehensively*) I don't know what you'll think about this. But I guess I can trust you. I just can't live with this anymore. (*Pauses.*)

CW: (*suspecting from previous indicators what is coming*) Whatever it is, I can see how deeply troubling it is and how difficult it must be. I am here to listen and try to understand. Whatever it is, I want you to know that you will still be the same Heather, and that person is not going to be any different in my eyes. I hope what I've just said makes it easier for you to get it out.

Heather: (*starts sobbing*) This is really bad.

CW: Heather, I am going to reach over and hold your arm, is that OK? (*Heather nods. Counselor softly touches Heather's arm and speaks gently.*) I'm guessing this is about something that somebody did to you or that happened to you, and it's OK, really OK, to talk about it.

Heather: I had sex with my stepfather. (*Relates a long history of sexual and physical torment by her stepfather and mother, with the counselor listening and empathi-cally responding.*)

Heather: (*gently weeping*) I know you're a counselor and all, but you must think I'm horrible.

CW: I understand how terribly difficult that was. I also want you to know that I believe what you said. I don't think you're horrible at all. What I think is that you were a victim and that you are a survivor of those terrible things that shouldn't have happened and did. I want to correct one thing you said. You did not have sex with your stepfather. You were 8 years old and had no choice. He had, and he forced sex on you. That's a big difference.

Now I want to give you an idea of what is happening to you, why these bad memories keep coming back, and what they do to disrupt your life.

The crisis worker uses affirming and supportive statements throughout this opening scene. She touches the client only after being given permission because touching can sometimes be construed as anything but supportive by the client.

There are three general phases to this treatment. The first is safety; the second is processing, remembering, and mourning; and the third is reconnecting and reintegration (Courtois, Ford, & Cloitre, 2009; Mitchell & Morse, 1998, pp. 184–195). The first order of business is keeping the client safe and in full knowledge of what is going to occur. There have been far too many secrets in these clients' lives. There are no secrets here.

Psychoeducation. Psychoeducation about the role that PTSD plays in incest trauma is important at this point because it can help allay clients' fears that they are "different," "dirty," or "mentally ill," and it assures them that PTSD is responsive to treatment. Education about PTSD also removes the mystique, confusion, and "craziness," anchoring present maladaptive behavior as purposive and reasonable given the survivor's traumatic history. It also allows the client to believe that something can be done through treatment (Courtois, 1988, p. 173).

CW: (*after an explanation and showing Heather the DSM-5 PTSD classification*) So you are not "nuts." Those are the reasons these things are currently happening. We can treat this. It is a long road, and at times it is going to seem as if things are getting worse instead of better. We will have to go back and dig into those memories, and they are going to be painful. I want you to think about this because it is not an easy task. It is something you will need to choose. If you choose to do so, I want you to know that we'll go through this together. (*The counselor then explains what the treatment procedures will be and answers questions the client has about different components of the treatment.*)

Grounding

Grounding refocuses clients' attention onto the immediate therapeutic environment or, when over the phone or Internet, on the physical surroundings they are presently inhabiting as opposed to flashbacks, intrusive thoughts, and dissociative states that are beginning to overwhelm them (Sanderson, 2013, pp. 167–174; Briere & Scott, 2006, pp. 96–97). They propose the following five steps:

1. Attempt to focus the client's attention on the therapist and the therapy. "I am right here. We're together in this room and we are doing exposure therapy. You are not back in the bedroom 20 years ago" are typical verbal responses to a client "going into the wind." At times, gentle touching may also be appropriate.
2. Ask the client to describe the internal experience he or she is presently having. "Describe what's going on right now." If the client has difficulty or appears frightened or otherwise unequal to the task, then move to step 3.
3. Orient the client to the immediate environment that he or she is in—the room with the worker, where it is, how it looks, what's in it, and how safe it is, and that it is not in the bedroom 20 years in the past.
4. If the client is still indicating stress, start deep breathing and relaxation techniques (which we recommend teaching to these clients).
5. Repeat step 2 and assess the client's ability to return to therapy.

Grounding is a critical component of this therapy, in which clients are taught to literally put their feet on the ground, get physically and psychologically anchored, and stop the fragmentary thought processes and heightened affect that lead to depersonalization, flashbacks, and overpowering emotions (Matsakis, 2003, pp. 57–58; Mitchell & Morse, 1998, p. 198). Sutherland (1993, p. 23) proposes that focusing on gravity in relation to the body starts to make the client aware of the numbness and disowning of various body parts that she uses to dissociate from the trauma. The client is asked to find and identify a "spot of safety" where she can practice grounding. That spot of safety is a place the client can go and feel absolutely safe. One anchor that grounds clients is carrying a talisman with them, something that can literally be touched to connect them with reality. Coins, charms, key chains, totems, worry stones, and so on can all serve this purpose. Your authors use this technique with abused and neglected foster children a lot and see no reason it shouldn't work with adults as well. Matsakis (2003, p. 58) proposes physical grounding, such as holding a familiar or safe item like a teddy bear; emotional grounding by writing oneself an e-mail or leaving a message on one's answering machine and then reading or listening to it; or mental grounding by describing aloud the room one is in, singing, or reading out loud from a magazine.

CW: So the safest place in the house is the bathroom, with you sitting on the commode. Fine! When some of these cues that we've talked about start happening and you start to feel things sliding away, I want you to go into the bathroom, put your feet flat on the floor, and with the toilet lid down, have a seat, pick up a copy of *Car and Driver* (or any other magazine), and say to yourself, "It is 9:15 P.M., Tuesday evening, January 25, 2016. I am sitting on the toilet in my home, reading *Car and Driver*, and I feel a little silly sitting on the toilet lid, but I am quite safe." So just relax and enjoy that. Just notice your eyes scanning over the articles and looking at the pictures.

At times when the client is in crisis and away from the worker, grounding the client over the telephone is critical. This can be done by reassuring her she is safe and asking her to describe what she sees and hears around her. Ask her if she can feel her feet on the floor and if not, press down with her feet and grip something with her hands. Finally, she should keep a list of people she can call and go through the grounding exercise with (Mitchell & Morse, 1998, p. 199).

Mindfulness. A variation on stabilizing a person who is dissociating and derealizing is using mindfulness exercises. Mindfulness is the art of relating to one's experience in the present moment with full awareness and accepting whatever comes to mind (Brown, Marquis, & Guiffrida, 2013). Using mindfulness techniques can significantly reduce distress (Sass, Berenbaum, & Abrams, 2013) by opening attention to one's experience and keeping an open mind to whatever one encounters (Bishop et al., 2004). This is not a "just do it" exercise but takes practice and should not be done until an individual receives a good deal of psychoeducation (Williams et al., 2007), practice, and tryout with the technique. The major idea is that thoughts are just thoughts—not fixed and immutable facts that can't be changed (Greason, 2015).

CW: So sit on the toilet and focus your attention on the lavatory and just tell me what you see on the countertop as you see it.

Heather: All my hand lotions and pills and stuff and shit! My frickin' razor!

CW: OK, the razor's there, but for the moment focus on something else.

Heather: It's that new oatmeal soap I got at the healthful food store.

CW: Tell me what's going through your mind as you look at it.

Heather: Well erh, ah. It's suppose to really clear your complexion up; deep scrubbing gets the oil out and that. I could sure use that after the day I've had and . . . oh man! I am starting to lose it again.

CW: That happens, but now remember the exercise of watching those thoughts we did and how we moved them. You can just watch them float away.

Heather: Ha! I did! By golly I did it! Ha! They just sorta went down the shower drain.

CW: Good! Now let's try something. Get a washcloth and soap up and wash your face. Can you do that?

Heather: (*Gets up, wets washcloth, and goes back on the stool and starts soaping her face.*) OK I'm washing my face. I did it with cold water. It's rough but it feels kinda good. Cool and like scrubbing you know. Like maybe I could just take a shower and feel clean.

CW: So you have that in your mind, what your face feels like and can start to imagine how that would feel like if you did take a shower and could just feel that sensation of cleanliness.

Heather: I umh, yeah, I think I could. I am back together pretty much. Thanks Dr. J.

CW: OK! Are we good to go?

Heather: Yes!

The crisis worker uses the "watching" technique to shift the client's attention when she starts heading back down old ineffective trauma-filled paths to give her a sense of control and power over her thoughts (Greason, 2015). The face wash utilizes a different type of mindfulness technique called **body scanning** (Kabat-Zinn, 2013, pp. 75–97). In body scanning the individual monitors physical sensations throughout the body and gently allows himself or herself to feel, experience, and accept the physical sensations that emanate from various body parts. The crisis worker doesn't panic or attempt to get Heather to stop when she starts to dissociate again. Rather, he acknowledges that in a matter-of-fact way, but gently guides her back to ground. If you have ever been camping and got up on a frosty morning and washed your face in a cold mountain stream you surely understand how quickly you are grounded in that moment with all that cold freshwater on your face and very much aware of the world around you!

Validation

As the client starts through the process of therapy, numerous transcrisis points will occur as long-buried trauma is brought back to awareness. In an active, directive, continuous, and reinforcing manner, the human services worker (Courtois, 1988, pp. 167–170; Longdon, 1994; Mitchell & Morse, 1998, pp. 90–91, 184–188):

1. Validates that the incest did happen, despite denial of this fact by significant others; the client is not to blame, it is safe to talk about it, and the worker does not loathe the client for having been a participant.
2. Acts as an advocate who is openly, warmly interested in what happened to the survivor as a child and makes owning statements to that effect but still maintains neutrality and neither advocates for nor dismisses legal action. The worker also understands there is a high potential for transference/countertransference and is clear and consistent in maintaining boundaries.
3. Reinforces the resourcefulness of the victim to become a survivor.
4. Provides a mentor/reparenting role model to help with childhood developmental tasks that were missed.

Extinguishing Trauma

Extinguishing trauma means effecting a psychological extinction—that is, facilitating the reduction or loss of a conditioned response as a result of the absence or withdrawal of reinforcement. In practical terms, this means the reduction or loss of both Heather's negative beliefs about herself and her debilitating behaviors that were responses to her childhood sexual abuse. It also means getting rid of the perpetrator.

When the survivor is in therapy, there are always at least three people there—in Heather's case, there are four (Mitchell & Morse, 1998, p. 198): the worker, Heather, and the perpetrators—her mother and her stepfather. The crisis worker sought to extinguish Heather's negative beliefs and behaviors by systematically leading her to mentally refute her erroneous perceptions that she was responsible, culpable, or guilty and had her reframe her previous beliefs to help her gain a new insight that she was an innocent victim

and can now view herself more realistically as a guilt-free survivor.

When working through traumatic events, the client will experience a dramatic increase in affective and autonomic arousal (Ochberg, 1988). The human services worker must be very careful to provide palatable doses of the traumatic material that do not exceed the client's coping abilities (Courtois, 1988, p. 174) and prompt a crisis within the therapy session. Careful processing with the client before and after each session of extinguishing and reframing traumatic memories is important in preventing such crises.

CW: Let's take a look at what we did today.

Heather: I'm pretty scared. I didn't remember a lot of that stuff until we dug that memory up.

CW: That's pretty typical. Any reasonable person would bury that stuff. If you really start to feel like you're losing it, I want you to call me.

Heather: (*later that evening, calling*) I really hate to disturb you, but I've really got this urge to start cutting myself. I'm also having thoughts about killing my other pet bird. They're starting to get pretty real.

CW: (*very directively*) Do you feel like you're losing it enough that you need to be hospitalized?

Heather: I don't know. Maybe if I just talk this through.

CW: OK. Go get on the toilet seat, put your feet on the ground, and let's talk. (*Heather does so.*) OK, you there? Feet on the ground? OK! Remember what I said about this being rough. What you went through today brought back a lot of old memories and some ugly fresh ones. That's normal. It's nasty, but it is normal. Now I want you to think of how we changed that scene, how you told yourself all those negative things about yourself being dirty and no good, and what the reality of that scene is. (*A dialogue ensues that recaps the day's events. Heather is able to regain control, and after a 20-minute dialogue is able to feel secure enough to relax and go to bed.*)

The worker should be aware that extinguishing one traumatic event does not lessen the fear and trepidation of moving on to other events. This is particularly true in the case of adult survivors of childhood sexual abuse, who may experience increased intrusive behavioral symptoms and regress to former maladaptive behaviors even though they are making good progress in erasing bad memories (Cogdal & James, 1991).

Clients may appear to be getting worse instead of better—which is threatening and scary for both client and worker.

The worker should be prepared for this contingency, tell the client of its likelihood, and affirm that it is totally acceptable for the client to check in with the worker if these symptoms and behaviors reemerge between sessions. The worker's role when this happens is to be understanding, affirming, and calming. Constant validation is important because many clients will be discouraged at the length of treatment, afraid and angry over revictimization and extension of the traumatic experience's "life," and flee from therapy (Courtois, 1988, p. 177). The second phase of therapy involves reclaiming the self. It is a painful business to watch, and there is every urge to rescue the client. This must not happen! The work must be done by the survivor, and dependence cannot be allowed to occur (Mitchell & Morse, 1998, p. 190).

Prolonged Exposure/Cognitive Restructuring

Reframing the client's negative and distorted beliefs about himself or herself is critical in allowing the client to separate the fact and fiction of an abusive childhood (Courtois, 1988, p. 181). While imaginally flooding the most abusive childhood scene the client can tolerate, clients paste mental billboards under the scene (Cogdal & James, 1991). These billboards typically deliver all the myths and distorted messages that the abuser gave in addition to the client's own childhood negative self-talk. The image of the assault scene is enhanced though prolonged exposure or flooding by loading all the sights, sounds, smells, and noises as if it were happening in real time to the most distressing level the client can tolerate. The idea is to build the noxious stimuli to such an extent that it finally loses it malignant power over the client and becomes benign.

CW: (*with the client deeply relaxed, eyes closed*) Picture that videotape, the bedroom, the "game," him making you get on him and suck his "peter," almost strangling as you do so. Feel the pain and the disgust. But he makes you keep doing it until he gets off, and the semen is running all over, sticky and wet. Notice the messages underneath that scene. "This is what fathers do to educate their daughters to become women." "You aren't a good daughter if you don't do this." "I'll kill you if you don't keep our secret." Feel the confusion, the fear, and the repulsion as you do this. Put those messages in big block letters underneath that scene. Do you see them?

Heather: (*eyes closed and body twisting*) Yes!

CW: Freeze that scene and the billboards. Take a snapshot of it. Let it develop. Hold it in your hands.

The client is then asked to destroy the image along with the negative parental injunctions and her own negative self-injunctions (Cogdal & James, 1991).

CW: Now I want you to get rid of that scene. It is in your past, and it is gone, so now get rid of it from your memory also. Do that now, and tell me what is happening.

Heather: I set a match to it. It is burning. It's a huge fire now with yellow, sick-smelling smoke.

CW: Let it burn.

Heather: It's just a crisp cinder now, all gone.

CW: All gone? Is there anything else you want to do with it?

Heather: CRUSH IT!

CW: Do it! What's happening?

Heather: I'm grinding it up with my boot heel. It's nothing; he's nothing.

CW: Fine. Now relax and slip back into that soft, cool mountain glade. Just relax and feel the tranquility, calmness, and peacefulness.

The client then replays the scene, but this time substitutes positive, self-enhancing counterinjunctions based on the facts and not on the fictional messages of the event. The worker guides the image and reframes the stepfather in a truer psychological image (Cogdal & James, 1991).

CW: Go back to the bedroom with him now. Picture the scene, but change it. See him as small, very small, weak. He is a small, selfish, pouting boy, dressed up in a man's pajamas. He looks ridiculous. Put these billboards under the scene. "The only people he has power over are little girls." "It is his fault this is happening." "It is WRONG!" "It is criminal!" "I should have felt confused, fearful. I had the right to feel that way!" "I also have the right to be *angry* about it." "*Nobody* has the right to do that. Nobody!" Now freeze that picture and snapshot it. Let it develop. Look at it. What are you feeling and thinking?

Heather: (*yelling*) You asshole! You bastard! You are gone from my life, you puke! You lied to me, you scared me to death, and kept at it. You used me because you were afraid of everybody else. I was the only one you could use, you scumbag. You've got no power over me now, you pissant, or my memories. You are history!

CW: I want you to save that picture. Put it someplace else, safe in your memory, and every time that image starts to come back, pull out the picture and look at it. See that scene for what it really is, and see those billboards, flashing. Have you got it?

Heather: Yes. I've got it.

CW: How do you feel?

Heather: Better, relaxed, relieved maybe.

As the client works through a series of traumatic events, each one is set up as it happened with all of the negative distortions and self-talk that accompanied it. These negative self-attributions carry over into the present time and form maladaptive operating schemas for how the client lives. By rooting out these distortions and modifying them into more positive self-enhancing and enabling counterinjunctions, clients are able to compare "old" and "new" schemas and not only modify and rid themselves of the debilitating memories but also begin to incorporate those new schemas into their present-day lives (Cloitre & Rosenberg, 2006).

Relearning Feelings. Like combat veterans, survivors of childhood sexual abuse have developed excellent coping skills to deny and numb feelings. But this is even more problematic for survivors of childhood sexual abuse because learning to differentiate feelings is a skill that develops in childhood. For most of these survivors, their childhood environments were anything but nurturing, and their caretakers may have suffered from severe affective dysregulation, alternating between a flood of feelings and none at all. As a result, a condition called **alexithymia** develops in many survivors of childhood sexual abuse. Alexithymia is the inability to recognize and label feelings. Recognizing and labeling feelings is of utmost importance in helping clients give voice to shunted emotions and warded-off feelings. Heather's bitter and angry emotions are not unlike those of combat veterans as they relive and extinguish bad memories.

Developmentally, clients have to literally relearn and identify their emotional states. Cloitre and Rosenberg (2006) use part of their group format on skills training in affect and interpersonal regulation (STAIR) to teach clients to recognize feelings,

monitor emotional intensity levels, learn emotional triggers, and formulate coping/reaction responses. Many of the students in survivor groups have absolutely no idea what the visual cues are that others give them. For example, a professor who gives one of these women a quizzical look after asking a question might well be described as angry or mad by the woman. In work with survivors, one of your authors commonly uses an elementary school classroom guidance technique to train students to recognize feelings. Each student in his survivor groups gets a handout showing faces with different emotions and feeling words attached to them to help the students relabel feelings and discriminate emotional cues from others. Far from seeing this exercise as childish, clients report that they pull out and use these sheets on a daily basis to validate their present emotional state.

Grief Resolution

Beginning to recognize past, buried feelings is to start on the road to acknowledging feelings of anger and rage, as Heather does in the preceding dialogue (Courtois, Ford, & Cloitre, 2009, pp. 93–94). These feelings will ultimately end in sadness and grieving for the loss of a happy childhood, her loss of who she might have been without the trauma, and the loss of a psychologically healthy family instead of the malevolent one she grew up in (Courtois, 1988, p. 181). It is likely to be one of the most painful stages as the client comes to grips with the reality that there is no retrieving the past or changing it and that attempts to do so are fruitless. Only the future holds promise for her, and she can control only that (Hays, 1985). Grieving and resolution, particularly with perpetrators of the abuse, are other transcrisis points in therapy. At this time, the crisis worker will have to move into a grieving and loss mode (see Chapter 12, Personal Loss: Bereavement and Grief).

Heather: I had a call from my mother last night. I wanted to be assertive with her and tell her how I felt, like I had worked out in group. But when it came down to it, I just couldn't. I haven't got the guts. (*Starts crying.*) I'll never get rid of this. Why couldn't she have been different? Why does she still try that stuff of browbeating me? Wasn't what she did enough?

CW: You have every right to feel sad that she wasn't or still isn't what you'd hope a mother might be. I wish she could change, but I have my doubts. So if she won't, what will you do?

Heather: I guess she won't. I guess I'll just kiss her off.

CW: You survived with her battering you, and you've survived for 10 years without her. Perhaps it's time you did say good-bye. (*Patiently lets Heather silently weep.*)

Confrontation. The tremendous push–pull between love and hatred survivors feel for their perpetrators is a difficult issue to resolve. Role-playing with the empty chair technique, writing letters, drawing, and journaling may be ways of mourning the loss. Whether the survivor will ever actually confront the abuser is a question only the survivor can answer. There are a number of reasons it may be good for the survivor to confront the perpetrator, such as empowerment, closure, "setting the record straight," anger, grief, and forgiveness (Cameron, 1994). However, *this must be the survivor's decision*, and the crisis worker must remain scrupulously neutral in this debate. Confronting the abuser is not mandatory for healing (Mitchell & Morse, 1998, p. 162). Further, to believe that the perpetrator will "confess" to the abuse may be very wishful thinking indeed.

The following questions generated by Bass and Davis (1992, p. 134), or some variation of them, need to be asked and processed with the survivor before the decision to confront is made.

1. What is motivating you to do this, and are you prepared to do this?
2. What will you possibly gain, and what will you possibly lose?
3. Could you live with being excluded from family functions and risk losing contact with family members who did not abuse you?
4. Will you be able to handle it if you are labeled "crazy"?
5. Can you handle getting no reaction or denial?

Changing Behavior Through Skill Building and Reconnecting. Although coming to terms with past trauma and stopping maladaptive present behavior are critical to the adult survivor, changing behavior to more self-determining choices is the major end goal of therapy. The vacuum left by the removal of bad memories and the psychic energy previously expended to maintain control of those memories is not easily filled. Pearson (1994) and Mitchell and Morse (1998) recommend using several categories of techniques for skill building, listed earlier in this chapter.

Reeducation is necessary for survivor skill building, and the worker may assume a teaching role in transmitting basic life skills such as communication, decision making, conflict resolution, cognitive restructuring, and boundary setting (Courtois, 1988, pp. 181–182). Herman (1981) likens the survivor to an immigrant who must literally rebuild her life in a culture that is absolutely foreign to what she experienced as a child. From that standpoint, the crisis worker should not be unsettled by the emergence of some rather unusual and personal questions.

Heather: Er, ah, I was just wondering, Dr. James, how you treat your kids. I mean, if they act up do you ground them, or what? What do you talk about at dinner? And do you and your wife ever argue?

Although such questions may be construed as intruding on the private life of the worker or attempts by the client to shift focus from her problems or create dependency, it is important to answer these questions as honestly and succinctly as possible, without shifting the focus away from the client's personal concerns. The client is testing her perceptions against the most valid and stable validity check she currently has—her therapist. For that reason, it is important to urge survivors to join therapy or support groups so that new behaviors can be tested out and discussed with peers. Because many families of survivors such as Heather's are so completely dysfunctional, clients need education on what a functional family is and how it operates. Duncan (2004) has defined the characteristics of a functioning family (not the Hollywood ideal one), and we believe they are well worth spending time on in a support group.

As these survivors reconstruct their lives and start to become interested in developing meaningful relationships, Sheehan (1994) proposes five basic fears that they will have to deal with: abandonment, exposure, merger, attack, and their own destructive behavior. Fear of abandonment comes because there never were protectors in their young lives. Thus they avoid emotional encounters because they vow never to be hurt in the same way again and constantly test whether significant others are really committed to them. Fear of merger means fear of losing control and of losing one's selfhood. Survivors have to learn what personal boundaries are because parent/child boundaries were merged into sexual ones. Fear of attack has to do with real or imagined assault, something quite common in most survivors' backgrounds. The anger and rage that accompany the traumatic wake can make survivors wonder whether they can control their own destructive impulses and rage toward themselves or others. These are all topics that involve group work and support and can occasion many transcrisis moments for these people.

Support Groups for Adult Survivors

For victims, groups provide a number of potential positive outcomes and help them move from victim to survivor. Victims may be reluctant to participate, but they should be encouraged to do so, although not all victims may be ready or immediately able to participate in groups. Education as to what the group is about, who the members are, confidentiality issues, what kinds of problems members are working on, and the safety and support of the group format is a critical component in assessing, selecting, motivating, and committing survivors to group work (Courtois, 1988, pp. 253–262).

LO14

Courtois (1988, pp. 245–249) lists the following benefits of group treatment for survivors of childhood sexual abuse:

1. The individual's sense of shame, stigmatization, and negative self-image are reduced by meeting other survivors who appear "normal."
2. Commonality of experience raises members' consciousness about incest, so the experience becomes more normalized and may be seen from an interpersonal and sociocultural perspective rather than an "only me" perspective.
3. The group serves as a new "surrogate" family where new behaviors and methods of communicating, interacting, and problem solving can be practiced in a safe, accepting, and nurturing environment.
4. The group allows for safe exploration and ventilation of feelings and beliefs that have been denied and submerged from awareness.
5. Childhood messages and rules that were generated within the abusive environment can be challenged and dissected to determine how they still influence the survivor's maladaptive behavior patterns.

In summary, the case of Heather should make very clear that dealing with an adult survivor of childhood sexual abuse is a complex, tedious, meticulous, and stressful process that is filled with many crisis events. It should come as no surprise that one of the toughest customers a worker will face, the borderline personality disorder, runs rampant in this population. It takes a great deal of expertise, patience, empathy, and personal resiliency to work with such cases. The case of Heather should vividly illustrate why compassion fatigue, vicarious traumatization, and burnout are high probabilities in this kind of work.

Religiosity and Spirituality. In a just world where a benevolent and caring God is ever present, rape and childhood sexual assault never happen. Yet they do quite regularly, so what happens to a person who has a belief that there is that just God out there somewhere who has abandoned her or him? To examine the role religiosity plays in trauma, ter Kuile and Ehring (2014), queried 293 trauma survivors on their changes in religious beliefs as a result of their trauma. Nearly half reported changes, and as the researchers predicted, shattered assumptions about a just world and a fair God caused a decline in their religious beliefs and increased their chances of "catching" PTSD. Those who experienced increases in religious activities used them as a positive coping mechanism, and that finding has been supported in other studies as well (Baty, 2013; Glenn, 2014). This issue is covered extensively in Chapter 12, Personal Loss: Bereavement and Grief, and in Chapter 11, Family Crisis Intervention, but suffice it to say that if at all possible, it appears that finding meaning making in a higher power is a critical ingredient in getting though a sexual trauma.

Helping individuals who have been traumatized after traumatic events to find meaning in what has happened to them is probably the second most important thing after getting them stabilized (Altmaier & Prieto, 2012). Probably above all other traumas, finding forgiveness and resolution and obtaining posttraumatic positive growth are tremendously difficult particularly when the offender is a family member. For each member of the subset the crisis worker must assess the sexual abuse's impact and what part spirituality and religion can (or can't) play in helping them forward in a posttraumatic growth mode. To that end the crisis worker should attempt to determine whether the spiritual distress comes from God for not being there when the abuse happened or not giving the person the strength to get through it. This is a slippery slope, particularly when the person has been strong in his or her faith. At such times referral to a pastoral counselor with expertise in the area is highly recommended (Young, 2015).

Sexual Abuse in Childhood

The fact is that child sexual abuse has always been with us (DeMause, 1974; McCauley et al., 2001), but a variety of political, social, and cultural factors have kept child abuse—and most particularly, child sexual abuse—behind closed doors in the United States (Costin, Karger, & Stoesz, 1996) and throughout the world (Schwartz-Kenney, McCauley, & Epstein, 2001).

By the time one of your authors was a school counselor in 1966, mandatory reporting laws for physical abuse had been enacted in all 50 states (McCauley et al., 2001)—although there was considerable comment at that time on just how exactly one was to report such abuse and the still unclear question of whether one could get sued or fired for doing so no matter what the law said! (Indeed, no matter what the law says today, you should be aware that when the subject of child physical or sexual abuse rears its ugly head in a school building, there can be and often are repercussions when abusing parents are confronted.) Oftentimes legal, ethical, moral, and political considerations (see Chapter 15, Legal and Ethical Issues in Crisis Intervention) collide when child physical and/or sexual abuse is involved. (For that reason, you should know exactly what you need to do and how to substantiate it when making a report. We believe it is absolutely mandatory to consult with another professional and have him or her bear witness when doing so.)

However, it wasn't until the rise of the women's movement and child advocates in the 1970s and their lobbying efforts to open up the blinds that had been closed on this topic that the public really started to become aware of the extent of the problem. In 1974, the Child Abuse Prevention and Treatment Act was passed in the United States, and its definition of who might be covered under the law included sexual abuse. Just as Leontine Young's book *Wednesday's Children* (1964) raised consciousness levels about the physical abuse of children, David Finkelhor's book *Sexually Victimized Children* (1979) did the same for awareness about child sexual abuse.

The Numbers. Child sex abuse numbers are staggering. This compiled report from the National Sexual Violence Resource Center's (2015) compilation of child sexual abuse is mind numbing. One in four girls and one in six boys will be sexually abused before they turn 18 years old (Finklehor, Hotaling, Lewis, & Smith, 1990). Thirty-four percent of those who sexually assault children are family members (National Sexual Violence Resource Center, 2011). Twelve percent of women were age younger than 10 at the time of their rape, and a staggering 28% of men were age 10 or younger (Black et al., 2011). An estimated 325,000 children are at risk of becoming victims of commercial sexual exploitation each year (Adams, Owens, & Small, 2010). Michael Salter's (2013) book, *Organised Sexual Abuse,* provides a chilling look into all of the different groups that organize to sexually abuse children. The good news is that Finklehor and associates (2008) found a 58% decrease in the number of substantiated child sexual abuse cases in the United States between 1992 and 2008. Finklehor and his associates suggest that two decades of prevention, treatment, and criminal prosecutors may have caused this decline. However, we agree with Tabachnick (2013) that the change in the media's reporting of the graphicness of Jerry Sandusky's sexual assaults at Penn State moved the full light of media attention onto perpetrators and caused massive public revulsion of a person who was coach in the national spotlight and who was supposed to be a role model for young men being anything but that in one of the most repellant ways possible.

Dynamics of Sexual Abuse in Childhood

Manifestations of PTSD do not just spring forth full blown in adulthood (McLeer et al., 1992). Sexually abused children have significantly more specific PTSD symptoms than do physically abused and other psychiatrically hospitalized children (Deblinger et al., 1989; McLeer et al., 1992; Wolfe, Gentile, & Wolfe, 1989). Sexually abused children are at high risk for PTSD and symptoms of posttraumatic stress, anxiety, and depression in the immediate period after disclosure and termination of the abuse (McLeer et al., 1998). PTSD, aggressive behavior, and sexually related problems following sexual assault are greater for boys than for girls (Holmes & Slap, 1998). For example, Kuhn, Charleanea, and Chavez (1998) found that sexually assaulted male adolescents were more emotionally distressed, socially isolated, deviant (for example, lying and stealing), and likely to affiliate with deviant peers than males who did not report sexual assault. Even when considering clustering of other types of childhood traumatic caregiver events such as physical abuse, neglect, domestic abuse, emotional abuse, and noncaregivers' trauma such as natural disasters or severe medical problems, when sexual abuse was factored in child sexual abuse had a potent and additive effect on the duration and degree of trauma experienced (Kisiel et al., 2014). Probably the most ominous finding of this rogue's gallery of behavioral outcomes was a study that Fox and associates (2015) did on over 22,000 delinquent juveniles in Florida. They found that each additional adverse traumatic

LO15

event the child suffered on the Adverse Childhood Experiences Index increased their movement toward becoming serious violent and chronic offenders.

Even when rape and sexual assault on children and adolescents do not later result in full-blown PTSD, the emotional and behavioral fallout is far reaching and destructive. In addition, these children have a wide variety of other problems that include concentration difficulties, poor grades, aggressive behavior, social withdrawing, somatic complaints, overcompliance, depression, antisocial tendencies, behavioral regression, poor body image/self-esteem, eating and sleep disturbances, encopresis and enuresis (loss of bowel and bladder control), hyperactivity, suicidal ideation, and extreme, generalized fears (Conte & Schuerman, 1988; Knauer, 2000; Miller-Perrin, 2001; Sgroi, Porter, & Blick, 1982).

Although the foregoing symptoms may be indicative of many disorders of childhood, the following are not, and are rarely ever found with any stressor other than sexual abuse (Goodwin, 1988; Knauer, 2000, pp. 3–30; McLeer et al., 1992; Miller-Perrin, 2001; Salter, 1988, pp. 230–235). Sexually abused children come to school early, stay late, and are rarely or never absent. They barricade themselves in their rooms or otherwise hide and attempt to seal themselves off from their assailants. They may be "perfect" children to the world and to their teachers.

To the contrary, they may engage in inappropriate and persistent sexual play with peers. They may have a sexually transmitted disease. They will have a detailed and age-inappropriate understanding of sexual behavior. They may have physical and somatic symptoms with overlying sexual content such as vaginal or anal bleeding and odors. Sexual drawings, stories, or dreams are common occurrences. They may suddenly have money or gifts that can't be explained. They may display blatant sexually suggestive poses such as wide-open legs, rubbing of genital areas, and provocative dress. They may engage in excessive, compulsive, and even public masturbation, and may even approach other adults sexually. Small children may act out sexually with real or stuffed animals. Teenagers may run away and engage in prostitution.

They may engage in self-mutilation by either cutting or burning themselves. They may have a sudden dislike for someone or demonstrate inordinate clinging behavior. These behaviors provide a template with which varying patterns of psychopathology seen in adult survivors are drawn.

A particular subset of childhood PTSD are the effects of parental abuse and neglect that often occurs in the course of childhood sexual assault. The differences between how PTSD manifests in abused children with PTSD versus adults with PTSD has become profound enough that a team from the National Child Traumatic Stress network has designated a new disorder called developmental trauma disorder (DTD; DeAngelis, 2007). DTD is characterized by exposure to one or more developmentally adverse interpersonal traumas such as abandonment, betrayal, physical or sexual abuse, and emotional abuse. Emotional outcomes range across rage, fear, betrayal, resignation, defeat, and shame. A major marker of DTD is dysregulated development that affects physical health, behavior, cognition, relationships, and self-attribution. Negative expectations about caregivers develop because of their abusive history. As a result, these children stop expecting protection from others and believe future victimization is inevitable (van der Kolk, 2005).

Dynamics of Sexual Abuse in Families

The incestuous family may operate much like **LO16** an alcoholic or battered family does in developing a series of messages or rules that pivot around denial, duplicity, deceit, role confusion, violence, and social isolation (Courtois, 1988, p. 45). Children receive messages such as:

1. Do not show feelings, especially anger.
2. Be in control at all times; do not ask for help.
3. Deny what is happening, and do not believe your own senses/perceptions.
4. No one is trustworthy.
5. Keep the secret because no one will believe you anyway.
6. Be ashamed of yourself; you are to blame for everything.

Intergenerational Transmission of Sexual Abuse. Typically, there is high potential for intergenerational transmission of sexual abuse in these families. Parents who themselves have been abused often seem to have blind spots for what is occurring in front of them. Further, Knauer (2000, pp. 18–19) proposes that the original attraction to the abuser is because of the familiar traits that the person sees in him that ring true within her own abusive family of origin.

Incestuous fathers display inordinate amounts of jealousy and paranoia over their daughters' dating and relationships with other males and attempt to rigidly control behavior through threats and intimidation, and the same may happen with mothers who abuse their sons (Knauer, 2000, pp. 49–61; Rosencrans, 1997, pp. 69–83; Salter, 1988, p. 237). Abusive fathers are controlling tyrants who erect a facade of respectability in the community and often try to isolate their children and spouses or partners by forbidding them to socialize outside the home and refusing to let them have close friends. However, because of their sensitivity to power, they become meek and contrite when confronted with their abuse (Herman, 1981, p. 178).

Mothers are often oppressed and economically dependent, abused by their mates, and products of incestuous families themselves (Courtois, 1988, pp. 54–55; Herman, 1981, pp. 178–179). Mothers may be physically or mentally disabled, causing the eldest daughter to take on the role of "little mother," which extends to fulfilling the father's sexual demands (Herman, 1981, p. 179). Although some mothers may confront the abuse once they discover it, many others engage in denial and helplessness, and when confronted with the reality of the situation may revictimize the child by physical or verbal abuse (Salter, 1988, p. 209). In effect, the child becomes the scapegoat for the family's problems (Knauer, 2000, p. 18).

Female Abusers. Females who are abusers are not as much of an anomaly as one might think and are more than likely underreported as sexual abusers. Allen (1991) believes there are about 1.5 million victims in the United States, and Elliot (1994, p. 220) reports a figure of about 500,000 in Canada who have been abused by females. While these numbers may be outrageously high, they also may not be. A study of Latino and European American adolescents who had been sexually abused found that among male high school students, 52.8% reported that they had been abused by females (Newcomb, Munoz, & Carmona, 2009).

A few studies have reported on female sexual abusers and the outcomes for their victims (Allen, 1991; Elliot, 1994; Fehrenbach & Monastersky, 1988; Knopp & Lackey, 1987; Mathews, Mathews, & Speltz, 1989; McCarty, 1986; Nathan & Ward, 2001; Rosencrans, 1997). More often they are discovered as coabusers (Elliot, 1994; Rosencrans, 1997). The traumatic wake they leave is generally even more devastating because they are seen as the primary caregivers and the persons in whom most trust and nurturing are placed.

In particular, it is important to disabuse the myth that boys are not troubled by such sexual behavior

and "gain experience from older women." The research of Rosencrans (1997, pp. 245–253) indicates quite the opposite. The young man who has sex with an older woman is placed in a double bind. If any part of the experience felt good, the victim may believe it wasn't abusive. If it didn't feel good, then he may have all kinds of recriminations and start to believe that perhaps he is some kind of deviant homosexual (Lew, 2004, p. 61). Lew (2004, p. 61) believes that this causes male survivors to repress memories of abuse by women far more than they do abuse by men. And when those memories do return with a vengeance, they are far more devastating. That outcome is exponentially true when the perpetrator is the victim's mother.

"Motherfucker" is one of the most pejorative, vulgar, and demeaning terms in the English language and has all kinds of negative connotations for boys who might engage in such deviant behavior. That term presupposes the son is the instigator of such illicit sexual contact (Gartner, 2005, pp. 29–30). Research indicates that is anything but true. The Freudian notion of an Oedipal complex wherein the son lusts after the mother has little validity. The social myths and cultural artifacts that mask the true malevolence of female perpetrators on male children minimize this problem in much the same way as the issue of male perpetrators was minimized in the past (Speigel, 2003, p. 15). If we turn that term around as "son fucker," does that reframe your thinking on the matter and shed light on who the true aggressor is?

The sexual identity problem that boys face when they have been abused by female caretakers, and particularly mothers, is a psychological abattoir (Elliot, 1994; Mitchell & Morse, 1998; Rosencrans, 1997). Gartner (2005, pp. 106–120) proposes that it can be cataclysmic to the victim to acknowledge he is in an incestuous relationship with his mother. Yet, while the erotic excitement he feels is disturbing, it can also lead to a sense of sexual prowess that can plant the seeds of some very deviant and pathological beliefs about women. This is not a movie plot in which a young man becomes a mature and skillful lover at the hands of an experienced, beautiful, and competent woman. It is sexual abuse at the hands of a woman who is selfish and needy, has failed at marriage, and has severe relationship and pathological problems. Indeed, out of the bad seeds of these relationships may grow some very poisonous adult relationships for these boys. The bottom line is that adult female abuse of boys is extremely serious and can lead to ominous outcomes (Deering & Mellor, 2011).

As an example, the two adult males one of your authors has encountered in his own practice who were sexually abused by their mothers were potentially the most dangerous to women he has ever seen. They had wildly vacillating "madonna–whore" complexes about women they had targeted for their affection that could turn these women from the purest virgin to the sluttiest streetwalker in a moment, all because of some imagined travesty the women had committed. The really scary part of their delusions was that the women had no idea any of this was going on! Rosencrans's (1997, p. 252) informal interview with law enforcement officers tends to confirm that these abused males have a high potential for sexually related crimes.

Our overall knowledge of female sexual abusers probably compares to what we knew about male child abusers 30 years ago. Therefore, the astute crisis worker needs to ask the following when doing an intake interview with a sexual abuse victim who is male.

CW: We have talked about the perpetrator. Did anybody else sexually abuse you? I am wondering if there were any females who ever did those sorts of things to you?

Because of the high incidence of sexual abuse perpetrated on boys and their reluctance to talk about being sexually abused as children, tactful questions should be asked of any age male even when this is not the presenting problem. The plain and simple fact is that we still tend to dismiss sexual acts and the harmful aspects they present in males (Alaggia & Millington, 2008; O'Leary, 2009). A case in point is the filing of criminal charges against abusers of male children. While the cases filed against perpetrators when the child is female are woefully small in relation to the number committed, a study conducted by Edelson and Joa (2010) found that charges are even less likely to be filed against perpetrators when the victim is a male child.

Phases of Child Sexual Abuse

Sgroi (1982) found that the behavior of the abuser can be traced through five phases: (1) engagement, (2) sexual interaction, (3) secrecy, (4) disclosure, and (5) suppression. These phases apply to both intra- and extrafamilial abuse.

LO17

Engagement Phase. The abuser's objective in the engagement phase is to get the child involved in sexual activity with the abuser. Both access to the child and

opportunity (privacy) are needed if the abuser is to be successful. Therefore, if one were looking for possible instances of unreported abuse, one would identify times and situations when the potential abuser and the child were alone together. One must also look for different strategies that two different types of abusers (child molesters and child rapists) may employ.

Called **grooming,** molesters enter a seduction phase wherein they successively approximate a child to accept that the sexual abuse is okay, appropriate, educational, acceptable, and even a duty. This seduction phase is prior to actual sexual abuse and is not well defined, and there is a lack of consensus on what it actually entails (Bennett & Odonohue, 2014). However, molesters tend to use enticement and entrapment to get the child engaged in sexual activity. **Enticement** may include deceit, trickery, rewards, flattery, or the use of adult authority to tell the child in a matter-of-fact way that the child is expected to participate. **Entrapment** is used to manipulate the child into feeling obligated to participate through traps, blackmail, and so forth. Molesters may make pornographic pictures or videotapes and convince the child that there is no choice other than going along with the secret activity, and may also seek to impose guilt by making the child feel responsible for the abuse.

Online Grooming. The adage your grandmother told your parents, "Never talk to strangers!" really, really applies here except you don't talk to them on the Internet either. Whittle and associates (2013) examined both familial factors such as close parental supervision of Internet use when integrated with contextual and environmental risk factors (low income, poor schools, decaying neighborhoods) and found heightened risk for potential contact with potential molesters. If you've seen any police sting operations on television, you know how prominent this is and continues to be even with the stings! It is indeed illegal to proposition a child on the Internet for sexual interaction, even if that "child" is a 22-year-old police officer.

Factually though, and stings aside, not a lot is yet known about how molesters operate. In Seto's report (2013) the median year for online offender research is 2009 with the range from 2000 to 2009. Undoubtedly it has expanded a great deal since his study, but the problem is that molesters get tied in with child pornography, and that muddles the picture even more. Online offenders may engage in only Internet action or become **solicitation/traveling offenders**. Those are offenders who will attempt to entice a child to meet with them to have sex or encourage them to run away with them (Seto , 2013). It is undoubtedly safe to say that future editions of this book will have a lot more to say about the dynamics of online molesters.

Child rapists use threat (particularly the threat of harm) or the imposition of superior physical force to engage the child in the abusive activity. Typically, the rapist will threaten to kill or injure the child or someone dear to the child or destroy something the child holds dear like a pet or threaten to commit suicide himself, convincing the child that he or she will be blamed for the rapist's death if the child resists or reports the rape. In using superior force, the rapist may simply overpower the child, restrain the child by tying him or her, give the child drugs or alcohol, or physically brutalize the child into submission.

The vast majority (about 80%) of abusers use the first two strategies—enticement and entrapment. Abusers tend to repeat their engagement patterns and show little tendency to move from nonviolent to violent strategies. Molesters are apt to consistently entice or trap children, whereas child rapists tend to use threat or force almost exclusively. The strategy used by the abuser is an important issue in treatment, because survivors typically wonder throughout their lives why they permitted it to occur.

Sexual Interaction Phase. Types of abuse may include (blatant or surreptitious) masturbation (the abuser may masturbate prior to making physical contact with the child), fondling, digital penetration, oral or anal penetration, dry intercourse, intercourse, forcing or coercing the child into touching the abuser's genitals, forced prostitution, and pornography. Children may be coaxed into cooperating, though not consenting, because abusers—as adult authority figures—often command, engage, or enlist cooperation from the child. Children lack the maturity, experience, and age to be able to consent, but they may cooperate because of their subservient status.

Secrecy Phase. Abusers communicate to children that others must not discover the sexual activity. The objective of abusers is to continue the activity. This necessitates avoiding detection and maintaining access to the child while continuing the abuse. The techniques for maintaining the secrecy may involve incorporating "rules" or "games," implicating the child in the activity, and setting the child up to be responsible for keeping the secret.

Disclosure Phase. Sometimes the abuser is discovered accidentally. Other times the abuse is disclosed intentionally by the child or someone else. Intentional disclosure is usually made by the child. Intentional disclosure often enormously complicates the discovery and existence of sexual abuse, because parents and others refuse to face it or believe it. Accidental discovery may occur as a result of such consequences as pregnancy, STDs, sexual acting out, promiscuity, and physical trauma. The way the abuse is disclosed can affect the child's self-esteem and reaction to treatment. For instance, disbelieving adults sometimes respond by blaming and punishing the child—and allow the sexual abuse to continue.

Suppression Phase. The suppression phase may begin as soon as disclosure takes place. Suppression may be attempted by the abuser, the child, the parents, other family members, professionals, the community, or an institution. There are many reasons for suppression: fear of publicity; fear of reprisal; to protect the reputation of a family, an abuser, or an institution; to avoid prosecution; to avoid responsibility; to protect the child; to avoid embarrassment; to avoid the kinds of confrontation and intervention required to deal effectively with the difficult and sensitive situation; and fear of getting involved.

Survival Phase. On the basis of our own experiences and the reports of other writers (Besharov, 1990; Kendrick, 1991), we have added another phase, the survival phase. During this phase, it is important to implement strategies for helping the child and the family respond to and recover from the abuse as much as possible. This phase includes stopping the abuse, providing needed medical and psychological treatment for the child, and helping the significant others close to the child to overcome the trauma, fear, anger, betrayal, and despair caused by the abuse (Benedict, 1985). It also involves preventing further abuse (Bass & Thornton, 1983) and prosecuting and/or getting counseling for the abuser (Benedict, 1985).

Intervention Strategies with Children
Assessment

Assessment includes thorough documentation of the abusive events for possible legal use. Using anatomically correct dolls helps confirm what

LO18

actually occurred in the abuse. No specific measures currently exist for measuring the effects of psychological abuse in young children, although a complete psychological evaluation may be useful in gauging the child's overall level of functioning (McLeer et al., 1992; Wheeler & Berliner, 1988, p. 235). The previously mentioned behavioral indicators of childhood sexual abuse and PTSD criteria for children are currently the best indicators that sexual abuse has occurred.

Peterson and Hardin (1997) have developed a guide for screening children's art for sexual abuse. The child is asked not to verbally disclose but rather illustrate different subjects and situations. Different indicators of sexual abuse may appear as the child illustrates the requested subject matter—such as a picture of people doing something at home. Assessment includes an analysis of style, treatment of figures, and actions with negative aspects. Point values are awarded for a variety of criteria commonly found in abused children's drawings. Once the point value reaches a certain level, child abuse should be suspected (Peterson & Zamboni, 1998). However, it doesn't take a doctorate in projective techniques to see how different the drawings of children who have been abused are (Kaufman & Wohl, 1992). We would propose that most children do not draw families that are joined by penises and vaginas or have clubs growing out of their arms that are raining blows down on other family members—but sexually and physically abused children do because that's the way their families interact.

Therapeutic Options

Because of the complex nature of child abuse, interventions should comprise multiple components targeting a variety of problem areas (Miller-Perrin, 2001). The first component is play therapy (Gumaer, 1984; Malchiodi, 2008; Webb, 2007; White & Allers, 1994). White and Allers (1994) have identified several characteristic behaviors that maltreated children may manifest during play therapy: developmental immaturity, opposition and aggression, withdrawal and passivity, self-deprecation and self-destruction, hypervigilance, inappropriate sexuality, and dissociation.

The second component is cognitive-behavioral therapy that is trauma focused (Cohen, Mannarino, & Deblinger, 2006; Neubauer, Deblinger, & Sieger, 2007). Farrell, Hains, and Davies (1998) found that selected cognitive-behavioral interventions (skills learned through procedures such as relaxation training, positive self-talk, cognitive restructuring, stress inoculation, and emotive imagery) may effectively decrease the anxiety and depression levels in sexually abused children ages 8–10 who exhibit PTSD symptoms. Deblinger, Thakkar-Kolar, and Ryan (2006) propose a cognitive behavioral approach that involves:

1. Psychoeducation that teaches children about faulty misconceptions they may have and offers new information to help children understand they are not so isolated and alone.
2. Behavioral rehearsal and modeling skills that are taught to both children and nonoffending parents to teach them how to regulate emotional expression and develop new cognitive coping skills.
3. Relaxation training and graded exposure treatment to the trauma that allows the child to learn that his or her fears and avoidance of the feared situation, object, or person are not nearly as frightening or upsetting as previously thought.

The third component is a trauma systems approach (Saxe, Ellis, & Kaplow, 2007). Incorporating an ecosystemic approach that involves not only children and parents, but community systems such as social services agencies, mental health facilities, and schools, increases the chances of stopping emotional and behavioral dysregulation across the entire system where the trauma operates. Saxe and his associates propose that two major components are operating with a traumatized child. First, a traumatized child has difficulty regulating emotional and behavioral states. Second, the social environment and system of care are not able to help the child regulate these emotions and behaviors.

Saxe, Ellis, and Kaplow (2007, pp. 95–108) propose 10 principles of treatment if the system is to be changed.

1. Fix a broken system, not just the identified client. Relentlessly attack the whole trauma system.
2. Put safety first. Nothing takes precedence over safety.
3. Create clear, focused plans that are based on facts and target specific components of the child's emotional dysregulation and the level of instability in the child's environment and system of care.
4. Don't "Go" before being "Ready." Build an alliance with the family, understand logistical problems such as child care and transportation, and create an understanding of what treatment will involve and who will be included.
5. Use resources to gain maximum benefit. Carefully plan and coordinate the tactics and strategy with

the system's players for the best possible outcome. Time and money are scarce in the treatment world. Plan carefully so neither gets wasted.

6. Accountability is critical. Accountability has two parts. First is the worker's ability to put words into action and evaluate how well those actions are working and change them if they aren't. Second, and more daunting, is requiring that children, parents, and others in the social ecosystem be accountable as well.

7. Deal with the reality of the situation. If resources aren't there, if family systems are compromised, if children are developmentally delayed, then understand the reality of the situation and adjust goals and expectations to it.

8. Take care of yourself and the treatment team. All the king's horses and all the king's men do not put Humpty-Dumpty back together again if the horses and men are broken themselves. There's a chapter ahead of you in this book on burnout. Guess what one specific area of crisis intervention has high burnout rates? That chapter is the real deal if you are going into this business, so read it carefully.

9. Look for the strengths in the system. The trauma system of the child is rife with pathology and failure. It is easy to find things wrong. Yet there is resiliency and strength within this system. It is your job to keep a positive view of it and make lemonade out of the lemons.

10. Leave a better system. As with all crisis intervention, you are not an adoption agency taking on children and families to raise forever. Teaching families how to take care of themselves is the end goal.

You'll soon meet crisis workers from the Carl Perkins Child Abuse Center, who operate out of Jackson, Tennessee, and cover much of rural west Tennessee. They operationalize all of the foregoing 10 principles and then some! When the entire ecosystem of the child is brought into play, involving all of the players in the treatment using combinations of play and cognitive-behavioral therapy, outcomes for parents include better parenting practices, improvement in depressive symptoms, reduction in abuse-specific emotional distress, and greater support for the child. Children have less externalization of problems, fewer depressive symptoms, reduced behavior problems at home and school, and feel less shame, guilt, depression, and anger due to the abuse. Perhaps even more important, social services, schools, law enforcement, judiciaries, and mental health services all play well together. When this happens, the sum is indeed greater than its parts.

Need for Affirmation and Safety

Initial intervention techniques call for intentionally and positively managing the crisis of disclosure and the resulting fear and anxiety. Affirmation and validation are crucial in regard to what has happened, what is happening, and what will happen to the child, the offender, and significant others. The admonition in the PTSD chapter on *not* using flooding techniques with children holds even more firmly with sexual abuse. If prolonged exposure techniques are to be used, they should be done with gradual and graded exposure to the aversive stimulus, with plenty of time for processing between exposures. Children should also be taught progressive relaxation techniques so that they can learn how to remove themselves from the feared stimuli. Because small children are not fully developed cognitively, most instrumental and operant behavioral techniques that may be used with adult survivors are also not efficacious. Yet anxiety about and fear of the abusive events and the abuser need to be reduced, and this calls for reexposure to the trauma.

Contrary to most popular professional opinions (there are a lot of cognitive behaviorists out there!), your authors believe this work is best accomplished by the use of play therapy, in which the child is given puppets, dolls, and drawing materials to safely distance himself or herself from the trauma. By gently and directively encouraging reenactment and discussion through the safety of the play material, the therapist may enable the child to gradually extinguish fear and anxiety feelings and develop skills in communicating healthy inner feelings and experiences without revictimizing the child (Baker, 1995; Gil & Johnson, 1993; James, 2003; Malchiodi, 2008; Merrick, Allen, & Crase, 1994; Oates et al., 1994; Pifalo, 2002; Sadowski & Loesch, 1993; Webb, 2007).

Regaining a Sense of Control

Anger and grief are emotional by-products for children of sexual abuse. Venting of these feelings should be encouraged, particularly because most adults are not comfortable with them and may attempt to repress such feelings when children exhibit them (Wheeler & Berliner, 1988, p. 237). Drawing, painting, modeling clay, sand play, writing, and learning to verbalize emotions are all therapeutic vehicles to ventilate angry feelings and loss. Play techniques can also give the child a renewed sense of empowerment by allowing play figures to be acted on, thus reducing long-standing feelings of helplessness (James, 2003; Malchiodi, 2008; Sadowski & Loesch, 1993; Webb, 2007). Punching out a Bobo doll or picking up a play telephone and calling the police can give children a sense of control in a situation in which they have little (Salter, 1988, p. 215). Along with relaxation and other stress reduction measures, play techniques such as sand tray therapy can be used to teach the child to control anger when the child constantly acts out with peers or significant others.

Education

Education about adult sex offenders and sex itself is important for children because they will have little if any knowledge of why or what has happened to them. Shame is a predominant feature of the child's response to abuse (Knauer, 2000, pp. 74–82). Children need to know that it is the adult and not the child who made the mistake. Children who have been physically injured need to have these injuries explained and be told that their bodies will be okay. Many children believe that others will be able to tell what happened by looking at them. Children need to know that although they may feel different, sexual abuse does not make them look different.

Understanding developmental stages is critical in what kind of education is provided and how therapy is delivered (Saxe, Ellis, & Kaplow, 2008, pp. 7–12). Cognitively, young children usually have little understanding of sexual functions. Typically they will not initiate questions about sex, but when workers initiate education about sex through slides or books, children will respond with their own questions. Every child who has been sexually assaulted needs some type of sex education and information on what the assault means (Baker, 1995; McLeer et al., 1992; Oates et al., 1994; Salter, 1988, pp. 217–218).

In addition to the play therapy techniques (such as drawing, painting, modeling, and sand play, mentioned earlier), a highly effective means of teaching important social and survival lessons to children is through outreach services into schools, churches, and community centers with professionally developed puppetry programs. One example is the Kids on the Block (1995) system, which uses the unique and dynamic medium of puppetry to educate children and their adult caregivers on how to think about and respond to important and emotionally charged issues that impact children's lives. Trained volunteers perform with puppet characters designed to realistically represent children and the dilemmas they may face. Through carefully researched and scripted dialogues, these puppets ("children") talk about important issues and then engage in interactive question-and-answer periods with children in the audience, who converse directly with the puppets. This form of puppetry has proved to be an effective strategy for expunging children's myths and misconceptions about physical and sexual abuse and replacing them with facts and sensitivity (Sullivan & Robinson, 1994).

Assertiveness Training

Assertiveness training may be seen as more a preventive measure to keep children out of harm's way than a remedial measure for sexually abused children. Yet, sexually abused children have learned to be compliant to deviant requests and clearly need to learn how to "Just say NO!" (Salter, 1988, p. 219). Because abused children are at greater risk for revictimization, teaching them cues and warning signs and appropriate assertion responses is important so that they can avoid future abuse (Miller-Perrin, 2001; Wheeler & Berliner, 1988, p. 242).

Intervention Strategies for Child Sexual Abuse: The Case of Elizabeth

Elizabeth, age 8, is the middle child in the family. She, her 11-year-old brother, and a 5-year-old sister live with her mother and stepfather, whom her mother married nearly 2 years ago. Elizabeth's mother, Mona, and father divorced when the youngest child was about 1 year old. Elizabeth's stepfather started off by fondling her. This went on for several weeks. Although Elizabeth was bewildered, scared, and intimidated, no one else knew about the abusive activity. Recently, while everyone else was out of the house, her stepfather raped her. He threatened to kill Elizabeth, Mona, and her sister if she told anyone. The following morning Elizabeth confided in her brother, who in turn, told Mona what had happened.

Incredulous over this discovery and paralyzed as to what to do, Mona called the child abuse hotline that she remembered seeing advertised on TV and in the local newspaper. The following dialogue and discussion is representative of what an absolutely outstanding child advocacy agency, the Exchange Club–Carl Perkins Child Abuse Center of Jackson, Tennessee, does.

Disclosure

Mona: (*calling the child advocacy hotline; angry, crying uncontrollably, barely in control*) Hello. Hello! I want to report a (*choke, sob*) rape. He ... that bastard ... he raped my baby. That sonofabitch raped my daughter. Oh, how could I have not seen ... How could I have let this happen? (*Continues ranting and raving in hysterics, beseeching the hotline worker for help and railing at her husband.*)

CW: OK, I understand you're extremely upset and have every right to be, but I need for you to be in control right now. My name's Delaine. I need to know your name, where you live, and whether you're safe from who did this to your daughter.

Mona: (*Regaining a bit of control, gives her name and address.*) It was my ... It was ... my husband ... Leon. Her asshole stepfather ... I found her underwear. It was all bloody ... Oh my God! My baby ... My poor baby. He's gone in his truck ... He's headed for Chicago on a run ... I'll kill him ... By God! I will kill him if it's the last thing I ever do!

CW: So you are safe, and he's not in the house. How badly hurt is your daughter? Does she need an ambulance and medical attention?

Mona: I don't know. She's kinda in a daze. Just walking around holding on to her teddy bear. Oh, that bastard! I'll castrate that bastard before I kill him!

CW: Mona, I hear how angry and shocked you are, but I need for you to follow me very closely. This is extremely important. I want you not to do anything with Elizabeth. Don't wash her up or change her clothes. I want you to take her to Madison County General Hospital and bring her underwear with you in a plastic baggie. Do you have a way to get to the hospital? Are you OK enough to get to the hospital? (*Gets acknowledgment from the mother that she can get to the hospital.*) There are going to be people at the hospital who are going to want to talk to you and Elizabeth, and we're going to need to do a medical exam of her. This is not going to be easy, but we know how to do this. You did the right thing. I'll meet you at the hospital, and I'll help you get through this. We will get through this! Do you understand? Now tell me what you're going to do and when you'll get to the hospital. (*Mona restates what the crisis worker has told her and assures the worker she can do those things.*)

The initial shock that accompanies discovery and disclosure is invariably highly dramatic and volatile for parents who have been blind to the perpetrator's intent. Because rape is a violent crime, the primary consideration of the crisis worker is to determine if people are now safe from the perpetrator and if they need medical attention. The initiating crisis is multifold. The crisis worker needs to make sure that there is no physical injury to the child and that the out-of-control parent is sufficiently functional to take care of the child and do the things necessary to preserve evidence. She will also need to restore the mother to equilibrium. Exacting revenge by assaulting the perpetrator would put both mother and daughter in jeopardy. The scene at the hospital can be extremely threatening, and the crisis worker does all she can to indicate that the mother has done the right thing and that, as difficult as it may be, the crisis worker will be there with her to the conclusion. The crisis worker's initial job will be to do crisis intervention with the mother by making sure everyone is safe and helping her get back in control of her emotions and actions (Bottoms, 1999; Knauer, 2000, pp. 31–47).

Immediate Aftermath

In cases where there is physical injury, the survivor will need immediate medical evaluation and care. The crisis worker, after determining that the mother can get herself and her daughter to the hospital, immediately makes other phone calls to the Department of Human Services and the police department. She also calls the hospital and informs them that a child sexual assault victim is on her way and that a sexual assault team needs to be assembled. After making these phone calls, she immediately leaves for the hospital.

Mona: (*at the hospital, in a room with the crisis worker*) All I can think about is that no-good lying creep. He's lucky he's on the road, or he'd be dead now. I'd shoot the asshole's balls right off of him. I've got a .38 Special, and by God ... as God is my witness ... I will do it. What's happening to my daughter? They took her away. Is she going to be all right? I've read some stuff on this. It's not just him raping her now, but she'll be scarred for life! How could it happen? How could I be so stupid? What in the hell is wrong with me? He was so nice to her, to all of us! How, oh how could I have been so stupid? (*Starts uncontrolled sobbing and pacing, slamming her purse down again and again.*)

CW: You've certainly been through a lot in the last few hours. And you've done a remarkable job of taking care of Elizabeth. Your concerns about her physical injuries now and her psychological injuries later are certainly justified. I'm not going to sugarcoat this. You're obviously a very good mother who has suddenly been thrust into this—nothing you or Elizabeth did caused it. It was perpetrated on her and you. We are here to assist you in any way we can. We want to provide someone to be with you and Elizabeth during these critical hours, as well as providing aftercare and follow-up counseling.

But right now, even though your husband is away, I'm concerned about your anger. It's certainly justifiable, but what Elizabeth needs is for you to be the best mother you can be right now. If you shoot your husband, how will you be able to support your daughter when she needs you most? You won't! You will be in jail. That's where your husband deserves to be, not you. Let the police handle your husband. What we need to do is handle this and care about Elizabeth. Can you do this? That's really what you want, isn't it, to help your daughter get through this?

Mona: I . . . I . . . I guess so. I appreciate it. Everything happened so fast! I don't know how I managed without falling apart. It's like a wild, awful dream—an ugly nightmare. I don't know how I'll handle it when the dust settles. I'm so mad—I could kill him! I feel like I've been raped too. There's so much on me right now. I don't know if I'm capable of bearing up under all that's got to be done. Damn, damn, damn that man! Excuse me, I shouldn't blow up like that.

CW: That's all right. You have a perfect right to be angry and to say it. It's good that you care enough to be upset, and it's good to see you direct your anger at him—the real cause of Elizabeth's hurt and your anger. Both of you deserve better treatment than he gave you, and no child asks to be raped.

Mona: That's right. I trusted him! And he took advantage of her. She was helpless—a helpless child. I've got to show her where I stand on this. First, I'm going to take good care of her, and then I'm going to send that rotten louse to jail for good!

CW: Mona, I know things are really crazy right now, and you don't know what's happening. I want to take care of that by telling you what's going to happen and how things are going to be done, so you know what's going on and don't feel so out of control. I'll go through each step of what is going

to happen today and what we can do to ensure that Elizabeth gets through this in good shape. I'm going to explain what will happen very carefully to you. If you have any questions, stop me. There are no stupid questions about this. I want you to fully understand what's happening, so you can start to get back in control. Mona, the important thing is that you gain control. Right now, I'm being very directive, and will be doing so until you get past this emergency and back on top of things. You have choices, and if, at any time, you feel like making any of the choices yourself, please feel free to do so. You can stop me at any time, and that will be OK. (*The crisis worker patiently goes through all the details of what is going to happen, stopping whenever Mona has questions, and checking to see that she understands what she's being told.*)

The crisis worker permits her to express her anger, isn't threatened by Mona's outburst, encourages her to keep owning and expressing her feelings, and lets her know that neither she nor Elizabeth was to blame for the assault. That strategy is important in letting Mona know that she can be in control and that the worker believes in her, without the worker's jumping in and expressing the anger for her. This is no place for the human services worker who is not calm, cool, and detached in her or his professional demeanor. That the worker must be as solid during a crisis as the rock of Gibraltar is never more true than here. There is probably nothing more heart wrenching and sickening than the aftermath of a severe sexual or physical assault on a child. Intervention here clearly calls for a strong constitution. But more important, if the worker manifests her or his own anger directly at the parent or the perpetrator, then that anger may be misinterpreted as being directed toward the victim.

At times, when the perpetrator is still an immediate threat, the worker must take on the trappings of a crisis worker who deals with battering victims. The family may need to be moved to a safe place until the perpetrator is apprehended. The crisis worker continuously reinforces the mother for doing the right thing and for caring about her daughter. This is an extremely important strategy, because adult caregivers may engage in severe guilt and recrimination because they believe they should have been more vigilant. The crisis worker also must make sure that the mother will not exact revenge on the perpetrator and put herself in jeopardy with the law (Knauer, 2000, p. 46). It will indeed do Elizabeth little good if her mother is facing a charge of assault with intent to commit murder. Finally, the crisis worker patiently educates the parent on what is going to happen. Education about the aftermath of a child assault is critical in giving parents back the sense of control they feel they have lost.

Two components of education are important. First, detailing what the legal proceedings are and what the mother and child need to prepare for allows them to know what is ahead of them and not be blindsided by all the legal, social, and psychological ramifications of a child sexual assault. Second, giving the parent information on how to deal with the child in the immediate aftermath of the discovery is critical in ensuring that the child is not revictimized and that the parent does not feel guilty for doing or saying the wrong thing (Bottoms, 1999). An even more shocking revelation may occur during the initial disclosure and interview. That is, it is not uncommon for the parent to disclose that she was also sexually abused as a child and swore this would never happen to any of her own children.

Mona: (*head in her hands, slumped over*) It's my fault. I let this happen. God knows I should have known. Uncle Ralph did the same thing to me when I was 14. I tried to tell Mom, but she just blew it off 'cause Uncle Ralph helped us out when Mom went through her divorce. And now my own daughter . . . I couldn't even protect her. I'm no better than my mother.

CW: (*reacting coolly, letting Mona talk through her own sexual assault*) There's a big difference. As I hear you say it, your mother didn't follow up because she was afraid and dependent on your uncle. You weren't afraid, and when you found out you took immediate action. See the difference? A big difference! Right now you are being the best mother in the world. Do you see that difference?

The worker, although taken aback, immediately discriminates between what Mona's mother didn't do and what Mona did do. She underscores and reinforces Mona for taking action and reaffirms her as a fit parent.

Prosecuting the Perpetrator
Interviewing the Child

Whenever a child is sexually assaulted, there **LO19** are two primary concerns. First is taking care of the child and seeing that she or he is safe. Second is

obtaining evidence to prosecute the perpetrator. If the child has not been injured or if the discovery is made a good while after the assault, then an interview needs to be conducted that will allow the necessary evidence to be obtained. In the past, report of a child assault would entail numerous interviews with medical staff, police, and social services. The intimidating circumstances and the necessity to repeat the story over and over have a high potential for making the child feel terrorized, guilty, confused, and unequal to the task of meeting the demands of a variety of strange and threatening adults. The potential for revictimizing the child and the parent while going through this procedure is extremely high if not handled appropriately (Bottoms, 1999).

To stop this from happening, the Carl Perkins Center uses an interview procedure that many other child advocacy agencies employ. This approach is a good model for dealing with cases of sexual or severe physical assault on children and is now starting to be instituted across the country. One *trained* forensic interviewer with a listening device in her or his ear conducts the interview and tape-records it at a safe house. Other agencies' staff are behind a one-way mirror. If they need more information on a particular part of the assault, they transmit that information to the worker in the room via the worker's earpiece. Note here the emphasis on *trained*. Because this is a criminal matter, the worker needs to be able to obtain information without biasing the child's testimony. In other words, the typical mental health worker will not have the expertise to do this. However, the psychological well-being of the child is critical in the aftermath of disclosure, and a typical police interrogation would likely put the child under severe duress. Therefore, whoever does the interview should be skillful not only in obtaining evidence, but also in making the child feel safe while the interview occurs. At Carl Perkins the interview is conducted in a pleasant, child-friendly room by a very caring child-centered forensic worker at the center, not in the stark confines of a police interrogation room (Bottoms, 1999). The worker may also use "good touch–bad touch" with a doll or a figure drawing to have the child indicate where on his or her body (e.g., genitals, mouth) the assault took place. (Note: *Mouth* is included here because oral sex is a common occurrence in child sexual abuse [Knauer, 2000, pp. 5–6].)

If there is no prior knowledge of abuse and the child discloses an assault in a spontaneous manner, then the crisis worker needs to be cool-headed, listen to the child, and be prepared to make an immediate referral. Often the workers at the Carl Perkins Center have staged a Kids on the Block puppet show at a local school. After the presentation on prevention, they invite children who may have been victimized to come down and talk to them about their experiences. At times they have been flooded by children! In that case, the worker needs to write down pertinent information in a calm manner and make an immediate referral to Children and Family Services (Bottoms, 1999).

After the examination, the crisis worker needs to affirm to children that they are okay physically, that some part of their body is not "broken," that they do not now have AIDS, that they will not die, and in the case of a girl, that she is not pregnant (Bottoms, 1999).

CW: (*Very empathic, sits down beside Elizabeth and takes her hand.*) Elizabeth, I'm Delaine from the Carl Perkins Center for Children. I'm guessing some pretty scary things have happened, and you're probably having some pretty scary feelings right now. I want to talk to you about some of those scary things. It's OK to be scared, because it was a pretty scary deal. But you're safe now, and your mom and we are going to make sure you stay safe. So if you'd like, I'll try to answer any questions you have about what happened and what's going to happen.

Elizabeth: (*after the examination and the initial interview by a forensic expert*) When Leon did this to me and he stuck his peter in me, it really hurt. Am I gonna die, 'cause I started bleeding? Will I get pregnant?

CW: No, you're not going to die. It's normal to feel sore after all that and to bleed some. But the doctors said you were OK, and Dr. Ann will be back to see you and tell you you're OK. I checked with the doctor, and you're not old enough to get pregnant yet. Dr. Ann will tell you about all this, so don't worry about that.

It is extremely important for young children who have little information about how their body functions to immediately allay fears of what may happen to their body as a result of the assault. A somewhat controversial issue is whether the initial examination should be done at the child advocacy center, as opposed to a hospital. Many times the child-friendly atmosphere of the center is much more conducive than a hospital for examining victims. The counterargument is that examinations should not be done at the center because the child might associate that frightening procedure with the center's physical environment and generalize it to the staff's subsequent attempts to work there with the child (Bottoms, 1999).

Preparing the Child for Testimony

Interviewing children about their potential sexual abuse is a tricky business and best done by practiced forensic examiners. There is no set protocol free of trail ramifications, so the goal is to elicit reliable and complete information without tainting it (Saywitz & Dorodo, 2013). The last thing that needs to happen is raising the specter of "false memories." Sexual assault is a criminal matter, and at some point the child will probably have to testify in a courtroom. That appearance may be terrifying to a small child who will have to give testimony against a caretaker who may have either been very nice to the child or made threats against the child and his or her family. Depending on the age of the child, the Carl Perkins Center uses puppets, books, and videos to educate the child on what testimony in a courtroom entails. Immediately before the child's appearance in court, a staff member from the center will take the child to the courtroom to acclimate him or her to what may be perceived as a frightening experience. The staff explains about everybody's role and how things will happen. He or she will role-play traffic court so the child gets an idea of how courts operate. Children can explore the courtroom, ask questions, and sit in the judge's and witness chairs, so that they become familiarized with a courtroom and are not terror stricken when they are asked to engage in the real situation.

Another problematic area is time of court appearance. Courts are notorious for not starting on time. Sitting all day on a bench outside a court waiting for it to convene while the perpetrator is seated on an adjacent bench is clearly not conducive to the child's or the family's good mental health. As a result, the Carl Perkins staff keeps the child and the family at the center until a call is received from the courthouse that court is about to convene. Only then are the child and family transported to the courthouse. After the court appearance, the child is brought back to the center and debriefed. Questions such as "How did that feel?" and "What was that like for you?" are posed to alleviate the residual fears of having confronted the perpetrator at close range (Bottoms, 1999).

The span of time from disclosure and discovery of the assault to court appearance may be up to a year, and there will be lots of transcrisis points as time seems to drag on interminably. It is important that each one of these crisis points be met head-on by crisis workers. Thus the Carl Perkins Center staff immediately swings into action in dealing with the child and the family and stays with them in support and therapeutic roles for at least a year after the initial contact is made (Bottoms, 1999).

Aftermath

It should be a given from all you have read **LO20** in this chapter that any child who has been sexually abused needs counseling (Knauer, 2000, p. 46). Discovery of an incestuous relationship throws the entire family into crisis. The father, and possibly the mother, faces loss of what has become an addictive behavior, possible criminal sanctions, loss of his or her family, and social stigmatization. The nonoffending parent finds herself or himself torn between her or his partner and the assaulted child. The child may find herself or himself discredited, shamed, punished, and still unprotected (Herman, 1981, p. 183). The worker will also face a crisis in deciding what to do and whether or not to believe the child's story. However, discovery of child sexual abuse is no different from discovery of any other physical abuse, and state laws mandate that it must be reported (Sandberg, Crabbs, & Crabbs, 1988). It is a criminal activity and should be dealt with in that manner. For those workers who are unsure of themselves, it may be reassuring to know that fewer than 5% of complaints of child sexual abuse are false.

Conversely, it is not uncommon for children to retract their complaints under pressure from the family (Goodwin, 1982). Therefore, until clearly proved otherwise, the child's allegations should be accepted as valid, and the worker's primary consideration should be reporting the abuse to Child Protective Services and obtaining safety for the child (Sandberg, Crabbs, & Crabbs, 1988).

Because the behavior is both criminal and addictive, treating the problem via family therapy is fruitless. What is called for is immediately referring the problem to and cooperating with family services and law enforcement agencies that do not subscribe to a family reunification policy (Sandberg, Crabbs, & Crabbs, 1988). It then becomes much more possible to remove the father from the home through a court order. Removing the child from the home has negative ramifications because it may be construed as banishment and may also serve to strengthen parent bonds against the child. The child needs assurance that she is not to blame for the incest; she should be praised for her courage and clearly told that she is helping, not hurting, her family and will not be abandoned even if she retracts her story (Herman, 1981, pp. 184–185).

Counseling

Aftercare is critically important to prevent a host of maladies from appearing in later childhood and carrying on into adulthood. Universal characteristics such as lying, stealing, fighting, verbal and behavioral oppositional defiance, and promiscuity are typical aftermath behaviors that will assail children who have been sexually victimized.

Boys will typically perpetrate sexual assaults on other children, bully other kids, vandalize property, and generally direct their anger outward. Girls typically turn their anger inward and engage in alcohol and drug abuse, eating disorders, and promiscuity. Reducing problem behavior is important along with dealing with the trauma (Miller-Perrin, 2001). The Carl Perkins Center attempts to deal with these issues before they become major behavioral problems, through play therapy, therapeutic games, and role plays that deal with the inappropriate behavior in both group and individual counseling. The Center follows a variation on the trauma systems approach (Saxe, Ellis, & Kaplow, 2007), including trauma-focused cognitive-behavioral therapy (Neubauer, Deblinger, & Sieger, 2007), play therapy group work (Haen, 2008; Malchiodi, 2008; Nisivoccia & Lynn, 2007), and work with the family, school, and social service systems (Saxe, Ellis, & Kaplow, 2007; Steele & Malchiodi, 2008). This comprehensive approach is all part of the postvention package of a 1-year follow-up (Bottoms, 1999).

Group Counseling

Group counseling is used to normalize the assault and help children understand they are not alone. The group breaks the isolation as children start to share their fears and feelings of shame and guilt. Peer interaction leads to expression of shared feelings, bonding, and higher self-esteem. By validating their experiences, the group helps shift the focus of responsibility off children and onto the perpetrators. Further, the typical parameters of group rules help children learn behavioral limits, identify appropriate interpersonal boundaries with others, and learn to express feelings appropriately (Knauer, 2000; Nisivoccia & Lynn, 2007). Children meet in groups twice a month for a year.

These issues are not sugarcoated. Group leaders discuss these problems in a straightforward manner and teach children how to deal appropriately with the feelings, behaviors, and thoughts that are likely to confront them as they work through the trauma they have experienced. The idea is that if these problems are talked about openly and honestly, then survivors will not be further victimized and will be empowered to start taking control of their lives back (Bottoms, 1999).

The assaulted child may have been told, not only by the perpetrator but also by other family members, that the child himself or herself is the cause of the family's breakup. Constant reinforcement is used to convey to children that the assault wasn't their fault. Workers who are not versed in dealing with sexually abused clients will not understand the importance of driving this point home. The fact is that many, many sexually abused clients will believe it is their fault and that they, and they alone, as a result of their disclosure, have caused all the problems that have occurred for the family (Bottoms, 1999).

Groups are set up in age ranges of 2 to 3 years. Groups are not run for 3- to 5-year-olds because of their short attention span and lack of mature cognitive development. The 3- to 5-year-olds receive only individual counseling. Because of the curriculum and techniques used, groups are also divided into readers and nonreaders. Group participants also receive individual counseling, twice a month on alternate weeks from when groups meet. Different children manifest different problems as they work through the trauma of the abuse. When a child starts to manifest a particular characteristic, such as stealing, then individual counseling is tailored to fit that child's specific needs (Bottoms, 1999). Particularly for younger children, any group therapy should not be entirely devoted to "talking" therapy. Play is the medium that gets the message across; puppets (Webb, 2007), dramatic enactment (Haen, 2007), bibliotherapy (Malchiodi & Ginns-Gruenberg, 2008), sand play (Carey, 2006), art (Malchiodi, 2008), and particularly for older children, board games (Schaefer & Reid, 2001) all provide mediums to get the message of abuse across and teach children cooperative, prosocial behaviors that many of them lack.

Boundary Issues

Boundary issues are endemic to this population. The positive feedback and attention these children receive from engaging in sexual activities with long-term perpetrators transfer over to and generalize to a variety of other situations and people. Thus one of the primary thrusts of counseling at Carl Perkins is to reestablish appropriate personal and interpersonal boundaries.

Sexual assault turns understanding of normal developmental boundaries upside down and children may become erotized, meaning that psychologically the children may believe that the only way to gain attention is to be sexual. Physically, the feeling may have been enjoyable and they do not perceive it as abuse (Knauer, 2000, p. 10). An example of the lack of understanding that sexually assaulted children have of interpersonal boundaries is related by the Assistant Director of the Carl Perkins Center:

Assistant Director: I was on a home visit working with the mother of a young girl who had been sexually abused. My purpose for the visit was to work with the mother in teaching her parenting techniques to use with the daughter. I really wasn't there to deal with the young girl, but she incessantly demanded attention from both me and the mother. Providing her with alternative activities such as coloring books and dolls didn't satisfy her demand for us to attend to her. The little girl left the room and then reappeared with a negligee on and tried to get me to look at her. When that didn't work, the girl got up and sat as close to me as she could. When I still continued to attend to the mother, she climbed in my lap. When I still did not attend to her, she started kissing me, and finally attempted to stick her tongue in my mouth. In her attempt to get my attention and affection, she knew no interpersonal boundaries. It doesn't take a rocket scientist to figure out how that had come to be. Love, attention, and sex are all rolled into one as far as these kids are concerned. I can't tell you the number of times we have discovered these 6-, 7-, and 8-year-olds having sex with other kids when they should be playing with dolls and trucks with those kids. So a lot of time is spent on talking about what appropriate boundaries are.

Group Support Work with Nonoffending Parents

For mothers, the notion of entering a support/therapy group may be very threatening. However, it is quite possibly the only way they will be able to get their families back together. Mothers should be told this fact in plain and simple terms and should be strongly encouraged to join such groups. Groups for spouses of abusers enable members to come to terms with doubts of their own womanhood, regain a sense of control and empowerment in themselves and their families, reduce blame and guilt in themselves, and restore mother–daughter bonds (Brittain & Merriam, 1988; Salter, 1988, p. 211).

Preventing Revictimization

Perhaps most tragic of all the issues that assail a family is revictimization of the child by the nonoffending parent. Often a role reversal occurs whereby the child not only is the sexual object of the perpetrating parent, but also becomes the chief confidant and comfort provider for the nonoffending parent. She or he takes on the role of being the real partner of the nonoffending parent and usurps the nonoffender parent's role. This role reversal may be completed by the nonoffending parent's psychologically taking over the child role.

Therefore, crisis workers spend a good deal of time with nonoffending parents, teaching them to reassume the role as head of household and to stand their ground when the child attempts to reassume her or his pseudo-adult role. Finally, time is spent on talking about the nonoffending parent's not falling into another relationship that has the same outcome, as the parent may be highly likely to do (Bottoms, 1999).

What the Carl Perkins Center does with families who have been involved with sexual abuse is not short-term, brief therapy. The multiple crises that erupt after disclosure should make it readily apparent that there are no quick fixes to this horrific problem. At least a year of continuing crises may be expected as the family attempts to restabilize and reinvent itself, and to be successful, it will need help every step of the way.

Individual Counseling

There are two major purposes in individual counseling following childhood sexual abuse. The first is making it safe enough for the child to discuss the assault. Avoidance is typically a hallmark of a traumatic event for children and children are generally reluctant to discuss it (Webb, 2007, p. 51). Second is reenactment of the trauma and cognitively restructuring it so that it no longer is the axis on which the child's life turns.

Intervention with abused children should never be done in isolation but should include the nonoffending members of the family (Mohl, 2010). Neubauer and her associates (2007) and Saxe and his associates (2007) propose that trauma therapy with children should have parallel parent training and therapy occurring at the same time. Neubauer and her associates propose that individual therapy should progress with the nonoffending parent and child seen separately first. The reason for doing so is to create a safe atmosphere for both the parent and the child to start to openly discuss their thinking and feeling about the abuse, which will not be easy to do under the best of circumstances. Later on, when both the child and the parent have received a good deal of processing and training, they are brought together in conjoint therapy. At this time the child tells the complete story of the abuse, and the parent openly discusses her or his own feelings and reinforces the child's proactive behavior. The end result is that emotional and behavioral dysregulation is first stabilized and then, through the course of therapy, psychoeduction, and parent training, both parent and child can transcend the abuse and move on with their lives (Saxe, Ellis, & Kaplow, 2007).

Session 1: Establishing Safe Ground. In this opening session the worker seeks to establish safe therapeutic ground for the child by asking him or her to talk about something they like or want to do.

CW: Elizabeth, I am pleased to meet you. My name is Delaine Uptown, and I am a counselor here at the center. You and I are going to be spending some time together, so I'd like to get to know you a bit better. I'm wondering if you could tell me a bit about things you really like to do or, in fact, might want to do. Perhaps something you did this weekend or today? Which would you like to choose?

Elizabeth: Well, I mostly stay at home now, but I like to ride my bike and go over to my best friend Cindy's and play in her tree house, it's really neat. We play dolls and stuff up there.

CW: OK, great, so you've got a good friend and pal that you can depend on and can go play dolls with. I also know that it's a lot easier for kids to sometimes use toys and drawings as ways to express feelings. Take a look around the room, Elizabeth. There are a variety of toys and art supplies here that you can use. There is even a sand tray over here that we can use if you want. The choice is yours, so where would you like to start?

The worker sets the scene with the child in a benign, nonthreatening way. She also introduces Elizabeth to the play materials in the room.

Concurrently the worker will start educating the parent on symptoms and behaviors the child is likely to display as they move through therapy, which will undoubtedly have transcrisis points as the child begins to regulate emotions and behaviors and parents learn new communication and behavior management skills. As the child and the worker begin bonding, the worker will move to trauma.

Session 2: Introducing Traumatic Material

CW: I think you are pretty good at expressing your feelings and ideas about stuff. I think you also are a pretty smart young woman and know that we are here to talk about stuff that happened that doesn't make you or your mom feel good. You know what I mean?

Elizabeth: Like what Leon did to me.

CW: Yes, that's right. We could either talk about it or you could show me what happened. I know you like to draw things.

Elizabeth: Well, he sorta touched me in places where he shouldn't have. (*Takes markers and starts drawing randomly with no apparent meaning or form.*)

CW: OK. Did he do anything else?

Elizabeth: (*Continues to draw and says nothing.*)

CW: OK, thank you so much for sharing that with me. So what are you drawing? It looks extremely busy with all those lines.

Elizabeth: Like it's all the lines running everywhere and they don't connect to anything.

CW: Is that perhaps the way maybe you feel sometimes?

Elizabeth: Maybe.

CW: That makes perfect sense to me. Kids who have been abused by people who should take care of them but abuse them would leave anyone pretty jumbled up.

Elizabeth: I guess maybe that's so. The kids in my group talk about that a lot. You wouldn't hurt something you loved like my cat. And my stepfather hurt me.

CW: That is correct, Elizabeth, and that's why he is going to jail. You know I think you ought to write a book about this experience complete with the pictures you have drawn.

This exchange indicates that the worker is moving ever forward in getting Elizabeth to recount and capture the whole episode. Saxe and associates (2007, pp. 269–271) propose that children write a book about the episode that they can then share with their caretakers. Saxe and his associates believe book writing allows the child to narrate in both words and pictures the sequence of the assault. They propose chapter titles like "All About Me," "My Family," "Something Bad Happened to Me," "Things Changed After the Bad Thing Happened," "Some Things Stayed the Same," "People Who Care About Me," "What I Can Do to

Protect Myself in the Future," and "Skills I Have Used When My Bad Thoughts Get in the Way." These chapter headings can, in fact, be the topics of counseling sessions. Once recorded, Elizabeth can immediately refer to her chapters so that the behavioral and cognitive sets she will learn—such as deep breathing and relaxation training, sensory and verbal cueing, catching oneself, and setting up cognitive "stop" and "go" signs before things go awry—are readily available and in her own voice rather than the therapist's or what a book says to do.

This initial foray is met with some resistance, but it is a start and the mass of twirling lines apparently do represent a central part of this youngster's thinking. Concurrently the worker has given Mona a homework assignment and discusses her progress in reinforcing Elizabeth and also using natural consequences of actions when she becomes rebellious. The focus here is not on Elizabeth but on Mona's responses.

CW: So, you've gotten through the first part of Becker's *Parents Are Teachers* [Becker, 1972] and have really upped the verbal M&Ms, reinforcing her a lot more than you did. You have even kept a diary. Wow! That is really great. That tells me that you are into changing behavior big time, and not just your kid's. What about timeout when she acts out?

Mona: I'm having some trouble with that. I feel so bad about sending her to her room after all that has happened. I love that girl so much, and it tears me up to have to come down on her and ground her when I know it's all from that no good bastard.

CW: So pick a time last week when things were REALLLLLY good and when they were REALLLLLY bad. What were the billboards going through your head that made you continue doing the reinforcement and reading the *Parents Are Teachers* book, and what were the negative ones that made you want to throw in the towel?

Just as she will do with Elizabeth, the worker is not only training Mona in new ways of parenting, she is also teaching her to catch the positive self-enhancing statements she is giving herself and the negative ones that help extinguish attempts at new behavior. In short, she is teaching Mona how to regulate her emotional behavior as well.

The Carl Perkins staff meet with the nonoffending parent twice a month for a year. After the abuse has been discovered, children tend to behave differently. Without knowledge and training, parents are likely to be shocked by these previously unseen behaviors as the child acts out (Knauer, 2000; Miller-Perrin, 2001).

Thus, home visits and parent training to educate and normalize the behavioral changes that are likely to occur are critically important. If such training does not occur, then warfare between the parent and the child will create another crisis. Forewarned is forearmed, and if parents start seeing these behaviors, the center staff immediately start tackling these issues with the child. Therefore, center staff keep close contact with the home to catch and stop inappropriate behavior before it gets started (Bottoms, 1999).

A classic example of acting-out behavior is stealing or shoplifting. The immediate knee-jerk reaction of many parents is to use shame as a way of modifying the behavior. Yet using shame to extinguish behavior compounds all kinds of shame-based issues the child may already have. Another example is sexual acting out. A parent who has started to date again after removal of the perpetrator will be horrified when the child attempts to become intimate with this new person. Because of the vacuum left by the removal of the perpetrator, the child's need for love and affection, and her or his confusion over boundaries, the parent's new boyfriend or girlfriend may become a target for the child's commingled notions of how love and sex are intertwined and how she or he can obtain that love through sexual gratification (Bottoms, 1999).

We will speak a good deal about making home visits and their potential for violence in Chapter 14, Violent Behavior in Institutions. However, you should clearly understand that even though one perpetrator has been removed from the home (or thought to be removed) you still need to be cautious and planful when making a home visit, and that plan includes your own personal safety. Saxe and his associates (2007) propose an "On-the-SPOT" decision tree (p. 179) that dictates what you will do if you enter a home that is in crisis and violence boils over. The first question to ask yourself is "Is everything cool and calm here, or is something unusual happening that appears headed toward a crisis?" The very next question is "How safe am I?" If the answer to that question is "I'm not sure" or "Not very," then get out now!

Home intervention also includes many case management activities. Getting ready for court, obtaining an attorney, looking for alternative living arrangements and transportation, dealing with school issues, and applying for victims' compensation and other state support mechanisms for families are but a few of the many support activities that will be needed to help the family restabilize (Bottoms, 1999). As Saxe and his associates propose (2007), this is a systemic effort, and nothing less than dealing with the whole system will do.

Crisis Session. All of the foregoing sounds swell, but the fact is that the therapy of child sexual abuse rarely progresses in a nice, linear, ever upward, ever onward manner. There are transcrises aplenty with which to reckon.

Elizabeth: (*Tears up the carefully made new family she has been building in the sand tray and breaks down in tears.*) This won't ever come true! Some kids at school said Leon's gonna get out just like their daddies did and will be right back at home. I HATE THIS STUPID SAND TRAY! THIS IS HOPELESS. WE'LL NEVER BE SAFE, AND I HATE THERAPY, AND YOU TOO, MISS DELAINE, so you can just kiss my ass goodbye! (*Stands defiantly as an 8-year-old can, tearfully regarding Delaine with as evil a look as she can muster.*)

CW: (*Says nothing but picks up some modeling clay and popsicle sticks and starts constructing something.*)

Elizabeth: (*Sits over in the corner staring balefully at the worker. Slowly comes over to the worker.*) Whatcha doing with that clay and those stupid popsicle sticks?

CW: I am going to build something I think might help when things are really down. I guess you are so hopeless and helpless right now you couldn't help me.

Elizabeth: I didn't say that. What is it?

CW: (*Sweeps the sand away in the sand tray and parts it to reveal a broad swath of blue board.*) It is a bridge. I am building a bridge over troubled waters. But it has to be a strong bridge with good foundations, strong girders, and support wire because it has to stay solid and mustn't fall in. It carries very important people on it . . . like your mom and you.

Your stepfather may get out some day, but you will be a grown woman by then. But there are going to be other troubles that will get you down and things that will appear just as hopeless, maybe things you do, or your mom does, or maybe what other people say or do. So it's got to be a strong bridge. I'd like to put this family on the other side with palm trees and beach chairs and sunshine, not on this side with the swamp and all the nasty swamp things that live in it. But I can't build this alone. It is your bridge.

Elizabeth: (*Grudgingly starts to help mold pillars for the bridge.*) I guess so.

CW: (*after bridge is done*) How do you feel? You see you have a real way to get out of the swamp. I am going to take a picture of this, and I want you to put it in the book. This is very important because it shows that you can get to the other side and you can make your own bridge to get you there. So remember where you have come from. You have indeed crossed over that bridge with all the work we have done. There is no going back, you are across, but every once in a while when things get tough it's good to remember that this bridge we just built really is your bridge, Elizabeth. It is something you now own and can use forever. Now stand over there by the bridge and give me a big cheesy smile!

Drawing or constructing a bridge lets clients concretely fill in gaps when they see little way across "troubled waters." Bridging exercises are mainly used for assessment to determine where people have been and where they are going (Martin, 2008). Here we use bridging as a therapeutic vehicle to get Elizabeth mobilized again and show her where she has been, whence she has come, and where she is going. Here the crisis worker takes action and very actively and directly gets into the game, but as soon as Elizabeth mobilizes herself, the

crisis worker assumes a collaborative mode and then becomes nondirective as Elizabeth regains control.

Last Sessions: Transcending. What Saxe and associates (2007) call the transcendent phase of intervention occurs when the caregiving parent and abused child are brought together in conjoint therapy. The notion is that both caregiver and child are now able to talk openly and honestly about the abuse. The worker may start these sessions by acting as a game show host and asking both clients questions about sexual abuse (Neubauer, Deblinger, & Sieger, 2007). As survivor and caregiver reaffiliate, the child is encouraged to read passages from her book; Saxe and associates (2007, p. 276) recommend about three chapters per session. As the child reads the chapters, the caregiver expresses his or her own thoughts about what the child has written and gives the child a whole lot of reinforcement for having done such an awesome job of getting her feelings, thoughts, and behaviors about the sexual abuse down on paper (Neubauer, Deblinger, & Sieger, 2007).

SUMMARY

The sexual assault research consistently finds that the incidence of sexual assault is greatly underreported. The majority of reported rapists and other sexual abusers are males, and they come from all walks of life. Most abusers appear to perceive those they attack as objects of prey rather than as people. They usually assault not out of lust or desire for sexual gratification but out of a perceived need to control, exert power over, punish, vanquish, defeat, hurt, destroy, degrade, or humiliate others. Typically, abusers deny, minimize, and/or rationalize their behavior to the extent that they themselves rarely define their attacks as abuse. Instead, they usually claim that the survivor asked for, deserved, seduced, wanted, needed the experience in order to grow up, or somehow caused the abusive activity to occur.

Rape is a complex phenomenon that encompasses and affects the psychosocial, cultural, and personal aspects of society. There are no cause-and-effect formulas that explain why one person sexually assaults another. Consequently, many erroneous assumptions, beliefs, and myths about rape are held by different people, and women and men often differ in their perceptions about rape.

Date and acquaintance rape, especially on college campuses, has become a pressing problem. The problem is exacerbated by the use of drugs and/or alcohol that is usually found to be associated with date rape. One impediment to preventing date and acquaintance rape is the differential perceptions between men and women. The research consistently reveals that men are more tolerant of rape than are women.

Recently, the human services professions have directed a great deal of attention to rape and sexual assault on children. Substantive work has been done in the areas of crisis work, counseling, legal, social, and psychological interventions to help children and to prevent child sexual abuse. Such intervention and prevention have been made even more urgent in light of recent findings that child sexual abuse extends debilitating traumas far into the adulthood of survivors. An enormous amount of research has shown that adult survivors of child sexual abuse often suffer a wide diversity of emotional, physical, psychological, and social pathologies that manifest themselves in various degrees of transcrisis and PTSD symptoms later in adulthood. These findings have produced greater urgency than ever before to help victims of sexual abuse and to stop offenders from assaulting.

Crisis intervention and other human services work in the area of rape and sexual assault of children require unique and specialized knowledge and strategies. Children are vulnerable to many kinds of pressures, and perpetrators of child sexual abuse know all the angles needed to ensnare child victims. The legal, medical, social, mental health, law enforcement, and human services professions as well as the court system are becoming increasingly integrated in attempting to stop the abuse and to work with abused children and their families. There is ominous research on sexual predators' use of the Internet, and that arena will surely deserve even more attention in studies on controlling and containing child sexual abuse.

In recent years the public, too, has become increasingly aware of the phenomenon of rape and other forms of sexual abuse, and that new awareness appears to have ushered in a greater sensitivity to and advocacy for the rights and needs of survivors. However, much remains to be done. Society still needs to overcome a number of long-standing myths about rape and other forms of sexual abuse. And survivors' families, friends, and coworkers need to be willing and able to respond to survivors with openness, genuineness, acceptance, understanding, and respect, all of which are key attitudes or conditions for nurturing recovery from the debilitating trauma and effects of sexual assault. Given the high incidence of sexual assault and its underreporting, it is highly likely that a number of you—both male and female—may have experienced this crisis. As a result of reading this chapter, you may experience or be experiencing some of the repercussions this chapter speaks of in people who have been sexually assaulted and abused. We urge you to not be ashamed, embarrassed, or guilty but to understand that this crisis is common to a whole lot of people and to get help! If you don't feel there is help in your community or you are too embarrassed to ask, call the National Office on Violence Against Women's hotlines: the Rape, Abuse, and Incest National Network Hotline at 1-800-656-HOPE (4673), the National Sexual Violence Resource Center at 1-877-739-3895, or the National Teen Dating Abuse Helpline at 1-866-331-9474. If you are attempting to recover on your own from a sexual assault, get Aphrodite Matsakis's *The Rape Recovery Handbook* (2003). It is a step-by-step help program for survivors of sexual assault. It's user friendly, talks straight to you, and has really helpful exercises in it.

Visit CengageBrain.com for a variety of study tools and useful resources such as video examples, case studies, interactive exercises, flashcards, and quizzes.

Partner Violence

10

LEARNING OBJECTIVES

After studying this chapter, you should be able to:

1. Understand the pervasiveness of partner violence that cuts across all cultures and socioeconomic classes.
2. Understand that approaches to partner violence are changing in the 21st century.
3. Know the dynamics of partner violence.
4. Understand the psychological factors that contribute to partner violence.
5. Understand the stressors that lead to partner violence.
6. Know the myths that surround partner violence.
7. Know the different types of batterers.
8. Understand the cycle of violence.
9. Understand the realities that militate toward staying in a battering relationship.
10. Understand assessment strategies for battering relationships.
11. Know the intervention components for battering.
12. Understand the dynamics of living in a shelter.
13. Understand what occurs in follow-up after leaving the shelter.
14. Know how to intervene with children who live in a battering environment.
15. Understand the dynamics of courtship violence.
16. Understand the dynamics of stalking.
17. Understand the dynamics of gay and lesbian battering.
18. Understand how treatment for batterers occurs.
19. Know how a typical domestic violence reduction group operates.

Introduction

The pervasiveness of domestic violence is **LO1** so great that it cuts across social, economic, religious, ethnic, cultural, racial, and geographical boundaries (Ahrens et al., 2010; Arai, 2004; Archambeau et al., 2010; Browne & Herbert, 1997; Hague & Sardinha, 2010; Haj-Yahia, 2003; Hotaling & Sugarman, 1986, 1990; Kasturirangan & Williams, 2003; Lee, 2002; Levinson, 1989; Maziak & Asfar, 2003; Murdaugh et al., 2004; Robinson, 2003; Santiago, 2002; Sev'er, 1997; Weitzman, 2000; West, Kaufman Kantor, & Jasinski, 1998; Witko, Martinez, & Milda, 2006; Yoshioka et al., 2003; Zanipatin et al., 2005). Indeed, a review of the American Psychological Association abstracts reveals that almost every country the *National Geographic* covers has had a study done on domestic violence. Culture plays a large part in what is defined as domestic violence or if it even exists. Further, if we define culture in terms of the social locations that Laura Brown (2008) speaks so eloquently to, we need to look at being pregnant (Suglia et al., 2010), homeless (Yeater et al., 2011), HIV positive, or a sex worker (prostitute) (Ulibarri et al., 2010) as some of the many locations that lead to physical violence between intimates (Bryant-Davis, 2010).

Certainly, physical abuse in domestic situations is not limited to husband-and-wife relationships. Indeed, single, separated, and divorced women are actually at greater risk for battering than are married women (Stark & Flitcraft, 1987). Furthermore, battering is not confined to heterosexual relationships: lesbians, gays, and bisexuals also batter one another (Kanuha, 2005; Peterman & Dixon, 2003; Randle & Graham, 2011; Ricks, Vaughan, & Dziegielewski, 2002; Stanley et al., 2006; West, 1998). Men are also assaulted by women (Langhinrichsen-Roling, Neidig, & Thorn, 1995; Randle & Graham, 2011; Stets & Straus, 1990; Straus & Gelles, 1990; Wiehe, 1998). Therefore, it should be clearly understood that the concepts discussed in this chapter apply to *all* partners or people involved in any established current or former cohabiting relationship. To further amplify the cross-sectional aspects of battering, the politically correct term has now become **intimate partner violence (IPV)** to encompass all types of couples. Because women form the major target group of severe domestic violence, however, this chapter focuses mainly on crisis intervention with women who are involved in domestic violence and the men who batter them.

The terms *battering*, *abuse*, and *assault* are often used interchangeably in the literature. In this chapter, **battering** indicates any form of physical violence perpetrated by one person on another and typically includes a life-threatening history of injuries and psychosocial problems that entrap a person in a relationship. **Abuse** is a more general term that indicates that physical violence is only one weapon in an armory of coercive weapons. Abuse denotes the unequal power relationship within which the assault occurs and further suggests that a presumption of trust has been violated. **Assaultive behavior** can include not only harmful acts against a person but also both verbal and behavioral threats to significant others, pets, or property. **Domestic violence** subsumes any act of assault by a social partner or relative, regardless of marital status (Stark & Flitcraft, 1988).

The Incidence of Partner Violence

The history of spouse beating in Western society goes as far back as the patriarchal system does. Whereas an assault on or rape of another man's wife caused and still causes immediate and severe legal punishment and moral outrage, abuse by a man of his own wife is quite another story (Pleck, 1987). Common law in the United States early acknowledged the right of a man to chastise his wife for misbehavior without being prosecuted for doing so (*Bradley* v. *State of Mississippi,* 1824). Indeed, the law's attitude toward wife beating to the current day is aptly summarized in the case of the *State of North Carolina* v. *Oliver* in 1874. The court ruled that "if no permanent injury has been inflicted, it is better to draw the curtains, shut out the public eye, and leave the parties to forgive and forget." The implications of such "blind" justice are ominous.

There is no more anxiety-provoking call for a police officer than a domestic disturbance call. Furthermore, domestic disturbance calls far outnumber other types of police calls in which the possibility of violence, injury, and death exists to both civilians and police (Benjamin & Walz, 1983). In the last comprehensive survey on domestic violence, it was estimated that about 1.5 million women and 830,000 men were victims of intimate violence in the United States (Tjaden & Thoennes, 2000). The Centers for Disease Control's report on homicides in the United States from 1981 to 1998 found that approximately one in three murders were intimate partner homicides (Centers for Disease Control, 2001). The good news is that these rates are apparently decreasing (Agency for Healthcare Research and Quality, 2010); however, those most likely to suffer IPV are, like many of you reading this book, women in their 20s to early 30s. A summary of all violent crimes reported that around 500,000 were perpetrated by intimates in 2002, down from the 1.1 million reported to authorities in 1993 (Bureau of Justice Statistics, 2003). Incidence studies report that 25% to 44% of women and about 7.6% to 13.8% of men in the United States have experienced a violent incident with a partner during their adult lifetime (Black et al., 2011; Thompson et al., 2006; Tjaden & Thoennes, 1998a). The foregoing figures should be viewed as very conservative estimates. Other estimates place the number of domestic violence incidents at anywhere from 4 to 8.7 million! Worldwide, it is estimated that between 8% and 67% of women are physically assaulted in their lifetime, with most countries reporting lifetime prevalence rates of 20% (Aldarondo & Castro-Fernandez, 2011). These latest figures probably underestimate the magnitude of the problem, for several reasons: cultural norms tolerate and in some instances condone family violence; confidentiality keeps violence a family secret; poor and non-English-speaking women are underreported; women who are institutionalized or hospitalized are often not included; elderly, gay, and lesbian incidents of violence are often not reported; and gender roles based on power differentials that are still sanctioned keep a number of domestic violence cases out of the legal system (Browne & Herbert, 1997; Lee, 2002; Pence & Shepard, 1999; Ricks, Vaughan, & Dziegielewski, 2002; Santiago, 2002; Wiehe, 1998). If there is possibly a worse number in these statistics, it is that an estimated 15.5 million children live in families where violence has occurred and about 7 million have witnessed severe violence (McDonald et al., 2006). What that kind of problem-solving behavior models for children and begets in adulthood should give you an idea why this type of crisis has been so intractable.

One of the major reasons much domestic violence is not reported is that the medical system fails to do so (Hampton, Vandergriff-Avery, & Kim, 1999; Roberts & Roberts, 2002). The American Medical Association, the American College of Obstetricians and Gynecologists, the Institute of Medicine, the U.S. Preventive Services Task Force, and the American Nurses Association all recommend counseling and screening for domestic violence, and the Affordable Care Act includes screening and brief counseling for IPV as part of required free preventive services for women (Boes & McDermott, 2002; Miller et al., 2015). Using a trauma screen to determine how the physical injury has occurred, researchers found that the single most common cause of a female injury brought to medical attention was abuse. In emergency room settings, an estimated 20% to 35% of female patients seek treatment for domestic violence, and in family practices, between 25% and 40% of women report abuse. However, only 2% to 10% of battered women are commonly identified as such by physicians (Hamberger, 1994). The failure of health care professionals to adequately detect partner violence stems from a fear of offending patients, lack of training and knowledge, inability to cure the problem, lack of time, and lack of insurance coverage (Tilden et al., 1994). This failing should not be too surprising because little emphasis on domestic violence has been given in medical schools or nurses' training (Sassetti, 1993). Compounding the problem are state reporting laws that are not nearly as stringent as child abuse laws in requiring health care professionals to report injuries from suspected partner violence (Chalk & King, 1998, p. 173). However, during the 1990s the American Medical Association started an education campaign for its members and started teaching them how to ask appropriate questions to women who appeared to be battered. More recent data suggest that women are more likely to report abuse if they seek out treatment and are asked appropriate questions in an empathic and supportive manner. The problem is that it is still unclear how many women do not seek out treatment (Walker, 2000, p. 31).

Another culprit in the helping professions is the clergy. Many clerics who deal with family violence have a great deal of difficulty with the issue, and a number were found to place the blame on the woman (Wood & McHugh, 1994). However, other human services workers should not feel smug. Research indicates that they, too, may have biases against and stereotypes about abused women that interfere with

and hinder treatment (Ross & Glesson, 1991). But it is noteworthy that although crisis workers are not contacted as often by abused women as other professionals are, they were reported to be the most helpful (Hamilton & Coates, 1993).

Emerging Approaches to Partner Violence

Despite the long history of partner abuse, only LO2 since 1974 has there been a consistent and planned systematic approach to the problem. Erin Pizzey's book *Scream Quietly or the Neighbors Will Hear* (1974) was responsible for the start of the first women's shelter in England. Subsequently, in the United States, the National Organization for Women, along with grassroots organizations such as the Massachusetts Coalition of Battered Women Service Groups, has come to the forefront in developing funding sources, shelters, support groups, organizing and training manuals, and legislation for battered women. Such increased public awareness and the efforts of feminist and other citizens' groups resulted in the formation of the National Coalition Against Domestic Violence to promote a national power base for battered women (Capps, 1982). This group has exerted a good deal of social and legislative pressure to combat the problem of domestic violence. The Domestic Abuse Intervention Project in Duluth, Minnesota, has become internationally known as the Duluth model for its integrated approach to the problem (Pence & Shepard, 1999). The Duluth model has become internationally known because of its massive and sustained effort to get every agency that comes in contact with a battering incident—from 911 dispatch that receives the first call to the last judge, probation officer, or therapist who signs off on the batterer as finished with intervention—involved in a systematic and integrated manner so that no battered person or batterer falls through the cracks (Home of the Duluth Model, 2011).

Thus, over the last 30 years, the country's approach to domestic violence has changed dramatically. First, there has been a shift in police procedures, increased prosecution of partner violence, and enhanced legal protection through tougher protective orders and warrantless arrest. In many cities and states, a police call to a domestic dispute in which battering is involved now results in a mandatory arrest; and if convicted, the batterer is mandated by the court to either participate in counseling and a batterer intervention program (BIP) or go to jail (Goodman & Epstein, 2011;

Pence & Shepard, 1999; Shupe, Stacey, & Hazlewood, 1987). Second, as a result of lobbying efforts by activists, state legislatures have enacted protection laws with teeth in them that allow judges to tailor-make orders of protections suited to individual cases (Goodman & Epstein, 2011). Third, countywide coordinated community responses on the order of the Duluth model have been formed (Goodman & Epstein, 2011). Fourth, domestic violence units have been formed in police departments, probation and parole offices, states attorneys' offices, and domestic violence courts, which all coordinate efforts to reduce domestic violence (Chalk & King, 1998, p. 172; Pence & Shepard, 1999).

A growing number of women have entered academia in the past 30 years, particularly in the social sciences. Their research on family violence, gender roles, and male dominance has resulted in social activism that has debunked the "safe haven" notion of the family (Jasinski & Williams, 1998, pp. vi–vii). The Violence Against Women Act of 1994 provided $1.2 billion for the improvement of services and community support for domestic violence victims, the criminal justice system's response to violent crimes against women, safety for women in public transit and public parks, assistance to victims of sexual assault, and support for a variety of educational, health, and database services. This bill was reauthorized in 2000 with an increase of $3.3 billion over 5 years to community services to aid survivors of domestic violence, sexual assault, and stalking. It was reauthorized again in 2005 and has received continuous funding. An overview of its many activities can be found at the website of the Department of Justice's Office of Violence Against Women (www.ovw.usdoj.gov).

Media attention about the severity of the problem has raised public consciousness. Television documentaries, newspaper articles, and media coverage have attracted attention, changed public perspectives, and removed some of the cloak of secrecy from domestic violence. Stories such as those of Francine Hughes (subject of the movie *The Burning Bed*), who suffered prolonged and severe beatings by her husband and who finally killed him by pouring kerosene around his bed and setting it on fire, have had an impact on the courts by challenging legal precedents and assumptions about homicide and self-defense (Edwards, 1989). Indeed, psychologist Lenore Walker's (1989) book *Terrifying Love* is a chilling and eye-opening account of her experiences as an expert witness in murder trials of battering victims who have killed their assailants. The result has been the recognition of

a history of abuse called the **battered wife syndrome** (PTSD-like symptoms due to battering) (Walker, 2000, pp. 160–161) as a valid part of a legal defense for battered women who kill their husbands (Chalk & King, 1998, pp. 171–172).

Once arrested, batterers are required to go through a variety of different educational programs to teach them not to batter (Geffner & Rosenbaum, 2002; Mederos, 1999; Rosenbaum & Kunkel, 2009; Sonkin & Dutton, 2003). Treating batterers has become a big-time business. For example, as of 2006 there were 450 registered batterer programs (BIPs), serving more than 25,000 batterers in California alone (California State Auditor, 2006). All states now have laws on the books that make IPV a crime and domestic violence courts that may mandate sentences ranging from jail time to BIPs (Rosenbaum & Kunkel, 2009).

Although no national register of BIPs exists, Price and Rosenbaum's (2007) survey found 1,750 programs nationwide. That is undoubtedly low because it didn't take into account many of the private programs that exist in addition to those run by local community agencies. It is safe to say that hundreds of thousands of men and women have now gone through some kind of BIP in the United States. In Tennessee, batterers are required to pay for their group treatment from a certified leader. But the philosophy and treatment approaches of these programs vary a great deal, and by no means is there a common, unitary approach.

In their 10-year follow-up study of family violence in 1985, Straus and Gelles (1986) found an overall decline in husband-to-wife violence of 6.6% and a decrease in severe husband-to-wife violence (battering) of 26.6%. Overall violence reduction has continued to the present, which would lead one to believe that the massive effort by the judiciary, law enforcement, education, social services, and media attention has started to have an impact. However, what was perplexing in their study was that wife-to-husband violence had increased to a rate higher than that of husband-to-wife violence. Other studies support this increase, particularly when courtship is involved (Carrado et al., 1996; Fiebert & Gonzalez, 1997; Morse, 1995). In fact, a number of more recent reports have found comparable levels of female-versus male-initiated violence (Bowen, 2009; Dutton, 2007; Hines & Douglas, 2011; Randle & Graham, 2011). Needless to say, the veteran feminists who were in the forefront of the fight to get domestic violence out into the light of public scrutiny have hotly disputed these findings.

Clearly, a great deal of violence by women against men is retaliatory, or in self-defense, as opposed to male batterers' attempts to terrorize, control, or intimidate. Also, when women are the victims of assault, it usually means more serious injury than when the opposite occurs. Furthermore, no research places men in the same systematic victimization status of women who are literally terrorized into attempting to escape the relationship (Kaufman Kantor & Jasinski, 1998, pp. 9–10). The apparent statistical decrease in women reporting domestic violence is puzzling given that the number of shelters for abused women has grown from none in 1975 to more than 2,000 shelters in 2002 (Roberts, 2002), and those shelters are constantly beyond capacity and must turn people away.

Dynamics of Partner Violence
Psychosocial and Cultural Dynamics

The overarching dynamic that has held sway **LO3** over the battering of women is the belief in male supremacy. This belief is the natural result of a long-term sexist, paternalistic social order that rewards aggressive behavior in men but expects women to be passive and submissive (Benjamin & Walz, 1983, p. 65; Pence & Shepard, 1999). This stereotypical and dated view has produced a volatile mix of personality dynamics between the "traditional" male and the female. The flash point of such a mix occurs when the man who lives the traditional male image of chief breadwinner and director of the family perceives himself as losing power in the conjugal relationship.

The question of power is the fuse that ignites this explosive mixture. In this view, the woman's position is to obey, conciliate, perform traditional domestic duties, and, in general, be subservient. Any attempt to establish herself in her own right is likely to be met with punishment for overstepping her bounds (Benjamin & Walz, 1983, pp. 74–77; Pence & Shepard, 1999). Violence, though, is not something that develops only in families. It involves a complex interplay of social, cultural, and psychological factors, and to say that a patriarchal system alone is responsible for battering would seem to fall far short of the mark (Dutton, 1995, pp. 27–62).

The fact is that a great many men who have patriarchal attitudes go through their entire married lives without assaulting their wives, and the sociopolitical beliefs of abusers don't discriminate them from nonabusers (Hotaling & Sugarman, 1986; Straus & Gelles, 1986). So is there one true theory of the abusive/assaultive personality that leads to partner violence? The answer to that question is a resounding "No!"—although most of the following theories have their rabid supporters who would vehemently disagree with that statement. The following theories encapsulate past and present thinking about the causes of battering.

Attachment/Traumatic Bonding Theory. Disruptions of attachment in early life arouse intense anger, grief, sorrow, and anxiety in the child and diminish the child's ability to form mutual and trusting relationships as an adult. High correlations appear among spousal violence, the number of separation-and-loss events abusers and their families of origin experienced, and the erratic caregiving patterns of batterers' parents. Thus, men whose parents were unreliable, abusive, needy, or otherwise unequal to the task of child rearing may be very sensitive to fears of abandonment and enmeshment. The partner may contribute to these fears by her own fears of abandonment. Each partner creates ways to control the other to avoid being abandoned. One of those ways is through violence. Traumatic bonding may explain why some women stay with or return to their abusive partners (Bowlby, 1980; Brewster, 2002; Sonkin & Dutton, 2003).

Coercive Control. Morgan (1982) used the term **conjugal** or **intimate terrorism** to describe a tactic akin to brainwashing and political terrorism, whereby violence or the threat of violence is used to break the victim's resistance and bend her to the will of the terrorist (batterer). Typical brainwashing and terrorist tools such as social and physical isolation, torture, sleep deprivation, malnourishment, dictating the use of the victim's time, bondage, false confessions, and denouncing and belittling the victim to significant others are all standard operating procedures of abusers to enhance the victim's dependency on them. Johnson (1995) identifies this type of batterer as indeed a terrorist, representative of the type that women who seek out shelters describe. Women who are battered by these men have more injuries, take more painkillers, have more PTSD symptoms, are attacked more frequently, and are less likely to have the violence stop (Johnson & Leone, 2005). This pathological male is very different from the general population of situational batterers and is extremely dangerous.

Cultural Reinforcement. Sociological theories cover a wide gamut of specific theories that are psychosocially and culturally bound. These theories find the roots of violence in institutions ranging from the culture at large down to the family unit. Societal attitudes about the legitimate use of violence to achieve personal ends have their roots in a tradition of perceived "national interest." As a nation, we promote and glorify the controlled use of aggression for protection, law and order, self-defense, and national interest (Benjamin & Walz, 1983, pp. 64–66). Force is a major resource in maintaining the existing social structure and projecting national presence. This notion has been extended to the family by at least implicit permission of the state. For the state, the family is the basic disciplinary agent—family over individual, male over female, adult over child. Control is direct, continuous, personalized, and an efficient way of keeping intact the past social order of the state (Capps, 1982).

Exchange Theory. Exchange theory (Gelles & Cornell, 1985) is a variant of a learning theory approach. It proposes that batterers hit people because they can (Carden, 1994). As long as the costs for being violent do not outweigh the rewards, violence will invariably be used as a method of control (Hampton, Vandergriff-Avery, & Kim, 1999). Particularly when social control agents such as the police, criminal charges, imprisonment, loss of status, and loss of income are not used as negative sanctions that increase the cost of the behavior, batterers will continue to batter. Gender inequality in physical size, financial resources, and social status allows batterers to become violent without fear of retribution. Although there may be loss of status in the larger society for being a child or wife beater, there are certain subcultures in which aggressive and violent behaviors are proof of being a "real man." Finally, exacting "costs" from a partner to pay for her or his supposed "sins and transgressions" is itself satisfying to the batterer (Gelles & Cornell, 1985, pp. 120–125).

Feminist Theory. Feminist theory views social phenomena as determined by the sexist, patriarchal structure of our society and battering as merely one outcome of a structure that allows rape, incest, prostitution, foot binding, and a host of other sexist restrictions to keep women in servile positions (Schechter, 1982; Stark & Flitcraft, 1988). Feminists believe that women have not achieved the political, economic, and social independence that would empower them to leave abusive relationships (Bograd, 1992; Dobash & Dobash, 1992; Pagelow, 1992). They do not believe that a woman has any culpability in promoting or maintaining a violent relationship because the perpetrator alone commits the act; he alone is morally and legally responsible for it and should be the one to suffer the consequences (Avis, 1992; Bograd, 1992). A strict feminist view categorically separates woman battering from other forms of intrafamily violence, or at the most sees the other forms of family violence as a by-product of how women are brutalized (Okun, 1986). The feminist view also holds that until women are seen as other than subservient, compliant victims, little will change. Feminists criticize the mass media for romanticizing violence, male dominance, and female submissiveness (Dines, 1992; Jarvie, 1991). Feminist theory calls for a complete restructuring of society to eradicate the power differential that males enjoy that allows them to batter.

Intraindividual Theory. There is evidence that psychopathology and neurophysiological disorders may play a greater part in some perpetrators of battering than was previously thought. Personality disorders, attention deficit disorder, psychosis, internal head trauma, and substance abuse have been identified as possible contributing factors that lead to aggression and rage reactions (Browne & Herbert, 1997, p. 61; Dutton, 1994, 1995, pp. 26–29; Jasinski & Williams, 1998, p. 42; Stuart et al., 2006). Both male and female adolescents with psychiatric disorders are at greater risk for becoming involved in abusive adult relationships (Ehrensaft, Moffitt, & Caspi, 2006).

Learned Helplessness/Battered Woman Syndrome. Learning theory approaches operate on the principle that both perpetration and acceptance of physical and psychological abuse are conditioned and learned behavior. A great deal of research indicates a strong relationship between being abused by parents and/or witnessing interparental violence as a child and being violent toward a partner as an adult (Astin et al., 1995; Barnett & Hamberger, 1992; Jouriles & Norwood, 1995). Foremost among these theories is Lenore Walker's (1984, 1989, 2000) theory of learned helplessness, which she adapted from animal studies conducted on random, noncontingent punishment.

Applied to battering in particular, the theory proposes that battered women stay in abusive relationships because they have been conditioned to believe they cannot predict their own safety and that nothing they or anyone else does will alter their terrible circumstances. Over time, through continuous conditioning, a battered woman syndrome emerges that causes the woman to lose hope and feel completely incapable of dealing with the situation (Brewster, 2002).

Walker (1984, 1989, 2000) proposed a number of factors in childhood and adulthood that are building blocks for learned helplessness. Childhood factors include witnessing or experiencing battering, sexual abuse or molestation, health problems or chronic illness, stereotypical sex roles, and rigid tradition. Such experiences teach the child that external, autocratic, and often whimsical forces dictate outcomes. In adulthood, factors that are instigated by the batterer include an emergent pattern of violence, sexual abuse, jealousy, overpossessiveness, intrusiveness and isolation, threat of harm, observed violence toward other people, animals, or things, and alcohol or drug abuse. Given these conditions, the victim cannot escape the noncontingent punishment and thus loses any effectiveness in being able to control what happens to her (Walker, 2000, pp. 10–12).

The term **helplessness** has caused a great deal of furor from feminists because they see this pejorative term as casting women in a victim role with few resources or little empowerment. However, according to Walker (1989), women are not helpless in the standard sense of the term. What **learned helplessness** means is that battered women choose behavioral responses that have the highest predictability of causing them the least harm in the known situation (pp. 50–52), or what Gondolf and Fisher (1988) call the survivor hypothesis, wherein women become very active and resourceful in protecting themselves and their children (Browne, 1997). Because of the extreme and often lethal violence that occurs when these women attempt to leave, and the lack of social support for making any attempt, it is understandable that a "Better the devil I know!" philosophy predominates for many abused women.

Masochism. Psychoanalytic theory, which has held masochism to be the primary motivating factor in abusive relationships, is now mostly obsolete in the therapeutic community. There is no empirical research to substantiate the notion that erotic enjoyment of pain through battering is a trait found in abused women (Okun, 1986; Stark & Flitcraft, 1988). That being said, one has to wonder why *Fifty Shades of Gray* was a best-selling book and movie if there isn't at least a grain of truth in what the Freudians extolled. From a feminist point of view, this theory held sway

for a long time because the male-dominated field of psychiatry found it a convenient pigeonhole for a troublesome problem. Until interest in the problem was generated in the 1970s, little research was presented to refute the idea.

Nested Ecological Theory. Because no single factor theory has effectively explained the battering phenomenon, an integrated, multifactor approach may be the best way to understand the complexities of battering (Brewster, 2002). Dutton (1985, 1995) proposed an ecological theory that integrates many of the foregoing theories. Four layers of variables operate within the ecosystem. First is a core of individual experience composed of intrapersonal psychological factors such as shame, denial, and hostility. Second is a family system layer, in which the individual experiences such negative actions as abandonment, neglect, and abuse. Third is a community/peer layer, which inculcates fundamental religious training, alcohol and drug use, and rigid gender role socialization. Finally, in a larger societal context, the individual is exposed to sociopolitical gender inequities, media portrayal of subjugation and violence against women, and racial/ethnic prejudices. As a result, it is not just one but many factors that operate within the individual, in interpersonal relationships, and throughout the larger social environment that are communicated and synthesized to make battering a viable option (Hampton, Vandergriff-Avery, & Kim, 1999).

Psychological Entrapment. Psychological entrapment proposes that the woman does not leave the relationship because she feels she has too much time, energy, and emotion invested in it (Brewster, 2002), or she would feel shame if her terrible secret were found out (Buchbinder & Eisikovits, 2003). She engages in wishful thinking that some miracle will occur or that she can somehow change the significant other and a nonviolent, intimate, and loving relationship will emerge. For some women, the shame of their battering and the failed relationship is so great that they will do anything to keep it from public view.

Sociobiology. Sociobiology proposes that evolutionary adaptation requires aggression for survival. Thus, there is the inherited tendency to aggress against someone who threatens the chances of survival and, deductively, procreation of the species. If the foregoing is true, then it would be reasonable to expect that males would aggress against other real or imagined males who were trying to take away the female. The question then arises: Why would the male assault the object he wishes to possess instead of other intruding males? The sociobiologists have no clear answer to this question (Dutton, 1995, pp. 29–34).

Stockholm Syndrome. (For a complete description of this syndrome, see online Chapter 19, Crisis/Hostage Negotiation.) Akin to being held hostage, the woman is completely isolated and subjugated by her abuser, and her survival is entirely dependent on his whims, desires, or purposes. Because she is shown occasional kindness and is completely isolated from other support systems, she develops a strong emotional bond with the abuser (Brewster, 2002).

System Theory. System theory posits that battering is not attributable to the standard victim–abuser dichotomy. Rather, **conjugal violence** and **battering relationship** are more appropriate terms to depict battering as part of a violence-prone system. The violence is a maladaptive but efficient way to keep the system in homeostasis. Through learning history and rigidly polarized roles for both parties, the system is able to maintain itself (Wiehe, 1998, pp. 87–90).

Although each of the preceding theoretical stances has merit, to this point none has proven able to completely explain the phenomenon of battering. Certainly, there is much to be said for a feminist perspective couched in paternalistic sociocultural terms. If it had not been for the feminist movement's willingness to take on battering as a social issue, it would probably still be "behind drawn shades." There is also clear evidence that at least one factor contributing to our bulging prison population is that certain people will attempt to get away with anything they can with little regard for the cost to others, as long as they believe they can escape the consequences of their actions. Similarly, evidence exists that legions of people with personality disorders would think nothing of manipulating anyone in any manner to satisfy their insatiable narcissistic or dependency needs. There is also clear evidence from a national perspective that Teddy Roosevelt's admonition "Speak softly and carry a big stick!" is extremely effective and has trickled down to the family unit. It doesn't take a doctorate in sociology to figure out that ecological and cultural variations may have profound effects on the kind and incidence of partner violence. Finally, it is hard to argue against the contention that the founding fathers' belief that "a man's home is his castle" has much to do with society's refusal to intervene in the sacrosanct realm of the home.

Psychological Factors

Psychologically, both parties to a battering situation may have certain identifiable characteristics. You should clearly understand that these are not just separate and individual ingredients, but complex forces that interrelate with one another and thus increase the odds of IPV. As an example, Bornstein (2006) has provided an in-depth examination of how emotional dependency in males and economic dependency in females, when combined, become an extremely dangerous mix that can lead to violence.

Men in a battering relationship may:*

1. Demonstrate excessive dependency and possessiveness toward their women—although they deny it.
2. Be unable to express any emotion except anger and generally have poor communication skills where emotional issues are concerned.
3. Have unrealistic expectations of their spouses and idealize marriage or the relationship far beyond what realistically may be expected.
4. Have a lack of self-control and, paradoxically, set up rigid family boundaries for everyone else.
5. Be alcohol or drug abusers.
6. Have been abused as children or saw their mothers abused.
7. Deny and minimize problems, particularly battering, that they generate in families.
8. Emotionally cycle from hostility, aggressiveness, and cruelty when they do not get their way, to charm, manipulation, and seductiveness when they do.
9. Be characterized as jealous, denying, impulsive, self-deprecating, depressive, demanding, aggressive, and violent.
10. Feel a lack of comparative power to the woman in economic status, decision making, and communication skills.

Women in a battering relationship may:†

1. Have a lack of self-esteem as a result of being told over and over that they are stupid, incompetent, and otherwise inadequate.
2. Experience a lack of control and little confidence in their ability to take any meaningful steps to improve their marriage.

---

*This list was derived from Babcock et al., 1993; Barnett et al., 1980; Bornstein, 2006; Ehrensaft et al., 2003; Finkelhor et al., 1983; Gelles & Cornell, 1985; Okun, 1986; Schumacher, Fals-Stewart, & Leonard, 2003; Shupe, Stacey, & Hazlewood, 1987; Walker, 1984, 1989, 2000.
†This list was derived from Benjamin & Walz, 1983; Bornstein, 2006; Ehrensaft et al., 2003; Finkelhor et al., 1983; Gelles & Cornell, 1985; Hage, 2006; Ibrahim & Herr, 1987; Okun, 1986; Roberts, 2002; Walker, 1984, 1989, 2000.

3. Have experienced a history of abuse that leads them to accept their role as victim, or saw their mothers abused and accepted it as their lot.

4. Be so ashamed that they hide their physical and emotional wounds and become socially and emotionally isolated.

5. Lack personal, physical, educational, and financial resources that would allow them to get out of the battering situation.

6. Be extremely dependent and willing to suffer grievous insult and injury to have their needs met.

7. Have an idealized view of what a relationship should be and somehow feel they can "fix" or "change" the man.

8. Not have good communication skills, particularly in regard to asserting their rights and feelings.

9. Have learned stereotyped sex roles and thus feel guilty if they do not adhere to a rigid patriarchal system.

10. Be unable to differentiate between sex and love and believe that love is manifested through intense sexual relationships.

In one way or another, all the concepts just enumerated have to do with power, and all point back to this basic enculturated dynamic. If men acted on impulse or some other drive, they would beat up their bosses, secretaries, friends, or neighbors as often as they do their mates and children. Although some sociopaths might fit this category of indiscriminate violence, they are in the minority (Gondolf, 1985; Hastings & Hamberger, 1988; Holtzworth-Munroe & Stuart, 1994). Only in a conjugal relationship do many men generally believe in and exercise their ability to coerce, abuse, and beat women and children (Hart, 1980).

Stressors

If power is the fuse, then stress is the match that lights the fuse. As the idealized image of the relationship breaks down and environmental stresses build up, couples become engaged in an ever-increasing spiral of violent interaction (Barnett et al., 1980). Although they are not generic to all battering, a list of factors that seem to appear over and over in domestic violence follow (Barnett et al., 1980, pp. 7–9; Benjamin & Walz, 1983; Bograd, 2005; Brown, James, & Taylor, 2010; Finkelhor et al., 1983; Gelles & Cornell, 1985; Halbsgut, 2011; Jasinski & Williams, 1998; Koverola & Panchanadeswaran, 2004; Okun, 1986; Parker et al., 1993; Stuart et al., 2006; Walker, 1984, p. 51). These factors may be introduced by the batterer to control the

LO5

situation, may occur as a product of the relationship itself, or may be environmentally introduced from outside the relationship.

1. *Geographic isolation.* Because of geographic location, the victim has no friends nearby who can provide a support system. A farm woman who cannot drive is an example of the worst case—literally being marooned and held captive by an abusive husband.

2. *Social isolation.* Because of extreme emotional dependence, the woman expects all needs to be met by her partner and has no significant others to turn to when she is assaulted.

3. *Economic stress.* When a woman is unemployed or underemployed, has inadequate housing, is pressured by creditors, and cannot feed and clothe her children by herself, she becomes human chattel to her abusive partner.

4. *Medical problems.* Long-term, chronic medical problems for either spouse or children exact tremendous financial and emotional costs.

5. *Inadequate parenting skills.* A lack of knowledge of parenting skills and conflict over parental roles can lead to situations that start as minor disciplinary problems and escalate into violence in the family.

6. *Pregnancy.* Ranging from heralding an unwanted child through creating anxiety over providing for the new baby to arousing jealousy over a wife's attention to a newborn, pregnancy is an especially acute crisis point for potential abuse.

7. *Family dysfunction.* A veritable kaleidoscope of problems causes dysfunction in the family. Some of these problems are related to age and number of children, presence of stepchildren, loyalty conflicts, death, desertion, and career change.

8. *Alcohol and drug abuse.* Chemical dependence serious enough to cause economic chaos and severe emotional disturbance characterizes addictive families and has spin-offs that commonly include spouse abuse. The insidious problem with alcohol and drugs is that they are often used as an excuse for behavior (battering) that is normally prohibited by societal norms and standards. Interestingly, there appears to be a significant relationship, at least in Australia, between the number and proximity of liquor stores and the incidence of domestic violence (Livingston, 2011).

9. *Educational and/or vocational disparity.* When a female in a relationship has higher educational attainment or higher vocational status than the male, this may raise questions of adequacy and

responsibility with both parties. Furthermore, if the man is unemployed and the woman is employed, the man has a great deal of time to brood on his inability to function as the head of household, which males already suffering from feelings of inadequacy may find extremely demeaning. The role of occupational therapy in domestic violence has become important enough that a book has been devoted to that connection (Helfrich, 2001).

10. *Age.* One of the most consistent risk factors of battering is age. Approximately 20% of men in the age range of 18 to 25 and 17% of men in the age range of 26 to 35 have committed at least one act of violence in the past year.

11. *Disenfranchisement.* Seeking help from the authorities for battering may be very aversive to persons of color, same-sex orientation, minority status, immigrant status, and other marginalized groups because of their previous negative experiences or fear of retribution from the system.

12. *Rejection.* The batterer's perception of rejection is an antecedent to abuse. Men with a family of origin where rejection occurred become extremely sensitive to any behavior construed as rejection. Their response is likely to be aggressive.

13. *Threat to masculinity.* Some men who perceive themselves as less masculine see their use of battering as affirming their masculinity in comparison to males who have good self-concepts who do not batter.

Myths About Battering

The following myths encapsulate numerous **LO6** arguments used by those who would submerge, camouflage, and diminish battering (Gelles & Cornell, 1985; Hampton, Vandergriff-Avery, & Kim, 1999; Massachusetts Coalition of Battered Women Service Groups, 1981; Okun, 1986; Roberts, 2002; Stark & Flitcraft, 1988; Straus, Gelles, & Steinmetz, 1980; Weitzman, 2000).

1. *"Battered women overstate the case."* Any person who has contusions, lacerations, and broken bones is not overstating anything. In any other instance, such outcomes are referred to as *assault and battery*.

2. *"Battered women provoke the beating."* Although some women may be classified as the stereotypical "nag," there can certainly be many significant others in a man's life who fit into the "nag" category who are not beaten.

3. *"Battered women are masochists."* If such women did have masochistic tendencies, they would find a variety of ways to suffer pain, not just an abusive mate.

4. *"Battering is a private, family matter."* When beaten women are disenfranchised from their homes and the children of battering relationships learn the pathological roles a battering father models, battering transcends the home and becomes society's problem. All 50 states now have warrantless arrest policies for battering. Battering is anything but private.

5. *"Alcohol abuse is the prime reason for wife abuse."* Although alcohol plays a part in many cases of abuse and is present and used by both men and women who engage in violent relationships, it may be only an excuse for, and not the cause of, violent behavior. There are many violent relationships where alcohol is not present.

6. *"Battering occurs only in problem families."* The dynamic representation of stress factors that assail families shows that any family, at any given point, may be classified as "problem."

7. *"Only low-income and working-class families experience violence."* Members of those socioeconomic classes do come to the attention of the police and welfare agencies to a much greater degree than middle- or upper-class members, but statistics from shelters, police calls, and crisis line calls indicate that battering has no class boundaries.

8. *"The battering cannot be that bad or she would not stay."* The host of personal factors that tie a woman to the relationship militate heavily against simply picking up and leaving.

9. *"A husband has patriarchal rights."* What a man does in his own family is not his own business when the emotional overflow of what he does spills over into the community. No amount or kind of justification from the Bible or any other authority—be it person, institution, or book—can excuse spouse abuse.

10. *"The beaten spouse exaggerates the problem to exact revenge."* Reporting a beating—whether committed by a total stranger or one's spouse—is no exaggeration. If revenge were the motive, there would be a host of ways of going about it that would be far less traumatic than calling or showing up at an abuse shelter.

11. *"Women are too sensitive, especially when they are pregnant."* If a person is too sensitive because she objects to being kicked in the stomach or vagina, thrown down a flight of stairs, or hit in the face with a lamp, then we would suppose that everyone is overly sensitive.

12. *"Battering is rare."* The statistics reported in this chapter clearly indicate otherwise. Family violence is endemic in society.

13. *"Battering is confined to mentally disturbed or 'sick' people."* It appears that less than 10% of family violence is caused by mental illness. Although continued physical and psychological abuse may cause many victims to suffer serious emotional distress and posttraumatic stress disorder, they did not enter the relationship "sick." Furthermore, most perpetrators are not mentally ill by any DSM-5 (American Psychiatric Association, 2013) definition.

14. *"Violence and love cannot coexist."* Strange as it may seem, members of violent families may still love one another. This paradoxical aspect is most problematic because children in such families grow up believing you hit the people you love.

15. *"Elder abuse between intimates is neither prevalent nor dangerous."* Because of the debilitating factors that come with aging, the potential for physical abuse becomes greater and more lethal as partners become more frustrated, angry, and depressed over the declining physical and mental capabilities of both themselves and their partners.

Profiling the Batterer

Researchers have examined multiple personality and behavioral typologies of batterers. Dutton (1995), Fowler and Western (2011), Gondolf (1985), Hastings and Hamberger (1988), Holtzworth-Munroe and Stuart (1994), Holzworth-Munroe and associates (1999, 2003), and Saunders (1992) have all developed typologies of batterers based on clusters of demographic, personality, and abuse variables. Holtzworth-Munroe and Stuart (1994) and Holtzworth-Munroe and associates (1999, 2003) have compiled three major groupings—family only, dysphoric (anxious)/borderline, and generally violent/antisocial—and a fourth subgroup, low-level antisocial. Characteristics of the **family only batterer** include high dependency, impulsivity, poor communication skills, and family-of-origin violence. The **dysphoric/borderline batterer** has a history of parental rejection and child abuse, delinquent acts, poor communication and social skills, violence-as-a-solution ideation, extreme fears of abandonment, and low remorse. The **low-level antisocial batterer** has antisocial behavior and moderate levels of domestic and general violence. Fowler and Western's (2011) typologies conform closely to the foregoing types with psychopathic, hostile/controlling, and borderline/dependent. The **generally violent/antisocial**

LO7

batterer has all the foregoing characteristics, but to a much more profound degree and probably falls into what Jasinski and Williams (1998, p. 1) call the **terroristic batterer**. Such people are extremely aggressive and impulsive, and view violence as appropriate to any provocation inside or outside the home.

The family only batterers are the largest group, and their behavior is consistent with Walker's (1979) cycle of violence. Its members are likely to be contrite and apologetic after battering incidents. Gondolf (1985) reports this group type to be most prevalent, with a 52% occurrence rate. The dysphoric/borderline and antisocial types are typical of how women who flee to shelters describe their batterers. They are the most dangerous and according to Gondolf make up about 41% and 7% of batterers, respectively. Differences in these groups in regard to their level of violence appear to remain somewhat stable over time, and they do not appear to move from one group to the other (Cavanaugh & Gelles, 2005). Thankfully, not all marital violence escalates nor does it evolve to more dangerous personality types (Holtzworth-Munroe et al., 2003).

There is a good deal of debate over the use of profiling because of the diversity of typologies in battering populations. However, Gibbons, Collins, and Reid (2011) used the Millon Clinical Multiaxial Inventory with a sample of 177 batterers and found that 54% fell into a personality disorder category and 37% could be characterized as having severe pathology. Taking the foregoing typologies together with an assessment device like the Millon, consider that Eke and associates (2011) found that of their sample of men who had murdered or attempted to murder an intimate partner, 42% had previously committed crimes, 18% had a psychiatric history, and 15% had both. These individuals were given the Ontario Domestic Assault Risk Assessment. Their mean score was in the 80th percentile of "at risk" for domestic violence. The researchers concluded that the use of validated risk assessment data for batterers and indicators of pathology and/or criminal behavior would increase the ability to predict who would violently assault an intimate partner and hopefully aid in intervention and prevention of homicidal acts toward intimate partners. Loinaz (2014) used the Brief Spousal Assault Form for the Evaluation of Risk (B-SAFER) to classify offenders and predict recidivism. His study on incarcerated batterers in Spain found high predictive validity with both the nonpathological group and the antisocial/pathological group. He further found that the antisocial pathological group had about a 2 to 1 recidivism rate. We believe some fine-tuning of these instruments, applied to all batterers, would be of some worth in determining their degree of potential lethality and guiding judicial disposition as to what kind of intervention they should receive.

The Cycle of Violence

Barnett and associates (1980) schematically represented the phases leading to the explosion of violence in the family. Walker's (1984) cycle theory of violence—(1) tension building, (2) battering and abuse, (3) contrition and loving respite—closely parallels these phases, and her research supports the theory (p. 95).   **LO8**

> *Phase I. Tranquility prevails.* The relationship may have been characterized as calm to this point, with no previous violent incidents, or a period of calm may follow an earlier violent episode.
>
> *Phase II. Tension starts to build.* A variety of stresses impinge on the relationship. They may come in combination or singly from the common group already mentioned. However, there is no reduction of tension, and the situation grows more strained.
>
> *Phase III. A violent episode occurs.* The episode may range from harsh words to a severe beating. At this phase, communication has broken down, and the situation is out of control.
>
> *Phase IV. The relationship takes on crisis proportions.* A variety of options becomes available.
>
> A. The abuser becomes remorseful and asks forgiveness. Sooner or later the victim forgives the abuser, and calm is restored.
>
> B. The abuser is not remorseful and feels his control over the situation has been established. The victim gives in and relinquishes control, and calm is restored.
>
> C. The victim takes new action. Within this option are two possibilities: the abuser negotiates the situation, and, given that the negotiation is agreeable to the victim, calm is restored; or the abuser rejects the new action and a crisis state continues.

It is at this last point, in which no possibility of resolution exists, that the victim is most likely to seek help by contacting an abuse center. Walker found that as the battering continues, the loving contrition phase diminishes and battering becomes more prevalent

(2000, p. 128). If effective assessment and intervention do not occur when the violence emerges (Phase III), the likelihood that the violence will recur and will be of greater intensity is dramatically increased (Barnett et al., 1980, p. 34). Dutton (1995, pp. 126–139) has demonstrated that this cycle closely fits that of the borderline personality disorder type of abuser.

Not all battering relationships fit the cycle of violence. Battering between partners may be a once-in-a-lifetime affair. But many women have reported being constantly terrorized and assaulted with no intermittent periods of relief (Dutton & Starzomski, 1993). These are most probably the victims of the antisocial, psychopathic type of batterer, who sees little need for contrition or remorse in his dealing with a partner—or anybody else, for that matter.

Realities for Abused Women

Why, then, do women stay in an abusive relationship? For those who have no experience with violence in a relationship, it is an easy thing to say, "Throw the bum out!" or "I wouldn't tolerate that. I'd call the cops and have him arrested!" or "Forget you, nobody does that to me, I'm leaving!" In actuality, most women who are in battering relationships do leave, and this in itself is a courageous act because it is one of the most dangerous things a woman can do. The batterer tends to do poorly on his own and would often rather kill or die than be separated from the woman, because he is more terrified of abandonment than violence or punishment (Walker, 1989, p. 65). It is remarkable that a number of women do leave, given their clear understanding that lives hang in the balance—their own, those of their children, and even the batterer's.   **LO9**

The same question could be asked of men. Why do they stay? Henning and Connor-Smith (2011) examined more than 1,000 men who had been adjudicated for battering their partners. More than half said they were planning on staying in the relationship. Their reasons included being older, caring about their children, attributing less blame to the female for the alleged offenses and their arrest, and coming from a family where they saw the same thing as children and regretted modeling their parents' assaultive behavior. Ominously, the researchers also found that some men who were continuing the relationship had low relationship satisfaction predictors: having children, expressing hostile attitudes toward women, being jealous, blaming the victim for the arrest, and describing the victim as being aggressive.

Most women leave a battering relationship an average of three to six times, but do so with varying degrees of permanency (Dobash & Dobash, 1979; Walker, 1979). The following reasons for staying in the relationship have been gleaned from a number of researchers (Benjamin & Walz, 1983; Bograd, 2005; Koverola & Panchanadeswaran, 2004; Okun, 1986; Pagelow, 1981; Walker, 1979, 1984, 1989, 2000), and these realities have nothing to do with the myths listed previously.

1. The woman has a fear of reprisal or of aggravating the attacks even more.
2. Even though the situation may be intolerable for the woman, her children do have food, clothing, and shelter.
3. The woman would suffer shame, embarrassment, humiliation, and even ridicule if her secret got out.
4. Her self-concept is so strongly dependent on the relationship and perceived social approval that leaving would be very destructive to her.
5. Early affection and prior love in the relationship persist and, by staying, the woman hopes to salvage them.
6. If financially well off, the woman is unable to forgo a reduction in her financial freedom.
7. In the cyclic nature of abuse, her mate may not be terrible 24 hours a day, 7 days a week. The victim may tend to forget the batterings and remember only the good times.
8. Early role models of an abusive parent may lead her to believe that relationships exist in no other way.
9. The woman may hold religious values that strongly militate against separation, divorce, or anything less than filial subjugation to the man's wishes.
10. The woman may be undereducated, have small children to raise, and have no job skills.
11. She may be kept so socially, physically, geographically, and financially isolated that she has no resources of any kind to help her get out.
12. She may be so badly injured that she is unable physically to leave.
13. She may believe the man's promise to reform.
14. She may be concerned for children who are still at home.
15. Love or sorrow at the mate's professed inability to exist without her may impel her to stay.
16. Because of previous negative experiences with the authorities, she may believe she has no options.
17. Due to language barriers or immigration status, she may be unable to communicate her abuse, or she may be afraid to seek help.

Secondary victimization may result by labeling battered women as hysterical, depressed, schizophrenic, alcoholic, or child neglecters and abusers. Such labeling may provide professionals with "reasons" to do things to battered women ranging from overmedication with psychotropic drugs to sending them to jail and removing their children from the home. Any one of the revictimizations by well-meaning or not-so-well-meaning institutions undermines assertiveness and reinforces submissiveness and compliance, which in turn increases vulnerability to abuse (Stark & Flitcraft, 1988; Walker, 1989). It is little wonder that a woman making her first call to an abuse center may be taking only an initial step in a series that sometimes goes on for years before she can make a complete break from the battering relationship.

Intervention Strategies

In the past 35 years the raising of consciousness that domestic violence is epidemic and that it extracts tremendous financial and emotional costs from society has caused an exponential rise in attempts at intervention. To that end, intervention strategies for battering are different from other types of crises, because they target both victim and victimizer.

Assessment

Assessment in battering and domestic **LO10** violence is complex and is subject to controversy and many unanswered questions in regard to its precursors, onset, and outcomes for both victims and victimizers. Assessment is also problematic because of the transcrisis nature of battering. Both batterers and those who are battered do not present themselves in a "steady state" that is amenable to stable and consistent measurement.

Personality Measures. Assessment of battered women by personality measures is somewhat confounding and contradictory to what one might logically expect. One never really knows whether the personality factors found in battered women were present before they were battered or are the result of the victimization (Gelles & Cornell, 1985, p. 71). However, Walker (1989, p. 105) reports that as the battering progressively becomes worse, Minnesota Multiphasic Personality Inventory (MMPI) profiles change notably.

The question arises: Are there particular attributes, traits, or psychological profiles that will indicate those women who are potential victims of batterers? In an extensive review of characteristics of battered women, Hotaling and Sugarman (1986) found only one characteristic—having witnessed or been a victim of personal violence as a child—as a consistent characteristic. When they reviewed the responses of 699 women who participated in the first National Violence Study, the researchers could not find even that characteristic (Hotaling & Sugarman, 1990). Thus, there appears to be little empirical evidence that there are any consistent predisposing factors that predict who will and who will not become a victim of abuse.

The Attitude Towards Women Scale (Spence & Helmreich, 1972) measures the traditionality of a woman's attitude about her role as well as her perception of significant others' views of women. Walker found that battered women viewed their father's perception of a woman's role much more traditionally than did a nonbattered control group (2000, p. 105).

The Battered Woman Scale (Schwartz & Mattley, 1993) is used to measure traits that arise as a result of experiences in battering relationships. Overall, battered women present many of the symptoms of posttraumatic stress disorder and can be placed for diagnostic purposes within the PTSD category of the DSM-5 (American Psychiatric Association, 2013; Astin, Lawrence, & Foy, 1993). Weaver (1998) found in her study of women who had been either sexually or physically abused as children, raped as adults, or battered that only battering was a common marker for PTSD. Thompson and associates (1999) found that suicide, PTSD symptomology, and physical partner abuse go hand in hand. Women incarcerated for killing or seriously assaulting their partners also show increased levels of PTSD symptomology (Hattendorf, Ottens, & Lomax, 1999; O'Keefe, 1998). Indeed, Walker (1989, pp. 48–49) proposes the battered woman syndrome as a subcategory of PTSD. Therefore, if PTSD symptoms are present, then partner violence should always be suspected.

Clinical Interview. Probably the best assessment device for partner abuse is a clinical interview. Any family history taking should include questions about hitting, threats, controlling, destruction of property or pets, forced sex, alcohol and drug use, and the partner's hypervigilance and paranoia about the client's actions (Jasinski & Williams, 1998, p. 37).

Walker (1984, p. 122) also has one major rule of assessment that supersedes all others and to which your authors strongly subscribe: *When a woman calls or comes in to report a battering, believe her and start intervention immediately.* It is a safe bet that whenever a battered woman seeks help, she is not carrying out the act as some impetuous, hysterical, spur-of-the-moment way to get back at her mate. Battered women refer themselves only after their problems have become exceedingly serious.

Walker (1984, p. 26) found that only 14% of battered women surveyed would seek help after a first incident, 22% would seek help after a second incident, and 49% would seek help only after a series of incidents had taken place. Given the length of time that passes and the degree of severity of the crisis that is typically reached before help is sought, triage assessment of the battered woman should look first and foremost to her safety and the safety of significant others, such as her children. We can assume that a battered woman making an initial call to a crisis line will be at the extremely high end of the assessment scale. She will be behaviorally out of control because of the beating she has just had. She will be affectively out of control because of the trauma she has just suffered and the threat of more to come. Cognitively, she may be just holding together and may not be far from dissociating from the terrible reality of her situation.

Sadly, many in the helping professions still confuse the effects of domestic abuse with symptoms of other diagnoses. It is extremely important to be aware of these masking symptoms. Compared to women who are not abused, battered women are 5 times more likely to attempt suicide, 15 times more likely to abuse alcohol, 9 times more likely to abuse drugs, 6 times more likely to report child abuse, and 3 times more likely to be diagnosed as psychotic or depressed. It is little wonder that these women experience low self-esteem (Aguilar & Nightingale, 1994).

Crisis workers typically encounter battering victims in the following four settings: in hospital emergency rooms and other medical care settings, on telephone crisis lines, in police follow-up operations on domestic violence calls at crisis centers, and at shelters (discussed later in this chapter). The operational strategy in all of these settings should be twofold. First and foremost: Ask! Ask if the person has been battered, even if the presenting problem appears to have little to do with battering. Chang and associates (2005) advise that workers give a reason for why they are asking about IPV, to reduce women's suspicions and minimize stigma, and that they provide information, support, safety, and access to resources whether or not the woman discloses IPV. By doing so, workers are not seen as trying to diagnose a pathological condition, but communicate compassion, provide valuable information, and open the door for women to self-disclose IPV and consider seeking services.

That show of concern creates increased levels of trust when questions about battering are asked in an empathic manner, confidentiality is discussed, and nonjudgmental and supportive responses and concern for the person's safety are made with offers to provide help, even if IPV is not the basic issue that brings the woman into counseling (Battaglia, Finley, & Liebschutz, 2003). The smorgasbord of symptoms presented in this chapter all come out of battering. While there may be other reasons, one of the biggest mistakes a worker can make is to not empathically query a person about battering and validating their experiences (Day, 2009; Spangaro, Zwi, & Poulos, 2011). When a woman is validated by an external source that she is being battered and that it is unacceptable, that act is a major contributor to her taking action to remove herself from the battering (Day, 2009). Congruent with validation is her sense of support from community resources in providing her with information and supporting her in making the myriad decisions that range from career and geographic moves to religious and moral qualms she has over leaving (McLeod, Hays, & Chang, 2010).

Medical Settings. Contrary to recommendation after recommendation by a variety of medical groups, including the surgeon general of the United States, abuse assessment is still not routine in hospital ERs, maternity wards, obstetrics, and family practices (Boes & McDermott, 2002). Many battered women will not acknowledge abuse no matter how empathic and supportive the medical worker is. Therefore, when physical abuse is suspected, the worker should state that this is just a routine part of any medical examination and that the supportive service information the woman is about to get is also routinely provided. In that way, the woman is given control of the situation, is given support by the worker, and her autonomy is respected (Hamberger, 1994). No one else should be present in the interview for the sake of the patient's safety. The worker needs to ask specific and direct questions while walking a tightrope of not being confrontational or antagonistic.

The following questions are abridged from Snyder's (1994) and Hamberger's (1994) protocols for hospital emergency room staff.

CW: Lots of times people get into arguments, and they get physical with one another. I'm wondering if some of your bruises occurred that way? When you and your husband or boyfriend argue, does he get angry? Do you feel afraid? I'm wondering if he ever loses his temper with the children, and when you step in he loses it with you and maybe winds up hitting you. How does he act with you if he's been drinking or using drugs? Sometimes when people get jealous they overreact and get physical. Did this happen with him? Have you ever been with someone who tried to really control you by hitting you or threatening to hurt you? Are you in one of those relationships now?

By raising the issue of arguing, the worker normalizes the situation and opens the door for the client to talk about the reasons that brought her to the medical facility. By asking about her fears, the worker validates her affective and cognitive bases regarding the situation. These and other questions move from general relationship issues to what Hamberger (1994) calls "funneling" to more behavioral specifics about the abuse, such as number and severity of incidents, types of weapons used, and who did the battering.

Juanita: Well . . . I sorta got hit with a broom handle.

CW: (*empathically but assertively*) A broom handle has to be attached to somebody's hand. Whose hand was it? Is he the man who brought you here?

Specific information about what she can do and what the hospital can do should be given if the patient admits she has been physically abused. Medical staff should be well acquainted with local and state laws governing abuse so they can know what legal obligations they have and what can be done to keep the woman safe. Very specific step-by-step protocols should be formulated and made available to all staff, along with inservice education on domestic violence and its signs. Brasseur (1994) abstracted a typical protocol from Chicago's Rush–Presbyterian–St. Luke's Medical Center to be followed once a battered woman has been identified:

1. Assign a primary nurse.
2. Notify appropriate support services within the hospital.
3. Give a complete physical exam, along with a neurological exam and X-rays.

4. Document statements about who caused the injuries.
5. Make a body map of old and new injuries.
6. Depending on the jurisdiction, make a call to the police, identify the assailant, and have him arrested, if possible.
7. Take photographs of the victim's injuries.
8. Inform the patient of her right to access her medical files and how to do it.
9. Discuss with the woman a posthospital plan that will include shelter or other referral, safety plans if she is not leaving the abusive situation, and community support services.

When a protocol such as the foregoing is followed, identification rates of victims of partner violence go up (McLeer & Anwar, 1989; Olson et al., 1996; Tilden & Shepard, 1987).

Crisis Lines. Of all the dilemmas a crisis telephone worker faces, battering is one of the worst. Women may present emotions that range from icily detached to hysterical to white-hot anger. No matter what the woman's emotional response, the worker's job is to try to help the woman cope with the immediate situation (Roberts & Roberts, 2002). That immediate situation may include the batterer being present while the woman makes the call. The woman may call a crisis line instead of the police in hopes that the police will not have to become involved but the publication of the abuse to an outside agency will make the batterer stop.

At times the woman may ask the worker to talk to the batterer. In almost all cases that is not a wise choice. The woman should be asked if she is in danger and needs police assistance. The focus is on the caller and the caller's safety, not attempting to defuse the batterer. If the batterer truly wants to be defused, then he may call the crisis line. Although the threat of further injury or death to the woman may be extremely high, unless the crisis worker feels danger is imminent and can get the woman to give her name and address so that a 911 call can be made, the best the crisis worker can do is offer short-term assistance to help ease physical pain and calm the emotional state of the client. Duty to warn certainly takes precedence over confidentiality, but deciding whether the danger is sufficiently imminent and lethal to necessitate a call to the police is tricky and has future ramifications. Even then the crisis worker may have raging internal debates about what to do. If the client is helped to a safe place, will that only enrage her mate even more? Is the woman really ready to make such a move? What assets does the battered woman have so that she can leave? What are her debits? That is why the worker should carefully go over each area, making sure that all pertinent information and all possibilities of available action have been carefully considered. No other type of crisis presents as critical a need for comprehensive yet fast assessment.

It is also worth remembering that if the worker calls back a week later, the client may be going through a "honeymoon phase" and may seem not to have a care in the world, only to turn around later at the next battering and beseech the crisis worker to help her. These situations, oscillating from extreme need one day to little if any need the next, can make workers cynical and uncaring if they do not carefully manage their stress levels. Yet such ambivalence is more typical than not as clients slowly come to grips with the risks and realities of leaving the situation or quite possibly facing death there.

Components of Intervention

As a call comes in to the abuse center and the crisis worker picks up the phone, the assessment process begins with active listening. The crisis worker immediately has to be concerned with a variety of roles. The worker must be not only a good listener but also supportive, facilitative, and concerned with the caller's safety and must act as an advocate (Barnett et al., 1980, p. 44).

LO11

Listening. Facilitative listening and responding are crucial. The victim must know that the crisis worker understands and accepts her present situation in a nonjudgmental, non-value-laden way. Only then will the battered woman be able to open up and share her feelings about her predicament (Heppner, 1978). The crisis worker also immediately reflects that she understands the difficulty and urgency of the situation by positively reinforcing the battered woman for calling and taking a first step toward resolving her problem.

CW: You did the right thing by calling. No matter how bad it seems and what terrible things have happened, you've made a big step on the road to straightening it out. We're here to help, and we'll stick with it as long as it takes.

Juanita: I . . . I . . . don't know. It's gone on so long. I feel so ashamed. I don't know what to do! It's so confusing.

CW: I understand how you feel and how difficult it was to make this call. The hurt, the fear, the uncertainty of it all. So start anywhere you want. We won't do anything unless *you* decide it's best for you. Right now, I want to listen to what you have to say. I'll listen for as long as it takes, so take your time and tell me what's happened.

Supporting. The caller is given both explicit and implicit permission to ventilate. The free flow of the victim's anger, hurt, fear, guilt, and other debilitating feelings may take from a few minutes to 2 hours to an extended period of months. Supportiveness means empathizing but not sympathizing with the victim. A sense of lack of social support is one of the major factors for battered women (Perrin et al., 1996), and this lack may be particularly severe for immigrants with different cultural backgrounds (Sev'er, 1997, pp. 3–5). Many victims are only partially mobile, and any action steps they take may be months away from happening. Thus, supporting a victim does not mean intervention on a one-shot basis. The crisis worker may have to exert an excruciating amount of patience over a long period of time as the victim slowly moves toward making a decision to take action. No matter how bad the victim's situation looks to the worker, only the victim herself can decide when she is ready to take action to alleviate her traumatic circumstances (Dagastino, 1984).

CW: OK! I understand it's a hard decision to make—getting out. Your marriage has had some good times, and you'd really like to hang onto that part of it, even though the beatings are happening more often. You say you want some time to think about it. That's OK! It's your decision, and we'll help whenever you need us.

Breaking away from a battering relationship is a slow developmental process. The crisis worker cannot move the victim any faster than she is willing to go. The worker must be acutely aware of being manipulated into becoming sympathetic to the victim's needs and attempting to "fix" things for her. Many times the victim will project anger onto the police, a minister, or other significant persons. At some point the victim needs to see that displacement and shifting of responsibility to others are not going to solve the problem. The crisis worker must be aware of this possibility and not get trapped into proposing external remedies.

The victim is actually demonstrating what Heppner (1978) calls the *wishing and hoping syndrome*. The victim wishes the situation would change, that her spouse would treat her the way he used to, and hopes the crisis worker can effect a change in her husband. However, cessation of battering by the abuser rarely happens without legal or therapeutic intervention (Dagastino, 1984). Under no circumstances should the crisis worker attempt to rescue the victim by talking to the batterer. It is dangerous and takes responsibility and autonomy away from the victim. Instead, the conversation should be redirected away from what can be done to "fix" the batterer and toward what the victim is now able to do.

CW: Although I hear you wanting me to come and straighten your husband out and make things the way they were, I can't do that. I wish I could, but I'm not a marriage counselor. If you think marriage counseling would work, I can give you some names of people who do that. What I can do is help you make some decisions about what you want to do right now.

A typical response to the crisis worker's refusal to fix the problem is anger.

Juanita: You're no damn help at all. You're just as bad as the rest. You're a horrible counselor. I'm gonna have to go back to him, and he'll kill me, just because you wouldn't do anything.

Because abuse workers do not want to lose clients, such ploys often rub a raw nerve in the workers and propel them to do something they may later regret. The crisis worker should realize that when a victim doubts the worker's ability, she is also doubting her own ability. She is probably looking for a way to resume the relationship and may be displacing her own incompetence to make changes by blaming the worker (Dagastino, 1984). The best response the crisis worker can make is not to be confrontive but to be empathic, realizing that right now the woman is looking for a way to go back to her mate.

CW: I'm sorry you're angry with me because I won't talk to your husband. I realize the frustration you feel. Yet I'm also not like the others who'll tell you how to act and what to do. I want you to know I'd be happy to work on a plan of action you want to take.

The excerpt typifies the response of a crisis worker who is being supportive yet not taking over for the victim. Usually abuse victims have not been independent to any degree and quickly fall back into a dependent state. If the crisis worker keeps foremost in mind that the woman he or she is now talking to is ultimately going to have to be her own defender and protector, then the crisis worker is not likely to fall into a sympathy trap. The crisis worker who becomes angry or engages in denouncing or criticizing the husband is making a fundamental mistake. The worker may provoke the victim to defend the violent batterer and to attack the crisis worker (Dagastino, 1984).

Facilitating To facilitate the movement of a victim to action takes a great deal of tenacity and patience. Typically the crisis worker will have to deal with feelings of dependency, ambivalence, and depression, which are all clear-cut signs of the client's immobility. Overarching these immobilizing feelings is the learned helplessness referred to earlier. To generate movement in the victim, the crisis worker strongly reinforces the victim's attempts at rational decision making, self-control, and statements of personal power (Heppner, 1978).

CW: You said that you couldn't do anything, but that's not true. You called here, didn't you? When you first started talking, you were crying uncontrollably, and now you're speaking in a rather level, controlled voice. I also notice a lot of "I" statements, which say to me you're starting to take responsibility. Maybe you don't know it, but those are all signs that you're starting to feel some personal power for the first time in a long while, and I think that's great!

Ambivalence about the situation is predominant in most women who seek help from abuse centers. Ambivalence is particularly strong with regard to the man who, after beating the woman, apologizes, showers her with gifts, and tells her what she wants to hear and what society leads her to believe (Conroy, 1982). To deal with this ambivalent state, the crisis worker cycles between asking open-ended questions and reflecting and clarifying the victim's feelings as an effective means of helping the victim begin to examine previously denied feelings and thoughts.

CW: What were you thinking and feeling while he was beating you?

Juanita: It was like I was standing off to the side watching a movie of this. It was like this can't really be happening, especially to me.

CW: So that's how you cope with it. Kind of separating yourself from the beating, as if it's happening to someone else.

Juanita: Yes, I guess I've done it that way for a long time. I'd go crazy otherwise.

CW: What is your understanding of why you're being battered?

Juanita: I don't know. I guess I'm just not a good wife.

CW: You're not living up to his expectations, then. How about your own?

Juanita: I'm not sure. I mean, I've never thought of that. It's always been what he wants.

CW: How do you cope with the beating other than just kind of separating yourself from the situation when it happens?

Juanita: I try to do what he wants, but when it starts to build—the tension—I just try to stay out of his way and be nice, although I know sooner or later I'm gonna get it. I dread the waiting. Actually sometimes I push the issue just to get it over with. I know he'll always apologize afterward and treat me nice.

CW: So you do what he wishes even though you know the bottom line is a beating. Yet because of the anxiety you may even push things to get it over with. Seems like you're willing to pay a steep price to get his love back.

Juanita: When you say that, I can't believe I'm letting this happen to me. What a fool . . . a stupid fool!

CW: Then you feel foolish about paying that price. What's keeping you in the relationship?

Juanita: God! I don't know. Love! Honor! Obey! The kids. The good times. Martyrdom. I don't have a job, and I'm pregnant again. I've got to get out. He'll wind up killing me.

Using open-ended questions, restatement, and reflection, the crisis worker relentlessly hammers at the victim's faulty and illogical perception of the abusive situation. Only by looking and listening through the victim's eyes and ears can the crisis worker form an accurate perception of what steps to take and how the crisis worker will operate on the nondirective-to-directive continuum of intervention. Women who have been abused also have in common the feeling of depression. Invariably, once a victim has related the details of the assault, her affect becomes flat. Depression has taken over. Beneath the depression is a volcano of residual anger that is trying to find an outlet. The crisis worker's job is to help move the victim out of her depressed state and let the angry feelings out (Dagastino, 1984). This is the first step toward taking action.

CW: As you relate the details, it sounds like you're reporting it but not living it. I wonder if that's a typical way you hold it in . . . control it.

Juanita: I guess . . . if I really thought about it, I'd kill the SOB. How could the bastard do this to me?

CW: How does it feel to let some of those angry feelings out?

Juanita: Scary! I'm really scared I would kill him if I got the chance.

CW: That is a legitimate feeling after what you've been through, but that won't get you where you want to go. Let's take a look at some of the alternatives between killing and being killed.

In summarizing the facilitation of the victim's movement from an immobile to a mobile state, the Massachusetts Coalition of Battered Women Service Groups (1981, pp. 25, 67) has made the following recommendations for crisis workers.

1. *Be real.* Don't hide behind a role. You are what you are. To pretend to be something else makes the crisis worker false and discredited in the eyes of the victim.

2. *Set limits.* The crisis worker is not Superman or Superwoman. Owning feelings of puzzlement, anger, stupidity, tiredness, and so forth allows the crisis worker to stay on top of the game. If the worker is tired, is taking on a lot of anger, and cannot work it through with the victim, the worker should own the feelings, ask for time out, and get out of the situation until the problem can be gone over with a fellow professional and a fresh start can be made.

3. *Give the victim space and time to "freak out."* Remember that the victim is experiencing a flood of emotions that have been building over a long period of time. Knowing that anger is one step on the way to becoming her own person can be reassuring and empowering to the victim. Give her time to ventilate before settling down to a plan of action.

4. *Allow the victim to go through the pain, but stay with her.* Your first response may be to become a psychological crutch because the victim is so fragile that she cannot hold together. The crisis worker who remembers that the victim has been down a long road of pain and is just now beginning to experience that pain will realize that the victim possesses a lot of staying power. Belief in the victim's ability to get out of the mess she is in is of overriding importance.

5. *Maintain eye and ear contact.* Both nonverbal and verbal responses of the victim are important; they tell the crisis worker whether what the victim is saying is congruent with what she is doing. Reading nonverbal responses may be difficult over the phone, but the worker needs to be aware of intonations, pauses, and sighs. How something is said may be as important as what is said. Also, what is not said may be as important as what is said.

6. *Be respectful and nonjudgmental.* The victim's actions must be carefully separated from the victim herself. What the victim does may seem asinine; that does not mean the victim is an ass. That is especially true of the religious and moral issues that go with leaving.

7. *Restate and reflect the victim's thoughts and feelings.* As simple as this sounds, it is often extremely difficult. There is no greater therapeutic help than manifesting these skills.

8. *Set priorities together.* Two heads are better than one. This is why the crisis worker is there. If the victim could handle the problem alone, she would. Likewise, the abuse worker is not in business to run the victim's life for her.

9. *Look at options.* Brainstorming can uncover a variety of previously hidden ideas and actions.

10. *Stay away from "whys."* Asking *why* a person does something like staying in a battering relationship often leads the victim, rightly or wrongly, to assume she is being judged. When a victim feels she is being judged, she is apt to respond in defensive ways that do little to help her or her situation.

11. *Give the victim time to experience catharsis, but do not let her get stuck in self-pity.* The client needs to accomplish movement, and the crisis worker needs to move gently from nurturing emotional release to helping the client start to make plans, however small, concerning her own predicament.

12. *Get back to the victim.* Even if the battered woman says, "I guess I can make it now," get her phone number and call a few days later to make sure she is getting along all right. Many abused women are so embarrassed by their plight and their own self-assessed stupidity that they cannot bring themselves to make another call and admit they have failed again. (Note: It is important to determine when the abuser will *not* be home. Furthermore, it is important to determine whether the phone has caller ID or call-back features so the victim's safety will not be compromised.)

13. *Peer supervision and feedback are essential for domestic abuse workers.* The intensity of partner abuse is such that few, if any, crisis workers can remain totally objective all the time. Cross-supervision by trusted coprofessionals keeps the worker on track, reduces personal stress, and helps avoid burnout.

Ensuring Safety. The crisis worker's first job is to determine how critical the situation is (Roberts & Roberts, 2002; Walker, 1984, p. 122). Is this a crisis call where danger is imminent or the woman just needs a chance to cathart? All the listening and responding skills known to humanity are of little use if the victim has multiple fractures or if her significant other has threatened to come back and kill her. The crisis worker calmly and cautiously makes an assessment of how bad the situation is. Does the victim need and want medical attention, shelter, a place to send her children, a way out of the house if her husband returns?

All these questions are posed in a measured, deliberate way to avoid adding to the panic the victim already feels. Although the situation may be critical and the best alternative may be for the victim to come directly to the shelter, the crisis worker has to remember that the woman cannot be forced into making that choice. This does not mean, however, that the worker cannot make such a recommendation.

CW: From what you've said, it sounds like the situation is pretty bad. Bad enough that you might consider leaving and coming to the shelter. Do you feel as if you or your children are in danger now? Is he there now? Do you want me to call the police? Do you need medical attention?

Because of a fear of the unknown, the victim may balk at this alternative (Dagastino, 1984). Patiently, the crisis worker explains the role and function of the shelter, answers any questions the victim has, and tries to allay her fears. If, after all this, the victim is still unwilling to make a decision, the worker does not push the issue. In initially reporting the battering, victims often appear to feel that it is an isolated incident and not abuse. They refuse to see it on an ever-escalating continuum. They delude themselves with the belief that "He really does love me, and if I'm a better person, it'll never happen again." As the crisis worker intervenes, he or she should be aware that such incidents are not isolated. Indeed, there is a consistent pattern leading up to the climax of battering (Walker, 1984, p. 24). The crisis worker

endeavors to lay that pattern out so that the victim sees it not as isolated but as continuous and predictable. Seeing the pattern is particularly important when the victim is not sure whether to leave or stay. Walker proposes that instead of speaking about the cycle of violence, the worker should lay out the escalating behavior in graphical form. Having the woman draw a graph of the ever-escalating violence and the shorter periods of tranquility can be an eye-opening event that allows her to decide to get out (Walker, 2000, pp. 136–137).

CW: As you tell me about it, I hear a sort of pattern. For about a week he gets surly, starts criticizing the way the house looks, the way you look, the food you cook, and your control over the kids. Those criticisms start out mild but become more severe, until you finally have had enough and say something to the effect that he ought to take more responsibility if he doesn't like things. That winds up with your getting beat up. I wonder if you can look back and see how the situation has repeated itself. Just take a pencil and piece of paper and make a graph back for the past couple of months. Put down the length of time when there has been peace and tranquility. Then put down how many hours or days the tension builds and he gets psychologically abusive, then put down when the fights start and how long they go on before he comes back and says he's sorry.

Juanita: Well, I don't know. I really think it was different this time. I mean this was the first time I needed emergency treatment. He was really sorry afterward. *(draws out graph)* Well, maybe it is getting worse. He seems to be getting madder faster.

CW: OK. So you see! What's different is that the pattern seems to be repeating itself more frequently, and it's getting more intense.

Juanita: Damn! I do see! I just don't know, though.

Often the client may be very immobile and may not even hear the question, so the worker may need to pose it again (Dagastino, 1984).

CW: When did he say he'd be back, and what'd he say he'd do?

Juanita: I just don't know whether to take it anymore. I love him, but I'm really scared.

CW: OK, I understand you are afraid, but I need to know how much time we've got and what threats he made.

By gently guiding the victim back to immediate and pressing issues, the crisis worker keeps the session on track but does not deny the emotional hurt and confusion the victim is experiencing.

By the time the battered woman becomes desperate enough to make the call for help, she does not have time to be analyzed. What she needs is some behavioral action-oriented techniques she can use on a short-term basis (Walker, 1979, pp. 75–77). Just having a plan allows the victim to regain some composure and feel she has obtained some control over the situation. The whole focus of the conversation is to prepare her to get through that one day. At this time, the worker does not worry about tomorrow or any other time. Tomorrow, the worker may call the victim and talk about the next day. If the worker attempts to deal with future events that extend beyond a week, the victim gets lost (Dagastino, 1984).

Because of the flood of critical needs the victim faces, the worker must realistically judge which needs may require immediate action and which ones can be deferred. To help make sense of the heavy flow of information, the crisis worker writes down what the victim tells her so that she can quickly identify and set priorities on the very practical concerns that are pressing at the victim.

Logs that are preprinted and pose a structured set of questions and information ensure that crisis line workers cover critical needs of battered women and provide them with consistent information (Dagastino, 1984; Roberts & Roberts, 2005). Immediate actions and follow-up actions need to be covered and checked. Issues such as getting enough money for the children's lunch the next day may be just as important as taking care of a broken nose, and the worker will need to remember this. By calmly, clearly, and concisely feeding back to the victim her written summary, the crisis worker takes the victim step by step through a review of her most critical needs. By dissecting the crisis in this manner, the worker assures the victim that her problems can be broken down and managed (Dagastino, 1984).

CW: Here are all the things I hear happening to you right now. No wonder you're feeling paralyzed; anyone in that situation would feel the same. You've said you have no job, the children don't want to leave, and that he might kill you. You also indicated that it was against your faith to get a divorce, and particularly coming from Colombia there are some really strong cultural prohibitions. That's a load. Let's take them one at a time and sort through each problem and put them back together.

A careful examination of the woman's fears about these problems, what priorities need to be set on them, and the options she has in dealing with them is extremely important. Until the abused woman can confront such fears openly, she cannot begin developing strategies to deal with her problems (Heppner, 1978).

CW: You're afraid to leave because you feel sure he will come after you when he comes back, and you're not sure what he might do, so that causes tension to build. Yet I really believe if we make a plan right now you'll feel better, even if you don't have to use it.

If the victim states that she does not know what to do, the crisis worker immediately looks at the two basic alternatives—staying and leaving. What has she done before? How is this time different, if at all, from the times before? If so, what different action needs to be taken now? A key ingredient is determining the level of danger at home. Is the abuser really going to act out, or is the fear of his acting out propelling the woman into making the call? To learn what has happened before, the crisis worker asks questions such as "When he's gone out and gotten drunk before, what has he done?" "What have you done?" From the answers, the crisis worker gains a realistic assessment of the danger level of the situation. If the victim is unwilling to leave the house, then the crisis worker role-plays the scene of the drunken abuser returning home.

Assuming the role of the abuser, the worker goes through, in a systematic way, each situation of potential confrontation and then discusses the potential positive and negative outcomes of the victim's attempt to handle the confrontation (Dagastino, 1984).

CW: (*in role*) Hey, honey, come in the bedroom, I need you real bad.

Juanita: (*typical response*) I can't stand having sex with you when you are drunk.

CW: (*as self*) Now, look at how you responded to that. When you shut him off like that, he gets angry, right? What could you do or say differently? How could you change things? How about turning the tables so he had no desire for you at all? What would happen if you had a facial on and your hair up in curlers and had on a frowzy housecoat? Although that might not make you very alluring, would that turn him off?

By looking at options and posing alternative ways of behaving, the worker attempts to provide coping techniques that may defuse the crisis. By the time the worker is done, the victim is feeding back a plan, point by point, either for staying in the house or for moving out. Having an escape plan is critical (Walker, 1984, p. 122).

CW: All right! You've figured out how to get out of the house. You'll keep the back door open. You've given the kids a note to go over to the neighbors. You've got our number, and you know you can get to your car, parked out back, and get to a phone booth and call us.

As indicated in Chapter 6, Telephone and Online Crisis Counseling, computers and electronic technology play a larger and larger role in the lives of young adults. Therefore, the following study would seem to have some potentially important ramifications for younger women who are battered and have access to a computer. A computer program that has been field-tested with a group of battered women currently residing in a shelter holds promise for both keeping women who are abused safer and encouraging them to risk leaving (Glasser et al., 2010). This English/Spanish program was tested on women who had experienced severe threats to their safety. It provides feedback about risk for lethal violence, options for safety, assistance with setting priorities, and a safety plan personalized to the user. From their scores on the Danger Assessment component, 69% of the subjects discovered that they were in extreme danger. After using the safety decision aid, the women felt more supported in their decision to leave and had less decisional conflict about doing so.

In summary, both short- and long-term safety depends on helping abused women take action steps rather than remaining immobilized. For many victims, it may not be a question of returning to a precrisis equilibrium. The equilibrium was never there in the first place. Therefore, for many women, taking first, tentative steps toward action is likely to be extremely frightening, confusing, and full of trepidation.

The following points seem worthwhile for crisis workers to know and understand in helping abused women make such decisions and take action (Massachusetts Coalition of Battered Women Service Groups, 1981, pp. 25, 67).

1. Help women think and act on their situation by providing legitimate reinforcement for their efforts.
2. Help women figure out what they want by providing a sounding board for examining ideas and alternatives.
3. Help women identify feelings that prevent them from making decisions.
4. Be honest. The worker cannot tell a person what to do but can clearly state from her own life how the situation would affect her.
5. Help women to things for themselves, but do not let them become dependent on the worker.
6. Know and offer resources from which battered women can get specific kinds of assistance: Spell out *who, what, where, when,* and *how.*
7. Help women gain a sense of self-confidence and ability to take care of themselves.
8. Be challenging. Support women, but do not be afraid to push them toward a decision-making point.
9. Be open to choices. Each woman has control over her life; the crisis worker must not attempt to assume control for clients.
10. Hear and understand what women have to say, particularly if it does not run parallel to the worker's own beliefs, attitudes, and outlooks.
11. Build on the commonalities that women, particularly battered women, share, but recognize the worth of the individual differences of each person.
12. Assess lethality. "I'm fed up and whipped" may really mean "I'm ready to commit suicide."

The following crisis worker's response to a battered woman, who after 2 hours of talking on the telephone still could not make up her mind about what to do, aptly illustrates the application of the 12 points just made.

CW: I understand your mixed feelings of wanting to stay and wanting to leave; also the constant fear you live with while waiting for the next time, maybe even wishing it would happen quickly so the tension will ease off. But my guess is that tension reduction only occurs for a short period and then starts to build all over again. I also understand that you feel like you're locked into this, but there are some alternatives, which we have gone over. I want you to pick at least one of those, whichever seems best for you, and do it. I won't take no for an answer. Do something that will make you feel better right now. Go take a hot bath if that'll help, and don't spare the bath oil. I think it would be safer for you to come to the shelter right now, but if you don't really feel you can do that, I understand. However, if you feel the tension start to rise and feel like you just can't take it anymore, I want you to promise to call back here.

I won't take no for an answer. I'll call you tomorrow afternoon to see how things are going. What would be a good time?

Advocacy. Because battered women have been isolated for much of their lives, they generally have little knowledge of alternatives open to them. This is especially true with respect to their rights and options with both legal and welfare systems. Providing court advocates who understand the laws and how to weave through bureaucratic obstacles and how to cut through the red tape that often interferes with someone seeking help from the system is of paramount importance. Weaving one's way through the state employment and welfare system to obtain financial aid and job training requires support and advocacy (Shepard, 1999). The worker needs to have an excellent networking system to tap into and get immediate help for a variety of problems these women will face.

Transcrisis Perspective. All the preceding intervention procedures cannot be accomplished in a 20-minute phone call. Even minor crises may require two or three calls to get the client stabilized, in touch with her feelings, and into some semblance of preabuse equilibrium. The crisis worker is not providing a short-term elixir that merely calms the victim and then blithely sends her on her way. What is being provided is a blend that not only deals with the immediate crisis but also has a long-term application. Many battered women need to go through a complete reeducation process about who they are and what they can do. This process should not be hurried even if it takes a year to accomplish this goal.

Indeed, the transcrisis of the battered woman does not end when she gets off the phone and decides to come to the center or go to the shelter. The initiating interview or hotline call is only the first part of the crisis resolution. Other crises will continue to plague the victim. Ibrahim and Herr's (1987) work with battered women who were involved in a group counseling format that concentrated on vocational exploration and economic independence is an excellent example of a transcrisis point. When these women reached the stage of vocational implementation, ready actually to go out into the world of work and test their skills, they experienced all kinds of threatening and anxious feelings and became immobile and paralyzed. The women needed 15 two-hour sessions of intensive support by the group leaders to work through this stage!

Shelters

A center and a shelter are generally two different entities within a domestic abuse program. The center deals with telephone and on-site, short-term crisis intervention and counseling. The shelter is a longer-term facility where women and their families can stay for short or extended periods of time. A comprehensive program will have both a center and a shelter and will be staffed around the clock with a 24-hour hotline and an open door policy for walk-ins (Barnett et al., 1980). Shelters generally provide two other important ingredients, individual counseling and peer support (Hampton, Vandergriff-Avery, & Kim, 1999). There will be tie-ins to other social services agencies: police, free or sliding-scale legal services, hospitals, medical staff and mental health facilities, mobile crisis teams that provide transportation for abuse victims, and direct links to emergency housing facilities with follow-up services (Benjamin & Walz, 1983, p. 83).

The typical shelter is linked to the abuse center and is well publicized, but for security reasons its location may not be made public. For the same reason, it will be well patrolled by the police and will be secure. Staffed by both professionals and volunteers, it will have adequate cooking, sleeping, bath, and child and infant care facilities for a number of families and funds for clothing, food, and transportation (Langley & Levy, 1977). It should also provide a variety of counseling services to help women ventilate feelings, explore alternatives, and make immediate plans for what they will do next (Benjamin & Walz, 1983, p. 84). It should also have comprehensive services for children (Roberts & Roberts, 2005). This ideal shelter is a rarity due to lack of funds, although in the authors' home state of Tennessee, a portion of every marriage license fee goes toward support of shelters.

Counseling Women at Shelters

Women who enter the shelter fit into two categories: those who are unsure about leaving the battering relationship and those who have made a definite commitment to leave it (Dagastino, 1984). Women who fall into the first category need to be monitored on an hour-by-hour basis and are the more critical of the two categories. The crisis worker maintains constant contact with these women and reinforces them for having had the courage to come to the shelter.

CW: I'm glad you made it. I know it took a lot of courage.

CW: (*10 minutes later*) Getting settled in? Come on with me. There are some other women I would like you to meet.

CW: (*2 hours later*) How are things going? Got the kids settled in? They're great-looking children. Want to have a cup of coffee and talk?

Vacillation between going back and staying is characteristic of these women. The longer the women stay at the shelter, the greater the probability is that they will not return to their mates (Hilbert & Hilbert, 1984). However, until women can recover their self-esteem and come to understand that they are not the cause of the abuse, they are at risk to leave and go back (Schutte et al., 1986). The worker does not try to force women to stay at the shelter but does try to get them to take some psychological "time-out" to review their situation in a more objective way (Dagastino, 1984). The foregoing is particularly true of women who have suffered childhood sexual abuse, who are far more likely to return to the batterer because of their emotional attachment (Griffing et al., 2005). Knowing this kind of information is critical to worker intervention and keeping women from leaving before they have a chance to start gaining back their self-esteem.

Juanita: I'm all mixed up. I don't know if I'm wrong or not. I'm Catholic, and I'm Hispanic. Women in my family just don't walk out of a marriage. The church and my family both say we just need to work things out, but I really think he'll kill me.

CW: Let's assume you're taking a 1-day vacation, so you can get some rest before you go back and deal with it. It's fine if you want to go back home, but do this much for me—just take it easy for a while. I can see that you're physically all right and not hurt, and I'm relieved. This is a great time to talk about what you can do if you do or don't go back.

The shelter worker checks repeatedly with the new arrival and reinforces her decision to come. She conveys her concern for the victim and, with the help of other women in the shelter, sees that the victim and her family are settled. The focus is on the here and now. During the first few hours of the victim's separation from her abuser, the worker will probably have to be very directive. Few women at this time have the ego strength to stand on their own, and most need an abundance of support and help. The objective is to keep the victim moving, thinking, and acting so that she is preoccupied and does not have time to let

fear, guilt, or any other debilitating and anxiety-ridden emotions overcome her. Domestic chores such as cleaning and cooking seem to be particularly helpful in this regard. In all instances, the worker should be carefully attuned to the victim's needs. Some may find help sitting, talking, or crying with a worker or a group of other women. Others may be so exhausted that they need to go to bed and sleep. Whatever the victim needs, the worker should be adaptable to those needs and flexible enough to change as circumstances demand (Dagastino, 1984).

Shelter Dynamics. A variety of positive dynamics occur at shelters. There is substantial support from other women who have experienced the same kind of trauma. This support enables victims to begin gaining the courage to face people, recovering their lost self-esteem, and learning that the beatings were not their fault (Schechter, 1982, pp. 55–60).

Wife abuse shelters are not vacation spas where one's every whim is catered to. Although an abundance of caring and sharing occurs, women who live in shelters are encouraged to start trusting themselves to make decisions. Part of the decision-making process includes determining what is best for the shelter. This is not an easy task. Limits have to be set with respect to pets, children, cooking, and so on (Schechter, 1982, pp. 63–64). Women get bored, boss each other around, miss their men, miss sex (pp. 55–60), and have problems relating to people from different ethnic and racial backgrounds and sociocultural milieus (Massachusetts Coalition of Battered Women Service Groups, 1981, p. 28).

Shelter user: Getting used to a shelter is overwhelming. You like it, but you don't want to be there, 'cause it isn't home. You've got to put together all your psychological know-how in getting along with different types of people. Wondering if you're going to make it, especially when you see all the pain and confusion and don't know whether it's yours or theirs or what, and hoping nobody finds out you're here. Trying to be understood and feeling like you are a blabbermouth here when you couldn't talk at home. Trying to look forward and all the time wanting to forget . . . wanting to forget . . . wanting to forget (Schechter, 1982, pp. 59–60).

At a shelter, everything is not always as it seems. Many women who come to the shelter are extremely dependent and exceptionally adept at manipulating the workers there (Walker, 1984, p. 126). A statement like "You really understand—you've made my whole life better" is reinforcing to the worker but may actually be manipulation. The woman is using the house and the worker as a security blanket and is not making any progress toward getting out on her own (Dagastino, 1984). The wise shelter worker comes to see the manipulation for what it is, a refusal to take responsibility for oneself and a shift from dependency on an abusive partner to dependency on a caring shelter worker (Weincourt, 1985). Gently but firmly, the worker extinguishes such behavior.

CW: I appreciate what you said, and I appreciate your wanting to cook my dinner and all the other things you want to do for me. Yet I believe your time and mine could be better spent working on getting you set up in an apartment and looking for a job.

Grief. Besides being dependent, many abused women go through a grief process. Sorrow and depression, guilt and self-blame, and decision-making difficulty are all hallmarks of the grieving process. What would be viewed as normal in a woman who suffered the death of a spouse may be viewed as pathological in an abused woman. However, these responses are just as legitimate for an abused woman who is trying to come to terms with the loss of a significant relationship, shared parental responsibilities, and a clearly defined role as a wife (Campbell, 1989).

There are a lot of *yes, buts* as workers start to confront abused women with making a new future. As victims shift from a depersonalized view of their situation to depression over it, the process can be extremely frightening to a shelter worker unless she knows that this, too, is another step in the transcrisis that battered women go through (Dagastino, 1984). The woman's grief often puzzles those trying to help her. Many human services workers may be threatened by these feelings and deny the woman's need to mourn by concentrating on dealing with concrete aspects of the woman's dilemma, such as providing food, clothing, and housing.

Her grief can be understood, however, if one asks the question "For what is she mourning?" In most cases, she has defined herself in terms of her relationship with the batterer, and if that relationship ends, she feels as if she has lost everything—including her sense of self (Turner & Shapiro, 1986). She clings quite tightly to the dreams she has for the relationship—including the expectations with which she entered

into it. When the relationship ends, she must come to terms with the fact that these dreams will never materialize. Therefore, she is not grieving so much for what was, but for what she hoped could have been (Spanno, 1990). A crisis worker can and should validate that the woman's loss is very real and that she has a legitimate right to mourn and experience the feelings she has over the loss (Russell & Uhlemann, 1994). At this point, the counseling process is little different from grief due to death of a loved one (see Chapter 12, Personal Loss: Bereavement and Grief).

Juanita: I wanted this to work so much. We could have had it so good, but I couldn't take him beating on me and the kids too. What went wrong with that good-looking, happy couple in this picture? He was so handsome and so good to me in the beginning. Then it just slowly went to hell, and now this. (Weeps while slowly turning over in her hands a wedding picture that she brought with her to the shelter.)

CW: It's really hard to say good-bye to all those things that were and might have been. It must hurt even more than the beatings to know that all those hopes and dreams won't come to pass.

Juanita: It tears my heart out, but I know I did the right thing. Sooner or later he would have killed me or the kids in one of his rages. It's so weird! I still love that SOB.

CW: The grief you're feeling is as real as if a close friend or a relative had died. Perhaps even more tragic because when this relationship died, a part of you died with it, Juanita. The part of you who struggled out of the barrio, went to college, got an education, made a success of herself, married the perfect man, and then had all those expectations dashed because of the way he treated you and the children.

Juanita: I can't let that stop me. Nothing else did. I made the right decision coming here. I also made the right decision getting a warrant on him. Maybe that last act of love will get him the help he needs or the jolt he needs to wake him up so he doesn't do it to somebody else.

CW: As you say that, I see so much determination coming through the tears. I also see a new, different, stronger person as you say those farewells, as tough as they are.

A woman who has been involved in an abusive relationship needs to grieve and to have her grief validated. The crisis worker does this while reinforcing that although there is now an altered future, it has potential to be a good one. It is through this process that the battered woman can come to see the relationship for what it really was—abusive. The crisis worker will make a very bad therapeutic mistake if she expects the woman to rejoice. If she is expected to be happy for leaving and is discouraged from feeling her sense of loss and expressing it, she may never confront the truth about the relationship. The end result may well be a return to the partner or one just like him (Spanno, 1990).

Depression. Depression comes in many guises. Many women who come into the shelter sleep much of the time. On first appearance, they may seem to be lazy. Actually, they may be going through a stage of trying to regroup their psychic energy. The worker's task becomes one of trying to help them move past their inactivity, but not by pressuring them or taking them on a guilt trip (Massachusetts Coalition of Battered Women Service Groups, 1981, p. 27).

CW: I've noticed you pretty much sticking to your room and sleeping a lot. I was a little concerned and was wondering how you were feeling. I wonder if you've had a chance to talk to anyone about how you feel since you got here.

Juanita: I feel so guilty. It seems like I have slept ever since I've gotten here, and the other women have been so good to take care of the kids. I'm not really like this. I just don't seem to have any get-up-and-go. I'm really sorry to be so much trouble.

CW: What you are doing is exactly what you should be doing, getting your energy back. You burned up a tremendous amount of it making the decision to get out and get here. The other women have felt the same way, so they understand. In a few days you'll do the same for somebody else. If you want to talk, we're here. If you want to rest, that's just fine too. The main thing is you're safe, and that's what's important right now.

Terror. For many women, a stress-related syndrome similar to agoraphobia arises after they have been in the shelter for a while (Massachusetts Coalition of Battered Women Service Groups, 1981, p. 27). They may have extreme and unexplainable attacks of terror that are touched off by seemingly innocuous incidents. These incidents greatly restrict their activities and new freedom. Fear of their mates, fear of their predicament, fear of their separation from a definable

past, and fear of an undefinable future can all cause the onset of terror. Under no circumstances should the shelter worker allow it to continue. Victims must be encouraged and helped step by step to pull themselves away from the security blanket of the shelter and out into the real world.

Such progress may take place in very small, slow steps, but the steps must be taken. As women take these steps, they receive very specific, positive reinforcement for what they have accomplished, enabling them not to fall back into learned helplessness but instead to take responsibility for their behavior (Weincourt, 1985). Invariably, victims will not be able to see that they have done much of anything, or they tend to diminish their successes. For women who are faced with leaving a relationship with no means of support, structural change in their economic environment is imperative. Independent housing, job training and opportunities, affordable child care, and social support services are critical. Programs such as the Job Readiness program that is run in a number of Kentucky shelters provide job training to make women employable (Websdale & Johnson, 2005). However, such preparation may bring on its own developmental crises as these women venture into new, unfamiliar territory.

CW: I know you're still scared to death to go down and talk to them at Federal Express about that job. It's a big step, but a week ago you couldn't walk down to the grocery store, and now you're doing that fine. So let's take it a step at a time. Look at what you overcame. We can go through the job interview, play it a step at a time, talk about those steps right here where it's safe, and give you a chance to really become confident about going down there.

Those Who Have Decided to Leave. The second category of women who come to the shelter are in for a long haul and are not going back to the battering situation. For women who are in for the duration, the crisis worker deals with immediate specifics such as finding a place to live, financial aid, and child care. Emotional support has a low priority because these women are so busy that all they want and need is very practical advice and help. These women are very different from those experiencing acute crisis because they are highly motivated to change their lives. They are much easier to work with, because they have made a decision to get out of their domestic pressure cooker (Dagastino, 1984).

Follow-Up

Once women leave the shelter, they should be provided with follow-up care (Tutty & Rothery, 2002). As immediate demands are relieved, the emotional impact of their decision should be dealt with over the long term. These women are urged to go for counseling with the idea that no one can be beaten even once without suffering some psychological damage. It is not uncommon for a woman to be so busy getting her act together that her emotional reactions are delayed. The victim may be out on her own, well established, and watching television at the time that she experiences a sudden emotional breakdown. The crisis worker apprises the victim of what to expect in the way of emotional aftershocks. Such residual psychological trauma seems to be particularly characteristic of women who initially appear to be very much in control (Dagastino, 1984).

CW: Even though you feel like you've made the break from your husband, don't be surprised if later on you get depressed and really feel like you need and miss him. That's to be expected. We know that, and we're here to help then too!

Indeed, in the worst of scenarios, the victim may become lonely, forget about the terrible abuse she suffered in the past, invite her ex-mate over for dinner, and get beaten up again. Or because of urging from children or the ex-partner, she may feel pressured into reuniting (Tutty & Rothery, 2002). Therefore, in following up with the victim, the crisis worker should understand that there may be relapses and that the victim may fall into old ways of behaving. Or, the victim having made the break, the batterer may seek her out for revenge. Thus, crisis workers not only may have to check up on their clients but also may have to be indirect about it, so the women do not become dependent on them (Dagastino, 1984).

CW: Hello, Juanita. Just called to see if you've been able to make that appointment for counseling at the Human Services Clinic. I know it's hard to get in there at times and thought if you hadn't, I could call the clinic, and we'd have one of the people here drive you down and help you get started.

The crisis worker continues to be a support system until the victim is well connected to a long-term support source (McLeod, Hays, & Chang, 2010), and only then does the crisis worker fade from the victim's life. Long-term support is particularly critical for abused women. Research indicates that women who leave the shelter and strike out on their own continue to undergo emotional changes for at least 6 months after leaving. Therefore, support and advocacy are critical during this time frame. Those who have a support group and advocates who help them access services do significantly better in reaching their goals than do women who lack such services (Sullivan et al., 1994). Support services also build self-esteem, increase locus of control, reduce stress, and enhance feelings of belongingness and support (Tutty, Bidgood, & Rothery, 1993). Follow-up and support are particularly important for women who have little education, few job skills, and minimal financial support (Webersinn, Hollinger, & Delamatre, 1991).

Do the shelter experience and its follow-up services significantly alter a woman's chance of not becoming involved in an abusive relationship again? The data are not clear on this issue. Research indicates that the greater the number of times a woman leaves an abusive relationship, the more likely she is to leave permanently (Schutte, Malouff, & Doyle, 1988). Going to a shelter without benefit of follow-up and other support services may actually *increase* violence (Berk, Newton, & Berk, 1986). Finally, because shelters tend to be based on Western forms of feminism, ethnic minorities with different cultural backgrounds report difficulties in adapting to a shelter environment (Hamby, 1998, p. 238). Clearly, entering a shelter is a major step and not one to be taken lightly. While entering a shelter may be necessary, based on the foregoing it is not necessarily sufficient by itself and is but a first step on a long road (Tutty & Rothery, 2002).

Intervention With Children

There has been a tendency in the battered **LO14** women's movement to look at children as "secondary" victims (Lehmann & Rabenstein, 2002; Peled, 1997). They are not. Remember that there are an estimated 7 million children who have been exposed to violent abusive conditions in the United States alone (McDonald et al., 2006). First and foremost, children often receive physical abuse along with their mothers (McMahon, Neville-Sorvilles, & Schubert, 1999). Statistics on family violence identify that at least half the homes that suffer domestic violence have children under 12 years of age living in them (Greenfield, Rand, & Craven, 1998). Children are often lost in the shuffle of domestic violence, but that violence has a direct impact on their lives both in the present and in the future (Wolak & Finkelhor, 1998, pp. 73–111).

Lehmann and Rabenstein's (2002) review of research outcomes on children who have witnessed domestic violence indicates a variety of behavioral and emotional problems that range from academic difficulties to approval of violence as a problem-solving method. In adulthood those same children are likely to experience poor interpersonal relationships, use and accept violence as a way to solve problems, have chronic depression and low self-esteem, and engage in criminal behavior. In that light, crisis workers need to be as concerned for children as they are for the women who are immersed in battering relationships.

Of primary concern is the safety of the children, so a lethality assessment should be conducted to determine where the children should reside and who will supervise them during visitation and other occasions on which the perpetrator may be present. For children who are old enough to take action on their own, a safety plan should entail how to determine whether the situation is becoming lethal, how to get away from the perpetrator, and where they can go to be safe. If they are in a shelter, they need to know how to keep the location a secret not only from the perpetrator but also from other relatives and acquaintances. If there is evidence of abuse toward the children, which is highly likely in partner violence, then the crisis worker is mandated to refer the case to a state welfare agency (Wolak & Finkelhor, 1998, pp. 100–101).

Children who have witnessed partner violence or have just fled or been removed from a home can benefit from immediate crisis counseling to stave off typical PTSD symptoms (Lehmann & Rabenstein, 2002) that can follow them into adulthood (Anderson, Danis, & Havig, 2011). (See the sections on children in Chapter 7, Posttraumatic Stress Disorder, and Chapter 9, Sexual Assault, for more detailed assessment and intervention strategies.) Specific immediate intervention with a trained crisis worker should first do a safety assessment, then allow children to recount the events and their feelings about them, correct negative misattributions about self-blame, and work through overwhelming negative feelings (Wolak & Finkelhor, 1998, p. 101). Specific problem-solving strategies need to be developed in which the child's affect is normalized and she or he learns how to anticipate and deal with uncomfortable emotions (Lehmann & Rabenstein, 2002).

There is probably no age too early to start therapy for children who come from abusive home settings.

Roberts and Roberts (2005) report that the Jersey Battered Women's Service in Morristown, New Jersey, has developed coloring books that are used during initial contact with the children. The books encourage children to identify feelings, provide assurance of safety, give them information to understand what is happening in their families, provide information to help the children adapt to the shelter setting, and begin to assess the children's needs and concerns.

Therapeutic work done conjointly with caregivers is critical. First, a parental interview should be conducted with the battered parent to determine safety issues, developmental history of the child, a history of the traumatic exposure, what current symptoms are being manifested, and how well the child is handling separation issues, and to provide psychoeducation about children's symptoms as well as hope that things will improve (Weinreb & Groves, 2007). Douglas (1991) used conjoint therapy with mother and child, employing attachment theory to help toddlers ages 15 to 36 months work through traumatic battering events they had witnessed. Hughes's (1982) brief intervention strategy includes intervention with children, mothers, schools, and shelter staff members. Her model is comprehensive in that it provides individual counseling; initiates group meetings for peers, siblings, and family; teaches parenting skills to mothers; establishes a liaison with school personnel; and trains shelter staff members in child advocacy and child development issues.

Malchiodi (2008, p. 254) recommends art and play therapy as a primary therapeutic mode because many children will not want to talk about the violence they have witnessed. Further, children will have difficulty because of their immature cognitive development in verbalizing the complex issues that undergird domestic violence (Weinreb & Groves, 2007).Treatment goals for children and the victimized parent include (Malchiodi, 2008; Weinreb & Groves, 2007):

1. Creating an alliance with the parent to help the child heal.
2. Providing psychoeducation to both parent and child about the trauma and therapy.
3. Restoring the parent's self-esteem and confidence to parent.
4. Establishing a safe therapeutic environment for the child to express thoughts and feelings.
5. Relieving the child's symptoms, including difficulty with living transitions, sleeping, nightmares, and other trauma symptoms.

6. Reestablishing the child's previous level of cognitive functioning and strong attachment with the caregiver.
7. Reassurance that what has happened is not the child's fault and the child is not guilty of anything.
8. Helping the child express thoughts and feelings and regain cognitive and emotional regulation.
9. Providing stress reduction strategies to aid in stopping emotional dysregulation.

Weinreb and Groves (2007) provide an excellent example of why using play therapy is effective with children coming out of domestic violence situations. In this instance a 7-year-old girl had witnessed severe beatings of her mother by her father. She was introduced to therapy by being brought into a play therapy room and invited to play. She used drawing and playing with figurines that represented her violent environment to work through a constellation of conflicted feelings about the traumatic events and separation of the family. She expressed that she was afraid of, yet missed, her father, which are all too common ambivalent feelings about the offending parent. Trying to verbalize these ambivalent, conflicted feelings and integrate them is extremely difficult for an elementary school age child. Working them out through play and anchoring them with drawings, models, and other concrete representations isn't.

Many times group work (Malchiodi, 2008, pp. 252–263) may be used with children; benefits include decreasing isolation, bonding with other victims, and seeing others moving forward from the trauma of the domestic violence they experienced. Malchiodi (2008, pp. 258–261) has adapted Herman's (1992) three-phase trauma recovery model to her groups, which generally meet for 90 minutes for up to 12 sessions. Phase 1 is about establishing safety rules, confidentiality, personal space, and boundaries, which may be put on a colorful poster and signed by the children as part of their behavioral contract. The group engages in activities such as making feeling thermometers; reading about Brave Bart, the traumatized cat who gets into a group of other traumatized cats; creating safety hands with "safe" adult names and phone numbers on it; learning relaxation and yoga activities; and free drawing and play time. Phase 2 is about telling the trauma story and includes activities such as creating collages of being powerless and powerful, making "how hands can hurt" posters, drawing a picture of "your family," reading therapeutic storybooks, engaging in relaxation and stress

reduction activities, practicing scaling techniques with feeling thermometers, learning simple cognitive-behavioral techniques to reduce negative thinking, and free play and art time. The final phase has to do with returning to the community and reconnecting with significant adults in the child's life who are central to his or her emotional recovery. These caregivers are asked to participate in the final two sessions. Children can share their artwork and have parents engage in reconstructing artwork, cooperatively creating or adding to safety hands to reinforce the child's sense of security and creating past, present, and future collages to show where they have been, where they are now, and the hopeful future they are moving toward.

Outcomes for the children should include the following (Malchiodi, 2008, p. 261):

1. Increased knowledge of the emotional and physical effects of family violence
2. Understanding that violence in the family is not okay and it is not their fault
3. A reduction in stress-related or PTSD symptoms; increased ability to self-regulate emotions
4. Decreased negative self-talk
5. Improved ability to identify feelings, and the ability to communicate those to peers and adults
6. Increased sense of social support
7. Stronger connection with the nonabusive parent
8. Resilience to cope with future crises

Finally, many children are still involved with both parents, and long-term monitoring and intervention are needed. The Duluth Family Visitation Center operates on the premise that this will occur and that parent training is critical for both parents so that children will not be used as messengers, negotiators, or witnesses to further verbal or physical abuse. As such, the Center staff members attempt to remain neutral and to act as advocates for the children with both parents by providing a safe place to exchange children, helping parents develop good parenting relationships with their children, and providing valid information to courts regarding custody and visitation rights (McMahon, Neville-Sorvilles, & Schubert, 1999).

Courtship Violence

To believe that only women who are partners in a conjugal relationship are victims of violence is to be badly mistaken. Studies on courtship violence estimate that it occurs in anywhere from

LO15

22% to 67% of courtship relationships and cuts across college, high school, and nonschool dating populations (Burcky, Reuterman, & Kopsky, 1988; Henton et al., 1983; Makepeace, 1983). A conservative estimate is that violence occurs in approximately 25% of courtship relationships. As simplistic as the following may sound as a predictor of violence, Bergman (1992) found that number of dating partners and dating frequency had the highest positive correlation and that grade point average had the highest negative correlation. As one might expect, adolescents who come out of violent families carry their experiences into their dating behavior (Foshee et al., 2015; Kaukinen et al., 2015; Laporte et al., 2011). All of the foregoing researchers found that indeed family of origin violence is a risk factor in dating and aggression. Females who had been victimized by either parent were at greater risk for revictimization but not increased aggression. High-risk males reported being aggressive toward girlfriends, particularly if they had been harshly disciplined by their fathers. For both males and females, but particularly for girls, the extent of their aggression toward their parents predicted their aggression toward partners (Laporte et al., 2011).

If you then also consider living in violent neighborhoods and attending violent schools, dating violence is just part of the culture (Black et al., 2015; Niolon et al., 2015). However, as old fashioned as this sounds, East and Hokoda (2015) found that mothers' early strictness, close monitoring, and conservative sexual attitudes predicted a lower likelihood of subsequent dating violence in low-income Latinas /os and African Americans. So it appears that what goes on within the family can buffer environmental effects.

Perhaps, even more ominous, in a study of high school students by Burcky, Reuterman, and Kopsky (1988), dating violence affected girls as young as 12. These researchers also found that assaultive behavior was not just shoving and pushing. Among those experiencing dating violence, 37.5% reported that the minimum assaultive behavior was being punched, and approximately 9% reported having been assaulted with a gun or knife! It is noteworthy, and may presage the future of these relationships, that the percentage of violent incidents reported closely parallels that found in samples of married couples and that this violence is reciprocal in nature (Jasinski & Williams, 1998, p. 30; Straus & Gelles, 1986; Straus, Gelles, & Steinmetz, 1980). What is truly astounding is that, in a study by Henton and associates (1983), 25% of victims and 30% of offenders interviewed

interpreted violence in courtship as a sign of love! Research study after research study indicate that violence invariably escalates the longer people are in an abusive relationship. Further, each subsequent year that women experienced violence as adolescents increases their risk for revictimization compared with those who did not have that experience. Across all years, women who are physically assaulted are significantly more likely to be sexually assaulted in that same year (Smith, White, & Holland, 2003). To think that people will give up violent behavior for "love" or any other reason is to think wrong. Worse, to think that one has the power to get a partner to give up an addictive behavior such as battering is patently false!

In that regard, the best directive your authors can offer to anyone who is physically assaulted even once in a dating relationship is, no matter how great the love, how great the good times, how great the sex, how many flowers, apologies, and promises to change are given after an initial assault, *get out of the relationship now!* No battered woman we have met set out with the intention to go with or marry someone who would beat her. However, by letting such behavior occur early in courtship, many battered women unwittingly set the stage for some terrible consequences of their early tolerance.

And if *you* have assaulted someone in a dating relationship, *get help now!* "Assaulted" doesn't necessarily mean that you put the person in the hospital. It may have been a series of hard shakes, a shove or two, or a slap in the heat of an argument or a moment of jealousy. Although you can easily rationalize this behavior away, the chances are good that this behavior will increase in the future. Besides the harm you do to someone you profess to love, the changes in the law and increased judicial sensitivity to battering mean that you will probably spend some time in jail if you are convicted of an assault on your girlfriend or boyfriend. If your school counseling center doesn't conduct anger management groups, there are therapists who do. The section on treating batterers will give you an idea of what you need to look for in a therapist.

Stalking

LO16

Epidemiological studies of stalking prevalence range from 8% to 16% of women and 2% to 7% of men who will be stalked during their lives (Dressing, Kuehner, & Gass, 2006; Tjaden & Thoennes, 1998b, 2000), with the National Intimate Partner and Sexual Violence Survey pegging the stalking rate at 15.2% for women and 5.7% for men (Breiding, 2015). That percentage is most likely a lot worse on college campuses. Shorey, Comelius, and Strauss (2015) found that in their study 38% of men and women in a current dating relationship had been stalked in the previous 6 months. But those cases often go unreported because of fear of violence, gender norms, and shame (Cass & Mallicoat, 2015). So for those who are victims, the official definition of stalking is "the willful or intentional commission of a series of acts that would cause a reasonable person to fear death or serious bodily injury and that, in fact, does place the victim in fear of death or serious bodily injury" (Office for Victims of Crime, 2002, p. 1).

Stalking is generally defined as repeated harassment, following, and/or threats that are committed with the intent of causing the victim emotional distress, fear of bodily harm, and/or actual bodily harm. Fantasy stalkers who typically target movie stars may send out hundreds of e-mails, letters, or phone calls. Most of these stalkers are not targeting their victims for murder, as opposed to stalkers who are strangers to their victims who demonstrate a variety of pathologies, are angry, and want power over their victims, and are extremely dangerous sexual predators and murderers (Dressing, Kuehner, & Gass, 2006; Mester, Birger, & Margolin, 2006; Schlesinger, 2006). However, as evil as those stalking strangers may be, they are less likely to cause a woman injury as opposed to those who are familiar with the person. Tjaden and Thoennes (2000) reported that injury rates were four times higher among women stalked by acquaintances as opposed to strangers. To top it off they also have more severe mental health problems (Cole, Logan, & Shannon, 2005). It may interest you to know that the first state stalking law in California didn't come into existence until 1990 although all 50 states in the U.S. now have stalking laws (Lawson, 2013).

Stalking is not just a problem in the United States but apparently is worldwide (Maran et al., 2014; McKeon, McEwan, & Luebbers, 2015; Pengpid & Peltzer, 2014), and as McKeon and associates (2015) found out in Australia, males minimize the problem by believing stalking isn't really serious, that it's romantic, and victims are to blame when it happens. Indeed, better you are stalked by a stranger from that standpoint because Scott and associates (2014) found that the victim was perceived more responsible when the stalker was known to her as opposed to a lurking stranger.

Cyberstalking. There is probably no more terrifying experience than being stalked. A new phenomenon is stalking over the Internet. Cyberstalking allows the stalker to collect information about the target and then, when communicating with the target, reveal these personal facts. Interestingly, in a study of cyberstalking among college students, Alexy and associates (2005) found that males were more likely to be stalked than females by this method, and that was also found to be true in Strawhun and associates' research (2013). Cavezza and McEwan (2014) found that while cyberstalkers were more likely to be ex-intimate partners and less likely to approach their victims, the majority still combined off-line stalking as well, and this behavior was also affirmed by Strawhun and associates (2013). The field of cyberstalking has now grown to the point that a test, *Fear of Online Interpersonal Victimization Measures* (Henson, Reyns, & Fisher, 2013), has been developed to measure three different forms of online victimization. The test measures online harassment, cyberstalking, and online threats of violence by a current/former intimate partner, a friend/acquaintance, or a stranger.

Stalking targets have many of the same PTSD-like symptoms that battered individuals do and resort to the same kinds of strategies when the stalking becomes intolerable, such as changing one's address, moving away, quitting one's job, changing one's name and appearance, and going underground (Knox & Roberts, 2005).

Stopping stalking can be highly frustrating because the authorities will not likely intervene unless the individual has some proof that she or he is being stalked (Brewster, 2002). Persons who are being stalked need to keep a recorded log of sightings, phone calls, copies of e-mails and letters, and any witnesses to the stalking. The Stalking Behavior Checklist (Coleman, 1997), which is available through many advocacy groups, measures unwanted harassing and pursuit-oriented behavior and can be used to provide excellent documentation. If you are being stalked, you need to call the police now! You need to get in touch with victims' advocacy groups that know how to deal with this problem and have them go with you to the authorities. Federal antistalking legislation was implemented as part of the Violence Against Women Act in 1996, and all 50 states now have laws regarding stalking (Knox & Roberts, 2005). While many jurisdictions have paid little heed to stalking problems in the past, increased awareness has caused the instigation of counterstalking programs like the Nashville Metropolitan Police Department's Counterstalking Plan, which uses a wide array of technology to trap and prosecute stalkers (Roberts & Kurst-Swanger, 2002). Michele Path (2002) has written an excellent survival manual for stalking victims.

Gay and Lesbian Violence

LO17

Although statistics indicate that same-gendered sexual orientation is prevalent in about 10% of the people in the United States (Gebhard, 1997), even though the Supreme Court has ruled favorably on same-sex unions, the attitude of the general public is often highly negative, scornful, and openly hostile to gays and lesbians. This prevailing attitude keeps many same-sex relationships under wraps, so when violence occurs, no report is made. There is also reluctance on the part of same-sex partners to report violence because of the added stigma attached to an already stigmatized perception that gay and lesbian relationships are unhealthy (Bograd, 2005; Elliot, 1996; Kanuha, 2005). Finally, unless they themselves are gay or lesbian, few service providers or researchers have the inclination, resources, or education about same-sex relationships to provide meaningful help (Island & Letellier, 1991; Renzetti, 1996). The bottom line is that while same-sex relationships can become violent as easily as heterosexual ones, figuring out how to help both the victim and the batterer is a tough proposition since there is not much evidence-based practice or support systems specifically designed for them. Indeed, the question arises in regard to whether the Duluth model for battering intervention, which has come to be seen as the gold standard intervention, works for same-sex battering (Buttell & Hamel, 2014).

Prevalence of Violence

The sparse statistics on gay and lesbian relations indicate that same-sex relationships are no more immune from partner violence than heterosexual ones. What has slowly come to light is that battering is an equal opportunity malady that affects gay men and lesbian women in the same staggering numbers as it does those in heterosexual relationships (Mederos, 1999; Peterman & Dixon, 2003; Ricks, Vaughan, & Dziegielewski, 2002). From 25% to 50% of lesbians report being in a battering relationship (Barnes, 1998; Friess, 1997; Lie & Gentlewarrier, 1991; Lockhart et al., 1994; Oatley, 1994). In one study, when all former relationships were considered, the figure moved up to 64% (Bologna, Waterman, & Dawson, 1987). In gay relationships, the data are even more sparse. Estimates

are that about 10% to 20% of males in gay relationships are assaulted each year (Island & Letellier, 1991). When all previous gay relationships are taken into consideration, the figure moves up to 44% (Bologna, Waterman, & Dawson, 1987). The bottom line is that it appears that a great deal of violence occurs in such relationships (Bartholomew, 1999; Gillis, 1999; Ristock, 1999; Stanley, 1999). Interestingly enough, in a study by Toro-Alfonso and Rodriguez-Madera (2004), while 48% of the gay men interviewed reported emotional abuse, they didn't consider it as interpersonal violence. From your authors' experience of crisis intervention with women and men of same-sex orientations, their presenting problems usually revolve around "outing" (revealing to others, such as parents and employers, of the victim's same-sex orientation), jealousy and mistrust, unwanted breakups, and feelings of loss, grief, and betrayal over dissolved relationships—all of which have the potential for violent confrontations.

Complicating Factors

Although many of the same coercive controls used by heterosexual batterers are employed in the homosexual community, there are differences. Positive-HIV status can be used as a coercive control. Failing health or threat of infection may be used to make the partner feel afraid or guilty. If the victim is infected, the coercive partner may refuse to provide support or get medical care for the victim, or double "out" the partner (tell people she or he is both homosexual and HIV positive; West, 1998, p. 170). Indeed, the coercive partner often uses "homophobic" control by threatening to "out" the partner and by constantly reminding the partner that no one in a homophobic world (particularly the police) will believe her or him or will dismiss the violence as inconsequential or what the person may "deserve" (Hart, 1986).

A further complicating factor is that battering may be seen as "mutual." That is, in a same-sex relation there is no clear "identifiable" assailant and victim. Thus, the assaulter can discount the victim's accusations by claiming that both were equally responsible for the violence. The foregoing is particularly true of gays who may be made to feel inadequate for "not taking it like a man" (Stanley et al., 2006; West, 1998, pp. 169–170).

To date, what research there is seems to indicate that many of the factors that influence violence in heterosexual partners are contributors to violence among same-sex partners. Intergenerational transmission of violence, alcohol abuse, dependency, autonomy issues, and power imbalances seem to contribute to same-sex partner abuse (Cruz, 2003; Peterman & Dixon, 2003; Ricks, Vaughan, & Dziegielewski, 2002).

Crisis Intervention Involving Gay and Lesbian Violence

Gay and lesbian battering is no different from heterosexual battering in that power and control are the key motivating factors. Gays and lesbians are also much the same in their reluctance to admit that abuse and violence can occur. However, gay men rank domestic violence third, behind substance abuse and AIDS, as their most pressing health problems (Island & Letellier, 1991). An even more dismal outlook may be forecast for elderly homosexuals, who may be entirely at the economic mercy of their partners and be extremely isolated from other support systems (Peterman & Dixon, 2003).

Sensitivity. Your authors' own experience indicates a number of issues that make crisis intervention difficult and sensitive with same-sex partners who have engaged in violent acts. First is the person's reluctance to talk about the problem because of trust issues with the crisis worker and the fear that the client will be held in low esteem for his or her sexual orientation. The worker must show a great deal of sensitivity and unconditional positive regard for the client to establish safe ground for the client to talk about such traumatic personal issues. This means that heterosexual workers must acquire knowledge and skills for work with this clientele and not allow their own homophobia to harm clients (Morrow, 2000) by obtaining training in counseling gays and lesbians (Matthews & Lease, 1999).

Precipitating Factors. Dependency versus autonomy, jealousy, and the perceived balance of power are major precipitating factors in battering in same-sex relationships (Renzetti, 1992). Balancing closeness and attachment with one's partner with independence and autonomy is difficult in any relationship, regardless of sexual orientation. In same-sex relationships, an absence of support outside the relationship may cause couples to turn more intensely to one another. Such dependence on one another may cause major stressors when one partner perceives the other as having become too autonomous, and fears abandonment.

Jealousy is certainly not exclusive to same-sex relationships. However, it may be more pronounced in same-sex relationships because another person of the same sex may pay attention to one partner and not to the other. As a result, such envy and jealousy may promote possessiveness and attempts to restrict and control the freedom of the other person, much as in a heterosexual relationship (Peterman & Dixon, 2003).

Distrust also tends to be much more pronounced in same-sex relationships than in heterosexual ones (Wiehe, 1998, p. 79). This is true because it is not uncommon for former lovers to still be in the support system of same-sex couples (all the same-sex people in a community may constitute each other's support system), whereas it is much easier to terminate those relationships in a heterosexual world (Kurdek, 1994). In summary, Craft and associates (2008) have found that some of the same issues of dependency and attachment theory that are abundant in heterosexual battering are also present in homosexual relations for both gay men and lesbian women. When stressors accumulate and escalate for those who have insecure attachment with their significant other, the threat of violence goes up.

Finally, the term **balance of power** refers to the ability of the person to influence and get others to do what he or she wants. Although heterosexual couples may have a division of labor in regard to household chores divided along stereotypical male–female lines, same-sex couples may have terrible conflicts over such domestic duties because they may perceive an inequity of power in doing these chores (Wiehe, 1998, p. 80).

Specific Issues. Any exploratory assessment should deal with issues specific to same-sex couples. That is, threats of "outing" the other person's sexual orientation or his or her HIV-positive status, exploration of internalized homophobia, degree of closeting (hiding same-sex orientation from others), and acceptance of sexual orientation are all components that adversely affect gays and lesbians and may be used for coercion.

It should never be assumed that one person is the victim and the other the perpetrator. It is also a myth that same-sex battering is mutual because both partners have equal strength and the ability to fight back (Peterman & Dixon, 2003). Thus, for both the police who respond to the assault and crisis workers who counsel the victims, sorting out the truth is even more complicated than it is in heterosexual battering.

Marrujo and Kreger (1996) found that a third of the lesbian battering relationships they investigated fell into what they call a "participant" category. Although they didn't initiate the aggression, participants did fight back, and once engaged, gave as good as they got. Hopefully, the worker can sort out who did what by the partners' responses. Aggressors may paradoxically propose that they are the real victims, participants may see themselves as righteously justified in retaliating, and victims may express a desire to end the conflict and be safe. Indeed, some lesbian abusers have shown up at shelters claiming to be the abused partner in hopes of finding the person who has left them (Leventhal & Lundy, 1999).

Severity. By the time a gay man or lesbian woman seeks therapeutic help with a relationship that involves battering, it is likely that a triage rating will put them in the highly impaired range. Interestingly, the person who seeks out therapy in a violent same-sex relationship may be the *batterer*. He or she may have typical feelings of conjugal paranoia that involve jealousy, betrayal, and fears of abandonment over some new or old partner (Peterman & Dixon, 2003; Ricks, Vaughan, & Dziegielewski, 2002). These feelings may rapidly escalate to guilt, contrition, self-doubt, and self-disparagement as the client attempts to repair the damage to the relationship. The person may be dominated by an "all or none," "If I can't have him/her, nobody will," cognitive set, and be constantly attempting to keep the relationship intact and out of the arms of some other real or imagined threat (Bartholomew, 1999). At this point, lethality becomes a high probability.

Safety and Support. A major concern is establishing a safety net and a support system because the client will believe that support people or resources are not available to him or her (and in fact they may have few, if any). Locating a support system or a safe place may be very difficult for gay or lesbian clients because a majority report they would not use support groups or go to a shelter and feel they are silenced and isolated when they do try to reach out for help (Lie & Gentlewarrier, 1991; Walters, 2011).

Treatment Issues. Complex issues revolve around treatment delivery. Although heterosexual battered men have few places to find shelter, there are even fewer places for gay battered men to go—although a few shelters will offer hotel vouchers (Friess, 1997). Lesbians may not be welcomed with open arms by heterosexual women at shelters (Ricks, Vaughan, & Dziegielewski, 2002). Group therapy may be helpful for victims because it reduces feelings of isolation and provides a safe place to work through their issues with empathic others. It may also be helpful for perpetrators, because of the same isolation issues, and it may also offer a place where the peer group can confront the batterer. The problem is that mixing homosexuals with heterosexuals in groups is not recommended (Margolies & Leeder, 1995), and it may be very difficult to generate an intact gay or lesbian group.

Couples therapy, mediation, conflict resolution, or any other approach that brings the two warring parties together is debatable from the standpoint of safety. Further, the abuser may heartily endorse this as a way of keeping the relationship going and shifting blame onto the abused partner (Ricks, Vaughan, & Dziegielewski, 2002). Setting aside the foregoing factors that differentiate homosexual from heterosexual battering relationships, the crisis worker still operates pretty much in the same manner of providing for immediate safety needs, obtaining support, and empowering their clients to leave the relationship (Peterman & Dixon, 2003; Ricks, Vaughan, & Dziegielewski, 2002).

Treating Batterers

Couples Counseling. Hamel (2014) proposes that same-sex psychoeducational, one-size-fits-all group formats are limited in reducing recidivism, and rigorous studies using cognitive-behavioral therapy prove superior to the Duluth model (the gold standard you'll soon read about) and that couples counseling is safe and effective. This approach flies in the face of the prevailing feminist view as blaming the victim as being partly culpable. However, McCollum and associates (2012) argue that it is becoming clear that all batterers are not the same and that same-sex-only group programs have very high dropout rates. To that end Stith, McCollum, and Rosen (2011) have developed a solution-focused brief domestic violence therapy program for couples. How this will turn out remains to be seen, but it is a noteworthy shift in how perspectives are changing in trying to crack the tough nut of domestic violence.

During the early 1980s, the Coalition **LO18** for Justice for Battered Women in San Francisco was instrumental in getting police to redefine how they handle domestic disputes and how the district attorney prosecutes domestic assault cases (Sonkin, Martin, & Walker, 1985, p. 25). Police do not mediate but arrest, and district attorneys do not dismiss but prosecute. In short, batterers need to realize that domestic violence is a punishable crime (Sonkin, Martin, & Walker, 1985, p. 41), and in more and more cities and states it is becoming exactly that.

Although arrest may deter battering while the perpetrator is in jail (Gondolf, 1984; Sherman & Berk, 1984), that same perpetrator will come back to his family, or at least be in close proximity or inevitably form a relationship with another woman. While many believe that "throwing the bum in jail" is justified because of the battering, jail will not have changed the batterer's attitudes and behavior in any way, and he will continue to be a threat (Bent-Goodley et al., 2011).

Many communities and most states have adopted some form of diversion program modeled along the lines of the program the Coalition for Justice for Battered Women in San Francisco and the Domestic Abuse Intervention Program intervention model developed in Duluth, Minnesota (the Duluth model). These are *intervention* models as opposed to *treatment* models. Note the distinction between *intervention* and *treatment*. As with many systemic crises, there are philosophical issues between grassroots activists who organized and lobbied for aggressive intervention with batterers and mental health professionals, who came after them, who focus on the underlying pathology of the batterer and seek to provide treatment to change the personality structures that cause the battering (Rosenbaum & Kunkel, 2009).

Whereas treatment of any psychological issues is generally considered private and confidential, the Duluth model is not concerned with confidentiality and in many ways, according to its critics, goes out of its way to publicize batterers and their issues, in clear violation of the confidentiality rules that all psychological treatment programs we know of abide by. Because it sees battering as a public matter, this stance has invoked the ire of many professionals, who see real ethical dilemmas in approaching treatment of batterers in that manner. They further see the model as based not so much on evidence-based research as on emotion and political pressure (Corvo, Dutton, & Chen, 2009; Dutton, 2007; Dutton & Corvo, 2006, 2007; Rosenbaum & Kunkle, 2009). Supporters of the model, in turn, point to the critics' own research biases and maintain there is psychological theory and criminal justice research that support the Duluth model (Gondolf, 2007). The data are indeed conflicting as to what, if any, good any one of these models does in stopping recidivism of batterers.

There is also wide divergence in the length of programs, which range from one meeting a week for 12 weeks up to a full year. There is also wide divergence in the education and training that facilitators must have. In a number of states, no college degree or professional licensure is required, although most states do mandate that some sort of training in domestic violence must be completed. Policies regarding absences and termination for conduct and absenteeism are also extremely variable. The same is true of fees. Many batterers are of lower socioeconomic status and cannot afford the programs, so most states provide for a sliding fee schedule based on income. However, most states do demand that batterers pay some fees so that value is attached to the service (Rosenbaum & Kunkel, 2009).

Intervention Models

These models are feminist based, have highly integrated coordination between a variety of agencies, provide support to survivors of IPV across a range of issues, and provide psychoeducational treatment to batterers. That treatment focuses primarily on power and control issues (Rosenbaum & Kunkle, 2009).

The Duluth model requires a tremendous amount of commitment and integration of community agencies, mental health facilities and institutions, police, and judiciary to provide services for battered women. In Duluth, more than 10 agencies, five distinct levels and types of government, and dozens of workers of those institutions will be involved. As you might well imagine, getting all these agencies and institutions working on the same page is equivalent to herding cats. Lindsay and Brady (2002) acknowledge and discuss some of these issues when such massive integration of services is undertaken. The treatment aspect of the model does have a cognitive-behavioral component to it. However, it also examines the historic separation of roles and power for men and women and seeks to knock down those stereotypes. The program's aim is to give batterers insight into their mistaken beliefs and goals based on these age-old stereotypes about marital roles and functions and to change their belief systems in regard to marriage, relationships, women, masculinity, and the use of aggression to solve problems (Aymer, 2008; Miller, 2010; Pence & McDonnell, 2000).

Most other models have a cognitive-behavioral basis that focuses on cognitive restructuring of batterers' irrational thinking (Rosenbaum & Kunkle, 2009). Models that emphasize batterer strengths rather than deficits are being tried (Lehmann & Simmons, 2009). Other models provide skill building through self-empowerment strategies. This model works off the notion that targeting self-empowerment can revise and regulate feelings of powerlessness and worthlessness, which are hypothesized as core values that lead to the abuse. In this model, then, abuse is seen as a problem not of the woman, but rather of the abuser's own feelings of inadequacy and failure to develop compassion for loved ones (Stosny, 1995).

From a therapeutic treatment viewpoint, cognitive-behavioral treatments are seen as the preferred mode of operation. Indeed, treatment professionals take umbrage at the notion that this is "anger management training" because they see the issues that batterers are attempting to overcome as far more complex than that. Thus, it will probably come as a surprise to you that most programs and many states prohibit "anger management" as a primary treatment because they see it as an excuse to rationalize a controlled behavior (Rosenbaum & Kunkel, 2009). The fact is that in many instances the Duluth model has been combined with cognitive-behavioral therapy for batterers, so there is a great deal of variance between programs that claim to follow the Duluth model (Bennett & Vincent, 2001; Healy, Smith, & O'Sullivan, 1998).

Hybrid Models

A variety of models have been operationalized in same-sex domestic violence treatment programs that range from mind–body bridging (Tollefson & Phillips, 2015), to *Violent No More* (Paymar, 2015), a book that uses stories to illustrate how batterers were able to stop their use of violent behavior and emotion-focused therapy for incarcerated offenders (Pascual-Leone et al., 2011). These are a few examples of a lot of different types of programs seeking to reduce battering.

In our own community of Memphis, an adjudicated batterer is given a thorough assessment and diagnostic interview after adjudication. Although specific treatment recommendations such as parent training, drug abuse treatment, and individual mental health counseling are generated for each person, the vast majority will be recommended for anger management. Certainly, most batterers, particularly those so adjudicated, do not willingly come to a treatment program, nor are they willing to admit that they have problems. People who enter counseling for abuse often manifest outright denial, minimization, or justification and projection of blame to escape owning their abusive behavior (Shupe, Stacey, & Hazlewood, 1987, pp. 26–28).

Denying batterer: I never touched her. Sure, I'd been drinking a little, and we had an argument. She must have fallen, because she was pretty drunk too! (*The complainant had three broken teeth, a fractured jaw, and two broken ribs, plus numerous contusions, cuts, and abrasions.*)

Minimizing batterer: Well, I might have pushed her when we were arguing at the top of the stairs, but I'd never hit her. (*The complainant had a broken nose, a bruised kidney, and two black eyes from the "push."*)

Projecting batterer: Listen, she ain't no rose. She gives as good as she gets. Besides, I got some rights, like dinner when I get home from work, instead of a drunk sittin' in front of the TV suckin' on a drink. She deserved a lesson! She always gets the kids to stick up for her. (*Both the woman and her two children were treated at an emergency room for contusions and lacerations from being whipped with a power cord.*)

Although individual counseling, partner counseling, and partner counseling in groups have been attempted (Shupe, Stacey, & Hazlewood, 1987, pp. 26–27; Stith et al., 2004; Tolman & Bennett, 1990), the prevalent mode of counseling for batterers is court-ordered group counseling. Generally, couples counseling is not recommended until the batterer has made a great deal of progress on anger management and other personality issues, and only if both parties truly wish to reconcile (Hamberger, 1994; Lawson, 2003). Groups provide opportunities for social learning and retraining that would be nearly impossible in individual or couple therapy (Adams & McCormick, 1982). The group also provides a support system for what are typically emotionally isolated individuals and enables these men and women to start to learn how to depend on others in times of stress.

Treatment Goals

Group treatment formats, however they are configured, have four major purposes: (1) ensure the safety of the victimized partner, (2) alter the batterer's attitudes toward violence, (3) increase the batterer's sense of personal responsibility and teach him about equity issues, and (4) help the batterer learn nonviolent alternatives to past behaviors (Edleson & Tolman, 1992; Mederos, 1999). Groups typically use either the Duluth model (Pence & Paymar, 1993), which operates with a power and control focus, or an anger management model, which seeks to understand and control anger (Hamby, 1998, pp. 223–225). There appears to be merit in both approaches.

To accomplish these goals, most groups use a combination of anger management, stress reduction, communication skills, and sex role resocialization components (Dutton, 1995; Gondolf, 1985; Hamby, 1998; Mederos, 1999). Therapeutically, most programs use some form of cognitive-behavioral approach that deals with batterers' irrational thinking and also provides techniques to restructure maladaptive cognitions, overreaction to violent urges, self-sabotage, setting oneself up for violence, and selective forgetting; offers assertiveness training and teaches problem solving; and handles premature "cures" (Dutton, 1995; Hamby, 1998; Hanson, 2002; Lawson, 2003; Mederos, 1999). Programs typically are psycho-educational, structured learning experiences with some time reserved for role play, discussion, and processing concepts and ideas (Edleson & Syers, 1990; Scales & Winter, 1991). Coleaders are generally used so that they can model together the types of behaviors the batterers need to learn, and any interactions between one leader and a member can be facilitated by the other group leader (Sonkin, Martin, & Walker, 1985, p. 98). Groups typically meet once a week for 2 hours and range from 8 to 32 sessions (Tolman & Bennett, 1990). Before a batterer is inducted into a group, an assessment and intake interview should be conducted to obtain a profile of the battering behavior, incidence of other psychological problems, and motivation to participate in counseling.

Assessment

The Conflict Tactics Scale (Straus, 1979) has been the only instrument used on any wide scale to measure intrafamilial conflict. The scale looks mainly at physical means used to resolve conflicts, does not adequately account for verbal abuse, and entirely ignores the emotional, social, sexual, and economic forms of abuse. It also does not look at power differential—one of the key ingredients in domestic violence (Poynter, 1989). It certainly was not meant to—nor does it—predict who will be violent or who, after being arrested or completing counseling, will recidivate.

One test that should always be given is an alcohol screening test such as the Substance Abuse Subtle Screening Inventory (Miller, 1983), with follow-up interview questions. Determining alcohol abuse is important for two reasons. First, numerous studies have shown *chronic* alcohol abuse to be a strong predictor of more violent behavior (Blount et al., 1994; Heyman, Jouriles, & O'Leary, 1995; Stuart et al., 2006; Tolman & Bennett, 1990). Second, any individual

who is under the influence of a mind-altering substance needs to get dried out first.

Probably the worst "bets" for success in anger management and those most likely to recidivate are those individuals who fall into personality disorder categories. Therefore, tests like the Millon Clinical Multiaxial Inventory (Millon, 1987) may be used to determine borderline, narcissistic, depressive, somatoform, antisocial, and other pathological types. If elevated scores on the Millon indicate psychopathology, these individuals may be served better in individual therapy that targets their pathology rather than in a generic anger management group (Hanson, 2002; Lawson, 2003; Mederos, 1999). Dutton (Dutton, 1994, 1995; Dutton & Starzomski, 1993, 1994) has extensively examined borderline personality disorder (BPD) as a unifying personality construct in domestic violence. Dutton's research seems to indicate that the individual who batters looks much more like a full-blown BPD than a normal individual who does not batter. His research presents a strong argument that there are at least some batterers whose major problem is intimacy anxiety and fear of abandonment, hallmarks of the borderline personality, as opposed to the more universal and feminist notion of domestic violence as being an attempt to reinforce male dominance and preserve a patriarchal order (Dutton, 1995, p. 138). This "either/or" view has much to say about how treatment for batterers should be conducted and has bred a great deal of controversy in regard to treatment approaches.

The Intake Interview

The worker should conduct a comprehensive intake interview to assess the batterer's psychological status and motivation and provide information on what may be expected from a counseling group (Sonkin, Martin, & Walker, 1985; Tolman & Bennett, 1990). First, the worker should assess lethality, for both suicidal and homicidal ideation and/or behavior. As paradoxical as it may seem, many batterers are so dependent on their partners that the thought of being without them is worse than death, so suicide and murder may seem viable and realistic options.

There are apparent relationships between lethality and a number of factors common in battering relationships, such as frequency of violent incidents, severity of injuries, threats to kill, suicide threats by the woman, length and incidence of the batterer's drug use, frequency of intoxication, and forced or threatened sexual acts (Sonkin, Martin, & Walker, 1985, p. 73). A fast assessment of the history of the violent relationship would seek details on the first, last, worst, and typical episode to provide a comprehensive profile of the kind, degree, and length of abuse. Assaults and violence on other family members, previous criminal activity, violence outside the home, increased social proximity of victim, attitudes toward violence, life stresses, general mental functioning, physical health, and physical and emotional isolation are important background information on the potential for future violent behavior. The more these indicators appear, the more likely the client is to engage in lethal behavior (Sonkin, Martin, & Walker, 1985, pp. 75–83).

It should be remembered that these men and women are in crisis, and appropriate measures should be taken to ensure everyone's safety. Bodnarchuk and associates (1995) estimate that, based on the National Family Violence Surveys, their domestic violence clients fell into the most dangerous 1% of the U.S. population. During intake interviews, such people should be given clear messages about expectations inside and outside the group and what the consequences of inappropriate behavior will be. Finally, there is evidence that clients who are apprised of the procedures, purpose, and goals of the group are less likely to drop out and less likely to recidivate (Tolman & Bennett, 1990).

Motivation

Motivation depends on a number of variables. Men who are younger, are less educated, have lower incomes, were abused as children, and are minorities drop out at a significantly higher rate (Tolman & Bennett, 1990) than do those who are older, have no arrest record, are better educated, are employed, have more children, and witnessed abuse but were not abused themselves as children (Demaris, 1989; Grusznski & Carrillo, 1988). Tolman and Bennett (1990) report that structured groups tend to be more effective, and it appears from the Memphis Family Trouble Center's low attrition rate (10%) that the threat of having probation revoked and spending up to a year in jail is a strong external motivator for obtaining the points necessary to complete the program (Winter, 1991).

A Typical 24-Session Domestic Violence Reduction Group

The following profiles the highlights of **LO19** a typical 24-session group counseling format for batterers. The content of the course is taken from the Memphis Police Department's Family Trouble Center (FTC) anger management program. The

counselor dialogue is abstracted from Betty Winter (1991), director of the program and facilitator of numerous anger management groups.

It would be an error to think that only men go through treatment for perpetrating domestic violence. Although better than 90% of those who go through the FTC program are men, the percentage of women adjudicated for anger management is increasing. Therefore the generic terms *clients*, *members*, and *participants* will be used in describing the FTC anger management program because both genders are represented.

Starting the Group. A great deal of anger is ventilated over being arrested and adjudicated to the program. The batterers are mad and hostile about being there. The crisis worker starts the group by sitting in the middle of it and letting the group interview her. She responds to any professional and personal questions she deems appropriate.

CW: (*after giving qualifications*) One of my major credentials is that I get angry a lot, but I've never been arrested for it. Now that I've given you my credentials, I'd like you to give me your credentials, the ones that got you here. I'd like you all to pair off, and I'd like for each pair to share with one another what caused you to get here. Then I'd like each pair to report back to the group.

By putting herself at risk with this group and letting them interview her, the crisis worker turns the tables on these angry clients. It is very difficult for these "macho" clients not to own up to what brought them here when a woman can face up to their angry and caustic interrogation of her and her credentials. The rules of attendance and conduct are reviewed, and positive and negative consequences of appropriate and inappropriate behavior are explained. For many of these individuals, it will be the first structure they have experienced since high school, so they will need to know very clearly what is expected of them. The major purpose of this counseling is corrective and remedial. It is counseling within the criminal justice system. As a result, initially trust is not high, and in these early sessions the therapist meets the issue head on.

CW: I don't expect you to share everything in this group. Take some time to see how safe you feel in here. Although what you say will be held in confidence within the bounds of the legal and ethical standards I've talked about, you're undoubtedly feeling pretty victimized by the system right now. Nobody will force you to say anything you don't want to.

Paradoxically, the admonition to not trust probably does much to establish trust and breaks down some barriers and paranoia about the group.

Making Choices. The group is given an explanation of what taking an anger time-out is and is given a homework assignment of taking practice time-outs at home. Finally, the concept of choices is introduced.

CW: You'll think this is crazy, but you did have a choice in coming here. If you don't like what we're about, you can leave. (*Gets up, walks to the door, and opens it.*) Of course, you will have chosen to violate your probation terms and will probably go to jail.

Batterer: That's no damn choice.

CW: Granted, it's not a good choice, but it is a choice, just like what got you here. Battering was a bad choice, but it was one you made. During the course of the time we're here, we'll be looking at a lot of those choices you make.

Most of the clients do not realize that when they do something, they are making choices. Furthermore, they don't realize the variety of choices open to them. The concept of decision making and choosing wisely will be woven throughout the 24 sessions.

Support and Confrontation. Another key component of the group is instituted in these first sessions: dyadic interaction—"that pairing crap," as participants call it. Clients are immediately paired off and start working with one another in pairs. Pairing off starts to generate closeness and bonding in the group. It also conveys early on that there is interest in hearing their story.

Open-ended questions and reflective responses alone are not conducive to facilitating the start-up phase of a group of hostile and anxious batterers. Therefore, a combination of both open-ended and closed-ended questions and supportive and confrontive statements is needed to break through defense systems, reflect threatening feelings, and reframe irrational thinking (Sonkin, Martin, & Walker, 1985, pp. 64–65).

CW: (*indirectly confrontive*) How did you come to be here?

Batterer: I sorta hit my wife.

CW: (*directly confronting the minimization with a semiopen question*) I don't understand "sorta"! What do you mean?

Batterer: (*projecting and blaming*) I mean she made me mad. She was running her mouth, so I had to hit her.

CW: (*confronting all-or-none thinking*) You say "had to" as if there were no options other than to smack her.

Batterer: Not really—she was really being a bitch!

CW: (*proposing consequences and obtaining facts*) So your choice for stopping her bitching was breaking her jaw. That choice also got you arrested. What happened?

Batterer: She swore out a warrant, and I got sent to jail.

CW: (*confrontive closed question*) Had you ever been in jail before?

Batterer: Lord no!

CW: (*empathically reflecting feeling*) I'm betting that was a scary experience.

Batterer: You better believe it. There were some bad dudes in there. I didn't know if I was gonna get out of there in one piece.

CW: (*reflecting feeling and exploring affect*) So you were feeling pretty alone and helpless. I'm wondering how you're feeling right now?

Batterer: Madder than hell that I got to be here.

CW: (*closed question that seeks to elicit defensive responding*) Do you understand why you're here?

Batterer: (*projecting*) 'Cause she swore out a warrant on me.

CW: (*confronting projection by making client own behavior*) No! You are here because you put your wife in the hospital by beating her. That's criminal assault. The judge gave you a choice, and you are still free to exercise it. You may come here to 24 group sessions for people who have battered. You have the opportunity to learn some things here that may help you with future relationships and that may also keep you out of harm's way in the future. Or you may walk out of here right now.

Batterer: That's not much of a choice.

CW: (*confronting batterer with consequences of his behavior*) Maybe not, but it's more of a choice than you gave your partner.

The responses are typical of a batterer's way of defending himself with denial, externalization of blame, and black-and-white kinds of statements that give little consideration to behavioral options and long-term consequences of behavior. The crisis worker gently but firmly wades into the client's defense system while at the same time attempting to establish rapport. This is not an easy job.

Managing Stress. The time-out assignment is discussed. Participants start looking for physical anger cues, and are asked to write down the signs as warning signals and learn to use those cues to time themselves out of an escalating dialogue that has the potential to turn violent. Basic stress management skills and relaxation techniques are taught and practiced. The worker gives a homework assignment that combines recognizing physical cues of anger with the use of relaxation techniques.

The prevailing pragmatic philosophy of the FTC program is that it is extremely difficult if not impossible to change ideology. Rather, the notion is that the batterer's sex role expectations may differ from his or her partner's and that he or she can be taught how to negotiate those differences. That notion is much more palatable and makes much more sense within clients' social and work environment than attempting to reindoctrinate them into a more feminist view of role expectations.

Understanding the Cycle of Violence. The idea is to make batterers aware of Walker's (1979) cycle and its commonality to all relationships, both at home and in the workplace, and to help them gain some dynamic insight into their own behavior and that of their partners as they go around in this destructive cycle. Clients are apprised of the difficulty of getting out of the cycle because of how long it has been going on and its familiarity. Anger diaries are started. Anger diaries help to identify instigators of anger and the physical and cognitive responses to it. They also help batterers start to identify feelings that support anger, such as guilt, shame, and depression. The diaries start to condition responsibility, because the person must constantly attend to diaries as he or she monitors anger.

Costs. Few batterers have stopped to think of the costs. Costs vary, but it is not uncommon for a group to average a minimum of $10,000 per person in financing his or her anger.

CW: Add up all the money you've spent on lawyers, work time lost, furniture broken, hospital bills, bail, fines, motel rooms, not to mention divorce proceedings and alimony as a direct or indirect result of violence. What could it have bought you? Wouldn't it be great to never have to spend another dime on your anger? You see, learning to control your anger will make you money. How many of you would be against that?

Time is also spent on the emotional cost to victims. These factors paradoxically start to describe some of the background of batterers because they have also become victims, albeit of their own behavior. Indeed, once they can start to see themselves as victims, they gain insight into how their victims feel. This is the start of empathic understanding for these clients.

CW: Add up all the emotional costs: the guilty, angry, hurt, depressed, dependent, hopeless, helpless feelings. Wouldn't it be great to never have another lousy feeling like that? How does that fit with your partner's notions of being your victim? Is there any difference between how your partner may feel about you after a beating and how you feel about the court system?

Shoulds, Oughts, and Musturbatory Thinking. Members are asked to write down three bad choices and three good choices they have made in their relationships. Anger diaries are used to help the batterers identify the emotional toll that their choice of anger and violence takes on them. The leader introduces the topics of irrational thinking and the maladaptive behavior resulting from it. Cognitive-behavioral techniques from Albert Ellis's (1990) *Anger: How to Live With It and Without It* are illustrated. Specific emphasis is placed on absolutist thinking and *should, must,* and *ought* statements. Discussion focuses on how these statements get constructed, what environmental cues set up "*must*urbatory" thinking ("I must have my self-gratification or it will be absolutely intolerable"), and how irrational, self-defeating thoughts and subsequent maladaptive behavior are tied together.

Violence and Families of Origin. A violence and abuse assessment is made of the family of origin. Leaders ask members to respond to such questions as "Did your father hit your mother, or vice versa?" "How were disagreements handled?" "How did you feel about your parents?" "How were you disciplined as a child?" "How do all those events that you learned from early childhood carry over into your present family?" "How do you feel about that?" "How do those irrational beliefs we talked about earlier in the session relate to the behavior that you saw and learned as a child?" Members are given didactic instruction on how transgenerational violence occurs.

Processing the following discussion questions generally results in a shocking and nasty insight, because the very thing the batterers hated most about their own parents they may now be perpetrating on their children. This will be the first time that many of the batterers have ever talked about their childhood experiences with domestic violence, and it is usually a very emotional experience.

CW: What was your feeling as a child in regard to the abuse you saw? How do you suppose your kids are affected by your violent behavior? Do they feel any different from the way you did? Guess at their feelings and what they might be thinking about you and why they might feel and think that way.

The homework assignment is to start changing members' ways of responding to stressful situations by (1) watching out for environmental cues that start *mus*turbatory thinking and (2) using cooler cognitions, such as "It'd be nice, convenient, if XYZ happened, but it doesn't *have* to happen."

Feelings. Participants are asked to list several positive and negative feelings they have. Usually most of them will have a great deal of difficulty with this task, because they have never had to identify any feelings they have. Feelings generally get lumped into two categories, angry and happy. A lecture is given on how males, in particular, are taught at a very early age to "stuff" their feelings and not acknowledge them as real. The anger diaries are used to expand their ability to label and identify the many feelings that support anger.

Outcomes from denying feelings are discussed. Examples are given from Stoop and Arterburn's (1991) *The Angry Man: "Why Does He Act That Way?"* This session is very difficult, because members will be asked to share feelings—a very threatening experience for most of them. Leader statements such as the following are designed to minimize the threat.

CW: Although there are risks when you tell someone how you feel because you become vulnerable, you also become a lot more real. You become much more lovable and find it easier to love when you tell someone how you feel. You need to be prepared for them to do the same and understand that there is the possibility of feeling some pain and hurt from what is said. You don't tell someone your feelings just to get their sympathy. You share your feelings with significant others as a way of

taking care of yourself, so you don't have to stuff feelings anymore until they finally boil over and get you in trouble or hurt you.

Outcomes may be very dramatic as clients start to talk about their feelings, relive their experiences as children, and grapple with feelings of guilt, helplessness, dependency, and insecurity that they have had since childhood. It is not uncommon for some highly charged emotional catharsis to occur at this point and, as these feelings emerge, for some strong bonds to form as clients start, for the first time, to share deeply but closely held feelings with another person.

Power and Control. The attempt to convey verbally both positive and negative feelings is discussed and leads into issues of power and control. Power and control are the focus of the session, discussed in relation to faulty belief systems. The stereotypical concept of power in batterers' issues develops out of a mistaken concept of independence: "I've got it, so you don't!" A new way of looking at power is interdependence: "The two of us together are more powerful than any one person!" Questions are posed about how they can form a team with their partner to reduce those powerless feelings. It is interesting that many of these clients who are physically strong may feel extremely powerless and frustrated when they are dealing verbally with others and when they are being "outtalked" in a relationship and may regress to their only way of regaining power and control—violence.

CW: When you allow someone else to push your button, who is in control? How do you use anger as a control tool? Abuse is a last-ditch effort to gain control back in a relationship. Why is that so? Do you believe that you try to get power and control only when you feel you don't have any? If power and control are the bottom line, do abuse, anger, and battering get the job done for you? If they really do get the job done, then why do you still have to rely on them?

Assertion. Closely allied with different ways of obtaining power and control are the concepts of aggressiveness and assertiveness. Because of their inability to use words in powerful ways, most of the participants have difficulty making clear assertions about what their wants and needs are. Furthermore, they have an overriding fear that they will be rejected if they ask for something, and their insecurity does not handle rejection well at all. As a result, they use aggression to meet their needs. The group is taught how to construct assertion statements and given an assignment of using them at home.

The most difficult part of an assertion statement for the group is the "I" or owning part. On the board, the leader puts up "I" or assertion statements and "you" or aggression statements so members know what they sound like, how they differ, and what can happen when each is used. Each member is asked to formulate a problem in terms of "I" and "you" statements and practice with a partner. Using a describe, express, specify, and consequences script (Bower & Bower, 1976), members are asked to identify what behaviors in others bother them, to express how those behaviors make them feel, to specify what new behaviors they want, and to be able to positively reinforce others if those behaviors happen. Careful construction of these clear, precise, and owned assertive statements is practiced through role plays.

Because jealousy is common to most of the stories that have brought members here, time is devoted to members' retelling their original story using the skills they have learned in their first 16 sessions. As these stories are reprocessed, other feelings undergirding the jealousy begin to surface. Hurt, betrayal, insecurity, lack of trust, and dependency are all threatening feelings that are denied and replaced by jealousy, which allows batterers to place blame on their partners for "transgressions," thus providing a face-saving way of not having to deal with their own problems.

Batterer: I hate to admit it, but all that stuff makes sense. Still and all, I don't believe I can trust her.

CW: Maybe you know she can't trust you, so you don't trust her. Could you use some of those "I" statements and discuss it with her, and no matter what she said, not use "you" statements?

The homework is to name a time in their lives when jealousy turned to violence. The members are also asked to mentally substitute a new feeling every time they start to feel jealous and to report back on their experience.

Alcohol and Drug Effects. Because alcohol and drugs play a predominant role in the vast majority of battering incidents, members are educated about how these issues apply to battering—specifically, that alcoholism and drug abuse are not necessarily the cause of battering but release inhibitions enough that batterers can give themselves permission to become violent. Results of the Substance Abuse Subtle Screening

Inventory (Miller, 1983) are given to each participant. Participants are shown how alcohol or drugs can be a trigger for violent behavior and an excuse for making violent behavior acceptable.

Sex. Sex is an overriding concern because of all the myths that surround it. Much of the need of the batterer to feel superior, confident, and capable is tied to sex and, particularly for men, their concept of manhood. Many times, particularly with young female leaders, members will say things and use language designed to shock and embarrass the leaders. Although X-rated language just for the sake of X-rated language is not tolerated, some leeway is given for the street vernacular that is commonly used. The ability of group leaders, particularly young women, to weather the language goes a long way toward establishing their credentials with these men.

Batterer: So she wouldn't give me a blow job, so I smacked her. That's part of earning her keep, to blow my pipes, man!

CW: (*young female graduate student*) So forcing oral sex on her keeps you in control. I wonder if the way you said that isn't designed to shock and embarrass me and kinda control me through verbal sex like you control her physically through sex.

Batterer: Hey, I thought we was supposed to be talking about the real stuff in here.

CW: (*very calmly, with eyes leveled at the batterer, avoiding the taunt*) I'm wondering how you'd like it if Harold (*240-pound ironworker in the group*) were to request oral sex of you, and if you didn't comply, start pounding on you, particularly in your groin. Do you start to get some of the feelings your partner would get? (*The group members nod their heads in agreement.*) I wonder if you can respond to that?

The many myths that hold men up to impossible Hollywood "stud" or women to "love goddess" standards are discussed and debunked. For many of the clients, this will be the first valid information they have ever received about sexual behavior. They will typically experience relief after being told that no man or woman could live up to some of the performance expectations they have self-propagandized for themselves. Homework assignments focus on irrational and negative thoughts clients generate for themselves in their sexual relations. They are asked to watch for and write down some of their unrealistic expectations of themselves. They are also asked to try using assertion statements when asking for sex. Coming to understand that making requests for sex ("I'd like to make love to you") rather than demanding sex ("You get in here and do it") may not only get them sex, but better sex, is a revelation. Finally, the leader asks each member to pick one of the subjects already covered in the group and be prepared to teach a review on it next session.

Summing Up. Amazingly, many of these groups bond. Members express that this is the first time in their lives they have been able to openly express feelings and feel they have been listened to by someone. Participants may actually form friendships as a result of the group.

CW: If you had to tell the judge anything about this program, what would it be? What did you like best and least? What would you like to see changed? What techniques seemed to work for you, and what didn't?

Members then discuss how they are putting their comprehensive anger management plans into action. They also indicate the strengths they now see in themselves and positively reinforce one another for their efforts. Depending on how cohesive the group has become, it is not uncommon for the clients to bring food, exchange phone numbers, and have a graduation party for one another at the last session.

Program Success

Do battering programs work? The results are equivocal. Overall, batterers report that such programs help them gain control of their anger, enable them to communicate better with their partners, and reduce their violence. Shupe, Stacey, and Hazlewood (1987) found that battered women in approximately 7 out of 10 cases reported that physical and sexual violence stopped after their partners went through an anger management program. When violence did recur after the men graduated from these programs, it was almost always remarkably reduced. Relationships were also improved, and many women who had not attended indicated that they had picked up pointers that their partners brought home from the sessions (pp. 113–117). The following have all been found in a variety of studies involving battering groups with different cultural, racial, and socioeconomic backgrounds: increases in self-esteem (Kriner & Waldron, 1988) and assertiveness (Douglas & Perrin, 1987); decreases in depression and anger (Hamberger &

Hastings, 1986), in jealousy and negative attitudes toward women (Saunders & Hanusa, 1986), and in overall psychological symptoms (Hawkins & Beauvais, 1985); reduction in both self-reported and corroborated physical and psychological abuse on postcounseling follow-up (Edleson & Syers, 1990; Poynter, 1989); and more cohesive, expressive, and less conflict-ridden family life (Poynter, 1989).

Other researchers have found little evidence to indicate that rates of violence by perpetrators who obtain and complete treatment are very different from those who do not (Rosenfeld, 1992; Tolman & Bennett, 1990). More recent meta-analyses of batterer prevention programs have indicated less than satisfactory results (Babcock, Green, & Robie, 2004; Stover, Meadows, & Kaufman, 2009). Babcock and associates conducted a comprehensive meta-analysis of battering programs and found small effect size in overall success for programs. They also found little difference between programs that used the Duluth model and those that used CBT programs. What these results mean is that the programs appear to have little impact on recidivism. Stover and her associates found that the recidivism rate for both perpetrator- and partner-focused treatments was about 30% after 6 months.

However, there are some important footnotes to these sobering statistics. There are probably as many different programs and different styles of intervention as there are programs. Also, the expertise of individuals providing the treatment may vary a great deal. A critical prerequisite for batterers' not recidivating is the imposition of severe consequences for not completing the program or for battering again. Such consequences are not always enforced. Tracking batterers is difficult. Many of these people are very transient, moving from jurisdiction to jurisdiction, and there is no good way to determine if they have recidivated when they are halfway across the country. Frankly, because of the severity of their pathology, some people do not or cannot profit from group programs.

It appears that close follow-up supervision of batterers makes a large difference in recidivism (Barber & Wright, 2010), so it may be that besides treatment, close follow-up may be a critical variable either from the standpoint of feeling supported or threat of punishment. Where and to whom treatment is rendered also appears to make a difference. Smith (2003) reported that the Duluth model and the Military Family Advocacy Program LEAD model were both effective in reducing domestic violence, with only a 5% recidivism rate, in the U.S. Marine Corps. The fact that noncompletion of such a program in the Marine Corps could ruin one's career may be a potent consequence in ensuring completion. Sartin (2005) found differential effects by clustering batterer types. Not surprisingly, family-only batterers were better program completers than antisocial and borderline cluster types. He also found that being employed was the only significant demographic variable predicting program completion. So, keeping a job by not going to jail may be an important motivator.

Another issue is motivation to change. Walker and her associates (2010) developed the Perceived Consequences of Domestic Violence Questionnaire to assess the consequences of intimate partner violence as perceived as the perpetrator. They found that the scale would significantly predict motivation to change and treatment-seeking behavior. Thus, it may be that screening instruments that separate out more pathological types may produce better results in terms of program completion and reduced recidivism. Research indicates that batterers must attend at least 75% of the sessions in anger management groups to have a chance of avoiding recidivism (Chen et al., 1989). What is clear is that arrest alone will not change much of anything in a domestic violence situation without concomitant treatment for the batterer (Gelles, 1993; Hirschel, Hutchison, & Dean, 1992).

Although most clients come to battering programs angry and hostile because they are pressured or required to be there, the majority report that they learn from and even come to enjoy the camaraderie of the group (Scales & Winter, 1991). Whether the programs truly change their participants or whether they work in other ways, as graphically described in the following excerpt, clients who complete a battering program are not reported to the police nearly as often as those who have nothing happen to them.

Batterer: Man, I ain't never gonna beat up on a woman again. Nothing will ever make me go through this crap twice! (Shupe, Stacey, & Hazlewood, 1987, p. 103)

Although research indicates that witnessing battering as a child is a primary modeling factor for both the abused and the abuser, as innocuous an event as one's favorite professional football team winning a game (White, Katz, & Scarborough, 1992) or watching World Wrestling Entertainment (Butryn, 2003) may have an impact on battering. Carden (1994) states that "Seventeen years after the founding of the first program designed to eliminate wife abuse by working with the wife abuser, we have only the most primitive notions about what works, why and how it works, or even whether in the long run, it does work" (p. 573). Sadly, after another 17 years and more, we are still only a little further along in our understanding and prevention of domestic violence.

SUMMARY

Battering has deep roots in the psychological, sociological, and cultural makeup of the United States and many other countries that go back to the beginnings of their patriarchal systems. Battering is pervasive through all socioeconomic levels of society and knows no ethnic, racial, or religious boundaries. Same-sex relationships are also not immune from domestic violence. Dynamically, battering may be seen as having much to do with the concept of power. A number of stressors that insinuate themselves into a relationship can escalate relational problems to violence.

A variety of theories have been proposed to explain why battering occurs. However, it is still unclear what propels people into battering relations, why people batter, and what will keep them from battering again.

Domestic violence is sequential, developmental, and dynamic. The situation of the battered client is unlike that of many others in crisis in that it is almost always transcrisis in nature; that is, it is cyclic, reaching many peak levels over extended periods of time. For a variety of reasons, it is the rare person who leaves a violent relationship for good after the first battering. Continued and increased violence over a period of years is the typical pattern of battering relationships.

In the last decade, crisis lines, shelters, and programs for battered women and their children have grown exponentially across the United States. Courts and law enforcement agencies have become much more proactive in protecting the rights of these women. However, the number of battered women still far exceeds the capacity of human services to deal with them comprehensively and effectively. One of the most frustrating components of intervention with clients who are victims of domestic violence is their seeming inability to extract themselves from the terrible situations they face.

Providing counseling in such trying circumstances calls for a great deal of empathic understanding. The worker's job is to help keep the client as safe as possible, provide options, and, working patiently with the victim, help her or him explore alternatives and choose a plan of action. Recently, the focus on domestic violence has shifted to include comprehensive and integrated intervention and treatment programs that involve social services agencies, law enforcement, and the judicial system. IBPs operate throughout the country. Typically sent to such groups by court order, batterers learn to understand the factors that lead them to violence, learn to recognize and communicate their feelings, and learn to avoid or stop confrontations that lead them to act out their feelings in violent ways. If you are being battered and don't know what to do, and there don't seem to be resources in your community, call the National Domestic Violence Hotline at 1-800-799-SAFE or 1-800-787-3224 (TTY). If you are suffering from dating abuse, call the Helpline at 1-866-331-9474 or 1-866-331-8453 (TTY). If someone is stalking you, call 1-800-394-2255 or 1-800-211-7996 (TTY).

Visit CengageBrain.com for a variety of study tools and useful resources such as video examples, case studies, interactive exercises, flashcards, and quizzes.

Family Crisis Intervention

11

Rick A. Meyer
University of Texas, El Paso

Richard K. James
University of Memphis

LEARNING OBJECTIVES

After studying this chapter, you should be able to:

1. Define crisis as it applies to families.
2. Define transcrisis as it applies to families.
3. Describe areas of research that have focused on family crisis intervention.
4. Summarize different models of crisis intervention with families.
5. Categorize types of crises families experience.
6. Understand the dynamics in a family crisis.
7. Explain changes in family dynamics resulting from crises.
8. Apply the hybrid/task model for crisis intervention with families.
9. Use the stage model for family recovery in crisis intervention.

Introduction

Everyone probably knows a family that seems to be in a constant state of chaos. For these families as soon as one chaotic situation is rectified or averted, another pops up to take its place. A family member loses his or her job, another family member is diagnosed with a chronic medical condition, and that is followed by someone causing a car accident. Topping it all off, another family member is arrested for some alleged illegal activity, and the family continues to spiral out of control. One frenzied situation after another produces an unremitting sense of pandemonium; and in these families a dull moment never happens. You very likely shake your head, wondering what is needed to get their collective act together. The thought crosses your mind that a reality television series or daytime soap opera could feature this family.

A few families are like this, but the vast majority are not. Most families live in a stable, predictable manner, following the same routine day in and day out. However, even for stable families, crises are a fact of life. No family is immune (Hoff, Hallisey, & Hoff, 2009; Rolland, 2012). All families bump or maybe crash into something that taxes them and disrupts routines. Some crises come suddenly and unexpectedly, disrupting day-to-day life. Other crises can be the result of fatigue that develops from a series of events that have worn down a family's resilience (Golan, 1987; Walsh, 2012a). When this occurs, the usual way of coping no longer works and families scramble simply to survive. Still other crises are insidious, creeping up on families, and suddenly they find themselves besieged with

decisions they are not prepared to make. These families may not even realize they are in crisis until things start crumbling around them. Even if your practice is exclusively with individuals, individual crises always entangle family members (Rosenfeld, Caye, Ayalon, & Lahad, 2005; Walsh, 2012a). In fact, understanding the effect of a crisis from a family perspective may just be the way to ease the pressure and facilitate the ability to restore an individual's coping mechanisms. Using an intervention model designed for family crisis situations is critical (Walsh, 2012a). Just as personal theories and intervention models fall short in individual crisis intervention, family therapy models also may not be effective in these situations.

Not everyone who works in the field of crisis intervention is a professional counselor, social worker, psychiatric nurse, or psychologist. Other professional service providers also are called on to offer support for people in crisis. Many times the determination of who is on the front lines handling crisis situations depends on the setting. On the streets, Crisis Intervention Team police officers are called on a daily basis to help people in crisis. They handle a wide range of situations from someone getting ready to commit suicide to people who may need temporary support after an accident. Another group of professionals called upon to provide crisis intervention services are chaplains and pastoral counselors. These individuals as well as other faith-based organizations are often called on to provide and coordinate the crisis intervention process for families who need support as they wind their way through the complexities of a crisis (Phillips & Jenkins, 2010; Walsh, 2012b). The Association for Clinical Pastoral Education trains ministers as chaplains for work in hospital settings. Chaplains are often the first person to meet families of individuals who are in need of emergency medical care. Through training, chaplains learn how to help families cope with a medical crisis by listening to and supporting families and patients while hospitalized. The American Association of Pastoral Counselors (AAPC) is like most professional organizations that have training standards, a code of ethics, and guidelines for membership. The organization is nonsectarian with members coming from all faiths and educational backgrounds. Members of AAPC include not only ministers but also medical doctors, psychologists, social workers, professional counselors, and family therapists, with most being licensed as mental health service providers in their respective states.

In this chapter you will meet Chaplain Hamill and a pastoral counselor named Paul Johnson. Together these two professionals work together to support the Taylor family as they adjust to a crisis involving the Taylor's youngest daughter, Dianne. Dianne was severely injured in an automobile accident while on her way home from school and had to be rushed to the hospital. In the first few hours and days following the accident the Taylors must make decisions about surgeries and treatment that have the potential to speed up the recovery or possibly result in Dianne never being able to walk again. Chaplain Hamill will help the Taylors navigate a series of decisions regarding Dianne's condition as well as sort through the initial changes to their family caused by the crisis. In these first few days and weeks, the Taylor's faith is challenged as they struggle to survive. After being discharged from the hospital to start rehabilitation, the Taylors discover the crisis is not over. Over the next several months the Taylor family will need to make many more decisions that have both short- and long-term effects on their family life as Dianne goes through rehabilitation. During Dianne's recovery the family's ability to function will be tested as they strive to maintain some semblance of family life and realize they must battle with anxieties about their spirituality. During this time the Taylors talk with Mr. Paul Johnson, a pastoral counselor. Mr. Johnson works with the Taylors to help them cope with the new reality of their lives and find the support they so desperately need. As you will see, crises in families have the potential to not only bring out the best but also the worst in family life as the status quo is challenged and changed.

This chapter begins by presenting information that forms the foundation for working with families in crises. We begin by defining family crisis and transcrisis. The next section provides historical context for family crisis intervention by summarizing research on family crisis followed by a discussion of various models for understanding families in distress. The models discussed in this section trace the development of family crisis intervention since World War II. As you will see, the models have evolved over time and now emphasize resiliency. The next section discusses the types of crises families encounter followed by an introduction of the Taylor family. The remainder of the chapter uses the Taylor family to illustrate "hands on" practical information for helping families in crisis.

Definition of Family Crisis

The effect of crises on families is mentioned **LO1** in many chapters in this book. Chapter 18 (online) on addictions talks about "family rules and addictions" and "children in alcoholic families." Chapter 10 on partner violence obviously involves a family crisis. Chapter 18, Chemical Dependency: The Crisis of Addiction (online), Chapter 9, Sexual Assault, Chapter 10, Partner Violence, Chapter 12, Personal Loss: Bereavement and Grief, and Chapter 17, Disaster Response, each discuss family issues related to those crises. In each of these chapters, the focus is on understanding and helping the individual having the crisis. The chapter on partner violence focuses on Juanita and helping her. The crisis intervention with Heather in the chapter on sexual assault addresses her working through feelings about being assaulted by her stepfather. While the Benefield family are the targeted characters in the disaster chapter, the focus is still on how each one of those members copes with the trauma they have been through rather than looking at the total family system as they struggle to regain predisaster homeostasis. Yet, all of these crises affecting individuals have the capacity to significantly change the family system. Understanding the effect of crises on families begins by defining a family crisis.

Chapter 1 introduced our definition for a crisis as individuals being overwhelmed and unable to marshal the resources needed to at that moment to attend to what has happened. Included in the discussion was a brief description of systemic crisis that applies to families, organizations, and communities. That discussion is an excellent foundation for shaping a definition of family crises. However, coming up with a definitive definition of a family crisis is like trying to grasp a handful of mud. The more you squeeze the mud, the more it slips through your fingers. You might ask why a definition for family crisis is so slippery. First, the different starting points and intensity levels for a family crisis make it difficult to pin down an all-encompassing, perfect definition. No matter the starting and ending points, something always seems to be missed. Second, attempting to understand family crises from the reactions of individual family member's reactions is an exercise in futility (Ectherling, Presbury, & McKee, 2005). A systems understanding is needed because the "whole is greater than the sum of the parts." Understanding individual reactions is essential, but when working with families a broader more comprehensive view is needed in order to be effective.

As suggested in Chapter 1, some family crises start with one family member experiencing a personal crisis that ripples through the family causing a larger crisis (Walsh, 2012a). These crises leach into the family, pulling in all members one at a time. An individual crisis generally takes the path of least resistance in families, seeping at the most vulnerable places. Take, for example, the crisis of a family member losing a job. While only one family member lost a job, the crisis has the potential to affect the family in many ways such as changing spending patterns, causing others to get jobs to make ends meet, or disrupting relationships in the family. Other family crises begin outside the family and come without warning, affecting family members simultaneously, such as the sudden accidental death in the family (Hoff, Hallisey, & Hoff, 2009). This type of crisis hit the family all at once. Like a head-on collision, all family members feel the brunt of the crisis instantaneously. In general, natural and technological disasters fall into this category and are a major cause of family

crises causing relocations, injuries, major financial issues, and so on (Everstine & Everstine, 2006).

The intensity with which a family experiences crises must also be considered. For some family members the crisis might be quite intense while for others the situation might be a minor disruption (Myer & Moore, 2006). Members of a family in which someone has sustained a debilitating injury causing extended rehabilitation and physical therapy might experience different levels of intensity. Some members of the family might have their entire schedule disrupted taking care of the person, taking them to appointments, and caring for them in the home. Others in the family might only experience minor inconveniences, having to alter their lives occasionally to help and support the injured person. Taking this a step further, a complicating factor for family crisis is when some members of a family believe a crisis is occurring and other family members do not even acknowledge a crisis exists (Al, Stams, van der Laan, & Asscher, 2011). When family members are not on the same page with respect to the crisis, intensity is difficult to gauge. Many times this situation involves making a decision of some kind such as placing an older family member in a nursing home or other similar care facility. Some family members may get caught up struggling with ways to address the crisis, while others may ignore or discount there is even a problem. The latter simply want to make a decision and move on. Working with these families calls for crisis workers to use the patience of Job to help family members find a common ground in order to address the crisis.

We found several definitions that shed light on just exactly what a family crisis is. These definitions are like a diamond with many facets. Each facet offers a different perspective on family crises.

1. Family crisis occurs when a disaster or trauma damages the bonds that connect people and destroys the basic tissues of social life and the prevailing sense of community ("Rosenfeld et al., 2005"?)

2. A crisis results when a stress comes to bear upon the system and requires change outside the systems' usual repertoire causing nonspecific changes in the system (Pittman, 1987).

3. A crisis results from families feeling dismemberment (loss of family member), accession (unexpected addition of a member), demoralization (loss of morale and family unit), or a combination of the three (Hill, 1965).

4. A crisis occurs depending on how a family defines an event that disrupts the social networks of a family changing its configuration (Hoff, Hallisey, & Hoff, 2009).

5. A crisis takes place when traumatic events wreck a family's homeostatic balance and render the system nonfunctional (Everstine & Everstine, 2006).

6. A crisis is an unexpected, negative event that does not allow the family to continue functioning in their usual manner; further most families are unprepared for the crisis and find addressing such circumstances both challenging and stressful (Webb & Dickson, 2012).

Just as with the definitions for individuals in crisis, clearly different perspectives are used to define family crisis. These definitions focus on various aspects including structural changes in relationships, lack or deactivation of coping mechanisms, a sense of loss within the family, family communication, inability to function in the usual manner, and balance within the system. Integrating components of the definitions above with the one in Chapter 1 for individual crisis shapes our characterization for family crisis. Our definition of a **family crisis** is: *A crisis occurs when perceptions or experiencing of an event comes to bear on the family as a whole, testing the family's structural integrity, because the usual repertoire of problem-solving skills and communication styles are not adequate or have been exhausted. Unless relief is obtained the crisis jeopardizes family homeostasis and has the potential to strip family resilience.*

Transcrisis

Transcrisis is a concept that recognizes crises may at times not be fully resolved and what van der Kolk and McFarlane (1996) identify as the black hole of trauma. If not fully resolved, the feelings, behaviors, and cognitions may become submerged and out of awareness. These feelings, behaviors, and cognitions can lay dormant for extended periods of time and have no effect on day-to-day living. However, when new stressors occur, the feelings, behaviors, and cognitions surface, resulting in a reaction similar to the original crisis. Unlike posttraumatic stress disorder, **family transcrisis** is not a diagnosable DSM-5 disorder. Rather, transcrisis is present as more of a low-level, lurking, residual state that surfaces when the situation activates the suppressed feelings, behaviors, and cognitions associated with the original crisis.

The way a family addresses and attempts to resolve a crisis has a significant impact on the development of issues that lead to a transcrisis state. Families can stifle a crisis, hoping it simply will evaporate, ignore it thinking it will go away, or hide from it hoping the storm will blow over. Regardless in the end, the issues related to the crisis fade, receding to a point these are below the awareness and not affecting day-to-day functioning. The issues are an undercurrent swirling just below the surface seemingly waiting for the opportunity to erupt when a new stressor is encountered. Just as with individuals, the eruptions into a transcrisis state are not predictable and may not occur for weeks, months or even years after the original crisis. Between the flare-ups, families attain a homeostasis behaving as if nothing is wrong. Interactions of family members between the outbursts are typically filled with usual everyday customary activities. Family members understand the expectations and function in a consistent routine manner. However, the experience of a novel stressor can catapult families into a transcrisis state and reopen old wounds. Issues not resolved from the original crises rocket to the forefront leaving families wondering what is happening. Families might experience an empty, sinking feeling that nothing has changed from the original crisis event and they are just experiencing another setback in a long line of aftershocks, which they attempt to survive while waiting for the next aftershock because the original issue has never been resolved.

Interactions among family members often provide a window into identifying a transcrisis state in families. These interactions can be obvious or subtle, but almost always refer back to previous experiences when families were not able to satisfactorily resolve a crisis. Obvious transcrisis statements are relatively easy to detect. A family member might say something like "Here we go again, just like before." Other obvious statements include "This is just like before, you did not listen to me then and you are not listening now," "You keep saying the same thing, over and over and over, you never change," or "We just cannot get this right." Each of these statements refers back to previous experiences that are clues for considering if families are in a transcrisis state. Many times less obvious, subtle indicators are seen in the form of nonverbal behaviors. Family members may shake their heads as if saying "Here we go again," or roll their eyes communicating "Not the same thing we did before." Recognition of the transcrisis state means crisis interventions strategies are needed to facilitate families' satisfactory resolution of the original crisis.

Research on Family Crisis

The framework of crisis intervention for **LO3** working with families is somewhat unclear ("Al et al., 2011"?). A possible reason for the ambiguity is that much of the research in this area has concentrated on identifying specific factors associated with families in crisis such as economic factors, individual family member history, race or ethnicity, spirituality and beliefs, stage of the family life cycle, parental behaviors, education level, recovery, and so on (Gil-Rivas et al., 2010; Price, Price, & McKenry, 2010; Rosenfeld et al., 2005; Yorgason, 2010). Research has also focused on specific situations that tax the ability of families to respond (Price, Price, & McKenry, 2010). The results of this research provide a model for identifying risk factors and issues related to families in crisis. Keep in mind that this research is just the framework, not a complete grasp of the nuances of the unique ways individual families react to and cope with crises. Like using the same blueprint to build two houses, the basic frame of the houses is the same yet the insides are very different. One house might have smooth walls while the other might have textured or paneled walls. Soft pastel colors might be the color scheme for one house while the other house has bright bold colors for the walls. The two houses have the same floor plan, yet each is very different. Similarly, two families might have the same or similar risk factors and have experienced the exact same crisis situation, but the reactions are very different. The findings of the research allow crisis workers to sort through relevant and not relevant issues, but does not address the intervention process.

Medical Crises

Probably the most extensive research with families in crisis situations involves the disruption of family life because of medical issues (Metha, Cohen, & Chan, 2009; Gonzalez, 2013; Lutz et al., 2011; Tunick et al., 2013). A catalyst for much of this research has been advances in health care that extend life beyond what was previously possible even a few years ago (Rolland, 2012). This emphasis is not surprising since the question is not if families will face a medical crisis, but when and what type of medical crisis. Sooner or later all families face decisions about medical treatment such as end-of-life issues, management of chronic illnesses, choices regarding critical care, and/or supporting family members who are not able to care for themselves. Research on decision making has examined family processes regarding end-of-life issues (e.g., Metha, Cohen, & Chan, 2009; Gonzalez, 2013; Haley et al., 2002), elderly care (e.g., Buhr, Kuchibhatla, & Clipp, 2006; Ducharme, Couture, & Lamontange, 2012), choices involving critical care (White et al., 2012; Tunick et al., 2013; Williams & Koocher, 1999), treatment of chronic illness (e.g., Hickman & Douglas, 2010; Yorgason, 2010), and aftercare (e.g., Lutz et al., 2011). Situations such as these can cause family members to struggle and sometimes battle over limited choices, none of which are optimal. Reactions range from cooperative coordination of efforts to chaotic and even mean-spirited attempts at taking advantage of the disorder surrounding the situation. Emotions bubble up, maybe even exploding into full blown non-politically-correct name calling. Behavioral reactions might be smooth and well coordinated or restrained to the point of being paralyzed with no one willing to do anything. Behavioral reactions also can erupt into something less than appropriate to the point of physical altercations at times. Family members might scheme and/or conspire to deliberately manipulate the situation in order to cause other family members' feelings of guilt or to take responsible for all the ills ever experienced by the family. They may attempt to sabotage efforts to address the crisis in order to punish or finagle an advantage for themselves. Forewarned is forearmed in order that you are not blindsided as families grapple with medical crises. Simply stated, the variety of reactions is limitless.

Disaster Recovery

Risk factors, resilience, and recovery from disaster are another area that has been the focus of crisis intervention with families (Knowles, Sasser, & Besty Garrison, 2010). Research in this area typically takes place in the aftermath of disasters such as the Three Mile Island nuclear accident (Handford, Mayes, Mattison, Humphrey, Bahnato, Bixler, & Kales, 1986), the terrorist bombing in Oklahoma City (Sitterle & Gurwitch, 1999), the terrorist attacks of 9/11 (Devoe, Klein, Bannon, & Miranda-Julian, 2011), and Hurricane Katrina (Gil-Rivas et al., 2010; Knowles, Sasser, & Garrison, 2010; Shanhinfar et al., 2010). These situations can shatter the day-to-day activities of families in an instant, resulting in considerable change (Everstine & Everstine, 2006). The result is that families are thrust into a novel and stressful situation that is often chaotic without forewarning and/or experience to manage all that needs to be accomplished. Many times resources are scarce and families have difficulty accessing these in a timely manner (Rosenfeld et al., 2005; Webb, 2005).

Much of the attention in the research on families in disaster recovery addresses the role parents and caregivers have in family members' reactions, specifically children and adolescents (Gil-Rivas et al., 2010). This research found that caregivers significantly influence children's and adolescents' adjustment positively or negatively following a disaster (Devoe et al., 2011; Felix et al., 2015; Polusny et al., 2011). As would be expected, negative reactions to a disaster such as increased anxiety or chronic unwanted thoughts in caregivers had high transference to youth in their care. On the other hand, caregivers who demonstrate resilience and growth after a disaster had high transference value to children and adolescents in their caregiving as well. Researchers have also discovered a critical factor following a disaster involves the capacity of communities to meet the ongoing needs of families following a disaster (Kilmer & Gil-Rivas, 2010). Kilmer and Gil-Rivas believe that communities must go beyond traditional mental health intervention and develop comprehensive disaster response services that address families' needs in the longer term.

Family Crisis Models

Theoretical explanations of families in crisis **LO4** have been in existence since 1949 (Weber, 2011). These models describe families' reactions to distress or stress depending on the developer's experience with and observations of families experiencing hardship. For example, the ABC-X model was developed to explain families' experience of absences due to military deployment and reunion of families (Price, Price, & McKenry, 2010), whereas the family distress model builds on the developers' experience in family medicine and was created to explain families who need but are reluctant to seek external support (Weber, 2011). The models offer different vantage points to view families' crises with each one presenting valuable insight to understanding the experience of crises as they impact families.

ABCX and Double ABCX Model. The first and one of the better known family crisis models is the ABCX formula (Boss, 2002). The catalyst for the development of this model was the return of soldiers following World War II (Price, Price, & McKenry, 2010). Since the model's inception in 1949 and initial reconsideration in 1958, many researchers in the field have adjusted and adapted the model for a wide variety of crises (Boss, 2002). The most significant change in the

model was made by McCubbin and Paterson (1983), who expanded the model to include risk and protective variables that influence the crisis following the event to explain ways families adapt. The expanded model, known as the double ABCX model, is used to explain families' reactions to and recovery from events ranging from internal and external disruptions to family functioning.

The elegance of the ABCX and double ABCX model is its simplicity. The model starts by focusing on precrisis with the "A" being the precipitating event and/or stressor (Weber, 2011). These events are ones for which families have little to no prior experience. As a result families experience hardships they are not able to manage because of the lack of competence and/or resources (Rosenfeld et al., 2005). "B" represents the resources available to families to cope with the event (Price, Price, & McKenry, 2010). If adequate resources are available, families avert falling into a crisis. If resources are not accessible, a crisis may occur depending on the interpretation of the event. This brings us to the "C" in the model that stands for families' interpretation of the event (Weber, 2011). When families interpret the event as a crisis producing problems that exceed their physical and psychological resources, a crisis "X" is experienced requiring potential changes in structure and interactions to restore stability (Rosenfeld et al., 2005).

The double "aA" refers to the immediate stressor plus the demands and shifts that occur in families and individual family members resulting in a stacking of stresses one on top of the other (Boss, 2002). As the stresses continue to stack up, families feel even more squeezed, thus increasing the severity of the crisis. The "bB" in the equation concerns activating existing resources as well as seeking additional resources from outside the family (Price, Price, & McKenry, 2010). The double "cC" of the model involves families' perceptions about the way to restore balance (Rosenfeld et al., 2005). For example, if the primary breadwinner losses his or her job, a family might decide that other members in the family need to secure jobs in order to offset the loss of income. The family might also cancel planned vacations to cut cost, change eating habits such as dining out, and so on. All these measures are perceived methods to restore balance to the family. "xX' refers to families' adaptation process to crises. Successful adaptation is termed **bonadaptation**, whereas the lack of balance is called **maladaptation** (Rosenfeld et al., 2005). Bonadaptation is considered to be good, useful, and healthy, whereas maladaptation is negative, ineffective, and unhealthy. Understand that what is bonadaptation for one family may not be the same for other families. The same is true for maladaptation. Also bonadaptation in one situation is not for another and the same holds true for maladaptation.

Contextual Model. The **contextual model** of family stress builds on the ABCX model (Weber, 2011). Introduced by Boss (2002), this model recognizes that families are unique and that events, the same or similar, will be experienced in distinctive ways. As a result, this model considers families' internal and external context as major factors in shaping reactions to stress and crisis situations. Internal context refers to things families can control and are divided into structural, psychological, and philosophical context (Boss, 2002). The structural context of families includes issues around boundaries and communications patterns that can be manipulated by families. Issues related to families' psychological context concern affective and cognitive perceptions of the stressor or crisis (Weber, 2011). Philosophical contextual issues concern values and belief systems held by families (Boss, 2002). Boss believes that because internal contextual issues are regulated by families, these should be addressed in the intervention process.

However, many external contextual issues are beyond the control of families. Issues such as history, macroeconomic human development, heredity, and culture fall into this category (Boss, 2002). Families cannot control historical events nor can they control global finances, for example, whether a recession takes place. These issues are global and are a result of a multitude of interacting factors. Aging is another external factor over which families have no control although some try through cosmetic surgery or antiaging products. The biological and genetic makeup of families is an external factor (Boss, 2002). Boss contends that we are born into families not by choice and that some families' genetic makeup is stronger than others. The final external factor concerns culture and the way it interprets events (Boss, 2002). Research supports this concept by examining cultures and studying the way some cultures react to traumatic situations (deVries, 1996). External contextual factors should be recognized as contributing to family reactions and used as a framework for understanding families' experiences (Boss, 2002).

Family Distress Model. The **family distress model (FDM)** was first introduced in by Cornille and Boroto (1992) and later was enhanced by the **family outreach model (FOM)** (Cornille, Meyer, Mullis, Mullis, & Boroto, 2008). The purpose for the model is to identify families' patterns of coping in order to develop interventions designed to support attempts at managing the situation (Weber, 2011). FDM states that when in distress, families use strategies that are different from their daily predictable patterns (Cornille et al., 2008). If the changes in routine are not successful in reducing the stress, crises arise. FDM was broadened by the formation of FOM that added a practical intervention component. FOM goes beyond traditional family intervention models based on conceptualizations of pathology that must be diagnosed or dysfunctional families that require expert assessment (Cornille, Meyer, Mullis, Mullis, & Boroto, 2008). According to the developers, this model can be used to identify families' needs and direct the intervention process from collaborative to directive approaches.

FDM consists of five phases that move from the initial encounter with a stressful event to the tools for assisting families. Phase 1 of FDM assumes families have predictable patterns that are typical and desirable and include routines, rituals, and rules used for decision making (Weber, 2011). Decisions can be conscious or automatic, occurring with little to no thought such as when dinner is served, who is responsible for cleaning bathrooms, who drives the family car, and so on. However, situations arise, either internal or external, that disrupt day-to-day patterns resulting in families moving to Phase 2 of FDM (Weber, 2011). Tried and true strategies to correct the disturbance are attempted in this phase. These strategies have been successfully used to manage previous disturbances and are designed to reduce stress, therefore returning families to normal functioning. If these methods are not successful a family crisis occurs. Phases 3 to 5 involve families organizing around the crisis, seeking resources to manage the situation, and finally reorganizing to create a new pattern of stability (Cornille et al., 2008). In these phases families become preoccupied with the crisis and a great deal of collective energy is used to control the disruptions (Weber, 2011). Weber states that unless families are able to access support to manage the crisis, patterns will adjust to accommodate the crisis state. If, however, support is found, families will regain stability through activating old patterns or developing new patterns.

When families enter into Phases 3 to 5 of FDM, FOM can be used to understand the crisis and direct the intervention. FOM also has five phases. These phases mirror the phases in FDM but add an applied element that directs the intervention process. The model is built on clinical or empirical observations and is meant to describe the crisis so that plans can be made to solve it. FOM is a strength-based model that engages families in collaborative problem solving consistent with family goals and values with the goal of returning families to former, stable, and predictable precrisis patterns of living (Cornille et al., 2008).

Family Communication Model.

The **family communication model** depicts an approach for families to cope with and prevail during crises using internal and external verbal interactions. The model makes the assumption that the root of family crises is communication (Webb & Dickson, 2012). According to this model communication patterns change in order to discuss challenging topics that are not typically discussed. Examples of topics challenging to discuss are a family member's terminal illness and the effect on everyone in the family or the excessive consumption of alcohol or use of illegal substances by one or more members in the family. Generally issues such as these are not the average topic for day-to-day conversations; rather, they are discussed as needed and in extraordinary circumstances. The authors add that communication can be internal discussion with only family members and/or external communication with others. Dickson and Webb stress that these difficult conversations are the key element for coping with crises. The goal of this communication is the co-construction of a rational explanation that makes meaning of the experience in order to create a positive view of the ultimate outcome for crises. Dickson and Webb do caution that any change in communication patterns be strategic, rather than unregulated disclosure. According to them, discussion should be tailored for individual family members with respect to the amount of information given and to whom it is shared and how it can be handled.

Webb and Dickson (2012) further state that effective family coping with crises involves two types of communication. The first type of communication is instrumental and concerns the exchange of information. Instrumental communication involves discussions that are unique to crises and are deliberate in nature. For example, in the case of weather-related crises such as hurricanes, floods, or tornadoes, families would discuss issues such as evacuation plans and locations to meet in case members are separated. Instrumental communication is based on a "need-to-know" basis with not everyone being given the same information. The second type of communication is emotion based. These discussions can involve sharing of feelings previously not disclosed that relate to the crisis. According to Dickson and Webb, communication of emotions is vital in helping family members to develop healthy coping mechanisms.

Resiliency Model.

The **resiliency model** represents a current focus of family crisis intervention and views families not as damaged, but rather challenged by adversities (Walsh, 2012b). This model concentrates on the potential for recovery and restoration functioning rather than pathologizing families' reactions while experiencing adversity. Through activating families' belief system, organizational patterns, and communication process, families have potential for personal and interaction transformation and growth (Walsh, 2012b). According to Walsh, when adversity strikes families, a dynamic process occurs that sets a trajectory for families' reactions to the situation. Belief systems involve families' ability to make meaning of the crisis, developing a positive outlook, and culture including spiritual traditions. These elements create a perspective families employ to approach crises. Organizational patterns include the capacity of families to be flexible, feeling a sense of connectedness, and the ability to access social and economic resources. These elements must be clarified and marshaled in light of modern families' structures and resources. Walsh states there is no common configuration and therefore organizing crises will be unique for families. Finally, communication involves problem solving and includes clear messages, open emotional expression, and collaboration. Walsh recognizes culture is important and significantly influences the communication process. This influence includes the way emotions are shared along with what feelings are acceptable to communicate.

Although other models for family crises can be found, the ones presented in this chapter are representative and practical in planning and coping with a family-wide crisis. Each model provides a different perspective in working with families in crisis.

Types of Crisis Families Encounter

LO5

Family crises come in all shapes, sizes, and forms with each having idiosyncratic qualities. Generally, the types of crises families experience mirror the types described in Chapter 1 such as developmental, situational, and so on. Just as with individuals, some crises come from seemingly nowhere, shattering a family's homeostasis, while others creep up insidiously on families and before they know it a full blown chaos reigns. With families, however, several special types of crises can occur. These crises develop because as a system, stressors placed on families have an effect on the collective whole, as well as individual family members (Myer & Moore, 2006).

Knowledge of the types of crisis experienced by families is critical for identifying possible issues that may be causing problems and is important for understanding effective approaches for helping them climb out of the crisis. Recognize that although the types of crises families experience will be discussed as separate types, crises are not usually that distinct. Some issues and problems are common to all types of family crises. The most distinguishing aspect of family crises is their origin. Also you need to appreciate that families may present a crisis situation in such a way that makes it difficult to identify the type. The watch words here are "be flexible" and willing to adjust as you find out more about what is happening.

Developmental Crises. As families develop and mature, crises are inevitable (Pittman, 1987) because the transitions brought on by development strain family coping and resilience, creating the potential for stressors to accumulate and disrupting their ability to function (Bonnefil & Jacobson, 1979; Peterson, Hennon, & Knox, 2010). Crises falling into this category in many ways are governed by families' culture. In fact, the concept of family is greatly influenced by culture (McGoldrick & Ashton; 2010). For example, in many cultures family refers to the nuclear family while in others family has a multigenerational connotation. For traditional Eastern families, a crisis might occur if a member of the family eschews a collective identity and strikes out on his or her own, leaving customs behind. In contrast, a family in the Western culture might have a crisis because of the "failure to launch" that happens when young adults do not separate from parents and do not leave home. More will be said about culture later in the chapter.

Most **developmental crises** can be anticipated and therefore planned, while others cannot (McGoldrick & Shisbusawa, 2010; Pittman, 1987). Getting married, having children, children beginning school, midlife transitions, retirement, and so on are all examples of predictable situations that may cause developmental crises (Cowan & Cowan, 2012).

These situations have the potential to shift a family's day-to-day functioning (Peterson, Hennon, & Knox, 2010), straining its coping abilities and resources. If stretched far enough, a crisis occurs. **Off-time developmental crises** occur when transitions are out of sequence, not happening in the expected order (McGoldrick & Ashton, 2012). By nature, these situations are particularly troublesome as they can be extremely disruptive to families' resilience and capacity to cope (Peterson, Hennon, & Knox, 2010). Examples of off-time developmental situations are the untimely death of a parent, unplanned pregnancies, forced retirement, disability due to chronic illness, and so on. Families may not be prepared to mobilize the resources needed to manage the demands and could spiral into crises (Cowan & Cowan, 2012).

Bolts From the Blue. Bolts from the blue family crises (Pittman, 1987) are akin to individual situational crises in that these are unexpected, resulting in families feeling as if they have smashed into a brick wall at full speed. No matter how prepared families might be, these crises fracture the family homeostasis, disrupting the day-to-day functioning of a family. This category of crises includes, but is not limited to, off-time developmental crises. Most of the crises falling into this category are largely universal in nature crossing cultural boundaries. These crises are generated both internally and externally to families (Weber, 2011). Examples of internally generated crises of this nature include infidelity, mental illness, desertion, chronic gambling, and diagnosis with a chronic illness. Externally generated crises include loss of job, disasters, sexual assault, victim of a crime, and lawsuits.

Pile Up Crises. Pile up crises for families take place when stressors accumulate to the point that these derail families' ability to function (Walsh, 2012b). The idiom "the straw that broke the camel's back" captures the essence of pile up crises. Pile up crises occur when families experience a series of internal and/ or external stressors over a short period of time (Patterson, 2002). Initially, families cope well, but as the stressors accumulate the capacity to cope falters and breaks down, plunging families into a crisis. Families may not be aware they are experiencing a pile up crisis. Instead, families may perceive the situations as isolated events that unfortunately have come all at once. Families may ask for assistance with just the latest of the series of events. Yet the persistent challenges eventually drain the available resources and coping mechanisms. The refrigerator stops working one day, which may not have been a major surprise. However the same day the family car has a flat and you discover while getting the flat fixed a new set of tires are needed, not to mention the brake pads are too thin to drive safely and both must be replaced immediately. The financial strain is great, but manageable with effort. Later in the day the family discovers that an extended family member with whom they have been close has been diagnosed with a potentially fatal medical problem. Following this comes a revelation that one of the children in the family is not doing well in school and in fact is close to flunking. One situation after another ensues, none of which on its own is insurmountable, but combined eventually overwhelms families' capacity to bounce back. The breakdown of coping mechanisms and the rapid depletion of resources send the family into a nosedive and a pile up crisis is the result.

Exhaustion Crises. Exhaustion crises are similar to pile up crises but instead occur over a more prolonged period. These crises occur when families experience stressors over an extended period of time. Unlike pile up crises that involve multiple stressors, crises of this type may be due to one stressor that has unrelentingly beleaguered families over an extended period of time. Take for an example a situation where a child has a medical condition that requires repeated attention. The medical condition is not life threatening but requires numerous visits to a physician and periodic stays in the hospital. Initially families may find this situation manageable, but after a few months fatigue begins to take its toll on the family, disrupting its day-to-day function. As resilience wears down and exhaustion sets in, a crisis of some type surfaces (Patterson, 2002; Walsh, 2012b).

Perpetual Crises. Some families roll from one crisis to the next with virtually no time between the crises (Kagan & Schlosberg, 1989). Crises for these families are a way of life as they are unable to cope on a day-to-day basis because the threshold for tolerating even minimal stressors is so low almost every situation evokes a crisis response. Families in perpetual crises specialize in getting others involved, including welfare offices, schools, child protective services, and so on (Kagan & Scholsberg, 1989). Families in this category may have structural problems that constantly intentionally or unintentionally cause crises (Pittman, 1987). Examples of structural issues that cause continuous crises in families include members who are alcoholic and disrupt family functioning or family members in persistent trouble with the law resulting in families living in a constant state of uncertainty, not knowing if the sheriff will be knocking on the door. These families live as if they are not at the edge of the cliff, but have already taken a step off that cliff.

Crises for these families are different from metastasizing crises discussed in Chapter 1. Metastasizing crises can be traced back to an isolated catalyst that spreads into other areas of families' day-to-day life. That is, you can trace a starting point to the series of crises that are linked together. However, there seems to be no starting point for families in perpetual crises. These families act out themes over and over again caught in a loop that never stops (Kagan & Scholsberg, 1989). The situations causing the crises are separate and unrelated yet the same modus operandi is used regardless of its appropriateness. The families may be able to acknowledge the futility of the situation but lack the energy, knowledge, or will to do anything different. Instead they rely on others to rescue them from crises.

Ambiguous Loss. Ambiguous loss is a special type of family crisis worth mentioning (Boss, 2006). Families having an ambiguous crisis experience the incongruity between physical and psychological presence and absence of family members (Price, Price, & McKenry, 2010). Clearly an ambiguous loss involves families with a member who is a soldier listed as missing in action or families of passengers of the Malaysian flight 370 that crashed and no wreckage or bodies were found. Yet family crises of this nature also involve times when someone may be physically present but not psychologically or emotionally, such as family members with dementia or possibly a chronic mental illness (Price, Price, & McKenry, 2010). According to Price, Price, and McKenry, these crises unsettle the functioning of families because of the lack of clarity to the situation. The lack of clarity prevents families from reorganizing the relationship with absent family members and completing social rituals that enable adjustment to the loss (Weber, 2011).

Dynamics of Family Intervention

LO6 and LO7

Families create systematic patterns of relating to one another and the world around them in order to maintain equilibrium as they live together (McWhirter et al., 2013). These patterns establish the instrumental and expressive dynamics within the family that ease daily life so that families function effectively (Knowles, Sasser, & Garrison, 2010). Instrumental dynamics include roles family members assume in order to meet the functional needs of day-to-day living (Cochran & Niego, 2002). Think about your family; everyone has a pretty good idea of who is responsible for what and when tasks need to be completed. You do not have to consult about who takes out the trash; you know who has that responsibility. You also know the rules about whose turn it is to set or clear the table. Your family might take turns, but it may be that the person who cooks does not have to help clean up after dinner. Boundaries are also part of instrumental dynamics and manage the interactions within and outside the family (McLendon & Petr, 2005). In your family, what can you say and who can you say that too? Are you supposed to talk with your friends about the argument that happened the previous evening? Can you tell mom, dad, or others in the family about problems you are having with school, relationships, or other issues? These are the boundaries for your family.

On the other hand, expressive dynamics of families involve the ways family members interact with one another (Pierce, Sarason, & Sarason, 1996), how conflicts are negotiated (Knowles, Sasser, & Garrison, 2010), as well as values and goals held by families (Myer et al., 2014). In your family, you know the person best able to provide emotional support and comfort. You probably have a good idea about how differences of opinions or conflicts are resolved in your family. Some families might get quite loud when clashing with one another whereas other families might know that discussing differences is forbidden or limited to certain times of the day. You also know that ignoring family values will cause trouble, possibly resulting in punishment of some type. However, when families face a crisis these dynamics, instrumental and expressive, are turned upside down and become confusing (Ectherling, Presbury, & McKee, 2005; Peterson, Hennon, & Knox, 2010). The usual way of doing things no longer works and families are forced into making adjustments (Rosenfeld et al., 2005). This discontinuity can be a turning point for families (Patterson, 2002). Understanding these dynamics is critical in order to work with families who are in a crisis (Myer et al., 2014).

Based on the family crisis intervention models discussed previously, six dynamics are particularly sensitive to the break of family dynamics (Myer et al., 2014). Crises seem to weave their way through these dynamics causing distractions, disturbances, and interruptions as families work to overcome the situation. However, resolving a family crisis is not easy and in fact is very complicated. Often the changes in dynamics hamper, stall, and otherwise thwart the resolution process as families struggle to right themselves. In fact, the modifications to dynamics may cause other crises to surface. Therefore, a critical aspect of the crisis intervention process is recognizing the shift in routine functioning in order to help families bring this shift into focus.

The Taylor family will be used to illustrate changes to family dynamics that occur when families face crises. You will see that Dianne's accident and subsequent hospitalization and rehabilitation is the catalyst for a myriad of changes in the family. It is like everything is turned upside down in the family as they are forced to make tough decisions about Dianne and modifications to their lives as a result of the accident.

Roles. Probably the most visible dynamic altered by a crisis is the roles family members play. Customary roles are no longer performed, leaving gaps in families' capacity to function (Price, Price, & McKenry, 2010). A wide range of alterations in roles can take place, but generally fall into two categories. First, a family member develops a chronic illness or an accident occurs and is no longer able to fulfill a role because of not being able to go up and down stairs. Someone else in the family must assume the roles the debilitated family member fulfilled. Or the family's primary "breadwinner" is fired or furloughed leaving finances uncertain. Other family members must pick up the slack and possibly adolescent family members must find jobs to make up for the loss of income. The second way roles change in the wake of crises involves the creation of new ones. For example, new roles are created when crises incapacitate members, resulting in the need for a caretaker. Both of these changes occur because families are trying to maintain homeostasis while coping with crises.

A **role** is defined as a practical function taken on by someone within the family (Goldenberg & Goldenberg, 2013). Roles within the family may be assigned because of the status of individuals within the family such as "mother," "father," "oldest," and "youngest." However, roles may also be assigned because of an individual's abilities or availability to perform certain tasks. For example, someone who is very good at organization may be assigned to manage paying the bills. An individual who has a talent for cooking, regardless of traditional gender roles, may take the role of planning and preparing meals. Families learn to expect that the roles assigned to specific members will be carried out (Gladding, 2010). In the face of a crisis, roles within families become blurred or performed inconsistently (McLendon & Petr, 2005; Price, Price, & McKenry, 2010). The absence of one or more family members due to the crisis may result in another member assuming the absent member's role (Price, Price, & McKenry, 2010). At times, a shift in roles is in some ways socially sanctioned—for example, in the case where a parent leaves the family either through divorce or death and the oldest same-gender child is expected to assume the departed parent's roles. The often voiced, well-intentioned statement "Now that your father has gone, you are the man of the family" signifies a shift in roles for the adolescent male who hears this statement. Shifts in the roles can be viewed as a family system's attempt to survive and adapt to the crisis (Gillespie & Campbell, 2011). The number of role shifts and the degree of those shifts in roles compared to prior role functioning can be used as one measure of a family's reaction to a crisis. Generally speaking, the greater the number and the more pronounced the shifts in roles, the more severe the crisis. Thus, assessment of the nature of the changes to roles within the family is critical for effective crisis intervention as it offers an understanding into one aspect of the chaos and conflict that may be observed in a family system during a crisis.

Assignment of roles during a crisis can be negotiated and agreed on by families, or they can be presumptuous, with specific family members being aggressive and forcing their way into certain roles or imposing roles onto others. Roles may also be assigned with a family member taking control and dictating the roles family members should fulfill. Often, conflicts will arise regarding who in the family takes various roles. These conflicts limit a family's ability to adapt and adjust to a crisis (Rosenfeld et al., 2005). Navigating through these conflicts can be treacherous as family members vie for their preferred roles. Sorting through these situations must be carefully done and caution exercised not to take sides. Even though family members may not agree on their roles, interference can result in an immediate attack if this is from someone outside the family.

Boundaries. Family boundaries are used to manage internal and external interactions (McLendon & Petr, 2005). Boundaries help to create order as families manage daily activities by setting up subsystems and coalitions, controlling relationships and contact with others. According to Brown and Manning (2009), boundaries can be physical and psychological. Physical boundaries shape interactions within the family as well as outside the family. These can restrict or encourage interactions. An example of a typical physical boundary is that between parents and children. Another traditional physical boundary is between the men and women in families. Psychological boundaries serve as an injunction/expectation for when and how family members interact with others (Brown & Manning, 2009).

In crisis situations, families find themselves in unfamiliar territory as they face forces pushing families and individual family members in many directions (Price, Price, & McKenry, 2010). Families' status quo with respect to organizational patterns is tested in ways never before encountered. The result is that new organizational patterns may be formed to meet the needs of the current situation (Myer et al., 2014). In crises boundary shifts can become more permeable or rigid depending on families' perceptions (Carroll, Olsen, & Buckmiller, 2007). Families might find these shifts in organizational patterns necessary and advantageous as they adapt. However, some families and possibly individual family members may resist modifications and be either unable or unwilling to make changes.

A key issue for families in crisis is flexibility in organizational patterns (Walsh, 2012b). Families that are able to adjust boundaries in the wake of crises situations fare better than those whose organizational patterns become more rigid. Families with rigid boundaries can lose their sense of connectedness as they work to overcome the challenges presented by crises (Walsh, 2012b). This connectedness permits mutual support and collaboration, and respects individual family members' needs and differences.

Communication. Communication is another dynamic often altered as families struggle to cope with crises (Webb & Dickson, 2012). These authors state that changes occur because families are challenged to make sense of crises necessitating disruptions in communication patterns. These changes can be disruptive or beneficial depending on families. Disruptive communication in families is commonly experienced because of uncertainties embedded in crises (Tjersland et al., 2006), disagreement about what actions are needed (Sofka, 2004), and the desire to regain a sense of control (Hoff, Hallisey, & Hoff, 2009). Troublesome communication following crises can become either truncated or expanded (Ratnarajah & Schofield, 2008). Truncated communication is generally to the point without embellishment, including only facts, whereas expanded communication can involve enhancing stories with great bravado, including emotional details and minute details. While neither of these two patterns is inherently negative, these can lead to misunderstanding and annoy other family members. Often these are a gauge to families' reactions to crises situations. The more severe the reaction, the more difficult it will be for families to work through and adapt to the new situation.

On the other hand, good communication has the potential to facilitate positive outcomes in the resolution of families' crises (Yorgason, 2010). Open communication seems to be a key factor in facilitating families working through crises (Webb & Dickson, 2012). Clear consistent messages and clarity of information is indispensable for families weathering crises (Walsh, 2012b). In addition, open emotional expression and collaborative problem solving help families adjust as they live through the demands placed on them by crises (Knowles, Sasser, & Besty Garrison, 2010; Walsh, 2012b).

Rules. **Rules** govern families' day-to-day behaviors and are negotiated in the formation of families (Imber-Black, 2012). Rules fall into two categories: (1) procedural and (2) ritualistic. **Procedural rules** set the basis for family structure and provide consistency. When followed, procedural rules result in families maintaining a state of equilibrium. These rules/processes determine internal and external interactions of family members as well as set the standard for topics for conversation (Murray, Toth, Larsen, & Moulton, 2010). Breaking procedural rules has the potential to destabilize by undermining the foundation on which a family is built. Behavior of family members is not predictable and families must try to reestablish stability. Another type of rule involves expectations involving rituals within families. Rules around rituals are ever present in families' lives and create meaning as they remember special times in their lives (Imber-Black, 2012). **Ritualistic rules** can be as mundane as kissing your partner as you leave for work or tucking in children at bedtime. Celebrations at birthdays, anniversaries, holidays also are covered by ritualistic rules. For example, birthday cakes must be purchased at a bakery or maybe instead of a cake the ritualistic

rule is that someone bakes a favorite kind of pie. Holiday ritualistic rules are even more easily identified. On Memorial Day the extended family gathers for a backyard barbeque or at Christmas, breakfast always entails baking homemade pecan caramel rolls. Abiding by ritualistic rules symbolizes families' connectedness with the past, gratitude for the present, and hope for the future (Imber-Black, 2012).

Crises can result in changes for both procedural and ritualistic rules. Families become sidetracked and embroiled in addressing the immediacy of crises and might neglect, forget, or otherwise ignore family rules (Myer et al., 2014). Procedural rules may no longer be effective given the demands of the crisis situations. Generally speaking, the more severe the crisis, the more likely procedural rules will be broken. For example, even though a procedural rule is not to talk about family matters with someone not in the family, this rule may be ignored as family members seek support. At times crises force a change in procedural rules. Some family members might perceive these as beneficial, whereas others in the family might have a very different perception. Other times families choose to alter these rules by making deliberate decisions to change these.

Ritualistic rules are also at the mercy of family crises. Birthdays might be forgotten or celebration of holidays could be postponed. Emotions can run high if celebrations such as these are forgotten or missed even though families are struggling through a crisis. Cognitions can also run hot because expectations were not met regarding rules around rituals. However, ritualistic rules can be an important anchor for families in certain types of crises. The reason is that many of these rules revolve around faith-based functions and beliefs (Rosenfeld et al., 2005). These can help families ground themselves and give security as they work through crises (Imber-Black, 2012). Ritualistic rules support family members' efforts coming to terms and finding meaning in crises.

Values. Arising out of families' belief system, **values** are those things deemed important for morale (Greenstone & Leviton, 2011) and drive families' perceptions. As such values play an important role in crises (Boss, 2002) influencing families' reactions as they attempt to make sense of the situation (Walsh, 2012b). Two different aspects of values are involved in families making sense of crises. First, values play a critical role in the way families interpret crises. Families use casual or explanatory attributions based on their values to assign meaning to crises. Cultural heritage, faith-based beliefs, beliefs held because of ethnic background, political beliefs, along with others (Boss, 2002; Robert & Kelly, 2015; Rosenfeld et al., 2005; Humphrey, 2009; Walsh, 2012b) all contribute to families' perceptions of crises situation. Some families might attribute crises to being "God's will," while others might explain the situation as an "act of nature." Still other families might attribute crises to simply having bad luck. It is important to remember that families are unique with respect to the way and degree belief systems influence their values (Boss, 2002). Second, families use values to determine their ability to handle the situation. Values help to create a sense of coherence that allows families to tackle crises together (Hansson & Cederblad, 2004). Families whose values lead them to be optimistic and positive tend to have greater success in facing crises (Walsh, 2012b), whereas a fatalistic perspective can be a barrier for coping with these situations (Boss, 2002). Some families rely on their faith to see them through crises. Other families might trust their political beliefs, feeling the government will come to their rescue.

Crises often challenge and even alter families' values (Schmidt & Welsh, 2010). The challenge comes when values are unable to provide guidance on how to make sense of crises. Families may feel as if they are trying to fit a square peg into a round hole or a round peg into a square hole. No matter what there will be gaps. Families struggling to make sense of crises will try to fill in the gaps in order to maintain allegiance to their values. If these efforts fail, families will look for ways to rationalize the experience. In these situations, some values may take precedence over others. Values can also change because of crises. Values prized by families may no longer be practical or functional because of crises. Values such as education, leisure, political involvement, religious affiliation, and community service may be reconsidered as families grapple with the consequences of crises.

Goals. **Goals** motivate families in their desire to attain or achieve something (Rosenfeld et al., 2005). Obviously some goals involve physical objects such as having the biggest house or new vehicles every year. Other goals are intangible and might include contributing to retirement funds or being a member at a prestigious country club. Not all family goals are expressed—some may be unspoken. Expressed family goals might include stable employment that provides income or becoming a home owner. Unspoken family goals can help children become independent or maintain a healthy lifestyle and live a long happy life. Regardless of the type of goal, crises bring into focus the uncertainty of the future (Galvin et al., 2012). Families might reconsider the goal of living to a ripe old age when medical crises arise. Disasters might cause families to learn to appreciate health rather than focus on obtaining material possessions (Rosenfeld et al., 2005). Faced with changes brought on by a new reality, families are compelled to reexamine goals making changes as required (Myer & Moore, 2006).

In crises situations families' goals may undergo dramatic and unexpected changes (Rosenfeld et al., 2005) and interrupt families' ability to reach goals (Weber, 2011). Collective and individual ambitions are at stake as families struggle to weather and resolve crises. Goals are put on hold or abandoned altogether as crises send shock waves through families. Shock waves have the potential to stir up issues that can either be beneficial or detrimental to working through crises. More often than not, family members initially rally around each other for support. Differences are put aside and families work together to get through the crisis. Yet as the crisis wears on, those differences have the tendency to resurface. Families with positive stable, lasting supportive interactions will fare much better (Boss, 2002). In fact, these families have the tendency to get stronger. Unfortunately, the same happens with families who have a history of uncooperative dealings. These families often experience an upsurge of these types of interactions as crises cause friction among family members.

Although these dynamics are discussed as distinct and separate, in reality these are interrelated. Changes in one of the dynamics listed above generally cause changes in one or usually more of the others. Later in this chapter, we will introduce a modification of the Triage Assessment Form that can be used with families. The form for families was developed based on the dynamics listed above and can be used much in the same way as the original.

Case Vignette

Meet the Taylor family, a typical middle-class blended family. The Taylors will be used throughout the remainder of the chapter to illustrate crisis intervention with families. The case will be discussed at various points in the family's journey after Dianne is involved in a terrible car accident while getting a ride home after school. Below is a brief history of the Taylor family as well as the accident that throws the family into a full blown crisis.

David, the husband, is 45 and works as an account executive in a small advertising firm. David's first wife tragically died in a car accident leaving him to raise their daughter, Christina. Christina was 7 years old when her mother died but is now 19 and attending a nearby university and living on campus. Elizabeth (Liz), the wife, is 41 and works as an executive administrative assistant. Liz has two children, Dianne age 14 and Wesley 16, both living within the home with David and Liz. Liz divorced her husband 1 year before she met David. After a whirlwind romance David and Liz were married 10 years ago. At the time of the wedding, Christina did not seem very happy about having to share her Dad with two strange kids but was happy about having a stepmother who could help her. Wesley was not happy about the remarriage and told his mother she should get back with his Dad. On the other hand, Dianne was excited about having an older sister and said she wanted to hang out with her as much as possible. After a few months of marriage, David and Liz decided to have a child in order to solidify the family. They gave birth to William who is now 8 years old.

Dianne has been rushed by ambulance to the emergency room because while leaving the school parking lot the car she was in was slammed into by another vehicle. The scene was horrific, with the driver of the car killed and Dianne severely injured. A teacher at Dianne's school contacted Mrs. Taylor and told her about the accident, telling her to get to the emergency room as soon as possible. On the way to the hospital Mrs. Taylor (Liz) called her husband and asked him to pick up William and Wesley and meet her at the hospital as soon as possible. Upon arriving at the emergency room, Mrs. Taylor is met by Chaplain Hamill. She is frantic to see her daughter and the chaplain quickly assesses her on the TAF as 9 on the affective scale and 8 on the behavioral and cognitive scales. The chaplain escorts her to a private room and works to calm her. Chaplain Hamill assures her that Dianne is in good hands and the doctors are doing everything they can. He says that Dianne is in surgery and based on experience the doctors will send someone out on a regular basis to give updates. Chaplain Hamill says he will stay with her as long as needed and also help her contact family and friends to come sit with her.

After 4 weeks in the hospital Dianne was released to continue rehabilitation as an outpatient. David

and Laura Taylor were referred to the Midtown Pastoral Counseling Center by Chaplin Hamill. They did not immediately follow up on the chaplain's referral. The most serious injury was the head trauma that resulted in Dianne needing occupational therapy to regain some skills needed for daily living. Although a full recovery was expected, the Taylors were told this would take several months and possibly longer. The Taylors became increasingly distressed after their first three visits to the rehabilitation center. On one occasion, Dianne sat for 45 minutes before being picked up after her appointment. Mr. Taylor apologized profusely, saying there is just so much going on and he just could not get there any sooner. Mrs. Taylor also peppered the occupational therapist with questions and confided that things were terrible at home. In Mrs. Taylor's words, "things were going to hell in a hand-basket," at which time she began to cry. The occupational therapist said families in their situation sometimes need help sorting everything out and recommended that Mrs. Taylor find someone to talk to about the psychological fractures they were now having that followed Diane's physical fracture. These psychological fractures were the catalyst for the Taylors to follow through on Chaplain Hamill's referral.

Hybrid Model Applied to Families

Chapter 3 introduced the hybrid model for crisis intervention. The flexibility of this model makes it extremely useful while working with families in crisis. The seven tasks imbedded in the model can guide the process of helping families in crisis. Three tasks: (1) safety, (2) assessment, and (3) support are continuously being worked on throughout the intervention (Myer, Lewis, & James, 2013). The other four tasks: (4) making contact/predispositioning, (5) examining the problem, (6) reestablishing control, and (7) follow-up are incorporated into crisis intervention as needed (Myer, Lewis, & James, 2013). Once these tasks are completed, crisis workers can move to another one. However, the chaotic, fluid nature of crisis may cause crisis workers to return to these tasks several times during the intervention.

In this chapter the focus is primarily on the tasks rooted in the model, not the model itself. Although the application is very similar to the one with individuals, differences do occur when working with families. These differences are analogous to the application of basic counseling techniques with individuals and families or groups. The techniques are the same, but because more than one client is involved the application is altered. The excerpts from sessions used to illustrate the tasks take place in the first few days following Dianne's accident. As often happens in hospitals, the sessions take place at various locations. These locations include the emergency room, a consultation room near the Intensive Care Unit (ICU), Chaplain Hamill's office, and the ICU waiting room.

Making Contact/Predispositioning. **Making contact/predispositioning** as a task with families in crises involves placing yourself in a position of being helpful. Kanel (2011) views making contact as the foundation for being able to assist families in crises. Ectherling, Presbury, and Mckee (2005) echoed this sentiment, stating that making contact is a fundamental connection that demonstrates a genuine commitment by the disaster counselors' willingness to stand by the client. This process of making contact/predispositioning is very different than traditional rapport building (Myer, Lewis, & James, 2013). Rapport develops over time often taking several weeks whereas making contact/predispositioning is established in the first few moments of the crisis intervention process. The goal of this task is to quickly connect and bond with families in a way that makes them receptive and cooperative to the intervention process.

As with individuals, making contact/predispositioning begins before the first contact. The crisis worker should position himself or herself as someone who has the family's best interest at heart and acts as an advocate. This mind set is particularly important when the family runs head on into the bureaucracy of a large institution like a regional trauma unit hospital as the Taylors are about to do. They are going to be confronted with every one of the hybrid model's tasks, and they are now going to be doing it on what may be considered alien territory. As such, if the crisis worker is seen as a representative of a bureaucratic system, this can derail at worst, or set back, at best, the entire intervention. Instead you must communicate being knowledgeable yet not subservient to the system. As stated in Chapter 3, the way introductions are made is critical. Long-winded introductions listing your degrees, licenses, and certifications only serve to make you seem important and do not necessarily help families. If requested, by all means provide these. However, in the initial contact tell families your name, your profession, and that you are sorry for what is happening. You will also want to allow them to introduce themselves to you and if possible greet family members individually. This process helps to connect with everyone as well as the families as a whole. Clarify your intentions by telling families the purpose of you being with them and then start employing the basic listening and responding skills detailed to you in Chapter 4, The Tools of the Trade.

Although the task begins with the initial contact, making contact/predispositioning may need to be repeated periodically. One reason for repeating this task is because family members may arrive at different times. As family members arrive you will need to recycle back to this task and introduce yourself and allow them to do the same. Take time to listen to the new arrivals' concerns as well as bring them up to date with the discussion to that point. This process validates their participation and incorporates them into the discussion. Another reason for returning to this task is the fluid, chaotic nature of crises. As crises evolve, families or individual family members may question the relevance of the presence of crisis workers. Their perception may change and cause them to question the purpose of a crisis worker's presence. Care must be taken not to overreact or become defensive. When this situation occurs, crisis workers must for a second, third, and fourth time make contact and predisposition themselves with families. Revisiting this task is also needed as families move through the recovery stages. Crisis workers must redefine, that is, predisposition, themselves as families move through the recovery process. The need for revisiting predispositioning is the changing role and function of crisis workers as families move through recovery. As families begin to adapt and stabilize, the role of crisis workers shift from being the "go to" person to more of a "guide," steering them on an as needed basis. Stages of recovery for families will be discussed in the next section of this chapter.

The following exchange takes place in the first few minutes after Mrs. Taylor arrives at the hospital. Mrs. Taylor had gone by the high school and seen the mangled car in which Dianne was riding. She also saw the police officers doing their investigation and noticed a dark stain on the sidewalk, which she assumed was blood. After arriving at the Emergency Room, the receptionist and a nurse guided her to a private room. Both the receptionist and nurse assured her someone would be coming to talk with her as quickly as possible. A couple minutes pass and Chaplain Hamill knocks on the door.

Chaplain Hamill: (*opens the door slowly*) May I come in?

Liz: Are you the doctor?

Chaplain Hamill: No mam, I am a chaplain at the hospital . . . Chaplain Dan Hamill.

Liz: Oh my god, she is dead!

Chaplain Hamill: No Dianne is not dead. She is in surgery right now.

Liz: Are you sure?

Chaplain Hamill: Yes I am sure. I am Chaplain Hamill and you are Mrs. Taylor right?

Liz: (*shakes her head affirmatively*) Yes . . . call me Liz.

Chaplain Hamill: I go by Dan. Dan Hamill. I am going to be your advocate and information center for a while. OK?

Liz: Where is the doctor, I want to see the doctor.

Chaplain Hamill: (*gently*) I know you do, I would want the same, but right now the doctor is in surgery with your daughter. I'll be getting information from the surgery center and immediately relay it to you. I wonder if you heard what I said.

Liz: OK. I heard. I just have to know she is alive. (*cries*)

Chaplain Hamill: Mrs. Tay . . . I mean Liz. Dianne is alive. I saw her when the ambulance arrived. The doctors asked that I come down and meet you when you arrived. Then they took her immediately to surgery.

Liz: Oh my God, it must be awful. (*visibly shaking and cries more*)

Chaplain Hamill: I am not sure what injuries your daughter has. The doctors thought you might need someone to sit with you until they can determine the extent of the damage and talk with you. That's the only reason I'm here. That's part of my job. OK. Liz, the doctors wanted me to here to help you be as comfortable as possible. They are really good doctors and knew whoever came would need someone who understands how hospitals work . . . (*pause*) . . . Can I get you some water or anything?

Liz: Oh yes please water would be great.

As soon as Chaplain Hamill arrives, he begins working on the task of making contact/predispositioning. He begins by introducing himself; however, Mrs. Taylor immediately jumps to the conclusion her daughter has died. Chaplain Hamill quickly assures her Dianne has not died but is in surgery at the moment. At this point he confirms that Mrs. Taylor is Dianne's mother. After the initial few exchanges, notice that the Chaplain begins using Mrs. Taylor's first name. He checks to make sure she is hearing him particularly as to his purpose and not just as the death messenger she first makes him out to be. This helps to personalize the interaction, communicating to them they are not just another family of a patient but rather are people with names. Chaplain Hamill also lets the family know his role in being with them at this time. He is with them to make sure they are comfortable by anticipating their needs. By communicating this purpose to the Taylors, Chaplain Hamill sets boundaries on his role yet at the same time soothes the situation.

Safety. **Safety** is a default task and particularly important when working with families in crises (Rosenfeld et al., 2005). Automatically, many of you will think, of course, client safety (for this chapter that means families) is essential and the first item of business in crisis intervention with families. To a point you would be correct, but only to a point. As we stated in Chapter 3, this task includes *your* safety, not just the families' safety. The first consideration is your safety when working with families in crisis. You must first and foremost consider your safety as the priority. Do not place yourself in a situation that compromises your safety. We repeat, under no circumstances should you put yourself in situations that place your life in danger. Why you might ask? First, your training will almost assuredly not prepare you for those situations. Second, crisis intervention is not a video game that gives you multiple lives to keep playing. Third, although you mean well and are a caring, sharing, wonderfully empathic human being, families in the chaos of crises can suddenly without clear provocation lash out at anyone perceived as a threat whether that is accurate or not. For example, you might be called to a home to work with a family in crisis. Even though you are there to help, individual family members may not appreciate your presence. Family members might think you are sticking your nose where it does not belong. Some individuals could look for chances to sabotage your attempts to help. Something that is said could be interrupted negatively, taken as an affront to the family or individual members. A comment might be construed as a derogatory and felt to question the family's integrity or their intelligence. In an instant, families as a whole or individual members can lash out at you unexpectedly. Therefore, safety for crisis intervention means being mindful of your well-being at all times and this is particularly true in the present situation where highly distraught family members and supporters are coming into a hospital after a traumatic injury has occurred.

Prevention and preparation are key aspects for safety. A guideline is to have two crisis intervention workers present when working with families if possible. Two crisis workers allow one to take the lead in the intervention while the other is watching and alert for changes in milieu and interactions in the family. Understandably having two crisis workers is not always possible, but when possible it is recommended. Being aware of surroundings is also essential when working with families in crisis. Awareness of surroundings is especially important if you are asked to make home visits. Gather information and know the nearby area if working with families on their home turf so to speak. Where is the closest place to get help if needed? Is there a fire station nearby? Is a police substation close by? What other places could you get to quickly if needed? Being able to communicate with the office is important. Let someone know not just where you will be, but also when you expect to return. Set check-in times so that if you are unable to, someone will contact you. Also have a signal so that if you call and use a word or phrase they are alerted that you need assistance immediately. While seemingly common sense, prevention and preparation creates a measure of safety for you as well as families.

Throughout the intervention process vigilance is needed to guard your and the families' safety. This means being constantly mindful of the environment through observing verbal and nonverbal behaviors of all family members. What are family members saying? Is anyone making threats, directly or indirectly? Has someone said something that might be considered a veiled threat? **Veiled threats** are circuitous statements that do not express a direct warning but contain a menacing message beyond the words (Braverman, 1999). Are any intimidating statements pointed at individuals or groups of family members. Being mindful of nonverbal communication is also vital. Threatening moves such as shaking a fist at someone or making a slight lunge are moves that might put safety at risk. Have family members raised their voices, speaking louder or more rapidly? Anger or fear can be a catalyst for threatening behavior that jeopardizes safety. Relentless and continual watchfulness is central to providing safety for yourself and families as well as allowing you to gather the information needed to help.

The following exchange takes place approximately 45 minutes after Mrs. Taylor arrived at the hospital. Chaplain Hamill was there to meet her and has been with her the entire time. Mrs. Taylor was distraught when she arrived and has vacillated between sitting and pacing the floor. Mr. Taylor has just arrived after picking up Wesley and William. They were shown to the room by hospital security. The door is open and they walk into the room. Wesley and William immediately go to their mother, giving her a hug.

Wesley: Mom, what is going on?

William: (*staying close to his Dad and holding his hand*)

David: (*looks at Chaplain Hamill*) Hi, I am Liz's husband. Who are you and what's going on with my kid?

Chaplain Hamill: Nice to meet you. Thanks for coming so quickly. I am Dan Hamill the chaplain here but more importantly I guess, the guy who is going to help get you through this.

David: Liz, are you okay?

Liz: (*shakes her head no, big tears in her eyes*)

Chaplain Hamill: Let's sit down and I will tell you what I can.

Liz: I don't want to sit down. I want to see my baby girl.

Wesley: What happened? Where is she?

Chaplain Hamill: Please let's sit down so I can fill everyone in.

David: What . . . Liz, have you seen her?

Liz: (*says softly*) They won't let me. I want to see my daughter, please! I have to know she is alive!

Wesley: (*voice raised*) Who in the hell won't let you see her?

Chaplain Hamill: (*uses a soft steady tone*) Let me explain.

David: (*his voice raised*) Explain what, Liz needs to see her. Why can't she, she is her mother.

Chaplain Hamill: I realize this is beyond distressing and you are frantic with worry, so please take a seat and let me explain.

Wesley: (*turns toward the chaplain*) Explain nothing, let her see my sister now. (*stands straight as a board, his face becoming flushed*)

Chaplain Hamill: Your sister is in surgery. I know this is difficult, but I need for you to be patient.

Liz: I have been waiting and waiting and no one will let me see my daughter. (*cries hysterically*)

David: She is in surgery?

Wesley: What the fuck! You let her see my sister now! Come on Mom let's go find her.

Chaplain Hamill: (*says quietly but with assertion*) I need for you to hear me carefully. I need for you to sit down and listen to what I have to say. If you can't, the police will escort you from the building and I don't believe you want that. I need to know that you understand what I said. I want to help you see her as soon as possible, but I need for you to cooperate with me now

David: Hold on Wesley. *(looks at the chaplain and in a caustic voice)* OH. I get it. You want to know if we got insurance. Can we pay? Well hell yes. Get the frickin' forms and I'll fill the damned things out.

Chaplain Hamill: There are plenty of forms. The last thing you want to hear and I'll get you the help to take care of them when time comes, but right now, I am going to stay with you for a while. She was pretty banged up when she arrived. The doctors had to do surgery immediately. I was told she was bleeding internally, so you understand the surgery unit is off limits, right! The risk of infection and all. You can see her when she is in recovery, Mrs. Taylor. I'll be your conduit of information until the surgeon is done and then she'll talk to you. She is in good hands with Dr. Melton. She is an excellent surgeon. I'd want her working on my own child if it came to it. So would you all please have a seat. I can have one of the attendants get you something to drink if you want. I will give you updates as I get them

David: *(still standing and pacing back and forth agitated)* Bleeding internally, no one said anything about that, is she dying? *(said in a demanding voice)* I want to speak with the doctor now . . . make . . . it . . . happen.

Liz: She is dying? *(cries more but sits down)*

Chaplain Hamill: Thank you for sitting down, Mrs. Taylor. No one said that . . . was just your husband's question.

Wesley: If she dies someone will pay for that—that is for damned sure.

Chaplain Hamill: Let's all sit down. Let me get someone who can sit with you and see if I can find out what is happening. I do need for all of you to sit. I understand your frustration, but if you can't help me help you, I'll have to call the police and they will escort you from the building . . . the last thing you want. So please have a seat.

Wesley: *(muttering and sits)*

David: *(sighs)* OK, just get us some information please. *(sits)*

Chaplain Hamill: Thank you. I will. You can stay here or I have an intern who can go down to the chapel with you. I will be right back as soon as I have some information on the progress of Diane's surgery.

Throughout the exchange, safety is the first and foremost concern. Chaplain Hamill uses a soft calming voice to ease the Taylor's anxiety level. Reduction of their anxiety is essential in order to maintain everyone's safety. Several times he uses owning statements to express his compassion and concern in order to make a connection with the Taylors. The owning statements are straight out of Chapter 4, The Tools of the Trade. These statements are used to express understanding and engender trust. The goal is that if trust is built the Taylors will find a way to compose themselves and not do anything that would endanger their well-being. Chaplain Hamill also uses limit setting and assertion statements with the Taylors, stating if they attempt to enter the surgical area Dianne's safety is compromised as well as the need to call security. These limits are set to protect the Taylors as well as others. He immediately reinforces Mrs. Taylor for sitting down in hopes of successively approximating her husband and son to do the same. He also uses "I understand" statements to acknowledge their affective state. All of these people are high on the triage scale, and he cannot let them remain there for their safety and everyone else's for that matter.

Assessment. When working with families in crisis, you will have to sort through an overwhelming amount of data (Bonnefil & Jacobson, 1979). The ability to shift through this information quickly and efficiently is critical. This assessment should focus on gathering information needed to assist families as they work their way through crises. This means having criteria or a model to use to organize the information (Bonnefil & Jacobson, 1979). The model should be flexible enough to use with various crises and should also be adaptable to use with families that have different structural configurations. The assessment process should also provide real-time information that can immediately be used in the intervention process.

Family assessment has come a long way since the early days of family therapy (Lebow & Stroud, 2012). Among the various methods are self-report instruments such as the Family Environment Scale, F-COPES, FACES IV (Family Adaptability and Cohesion Evaluation Scale IV), and Sources of Stress Scale (Lebow & Stroud, 2012). These instruments provide an insider's perspective to the way families are functioning and seem relevant in crises. Yet self-report instruments have limitations when being used in family crisis situations. Can you imagine the challenge of completing self-report instruments when families

Crisis Date: _____   Office Visit Date: _____

Family Members: Name, Age, and Role (present and not present) _____

_____

_____

Crisis Description _____

_____

Attempt/s at Resolution: _____

_____

Observations and Reported Behaviors (Check as many that apply**)**

___ inability to provide daily needs (___food ___clothing ___shelter ___ utilities)***

___ self-medication by one or more members

___ major health concerns reported *

___ family violence ***

___ neglect of children (emotional, physical)***

___ verbal threats to self or others

___ suicidal/homicidal thinking/verbalizing *

___ suicidal/homicidal gestures/behaviors *

___ suicidal/homicidal plan clear *

___ disagreements within family

___ family members disengaged

___ lack of energy within family

___ isolation from social support systems

___ approval seeking by family members

___ refusal to communicate with other family members

___ demanding special attention by family members

___ tension among family members

___ denial by family members

___ family members nonresponsive

___ family members responses guarded

Notes: _____

_____

*** Referral to Social Service Recommended *Referral for Specialized Support

TRIAGE ASSESSMENT

Feelings	**Behavioral**	**Thinking**
___ Anger ___ Fear ___ Sadness	___ Approach ___ Avoidance ___ Immobile	___ Transgression ___ Threat ___ Loss
1 2 3 4 5 6 7 8 9 10	1 2 3 4 5 6 7 8 9 10	1 2 3 4 5 6 7 8 9 10

Total Score: ___

FIGURE 11.1 Triage Assessment Form: Family Therapist

Digital Download Download at CengageBrain.com

SEVERITY SCALES

	1 No Impairment	2/3 Minimal Impairment	4/5 Low Impairment	6/7 Moderate Impairment	8/9 Marked Impairment	10 Severe Impairment
A F F E C T I V E	○ Stable mood, control of feelings suggesting family resiliency.	○ Brief periods of elevated negative mood with little effect on family resiliency.	○ Evidence of negative mood noticeable causing family resiliency to fluctuate.	○ Mood primarily negative causing family resiliency to be ineffectual.	○ Mood is negative causing family resiliency to be fail.	○ Mood is shutting down ability to respond to the crisis causing family resiliency to disappear.
	○ Affect is appropriate with no effect on boundaries.	○ Affect elevated but generally appropriate with little effect on boundaries.	○ Affect intensity is longer than situation warrants causing boundary disruptions.	○ Affect control is difficult and not always successful causing changes in boundaries.	○ Affected not controlled with significant boundary shifts.	○ Affect control absent causing danger to family or others and boundaries to be ignored.
	○ Emotions are under control with no impact on family values.	○ Emotions are substantially under control with no effect on family values.	○ Emotions are controlled but influenced by crisis with minimal effect on family values.	○ Emotions not under control and focused on crisis and influencing family values.	○ Emotions generalize from crisis event to other situations and changing family values.	○ Emotions of the crisis are generalized to situations substantially changing family values.
	○ Responses to questions/ requests are calm and composed.	○ Responses to questions/ requests are emotional but composed.	○ Responses to questions/ requests vary from rapid and agitated to slow and subdued.	○ Responses to questions/ requests are emotionally volatile.	○ Responses to questions/ requests noncompliant due to interference of emotions.	○ Cannot respond to questions/ requests because of interference of emotions.
B E H A V I O R A L	○ Behaviors are socially appropriate.	○ Behaviors mostly effective, outbursts if present are inconsequential.	○ Behaviors are ineffective, yet not dangerous.	○ Behaviors are maladaptive but not immediately destructive.	○ Behaviors are likely to intensify crisis situation.	○ Behaviors are ineffective and accelerate the crisis.
	○ Family rules unaffected.	○ Family rules mostly followed.	○ Family rules recognized but adjusted.	○ Family rules altered.	○ Family rules suspended	○ Family rules abandoned.
	○ Daily routine unimpeded.	○ Daily routine mostly followed with minimal effort.	○ Daily routine experiencing periodic disruptions.	○ Daily routine noticeably compromised.	○ Daily routine experiencing significant disruptions.	○ Daily functioning not preformed.
	○ Behaviors are not a threat or danger nonexistent.	○ Behaviors demonstrates frustration, but is nonthreatening.	○ Behaviors minimal threat to family or others.	○ Behaviors are a potential threat to family or others.	○ Behaviors are impulsive and harmful to family or others.	○ Behaviors are highly destructive possibly to cause injury/ death to family or others.
	○ Roles are stable.	○ Roles mostly stable but still functional for daily living.	○ Roles fluctuating but still functional for daily living.	○ Roles fluctuating and not functional for daily living.	○ Role overlap interrupts functioning for daily living.	○ Role breakdown prevents functioning for daily living.

FIGURE 11.1 (*continued*)

Digital Download Download at CengageBrain.com

SEVERITY SCALES (continued)

	1 No Impairment	2/3 Minimal Impairment	4/5 Low Impairment	6/7 Moderate Impairment	8/9 Marked Impairment	10 Severe Impairment
C O G N I T I V E	○ Decisions are considerate of family members.	○ Decisions are not consistently considerate of family members.	○ Decisions are inconsiderate of family members.	○ Decisions are arbitrary and antagonistic of family members.	○ Decisions are random with a potential to be harmful to family members.	○ Decisions are a clear and present danger to family members.
	○ Decisions are logical and reasonable.	○ Decisions are indecisive but only with respect to crisis.	○ Decisions are inconsistent and sometimes unreasonable.	○ Decisions erratic and reality and interfering with daily functioning.	○ Decisions are illogical, have little basis in and generalized beyond crisis.	○ Decision making frenetic or frozen and not based in reality and shuts down daily functioning.
	○ Discussion of crisis event substantially matches reality with communication being normal within the family.	○ Discussion influenced by crisis, but communication not effected.	○ Discussion focused on crisis but with prompting still able to consider other issues within family.	○ Discussion is limited to crisis situation disrupting communication within family.	○ Discussion about crisis intrusive to communication within family.	○ Discussion is chaotic shutting down communication within the family.
	○ Accept views of others in family.	○ Acknowledge views of others in family.	○ Acknowledging views of others in family difficult.	○ Disagreement with views of others in family.	○ Antagonistic of views of others in family.	○ Aggressively confronting views of others.
	○ Problem solving strategy agreed on.	○ Problem solving agreed on with minimal dissent.	○ Problem solving inconsistency within family.	○ Problem solving disputed with no agreement.	○ Problem solving argued with no consensus.	○ Problem solving not observable with no ability to focus.

CIP-Solutions, March, 2009

FIGURE 11.1 (continued)

Digital Download Download at CengageBrain.com

are in the midst of crises? The emotional or cognitive disruptions from crises can make completing any assessment instruments problematic. The question of reliability also surfaces since it is not known if individuals are responding based on only their perception or based on the collective functioning of their family (Lebow & Stroud, 2012). In addition, measures of functioning from these types of instruments are partial and are not able to examine all aspects of families in crisis (Lebow & Stroud, 2012). Another problem is that these instruments must be scored and the data deciphered into information useful for the intervention process. While useful, these instruments may not be the best choice for crises. So the default option is the triage scale (Figure 11.1), which Chaplain Hamel uses to make his determination whether it is safe to leave the Taylors for a while.

We have adapted the Triage Assessment Form: Crisis Intervention (TAF:CI) described in Chapter 2 for use with families. The Triage Assessment Form: Family Therapist (TAF:FT) uses a similar format as the TAF:CI and is based on crisis workers' observations and interactions with families. Just as with the original form, the severity of families' reactions to crises are rated in affective, behavior, and cognitive scales. Anchors for ratings were developed using the six dynamics described earlier (i.e., roles, boundaries, communication, rules, values, goals). Figure 11.1 is the TAF:FT. As with the original form a rule out method is best for rating the severity of families' reactions. Assume all families in crisis are a 10 on each of the scales. Does a family fit any of the anchors for a rating of 10? If not, move to the 8/9 anchors of marked impairment. Do any of those anchors describe your observations? Again, if not, move to 6/7 and keep moving down the scale until at least one of the anchors match your observations. If families match half or more, the higher number in the category is most likely correct; if less than half, the lower number is probably accurate. Scores on individual scales suggest the reaction needing attention at the moment with the highest being the reaction needing attention at that moment. The composite or total score indicates the directedness of the intervention whether that be a nondirect, collaborative, or direct. The higher the total score, the more direct the intervention should be.

Assessment can be confusing when working with families. The confusion involves assessing family members individually and the families as a whole. What happens if one family member seems rather calm and collected while another person in the family is reacting just the opposite and is particularly disturbed to the point of hysteria? What and how do you assess these situations? Simply assess individual families using the original TAF:CI and the family using the TAF:FT. Crises causing a wide range of reactions among individual family members mean you attend to individual family members with extreme reactions while simultaneously helping families address the hardships caused by the crisis. These situations call on crisis workers to do a juggling act, moving between addressing individual needs and helping families deal with crises as a unit. A general guideline is to attend to individual's reactions if these are interfering with helping families as a whole.

This excerpt shows Chaplain Hamill switching between helping the Taylor family and concentrating on reactions of individual family members. In this excerpt, Chaplain Hamill bumps into the Taylors in the ICU waiting room. During the exchange, Mrs. Taylor becomes overwhelmed cognitively as she confronts the reality of Dianne's injuries. She becomes caught in a loop of thinking that does not let her or other family members address the pressing issues caused by the crisis. The severity of her reactions on the TAF:CI are 6's for the affective and behavioral scales while the cognitive scale is an 8. Chaplain Hamill must take steps to help Mrs. Taylor stop her merry-go-round thinking patterns before he can address family issues. William, the youngest in the family, feels the mounting pressure and is crushed under the weight of his emotional reaction which at times reaches an 8 or even 9 on the affective scale. Chaplain Hamill understands William is feeling abandoned and needs support

from his parents. Chaplain Hamill weaves in and out of focusing on these two family members while also addressing family dynamics within this session.

Chaplain Hamill: Hi, how are things going since we talked yesterday?

David: Well not so good, the doctors told us Dianne will need surgery again.

Liz: (*looks down and sighs loudly*)

Wesley: (*pats his Mom on the back*). It will. OK, Mom, don't cry.

David: (*reaches over and pats her knee*)

William: (*sits still with his back straight and breathing in a measured manner but his lips are quivering*)

Chaplain Hamill: I heard that the surgery has stabilized her and she is off the critical list, but to get her walking and running again there's going to have to be some more work down the line. How about we go to the room down the hall and talk about what's coming. We can talk there and I can give you some information on the rehabilitation process she'll go through.

Liz: What if the nurses or doctors come looking for us? I can't miss that, you go I will stay here.

Chaplain Hamill: I think we all should go. There will be more privacy there. I'll let them know at the desk. We have to walk right by there.

Taylors: (*stand and follow the chaplain down the hall*)

In this brief exchange Chaplain Hamill recognizes the Taylor's reactions are in the moderate to marked category. Using his knowledge of the TAF:FT, he wisely decides to take control of the situation, suggesting they regroup in a more private location. He uses a directive approach, asking the Taylors to follow him down the hall. He also responds directly to Mrs. Taylor regarding her concern of the nurses not being able to find them. In the exchange Chaplain Hamill is firm but also expresses concern for the Taylors. David's daughter, Christina, has now arrived at the hospital from college.

Chaplain Hamill: (*looks around with his eyes falling on everyone for a moment*) Sounds like you got some bad news.

David: (*looks sad and worried*). She [Dianne] needs surgery again. They need to do something to her hip and pelvis I think he said. But that is not the worst of it. (*starts crying*)

Christina: Dad, don't cry, the doctors are doing the best they can. (*tears well up in her eyes*)

William: (*breathing faster and legs begin to shake*)

David: I know but . . .

Chaplain Hamill: What did the doctors say exactly?

Liz: (*blurts out*) Dianne may not ever be able to carry a child because of all this. (*jaws tightened*) I will never be a grandmother and that is that.

Chaplain Hamill: I am so sorry. (*silence follows*)

Liz: What did I do to deserve this? I have prayed and prayed.

Wesley: We all have, Mom. Everyone is praying . . .

Chaplain Hamill: My guess is you are wondering why can't something be done. Maybe why this is happening?

David: Yeah! I mean I thought . . . never mind what I thought, we just want Dianne to get better.

Chaplain Hamill: How is everyone else feeling? Sounds like you are angry.

Chaplain Hamill recognizes the Taylors are barely able to regulate their feelings. He also realizes anger is lurking just under the surface as the Taylors start asking the question of "why" all this is happening. Mr. Taylor's statement also suggests feelings could be swinging toward sadness and they feel helpless to do anything more. Chaplain Hamill continues to assess the reactions while also offering support. Note that he does not try to explain the situation but instead lets the Taylors express their feelings. At this point, Chaplain Hamill must be cautious. The Taylors should be allowed to express their feelings, but in a controlled manner. A "safety valve" must be used with the Taylors as they express their feelings because unbridled expression of emotions in crises can backfire (Myer, 2001). If left unchecked, the Taylors could spiral into an intense, counterproductive expression of feelings. Chaplain Hamill must help the Taylors express their feelings in a constructive and appropriate manner.

Chaplain Hamill: I can see everyone is on edge. I guess I would feel the same especially when nothing seems to be going right.

Liz: Yeah nothing is going right. All the doctors do is give us double talk. (*gets louder and speaks faster*) First they say this and that and use all the big medical words!

Wes: They [*doctors*] talk to us like we are stupid.

William: (*squeaks out*) Yeah, asked one if he could tell me how my sister was . . . (*sniffs*) . . . and she did not even answer.

Chaplain Hamill: Aw I am sorry William. That probably made you pretty mad.

William: (*shakes head affirmatively*)

David: And then there is all this other stuff they told us with the rehab and . . .

Liz: Right now we need to think about Dianne and her life. I mean who will ever marry her.

Wesley and Christina: (*at the same time*) What? She's like 14. Why are you saying that?

Liz: (*angrily*) What nothing . . . who will want to marry a woman who cannot have children?

David: Liz, we don't know . . .

Liz: Yes we do. We have to plan on that and my daughter will never get married.

Chaplain Hamill: Let's try to slow down for a moment. (*looks around the room*)

Wesley: Mom, how do you know what will happen?

William: (*tears welling up in his eyes and no one seems to be noticing*)

Chaplain Hamill: Liz, try to slow down...

Liz: (*interrupts*) I sat up all night figuring this out. You cannot tell me any different . . . no uterus, no children, no marriage. What could be more . . .

David: Stop Liz, the doctors . . .

Chaplain Hamill: Let's everyone take a time-out for a moment.

William: (*breaks into tears*) What about me? No one even talks to me anymore. All I get is to go to the lady's house down the street. No one loves me as much as Dianne . . .

David: (*reaches over to William*) Hey, you are my little man, I still love you.

Wesley and Christina: (*both shake their heads affirming the statement*)

Liz: (*sits still with a glazed look as if she has shut the world out*)

Chaplain Hamill: Nothing seems to be going right for anyone at the moment. I am sure there is some way to get some better answers. Let's see if we can figure that out...Is anyone thirsty? I will get the nurse's aide to bring us some water bottles.

As the session unfolds, Chaplain Hamill sees the situation beginning to unravel. Mrs. Taylor's cognitions are circular and keeping the family im-mobile with respect to focusing on more urgent con-cerns. William's feelings surface and possibly could be an attempt to redirect the attention to him. Fam-ily dynamics involved at this time are that the bound-ary issues have been altered, communication has been disrupted, roles have been changed, and values have been compromised. Chaplain Hamill listens carefully to everyone, even to William, the youngest of the Taylors. He uses an owning statement to communicate support and empathy for the family. Chaplain Hamill acknowledges the building emotions but guides the family into focusing on ways to get the information they want rather than get caught in an unproductive diatribe of criticizing doctors and feeling sorry for themselves. His request for water at the end serves as a break, allowing the Taylors to shift gears to a more productive mindset.

Ratings for the TAF:FT vary from the moder-ate to marked range of severity. The affective rat-ings are at least a 7 and at times may move up to an 8. The Taylor's values and boundaries both are be-ing disturbed as they cope. Their daily routine is in flux as they attend to Dianne at the expense of other family members. The Taylor's behavioral reactions are in the low marked severity range as the family copes with the consequences of Dianne's accident. Family rules are ignored or completely dismissed, causing significant changes in the way the Taylors interact with each other. Dynamics associated with cognitive reactions are in the moderate range as communications have broken down and deci-sions about family goals are being challenged. Chaplain Hamill works to interrupt Mrs. Taylor's repeating thoughts and directs support to William while also helping the Taylors address the collective hardships.

Chaplain Hamill: Let's look at this one thing at a time. (*looks around*)

Taylors: (*look at each other and shake their heads affirmatively except for Liz and William*)

Chaplain Hamill: (*looks over at William and speaks in a soft voice*) William, what is going on? Can you tell me?

William: (*sniffs and look up*) Nobody talks to me any-more. They all whisper and when I come they stop . . . I just know they want to send me away so they can take care of Dianne.

David: (*surprised*) Oh no way little man. (*reaches over and pulls him close*)

Chaplain Hamill: William, what do you want to hear from your Dad and Mom? (*looks at Liz who is still sitting staring*)

William: (*in a soft voice and hesitantly*) That . . . that they are not going to send me away.

David: No way, we would never do that.

Liz: (*says nothing and still staring*)

Chaplain Hamill: Liz?

Liz: Yeah sure, I love you sweetie. (*staring and not look-ing at William as she says this*)

David: (*rolls his eyes*)

Wesley and Christina: (*sitting quietly and watching*)

Chaplain Hamill: (*using a soft voice*) Liz, where are you now?

Liz: Oh sorry, I was just thinking.

Chaplain Hamill: Thinking what?

Liz: (*looks over at Chaplain Hamill*) Well, you know, that Dianne will not get married. I thought maybe she can go to med school or something, maybe be a lawyer.

Chaplain Hamill: I see. What makes you think she will not get married?

Liz: (*raises her eyebrows*) Haven't you been listening? She can't have children.

Chaplain Hamill: Have the doctors said that is certain?

Liz: No . . . but I know that will happen.

David: Liz, you don't know that for sure . . .

Chaplain Hamill: Liz, you seem to be jumping to conclu-sions. How about I go with you to talk with doctors?

Liz: Sure, but they will say the same thing.

Chaplain: Probably but sometimes someone from outside the family hears things a little different.

David: That would be great, thanks so much. Liz, don't you think so?

Liz: Sure I guess it would be okay.

Chaplain Hamill: OK, at the end of the session we can set a time for that. Right now let's talk about ways everyone can be a part of helping while Dianne is in the hospital. (*looks at William and smiles*) That in-cludes you too, William.

William: Cool.

As the session continues, Chaplain Hamill takes control by asking the Taylors to consider the is-sues one at a time rather than dumping everything out at once. He addresses boundary issues being encouraging the Taylors to communicate with each other. Chaplain Hamill begins by talking with William and helping the rest of the family become aware of his distress. The goal is to bring all family members into the discussion and help them support each other. Chaplain Hamill also quietly confronts Mrs. Taylor's catastrophizing the situation, asking her to share her thoughts, and does not allow her to pull him into discussing long-term decisions such as career choice. He offers to accompany Mr. and Mrs. Taylor as they talk with the physician. That seems to help them as they may have misheard what they were being told.

Support. Plain and simple—families in crisis need **support**. Discussed in Chapter 3, crisis workers must be able to communicate a sense of caring in order to help clients in crisis. The same holds true for families. In fact, the crisis intervention process may be the best opportunity for families to find the needed support. Often families believe they are alone, marginalized, and otherwise not deserving of support when faced with crises. The pioneer mindset of self-sufficiency might emerge with families believing no support is needed, that they can do it themselves, that they are self-sufficient. While this attitude is admirable and often allows families to weather crises, sometimes this belief is not enough. Everyone, including families, needs someone to lean on from time to time.

Support can be considered the cornerstone of crisis intervention. Support provides a foundation on which family can rebuild their lives following crises. This means listening to families as a group talk about their experience (Ectherling, Presbury, & McKee, 2005). As individual family members share their experience, group understanding or "knowing" will evolve. "Knowing" refers to the family forming a meaning of crises as collective apart from individual family members (Boss, 2002). The support that is needed comes in four different forms: (1) psychological, (2) logistical, (3) social, and/or (4) informational. Each of these types of support is important in the intervention process. Families almost always need more than one of these supports to face the adversities brought on by crises. Psychological support for families involves crisis workers joining the struggle of families as they search for ways to overcome the hardships brought on by crises. Joining with the family conveys you are connected with families and you will be with them through crises (Peterson, Hennon, & Knox, 2010). The connection ranges from being a

sounding board for mild crises to taking a direct role in decision making with families with more severe reactions.

Logistical support comes in the form of helping families access resources (Myers & Wee, 2005). Resources may involve referring families to appropriate agencies that give assistance to actually contacting and possibly arranging transportation for families to access the resource. For example, families may need logistical support following a fire that destroyed their home and most of their belongings. Crisis workers can help these families locate resources for clothing, shelter, and so on. If they do not have transportation, you might have to arrange for that as well. Social support concerns connecting families with others with a shoulder to lean on. This may be with families having similar experiences or to organizations (e.g., church, community centers) that can provide ongoing, longer-term support. Social support has been shown to be very important for families experiencing crises, creating a network of families to talk with about their experiences (Cohen, 2004; Myers & Wee, 2005). Helping families to recognize they are not alone by connecting them with others having similar experiences is a powerful tool to facilitate recovery. Informational support involves facilitating families in gathering the data needed to make decisions. Because crises are not planned, families more often than not do not have the experience or knowledge base to face the effects of crises. Educating families through informational support gives families the knowledge needed to work toward a positive resolution to crises.

The Taylors are in desperate need of support as they struggle with the meaning of Dianne's injuries. The family members fall into disarray as their routines are disrupted and Dianne's accident has challenged the Taylor's values. The excerpt below takes place in a small room off the Intensive Care Unit a couple days after the accident. Chaplain Hamill is with Mr. and Mrs. Taylor, Wesley, and William. Cristina is not there because of a test in one of her classes. In this exchange Mr. and Mrs. Taylor lament over the prospects of Dianne's injuries that might result in permanent damage or possibly even death.

Liz: (*crying*) Why did this happen? We go to church all the time, I just don't understand. What did I do to deserve this?

Wesley: (*rubs his mother's shoulder*) Come on, Mom, it is going to be OK.

Chaplain Hamill: You sound really worried.

Liz: That my beautiful daughter is going to die (*cries uncontrollably*).

William: You mean sis going to die? I thought you said...

David: (*interrupts*) Well the doctors did not say that exactly. They said that they just don't know.

Chaplain Hamill: Let's slow down a little . . . Liz, what are you thinking about?

Liz: I don't know, I wonder why this happened? What did I do?

William: (*looks puzzled*) Mom, I don't understand you said . . .

Chaplain Hamill: Liz, what have you been thinking?

Liz: (*turns to David and does not say anything*)

David: (*takes a deep breath*) I am not sure I understand everything, I mean all the doctor talk. Basically they said Dianne needs surgery to speed up recovery. But they said it is risky and without the surgery she may not walk again. (*sighs*) But she might not make it through the surgery. We have to make a decision. I just don't know. (*looks down*) We have always tried to be good parents but then this happens. Dianne is a straight A student and this happens. What did we do wrong? Why are we being punished?

Liz: Dianne will be at least a year behind in school. (*wipes tears from her eyes*) That is even is she even able to go back to school. The doctor said they still cannot tell the extent of her brain injuries. Christina will have to drop out of college in order to help in taking care of things around the house.

David: Let's hope it does not come to that.

Chaplain Hamill: Let's go back just a bit. Liz, you asked something about why are you being punished?

Liz: That just keeps going through my mind. I just cannot figure it out. Over and over again I think I have done something wrong or bad.

Chaplain: Let me see if I understand . . . (*sighs . . . you think you caused the accident or that you are being punished?

Liz: I cannot think of any other explanation. I mean . . .

William: But, but you are good, Mom.

Wesley: Yes, the best.

David: Yea, the best, but still I have thought kind of the same thing . . . I mean did I do something wrong?

Chaplain Hamill: Both of you seem to have lots of questions.

Liz: David, you are great Dad . . .

Chaplain Hamill: Are you all listening to what each other is saying?

In this exchange Chaplain Hamill listens to the questions the Taylors are asking and tries to get the Taylors to simply listen to each other in the hopes of them finding encouragement from each other. The values of the faith, their ability to be parents, and education all come into question in this exchange. These questions indicate that their values are unable to provide a rationalization for the accident. Initially, Mrs. Taylor searches for an explanation for the accident. In this effort, she begins by alluding to the importance of her faith but quickly says she may be the cause of the crisis because somehow she failed as a parent. Chaplain Hamill attempts to allow her to explore these issues but gets distracted by a statement made by Mr. Taylor. Mr. Taylor also questions their ability at parenting. His question about why are they being punished suggests the family's values are being challenged. Chaplain Hamill notices the conversation shifting and makes a statement bringing the Taylors back to the issue of values. Questioning these values leads to Wesley trying to console his mother. William is confused and not sure what is happening. Both Wesley and William affirm their mother's ability to be a parent. In the same way, Liz supports her husband's parenting ability.

Reestablish Control. **Reestablishing control** is an essential, recurring task as families search, sometimes desperately, for ways to regain stable, predictable functioning—essential because reestablishing control is the basis for climbing back to a sense of normality and recurring because of the unpredictable nature of crises that cause setbacks as families labor to regain equilibrium. The immediate goal is to stop families' downward spiral because familiar methods of functioning become increasing ineffective when in a crisis situation. Once the downhill slide is halted, the objective becomes one of rebuilding families' capacity to maintain the restored stability and begin a steady climb back to functioning, as much as possible, in a routine manner. Short-term, concrete goals are generally the most effective to helping families reestablish control. These goals might be set for the next few minutes, hours, or possibly for a day or two. The time frame greatly depends on the severity of families' reactions to crises. Typically, the more severe families react, the shorter the time fame for goals. Accomplishing the goals helps families regain control and create a foundation on which to restore day-to-day functioning.

Reestablishing control often means helping families to simply slow down, to calm themselves. Families in crisis may find themselves going at full throttle as they scramble to maintain order and manage the aftereffects of the situation. The frenetic pace may be thought of as the only way to survive and manage the chaos. Often, families might believe that with just a little more effort, normality with reemerge. Yet from the outside, the frenzied pace suggests families are in disarray with limited to no ability to manage the fallout from crises. Slowing down families creates a situation that will allow them to take one thing at a time rather than trying to untangle a jumbled mess all at once. Taking things one at a time is central to reestablishing control. Helping families prioritize the order lets them address the situation in manageable chunks, little by little.

Reestablishing control also helps families sort through the chaos to discover and create a new foundation to regulate the effect of crises. Generating a new base allows them to start the climb to a reliable, routine day-to-day functioning that may not be the same as prior to experiencing a crisis. An aspect of reestablishing can involve a psychoeducational component. Information is a powerful tool to allay fears that they are dysfunctional in some way or another. Providing information on typical reactions, what to expect, the potential for setbacks, and so on all ease the anxiety of not knowing what is happening. This newly established level of functioning can be the basis for new ways of coping and developing resilience (Boss, 2002).

The chaos brought on by Dianne's accident is mushrooming and the Taylor's ability to maintain control is steadily decreasing. In this exchange Chaplain Hamill sees that family boundaries and communication are being affected. In an attempt to slow down the merry-go-round the Taylors find themselves on, Chaplain Hamill works on the helping them reestablish control. He recognizes that better communication is needed in order for the family to find a way to address the crisis. Notice how communication is limited and somewhat truncated. In this exchange you see that decisions are being made without including all family members affected by the decision. This situation has the potential to spiral out of control unless Chaplain Hamill can find a way to open communications lines.

Chaplain Hamill: David and Liz, how are things going? I see you brought Christina with you. Nice to see you again.

Liz: Good to see you and thanks for all your help . . . (*takes a deep breath*) . . . I, we, have to talk with you. Something has come up.

Chaplain Hamill: Sure I am happy to help. What is going on?

David: (frowns) It is like this (*looks at Christina*). We need help because Liz has to be at the hospital with Dianne. I have to work and well, we need someone to help out with the other kids.

Christina: (interrupts) Dad, you know I want to help but . . . well I just can't all the time.

Chaplain Hamill: Hold on what are we talking about?

Liz: Let me explain. (*sighs*) Christina is in college about 50 miles from here. We need her to be at home more, you know, to pick up the slack.

Chaplain Hamill: Slack? What do you mean?

Liz: You see since Dianne is still in the hospital we need someone to be at home when William gets out of school. Like David said I have to be at the hospital and he does not get off work until after 6 sometimes. How can I expect Wesley to do it because he has track practice every day and sometimes he does not get home until way after 6. (*sighs and pauses*) We have imposed on the neighbors enough to watch William and now I think it is Christina's turn. (*looks at Chaplain Hamill for support*)

Christina: Why me, it just isn't fair that should I give up my stuff and not Wesley? You always think he is the best. It just isn't fair! Dad, can't you do something, find someone else to do it? Please.

David: I know it does not sound fair, but . . . well I think Liz has come up with an OK solution.

Chaplain Hamill: Sounds like everyone doesn't agree about what needs to happen.

David: You can say that again. (*rolls his eyes*) We have been round and round about this. Every time we end up at the same place.

Liz: (*glances over and bites her lip*) We have talked this through and I thought you agreed.

David: I know, I know. But every time you always say it has to be Christina. Why not Wesley? I know he is your son, but Christina is my daughter. She is in college and is just as important.

Chaplain Hamill: Hold on let's . . .

Liz: (*interrupts*) Are you saying that it is just because he is my son? That I favor him more than your daughter? I am just thinking of Dianne is all. (*tears fill her eyes*)

Chaplain Hamill: (*hold up his hand making a "T"*) Time-out, let's each take a turn. Help me understand what is going on.

David: (*looks at both Liz and Christina*) Last night in the hospital cafeteria Liz and I talked about how we were going to manage everything. I mean we all are busy.

Christina: (*interrupts*) Yea right, I was not even included and you . . .

Chaplain Hamill: (*interrupts*) Hold on, everyone will have a turn to say something.

David: OK, well Liz and I tried to figure this all out. I mean we never had to deal with anything like this. We are at the end of our rope and barely hanging on. So Liz thought it best for Christina to move back home and help out with William until things settle down. To be honest I am not so sure, but she seems so certain this is best.

Liz: (*looks tired*) David, we talked about this and you agreed. I know we usually involve everyone on big decisions but we just don't have the time right now.

David: I know but we can't ignore the kids. What do you think, Chaplain Hamill?

Christina: Yea, what do you think? (*looks at Liz and glares*)

Chaplain Hamill: OK, wait a minute. Let me see if I got this straight. Liz, you and David discussed this last night while having dinner here at the hospital. And Christina was not there. You just told her she had to move home?

Liz: Well, yeah. I mean I thought David liked the idea. William sure did when I told him.

Chaplain Hamill: I don't understand . . . you told William.

Liz: Yeah, I asked William if he would like Christina to help and he said that would be cool.

Chaplain Hamill: So does Wesley know what is going on?

David: Well, not yet . . . and that could be a problem too, because he is using Christina's bedroom now.

Through this exchange Chaplain Hamill works to de-escalate the rhetoric that is growing increasingly heated and unproductive. This process involves helping the Taylors sort through the logic of the decisions that are being made. He suspects, and rightfully so, that the Taylors are not in control and decisions are being made in almost a random way without thinking through ramifications. Several times in this excerpt, Chaplain Hamill tries to clarify exactly how and what decisions are being made and to slow things down. The goal of these clarifications is to create a better understanding of the decision as well as slow the process down. In this way, he is working to assist the Taylors to regain a sense of control.

Problem Exploration. Problem exploration is critical with families because of the inclination to compartmentalize the effect of crises (Myer & Moore, 2006). The tendency is to define and understand crises on an individual basis, not the families as a collective unit. The impact of crises on families as a system is an afterthought, and sometimes disregarded. Attention is concentrated on helping individual family members, while intervening with families as a unit is neglected. (Myer, Lewis, & James, 2013). Consequently, families' dynamics and issues are not addressed. Not addressing these issues can be the seed of problems emerging in the future.

Problem exploration involves listening to all family members. All family members are affected although the impact may be experienced in a different way (Myer & Moore, 2006). Every family member should have a voice in this task. Care must be exercised not to allow a single family member to dominate and arbitrarily assign meaning to crises or to demarcate the boundaries of the resolution process.

Problem exploration means focusing on the immediate effect of crises on families' ability to function. Digging up skeletons of past problems or dissecting the causes and undercurrents of families' misfortunes is not the goal of crisis intervention. Although these issues influence families' reactions, attention should remain on identifying and addressing the issues surfacing because of the current crisis. Problem exploration should be directed at recognizing the dynamics being affected, identify potential actions leading to a positive resolution, and channeling families' energies in that direction. How have families' dynamics changed in the aftermath of crises? Are the changes beneficial or detracting from families' ability to work through crises? These questions help in appreciating the effect of crises on families. What are some actions families can take to manage the current circumstances? How do these actions affect and/or influence family dynamics? Brainstorming can be helpful to facilitate families' movement at identifying possible actions to take in the midst of crises. Another techniques is "priming the pump." In times past, priming the pump was needed if you could not get water out of a pump. No matter how hard you pumped the handle no water would come up. However, by pouring a little water into the pump and then pumping the water created a suction making the pump work. In crisis intervention this method means crisis workers offer a few suggestions, priming the pump in a manner of speaking, which will hopefully kick-start families to coming up with their own solutions. Helping families channel energies into constructive solutions and actions is also part of problem exploration. At times this means crisis workers taking the lead while at other times this involves pointing families in the most practical and beneficial direction.

In the days following Dianne's accident, the Taylor family is trying to come to terms with the changes in their routine. The accident caused their entire schedule to be altered to the point no one is able to get things done. Chaplain Hamill sees the turmoil and begins to help the Taylors sort through things in a more reasonable manner. Note the way Chaplain Hamill offers suggestions without imposing these. This strategy works well with families and jump-starts their ability to use common sense in coping with practical issues that often are a part of families' crises.

David: Thanks for talking to us again, Chaplain. I feel like we are becoming a pain in the you-know-where.

Chaplain Hamill: What makes you say that?

Liz: It seems like we are in here almost every day. I know other people have problems too.

Chaplain Hamill: Thanks for considering me, but don't worry. (*He looks around the room at the family. David and Liz are sitting on the couch with William next to her; Christina and Wesley are sitting in chairs.*) What's bothering you?

David: I don't know how to start but . . . you see we have this problem. The costs are beginning to mount up. And well, I had to take off work to pick up William from school and well now they are beginning to dock my pay. Not much, but some. I even had to cancel a business trip.

Liz: And yes, I have not been to work since the accident. So I am not getting a check either. And I know they are cutting back at the office so they may just decide to let me go.

Chaplain Hamill: Sounds like things are not going well.

David: I guess so . . . we are doing OK but if this keeps up our savings will be gone.

Chaplain Hamill: You seem to be stretching things pretty thin just to keep your head above water?

Liz: Yes, but not for long. Soon Christina's tuition for next year will be due, that is if she stays in school (looks at Christina).

Christina: (*interrupts*) But I thought that . . .

Liz: (*Liz looks over and continues talking*) David and I talked about dipping into retirement funds and well . . . we know that is not a good idea but I think we may have to pay for Christina's tuition.

Chaplain Hamill: Wow, everything seems to be piling up with no sign of relief.

David: Yes, you could say that. I was hoping to retire early but now who knows. And well I was up for a big promotion and now that's not going to happen. I mean everyone at work is supportive and knows I am having a tough time. But the promotion would involve a lot of travel that I just can't do now.

Wesley: Well, what about me, I want to help but I have a chance to go to the state track meet and get a scholarship offer. If I have to get a job even part-time like David said I won't be able to train. (*crosses his arms and looks at his mother*)

Liz: When did this come up?

David: I am just trying to figure things out.

Liz: Without me?

David: You are always at the hospital, and it came up.

The Taylors are bombarding Chaplain Hamill with all the problems that have come about since Dianne's accident. The family is overwhelmed and unable to see the separate issues. Their world is crumbling up and crashing around them. While all of the problems stem from the accident, each needs to be tackled individually. Chaplain Hamill must take control of the exchange so that the Taylors can begin the process of addressing the practical fallout from the accident.

Chaplain Hamill: Slow down, sounds like some big decisions need to be made, let's see if we can sort those out . . . let me think. . . . (*pause*). . . . what is the most pressing thing that needs to get done right now?

Liz: Well, for Dianne to get better and come home.

Chaplain Hamill: Yes, that's the most important thing, I agree, but what needs to be done right now? What do you have control over?

David: (*looks around at everyone*) I guess I just cannot take off work so much? Liz, what do you think?

Liz: I suppose but you can't because someone has to pick up William from school and stay with him. We have talked about that. You know I just can't right now.

Chaplain Hamill: Wait, you said something really important. Someone has to pick up William at school and be with him at home.

David: Yea, we live too close to the school so he cannot take a bus. And we live far enough away that he can't walk home, too may busy streets. And the only one who can is me, which means (*shrugs shoulders*), I have to get him.

Chaplain Hamill: Mmmmm, yes I guess that's a problem . . . I wonder if there is an afterschool program. Do you know if the school has that?

Liz: (*looks at her husband and her eyes widen*) Do you know? I think I remember something about that . . . but just never thought about it.

David: Yes, maybe, I remember a letter or something about. Why didn't I think of that before?

Chaplain Hamill: You both have been very busy and worried about Dianne. Don't blame yourselves. Maybe looking into an afterschool program is something to consider?

Liz: (*shakes her head yes*) I bet they would also help him with his homework, like I usually do.

David: Thanks! I don't think we ever considered that. I bet I would not have to leave the office early then.

Chaplain Hamill: (*smiles*) Sounds like a plan. When do you think you could find out about the program?

Liz: First thing in the morning I will call.

Chaplain Hamill: What time does the school office open?

Liz: I am sure it is at 8 in the morning. I think I'll call then or a few minutes later.

Chaplain Hamill: Sounds good. I'll stop by first thing in the morning to see how it goes, is that OK, Liz?

Liz: Sure!

Chaplain Hamill: OK, that takes care of two things, David taking off work and someone being with William after school. What is next? Maybe we can see what can be worked out about your job, Liz, or maybe Christina's tuition?

In this exchange, Chaplain Hamill deftly directs the discussion to practical issues rather than allowing the Taylors to wallow in what seems to be a morass of problems. By offering one suggestion about an afterschool program two problems are taken care. The Taylors react enthusiastically and feel empowered by the process. Notice how Chaplain Hamill gets a commitment about contacting the school concerning the afterschool program. This step is important because families may need that in order to remember. Chaplain Hamill then gives the Taylors a choice about the issue to talk about next.

Follow-up. Follow-up as a task occurs periodically during the intervention, not just at the end or after a few days. Crisis workers should periodically check with clients in crisis to ensure they are aware of what is happening. Attending to this task can be seen as boring and almost tedious. However, remember that families' awareness of immediate circumstances is often compromised and as a group or individual family members are preoccupied thinking about the crisis (Myer, Lewis, & James, 2013). Families may seem to be paying attention, yet the focus on the crisis impairs their ability to respond to questions and follow simple instructions. Periodically "checking in" allows crisis workers to monitor families' attentiveness to the current situation and ability to take action on plans to resolve the crisis.

A second type of follow-up is short-term follow-up (Greenstone & Leviton, 2011) and may be either formal or informal (Roberts, 2005). Short term does not mean weeks or months, but rather hours and days. Depending on the situation, accomplishing this task ranges from easy to impossible. Chaplain Hamill can easily follow up with the Taylors by occasionally stopping by the ICU. This type of informal follow-up allows Chaplain Hamill to assess the Taylors to determine if a more formal meeting is needed. Formal follow-up means setting a time to meet and talk about progress being made on the road to recovery. In other situations, short-term follow-up is more difficult because families are not easily accessible. These situations might require setting a meeting time for families to come to an office or visiting them in their home. Phone contact might also be useful to check in with families.

Long-term follow-up is a third type that is useful with families. Long-term follow-up involves monitoring families for mental health issues that could emerge a few months or longer after disasters. These problems may be seen because families fail to adjust to life after a crisis. The result is continued strife in the family as they strive to reconcile the changes in their dynamics. Long-term follow-up also allows crisis workers to check for symptoms related to a diagnosis with a mental health disorder (Myer, 2014). If these surface, referral for personal counseling is recommended (Kolski, Jongsma Jr., & Myer, 2012).

The morning after Chaplain Hamill makes the suggestion for the Taylors to look into afterschool programs for William he checks in with Mrs. Taylor. Mrs. Taylor is in the ICU waiting room reading a book and he stops by.

Chaplain Hamill: Liz, good morning.

Liz: (*looks up from her book*) Oh, hi.

Chaplain Hamill: Sorry, I did not mean to interrupt your reading.

Liz: No . . . please sit down. It is OK.

Chaplain Hamill: Thanks. (*sits in the chair across from her*) How are things this morning? How is Dianne doing?

Liz: Thanks for asking, you have been so much help. Dianne . . . (*takes a deep breath*) . . . not much change but the doctors are more hopeful now.

Chaplain Hamill: Great news, I am sure that is a relief.

Liz: Yes, I just keep praying. Oh I almost forgot. You were so helpful yesterday. (*smiles*) I got William set up for the afterschool program. The school was really helpful and William is really excited. He can't wait for school to be over so he can be with his friends.

Chaplain Hamill: I am really happy that worked out.

Liz: Me too, you were so helpful. I don't know why I didn't think of that myself.

Chaplain Hamill: You have had other things on your mind.

In this brief exchange, Chaplain Hamill follows up on the conversation from yesterday. Mrs. Taylor followed through on her commitment to contact the school and got William enrolled in the afterschool program. If Mrs. Taylor had not made the phone call, Chaplain Hamill's follow-up could have been a reminder for her to make the call.

Crisis intervention with families involves working on these tasks. Sometime the process moves very

quickly, while at other times moving through the tasks takes more time. Safety, assessment, and support are continuously worked on through the intervention process, whereas the tasks of making contact/predispositioning, reestablishing control, problem exploration, and follow-up are addressed as needed. Periodically during the intervention these later four tasks may need to be worked on when families are sidetracked.

Stages of Family Resolution of Crises

Historically, crises were typically considered **LO9** to be resolved in 6 to 8 weeks. However, over the past decade it has been recognized that the impact of crises can be longer (Myer & Moore, 2006). Depending on the specific crisis, families' recovery may range from months to years. This section continues to follow the Taylor family as they struggle with the consequences of Dianne's accident. Up to now, only Chaplain Hamill has been involved in helping the Taylors in the few days following Dianne's accident. However, Dianne's discharge is imminent, which means the Taylors will be confronted with a new set of hardships. Mr. Paul Johnson, a local pastoral counselor enters into the Taylor's life as they continue to grapple with the consequences of the crisis.

Families go through a predictable series of stages as they work to resolve crises. What is not as predictable is the time frame through these stages. The number of stages families experience following a crisis varies among the assorted models (Weber, 2011). A condensed three-stage model seems most practical for working with families experiencing crises. The stages are survival, adjustment, and adaptation (Myer, 2014). Each of the phases presents a unique set of issues and challenges for helping families (Walsh, 2012b). As a result, crisis intervention strategies fluctuate depending on the phase of recovery. Some families race through the stages, barely missing a beat or experiencing much disruption. Other families seem to move through the stages as if their feet are stuck in molasses while going uphill with weights dragging them back. Both internal and external factors have a significant role as families work to recapture their ability to move on and function on a day-to-day basis (Boss, 2002). Among these factors are families' experience with similar situations (Boss, 2002), the amount of change resulting from crises (Myer & Moore, 2006), family cohesion (Olson, 2000), resilience (Rosenfeld, et al., 2005), and their reliance on their faith and spirituality (Robert & Kelly, 2015; Walker, Courtois, & Aten, 2015). It is important to recognize the stage families are in in order to match the intervention process accordingly.

Survival Stage. The survival stage of recovery occurs from the first few hours through possibly 3 to 4 weeks following crises (Rosenfeld et al., 2005). Initially, the primary focus of this stage is to meet the physical needs of families if needed (Snider et al., 2010). For example, families in crisis following disaster might need assistance locating shelter, food, and clothing. If physical issues are not a concern, the survival stage involves helping families recognize and acknowledge a new reality brought on by the crisis. While this is easily said, in some situations it is not so easily done. Families may cling to and long for familiar ways, ignoring and resisting change in order to ward off uncomfortable thoughts and feelings (Walsh, 2012b). A family may long for walking the dog around the block like they did almost every evening. They may seek "comfort" food such as mom's meatloaf and mashed potatoes smothered in gravy or a pot of collard greens with pork loin and corn bread. Families will want to find anything familiar that reminds them of fond memories of better times.

Many families will also seek guidance and comfort through connections in their spiritual tradition (Walker et al., 2015; Walsh, 2012b) in the survival stage. Crises can be a catalyst for families to find the strength in their spirituality to withstand the hardships resulting from crises (Boss, 2002; Richards et al., 2015; Walsh, 2009). However, some families might not find solace in their spiritual tradition or culture. Instead crises may cause them to have reservations about their spirituality and cultural traditions (Public Broadcasting Service, 2002). Addressing these issues in crisis intervention depends on the setting and should be done with care. The setting plays a major role in the way spirituality is discussed. For example, Chaplain Hamill is in a position to introduce spirituality into the sessions with the Taylors. His training also gives a strong foundation and understanding that can be used when discussing spirituality. However, crisis workers who are not housed in a faith-based agency or does not have training in this area may need to be more careful about discussions in this area.

Patience is critical as you listen to families as a group talk about their experience (Ectherling, Presbury, & McKee, 2005). They may need to tell their story not just once, but multiple times as they attempt to make meaning of the crisis. As individual family members share their experience a group, understanding or "knowing" will evolve (Boss, 2002). Allowing families to tell their story is very important in this stage (Rosenfeld et al., 2005) as new feelings and thoughts are uncovered with each telling of the story as they try to make meaning from all that happened (Echterling, Presbury, & McKee, 2005; Williams, 2004). As this attempt to make meaning unfolds, watch for a hierarchy of suffering that alienates family members (Myer, Moore, & Hughes, 2003). Family members might try to play one-upmanship on others in the family either directly or indirectly. Family members may say something like "I was more scared than you [another survivor] because I saw this or heard that." Or "You can't be as stressed as me ... you weren't even around when the disaster happened, you were out of town." Indirectly they may say "No one knows how much I suffered, I don't even know yet." Defusing interactions that create hierarchies of suffering involves carefully listening and facilitating respect for everyone's experience. A second word of caution concerns family relationships and interactions. Initially families will typically "circle the wagons" and let bygones be bygones. However, after the initial coming together, the relationships that existed prior to the disaster will most likely be exaggerated. Families with healthy relationships and interactions will tend to become healthier. At the same time, families with destructive or unhealthy relationships and interactions will move more in that direction. Of course, this situation does not happen 100% of the time; exceptions do exist.

Another aspect of crisis intervention in this stage involves preparing families for postcrisis experiences (Rosenfeld et al., 2005). Using a psychoeducational approach helps prevent discouragement and frustration from setting in (Kolski, Jongsma, & Myer, 2012). Knowing what to expect strengthens families' resilience in the wake of setbacks. Guidance and ordering are both useful strategies for organizing families' thoughts about life after the crisis. Some families might simply need a gentle push while others will need their hands held during the survival stage. A special case occurs when the death of a family member is involved. Families that have lost a love one might need to be prepared for identifying the body at a morgue (Rosenfeld et al., 2005).

The following excerpt involves Chaplain Hamill preparing to refer the Taylors to Mr. Paul Johnson. Dianne has recovered to the point where she is ready for rehabilitation.

Chaplain Hamill recaps the past several weeks and also offers suggestions to the Taylors. The entire Taylor family is present and expresses their gratefulness to the chaplain. He also reads them a letter he is sending to Reverend Johnson. This letter is the hallmark of solution-focused brief therapy (SFBT) (de Shazer, 1994). It first lists the accomplishments of the Taylor family, then has a bridging statement to a task, and finally the task itself.

Chaplain Hamill: Good afternoon, nice to see everyone again.

David: Thanks for seeing us again.

Chaplain Hamill: This is a big day, one you have been hoping and praying to happen.

David: Yes, it has been a long time coming.

Liz: Yes, I thought it would never end. *(sighs)*

William: (moves closer to his mother)

Chaplain Hamill: How are you today, William?

Liz: He is OK, glad his sister is better.

Chaplain Hamill: Is that right, William?

William: (shakes head yes)

Chaplain Hamill: Wesley, Christina, how are you?

Wesley and Christina: (respond at the same time) OK . . .

Wesley: Just a lot of changes still going on.

Chaplain Hamill: Yes, I wanted to talk with you about that.

David and Liz: (look at one another)

Liz: What do you mean?

Chaplain Hamill: All of you have been through a lot. And have done very well . . .

David: Thanks to your help. *(smiles)*

Chaplain Hamill: From what you have told me there is still some things to think about.

Liz: Well yes, but that will be easier than worrying if Dianne will be alive.

Chaplain Hamill: Yes, early it was pretty difficult, but now you have other issues to consider.

David: (sighs) Yes, we know but everything will be fine when Dianne comes home after rehab.

(Wesley and Christina look at one another.)

Chaplain Hamill: Will things be OK?

Liz: There will be some changes, but we are a family and will stick together.

Chaplain Hamill: What kind of changes?

David: We have talked about this before. Dianne will need some extra care and we have to do some remodeling because, well, you know, she will have trouble getting around.

Chaplain Hamill: What about her head trauma?

Liz: (tears well up in her eyes) The doctors said they really cannot tell how much she will recover from that . . . it may take a year before she recovers as much as she will.

Chaplain Hamill: Yes, you told me. It sounds like there are still many issues after she goes to rehab.

David: Yea, we know.

Chaplain Hamill: I was wondering if you might want to keep talking with someone after Dianne is discharged?

David: (looks at Liz) I never thought about that. We were so intent on her getting out of the hospital. Liz what do you think?

Liz: Can't we just keep talking with you?

Chaplain Hamill: I would like that but the hospital wants me to talk with people in here.

Liz: Oh, OK.

Chaplain Hamill: I do know someone who has helped families in your situation. I have referred families to him. He is a pastoral counselor, Rev. Paul Johnson, and has an office close to where you live. I'll give you his card.

Liz: David, what do you think?

David: Might be a good idea I guess . . . kids, what do you think?

Wesley: (shrugs his shoulders) Whatever . . .

William: (shakes head affirmatively)

Christina: (frowns) Sure, whatever . . . I just cannot miss school anymore.

Chaplain Hamill: OK, let me give you his card. I also have a letter I will send that introduces you. I'd like to read it to you if you don't mind.

Taylors: (sort of in unison) Well um OK we guess OK so go ahead . . . umh read it.

Chaplain Hamill: (reading) Paul: This letter will introduce you to the Taylor family. *(POSITIVE, CHEERLEADING MESSAGE)* They are a remarkable blended family who have really pulled together during a long grueling ordeal with their daughter and sister Dianne's accident. Each one of these family members have had to make sacrifices to keep the family going while Dianne recovered.

It has not been easy, but they have adapted and persevered. Frankly I think that their commitment to pull together has had a great deal to do with Dianne's recovery because of their unconditional love for her and each other. They have used me as a sounding board as they struggled with some difficult life changes while Dianne recovered here at the hospital. Dianne is now ready to leave and go into rehab.

(BRIDGING STATEMENT) Because of that love and sacrifice I believe they are ready to meet the challenges that will come with Dianne's rehabilitation journey. *(HOMEWORK ASSIGNMENT)* Since they have found me to be useful to bounce ideas off of, I believe you can serve the same useful function to them outside the hospital as Dianne and the family go through rehab, so I have urged them to seek out guidance and help. Yours, Father Dan Hamill, Chaplain, St. Dominic Hospital

Liz: Oh my! You have been far more than just a sounding board. You have been our anchor and lifeline while we've been here.

David: Amen to that Father Dan. You have kept us from killing each other and focused on Dianne. You are as good as any surgeon here when you operate. *(rest of Taylors laugh)*

Chaplain Hamill: Great! Thank you. Now get your kid and get out of here!

In the exchange, he validates the Taylor's ability to cope to this point. He also recognizes the Taylors have also focused all their energy on Dianne being discharged from the hospital and have not thought of the changes their lives will have afterward. He helps the Taylors understand that although the immediate emergency and fear of Dianne not surviving has past, the Taylors still have many issues with which to cope. Notice the way he works to include all family members in the conversation even though Mrs. Taylor answers for William. Chaplain Hamill suggests the Taylors continue talking about the hardships with another person. In making the referral Chaplain Hamill predispositions the Taylors, telling them a little about the person and setting them up with a positive mental set to go on that is characteristic of SFBT (de Shazer, 1994).

Adaptation Stage. The adaptation typically starts a few days up to 3 weeks after crisis and spreads over several months and in some situations longer. In this stage families will assess their ability to carry on and search for explanations (Weber, 2011) and recognize recovery may be a daunting task that will not happen overnight (Price, Price, & McKenry, 2010). A stark realization floods into consciousness as people see their world has been turned upside down, and righting it will take hard work. Victories as well as defeats will be weathered as families work through this stage. Although the experience of families in this stage is idiosyncratic, several general types can be described. Some families rise to the challenge, not being afraid to take the first step on the long road of recovery (Echterling, Presbury, & McKee, 2005). Families reacting in this manner generally view the crisis as a shared problem and may only need guidance and a little support (Walsh, 2012b). Other families will react as if they hit a brick wall, giving up and deciding the work is too much. These families become immobile and will need support and inspiration as they work to overcome the challenges brought on by crises. Still other families are slowly worn down as they seemingly trudge through adjusting to hardship that beset them (Rosenfeld et al., 2005). These families will need encouragement and caring in order to sustain their efforts at resolving the crisis.

Be on alert for families that the crisis has reignited past unresolved crises in their lives. As we said earlier, families may have "unfinished business" about a crisis submerged below their awareness that can be triggered by a current crisis. The new crisis causes unresolved issues to emerge resulting in a roller-coaster-type experience. This situation is very possible during the adjustment stage as families are faced with numerous challenges as they put their lives back together.

Although all the strategies are useful during the adaptation phase of recovery, a few merit special attention. **Mobilization** is one of those strategies. According to Myer and James (2005), mobilization involves helping survivors activate internal strengths and trigger dormant coping mechanisms. The amount of involvement depends on the severity of families' reactions. The more severe survivors' reactions, the more direct you will be as a disaster counselor. You may find yourself being a cheerleader when using this strategy. From an SFBT standpoint the worker will be encouraging and cheering families along as they struggle to regain a daily routine (Walter & Peller, 1992). Indeed the Taylor family has done a magnificent job of blending two families together over a long period of time. From an SFBT standpoint Dianne's accident and the subsequent struggles they are having with it are an exception to the constant success they have of engineering and effectively running a blended family. Thus, the worker needs to point out that this is one exception in an extremely long line of successes and hammer that point home (Guterman, 2013). In addition, this strategy can be used as a catalyst to marshal families' energy to locate external resources.

Families who seem adrift and scattered, not able to concentrate on what needs to be done in this stage, will benefit from focusing (Myer & James, 2005). Families may be collapsing under the weight of the tasks being heaped on them in the recovery process. They might think all is lost and feel a sense of helplessness. **Focusing** helps families sort through what seems like a junk pile of responsibilities in order to focus on the most important ones at that moment. A direct approach may be indicated for survivors who are floundering and not able to even know what needs to be done. A less direct approach is required for families who may have a list of things that need to be done but simply cannot decide where to start. Leading these families involves helping them make that decision by listening patiently and getting them to focus on the most important issues. Setting and meeting short-term goals builds confidence for these families.

The flip side of the coin from focusing is expansion (Myer & James, 2005). **Expansion** allows families to see alternative perspectives to understand and recover from their experience. Families with a restricted, narrow perspective may need to have their view expanded to see other approaches to recovery. Expansion is effective with families who find themselves in a velvet rut, thinking only one way will work to help them dig out from the aftermath of crises. Although comfortable, the rut hinders recovery because it is inefficient at best and counterproductive at worst. Helping families entertain other viewpoints lets them reframe their experience and consider additional paths to recovery.

A final strategy useful in this stage is **ordering**. This strategy is used to help survivors rank order a list of what needs to be done and in what order this should be worked on (Myer & James, 2005). Some families may be stuck not knowing where to start. Other families may know what needs to be done but confused about what needs to be done first. An important part of using this strategy with families is to help them understand that the most important things needing attention are not always what needs to be done first. Many long-term goals fall into the category of important tasks. For example, recovery for some survivors involves rebuilding a house or returning to work in order to have a paycheck. Arguably these are tremendously important; however, they may not be the first thing that needs to be done. Helping families rank the issues enable them to break these into manageable portions so that they can move forward and reestablish a routine in their lives.

This following excerpt is with Rev. Johnson, the pastoral counselor who is working with the Taylors as they sort through everything that must be done during Dianne's rehabilitation. The Taylors have seen Rev. Johnson several times over the past 2 months. The sessions have focused on changes in the family caused by Dianne's accident and recovery. In this exchange Rev. Johnson directs the session to an issue that is disturbing the Taylors the most—that of Dianne's return home. Dianne is being discharged from the Rehabilitation Center but will continue to need outpatient therapy for several months. This situation along with her cognitive challenges are concerning the Taylors.

Rev. Johnson: Good to see you all again. And Christina, thanks for coming all the way from college.

Christina: (*smiles*) Thanks, I can't stay because finals are coming up . . . but Dad thought I should be here.

Rev. Johnson: Glad you could come . . .

David: Thanks for coming, Christina. I know it is hard but there is a lot to talk about and figure out.

Liz: Yes, Dianne comes home next week. (*takes a deep breath*) I am so worried.

Rev. Johnson: OK, let's recap where we are . . . Dianne is being discharged from rehab . . . when is it?

David: Next Thursday.

Rev. Johnson: Right. She is still having to use a walker but can get around by herself most of the time. How about the occupational therapy? How is that going?

Liz: She is doing really good according to what they told us . . . but she is just not the same.

Wesley: Yea, she still has problems doing some things.

William: (*giggles*) Yea, sometimes she kind of has trouble eating.

Liz: William, don't make fun of your sister.

Rev. Johnson: You all have been really nervous about that. How is the speech therapy going?

David: Well, pretty good. Most of the time she does good and gets things out. But when she can't she gets really frustrated.

Rev. Johnson: She must really be upset when that happens. How is the work on the house?

David: The contractor said it will done in a day or so.

Liz: I am just so worried.

Rev. Johnson: Tell me more.

Liz: I just don't know what I will do. I am not sure I can handle it. It's like God has dumped this dumpster load of stress on me and it's all on me to decide. (*wrings her hands and fidgets while tears well in her eyes*)

Rev. Johnson: Liz, you sound really worried. What about the rest of you? What is going on with you?

David: Well, I am worried.

Christina: Yes, I guess I am too, but when I come home in 2 weeks what is going to happen? Liz keeps saying I can take care of things, but I have no clue.

Liz: Christina, she is your sister. You should help.

Christina: My stepsister, not . . . my . . . sister.

Liz: (*starts crying*) See what I have to deal with? David, do something, say something, please!

David: Like what Christina is a . . .

Rev. Johnson: Seems some things need to still be worked, like everyone is not ready for Dianne to come home.

William: But I want her to come home, then Mom will not be away so much, and she can start cooking again, not Dad. (*look of disgust*)

Rev. Johnson: Things are still upside down sounds like. Have you been able to talk about this, I mean as a family?

Wesley: You can say that again about the upside down part.

Liz: Everyone listen. Dianne should be the focus, not us.

Rev. Johnson: (*says thoughtfully*) Liz, you are a 100% right. But let's see if everyone can get on the same page. The remodeling is almost done. But still everyone is worried about Dianne coming home. Sounds like things are not settled about who will be taking care of Dianne and what to do when she gets upset. Is that about right?

David: I guess in a nutshell. (*looks around at the rest of the family*)

Liz: Yes, that is about right . . . (*looks at Christina*) . . . I am sorry, I am just not thinking right.

Christina: (*smiles*) Thanks, Liz, just so you know I am really stressed about this too. (*reaches out to take Liz's hand*)

Rev. Johnson: OK, let's get started. What should we work on first? William, maybe we should talk about dinner . . . (*smiles*)

William: Yeah! I am getting tired of spaghetti with sauce out of a jar.

The Taylors are very much on edge. The impending discharge of Dianne from the Rehabilitation Center is bringing back many of the issues they faced during the survival stage. Now in the adaptation stage the Taylors are once again adrift, trying to find solutions and ways to cope given the reality of Dianne's condition. Notice the way Rev. Johnson works to help them identify the issues that are troubling the family. He starts by checking on and summarizing the issues they will encounter when Dianne returns. Rev. Johnson allows them to vent feelings. The feelings are brought on because the dynamics of roles, boundaries, and possible rules have changed. He invites the Taylors to explore these changes. He starts by giving permission for William to talk about his concern about dinner. This tactic is deliberate as Rev. Johnson wants to start in a nonsmall, nonthreatening way. The Taylors can work something out with respect to planning meals more effectively, which will set the path to effectively deal with other issues.

Adjustment Phase. As families adapt to the changes brought on by a crisis the adjustment stage begins. This stage involves the integration of changes resulting from crises into their day-to-day functioning although they may have periodic setbacks, especially at anniversaries or holidays. Typically, adjustment begins in the first few months following a crisis, but the time frame for this stage to begin depends on individual families. Some families move into this stage quickly while others take time to adjust (Price, Price, & McKenry, 2010). A key element in the amount of time needed to adjust is the amount of change experienced by survivors (Myer & Moore, 2006). Crises causing significant shifts in families' priorities generally result in this stage being prolonged. The more severe the crisis, the more likely families will need extra time to fully adjust to the new realities brought on by crises.

An important aspect of the adjustment stage is watching for the emergence of symptoms related to mental health disorders. Yet care must be exercised not to overdiagnose even though survivors seem to be experiencing symptoms consistent with a diagnostic label (Violanti, 2000). Myer, Moore, and Hughes

(2003) caution that a diagnostic model is not always the most beneficial for understanding reactions to crises. Ectherling, Presbury, and McKee (2005) seem to concur, saying that reactions to crises cannot only be viewed as mental health problems. The most important consideration is what will help you to understand and provide interventions that will facilitate families' process of recovery (Myer, Moore, & Hughes, 2003). A strength-based rather than symptom-based approach may be more therapeutic in this stage (Stuhlmiller & Dunning, 2000). Being open to creative approaches that are based on research and innovation is valuable in the adjustment phase of recovery.

During this stage of recovery anniversaries and holidays are important (Myer & Moore, 2006). At these times families will remember and reminisce about the way life was before the crisis. Some families may express regrets about lost opportunities with respect to what they wish they had done or said (Eliason, LaPore, & Myer, 2008). Listening and validating these expressions is important for families as they move forward. At these times families will re-experience the same feelings, behaviors, and cognitions suffered at the time of the crisis. Reminiscing at these points is a way for families to integrate the new reality and make meaning of the hardships faced during the crisis. Take care not to allow families to become too melancholy and sink into a pit of self-pity as they reflect at these times. If this situation occurs, families will slip back into a crisis requiring a new round of crisis intervention services.

Five months after Dianne's accident the Taylors meet again with Rev. Johnson. This meeting is the first time that Dianne is present. School is about to begin and the Taylors believe another meeting is needed. The entire family is present. Mrs. Taylor introduces Dianne and Mr. Johnson catches up on what is happening. This excerpt begins several minutes after the session begins.

Rev. Johnson: Let me see if I have everything right . . . Dianne is going back to school in a few weeks, Christina is going back to college but she will have to take out a loan to stay in the residence hall . . . David is back at work but had to turn down a promotion, and Liz you are planning on finding a part-time job as soon as Dianne starts school. Is that about right?

William: Hey, you forgot about me?

Rev. Johnson: Oh yes, you got promoted to the fourth grade, congratulations. And Wesley, you are starting soccer this fall as a senior.

Liz: That seems to capture everything...we have been talking. And . . .

David: You need me to tell him?

Liz: (*shakes head yes and tears well up*)

David: You see, Dianne was always a really good student, you know in the band and was going to be on the volleyball team this year. But now given everything she may not be . . . you know, able to do everything.

Rev. Johnson: What do you mean? Help me to understand.

Dianne: (*looks down*)

David: Remember when we talked about what the doctors said about the brain injury. Well it is better but sometimes Dianne still gets frustrated when she has trouble saying things and remembering stuff.

Liz: (*pats Dianne's knee*)

David: We all know how to handle it now so she does not get upset that often. But at school? I mean kids can be cruel. And then she has to use a cane most of the time. You saw she can walk pretty good, but still.

Rev. Johnson: Let me see if I am getting this right. You all are worried about Dianne and that school will be really tough for her.

Liz: Yea.

Dianne: (*speaks slowly*) Mom . . . I . . . want . . . to . . . go . . . to...school. I . . . will . . . be . . . OK.

Rev. Johnson: (*smiles*) What have the doctors said?

David: They said it is OK and will be good for her. Her speech is a little impaired and her fine motor coordination is still a bit off, but intellectually she is no different than she ever was.

Liz Yes . . . but . . .

Rev. Johnson: Mmmmmm, sounds like the issue is more with you (*looks at Liz and David*) trusting the doctors but are scared about what might happen.

Liz: Trusting the doctor? Of course we trust them, but this is my daughter.

Rev. Johnson: Maybe it is more trusting Dianne then?

David: I never thought of it that way.

Rev. Johnson: What needs to happen for you to trust Dianne? Why don't you tell them what you told me, Dianne.

Dianne: (*red-in-the-face but holding her temper and speaking in a commanding voice*) I . . . have . . . given . . . this . . . over . . . to . . . the . . . Lord . . . and Mr. Styles . . .

the . . . school . . . counselor . . . who . . . talked . . . to me . . . and . . . is putting me . . . in . . . his . . . Stylin' . . . peer . . . leader . . . group and Miss . . . Shoate . . . the speech . . . therapist . . . will . . . work with me . . . and Mr. . . . Isenogle, . . . the . . . band . . . teacher says I can . . . come and . . . help him . . . until I get . . . my trombone . . . lips . . . back . . . so . . . I am . . . really OK . . . and it's . . . going . . . to be . . . OK so just . . . worry . . . about . . . the regular . . . stuff . . . and not . . . me. I . . . am sick . . . of it . . . Mom . . . I . . . don't want to be . . . coddled anymore . . . If . . . I fall . . . down . . . I can . . . get back . . . up. I . . . think . . . you . . . need . . . to talk . . . to Rev. Johnson . . . yourself.

Recognizing the Taylors are having difficulty both affectively and cognitively with allowing Dianne to return to school, Rev. Johnson has been meeting with Dianne at her request. Dianne is frustrated and angry with the family's continued focus on her. Unknowingly, the family has dropped into pathological homeostasis as a result of the aftermath of Dianne's accident and much like an alcoholic family with a big pet pink elephant in the room (the alcoholism) steer completely around it. In the case of the Taylors, Dianne's disability is the elephant and she is the identified patient. She has been on a familiar path well known in alcoholic families, and that is Karpman's (1968) drama triangle where there is a victim, savior, and persecutor. While Dianne is the victim and mom functions heroically as the savior, mom is also victim and feels abandoned and empty with her faith. She is the prosecutor of other members of the family who at times are victims and at times saviors and at times prosecutors as well. By staying on this pathological triangle, people get their needs met without having to come to grips with the big pink pet elephant, the dysfunctional component now present and operating in the family. Rev. Johnson is aware of this and in a rather paradoxical twist, Dianne, with Rev. Johnson's help, has decided to break the triangle and let it fall apart by refusing to be the victim any longer. The motivations of the rescuer, mom, on the surface, appear to be obvious—that is, protecting or overprotecting her daughter. However, there may be a much more devious and egocentric reason for Mrs. Taylor to keep the triangle intact, which is that she gets an increasing payoff for being the heroic martyr and assuming the rescuer role. As such she needs to keep the triangle upright, much like an enabler in an alcoholic family. Rev. Johnson has become aware of this family system

problem and with Dianne's help seeks to break the triangle by having Dianne refuse to be rescued. This will create a crisis for Liz Taylor and it will come to light that she is having a big problem with her creator.

(A long silence ensues as family members are first shocked and then think on Dianne's statement.) Rev. Johnson revisits the Taylor's concerns regarding their spirituality. Notice how he does not impose a specific structure on their beliefs, but rather lets the Taylors explain from their perspective.

Rev. Johnson: We have a few more minutes, but before we end I have one more thing. When Dianne had the accident everyone seemed to be having questions about spiritual issues. Where is everyone with that? (*The Taylors look at each other, seeming to wait for someone to start.*)

Liz: I guess I can go first . . . I did have lots of questions, and well, still do I guess. Frankly, I don't know where God is anymore. I still cannot find answers, at least ones that are OK.

David: Yes, I guess we all wondered why and could not figure it out. I am not sure I still understand but we've come out of and I thank the Lord we did.

Liz: (*looks at David*) Our minister has really helped by listening to us and stopping by to see how Dianne is doing . . . *reaches out to rub Dianne's arm*) . . . And to be honest I don't know what would have happened if you and Chaplain Hamill had not been there. You both really helped. But I'm not so sure, at the least God went on vacation for this to happen and at the most just abandoned me. I don't know what I believe anymore.

Rev. Johnson: Would you like to spend some time talking with me about faith, or the losing of it and what that means for you?

Liz: I believe I would. Maybe it's what's been eating at me all along. And I'm truly sorry I've been a mother hen, Dianne. I know you are strong. Always have been a rock. You go girl!

Spirituality. Pervasive throughout traumatic events that slam into and wreak havoc with most family systems is that the family's belief in a higher power is questioned. The degree of the higher power's involvement in the traumatic event itself and the traumatic wake of the event's aftermath result in questions with which many families struggle. Denied by, unsure of, and embarrassed by it, many therapists deflect or attempt to ignore it as a topic to be included in therapy (Walker et al., 2004). Walker and associates (2015, p. 5) report that the gap between how important spirituality and the validity in using it as an integral part of therapy is and the validity the general public places in it is huge. This gap is further exacerbated by the fact that few psychotherapy training programs address spirituality or religion. We hold that is not a viable option. There is good reason that spirituality appears in the Triage Assessment Form under the cognitive domain. For most people, when they come to grips with a trauma and try to make meaning from it, spirituality, religion, and how one communicates with a higher power are critical in finding peace and resolution toward traumatic events (Humphrey, 2009; Slattery & Park, 2015; Van Deusen & Courtois, 2015). A **spiritual crisis** occurs when a previously held religious or spiritual belief is called into question or completely abandoned (Richards et al., 2015, p. 85).

Throughout this chapter, Liz Taylor's faith has been tested and indeed found to be wanting by her. Her daughter's calling her out was not intended to target her belief system, but that belief system is so inextricably tied to her self-concept. Liz's crisis is indeed spiritual as she seeks out Rev. Johnson. As Rev. Johnson works with Liz Taylor, care needs to be taken in regard to transference and countertransference issues. Trauma brings with it a Pandora's box of psychological hornets that once opened can sting the most experienced therapist (Courtois, 2015; Miller, 2015). Rev. Johnson has to decide on a treatment plan. Is the martyr/rescuer role Mrs. Taylor is playing hooked to her loss of faith and misgiving about God? Is this loss letting a person who has spent her life honoring and praying to God the principle ingredient that has fueled her pathological role in the crisis? Does he in fact become her spiritual director, helping her reconcile her faith issues and guiding her back into a meaningful relationship with God without pushing his values off on her (Miller, 2015).

Among the issues that Rev. Johnson will have to deal with are the person's attachment styles to God. Is this a close, loving relationship and reliable God who is always present; a God who is loving but pretty unreliable for help and guidance; a God distant and remote and not to be relied on; or a God who may be a fearful and threatening one to be avoided if possible (Griffith, 2010, p. 108). Anger toward an unjust God is often an outcome of trauma and that anger has been found to be associated with poorer mental health outcomes for survivors (Walker et al., 2015). Johnson knows that and his treatment plan will be to reconcile Liz's understanding of God (loving or vengeful)

with her self-concept (worthy or unworthy in God's eyes) (Slattery & Park, 2015). This will not be an easy process, particularly if the individual's faith has been deep and abiding before the trauma and is now in shambles. As with any loss counseling (see Chapter 12, Personal Loss: Bereavement and Grief), Rev. Jackson gently listens and empathically responds to her questioning as she tries to make meaning of the traumatic experience. There is no proselytizing. This will be a journey of self-exploration in finding her answers (Brown, 2008). Rev. Johnson may offer guidance in finding materials to pursue her quest, but if spiritually oriented therapy for trauma is to work, it will be Johnson acting in a very client-centered, nondirective way as Mrs. Taylor searches for her answers.

(Two months later after Liz has spent several sessions with Rev. Johnson getting squared away as much as she possibly can with her God.)

Christina: You know at first things were really bad. Everyone seemed on edge or angry about something. But we actually seem to be closer now. I mean everyone has found a way to help. I know Liz and I talk more now. *(looks over and smiles at Liz)*

Liz: Thanks. We have learned to talk about our feelings more. Although I would not want anyone to go through this. The accident brought us closer together and trust each more. And to trust our faith. Don't get me wrong. I still have questions but don't worry about not having all the answers as much.

Wesley: Yea, Mom, you seem less stressed most of the time . . . me I like that we talk more. Even David seems to listen and respect me more. I am not sure about the faith stuff, but I am open to it more now.

David: Thanks.

Rev. Johnson: Everything seems to be better now. What about you, William?

William: I guess so. I don't get left out as much. And we do more things as a family. Are we going to get ice cream after this like we always did before?

Liz: Sure.

Rev. Johnson: What about your spirituality and your faith? Where is that for you now?

David: I think at first everyone questioned it, at least I did. *(Liz and kids all nod in agreement)* I, or we, had lots of questions but no answers. I think we all were kind of angry, really mad about that. And no one could give us an answer, which made it worse. Now we seem to know that questions are OK and we have to find our own answers.

Liz: Yes, and that will take time.

Rev. Johnson: You seemed to have come a long way, learned some important lessons for your family. As bad as a crisis may be, there is always the opportunity to find growth from it, and I believe you all have. I think we are finished. God's speed to you all. (*brings the family together in a circle holding hands, asks a prayer of gratefulness, and bids the Taylors good-bye*)

Rev. Johnson is following up on an issue that plagued the Taylors in the survival and adaptation stages of recovery. His goal is to help the Taylors recount their journey in order to ground them with respect to the meaning of the experience. The questions enable each family member to voice his or her perspective without fear of being judged. Throughout the exchange Mr. Johnson stays neutral and supports the Taylors. His statements are used to reinforce the journey as well as where they are at this time and where they are headed in the future.

Cultural Issues

Up to now issues related to families' culture and ethnicity have only been touched upon, yet these play an important role in crisis intervention. Chapter 2 discusses in detail about the importance of culturally effective helping, especially with respect to the concept of social locations (Brown, 2008). Just as with individuals, families have social locations (McGoldrick & Ashton, 2012). Social location for families uses a multidimensional perspective that helps to avoid the stereotyping that often occurs when using a one-dimensional viewpoint. Instead of just using ethnic background or racial origins, the concept of social location incorporates many aspects of families' lives. In addition to typical things such as race and ethnicity, social location for families can also include such things as education levels, spirituality, socioeconomic status, generational status, geographical location, family structure (e.g., blended, divorced), and so on, as ways to understand families.

A useful way to understand families is to begin at home by looking at the dynamics in your family. What did your family value? What were your family's goals? What roles did family members fill? How were rules viewed and enforced? What boundaries did your family use, and how did your family communicate? This knowledge gives you a foundation for how families in crisis are similar or different from yours. The awareness and insight gained from looking at how your family functions will be invaluable in understanding families in crises.

In crisis intervention, situations may occur when doggedly sticking with cultural values and beliefs can hinder or even prevent families' recovery. In these situations, crisis workers may need to help families look beyond and possibly suspend devotion to their culture values and beliefs in order to help them find the support needed to recover. A judgment will need to be made whether or not families' culture is preventing or just slowing progress toward recovery. This situation is especially true when families' safety and/or immediate well-being is jeopardized. Some medical crises might also fit the category with cultural values and beliefs that impede families' recovery. Take, for example, a family member with dementia who has become a danger to self and others. Although cultural values and beliefs maintain that families should care for this family member, the family member would be safer and better served in a setting with people trained to work with people who are suffering from this condition.

SUMMARY

Working with families in crisis can be both challenging and rewarding. The challenge centers in trying to understand and then help families stabilize their lives. Families have been thrown into disarray by a tragic event and are unable to manage what is happening around them. Regardless of the severity of families' reactions, helping them weather, overcome, and grow from the experience involves understanding not just the effect on individual members, but the system as well. The information in this chapter furnishes a strong foundation for understanding the changes that occur when the typical ways of coping are ineffective. These changes generally occur around the six dynamics (i.e., roles, boundaries, communication, rules, values, and goals) discussed earlier. Combined these dynamics interact making each family's reaction unique. The Triage Assessment Form: Family Therapist introduced in this chapter gives crisis workers the ability to assess these dynamics quickly and effectively in order that interventions can address families' reactions needing attention. Spirituality is often a key component in dealing with a crisis and should never be arbitrarily dismissed as unimportant or not within the purview of crisis intervention.

The reward comes when you see families overcome the hardships and establish a new routine. The tasks imbedded in the hybrid model can guide the intervention as you work with families to survive, adapt, and ultimately adjust to the new reality they are facing. Patience and time are generally key elements helping families work toward the goal of resuming a day-to-day routine. While the pace of recovery for families varies, eventually families are able to function hopefully for the better.

Visit CengageBrain.com for a variety of study tools and useful resources such as video examples, case studies, interactive exercises, flashcards, and quizzes.

Personal Loss
Bereavement and Grief

12

Introduction

One of your authors is about to fill his gas **LO1** tank at a self-serve when he notices an elderly woman struggling to fill her tank. It becomes apparent to your knight-in-shining-armor that he needs to render assistance to this clearly distraught and frustrated woman. He does so and immediately gets into a grief counseling session as the woman has an emotional come-apart at the gas pump. Her husband, you see, took care of all the "mechanical" issues in their lives, including filling the car with gas, for 50 years of marriage. After he dropped dead from a heart attack 2 months ago, this woman's world turned from a very secure, knowable, and predictable life into a fairly good working analysis of what we describe in Chapter 1 as chaos theory. A hour and a half later your chivalric, somewhat disheveled author, now late for a meeting with the dean, who, while sitting in a car in a strip mall parking lot, has experienced a range of emotions from his unintended client that range from hysterical grief to rage against her husband's chauvinism that has left her helpless with things "mechanical," gets her somewhat stabilized after a cell phone call to a friend of the woman to come and take her home and a commitment from this bereaved and grief-stricken woman to go to a church in town that has workshops and counseling for the newly widowed.

One of your authors is not a good one-trial learner. A number of years ago when he was a junior high school counselor who had become a self-styled expert in parent training (subject of his doctoral dissertation), he decided to really show how astute he was at ferreting out parenting issues after he invited a school psychologist over to see how his revolutionary communications/behavior management parenting class

LEARNING OBJECTIVES

After studying this chapter, you should be able to:

1. Understand that loss is universal and you will have to deal with it in its many manifestations if you go into the human services business.
2. Learn the terms necessary to speak the language of loss.
3. Understand the cultural dynamics that influence how people deal with loss.
4. Understand the role of spirituality and religion in loss.
5. Know the different models of loss.
6. Know the basic instruments for assessing loss and complicated grief.
7. Understand the different types of loss.
8. Know the principles of treatment for loss in different subgroups.
9. Know the criteria for complicated grief.
10. Know the treatment techniques for complicated grief.
11. Understand how to deal with different types of loss.

(it was 1971) worked. A mother was talking about her seventh-grade daughter who was acting rebellious and oppositionally defiant since her father passed away more than a year ago. It was about 8:30 P.M. with another half hour to go in the meeting. Dr. Freud decided to make an astute interpretation of the mother's complaints and reflected to her that it appeared it was not just the daughter, but she who had not gotten over the death of her husband. That keen insight started a delayed grieving process that was not the highlight of the evening for the other parents, who would have rather been almost anywhere than the teacher's lounge of Jefferson Junior High School at that point in time. The ending of this story occurred at about 10:30 P.M. when your now thoroughly ego-deflated and wrung-out author drove the parent back to her home in a small rural community 15 miles from school and had to listen to his school psychologist friend, who had to follow him out to her farm, needling him about his therapeutic insight on the ride back to town. This is a trilogy, as most tales of wisdom are, so there is one anecdote more to go.

At one point in his life, your self-same author was thoroughly burned out with education and counseling and decided to get into the oil business. He ran a bulk petroleum products plant in Wisconsin. In that capacity he served a number of dairy farmers by making home deliveries of gas and diesel fuel in his tank delivery truck. One farmer in particular was a jovial if somewhat rowdy individual who had a reputation for wrecking bars when he got a little too much beer in his system. As a result, this robust young dairy farmer had a good deal of respect and some bit of fear from his neighbors. One spring day he was gearing up to cultivate for spring planting. His 5-year-old son was badgering him to ride on the tractor, but dad thought it too dangerous so he was sent back into the yard to play. Somehow the 5-year-old was able to get over the locked gate into the feed lot. There, he turned on the automatic feeding system, got caught on an auger and was chewed to pieces. This was a horribly traumatic death with a closed casket. Empty words or no words of condolence could be said to the devastated parents. Your author had a Ph.D. in counseling psychology, but had little experience in grief work, as the previous anecdote would indicate. No one knew what to say, or indeed was afraid to say anything to attempt to assuage his grief and self-blame for his son's death. Finally, after watching this desolated and isolated young man for a month after the funeral, your author sucked up his courage, made plans to finish his route early, walked into the milking parlor, and told the aggrieved farmer that in another life he had been a counselor and was willing to talk and listen to him about his son's death and the circumstances surrounding it. That conversation went on for 2 hours. It was one of the toughest counseling sessions your author ever had. It was also a turning point, because it convinced him that he didn't want to be a millionaire oil baron, but needed to get back into the business of counseling. So the point of this long-winded opening is . . .

To be human in the world as we know it is to experience loss. While you may, if you are really lucky, never experience any of the other crises in this book, you are going to experience loss. Almost every chapter in this book has statistics about the chapter's affliction in it.

This one doesn't, because sooner or later you are all going to experience at least one loss—your own! Besides that ultimate loss, you will also experience loss in two other ways. First, you will lose something near and dear to you. Second, and just as important, if you go into the human services business, you are also going to experience dealing with clients who have experienced loss. Actually, you are going to deal with it a lot more than you think because it's not just death you are dealing with, but almost any other kind of loss you can think of having. Therefore, this chapter on loss is indeed about you, and perhaps your denial and fear of it.

Of all the tough issues that crisis workers face, probably none is more difficult than dealing with individuals who have suffered a traumatic loss. People who are assailed by a violent loss have significantly higher symptom levels of prolonged grief disorder, PTSD, and depression compared to persons bereaved by nonviolent losses (Boelen, de Keijser, & Smid, 2015). Boelin and his associates found in their study of 496 bereaved individuals that indices of unrealness, negative cognitions about self and the future along with catastrophic misinterpretations about the world and depressive avoidance of the traumatic loss were all significant mediators of prolonged grief, PTSD, and depression. The Dyregrovs (2008) capture the essence of this in a father's response to the traumatic death of his child: "We are taught to handle most situations, but whenever sudden, traumatic death occurs, we are completely helpless both in terms of handling it personally and giving others support" (p. 47).

Our students, who are required to do "volunteer" work, avoid hospice like the plague for the most part. However, the unlucky few whose schedule won't fit other programs are practically gang-pressed into it. Scared pea green going in, they invariably come out changed and report it is one of the most positive, life-changing experiences they have had. So while you might enjoy a root canal more than reading this chapter, know full well that you will need it, and perhaps, like others, you will come to find satisfaction in doing a job few others care to do or in fact can do very well.

It is not uncommon as you read and discuss this chapter to experience some potent feelings regarding loss that you thought were pretty much buried. As we indicated in Chapter 7, Posttraumatic Stress Disorder, when we use Charles Figley's (1985) traumagram we always ask people to graph their losses as well as their traumas. Lots of times when we are absolutely perplexed as to the reasons people are manifesting the problems they do, the reason lies with an unreconciled loss. So understand that what you read here may well cause some of the same feelings to arise in you. For that reason, our course syllabus in crisis intervention specifically states that if you have suffered a recent or unreconciled loss, this is probably not the best time for you to take this course. That being said, if you are experiencing discomfort in reading this chapter, we urge you to talk to your professor or supervisor to find a grief counselor and talk though your loss.

Recovery from major **primary losses**, such as the death of a friend, child, parent, or spouse, may require several years, and the traumatic event may have a profoundly lasting effect on the remainder of one's life (Costa & Holliday, 1994; Finkbeiner, 1998; Lerner, 2000; McCown & Davies, 1995; Morse, 2000; Pearlman, Schwalbe, & Cloitre, 2010). Although generally not as catastrophic as death, other loss events—job loss, bankruptcy, physical paralysis, job disability, a forced move to a different residence, chronic illness (both physical and mental), geographic and school change, limb amputation, divorce, or loss of one's home or possessions from flood or fire—can have many or all of the same ramifications (Colgrove, Bloomfield, & McWilliams, 1991, p. 2; Farina, 2000; Lerner, 2000; McCown & Davies, 1995; Michaels, 2009; Morse, 2000; Schliebner & Peregoy, 1994).

Probably in no other area of crisis does one's belief (or lack of it) in religion and a higher power come into play (Walker et al., 2015) and attempts to make sense of it and derive meaning from the loss (Slattery & Park, 2015). To that end, the questions that spirituality and religion bring to the table tend to cause most crisis workers indigestion and heartburn as they struggle deal with it—both for the individual and themselves. To that end, besides what else we have to say on the subject in this chapter, the list Aten and associates (2015) propose crisis workers use when dealing with religion (see Chapter 17, Disaster Response) is well worth memorizing.

Terms Critical to Understanding Loss

The objective of this chapter is to provide a **LO2** general survey of ways in which crisis workers may help clients understand and cope with losses without attempting to deal with the infinite ways in which loss occurs and clients attempt to resolve it. To that end, it is important to understand a number of terms that coexist with crisis intervention involving loss.

Bereavement is a period of sorrow following the death of a significant other (Humphrey, 2009, p. 6) and is a common life transition rather than a clinical disorder (Neimeyer & Kosminsky, 2014). It is an objective state or condition of deprivation that is especially caused by death and is then followed or accompanied by grief (Pine, 1996). In Rubin's (1999) two-track model of bereavement, the first track is the individual's own adjustment (or lack thereof) in overall biopsychosocial functioning—affective, behavioral, cognitive, social, somatic, and meaning-making systems. The second track involves the individual's affective-cognitive relationship to the deceased and how that is reconciled over time.

Uncomplicated bereavement is the process that occurs as the bereaved individual works through a variety of tasks to integrate the reality of moving forward in life without the person who died (Cohen et al., 2002, p. 309). Those tasks include (1) moving from an interactive, living relationship to memories that establish continuing bonds with the deceased; (2) coming to terms with the reality of death; (3) experiencing and working though the painful, negative emotions associated with the loss; (4) finding meaning in the loved one's death; (5) adjusting to life without the loved one and forming new relationships with other peers; (6) becoming open to the possibility of changing negative attitudes such as fear, sadness, anger, and bitterness about life and one's loss into joy and happiness as new opportunities, relationships, and transformations evolve and develop (Cohen, Mannarino, & Knudsen, 2004; Van Praagh, 2000; Worden, 1991). For most individuals, bereavement is transitory with resilience and they return to former levels of functioning over the course of several months (Neimeyer & Kosminsky, 2014).

Grief is a psychic state or condition of mental anguish or emotional suffering and a result or anticipation of the bereavement (Pine, 1996). Grief is highly unique and multidimensional; a person's affective, behavioral, and cognitive makeup and the contextual and ecosystemic influences that operate on it dictate what the grief experience will be. Grief and grieving may apply to both primary and secondary losses. Although grief is a universal experience, there is no universal agreement on what it is, and considerable controversy exists over its "normal" duration (Howarth, 2011). *Complicated grief* and *prolonged grief* are interchangeable terms, although the latter term now seems to be prevalent. This disorder has been reviewed by the fifth editon of the *Diagnostic and*

Statistical Manual of Mental Disorders (American Psychiatric Association, 2013) work groups, who have decided that it be called *persistent complex bereavement disorder* and placed it in the chapter on Conditions for Further Study in the new DSM-5.

The majority of people who suffer loss and grieve do not manifest complicated or prolonged grief. While grief itself is not a sign of mental illness, prolonged grief is if we define it as a personality disorder, which many researchers and practitioners hope will happen, although some critics argue that it is only grief along the extreme end of the continuum of grieving (Humphrey, 2009, p. 12). Persons suffering from complicated or prolonged grief are preoccupied with the deceased and may have recurrent, intrusive images or thoughts of the death. Common symptoms include shock, disbelief and anger about the death, loneliness and isolation, a feeling that a part of the self has died along with the deceased, and a feeling that the future holds little worth (Neimeyer & Kosminsky, 2014). People with complicated grief experience prolonged grieving that causes distress and impairment that can affect both physical and mental health (Shear & Mulhare, 2008).

Traumatic grief is generally subsumed under complicated or prolonged grief, with the additional requirement that the person witnessed or was in close proximity to the violent, sudden, unexpected, horrifying death of a loved one (Cohen, Mannarino, & Deblinger, 2006, p. 15). In such cases, PTSD symptoms generally go hand in hand with the grief.

Disenfranchised grief occurs when a person has experienced a deep and meaningful attachment, experienced loss, and cannot openly acknowledge or grieve the loss or have it validated by others (Doka, 1989; Stroebe et al., 2008). It might be erroneously thought that disenfranchised grief occurs only in clandestine relationships involving gay or lesbian lovers who have not come out or two married people carrying on an affair. However, cultural and societal norms may also forbid—or at least not sanction—displays of grief between coworkers, men, various types of professionals such as medical doctors, and other people who should "keep it together" or "not care all that much."

Further, individuals may feel ashamed about the relationship, be afraid that an overt display of emotion could hurt them professionally, or just experience emotions that inhibit the grieving process (Doka, 1989). Many people would believe it "silly and overemotional" to grieve over a pet. They may keep

their feelings of grief closely to themselves unless they feel they are absolutely safe in sharing them. Yet to act as if the death means nothing for the sake of "having a stiff upper lip" can be a harmful variation of disenfranchised grief—particularly for children and older adults (Doka, 1994).

Loss is a universal human phenomenon, but people respond to it with varying degrees of grief and mourning (Howarth, 2011). Any loss is some form of death. Death of a loved one, death of a relationship through the breakup of a marriage or a friendship, leaving a job, putting down a pet, repossession of a home, geographic moving away from friends and family, even the loss of precious keepsakes can constitute a loss that becomes a crisis. All losses produce some degree of grieving (Giunta & Giunta, 2002, p. 4).

Primary loss is a significant event such as a death. **Secondary loss** is a consequence of a primary loss. Death of a spouse may cause loss of status, social contacts, financial security, and sexual intimacy, which are secondary losses. Primary loss of a job may cause financial insecurity, reduced self-esteem as family provider, and lack of self-confidence in vocational ability, which are secondary losses (Humphrey, 2009, p. 20).

Ambiguous loss is of two types. The first is when a person is physically absent but psychologically present, as in the case of a missing person. The second is when a person is physically present but psychologically absent, as in the case of dementia or schizophrenia (Boss, 2006).

Mourning is a social or cultural state or condition expressing grief or feeling because of bereavement (Pine, 1996). Mourning is a communal rather than an individual reaction to loss, generally prescribed by cultural protocol and the time frame in which it occurs (Bedikian, 2008; Humphrey, 2009, p. 5; Morgan & Laungani, 2002; Stroebe et al., 2008). The public appearances one makes, the clothing one wears, the music one listens to, the religious rituals one performs, and even the food one eats are many of the artifacts prescribed for mourning. Mourning can apply to both death and nondeath losses (Humphrey, 2009, p. 10).

Thus, when dealing with the crisis of personal loss, crisis workers are likely to encounter a variety of issues. First are the individuals suffering the loss, which may range from a terminal illness to the breakup of a teenage romance to the loss of a job to the loss of a pet—all of which may be perceived as intolerable and catastrophic. Second are their caregivers, who must provide help and succor not only for those experiencing the loss but also for themselves (Allen et al., 2006; Okun & Nowinski, 2011). Third are survivors who may be experiencing problems that range from shame, sorrow, guilt, and anger to prolonged grief, depression, substance abuse, serious physical illness, and suicidal behavior (Boelen & Prigerson, 2007; Giunta & Giunta, 2002; Parkes & Prigerson, 2010; Rosenblatt, 2010; Wakefield, Schmitz, & Baer, 2011). Further complicating the issues that confront workers who are dealing with grieving individuals are the cultural contexts within which their clients operate.

Dynamics of Bereavement

Cultural Dynamics

No area of crisis intervention is quite so culturally sensitive as mourning and bereavement after a loss. While grief responses are largely biological and common across all societies, mourning and bereavement are culturally based and vary greatly from society to society (Morgan & Laugani, 2002, 2003, 2004a, 2004b; Morgan, Laungani, & Palmer, 2009; Stroebe et al., 2008; Weiss, 1998). Humphrey (2009, pp. 8–9) exhorts us to recognize that loss and grief occur in the multiple and fluid context of personal, familial, social, cultural, and historical influences. Humphrey proposes that an individual's grieving is a continuous negotiation process among a wide array of sociocultural influences specific to the person and the environment in which he or she lives. These influences range from beliefs and values about meaning, to rules and conduct for behaving, to support networks to religious practices and healers, to an individual or collectivist society, to traditions and rituals, to communication style, to levels of acculturation and assimilation, to ethnicity (p. 8). Suffice it to say that Brown's (2008) social locations you read about in Chapter 2 play a huge role and act in infinite ways to form the individual's response to loss.

Consider the term *culture* in the broadest possible context. Race, religion, gender, geographic region, sexual orientation, disabling condition, socioeconomic class, and temporal context all factor in multiple ways into the loss experience (Doka & Davidson, 1998). The manner in which humans grieve differs from culture to culture and from time to time. As Bedikian (2008) suggests, the ecosystem within which we operate has a great deal to do with how we mourn and grieve. The prolonged grief that

Queen Victoria felt for Prince Albert in late-19th-century Great Britain translated into rigid rules of mourning for women that included heavy black costumes and black crepe veils for up to 4 years after the dearly beloved's demise to show their grief. The advent of World War I brought that practice to a screeching halt because women went to work in factories and formal mourning etiquette gave way to the necessity of showing up for work in work clothes. That somber and extended approach to mourning has given way to wearing a dark dress or suit to a visitation or memorial service of a half hour and going back to work that afternoon.

Thus, each culture develops its own beliefs, mores, norms, standards, and attitudes toward death, and these can change over time to meet changing conditions (Dutro, 1994). Further, groups from differing backgrounds within a particular culture may have vastly divergent attitudes and perceptions about death (Dutro, 1994), and individuals within that group may further differ dramatically in how they construct and make meaning from the loss (Neimeyer, 2001).

Rando (1984) stated that "for all societies there seem to be three general patterns of response: **death accepting**, **death defying**, or **death denying**" (p. 51, bold added). Joffrion and Douglas (1994) characterize modern Western society as a death-defying culture. Kübler-Ross (1975) writes that in our culture "death has become a dreaded and unspeakable issue to be avoided by every means possible," noting "that death reminds us of our human vulnerability in spite of our technological advances" (p. 5). Do you suppose that is why there are drive-by funeral homes in California where you can view the body from your car without ever having to get out? Ramshaw (2010) proposes that while postmodern Euro-American Protestant funerals have become highly impersonal, there still exists a desire and a need to personalize rituals as a celebration of the person's life.

Contrast that drive-by visitation to being in the second line at a New Orleans funeral procession (the mourners following the funeral band) as the body is carried to the cemetery. Do you believe you would see a very different view of how death is dealt with in Louisiana and how emotionally involved you were in it? Let's suppose you were the main object of attention. Would you prefer the drive-by visitation (barely in sight, quickly out of mind) or an African American family's 2-hour funeral ritual in Kentucky that was full of reverence, respect, open grief, and spiritualism for the departed plus a lot of singing, music, and dinner on the church grounds (Collins & Doolittle, 2006)?

Contrast that last image with what Westerners view as utterly incomprehensible—Muslim suicide bombers, who are seen as martyrs absolutely merged with God and God's will in their own willingness to sacrifice themselves. Indeed, for Muslims in general, prolonged public mourning and expression of grief are discouraged because of the great value placed on acceptance of God's will with restraint and understanding. While Muslims may cherish memories of the departed and grieve mightily in private, their return to public functioning after a loss is strongly encouraged (Rubin & Yasien-Esmael, 2004).

Contrast that notion again to Mexican American families as they handle traumatic grief. Perhaps because of the mingling of Aztec and Catholic beliefs about death as a way into a new life and beginning, along with the strong family bonding that predominates in the Mexican culture, death plays a prominent role. Besides the famous Day of the Dead, when parades and festivities honor deceased family members, living family members honor and maintain a strong bond to the deceased through storytelling, dreams, keepsakes, ongoing faith-based altars at home, and rituals through church (Doran & Hansen, 2006).

Finally, consider how two very different cultures half a world apart process grief. Bonanno and his associates (2005) measured grief processing and deliberate grief avoidance in the United States and the People's Republic of China. How people in both cultures grieved initially predicted how they would process their grief later on. However, contrary to how those in the United States fared, continued grief processing or avoidance did not predict negative psychological consequences for the Chinese.

What needs to happen as far as grieving is concerned and what the culture expects to happen often butt heads. Van der Heijden and Swartz (2010) investigated a peer-led HIV/AIDS prevention strategy in South Africa for vulnerable children who had lost parents to the disease. The intervention ran into trouble because attempts to talk about death and elicit memories of loved ones ran counter to the cultural practice of maintaining silence about the deceased and protecting children from unpleasantness. What all of the foregoing boils down to is that loss and its reconciliation constitute one of the most culturally sensitive areas into which a crisis interventionist ventures. To say that one must tread lightly here and be very observant when dealing with cross-cultural loss is one of the bigger understatements made in this book!

Sociocultural Mores

Schoenberg (1980) describes how societal mores and attitudes toward life, death, and dying in the United States have changed over the years. As the country has shifted from a rural to an urban orientation and lifestyle, there has been a shift from a death-defying culture to a death-denying culture (pp. 51–56). Whereas farm families usually came in contact with birth, life, and death of animals as well as of people, city dwellers rarely encountered dead animals or dead people. People in rural communities cared for their own dying relatives and friends. They prepared the corpses for burial and dug the graves by hand. They laid out the bodies of the dead in the parlor and commemorated the lives of the departed; then they buried them in the family or community cemetery. That's quite a contrast to the way dying, death, grieving in public, and funerals are carried out in most communities in the United States today. Death in modern Western societies has been sanitized and generally removed from the context of everyday life (Crase, 1994; Joffrion & Douglas, 1994; Morgan & Laungani, 2003; Schoenberg, 1980).

The social organization of bereavement and the social reaction to the loss of loved ones have changed partly because of shifts in age-specific mortality patterns (Osterweis, Solomon, & Green, 1984). In former times, adult life expectancy was short and infant mortality was high. Epidemics and famines frequently wiped out large numbers of people. Communities were small and close-knit. Death was taken personally by everyone in the community, and mourning rituals were community-wide events (pp. 199–200). People saw death every day, and fiery sermons about hell, death, and eternal damnation made people acutely aware that they were always one step away from the grave. Changes in families, geographic mobility, urbanization, information technology, aging patterns, the job market, birth control and child-rearing practices, medical and nutritional improvements and advances, and information dissemination and processing have greatly affected the way society views and deals with death, loss, and grief (Green, 2008; Morgan & Laungani, 2003, 2004a).

In modern times, the bereavement process has tended to become standardized by laws, regulations, and the development of specialists who carry out these laws and regulations. Death usually occurs in a hospital or nursing home. Frequently, the deceased are older people who have been out of the mainstream of community activity for a number of years; as a result, they are not as widely known as they were in their younger years. Mourning has tended to move out of the home and into funeral parlors and hospital chapels. Laws affecting the role of funeral directors and the policies of employers have influenced the ways society mourns. Workplaces have established rules governing the time employees can take off from work following the death of a close family member or loved one. Many institutional constraints on behavior have tended to impose social uniformity on the previously diverse patterns of grief and bereavement (Green, 2008; Morgan & Laungani, 2003, 2004a).

Grief that follows a death has become much more institutionalized (Osterweis, Solomon, & Green, 1984, pp. 201–202), but such institutionalization is not necessarily negative. For example, some funeral homes offer professional grief counseling programs for their clientele and communities (Riordan & Allen, 1989). Thus, the sociocultural changes that occurred between 1900 and 2000 brought about important changes in reliance on such helpers as physicians, nurses, psychologists, social workers, counselors, rehabilitation specialists, hospice workers, and caregivers for survivors of loss (Dershimer, 1990, pp. 14–36; Huber, 1993; Schneider, 1984, p. ix). Indeed, Morgan and Laungani's (2002, 2003, 2004a, 2004b) multivolume set on a global perspective of death and bereavement looks like a Dictionary of Occupational Titles search in regard to the wide array of occupations that are represented in the contributing authors.

Spirituality and Religion

One of the major reasons religion exists is **LO4** to make meaning of and understand death (Slattery & Park, 2015; Walsh, 2009). Whether you believe in Zeus, Odin, God, Buddha, Isis, Allah, the Great Spirit, or Charlie Brown's Great Pumpkin, the human quest for meaning in life and death has looked to some deity to provide the answers. Whether you believe in Valhalla, heaven, Nirvana, paradise, reincarnation, that great NASCAR racetrack-in-the-sky, or anything else that means a secure, happy, peaceful place in the hereafter, humans have continuously attempted to cheat the finality of death by creating an afterlife and making sense of why bad things happen to good people and why the good die young (Drescher & Foy, 2010; Giunta & Giunta, 2002; Green, 2008; Walsh, 2009). Faith, beliefs, and religious practices are the foundation stones for dealing with life's end and the loss of loved ones. They offer comfort, hope, support, and connection when one feels hopeless,

unsupported, and disconnected. Spiritual resources provide guidance to family members and friends in how to honor the deceased and mourn their loss, across the world and through the millennia (Walsh, 2009). To that end, Kaut (2006) proposes that any end-of-life assessment and counseling should include a bio-psycho-social-spiritual network.

However, religion, spirituality, and supreme beings are a double-edged sword. What they bequeath as far as hope is concerned, they can also snatch away. One of the biggest problems people face when faced with loss is making meaning structures that work and help them move through the grief. That's fairly easy in a just and equitable world, but in the world of crisis intervention, as you should know by now, very often it is anything but fair and equitable. That can put people out of sorts with their particular deity of choice when their beliefs, attitudes, assumptions, values, and everything else they hold dear to make sense of the world become ruptured, disjointed, and chaotic (Gillies & Neimeyer, 2006). If the Great Pumpkin continues to dash Charlie Brown's hopes for a meeting, then it may challenge one of his deepest held beliefs and then lead him to question whether this whole "spiritual" thing is just one giant house of cards and he needs to find another vegetable deity or just go worship Lucy!

So it should become clear that attempting to make sense and meaning of a loss can challenge one's most deeply held religious and spiritual beliefs (Humphrey, 2009, p. 26), and that is especially true when the loss is traumatic, interpersonally caused, chronic, and occurs over time during significant developmental stages of a person's life (Walker, Courtois, & Aten, 2015). On the other edge of this spiritual sword, the Giuntas (2002) are among a multitude of authors who spend a great many pages of print hooking all of the many facets of grief up with why God has not left the building with Elvis and is still a shoulder to lean on. The process of making sense or meaning out of loss, then, involves examining those constructs that help make sense out of life up to the point of the loss and then renewing, redefining, or revising them to restore homeostasis and equilibrium (Humphrey, 2009, p. 26).

In that regard, in the areas of death and major losses, a significant proportion of people (in all societies, including ours), perhaps a majority, find faith to be their most important resource for coping, recovery, and growth. Crisis workers must be comfortable in allowing grieving clients to find healing in their faith and spirituality (Culliford, 2002). This stand does not, of course, mean that crisis workers should inject or impose their own religious beliefs on their grieving clients.

Conceptual Approaches to Bereavement

There are a variety of models, ranging from [LO5] psychodynamic to constructivist to cognitive-behavioral approaches, that seek to deal with loss (Bowlby, 1969, 1973, 1980; Cohen, Mannarino, & Deblinger, 2006; Gillies & Neimeyer, 2006; Neimeyer & Levitt, 2000; Osterweis, Solomon, & Green, 1984; Powers & Griffith, 1987; Raphael, 1983). Historically, stage/phase models (Bowlby, 1969, 1973, 1980; Kübler-Ross, 1969; Kübler-Ross & Kessler, 2005) have achieved a great deal of fame and notoriety.

Stage/Phase Models

Kübler-Ross's Stages. Probably the loss model best known to the general public is that of Elisabeth Kübler-Ross (1969), which views loss as a series of five stages—denial, anger, bargaining, depression, and acceptance—that people go through as they come to grips with their own imminent death. She later used these five stages to describe grief and the grieving process (Kübler-Ross & Kessler, 2005). While never intended as a strictly linear, stepwise model, it has come to be perceived as such. As popular and valid as this model has become in the general public's mind, there is little research to substantiate its validity (Konigsberg, 2011). Thus, while its simplicity gives it a lot of curb appeal to the public, there is little empirical evidence to substantiate its use, and it causes problems when people stubbornly refuse to move though its stages as Kübler-Ross proposed. No matter how much people want a neat ribbon-wrapped package that sets out simple rules and stages for grief, there are simply no stages of grief that fit all persons (Friedman & James, 2009). As a result, Kübler-Ross's and most other stage models have been pretty much consigned to history's dustbin.

Bowlby's Attachment Theory. Probably most widely known in the therapy field is Bowlby's attachment theory (1969, 1973, 1980), which was generated from his studies of separation and reunion of young children with their parents. Attachment theory is a linear phase model that focuses on the nature of the griever's relationship to the deceased. The breaking of affective bonds and the disruption caused by the loss require grieving. Failure to grieve intensely is seen as problematic in not coming to terms with the loss of the object. The need to emotionally turn loose or "detach" from the person or object is the end goal of the grief process. This phase model also has its share of controversy and criticism. Grief may not follow a prescribed set of stages the way Bowlby proposes. Moreover, failing to grieve intensely may be a sign of resilience rather than pathologically avoidant suppression of feelings. Finally, detachment may not necessarily be preferable to continuing to keep bonds and memories of the lost object (Shaver & Fraley, 2008).

Schneider's Growth Model. We feel that one of the better stage/phase models is Schneider's (1984) eight-stage process model of loss. It is a holistic, growth-promoting model designed to nurture as much personal growth as possible within a context of stress, loss, and grief (p. x). Its focus on growth from loss is currently attracting a great deal of attention in the study of the potential positive aspects for growth in the wake of a trauma (Cann et al., 2011a, 2011b; Triplett et al., 2011).

The model includes the following stages (Schneider, 1984, pp. 104–226): (1) initial awareness of a loss, which is generally a significant stressor; (2) attempts to limit awareness of the loss, holding on by means of concentrating one's thoughts and emotional energy, for a period of time, on whatever positive aspects of the loss one can recognize and making use of whatever inner resources one has to immediately stave off immobility and disequilibrium; (3) attempts at limiting awareness by letting go, which involves recognizing one's personal limits with regard to the loss and letting go of unrealistic goals, unwarranted assumptions, and unnecessary illusions; (4) awareness of the extent of the loss, recognizable as mourning—the most painful, lonely, helpless, and hopeless phase through which the loss sufferer goes; (5) gaining perspective on the loss, reaching a point of accepting that what is done is done and providing time to make peace with the past; (6) resolving the loss, which occurs when the bereaved can see and pursue activities unconnected with the loss without its being a reaction against (letting go) or identifying with (holding on) the lost person or object; (7) reformulating loss in a context of growth, which involves discovering potential rather than limits, seeing problems as challenges, being curious again, and seeking a balance between the different aspects of self; and (8) transforming loss into new levels of attainment, which involves an integration of the physical, emotional, cognitive, behavioral, and spiritual aspects of the person and is an integral part of the process of reformulation to higher levels of understanding and acceptance of the loss.

A Counterpoint to Traditional Models

Dutro (1994) has described how our concepts of grief and loss have become more dynamic, moving from the medical or pathology theories to more interactive models. Dutro's comprehensive and dynamic model views grief and loss from the perspective that each individual experiences loss according to psychophysiological, affective, and cognitive-behavioral factors, such as the mode of death, relationship of the deceased, prior losses experienced, and dominant subcultural norms. These factors figure into a dynamic structural model of grief that, according to Dutro, is in sync with sociocultural life in the 21st century. His and others' dynamic, individualistic grief models (Dyregrov & Dyregrov, 2008; Humphrey, 2009; Konigsberg, 2011; Neimeyer, 2000; Worden, 2002) refute many ideas about grief that have been associated with older stage theories:

1. The common assumptions concerning "stages" of grief are not supported.
2. Placing time limitations on grief is inappropriate.
3. The withholding or suppression of sadness in response to bereavement is not necessarily pathological.
4. Insistence on severing ties or detaching oneself from lost objects denies lifelong bonding and usefulness of positive memories.
5. One-size-fits-all models don't work because each individual griever's experience is unique. Grief is not a unitary phenomenon but rather a multidimensional, interactive, individual experience for every bereaved person, based on a complex set of interwoven variables.
6. There are no fixed beginning and ending points in grieving.
7. While grief does not end, it does change.

From that standpoint two current models, the dual process model (Stroebe & Schut, 2001; Stroebe et al., 2008) and the adaptive grieving model (Martin & Doka, 2000), seem to best represent current thinking (Doughty, 2009; Humphrey, 2009) on the fluid, idiosyncratic nature of grief and grieving and how the crisis worker should consider approaching them.

The Dual Process Model. The dual process model may be characterized as an approach-avoidance model

that has two components: loss orientation and restoration orientation. **Loss orientation** stressors are associated with the loss itself, which may be experienced in ruminating about it and having behavioral, emotional, and cognitive reactions to it that oscillate between avoiding and confronting the disrupted bond with the object of the loss (Stroebe & Schut, 2001; Stroebe et al., 2008). Stroebe and Schut see this process as a normal and natural process of loss adaptation. For instance, a college athlete may feel sadness and anger over the loss of a girlfriend (confronting the stressors), but redouble workouts and increase his study time (avoiding the stressors) in efforts to put lost love out of his mind. As the loss recedes in time, and in line with how processing models are supposed to operate, a restoration orientation begins. So both avoidance and confrontation are to be seen as a normal and natural process of loss adaptation (Humphrey, 2009, p. 47).

Restoration orientation occurs when grievers start to come to grips with the consequences of the loss and begin to form new roles and identities, develop new relationships, make life changes, and engage in new activities that distract their grief. The newly aggrieved widow we met at the gas pump at the beginning of this chapter may start to engage in restoration orientation by alternately avoiding her confrontation with loneliness by sitting in front of the TV for hours on end and deciding to confront it by joining a church renewal group that her newly met crisis counselor and pump jockey told her about. The primary task of restoration orientation is attending to rather than avoiding life changes, doing new things, seeking distraction from grief, and dealing with new roles, identities, and relationships (Humphrey, 2009, p. 48). One of the major advantages of this model is that it recognizes that grief is not static, but is a series of waves with crests and troughs that ebb and flow at their own pace but gradually move into more quiet, placid, and calm affective, behavioral, and cognitive waters that nourish growth. However—and this is a big "however"—these researchers propose that the griever can get into hot water and move into prolonged grief if this ebb and flow does not occur (Stroebe et al., 2008). So the crisis worker who uses this model should understand that it will make absolute sense when the griever bounces back and forth between a loss and a restoration orientation that operates on an approach-avoidance continuum and gets the worker's undivided attention when it does not. If you understand this model, then, it is not upsetting but rather understandable that people are not static or stable as they grieve, but move back and forth as they attempt to bring equilibrium and homeostasis back into their lives.

The Adaptive Model. Martin and Doka (2000) identify grieving as three basic styles that operate along a continuum, with *intuitive* grieving on one end, *instrumental* grieving on the other, and an infinite number of variations between the two. Intuitive grievers respond to loss mainly in terms of emotion, while instrumental grievers think through their grief and/or act on it. Most people, Martin and Doka believe, operate somewhere in the middle and have a blended style. The other component of the adaptive model targets the preferred affective, behavioral, cognitive, and spiritual strategies that grievers use to adapt to the loss. Martin and Doka place a heavy emphasis on spiritual components because of the model's strong theoretical basis in Jungian psychology and the fact that many people place a great deal of emphasis on the spiritual aspects of adaptive grieving.

It is important to note that adaptive strategies are a good deal more than, and different from, coping strategies. Coping implies "getting along" or "bearing up," while adaptation means engaging in behavior that will result in change. Interestingly, the same adaptive strategies may be used by persons at both ends of the intuitive-instrumental continuum but for entirely different reasons. For example, the common practice of going through a photo album of the deceased and reminiscing about happier times may be used by both intuitive and instrumental grievers. For intuitive grievers, it is a cathartic release of emotions as memoires flood conscious awareness and are relived. For the instrumental griever, the photo album may be a way of remembering, organizing, and planning activities. So for the intuitive griever, pictures of riding horses on the family farm bring back memories of Sunday afternoon rides, picnics by the river, the smell of horses and harness leather, and grandfather's wide-brimmed Stetson cowboy hat bobbing along in front on his horse Whiplash. For the instrumental griever, the same photos may remind him or her that the upcoming sale of the farm equipment needs to be inventoried and favorite items parceled out according to requests from brothers and sisters.

It should be clearly understood that adaptive styles do not necessarily mean a rose-covered remembrance path down memory lane. Adaptive styles that are useful in the short term may be counterproductive in the long run. Emotional catharsis verging on hysteria may be fine at the funeral, but level-headed business sense is called for when the family farm is put on the auction block. Also, if primary grievers have different grieving styles, they may butt heads. An instrumental griever who throws herself back into her work may be confounded by a husband who continues to emote at any small remembrance of a daughter who has died in an auto accident. Likewise, he may be appalled that she is so callous and cold as to start packing their beloved daughter's clothing to give to Goodwill 6 months after the funeral. While they are both using adaptive strategies that serve them well, the interpersonal divisiveness that may occur is something else to behold.

People get into trouble with the adaptive model by employing **dissonant response** modes that are consistent with the opposite grieving style. This sets up a discrepancy between people's inner experience and their outward expression of grief so that persons with intuitive grieving styles tend to act like people with a more instrumental style. When that happens the person has taken a large step toward complicated grief (Humphrey, 2009, p. 42).

It should become readily apparent to you as the crisis worker that being able to ferret out and understand these styles can be critical in helping grieving individuals move through grief and, even more important, in helping significant others understand that the bereaved's grief is not some weird, aberrant pathology but a highly functional, idiosyncratic adaptive measure that works for him or her.

Assessment Tools

The Texas Revised Inventory of Grief (TRIG). LO6
The TRIG (Faschingbauer, Zisook, & DeVaul, 1987) is probably the most widely used inventory to measure grief. It has two scales, Current Grief and Past Disruption. Because of their temporal nature, the two scales allow the worker to determine what kind of progress in grief resolution has been made. The inventory asks respondents to rate themselves on a Likert scale (1 = completely false to 5 = completely true) in response to 8 questions about past behavior at the time the person died (I felt a need to do things the deceased had wanted to do; I was angry at the person; I found it hard to sleep) and 13 questions about how the person presently feels about the person's death (still cry when I think of the person who died; I cannot accept this person's death; I hide my tears when I think of the person who died). It has few validity studies, and

some of the items ("crying") are replicated while other well-known concepts such as guilt are left out. Yet it has been used with a wide variety of groups, providing good cross comparisons and a wealth of normative data.

Grief Experience Inventory (GEI). The GEI (Sanders, Mauger, & Strong, 1985) assesses the longitudinal course of grief. Self-descriptive items that are answered true/false compromise the inventory. Nine clinical scales cover Despair, Anger/Hostility, Guilt, Social Isolation, Loss of Control, Rumination, Depersonalization, Somatization, and Death Anxiety; six research scales include Sleep Disturbance, Appetite, Loss of Vigor, Physical Symptoms, Optimism–Despair, and Dependency; and three validity scales cover Denial, Atypical Response, and Social Desirability.

Hogan Grief Reaction Checklist (HGRC). The HGRC (Hogan, Greenfield, & Schmidt, 2001) is designed to discriminate grief reactions from depression or anxiety. Its 61 items target categories of Despair, Panic, Blame/Anger, Disorganization, Detachment, and Personal Growth. It can discriminate variability in the grieving process as a function of cause of death and time elapsed since death.

Inventory of Complicated Grief (ICG). The ICG (Prigerson et al., 1995) specifically targets symptoms of grief that are distinct from bereavement-related depression and anxiety, and predicts long-term functional impairments. Its items are rated on a Likert scale from "never" to "always." Items target long-term grief, such as not accepting the death, feeling anger or disbelief, avoidance, and auditory and visual hallucinations of the person.

Quality of Object Relations (QOR). The QOR is a structured interview that measures the recurring pattern of relationships over the course of the individual's life span. It assesses relationship patterns that range from primitive (unstable and destructive) to mature (reciprocating and mutually involved). A person operating at a primitive reacts to perceived separation and loss, or disapproval and rejection from the preferred object with intense anxiety that affects their functioning in deleterious ways as they try to grieve the relationship. They become candidates to meet a grief therapist. At the mature end of the continuum, the person has good social relationships that are marked by affection and tenderness. Individuals assessed on the mature end can effectively mourn loss relationships and tolerate unobtainable relationships (Piper et al., 2011).

Types of Loss

People may encounter many different types of LO7 loss that produce stress, trauma, and/or grief. Following are several types of loss that crisis workers may encounter. It is not the purpose of this text to provide crisis intervention techniques for dealing with every specific type of loss. What is shown here is that loss covers a broad scope, and that certain fundamental helping skills and strategies apply in a generic way to helping individuals who are suffering from loss.

Death of a Spouse

An unimaginable, indescribable loss has taken place and the numbness and excruciating pain is so deep because someone you love has died and it is unmatched for its emptiness and profound sadness (Kübler-Ross & Kessler, 2005, p. 29; Parkes & Prigerson, 2010). The death of a spouse is one of the most emotionally stressful and disruptive events in life (Cramer, Keitel, & Zevon, 1990; Daggett, 2002; Leahy, 1993). Camelley and associates (2006) studied the long-term effects of widowhood. They found that the widows continued to talk, think, and feel emotions about their lost spouse decades later. Twenty years postloss, they would still reminisce about their spouse every week or two and had a conversation about their spouse once a month on average. Twelve and a half years postloss they reported still feeling upset between "sometimes" and "rarely" when thinking about their dead spouse.

Based on this research, does it surprise you when at the end of a year your surviving parent is not "over it"? Losing a mate is in a way as if part of yourself has died. You are now alone when you need your significant other the most, and you are stricken to think that what you have built over your entire life is now pretty meaningless (Van Praagh, 2000, p. 96). As James Van Praagh states, "On the day my mother died my father was not the man I had known all my life" (p. 97). That simple statement is as well put as we can find and pretty much encapsulates what is going to take place as the widow/widower attempts to put life back together. Van Praagh's statement makes two points. First is clearly what will happen with dad and how he will come to grips with his loss. The other component is not only how the family will handle their grief over the loss of mom but also how they will handle dad. This issue becomes even more critical if dad is now responsible for raising young children alone (Glazer et al., 2010).

There are more women survivors (widows) than men (widowers), and the bereaved spouse typically faces a number of problems and stages of bereavement alone (Kübler-Ross, 1969; Kübler-Ross & Kessler, 2005). In addition to the immediate shock and stress, many survivors face serious personal, physical, emotional, economic, social, career, family, and community problems (Buckley et al., 2010; Johnson, 1977; Khosravan et al., 2010; Osterweis, Solomon, & Green, 1984, pp. 71–75; Pizzetti & Manfredini, 2008; Rando, 1984, pp. 144–149; Vahtera et al., 2006). More ominous for the elderly, the death of a spouse increases the mortality rate for the surviving spouse (Elwert & Christakis, 2008; Hart et al., 2007).

It appears that other variables intrude into mortality rates of surviving spouses as well. Elwert and Christakis (2006) found that race played a significant role in mortality rates of surviving spouses, with Caucasians suffering a large and enduring effect of mortality while African Americans did not suffer a detectable effect. Religion may also affect how long people live after a spouse dies. Abei and Kruger (2009) found that Catholic men lived 2.2 years longer than Jewish men after a wife died and Catholic women lived 1.5 years longer after their husbands died than Jewish women.

So should you be calmed if you are an African American Catholic and anxious if you are a Caucasian Jew? Not necessarily, but you should understand as a crisis worker that a multitude of variables go into survivorship and realize that some pretty mundane demographics go into what you need to be observant of when dealing with grief and bereavement. Further, while some may argue that bereavement and grief should not be classified as mental illness, an abundance of research indicates that there is a Pandora's box of evil hornets that can sting some survivors in multiple ways, and if some of those survivors do not have good immune systems, it can hasten their deaths. Therefore, it would appear important that crisis workers and medical health care workers in particular be aware of the part bereavement and grief play in physical health issues.

Loss Due to Caregiving

Caregiving is a major issue for spouses and parents. Long-term care causes radical changes not only in

attitudes toward the receiver, but in the provider as well. You might stereotypically think in terms of someone in this category as providing heroic years-on-end efforts in caring for a bedridden individual with some terminal disease or chronic disability. Think also about the parents of a 28-year-old son with schizophrenia who has delusions of persecution to the extent that he is on a first name basis with the local CIT, goes off his medication, and becomes dangerous to the extent that his parents sleep in watches and have a heavy-duty reinforced deadbolt on their steel bedroom door. In other words, there are many brands of caretakers, there are a lot of them, and there are going to be even more as the baby boomer generation ages and continuing advances in medical science prolong more lives, saving those who otherwise might have died but are profoundly and severely mentally and physically disabled.

Grief and bereavement over lost relationships are compounded by frustration over the ambiguousness of the loss. The receiver of care is alive but not there for the caregiver either mentally, physically, or both, so that former behavioral duties (who takes care of the taxes, bills, car, kids' lunches), affective relationships (emotional support, sexual activity), and cognitive abilities (figuring out job moves, college decisions, buying a house) are no longer functional (Betz & Thorngren, 2006). Caregivers often report a sense of loss of their identity (Dickson et al., 2010)—for example, from former spouse and lover to caregiver and nurse—as they move farther and deeper into caretaker roles.

Bad things happen to good caretakers who take care of individuals with spinal cord injuries, internal head trauma, multiple sclerosis, end stage cancer, renal disease, Alzheimer's, dementia, the profoundly mentally and physically challenged, the mentally ill, and others who are so incapacitated by their maladies that they require constant care and or vigilance. Those who wound up having complicated grief reported that there were more intense end-of-life family conflict and problems dealing with other family members who refused to accept the illness or manner of care (Kramer et al., 2010).

Caregivers reported a kaleidoscope of problems. They suffer depression, sadness, anger, guilt, worry, isolation, resentment, financial difficulties, frustration, relational deprivation, loss of employability, worry about the future of the person they care for if they are older, and have their own physical health problems that are often exacerbated by the constant physical and psychological stress of caregiving (Adams, 2006; Morgan, 2009; Ott, Sanders, & Kelber, 2007; Taylor et al., 2008). Length of time in dying also has an effect on the surviving caregiver. Keene and Prokos (2008) found that compared to spouses who were noncaregivers or short-term caregivers, long-term caregivers reported more relief and less depressive symptoms than their counterparts. As coldhearted as it may seem, relief from long-term care of the terminally ill seems to allow caregivers to cope with their loss better.

It is a safe bet that the caregiver population is going to grow in the United States as the baby boomer population ages into degenerative disease territory. Other countries provide supportive services at the national level; how well these programs are working is still an open question. In the United States, this population is underserved and depends on charitable organizations such as the Alliance for the Mentally Ill, the Alzheimer's Association, and other malady-specific support groups. Most caregivers constantly live in subtranscrisis or transcrisis states due to the ever-present threat of medical or financial crises for the disabled person and their own continual stress in caring for them.

These caregivers and the people they care for often come to the attention of first responders such as CIT officers. Helping these individuals find support groups, get relief through time off/out programs, plan for future events, obtain psychological first aid or supportive psychotherapy, normalize negative feelings, find outside help, obtain financial, medical, and legal advice, acquire psychoeducation about caregiver issues, and develop meaningful narratives about their losses are all program components that crisis workers might well provide (Adams, 2006; Dillenburger & McKerr, 2009; Haley et al., 2008; Morgan, 2009).

Death of a Child

Regardless of the ages of parents or children, the death of a child is always a major loss (Edelstein, 1984; Finkbeiner, 1998; Kübler-Ross, 1983; Rando, 1986; Romanoff, 1993; Silverman, 2000). The death of a child is perhaps the ultimate loss for a person to endure. Parents are left to deal with the incomprehensible fact that their child died before they did, and often feel enormous guilt that they should have done something differently to have prevented it (Van Praagh, 2000, pp. 154–155). Death of a child is another type of loss that survivors don't "get over" quickly. McCarthy and associates (2010) studied parents whose children

had died from cancer. While few of the parents suffered from complicated/prolonged grief disorder or depression, after an average of 4½ years they still reported significant separation distress associated with persistent longing and yearning for their children.

Every parent is unique in terms of needs, history, personality, coping style, relationship to others, social concerns, family situation, and sense of meaning regarding the death of a child (Braun & Berg, 1994; Finkbeiner, 1998; Romanoff, 1993). Therefore, every parent suffers the loss of a child somewhat differently. The death of a child is traumatic for parents, whether it occurs as stillbirth or sudden infant death syndrome (SIDS) or follows accident or illness in adolescence or young adulthood (Osterweis, Solomon, & Green, 1984, pp. 75–79). It is equally traumatic for aged parents to lose their children who may be middle aged or older.

Ann Finkbeiner (1998, pp. xxi, 37, 44, 54), after several years of grief and healing, shared her deep personal meanings regarding the loss of her only child, an 18-year-old son who was killed in a train accident. Her comments cut to the core of what it means to lose a child.

> I learned two things about the long-term effects of losing a child. One is that a child's death is disorienting. The human mind is wired to find patterns and attach meanings, to associate things that are alike, to generalize from one example to another, in short, to make sense of things. Your mind could no more consciously stop this than your heart could consciously stop beating. But children's deaths make no sense, have no precedents, are part of no pattern; their deaths are unnatural and wrong. So parents fight against their wiring, change their perspectives, and adjust to a reality that makes little sense.
>
> The other thing I learned is that letting go of a child is impossible. One of my earliest and most persistent reactions to T.C.'s death was surprise. I had no idea whatever how much he had meant to me. All I knew was that I hadn't wanted to think about it. Our children are in our blood; the bond with them doesn't seem to break, and the parents find subtle and apparently unconscious ways of preserving that bond.

Bereavement in Childhood

Children who experience the death of a parent or sibling may show overt signs of bereavement, but sometimes their grief may be covert, leading caregivers to assume that the children are not affected by the loss. Norris-Shortle, Young, and Williams (1993) have documented the fact that *young children do grieve*. Most children who experience loss of a loved one go through mourning as a normal process and do not necessarily end up with pathological responses (Glazer, 2010). However, the death of a parent, the death of a sibling, or the death of a friend can bring about disenfranchised, traumatic, and complicated/prolonged grief (Cohen & Mannarino, 2011; Cohen, Mannarino, & Deblinger, 2006, pp. 199–203; Cowan, 2010; Crenshaw & Lee, 2010; Howarth, 2011). Because the majority of time that children spend outside of the home is at school, it necessarily follows that strengthening school support systems that can deal with traumatic grief in childhood is important (Cohen & Mannarino, 2011; Heath & Hudnall, 2011; see Chapter 13, Crises in Schools), particularly in supporting caregivers who may be having their own difficulties resolving grief issues.

Studies by Gudas (1990) suggest that signs and symptoms of behavioral and psychological difficulty occur differently between bereaved preschool and school-age children. Older children, with concepts of permanence of death and personalization of their own mortality, experience more anxiety, depression, and somatic symptoms than do younger children (p. 7). Depending on the age and cognitive development of the child, his or her understanding about death may be very different and unsettling. From a Piagetian standpoint, the preoperational child's egocentric view of death may be laced with magical thinking and fantasy with no clear view as to death's finality (Brown, 1988, pp. 70–74). Children at the concrete operational stage may understand the "why" of death as a specific cause-and-effect event, whereas children at the formal operational stage can understand the finality and irreversibility of death and have all kinds of questions concerning the "whys" (Brown, 1988, pp. 7–81; Matter & Matter, 1982).

Toddlers. Toddlers ages 18 months to 3 years do not understand how death differs from going away. Because they live in an egocentric world, they may well assume that they caused the death to occur. While death does not have meaning as such for them, they do understand when something is lost, and that loss may be very distressing. They may exhibit high levels of anxiety, seen in agitated/restless behavior, excessive

crying, thumb sucking, biting, and tantrums. While it is unlikely they will retain a strong memory of the traumatic event of the person's passing, they may have some physical memoirs (Giunta & Giunta, 2002, p. 244).

Preschoolers. Children ages 3 to 5 also experience profound reactions to loss and may display feelings of sadness, anger, crying spells, feelings of remorse and guilt, somatization, and separation anxiety (Gudas, 1990, pp. 1–2). At about age 4, children have a limited and unclear understanding of death. Because they are still ego centered, they may believe they caused the death. They are not yet able, for the most part, to understand the permanency of death (Webb, 2007). While they are much clearer about who died and the sense of loss in their lives, they are usually quite literal about their interpretation of what it means to go to heaven, perhaps wondering "Does Bobbie get to have pizza and birthday cake and other little angels over to his house on his birthday?" Because of their egocentric stage of development, they also may feel that they caused the death (Webb, 2011): "Bobby gets everything, mommy and daddy love him most, and I wish he was dead."

At this age, children will start to play the event out, often to the dismay of parents who, horrified and distressed from their own grief, forbid children to do so. There is likely to be severe separation anxiety from caretakers, including excessive clinging and crying on separation, needing to be held, and not wanting to sleep alone. Children this age may see a change in daily routine as a threat and feel angry and rejected for no apparent reason. They may become mute and withdrawn, with extended periods of sadness. There may be noticeable regression in physical independence such as inability to dress themselves, tie shoes, go to the bathroom, or eat with utensils. Bed-wetting and night terrors may occur (Giunta & Giunta, 2002, p. 245). Because their vocabulary is still very limited, when preschoolers hear such words such as "passed," "lost," "gone over," and other euphemisms for death, these words will be taken quite literally (Webb, 2011), so if dad is "lost" it is the family's or police's duty to go find him.

Primary School Age. At about age 6 or 7, most children understand the universality and irreversibility of death. Death is now more specific, precise, and factual. Elementary school-age children operate in the concrete stage of development. As such, they may report matter-of-factly the gory details of a pet getting run over and thus be seen by adults as cold and uncaring (Gudas, 1990.) Conversely, because of their sensitivity to pain, they may become quite agitated if they hear the gory details about how mutilated the body was and will attempt to avoid such conversations (Webb, 2011). They may also be able to run a balance sheet and see that while their sister's death is a sad thing, their parents will now be able to spend more time and money on them.

Play is used extensively to attempt to work though the trauma. If play becomes both extensive and intensive and is focused on the trauma, it has now moved into traumatic childhood grief (Terr, 1981; see Chapter 7, Posttraumatic Stress Disorder). At this point there will be difficulty concentrating in school, with commensurate behavior and/or academic problems. Numerous somatic complaints may arise (headaches, stomachaches, dizziness, unspecified malaise with numerous school absences). Primary school–age children may have increased difficulty controlling their own behavior and may exhibit radical changes from quiet and shy to verbally aggressive and acting out, or vice versa (Cohen & Mannarino, 2011; Giunta & Giunta, 2002, p. 245).

Intermediate/Middle School Age. While children at this age will generally understand the permanence of death, they may exhibit a good deal of anger and rage at the unfairness of it. They may develop a sense of foreboding and doom about a foreshortened future and see their existence as now pretty meaningless. They may alternately feel euphoria and excitement at having survived, then guilty feelings for having survived when others didn't. Such mood swings may occur often and dramatically as they attempt to cope with emotional dysregulation. They may become highly judgmental about their own and others' behavior, particularly in regard to the deceased or the handling of events surrounding the trauma (Cohen & Mannirino, 2011; Giunta & Giunta, 2002, p. 246; Webb, 2011).

However, to suppose that a child's concept of death progresses in an orderly chronological manner is to suppose wrongly. Life experiences have much to do with a child's perspective and understanding of what death is (Silverman, 2000, pp. 47–53). One can only imagine the difference in perspective and view of death between the average 6-year-old in Baghdad, Iraq, and an average 6-year-old in Des Moines, Iowa.

Intervention and Treatment. Children's affective, behavioral, and cognitive responses must be **LO8** approached not in terms of adult perspectives but in terms of each child's understanding and developmental stage (Rando, 1984, pp. 157–162). Children are especially vulnerable during periods of major loss because their inexperience and their undeveloped personalities can easily lead to confusion and misinterpretation of events and lack of grieving (Schoenberg, 1980, p. 200). Because children's personalities are growing and absorbing social stimuli at a very rapid and concentrated rate, care must be taken to provide reassurance and support during family bereavement (Schonfeld, 1989). They may ask the same questions over and over about the loss, not so much for the factual information, but for reassurance that the adult view is consistent, that the story has not changed, and that the grieving adults and children are safe. Children need to hear, over and over again, the simple, truthful, reassuring words of adults who are relatively secure and who show genuine concern for the children's feelings (Osterweis, Solomon, & Green, 1984, p. 100).

Some people believe that children should be shielded and protected from exposure to death and loss. Sugar-coating death, such as daddy having gone away, should not happen. While death is indeed a dirty word in contemporary society, it is one that needs to be used to honestly convey what has happened. The research suggests very strongly that bereaved children will make healthier adjustments to loss if they are informed about the loss truthfully and permitted to participate actively in mourning (Osterweis, Solomon, & Green, 1984, pp. 99–127; Rando, 1984, p. 155; Schoenberg, 1980, pp. 151–154). Even though children may exhibit behavioral responses during the bereavement process that adults may interpret as "not caring" or "not understanding," children should be permitted to proceed with mourning at a level and pace appropriate to their development. Children should not be forced to participate in activities when they decline to do so, but should be included when they request to do so.

Cohen and Mannarino (2011) indicate that treatment models should include five tasks that incorporate *gradual* exposure to the loss and the traumatic grief:

1. Resilience-building stress management skills help children re-regulate feelings, behaviors, and thoughts related to the traumatic death. Techniques include use of positive reinforcement, encouragement, and selective attention for

positive behaviors by both parents and teachers, and teaching relaxation skills such as focused breathing and muscle relaxation to stop and reverse physical manifestations of stress.

2. Affective expression skills development helps children and parents accurately label and express different feelings without passing judgment on negative feeling states. Children should be encouraged to share feelings rather than deny them. At times both parents and children may be terrified at the variety and intensity of their feelings, so it is important to teach both parents and children affective modulation skills so that they feel confident of not only speaking to their feelings, but also controlling them as well.

3. Cognitive coping skills aid both children and parents in hooking up connections among thoughts, feelings, and behaviors. Children and parents learn how to assess how their thinking is adaptive or maladaptive and to change maladaptive thinking through thought stopping, reframing, and cognitive restructuring techniques.

4. Trauma-specific interventions focus on building a trauma narrative, which is usually started after resiliency skills have been developed in children and parents. This narrative may take several forms, including stories, poems, artwork, and play. The purpose of the narrative is to decrease avoidance behavior, directly confront the feared trauma, make sense of it, and put it in the past. Concomitant with exposure to the feared trauma, safety issues may be dealt with if the traumatic event involved violence in which the child was involved or an observer.

5. Grief-focused interviews help children and parents develop more adaptive grieving processes and include many of the conflicting and ambivalent emotions they may have about the deceased.

Webb (2007) recommends directed play therapy as a vital adjunct to cognitive restructuring (Cohen, Mannarino, & Deblinger, 2006) of the traumatic event in tackling the issue of avoidance. Webb lists the following reasons for doing so:

1. Play therapy provides cathartic relief from tensions and anxiety.
2. It provides ways for the child to symbolically review in play what happened, and build armor plate against the feared feelings of the traumatic event in concrete form through manipulating the play media. Through manipulation of the play

material, the child and therapist can safely rehearse plans, problem-solve, and gain resolution.

3. It permits role rehearsal to strengthen the child's feeling of competence in handling the future.
4. It can provide a restorative function and transformative experience that moves the child from despair, hopelessness, and lack of self-confidence to reconciliation, hope, and self-confidence. (p. 48)

It is also critically important to carry out intervention in a team approach that integrates home and school (Cohen & Marinnarino, 2011). Teachers, school counselors, psychologists, and social workers can all serve as supportive personnel that aid and abet therapeutic endeavors by knowing what is occurring at home and in therapy and by providing backup or indeed serving as the primary therapeutic agent.

Bereavement in Adolescence

Kandt (1994) cites research indicating that 90% of middle and high school students have experienced a loss associated with death. Almost half have experienced the death of a friend, and one out of five has witnessed a death. Adolescents today are encountering death and loss more frequently than ever before, and this presents a challenge to both adolescents and their caregivers. Other crises such as destabilized families and parents' job loss create in adolescents feelings of pessimism, futurelessness, confusion, depression, and isolation (Schliebner & Peregoy, 1994). A peer death can be a particularly traumatic experience for an adolescent because it is a nonnormative experience that shouldn't happen, often is violent, and may be seen as preventable. Peer deaths can foster school problems, depression, substance abuse, suicidal ideation, and delayed developmental processes (Balk & Corr, 2001; Balk, Zaengle, & Corr, 2011; Malone, 2011).

Value of Connectedness. Hansen and Frantz (1984, pp. 36–47, 62–72) describe adolescents who are in bereavement as needing to be included (involved) in the family's grief, while at the same time needing periods of privacy. Often the adolescent may feel excluded, for example, at the sudden death of a grandparent. Bereaved adult family members may erroneously assume that the adolescent's perceptions of events are the same as theirs. At such times, adolescents may not know how to behave because they do not have a sufficient understanding of death, the circumstances surrounding it, the appropriate mourning role, or life experience in general (Brown, 1988, pp. 77–79).

Adolescents may feel a deep sense of pain, fear, anger, guilt, helplessness, confusion, loneliness, and grief (Balk, 2009), yet they may not know how to express or feel comfortable in expressing these emotions. They need opportunities to be included in discussions, planning, mourning, and funeral and commemorative activities (Hansen & Frantz, 1984, pp. 62–67). Guerriero-Austrom and Fleming (1990), researching the effects of sibling bereavement on adolescents, found that physical and emotional symptoms fluctuate over time, showing the most severity at 6 to 12 months following the sibling death and emerging again at 18 to 24 months. Females exhibited more death anxiety and health-related problems than did males. Adolescent grief reactions were documented as long as 3 years following the death of the sibling (p. 11). The problem with these reactions is that death brings a stark reality to an already cynical teenager who may act out his or her anger and depression in dangerous, life-threatening ways (Brown, 1988, pp. 79–81).

Intervention and Treatment. One of the key components in promoting resiliency to a parent's death has been positive parenting (Sandler et al., 2003; Worden, 1996). While adolescents reported themselves as fearful and anxious over a parent's death (Worden, 1996), they also reported themselves as more mature when assuming parental responsibilities and grew up faster. Effective parenting cannot be done in hindsight, but interventions that include parents individually or in treatment groups can be effective in supporting both adolescents and surviving parents in moving forward.

While less is known about the effect of good parenting practices on adolescents when a peer dies, it is important that parents understand and acknowledge the importance of that loss and avoid discounting the loss and turning it into disenfranchised grief. Oftentimes the traumatic death of peers comes from making typically dumb teenage decisions: the daredevil stunt that goes horribly awry and results in a broken neck and quadriplegia; alcohol, fast driving, and a victory celebration over an archrival that end in vehicular homicide and injury to friends; any of a variety of videotaped we'll-put-it-on-YouTube stunts that go wrong, causing injury, death, and lawsuits; the aftermath of the accident leading to the instigator's depression and suicide. These classic examples of immature adolescent behavior resulting in accidental deaths are vilified by parents.

Parents need to be cautious about knee-jerk critical reactions about the stupid behavior of their children's peers or the inconsequential nature of their children's loss. When parents dismiss or criticize adolescent peer friendships, first loves, and high school bonds as transitory and insubstantial, they are essentially telling adolescents their friendships don't mean much and their feelings don't count for much either (Balk, Zaengle, & Corr, 2011). Nothing could be further from the truth, and wise parents will react sensitively to their adolescents' grieving over lost friends and relationships.

Finally, school is a major source of support for adolescents (Balk, Zaengle, & Corr, 2011). Chapter 13, Crises in Schools, provides a good deal of information on the part that schools play in helping adolescents move through the loss of a peer.

Bereavement in Elderly People

The fact is that older adults may experience considerable difficulties with bereavement (Hansson & Stroebe, 2007; Hinrichsen & Clougherty, 2006). O'Connor and associates (2015) found that when bereavement complications turned into prolonged grief that in turn potentiated posttraumatic stress. As medical advances extend life and retirement becomes prolonged, commensurate issues arise involving finances, health, cognitive difficulties, and social support systems that often include loss of independence. Independence is a precious commodity and older adults do not lose their desire for it (Langer, 2011), as most children become aware when they deal with aging parents who become obstinate and rebellious over suggestions about quitting driving or going to a retirement center. For older adults, losses of friends are a continual degradation of their support system, and as these losses pile up, when ultimate loss—the death of a spouse—arrives, the potential for loss to cascade into prolonged grief and bereavement increases exponentially. Indeed, the most profound and devastating loss older people may encounter is the loss of a spouse (Schoenberg, 1980, pp. 211–214). Demographic data indicate that the elderly population, age 65 and older, is growing at an increasing rate. It is predicted that by 2030 there will be about 70 million older adults, more than double the number now, and that number will represent 20% of the U.S. population (Schwiebert, Myers, & Dice, 2000, p. 123), so it is clear that this potential problem is going to grow . . . a lot!

From a developmental standpoint, bereavement among elderly people is compounded by decreases in sensory acuity, general decline in health, and reduced mobility. Having a lower income and fewer support people available to them than in their younger years also represent changes that are detrimental to their psychological well-being. Elderly people generally experience more losses than do their younger counterparts: loss of relatives and friends; loss of job, status, and money; loss of bodily functions and abilities; and loss of independence and self-respect (Freeman, 1978, p. 116). It appears that advancing age tends to correlate with a decrease in coping strategies, but it is not known whether this decrease is related to one's greater awareness of impending death, decrease in physical stamina and function, or other factors (Schoenberg, 1980, pp. 221–223).

Schoenberg (1980, p. 230) summarizes four conclusions that may be drawn from the literature on bereavement and age:

1. Elderly people present more somatic problems than psychological problems.
2. There is no indication that the intensity of grief varies significantly with age of the elderly person.
3. Evidence suggests that grief among older people may be more prolonged than among younger people.
4. Elderly people tend to be lonelier and to have far longer periods of loneliness than do their younger counterparts.

Crase (1994) found that the ways the older generation generally deals with loss fall into the following three broad categories.

1. One group totally ignores the inevitability of death and makes no preparation for it. People—especially men—in this category engage in little or no open discussion of death. By ignoring death issues, these elderly individuals attempt to avoid negative feelings, using denial as a defense mechanism. They are vulnerable to being unprepared when struck by disabling disease, crisis, disaster, or the death of their spouse.
2. A second group thinks about death and dying excessively and makes unusual preparations for death's inevitability. These individuals go overboard in making meticulous plans for every detail of their decline, death, and funeral.
3. A third group demonstrates a healthier balance. They are attuned to the developmental implications of total loss, making appropriate plans and decisions, and going on with their normal lives.

The realization of disease, suffering, and eventual loss of life should foster the motivation to look ahead to our death with intelligent preparation, just as we would prepare for any of life's major stages or events (Kaplan & Gallagher-Thompson, 1995). When we don't do this, it is an open invitation for the crisis worker to enter the picture.

HIV/AIDS

Since the 1980s, acquired immune deficiency syndrome (AIDS) and the human immunodeficiency virus (HIV) that precedes and accompanies AIDS have become pandemic. What HIV/AIDS has shown us is that health epidemics are rarely, if ever, just about disease. The psychological milieu that accompanies an epidemic is different from that of other diseases, and HIV/AIDS is different from other epidemics. While a person with AIDS may have many terrifying, uncontrollable physical problems and psychological issues similar to those of cancer patients, the complex sociocultural aspects of HIV and its transmission set it apart from any other modern-day disease (Hoffman, 1996). The worker must be prepared to consider a variety of the client's secondary losses, such as stigmatization, personal rejection, prejudice, religious rejection, job loss, economic deprivation, discrimination, legal oppression, fear of contagion, guilt, shame, and loss of self-esteem.

The AIDS pandemic affects millions of victims and their families and is the epitome of the multiple ways that a pernicious disease can bring loss and grief to its victims, significant others, and families (Morgan, Laungani, & Palmer, 2009). Shelby (1995) and Miller (1990, pp. 189–195) have noted that emotional trauma commences when the client first receives notification of seropositivity (HIV-positive status). Typically, expected clinical reactions include disorganization of self, particularly in the initial weeks after notification of results, episodic periods of anxiety, depression, self-blame, shock, denial, suicidal ideation, demoralization, psychosomatic symptoms, low self-esteem, exacerbation of premorbid relational conflicts, and social withdrawal in the months following discovery.

Diagnosis results in immediate and powerful emotional responses, often long before any physical symptoms occur. Victims may feel emotional and physical abandonment, romantic betrayal, and face medical treatment issues that spread a sense of loss and grief across multiple dimensions of their lives (Mphande-Finn & Sommers-Flanagan, 2007). The

HIV-positive person may experience any number of severe physical and emotional manifestations such as nausea, panic attacks, diarrhea, dizziness, skin rashes, lethargy, tremors, visual disturbances, sweating, depression, and sleeplessness. It is difficult to distinguish whether and to what extent these symptoms are related to the HIV infection itself or to its cognitive effects on clients (Miller, 1990, p. 190).

Further, HIV/AIDS clients have many legitimate reasons for developing anxieties as the disease manifests itself in physical symptoms. Their short- and long-term medical prognosis may be grim. HIV/AIDS clients are particularly at risk of infection as well as being subject to the burden of stigmatization, marginalization, and social, occupational, domestic, and sexual hostility. They face potential abandonment, isolation, and physical pain (Nord, 1997, pp. 43–64). HIV-infected people may feel it is impossible for them to alter their circumstances. It is difficult for them to maximize their future health prospects, and they have little control over helping loved ones and family members cope. Adequate medical, dental, and welfare assistance may be very difficult to obtain. They may face negative social pressures and ostracism because they have been identified as homosexuals, drug users, prostitutes, or unfaithful. Further, Theuninck and associates (2010) found that when gay men start to experience symptoms, see others die from AIDS, and undergo the rigors of medical treatment, they became excellent candidates for traumatic grief and PTSD.

AIDS squarely impacts the families and support system of its victims (Duggan, 2007). The epidemic of AIDS in Africa has caused the disintegration of families and turned children and grandparents into major providers and caretakers for HIV-infected parents, with all the inherent crises, grief, and loss that entails (Boon et al., 2010; Nkomo, Freeman, & Skinner, 2009; Van der Heijden & Swartz, 2010; Wood, Chase, & Aggleton, 2006).

The HIV-positive person may also suffer from lack of privacy and confidentiality, feel the loss of dignity with increasing physical dependency, experience sexual unacceptability, and lose physical and financial independence (Nord, 1997, pp. 43–64). All these factors militate against clients' coping mechanisms and are fertile fields in which crises may develop. Kübler-Ross (1987), Miller (1990), Ostrow (1990), Hoffman (1996), Shelby (1995), and Sikkema and associates (2003) have documented a variety of difficult psychological as well as physical obstacles that people with

HIV diagnoses face. They may view their entire physical being as transformed and obsessively search for new bodily evidence of the disease progression; they may relentlessly pursue fads related to health and diet regimens; and they may become preoccupied with illness, death, and avoidance of new infections.

Compounding the problem, AIDS strikes a disproportionate percentage of people who have fewer resources to combat it. In the United States, the poor, minorities (especially African Americans and Hispanics), women (especially women of color), youth, gay and bisexual men, drug addicts, and people who are homeless or mentally disabled are all at higher risk (Britton, 2001; Meris, 2001).

The unique issues related to AIDS define it as a disease of crisis events. The stigma associated with it cannot be dismissed because it colors every facet of the client's life. The isolation caused by the disease can result in extreme problems in maintaining intimate relationships—both sexual and platonic. Its unpredictability makes decision making—concerning such things as jobs, relationships, and even planning for one's end—a hellish emotional roller-coaster ride. While a 75-year-old may have a pretty fair psychological reconciliation with his or her coming demise, a 25-year-old who is grappling with career and other life-planning issues is ill prepared to be faced with the grim news of being HIV positive (Britton, 2001).

Whether or not one's view of AIDS is biased by a moralistic judgment about its victims' sexual or other "sinful" habits, HIV infection drains intrapersonal, interpersonal, and material resources and cannot be thought of as a single stressful life event (Kalichman, 1995, p. 1). It is unremitting, with an uncertain course, and is a transcrisis of pervasive loss in every sense of the word. There is probably no other crisis work that is more important, challenging, or necessary than that done with the AIDS/HIV-positive clientele, a group that is growing throughout the world. The special knowledge, training, and attitudes of workers who counsel and help people in this underserved population deserve special consideration and commendation, and these workers have a high potential for countertransference and burnout (Gueritault-Chalvin et al., 2000; Kuhn, 2008; Van Dyk, 2007).

Job Loss

We are pretty much defined by our jobs. If you don't believe that, consider the first question you generally ask a stranger at a party after you find out the person's name. We would wager that it's something on the order of "What do you do for a living?" Jobs and one's identity with a job have far more than work and wage ramifications. Besides the fact that jobs determine how much money we will make and what our earning potential may be, jobs structure our day and delineate a regular and required set of activities as we prepare for, go to, and finish our day's work. Our jobs account for our status and identity, our sense of participation and purpose, and the social interaction and network that work brings (Jahoda, Lazarfield, & Zeisel, 1933/1971). While losing one's job under any circumstances can certainly be a crisis, losing one's job for no reason, or one that has nothing to do with job performance, absolutely is. For those it happens to, what they experience looks and feels very much like grief (Vickers, 2009).

Technological progress and a free market economy have changed the American workplace dramatically. A major ramification of that change has been the loss of millions of well-paying white- and blue-collar jobs that provided a wage earner with income, job security, and the hallowed, and much aspired to, middle-class existence (Lerner, 2000). In the new economic millennium, the possibility of economic restructuring and job loss is ever present no matter how diligent and faithful employees are (Newman, 1993).

The ripple effects stretch out to the families of those employees and result in a variety of pathological reactions as the primary breadwinner comes to realize that he or she is now downwardly mobile, with little chance of regaining his or her former job status. Alcoholism, drug use, battering, child abuse, divorce, suicide, and murder are but a few of the family handmaidens of job loss. On a personal basis, depression, anger, blame, projection, loss of self-esteem, loss of personal identity, lower self-concept, loss of social support systems, stigmatization, loss of control, disintegration of ego integrity, and overall negative mental health are emotional outcomes for someone who may now also suffer secondary victimization not unlike rape or other assault victims (Price, Friedland, & Vinokur, 1998).

That victimization may occur at the hands of others who need to rationalize that the person is somehow incompetent, lazy, or otherwise unequal to the job. To acknowledge otherwise would put themselves in peril and say very clearly that they had no control over their own destinies any more than the coworker who was let go (Reichle, Schneider, & Montada, 1998). Further compounding the problem, the victim often reacts in the same way as the victimizers, casting

about in a futile attempt to make sense out of what has happened (Lerner, 2000). When whole industries shut down, outsource, or downsize, entire towns are put at risk, and we now have a systemic crisis.

The negative effects of unemployment on both physiological and psychological well-being are well documented, while job loss as it pertains to grief is relatively new and unknown. Much like those bereaved who suffer traumatic loss due to death, the assumptive world of the newly unemployed is shattered, their view of a just world is challenged, and views of themselves as valuable and worthy are invalidated (Harris & Isenor, 2011). Brewington and associates (2004) studied factors hypothesized to relate to job loss grief. Grief scores correlated positively with time since job loss and number of dependents and negatively with length of notice of termination. Income loss and lack of perceived reemployment prospects related positively to grief subscales. Donahue (2010) compared a job loss group to a bereaved group. The job loss group demonstrated similar levels of hopelessness, tension, stress, confusion, and physical symptoms and had higher degrees of irritation, guilt, withdrawal from social responsibility, oversensitivity, and brooding than the bereaved group.

Therefore, to say that career counseling is a dull and humdrum job when dealing with job loss is to have one's head stuck in the sand. Vocational outplacement counselors often have to dance between helping individuals look for work and engaging in crisis support therapy for grief, anxiety, depression, and stress (Harris & Isenor, 2011). The ramifications of job loss can be far-reaching and devastating. As we saw in Chapter 8, Crisis of Lethality, in the example of the outplacement job counseling that turns into a suicide intervention, the potential for crisis when job loss occurs is ever present and often blindsides the unwary human services worker.

Another issue that is often overlooked is how grief is handled in the workplace. Sooner or later, people who lose significant others need to go back to work. Generally it is sooner; there is nothing like a pregnancy leave of absence for grief-stricken workers. Grieving workers can make poor business decisions, miss business opportunities, have accidents, and cause financial losses (Hazen, 2009). For all these reasons, it is in the best interests of management to pay attention to the human reality of death and bereavement in the workplace (Charles-Edwards, 2009). With increased knowledge about the negative effects of complicated/prolonged grief, it should be apparent that businesses need to look beyond the obligatory floral arrangement for the deceased in making provisions for valued employees who have suffered the loss of a loved one.

Separation and Divorce

Better than 50% of all marriages in the United States end in divorce after 20 years, and this statistic has held steady for quite a while (National Center for Health Statistics, 2012). It is devastating to adults and children alike when the relationship dies but the person is still living (Harris, 2011). It doesn't take an expert in marriage and family counseling or a grief specialist to understand the heartache, sense of loss, and all of the accompanying bad emotions that go with a divorce. The crisis of separation and divorce followed by acrimonious custody fights often places children in untenable positions, causing them to feel confused, insecure, fearful, trapped, angry, unloved, and guilty (Karkazis & Lazaneo, 2000). Bruce and Kim (1992) found that major depression is prevalent among both men and women experiencing marital disruption. According to Johnson (1977), the most common experience that marriage partners have regarding separation is intense and disturbing fear and emotional turmoil.

Almost all separations produce negative feelings and outcomes that were not anticipated by either party. Even when the separation is desired and sought, it precipitates a sense of frustration, failure, loss, and mourning. Schneider (1984) reports that people suffering from loss due to divorce or widowhood "show significant and consistently higher vulnerability to almost every major physical and mental disorder, particularly to heart disease" (p. 19). Colgrove and associates (1991) advise that surviving and healing following such loss begin by recognizing and facing the loss immediately and doing the mourning now (pp. 1–2).

Death of a Pet

It is estimated that in the United States there are 57 million dogs and 62 million cats kept as pets (to say nothing of other pets such as horses, snakes, gerbils, and so on). As many as 63% of American households have pets. There are good reasons for pet cemeteries and the expense to which pet owners will go to keep a dying pet alive. The human–animal bond is now recognized as an integral part of pet owners' lives, and it is important for us to recognize and validate the grief that pet owners experience when their beloved

companion animals die (Lagoni, Butler, & Hetts, 1994; Nieburg & Fischer, 1982; Planchon et al., 2002). Weisman (1990–1991) and Reitmeyer (2000) compared bereavement following the death of a companion animal to the experience of the loss of another human.

Smith (2009) speaks of individuals who have suffered the loss of a pet as manifesting profound grief and depression. Smith notes, somewhat tongue-in-cheek, that there is good reason for such severe reactions. Unlike humans, dogs are absolutely loyal, they keep our secrets, they don't complain, clearly communicate their needs, and are pretty patient unless they have to relieve themselves and need to go out or haven't been fed all day.

When pets die or suffer terminal illness and have to be "put to sleep," the owners may suffer grief, guilt, and other emotional reactions similar to those experienced at the death of human family members. Hsu (2010) found that pet owners she examined could be partitioned into high and low grief groups. High grief groups were distressed by dreams of their pets, were distressed by fond memories, kept their pets' belongings, erected shrines and memorials, and felt more social constraints, feelings of alienation, and lack of support for their grief. Low grief participants, on the other hand, were comforted by dreams of their pets, gave their pets' belongings away, and were comforted by fond memories of their pets. These feelings and responses may be especially acute in the elderly whose main object of affection is a pet (Brooks & Martinez, 1999) or those who live alone (McCutcheon & Fleming, 2001–2002).

The death of a pet may provide a naturally occurring opportunity for adults in the family to introduce children to the concept and experience of death and dying (Koocher, 1975; Nieburg & Fischer, 1982; Schoenberg, 1980, pp. 203–204). Recently, pet loss counseling has become widespread in the United States. The Delta Society publishes a national directory of pet loss counselors. These counselors are a legitimate and growing occupation and are now affiliated with schools of veterinary medicine, local humane societies, and private practices (Reitmeyer, 2000).

Complicated/Prolonged Grief, Bereavement, and Mourning Reaction

LO9

When a person is unable to mourn a loss and move on in a context of renewal and growth, the possibility of delayed or chronic grief arises (Middleton et al., 1998; Raphael & Minkov, 1999). According to Shear and associates (2011), the following criteria are necessary for a diagnosis of complicated/prolonged grief: The person has been bereaved (i.e., experienced the death of a loved one) for at least 6 months. At least one of the following symptoms of persistent, intense, acute grief has been present for a period longer than is expected by others in the person's social (or cultural) environment:

1. Persistent intense yearning or longing for the person who died.
2. Frequent intense feelings of loneliness, or that life is empty or meaningless without the person who died.
3. Recurrent thoughts that it is unfair, meaningless, or unbearable to live when a loved one has died, or a recurrent urge to die in order to find (or join) the deceased.
4. Frequent preoccupying thoughts about the person who died; for example, thoughts or images of the person intrude on activities or interfere with functioning.

At least two of the following symptoms are present for at least 1 month:

1. Frequent, troubling rumination about the circumstances (or consequences) of the death (concerns about how or why the person died, about not being able to manage without their loved one, thoughts of having let the deceased person down, etc.).
2. Recurrent feeling of disbelief or inability to accept the death.
3. Persistent feeling of shock; feeling stunned, dazed. or emotionally numb since the death.
4. Recurrent feelings of anger or bitterness related to the death.
5. Persistent difficulty trusting or caring about other people, or envy of others who have not experienced a similar loss.
6. Frequently experiencing pain (or other symptoms) that the deceased person had, hearing the voice of (or seeing) the deceased person.
7. Experiencing intense emotional or physiological reactivity to memories of the person who died or to reminders of the loss.
8. Changes in behavior due to avoidance (or its opposite, excessive proximity-seeking—refraining from going places, doing things, or having contact with things that are reminders of the loss; feeling drawn to reminders of the person—wanting to see, touch, hear, or smell things to feel close to the

person who died). Both symptoms may coexist in the same individual.
9. Duration of symptoms and impairment of at least 1 month.
10. Symptoms cause clinically significant distress or impairment in social, occupational, or other major areas of functioning, where impairment is not explicable as a culturally appropriate response.

These are the precursors to a complicated or prolonged grief, bereavement, and mourning reaction, which involves continuous distressed yearnings, pangs of severe separation anxiety, intense intrusive thoughts, feelings of increased aloneness and emptiness, excessive avoidance of tasks related to the deceased, loss of interest in personal activities, and disturbances in sleeping, eating, and other daily living patterns present more than a year after the loss (Horowitz et al., 1997). Complicated/prolonged grief is persistent and does not tend to go away (Ott, 2003). There is a continued and increased sense of and binding to the deceased that hampers the griever's ability to function in a normal social and occupational manner (Rando, 1993, p. 175).

Kersting and colleagues (2011) found that the incidence of complicated/prolonged grief in a representative sample (N = 2,520) was about 3.7% in the general population and the potential for developing it after major bereavement was 6.7%. High-risk predictors for developing it were female gender, low income, older age, having lost a child or spouse, or cancer as the cause of death, although there appear to be limitations to these particular subsets due to small cell sample sizes.

Some people don't begin to have complicated/prolonged grief symptoms until 6 months after the loss. Others experience acute symptoms immediately that continue for a year or more. They also tend to experience co-occurring disorders such as major depression, posttraumatic stress disorder, and generalized anxiety, although researchers contend that prolonged grief is distinguishable from those disorders (Boelen et al., 2010; Horowitz et al., 1997; Prigerson & Jacobs, 2001). People in both time frames do have a higher risk for a major depressive disorder, PTSD, or generalized anxiety disorder than those whose grief runs a more conventional course or who are treated (Kersting & Kroker, 2010; Prigerson, Vanderwerker, & Maciejewski, 2008; Shear & Mulhare, 2008). More ominously, they have a higher incidence of suicidal ideation and risk of suicide (Shear & Mulhare, 2008). Indeed, people with complicated/prolonged grief appear to have an incidence rate of these disorders and behaviors that is equal to or higher than psychiatric outpatients with other known disorders, those bereaved by suicide, survivors of disaster events, caregivers of people with dementia, and older adults (Piper et al., 2011).

In all complicated or prolonged grief, two dynamics predominate and do not allow the individual to move forward. First, the person denies, represses, or avoids aspects of the loss, its pain, and the full realization of its implications for the mourner. Second, the individual holds onto and avoids relinquishing the lost loved one (Rando, 1996). The contrast with normal grief reactions and typical bereavement patterns, in terms of period and intensity of mourning, is so pronounced that practitioners and researchers proposed including distinct diagnostic criteria in the fifth edition of the American Psychiatric Association's *Diagnostic and Statistical Manual of Mental Disorders* (Shear et al., 2011). That did not happen to the chagrin of many professionals in the field. What many therapists label as **complicated grief** or **prolonged grief** got classified as a depressive disorder in the fifth edition of the *Diagnostic and Statistical Manual of Mental Disorders* (American Psychiatric Association, 2013). One reason that grief therapists have become so angry with that decision is that it implies that a person who is experiencing profound and extended grief is mentally ill.

The work groups that determine what goes in and out of DSM-5 decided that it would be called **persistent complex bereavement disorder** and placed it in the chapter on Conditions for Further Study in the new DSM-5. That term has been given its fair share of criticism (Boehlen & Prigerson, 2012; Melhem et al., 2013) by grief researchers who believe the authors of the DSM-5 are waffling because they are in essence saying there is enough evidence to classify it as a new disorder, yet they believe the evidence-based criteria is still to ambiguous to classify it when, in fact, the evidence is there. So for the present, if you or a significant other are experiencing prolonged grief, and you seek therapy for it, the therapist needs to classify the problem as an adjustment disorder with depressed mood to get paid by an insurance company.

Proposed criteria for prolonged grief as a personality disorder in the new DSM-5 include distressed yearning to be reunited to the extent that it causes physical or emotional suffering, preoccupation with the deceased, intrusive recurrent images or thoughts of the death, as well as a number of the following symptoms still being experienced 6 months or more after the loss: (1) emotional numbness; (2) a stunned, dazed, or shocked feeling; (3) a feeling that life is meaningless; (4) bitterness or anger over the loss; (5) estrangement from and mistrust of others; (6) difficulty accepting the loss; (7) avoidance of reminders of the deceased; (8) difficulty moving on with life; (9) a feeling that part of oneself has died; (10) excessive avoidance of tasks reminiscent of the deceased; (11) unusual sleep disturbances; (12) loss of interest in usual activities; and (13) hallucinations of the deceased (Forstmeier & Maercker, 2007; Horowitz et al., 1997; Prigerson, Vanderwerker, & Maciejewski, 2008; Simon et al., 2011).

Traumatic Death/Traumatic Grief. When death occurs by traumatic means, such as a vehicle accident, murder, or natural or human-made disaster, the potential for complicated mourning increases exponentially (Figley, 1996; Lord, 1996; Rando, 1996; Redmon, 1996). The degree of trauma is increased by (1) the suddenness and lack of anticipation, (2) violence, mutilation, and destruction, (3) preventability and/or randomness, (4) multiple deaths, and (5) the mourner's own confrontation with death or witnessing of violence or mutilation (Rando, 1996, p. 143). Besides type and degree of violence in the death, the relationship, both in regard to kinship and emotional connection, and what social support systems are available are external variables that play a large role in how and whether traumatic grief will turn into complicated/prolonged grief (Hibberd, Elwood, & Galovski, 2010).

Survivors who have not initiated or finished grieving for their lost ones are vulnerable to suffering from residual trauma, transcrisis, impaired functioning, or worse. It is not uncommon in traumatic deaths for the griever to be reexposed over and over to the traumatic death if the legal system becomes involved through either civil or criminal actions (Rynearson, 2010). The differentiating factor between traumatic grief and complicated/prolonged grief appears to be that complicated/prolonged grief is a function of one's degree of emotional relationship with the loss object, whereas in traumatic grief the degree of distress has more to do with situational factors such as degree of violence, extent of maiming of the body, and physical proximity to and witnessing of the death (Holland & Neimeyer, 2011). If the foregoing is now starting to remind you of PTSD stimuli, you are right! In fact, when a complicated/prolonged grief reaction occurs, they may be considered co-occurring disorders and treatment for PTSD is generally recommended concurrent with bereavement counseling (Figley, 1996; Rando, 1996).

Clues for Identifying Complicated Grief Reaction.

Rando (1996) and Worden (1991) have constructed clues for identifying complicated/prolonged grief reaction that may prove useful to crisis workers in cases in which survivors of loss are in serious denial. Examples might be a parent who has experienced the loss of a child and refuses to face the fact that the child is gone, keeping the child's room just as it was years after the death; a spouse or partner whose mate has either died or left for good, and the survivor carries on as if the partner has simply stepped out to the corner convenience store and will return shortly; or an adult child angry over the death of a parent with whom he had unfinished business that cannot now be resolved who projects his rage onto everyone else. Rando's (1996, pp. 145–146) and Worden's (1991, pp. 75–77) list of clues may help crisis workers identify and offer help to people who manifest such severe denial or other debilitating reactions.

Crisis workers and other caregivers should take note of and attend to clients when:

1. The person cannot speak of the deceased without experiencing intense and fresh grief.
2. Some relatively minor event triggers an intense grief reaction.
3. The survivor cannot remove material possessions or belongings of the deceased.
4. Loss themes continually come up during interviews.
5. The griever manifests the same physical symptoms as those the deceased had.
6. The individual exhibits radical changes in lifestyle following the death or excludes family, friends, activities, or visitation of places associated with the deceased.
7. The person experiences a long history of depression following loss, often marked by persistent guilt and lowered self-esteem.
8. There is a compulsion to imitate the dead person.
9. The person exhibits self-destructive impulses or suicidal ideation.
10. There is unaccountable sadness at certain times of the year.
11. The person has phobias about illness or death.
12. There is definite avoidance of death-related rituals or activities.
13. There is obsessive reconstruction of events surrounding the death.

14. The person focuses on what was happening in the relationship at the time of death (usually negative) to the exclusion of the complete span of the relationship (more positive).
15. Secondary losses, such as the loss of a house or savings due to a lack of planning, impetuous spending, or vulnerability to scams, occur and cause financial problems.
16. There are compulsive and obsessive attempts to fix blame and assign responsibility if the death was caused by humans.

Workers are reminded that relatively few grievers display all of the clues on the list. The value of this list lies in the fact that such grievers are encountered more often than one might think and workers need to be prepared, and not show surprise, when faced with such behavior in grievers whom they counsel (Worden, 1991, pp. 65–78). Indeed, many times clients who have complicated grief reactions have submerged the loss experience from conscious awareness or summarily dismissed it as "part of life." When you are faced with a client who is in crisis for no apparent legitimate reason, you should always assess for unresolved grief and loss issues. These issues may not necessarily have to do with unreconciled loss and sadness over a loved one; they may involve anger over unfinished business with the deceased, the departed lover, or the lost job. Under circumstances in which parting was anything but sweet sorrow, the aggrieved individual must be able to forgive and let go, which is not an easy task (De Moss, 2003).

Intervention Strategies

If we believe the current research that tells **LO10** us the stage theories that have held sway for so long in the field of loss and grieving are not very workable, then we are faced with the business of tailor-making and custom fitting an intervention for every person who has a grieving problem. Further, when we dichotomize normal against complicated/prolonged grief, we are faced with another dilemma because they are essentially two different constructs. So how in the world do we go forward? Even though a huge volume of research has been done on the concepts underlying this chapter and on demographics such as age, race, and sex in describing grieving characteristics, the actual testing of interventions as to how effective they are is pretty sparse.

To complicate matters even further, it appears that what is presently being done in the field of grieving and bereavement isn't working very well. Meta-analyses of outcome studies have consistently shown that, in general, grief intervention outcomes don't measure up to outcomes for most other psychotherapy issues. Essentially, most people with grieving problems don't get better as a result of intervention and in fact may get worse (Allumbaugh & Hoyt, 1999; Currier, Holland, & Neimeyer, 2007; Currier, Neimeyer, & Berman, 2008; Kato & Mann, 1999; Neimeyer, 2000; Rosner, Kruse, & Hagl, 2010).

There is a caveat to these findings. While intervention with normal grief reactions is generally unproductive, individuals with complicated/prolonged grief may indeed derive some benefits equivalent to other areas of psychotherapeutic intervention. It also appears that when individuals self-select for intervention they do much better than do those selected by the researchers (Currier, Neimeyer, & Berman, 2008; Rossner, Kruse, & Hagi, 2010). That finding seems to resonate pretty clearly with the entire area of loss; that is, you can't push grieving people into action until they are ready to do something about it.

What we do know about the business of counseling, though, is that more than anything else, the quality of the relationship between a client and a counselor is probably the best basis for determining how effective the counseling is going to be. From that standpoint, we believe that Altmaier's (2011) view of best practices in grief work that focuses on the relationship has a great deal to say about how effective workers can be in dealing with normal grief.

Being There for Grievers: A Worker Imperative

Particularly as the news of a death is received, "being there" is as important as anything the crisis worker does. Being there manifests the qualities of *empathic presence, gentle conversation, providing available space,* and *eliciting trust* (Altmaier, 2011).

Empathic presence involves listening, silence, and support through accepting and encouraging the expression of feelings, allowing pain to be expressed, and responding in a noncritical, nonjudgmental manner in allowing the grief-stricken to tell their story (Altmaier, 2011). Above all else in grief work, empathic listening to the bereaved and their families appears to be the single most useful skill or strategy available to crisis workers (Rando, 1984). Studies by Balk (1990) confirm the value of empathic listening. He found that bereaved college students identify "attentive listening and presence" as being the most helpful to grievers and "avoidance" as being the least helpful.

Avoid cliches, easy answers, and phrases meant to comfort survivors (Altmaier, 2011; Aten et al., 2015). "She's in a better place." "It was God's will." "The good die young." "He's at home now." "You're a strong person." "There's no more pain." "God loves those who suffer most." "Better days are ahead." All these pat phrases are discounting at best and demeaning at worst. They are cliches that people use who are absolutely confounded as to what to say to the griever. What they really mean is: "I haven't a clue as to how to help you assuage this grief and am really embarrassed to try, but I'll mumble this and maybe I'll feel better and can get out of this uncomfortable situation." Trying to smooth things over such as "It could be worse, It'll be OK" are discounts on the depths of feelings. It's up to the survivor to decide when things will be "OK."

Likewise, stay away from "Don't cry! "Don't worry!" Don't be blue!" "Don't feel bad." "Don't swear!" (Aten et al., 2015). Survivors have every reason to "Do" all those things. "Don't" generally says more about the anxiety of the speaker than it does about the survivor.

Gentle Conversation. Gentle conversation allows for memory sharing, telling and retelling stories, and owning statements from the worker such as "I am sorry. I don't have words to begin to touch the feelings you must have, but I am here, and I will stay here and listen if you care to talk." Use active and reflective listening skills (Aten et al., 2015). "I can really sense the caring and feeling you had for your grandfather as you talk about those Sunday afternoon rides down to the lake."

Providing available space has to do with what contemporary research and practice in the field of loss keep harping about—that is, helping the client find support, doing things clients can't do for themselves right now (pumping gas), but letting them tell us what they can and can't do so they have at least a modicum of control in their lives. Providing available space also has to do with time. Since each client's grieving process marches to its own drummer, patience is a huge virtue for the worker (Altmaier, 2011).

Eliciting trust is a keystone that communicates that clients have the ability to get through tough times, recover, and grow (Altmaier, 2011). It is not cheerleading, but it is gentle encouragement and trust that the client can engage the grief and not avoid it. "I'm in this for the duration as long as it takes. You want to cry, I'm here. You want to swear I'm here. You want to sleep I'm here. You want to talk, I'm here. I know you have strength and I have strength and we will get through this together." Hughes (1988) believes that grieving clients' expectations of the worker's abilities are crucial in facilitating the healing process. Hughes stated that the worker's expectations are always communicated directly or subtly to the client and that clients heal when they are "informed" by the worker that they are never helpless victims, but instead are powerful and capable of healing themselves (p. 77).

We agree that by being there, the crisis worker is an empathic, nonjudgmental pillar of support who provides emotional understanding and allows the client to feel *felt* (Wylie, 2004, p. 33). As odd as that sounds, "feeling felt" ribbon-wraps the total package of "being there." As Schuurman and DeCristofaro (2007) state, "It is that simple, and that complex" (p. 174).

We also believe that a critical component that does much to lend the worker credibility is much like intervention in a disaster area; that is, one builds up sweat equity with clients by doing some very pedestrian and mundane activities. These may include calling relatives, helping make arrangements for organ donation, contacting funeral homes and flower shops, finding legal papers, contacting charitable organizations, and attending to other basic necessities that go with the death of a loved one. If no relatives or friends are present or capable of doing this, it is reasonable and proper for the workers to offer their services in that regard.

Fitting Technique to Style of Grief

The Dual Process Model. When workers operate with contemporary grief models, they are going to have to be nimble, fluid, and adaptable as clients oscillate back and forth between a loss orientation and a restoration orientation. In Stroebe and associates' (2005) dual process model, the griever sometimes confronts and sometimes avoids the stressors of both orientations (Humphrey, 2009, p. 49). In fact, one of the primary jobs of the worker is not only to tolerate but also to encourage such oscillation (Stroebe & Schut, 1999). Humphrey (2009, p. 51) lists the following recommendations for using the dual process model:

1. Identify and explore both loss and restoration stressors and the specific avoidance and confrontation responses the client uses.

2. Keep in mind that an initial period when the client is fixed in a loss orientation is normal. Identify evidence (or lack thereof) of oscillation as time moves forward.

3. Normalize and validate the dual process model by explaining how it works and why it applies to the client's particular situation.

4. Address problematic avoidance such as excessive alcohol/drug use, extreme denial, suppression of emotion, or acting out.

5. Do not push clients toward restoration. Let the oscillation work.

To Humphrey's recommendations we would add another, which we feel is critical to effective resolution of any situation where families or significant others are interwoven in the fabric of the grief. That recommendation is psychoeducation with family and other support systems as to how this model works. Otherwise, there may be some very frustrated and unhappy significant others who, on the surface, see little progress and indeed regression. In that regard, we feel it is highly important to include significant others in progress assessments and support meetings that reinforce them for "sticking in there."

The Adaptive Grieving Model. The same flexibility and ability to operate in a fluid manner is called for from the worker in Martin and Doka's (2000) adaptive model. In our experience, clients seldom remain fixed at one point on the model's intuitive–instrumental continuum. In our opinion, this model calls for a fairly high degree of ability and skill to operate in an eclectic manner across a wide array of therapeutic modalities to fit with affective, behavioral, cognitive, and spiritual reactions of clients. Note the addition of *spiritual* to the usual triad of intervention strategies. While we don't necessarily believe you have to be able to quote directly from the Bible, Talmud, Koran, or any other spiritual source, we do believe you had better know something about this area and be able to work in it. To not know about spirituality and faith when working with loss, grief, and bereavement or, worse yet, discounting them is akin to not knowing or discounting any of the affective–behavioral–cognitive triad modalities when involved in other therapeutic endeavors. Given the foregoing admonition, the following strategies from Martin and Doka (2000) can serve as starting points.

Affective Strategies. Affective strategies should initially allow for emotional catharsis through a range of what may be construed as negative emotions from crying to angry swearing. Because emotional dysregulation is seen as a major problem in problematic grieving, setting the stage for emotional exposure is important in regaining regulating abilities. Successive approximation to full emotional regulation through carefully graded, stepwise exposure to experiencing painful feelings is important. Likewise, carefully planning and choosing times, places, and people with whom to field-test affective interaction with others moves the grief from the counseling session into the real world. Assessment and revision of these field experiments is important in determining abilities, skills, and limits and also reinforces the idea that plans fail but people don't.

Behavioral Strategies. Behavior strategies involve a variety of actions that may include substituting a range of positive addicting behaviors, such as running, quilting, fishing, gardening, singing, biking, or building something, for static behaviors such as sitting trancelike, watching television for hours on end, and ruminating about the loss. Making plans that deal with current problems and tasks, such as disposing of the deceased's belongings, locating a retirement center, starting a job search, and reviewing financial plans, are all examples of concrete, forward-looking behavioral strategies. Confronting and motivating new adaptive behaviors that deal with negative addictions such as alcohol and drug abuse, overeating, anorexic tendencies, or gambling are also part of the behavioral game plan for the crisis worker.

Cognitive Strategies. Cognitive strategies deal with changing maladaptive thinking. Workers help clients create positive counterinjunctions and positive mental billboards in place of negative self-defeating thoughts. Workers aid clients in reframing and restructuring hot, all-or-none, intolerable, catastrophic thinking into cooler, less absolutistic, more preferable and tolerable thoughts. They also caringly confront clients on cognitive avoidance, denial, and minimizing or discounting the impact of the loss.

Spiritual Strategies. Spiritual strategies are about transcending the loss through faith-based activities. This is a sensitive and tricky area to operate in because of each person's idiosyncratic interpretation of the part that spirituality and faith play in both the loss and its resolution. This is so because a secondary loss may indeed be a loss of faith over the perceived

injustice or the uncaring of God in the primary loss. The worker needs to be extremely sensitive in regard to what will help the client deepen, renew, or discover new or old spiritual wellsprings. So whether through prayer, meditation, reading scripture with a group or on one's own, burning incense at an altar, hugging a large Douglas fir tree, or spending time stargazing, the idea is to activate spiritual resources. The worker does not have to be an ordained minister to do this.

Perhaps the best prototype for this area is the work of the Christian Stephen ministry, which trains laypeople to administer spiritual psychological first aid to persons who are experiencing all kinds of trouble. Named after Saint Stephen, the first Christian martyr who cared for the poor, they provide a complete system of training and equipping laypeople to provide quality Christian care to hurting people (Stephen Ministries, 2011). We think the analogy of them being the spiritual equivalent of community emergency response workers (CERTs; see Chapter 17, Disaster Response) is an apt one, and crisis workers who do not have in-depth spiritual training might do well to go through the Stephen Ministry's workshop or its equivalent with other religions. Barring that, we heavily endorse forming a relationship with a trusted cleric with whom the worker can coordinate this facet of grief recovery.

Cognitive–Behavioral Approaches

Cognitive-behavioral therapies, which focus on changing maladaptive thinking, are the most commonly used therapies for those who suffer from complicated/prolonged grief (Cohen, Mannarino, & Deblinger, 2006; Humphrey, 2009; Shear & Frank, 2006). Cognitive-behavioral strategies are used in dealing with both loss and restoration orientations (Shear & Frank, 2006). A variety of cognitive-behavioral techniques, including relaxation training, desensitization, thought stopping, cognitive restructuring, depropagandizing and disputing irrational beliefs, guided imagery, and in vivo imagery, are used to deal with the emotional dysrgulation, behavioral dysfunction, maladaptive cognitions, and avoidance issues that are characteristic of complicated/prolonged grief.

Added to basic cognitive-behavioral therapy are the postmodernist constructivist therapies (Neimeyer, 2001, 2010b; Neimeyer et al., 2007) that focus on one of the major tasks of complicated/prolonged grief counseling—meaning making (Slattery & Park, 2015). Meaning making has to do with one's interpretation of reality and truth as the central process of one's life (Humphrey, 2009, p. 62). Certainly one of the core issues of loss is making sense of it in such a way as to reformulate one's life, develop a new sense of purpose, and move from the past to the future.

Narrative Therapy

Narrative therapy is a postmodern social constructivist approach that emphasizes the stories or narratives of people's lives (Humphrey, 2009; Monk et al., 1997; White, 1989). Narrative therapy is particularly important in grief work because it involves the telling and retelling of stories that thematically represent the meaning of the loss in the person's life. It brings to light and helps clients challenge the underlying beliefs and assumptions of dominant, maladaptive narratives that they have created in an attempt to make sense and meaning of the loss and challenges negative descriptions of themselves as guilty, weak, ruined, wasted, broken, guilty, shamed, cowardly and so on, that are often a complicating factor in loss adaption (Humphrey, 2009, p. 175). Narrative therapy also helps reconstruct, rather than relinquish, the relationship of the deceased and gives voice to the unspeakable thoughts and feelings of dog grievers' attempts to reclaim their lives and make meaning of them (Neimeyer, 2010a).

Attachment Theory and Therapy

Attachment theory is one of the oldest theories to deal with grief. While it has origins as a phase theory, it still has a great deal of utility and is a basic premise of grief and loss. Attachment creates bonds that are rooted in the core of our existence, and when those attachments are broken, severe fractures and breaks can occur in the personality. Attachment theory emphasizes separation anxiety arising from the griever's attachment to the deceased, the breaking of bonds of affection, and the need to emotionally detach from the lost object. Attachment theory proposes that human beings form close affiliation bonds (emotional attachments) from birth because close attachment between parent and child is an evolutionary adaption that keeps infants secure and safe, and the resulting close physical contact with the parent enhances physical, emotional, and cognitive development (Bowlby, 1969, 1980, 1988).

The key component in understanding attachment theory comes from Main's (1996, 2000) research on "coherent narrative," which is the way parents told the stories of their lives. It was the most potent predictor of whether their own children would be securely attached to them. In other words, it wasn't what actually happened to them as children, but how they made sense of what happened to them. Thus, making meaning of one's childhood, regardless of the actual event, corresponded positively with emotional integration and better parenting (Schuurman & De Cristofaro, 2007). When Bowlby's and Main's research is translated to loss and grief, it is thus not how one actually lived with the deceased, but how one *thought* about how one had lived with the deceased that really matters. As such, how the narrative of that thought process unfolds has a great deal to do with whether one moves through the loss and grief well or not. If the narrative is maladaptive, then it follows that the griever will be maladaptive as well. At that point, narrative therapy's ability to change the story comes into the therapeutic picture. Thus, attachment theory can blend well with narrative therapy (Dallos & Vetere, 2009).

Dealing with Loss
Sudden Death of a Spouse

Stuart Wynn, a 44-year-old machinist, his **LO11** wife Kate, a 42-year-old bookkeeper, and daughter, Anne, an 18-year-old high school senior, were a stable, middle-class family living in a quiet neighborhood in a large city. On her way to work one morning aboard a commuter train, Kate Wynn suffered a severe stroke and was taken by ambulance to a hospital emergency room, where she died. As far as Stuart knew, Kate had been in good health and had had no medical history to indicate that she might have had a health problem.

Sudden deaths have their own constellation of problems, and survivors' ability to use adaptive coping mechanisms is often overwhelmed (Redmon, 1996). The sudden death is often violent, which means that authorities, autopsies, inquests, identification and return of remains, and a variety of other state and legal activities will often be involved. The news media and the criminal justice system can be intrusive and dramatic in clients' lives. Survivor reactions may be equally dramatic (Cummock, 1996). Because sudden death often occurs when significant others aren't present, questions arise as to how much the deceased suffered. There may be a desire for retaliation and revenge if the death was violent and human caused. The unpredictability of sudden death challenges assumptions about what the world is and how it operates. All of these disruptive negative cognitions can complicate grieving of sudden losses and leaves survivors with unfinished business (Humphrey, 2009, p. 23). Cognitive dissonance in sudden—and, in particular, violent—death is almost always high. The death makes no sense, and the mind cannot comprehend the reality of it. Emotions and many times behaviors are completely out of control because of the blame, accusation, and fault finding that the aggrieved erroneously believes will somehow make sense out of this impossible event (Redmon, 1996).

On the Triage Assessment Form, the worker mentally computed Stuart's profile: affective, 5 (emotionally shocked but substantially under control); behavioral, 8 (minimally able to perform tasks relevant to his wife's death); cognitive, 3 (thought processes affected by the crisis but under volitional control and congruent with reality); total, 16 (moderate impairment). Stuart's actions are not atypical in a situation involving sudden death by heart attack or stroke (Hersh, 1996). Despite the immediate disequilibrium following the sudden death of his wife, at that moment Stuart was maintaining psychological equilibrium; only later would the impact of the loss catch up with him and would he experience severe affective, behavioral, and cognitive impairment. But for the moment he could cope, even though the help of a crisis interventionist was needed and welcomed.

His daughter, Anne, was triaged as being much more substantially out of control. Her affect was rated as 10. She was decompensating and highly agitated and could not keep her emotions under volitional control. Behaviorally, she was erratic and unpredictable. She had accused the ER staff of not keeping her mother alive and had to be contained by security. Her behavioral rating was also 10. Her problem-solving skills were barely adequate to the situation. She could barely contain herself after the intervention of security. Her cognitive rating was 8, for a full-scale score of 28. The attending physician suggested that Stuart might wish to have his daughter kept in the hospital overnight and that she be given medication to de-escalate her extreme agitation. It was also recommended that a staff psychiatrist evaluate her due to her extreme agitation and the fact that her triage assessment put her in the potentially lethal range. While Anne is certainly a critical part of the case, here the focus will be specifically on Stuart as the surviving spouse. The case of a surviving child and the problems he or she may encounter will be dealt with later in the chapter.

The first intervention session was a very brief meeting that included only the crisis worker and Stuart. The second meeting, approximately 20 minutes later, was also a short-term intervention session that featured a meeting between Stuart and his daughter and a multidisciplinary care team consisting of the crisis worker, the attending physician, a psychiatric nurse, and the hospital chaplain.

Care teams are important because they are a response to complex biological, psychological, and social problems in sudden death situations that call for experts from more than one profession (Larson, 1993, p. 199). These initial short-term sessions were aimed at providing the following:

1. Empathic understanding and acknowledgment of the special problems related to Kate's sudden death
2. Assurance to Stuart and Anne that all appropriate emergency medical measures had been attempted in efforts to save Kate
3. Emotional support for both Stuart and Anne by the worker and by the other members of the multidisciplinary team
4. Assurance that Stuart and Anne would have time alone with Kate's body prior to its being picked up for autopsy
5. Referral resources that Stuart needed immediately to make arrangements for the funeral, notification of kin, and other matters
6. Information about autopsy rights and procedures, in case Stuart requested it (which he did)
7. Contact with the family minister, at Stuart's request
8. Immediate medical and psychological assistance for Anne

The care team laid out a long-term treatment plan that included the following intervention strategies to be provided during the initial hours and days immediately following Kate's death. Under no circumstances should you suggest that the person immediately seek out a survivors' group or grapple his or her way through stage models of loss and bereavement. These activities will occur on the person's own mourning timeline and not some "hypothetical" or "scientific" timeline (Humphrey, 2009, p. 6; Shallcross, 2009).

1. *Immediate crisis intervention.* Dealing with the immediate practical necessities of Kate's death, such as autopsies, organ donation, funeral arrangements,

contacting her employer, contacting family members. Continued assessment of Stuart's coping ability. Provision of support persons from the hospital, church, family, and friends. Discussion and recommendation to Stuart of immediate temporary hospitalization for Anne due to assessed potential to do injury to herself or others.

2. *Transcrisis individual counseling and intervention.* Identification of Stuart's grieving style on the adaptive model intuitive–instrumental continuum and tailoring intervention to that style (Martin & Doka, 2000) because research indicates that close emotionally tied marriages like Stuart's tend to result in greater yearning 6 months after the loss may think they are moving on and then be blindsided as the full impact of their soul mate's loss washes over them (Piper et al., 2011, pp. 97–98). Issues of loneliness and bereavement related to Kate's absence (Giunta & Giunta, 2002, pp. 125–146). Implications for regaining equilibrium and going on with his life. Identification of functions and roles in the family that were previously carried out by Kate and that must be reevaluated or reassigned. Dependence on the deceased spouse for instrumental task increased postloss yearning and anxiety (Piper et al., 2011, p. 97). Grief work regarding Stuart's new identity without Kate: "I, Stuart," instead of "We, Stuart and Kate" (Van Praagh, 2000, pp. 95–153). Identifying and dealing with Stuart's areas of vulnerability created by Kate's death. Assessment of ways to remember and use the positive strengths of Kate's life in a healthy and growth-promoting way for both himself and Anne through the use of attachment theory and constructivist meaning-making strategies.

3. *Spouse-survivor support group work.* Assessment of overall implications of Stuart's widowhood, such as loss of social connections. Suggested referral to a support group, when Stuart and Anne are ready. Group-generated alternatives available to Stuart and others who had recently experienced the death of a spouse. Suggestions from the support group on Stuart's responses to his new single-parent role with his daughter. Group focus on ways to cope with the loneliness and other emotions brought on by the absence of one's spouse. Most group therapy for loss addresses immediate losses and those who are devoid of clinically significant symptoms (Currier, Neimeyer , & Berman, 2008).

4. *Conjoint child–parent sessions.* Given Anne's extremely agitated reaction, she is most likely going to have some severe problems working through from a loss to a restoration orientation. Different family members grieve differently, and they are going to need to negotiate and understand that each person's grieving style needs to be recognized and honored. Differential family member grief, if not dealt with after a traumatic death, can cause severe family problems as the family attempts to reorganize and redefine itself (Humphrey, 2009, pp. 52–53). Both parent's and child's reorientation may prove to be difficult as they come to grips with a new family system that does not include a wife and mother. To that end, each is going to need to develop loss narratives that move deceased mother and wife from active presence to bonded memory. While father and daughter may develop their loss narrative individually, at some point they need to come together in conjoint therapy and compare those narratives (Cohen, Mannarino, & Deblinger, 2006, pp. 153–156).

On the afternoon of Kate's sudden death, the crisis worker met individually with Stuart. The following segment illustrates a part of that first intervention session.

CW: (*holding Stuart's hand*) Stuart, I realize your wife's death has been sudden and overwhelming to you. I want you to know that I am here to help you with whatever you need done. (*Silence. Still holding Stuart's hand.*) I'll be with you and assist you in whatever way I can. (*Silence. Still holding Stuart's hand.*)

The crisis worker's assessment is that Stuart's emotional status is one of shock, denial, or disbelief.

Stuart: (*After a long pause, during which the worker waits patiently, Stuart gathers himself and responds.*) This is so unreal! I just can't believe she's gone. It's such a sudden blow to me. Right now all I can think about is Anne, my daughter, and how she is. My God! What will I tell her? My sister-in-law just brought her here.

CW: I will be there with you for as long as you need me. Certainly we both can talk to Anne and your sister-in-law. We have a whole team that will help you now.

Stuart: I want to be with Kate—to be alone with her some before they take her away. Anne, too, if she wants. Can you arrange for us to do that?

CW: Yes, we'll arrange for that right now.

Stuart: I'm afraid I'm going to be in pretty bad shape after I've seen her. Her sister will be too. I just don't know about Anne. Could you arrange for us to sit in the chapel a while after we get back? And is there a chaplain around who could be with us for a few moments? I left a message with our minister at the church, but I don't know when he can get here.

CW: I'll phone Chaplain Myer again. He's aware of Kate's death, and he said he'd be available anytime, if you want him. I'll go with you and leave you alone with Kate's body and then, when you're ready, I'll go with you to the chapel.

The work with Stuart was immediate and intense. Such a cascade of events, problems, and emotions is typical in a sudden death. Particularly seeing and/or touching the body is important to verify that the loved one is actually dead (Hersh, 1996). Stuart manifests very well the initial impact of Stroebe and Schut's (2001) dual process model of an initial loss orientation. Thus, the worker's primary goal was to help Stuart deal with rapidly emerging needs an hour at a time or a day at a time.

The worker kept in mind that as time evolved Stuart and his daughter would need to start moving toward restoration. But for the moment, the short-term intervention focused on Stuart's need to deal with his initial shock. The worker was also sensitive to allowing Stuart to become aware of his own loss. The worker never tried to or considered trying to manage, defer, speed up, or otherwise intrude on Stuart's grief process. Note the patience and use of respectful silence as a primary intervention tactic and the worker's ability to model strength and acceptance of the client's emotionally distraught state. From that standpoint, while the worker assumed a **facilitator role** in helping make immediate post-death arrangements, the worker provided only the degree of structure necessary and appropriate to client needs, goals, and preferences. The worker's main function at this time was to serve in a **witness role** to observe, listen, and not do anything other than "be with" the client and allow the client to feel "felt" (Humphrey, 2009, pp. 213–214; Wylie, 2004, p. 33).

About 2 weeks later, after initially taking the death in stride, Stuart was hit with the full impact of Kate's loss. Stuart's grief and his feeling of helplessness regarding emotional support for his daughter were reflected in a rapid escalation of his observed triage assessment scores: affective, 8; behavioral, 7; cognitive, 8; total, 23. This later assessment prompted an immediate referral of Stuart to a long-term therapist for grief work. Such a rapid escalation is a frequent occurrence among clients who have experienced the sudden loss of a loved one.

Stuart's condition was rapidly turning into complicated grief as was his daughter's. The crisis worker suggested that both needed more than a support group. As a result both entered a complicated grief group that focused on meaning making. One component of this group was to use narrative therapy to help tell their stories and make sense of Kate's death (Monk, Drewery, & Winslade, 2005) as they struggled to reconcile discrepancies between pretrauma beliefs (this cannot happen) and posttrauma beliefs (This is a bad dream. I can't handle this. I need to move on but can't or won't). This group has two purposes to help members oscillate between restoration and loss and to start revising pretrauma global meanings (generally very good) and reconciling them with their postappraisal of the trauma (generally very bad). Such meaning making helps people restore their sense of the world as a meaningful place and their lives as worthwhile and having renewed purpose (Slattery & Park, 2015).

Traumatic Death of a Child

Brad Drake, age 34, a farmer, and his wife Helen, age 30, had twin sons, Gene and Jerome, age 6. Late one afternoon, while Brad was doing the chores at the barn behind their house and Helen was preparing supper, Gene tried to cross the highway in front of their house to catch a runaway goat and was struck by a grain truck. Gene was airlifted to a regional trauma unit hospital 52 miles away, but was pronounced dead on arrival. The death of Gene left his parents feeling a soul-deep sense of shock, grief, hurt, bewilderment, guilt, powerlessness, psychological immobility, and vulnerability, and searching for answers and meaning.

The death was ruled accidental; the driver of the grain truck that struck Gene was a local farmer, a friend who was as grief stricken as the Drakes. Approximately 2 weeks after Gene's burial, Brad and Helen together sought counseling. The crisis worker saw them immediately following the intake interview. The worker decided that crisis intervention could do four interrelated but equally important things: (1) facilitate the release of their grief energy, (2) reassure them that their feelings were normal,

(3) put them into communication with other grieving parents, and (4) assess for posttraumatic stress disorder and complicated grieving and mourning reactions. These goals of intervention, described by Hansen and Frantz (1984, pp. 21–22), Cable (1996), Redmon (1996), and Rando (1996), formed the basis for starting grief work with Brad and Helen Drake.

This case is an example of long-term intervention. The following strategies were provided and issues explored with Brad and Helen during the days and weeks following Gene's burial.

1. *Assessment for posttraumatic stress disorder (PTSD) and suicide.* Gene's death fit several of Rando's (1996) criteria for traumatic death. It was sudden, it involved a child, there was traumatic and disfiguring physical injury, and it was preventable. These are excellent growing conditions for Horowitz's (1986) stress response syndrome. A very grave mistake in loss counseling is to not deal with the potential for PTSD that arises out of stress response syndrome and overlays mourning. When this occurs, full-scale intervention for PTSD must be instituted before mourning can even begin (Rando, 1996). Thus, assessment for PTSD, as described in Chapter 7, Posttraumatic Stress Disorder, should be considered. Perhaps more ominous is the research of Zetumer and associates (2015) who found that death of young children caused more intense increased complicated grief with self-blame and suicidal ideation in their surviving parents.

2. *Couple counseling and intervention.* The situation surrounding Gene's death made it a good bet that one or both parents would blame themselves (Redmon, 1996). Also, the impact of the death on the twin brother, Jerome, would require appropriate parental handling so that Jerome would not be neglected as they grieved, or overprotected because they feared he would also die (Brown, 1988, pp. 66–68; Silverman, 2000, p. 159). Brad and Helen were reassured that they were not going crazy, because for many couples suffering the traumatic loss of a child, the recrimination, guilt, questioning, vulnerability, and incomprehensibility will make them think they are (Redmon, 1996). They received affirmation that they were the best parents they could be and that their parenting should not be blamed for the accident.

3. *Assessment of family problems and potentials.* This included assessment of marital and family systems relationships following Gene's death and exploration of ways to cope with the effects of the bereavement on the marriage and family. When a child dies, there is a high probability there will be serious marital problems within months following the death (Brown, 1988, pp. 57–65). Parents may attempt to support each other by telling the other person that he or she was not at fault, only to have the other parent even *more* sure that the spouse is merely attempting to assuage his or her own feelings and placate them. Or, if blame is assigned, the whole system will deteriorate (Redmon, 1996). A good deal of psychoeducation was conducted with both parents and Jerome. Brad and Helen were reassured that the grief and pain would continue for a long time and that this is normal; that they'll always have memories of the loss; that they will, in time, let go of the pattern of holding onto their grief and move on; and that there is no set timetable for them to finish their grieving.

4. *Parent survivor and support group work.* Brad and Helen became involved in a group whose common focus is the loss of a child. Social support is critical in traumatic loss and needs to remain in place long after the funeral (Pine, 1996). Putting the parents in touch with intervention supports such as parental self-help bereavement groups (Bordow, 1982; Dickens, 1985) is an important social support. Group-supported talk, reminiscence, sharing, grief, and tears will help the Drakes bond with members who have had similar experiences. It will also give them a point of reference as they see older group members making progress and newer members struggling with issues they have already overcome (Cable, 1996).

5. *Reading and media material.* The Drakes were provided with books, other reading materials, and CDs.

First Crisis Session 3 Months After Gene's Death

The first crisis intervention session with Brad and Helen took place when both were still in a stage of denial, isolation, and depression. They were clearly stuck in a loss orientation and were regressing even further into it. They were given the Texas Revised Grief Inventory, which showed that both had not moved past their initial response to the loss.

Helen: But my words are nothing compared to my thinking since this happened. I'm thinking I may be going insane or something. I keep going to Gene's side of the bedroom and cleaning it up. I got on Jerome for going over there and messing with Gene's stuff the other day

CW: Helen, you're not going insane. You're responding in a way that makes perfect sense to me. You have both lost the most important and precious gift a mother and father can lose. It is natural and typical for you to experience unusual feelings and grief. You're doing a very good thing by talking openly about your thoughts and feelings. That's why I'm glad you came and reached out to me today. Nobody can erase your hurt or bring your son back, but I will help as best I can.

Brad: I don't know anything anymore. Everything I knew about dealing with problems doesn't even begin to deal with this.

CW: First of all, there is nothing to compare with the tragedy of Gene's death that you have encountered. As bad and terrible as your feelings are, they are absolutely typical for parents I have dealt with who are going through what you are. You are not going insane, and there are things we can do that can help you get unstuck, because the inventory you took tells me that you are, in fact, stuck. I want to take some time and let you both tell me the events that got you from Gene's death 3 months ago to my office today. I may ask some questions from time to time, but mainly I am going to listen and understand the emotions, thoughts, and behaviors you are dealing with right now. I want to take time to understand this, so start where you would like.

The crisis worker reaffirms that the abnormality they are experiencing is to be expected. The death of a child has been likened to an amputation. A part of the parent has been cut off much like an amputated limb, and the missing part will always be missed and mourned (Klass, 1995). The worker acknowledges this terrible and everlasting hurt and in the same breath issues the parents an offer of her help. Later in the same session, the crisis worker facilitated their release of grief energy and suggested that they contact an ongoing support group, the local chapter of Compassionate Friends (2015), a national organization for parents who have lost a child.

The worker uses basic client-centered therapy. By demonstrating empathy, acceptance, unconditional positive regard, congruence, and concreteness, the worker provides a nurturing, trusting, and safe environment. That environment is particularly important when the griever's reactions are still very strong and he or she feels anything but safe and in control (Cable, 1996).

The crisis worker noted that they exhibited signs of being physically and emotionally drained; they vacillated between moping and benign circumspection but showed no indication of movement from a loss orientation to a restoration orientation. The crisis worker's goal was not to push them; rather, the aim was to understand their current inner concerns and to provide them with opportunities to identify and express their immediate and deep feelings openly. Narrative therapy calls this listening to the *problem-saturated* story (Humphrey, 2009, p. 180).

CW: (*after listening for half an hour to the Drake's story*) I get the sense that you are both feeling drained of your emotional energy—like you're stuck there and cannot seem to move on after Gene's death.

Brad: Yes, *stuck* is the word. I don't want to talk about this, just get on with it. Helen talks all the time about it and I can't stand that. But just sucking it up isn't doing me any good either. (*awkward silence*) It's like a fog that won't let up that chills you to the bone. It physically hurts, and hurts terribly.

CW: So you are hamstrung, Brad. You don't want to hear about Gene's death, but trying to shut it out isn't working either. Where are you with the problem?

Helen: We've just about stopped talking about it. We've become two lonely recluses in the same house. That scares me and hurts almost as much as the accident. I never, ever thought about us ever getting a divorce, but we can't go on like this. This is almost as bad as Gene's death. At least we could put him to rest. We can't seem to do that with this. It just grows and grows.

CW: Helen, what would you like to be doing right now, instead of being stuck and isolated?

Helen: I'd like to be more open. I'd like to know what's going on with Brad, and I'd like to be able to share feelings—even though they may be sad. I have this need to talk about it, but Brad doesn't seem to want to.

CW: If we were to give the problem both of you are having a name, almost as if it were an invasive weed that had come onto your farm, what would it be?

Helen: Paralyzed.

Brad: Mired.

CW: OK, Mired and Paralyzed. How has that kept you from doing something?

Brad: Every time I go out, I seem to just go through the motions. Not getting anywhere or anything much done.

Helen: I get up and do pretty much the same thing every day. Go through the motions. Go to bed. Can't think of anything in between. Neither one of us sleeps much. I know it's bad for Jerome. He has his own problems, he feels guilty over letting the goat get out, but I can't seem to talk to him about it. Whenever I do, he just takes off. (*starts to sob*)

CW: (*hands Helen a tissue*) So what do Mired and Paralyzed do for you?

Brad: Nothing. We have never been like that. Always faced hard times, drought, floods, hail, wind, insect invasions, you name it. Put your shoulder to the wheel and git 'r done.

Helen: Yes. Nose to the grindstone. Even though it hurts, you move through it, knowing there will be better times. That has always seen us through until now.

CW: I wonder if that's the problem, that you are putting your shoulder to the wheel and nose to the grindstone but it's a pretty immovable object and something you can't sharpen and get an edge on. So how are Mired and Paralyzed causing you to be motionless? I want you to picture Mired and Paralyzed. What would they look like?

Brad: Just gumbo earth like I can't get though in the south 40 acres. I track the stuff around, can't get it off my boots.

Helen: It's like I have a 100-pound backpack on.

CW: Those are really good examples. Could you see those boots and backpack sitting in the foyer? I'd like you to imagine taking both things off for a minute and just sitting there. How would that feel?

Brad: Different. I dunno. You mean just setting it aside.

CW: Gene will never be out of your life, and I feel like you are trying to slug your way through this and keep him in it in a way that can't be anymore, when it might be OK to just set the Mire and the Paralysis in the foyer. I wonder if you both could go home and just literally say to one another,

boots off here, backpack off here. You might even want to get a backpack and muddy boots to really make those feeling concrete. If you need to pick them up and wear them tomorrow, OK, but right now they are off. What do you think?

Brad and Helen: (*in unison*) Like it was a dead weight off of us.

The worker's opening statement uses the most profane of contemporary words—"death." Using this word, as opposed to "passed," "went to his reward," or other analogies that deny and soft-pedal the death, acknowledges exactly what has happened (Cable, 1996). The grievers must learn to deal with the painful aspects of the loss, and supposedly kinder, gentler words are a trap the worker must not fall into.

Initially, the worker is attempting to respond in a way that would give both parents the autonomy to experience their current state of bereavement and, at the same time, encourage them to open up and provide mutual support for one another. The worker is also using a series of narrative therapy strategies to help this couple start to oscillate from loss to restoration. After the worker listens to the problem-saturated story, he **externalizes** the problem and gives it substance by having the couple give names to it (Winslade & Monk, 1999). In most counseling the last thing we want is to externalize the problem, as in the drug addict who complains that "The crack does this to me" and take no responsibility for his use of crack cocaine. With the Drake's grief, however, they are so enmeshed in the problem they need to separate from it. By naming the problem and giving it substance, such as muddy boots or a rock-filled backpack, it is something that can be set down. The crisis worker does not get rid of it, because grief is not abnormal nor something to be eliminated (Humphrey, 2009, p. 181). By attaching a name to it, it can be put in its proper perspective as a problem, but one that can be set down as well. Notice that the worker says they may choose to put those emotions back on, but they can indeed take them off too.

The worker also uses a constructivist narrative technique by using client-generated metaphors. Metaphors are helpful because they reduce resistance and provide a safe way of talking about threatening material (Romig & Gruenke, 1991). The worker uses the client metaphors of how they have lived their lives and hooks it to how they continue to strive mightily against the Mire and Paralysis of their grief but sink deeper in it. What the worker does is explore the metaphors with the clients and attempt to extend them (Humphrey, 2009, pp. 132–133) by changing the metaphors to their antonyms.

CW: I am going to give you a DVD to watch that we can talk about, and a couple of books as well. *Always* (Spielberg, 1989) is about grieving and processing of bonds. It may be difficult to watch, but I think it is worth seeing and talking about to get this process started. I also think it is critical you get in a support group. There is not one here in Brighton, but there is one in Memphis called Compassionate Friends. There are chapters all over the country and you can google it up to see what they are about, but above all else the research shows that a support system is critical to your getting through Gene's death, and as tough as it may be, you need to talk about this with other people who have gone through trauma.

Brad: I'm glad we came today. We would like to come in again. The group of parents you spoke about is a good idea. I think we need that now, and we are going to need it more.

Helen: We didn't know about Compassionate Friends. I'll call them this afternoon. It's good to know that such a group exists. It sounds like a wonderful thing.

CW: I think you will both be glad you discovered Compassionate Friends. I'm truly glad you came, and I look forward to seeing you again.

Compassionate Friends has more than 650 chapters in the United States and Puerto Rico. It exists to support bereaved parents, siblings, and family members in the positive resolution of their grief and to foster physical and emotional health. The Compassionate Friends' credo suggests the unifying sense that bereaved parents can gain from joining a support group: "We reach out to each other with love, with understanding and with hope. Our children have died at all ages and from many different causes, but our love of our children unites us. Whatever pain we bring to this gathering of the Compassionate Friends, it is pain we will share just as we share with each other our love for our children. We need not walk alone" (Compassionate Friends, 2007).

The worker also gave Brad and Helen *After the Death of a Child: Living With Loss Through the Years* by Ann K. Finkbeiner (1998), one of the best books your authors know in regard to loss of a child, and Harold Kushner's (1983) paperback *When Bad Things*

Happen to Good People, which is a classic in the field and a best seller. The two books together represent comprehensive guidelines for surviving the death of a loved one. The crisis worker was employing a strategy of grief bibliotherapy (Becvar, 2001, pp. 237–239), which is an effective way of providing information, reinforcement, and support through reading and other media that can be used to help clients on the path to restoration.

Second Crisis Session 1 Week Later

CW: How are things going?

Brad: It's strange. I did get an old pair of boots and we got one of Gene's old backpacks and set it on the back porch. With mud on the boots and rocks in the backpack. Jerome thinks we have really gone nuts. We finally told him what we were doing. Lo and behold, the goat collar and rope appeared out there yesterday. We didn't ask him why and he didn't tell us, but clearly he is trying to set something down too.

CW: So how does it feel to merely set that Mire and Paralysis down and watch the world go by and just let things happen?

Helen: You know we went back home and did that after dinner. We went back into the living room and sat down, looked at each other, and sorta goofily smiled at one another.

Brad: Yeah, then we laughed cause we both thought Gene and Jerome would be shocked that we just set the stuff down and didn't work our tails off. We both talked some, did a little reminiscing, and then started to talk a little bit about establishing a scholarship with the Future Farmers of America in Gene's name. Helen knows I want to do that and listened to me. That instrumental thing you talked about, I guess.

Helen: I cried some at the thought, but it is something Gene wanted to be in when he got to high school. I suppose we are getting to understand each other's style of grieving a bit more after what you told us. I do feel like maybe we have started into the restoration part of this wretched business. I slept pretty good that night, and I know Brad did from his snoring. (*smiles at Brad*)

It is not uncommon for two parents to have entirely different views and coping mechanisms (Brown, 1988, pp. 58–59). Helen's need to continuously talk about the accident and weeping at a moment's notice is a common example of catharsis (Lord, 1996). She personifies a largely intuitive grieving style, while Brad's "git 'r done" attitude operates more from an instrumental style. Getting Brad and Helen to understand that they use these different styles is an important issue, so the worker spends time giving them information about adaptive and dual model processes. The change in this session may be considered in terms of the narrative therapy steps of mapping. Mapping the influence of the problem on the person lets clients understand how the problem has been affecting them. The turning point from a complete loss orientation to one that oscillates between loss and restoration is reversing the mapping to focus on the influence of the person on the problem (Humphrey, 2009, pp. 182–184).

CW: So how did all that happen? I mean, I am good but not *that* good. (*A little self-deprecation and humor when clients are able to handle it is never a bad thing, in our opinion.*)

Helen: Well, I was filling the backpack with rocks and it really felt like I was taking the damn thing off my back, and I dunno. . . . Then Brad said he didn't feel so mired down, and so we decided to go for a walk back to the river, which we used to do a lot, but it kinda reminded us of taking the boys back fishing and we stopped doing that, and we just sorta decided to get out, and I dunno. . . . It just sorta happened.

CW: So taking some time to be with one another, and that hasn't happened for a long time. How did that feel? What was different?

Brad: It felt pretty good, and we talked some going down to the river. Like old times, talking about crops, neighbors, and stuff. Once we got to the river, maybe we put the backpack on and boots on for a while remembering, but we did make the walk, which was impossible before that, and (*smiles sheepishly*) we did hold hands on the way back.

CW: I would really like to have you take those instances apart so you know really clearly what the alternative story line you are now writing it is and can continue to build on it. It's called **deconstructing.** Deconstructing means taking apart those disrupted meanings you have created since Gene's death that get in the way of some of the core values you have had up to that time. As for instance, when you started to put the boots and backpack on down at the river, you took them off

on the way home. I am interested in your holding hands. Could that be a cue that might allow you to refocus when the problem arises and you want to put the boots and backpack on again? Maybe you could think of a new name for yourselves, too, as you work through Mired and Paralyzed.

Here the worker uses constructivist strategies by taking apart (deconstructing) the disruptive meanings and attempting to use refocusing (Malkinson, 2007) from the symbols of the disrupted meanings (boots and backpack) to older core meanings (holding hands)—starting to realize that when they put the disrupted meanings back on, they can use that as a cue to stop the disruption and substitute an old positive behavior. The worker also attempts to install a positive external name for their efforts to readapt.

Third Crisis Session a Week Later

Helen: We have a new name for us. Peace and Harmony.

CW: Wow, that is different! So Peace and Harmony is now in charge. What will that look like in a month? Six months? What would people at your church say about Peace and Harmony as opposed to what they are saying now about Mired and Paralyzed?

Working out the alternative story is not easy. One way of reinforcing the new story line is to create a support system of significant others to bear witness to the change or to create an imaginary audience to give voice to their efforts at restoration. Indeed, at some point in the future, Brad and Helen may invite witnesses to bear testimony to their change (Humphrey, 2009, pp. 188–189).

Testing One's Faith. Brown (2008) has written at length about the complexity of the relationship between faith, spirituality, and trauma. Faith, or the absence of it, is of critical concern in most traumatic deaths. Trauma survivors who run into trouble with their faith generally fall into Fowler's (1991) faith development model stages of **mythical literal**, which is a one-dimensional view of God as an entity that doles out rewards and punishment based on how rigorously one practices one's faith and follows its commandments (typical of children 8–12), and **synthetic-conventional**, which conforms to the community's basic cultural standard of moral behavior, normative beliefs, values, and religious practices (typical of 12 years of age to early adulthood). When losses occur, people in these stages may do three things. They may adhere to these stages and do nothing but pray harder and accept God's will that they are sinners and must atone by hard sacrifices, as their recent loss illustrates. Alternately, they may reject any and all faith, feel that their religion and their God have abandoned them, and become embittered at their faith and the community that supports it. However, through a spiritually focused trauma approach (VanDusen & Courtois, 2015) individuals may move beyond these regressive spiritual states toward Fowler's (1991) stages of **individuative/reflective faith** where one is able to reflect critically on one's story and values and disregard personal myths about self, God, and one's relationship with the world; and **conjunctive faith** wherein an individual can hold two differing beliefs and can deal with the paradoxes and polarities of those beliefs. Finally, they may conduct a critical examination of their religious faith, move into progressively higher stages of introspection, and become even more grounded in their faith.

Brad: We just don't know where to turn. We take our religion seriously, and we've talked to our minister. That doesn't seem to help us. I keep on asking, "Why, why, why?"

Helen: We know the story of Job and such as that. We know tragedy strikes anywhere and anybody. Still, we don't know—we can't see—that a God of love or a God of justice can condone or permit the life of a good and innocent child like that to be snuffed out. I'm amazed at myself for talking like that. There is no justice, no fairness in this. No just God allows a sweet child like Gene to die so horribly.

Attempting to find meaning in the tragic accidental death or murder of a child tests the most dedicated believer. The notion that a life lived according to one's religious precepts, particularly that of a child, is seemingly for naught causes a tremendous amount of anger at God and can cause a severe secondary loss in regard to the person's religious beliefs (Becvar, 2001, p. 235). Religion is not an insurance policy against the outrageous slings and arrows of death, nor does it preclude suffering. Doubting is part of the cycle of faith (Grollman, 1996).

It is not the worker's job to move people from one developmental stage to the next (Humphrey, 2009, p. 30). What discussion of their faith does is allow the worker to assess another significant component of the clients' story and determine whether faith is part of the problem saturation.

CW: I don't begin to have answers, and I would submit that no one but you does have the answers to what part God and your faith play in this tragedy and if you can find solace in your faith. What I might ask you to do as part of the narrative you are creating is to write down your thoughts on these questions that Chaplain Ray Giunta, who is well known for his work in a variety of traumatic events, has posed. You can discuss them with me or your minister or just consider them and talk with one another. At the least, writing this out will allow you to get your thoughts out in the open. These are the questions (Giunta & Giunta, 2002, pp. 13–14):

Think about the loss you have experienced. If you listen to your heart, why did it happen and who is to blame?

What do you think your head might be telling you about your perspective that your grieving heart might not be able to hear?

How do you think God is seeing you in your loss?

How do you see God right now? Do you see him as raising his hand against you or as a loving Father with arms wide open wanting to help your hurt?

Pastoral counselors, in particular, must be very careful how they use their religion and spiritual beliefs to deal with grieving. "It's God's will" or "She is in a better place now" may be very little consolation to a mother whose heart is breaking because she so badly wants to hold her dead 7-year-old daughter again and sit down to tea with her after school. It follows, then, that rather than attempting to provide spiritual answers (which the authors of this book most certainly do not have), our goal must be to find ways of providing encouragement and support in searching for meaning (Wheeler, 2001). Given the foregoing qualifiers, it still appears that there is a tremendous amount of power and healing in prayer, religious ritual, religious ideation, and spiritual faith (Walsh et al., 2002). Your authors firmly believe bereaved individuals should be encouraged to explore this as one of their options.

Bereavement in Childhood

Thadeus and Latoya Kirk, ages 36 and 38 respectively, were spending all the time, energy, and money they could in their attempts to cope with the terminal illness of their son, Charles, 5 years old. They spent

2 years in and out of the children's research hospital, and the family was exhausted physically and emotionally by the time Charles died. Their only other child, Makeena, age 7, felt sad, bewildered, lonely, and neglected. The whole family was consumed with grief the day Charles died. In addition to grief, Makeena suffered from guilt. She felt guilty because for several months she had dared to wish that Charles's illness would just end and get it over.

Somehow Makeena believed that her wish had contributed to the death of her brother (Brown, 1988, p. 85). She also felt guilty because she was alive and didn't deserve to live as much as Charles. She was also afraid because she was sure she would "catch" the cancer her brother had. Overridden by guilt and fear that she was now an "endangered species" (Becvar, 2001, p. 129), Makeena became isolated both at home and at school, and her grades plummeted. She also started to have physical symptoms similar to what her dead brother had, which is not an uncommon occurrence (Bernstein, 1997). The school counselor, who had a good deal of experience in workshops for trauma and grieving children, was asked to intervene with Makeena.

Little attention has been given to siblings, who often get lost in the shuffle—both during the illness and afterward in the parents' grief—to the point that the siblings may feel abandoned (Brown, 1988, p. 67). Parents may also establish rules that prohibit talking about the deceased sibling because it is too painful. Relatives may ask siblings how well their parents are holding up and completely neglect how the sibling is feeling. Family discipline may disintegrate, leaving the surviving children with the sense that they really don't count for anything because nobody cares what they do.

Further, if they are afraid they will suffer the same fate as the deceased sibling, they may become paranoid or obsessive in their behavior to "not step on a crack and break my back." Finally, siblings may fear that their parents are too vulnerable and are not able to bear the burden of the surviving child. As a result, they may act out or attempt to become perfect (Becvar, 2001, pp. 129–135). These feelings will almost always be present in such instances. Siblings may have big problems if those feelings are not dealt with in a timely manner, and those feelings may follow them throughout their lives.

The following intervention strategies were provided and issues explored with the Kirk family during the days and weeks immediately prior to and following Charles's death.

1. *Individual counseling and intervention.* Assessment of Makeena's concept of death. Ensuring that Makeena has opportunities to participate actively and learn the medical facts relating to Charles's terminal illness in a truthful and realistic manner (Griffith, 2003). Use of child-centered play therapy counseling approaches in helping Makeena deal with and refute her guilt feelings related to her brother's death. Assessment of the impact of Charles's death on both parents and Makeena. Including Makeena in the funeral plans and commemorative activities. Providing opportunities for each family member to release grief energy. Assessment of the impact of Charles's illness and death on the marriage and provision of individual therapy for Thadeus and Latoya as needed.

2. *Family systems therapy.* Assessment of the family's stress level and coping resources. A variety of toxic responses can come as a result of a prolonged illness of a family member—particularly when it is a child. Scapegoating, stonewalling, detachment, guilt, and masochism are a few of the defensive responses that can occur (Johnson, 1987). Provision of opportunities for the family together to explore the important issues related to Charles's death: the meaning, the good times and memories, guilt, blame, anger, rejection, unfinished business, and new family alignments (Brown, 1988, pp. 74–77; Silverman, 2000, p. 161). Focus on Makeena: ensuring that she knows that she is loved and that the time and energy that Thadeus and Latoya have devoted to Charles in no way diminished their love and devotion to Makeena. Discussion of feelings openly and honestly, keeping in mind the developmental capacity of Makeena (Brown, 1988, pp. 74–77). Ensuring that all family members have permission to mourn openly. Assuming that Charles's death will have a lasting impact on Makeena and will be manifested through her play, her fantasy life, and her relationship to both Thadeus and Latoya.

Using puppets in crisis counseling with Makeena, the worker was able to help her dispute her irrational and magical belief that her covert wish had caused her brother's death. During two previous sessions with the crisis worker, Makeena had developed a great deal of trust in the worker and considerable facility and ease in using the raggedy puppets. At the third session, there were five puppets: Raggedy Ann, Raggedy Billy (Raggedy Ann's dying brother), Raggedy Mom, Raggedy Dad, and Raggedy Doctor.

CW: (*holding Raggedy Billy and Raggedy Mom—Raggedy Billy speaking*) Mommy, Mommy, Ann said I'm dying because she had bad thoughts—she wished I would die so you and Daddy could leave the hospital and come back home.

CW: (*holding Raggedy Billy and Raggedy Mom—Raggedy Mom speaking*) Oh, Billy! Wishing someone is dead can *never, never* make it happen! Your sister, Ann, has a perfect right to wish for this hurting and sickness to end. She is so lonesome for Mommy and Daddy and for you, too. It's normal for her to wish this sickness were ending. But Ann should never feel bad or guilty just because she wished something. Remember, *wishing* doesn't make it happen!

CW: (*holding Raggedy Billy and Raggedy Mom—Raggedy Billy speaking*) Mommy, I wish I could see my sister, Ann. I'd like to tell her it's OK.

CW: (*holding Raggedy Billy and Raggedy Mom—Raggedy Mom speaking*) Oh, Billy, my dear son! (*Raggedy Mom kisses Raggedy Billy.*) I love you, and I love Ann. Here comes your sister now. Why don't you talk to her? She's in the hospital to visit you.

CW: (*holding Raggedy Billy and Raggedy Mom—turning toward Makeena, Raggedy Billy speaking*) Hi, sister Ann. I'm glad you came to the hospital to see me. I wanted to tell you how much I love you and how much I will miss you when I die. I want you to know that you should not worry about the wishes and thoughts you had. My disease is making me die. Your thoughts cannot make me or anyone else die. I want you to know it's all right. I love you, Mom loves you, and Daddy loves you. We will always love you.

Makeena: (*holding Raggedy Ann and Raggedy Dad—Raggedy Ann speaking*) I'm sorry. I wish you wouldn't die. I'm very, very sorry. I hope you don't die.

CW: (*holding Raggedy Billy and Raggedy Mom—Raggedy Mom speaking*) Oh, Ann, we all hope he doesn't die. But I'm afraid he will. Then we will all be sad together. We will miss him. But we will have to learn to live without Billy when he's gone. We will still love him. But we will have each other and love each other. We will never blame you or ourselves for his death. His death will be caused by his sickness, not by your thoughts or wishes, nor by my thoughts or wishes.

Makeena: But then Raggedy Ann could catch what Raggedy Billy caught, and she could die. (*lays Raggedy Ann out as if in a casket*)

CW: (*takes Raggedy Doctor out, who picks up Raggedy Ann and gives her back to Makeena*) No she can't, and I know because I'm Doctor Feelgood. Raggedy Ann could catch some different kinds of bugs and get sick all right, but Raggedy Billy didn't have a bug. He had cancer. You can't catch cancer, so Raggedy Ann shouldn't worry about that. Raggedy Ann could never catch what Raggedy Billy had.

Makeena: (*looking wistfully at Raggedy Ann*) Well, maybe.

CW: (*looking at the doctor puppet*) Dr. Feelgood, do you suppose we could talk to that other doctor, who is a real cancer expert? He is a friend of yours, Dr. Degrott. He takes care of lots of kids who have cancer at St. Jude's.

Makeena: (*smiles and hops up*) Yes! Let's do that. He took care of my brother. I know him.

CW: OK! I'll go make a phone call and see if we can do that.

Although the segment cannot reveal all the preparatory work and dialogue that preceded and followed this brief encounter, it provides some idea of how versatile and effective puppetry can be. The crisis worker uses directive play therapy, as opposed to the nondirective approach used with most child therapy. The reason is that with the kind of traumatic material being dealt with here, the child may be very reticent to venture into this forbidding territory, and once there have no idea what to do. Directive, crisis/trauma-focused therapy can help a child to process anxious feelings and to learn methods to cope with these terrifying "bad" thoughts (Webb, 2007, pp. 50–51). The crisis worker is focusing here on only two dimensions of bereavement during childhood: Makeena's guilt feelings and her fear of dying from what her brother had.

Once the worker has moved though "forbidden" territory, the child can move forward and grieve the loss. Makeena's grief work could have been processed with equal effectiveness by a crisis worker skilled in using artwork, dolls, storytelling, modeling clay, sand play, or psychodrama (Brown, 1999; Corr & Corr, 1996, pp. 258–261; Johnson, 1987).

CW: (*Two pieces of poster board have large word balloons already colored in. A ground line is drawn, with some balloons anchored to the ground and others floating away.*) Makeena, I would like you to draw a picture of you and Charles doing something together that was fun for both of you. We can talk about that and other fun things you two did together. When you get done, we are going to put some words in the balloons. The balloons up in the air represent things you have lost with your brother. The balloons anchored to the ground represent all the things you still have of Charles, including your memories.

Makeena: (*draws herself and Charles fishing*) I like fishing, and Charles would always put the worm on and take the fish off.

CW: So that is something you remember that's really positive. Can you put that in one of the balloons floating away? I wonder, do you remember how Charles did that?

Makeena: Yes. He threaded the worm just on its head and let the rest of the worm dangle. He also pushed down and back on the hook while holding the fish's top fin down so it wouldn't stick him.

CW: So that is something you have learned. You can keep that right here in this balloon that is anchored right by the pier.

The whole purpose of the balloon activity is to contrast what has been and what is: while memories of the positive relationship remain, the real-life experiences of the past are now gone (Stubenbort et al., 2001). From a cognitive-behavioral standpoint, this work is necessary in mentally reworking or cognitively restructuring the loss (Cohen, Mannarino, & Deblinger, 2006). From a narrative therapy standpoint, it is part of the *restorying* (Zimmerman & Dickerson, 1996) process of creating a new storyline that she feels best about instead of the problem-saturated story she carried into therapy.

We are very big on "anchoring" those positive thoughts in the person's brain with an associated stimulus that is readily available to retrieve memories.

CW: Makeena, you can take this really nice drawing home and hang it up in your bedroom. Now I want you to put these balloons in an imaginary file drawer in your brain that you can pull out whenever you need to remember the good things and times you and Charles had before he died. So, picture a file drawer right up here in your head. Show me where it is. (*Makeena points to a spot behind her right ear.*) OK, that's where it is from the side. Where is it from the top? (*Mekeena points to the left side of the center of her head.*) Excellent, so I am going to take both your fingers from the top and the side and point directly where it is. (*Makeena points so there is*

an imaginary bisected line in her brain.) Excellent! You have it right there, and every time you need it you can pull it out. OK, now just shut your eyes and try it. (*Mekeena smiles and nods her head.*) Good! I believe Charles would be very proud of you the next time you go fishing with your family, because you can go right there and get those instructions and tell them Charles showed you how to do it.

Separation and Divorce

When Eric Ishitani, age 32, an automobile salesman, came home and announced to Nancy, age 30, a very successful lumber wholesale manager, that he was in love with another woman and wanted a divorce, it shattered Nancy's world. The marriage had been going downhill for a long time, and during the preceding months Eric had been staying out nights. Nevertheless, Nancy wanted to patch things up and to have a child. But Eric was adamant, and left. Nancy was extremely distraught, with feelings of grief, guilt, worthlessness, and failure. She felt her life was meaningless. She didn't want to face life alone; she was stuck in grief and felt that she was doomed to live the remainder of her life unfulfilled, without a husband or a child. She felt like a complete failure and blamed herself for not succeeding in the marriage. Nancy found herself frozen in a state of grief, remorse, guilt, depression, and self-pity.

The following intervention strategies were provided and issues explored with Nancy during the days and weeks immediately following Eric's announcement that he wanted a divorce.

1. *Individual counseling and intervention.* Assessment of Nancy's lethality level. Assessment of her coping skills and resources. Provision of a safe atmosphere for her to talk her grief out and ventilate her emotions. Assessment of available support people. Consideration of her feelings of worthlessness, fear, failure, guilt, anger, depression, self-pity, and lack of self-efficacy and self-confidence. Use of rational-emotive behavior therapy (Ellis & Abrahms, 1978) and behavioral modalities (Williams & Long, 1983) to help Nancy identify and successfully refute her negative and self-defeating beliefs and self-statements and start modifying her maladaptive behavior. Reprogramming her internal sentences and developing positive action steps that she can own, practice, and carry out independently of a helping person. Develop a new restoration narrative that no longer includes her ex-husband.

2. *Support group work.* Identification of divorce self-help groups for Nancy to use as supports. Assessment of her social needs on a time continuum from the present forward for several years. Use of the self-help group to assist her in making realistic plans for her personal and social adjustment to her new situation.

3. *Referral resources.* Assessment of Nancy's need for legal, vocational, and financial assistance. If necessary, identification of specific referral people for her to contact immediately. While interviewing her, careful assessment of statements reflecting her present autonomy and ability to attain her goals. For example, depending on her husband's attorney, banker, or accountant may not serve her best interests. Many newly estranged wives find that they need a different attorney, banker, and accountant from the ones used by their spouses. They also may need to find employment or training to enable them to become economically self-sufficient. Often this is a sudden and difficult switch. The worker must be sensitive, supportive, realistic, and assertive, because Nancy is so vulnerable during this phase of her separation.

The abrupt termination of a relationship by separation is frequently accompanied by emotional responses that are as traumatic as after the death of a loved one. People who experience the loss of separation may exhibit shock, disbelief, denial, anger, withdrawal, guilt, and depression. Attachment theory indicates that separation and the subsequent feelings of loss can occur in many ways (Bowlby, 1969, 1973, 1980), and emotional reactions to a divorce may be very similar to those to a death of a partner. Each person responds in unique ways. Some will cry for several days. Some will verbally ventilate for days on end—to anyone who will listen. Some will go into a state of withdrawal, described by one person like this: "When he came in and told me he was leaving, packed his clothes, and left, I got in the bed and didn't move. I intended to stay there until I died." The loss by separation may be the result of severance of a marriage, a heterosexual, gay, or lesbian love relationship, a long-term friendship, a business partnership, or any other close personal attachment.

Helping people overcome the emotional and behavioral results of the loss of a relationship requires crisis intervention skills similar to those needed in other types of grief and bereavement. In Nancy's case, the client presented herself for crisis intervention

several days after she had stayed in bed with the intention of crying and grieving herself to death. Nancy truly wanted to die after Eric told her he was leaving permanently. At first her denial was so profound that she thought to herself, "This can never be. I will never be a divorcee. My parents must never know. My friends must never find out." Nancy did not talk to anyone about Eric's leaving for several days. There was denial: "He really isn't leaving for good. He will be back. We will work things out." There was guilt: "What did I do to cause this? I must have been a terrible wife. I shouldn't have been so blind to his needs. If I just died in an accident, he could go on and marry the other woman and no one would ever have to know." There was anger: "I've got a good mind to find her and pay her back for all the misery she's caused me." Nancy experienced a flood of negative emotions before she brought herself to the point of presenting her problem to the crisis worker, who was a marriage and family therapist. As she presents herself, her thinking is full of all-or-none, catastrophic thinking. Her sentences start and end with words like "should," "ought," and "must." She believes that the activating event, Eric's request for a divorce, is causing the consequences of her depressed, angry, abandoned behavior, when in fact it is her irrational beliefs and automatic thoughts about the event that are causing her distress (Dryden & Neenan, 2004; Ellis, 1973; Ellis & Dryden, 1977; Liese, 1994; Malkinson, 2007).

CW: Well, Nancy, what brings you to see me today?

Nancy: My whole life is a wreck. It's really a mess. The main thing is that my marriage is breaking up. Well, I guess it has broken up. My husband's gone. Been gone for over 3 weeks. I have just got to get him back. That's all there is to it. I am nothing without him. We were high school sweethearts and this is supposed to be forever.

CW: You're feeling pretty hopeless about the marriage, but you don't want to give up on it. What has happened today, in relation to your marriage breakup, to impel you to come in right now?

Nancy: Well, I was tired of lying around feeling sorry for myself—thinking about killing myself or harming my husband's girlfriend. My intuition told me that neither one of those acts would solve anything, so I've come in here looking for better answers. There should be an answer to this, and I have absolutely got to have some answers to this or I'll go nuts or wind up alone in some old folks home with no one.

CW: Nancy, I'm really glad you decided to come today. What I want to find out first is whether you are in danger of suicide or homicide now. Is your intuition still keeping you safe? Do you have a means at hand to do it? And how close are you to suicide or homicide now?

The crisis worker's first concern was Nancy's immediate safety. It appeared from her verbal and nonverbal cues that she was hopeful and stable enough to have some mobility. The fact that she came to present her problem was another positive factor. However, the crisis worker still checked out her lethality level. Then, when Nancy told the worker that she didn't have a definite plan or a definite means to kill herself, the worker proceeded with other steps in the crisis interview. At one point, Nancy appeared to be in a stage of "holding on," which Schneider (1984) describes as having elements of anger, bargaining, and denial, some of the primary stages of Kübler-Ross's stage theory (1969) of loss.

Nancy: I just can't believe this is happening to me. My whole world has caved in on me. This is simply horrible. I just can't stand it. I just don't know what I'm going to do without him. I must be a total loser. I haven't told anybody, but I think everybody in the sales department knows because my sales are way down. Christ! I probably have LOSER tattooed on my forehead. And I am so ashamed to tell my mother, although I think she knows something's amiss. My God! I am so pitiful, I just want to crawl in a hole and never come out.

CW: I want to do a couple things that I think will help you get a handle on the situation. I want to tape-record our session, and I am going to give you a homework assignment that involves some more taping. I think this is a good assignment because I want you to hear what I call *automatic thoughts.* In just the few minutes you have been here I have heard a dumpster load of them, and those can get you in the kind of hot water you seem to be in now. Automatic thoughts result from people's underlying assumptions and beliefs. The most common type of automatic thoughts involve all-or-none statements like you're making. *Telling yourself* that you can't stand it and *believing* that it's horrible and that you're terrible seem to be exaggerations that are getting in the way. If you listen to all those "musts" and "shoulds," those are also indicators that your belief system is out of sync with what you need to do and is contributing to

what I am going to call a problem-saturated narrative you have been building that won't allow you any leniency from all those self-condemning statements your belief system is making. That is different from telling yourself that it is bad, you don't like it, you wish it weren't happening, but that you didn't cause it and that it isn't the end of the world—even though it may make your life very difficult for a while. I want you to see where your catastrophizing, exaggerating, and awfulizing color your thinking and get in the way of your clearly and objectively assessing not only what has happened but also what your real options are. Don't you?

Nancy: Well, I don't know if that's right. I mean, I am pretty logical and linear and rational. I didn't get to be sales manager of one of the biggest wholesale hardwood lumber companies in the world by being a witless twit.

CW: I understand that, but would it be fair to say this is a little different than a sales campaign and the outcomes are a bit different? I have a little exercise I'd like you to do. I'd like you to make a loss and grief map.

Nancy: Well, yes, but . . . OK, I guess that'll be interesting.

CW: Draw a circle in the middle of the page and put your primary loss in it. Think of all your thoughts and feelings associated with it and write them down around the circle. [See Figure 12.1.] Focus on the thoughts, the billboards that pop up when you think about the word D-I-V-O-R-C-E. Once you have the thoughts down, put the feelings down that go with it. Go back and look at feelings. As you think about them, see if others don't bubble up. Lots of times we have a feeling about a feeling. For example, "stupid" might lead to "regret."

Nancy: Yes. I see it. That's pretty bad. I guess I have come down harder on myself and on the problem than is necessary. I know it isn't the end of the world, but I feel, at the time, that it's horrible and awful.

CW: Then your *believing* it's horrible and awful is the real culprit, isn't it? There is a difference between your beliefs and how things really are.

Nancy: You're right! It helps just to look at it differently, even though it doesn't solve my big mess.

CW: You're right. It doesn't solve it. But we can objectively examine it and together begin to figure out options you can choose if we know on the front end,

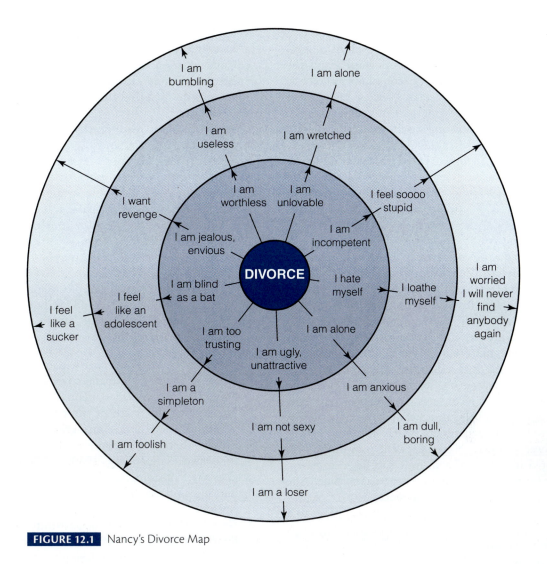

FIGURE 12.1 Nancy's Divorce Map

even though you're grieving over your hurt, that we are not dealing with a world-shattering catastrophe.

The crisis worker was intervening by using elements of rational-emotive behavior therapy (REBT) (Ellis, 1973) and cognitive-behavioral therapy (Meichenbaum, 1977). The worker was attempting to dispute the client's irrational beliefs about the separation and help her begin to direct her emotional energy toward the real issues. Nancy was an intelligent person who quickly responded to the rational ideas presented. But, as is typical in such cases dealing with the emotional state during loss, the worker knew that repetition, practice, support, and encouragement would be needed. A person in Nancy's state must have far more than just a one-shot session using REBT to get her beyond crisis and back to a state of equilibrium.

In addition to using REBT as a crisis intervention strategy, the crisis worker also used a self-managed behavioral technique (Williams & Long, 1983) to help Nancy expend her grief energy over a period of several weeks. What Nancy did was to make a series of audiotapes—alone, at home—in a sequential and systematic manner. The purposes for making the tapes were (1) to serve as a mechanism for self-catharsis; (2) to present to both her and the crisis worker her full story and form the basis for changing it from a problem-saturated story line to a restoration narrative; (3) to clarify, in her own mind, the loss and movement toward restoration she was going through; and (4) to document her progress in controlling her automatic thoughts and catching her "shoulds," "oughts," and other mustrabatory statements about love, marriage, and her self-concept.

The loss and grief map (Greenspan, 2003) is a concrete representation of all the absolutist, negative, irrational beliefs she has about herself and the divorce. Once she has those in conscious awareness, she and the worker will start working on positive counterinjunctions that cool these hot cognitions off. The worker will also set up a self-managed behavior model with her that will allow frequency counts of the number of times she makes those statement to herself in a day. He will use a thought-stopping procedure and cueing (Dr. James's magical rubber band-on-the-wrist-thought-stopper) to cue her to shift from those all-or-none irrational thoughts to cooler, more positive, self-enhancing counterinjunctions that are designed to start changing her narrative to one of restoration.

The audio recordings were quite useful to the crisis worker in verbally journaling her changing narrative as she worked her cognitive-behavioral plan. But the main value of the behavioral plan was providing Nancy the purpose and the experience of doing it. She described in detail her thoughts, feelings, and actions throughout several stages: shock and disbelief, denial, anger, withdrawal, guilt, depression, searching, and resolution. Nancy made eight recordings. She reported that the most valuable and helpful aspect of the activity was listening to her own recordings, which she found herself doing over and over. Nancy kept the recordings with the stated intention of continuing to listen to them. But she later reported that after her crisis subsided, she didn't need to listen to them anymore.

Nancy also contracted with the worker to go to a divorce support group at a local church. Such groups provide crisis support, role models for survival, adaptation pathways, and new social networks (Raphael & Dobson, 2000). You will note that over and over we advocate the use of these groups as part of a comprehensive crisis and transcrisis intervention treatment model. They are an important part of the response to bereavement, and there is evidence that they are effective as a social and healing process (Kitzman & Gaylord, 2001; Raphael & Dobson, 2000).

Death of a Pet

The Thompsons—Hollis, age 36, Faye, age 33, and their adopted daughter, Dawn, age 5—were grieving over the death of Tincup, their aged terrier. Tincup had been like a member of the family. He had been a faithful companion to the Thompsons since they were newlyweds; he had been the affectionate and protective playmate of Dawn from the day the Thompsons got her through the adoption agency. Lately he had developed severe health problems, and the veterinarian had finally told the Thompsons that Tincup's medical condition made it necessary to terminate his life. After making the painful decision, the Thompsons decided that they would all be present at his euthanasia.

While on a first reading, this may seem horrific for a small child, Butler and Lagoni (1996) make an excellent case that an honest discussion of the pet's condition and the need to put it to death is important. Children respond well to straightforward and concrete explanations. Note that we do not use the more palliative "put to sleep." As Butler and Lagoni (1996) suggest, small children may think that because they go to sleep every night, they may be "put to sleep" if they are bad and never wake up.

The following intervention strategies were provided and issues were explored with the Thompson family during the days and weeks immediately following the death of their pet.

1. *Individual counseling and intervention.* Assessment of the levels of grief, guilt, and stress in each—Hollis, Faye, and Dawn. Assessment of Dawn's understanding of the death of the pet. Provision of a period to grieve and release grief energy. Follow-up play therapy and ceremonial events as outlets for Dawn (Schoenberg, 1980, pp. 203–204) and display of meaningful objects that link Dawn to her deceased pet (Lagoni, Butler, & Hetts, 1994, p. 265).
2. *Group work.* Providing an opportunity for the family to talk about Tincup's death in a realistic, factual, and honest manner. Using the pet's death to help Dawn begin to develop her concept of death, free of misinformation. Providing opportunities and activities for the family to commemorate the pet's life and to reformulate the death within a context of growth.
3. *Bibliotherapy* about bonding with pets and coping with crisis and loss.

The pet counselor from the veterinary clinic met with the family 3 days after Tincup's death.

Dawn: I was a little scared at first, but Dr. Hobbs explained exactly what they were going to do to Tincup and how it wouldn't hurt. I really wanted Tincup to stay alive, but he would yelp every time I tried to pick him up, and I didn't want him to hurt anymore. I helped Dr. Hobbs get Tincup ready, and my parents did too. He just sorta relaxed, and

I petted him while they put the medicine in him. It was all done in a minute or so, and my parents and I petted Tincup for a while and then we took him home. He is buried out in the backyard, and I go visit him every day. I think I may want a new puppy for my birthday, but right now I just want to go visit Tincup.

As Butler and Lagoni (1996) suggest, getting new pets immediately is not always a good idea. Children, and for that matter adults, need time to grieve the loss of their pets just as they need time to grieve any other important loss. Schoenberg (1980) suggested that families use ceremonial events to help deal with their grief following the death of a pet (pp. 203–204). The Thompsons used a ceremonial event of pet burial to help open up opportunities for discussion, sharing of feelings, and explaining death to their daughter.

Faye: We had a small funeral in the backyard. I helped Dawn invite a few of her close friends to the funeral, and our next-door neighbors mailed us a sympathy card. Hollis and Dawn dug Tincup's grave, and we had a simple but beautiful grave-side service. There were flowers and friends, and we paid tribute and said good-bye to him. It was a good thing for our family and for the friends who came. We even had another small ceremony when we put Tincup's collar on the bulletin board in Dawn's room. We're still grieving somewhat over his death, but it has been a learning experience for all of us, and I think Dawn will have a more realistic and healthy view of death, loss, and grief as a result of these activities.

We also got *Zach and His Dog* (Meagher, 2009), which is a story about pet loss and bonding with children. We read that together and had some tears, but it helped put things in perspective too. So Dawn still touches Tincup's collar before she goes to bed, but I think probably by Christmas there may be a new puppy under the tree Christmas morning.

The strategies used in dealing with the loss of pets are aimed at the same goals as those used in any human loss: helping the grievers work through their various stages of grief in healthy and growth-promoting ways. Rituals for pets may seem a bit over the top, but their purpose for children as well as adults is to keep them from getting stuck (Reeves, 2011). It is recommended that people who work with clients who have lost pets read from sources such as *The Human–Animal Bond and Grief* (Lagoni, Butler, & Hetts, 1994) and *Pet Loss and Human Bereavement* (Kay et al., 1984).

Bereavement in Elderly People

Lenore and Robert Kizer, ages 82 and 85, respectively, had been living in a nursing home for 4 years. Robert had been there more than a year when Lenore had to join him. Their three living children resided in other states and were busy with their own families, so Lenore placed Robert in the nursing home when he was 80 and she was no longer able to care for him because he required 24-hour nursing care. Lenore was in the dining room eating breakfast when one of the medical staff members came and requested that she come to Robert's room because they couldn't rouse him. When Lenore arrived at the room, a staff physician met her and informed her that Robert had apparently died in his sleep. The following intervention strategies were provided and issues explored with Lenore during the days and weeks immediately following Robert's death.

1. *Individual counseling and intervention.* Assessing Lenore's level of grief and coping ability. Providing opportunities for Lenore to release her grief energy. Assessing Lenore's physical and mental capacities to cope. Assessing her children's ability to help. Examining her economic, medical, and legal needs. Using therapeutic strategies such as cognitive/spiritual, reminiscence, and constructive/narrative therapy to help Lenore revalidate herself as a worthwhile person separate from Robert.
2. *Group work.* Groups within the nursing home. Social groups outside the nursing home.
3. *Referrals.* Medical, religious organizations, legal assistance, Lenore's church, her children, senior citizens' agencies.

Lenore Kizer continued to live in the nursing home following Robert's death. Lenore had several assets, which the crisis worker, a pastoral counselor, used to validate her life as it had been lived and revalidate what her new life would be without Robert. She was physically mobile, she had lots of friends in the nursing home and in the community, she was an outgoing person with an optimistic outlook on life, and her children were supportive. Even with the positive factors she had going for her, Lenore experienced periods of denial, isolation, loneliness, fear, anger, bargaining, and depression that were profound. The crisis worker's goal was to help Lenore achieve a satisfactory degree of reconciliation with and acceptance of Robert's death, and to begin to reorient her postcrisis life as a worthwhile person who was not identified as Robert's wife or Robert's widow.

He did this by first tapping into her strong faith. He used cognitive restructuring (Meichenbaum, 1985) and existential therapy (Frankl, 1969) to reinvest her socially and inject new meaning into her life. Finally, he attempted to change her negative interpretations of the event by using a narrative/constructionist approach (Neimeyer & Levitt, 2000).

Lenore: Sometimes I feel it is terrible that I am so alone.

CW: On a scale of 1 to 10, one being absolutely awful and 10 being absolutely wonderful, where would you rate yourself?

Lenore: Probably a 2. Life isn't worth much anymore.

CW: I wonder if you might look back on your strong faith and see and say that a little differently, Lenore. Something like, "Robert is indeed gone, but God is still with me and so are my friends and my children."

Lenore: I know, and sometimes I forget that. God is always here. If I stop and pray a minute, God generally gives me a way to go. I get so moping around I forget that.

By reframing and proposing follow-through actions, the crisis worker attempts to cut through the ever-deepening vortex of isolation and despair that assails the grief-stricken when a longtime partner has died. Particularly with the elderly, creating resiliency and finding new meaning in life are critical. Many therapists are skittish about bringing spirituality into therapy. However, combining cognitive therapy with spiritual therapy can be extremely powerful (Ramsey & Blieszner, 2000). The worker is also setting Lenore up to engage in solution focused brief therapy (SFBT) for loss adaption (Humphrey, 2009), by using an SFBT scaling technique to lay the ground work to allow her to reframe her current despondent state and focus on finding positive solutions (de Shazer, 1985).

Lenore: A lot of times I just mope around. Some of the time I get to feeling sorry for myself. Then sometimes I forget and find myself walking down to Robert's room before I remember that he isn't there anymore. My life seems so meaningless without him.

CW: You're really missing him, and you're also having trouble remembering. What would you like to recall most, and when your life is better, how will it be like that? It's certainly fine to do that reminiscing, but also thinking about how you two worked through things together and how you can use his memories to do that.

While the worker uses reminiscing (described in detail in Chapter 14, Violent Behavior in Institutions), the focus is on marshaling positive assets Lenore has used in the past to cope with the present and the future. Together, the crisis worker and the client re-write the client's story line by deconstructing reality (Humphrey, 2009, pp. 184–185) into more positive self-descriptions that are much closer to her life, as opposed to the terrible exception she now faces (Ramsey & Blieszner, 2000).

Lenore: We were very active politically and socially conscious. We were also very active in our church.

CW: So if you were to write those down as the major narratives of your life, and have a conversation with the Lord about it, what do you suppose might come of that?

Lenore: Well, it isn't actually in the Bible, but it is a good saying. "The Lord helps those who help themselves." Robert used to say that, and I think it is true. I need to get off my rear end and help myself.

CW: So while this is a terrible exception to how you have generally lived your life, it is indeed an exception and not very representative of the strong and resilient Lenore who forged not only a great married life but also an exceptional independent life of her own.

Lenore: When you put it that way, there is more truth than fiction to it.

CW: So, suppose a miracle happened and indeed the Lord came down and in a vision tonight said, "Lenore, I am about to make a miracle happen with you. Tomorrow you will be as you were before. Robert will not be there, but you will be. What will I see happening, Lenore?"

Lenore: Well, you would see an old woman, but still full of a zest for living, taking the retirement van down to the church and going in the church van out to visit the shut-ins. I suppose you would see me also down at the local Republican Party headquarters doing some things there. I also haven't gone to my quilting group in a while, and I want to make every one of the grandchildren a quilt to remember me by. I have been putting that off, but time is flying by. I guess that is kinda egotistical, huh, Lord? (*A wry smile crosses her face.*)

CW: So, could you do that? And I wonder if you might relate what you have said with the women's group next week.

Lenore: Well, I expect I could do that.

The crisis worker uses the SFBT techniques of the miracle question, exception to the rule, and cheerleading (de Shazer, 1985) in a spiritual format to help Lenore recognize and reinforce the many positive attributes she has had and still has. By having Lenore look at this period in her life as the exception rather than the rule, the crisis worker reframes the loss narrative and seeks to reconstruct her view of life and its meaning. When life stories are rendered chaotic by narrative disruption due to the loss of a lifelong mate, reframing that narrative in more positive terms can foster healing (Neimeyer & Levitt, 2000). That healing may be made much more powerful by helping the client form or reform a spiritual foundation.

It may be argued that the foregoing is a "goody-two-shoes" approach to pacify and mollify the aggrieved and that no real change will occur. Further, it may be patently ridiculous to assume that disheartened old people who are only waiting for the grim reaper to appear could be uplifted by reviewing and hearing encouraging and joyous stories. We propose that this view is as negatively stereotypical of the elderly as one can be. Reconstruction of one's self-concept as a primary task of adaptation to spousal loss is a primary task no matter how old or young one is (Lopata, 1996), and research suggests that allowing older persons to discuss their thoughts and feelings (Segal et al., 2001) helps reduce a variety of negative effects. Further, the elderly are not helpless; they have the capacity to adapt and learn new coping responses even after suffering the loss of a mate (Hanson & Hayslip, 2000).

Bereavement in an HIV-Infected Client

Clint's partner of 6 years died of AIDS 18 months ago. Last week Clint lost his job as a bank loan officer and desperately needs a job. He is somewhat paranoid and suspects that the people at the bank found out that he tested positive for HIV last May, although his job performance had deteriorated considerably and his absences from work did not help. Normally, Clint is an intelligent, enthusiastic, energetic, outgoing, friendly, and positive individual. He is an exceptionally competent employee whom the bank was grooming for management work. Now he presents himself as unsure of himself, depressed, angry, nervous, and anxious. He is riddled with various somatic complaints, none of which has so far proven to be an actual AIDS-related illness. Besides the primary loss of his partner, he has suffered a secondary loss of his job and is further suffering from *stigmatized* loss, which

often jeopardizes or even prohibits the use of support systems (Humphrey, 2009, p. 22).

Clint: On top of everything else, I have never come out to my parents. I wouldn't mind telling my mom, but I would have real trouble revealing to my dad that I'm gay. I also worry that telling him that I've tested positive will be too much for his heart, because he's had two bypasses already. I may have to find a cheaper place to live, too. I have too many things to deal with right now. Not to mention the physical problems.

CW: Clint, I'm really glad you came in here today. I can see that you are feeling really depressed today. Are you to the point of thinking about killing yourself?

The first thing the crisis worker does is to explore Clint's lethality level. Because clients may be experiencing an enormous array of situational, medical, and environmental problems, workers must be diligent in defining the total scope of problems, ensuring physical and psychological safety, and providing emotional supports. Crisis intervention with HIV-infected clients must start with sensitive and empathic listening.

CW: I'm happy to know that you're safe for now. Clint, what do we most need to work on right now?

Clint: I just don't see how I can handle everything, how I can make plans, so much is happening.

CW: You're overwhelmed with all the issues you are facing, and you're needing some help, understanding, and supports right now.

Clint: It's been hard enough since my partner died. I still miss him terribly, and now I've lost my job—I have to tell my parents I'm gay—God! Gay and HIV positive, too! Sometimes I think I am going crazy, or then I worry, is it the onset of AIDS-related dementia? Then I wonder if I am not a sinner in the hands of an angry God, and I am getting my just desserts.

CW: Clint, all that would be overwhelming to anyone. I don't want to minimize this at all, but what I do want to do is see if we can't get a handle on this and start to manage these problems. You do not have an execution date, even though it may seem that way. Your HIV can be managed, like any other life-threatening disease. The question is, How do you wish to use your time while you are fighting it? I want to break this down into manageable components. You had huge responsibilities in the bank, so I know you can break complex issues down and plan what to do. This is an exception to what you are normally capable of doing, and I want you to see it that way. So let's use those considerable talents and brainstorm a list of the possible actions you can take, when they'll be done, and what resources and assets you have.

First, though, I want to get you into a support group of people who are HIV positive. This will do two things. It will give you good information and feedback for what is going on medically and how people cope with the physical problems. Second, it will get you out of the social isolation and all of the bad things that go with that.

The crisis worker acknowledges the continued losses Clint has faced, as well as the problem of revealing to his parents his HIV status and the difficulty he will face in the future. Concomitantly, the crisis worker begins to think about what concrete actions Clint will need to take immediately: employment counseling, support groups to help Clint regain a sense of control over his life, and medical services. He challenges the client in a typical REBT therapy manner to stop catastrophic thinking and start problem solving (Ellis & Abrahms, 1978); he also uses a solution-focused technique of cheerleading and pointing out that this is an exception to otherwise very competent behavior (de Shazer, 1985), stressing his abilities to solve complex problems. At this point the worker makes a decision that has more to do with crisis intervention than loss reorientation. He makes an assessment that Clint needs to divide his crisis into manageable pieces and seeks to break the multiple problems down into manageable issues.

Research by Williams and Stafford (1991) indicates that a fundamental form of intervention with partners and adult family members of persons with HIV/AIDS is the use of peer groups to break down the prevalent feelings of isolation, enhance sharing of personal grief, and promote healing (pp. 425–426). Support groups are absolutely critical in educating the person about the disease, sharing intense emotions, observing how others cope (effectively and ineffectively), coming to terms with the disease and its "dreaded" issues, and receiving help from and giving help to others (Hoffman, 1996, p. 72; Nord, 1997, pp. 233–235). They are also critical in helping those individuals who have stigmatized grief find a safe, supportive place to ventilate and get suggestions.

Clint agreed and was referred to an existing group at the Aid to End AIDS Center that could provide the help he needed in an environment of warmth, acceptance, professional competence, and healing. The crisis worker followed up by contacting the center director to make sure that Clint obtained the services he needed. The crisis worker also needed to break down the tidal wave of emotions that was rolling over Clint by validating the intensity of those emotions. The crisis worker attempts to reframe the cognitions about the disease by getting Clint to see that a good life and a long life are not inextricably linked (Hoffman, 1996, p. 80).

CW: So what's the first priority?

Clint: I would like to get clear with my parents. I would also like to do some things to honor my partner, Mark. I did nothing when his parents buried him. They don't want to talk to me. I was cut-throat ambitious in the bank business—the original Scrooge. I want to get another banking job, but I want to do it in a kinder, gentler way, perhaps doing finance work for Habitat for Humanity.

CW: So how do you want to plan on doing those things? I might suggest we role-play that conversation, both to give you practice and be sure how you want to get that over to your dad without upsetting him.

The worker assumes a collaborative role to get the client mobilized. Motivating HIV-positive clients to set goals and challenging them to achieve a meaningful quality of life are extremely important parts of counseling those clients. The crisis worker must not shy away from doing so out of fear that the client will not be up to the task (Hoffman, 1996, pp. 92–94).

Two other critical crisis issues need to be confronted. First is safe sex and general health-promoting practices. Stopping the spread of the disease is critical, and one of the major ethical dilemmas a crisis counselor faces is getting an infected client to practice safe sex. Whether clients are heterosexual or homosexual, the central issue is educating them about safe sex and disclosing their status to their partners or potential partners (Hoffman, 1996, pp. 100–112). Because of revenge, pride, ego, shame, loneliness, or sexual drive, getting a client to practice safe sex is not an easy issue. The psychological implications embedded in the destruction of the client's assumptive world have everything to do with the reason why some people continue to engage in risky behaviors and why public education campaigns to discourage risky behavior have been only marginally effective (Nord, 1997, p. 249). The last thing most young men want to do is admit to a potential sexual partner that they are infected.

CW: Sex may be the last thing on your mind right now, but it will come up. I am ethically and morally bound to say something about this because you would be putting another at lethal risk. I can't stop you from having sex, but I can help you to educate yourself about how to have sex and explore some of the reasons you might not feel you ought to tell somebody else. I want to refer you to Pete Endicott, a counselor at Aid to End AIDS. He can help you make some good decisions about sexual relations.

The complex and multiple loss issues that surround HIV infection and AIDS make it a horrific crisis. Initial crisis intervention generally means bringing runaway emotions to a halt and breaking the multiple issues of loss into discrete, manageable components. At the same time, the crisis worker is also tasked with dealing with clients' larger issues of attempting to find meaning from the disease and its effects, while living as good a life as they can.

Complicated Grief: Death of a Mother

These case examples end with the most difficult type of grief and loss issue—complicated grief reaction (Rando, 1993). Ann Marie is a 38-year-old legal secretary who went one-on-one with a bridge abutment and lost. Her car was totaled. She was unconscious and taken to the hospital for an examination. Luckily, her only injury was a concussion. However, her blood alcohol content was found to be 0.17—twice the legal limit. She was charged with a DUI and was ordered by the court to see an addiction counselor.

However, Ann Marie's case is not about addiction to alcohol but about a complicated and chronic grief reaction to the sudden death of her mother after a long bout with lupus. The problem is that neither she nor the crisis worker is aware of that at the moment. The crisis worker is a licensed addiction counselor who has also worked in bereavement.

CW: So what was going on before you had the wreck?

Ann Marie: I was angry at my father, and I finally decided to get out of the house and go out to a club with my girlfriend.

CW: Angry! How?

Ann Marie: (*starts weeping*) Look at me. I am 38 and taking care of my father. I never go out. I haven't had a date in forever. I don't know what got into me. I generally don't drink very much at all.

CW: What do you suppose *did* get into you to make you to decide to go drinking and driving? As I look at your record, this is your first offense. You don't have so much as a speeding ticket.

Ann Marie: I work all day. I come home at night and cook, wash, fetch, clean, sew for my dad and my brother Ralphie, who is 36 and living at home. I do everything for them. Ever since Mom died, they've expected me to take her place. I even moved back home from Phoenix, and now here I am. It is useless. I am useless.

CW: When you say "useless," I don't like the sound of that. You sound so down and out I am wondering if getting into that car and slamming into that bridge abutment was not a way of attempting to kill yourself without the stigma of suicide attached to it.

While it may appear that your authors continuously harp on this issue and you are tired of being nagged about assessing for suicide with every client, many suicides are accomplished by automobile. Mustering enough courage to do it by getting intoxicated is another common feature of suicide by automobile. Further, suicidal ideation is one of the markers for a complicated grief reaction. The addiction counselor immediately picks up on Ann Marie's hopelessness and helplessness, and pursues it. The addiction counselor has now shifted to crisis mode. Suicidal behavior is one of Worden's (1991, p. 76) complicated grief clues.

Ann Marie: (*cynical laugh*) If I was really serious about that, I'd have knocked Ralphie in the head and stuck him on the front of the hood. Kill myself? Not yet. Drink too much and do something stupid cause I feel sorry for myself? Yes!

CW: OK. I needed to check that out. You mentioned Phoenix. What was that like and how is this different in Pittsburgh?

Ann Marie: I had a great job with a great law firm in Phoenix 4 years ago. I had a great boyfriend there. I had a great life. I was going to get married. I just got a promotion to executive secretary. Then Mom got sick. She had always waited on Dad hand and foot. He was useless without her (*laughs cynically*), about like me now. I started flying home to help out, but the lupus got worse and Mom went to a wheelchair and then to a nursing home. I got a job out here. The boyfriend said I had to choose. I did.

A helluva choice. A dependent father and shiftless brother and a third-rate job. Maybe I did try to drive myself into that abutment. I don't think so, but I don't know anymore. I don't see much of a life for me anymore.

The client's losses are large and many. There is no rule that says grieving and bereavement must be over a death. The sacrifices the client has made career wise and in her relationships are profound. The isolation, loneliness, depression, anger, and sadness encapsulate all of the first five of McKenna's (1999) components of survivor grief.

CW: So you have sacrificed your life for your parents. What you have gotten from that is a smorgasbord of bad feelings and bad outcomes.

Ann Marie: (continues weeping softly) My mother died last year. Worked herself to death for them. (clinches her fist and pounds it into her hand) Christ! I wish she were back here. I miss her, but I would give her a piece of my mind for not standing up to those two jerks I am taking care of and make them grow up.

CW: How do you feel about your mother's death?

Ann Marie: Why . . . why . . . what do you mean? Terrible, of course. I loved her. We used to talk at least twice a week when I was in Phoenix.

CW: I am just wondering. You indicated your dad and brother were pretty dependent on her, and now they seem to be that way on you.

Ann Marie: Oh, Dad says he'll get a housekeeper. He's been saying that since Mom got sick, but he won't when he's got his daughter for an indentured servant. And that failure-to-launch brother of mine. "Yeah, I'll pitch in, Sis, right after I get back from the game. Say, mind washing my work clothes? I forgot and don't have any clean for Monday."

The crisis worker's content query moves immediately to the deceased mother. He is well aware that what clients say about their dead loved ones may be very different from how they feel. Unfinished business (Attig, 2000, pp. 112–117) can be a major problem in grief counseling. This is particularly true when the death is sudden (Cummock, 1996). Whether that unfinished business is guilt over having or not having done something, or having or not having said something, unfinished business is a common issue that is particularly problematic because of prohibitions against "speaking ill of the dead" or, indeed, the inability to speak to them at all.

In a very odd way, but anything but uncommon, what the client is manifesting is disenfranchised grief. It also has characteristics of rational-emotive behavior therapy's mustrabatory behavior (Ellis & Dryden, 1977) in that the client is duty bound and "must" absolutely take over for her mother no matter the cost to her because that is what "good daughters" do. This **mustrabatory behavior** segues into and goes a good deal beyond the client's primary loss of her mother to secondary losses of a love life, career, and her independence. When these are piled one on top of the other, they are an excellent recipe for complicated/prolonged grief. Ann Marie meets the proposed criteria (Prigerson, Vanderwerker, & Maciejewski, 2008; Zhang, El-Jawahri, & Prigerson, 2006) for complicated/prolonged grief in the following ways:

Criterion A: Yearning, pining, and longing for the deceased to a distressing degree (although she hasn't verbally acknowledged it yet because of her anger).

Criterion B: Experiencing four of the following in the last month as marked, overwhelming, and extreme: (1) trouble accepting the death; (2) inability to trust others since the death; (3) excessive bitterness or anger over the death; (4) feeling uneasy about moving on with one's life; (5) feeling emotionally numb or detached from others since the death; (6) feeling life is empty or meaningless without the deceased; (7) feeling the future holds no meaning or prospect of fulfillment without the deceased; (8) feeling agitated, jumpy, or on edge since the death. Ann Marie clearly meets Criterion B.

Criterion C: The above symptoms and disturbances cause marked dysfunction in social, occupational, or other important domains. Ann Marie's social and work life have been seriously impaired by the death.

Criterion D: The above symptoms and disturbances must last at least 6 months. A period of 4 years definitely meets this criterion.

Ann Marie: (pounding her fist into her hand) I told Mom again and again to make them be independent. She'd just say, "Oh, you know your dad, he likes to be taken care of, and your brother's had tough luck."

CW: But now it is you who is taking care of them. If you could speak to your mother about what you are now feeling, what would you say to her?

Ann Marie: That's crazy. She's dead. I can't speak to her.

CW: Do you visit her gravesite or memorial?

Ann Marie: I go there every morning and pray in the mausoleum. I am a good Catholic. I also light a candle at Mass. My old girlfriend from high school says I am going too much and can't get over it. It has been almost a year now. She was the one I went drinking with the other night. The only friend I've got . . . from high school! My God, but I am pitiful!

CW: I understand you care very deeply for your mother, but sometimes there are things that are left unsaid or undone. If your mother were sitting right here right now, what might you say to her?

The crisis worker uses a tried-and-true Gestalt therapy technique of the "empty chair" to attempt to allow some of the client's powerful and buried affect about the predicament her mother has left her in to come out (Cable, 1996; Humphrey, 2009, pp. 154–166). While it may seem this technique is used in a lot of situations in this book, it is one of the best for objectifying emotions—and many, many seemingly intractable crises call for just that.

Ann Marie: (*tentatively*) I guess . . . like always, that I loved her.

CW: Speak to her as if she were here right now in that chair over there!

Ann Marie: I love you, Mom. I wish you were still here. I miss you so much sometimes.

CW: What would you tell her about the situation with your dad?

Ann Marie: Not much, I guess, just I am bearing up.

The crisis worker gently reflects and confronts the buried anger he guesses she is feeling and calls her on her behavior.

CW: I sense some anger about that, not just your dad's demands and needs and your own lack of a life. Bearing up under her load. A load she left you with. Did she ask you to do that?

Ann Marie: Well, sorta. She never asked me to come back home, but she asked me to look after Dad.

The crisis worker now makes an owning statement targeted directly at the anger in an attempt to get the client to speak to the affect. This is not a one-step process; it calls for repeated attempts to uncover the pent-up emotion. This process may take considerable

time—or perhaps never happen with some clients who are so deeply mired in it.

CW: If it were me, I might feel a great deal of resentment. I wouldn't quite know how to deal with it, but I would surely feel it. I might even be afraid of some of those feelings that would not seem right, forbidden even. It wouldn't be right to be angry with my mother who died heroically trying to take care of my father, yet I would be angry about the predicament I was in and the loss of my own life—love life, career goals, a chance for a family. I would be very angry about that. If you were that angry, what might you tell her? I have an assignment, if you are up to it. I want you to go back to the mausoleum, and I want you to tell her how you feel. I will go with you if you want, but you need to do this.

Many times people will go out of their way to avoid returning to the gravesite or memorial site because of the fear of their inability to control their feelings. Or alternatively, their feelings will be so out of control that they practically deify the gravesite, they are there so often. The client should be willing to make the visit and should never be forced. Having an agenda such as Ann Marie's is important. When the grief is complicated, it is important that the crisis worker be willing to go with the client. While there, the client may write a letter and burn it, or put a message in a helium balloon and let it fly away. After the gravesite visit, it is helpful if the client does something positive, rests, and is reinforced for the accomplishment of the visit. The summation of this visit is to literally put the body to rest and bring closure (Johnson, 1987, p. 181).

Ann Marie: (*7 A.M. at the mausoleum by her mother's crypt*) I feel so stupid. I . . . I can't . . . I don't know what to say.

CW: Just say what is in your heart.

Ann Marie: (*struggles with long pauses*) I miss you. I . . . love you. I wish . . . you wouldn't have let Daddy and Ralphie be so dependent on you because they are on me, and I don't know how . . . what to do. I am kinda angry with you about that. . . . In fact, I am VERY ANGRY WITH YOU! How could you have done this? You always encouraged me to go out and be independent. To seek my own life, and I did . . . but then you hooked me and reeled me back in. Damn it! How could you! How could you do that! (*leans against the crypt and wails while the crisis worker holds her*)

CW: (*very gently while holding his arm around Ann Marie's shoulders*) Is it possible that underneath that anger is a lot of loneliness for your mom? That the real anger is that she left you without your main support, her wisdom, and the talks you had about your hopes and dreams? I wonder if you can forgive her for that.

Ann Marie: (*sobbing*) Oh, Momma, I do miss you, and not just for having to take care of Daddy and Ralphie. For always encouraging me and supporting me. I feel so selfish. I do forgive you and hope you can forgive me.

Forgiveness is a difficult thing to do. The anger that overlays her frustration also overlays her fears of now being on her own, of her deep personal insecurity now that her main support system is no longer there. Forgiveness is critical to letting go. By understanding and getting past the subtle fears that prevent forgiveness of real or imagined past indiscretions, injustices, hurts, failures, and insults, clients are finally able to move forward (De Moss, 2003).

CW: (*waits for her emotions to pour out*) Your mother wanted you to be independent. What do you suppose she might say to you about exerting some of that independence with your dad and Ralphie?

Ann Marie: (*regaining some composure*) I guess . . . I . . . guess . . . maybe . . . she would . . . say, "Ann Marie, you know good and well that is not what I meant. You must lead your own life. Now you sit down with them and tell them there are going to be some new rules. I took care of your dad and Ralphie, but I wasn't a babysitter for them. You know I didn't mean for you to do that either." (*continues dialogue with her mother*)

CW: I would like you to write up a list of "new rules" for your dad and Ralphie, and describe how you are going to behave toward them. I would like you to come and visit your mom tomorrow and discuss those rules with her.

While it may seem strange to have a conversation with a dead person who most assuredly will not answer, the fact is that clients may well have a fruitful dialogue and begin to concretize diffuse and abstract feelings that were heretofore unreachable.

We can objectify unfinished business in many ways, such as writing letters, having dialogues, playing music, drawing and painting pictures, creating scrapbooks, sculpting, or creating other symbolic ways to relieve our hurt and anger with the unfinished business (Attig, 2000, p. 116). By doing so, Ann Marie was able to start letting go of the complicated grief reaction she had developed, and forgive her mother for dying on her so suddenly and leaving her with two dependent men.

While prayer can be positive and helpful in many circumstances, prayer in this case served only to punch back the real feelings Ann Marie was holding toward her mother for having the audacity to leave her with a very dependent father. Until she was able to express her feelings and vent her anger, Ann Marie would continue to have transcrises in her own life, which could indeed become lethal for her. Ann Marie is representative of many people we see in crisis who appear to have one kind of crisis, yet have a different one underlying it. This underlying crisis is often complicated grief and unreconciled bereavement.

Indeed, while Ann Marie's DUI is most assuredly a problem, and her drinking may be a problem as well, the undergirding crisis is her sense of loss—loss of a job, loss of a romantic relationship, loss of her independence, and finally loss of a parent—none of which she had adequately grieved but over which she had instead built up a tremendous amount of unconscious resentment. Complicated grief is a delicate, sensitive, and troublesome issue that is surrounded by emotional minefields and taboo cultural totems (Rando, 1993). Yet if a crisis worker suspects an unresolved grief problem, much as our addiction counselor did, then this is the very place that intervention must go. If you do not feel comfortable in doing this, and even we "experts" sometimes don't, then refer the client.

Ann Marie was able to move forward and confront her father and brother. She was also able to engage some effective support systems to help her father and brother become more independent. None of these steps was fast or easy. She no longer visited her mother every day, but still remembered her by lighting a candle for her at Mass once a week. She completed her DUI course and got her driver's license reinstated. At last report she was actively engaged in a number of community activities and hobbies, and had moved to another, larger law firm with more responsibility. Although she has yet to find true romance, she has accomplished a great deal. She has mourned the loss of her mother, removed the unresolved grief that was an emotional anchor around her neck, regained some of her independence, and started to reinvent and reinvigorate her life.

The Crisis Worker's Own Grief

Before workers engage in grief work with others, they must first take care of themselves. This means becoming proactive in maintaining their own vitality. Failure to do so can result in the phenomenon known as *vicarious traumatization* or *compassion fatigue* (see Chapter 16, Human Services Workers in Crisis). Indeed, working with loss and bereavement has high potential for burnout. The 9/11 World Trade Center disaster resulting in a large population of disaster workers needing psychological assessment and treatment is standing testimony to this fact. The traumatic wake of that disaster resulted in the first large-scale screening and use of evidenced trauma practices on disaster relief workers (Olden et al., 2015) and the lessons learned from that disaster, the Oklahoma City bombing, and Katrina have lead to large-scale development of debriefing, screening, and treatment protocols for disaster workers (see Chapter 17, Disaster Response).

Schneider (1984) reminds us that "it is not possible to be a facilitator of the growth aspects of bereavement if the helper is not also experiencing growth in relation to personal losses" (p. 270). The knowledge and perspective gained from one's own growth following grief should serve as a quiet reservoir of strength for workers. But the worker's own grief experience should not be projected or imposed on clients. Both Rando (1984) and Schoenberg (1980) challenge caregivers to come to grips with their own personal and professional attitudes toward death, grief, and bereavement before venturing into helping relationships with clients who are in grief. According to Rando (1984), there are several reasons why caregivers should ensure that their own grief and attitudes about grief are not allowed to intrude on their strength and vitality for helping others (pp. 430–435).

1. *Emotional investment in the client.* A certain degree of emotional investment in clients is normal and needed. Overinvestment in those whom they help may require crisis workers to expend an inordinate amount of energy on their own grief responses in cases of dying and bereaved clients.

2. *Bereavement overload.* If the worker forms close bonds with several clients, the emotional load may involve too many risks and grief responses on the part of the worker. Workers can deal with their own bereavement overload provided that they are aware of it while it is happening to them and that they act on their internal signals to get help and/ or take steps to effect their own renewal before several client losses get them down.

3. *Countertransference.* Sometimes crisis workers engaged in grief work with others find that such work awakens their own feelings, thoughts, memories, and fantasies about losses in their own lives. Solomon, Neria, and Ram (1998) report on the tremendous countertransference issues that Israeli mental health workers had in dealing with Holocaust survivors and the equally tremendous problems that caused for them and their clients. Workers who experience such countertransference will be severely impaired in helping others. To deal with countertransference, caregivers who regularly work with loss-related clients should be involved in peer supervision, case staffing, psychological autopsies, and debriefing groups for reducing emotional overload caused by constant involvement with client grief.

4. *Emotional replenishment.* Caregivers in the area of grief and bereavement work must take special care to minister to their own emotional needs. Caregivers need support systems to provide for their physical, emotional, and psychological wellness. Emotional replenishment involves both taking care of oneself internally and having environmental supports from significant others—a supervisor, friends, family, colleagues—and meaningful physical and emotional activities that take the person completely away from loss and back into a positive emotional and physical state.

5. *Facing one's own mortality.* One of the important aspects of loss work is that it may arouse existential anxiety over one's own death. Support groups, supervision, inservice training, and reading are suggested coping mechanisms. Spiritual growth activities are worthwhile alternatives for many caregivers.

6. *Sense of power.* Caregivers, like all other people, need a sense of power or control. Working with clients in dying, grief, and bereavement may cause workers to identify vicariously with the losses of their clients. Such identification may result in a sense of loss of power or control on the part of workers. Strategies for preventing feelings of loss of power are essentially the same as those recommended for dealing with countertransference.

7. *Tendency to rescue.* It is essential that workers relinquish the rescue fantasy, especially when dealing with grief and bereavement, because

rescuing someone who has experienced or is about to suffer loss is to deny the inevitability of the loss.

The seven proactive points just noted are good starting points for worker vigilance in preventing vicarious trauma, compassion fatigue, and burnout in themselves. It is highly recommended that you thoroughly read Chapter 16, Human Services Workers in Crisis, for further coping strategies if you are going to do this work.

Humphrey (2009, pp. 218–219) has posed some hard questions for professionals in human services interested in doing this work. They are abridged, encapsulated, and stated here with our own additions. Think carefully about them and see what your answers are!

1. Can I see the differences between my own grief experiences and those of my clients?
2. Am I aware of my own unresolved issues of loss, do I have unfinished business with them, and do they spill over into my work?
3. Do I rescue clients from their grief because it is too terrifying for me or I can't handle their pain?
4. Do I have to expend so much of my energy controlling my own emotions that I am ineffective with my clients?
5. Do I avoid, deny, or otherwise sidestep certain grief-related issues because of my own issues with them?
6. Am I unwilling to let my clients experience the pain of grief because I don't believe they can handle such emotion-laden topics?
7. Does the mere mention of the topic of death or dying make me apprehensive or anxious and start dreading the counseling session?
8. Are my own losses so new and raw as to not allow me to work effectively with someone else's loss?

Is There Any Lemonade in All These Sour Lemons?

Of all the chapters in this book, Personal Loss: Bereavement and Grief is one of the most difficult and depressing, at times, to write. The question becomes: Given the overwhelming nature of most losses, can we hope for anything better than just getting back to some level of homeostasis and equilibrium? And if so, then what? Richard Tedeschi and Lawrence Calhoun are two researchers in particular who have been working on this problem for more than 15 years (Calhoun &

Tedeschi, 2001; Tedeschi & Calhoun, 1995, 2003, 2004, 2006, 2009; Tedeschi, Park, & Calhoun, 1998). They have been very interested in personal transformation (Tedeschi & Calhoun, 2012) and the potential for **positive traumatic growth** that comes out of any personal transformation that occurs as a result of trauma (Tedeschi & Calhoun, 2010) or the ability to not just survive a traumatic incident, but grow from it (Taku et al., 2008, 2015). One of the keys to understanding how that happens is the ability for individuals to change **intrusive rumination**, unbidden terrifying thoughts entering the person's mind about the trauma to **deliberate rumination** wherein the person deliberately thinks about the trauma and attempts to make meaning of it and reconcile it into passive memory (Triplett et al., 2012). Here's the good news: It doesn't happen to everybody, but overall there is a fair amount of research to indicate that people can grow out of trauma and bereavement and do so for the better (Armstrong & Shakespeare-Finch, 2011; Caserta et al., 2009; Cryder et al., 2006). Zhou et al. (2015) found that intrusive rumination indeed challenged core beliefs of Chinese middle school students who had experienced a devastating earthquake. On the other hand, deliberate rumination tended to mediate core beliefs towards posttraumatic growth.

Thus, when people are able to start to control their thinking and make meaning of the event, they do better than just adapt, but indeed experience positive growth beyond what and where they were before their losses and the ensuing crises. What is probably most interesting is that the more severe the loss reported, the higher the levels of growth (Armstrong & Shakespeare-Finch, 2011). So take heart! There is lemonade!

It also appears that crisis workers can experience positive growth out of dealing with trauma and loss (Arnold et al., 2005). So we end this chapter by finishing the horrific story of the Wisconsin dairyman you met at the beginning of the chapter. The whole community pitched in to take care of the farm so our dairyman could take his family and get away for a vacation (very hard to do when one milks twice a day and shovels a lot of fertilizer in between). That in and of itself was extremely moving and growth promoting for the whole community. One farmer told your author while the two were shoveling fertilizer at the dairyman's farm, "We used to do this a lot. It's the right thing to do and by God, we did it for Lutherans, Catholics, and even that Methodist family! It didn't make any difference. We helped people when they were down and hurting, no matter who. I personally feel damn good about this, and my guess is everybody else does too."

The dairyman took his family to Disney World, where his deceased son had wanted to go. A week after they returned, your author pulled his truck into the farm lot on his regular Friday route. The dairyman came out of the milking parlor and said, "Ah, come on inside, I got something for you. It isn't much but it just, umh, ah, my way of, I guess, well, umh, sorta saying thanks for listening to me. It helped a lot." With that he gave your author a cigarette lighter from Disney World. Your author doesn't smoke anymore, but he still has that lighter and that was in 1976.

But he got more than that from going into the jaws of this terrible death. He made a decision to get back in the business of counseling, which ultimately led to the University of Memphis, helping give birth to the CIT program that has become international in scope and the gold standard for police training for crisis intervention with the mentally ill; training more than 3,000 counselors, and writing an eighth edition of this crisis book that we humbly believe has affected thousands and thousands of students and, in turn, hopefully has helped them deal effectively with thousands more clients. So from the dread of walking into that milk house 38 years ago, it is safe to say one of your authors grew more than he could have possibly imagined.

SUMMARY

The stage models of death, dying, grief, and bereavement have become outdated due to a lack of research to prove their viability. Newer models of loss picture grief as highly individualist and not progressing neatly through linear stages. The adaptive model proposes that grieving over loss occurs along a continuum of styles and that no particular style is the one, right, true path to resolution. The dual process model promotes grieving as oscillating back and forth between a loss orientation and a restoration orientation over an extended period of time.

Several different types of loss typify the kinds of human events or tragedies that might bring crisis workers into contact with persons experiencing grief. All of these losses are the same in that they may strike individuals with grief and all that grief entails. Examples of such losses are (1) the death of a spouse, (2) the death of a child, (3) bereavement in childhood, (4) job loss, (5) separation and divorce, (6) the death of a pet, (7) bereavement in elderly people, and (8) the trauma associated with HIV and AIDS. However, loss is also different in that persons may suffer from a primary loss, secondary loss, multiple loss, ambiguous loss, and stigmatized loss.

Every human being will, at one time or another, suffer personal loss. During our lives most of us will encounter numerous people who are experiencing bereavement or grief as a result of some personal loss. What may be clearly perceived as a personal loss ranges from a devastating occurrence, such as the death of a spouse or a child, to what many people might view as a minor loss, such as that of a pet or a family heirloom. In any event, it is an important loss if the individual perceives it as such, and workers must treat each client's loss with empathy, caring, and sensitivity. Although the bereaved can never forget the loss and return to a state of complete precrisis equilibrium, he or she can be helped to reformulate the loss within a context of growth and hope.

Most loss is resolved by grieving and mourning that help the person place the loss in memory and move forward with living. Complicated/prolonged grief is a manifestation of loss that has not been resolved, grief that has gone unreconciled, mourning that hadn't been completed, and as a result is now pathologic. Complicated/prolonged grief may occur after an extended period of time in regard to a nontraumatic loss and have coexisting disorders such as depression and anxiety. It may also result from a traumatic loss and be classified as traumatic grief with the possible coexistence of PTSD. Complicated/prolonged grief is transcrisis in nature and, if not dealt with, can cause serious to lethal physical and psychological problems for the individual suffering from it.

Intervention strategies, techniques, and skills that crisis workers need for helping people in these categories of grief are focused on cognitive-behavioral and constructivist approaches, but may be highly eclectic when interventions are tailor-made to fit the idiosyncratic needs of the individual's grief process.

Crisis workers who work with grieving clients, and particularly clients with complicated/prolonged grief who do not take care of themselves emotionally, physically, and spiritually, become vulnerable to vicarious traumatization and compassion fatigue, particularly if they have not resolved their own losses.

Visit CengageBrain.com for a variety of study tools and useful resources such as video examples, case studies, interactive exercises, flashcards, and quizzes.

13

Crises in Schools

The New–Millennium, Violence–Proof School Building

Welcome to the (pretty much) violence-proof **LO1** school building of the new millennium. We are not spending any money on landscaping, because people can hide behind shrubbery and we want every square inch of the exterior in plain view of security vehicles that will patrol the perimeter on a 24-hour basis, 7 days a week. We really don't want taggers making their artistic statements on the school or common juvenile delinquents vandalizing it, so we have floodlit the whole facade and built a 10-foot chain-link security fence around the grounds. We maintain a vehicle path around the perimeter so that security vehicles or police cars can easily keep surveillance on the building.

We prefer that all students come to school in buses equipped with video monitors and two-way radios. For those few who drive, the student parking lot is enclosed by a 10-foot chain-link fence with razor wire on top. The lot is gated, so all student drivers need passes and hanger tags to get in with video surveillance. A security guard will check all students and parents who come into the parking lot. We also have concrete median dividers angled so that there can be no straight-on assault by individuals intent on drive-by shootings or school bombings.

We have only one student entrance into the school where all students must go through a metal detector. Only see-through backpacks are allowed and will be run through an x-ray machine. School uniforms are mandatory. Once students are in the building, all entry and hall doors will be electronically locked down. Teachers have swipe cards so they can move through the building. Closed-circuit TV and a call box at the front entrance enable parents to gain access.

Although uniforms are mandatory, you can have your choice of school colors—as long as those colors are not used by any known gangs operating in or around the school. All students must have holographic ID cards attached to their uniforms, as must the faculty. Students also must have GPS locaters, either carried or skin-implanted. All faculty are equipped with panic alarms and carry cell phones with speed-dial numbers preset to call security.

Kevlar bulletproof vests in the school colors will be issued to all staff. The building itself has almost no windows; the few, very small windows are made of bulletproof glass. Walls are double-brick thick (newer munitions can fairly easily penetrate a single-brick thickness). A central monitoring station is capable of visual, auditory, and motion surveillance of the entire school building—both inside and out. All classroom doors are equipped with timed electronic locks that can be operated only through a computer program or be overridden from the central monitoring station. Hallways also have locked electronic doors at strategic locations for crowd control and isolation of intruders.

The real savings is in building architecture. First, we have downsized the gymnasium. We don't need bleachers, because crowds are hazardous. Any pep assemblies, sporting events, plays, or pageants will be piped back into classrooms via TV monitors. Athletic events will be played on isolated fields, and spectators can watch via community cable television. As a result, we do not need showers or locker areas. In addition, we have also cut the width of hallways, because there are no lockers in this school—lockers are conducive to hiding contraband. There is no need for a cafeteria. Lunches can be either microwaved in classrooms or hot-packed from a central food preparation facility. Cafeterias are places where students congregate, and a congregation of students provides a setting for dangerous behavior. Thus, cafeterias are becoming as extinct as the little red schoolhouse.

There are no faculty bathrooms. Student bathrooms are dangerous settings and must be policed. So while faculty are relieving themselves, they can also watch students. Finally, the administrative area is now a command-and-control center that is target hardened with maximum security measures for its protection as the school's nerve center. Because most interaction between administrators and students and teachers is by video, there is little if any need for students or teachers to access this area. Therefore, only staff who require access to the administrative area have electronic card keys. The central staff are a little different from the staff of schools in the last millennium. Besides the administrative staff, secretaries, and support personnel such as crisis workers, four school police officers specially trained in dealing with school violence operate from a police-ready room. A central communications staff is in charge of all electronic surveillance and media from the central monitoring station.

The principal in this new-millennium school plays a somewhat secondary role. The coadministrator is the chief of security. She has a criminal justice degree and experience in law enforcement, as well as a thorough understanding of computer and security systems. In any emergency, she is the primary decision-making authority. This will happen because the principal does not have the necessary expertise to coordinate security, any more than he would have the ability to operate a nuclear power plant! If you are having trouble picturing exactly what this new-millennium school looks like, a reasonable facsimile would be any correctional facility built in the past 10 years and a number of schools.

Universities will change also in the 21st century. Because campuses are spread out over many buildings, the preferred method of security will be a large compound with carefully guarded entrances and high, blast-proof walls topped with razor wire running along the entire perimeter. Access will be carefully controlled; students not only will have to show IDs, but they will also be subjected to iris, handprint, or voice recognition checks. No part of the university campus will be without surveillance cameras, which will be linked to a central command post. If any suspicious activity is spotted, a blue light will start flashing in that area and heavily armed police will be dispatched. Students will also have GPS transmitters that will immediately give their location anywhere on campus to central security (optional at the university level but definitely required in K–12). Students will be required to carry cell phones, and those cell phones must be turned on and keyed to a university threat and warning system that will automatically page the entire student body if a threat is imminent, followed by text message information telling students what to do. Faculty will not like this safety feature, because students' cell phones will often ring in class when students forget to put them in vibrate mode. Loudspeakers and intercoms all over campus will ensure that every person will hear warnings and evacuation instructions. All buildings will have electronic locking systems, which can be activated immediately upon a threat announcement. All faculty and residence hall staff will be trained to recognize any early danger signs and threats of violence. There will be few commuter students because of the hassle of getting through the checkpoints at the school compound entrances. Most students who do not live on campus will take courses by distance learning or online. Indeed, cars will be parked at least a quarter mile away from university buildings to reduce the threat from car bombs. The campus police chief will be much higher up in the chain of command and will operate out of a hardened command center with a number of technologists to keep all the security apparatus running.

Are you appalled at the idea of a school that is in effect a penitentiary? Although we have not seen a school with every one of the attributes just described, we *have* seen each component just mentioned in at least one school building in the United States. In fact, many experts in school safety have recommended the foregoing features (Astor, 1999; Blauvelt, 1998; Brock, Sandoval, & Lewis, 1996; Dorn & Dorn, 2005; Giduck, 2005; Haynes & Henderson, 2001; Jimerson & Furlong, 2006; Nadel, 2004; Poland, 1999).

Since the advent of the new millennium, school violence has been a hot topic among the media, politicians, parents, academics, and the general population. During that time voluminous amounts of research, theory, and debate on both prevention and intervention have emerged on major topics of school violence such as shootings, suicide, and bullying (Page et al., 2015). This chapter is indeed concerned about those "hot" topics, but it is also concerned about the everyday crises that afflict students, teachers, administrators, and parents and how to plan for them.

The National Center for Education Statistics (2010) reports that between the 1999–2000 and 2007–08 school years, there was an increase in the percentage of public schools reporting the use of the following safety and security measures: controlled access to the building during school hours (from 75% to 90%); controlled access to school grounds during school hours (from 34% to 43%); students required to wear badges or picture IDs (from 4% to 8%); faculty required to wear badges or picture IDs (from 25% to 58%); the use of one or more security cameras to monitor school (from 19% to 55%); the provision of telephones in most classrooms (from 45% to 72%); and the requirement that students wear uniforms (from 12% to 18%). Between the 2003–04 and 2007–08 school years, there was also an increase in the percentage of public schools reporting the use of drug testing for student athletes (from 4% to 6%), as well as for students in other extracurricular activities (from 3% to 4%). During the 2007–08 school year, 43% of public schools reported that they had an electronic notification system for a schoolwide emergency, and 31% of public schools reported that

they had a structured, anonymous threat-reporting system. Seven years later while we have no hard data available, if articles in the *School Safety Advisory Council* newsletter and what exhibitors are showing at the National Conference School Safety Conference are relevant, we have reason to believe that has increased significantly after the Sandy Hook shootings (School Safety Advisory Council, 2015).

Our somewhat tongue-in-cheek new-millennium school building or college campus may seem patently ludicrous in Carmi, Illinois; Red Lake, Ontario; Truth or Consequences, New Mexico; or your own hometown. But to say that such a school building or college campus will never be built is to be so unaware of school violence in the United States that one would believe you have been living on another planet for the past 20 years. The violence that has arisen in schools is the reason many of these building modifications and security measures are being deemed necessary by more and more school districts and universities. In part, that is what this chapter is about.

School systems are generally able to deal with developmental crises because they are squarely in the middle of one of the greatest developmental crises of all, growing up! But they have not been prepared to deal with situational crises that arise unexpectedly and violently. Why is this so? First, it has simply not been deemed cost expedient to provide all the material and human support needed (Pitcher & Poland, 1992). Our new-millennium, violence-proof school building is not cheap, and the support personnel to staff it will not be cheap either! However, besides the many tips and plans on the Internet (search "school security"), the Department of Homeland Security (Homeland Security Administration, 2015) has planning grants available to put school security systems in place.

Conflicting Statistics

The Clery Act requires colleges and universities to report all the crime that happens on their campus, so you might suppose we would have pretty good statistics on what happens in K–12 schools as well. Unhappily, that is not the case because police jurisdictions around the United States do not report crime to the FBI in the same way, nor should you believe that K–12 school administrations, fearful of bad publicity, necessarily report all the crimes that occur in their buildings, nor do students report those crimes out of fear for their own safety. A great deal of debate occurs around whether crime is going up or going down in the more than 90,000 schools in the

United States with nearly 50 million students in attendance (National Center for Education Statistics, 2005b).

Some research indicates that there has been an increase in school violence; a study from the School Violence Resource Center, for example, showed that the percentage of high school students who were threatened or injured with a weapon increased from 1993 to 2001 (School Violence Resource Center, 2003). Other research, however, notes decreases in student victimization rates for both violent and nonviolent crimes during a similar time period (1992–2002; National Center for Education Statistics, 2004). Perhaps more problematic is that the sensational crimes, such as those at Columbine and Virginia Tech, get far more attention than the tens of thousands of mini-aggressions that occur every day and create a climate of fear and hostility in schools (National Center for Education Statistics, 2005a; National Institute of Justice, 1998).

Violent Crime Rates. In summary, the FBI's comprehensive study of crimes in schools and colleges over a 5-year period (Noonan & Vavra, 2007) found that 3.3% of all incidents reported through the National Incident-Based Reporting System involved school locations. The following statistics represent the latest report from the National Center for Education Statistics (2010). Preliminary data on the 2008–09 school year show that there were 38 student, staff, and school-associated nonstudent violent deaths from July 1, 2008, through June 30, 2009, of which 24 were homicides and 14 were suicides. In 2008, among students ages 12–18, there were about 1.2 million nonfatal crimes at school, including 619,000 thefts and 629,800 violent crimes (from simple assault to serious violent crime). In 2009, 8% of students reported being threatened or injured with a weapon, such as a gun, knife, or club, on school property; 10% of male students in grades 9–12 reported being threatened or injured with a weapon in the past year, compared to 5% of female students (National Center for Education Statistics, 2010).

Incidents of Crime. During the 2007–08 school year, 85% of public schools recorded that one or more incidents of crime had taken place at school, amounting to an estimated 2 million crimes. This figure translates to a rate of 43 crimes per 1,000 public school students enrolled in 2007–08 (National Center for Education Statistics, 2010).

Eleven percent of public schools reported that student acts of disrespect for teachers other than verbal abuse took place on a daily or weekly basis. With regard to other discipline problems reported as occurring at least once a week, 6% of public schools reported student verbal abuse of teachers, 4% reported widespread disorder in the classroom, 4% reported student racial/ethnic tensions, and 3% reported student sexual harassment of other students. Interestingly, the percentage of students in grades 9–12 who reported that drugs had been offered, sold, or given to them decreased from 32% in 1995 to 23% in 2009 (National Center for Education Statistics, 2010).

In 2009, 31% of students in grades 9–12 reported they had been in a physical fight at least once during the previous 12 months, and 11% said they had been in a fight on school property. Between 1993 and 2009, the percentage of students who reported carrying a weapon at least one day anywhere during the past 30 days declined from 22% to 17%, and the percentage who reported carrying a weapon at least one day on school property also declined, from 12% to 6% (National Center for Education Statistics, 2010).

Fear and Avoidance. In 2007, approximately 5% of students ages 12–18 reported that they were afraid of attack or harm at school, and 3% reported that they were afraid of attack or harm away from school. Smaller percentages of white students (4%) and Asian students (2%) reported being afraid of attack or harm at school than their black (9%) and Hispanic (7%) peers. Seven percent of students ages 12–18 reported that they had avoided a school activity or one or more places in school in the previous 6 months because of fear of attack or harm (National Center for Education Statistics, 2010).

Threats to Teachers. During the 2007–08 school year, a greater percentage of teachers in city schools (10%) reported being threatened with injury than teachers in town schools (7%) or suburban or rural schools (6% each). A greater percentage of teachers in city schools (5%) and suburban schools (4%) reported being physically attacked, compared to teachers in rural schools (3%). A greater percentage of secondary school teachers (8%) reported being threatened with injury by a student than elementary school teachers (7%). However, a greater percentage of elementary school teachers (6%) reported being physically attacked than secondary school teachers (2%) (National Center for Education Statistics, 2010).

Disciplinary Action. Forty-six percent of public schools (approximately 38,500 schools) took at least one serious disciplinary action against a student during the 2007–08 school year. Of the 767,900 serious disciplinary actions taken, 76% were suspensions for 5 days or more, 19% were transfers to specialized schools, and 5% were removals with no services for the remainder of the school year. Although the overall percentage of public schools taking a serious disciplinary action declined between 1999–2000 (54%) and 2003–04 (46%), there has been no measurable change since then (National Center for Education Statistics, 2010).

While those are big numbers, in comparison to the 90 million children going to school over that 5-year span, it really isn't a lot—unless, of course, you or your child was one of those statistics or was subject to a microaggression that was never reported. Schools have long been prepared for disasters such as tornadoes and fires, but preparing for these kinds of disasters is relatively simple. The situational crisis that involves violence perpetrated by others on students or teachers is not. Schools are relatively safe places as far as lethality is concerned, with school-associated violent deaths representing less than 1% of all homicides that occur among school-age children (Anderson, Kaufman, & Simon, 2001).

However, that does not mean schools are absolutely safe havens for learning. Assaults, threats, intimidation, property destruction, bullying, and physical injury occur, and they occur fairly often. They do occur more often in large urban schools, and perhaps more alarmingly they occur more often in middle schools (Kaufman, Chen, & Choy, 2002), but they also occur in rural and suburban schools, and when the media portray those incidents the public is shocked and alarmed that such things could happen (Stewart & MacNeil, 2005).

It is not enough that schools must be prepared to deal with the direct effects of a crisis such as a suicide or homicide. School staff must also be prepared for a variety of ripple effects. How to deal with huge numbers of other students affected by the crisis? How to deal with critical and concerned parents? How to keep the school safe without trampling on the rights of individuals who may be under suspicion or alleged to have committed violent acts? How to deal with the media that may descend vulturelike on the school in the event of a crisis? In short, few if any institutions have as many issues to deal with when subjected to such a crisis as a school district does.

This chapter will not deal with the potential for terrorist attacks on a school or the effects of a terrorist attack on a community, but you should certainly not disabuse yourself of that notion. The parents, teachers, and students of School Number One in Beslan, Russia, know all too well what the ramifications are, and crisis interveners in the United States have certainly been thinking and planning for just such an occurrence (Dorn & Dorn, 2005; Giduck, 2005; Jimerson & Furlong, 2006; Thompson, 2004; Webber, Bass, & Yep, 2005).

The opening of this chapter sounds more like an introductory course in criminology than in crisis intervention. However, you are going to meet some principal players in school crisis intervention who don't look anything like your U.S. history teacher or school counselor, or at least have very different roles than teaching you about government branches or filling out course schedules.

Violence and Youth

Why have today's youth become more violent? Poor parenting practices, an ineffective welfare system, marginalization of minorities and other disenfranchised students, availability of high-powered automatic weapons, racism, the growth of gangs, violence in homes, bullying, lack of male role models, hate crimes, physical abuse, and drug involvement are but a few of the ills that spill over into schools (Blauvelt, 1998; Collier, 1999; Goldstein, 1991; Goldstein & Kodluboy, 1998; Grossman, 1995; Hazler, 1996; Miller, Martin, & Schamess, 2003; Pledge, 2003; Poland, 1994; Soriano, Soriano, & Jimenez, 1994).

Media Violence. Perhaps the most chilling reasons, though, are proposed by David Grossman in his book *On Killing* (1995, pp. 302–305). He proposes that there are three learning theories at work: Classical conditioning is at work when one sits comfortably in front of a movie or television screen watching mayhem and carnage while eating popcorn and drinking a soda. Operant conditioning thrives at video arcades, which provide immediate feedback and rewards for killing and maiming. Social learning enters the scene when a whole new series of role models, such as Freddy Krueger, do not end up saving the girl and kissing the horse, but slash the girl's throat and the horse's, too. Glorification of a thug culture interlaced with weapons, women as sexual objects, and drug use are cornerstones of contemporary music and media that cater to youth. Even the movie and television heroes are antiheroes and operate outside the law because the justice system is seen as weak and powerless.

It doesn't take a great deal of imagination after reading Grossman's book to understand why

Westside Middle School in Jonesboro, Arkansas, and Columbine High School in Littleton, Colorado, became killing fields, and why drive-by shootings occur at any number of other schools across the United States. There is a continuing debate on how much influence experiencing vicarious violence via television and video games has on the manifesting of that violence in children (Azar, 2010). We believe there shouldn't be. Brain imaging studies show a clear relationship between brain areas that regulate and govern emotion and images of violence (Bailey, West, & Anderson, 2011; Brummert-Lennings & Warburton, 2011; Englehardt et al., 2011; Hummer et al., 2010; Krahe & Moller, 2011; Krahe et al., 2011; Sestir & Bartholow, 2010). A large meta-analysis of violent media and aggression research by Anderson and his associates (2010) strongly suggest that exposure to violent video games is a causal risk factor for increased aggressive behavior. However, there are enough detractors (Ferguson, 2011; Ferguson et al., 2011; Ferguson & Kilburn, 2009, 2010) that the American Psychological Association reversed its 2005 (Price, 2007) stand that the research strongly suggested a link between violent media and aggressive behavior (Azar, 2010). As this chapter is being written, the powerful entertainment lobbies have essentially won out with a U.S. Supreme Court decision overturning a California law that prohibited selling M(mature)-rated video games to minors. It may be that there are mediating factors such as family domestic violence, competition, and different degrees of exposure (Zhao & Jiang, 2010), and older adolescents may not have as much reaction as younger ones (Bucolo, 2011), but the preponderance of research shows that the two correlate and almost any elementary school teacher can tell when students have been watching *South Park* the night before. In summary, while it cannot be said that media violence causes school shootings, Langman's (2009) in-depth examination of school shooters found that they often have a fascination with violent media and become obsessed with it (p. 8).

Modeling. Modeling is an extremely effective way to reinforce behavior. The field of counseling is a great example. Dr. James wants his students to understand empathic understanding. He first lectures his students on various techniques such as open-ended questions and reflection of feelings. The students ask questions, and a classroom discussion ensues. However, empathic understanding and the techniques that facilitate it have only been talked about, not demonstrated. So Dr. James models these techniques in real time in front of the students. The students watch him, ask questions, and then are turned loose to try the techniques out for themselves under his watchful eyes and tuned-in ears in the classroom. Modeling also facilitates violence. Peggy Noonan, columnist for the *Wall Street Journal*, put it well when she wrote, after watching the video of Seung-hui Cho, the Virginia Tech murderer, "We'll be seeing more of that from thousands of disaffected teenagers who watched and thought, 'Wow! I could do that! Boy, would that teach them a lesson. Everybody would know me then!'" (Noonan, 2007).

Cho's role models were Dylan Klebold and Eric Harris of Columbine High School infamy. Who will see Cho as a role model to emulate? The showing of Cho's tape by NBC and other networks over and over in the view of millions of children set him up as a role model for those children. Playing a violent video game such as *Grand Theft Auto*, putting "gangsta" pictures on MySpace, or watching videos of school shooters or slasher movies does not automatically make a child a schoolyard shooter. If that were true, every kid who played *Grand Theft Auto* would go on a murder spree. However, along with other contributing variables discussed later in this chapter, the potential for violence can grow until those biological, sociological, and psychological factors coalesce into a homicidal gestalt, and little Eddie Haskell turns into Freddy Krueger.

The lethality issues to be dealt with in this chapter include potential physical assault by gang members, bullies, the estranged violent student, and suicidal children. However, targeted violence against specific students is not the only crisis that schools face. In addition, natural disasters, terrorist assaults, drug abuse, physical and sexual abuse, medical emergencies, and classmate, parent, and teacher deaths are all seen as crises. Crisis in the context of a school, although similar to the definition in Chapter 1, has unique features because of the social structure of the school and the sense of community within the school (Allen et al., 2002). As such, a crisis affects more than one student. It has ripple effects that can tear at the very fabric of the school to the point of destabilizing it (Johnson, 2000, p. 18). Therefore, this chapter will also provide the basic elements of what a school crisis plan should entail as a best bet for prevention, intervention, and postvention, who the players are in that plan, and what their roles are when a crisis of any type strikes a school.

Gangs

Types of Gangs

Of all the other contributors to violent behavior, none appears to have the predictive validity and potential for violent behavior in high school as do gangs (Rainone et al., 2006). The 2009 FBI Gang Assessment reported about 20,000 gangs of different types in the United States with a total of more than 1 million members. They are not just the stereotypical Mafia or Hispanic drug cartels, and they operate from the inner city to the suburbs to rural areas to Indian reservations ("The Gang Threat," 2009). Twenty percent of public schools reported that gang activities had happened during 2007–08, and 3% reported that cult or extremist activities had happened during that school year (National Center for Education Statistics, 2010). There are basically five types of gangs that human services workers in school districts are likely to encounter.

Homegrown Copycats/Wannabes. There is more than enough media representation of gang members to let every student in the United States who has access to cable TV, movies, magazines, music, or the Internet set up a stereotypical Vicelords, Gangster Disciples, Crips, or Latin Kings–type gang (Goldstein & Kodluboy, 1998, p. 5; U.S. Office of Juvenile Justice and Delinquency Prevention, 1995). "Wannabe" status may make them more dangerous in their attempts to prove how tough and cool they are. Generally they are short-lived. Makeup is composed of any ethnic group resident in the population.

Homegrown Survivalist, Aryan Nation, Neo-Nazi, Extreme Right-Wingers. These gangs are based on political/religious philosophies inculcated by adults and in response to the perceived "browning" of America and the supposed threat that entails. They are often supported both financially and/or morally as "youth corps" by both local and national organizations. Members are typically related to or are friends of adults who espouse such views. They may be transitory or stable in terms of membership, depending on adult support available. They specifically target ethnic/racial minority groups for violence. They are almost always Caucasian and "Christian" (Goldstein, 1991, p. 24; Goldstein & Kodluboy, 1998, p. 7; U.S. Office of Juvenile Justice and Delinquency Prevention, 1995).

Transients from Megagangs. Offshoots of megagangs are started by gang members moved to supposedly "safe" rural havens by parents seeking to escape the problems of big-city crime or feeling extreme pressure from law enforcement agencies in their city of origin (Goldstein & Kodluboy, 1998, p. 7; U.S. Office of Juvenile Justice and Delinquency Prevention, 1995). Their children are already members of the gangs they try to escape. These transported gang members start their own gangs. Indian reservations receiving families out of big cities are a prime example of this transient population. Racial/ethnic makeup may be mixed, but these gangs are typically ethnic group or race based.

Megagangs Opening New Territory. Increased competition in large metropolitan areas forces gangs to seek new territory to sell their wares (mainly drugs). Interstate arteries and towns adjacent to them are primary targets because of ease of access (Goldstein, 1991, pp. 20–21; Goldstein & Kodluboy, 1998, p. 7). This is the most formidable type of gang organization. It has older adults who may derive their livelihood from its criminal enterprise. It has a clear hierarchy of members, sophisticated organizational plan and operating rules, large numbers, recruitment programs, financial backing, and the will to be very violent in pursuit of its interests. Racial/ethnic makeup of these gangs is predominately African American or Hispanic in the Midwest, but may be a variety of nationalities on the East or West Coasts. This is the stereotypical street gang of the media (U.S. Office of Juvenile Justice and Delinquency Prevention, 1995).

Smorgasbord Home Boys. Some small gangs are started for a variety of reasons, ranging from instrumental criminal behavior such as theft to expressive behavior such as hate crimes or responses to being perceived as social outcasts. The organizing themes of these gangs range from skinhead neo-Nazism to demonology and devil worship to auto theft to retaliation for perceived social injustices perpetrated on them. This gang type generally is transitory and short-lived, with small numbers of members. Depending on the type, it may avoid violence if theft is its major activity or may be extremely violent and sadistic if it is into racism, Satanism, or a response to social ostracism. It is mostly Caucasian in makeup (Goldstein, 1991, pp. 20–24; Goldstein & Kodluboy, 1998, p. 7; U.S. Office of Juvenile Justice and Delinquency Prevention, 1995).

Emergence of Suburban and Rural Gangs

Why have gangs or the threat of gang formation become problematic for suburban and rural areas? A variety of trends have emerged that make gang formation a probability for Opie in Mayberry, rural America. The development of diverse, multicultural communities in the United States will proceed at an accelerated rate in the 21st century, particularly in historically white farming communities of the Midwest (Goldstein & Kodluboy, 1998, pp. 63–91). We have generally not had a stellar history in welcoming and integrating newcomers in the United States who don't look, talk, act, and think like us, as witnessed by the contemporary debate over illegal immigrants. Cable television, the Internet, and other electronic information systems make the most pristine and rustic rural area a part of the global community. Glorification of violence and gangs through electronic media sends children who feel powerless against the world messages about how they can be powerful (Goldstein & Kodluboy, 1998, p. 7).

Chat rooms, websites, and e-mail provide gangs plenty of opportunity to talk to Opie. If Opie is feeling alone and powerless out on 1300 Country Road East, he is likely to talk back. All of the ills that assail dysfunctional families are as characteristic of suburban and rural families as they are of urban ones. Gang leaders are highly sensitive to these parentless, throwaway kids and, like Fagan in *Oliver Twist,* recruit them. The gang becomes a surrogate family (Grossman, 1995, pp. 303–305; Melton, 2001).

Gang Intervention/Prevention Programs

Although this book is about crisis intervention, the fact is that when dealing with gangs, prevention is far more likely to be effective than intervention. After a gang has taken root and grown, fear and intimidation become huge obstacles to constructive change. Changing gang members' attitudes about gang membership is anything but easy. Gang members typically fall into what are called "at-risk" student categories. By definition, "at risk" means that a young person is liable to be an academic or social failure when the potential for becoming a responsible and productive adult is limited by barriers at home, at school, or in the community (Fusick & Bordeau, 2004). At-risk students are truant; have trouble with the legal system; are characterized by impulsive behavior, self-doubts, anxiety, depression, drug use, and suicidal ideation; are poor learners; and have few bonds with the culture of the school. They are what Melton (2001) calls "phantom students" because, much like the Phantom of the Opera, they wear tough masks to hide their emotional scars and largely remain in the shadows of the school culture.

Because of the publicized school shootings in recent years, a great deal of interest has been generated in what are believed to be two of its root causes—at-risk students and bullying or being bullied. While not all at-risk students are gang members, many gang members are at-risk students, lost between the cracks and dropping out of school. Not all bullies are gang members, but the reverse is generally true, because bullies and gangs both gain power and control over others by fear, threat, and intimidation. Therefore, in discussing intervention methods with "gang" members, the same characteristics and procedures also apply to at-risk students and bullies. Violence prevention approaches are legion; they range from teaching students warning signs of impending student violence (Alvarez, 1999) to teaching body movement exercises for self-control (Kornblum, 2002). The following approaches have all been tried, with varying degrees of success, with children who make up the bulk of gang membership.

Counseling. Counseling, in the sense of having a continuing, person-centered, nonevaluative, nonjudgmental dialogue with a gang member, is one of the least effective intervention strategies (Lipsey, 1992). Given their past experiences with uncaring and punitive adults, alienated and disenfranchised gang members are suspicious and do not establish relationships easily. They are ultrasensitive to perceived threats and insults, and they are manipulative and reluctant to share information (Melton, 2001). John and Rita Sommers-Flanagan (1997) propose that challenging such kids is an excellent way to start establishing rapport and trust.

CW: So you don't want to be in here getting this counseling "crap." Is that about right?

Gangbanger: Yeah, that's right. I'm outta here.

CW: OK. I'll just call your probation officer, and he can make the arrangements for you to go to the Wilder Youth Facility if you don't want to do this. Now, you are adjudicated here for 12 sessions, but since you don't want to be here, I can see us doing this in, say, 6 sessions, if you are smart enough to catch onto this stuff and not give me a bunch of "crap," as you say, and work hard to get through this stuff. What's your choice?

Counseling that uses reality therapy (Glasser, 1965, 2000) and targets behavior and consequences of actions is more likely to be successful when gangbangers are constantly confronted with their actions and given choices as to what they want to do (Loeber et al., 1998; Sandhu, 2000). The same is true of victims.

Victim: (*Lucinda has been absent from school the last 3 days and is talking to the school counselor about her absences. Finally she breaks down sobbing and tells the counselor why.*) This is the fifth time the Rosebuds have taken my lunch money in the past 2 weeks, but they threatened to break my legs, and they can do that. I've seen Tina do that with a ball bat. She's crazy and scares me to death. They also told me not to snitch or they would hurt my little sister.

School Counselor: Lucinda, I'd really like to get Officer Bates in on this and have you tell him. It is not your fault that you are being mugged. You didn't ask for it, and you don't deserve it. It isn't normal, and it isn't OK. You don't have to face this on your own. I and other people will help you.

Victim: No way! No cops! I could get killed.

School Counselor: I understand that it's scary, and there are some real risks. We will keep this confidential, and no one will know but the three of us. But you are not the only one who is getting mugged. You can make a choice about helping to stop this. I have an idea you are pretty tired of getting assaulted. School should be a place to come and have fun with your friends and learn. It is not a place you should be afraid to come to. Officer Bates and I are working with a lot of teachers and other kids. If enough kids like you say "That's enough!" we can stop this. I won't force you to see the school police officer or even tell him. I think your parents need to know about this. If you want to have your parents come in and talk, we can do that too. The choice is yours.

The counselor acknowledges the danger to Lucinda as real. Attempts to coerce a student into informing are fraught with ethical peril and quite literally can be dangerous to the student if a great deal of care is not taken to keep the information confidential until the school and law enforcement are ready to act. However, if the counselor feels that the threat to Lucinda is high (see the definitions of low, medium, and high threats later in the chapter), her parents should be informed and so should the police.

School Resource Officer. The crisis worker **LO5** attempts to bring the school resource police officer (SRO) into the crisis because multidisciplinary school pupil personnel service teams that involve the SRO are critically important to stopping threatening and intimidating behavior (James, Logan, & Davis, 2011; O'Toole, 2003; Welsh & Domitrovich, 2006). Police in the schools can do much more than direct after-school traffic and monitor ball games. SROs go through a good deal of training beyond the initial police academy (National Association of School Resource Officers, 2011). Coordinating intelligence between the police department and the school, working conjointly with school human services workers in gang prevention programs, helping students problem-solve, finding resources and making referrals, deterring violence, obtaining information about illegal activities, role modeling, and mentoring are proactive measures that integrate police officers into the fabric of the school (Dogutas, 2008; Finn, 2006; Finn et al., 2005; Italiano, 2001; James, Logan, & Davis, 2011; Petersen, 2008; Vancleave, 2008).

If you read any of the statistics at the beginning of this chapter, it should be apparent why SROs are in school buildings. They are there not only to preserve the peace, but also to provide support to troubled students by building rapport with them, serving as empathic listeners, and eliciting information. As such they are excellent conduits to provide information to school officials that might not otherwise be forthcoming (James, Logan, & Davis, 2011). Because many SROs, such as Officer Davis whom you are about to meet, have Crisis Intervention Team training to deal with the mentally ill and emotionally disturbed, they make excellent first-line interventionists—particularly when the presence of an authority figure is needed with out-of-control students (James, Logan, & Davis, 2011). We strongly urge that human services workers and school administrators incorporate these police officers as part of a comprehensive pupil personnel services team that deals with violent and potentially violent students, because what they do works (Johnson, 1999).

Meet school resource and Crisis Intervention Team (CIT) officer Scott Davis of the Montgomery County, Maryland, Police Department (S. Davis, personal communication, February 18, 2007). Officer Davis is responsible for policing a high school, a middle school, and three elementary schools. Officer Davis's day starts with roll call at 6 A.M. He patrols the neighborhood and keeps an eye out for people or activities that don't belong and other potential problems. This past month one of those problems included a very large gang fight that brought a number of police officers to the scene to break up the melee.

Because those involved are "his kids," he takes a personal interest in the incident. He follows up with those who were arrested and looks for any others who might have been involved. Occasionally during the day he will hop in his cruiser and look for truants. He spends about 75% of his time at the high school and 20% at the middle school, with drop-in visits to his three elementary schools. His first task of the day is to meet with the high school principal in the morning, go over any potential problems that might be occurring before school, and greet the students as they come in the front door. Parents come to his office to talk about problems their kids are having. During the day he checks out a number of students who have been having problems and promotes his Boy Scout Police Explorer program.

At first glance his job appears pretty humdrum, but what isn't apparent is that Officer Davis is putting his considerable CIT skills to use every day with "humdrum" stuff and using the same skills when things are boiling over. Laura is 17 years old and a runaway. A social worker has been called to the school and is attempting to take her back to a bad home situation. Officer Davis has personal knowledge of the home because he has responded to a disturbance call there. Laura's mother is a drug addict and long gone from the home. Laura tried to hit her father with a brick in one argument, so it is clear that home is not workable. As Officer Davis makes the scene, tensions are rising between Laura and the social worker, who is threatening to have Laura arrested.

Officer Davis: (*in a calm but authoritative voice*) All right, let's just everybody cool off! First off, you can't have her arrested for a status offense. It's clear home isn't working real well, so Laura, let's you and me go to my office and talk about what's going on and what you think needs to happen.

As Laura explains her situation, Officer Davis asks numerous open-ended questions to allow her to ventilate. He finds out she has a drinking problem, but only occasionally uses others drugs. Home is intolerable, but she does come to school. He also finds out she is bipolar but not taking her medication because of the side effects.

Officer Davis: OK, let's try this. How about going to the crisis center with me. I've got some friends there who might be able to help both in regard to the medication and a place to stay. It may not be exactly what you want, but it beats going home and running away again, 'cause that doesn't seem

to be working real well for you. I'll stay there with you and see what they can do. How about it?

Laura: Hey! You're kinda different. Most cops push people around. OK.

Officer Davis takes her to the crisis center, where she is evaluated and indeed prescribed different medication. She is also placed in a short-term foster home until her medication can be regulated.

Laura: (*a month later, in school, waves to Officer Davis*) Hey! Remember me?

Officer Davis: Sure, Laura. How are things going?

Laura: Not real great, but I'm getting by. I went back home. The old man and I are sorta getting along.

Officer Davis: Hey! You're here, aren't you! Best place you can be! Here you've got options. The more you're here, the less you're at home. Thought about any after-school activities or sports? Get your grades up, and pretty soon the only time you are at home is to eat and sleep.

Officer Davis enthusiastically reinforces Laura for making it to school. Laura may not be a huge success story, but at least she is in school, has made contact with somebody, and feels like somebody is really interested in her. These are little victories in the everyday grind of working in a school, but added up they can win wars for hearts and minds in working with troubled kids. But Officer Davis's life is about to take an exciting turn, and we will return to him later in the chapter.

Guidance Programs. Passive, lecture-based guidance programs that target fear arousal, moral appeal, and self-esteem building have not proven to be highly effective (Gottfredson, Gottfredson, & Skroban, 1998) in dealing with gangs or bullying. Active guidance programs that provide direct student involvement through modeling, role play, and behavioral rehearsal in areas such as anger management, bullying, conflict resolution, and peer mediation are more helpful in tackling gang and bullying issues (Beane, 1999; Coloroso, 2003; Davis & Davis, 2003; DuRant et al., 1996; Embry et al., 1996; Feindler & Scalley, 1998; Gottfredson, Gottfredson, & Skroban, 1998; Hausman, Pierce, & Briggs, 1996; Hazler, 1996; Horne, Bartolomucci, & Newman-Carson, 2003; Larson, 1994; Lupton-Smith et al., 1996; Sexton-Radek, 2004). To be effective, these programs must not be a one-shot session but should have continuous behavioral rehearsal and feedback sessions built into them. They must also have clear, easily implemented practices, be intense, and continue long enough with follow-up sessions to reinforce and change some very resistant behaviors in both victims and victimizers (Gottfredson, Gottfredson, & Skroban, 1998; Sullivan, 2011; Willard, 2007; Zins et al., 1994).

Peer Counseling/Peer Mediation. One of the very *worst* approaches is to use peer crisis workers who are gang members or bullies, or for the crisis worker to attempt to run homogeneous counseling groups composed entirely of gang members or bullies (Goldstein & Kodluboy, 1998, pp. 107–110). The gang members or bullies will take over the group. However, there is some evidence that heterogeneous counseling groups, those in which students are chosen from a representative cross-section of the ethnic, social, and economic strata of the school, are useful in helping gang members look at alternative solutions and develop new behaviors. There is also some evidence that a peer counseling/leader program that provides mentoring, tutoring, and support functions keeps at-risk and marginalized students out of trouble and in school (Allen, 1996; Cohen, Kulik, & Kulik, 1982; Fatum & Hoyle, 1996; Scruggs, Mastropieri, & Richter, 1985).

Peer mediation (Cassinerio & Lane-Garon, 2006; Day-Vines et al., 1996; Schrumpf, Crawford, & Bodine, 1997) is another approach that uses students to deal with other students who have anger problems. While it may seem that the last thing a gang member or bully would be willing to submit to is peer mediation, it should be remembered that peer pressure and the need to conform exert a tremendous amount of pressure on all students.

Further, if a student is unwilling to submit to peer mediation, he or she is ratcheting up the consequences by essentially saying, "I am not willing to try to work this out." Institutional use of these programs should start in elementary schools and be continuously carried through middle and high schools so there is a clear, consistent, and longitudinal approach to providing support to alienated, angry, and disenfranchised students. In fact, elementary schools are the best place to stop bullying, harassment, prejudice, and other forms of problem behavior.

Anger Management. A variety of anger management techniques have been developed to work with adolescents and children (Davis, 2004; Efrid, 2013; Feindler & Weisner, 2006; Nelson, Finch, & Ghee, 2006; Smith, Larson, & Nuckles, 2006). Most of these approaches involve skill training and behavior rehearsal in prosocial behaviors, the social (reputation) and financial costs (jail and fines), teaching students cognitive techniques that cool off their hot cognitions about stressful situations. While anger management approaches are effective in reducing abusive verbal and physical responses (Humphrey & Brooks, 2006; Rosenberg, 2004; Sharp & McCallum, 2005; Smith, Larson, & Nuckles, 2006), the problem is their pervasiveness and the environmental variables from both the home and the street that oftentimes see control of anger as weakness instead of strength.

After-School and Community Outreach Programs. As Goldstein and Kodluboy (1998, p. 126) state, "Playing on a basketball team means you are not stealing a car while you're at the game, but it does not prevent you from stealing a car before or after the game." Research indicates that although such after-school programs may have recreational value, they are not highly effective in delinquency reduction. However, programs such as the Boys and Girls Clubs of America that have a comprehensive curriculum integrating recreation with academic and social skill building, and career and personal counseling, do have high potential for stopping delinquency and reducing gang activity (Sherman et al., 1997).

National Violence Prevention Programs. When violence reduction in gangs have been tried, a major problem has been that gang membership is a proximity and affiliation motivator where in the culture and the expectancies of the gang promote and encourage violent behavior (Van Brunt, 2015, p. 126). There are many national and commercially available anger management and violence reduction programs available that specifically target elementary, middle, and secondary school levels (Farrell & Camou, 2006). These programs have ranged from violence prevention curriculums (Prothrow-Stith, 1987) to computer-based conflict resolution (Bosworth et al., 1996) to making physical changes such as brightly lit hallways, limiting access to lockers and graffiti off walls (California Department of Education, 2002), and enlisting coaches in violence prevention programs (Jamie et al., 2015). The U.S. Department of Health and Human Services published a highly negative review of school violence programs that a lot of money had been spent on and pessimistically noted that nothing much in the way of manualized programs worked in reducing youth violence (USDHHS, 2001). One of the major problems that Farrell and Camou (2006) report is that little rigorous, evidence-based research has been done that could provide valid information on antiviolence programs in schools that actually work. While this research was reported 10 years ago, as of yet, little in the way of change has been reported. Pretty clearly, programs that appear to work need to have all the trapping of rigorous research such as control groups, reliable and valid assessment devices, and the ability to be replicated. Even then a one-size-fits-all approach is probably not attainable. It is more likely that successful programs will deal with specific populations and specific conditions and environments within which that population operates (Farrell & Camou, 2006).

Schools. Schools and school districts are not without culpability in the growth and development of gangs, bullying, and violence. Megaschools and megadistricts limit many students' participation in the academic and extracurricular activities of the school; because of the large numbers of students and the criteria that restrict who can participate, relatively few students in very large schools do take part in such activities as band or sports or even the chess team (Goldstein & Kodluboy, 1998, pp. 21–22). Schools can play an active role in the prevention and intervention of gang activity. Schools need to set a number one priority of inclusiveness, nurturance, school as community, and the philosophy that no student is left behind either academically and socially (Cypress & Green, 2002). This concept is particularly important in schools where heterogeneity (diversity) of race and culture is the norm. Fairness and consistency for everybody, with open communication among stakeholders, are essential.

Communication flows not only outward from the administration but inward to them. There must be fair rules and clear sanctions that are enforced evenly in school (Goldstein & Kodluboy, 1998, p. 22). There should be an expectation of success. The total philosophy of the system, starting in kindergarten and working its way up through high school, should not be "If you graduate," but "When you graduate" (Allen, 1996).

Gangs grow in a vacuum. A school is asking for trouble if it has unmonitored areas, such as parking lots and bathrooms; dismisses rumors about planned violence or weapons, drugs, or other contraband brought onto school grounds; excuses the violent behavior of "good kids"; or sees intervention in any of the foregoing areas as "not my job" (Dykeman, 1999; Remboldt, 1994). A school reduces violence when its staff and teachers have high expectations, care about and are involved with their students in inclusive ways, enforce rules and procedures, maintain buildings and keep classrooms neat and clean, and believe it's everyone's job to do so (Stephens, 1997).

School safety goes beyond high-tech security systems. School safety is a sense of not only physical well-being but psychological well-being as well. Schools can maintain or take back their turf when they cooperatively develop mission statements, share decisions about school policies, maintain buildings and remove graffiti, organize gang awareness and prevention programs, promote parental and student involvement, allow zero tolerance of bullying, harassment, or gang recruitment, and have school authorities that declare, "This is our turf, not yours" (Blauvelt, 1998; Brock, Sandoval, & Lewis, 1996). Instead of asking, "How do I know which students will shoot next?" the question might be, "What is the faculty doing to build quality relationships with students and open lines of communication, and to develop the type of climate that will foster a wholesome sense of self in each individual as well as respect for others?" (Cypress & Green, 2002). But preventing gang growth and violence is a task that is much too great for a single school counselor, social worker, psychologist, teacher, or principal—or even a school system.

The Community. It takes everybody in the community working as a team to combat gangs. Cooperation with other agencies such as the courts, corrections, probation, parole, mental health, public assistance, and housing is crucial. Civic and religious organizations must provide personnel and financial support. City and county government must be willing to put in place ordinances that say there is zero tolerance for this kind of behavior and back it up with law and code enforcement (Bemak & Keys, 2000; Miller, Martin, & Schamess, 2003; Schaefer-Schiumo & Ginsberg, 2003).

Louvre (2008) makes a compelling argument for integrating community action in school crises. She is puzzled why there is so little outrage over the 97% of child murders that occur outside of school walls every year. Louvre argues persuasively that rebuilding trust and a sense of community in a school after a crisis requires the total participation of the community. That is what SARA (scanning, analysis, response, and assessment; Eck & Spelman, 1987), the Justice Department's model for combating gangs, is about. SARA is not about getting rid of gangs in one day. It is about little victories, such as getting loiterers off school property and cleaning up graffiti. It gets all of the stakeholders in having a safe community involved in continuous and ongoing linkages that set goals and generate plans to achieve the continuous little victories that make SARA so effective. Turf guarding and political boundaries have no place in a fight to eradicate gangs (Roth, 2000). This approach benefits communities by not letting gangs gain a further foothold in the community, resulting in improved performance by students who went to school in fear each day; decreased teacher stress and burnout; decreased need for security staff/equipment; fewer injuries and lives lost; and most important, renewed freedom in the school and the community. You can find further information about SARA on this book's website (www.cengage.com /counseling/james).

Bullying

Probably no other topic has received as **LO6** much attention in the school counseling literature and at conferences in the past 10 years as face-to-face bullying and, more recently, cyberbullying (Chamberlin, 2006; Holladay, 2010; Howe et al., 2013; Munsey, 2012; Paterson, 2010; Sabella, 2010; Suniti Bhat, Chang, & Linscott, 2010)—its causes (Crothers & Levinson, 2004; Espelage, Bosworth, & Simon, 2000), effects (Carney, 2008; Sullivan, 2011; Willard, 2007), and intervention strategies (Bauman, 2011; Burnham, 2011; Burrow-Sanchez et al., 2011; Hicks, 2015; Leo, 2010; Newman, Horne, & Bartolomucci, 2000; Paterson, 2011; Ratts, Ayers, & Bright, 2009; Saufler, 2010; Shallcross, 2013; Sullivan, 2011; Willard, 2007). That is particularly true with regard to gay, lesbian, bisexual, and transgendered (LGBT) students (Callahan, 2001; Jackson & Harding, 2010; Jones Farrelly & Robles-Fernandez, 2011; McCollum, 2010; Windmeyer, 2009), who have little power or support systems in most K–12 buildings. Because of bullying, LGBT youth may greatly increase their risk of depression and suicide (Russell et al., 2011), and that becomes even more profound when cyberbullying occurs (Wiederhold, 2014).

The crisis dimensions this problem has taken on culminated in a White House Conference on Bullying in March 2011. That conference sought to establish replicable training and intervention programs that were cost effective and time manageable for teachers already stretched thin (Munsey, 2011). The fact that a number of elementary, middle, and high school students have committed suicide because of bullying and cyberbullying in the past few years has gotten the attention of the federal government and caused the Department of Education to assist in bully prevention. In December 2010 a technical assistance best practice memo highlighting comprehensive state antibullying laws was sent to state school officers and governors. The Office for Civil Rights at the Department of Education and the Department of Justice are working together and will vigorously pursue complaints of bullying and harassment. This information and much more is available at www .stopbullying.gov. (U.S. Department of Health and Human Services, 2015). The Office of Safe and Drug-Free Schools will offer competitive grants to measure safety by surveying students and then providing federal funds those schools identified through as having the greatest need of intervention. Schools will also be required to make the "safety scores" public so they can be held accountable for performance in providing a safe environment (Jennings, 2011). Besides the veritable tsunami of commercial and professional literature on bullying prevention, the U.S. Department of Education (2015) has a two-part tool kit available for free to anybody who wants to start an antibully program training toolkit at www.ed.gov/blog/tag /bullying.

Bullying and intimidation affect large numbers of students. One study found that 77% of junior and senior high school students in a Midwestern U.S. school survey reported being a victim of bullies (Espelage & Swearer, 2003). In 2007, 32% of U.S. students ages 12–18 reported having been bullied at school that year. In this survey, 21% of students said they had been made fun of; 18% reported being the subject of rumors; 11% said they were pushed, shoved, tripped, or spit on; 6% said they were threatened with harm; 5% said they were excluded from activities on purpose; and 4% said that someone had tried to make them do things they did not want to do or that their property had been destroyed on purpose (National Center for Education Statistics, 2010).

Bullying can take a number of forms (Shallcross, 2013). It can be direct, such as hitting, kicking, or pushing a person. It can be verbal, such as malicious teasing, threatening, or taunting. It can be social aggression, where the leader of a clique influences the group to target a specific individual. It can be overt or covert and involve physical or verbal aggression or more subtle approaches such as rumors, gossip, and social exclusion (Bauman, 2011, p. 18; Shallcross, 2013). It can be relational wherein individuals who have been friends cease to be so, and in their acrimony, maliciously attempt to exclude that person from social activities and spread disparaging rumors about the other person (Shallcross, 2013).

Langman (2009) defines bullying as having three components: First, the bully has more power than the victim, because of larger size, greater strength, or greater numbers (clique or gang). Second, bullying involves intimidation through threats, to the point that victims are made to fear for their safety. Third, bullying involves a pattern of behavior, not a onetime push (p. 12).

Bullies are proactive aggressors who use aggression methodically, subtly, and with increasing intensity until they achieve their desired goal of personal gain of some kind. Bullying is preplanned and calculated to instill fear and gain control over others with little remorse for its effects on them (Hubbard et al., 2001; McAdams & Schmidt, 2007; Vitaro & Brendgen, 2005; Vitaro, Brendgen, & Tremblay, 2002). An entire school can be affected by systematic bullying behaviors. If left unchecked, an atmosphere of fear, mistrust, and low morale, along with the academic and behavioral problems that go with a hostile work environment, can create a negative atmosphere for all students (Hoover & Hazler, 1991). Finally, if left unchecked, bullying as a form of aggression can lead to lethal behavior from either the bully or the bullied.

Cyberbullying

Cyberbullying, simply defined, means using technology to harass, humiliate, or threaten someone (Holladay, 2010). Cyberbullying is different from face-to-face bullying. In face-to-face bullying, the effects are immediately known, and the victim knows who the bully is and who his or her supporters are. Cyberbullying can be far more insidious because the bully can remain unknown (Shallcross, 2013). Effects can also be more disastrous because the messages can go to an audience literally in the millions (Bauman, 2011, p. 19).

There are eight types of cyberbullying (Bauman, 2011, p. 57; Willard, 2007, p. 2):

Flaming refers to angry offensive language. "You are a shit-brained hootchy mama slut."

Harassment is the technology version of discriminatory or hostile behavior toward someone based on gender, race, religion, disability, or sexual orientation. "Jay is a limp-wristed fag gimpy Yid."

Denigration is sending or posting defaming information about someone. "Jennifer Sonstegarrd is screwing every boy on the hockey team . . . and the coach too!"

Masquerading is using someone else's identity to send messages that are rude and inappropriate. "Leslie, you stink! Literally! Get some feminine hygiene products. Signed Phewwwie! Joey" (a guy Leslie is interested in, but so is Devonne who actually sent the e-mail).

Outing *or* **trickery** is a way of getting people to reveal personal information that might then be used against them. "Leslie, I really have been thinking you're the fox of the history class. I wonder if you'd like to go out for a pizza and movie Saturday night. INTERESTED A LOT, JOEY." When Leslie replies, Devonne then puts it out on the net: "Leslie thinks Joey is going out with HER on Saturday night. How delirious and out of touch with reality is she?"

Social exclusion is a means of deliberately excluding someone from a buddy list, chat room, discussion board, or game. "How many of you want Leslie off the discussion board and out of the game? Everybody who does, vote 'aye.'"

Cyberstalking is the electronic version of pursuing a person who is not interested in the personal attention he or she is receiving, but receiving it anyway. "Don't think I don't know when you come on the discussion board, because I do, and I am going to be here watching and listening."

Cyberthreats are clearly meant to evoke fear and imply that danger is imminent. "It'll be dark by the time you get out of cheerleader practice and this is the night you always walk home. Have a nice night . . . and . . . oh . . . I'll be watching . . . and waiting."

The crisis worker's intervention with these bullies is difficult and fraught with legal and ethical issues (Stone, 2015). Some school counselors and other human services workers in schools have set up websites where students can contact them to deal with bullying and other personal issues in the virtual world that students inhabit. However, because of fear of sexual predators, the Missouri legislature attempted to make it illegal for any person employed by a school to have an individual dialogue with a student over the net. A judge ruled against the law as unconstitutional, but it is a slippery slope and workers can put themselves at risk legally and professionally. The better road to follow, at least at this point, is having clear district policies in place in regard to the use of the Internet (Willard, 2007). Those policies should include the following (pp. 195–265):

1. A cyberbullying/cyberthreat and face-to-face bullying review policy for threatening materials sent over the Internet or hard copies found at school.
2. School actions and options that are taken in regard to misuse of the Internet by students.
3. Incident and report forms that track and record behavior so that a chain of continuity can be built.
4. A comprehensive district plan to assess cyber use and misuse.
5. Student needs assessment as to bullying and bullying prevention effectiveness.
6. Teacher needs assessment as to understanding their role in student bullying.
7. District use policy for the Internet and agreement signed by students and parents that includes netiquette guidelines, to be given to and discussed with both students and parents.

Systemic Intervention. To sum this up, just doing the foregoing and calling it "done" won't work. There has to be initiative across the board within the whole community and that particularly includes parents. Zero tolerance and one day "Stop Bullying!" programs don't work (Novotney, 2014). The school's philosophy and policy have to fit with their antibullying efforts or it is useless. There also has to be regular evaluation of the program and updating of it or it will wither and die (Burnham, 2011; Novotney, 2014; Sullivan, 2011). That evaluation should include (Professional School Counseling, 2012):

1. School-wide intervention policies that include peer groups that create a critical mass whereby bullying is absolutely "uncool."
2. Continuous assessment of bullying and dissemination of that data to parents.
3. Gain staff and parent support that ranges from bus drivers to superintendents and community organizations and civic clubs.
4. Form a group to coordinate the antibullying campaign and train them on how to do it.
5. Increase adult supervision in hot spots where it is likely to occur and enforce school rules on bullying and apply them consistently.

Ttofi and Farrongton's (2011) meta-analysis of school-based programs to reduce bullying found that when the foregoing points are implemented both bullying and victimization decrease by 20%. Note that the best they could do was only 20%. Intervention with bullies first and foremost should include a strict policy against harassment and intimidation (Kerr, 2009, p. 112), and that policy should be clearly spelled out with no loopholes (McAdams & Schmidt, 2007; Willard, 2007).

Remediation. Once a bully has been identified, Sullivan (2011) proposes three approaches to remediation. First is punishment, which can range from dealing with the criminal justice system to expulsion, detention, or other disciplinary procedures. We believe Sullivan's approach should be a last resort because it essentially has no remediation but is used solely to maintain the safety and integrity of the affected students.

Second is a consequences approach. Bullies are generally masters of manipulation and rationalization, so the worker needs to be wary of getting into debates with them or accepting excuses for their aggressive behavior. Bullies don't change overnight, so positive reinforcement needs to be used cautiously and only when prosocial behavior has started to occur consistently (McAdams & Schmidt, 2007). While negative sanctions are involved, they are more educative than punitive in nature. Consequences may be attending an anger management group or working with special education students if that was the target population of the bully; behavioral contracting social skills training can be used (Burnham, 2011).

Third is a feelings approach that focuses on stopping the dehumanization and discounting of target individuals and focuses on building empathy for one's fellow students. Bullies may develop considerable skill in avoiding the consequences of their actions, but have much more trouble when the focus is on feelings generated by their hurtful behaviors, so that bullies begin to comprehend that there may be consequences when others feel victimized (McAdams & Schmidt, 2007).

Joy Burnham and her associates (2010) have developed an innovative virtual world program model that the worker can use with both bullies and bullied students. Scenarios can be set up to teach different kinds of responding skills, hopefully making the bully aware that there are better alternatives and also teaching the bullied student how to respond more assertively.

Fulton (2015) proposes that separating boys from girls when conducting bully prevention programs is important because males and females experience bullying differently and a one-size-fits-all approach doesn't work. In the first lesson, she uses different film clips for boys and girls to demonstrate male and female bully types. In the second lesson she discusses role players such as the bully, sidekick, supporter, disengaged onlooker, possible defender, champion, and target in gender-specific ways. Lesson three focuses on becoming aware of the behavioral impact of bullying and also focuses on gossip and rumors for females. Males learn that teasing can be turned quickly to bullying, and "just only joking" is a rationalization of bad behavior that gets reframed by asking them if "just joking" is going to make the target's hurt go away. Lesson four focuses on actions of the supporters, disengaged onlookers, possible defenders, and champions. For both boys and girls, these roles are examined and specific strategies are discussed that could help target and combat the bullying behavior. An addition for females is a card game that ends up in the exclusion of one member and then the effects of the exclusion are processed with the whole group.

Bauman (2011) believes that with minor bullying cases brief solution-focused counseling can help both victims and bullies. This approach looks at bullying events as exceptions rather than the norm. It builds on both the victim's and the bully's self-identified strengths and develops strategies for similar situations in the future. For more severe cases she believes support groups can be effective. Supporters of the victim, other individuals involved in the incident, and the main perpetrator can come together to agree on a support plan for the victim. Bauman proposes for the most serious cases that a restorative justice program be undertaken. First the victim is allowed to express how he or she can be helped. Then the bully has the option of coming up with a plan to meet the victim's needs in trying to make amends. There is a prescribed procedure and a very formalized structure as to what and when things are done, which most likely takes some additional training.

Glasser (1969) believes that classroom meetings that target real-time school and peer problems are an excellent vehicle for bringing a great deal of peer consensus and pressure into play on problems such as the Rosebuds' strong-arm tactics. Once the majority of students in a school or a classroom decide that a particular behavior is "uncool," it tends to diminish very quickly. The major problem with bullying is that bystanders do not speak up. Mobilizing the masses stops bullying and intimidation in their tracks (Charach, Pepler, & Zeigler, 1995). Further, by using the democratic, participatory process of Glasser's classroom

meetings to problem-solve, students come to feel empowered and are able to stand up to bullying and intimidating behaviors (Glasser, 1969). Having students write out experiences with bullying can help make it safe for them to start talking about it.

School Counselor: (*Starting a classroom meeting with a sixth-grade class. The objective is to start shining a very bright light on the strong-arm tactics of the Rosebuds, but the counselor does not specifically mention them by name. Indeed, there are two probable gang members in the room.*) I want you all to write down four stories about bullying, using the following instructions.

1. Describe a time when someone's words or behavior hurt you.
2. Describe a time when you said or did something to hurt another person.
3. Describe a time when you saw or heard bullying but didn't do anything about it.
4. Describe a time when you saw or heard bullying and either got help or tried to stop it.

After the students finish writing their stories and share them with the group, the school counselor opens up a discussion centered on how students felt as they heard different stories. What did they think about what they heard? What would they do? And what would the consequences be if they did do something or changed what they did (Beane, 1999, p. 22)? Once students have started openly discussing threatening and intimidating behaviors, the counselor can use the hallmark of the classroom meeting and reality therapy, making a commitment (Glasser, 1969) to make their school a safer and more friendly place by pledging to do so and writing down specifically how that is going to happen (Newman, Horne, & Bartolomucci, 2000, p. 123). There are a number of effective antibullying programs, and if handled correctly, they can cut bullying and the potential violence that goes with it.

Finally, Paterson (2011) summarizes a number of researchers and practitioners in advocating for bullies to get counseling. Many of these bullies have themselves been bullied and need empathy and support as they themselves struggle with the effects of bullying. It may also be that while bullies see their approach as making them powerful, their thinking is distorted and will invariably get them in deeper trouble. As such, cognitive interventions that reframe their distorted notions of how they obtain and hold power over others may be effective. The problem is that for both offender and victim, if things don't straighten out and get better they run the risk of falling into the next section—and those are the lethal students who make headlines.

The Estranged Violent Juvenile Offender

The U.S. Department of Education (Dwyer, Osher, & Warger, 1998) has an excellent booklet that deals with safe schools in a general way. The booklet specifically mentions the school counselor as one of the lead professionals in helping prevent violence but says little about the specifics of the counselor's role, or the role of any other human services worker for that matter. Although gang violence is a major component of violence perpetrated by and among school-age children and is a major contributor to violence perpetrated by what Loeber and associates (1998) call the serious violent juvenile offender (SVJO), recent school shootings and subsequent homicides and injuries have been perpetrated by juveniles who do not typically fall into the "gang" SVJO category. The purpose of this section is to examine these different, potentially violent juveniles in regard to their psychological profile, screening mechanisms to detect them, and counseling methods to uncover their violent thoughts before those thoughts turn into action.

Peter Langman (2009) has written an excellent in-depth book on school shooters. He believes that most school shooters share some psychological symptoms. He further believes they fall within three general trait categories: psychopathic, psychotic, or traumatized. We believe that these three categories encompass what we call the EVJO. The term *estranged* violent juvenile offenders (EVJOs) is chosen because these juveniles typically are separated from their peers in distinctive ways and harbor a great deal of enmity toward their peers or the school system. We believe these individuals are distinct from their equally lethal SVJO counterparts-gang members. In contrast to a gang culture, in which violence is generated in order to bind its members together in perpetuation of the gang's growth and stature, the EVJO is typically isolated and has no allegiances unless to a very few others who are also experiencing the same estrangement. EVJOs can be partitioned into two major categories, those who are mentally ill and those who are not. Langman's (2009) two categories of psychopathic and psychotic shooter would most nearly fall under our mentally ill EVJO category, and his traumatized shooter would fall under our not mentally ill EVJO

LO7

category. Although it could be argued that anyone who would shoot a number of his fellow students is "crazy," that does not necessarily make him mentally ill under the American Psychiatric Association's (2013) DSM-5 classification system. Therefore, it is also important to discriminate between EVJOs who are and are not mentally ill because of differences in profiles, screening, and intervention. Although we do not arbitrarily exclude the potential for females in this group, the preponderance of offenders will be male. As a result, we will use the male gender to describe the potential offender.

A Comparison of Traits, Characteristics, and Behaviors of SVJOs and EVJOs

The following traits, characteristics, and behaviors have been compiled from a number of published sources and interviews with human services workers who deal with both the SVJO and EVJO (Carney et al., 1999; Corder et al., 1976; Cunningham & Davis, 1999; Duncan & Duncan, 1971; Dwyer, Osher, & Warger, 1998; Fein et al., 2002; Galatzen-Levy, 1993; Hardwick & Rowton-Lee, 1996; James & Dorner, 1999; Lempp, 1990; Levis, 1992; Loeber, 1990; Marohn et al., 1982; Myers & Mutch, 1992; National School Safety Center, 1998; O'Toole, 2003; Sage & Dietz, 1994; Sloan, 1988; Vossekuil et al., 2002; Webster & Wilson, 1994; Zagar et al., 1990). These characteristics fall within what the FBI's Critical Incident Response Group and the National Center for the Analysis of Violent Crime call the four-pronged assessment model that evaluates the likelihood of carrying out a threat of violence. The four-pronged assessment model considers the personality of the student, family dynamics, school dynamics, and social dynamics (O'Toole, 2003).

Understand that there are serious moral, ethical, and legal implications of attempting to label potentially violent students (Simmons, 2000). A heated debate rages on whether an accurate profile of a school shooter exists. There is a belief that such profiles are overinclusive, biased, stigmatizing, and can potentially violate the student's constitutional rights (Bailey, 2001; Reddy et al., 2001; Vossekuil et al., 2000, 2002). Mulvey and Cauffman (2001) argue that such profiling is not only unproven, but has limited usefulness and often does more harm than good, particularly when a false positive identification is made and the student becomes labeled as a "homicidal maniac."

Langman's (2009) profiling of infamous school shooters in the last 15 years is an eye-opener in regard to some of the stereotypical myths that make for good media sound bites. While the characteristics that follow may be present to some degree in all school shooters, it would be a severe mistake to suppose that any one factor, such as bullying, being a loner, or having a fascination with violence and guns, is *the* factor that causes students to become homicidal, nor is it very likely that the student will have all of the characteristics that profile the school shooter. It is much more reasonable to say that each school shooter has a mix of these potentially lethal ingredients that, when combined in the right amounts and cooked for the right amount of time in the right ecosystem, turn into a recipe for lethality.

Thus, there seems to be enough evidence that when these traits and characteristics are combined with specific behaviors that indicate an increased threat level, they are at least a preliminary screening device that crisis workers can employ if reasonable judgment and care are used. On the other side of the dilemma, to not recognize that there is a potential threat is also professionally unethical and morally indefensible. More ominously, there are growing legal opinions that unanticipated acts of violence in schools can be anticipated and courts will expect schools to have prevention programs in place (Capuzzi, 2002).

Summarizing these characteristics of the potentially violent juvenile, your authors would emphatically echo the U.S. Department of Education's *Early Warning, Timely Response: A Guide to Safe Schools* (Dwyer, Osher, & Warger, 1998, p. 3) and the Federal Bureau of Investigation's *The School Shooter: A Threat Assessment Perspective* (O'Toole, 2003, p. 30) in their warning that it is important to avoid inappropriate labeling, stereotyping, or stigmatizing individuals based on the following categories. None of the categories by themselves or in combination can absolutely predict who will become violent and who will not. However, if the child fits into multiple categories, the crisis worker should be aware that the *potential* for violence increases and that this is an extremely troubled person. What we are more interested in when conducting a threat assessment are the demonstrated behaviors and communications that are likely to indicate intent (Fein et al., 2002; Langman, 2009). Therefore, when reading the following categories, focus not so much on the categories themselves but on what behaviors are being manifested by the individual in his actions and communications. As these behaviors and communications stack up, the potential for violence increases.

Abusive Childhood. Sexual, psychological, and physical abuses in childhood are fertile fields in which the SVJO and EVJO take root and grow. Exposure to violent role models at home, maternal or paternal deprivation, frequent moves, loss of a parent, inconsistent and punitive discipline, and rejection are characteristics of both. There is little parental control or supervision of curfews, Internet access, or television. Both SVJO and EVJO may rule the roost at home, and parents may be intimidated and afraid of the child. For the EVJO who does have a positive and supportive family, his sense of integration into the family likely will be weak and alienated. He will express contempt for his parents and dismiss their role in his life. He will insist on an inordinate degree of privacy, and his parents will have little information about his activities, friends, or school life. Such alienation may be particularly true for the mentally ill EVJO, even though he has an extremely supportive family situation and has received a great deal of nurturing and care. Parents may be in a great deal of denial about the potential for violence in either type.

Academic Problems. The SVJO will probably have a history of school problems that includes truancy, poor grades, discipline problems, and trouble with teachers. A combination of ADHD and conduct disorder is a high predictor of future violent behavior for the SVJO. In contrast, the EVJO will likely be passively compliant in school and may even do well academically. Unless some traumatic incident causes him to act out, he may well go unnoticed, or even be respected by his teachers. Both may have mild to severe language disorders that, when they are placed under stress, will cause them to be more likely to act than talk. The mentally ill EVJO will be likely to experience many academic problems because of his difficulty in maintaining contact with the reality and demands of the classroom.

Altered States of Consciousness. Even if psychoactive substances are not ingested, their cognitive processes lead both the SVJO and the EVJO to limited reality testing. Typical reports after a violent incident include derealization, decompensation, and depersonalization. Statements such as "I was just seeing red and sort of blanking out," or "It's like I wasn't there, sorta watching a videotape, so it was like me but really not me," are characteristic of both the SVJO and the EVJO. The mentally ill EVJO may operate in a continued state of altered consciousness and have minimum contact with the reality of the situation if not controlled by medication. Abuse of street or prescription psychotropic drugs increases the potential for violent behavior.

Anger/Low Frustration Tolerance. Both types react to stress in self-defeating ways. The SVJO is likely to have a "short fuse" and immediately aggress in a stressful situation, whereas the EVJO typically will flee the situation or act in a more passive way. The low frustration tolerance of the SVJO is much more immediate and seen in highly observable ways. In contrast, the EVJO may have less observable behavioral manifestations because his anger is turned inward and sublimated. He may be erroneously seen to have a high frustration tolerance. In contrast, the mentally ill EVJO may have a very low frustration tolerance because of his tenuous grip on reality.

Bully/Bullied. The SVJO is the stereotypical bully. A bully at school, he is most probably a victim at home. The EVJO is the stereotypical bullied child. He may fall into one of two categories, the passive victim or the aggressive victim. The aggressive victim may be hot tempered and attempt to retaliate when attacked. Paradoxically, the aggressive victim may also be seen as a bully. Whereas the passive bullied child is depicted as lonely and socially isolated at school, the aggressive victim is one of the most disliked and notorious members of his peer group. Although the passive bullied child may be much slower to act than his aggressive counterpart, both may bring weapons to school to counterbalance their perceived inferiority to their tormentors.

Chemical and Substance Abuse. Both types may alter consciousness by using psychoactive substances and freeing themselves of psychological restraints to commit violent acts. With the mentally ill EVJO, discontinued use of prescribed psychotropic medication combined with illicit drug use has a high likelihood of precipitating a violent episode. Substance abuse markedly increases the potential for violence.

Criminal Behavior. In contrast to the gang member, who probably has a long history of contacts with the police and juvenile authorities, the EVJO most likely does not. The EVJO is as likely as not to be seen as a good and compliant student by his teachers. Comments from his neighbors are typically, "He's a real quiet, polite boy." He may have excellent church attendance and belong to the Boy Scouts or other socially appropriate organizations. If the EVJO has any contacts with the police, it will most likely be of a petty misdemeanor nature and involve passive acts against objects rather than aggressive acts against people. If the EVJO is mentally ill, he may have had contacts with the authorities through domestic disturbance or "mentally ill" calls. He will be on some type of antipsychotic medication and will likely have quit taking it because he doesn't like the side effects.

Delayed Cognitive and Affective Development. Both types may not have reached Piaget's formal operational or even concrete stage of development. Linear and logical thinking is stunted, and short-term emotional gratification overrules long-term behavioral consequences. Their notion of the finality of death or the realness and pain of bodily injury may be very much like a game of cops and robbers in which they are shot and killed over and over in the course of an afternoon. They may not relate their violent actions to any negative emotional outcomes for either their victims or themselves.

Emotional Lability/Depression. Whereas the SVJO demonstrates a quick temper, "short fuse," and rapid mood swings, the EVJO may show depressive characteristics in which anger is turned inward. The EVJO may be serious to the point of sullenness, and see little humor in his world, particularly if he has been the object of derisive humor by his peers or significant others in his life. The severely depressed EVJO may see the end point of retaliation against his tormentors as also the end point for himself and may see suicide as a viable option after he has exacted revenge. The mentally ill EVJO may have bizarre thoughts and emotions with correlative mood swings that range from rage to fear. He also may have suicidal ideation, depending on his emotional state and particular mental illness.

External Locus of Control. Fate, God, "The Man," and other external entities play a large part in the behavior of the SVJO and the EVJO. The SVJO may view himself as both the victimizer as a way of gaining power, and the victim because of his circumstances. The EVJO clearly assumes a victim status. Both blame others for their outcast state. The EVJO's external locus is tied to a low self-concept that is constantly reaffirmed as being inadequate by the world around him. The mentally ill EVJO may receive "messages" from "voices" that tell him to act against others.

History and Threats of Violence. One of the best predictors of violence is past violence. Particularly when threats of violence are coupled with a past history of violence, the probability of violence increases. Whereas the SVJO will more likely be clear, immediate, and direct with his threats, the EVJO's threats are likely to be more implied, conditional, and veiled for a longer period of time. The mentally ill EVJO may make threats that commingle reality with fantasy such that specific individuals may be symbolized as "monsters" or other objects that are threatening to him.

Hypersensitivity. Both the SVJO and EVJO are hypersensitive to criticism and real or perceived slights and threats. They will both be suspicious, fearful, distrustful, and paranoid in their worldview. Whereas the SVJO will be more overt in his manifestation of these characteristics through name-calling, swearing, and angry outbursts, the EVJO will be more passive. Both are overly sensitive to what they believe others think, feel, and act toward them. They are "injustice collectors"; they harbor resentment over past wrongs and will not forget them or the people believed to be responsible. The mentally ill EVJO will be exponentially more hypersensitive to imagined threats to his well-being and react angrily to them. Paradoxically, both may have little sensitivity or empathy for others.

Impulsivity. The SVJO is quick to act and wants immediate gratification. He has little consideration for the consequences of his actions, lacks insight, has poor judgment, and has little understanding of how his belief system filters actions and resulting consequences. He habitually makes violent threats when angry. In contrast, the EVJO may be slow to act. He may be hypersensitive as a result of past negative experiences that have been socially and emotionally punitive. His belief system will turn to a "them against me" view that continues to build until his frustration spills out and he aggresses against his real or imagined tormentors. The mentally ill EVJO may fall along a continuum of high to low impulsivity depending on the disorder from which he suffers.

Mental Illness. Hospitalization for mental illness alone is not an indicator of potential violence. However, when hospitalization of the mentally ill SVJO or EVJO is preceded by a history of violent offenses, it is an indicator. Violence potential is further exacerbated when psychotropic medication is stopped because of its side effects, the inability to obtain it, or inadequate supervision in administering it.

Negative Role Models. For the SVJO, local and nationally known gangbangers and movie and music "gangstas" may be role models. The EVJO may be drawn to malevolent historical figures such as Hitler, religious figures such as Satan, and antiheroes in books, videos, and game simulations. The mentally ill EVJO may create his own alter ego who tells him to do violent things.

Odd/Bizarre Beliefs. Odd or bizarre beliefs fall into two categories. Schizophrenic-type mental illnesses and personality disorders are defined by odd and bizarre beliefs and behaviors, which would characterize the mentally ill EVJO. The second category more closely typifies the EVJO without mental illness. His thoughts and behaviors may range from an interest in demonology, magical thinking, and satanic cults to extremely rigid political and religious views that promote violent solutions to society's problems, which he knows little about. He disregards facts, logic, and reasoning that might challenge these opinions. Joining splinter groups that advocate such views is a way of achieving the affiliation, status, and power that the EVJO craves.

Pathology and Deviance. A psychological smorgasbord of problems may be exhibited by both types of juvenile offenders. Fire setting, cruelty to animals, defacing and destroying property, temper tantrums, running away from home, and oppositional defiance to authority are some examples. When these behaviors have a long history, they are probably more characteristic of the SVJO. When they seem to occur spontaneously with no prior history, or are kept under wraps by parents who are in denial and concerned about the social stigma attached to these behaviors, they more aptly characterize the EVJO. Parents of both groups may be passive in regard to what most parents would find very disturbing and abnormal behavior. If contacted by school officials or law enforcement, parents may respond defensively and minimize or reject reports of obvious misconduct.

Physical Problems. Particularly for the EVJO, physical problems that range from stuttering to severe acne to delayed physical development may contribute to a poor body image and feelings of inferiority. Internal head injuries, congenital brain damage, and a variety of neurological problems may contribute to the potential for violence in the mentally ill EVJO.

Preoccupation with Violent Themes. Both the SVJO and the EVJO may become fixated on movies, books, television shows, videos, and music that glamorize violence. Interest in violent pornography, weapons collections, sadomasochistic paraphernalia, and instruments of torture allow the powerless EVJO, and particularly the mentally ill EVJO who is paranoid, to fantasize about dominance over his persecutors and plot very meticulously how to get rid of them.

Social Status. The SVJO may be ostentatious and gregarious in his social relations as a means of gaining status. He sees females as providers of "goods and services" and tends to use them for his own self-gratification. He may display a pathological need for attention, and have an overall attitude of superiority and an exaggerated sense of entitlement. A social assessment of the EVJO would generally depict him as a social isolate from the majority of his peers with affiliations that place him in outlier groups. However, there are EVJOs who are popular, participate in extracurricular activities, and would generally be seen as involved in the school community. If asked, his classmates might characterize the EVJO in terms such as "geek," "Goth," "nerd," "freak," "weird," and other terms that clearly set him apart from the social mainstream. His attempts to form relationships with the opposite sex will generally be clumsy and fraught with failure. Females who try to be kind to him may well have their kindness misinterpreted. When the EVJO makes attempts to move beyond "kindness" in the relationship and his romantic overtures are rejected, the isolation he feels is further compounded. Because of his bizarre behavior, the mentally ill EVJO will be extremely socially isolated from his peers and labeled as "nuts," "mental," or "crazy."

Suicidal Ideation. Both the SVJO and EVJO may have severe depressive episodes with significant mood swings. The result may be angry outbursts against others or self, with concomitant threats or attempts of suicide. Such threats or attempts may occur particularly after a real or perceived personal loss. The mentally ill EVJO may consider suicide a very viable option to get the demons out of his head or as a way to keep "them" from getting him and further persecuting him after he does away with his enemies.

Weapons. Both the SVJO and the EVJO may have an undue fascination with and knowledge of weapons. The family may keep guns or other weapons accessible in the home, or the SVJO or EVJO may have easy means of obtaining them on the street. Parents or significant role models may have a casual attitude toward weapons and see them as a useful or normal means of settling disputes. The SVJO may commonly carry or have access to a weapon for both "protection" and "revenge" against other gang members. When the EVJO carries a weapon to school, he is most likely getting ready to act out against his tormentors. The mentally ill EVJO may be much like the SVJO in carrying weapons for both protection and revenge against his imagined enemies.

Case Study: Seung-hui Cho

Now consider Seung-hui Cho at Virginia Tech in April 2007. How well do you think he fits the foregoing behaviors and characteristics?

Seung-hui Cho, the Virginia Tech mass murderer and suicide, is the personification of the mentally ill EVJO. The following behaviors, characteristics, and traits are gleaned from the video he sent to NBC and from a report by Michael Ruane (2007), who interviewed Cho's former suite mate, Andy Koch.

Cho clearly had altered states of consciousness as exemplified by his imaginary supermodel girlfriend "Jelly," whom he claimed he was making out with in his locked room. He had severe ego identity problems, as indicated by his alter ego, Ismail Ax, a name written in red ink on his arm, and by his signature "?" on a class role, which earned him the nickname of the "Question Mark Kid." Claiming to vacation with Russia's president, Vladimir Putin, and to live in the ominous room "666" when his hall had only five floors, boosted his weak self-concept and gave him power. Like most EVJOs he had no apparent history of direct threats to anyone, but his behavior was most certainly threatening to all around him. His plays were so dark, twisted, and threatening that they caught the attention of his English professors. They are characteristic of the commingling of reality and fantasy for a person with paranoid schizophrenia and cannot be passed off as the works of "another Stephen King in the making." Cho's stalking behavior, scrawling of scary lines from Shakespeare on a girl's residence hall door, and other antisocial and bizarre behaviors over an extended period of time were precursors of his ultimate acts of violence; those oblique threats would slowly grow and finally take form in the direct and methodical act of mass murder. His hypersensitivities to external threats were legion and ranged from girls to the "rich snobs." He had been involuntarily hospitalized, was found to be depressed but not a threat to anyone else, and was released. Numerous complaints brought the police to his door. His antiheroes Eric Harris and Dylan Klebold, the mass murderers at Columbine High School, were ideal role models for the rampage he was contemplating. Most likely another role model, Ismail Ax, his imaginary alter ego, urged him along.

Cho's physical problems included not being able to speak well, being small of stature, and being different, although at this writing it is unclear whether "being different" related to being Korean, bullied, a loner, or some other factor or constellation of factors that set him apart. His writings and Facebook illustration of himself as a Zorro-like figure with only a large question mark in an otherwise blank face portray the graphic images of the violence he was contemplating. Finally and tragically, these characteristics were known to numerous people, from his roommate to professors to the police. The psychological leakage that characterizes a potentially violent student was a veritable flood for Seung-hui Cho.

In summary, if you now look back through the traits, behaviors, characteristics, and screening factors for the mentally ill EVJO and compare them to Cho's, they should scream at you, "Do something!" However, "doing something" in the case of a college student, even one whose behavior is as blatant as Cho's, is not so easily accomplished, as we shall see in this chapter's section on legal and ethical issues of potentially violent behavior.

Screening the EVJO

Langman (2009) emphasizes that the key is **LO8** early detection and prevention because once an armed suicidal/homicidal student sets foot on the school ground with a plan of action, all the metal detectors in the world are not going to stop him from carrying out his intended plan. The problem with profiling the estranged violent juvenile offender who is not mentally ill is that any staff member in a school could probably identify at least 20% of the male population who might fit the foregoing profile and have many of the characteristics described in the foregoing section. How, then, can this population be screened for those students who might have such characteristics and, more important, the intent to carry out a violent act?

Leakage. Leakage occurs when a student communicates to a third party the intent to do harm (Meloy & O'Toole, 2011). In school, these intentionally or unintentionally reveals feelings, thoughts, fantasies, attitudes, or intentions that signal a violent act. A note given to classmates then dropped and found by teachers, texts and post-its, and social media sites all are possible leakage pints. They can be delivered through stories, diaries, essays, poems, drawings, doodles, songs, tattoos, videos, or other media that make boasts, threats, predictions, or ultimatums. Another form of leakage occurs when unwitting friends and classmates are coerced or deceived into helping in preparations for violent acts. Leakage can be cries for help, signs of inner conflict, or boasts that may presage a serious threat. Leakage is considered one of the most important clues that precede a violent act (O'Toole, 2003).

Writings, Drawings, Pictures, Videos, Texts, Social Media, and E-Mails. The writings, drawings, homemade pictures, and videos of EVJOs are often an open pathway into their troubled minds. In cases of potential violent behavior, artwork may make the point more vividly than a verbal description. Graphic themes of violence that pervade the writings, drawings, photographs, videos, and e-mails of EVJOs are a tip-off that the student may be contemplating violent action against school staff or fellow students. These hard-copy emotional messages should be taken very seriously when previous incidents of violent behavior have occurred and when such graphic displays of violent ideation are issuing from the "quiet kid" who has no history of disruption in the school. School crisis workers need to apprise teachers of these indicators of predisposition to violence, and such student-generated work should be passed on to the crisis worker (Duncan & Duncan, 1971; Hammond & Gantt, 1998; James & Dorner, 1999).

Being aware of and acting on threats are critical in the prevention of a violent act (Wattendorf, 2002) and leaks are one way of doing so. Training teachers to be aware of and report these types of leakage and not dismiss them as idle, out-of-hand comments is important (Van Brunt, 2015, p. 9). Bondu and Scheithauer (2015) found that when German teachers were trained to detect leaking they reported more improved knowledge about leaking and understanding more courses of action after training. While this may sound like overkill in regard to the cascade of notes teachers find (kids being notoriously sloppy and negligent in the art of getting rid of the evidence), let somebody with threat expertise determine how valid the threat is.

Peer Referral. There are very, very few instances in which the EVJO does not give some warning of his intentions to harm himself or others. Invariably, in psychological postmortems of situations that resulted in injury or death due to violence by an EVJO, students had heard statements or seen notes from the student indicating his intent to do harm but had generally dismissed them as just "talk" (Hardwick & Rowton-Lee, 1996; James & Dorner, 1999).

However, the problem with peer referral is twofold. First, other students are afraid of and repelled by the notion of "narking" or "snitching" on another student. This reticence to inform on another is particularly true when the student in question may be so threatening that other students fear for their own safety or dismiss the threat of a student they have known for years and in their opinion is absolutely harmless. Students need to feel safe in providing information about a potentially dangerous situation (Dwyer, Osher, & Warger, 1998, p. 4; Stewart & MacNeil, 2005).

One of the best ways to screen for potentially violent students is through a peer referral and notification system run by peers and coordinated by school crisis workers (Allen, 1996). Conflict resolution, peer mediation, peer leadership, and peer counseling are all programs that allow students to legitimately notify faculty of potentially violent students without becoming informers. Whatever type of peer program is offered should not be operated from the standpoint that its only purpose is to "catch bad kids." The primary purpose of peer programs should be to help other students resolve conflicts, mediate disputes, and provide support, help, and referral for common maturational problems associated with adolescence and acclimation to school. However, when in the course of providing such peer helping services, peer helpers gain information about fellow students in crisis who may be planning to commit violent acts, it is clearly appropriate for them to apprise the crisis worker of the information they have received (James & Dorner, 1999).

Peer helpers need to be carefully trained, monitored, and supervised by crisis workers lest they exceed their limits (Allen, 1996). Peer helpers should be selected from a broad cross-section of the school population (Day-Vines et al., 1996). It has been your authors' experience that students who represent the full spectrum of the student population are much more effective in reaching their peers and being accepted by them. That does not mean that there are lowered expectations of peer helpers either academically or morally. The best peer helpers have been able to demonstrate a willingness to work with and help all of their fellow students. Their very diversity allows the program to reach a broader constellation of students than it otherwise might (Allen, 1996).

Team. The other major step is establishing a threat assessment team much like those that now exist on many college campuses (Lovre, 2013; Myer, James, & Moulton, 2011; Van Brunt, 2015) and in some K–12 school systems. The team should be composed of at least an administrator, a counselor, an SRO, and enough teachers spread across all grades and all sections of the school to ensure that at least one team member has direct contact with each student. This in-house team would be considered a threat level I team. It meets on a regular basis to filter all potential threats and rate them as to seriousness of intent. If a potential threat is discovered by the team, then a threat level II multiagency team composed of mental health and law enforcement individuals who are specialists in threat assessment should be brought into the picture. However, assessment is only the beginning of the threat team's job. The real job comes in designing (Lovre, 2013) a plan to not only find potential threats but to make plans to stabilize and move them away from a lethal thinking and operating mode. As we have discussed in Chapter 8, Crisis of Lethality, the threshold that an angry person crosses from suicide to homicide can be very easy, thus the school system should have a comprehensive suicide prevention plan in place. The most effective threat assessment plan does not put that on the shoulders of the school system, but sees it as a community problem and brings community resources to bear on it (Lovre, 2013).

Interviewing the Potential EVJO

When interviewing the potential EVJO, the first two tasks of the crisis intervention/prevention model, Predispositioning and Problem Exploration, along with the default task of Safety, are particularly critical in getting the EVJO to start talking about a violent act. The third task, Providing Support, and the default task of Safety are critical in assuring the student that the overriding concern is the student's own safety and well-being and that the issues that brought him to this point are not going to be shoved in a file drawer and never see the light of day. Coordinated with these preliminary tasks is the three-level threat assessment model provided in *The School Shooter: A Threat Assessment Perspective* (O'Toole, 2003, pp. 8–9).

Low threat is one that poses a minimal risk to the proposed victim. The threat is vague and indirect. The information is inconsistent and implausible, lacks detail, or is unrealistic. The content suggests it is unlikely to be carried out. *Medium threat* is one that could be carried out, although it may appear to be unrealistic. It is more direct than a low-level threat. Wording indicates that some thought has been given to how it will be carried out. There is a general indication of possible place and time. There is little indication the threatener has taken preparatory steps or made solid plans. There may be a specific statement seeking to convey the threat is real, as in "I'm serious, and I mean it!" *High threat* poses an imminent and serious danger to the safety of others. The threat is direct, specific, and plausible. Concrete steps have been taken toward carrying it out, and there is a solid plan with means, opportunity, knowledge, and lethal methodology to carry it out.

Problem Definition. The school crisis worker who interviews a potential EVJO initially needs to proceed with basic listening and responding skills that deeply reflect the student's feelings and allow him to ventilate his angry feelings. It should be understood that other negative emotions are undergirding and supporting the anger the student feels. Suspicion, betrayal, embarrassment, grief, anxiety, inadequacy, threat, insecurity, and particularly, hopelessness and frustration, are but a few of the negative feelings that may be pushing the student toward violence. As indicated in online Chapter 19, Crisis/Hostage Negotiation, when an individual is contemplating an expressive crime, empathic listening with open-ended leads and deep reflections of thinking and feeling will allow vitriolic feelings to emerge.

Case of John. John is a 14-year-old high school freshman who was referred to the school counselor by a teacher who had screened out John's theme after she had been through a workshop on profiling potentially violent students. The counselor has read John's theme, which is filled with angry and violent threats about a group of girls who have been teasing him.

CW: John, I've read your theme Mrs. Smith sent to me. You seem really angry. Would you like to tell me about what's making you so angry right now?

John: I'm sick of the Tri-Beta Club. Particularly the girls. They ask me to do stuff, and I do it, but then they make fun of me.

CW: Sounds like you're not only angry but hurt too. How do they hurt you?

These feelings and their antecedent causes need to be fully explored by the crisis worker to make a clear determination of what is going on and with whom it is occurring. Exploration is important for two reasons. First, by allowing the student to ventilate, the crisis worker does much toward defusing the potentially violent situation and can start to help the student develop alternative coping and problem-solving strategies. The crisis worker wants to establish an open and trusting relationship with this troubled student. Hearing the student and affirming him, through summary clarification and restatement of the content of his problem and reflection of his feelings, go a long way toward doing that.

John: Yeah. I want to be friends, but I don't think they really want me for a friend. When they need somebody to build a float or put up posters, I'm just fine. But when I asked Sally Johnson if she wanted to go get a soda after the float was done, she laughed at me, said I was a loser, and then told the other girls, and they laughed too. I hate them!

CW: So they really put you down and embarrassed you when you did everything they wanted you to do.

Second, by adequately exploring the affective, behavioral, and cognitive dimensions of the student's problem, the crisis worker may gain valuable information about the *who, what, where, when,* and *how* of the student's proposed course of action. The worker stays away from *why* questions because of their interrogatory nature. John is already defensive, and the crisis worker does not wish to do anything that will further alienate him.

CW: John, it sounds like you'd really like to get back at them for the way they've treated you. How might you do that?

Ensuring Safety. Assessment of lethality is primary in any crisis intervention. Contrary to exploring issues by using open-ended questions, we subsequently assess the potential for suicidal or homicidal behavior by asking specific, closed-ended questions that are designed to get direct answers about the student's threat level. The questions we ask could come straight from a detective's homicide manual and fall within the following areas:

1. Is there a motive?
2. Is there opportunity?
3. What is the method or plan?
4. What are the means?

Most people in psychological crisis who have suicidal or homicidal ideation will talk about what they are going to do, and talking about their plan does not, contrary to popular myth, make them more likely to carry it out. Even though they may believe they have exhausted all other possibilities, their willingness to talk about their thoughts and contemplated actions is a positive sign and an indication that at least some part of them believes there is an alternative. The potential EVJO, in particular, fits this pattern because of his feelings of anger, hopelessness, and frustration and his need to vent those feelings. If questions are asked in an empathic, nonjudgmental way, the individual will be willing to talk about the four points just listed. There is one major exception, and that is the mentally ill EVJO who is paranoid about the behavior of others toward him. He is highly unlikely to voluntarily come to counseling or think that he needs it. After all, he believes it is the others who are all wrong and messed up—not him! Persuading him to talk may best be accomplished by eliciting talk about "them" and displaying a good deal of empathy in regard to injustices perpetrated on him.

As motive, opportunity, method, and means are covered, the threat assessment goes up as each becomes more concrete. The motive of the EVJO is often unclear, or muddled, and therefore may be dismissed as inconsequential. It would be a mistake to dismiss such ideation, however, because it is not just the motive itself but the intensity and the lability with which it is discussed that are important. The more emotive the EVJO is about the injustices done him, the more he clarifies and elaborates on his plan and the opportunity to carry it out, and the more lethal his means, the higher the threat assessment (O'Toole, 2003, p. 9).

It should be abundantly clear that if the potential EVJO has access to firearms or other weapons and knows how to use them, the threat becomes critical, and there is increased risk for violence (Dwyer, Osher, & Warger, 1998, p. 10; Langman 2009, p. 182). Thus the crisis worker should not hesitate to ask the student what he knows about firearms and if he has access to them. If the crisis worker does not know about types and use of firearms, the SRO should be consulted.

The following two scenarios, using John as an example, depict low versus high levels of threat.

Scenario 1

John: I wish they were all dead. It'd serve them right!

CW: So if they were dead, it'd pay them back for what they've done to you. How might that happen?

John: Well, I don't know for sure. I'd wish they'd get some incurable disease and really suffer a lot.

CW: So you'd like to see them hurt as much as they've hurt you. How might that happen?

John: Yeah. Well, I dunno for sure. Maybe they'd get that bird flu or food poisoning from the cafeteria.

Here, the student's wish for the death of his tormentors is couched in fantasy with no clear means or method for carrying out his plan. This fantasized revenge would not carry a high lethality level, but would certainly indicate that this student is in need of support and continued work with the crisis worker.

Scenario 2

John: I wish they were all dead. It'd serve them right.

CW: So if they were dead, it'd pay them back for what they've done to you. How might that happen?

John: It'd be easy. I'd wait for them after school. When they go out to work on the homecoming float at the bus barn, I'd be behind the incinerator. I could shoot them real easy.

CW: John, do you know how to use a gun?

John: Sure. My dad's got a 9 mm pistol. He showed me how to use it. He says I'm pretty good with it.

CW: Can you get your dad's gun?

John: Well, he's got it locked up in the gun safe, but I know the combination.

CW: John, when are you planning on doing this?

John: I don't know, but if they make fun of me one more time, soon.

In this second scenario, the student's motive, method, opportunity, and access to lethal means are much clearer and better defined. Such a response would indicate a much higher threat level and would call for clear and immediate action on the part of the crisis worker.

Providing Support. In any case in which a student's lethality level is high, we need to provide clear owning statements about what we will need to do to keep the client and others he may intend to harm safe. Parents must be informed, and a clear line of communication needs to be established with the school administration, law enforcement, and other agencies that may become involved (Dwyer, Osher, & Warger, 1998, p. 11).

CW: (*responding to scenario 2*) John, what you have said really concerns me. It sounds like you've really worked out the details, and if you carry this out, I'm afraid for you and the other students. I understand you're really angry and hurt by what they've done to you. I can certainly understand how you could feel that way, but I don't want to see you get hurt any more, either by the other students in what they say and do to you, or by the police. I don't want you to shoot anybody, and I don't want the police to shoot you. I need to get some help for you right now, and I need to be sure you're safe. I want you to stay with me until I can make sure you are safe. I need to talk to your parents because I'm sure they would be concerned for you. I also need to talk to the principal to make sure that she understands what's going on, so she can make sure that you stay safe. I understand that you might be upset with me for doing this, but I'm really concerned about you right now, John. I understand that right now you think this is the only solution you've got, but I believe there are other ways to handle this, and I want you to understand that I'll help you to figure some of those out. I'll stay with you and work with you until we do get things worked out and you are safe.

Many clients will not be happy when they are informed about what is going to happen to them. One of the best responses the crisis worker can make when this happens is to use a combination of what are called "I understand" statements and the "broken record" technique, which continuously and repeatedly acknowledges the client's unhappiness about our decision, but also reaffirms our concern and caring for him. If the student becomes angry or enraged over the worker's insistence that help is required, and becomes threatening, the worker needs to acknowledge the anger, but also set limits.

John: Hey, everything is supposed to be confidential in here. You tricked me. No way you tell my parents, my old man would beat me to death. Screw this. (*jumps up with fists clenched*)

CW: (*immediately rises from her chair as a safety precaution*) No, I did not trick you, John. You heard what I said about confidentiality when we talked about harming yourself or others. John, I totally get what you say, but don't you want some respect, don't you want to feel better about coming to school? Don't you not want to be tricked and made fun of anymore? These things can happen because you have not acted on that angry notion. So please sit down and let me go to work for you. Nothing has happened so far that says we can't get

some more positive results. So please sit down and let me do my job to help you out.

The worker first acknowledges his anger and sense of betrayal. She then uses a series of negative interrogative questions that ask for agreement and attempt to reframe his present cognitive and emotional state to what he desires to have happen. She also uses "these" things to gain psychological closeness as opposed to "that" notion which she wishes to distance psychologically. Finally, she also uses Fauteux's (2010) technique of showing there is still time because nothing has happened yet that would destroy the possibility of John's getting what he wants other than revenge.

If these techniques do not get John to calm down, then the worker needs to consider her own safety and follow our recommendations in Chapter 14, Violent Behavior in Institutions, to get out of the room and/or get help.

At other times, what may at first seem to be a high threat situation may not be and, in fact, may mask other crisis issues. Return now to Officer Davis whom you met earlier in the chapter, and see how his day is going to become very interesting indeed.

Officer Davis receives a call from the school secretary at his home (S. Davis, personal communication, February 17, 2007). She is very distressed. The school has received a phone call from some kind of a psychotherapist in California who has been communicating with and working with a student via the Internet, a Goth 16-year-old white male. The therapist is very concerned because the student indicates he is tired of being bullied and is making a bomb to blow up the school. She calls long distance and tells the school secretary this information after the school day is over and the students are gone. The student has put that information on MySpace and indicated he is going to blow up something or somebody. Through some good detective work on the part of the school secretary, she has determined that the boy is Paul Jones. Officer Davis discretely meets the boy at school the next morning and pulls him into his office.

Officer Davis: Talk to me, Paul. What's going on? You seem kinda depressed.

Paul: Not really. Some kids trash talking me is all, and I'm tired of getting bullied by them.

Officer Davis: Look, you're not in any trouble OK, but I gotta check this out. It looks like you put some stuff on the net about making a bomb. Want to show me what it was?

Paul: Well yeah! I put some of that stuff on there, but I'm not really making one.

Paul shows him what he put on the net. Officer Davis e-mails this information to the local bomb squad, who are sitting in unmarked cars outside Paul's house. They get very excited over the information and immediately want to search Paul's house for bomb-making material. Officer Davis calls the parents and informs them of what is occurring. A search of the house is quietly conducted, and nothing is found in the way of explosive devices, much to the relief of the parents and everyone else. However, Officer Davis's CIT training kicks in, and he feels something more is going on with this troubled young man. He continues to explore Paul's feelings with him.

Officer Davis: Look, I've done a lot of this stuff, Paul, and I get a good sense when things are really troubling people. You seem really down or maybe something else. I think it's more than getting trash talk for being Goth. You sure you don't want to talk to me about it?

Paul: OK. Look, this is weird. Like I have spiders crawling all over my arms right now. And there is a waterfall right in back of you. Plus my dad talks to me a lot in class, but like he's at work and not really there, but nevertheless, he is talking to me, and it really is distracting and scary. See I scratch my arms, but the spiders still come back.

Officer Davis: (*thinking to himself, "Holy mackerel! This kid is having schizophrenic episodes!"*) Paul, that certainly concerns me. Have you told your parents?

Paul: No, I'm too embarrassed. I don't want them to know. I keep thinking they'll go away. They don't come often, but when they do, it's pretty scary. That waterfall behind you right now is pretty real.

Officer Davis: I don't see or hear it. I know you do, and that needs to get taken care of. I've got a friend at the crisis center who deals with this stuff. I believe after I talk with your parents you need to meet him.

Officer Davis now calls the parents, who are at their home with the bomb disposal unit, and informs them of their son's hallucinating episodes. To say that this is a day they would like to soon forget is putting it mildly. However, Officer Davis calmly talks them though the problem and then drives Paul to the crisis center, where the parents meet him. Whenever Officer Davis has to take someone to the crisis center, he stays to make sure the person is being seen and treated before he leaves. This is particularly true of students, who need a friendly face when they are taken to a mental health facility and are under emotional duress. This tactic allows students to know that he is not abandoning them and pays off down the road when he encounters them again. They know they can trust him and that he really is interested in them as people.

It may be argued that a school counselor, psychologist, or social worker might be the best person to handle this situation. However, when a school resource officer like Scott Davis is also CIT trained, the fact that this is a potentially lethal situation with disaster ramifications makes him the very best qualified person to deal with Paul. You may wonder whether this is a rose-colored picture of a police officer. With the spread of CIT training across the United States, officers like Scott Davis are becoming more and more common and are, in every sense of the definition, crisis interventionists. Further, they certainly have ample opportunity to ply their trade in 21st-century schools (James, Logan, & Davis, 2011).

Acting

How the crisis worker acts depends on a continuous assessment of the student. If the crisis worker determines that the student is indeed a threat, then the worker's response should be to make an immediate referral and notify parents, administrators, and, if necessary, law enforcement personnel. If the crisis worker determines that the student's lethality level is not high, then the worker can move forward in the model to examining alternatives, making plans, and obtaining a commitment to work on positive actions that will help him become less alienated and angry. An investigation might indicate that the behavior was merely a "throwaway" statement that had no meaning other than ordinary misguided playfulness or a momentary pique of anger. Even then, it would be a proper educative and counseling activity to teach the student not to play this game. However, in today's school environment, threats against others should not automatically be discounted. Thus, the crisis worker needs to keep a record of the encounter and follow up with the student to ensure that those threats do not escalate into action (James & Crawford, 2002).

Punishment by expulsion is not the answer and in fact does at least two things we don't want to have happen. First, it likely increases the student's grudge against the school or those in it he feels are responsible for his misery. Second, it is likely to leave the student unsupervised at home and give him free license to plan and assemble the necessary weaponry to pay the school back (Langman, 2009, p. 186). What needs to happen is that the student is evaluated for psychiatric and/or behavioral problems, medicated if necessary, provided counseling, and placed in an alternative school that is well supervised.

A primary consideration is what to do if the student is carrying a weapon. If the crisis worker feels the relationship with the student is positive enough and the student indicates that he has a weapon in his possession, then the crisis worker may ask for it for safekeeping. In taking a weapon, the crisis worker should always be sure it is handed over butt first or, if a knife, haft (handle) first. If the crisis worker is unsure of the student's intent or if the student is resistant, the crisis worker should *immediately seek help and get out of the room*. If the student indicates he has a weapon in his locker or some other hiding place, the crisis worker should have another person go with him or her to the hiding place. *In no instance should the crisis worker attempt to be a hero and attempt to forcibly take a weapon away from a student* (Crews, 1998). There is no known formula for determining whether to attempt to get the weapon away from the student or leave the premises to get help. Probably the best rule to follow is whatever the crisis worker believes will be the safest course of action for both the crisis worker and the student.

School–Based Suicide Prevention and Intervention

Because adolescence is the most volatile period of transition in the human cycle of development, factors involving youth who are at risk for suicide are dramatically different from those affecting adults who kill themselves (Berman, Jobes, & Silverman, 2006; Capuzzi, 2009; Maples et al., 2005; Pfeffer, 2006). Suicidal thoughts and behaviors represent the most common mental health emergency among teenagers (King et al., 2013). Suicide ranks third (12%) behind homicide (15%) and vehicle accidents (31%) as one of the leading causes of death in adolescents. From 1952 to 1995, the incidence of suicide among adolescents rose 300%. From 1980 to 1997, the rate of suicide among persons aged 10–14 rose 109% (Centers for Disease Control, 2002). For youth between the ages of 10 and 24, currently suicide is the third leading cause of death. It results in approximately 4,600 lives lost each year (Centers for Disease Control and Prevention, 2015a). Given these figures there is an average likelihood that every year, every teacher in every

high school classroom in the United States can expect two girls and one boy to seriously contemplate or attempt suicide (King, 2000), and every principal in the average American high school can expect one completed suicide every 5 years and 170 attempts in any given year, although certainly most of these will never come to the school's attention (Brock, Sandoval, & Hart, 2006).

Further, unless they are ferreted out, these teenagers are not likely to seek mental health assistance. Husky and her associates (2012) followed up the adolescent supplement national comorbidity study. During the course of 12 months, 3.6% of adolescents reported suicidal ideation without a plan or attempt, 0.6% reported a suicide plan without an attempt, and 1.9% made a suicide attempt. Overall, two-thirds of adolescents with suicidal ideation (67.3%) and half of those with a plan (54.4%) or attempt (56.9%) did not have any contact with a mental health specialist in the past year.

Deaths from youth suicide are only part of the problem. Suicide and self-harm in young people are a major cause of life years of adjusting to a disability brought on by the attempt (De Silva et al., 2013). More young people survive suicide attempts than actually die. A nationwide survey of youth in grades 9–12 in public and private schools in the United States found that 16% of students reported seriously considering suicide, 13% reported creating a plan, and 8% reporting trying to take their own life in the 12 months preceding the survey. That means that essentially every school counselor, social worker, and school psychologist has someone who is actively thinking about, planning or trying to kill themselves. Each year, approximately 157,000 youth between the ages of 10 and 24 receive medical care for self-inflicted injuries at Emergency Departments across the United States (Centers for Disease Control and Prevention, 2015b). So when that doesn't work, those same human services workers are going to see those kids again, only this time they may be both psychologically and/or physically disfigured from the attempt, have solved none of the problems that got them to a suicidal state, and are likely worse off than before. To that end, many states, our own state of Tennessee being a pretty good example, now require training for all school personnel in detecting suicidal behavior (Capuzzi, 2009).

Suicide affects all youth, but some groups are at higher risk than others. Boys are more likely than girls to die from suicide. Of the reported suicides in the 10 to 24 age group, 81% of the deaths were males and 19% were females. Girls, however, are more likely to report attempting suicide than boys. Cultural variations in suicide rates also exist, with Native American/Alaskan Native youth having the highest rates of suicide-related fatalities. A nationwide survey of youth in grades 9–12 in public and private schools in the United States found Hispanic youth were more likely to report attempting suicide than their black and white, non-Hispanic peers (Centers for Disease Control and Prevention, 2015b). Suicide is a problem that is far more prevalent and far more lethal than all the school assaults combined—even though school shootings get far more publicity.

From these figures it would seem apparent that crisis response programs in schools should incorporate suicide prevention, intervention, and postvention components that are comprehensive and systematic (Austin, 2003; Capuzzi, 2002, 2009; Kalafat, 2003; Komar, 1994; Malley, Kush, & Bogo, 1994; Reis & Cornell, 2008; Webb & Griffiths, 1998–1999). If a school system does not have a written formal policy, the board and the community should require that suicide prevention/intervention/postvention procedures be developed and implemented (Malley, Kush, & Bogo, 1994, p. 135). School-based child and adolescent suicide prevention/intervention/postvention should include (Capuzzi, 2002; Kerr, 2009; Malley, Kush, & Bogo, 1994, p. 131; Maples et al., 2005; Thompson, 2004):

1. A written, formal suicide policy statement.
2. Written procedures to address and ensure the safety of at-risk students.
3. Faculty and staff inservice orientation and training in warning signs and referral of at-risk students.
4. Identification and training of mental health professionals on-site or readily available crisis teams.
5. Prevention materials for distribution to students, parents, and the community, and for classroom discussion.
6. Procedures for psychological screening, identification, and counseling of at-risk students.
7. Preplanned postvention responses and strategies that occur following any completed suicide.
8. Written criteria for crisis workers to assess lethality of a potential student suicide.
9. Written policies on how the school-based child and adolescent suicide prevention/intervention/postvention program is evaluated.

Kerr (2009, pp. 24–26) has taken these general procedures a step further and outlined what the response should be to a suicide threat, a suicide attempt on school grounds, a suicide attempt off school grounds or during a school-sponsored activity and reported to an employee, and a completed or suspected completed suicide.

Risk Factors/Predictors/Cues

Almost all adolescent suicide victims have experienced some form of psychiatric illness. These range across affective, conduct, and attention deficit disorders (Shaffer, 1988) to antisocial personality, substance abuse, and depressive disorders (Guida, 2001; Hacker et al., 2006; Shaffer, 1988). Adolescents who have questions about their sexual identity, have recently experienced a loss, suffered humiliation at school or home, been bullied or cyberbullied, had an interpersonal conflict with a romantic partner or a parent, a dramatic change such as the death of a friend, or a pregnancy, are heavily into alcohol or drug use, have been traumatized by sexual or physical assault, are depressed, have a physical illness, have made a major geographic move to a new school, engage in risky behaviors (parasuicidal), or are petulantly angry and impulsively act out are all candidates for suicidal ideation, threats, and acting (Capuzzi, 2002; Guida, 2001; Nelson & Galas, 1994). When faced with these conflicts, it appears that lack of family or peer support is a precipitating factor in generating suicidal ideation (Mazza & Reynolds, 1998). Interestingly, giftedness may also be a contributing factor (Nelson & Galas, 1994). The individual who comes from a home where suicide has been attempted or has had a close friend who has attempted suicide may be at greater risk (Capuzzi, 2002; Nelson & Galas, 1994). But probably the best single predictor is a previous suicide attempt (Nelson & Galas, 1994; Shaffer et al., 1988).

The clues and behaviors that are commonly found in the suicide indicators in Chapter 8, Crisis of Lethality, would hold true for most adolescents and children. For children and adolescents, however, warning signs also include a sudden change in friends or dress habits, cutting hair or changing hairstyles, difficulty concentrating, persistent boredom, sudden or increased promiscuity, reversal of valuation of prized objects, use of drugs or alcohol, and a decline in school achievement (Capuzzi, 2002; Greene, 1994; Maples et al., 2005; Nelson & Galas, 1994). Copycat suicides are particularly problematic for adolescents, particularly if the adolescents believe there will be notoriety for them. This phenomenon occurs after a suicide when peers, who may have had similar thoughts, also attempt suicide (Austin, 2003). Although most adolescents give cues to their attempts, not all do. Adolescents may verbally indicate their decision to kill themselves in clear terms, or they may be far less direct with such statements as "I wonder what death is like" or "I'm tired of all of this."

Preadolescent Suicide

There is a prevailing notion that young children do not commit suicide. Have a conversation with any elementary school counselor, social worker, or school psychologist who has been in the business for any length of time and you will be quickly disabused of that faulty notion. The problem is that while a ton of work has been done with adolescents, relatively little has been done with young children. Price (2010), in a brief overview, pointed this out. The experts he queried indicated that most young children who commit suicide have some kind of mental disorder and are likely to have been victims of physical or sexual abuse. However, that is certainly not true of every child.

The other major issue is that when children are found to be suicidal they tend to be treated as miniature adults rather than in terms of the cognitive and developmental stage they are in. Indeed, because of their level of cognitive development, many young children's thought processes that lead to suicide would not generally be considered reasons to kill themselves if they were adults. But, as with all suicidal persons, it makes perfect sense to them. Consider the following reasons: wanting to meet a friend or relative who died; feeling guilty that they are the cause of parents' getting a divorce; avoiding punishment or embarrassment they believe is worse than death; wanting to punish someone else (although this can certainly happen with adolescents and adults); believing they will be martyrs for some cause; and escape from an intolerable situation such as an abusive home or a concentrated cyberbully attack (Muro & Kottman, 1995, pp. 324–325).

Further, parents and teachers tend to dismiss clues that are common to suicidal ideation. Indeed, it is interesting that most child counseling and therapy books tend to lump a lot of what is known about adolescent suicide into their recommendations and counseling techniques for elementary age children. The bottom line is that young children who emit suicidal clues should be taken seriously, and the child counseling procedures that are depicted in other parts of this chapter and book should be used with them along with the general suicide prevention and intervention techniques that are used with adults. To that end, our own state of Tennessee mandates by law training for all school personnel in suicide prevention, and we believe that it should be part of the policy of every elementary school that parents are educated about suicide prevention.

Child and Adolescent Cases of Suicidal Ideation

Here are some strategies and suggestions (Capuzzi, 2002; Flemons & Grainik, 2013; Fujimura, Weis, & Cochran, 1985; Nelson & Galas, 1994) for anyone (crisis worker or layperson) who comes into contact with a child or adolescent suspected of being suicidal:

1. Trust your suspicions that the young person may be self-destructive.
2. Tell the person you're worried about him or her; then listen to the person in a nonjudgmental, supportive way.
3. Ask direct questions, including whether the youngster is thinking about suicide and, if so, whether he or she has a plan.
4. Don't act shocked at what the youngster tells you. Don't debate whether suicide is right or wrong, or counsel the person yourself if you're not qualified. Don't promise to keep the youngster's intentions a secret. Be calm and supportive and reinforce the person for talking about it.
5. Don't leave the youngster alone if you think the risk of suicide is immediate.
6. Do not be embarrassed or reticent about getting help from a competent counselor, therapist, or other responsible adult.
7. Ensure that the youngster is safe and that the appropriate adults responsible for the youngster are notified and become actively involved with the youngster.
8. Assure the youngster that something is being done, that the youngster's suicidal urges are not being discounted, and that, in time, the emergency will most likely pass. Apprise the youngster that survival is a step-by-step, day-to-day process; that help is at hand; and that calling for help in a direct manner is necessary whenever the suicidal urge gets strong.
9. Assume an active and authoritarian role as needed to protect the child at risk. This is a crisis and calls for applied, directive guidance and management. After the youngster has apparently resolved the high-risk crisis, monitor progress very closely.

Many persons have been known to suddenly commit suicide after they seemed to be renewed and strong.

10. Actively acknowledge the reality of suicide as a choice, but do not "normalize" suicide as a good choice.
11. Ask questions about the suicidal ideation, but balance them with interspersed empathic responses.
12. Construct a short-term safety plan. If the youngster is unwilling or unable to comply or there are no parents or guardians available, go to 13.
13. Consider hospitalization if parents are not cooperating, if the youth is highly agitated, or if the student has not been eating, is exhausted or dehydrated, or has some other exacerbating physical condition.
14. Refuse to allow the youth to return to school without an assessment and release by a qualified mental health professional. This assures that the youth will receive the necessary treatment and also protects the school from liability if a suicide attempt or completion takes place.

The following scenarios incorporate many of the suggestions just given.

Billy, Age 11. In a group counseling session, children ages 9 to 12 (including Billy) were engaged in relaxation training, emotive imagery, and self-esteem building. The children were taking turns disclosing a positive image each was experiencing. Billy had been rather quiet and complacent in previous counseling sessions.

Billy: I see myself beside the highway. There's a big 18-wheeler—going fast. I'm feeling like I'm gonna die. I want to die. I see myself jumping in front of it.

CW: Billy, that concerns me to hear you say that! Could you and I talk about that after the others leave? And Billy, I want you to know that I'm glad you didn't keep that image a secret from us.

The crisis worker was shaken and surprised at Billy's sudden description of his images. The worker assessed the suicide risk to be high because of the content and the context of the disclosure (the group activity had been clearly structured to facilitate sharing only positive, growth-promoting images, which other members of the group had done).

Billy's nonverbal body posture and profoundly serious facial expression communicated that he was not fooling. The crisis worker did not deny, refute, or admonish Billy. Recognizing that Billy was taking a great risk by disclosing his death wish, the worker responded by assuring Billy that he had received the message as sent and conveying to members of the group the worker's willingness to attend to and answer Billy's cry for help.

Lester, Age 14. Lester was an intelligent youngster who made good grades in school and had a reputation for being quiet, cooperative, and well behaved. Following his parents' bitter divorce, while living with his mother and a younger sister and brother, Lester began to get into trouble in school because of his overt acting out and belligerent behavior. He lost interest in his studies and school activities, and his grades began to tumble. He became rebellious with his mother, and his appetite decreased to the degree that he just picked at his food. He became very withdrawn—seldom leaving his room—in contrast to his previous behavior of being actively engaged in outside activities whenever possible.

Lester's mother and the school counselor decided to place him in a student support group consisting of male and female middle school students, all of whom were experiencing severe difficulty following the separation and/or divorce of their parents. At the conclusion of one of the group sessions, Lester asked to speak with the crisis worker.

CW: Lester, sounds like something happened in the group today that got pretty close to you.

Lester: (*hesitant, looking down, nervous*) I . . . I've been feeling weird lately. Strange. Like I'm somewhere else.

CW: You mean like you're outside your own body observing yourself?

Lester: Yeah. Even at night. I don't understand it. I've even thought I might be going crazy.

CW: (*closely observing Lester's body language*) Lester, it sounds like this is so serious you may have even been wishing you were dead.

Lester: Yeah. I've been scared. I've just thought about how it would be to just go to sleep and not wake up.

CW: Have you thought about making that happen? Killing yourself, so that you'd never wake up?

Lester: Thought about it, yeah. Thought about it more lately.

The crisis worker had sensed prior to the interview that Lester might be suicidal. At least six indicators on the risk assessment checklist pointed to the conclusion that Lester was at a high risk level: his changing family life, his changing behavior and attitudes, his body language, his eating habits, his social habits, and his grades. Any one of these would have been an important lethality signal (Curran, 1987, pp. 111–118).

Crisis workers and other adults who work with suicidal youngsters must pay careful attention to clues indicating that suicidal ideation is present. Hunt, Osten, and Teague (1991, pp. 20–21) found that classroom teachers who are sensitive to the emotional changes in and have a close relationship with their students can be primary identification, support, and referral sources for youth who are suicidal.

Lester's science teacher, Mr. Birch, overheard Lester talking to a classmate about giving him his "boom box" and some CDs. Lester had also taken a pair of scissors and chopped off his long hair. He had gotten in a shouting match with a girl in class and almost come to blows with her before the teacher intervened.

These behaviors were clearly uncharacteristic of Lester. Mr. Birch also knew from a staffing meeting with Lester's teachers that Lester had thoughts of killing himself. The teacher had a list of warning signs he had received at an inservice training on suicide (Maples et al., 2005). After he became suspicious of Lester's behavior, he looked over the warning signs and made an immediate referral for Lester to the crisis worker. The crisis worker called Lester's mother, who confirmed Mr. Birch's suspicions. The assistant principal also indicated that Lester had had two disciplinary referrals for fighting after school in the last 2 weeks.

CW: (*3 months after the initial intervention*) Lester, I asked for this conference because I'm worried about you again. I thought you were doing great! But now, frankly, I'm scared to death for you. Mr. Birch and your mom are worried too and asked me to see you.

Lester: Oh, I'm OK. Things are going great.

CW: (*in a calm, soft, caring, empathic voice—not a lecturing or agitated tone*) They may seem OK to you, but what concerns me right now is what you've been doing lately. Your mother is very upset and puzzled because you've given your CD player to a friend, and the principal is livid because you've picked two fights on the way home from school this week. I've noticed that the last 2 days in the hallways and cafeteria you've been like an entirely

different person. If these things say what they appear to say, I don't think I can leave here today until I can be sure you're safe. I don't want to wake up in the morning and hear that you're dead!

Lester: It's really not anything you should feel worried about. I'm OK, really I am.

CW: (*soft, empathic vocal tone continued*) Fine, then you can help me feel OK by discussing with me what's going on. I just want you to know that the clues I'm picking up spell danger and that I'm as concerned for you as I've ever been. And I need to know that you're safe, even though you say you're OK. I really care about you.

The crisis worker was empathic but confrontive and persistent even though it would have been desirable and comforting to believe that Lester was OK. As it turned out, Lester was indeed on the threshold of suicide again. The important thing was that the worker interpreted Lester's unusual actions as clues that called for help—whether Lester overtly called for help or not.

What is particularly helpful for them is decreasing their feelings of isolation and marginalization (Berman, Jobes, & Silverman, 2006). Including suicidal children and adolescents in support groups and other activities that make them feel like valued and contributing members to their school and peer group is an important part of moving them away from suicidal thinking and behaving. Berman and Jobes (1994) found that suicidal adolescents particularly need empathic therapeutic alliances to help them feel affirmed, valued, and understood.

Postvention

Clustering of Suicides. Cluster or contagion suicides occur when more than one suicide attempt or completion happens within a proximate geographic area, giving the appearance that these events are related (Gould & Shaffer, 1986; Kirk, 1993, p. 15; Webb & Griffiths, 1998–1999, pp. B43–B48). There is evidence that publicity about child and adolescent suicide completions and media programs depicting factual or fictional suicides have been associated with suicide attempts and completions in geographic areas reached by the publicity (Austin, 2003; Kalafat, 1990, p. 364).

Kirk (1993, pp. 15–16) likens such clustering to the infectious disease concept; that is, when a pathogen is introduced into a vulnerable population, the probability of infection is spontaneously increased.

Similarly, when an adolescent suicide occurs and is sensationally reported or somehow glorified, other adolescents who may already be in a state of despair, helplessness, or hopelessness may be influenced toward terminating their lives or see it as an excellent way to get a great deal of attention.

Contagion. Sandy Austin (2003) reported on a series of four suicides at her school in an 8-month period. The school crisis response team immediately responded to the suicides in the following manner. After each suicide, faculty were called and informed of a meeting the next morning where they were briefed. District mental health personnel were contacted for support. The principal, counselor, and SRO visited the deceased's family members and asked if a memo could be read that stated the student "took his own life" instead of "committed suicide" to convey the finality of the act and decrease the "glory" of it. Memos were drafted and read in each class. At the end of the day, faculty met for a debriefing to determine how students were doing. Students were invited to come into the counseling office for one-on-one or group counseling or just to come to a "safe room." Parent/community meetings were hosted with an expert to address the suicide issue. The media were asked to construct their stories in a "signs to look for" manner and "how to help someone access resources" to address the contagion effect.

The crisis team was then confronted with another problem. Instead of dealing in typical teenager fashion with the ruts and potholes of adolescence, the students started talking about suicide as a viable option for taking care of problems. The counselor and student representatives visited each English class and asked students to be observant and tell someone if a friend started talking about suicide or showed warning signs. Posters were created on the subject of getting help and watching for clues and placed throughout the community. Crisis line phone numbers were put on cards and passed out. Austin reported that for the rest of the school year there was at least one tip a day on a potential suicide. The toll went beyond the suicides and the grief felt for their loss. Two peer counselors became suicidal, and one school counselor had to take a month's sick leave due to stress. Thus, you should get a pretty clear notion that vicarious trauma, which you will read about in Chapter 16, is real.

The school district did everything by the book. They did everything they could possibly do and generally did it right, but still the suicides continued. Shaffer, Vieland, and Garland (1990) reported that among adolescent suicide attempters, "talking about suicide in the classroom makes some kids more likely to try to kill themselves" (pp. 3153–3155). Thus, "postvention" classroom programs designed for suicide education and prevention may be appropriate for the majority of adolescents who are not currently at risk, but may not be appropriate for the at-risk population. Or at least a massive effort will be needed to get all of the student body involved and willing to tell an adult about a peer's suicidal thoughts or threats without fear of being labeled a snitch.

Publicity and Contagion. Kirk (1993, p. 17), in his investigation about media effects on adolescent suicide, makes three interesting observations: (1) The more sensational the reporting of the suicide, the greater was the increase in suicides within the reporting area. (2) There was a significant increase in auto accidents involving teenagers following media reports of youth suicides. (3) There was an increase in adolescent suicides following certain made-for-television motion pictures that focused on episodes showing suicides in the lives of troubled and suicidal adolescents. That's why it is critically important for the media liaison to work closely with the media, as in the case of Sandy Austin's school district.

Imperatives for SCRTs in Suicides. School crisis **LO10** response teams (SCRTs) must be knowledgeable about suicide postvention so that clustering does not occur. Crises of suicide are different from other crises because of the self-instigating behavior that goes with them and because so many different emotional evaluations are placed on suicide. If SCRT members do not know about the dynamics of suicidal behavior, they need to get outside consultation that does, and they need to have it available immediately. The worst possible scenario is an insecure SCRT that does not want to "look bad" because it needs outside help to handle the crisis. In our own experience, we have witnessed an SCRT that did not know what it was doing and wound up with three more completed suicides and two attempts on its hands in the space of 2 months in the same high school! Thus, it is critical that parents, teachers, and students be given notification and information regarding warning signs of suicide—particularly after a completion (Maples et al., 2005).

Jennifer, Age 17. Jennifer was terrified. Although she had suffered from depression, loneliness, and low self-esteem for several years, she had managed to have a satisfactory social life, maintain average grades in school, and regain her equilibrium following each depressive episode. Several stressors during the past year had combined to complicate and disrupt her life. Indeed, one of the major contributors to child and adolescent suicide is the role of the family (Berman, Jobes, & Silverman, 2006; Wagner, 1997). Her parents' separation and divorce were unexpected and bitter. Her maternal grandmother, to whom she had been very close, died from rapidly progressing intestinal cancer. Jennifer was living with her mother and two younger sisters. The mother began dating a single man and permitted him to move in with them. Jennifer changed schools during the middle of the year when her parents' original home was sold. Because of her lack of social adjustment and academic achievement in the new school, Jennifer was placed in a support group at the school and was also seen regularly by an individual counselor.

Following a weekend episode of trauma over the suicide of a friend who attended another school, Jennifer showed signs of being upset, severely depressed, exhausted, and withdrawn. The crisis worker had been notified that Jennifer had missed school on Friday to attend her friend's funeral. Being wary of **contagion suicide**, sometimes called *copycat suicide* (Gould & Shaffer, 1986), the crisis worker knew that Jennifer's risk level was probably elevated because of her trauma over her friend's suicide, in addition to her already stressful family situation.

CW: Jennifer, it frightens me to see you this way. What's happening to cause you so much pain right now?

The crisis worker could see the physical and emotional devastation Jennifer was feeling. It was important to communicate to Jennifer the worker's affective concern and to provide a direct and open opportunity for Jennifer to feel safe and to respond (Patros & Shamoo, 1989, pp. 126–128).

Jennifer: (*after a long pause, in a very low, subdued voice*) I . . . I've never been this scared before in my life. (*pause*) All weekend I've been at the end of my rope. I've just thought, there's no use going on anymore. And ever since last Friday at Etta's funeral, I've wondered if it wouldn't be better if I just went like she did. They said such nice things about her. She and I were so close. It was so sad but so comforting to hear all the wonderful things they said about her.

CW: Jennifer, I'm glad you're here now. I can see how the death of Etta and her eulogy really affected

you. What frightens me right now is what you just said, that it would be better if you joined her. Does this mean that you're planning to kill yourself over this?

The crisis worker's questioning was aimed at swiftly making an assessment of Jennifer's lethality and quickly heading off the idea of contagion suicide. The answer to such a question drastically impacts and changes what the crisis worker does. Even though Jennifer's destabilized family situation would have been signal enough to inquire into any suicidal thoughts and plans she might have, the hint of contagion suicide served as a red flag, alerting the crisis worker to be assertive and direct in asking the suicide question.

The concept of contagion suicide is controversial. Skeptics and critics claim that there is little scientific proof of clustering and copycatting because it is difficult to prove that one suicide attempt or completion directly causes another. But according to Kirk (1993, pp. 16–17), there is too much evidence of recent contagion suicides in the United States to ignore or dismiss claims of clustering. We agree with his conclusions and believe from our own experience that it is extremely important for school crisis response teams that go into a school after a suicide to know that this phenomenon has a possibility of being activated if postvention is not handled correctly.

There is evidence that providing peer support such as a professionally led peer counseling group can help suicidal teenagers (King et al., 2006). One of the major support systems in schools to prevent initial and contagion suicides is a peer counseling system such as Allen's (1996) peer leader program. Allen's peer counselors meet weekly to talk about issues and problems that are occurring in their high school. They are the eyes and ears of the counselor and are privy to information of a far wider and current scope than school staff will ever be. By relaying information to the school counselor about peers who are severely affected by a school trauma, they enable intervention to happen much more effectively and quickly. As Allen says, "I have no idea what types of drugs or alcohol are currently hot. I don't know who is depressed because he broke up with his girlfriend, but my peer leaders do, and they are not seen as snitches for telling me. It is okay because the rest of the kids see it as the peer leaders' job."

Grief and Mourning After Adolescent Suicide. **LO11**
Kirk (1993, pp. 112–115) found that suicides of adolescents and other youth represent a type of death that

severely complicates survivors' mourning and adjustment. He cited the following reasons:

1. The adolescent suicide is generally unexpected.
2. The death of a young person is harder to accept than that of an older person who has lived a full life.
3. To many people, suicide is incomprehensible and perhaps even morally wrong.
4. The suicide completer's family and friends are left with guilt, anger, and a sense of unfinished business with the deceased, which mourners must work through.
5. There is less social support for a suicide completer's family than there may be for other bereaved families because people tend to unjustly ascribe blame to the family.

Kirk also stated that when a suicide occurs in a school setting, grief reaction is often further complicated by the group response of classmates and school personnel. Educators, school crisis response teams, parents, and others involved in designing prevention, intervention, and postvention procedures should be sensitive to the unique grief factors just mentioned. A suicide absolutely must not be glorified or made heroic. That doesn't mean that feelings are ignored or questions concerning the deceased are not answered as truthfully and honestly as possible. Survivors will be seeking answers to why the individual took his or her life. There will be many questions about who had responsibility or culpability in not preventing it. There will be questioning of oneself as to why it wasn't seen, or if seen then why wasn't it stopped (Capuzzi, 2009). Empathic understanding of these concerns from students, parents, and faculty is of primary importance, and no questions or comments should be summarily dismissed (Capuzzi, 2002).

As with other traumatic events, a room for counseling students should be set up, factual information should be disseminated, and an SCRT meeting should be held to determine whether other students may be at risk. Maples and her associates (2005) describe an adaption of a four-stage model (Brammer, Abrego, & Shostrom, 1993) that can be used to work with teenage survivors of a suicide. In *stage 1* there will be *shock* and *disorganization*. Typical responses are "It couldn't happen," and "No, not possible!" Initial intervention follows along the lines of the intervention responses described in Chapter 12, Personal Loss: Bereavement and Grief, and uses basic nonjudgmental listening and responding skills. *Stage 2* is the most

potentially volatile stage of this particular grieving process. It involves feelings of *anguish, remorse,* and *guilt* over not having done something to prevent the suicide. "Why didn't I see this coming?" "I could have stopped it!" are common themes of recrimination. Besides conducting a psychological autopsy on the order of the one in Chapter 8, Crisis of Lethality, using cognitivebehavioral strategies such as thought stopping and positive mental videotapes may be effective in helping students control their feelings.

Heather: (*16-year-old best friend of a suicide starting to shake uncontrollably and with tears streaming down her face*) I think I am going crazy. Every time I pass Sally's locker I come apart. We had been best friends since first grade. I could have, should have stopped this, and I didn't even know it. That's some kind of friend.

CW: Remember what we said in the psychological autopsy. It made perfect sense to her. It is a terrible tragedy, but neither you nor I nor anyone else can be, or should be, responsible for her suicide. You have that pink memory band on your arm. Every time you pass where her locker was [note crisis worker's movement to past tense], tap the band and say "STOP!" when those feelings start to flood over you, and remember that one great moment you said when the two of you won the sixth-grade talent show. Smile and remember how deliriously happy and goofy you looked in your Raggedy Ann and Andy costumes. Then move on. You need to do this every time you go by the locker. Don't avoid the locker like you have been, but just make it part of your normal routine. We are going to get that mental image squarely in your mind, so lean back, close your eyes, and let's practice that.

Stage 3 has to do with *reconciliation of the loss.* When faced with traumatic death for the first time, teenagers may struggle with existential questions such as the meaning of life or the futility of everyday living. "What's it all about?" and "Why bother with school?" are topics for group grief work that help students reconcile and move on with their lives. Spiritual components of these questions should be considered, and working alliances and referrals to pastoral counseling are good options.

Stage 4 has to do with *emergence of new goals* for survivors. Recommitment to established friendships or dedication to a worthy cause or a sport season are ways of helping teenagers move past the suicide. Typically this stage will mark the passing of the friend and recommitment to living by the surviving teenagers.

Suicide of a popular student or teacher is one of the most difficult challenges human services workers in schools face. The potential for interventions to go terribly awry is high, and thus interventions must be thought through and carefully applied. One of your authors witnessed one instance in which the faculty of a school assembled after school to engage in a debriefing with the SCRT of the district. The teachers had all sorts of questions and emotions to deal with concerning the suicide of a fellow teacher the previous night. They were told, "If you are having problems with your fellow teacher's death, we suggest you call your behavioral health service provider and talk with them." Then the SCRT leader dismissed the group, leaving the principal and school counselor to deal with more than 50 enraged and frustrated faculty members.

As in any crisis, being at the school of the completed suicide as soon as possible after notification is critical for planning and for making assessments about the emotional state of faculty and students, quelling rumors, assessing for other possible suicides, and depropagandizing and deglorifying the suicide by debriefing faculty and students. Capuzzi (2009) recommends that a single statement be prepared and read in each class rather than over the public address system so that everyone receives the same message but in the presence of teachers who can be watchful for students who are having a difficult time. It is fruitless and damaging for the SCRT to come straggling in late in the afternoon or the next day. Such dilatory behavior lets rumor and chaos run wild, and makes a statement that there is not a great deal of concern about the health and well-being of the school.

The following points are recommended when the death of a student or teacher is due to suicide (American Association of Suicidology, 1991, 1998; Capuzzi, 2009):

1. Don't dismiss school or encourage funeral attendance during school hours.
2. Don't hold a large-scale memorial to the deceased or dismiss school to do so.
3. Do provide individual and group counseling.
4. Verify the facts, and do treat the death as a suicide.
5. Do emphasize that no one thing or person is to blame for the suicide.
6. Do emphasize that help is available, that suicide is preventable, and that everyone has a role to play in prevention.
7. Don't build a tangible memorial such as a bench or a tree with a marker or dedicate a yearbook to the suicide.

8. Do not release information in large groups such as an assembly. Work by classroom or in small groups.
9. Do be on the lookout for delayed grief reactions.

Do suicide prevention/intervention school-based programs work? Results are variable. There is no clear, evidence-based comprehensive prevention strategy at present (Katz et al., 2013). Katz and associates found that most suicide prevention programs are designed to improve students' and school staffs' knowledge and attitude toward suicide. Of 16 programs examined, only 2 reduced suicide attempts, although several of the programs did reduce suicidal ideation, improve general life skills, and train gatekeepers to become more vigilant. De Silva and associates (2013) conducted broad-based mapping studies for suicidal and self-harm studies. They found some school-based programs with skills training components to be promising. Zenere and Lazarus (1997) studied a comprehensive suicide prevention and intervention program in a large, urban, culturally diverse school district. Students were tracked over a 5-year period. What they found was that although suicidal ideation remained stable, the rate of attempts and completions was dramatically reduced. Wasserman and associates (2015) conducted a very sophisticated cross Europe study of 15-year-old students assigned to three treatment conditions. The Youth Aware of Mental Health Programme (YAM) targeted pupils as opposed to screening by professionals and a gatekeeper training program for teachers. YAM was effective in reducing the number of attempts and severe suicidal ideation, although Brent and Brown (2015) noted in a comment that the specific components such as seeking help or using coping were not isolated or discussed. Brent and associates (2013) in their comprehensive review of interventions found that the most effective interventions appeared to have either family interactions or nonfamilial support, so it may be that any school-based program needs to consider the inclusion of support systems outside the school.

Planning for a Crisis

Federal Emergency Management Agency. The LO12 school crisis events in the 1990s caused a huge change in the way schools viewed security and the need for crisis response. As various state and local education agencies started scrambling to prepare emergency plans that included more than fire drills and tornado warnings, a planning guide for schools was created in

2003 by the U.S. Department of Education. *Practical Information on Crisis Planning: A Guide for Schools and Communities* used the Federal Emergency Management Agency (FEMA) four-stage model for schools, mitigation, preparedness, response, and recovery as a template for the guide (U.S. Department of Education, 2003). This guide is currently available at www2 .ed.gov/admins/lead/safety/emergencyplanning.pdf.

This plan fits with the FEMA national incident emergency model (see Chapter 17, Disaster Response), which allows for a common language between first responders, school personnel, and the community (U.S. Department of Education, 2013). Having consistency with terms is an important feature, as it allows the school districts and the community first responders to speak the same language. Another national school model has been developed by school psychologists.

PREPaRE Model. The PREPaRE (Prevent, Reaffirm, Evaluate, Provide, and Respond Examine) school crisis prevention and intervention model was developed by the National Association of School Psychologists and piloted in 2006. PREPaRE stands for *prevent* and prepare for psychological trauma; *reaffirm* physical health and perceptions of security and safety; *evaluate* psychological trauma risk; *provide* interventions; and *respond* to psychological needs; *examine* the effectiveness of crisis prevention and intervention. PREPaRE is an evidence-informed school crisis curriculum with a strong mental health component. While the model is based on the U.S. Department of Education's phases of crisis management and the Incident Command System, as proposed by the National Incident Management System, it also incorporates components of Mitchell and Everly's (1995) critical incident stress management (see Chapter 17, Disaster Response), which introduced "debriefing" and offers both planning for student behaviors in crisis and prevention in school safety (Brock et al., 2011).

PREPaRE follows a planned system to use in a crisis situation including the assembling of a team, evaluating the potential trauma to students, and offering crisis services. In addition, the PREPaRE model uses a three-tier approach as all students may receive services following a crisis situation. Tier 1 may be conducted in the form of a classroom meeting, while Tier 2 may advance to a more individual- based crisis intervention. Finally, students who were severely traumatized would receive psychotherapy, which would be categorized under Tier 3 (Brock et al., 2011).

One of the main components in the PREPaRE model is offering training opportunities in order to understand the work of crisis response. Given that the National Association of School Psychologists covers the United States and its members are in practically every school district in the country, it should not be too surprising that many districts use this (Brock et al., 2011). There are indeed a number of different models for crisis response in schools such as the National Organization Victim's Assistance (NOVA) program (2015), the integrated model by Jimerson and associates (2005), and Caplan's (1964) three-tier structure. All these models highlight the importance of tasks that need to be done before a crisis, during a crisis, and after a crisis situation.

Whatever the model, a crisis plan for a school system is not done overnight. It takes a great deal of planning and commitment by the school district and the staff (Brock, Sandoval, & Lewis, 1996; Duncan, Delisle, & Esquith, 2013; Kerr, 2009; Luna & Hoffman, 1999; Maples et al., 2005; Montano & Dowdall-Thomae, 2003; Newgass & Schonfeld, 2005; Petersen, 1999; Petersen & Straub, 1992; Rubin, 1999; Stephens, 1997). Crisis plans are both generic and idiosyncratic. Crisis plans of other schools and consultants can be extremely helpful in making a skeletal outline for what needs to be covered in containing a crisis. No matter whether the crisis occurs in Brooklyn, New York, or Brooklyn, Mississippi, many of the same needs and responses generic to all crises of lethality will be applicable to each. When a disaster hits schools the federal government encourages schools to follow the National Incident Management System (2011), which standardizes how a crisis response is organized. That's all well and good, but the professional responders will leave after the emergency is over and guess who gets to carry on? Also, they won't be there in the first few minutes or hours of the crisis when the chaos theory you vaguely remember in Chapter 1 is running rampant.

Further, each school district and each school building has its own peculiarities in regard to its physical plant, its staffing, its student population, and its community makeup. Each of these variables plays a critical part in how specific planning for a crisis will be conducted. To think that a crisis plan for the Los Angeles school district can be taken wholesale and applied to Waterloo, Iowa, would be misguided, to say the least. A crisis response in a school needs a delivery system. The chief components of any service delivery system are the written policy of what to do when a crisis occurs, the physical resources to carry out the policy, and the trained personnel to implement the service (Nelson & Slaikeu, 1990, p. 339). A crisis plan must cover safety and security; obtaining, verifying, and providing accurate information to the various constituencies of the school; and also deal with the emotional needs of those constituencies. If these three areas are not addressed concurrently as the crisis unfolds, none will be addressed effectively (Newgass & Schonfeld, 2005).

The Crisis Response Planning Committee

Initial planning should use a crisis response planning committee (Brock, Sandoval, & Lewis, 1996; Duncan, Delisle, & Esquith, 2013; Kerr, 2009; Montano & Dowdall-Thomae, 2003; Newgass & Schonfeld, 2005; Petersen, 1999; Petersen & Straub, 1992; Poland, 1999; Rubin, 1999; Stephens, 1997). A decision needs to be made on the size of the committee. If it's too large, it becomes unwieldy. If it's too small, it's not viable enough to meet a large crisis. The ideal is probably a two-tiered team if the district is large enough to support it and a super-tier regional team outside the district. The first-tier team is a district-wide effort that deals with the big picture of crises. This team should be composed of a wide variety of individuals representing a cross section of social services and government institutions that will have to respond to the crisis. The second tier is a building response team that is familiar with its physical plant and its constituency. These individuals represent the teaching staff and administration, the parents, and most important, the support staff (failure to include the custodian might mean that nobody knows how to shut off the gas or electricity in the building) (Brock, Sandoval, & Lewis, 1996, p. 31; Lovre, 2013). One of the critical ingredients is coordination between these two tiers. If these two levels operate at cross-purposes, not only will they hinder crisis resolution, they can make it worse. Coordination should be systemic and integrate partnerships among a variety of stakeholders that work with adolescents (Lubell & Vetter, 2006).

A needs assessment should be conducted to determine what the school staff needs in the way of training and, even more important, whether the constituency believes in and is willing to support the effort (Davis & Salasin, 1975). One might suppose that few people would be opposed to implementing a full-scale crisis prevention and intervention program in a school given the current publicity about school violence.

That supposition may not be true when it comes to the reality of passing a bond issue, providing release time for staff, or disrupting ease of access to school buildings. Therefore, fully apprising the community and determining their resistance or acceptance are critical to implementing an effective plan (Duncan, Delisle, & Esquith, 2013).

A clear system for dealing with a major school crisis should be established long before the need for intervention. It should ensure that all personnel are clear as to what is going to happen, when it will happen, who will be responsible for each component, how a report is made, who is to make the report, and subsequent follow-up action.

Such planning should include all the school staff and administration. Furthermore, because such interventions will undoubtedly involve law enforcement and perhaps other mental health agencies, they too should be involved in planning for violence intervention and know what part they are to play in it (Blauvelt, 1998; Brock, Sandoval, & Lewis, 1996, pp. 33–37; Montano & Dowdall-Thomae, 2003; Newgass & Schonfeld, 2005).

Your authors have seen a number of voluminous crisis plans developed by school systems that are quite impressive. One plan has 29 different leaders, directors, officers, and chiefs, with very detailed roles and functions for each! These plans are gathering dust on the principal's and superintendent's bookshelf. Any crisis plan should be usable, and it should be simple enough that everybody knows his or her role in implementing it (Blauvelt, 1998; Goldstein & Kodluboy, 1998, pp. 170–171). From that standpoint, while no school district goes without a tornado, earthquake, or fire drill on a regular basis, very few schools have drills regarding armed intruders or other kinds of crises. If staff are not trained to implement the plan, and if a school crisis plan is not practiced, evaluated, critiqued, reviewed, and updated on a regular basis (Brock, Sandoval, & Lewis, 1996, pp. 243–248; Duncan, Delisle, & Esquith, 2013; Poland, 1999, p. 4), it is pretty much useless.

The School Crisis Response Team (SCRT)

When a crisis is of such magnitude that local staff are overwhelmed or emotionally devastated because of personal involvement, then outside help should be summoned. Mobilizing this regional tier should be planned for a long time before the crisis occurs. In small rural school districts where the labor power and expertise for the following positions are beyond the district's capabilities, it is absolutely mandatory that linkages be established between districts and support personnel. It is even more important for these small districts that they have close linkages between county-wide, state, and federal disaster management teams that compose this super tier.

If the crisis can be handled with help from within the district, the community generally will be better served because these people will be familiar with the setting and their clientele and the district will know what level of expertise these people have (Brock, Sandoval, & Lewis, 1996, p. 61; Rubin, 1999). Not everyone is cut out to do crisis intervention work. Just because a person is a counselor, a social worker, a school psychologist, or a caring teacher or administrator does not automatically make her or him the best person to be involved with the team. Careful consideration should be given to team composition, and people who feel that they might not be capable of handling a severe crisis should not be discriminated against because they are truthful about their trepidation (Kerr, 2009, p. 35).

The following roles make up what would be a competent SCRT. There should be redundancy in these roles (Brock, Sandoval, & Lewis, 1996, pp. 74–75; Kerr, 2009, pp. 36–45; Poland, 2004). If the crisis response coordinator is a principal who is being held hostage, or the intervention coordinator is a school counselor who is injured in an explosion, there needs to be someone else familiar enough with that role to take over.

Poland (1999, p. 4) speaks of three waves in the aftermath of a disaster. The first wave is the medical personnel and police. The second wave is the media. The third wave is the parents. Therefore, it is not just the victims and survivors that a school must be concerned with, but a host of other problems as well. Therefore, an SCRT will need to have a number of other people on it who may not have any expertise at all in crisis intervention but do have the expertise to allow the SCRT to handle the crisis effectively.

Crisis Response Coordinator. This person should be someone with decision-making capability, most likely a school administrator who is knowledgeable about the school district and staff. He or she is highly knowledgeable about the crisis plan and has good communication links within and outside the system. This person is in charge of coordinating, implementing, and evaluating crisis response plans (Brock, Sandoval, & Lewis, 1996, pp. 67–68; Rubin, 1999).

This role is different from that of the person who would actually coordinate the intervention.

Crisis Intervention Coordinator. This person is responsible for implementing and carrying out the crisis plan. The intervention coordinator should have a thorough understanding of crisis intervention techniques and strategies. He or she should have a clear understanding of the objectives and methods of the crisis intervention plan and should be able to deal with a multiplicity of crises that range from individual suicides to natural and human-made disasters. This person also needs to be a good administrator and delegator who can coordinate a number of activities and people under very stressful and chaotic conditions (Brock, Sandoval, & Lewis, 1996, pp. 68–69; Petersen, 1999). It should be readily apparent that time should be allocated for the crisis intervention coordinator to plan and coordinate for crisis events, and not just have these "added on" as a supplementary task.

Media Liaison. It is one thing to deal with the local news crew that the SCRT leaders may have developed close personal relationships with over the course of time; it is quite another to deal with national news media. Imagine yourself as a school counselor in Anytown Middle School who has been designated as the SCRT coordinator. An assault at 8:30 A.M. by a person with paranoid schizophrenia leaves six children and two teachers dead, the school principal seriously wounded, and nine other children in the hospital with severe gunshot injuries. A panic ensues as frantic parents come to the school to get their children. You are attempting to get information out about who is hurt and dead, trying to coordinate psychological triage of survivors who witnessed the carnage, giving information to law enforcement personnel who are looking for the still-at-large perpetrator, attempting to reunite distraught students with equally distraught parents, plus a myriad of other tasks, when at 10 A.M. the first national news helicopter lands on the football field and is quickly followed at around noon by a convoy of national news trucks with satellite uplink capability. There is a horde of reporters attempting to interview anybody they can get their hands on. They are particularly interested in getting any school personnel to comment on who is responsible, why it happened, why the school didn't prevent this from happening, what the school is now doing, who the dead and survivors are, and how you personally feel about this, among other intrusive and invasive questions to which they are clamoring for answers.

It should become very clear from the foregoing scenario that dealing with the media is a major responsibility and should be the sole responsibility of one person specially designated and trained for the job. Such a person should be able to keep relationships with the media positive, but should also be able to effectively control them by determining how and what information should be shared with them through well-thought-out and well-prepared statements (Brock, Sandoval, & Lewis, 1996, pp. 69–70). One of the worst scenarios in a school crisis is to allow anybody and everybody to talk to the media. The repercussions from the innuendo, rumor, half-truths, and incomplete data can be extremely severe for survivors and further exacerbate the psychological trauma. Media need to be given press releases that indicate how the media can best help and be least disruptive to students. The media liaison provides written notification to parents on what happened as quickly and currently and with as much factual information as possible and also provides helpful literature and directories of support services to deal with the traumatic repercussions of the event (Newgass & Schonfeld, 2005). Kerr (2009, p. 74) has generated a list of media questions that are designed to obtain information that may well be used to cast the district in a negative light. She has also generated a list of dos and don'ts in regard to those questions that any media representative would do well to learn (p. 75).

Security Liaison. The security liaison should have close links with local law enforcement agencies and would coordinate responses to single events such as a bus accident or recurring events such as gang-initiated drive-by shootings. One of the major preventive tasks of the security liaison is training staff in implementing safety procedures across a wide array of potential crisis scenarios (Brock, Sandoval, & Lewis, 1996, p. 71).

Community/Medical Liaison. The medical liaison should have established close links between the local emergency, fire, medical, and mental health systems and the school. A critical component of her or his role is planning for medical triage of victims of a school crisis and communicating to parents and staff the medical condition of those involved in the crisis (Brock, Sandoval, & Lewis, 1996, pp. 71–72; Rubin, 1999). If there is a local emergency management

agency, the liaison should have a seat on its board so that he or she knows whom to contact and what kinds of resources are available in a disaster.

Parent Liaison. The parent liaison's job is dealing with parents, period! Keeping parents calm, providing them with information, and furnishing them support are critical in the containment of a crisis. This person works closely with the media liaison in determining what information, about the event itself and support services, is disseminated to parents and how it gets to them. Where part of the community is not fluent in English, provision will have to be made for translators, both oral and for all written information that goes out to parents. Because parents may need the services of other components of the team, this school official must have a good working knowledge of each member's role (Rubin, 1999).

Community Liaison. This person or persons need to be the direct link to community resources (Kerr, 2009, p. 37). An ideal member may be the local emergency management agency director, the mayor's community action officer, or a high-ranking member of the police or fire department.

Crisis Interveners. While direct service crisis interventionists are most likely to come from the ranks of school counselors, psychologists, social workers, and nurses, it is important to obtain interventionists who are directly linked to children. Thus, it is helpful to include teachers who have direct contact with a broad sample of the students who might be affected. In an elementary school, at least one primary and one intermediate teacher should be on the team, and in middle and senior high schools, teachers who represent many different subject matter areas or curriculum tracks should be part of the team (Brock, Sandoval, & Lewis, 1996, p. 72).

The school and district unit should be capable of handling a small crisis such as the suicide of a teacher or a gang shooting. In a large crisis such as a bus–train wreck, backup workers from the local mental health system should be available, and in a very large crisis such as the Columbine shooting, the crisis interventionists would be an even larger integrated team of school, local, state, and national interventionists. Incorporating students into the team is also a good idea. They can act as messengers, help identify which students are missing, provide information about the status of other students, and function as peer counselors (Rubin, 1999).

Resource/Facilities Person. This member will need to know where a variety of available supplies are and how to get them from point A to point B in a hurry. Depending on the size and type of the crisis, the resource person may need to know how to obtain everything from pencils and paper to a backup diesel generator. This is not a menial job. If the material supplies are not available, including provision of food and drink when a crisis is going full tilt, then everything grinds to a halt (Rubin, 1999). This person also has a working knowledge of building plans and the systems that operate them. Knowing how to shut off gas lines, knowing the location of electrical junction boxes, and being able to show others the opening to steam tunnels can be critical in a crisis where knowledge of building structures is involved (Kerr, 2009, p. 37).

Implementing the Crisis Plan

The following minimum requirements are critical to a school crisis plan (Brock, Sandoval, & Lewis, 1996, pp. 75–76; Brown & Bobrow, 2004; Conoley & Goldstein, 2004; Duncan, Delisle, & Esquith, 2013; Gerler, 2004; Montano & Dowdall-Thomae, 2003; Petersen & Straub, 1992; Rubin, 1999; Williams, 2004).

Physical Requirements

Counseling Locations. As many locations as possible need to be identified for crisis counseling offices. Crisis counseling will involve a wide variety of activities that will require different accommodations. Auditorium-size rooms will be needed to handle large groups of people for briefings of factual information about the crisis as it unfolds and psychoeducational information about what people can expect and need to do in the aftermath of the crisis. Classrooms will need to be designated to administer psychological first aid. Offices will be needed to perform psychological triage and provide individual counseling. If school is in session, a great deal of rescheduling and shuffling of rooms and assignments will be necessary and should be planned for ahead of time, or alternate buildings such as churches will need to be used.

Operations/Communications Center. In a very large crisis, a room that will become the nerve center for a crisis needs to be designated and equipped. All necessary equipment—additional phone lines, supplies, and furniture for additional staff, computers with Internet capability, emergency equipment such as portable phones, citizen band and police band radios, and portable generators—should be available here. This nerve center will become the key component of an efficient crisis operation. In it, people will monitor procedures to determine what staff is available, establish procedures for getting written messages to staff, screen outsiders, and disseminate and coordinate media releases and crisis intervention procedures.

Break Room. A place that is private and will allow workers time to relax, eat, and rest; it may also double as a debriefing room for SCRT members and other crisis personnel.

Information Center. A room large enough to handle a number of media personnel, it should be equipped with a sound system and other visual media equipment. It may also double as an information dissemination or briefing room for parents.

First-Aid Room. This room should be stocked with first-aid supplies for minor physical problems.

Logistics

On-Site Communications. Message boards, computers linked to central files, dedicated telephone lines, citizen and police band radios, and walkie-talkies should be accessible. Because telephone lines may be jammed or otherwise inoperable, a central message board should be available for announcements, bulletins, student lists, and other personal information. If possible, dedicated phone lines with the numbers known only to officials and staff responsible for handling the crisis should be available. Because there may be little or no communication on-site, walkie-talkies are vital. Portable "to go boxes" provide vital hardcopy data such as updated attendance lists, release cards, emergency numbers, parent/guardian names, and so on, and can be moved to an alternate site to check off names of students. All teachers should have a "to go box" in addition to a master main office "to go box."

Establishing a Phone Tree Among All Staff. In any size crisis, a redundant phone tree is absolutely imperative. All staff members of a school building need to be informed of a crisis event as soon as there is knowledge of it. The phone tree is critical so that all staff members can begin to operate in a crisis mode and assume preplanned positions and duties. Messages about the crisis should be written down by each person on the tree. Relying on memory and verbal transmission will guarantee that facts get commingled with fiction. One of the worst mistakes that can be made is for staff not to be aware of what is happening and go blundering into an ongoing crisis. We have experienced such lack of communication firsthand, and it is, to say the least, a nightmare.

Procedural Checklist. Although it may seem time wasteful to go through a procedural checklist when a crisis is in full swing, not to do so in a chaotic situation is asking for trouble. It is too easy to overlook a critical component of the intervention plan and assume it has been taken care of by somebody else.

Building Plans. Building plans are vital to emergency personnel and police. Blueprints of every building in the district should be quickly available. Someone with knowledge of the building should be available to interpret the plans to emergency personnel.

Provisions. Because crisis personnel may be involved for extended periods of time, food and drink should be provided or be delivered on-site.

Responding to the Crisis

The following points, in linear order, indicate what needs to occur in a crisis response (Brock, Sandoval, & Lewis, 1996, pp. 80–104; Gerler, 2004; Kerr, 2009; Petersen, 1999; Petersen & Straub, 1992; Poland, 2004; Poland & McCormick, 1999; Rubin, 1999). Kerr has an operational acronym that should be a general overall operating guide to all responders called BE CALM. It stands for:

Before you act be sure you have the facts.
Call for help, communicate instructions, and collaborate with other responders.
Anticipate what could happen next and adjust the plan.
Listen to your audience and learn what they need.
Manage the crisis and maintain the responders with food, rest, water, debriefing, etc., and modify the plan as needed. (p. 9)

Getting the Facts. The ability to quash the rumor mill that invariably starts up in a crisis is critical to calming fears and anxiety of the public and also to providing valid information to crisis workers on how many and which students were affected, what level of response will be required, what information needs to be disseminated, and to whom it will be given. Facts need to be checked and rechecked. Getting a team member to the scene of a crisis to make a factual report is critical. Distraught parents and hysterical children make for extremely unreliable sources of information. Especially in the case of a suicide, getting verification from the medical examiner is a must.

Impact Assessment. As soon as the facts are known, an SCRT meeting should be held and an assessment should be made of the impact the crisis will have on the school. Considerations in assessing the impact are popularity of the victim, degree of exposure by staff and students, history and recency of similar crises, resources currently available, and timing (a crisis during vacation is likely to be less traumatic than one during school time). At that time, a decision will have to be made as to the degree of mobilization of internal staff and what, if any, outside assistance will be needed.

Triage Assessment. Once the facts are determined and the possible impact of the crisis event is gauged, a triage assessment needs to be conducted to determine those individuals most affected by the crisis. The SCRT needs to compile a list of those who may be directly and indirectly affected and determine who is most in need of acute intervention and who may need less immediate, intensive attention. Once this list is compiled, interviews and paper-and-pencil tests such as those described in Chapter 7, Posttraumatic Stress Disorder, may be used to further divide individuals into primary- and secondary-care groups.

It should not be assumed that relatives, survivors, witnesses to the event, and close friends within the school are the only people needing immediate and intensive attention. Siblings and close friends in other schools may be just as traumatized, and efforts should be made to assess these individuals as well. Individuals who are known to be at risk due to other factors and students whose reactions are out of proportion to their involvement should also be considered as high risk.

Parents and teachers need to be given checklists and warning signs that will let them know whether their children are starting to develop the symptoms of acute or posttraumatic stress disorder and referral sheets and phone numbers that will enable them to refer those students who may have been missed by the SCRT. Embedded within these referrals should be questions on lethality. Any student who is expressing thoughts about harming himself or herself or others should immediately be assessed as high risk and in need of immediate crisis intervention.

Psychological First Aid. Psychological first aid (Aguileria, 1997; Slaikeu, 1990, pp. 105–129) is a first-order response that deals with all of the affected individuals no matter what their degree of involvement (see Chapter 1, Approaching Crisis Intervention). The components of psychological first aid are making psychological contact, exploring dimensions of the problem, examining possible solutions, gaining assistance in taking action, and offering follow-up services. Psychological first aid is intended as a method to provide support, furnish a platform to be heard and valued, dispel rumors, allow catharsis and ventilation of emotions, reactivate problem-solving abilities, reduce potential lethality, and restore general stability to the school. It is probably most easily done in classroom meetings with teachers who are trained and supported by the SCRT. Such classroom meetings are an excellent vehicle for providing factual information about the event, giving students information about the psychological effects they may encounter, and dealing with personal issues and problems students may have as they come to grips with and attempt to resolve the crisis.

The NOVA Model. For older students, the National Organization for Victim Assistance (NOVA, 1997) group crisis intervention model may be used. This model operates along the lines of the critical incidents stress debriefing (CISD) program of Mitchell and Everly (1995). However, it is not as tightly structured as CISD, and the facilitator is a great deal more interactive with participants.

These groups meet for usually no more than 2 hours. The session has a brief introduction detailing safety and security for the participants. Time is then spent on reviewing physical sensory perceptions, going over emotional reactions of shock and disbelief, and giving opportunity for ventilation and validation of these reactions. Typical questions posed are "Where were you when it happened? Who were you with? What did you see, hear, smell, taste, or touch at the time? What did you do? How did you react?"

Time is then taken to review the emotional turmoil that has been experienced and to allow ventilation and validation of these feelings.

Questions are asked in regard to the aftermath of the event. "What are some of the memories that stand out in your mind? What has happened in the last 48 hours? What do you remember seeing or hearing during that time? How have you reacted?" The facilitator validates the thoughts and feelings of the group members. No judgments are made as to right or wrong. Where applicable, the facilitator draws comparisons between members to create a common bond and normalize thoughts and feelings that go with the abnormal event (National Organization for Victim Assistance, 1997, pp. 8–10).

Questions are then posed to elicit expectations about the future, what coping strategies can be used, and help predict and prepare the group for what may happen over the near future. "After all that you've been through, what do you think will happen at school in the next few days and weeks? Do you think your family has been or will be affected? How do you believe you might deal with the problems and issues that have been raised?" As the members identify positive coping strategies, they are reinforced and given alternative strategies if they are generating negative coping methods. Referrals for more in-depth help are suggested. These components are then followed by a summary recapitulation to validate what has been said and reaffirm the validity of the participants' experiences. A postgroup session of about 30 minutes is used to distribute handouts, answer individual questions, and say good-bye (National Organization for Victim Assistance, 1997, pp. 9–10).

Conducting a large assembly of all the school to do this is not recommended. Although a large assembly may be deemed efficient and expedient, it does not begin to address the many personal questions and issues that students may have. Psychological first aid is a two-way street and, to be effective, should allow an interchange of information between staff and students. In and of itself, psychological first aid may be an excellent way of determining who may be in need of more in-depth crisis intervention by observing reactions of students as they talk about the crisis. This admonition is particularly important in the case of suicide where other students may have "caught" the contagion and need to be identified.

Crisis Intervention. Any student who is assessed as needing more than psychological first aid should be given a complete screening interview (Aronin & Ransdell, 1994).

That interview should consider what the student's exposure and recollection of the events are, whether the event is persistently reexperienced, whether there are attempts to avoid reminders of the event, increased levels of physical and mental arousal, feelings of survivors' guilt, failure of previous coping skills to ameliorate problems, somatic complaints, self-destructive or impulsive behaviors, and pre- and postevent comparisons on effectiveness of daily functioning. In short, the screening interview should look at the diagnostic criteria set forth by the DSM-5 (American Psychiatric Association, 2013) for the onset of traumatic stress disorder.

It is important to take the time necessary to completely discuss the crisis, and attempts to immediately reintroduce the academic regimen should be held in abeyance until this task can be completed. Although getting back to the standard humdrum schedule of school is important in normalizing the situation, very few students are going to be academically able to do so if they are struggling with attempts to resolve the crisis.

Classroom meetings can help students move from reaction to proaction. That is, students can move from talking about the event to planning how they can take action to solve the residual effects of the event. By moving to a proactive stance, students can begin to attain a feeling of empowerment and reinstitute control in their lives. They can also gain closure on the event by cooperatively planning memorials and memorial services (note the previously mentioned exception of memorializing suicide).

The worker should be especially watchful for client reports that perseverate on special details, worst moments, and violence or physical mutilation. These will be extremely potent points in the crisis and need to be thoroughly worked through and controlled (Pynoos & Eth, 1986, p. 309). If there are perpetrators involved in the crisis, one of the greatest fears of children is that the perpetrators "will get them." Whether these perpetrators are caught and punished or are still at large makes little difference. The worker needs to take time to clarify what happened to the perpetrators or what is being done to catch them. Feeling of self-blame for not having done enough and an inability to take action, desires to retaliate and punish the perpetrators, and fear that they will be revictimized need to be explored and worked through (Brock, Sandoval, & Lewis, 1996, p. 168).

Briefing and Debriefing. Each morning of the aftermath of the crisis, a morning briefing and planning session needs to be held to obtain updated information, review responsibilities, assign tasks, and plan interventions. At the end of each day, actions need to be reviewed, weaknesses and strengths need to be examined, and reviews of referred students, staff, and parents need to be made. Plans are then made for the next day and what staff and resources will be needed to accomplish the goals. Additionally, a nightly debriefing should be held to give the SCRT a chance to exchange information, obtain reassurance, and ventilate feelings (Berman & Jobes, 1991; Rubin, 1999; Williams, 2006). The Missouri School Counselor Association's (2002) *Crisis Manual* makes the following points for SCRT members:

1. Keep your life in balance.
   a. Eat well-balanced meals and get plenty of exercise.
   b. Balance work and rest.
   c. Stick to a schedule as much as you can. It provides stability and the comfort of a normal routine when your feelings are out of control.
   d. Avoid new major projects or decisions.
2. Be realistic about what you can do.
3. Recognize and acknowledge your own feelings of loss and grief. Give yourself permission to mourn. No matter what the nature of your relationship, there is loss. Give yourself the same latitude you give your students. Meet with fellow SCRT members and be supportive of each other or form a support group.
4. Be kind to yourself. You don't have to get it all together right away. You don't have to do it all, be strong for everyone, or take care of everything. Treat yourself with the same gentleness and understanding you would anybody else.

Demobilizing. Demobilizing occurs when the crisis is finished. It allows the SCRT to integrate the experience into their lives and go back to their regular jobs. An overall evaluation is conducted by the crisis response coordinator with the SCRT. The crisis intervention coordinator writes an after-action report that includes a description of the crisis event and the interventions conducted, an evaluation of the effectiveness of the intervention, and recommendations for future events. As such it provides the SCRT with a potent learning tool. Furthermore, if questions are raised in the future about what was done or not done, this report documents what happened (Brock, Sandoval, & Lewis, 1996, p. 100).

Bereavement in Schools

The sudden death of a student, teacher, or other school personnel may precipitate a bereavement crisis for an entire school or school community,

LO13

which can lead to posttraumatic stress disorder, high-intensity grief, and complicated mourning. The closer the friendship to the deceased, the more the foregoing is likely to occur. As such it is important to have a grief resolution program in place (Poijula et al., 2001). Many children will be dealing with the reality of death for the first time. They will also be struggling with the significance of the loss and grappling with the idea that life is no longer predictable or fair. Further, they may have no idea how to grieve and may receive little help if their parents are also grief stricken (Kraft, 2003). Many of the bereavement procedures in Chapter 12, Personal Loss: Bereavement and Grief, are appropriate for working with children and adolescents. However, because of the social community and culture of schools, there are some specific actions that need to occur when a member of the school community dies.

Individually or in groups, team members may focus on the grief of a specific grade level, provide group discussion for particular subgroups, temporarily relieve bereaved teachers of classroom responsibilities, staff mini-counseling centers, or work with parents. Two SCRT members may follow a deceased student's schedule. One member will talk with each class, provide factual information, answer questions, clarify misinformation, provide support, provide information on funeral arrangements, explain what funerals and visitations are like and what to expect, suggest what types of things can be said to family members, and encourage students to talk about their memories of the deceased student. While this class discussion is taking place, the other member can assess and identify students who are not coping well and escort them to a support room (Missouri School Counselor Association, 2002).

Assessing students' needs prior to returning to school may help lessen anxiety. A home visit or a phone call that empathically responds to the student's progress can be made. Questions might include "How are you feeling about coming back to school? What is the most difficult thing for you about returning? Is there something you would like me to do to help you? Are you worried about what other students will think?" All these questions are designed to allow the student to talk about his or her fears and trepidation and allow the SCRT member to help him or her start to feel less anxious. After the student has been back to school a few days, the crisis worker may discuss with the child how she or he is doing with questions such as "Now that you are back at school, what has been

the hardest thing for you? What has been on your mind the most? How has the death affected you at school?" These questions allow the worker to determine how well the child is making the transition back into school (Rubin, 1999).

Kandt (1994, p. 207) suggests that school human services personnel working with grieving adolescents should (1) educate themselves about the grief process; (2) give permission to grieve; (3) allow time to grieve; (4) listen, listen, listen; (5) understand that reminiscing is essential; (6) give support for a variety of feelings; (7) know they can't "fix" the pain; (8) draw the adolescents out, keep in touch, and don't abandon them; (9) design a support group; and (10) let them know that they are not alone.

Swihart, Silliman, and McNeil (1992) surveyed grieving students and listed the following issues that caregivers should be sensitive to:

1. Many students were affected by the loss, even students who were not close to the deceased; therefore, they were reminded of their own mortality.
2. Teachers should not expect peak performance from students who are still too numb the first week following the death.
3. Teachers should be allowed to express their own grief to students who are willing to simply listen.
4. Students should be allowed to grieve in different ways—some in groups, some in their individual ways.
5. After-school activities should be provided for students to work off their grief by expending physical energy.
6. Students should be brought together in commemorative activities so that students who were not very close to the deceased one are not excluded.
7. Students should be permitted to discuss grief issues; denial of the opportunity to openly discuss their thoughts and feelings may cut the teenagers off from an open forum of support.
8. School administrators should be cognizant of the deceased student's role in the school; if the deceased was in a leadership role, the school will need to have administrative leadership in filling the role vacated by the deceased.
9. The school should be prepared to respond to the loss for a considerable length of time.

Group Work

An accident following the prom in early May resulted in the deaths of four Cedar Grove High School students: Phil, age 16, the driver of the car; Jerry, age 17;

LaTara, age 16; and Tracey, age 17. A group of seven classmates at school, representing the four youngsters' closest friends, appeared to be stuck in their grief. Keena, Lee, Samantha, and Rashid, all 17, and Eddie, Amber, and Tarunda, all 16, requested the help of the school counselor in reaching some understanding and resolution of their feelings of anguish and grief.

The following intervention strategies were provided and issues explored with these adolescents by the school counselor during the days and weeks immediately following the burial of the four teenagers who died.

1. *Individual counseling and intervention.* Assessment of individual stress levels. Providing individuals a safe place to release stress energy. Helping adolescents feel comfortable in expressing how they feel. Providing death education for adolescents.

2. *Group grief work.* Providing an atmosphere for the seven adolescents as a group to deal with the deaths of their four classmates in particular, and with the area of death and dying in general. Providing for group sessions and projects that commemorate the deceased classmates. Group exploration of unfinished business through written or role-playing exercises. Provision for students to deal with the deaths outside the group within the school environment through peer support groups. (Samide & Stockton, 2002)

Gray (1988) reported that bereaved teens in support groups found peers to be "most helpful," compared to other school-related workers, and that bereaved adolescents did not want to be singled out or treated in special ways (pp. 187–188). In cases of sudden death, grief, and bereavement among adolescents, a great deal of shock, vulnerability, remorse, and other emotions quickly emerge. Because most adolescents lack experience dealing with the death of their peers and because social influence is powerful and pervasive in a setting such as a high school, the use of adolescent group grief work is an ideal strategy for controlling distortions and rumors and for helping young people release grief energy and begin to resolve their feelings of loss.

The counselor, meeting with the group in the group guidance room, served as the crisis worker. She met with several grief work groups during the days immediately following the deaths of the four students. The counselor set the tone by introducing the topic and encouraging members to share their emotional responses to the loss. Later during the session, after the release of students' grief energy, the counselor began to use structured techniques to help them sharpen their memories and focus on reality.

CW: I really appreciate all the expressions of your feelings you've given so freely. Before the session begins today, I asked Samantha to go by the yearbook office and pick up a copy of this year's *Wildcat.* I also asked her to pick up some leftover photographs that the yearbook staff did not use. Samantha, would you like to share some of them with the group?

Samantha: I put filing cards in the pages of the annual that I thought we'd like to look at. Oh, and I've got some great shots of LaTara, Jerry, and Tracey. I only found one of Phil, and that was in a group. But Phil's class picture is in there (*pointing toward the yearbook*), and all four of them look so real and alive and so happy in the activities section.

The students in the group showed a great deal of interest and released a great amount of stress energy while examining the photographs of the deceased students. The crisis worker let the students take their own individual time in reminiscing and talking about their grief from 2 minutes to 20 minutes. Because everyone grieves differently, allowing students to take as much time as they need is important in moving beyond the grief (Tillman & Rust, 2011). Later in the session, the group discussed death in general, the impact of death on the living, and their own deaths. The counselor then used a technique called Memory Moments. Students finished off sentences such as "When I heard you died, I . . . ," "Our last conversation was . . . ," "My head feels . . . ," "My heart feels . . . ," "I wish I had said. . . ." All of these sentence stems allow students to openly speak to the wide range of emotions they are carrying (Counce & Sommer, 2003).

The counselor was able to use another technique that is sometimes effective in group grief work—the epitaph exercise. Each group member was given four index cards and was instructed: "If you were given the responsibility for writing the epitaphs for Phil, Jerry, LaTara, and Tracey, write down the exact words on the cards that would appear on their gravestones." The group shared their epitaphs and discussed them. When it is difficult to say or write words about dead classmates, Tillman and Rust (2011) propose making Feeling Hearts by drawing large hearts and having students print their feelings inside it and then pass the hearts around and have the group discuss those feelings.

Eddie: I thought Tarunda's was really good when she wrote—about Jerry—"Here lies the Martin Luther King of Cedar Grove," because he really did like and care for everybody. (*Students nod in agreement.*)

Keena: I *almost* cried when I wrote Tracey's, and then I *did* when Amber read LaTara's. I just felt like I couldn't stand it. It's so true. I'm really going to miss that girl. (*Students nod in agreement. Long period of silence; thoughtful look on all faces.*)

CW: I think what we've done is to write down, in the briefest form, what we want to remember most about each of our beloved classmates.

Before the session ended, the counselor led the group in identifying the positive contributions that each of the deceased students had made and in verbalizing their good-byes to each of their departed classmates. Grief doesn't always have to be, nor should it be, only sadness. Having students remember the good times is a powerful way to balance memories of loved ones who have died (Tillman & Rust, 2011). The counselor was attempting to use the power and social influence of the group setting to enhance the emotional impact on each member and to prepare each member to say good-bye, let go of the deceased, and begin to get ready to go on living.

Ending any counseling group after a bond has been formed is difficult. Loss and grief groups are even tougher because they are now truly saying good-bye to the loved one. Saying good-bye should include some simple symbolic ceremony such as releasing balloons, setting small paper boats with candles in them adrift on a river, or writing good-bye letters. Generally, letting the group decide on what simple memorial service to do will work best (Tillman & Rust, 2011). Tillman and Rust propose discussing in age appropriate terms that endings are a natural part of the life cycle. They further propose that the group summarize and discuss what they have learned from the group. Our own group ending goes something like this: After summaries of the experience have been given, state specifically:

CW: I want all of you to stand up and clasp hands with one another so we have a circle. This group was about remembering our dead classmates who are gone but not forgotten from our lives. Because we are living, we owe it to them and ourselves to move on with our lives, just as they would if we were gone from theirs. We are going to say one last good-bye in the circle, then we are going to spread the circle until our hands drop, let the spirits of our friends go out of this circle and on their way as we do the same with our own lives.

Defining the Boundaries

Probably one of the toughest jobs of an SCRT and the school administration is to discourage parents, students, or various other interest groups in the community from honoring the death by conducting a commemorative service or other memorial at the school. Unequivocally, suicidal students should not be formally memorialized by the school because of possible copycats (Capuzzi, 2002). It cannot be overemphasized that the school administration and the SCRT should be the ones to make decisions about the response to school tragedies in which deaths occur. Overall, it is probably best for the school not to memorialize any kind of deaths in any fashion—assemblies, yearbooks, trees planted, rooms or fields named, and so on—because of the perception of differential treatment.

Bluntly stated, schools are in the education business not in the funeral home or memorial business (Trotter, 2003). Trotter recommends that after the funeral, all of the drawings and other eulogies and epitaphs be collected and given to the family and not kept on display in the school. She also recommends that the student's chair be left alone until the day after the funeral, but then all chairs in the room need to be rearranged. She proposes that immediately upon notification, a member of the SCRT should go to the student's locker and collect all personal items when students are not present and prevent memorializing the locker.

The student's locker should be left vacant for the remainder of the year, but then be merged into the standard locker assignment for next year's class. Louvre (2002) believes that with younger children, the desk should be left in the room until the other students want it moved out. She further proposes that a suitable memorial be constructed by the children such as positive epitaphs or a signed teddy bear that the class might give to the parents when they come to school to collect the dead child's things.

Transcrisis Intervention with Individuals and Total School Systems

LO14

For those children who are in need of assistance beyond psychological first aid, transcrisis intervention uses many of the approaches detailed in the chapters on PTSD and sexual assault. Use of drawings, modeling clay, and other manipulative play materials is particularly helpful in empowering children to take control of a situation that may seem beyond their ability to do so. Initially, the child should be allowed to use the materials to construct whatever he or she desires. The crisis interventionist uses this time to build trust and rapport.

Invariably the crisis will be manifested in the child's play and will provide clues to the source of the child's anxiety and means of coping (Pynoos & Eth, 1986, p. 307). At some time during the process, a child who has been numbing and repressing the crisis event is going to have an emotional release that may be shocking and unsettling to the crisis worker (Pynoos & Eth, 1986, p. 308). At that point, the worker must be calm, cool, and collected and be able to psychologically and physically comfort the child.

The use of guided imagery and the employment of superheroes as helpers in those images (Lazarus, 1977), conscious dreaming to help stop recurring nightmares (Garfield, 1984), and relaxation and desensitization techniques to teach anxiety control (Thompson & Rudolph, 1992, p. 173) are all potent ways of helping children empower themselves and take back control over their feelings, thoughts, and behaviors.

The Case of Josh

Josh is a 7-year-old second grader who has just recovered from a bite from a brown recluse spider (one of the most poisonous spiders in North America). Josh was bitten in the leg, and the necrosis that developed required reconstructive surgery. He now walks with a cane and a limp. He is embarrassed by his disability and feels his classmates are making fun of him behind his back. For a time, it was feared that Josh might lose his leg. What has compounded the problem is that recently thousands of brown recluses were discovered in the steam tunnels of Josh's school. This discovery set off a panic, because the children had seen what happened to Josh and had also viewed news items on television about the brown recluses' movement into their geographic area. Although the school district immediately hired exterminators to rid the school of the spiders, the children's fears were not allayed.

Josh is now hypervigilant in regard to any insects, is afraid to sleep in his own bed, has developed school phobia, and shrieks and screams in terror at going to school. He has recurrent nightmares about hoards of huge, hairy spiders covering his body. He is very sure he is going to die from a spider bite. His academic achievement

has fallen, and he is in danger of failing second grade. His parents have talked to him about switching schools, but he is sure that all schools now contain brown recluses. Most of his conversation is centered on insects. He avoids outdoor activities for fear of getting bitten. The duration of his symptoms is now into its sixth week. After an interview with the school psychologist, Josh is given a diagnosis of acute traumatic stress disorder.

Because many other children at the school are manifesting symptoms of traumatic stress due to the brown recluse infestation, the SCRT has a meeting and determines that intervention is necessary with both the student population as a whole and Josh individually. Josh's parents are called, and they agree to individual intervention. The team's media person prepares a number of press releases and goes on radio and television news shows to explain what is being done to control the situation. In coordination with the parent liaison, bulletins are also sent home to all parents.

The medical liaison has classroom meetings with every homeroom in the school. She provides detailed information about what brown recluse bites look like and what medical care is needed, and answers the students' questions in a truthful, no-nonsense manner. Another classroom meeting is held with the high school biology teacher, who shows the students what the spider looks like, describes its habits, and also indicates to them that although the brown recluse is poisonous, it is a very shy spider that tries to avoid contact with people. Question-and-answer sessions follow, and students get a good idea of what they need to do at both school and home to avoid being bitten.

Parents are invited to a special parent–teacher meeting where all the SCRT staff are present to provide information about helping children cope with the sudden siege of arachnophobia (fear of spiders and similar creatures). After completing the psychological first aid program, the SCRT staff poll the teachers, who indicate the students seem to have conquered their fears of spiders. But Josh has not!

The crisis worker goes to Josh's home and, after making Josh's acquaintance, sets up the following exercise:

CW: I want you to draw me the feeling of what "scared" looks like, Josh.

Josh: (Takes markers and poster board and draws a picture of a very large tarantula-like spider with huge dripping fangs about to pounce on a small boy cowering in a corner. While drawing, Josh gives the crisis worker a blow-by-blow gruesome description of what the spider is going to do to the little boy.)

CW: Boy! That's scary all right. I wonder what we could do to make that big nasty spider run away and hide?

Josh: I dunno. Nothin', I think.

CW: Well, that is pretty tough with a spider that big, but you know, I've got an idea. It takes a spider to catch a spider. And I've got just the guy to do it. (*pulls out a Spider-Man comic book*) Have you ever read a Spider-Man comic? He is way cool.

Josh: (*eyes light up and takes the comic book and starts looking at it*) Yeah, and I've seen him in the movie. He is cool!

CW: So let's get him to help us. Takes a Spider-Man to catch a spider, right?

Josh: Well, I guess that's right.

CW: All right! Let's jump Spider-Man off the comic book and onto your poster board. Can you draw him on there and tell me what's happening?

Josh: Well, OK. (*draws Spider-Man casting a big net over the spider*) Spider-Man throws this big net over him, see, and the spider doesn't like it. But the more it struggles, the more it gets tangled up. Ha! Ha! Caught in a spider net. That's cool! He can't get out, but he's still there, though. I don't like him right there.

CW: OK! How could we get rid of him?

Josh: Well, we could take him to the bug-man, and let him douse him with bug juice.

CW: Fine. Go ahead and do that. (*gives Josh another piece of poster board*)

Josh: (*continues to draw Spider-Man pulling the spider over to an exterminator who looks very much like Josh*)

CW: Now what?

Josh: I'm gonna douse him good.

CW: Good! Do that! What does that spider look like now?

Josh: He's gonna shrivel up and blow away. (*Continues to draw the spider all shriveled up; he and Spider-Man triumphantly hold the spider up as a trophy.*)

Over the course of the next several sessions, the crisis worker continues to use modeling clay and drawing to give Josh and Spider-Man increasing control over his environment (Webb, 2007). The crisis worker uses the superhero to help empower this frightened and traumatized little boy. The crisis worker now moves further to help Josh regain control over more of his environment by taking him outside to the backyard. Although Josh is somewhat timid about going outside, he goes with the crisis worker, one hand clutching the worker's hand and the other clutching a Spider-Man figurine.

CW: Boy! We're outside here. How do you feel?

Josh: Yeah, I think the backyard is where I got bit.

CW: And you're back out here. That's pretty courageous, almost like Spider-Man.

Josh: Well, it's OK 'cause Spider-Man's here with me . . . and well . . . you too.

CW: Josh, I wonder if Spider-Man could help us with those nightmares too. What I'd like you to do is just sort of have a daydream, you know like let your mind wander like there was sort of nothing to do and you were just kind of relaxing, and just shut your eyes and instead of having a nightmare, just imagine yourself and Spider-Man. Just you and Spider-Man out on patrol, saving the world from those huge spiders. Can you picture yourself and Spider-Man like that? Now just lie back and listen to me and just let yourself relax. (*The crisis worker deeply relaxes Josh and then helps him create an image of him and Spider-Man.*)

The crisis worker uses a combination of relaxation training and guided imagery to decrease Josh's anxiety and help him build a mental image of himself and his powerful friend taking control of the nighttime environment.

Josh: (*with his eyes closed*) Yeah, me and Spider-Man are scaling up a tall building, looking for big old hairy spiders. (*Josh goes on to explain how they are out on patrol catching all kinds of spiders.*)

The crisis worker helps keep Josh on track, and when he gets stuck trying to catch a really huge, fast, fluorescent chartreuse spider, the crisis worker gives him a can of superstrong glue, and Josh and Spider-Man spread it out and get the spider stuck in it.

CW: Good. Now what I want you to do is get that image real clear in your mind. You and Spider-Man giving each other high-fives for catching that really monstrous spider. If you start to have that same old nightmare tonight, I want you to change that nightmare, and do just what you and Spider-Man did. That's what I want you to dream. I'll bet you can do that! (*gives and returns a high-five from Josh*)

The power of suggestion and use of guided imagery to enable a child to change his dreams may seem farfetched, but it must be remembered that children work out their problems through fantasy and play. As the crisis worker continuously reinforces Josh for getting back in control of his environment through the help of the superhero, Josh can start to feel safe not only in his backyard, but also in his sleep.

Finally, to expedite Josh's return to school, the crisis worker sets up a classroom meeting with his classmates. Josh tells his classmates about his real spider bite and all the things that happened to him in the hospital. The rest of the children are very curious about all this and ask him many questions. Josh has been embarrassed about his scar and his limp, but now he's in the limelight and eagerly starts to tell them what went on while he was in the hospital and doesn't hesitate to tell them some of the more gruesome details with accompanying "Oohs," "Aahs," and "Ughs" from the class. He also shows them the pictures he drew and tells them, with the help of the crisis worker, how he's "not afraid of any darned old spiders anymore." An examination of Josh's drawings indicates just how potent serial drawing can be (Gumaer, 1984). Over a series of sessions, the spiders get smaller and smaller, and Josh and Spider-Man get bigger and bigger until the spider is in realistic proportion to Josh in the drawings, no more than a spot on the poster board. In the course of 8 weeks, Josh was able to return to school, his nightmares of spiders went away, and he was able to resume the life of a normal 7-year-old boy.

Epilogue

If you are planning on being a school counselor and are reading this book in a formal graduate class, you are probably ahead of most of your peers. That statement probably holds as well for social workers and school psychologists. There is a reason that the Council on Accreditation of Counseling and Educationally Related Programs (CACREP) is mandating crisis intervention in its new standards for school counseling. Wachter (2007) has done a comprehensive study on school counselors and crisis, and what she found is sobering. Although school psychologists, school social workers, police officers, other in-school staff, and community mental health workers may well be involved in crisis intervention, the typical first responder in a school will be a school counselor. Particularly in a school shooting, school counselors are most likely to become the leaders in their school building. Many are unprepared to take on such a task, but they get it anyway when a building or district has not done the preplanning it needs to do (Fein, Carlisle, & Issacson, 2008).

Wachter found that more than half the school counselors (53.1%) reported dealing with all the crises discussed in this chapter plus sexual and physical abuse. About a fifth of the counselors (21.7%) reported that they had received no training at all during their master's degree program for any kind of crisis intervention. Forty-four percent reported that after obtaining a master's degree they had picked up training in areas such as suicide intervention and critical incident stress debriefing on their own. Interestingly, these counselors perceived their on-site staff and resources to be more helpful than external sources of support. The school counselors identified assessment for suicidal and homicidal ideation and the provision of support for students who are at risk for both as critical knowledge components.

To further make the life of a school counselor more exciting, there will not only be the once-in-a-year, or 5 years, or once-in-a-lifetime megacrises to make one's life more self-actualized. There will also be the daily mini-crisis, the constant transcrisis, and each of these will have the ability to metastasize into really big ones.

To that end Robertson (2013) provides her counseling interns with a simple SRSR acronym to base their decision making when confronted with a crisis. S is for *safety*. Do I feel safe in this situation? Do I need help maintaining a safe environment? Is this person in danger of hurting himself or herself or someone else? Do I need to notify anyone else if the answer to the foregoing questions leaves a reasonable doubt in my mind about safety? R is for *role*. Is it within the scope of what you are professionally competent to do? You will be confronted with all kinds of human dilemmas and many will be beyond your scope of practice. While on the one hand, "It's not my job!" is not acceptable, neither is thinking you are a drug or trauma therapist. Don't be afraid, embarrassed, or too proud to refer.

Interestingly, Robertson (2013) adds *skills,* but emphasizes having faith in and using basic listening and responding skills to defuse and de-escalate most crisis situations. And sometimes, because you do have advanced crisis intervention skills from reading this book and or taking a crisis course, you may even use some of the "stuff" you have learned here. Finally, Robertson speaks to cultivating *resources.* Having a ready list of people and numbers you can call to get specialized help that ranges from getting food and clothing to a burned out family to finding out someone who knows how to do eye movement desensitization and reprocessing (EMDR) for PTSD should be a first priority when entering new territory.

Crisis and burnout go hand in hand. Fein and his associates (2008) found that indeed school counselors suffered from the stress of being leaders in an unknown and chaotic situation where they had to make fast decisions. They learned how to do debriefing on the fly, which would be unthinkable for emergency responders such as police, EMTs, or firefighters. They also engaged in decisions they had never figured they would be involved in doing and suffered traumatic symptoms as a result. While Wachter found no significant difference in burnout symptoms and individual exposure to crisis, she did find significance in higher burnout rates when physical abuse was the precipitating crisis event. Wachter also determined that master's level training in the kind of course you are now taking with this book is significantly related to *reducing* burnout rates in school counselors. Finally, Wachter noted that building internal support systems and getting continuing education in crisis intervention is helpful in preventing burnout.

While every school district in the United States most likely has at least some kind of crisis plan that goes beyond fire, tornado, and earthquake drills, and some of those school districts may go to great lengths to detail how crisis teams will operate in large-scale disasters, the simple fact is that school personnel who deal with the day-in and day-out grinding crises that afflict many students don't have a lot of resources to help them (Heath & Sheen, 2005). So if you are a school counselor or other school professional taking this course, you may find that Heath and Sheen's (2005) book, *School-Based Crisis Intervention: Preparing All Personnel to Assist*, and Kerr's (2009) book, *School Crisis Prevention and Intervention*, would be very helpful in training the people you most likely will have to count on, your fellow professionals. Heath and Sheen's book goes into specific detail about the basic, hands-on crisis intervention skills and activities that teachers, secretaries, custodians, and bus drivers will need to help you out. Kerr's book has more to do with laying out the larger operational picture. Along with Scott Poland's (1999) book, *Coping with Crisis: Lessons Learned*, which deals with the logistical, tactical, and strategic problems of a crisis, it is especially appropriate for administrators. And make no mistake about it, you will need their help. Going it alone in a school building when dealing with the kinds of "stuff" this chapter is about will make you an odds-on favorite to be what the burnout chapter in this book is about. So, if you are an aspiring school counselor, be assured that what's in this book is "stuff" you are going to need. The question is absolutely not "If" but "When?"

SUMMARY

The rise of school violence perpetrated by the estranged violent student has caused a great deal of public concern and received widespread media coverage because of its perceived senselessness and its occurrence in communities where residents previously thought they were immune from such horrific events. Although the focus has been on the tragedy of estranged students who act out their frustration and anger in lethal ways, the growth and spread of gang-initiated violence in urban, suburban, and rural communities far exceed the tragedies the estranged juvenile has perpetrated.

Homicides are not the only lethal malady to afflict schools and cause crises. The suicide rate has risen to epidemic proportions among children and adolescents. School personnel face a wide variety of crises that reach far beyond the normal developmental issues and crises of childhood and adolescence. Schools have been called upon to develop wide-ranging prevention strategies for profiling, screening, and preventing acts of violence both to oneself and to others. Contemporary crisis strategies in schools deal not only with prevention, but with intervention and postvention as well. Crisis workers interact with students, faculty, and parents who have been associated with, witnessed, or suffered from traumatic events originating within the school or with students.

Although no known intervention plan will guarantee that tragedies will not take place, there are approaches that hold promise in dealing with a variety of crises that can afflict schools. These approaches call for everyone—community service organizations, child welfare agencies, mental health facilities, local, state, and national governments, the courts, law enforcement agencies, and all of the staff in schools—to work cooperatively in developing and implementing crisis intervention plans. Most important, no school should be without a crisis plan and a well-trained crisis response team.

Visit CengageBrain.com for a variety of study tools and useful resources such as video examples, case studies, interactive exercises, flashcards, and quizzes.

On the Home Front
Crisis in the Human Services Workplace

Part 3 deals with helping the crisis worker cope with crises that might occur in the human services workplace. The world in which we live and in which crisis workers function is becoming increasingly dangerous and violent for clients as well as for human services professionals. Chapter 14, on violent behavior in institutions, provides information and techniques to help workers better understand and deal with both the volatile environment and the dilemmas of clients who strive to cope within that environment. Hostage taking is another phenomenon of the contemporary human services setting that has become increasingly prevalent. Chapter 15 deals with human services worker burnout, vicarious traumatization, and compassion fatigue. These are major crises that directly affect the crisis worker. Chapter 16 discusses the largely uncharted waters of legal and ethical issues involved in crisis intervention.

Violent Behavior in Institutions

14

LEARNING OBJECTIVES

After studying this chapter, you should be able to:

1. Understand the risks of being employed in the human services workplace.
2. Understand the role the institution plays in violence perpetrated on human services workers.
3. Understand the risk human services workers themselves instigate that causes violence.
4. Know that potential legal liability occurs when violent acts happen against human services workers.
5. Know methods of assessing for violent behavior.
6. Understand the bases for violent behavior.
7. Understand what intervention procedures are and how they are used.
8. Understand what a threat assessment team is and how it is used.
9. Know what kind of training is necessary for violence reduction.
10. Understand the stages of intervention.
11. Understand violent geriatric clients and specific therapies used with them.

Introduction

Be forewarned! This is not a chapter designed **LO1** to recruit you into the human services field. Very little class or supervision time in most human services disciplines is given to the topic of dealing with violent behavior in the human services field because of bad publicity and politics that surround it. We believe that, at the very least, that missing curriculum is morally, ethically, and probably legally wrong. The human services field is one of the most gratifying and rewarding fields a person can be in, but it is also one of the most dangerous. Therefore, training on recognizing and handling violent clients should be one of the highest priorities in this business. Dr. Phillip Kleespies, an imminent researcher, practitioner, and writer on behavioral emergencies has taken the whole human services field to task in regard to the abysmal teaching and training of health care professionals on how to deal with violence (2014, pp. 47–97). This chapter is an attempt to rectify that a small bit and give you knowledge to be SAFE! Thus, we believe there is nothing more important you will read in this book that will affect your career in this business.

According to the Bureau of Labor Statistics, 27 out of the 100 fatalities that occurred in health care settings in 2013 were due to assaults and violent acts (Occupational Safety and Health Administration, 2015). That doesn't sound like a whole lot unless of course you were one of the 27! Thus, to think that violence against caring and sharing human services workers has never existed or doesn't still exist is to be gravely mistaken (Flannery, 2009; Gabe & Elston, 2009; Slovenko, 2006).

However, the vast majority of workplace violence is composed of nonfatal assaults. In 2000, 48% of all nonfatal injuries from occupational assaults in the United States occurred in health care and social services (U.S. Department of Labor, Bureau of Labor Statistics, 2001, 2002). For mental health workers in particular, the average number of assaults was 68.2 per 1,000 (U.S. Department of Justice, Bureau of Justice Statistics, 2001). These results were chilling enough that the Federal Bureau of Investigation sponsored a workplace symposium on violence in 2002. To put those statistics in terms that tell you how dangerous the mental health services can be, you would be as likely to be assaulted if you worked in a convenience/liquor store (68.4/1,000). Besides law enforcement and corrections occupations, only bartending is more likely to get you assaulted (91.3/1,000) (U.S. Department of Justice, Bureau of Justice Statistics, 1998)! Things haven't changed much since those statistics. The newest reports show that between 2011 and 2013 workplace assaults averaged about 25,000 annually with 70% to 74% occurring in health care settings. These are big numbers that perhaps don't mean much, but note that 10%–11% of health care injuries that required sick leave were assaults as compared to just 3% of injuries that occurred in the rest of the private sector (Occupational Safety and Health Administration, 2015).

A best estimate is that the chance of human services workers being assaulted on the job during their lifetime is approximately 50% (Turns & Blumenreich, 1993, p. 5). Newhill's (2003, pp. 35–54) comprehensive review of violence studies on social workers in the United States found that between 20% and 50% of the professionals studied reported that they had been assaulted. If that isn't enough to make you consider skyscraper window cleaning as an occupation, assaults on human services workers have been found to be a major contributor to burnout (Hensel, Lunsky, & Dewa, 2012; Gascon et al., 2013) and added stress, fear, and decreased job satisfaction (Harris & Leather, 2012; Hutchison et al., 2013). Lanctot and Guay (2014) reviewed 68 studies on workplace violence and found that physical, psychological, and emotional well-being, effective functioning at work, relationship with and quality of care of patients, and general social and financial well-being were all affected by violence perpetrated on the workers. The foregoing is indeed part of a long list of the reasons why human services workers burn out, which you will read about in Chapter 16, Human Services Workers in Crisis.

So being a human services/health care worker anywhere with the possible exception of Antarctica is a perilous occupation. Other countries such as the United Kingdom (Brown, Bute, & Ford, 1986; Leadbetter, 1993; Rowett, 1986), Canada (MacDonald & Sirotich, 2001), Israel (Guterman, Jayaratme, & Bargal, 1996), the Netherlands (Harte, van Leeuwen, & Theuws, 2013), Australia (Koritsas, Coles, & Boyle, 2010), and the sub-Sahara (El Ghaziri, Zhu, Lipscomb, & Smith, 2014) confirm a high incidence of violence and threatened violence against human services workers. The problem has become so bad in Spain that April 20 is designated a National Day Against Aggression in Health-Care Facilities (Marlasca, 2014)!

Perhaps more ominous is the notion of threat. Newell found in her own study that social workers who do not suffer an assault may experience destruction of property or verbal threats. Those threats are not taken lightly given the violent histories of many of the clients with whom they are dealing (Newhill, 2003, pp. 46–47). Constantly wondering whether an emotionally disturbed or mentally ill client will make good on his or her threats every time a human services worker walks out of the office is not the way to have a fulfilling and rewarding work experience. So threat assessment and management are not just the purview of Homeland Security. To that end, in 2013, the American Psychological Association started the *Journal of Threat Assessment and Management* (Dingfelder, 2013).

In summary, the foregoing statistics should tell you one thing: Although you may believe that you are some combination of Jane Addams, Carl Rogers, Florence Nightingale, and Mother Teresa ministering charitably and caringly to the disenfranchised and outcast, your clients may have a different idea (Newhill, 2003, p. 206)! Why is this so?

Precipitating Factors

A variety of hazards now put human services professionals more at risk of being victims of violent behavior than they have been in the past. This problem has become so pervasive that the American Psychological Association formed a task force to report on education and training in dealing with behavioral emergencies (American Psychological Association, 2000). They found in a survey of the literature that between 35% and 50% of psychologists in clinical practice had reported being assaulted. The threat has become so compelling that the American Psychological Association (2002) incorporated in their ethical standards a section to specifically address psychologists' freedom to terminate therapy if they feel threatened or endangered.

The social work profession has become very interested in violence because social workers are invariably in the line of fire as frontline workers attempting to deal with some of the most economically, socially, and emotionally disenfranchised individuals in the human services business. Interestingly, the counseling profession has not seemed as concerned, although high school counselors in particular are in the line of fire with one of the most volatile and violence-prone age groups there is. The amount of violence that now occurs in K–12 schools in the United States is approaching epidemic levels.

Substance Abuse. Probably the most noteworthy trend in the upsurge of violence has been the increasing numbers of substance abuse clients (Blumenreich, 1993b, pp. 23–24; Occupational Safety and Health Administration, 2003; Monahan et al., 2001; Turns & Blumenreich, 1993, p. 7). Intoxication's disinhibiting effect (McNeil, 2009) appears to directly influence violence, particularly in those individuals who are aggressive and impulsive (Chermack, Fuller, & Blow, 2000) and those with diagnosed major mental disorders (Rach-Beisel, Scott, & Dixon, 1999).

Deinstitutionalization. Since the "least restrictive environment" movement and subsequent deinstitutionalization of patients in the 1970s, day care centers, halfway houses, and shelters have filled the gap left when the warehousing facilities of state mental institutions were emptied. Lack of facilities for transients, shortage of staff, lack of follow-up care, and inability to monitor medication closely have created a fertile breeding ground for clients to regress to their previous pathological states (Occupational Safety and Health Administration, 2003; Weinger, 2001, p. 4).

Mental Illness. The role of mental illness in violent behavior has been hotly debated. To say that all mentally ill people will become violent is patently ludicrous. However, there is some clear evidence that a subset of mentally ill people will and do become violent (McNeil, 2009; Newhill, 2003, pp. 96–104). Delusions (schizophrenics), hallucinations (multiple disorders), and violent fantasies (sex offenders, multiple murderers) are all cues to possible violence in the mentally ill. Organic issues such as internal head injuries, brain diseases, and dementia all have the potential for increased violence (McNeil, 2009; Monahan et al., 2001; Tardiff, 2003). The personality disorders are rife with the kinds of mental disorders that may become violent. Many of the personality disorders are marked by anger control issues, impulsivity, and inability to regulate or control emotions (Newhill, 2003, pp. 99–104). Most particularly, those persons diagnosed with antisocial personality disorders and those with explosive personality disorders

are prime candidates for acute onset of anger and violence (McNeil, 2009).

Furthermore, because society and the judicial system have become increasingly aware of the role that mental illness plays in crime, a number of people who would formerly have been incarcerated are now remanded to mental health facilities (Occupational Safety and Health Administration, 2003). Also, because of prison overcrowding, potentially violent people are released on early parole. Farmed out to halfway houses that are also understaffed, and assigned to parole officers who have tremendous caseloads, parolees do not always get the follow-up care and supervision they need. Police now routinely use hospitals for criminal holds on acutely disturbed, violent individuals. Thus, human services workers are now being asked to deal with a wider variety of felons than before (Hartel, 1993; Occupational Safety and Health Administration, 2003; Walker & Seifert, 1994).

Gender. The stereotypical notion that males are more aggressive is becoming dated (Weinger, 2001, p. 7). While young males account for the majority of assaults, women are catching up. In regard to equal opportunity violence, Lam, McNeil, and Binder (2000) found that females were as likely to assault staff on a locked inpatient unit as were their male counterparts. Ryan and her associates (2004) found in their study of assaults on staff by youths that gender did not differentiate between who would and would not assault staff.

Gangs. Gang violence can be found in settings ranging from emergency rooms to juvenile detention facilities. Gang members' extreme violence, either as a rite of passage into the gang or in retaliation for offenses against them, is without fear or remorse regarding any person, time, or place (Kinney, 1995, pp. 168–169; Occupational Safety and Health Administration, 2003).

Required Reporting. The development of child and elder abuse reporting laws and domestic violence laws have made human services workers into something other than Florence Nightingale in the eyes of those who come into conflict with the social services and legal systems. Most of the time field staff such as social workers for human services agencies and school counselors and school psychologists become the objects of offenders' ire (Weinger, 2001, p. 5).

Elderly. The increase in the number of elderly people now institutionalized in nursing homes and hospitals has created a whole new population of potentially violent individuals. Casually dismissed as infirm and incapable of rendering harm to anyone, geriatric patients commit a disproportionate percentage of violent behavior against human services workers. The assumption that elderly clients are passive recipients of care is misguided. Study after study indicates this clientele to be at risk for behaving violently (Astroem et al., 2002; Gates, Fitzwater, & Succop, 2005; Hillman et al., 2005; Petrie, 1984, p. 107; Snyder, Chen, & Vacha-Haase, 2007; Weinstock et al., 2008).

Institutional Culpability

By their very nature, most care providers `LO2` are readily accessible to clientele and have minimal security checks. Often unrestricted movement throughout a facility may be gained by agitated and distraught family members, gang members, boyfriends and girlfriends, and clients who are frustrated over long waits and seeming lack of service. Care providers are also easy prey to anyone who walks in off the street with intentions other than seeking services and may believe drugs or money is readily available (Occupational Safety and Health Administration, 2003; Turner, 1984, pp. v–vi).

Security training and security devices cost time and money. Administrators trained solely in handling the financial, logistical, and personnel functions of institutions with the responsibility of maintaining adequate patient care are unaware of what it takes to provide an adequately secure environment for their staff (Dyer, Murrell, & Wright, 1984). Physical features of mental health facilities built to deemphasize security and confinement as a reaction to the "snake pit" mental hospitals of old have paradoxically put the human services workers at greater risk (Turns, 1993). Emotionally "cold and uncaring" settings, unclear staff roles, poorly structured activities, downsizing of staff, and unpredictable schedules are all stress elevators for the potentially violent client (Blumenreich, 1993a, pp. 38–39; Occupational Safety and Health Administration, 2003).

Assessment of potential for violent behavior should be mandatory in institutions and clinical facilities that deal with the mentally ill and emotionally disturbed (McNeil, 2009). Instruments are now available that, combined with clinical judgment, do a good job of predicting violent behavior if—and that is a big if—institutions will use them.

Universities and Their Counseling Centers

We have been particularly concerned with safety issues at many university counseling centers we have toured and two we have worked in. In an effort to be open, warm, and accessible, the university counseling center typically has no choke point that controls access to counseling offices. Students are free to roam about the center. Yet many of the offices are separated from the reception area and are extremely isolated. Even if there are visual, sound, and code alarms, the reaction time for help to arrive will be slow, giving a perpetrator time and ease of egress to escape. Career counseling, academic advising, and personal counseling clients in the university counseling center may all be mixed together in a very egalitarian environment, but it is a situation that has security risks. As evidenced by Seung-hui Cho's rampage at Virginia Tech in April 2007, some of the individuals who frequent the university counseling center may not be there just because they are homesick (Grayson & Meilman, 2006; Myer, James, & Moulton, 2011).

Numerous studies indicate that university counseling centers are dealing with more severe psychopathology than they have in the past (Benton et al., 2003; Bishop, 2006; Erdur-Baker et al., 2006; Pledge et al., 1998) and that more students are on psychotropic medication (Schwartz, 2006). More than 1 in 10 students sought counseling center services in 2009, which is the highest percentage ever found in the long-running National Survey of Counseling Center Directors. Further, about 48% of the students seen in those counseling centers have severe psychological problems (Munsey, 2010). Those shifts appear to be true not only in the United States but in the United Kingdom as well (Waller et al., 2005). Are those changes due to the general population in the United States becoming more pathological, or is the on-campus population changing because of the Rehabilitation Act of 1973 and the Americans with Disabilities Act of 1990, which made college campuses more receptive and accommodating to people with existing mental illnesses? This question has become so important that the *Journal of College Counseling* devoted its Fall 2005 issue to the topic of severe and persistent mental illness on college campuses (Beamish, 2005).

The implications for safety issues overall in the university as an institution are sobering. One study

(Kelly & Torres, 2006) found that women students felt a "chilly campus climate" that had nothing to do with the weather and everything to do with their perception of being unsafe on campus. This issue is even more compelling in regard to "chilly" safety considerations in university counseling centers. It is interesting to note that extended searches for any studies analyzing safety issues in university counseling centers turned up no hits.

Rudd's (2004) summary analysis of why college counseling centers are looking more and more like community mental health clinics is sobering. Counseling centers and universities that do not become proactive in tightening their security, notification, and oversight procedures will put their general populations at risk. Rudd contends that if university administrations have not already identified a risk management officer to place in the counseling center, they will soon have to do so.

In 40 years of counseling in some tough public schools, a state mental hospital, and a federal penitentiary, and meeting lots of disgruntled and unhappy customers with Memphis Police Department Crisis Intervention Team officers, we have yet to meet more severely mentally ill and emotionally disturbed individuals who were not incarcerated for their own safety than we have in a university counseling center. Two of the three colleagues we have known who were killed in the line of duty died from assaults inflicted on them by clients at the college counseling centers where they worked. Given our history and background, we may clearly have a bias. However, we do not think the murderous assault at Virginia Tech in April 2007 was happenstance. Subjective evidence tells us that many of our colleagues in counseling centers around the country still wear rose-colored glasses when it comes to truly appreciating the potentially dangerous people who find their way to a college counseling center and the lack of security that characterizes those centers. Combining those two variables results in a lethal formula.

Denial

Because of the negative publicity that accrues from violent incidents, institutions are loath to admit that they occur (Lanza, 1985), and it appears that such episodes go largely unreported (California Occupational Safety and Health Administration, 1998, p. 3; Hartel, 1993; Occupational Safety and Health Administration, 2003). Indeed, the reticence of colleges and universities to report campus crime for fear of bad publicity was in large part responsible for the Crime Awareness and Campus Security Act of 1990, known as the Clery Act for Jeanne Clery, a 19-year-old Lehigh University freshman who was raped and murdered in her campus residence hall in 1986. A study conducted to determine whether parents were aware of the Clery Act and how to find information on crime statistics found their knowledge of the act to be low (Janosik, 2004). It seems somewhat ironic that the study was carried out at Virginia Tech. One can only wonder if the results of that study would be different today.

Institutional Fault Lines.   For over 30 years research has continued to target the following problems in health care settings. Understaffing, overwork, poorly maintained physical environment, poorly educated nonprofessional staff, high staff turnover, absenteeism, time pressure and deadlines, on-the-job accidents, lack of senior management and staff support, poor or incomplete communication between administration and staff, lack of staff training in recognizing and managing escalating hostile and assaultive behavior, no time for problem solving and debriefing, and lack of a unifying treatment philosophy allow frustration to build within the staff and disrupt the treatment routine. As the staff transfer their frustration to the clients, the clients in turn become more threatened and start testing the limits of what will be tolerated. When staff attempt to impose behavioral limits under these erratic conditions, the outcome is often violent behavior by clients (Blair, 1991; Jensen & Absher, 1994; Evans & Petter, 2012; Lancman et al., 2013; Occupational Safety and Health Administration, 2003, 2015; Piercy, 1984, pp. 141–142).

Finally, secondary victimization occurs when, after an injury by an assaultive client, there is the underlying belief that "It wasn't handled right by the worker" (Turns, 1993, p. 131). Thus, not only does the human services worker suffer physical assault and all the psychological ramifications that go with it, but he or she also becomes a scapegoat for an administration unable to handle the increased violence (Newhill, 2003, p. 209).

Staff Culpability

Staff members are also culpable. A prevailing philosophy is that because human services workers are caring, well-intentioned people, recipients of their services will act in reciprocal ways toward them (Newhill, 2003, p. 13; Turner, 1984, p. vii). The ostrichlike assumption that "It can't happen to me, and besides, there are so few violent incidents that I really don't need to be concerned" is fallacious (Dyer, Murrell, & Wright, 1984, p. 1). Madden, Lion, and Penna (1976) interviewed psychiatrists who had been assaulted and found that more than half could have predicted the assault if they had not been in denial and thought themselves immune from the threat.

From the client's viewpoint, becoming violent is invariably seen as a consequence of being provoked by the worker in some way (Rada, 1981; Ryan et al., 2004). Paradoxically, most staff members have little idea what they or the institution do that is provocative. For many clients, treatment may be perceived as coercive, threatening, or frightening. When a client feels little control over treatment conducted by an authoritarian staff, the client may feel the only option is to aggressively act out (Blair, 1991). Furthermore, if the staff treatment philosophy includes limit setting such as use of restraints, seclusion, medication, locked units, and assaults as "part of the territory" (Occupational Safety and Health Administration, 2003), then a self-fulfilling prophecy is likely to develop, with violent acting out as the norm and the only way to get attention. Conversely, a staff's failure to set limits in regard to appropriate behavior in a positive, firm, fair, and empathic manner, as opposed to dictatorially taking away privileges without defining how those might be lost or explaining how they can be regained, increases the potential for violence (Blair & New, 1991). The attitude of staff toward clients also plays a part in who gets assaulted. Staff members who are burned out are more likely to be assaulted than those who are not (Isaksson et al., 2008).

Experience also makes a difference. The great majority of assaults occur to people like you who are reading this sentence—that is, rookies in the field who don't know the lay of the land (Flannery et al., 2011). Guy, Brown, and Poelstra (1990) found, in a national study of psychologists who had been assaulted, that 46% of all assaults involved students or trainees and that the incidence of assaults decreased the more years of experience workers had. So you might want to personalize the contents of this chapter a little more than usual.

Legal Liability

Although health care providers may be the victims of assaults, they may also become legally liable for their actions, no matter how well intended **LO4**

those actions may be (Monahan, 1984). Such liability extends to the institutions and directors of those institutions, who may fall under a heading of "vicarious" civil and criminal liability (Dyer, Murrell, & Wright, 1984, p. 23). As paradoxical as it may seem, assaultive clients have held institutions and their employees liable for failure of "duty of care owed" to those selfsame clients (Belak & Busse, 1993, pp. 137–143). Numerous successful lawsuits also have been brought against health care providers for failure to properly diagnose, treat, and control violent clients or protect third parties from assaultive behavior (Felthous, 1987).

Workplace violence has become so serious that the Centers for Disease Control has declared workplace violence a national health problem (National Institute for Occupational Safety and Health, 1992), and the federal Occupational Safety and Health Administration (OSHA) has come to the conclusion that workplace violence can no longer be tolerated (California Occupational Safety and Health Administration, 1998, p. 5). OSHA has recently started issuing citations to employers who fail to adequately protect their employees from violence in the workplace and have developed a comprehensive violence prevention plan for human services institutions (Occupational Safety and Health Administration, 2015).

One of the better predictors of who will or will not be at risk to become violent is the pooled clinical judgment of human services workers who have come into contact with the clients (Douglas, Ogloff, & Hart, 2003; Durivage, 1989; Werner et al., 1989). One of the primary reasons that cases have been decided in favor of the plaintiff is the failure of one clinician to communicate with another clinician that a client has a history of violence and might present a future danger (Beck, 1988; Belak & Busse, 1993, p. 147). From that standpoint, the institution and worker who wish to avoid a court appearance would do well to flag records of violent acts or ideation and relay that information to other members of the treatment team for feedback and possible action (Blair, 1991; Martin et al., 1991).

Dynamics of Violence in Human Services Settings

The ability to predict who will be violent, when, and under what conditions has been notoriously unreliable (American Psychiatric Association, **LO5**

1974; Kirk, 1989; Monahan, 1988; Mulvey & Lidz, 1984; Palmstierna & Wistedt, 1990; Sloore, 1988).

There is a long history that proposes actuarial assessments (normed instruments with reliability and validity studies backing them up) are better risk predictors than individual clinical judgment (Meehl, 1954). The problem with that piece of information is that many times in crisis there is no time or inclination on the client's part to sit down and compliantly take a test!

Predictions are especially likely to be wrong when crisis workers have little background information on clients and may not have time to make more than an "eyeball" assessment of the situation before they have to act. Yet data do exist to present general profiles of clients who are more likely than others to become violent, given the right constellation of conditions. To that end, accurate behavioral information is the central core in assessment for violent behavior. Cawood and Corcoran (2009, p. 17) propose that the depth and accuracy of behavioral information obtained are directly correlated to the quality and accuracy of assessment of who may become violent, where, and under what conditions.

Violence Potential Assessment Instruments

A great deal of research has been conducted on prediction of violence and the assessment of it. As a result, Ronan and associates (2014) have compiled a comprehensive book of over 130 scales, questionnaires, and surveys to accurately assess at-risk clients. So how to choose what to use? Here are a few representative examples.

The *Violence Screening Checklist–Revised* (VSC-R) includes checkoff items that review history of physical attacks and fear-inducing/threat behavior during the first 2 weeks of hospital admission, presence or absence of suicidal behavior, schizophrenic or manic diagnosis, and male gender (McNeil & Binder, 1994). This instrument appears to be highly reliable, particularly in regard to the first few days of hospital admission (McNeil et al., 2003).

The *Violence Risk Appraisal Guide* (VRAG) (Rice & Harris, 1995) combined with the *Hare Psychopathy Checklist–Revised* (PCL-R) (Hare, 1991) is designed to predict whether incarcerates who are soon to be released will violently recidivate. It has 12 historical, biographical variables that range across school adjustment to alcohol use and then is combined with measures of psychopathology on the PCL-R.

The *Broset Violence Checklist* (BVC; Linaker & Busch-Iversen, 1995) checks for the presence or absence of six factors that are frequently seen as a prelude to violent incidents on acute psychiatric wards: confusion, irritability, boisterous acting out, verbal threats, physical threats, and attacks on objects. This device has been shown to have good predictive validity during 24-hour follow-ups if two or more of these items are checked. A large-scale study of geriatric patients who were violent as opposed to those who were not found the BVC to be a good predictor of violent episodes and a good discriminator between those who would and would not become violent (Almvik, Woods, & Rasmussen, 2007).

Structured Professional Judgment

While all of these instruments would seem to do a good job of predicting both short- and long-term violence risk in psychiatric populations, the problem is still predicting when it is happening "RIGHT NOW!" and doing something about it. From that standpoint, knowing the verbal and physical cues and using interocular and auditory analysis (eyeballing and having your ears on) are still the best bet for staying out of harm's way. Understanding and knowing the observable risk factors for violence you will read in the following section are known as **decision support tools** when combined with actuarial techniques (Kleespies, 2014, p. 109). These are not standardized psychological tests but risk factors that have been assessed to have high reliability and predictive ability in regard to violence risk.

In that regard, Kleespies (2014, pp. 108–109) has critically reviewed an alternative to either instant eyeballing or 4 hours of sit-down testing that involves what Borum and associates (2010) have termed **structured professional judgment** (SBJ). SBJ combines the art of clinical judgment with the science of the actuarial predictors. Van Brunt (2015, pp. 121–137) details the following steps to arrive at a structured professional judgment decision about an individual's potential for violent behavior:

1. Gather information via clinical assessment and comprehensive background information from family, school, community, law enforcement, and the workplace.
2. Determine the presence of risk factors (as detailed in this chapter) as they apply to the present situation.
3. What are the potential motivators, disinhibitors, and destabilizing elements present in the current

environment that could turn potential violence kinetic?

4. Given that the foregoing variables have reached a critical mass, develop potential scenarios as to how the violence might potentiate.

5. Construct case management of the individual based on the foregoing potential violent scenarios.

6. Communicate these findings to all parties that will play a part in the case management and have the formal report on file and readily accessible.

SBJ is now a well-established approach to risk assessment for violence and is used in psychiatric hospitals, forensic mental health services and criminal justice systems (Webster et al., 2014). As an example of how these go together, the *Dynamic Appraisal of Situational Aggression* (DYAS) checks for immediate risk of violence and is also a treatment plan aid that helps in reducing the risk of violence. When combined with professional observation, the DYAS was found to be a better predictor than clinical judgments alone (Ogloff & Daffern, 2006).

In arriving at a decision of potential risk of violence the clinician uses evidence-based risk factors combined with clinical opinion. These risk factors have been reduced to manual form in such instruments as the *Historical-Clinical–Risk Management 20* (HCR-20) (Webster et al., 1997). Singh and associates (2011) did a comprehensive meta-analysis of nine of the most commonly used structured violence assessment instruments. Out of 68 studies examined, they found the HCR-20 to be one of the better decision support tools for predicting who will and who won't become violent. The HCR-20 is a violence risk assessment rating device that asks clinicians to rate clients on 20 variables based on a variety of questions concerning clients' history of violence, clinical mental health status, self-management, and degree of risk upon return to society.

The ratings show good reliability in predicting who among forensic psychiatric clients will become violent both in the long term (Douglas, Ogloff, & Hart, 2003) and in the short term (McNeil et al., 2003), although it fared poorly when assessing incarcerated females in regard to who might commit a violent crime and had an inverse ability to predict which females had been convicted for murder (Warren et al., 2005)! So it is also not a perfect predictor. However, one of the interesting assets of the HCR-20 is that a *Violence Risk Management Companion Guide* has been developed (Douglas et al., 2001) that offers suggestions on treatment approaches based on the constellation of elevated clinical and risk factors presented. Following are some of the critical variables that are used as a bases for judgment in predicting risk of violence.

Bases for Violence

Keeping in mind the terms *general profiles* **LO6** and *right conditions,* the following bases for profiling violence are "best bet" predictors of "RIGHT NOW!"

There are biological, psychological, and social bases for violence. Biologically, low intelligence, hormonal imbalances, organic brain disorders, neurological and systemic changes of a psychiatric nature, disease, chemicals, intense and chronic pain, or traumatic head injury may lead to more violence-prone behavior (Fishbain et al., 2000; Hamstra, 1986; Heilbrun, 1990; Heilbrun & Heilbrun, 1989; McNeil, 2009; Newhill, 2003, pp. 107–108). Psychologically, specific situational problems, certain functional psychoses, and character disorders are predisposing to violence (Greenfield, McNeil, & Binder, 1989; Heilbrun, 1990; Heilbrun & Heilbrun, 1989; Klassen & O'Connor, 1988; McNeil, 2009; Newhill, 2003, pp. 94–106). Socially, modeling the violent behavioral norms of family, peers, homelessness, lack of social support, relationship with potential victims, and the milieu within which one lives can exacerbate violent tendencies (McNeil, 2009; Nisbett, 1993; Tardiff, 1984a, p. 45; Wood & Khuri, 1984, p. 60).

Finally, specific on-site physical environmental stressors such as heat, bad lighting and decor, crowding, noise, conflict, and poor communication can trigger violence (Anderson, 2001; Jensen & Absher, 1994; Newhill, 2003, p. 190; Vaaler, Morken, & Linaker, 2005). The problem is that when all these ingredients are mixed together, the results start to resemble the kinds of people and environments with which the crisis worker is likely to come in contact (Tardiff, 1984a, p. 45)!

Age.   Males between the ages of 15 and 30 tend to be the most violent subgroup (Blumenreich, 1993a, p. 36; Fareta, 1981; Shah, Fineberg, & James, 1991). Next come elderly clients, who are disproportionately represented in the population that may become violent (Astroem et al., 2002; Hindley & Gordon, 2000; Petrie, 1984, p. 107). Crisis workers tend to dismiss this group as being harmless, but in a study of 200 cases of assault at the Cincinnati Veterans Administration Medical Center, Jones (1985) discovered that 58.5% of the assaults took place in the geriatric facility. This statistic is noteworthy because the institution also had a large psychotic and substance-abusing population.

Substance Abuse. There is probably no psychotropic drug, either legal or illegal, that does not correlate with violence when it is abused. Whether the abuser is going on a meth high, coming off Valium, or experiencing the withdrawal of heroin, violence and drug use have a strong relationship (Blumenreich, 1993b, p. 24; Piercy, 1984, pp. 131–135; Rada, 1981; Simonds & Kashani, 1980). The foregoing statement most certainly includes alcohol. Alcohol has been associated with more than half of reported cases of violence in emergency rooms and one fourth of reported cases in psychiatric institutions (Bach y Rita, Lion, & Climent, 1971). The potential for violence is further increased when individuals who have a history of psychosis engage in alcohol or drug use (Klassen & O'Connor, 1988; Yesavage & Zarcone, 1983).

Predisposing History of Violence. A history of serious violence, homicide, sexual attacks, assault, or threat of assault with a deadly weapon is one of the best predictors of future violence (California Occupational Safety and Health Administration, 1998, p. 3; Fareta, 1981; Monahan, 1981). Any background that includes contact with the criminal justice system for aggravated felonies, weapons possession, threats against prospective victims, or a history of assaultive behavior while hospitalized should automatically put the human services worker on notice to be extremely cautious with the client (Blumenreich, 1993a, p. 37; Klassen & O'Connor, 1988). Of all the predisposing clues for violent behavior, probably there is none better than being brought to a facility for violent behavior as a part of emotional disturbance or mental illness.

Psychological Disturbance. A variety of mental disorders may be predisposing to violence: the antisocial personality type who has a history of violent behavior, emotional callousness, impulsivity, and manipulative behavior; the person with borderline personality who lacks adequate ego strength to control intense emotional drives and repeatedly exhibits emotional outbursts; the paranoid who is on guard against and constantly anticipating external threat; the manic personality with elevated moods, hyperactivity, and excessive involvement in activities that may have painful consequences; the explosive personality who has sudden escalating periods of anger; the person with schizophrenia who is actively hallucinating and has bizarre or grandiose delusions; the panic attack victim who is fearful, dissociative, and has extreme fight-or-flight reactions; and the depressed and suicidal person who is hopeless, agitated, and acting out suicidal plans (Blumenreich, 1993b, pp. 21–22; Grassi et al., 2001; Greenfield, McNeil, & Binder, 1989; Heilbrun, 1990; Heilbrun & Heilbrun, 1989; Klassen & O'Connor, 1988; McNeil, 2009; Murdach, 1993; Newhill, 2003, pp. 96–104).

Social Stressors. Loss of a job, job stress, breakup of a relationship, a past history of physical or sexual abuse, and financial reversals are a few of the social stressors that cause acute frustration and rage in an out-of-control social environment that leads to violence (Blumenreich, 1993a, p. 370; Munoz et al., 2000).

Family History. A history of violence within the family is often carried into other environments. An early childhood characterized by an unstable and violent home is an excellent model for future violence (Wood & Khuri, 1984, pp. 65–66). A history of social isolation or lack of family and environmental support also may heighten the potential for violence (Heilbrun & Heilbrun, 1989; Munoz et al., 2000). A nasty predictor of future criminal and violent behavior is cruelty to animals (Felthous & Kellert, 1986; Hellman & Blackman, 1966). It doesn't take too much imagination to predict that children who set cats on fire or do other cruel things to pets are capable of a lot of violence as they become adults. Predisposing family histories of witnessing family violence, being abused, enduring excessive physical punishment, abandonment, deprivation, and neglect, as explicated in the chapter on partner abuse, are all predisposing to adult aggression (Eddy, 1998).

Work History. A history of fractiousness and problems at a worksite is another correlate with violence (Newhill, 2003, pp. 110–111). Being fired at the post office is not the only situation in which workers exact revenge. Job loss and economic instability easily translate into paranoid "they did me wrong" thinking, which can then transfer over to social workers in unemployment offices and vocational counselors at employment services.

Time. In relation to a person's admission and tenure in a facility, time is critical. Admission on Friday or Saturday night during "party hours" significantly increases the potential for violence. In geriatric settings and mental hospitals, the evening hours, with the onset of darkness, change of shift, and decrease in staff, often lead to client disorientation and states of confusion (Occupational Safety and Health Administration, 2003). The effects of this time period have become so notorious that they have been labeled the **sundown syndrome** (Piercy, 1984, p. 139). Mealtime, toileting, and bathing are also prime times for violent outbursts (Barrick et al., 2008; Jones, 1985). Patients in both general and forensic psychiatric hospitals are more likely to be violent immediately after admission to the hospital (McNeil et al., 1991). McNeil, Binder, and Greenfield (1988) found that recent violent acts in the community are highly associated with violent acts in the first 72 hours of inpatient care. For most patients committed involuntarily, the possibility of assault is significantly increased during the first 10 to 20 days after admission, and for paranoids it remains high during their first 45 days (Rofman, Askinazi, & Fant, 1980).

Presence of Interactive Participants. Violent behavior may be contingent on those who bring the person to the institution (Occupational Safety and Health Administration, 2003). Family members or friends who bring patients in for treatment often interact in a volatile manner with admitting staff, particularly if the staff are seen as abrasive and callous (Ruben, Wolkon, & Yamamoto, 1980) and treat either the patient or support persons in a curt or uncaring manner (Wood & Khuri, 1984, p. 58). Arguments that may occur between the client and support persons are easily transferred to staff. Furthermore, when admonitions by distraught or intoxicated supporters to "fix" the client are not given immediate attention, they or the client may express grievances against the institution and staff by acting out. Any client who is accompanied to the institution by a police officer should be viewed as potentially violent (Kurlowicz, 1990; McNeil et al., 1991; Piercy, 1984, pp. 140–141).

Motoric Cues. Close observation by the human services worker of physical cues will often give clues to emergent states predisposing to physical violence (Kurlowicz, 1990; Petrie, 1984, p. 115; Weinger, 2001, p. 24). Early warning signs include tense muscles; bulging, darting eye movements; staring or completely avoiding eye contact; closed, defensive body posture; twitching muscles, fingers, and eyelids; body tremors; and disheveled appearance (Tardiff, 1989, p. 98; Wood & Khuri, 1984, p. 77). If the client is pacing back and forth, alternately approaching and then retreating from the worker, this may be a sign that the individual is gathering courage for an assault (Dang, 1990). The agitated client may have an expanded sense of personal space up to 8 feet in radius, instead of 3 to 4 feet, and may be extremely sensitive to any intrusion into that space (Moran, 1984, pp. 244–246).

A number of verbal cues are precursors to violent action by the client. Heightened voice pitch, volume, and rapidity of speech may occur, particularly if the client has been using amphetamines or other psychostimulants. Confused speech content can reflect confused thought and psychotic breaks. Clients may use profanity or verbally threaten significant others, the worker, or the world in general. Note that there is a high correlation between threats of violence and acting on those threats. The more specific the threat is to the person, method, and time, the more seriously the threat should be taken (Blumenreich, 1993a, p. 37; Tardiff, 1989, p. 99).

Multiple Indicators. The more the foregoing indicators are combined, the higher the potential for violence becomes (Klassen & O'Connor, 1988). Tardiff (1989) indicates that, if possible, the human services worker should attempt to assess all these factors; if they are present, the worker should clearly note the potential for violence on an intake form (p. 97) or on one of the violence prediction instruments previously mentioned. Tardiff further proposes that whether or not this information is available, one of the better verbal assessment techniques is to ask, "Have you ever lost your temper [in a violent manner]?" If the answer is "Yes!" the worker should proceed to ask how, when, and where this happened, and then perform an assessment much like that for suicide (p. 98). If any of the foregoing factors are apparent or are stated by the client, no matter how calm the client may appear to be, then a triage assessment of 10 on the interpersonal behavioral dimension should be made, the client's record should be flagged, and caution should be used in regard to the potential of the client to harm self or others. Does this mean you should not go into the human services business and go into something less stressful, like hauling explosives? Your authors would propose not, because about 85% to 90% of violence is preventable (Mack et al., 1988). The rest of this chapter will attempt to demonstrate how that percentage can be achieved.

Intervention Strategies

Because the institution itself plays such a **LO7** large part in the who, what, why, how, and when of treatment, it may be viewed as an equal and contributing partner in resolving problems with clients disposed to becoming physically and verbally assaultive. No two institutions are alike with respect to a number of variables that affect what the institution can do about the problem of violence. Yet when confronting clients who may be distraught, angry, fearful, and experiencing disequilibrium, all institutions have a common core of problems. Given the financial, legal, treatment, organizational, and philosophical limits idiosyncratic to each setting, the following intervention strategies should be viewed as a best "general" approach.

Security Planning

No antiviolence program can be accomplished without the commitment and involvement of top management such that everybody in the institution or agency understands that preventing violence is an absolute top priority (Barret, Riggar, & Flowers, 1997; California Occupational Safety and Health Administration, 1998, p. 6; Newhill, 2003; Weinger, 2001). The five main components of any effective safety and health program also apply to the prevention of workplace violence. These components are management commitment and employee involvement, worksite analysis, hazard prevention and control, safety and health training, and record keeping and program evaluation (Occupational Safety and Health Administration, 2003, 2015). The new OSHA *Guidelines for Preventing Workplace Violence* (2015) have very specific criteria and checkoffs for each of these general areas, and if these criteria are followed and implemented, there should be very little opportunity for workplace violence to occur.

Commitment and Involvement. One of the first steps in preventing violence is understanding what precautions the institution has taken to ensure the safety of clients and staff. Management commitment and employee involvement in a safe workplace are critical (Occupational Safety and Health Administration, 2003, 2015). The institution should have a zero tolerance policy for violence for both clients and providers. It should assign clear responsibility to all staff members so that they know what is expected of them, along with adequate resources to carry out those responsibilities and make them accountable for doing so.

Certain precautions can be taken to ensure that workers are not put at extreme risk by their clientele. First and foremost, management should conduct a security management analysis with experts in the security field (Ishimoto, 1984, p. 211; Kinney, 1995, pp. 47–50). Kinney (1995) urges that management recognize that the people with the most knowledge are the frontline workers who deal with the institution's clientele on a day-in, day-out basis, even though management may not want to hear from these workers for fear of what they might say. There should be channels for employees to bring their concerns to management and receive feedback without fear of reprisal or censure (Occupational Safety and Health Administration, 2003).

Worksite Analysis. A worksite analysis involves taking a step-by-step approach to addressing potential hazards, focusing on areas in which they may develop, and reviewing procedures put in place to curtail violence (Occupational Safety and Health Administration, 2003, 2015). There is a condensed security analysis questionnaire from Kinney (1995, pp. 211–216) and Ishimoto (1984, pp. 211–216) in the website exercises for this chapter, and you are invited to peruse the rather lengthy list of questions. This questionnaire analyzes and tracks records, generates screening surveys, and reviews workplace security (Occupational Safety and Health Administration, 2003, 2015). If such a survey is not taken, not only does the facility risk outbreaks of violence but also the staff will perceive management as not being greatly concerned about what happens to them (Lewellyn, 1985). Once the results of the survey are compiled, the organization should institute planning in hazard prevention and control.

Hazard Prevention and Control. All staff should have input into these questions, and a comprehensive security plan should be worked out and disseminated (California Occupational Safety and Health

Administration, 1998, p. 8; Occupational Safety and Health Administration, 2003, 2015). Such a plan should be comprehensive and simple, detailing who is responsible for what, under which conditions. The plan should cover the entire domain of the institution, starting with the parking lot, moving through the front door to admissions, and proceeding through the building to encompass day treatment facilities, staff offices, food services, pharmaceutical dispensaries, and client rooms (Ishimoto, 1984, pp. 209–223). Although the administration may view the initial costs in time and money for this service as burdensome, net cost will be minimal if this action avoids just one lawsuit by a client or staff member (Moran, 1984, p. 249).

Threat Assessment Teams

While consultants with different areas of **LO8** expertise in violence containment may be helpful, planning should start by forming a threat assessment team composed of a cross section of the staff and by naming a violence prevention coordinator. The duties of this team and coordinator will be to (1) outline the scope and activities of a threat management policy; (2) issue a clear and publicized statement against violence, even if the statement simply says, "This organization will not tolerate violence and aggression either from within or from outside the organization"; (3) identify a location and person for reporting threats; (4) determine when threats are serious enough to convene the team; (5) set training for all staff; and (6) establish a protocol for violence reduction that addresses unacceptable types of behavior as well as appropriate sanctions for that behavior (Kinney, 1995, pp. 73–80; Myer, James, & Moulton, 2011; Newhill, 2003, pp. 189–199; Nicoletti & Spooner, 1996; Weinger, 2001, p. 53).

Establishment of a threat assessment team is particularly critical on a college campus (Myer, James, & Moulton, 2011, pp. 256–267). Virginia Tech is a classic example where, for various political, logistical, legal, and ethical reasons, a silo mentality occurred and critical information was kept in separate units and never shared. It should be clearly understood that Virginia Tech was no different from any other institution in regard to the barriers erected and communication channels that were effectively blocked that could perhaps have mitigated the effects of a mass murderer before he got to the tipping point. In fact, thanks to changes in Virginia law, institutions of higher education and mental

health facilities in Virginia are now better able to communicate and exert sanctions and exclusions on individuals who fail to cooperate in assessment and treatment programs than in most other states (Mandatory Treatment of Mental Health Patients, 2007; Threat Assessment Team Formation, 2008; Threat of Violence, 2008).

An individual such as Seung-hui Cho may come to the attention of a variety of individuals, entities, and departments but never be so blatant and labile that he or she comes to the attention of anyone who can make a decision to place him or her in a psychiatric legal hold and nothing is done to proactively contain the person until a tragedy occurs. That's why a cross section of campus representatives from housing, recreation, food services, academic departments, the counseling center, and law enforcement all need to be part of a threat assessment team that meets regularly and sifts through all incident reports that occur on campus. The same holds true in other institutions where a cross section of workers are used. To that end, the office secretary because of his or her central location or custodian because of his or her movement throughout the building should not be overlooked as possible members of the team. That threat assessment team also needs a common language such as TASSLE (Myer et al., 2007), discussed in Chapters 3 and 13, so that they have a common set of terms and behavioral anchors to use in making dispositions of individuals that come to their attention (Myer, James, & Moulton, 2011, pp. 233–270).

Precautions in Dealing with the Physical Setting. Safety precautions should be taken that deal with the physical settings of the institution in which staff members are most likely to become involved in potentially violent situations with clients. Two critical areas important to all crisis workers are the admissions area and the worker's office. The reception area or waiting room should offer a television set, reading material, and accessibility to snack areas. Availability of entertainment and food and drink gives clients and visitors an opportunity to engage in a pleasurable activity that can offset the hostile feelings that may be engendered by the problems they are facing and can defuse the stressful situation of admission (Somers-Flanagan & Somers-Flanagan, 1997; Wood & Khuri, 1984, pp. 79–80). One admonition is necessary with regard to food and drink: Clients who are extremely rebellious about entering the institution may attempt to choke themselves on food or even swallow pull tabs from metal cans. The admissions staff should carefully monitor clients if they are allowed to eat or drink (McCown, 1986).

The admissions area should be clean and well kept, with furniture, carpet, and wall coverings well maintained. First impressions are lasting. If the client's first impression of a facility is that staff have little regard or respect for the facility, the client will have little reason to respect what goes on there either (Marohn, 1982). Suffice it to say that fire engine red paint is not a decorating choice. Bright, cheery, energizing decorations should not be used any more than the somber and depressing institutional grays and greens of many mental institutions and prisons one of your authors has worked in and visited (Newhill, 2003, p. 190; Vaaler, Morken, & Linaker, 2005). Subdued painting and decorating and comfortable, relaxing furniture do a lot to alleviate anger, tension, and pent-up agitated feelings and thoughts. No sharp, movable objects, including furniture, should be available as potential weapons (McCown, 1986). Clients should be given lockers in which to put their belongings (Munsey, 2008).

The area should be set up so that it is a choke point: only one way into the rest of the facility should be available from the admissions area. Video surveillance should be kept on this area to record everybody who comes in and out, along with a sign-in sheet that records everyone coming in and is checked to make sure that everyone has gone out (Annis, McClaren, & Baker, 1984, p. 30). There should, however, be another way out for workers, and a panic room where workers could secure themselves from intruders is not a bad idea (Munsey, 2008). Depending on how much security is needed, the reception area may also have electronically locked doors that separate it from the rest of the facility, identity check procedures, curved mirrors, and metal detectors (California Occupational Safety and Health Administration, 1998, p. 10; Munsey, 2008; Occupational Health and Safety Administration, 2015). Clients who are waiting for service should be treated in a courteous and friendly manner and updated on interview delays. Waits should be kept to a minimum (Weinger, 2001, p. 53). In that regard, is it any wonder that people become agitated and enraged in most hospital emergency rooms?

The admissions worker will make the first contact with the client and will engage the person during one of the most potentially violent moments the institution is likely to encounter. The admissions worker should be highly skilled in crisis intervention techniques and should have one primary job—*staying with and attending to the client being admitted*! Under no circumstances should a secretary, receptionist, or any other support person who is not professionally well versed in crisis intervention or who has other tasks to perform, such as typing letters or answering the telephone, be delegated to handle this important assignment. The admissions worker should not leave the client until all admitting procedures have been accomplished and the client is safely settled (McCown, 1986).

The admissions worker should also never be left in a position of isolation from the rest of the staff (Turnbull et al., 1990). Security support equipment such as a body alarm (a button-activated device that when triggered will automatically send an alarm and position fix to security), an automatic dialer preset to in-house security and 911, convex mirrors to monitor the whole waiting area, panic buttons, closed-circuit television monitoring equipment, button locks on elevators, and a metal detector at the entrance should be available. Initial interviews are critical in setting the tone for what will occur behaviorally. Therefore, the interview area should be open, yet afford privacy. At times, if the client is very agitated, other staff or indeed a police officer may need to be present (Doms, 1984, pp. 225–229; Jones, 1984; McCown, 1986; Weinger, 2001, p. 53; Wood & Khuri, 1984, pp. 79–80).

Now a word about what you need to look like. The following admonition is probably politically incorrect, and we are going to sound like your overprotective father to many of you young women reading this, because we are now going to tell you what you need to wear. Low-cut necklines may be all the rage right now but are a bad idea. If you are a male, t-shirts to show your six-pack abs should not be part of the dress code. This is not the setting to be a slave to fashion! Some clients have real boundary problems (Newhill, 2003, p. 191), and here is not the place for their impulsivity to take over and you to wind up being sexually or physically assaulted, because sexual assaults on staff do happen. Alink and associates (2014) investigated the amount and kind of violent acts perpetrated on 178 workers in youth facilities, and 81% experience violence. There was no difference in assault rate by gender. Put on professional work clothes that say "I am here to help you, but I mean business!" And if you are a guy and you are into grunge and you think that looking like a punk rocker will help you relate to your clients, you probably need to go into a street ministry. Conversely, you don't need to look as though you stepped out of *GQ* or *Vogue* magazine, but not looking like a professional conveys the impression that you aren't. It is called **face validity**. If clients don't believe you look as though you know what you are doing, you will probably not get the chance to demonstrate that you do.

Personal work environments should also be safe. Desks should be set up so that they allow for separation of client and worker, even though communicating across a desk is not the most desirable counseling setup. Furniture should be heavy and difficult to move. Space should be arranged to permit both the worker and the client clear access to the door and to allow the worker to leave the room without having to confront the client or cross the client's personal space. No potential weapons such as paperweights, letter openers, and sharpened pencils should be openly displayed or within easy reach of the client. The same personal warning devices and procedures recommended for the reception area should also be in place in workers' offices (Jensen & Absher, 1994, 1998; Occupational Safety and Health Administration, 2015; Tardiff, 1984a, p. 50).

The receptionist or others in the building need to be able to warn the worker if danger is imminent, and vice versa. There should be a common code word that is understood to mean a summons for immediate help. A panic button and a telephone that the worker can use to get in touch with the outside world should be available. These last two points are particularly critical because of the typical isolation of the human services worker with a client in a therapeutic setting (Jensen & Absher, 1994, 1998; Occupational Safety and Health Administration, 2015; Tardiff, 1984a, p. 50).

Training

Planning is of little consequence if no train- **LO9** ing follows. Staff who have been trained in the appropriate methods, techniques, and procedures have increased confidence in their ability to de-escalate violence and have reduced assaultive behavior (Thomas, Kitchen, & Smith, 2005; Turnbull et al., 1990). Training should include both knowledge and skill building and should be ongoing, with immediate training for new members of the treatment team and continuing education for veterans (Dyer, Murrell, & Wright, 1984, pp. 12–15; Newhill, 2003, p. 207; Turnbull et al., 1990; Weinger, 2001, pp. 52–53). Every employee should understand that violence should be expected but can be avoided or reduced through preparation (Newhill, 2003, p. 206; Occupational Safety and Health Administration, 2003, 2015).

Training should begin with the crisis intervention skills listed in Chapters 3 and 4 and additionally cover legal aspects, theories of aggression, reporting and recording of incidents, assessment of contextual and environmental variables, verbal defusing techniques, triggers of aggression, warning signs, use of safety and alarm devices, self-defense and restraint techniques, behavioral observation, consultation, follow-up staffing procedures, and debriefing (Blair, 1991; Kinney, 1995; Murray & Snyder, 1991; Occupational Safety and Health Administration, 2003, 2015; Turnbull et al., 1990). A critical component of training is not just talking about problems but gaining practice in solving them (Kleepies, 2014). There is no better way of doing this than in role-play and incident simulation situations, which can be videotaped for analysis and feedback by instructors and peers (Forster, 1994; Turnbull et al., 1990).

Antiviolence Intervention. Most approaches to antiviolence prevention in institutions involve the use of behavioral (token economies, shaping, modeling contingency contracting) or cognitive-behavioral intervention methods (reframing negative attributions, thought stopping, relaxation training, positive counterinjunctions) (Douglas, Nicholls, & Brink, 2009).

The **risk-needs-responsivity (RNR) model** is a procedure that is taken from the corrections field. The risk component proposes that high-risk individuals get more targeted, specific, and tailored therapeutic inputs before they go critical. The needs component focuses on the dynamic risk factors that when changed reduce recidivism. This procedure has been applied to antiviolence programs with the severely mentally ill and severely emotionally disturbed. RNR usually incorporates cognitive-behavioral therapy, social skills training, anger management, and behavioral techniques that apply role rehearsal, modeling, and shaping to prosocial behavior (Douglas, Nicholls, & Brink, 2009). While not perfect by any stretch of the imagination, it appears that RNR is at least somewhat effective with severely mentally ill and severely emotionally disturbed individuals (Lovell et al., 2001; van den Brink et al., 2010; Wong, Gordon, & Gu, 2007; Yates et al., 2005) who present with very tough, intractable, and chronic issues that are generally resistant to change.

Assumptions. Adequate training should endow the crisis worker with the ability to make certain assumptions and take certain precautions when dealing with potentially violent clients (Newhill, 2003, pp. 121–165; Turnbull et al., 1990; Weinger, 2001, p. 45; Zold & Schilt, 1984, pp. 98–99).

1. Assume the need to set limits and provide clear instructions with options that define what positive and negative consequences will occur.
2. Assume the client feels a number of debilitating emotions such as fear, depression, anxiety, helplessness, anger, rejection, and hopelessness, and demonstrate concern by encouraging verbal ventilation through *how* and *when* questions, showing empathic concern by restatement and reflection of the client's feelings, and reinforcing appropriate behavior and communication of feelings.
3. Assume frustration of normal activity and boredom when the client is in residence, and provide activities to keep the client fruitfully busy.
4. Assume a threat to the client's self-esteem, independence, and self-control, and provide choices and opportunities to help in carrying out medical and psychological activities.
5. Assume tension and arousal, and provide a calm and relaxing atmosphere, particularly in high-tension periods, by manipulating environmental variables and using a cooperative "we" approach.
6. Assume that there will be confusion, and provide a careful explanation of all procedures to be employed, being particularly sure that all staff are operating from the same frame of reference.
7. Assume responsibility, and provide for one primary staff member to act as chief caretaker and advocate of each client.
8. Assume disconnectedness and rootlessness if the client is to be institutionalized for any length of time, and provide familiarity and psychologically calming anchors associated with pleasant memories.

Precautions. While providing support through the preceding proactive behaviors, the wise human services worker should observe a number of precautionary measures (Blair, 1991; Forster, 1994; Greenstone & Leviton, 1993; Kleespies, 2014, p. 26; Moran, 1984, p. 244; Piercy, 1984, p. 143; Turnbull et al., 1990; Weinger, 2001, pp. 33–48; Wood & Khuri, 1984, p. 69). There are a lot of Don'ts to follow, but reviewing them every once in awhile may save you a trip to the emergency room!

1. Don't deny the possibility of violence when early signs of agitation are first noticed in the client such as restless pacing, grinding teeth, clenched fists, swearing, muttering threats, loud agitated responses, etc.
2. Don't dismiss warnings from records, family and peers, authorities, or fellow workers that the client is violent.
3. Don't become isolated with potentially violent clients unless you have made sure that enough security precautions have been taken to prevent or limit a violent outburst.
4. Don't engage in certain behaviors that may be interpreted as aggressive, such as moving too close, staring directly into the client's eyes for extended periods of time, pointing fingers, or displaying facial expressions and body movements that would appear threatening.
5. Don't allow a number of the institution's workers to interact simultaneously with the client in confusing multiple dialogues.
6. Don't make promises that cannot be kept.
7. Don't allow feelings of fear, anger, or hostility to interfere with self-control and professional understanding of the client's circumstances.
8. Don't argue, give orders, or disagree when not absolutely necessary.
9. Don't be placating by giving in and agreeing to all the real and imagined ills the client is suffering at the hands of the institution.
10. Don't become condescending by using childish responses that are cynical, satirical, or otherwise designed to denigrate the client.
11. Don't let self-talk about your own importance be acted out in an officious and "know-it-all" manner.
12. Don't raise your voice, put a sharp edge on responses, or use threats to gain compliance.
13. Conversely, don't mumble, speak hesitantly, or use a tone of voice so low that the client has trouble understanding what you are saying.
14. Don't argue over small points, given strong opposition from the client.
15. Don't attempt to reason with any client who is under the influence of a mind-altering substance.
16. Don't attempt to gain compliance based on the assumption that the client is as reasonable about things as you are.
17. Don't keep the client waiting or leave a potentially violent client alone with freedom to move about.
18. Don't allow a crowd to congregate as spectators to an altercation.
19. Don't use *why* and *what* questions that put the client on the defensive.

20. Don't allow the client to get between you and an exit.
21. Don't dismiss increasingly vociferous client demands as merely attention-seeking, petulant, or narcissistic behavior.
22. Don't enter a room ahead of unknown clients. Stay behind and visually "frisk" them as you go into the room.
23. Don't remain after hours with a potentially violent client unless proper security is available.
24. Don't fail to make contingency plans for violent incidents. Take your personal safety seriously by playing "what if this happens" scenarios in your mind and with others.
25. Most important, *don't attempt to be a hero.*

Outreach Precautions. In the rapidly changing world of mental health, much crisis intervention now occurs on-site (see Chapter 17, Disaster Response). With the recent passage of the *Patient Protection and Affordable Care Act of 2010* traditional health care delivery is increasingly shifting to private settings and in those settings home health care workers experience one of the highest rates of client violence (Campbell et al., 2014). Although outreach and "mobile go-out" teams give the crisis interventionist far more mobility and rapid response capability, on-site intervention also has the potential to put crisis workers in extreme danger as they operate in violent neighborhoods and households (Burry, 2002). Besides the foregoing warnings given for in-house operation, the following injunctions generated by your authors and a variety of others (Cawood & Corcoran, 2009; Greenstone & Leviton, 1993, pp. 31–33; Jensen & Absher, 1998; Kleespies, 2014, pp. 146–148; Newhill, 2003, pp. 199–204; Occupational Safety and Health Administration, 2015; Weinger, 2001, pp. 56–59) should be added to the repertoire of the crisis worker who operates outside the walls of the institution. Again, checking this list every once in awhile before you make a home visit may save you a trip to the emergency room.

1. If you are not familiar with clients, check records before ever making a home visit for incidents of violent behavior. If they are present, do not go by yourself.
2. If at all possible, go with a partner, or at least have a cell phone or other means of communication to get help in a hurry with a code word indicating you are under threat and need help.
3. Let someone else in the office know where you are going and when you will be back. Log in/log out with specific name and place of client visited, scheduled time and expected duration of visit, your car description and license plate on file. Ensure there is office contact after visit termination and management procedures when no log in occurs.
4. Check out your surroundings. Although time is of the essence in most crisis intervention, move into the situation slowly and carefully, and be fully aware of what is going on in the environment around you.
5. Plan what you are going to do before you go. Take time to gather in-depth and accurate behavioral information on the client and family. Note any incidents of violence, drug abuse, or other potentially threatening behaviors in the client's folder before the visit. Our Crisis Intervention Team officers for the Memphis Police Department rendezvous and plan who is going to do what before they enter a hazardous situation whenever possible. You should do the same.
6. Don't park directly in front of the place where the crisis is occurring. Check out the area as you drive by, and park just beyond it. If you have to leave in a hurry, this position allows you to leave without crossing the line of sight of a person who may be able to harm you.
7. Before knocking on a door or entering a building, listen carefully for a few seconds for clues as to what may be going on inside.
8. Never stand directly in front of a door. Knock and, as the police do, stand aside, so you are not assaulted or shot through the door. If the client hesitates in opening the door, be very wary of going inside. If you think that something is happening that is suspicious or that could be hazardous to your health, politely terminate the appointment and leave.
9. Consider what you are wearing from a safety viewpoint. A tie or a choke chain may make you look more professional, but it can also get you strangled. High heels are elegant, but you can't run in them. Loose-fitting, mobile, and nonflashy clothing is the watchword.
10. Once the door is open, immediately scan the room to determine who is in it and where they are. Compare these visual data to information you may have received previously on the situation. Don't take anyone for granted, particularly elderly people who may look harmless. Ask if there are other people in the house and

who and where they are. If they are not supposed to be there, politely postpone the appointment and leave.

11. Monitor the verbal and nonverbal behavior of all the people in the room. What are they doing, and what must you do to stabilize the situation? If there are intoxicated people present, politely postpone the appointment and leave.

12. Enter the room only a short distance so that you can first assess what's going on and can get out quickly if you have to.

13. Don't let a crowd of bystanders gather or let neighbors "drop in" to see what's going on. Politely ask them to leave. If they won't leave or refuse to disperse, get out or get the police!

14. Alert the client you are coming to visit, find out who else will be there, or if you are in a housing project, alert the building captain or housing authority police.

15. If a verbal dispute is going on, first and foremost consider your own safety. If necessary, leave and call the police. If you believe you can control the situation or don't seem to have any other choice, attempt to take control as quickly as possible. Separate disputants and have them sit down. Stay calm, and make clear, concise, assertive statements about what you want them to do. If that doesn't work, get their attention by making a tangential request: "Stop that! I need to use the telephone to call in." If all else fails, a police whistle gets everybody's attention.

16. Sit in a chair where you can observe what's going on. Seat yourself so you're leaning forward and can easily get out of the chair quickly! If you sense that the situation is deteriorating, leave. *Don't be a hero!*

17. Leave your credit cards, purse, jewelry (except your wedding band, which can be a deterrent to sexual advances), and most cash at the office. Carry only your identification and driver's license. You don't want to get mugged.

18. Stay out of kitchens. They have knives and other things that can hurt you. Interview in the living room.

19. Check and see if the client has used firearms. If there are firearms present, leave immediately.

20. Remember that you are not on your own turf, and the unexpected can happen at any time. Stay alert from the moment you enter the neighborhood until the moment you leave the neighborhood.

These injunctions are not a recipe for avoiding violent confrontations, but they are general working procedures that will help the human services worker move adroitly with the client through the intervention stages.

Record Keeping and Program Evaluation

As per Van Brunt's recommendation (2015, pp. 137), a threat analysis and management-structured professional judgment report should be on file and available to all the staff that will come in contact with Jason, a very angry young man you will soon meet who is not happy about being adjudicated to a closed ward mental heath facility. This report should be reviewed as soon after Jason's arrival as possible so that a threat management plan is in operation. Thus, employees follow a procedure that provides for reporting *all* incidents, with or without injury. They participate in a safety and health committee that receives information and reports on security problems, makes facility inspections, analyzes reports, and makes recommendations for corrections. Regular case conference meetings are used to identify potentially violent clients and discuss safe ways of handling them (California Occupational Safety and Health Administration, 1998, p. 7; Newhill, 2003, pp. 205–213; Occupational Safety and Health Administration, 2003, 2015; Weinger, 2001, pp. 49–55). Most important, good records allow for program evaluation.

Stages of Intervention

There are three primary levels of intervention **LO10** (dos Reis et al., 2003). At level 1, the primary objective is to prevent further escalation. Level 2 intervention aims to reduce the target symptoms. Level 3 intervention maintains the safety of the clients and staff. Within these three broad levels, management of potentially violent situations should proceed in a sequential manner, based on a nine-stage model developed by Piercy (1984, pp. 147–148). The stages are (1) education, (2) avoidance of conflict, (3) appeasement, (4) deflection, (5) time-out, (6) show of force, (7) seclusion, (8) restraints, and (9) sedation. The cardinal rule for all of these stages, as stated by Larry Chavez (1999)—a noted authority on violence prevention in the workplace—is "Never, ever deprive another human being of personal dignity, respect, or hope nor allow anyone else under your control to do so." For each of these stages, personal responsibility is paramount. Furthermore, whether by circumstance or design, the first person who comes in contact with the problem is the one most likely to be the agitated client's focus of attention (Moran, 1984, pp. 233–234).

Stages 1 through 5 all rely heavily on talking instead of acting, in accordance with one of the primary goals of crisis intervention with violence-prone individuals: getting them to talk out rather than act out. This approach may seem obvious, but it is difficult to achieve. The agitated client clearly has a limited ability to talk and think through problems, as opposed to acting on them and giving little thought to the consequences (Tardiff, 1984a, p. 52). While the immediate goal is to defuse and de-escalate clients' rapid movement toward violence, the overall end goals are to alter violent clients' motivation so that they can utilize nonviolent ways to reestablish their lost sense of control; monitor them and preempt their reengagement of violence; and model for and assure significant others such as peers, family, fellow patients, and staff that calmness and serenity will prevail and violence will not be tolerated (Cawood & Corcoran, 2009, p. 8).

As we move through the nine stages, we will follow Jason, a 15-year-old white male client, and Carol, a therapist who by most standards is an old pro. She has been at Seashore Village, a comprehensive mental health inpatient treatment facility, for 4 years. Jason is new to the business of institutions. However, he is not new to being angry, which he is right now as he sits with a deputy sheriff in the reception area waiting for Carol to come through the door.

Jason's teen years have been filled with petty larceny, truancy, conduct problems at school, alcohol and drug use, and parents who have gotten him out of one scrape after another. He is impulsive, has anger management problems, and has difficulty controlling his emotions. His latest escapade of stealing a car landed him in front of a juvenile court, and he was sent to Seashore as an alternative to the state juvenile correction system. His father, fed up with Jason's behavior and over the objections of Jason's mother, has pushed for this placement. Jason feels betrayed and is extremely angry at his father for doing so.

Seashore itself is representative of a broad sample of institutions. It is neither the best nor the worst in terms of clients, staff, resources, and security measures. The endeavor here is to paint as representative a picture as possible, so please withhold judgments about the efficacy and appropriateness of these strategies in every institution. Our hope is that the procedures used in the case of Jason will make you think carefully about your own present or future role in an institution, compare the ideas

proposed here with the requirements imposed on you, analyze the procedures used, and thoughtfully compare these techniques and the real world within which you operate.

Jason: (*thinking to himself, hands sweating, slight tremors racing through his body*) Man, this place is scaring the hell out of me. How'd I ever get in this fix? What are they gonna do to me? I'll be at the mercy of the rest of the crazies in here. I'll really go nuts if I stay here. I gotta get out of this place if it's the last thing I ever do.

Jason is extremely angry and anxious about what will happen to him, frustrated that he has lost control of his life and that what he has considered to be normal activity is going to be severely curtailed. He also feels extremely vulnerable, confused, bewildered, and alone. Jason's feelings are typical of those of a client who is being introduced to a long-term treatment facility for the first time (Blair, 1991; Zold & Schilt, 1984, p. 96). Anger generally comes out of frustration or hurt and is one way of creating an emotional wall that protects us from being vulnerable (Fauteux, 2010). To say that Jason is feeling very vulnerable right now is a big understatement.

As soon as Jason enters Seashore, someone from admissions immediately calls the adolescent unit. Carol comes quickly to the reception area and meets Jason. As she enters the room, she makes a fast visual assessment of Jason's verbal and nonverbal behavior and monitors Jason closely to see what his reaction to her initial query will be.

Carol: (*thinking to herself*) What's going on with this kid? Any signs he is agitated? Yes! He's pacing around, eyes darting to and fro, keeps cracking his knuckles, looking at the door and the cop. He'll run if he gets the chance! Muttering to himself. Who brought him in? Nobody else here but that cop over there. He keeps watching him. Must be an adjudication. If a cop brought him here, be careful.

Carol picks up the file the deputy has brought, quickly looks it over, and finds the boy's name and rap sheet. A fast review tells her that Jason has been in a series of escalating scrapes with the law, that his parents are fed up with his behavior and feel he's out of control, and that he has been involved in fights when his explosive personality got out of control. Carol then talks briefly with the deputy and finds out what kind of a trip Jason had from the juvenile detention center.

Carol: (*thinking to herself*) OK! Check him out and see how stabilized he is, and let him find out what's going to happen to him.

Stage 1: Education. Clients need to be educated about what is happening to them, and why and how it is happening, through reasoning and reassurance. One way of doing this is to assume the role of the client's advocate (Pisarick, 1981). As in most crisis interventions first contact is important (Somers-Flanigan & Somers-Flanigan, 1997, p. 35).

Owning statements that indicate concern over the client's welfare are a good opening gambit. It must be assumed that in this new, strange, and alien environment the primary feeling of the client will be fear and anger (Rada, 1981). Open-ended questions and reflection of the client's feelings are crucial to conveying that the client's feelings count for something and are being taken into consideration (Turnbull et al., 1990). Carol sees how unenthused Jason is about being at the facility and uses sarcastic empathy (Newman, 1994) to try and ease a hostile situation.

Carol: Hi! My name's Carol, and you must be Jason. I'm the person who'll be working with you. I'll bet you've been really looking forward to that!

Jason: (*gives a menacing look*) OH Yeah! So what? (*points to officer*) The cop got me in here, but I ain't gonna go any farther.

Carol: I understand how you feel. Most people who come here feel about the same way. Seems like everybody's against you, telling you what to do. I'd be angry too! I want you to know, though, that here at Seashore you're going to have some options about what happens.

Jason: Screw your options. I ain't stayin' here. (*makes a menacing move toward Carol*)

Carol: (*senses move and moves back and a little to Jason's left, giving him some increased space*) One of your immediate options is that I'd like you to come with me and meet some of the other kids here and have them tell you what's going on and see if what they have to say fits with what you're about. On the other hand, the court sent you here, and if you don't like the first option and want to fight it out, you could be carried back to the unit, and we can wait until you've got yourself together. I understand you're angry, and I'd be angry too, but I'd like to know if you feel that fighting or running is gonna make it better for you and improve your situation rather

than checking things out. So you've got a choice. I think you might be interested in meeting some of the other kids, but you'll have to show me you can handle that, starting right now.

In this initial meeting, the worker uses the technique of providing options (Newhill, 2003, p. 158; Turnbull et al., 1990). This opening statement includes acknowledging the client's feelings but also conveys expectations that the client can control himself. By doing so, Carol sets the tone for what the behavioral expectations are in a clear and caring, yet firm, way (Steveson, 1991). She is letting the client have some semblance of control of the situation but is also clearly outlining what the consequences of his choices are. As soon as possible, she is going to model option therapy (McCown, 1986). Option therapy, in simple terms, says, "You always have a choice. You need to start deciding as soon as possible who's going to have control over those choices, you or us."

The staff have reviewed Jason's records and in their Threat Assessment and Management Report (Van Brunt, 2015, pp. 124–130) have determined the motivators (arousal and adrenaline rush via bullying), disinhibitors (negative attitudes that see the world as a hostile place and lack of integration socially with peers), destabilizers (disturbed attention span, difficulty staying on task, obsessive thinking that misattributes blame with a tunnel vision view of the world and racing thinking where thoughts can't be controlled and jump to incorrect and paranoid conclusions) that are likely to instigate violence. Therefore, scenarios of his initial interactions with his peers would predict watchfulness and early intervention at the first sign of trouble.

Jason: Well . . . all right . . . lady, I'll give it a look-see, but I ain't promisin' nothin' after that.

Carol: I don't expect any more than that at the moment. What I want most for you is to see what's going on here and what some of the other kids think about what we do before you make any kind of promises. We don't lie, and we don't make promises we can't keep.

The worker has to make a quick judgment about how directive or nondirective to be. Telling Jason he needs to calm down is not an option. How do you react when you are upset and somebody tells you "Just calm down"? Doesn't work very well, does it, and probably upsets you even more, and goodness knows you handle your emotions pretty well. That statement would be telling the client he is not in control but someone else is, which affirms for him that he isn't in control so the behavior escalates even more (Fauteux, 2010).

Carol is directive only to the extent of setting boundaries equivalent to how out of control the client is. Her other mission is to establish rapport and credibility with the client. She does this by accepting and acknowledging the client where he is and in turn stating the same from the institution's perspective. She offers no platitudes or false promises (Turnbull et al., 1990). Jason has a chip the size of Mt. Rushmore on his shoulder so he is always looking for an excuse to argue and bully his way through life. Carol will assiduously avoid arguing with him so as not to reinforce his behavior (Van Brunt, 2015, p.178). Her technique of letting the client talk to other people on the unit is designed to let the client hear and see with his own ears and eyes what is going on without feeling he is getting a lot of propaganda. However, she will not provide a forum for him to act out, and if in her judgment Jason is not controlled enough to make a tour with her, she will summon assistance, and Jason will be escorted to an observation room (McCown, 1986).

Carol: We have a lot of activities, so if you don't clearly understand what's happening or you want to know some more about it, just ask. (*Carol outlines Jason's schedule.*)

Very little free time is available. For most people who enter a facility such as Seashore, a major problem has been too much free time and the inability to handle it well. Structuring the environment brings some badly needed discipline back into their lives. Particularly for adolescents, burning up energy in constructive ways is of paramount importance. Furthermore, too much free time is a fertile breeding ground for acting out behavior (Jensen & Absher, 1994).

Seashore is also on a behavior management program that makes use of levels. Part of that behavior management program is a risk-need-responsibility component that will be used to help Jason learn how to control his emotions. Jason will start at entry level. Depending on how Jason operates in his environment, he will go up or down on the level system and will concomitantly receive more or fewer privileges. At an entry level, he will have few privileges—early bedtime, no passes—and will be under fairly close supervision. By conducting himself in a responsible manner, he may increase his level designation and gain access to a broader array of recreational activities, later bedtime, ground privileges,

and weekend passes. The system is explained to Jason in a careful and clear manner, with emphasis on the fact that whether or not he moves to higher levels is his responsibility.

Educating a client about what is to happen medically and psychologically needs to be done slowly, methodically, and in nontechnical terms with numerous perceptual checks. Keeping explanations simple and helping the client gain understanding ameliorate the situation, whereas complexity only increases the chance for violent behavior to occur (Jensen & Absher, 1994; Moran, 1984, p. 234).

Jason: (*somewhat belligerently*) Like, what's this group meeting?

Carol: The group meets every day. The group decides how to tackle a community problem and then collectively makes a commitment to do something about it. Second, when problems between people arise, we all put our heads together and see how those problems can be solved. You don't necessarily have to accept an idea, but you must listen to what's being said.

Jason: I don't think I got anything to say to these nerds.

Carol: Maybe you don't. However, a lot of kids here do. Your behavior and your willingness to work say how long you're going to be here or be in a juvenile detention facility if you don't work. My guess is you want to get out of here as quickly as you possibly can. Right?

Jason: You got that right lady.

Carol: So are you willing to cut a deal with me? We look pretty hard at what's going on with you right now as you deal with other people here, how that behavior may or may not cause you problems, and what's down the road for you if you do decide to change some things in your life and what's likely if you don't. We don't ask you to love everybody here, but we do ask you to respect what they're trying to do, just as we ask them to respect you. You do that and I move you through levels faster than that Jeff Gordon #24 t-shirt you have on.

The human services worker's responses are from Glasser's reality therapy (1965, 1969) and focus on the issues of becoming involved, looking at alternatives, making value judgments, accepting no excuses, and assuming responsibility and consequences for one's actions. They also use Somers-Flanigans' (1997) motivational technique of "cutting a deal." You do what I want, "work hard!" and you get what you want "Outta here faster!" In this manner Carol goes over the entire schedule with Jason. While she explains the content of the program, she also makes sure to assess and reflect the emotional content of Jason's responses, again and again reinforcing the idea of options, responsibilities, and commitments.

Stage 2: Avoidance of Conflict. Conflict and confrontation are avoided whenever possible. Matching threat for threat is likely to obtain for the human services worker exactly the opposite of control and containment of the situation (Dubin, 1981; Fauteux, 2010). Workers who delight in continuously pushing and escalating issues are not practicing good therapeutic intervention techniques and are clearly asking for trouble (Blair, 1991). One week has elapsed since Jason's admission.

Jason: (*standing in the hallway, shouting, shaking, and trembling, face flushed*) If you think you or anybody else can make me stay in my room or in this place, you're crazier than I am. I just wanted a drink of water, and Mr. Richardson started yelling at me that it was past quiet time. Just try stopping me and see what happens.

Carol: (*quietly and calmly*) Jason, OK, sounds like you feel he put you down, but if it's a drink you want, then return to your room, I'll bring you a cup of water. Please go into your room. You can have your drink, and we can talk about it. While I do that I'd like you to be doing a little thinking about what you really want and how to go about getting it.

The worker reflects his feelings, which have now probably become more important than the drink he was going to get. However, by offering to get him a drink if he complies, the worker is giving him an honorable way out, reinforcing prosocial behavior, and also offering to listen to his concerns (Fauteux, 2010). If the client is fast approaching a point of no return, let him or her ventilate feelings. Although shouting, cursing, and yelling are not pleasant, they are better than hand-to-hand combat (McCown, 1986; Vinick, 1986). The worker rolls with the resistance (Van Brunt, 2015, p. 179), and does not meet it head on, but instead encourages the individual to start thinking in new ways about the situation.

The worker should attempt to remove the agitated client from the vicinity of other residents, who may aggravate the situation (Chavez, 1999; Turnbull

et al., 1990). This is best done by immediately asking the client to go to an area that is away from the other residents (McCown, 1986). If the client retains some semblance of control, the client's own room may be an appropriate place. If the client is fast losing control and cannot calm down, a better choice is a room devoid of stimuli. Such a place should be specifically prepared and reserved for this sort of occurrence.

Carol: What are you angry about?

Jason: (*still standing in the hallway, quite agitated*) He was treating me just like my old man, just making me feel like a baby.

Carol: And what were you doing?

Jason: Hey, I was just going to get a drink of water. I still had 2 minutes until quiet time. He made me so mad I wanted to pick up a chair and bust him. I still feel like going after that jerk.

Carol: What will that accomplish?

Jason: It'll show him he can't push me around like my old man does.

Carol: If you do that, it'll just confirm that you need to be here, that you can't control yourself. Is that what you want?

Jason: Maybe I just don't care.

Carol does not display anger or fear, even though the situation is potentially volatile. She speaks in a calm, controlled voice, lower and slower than Jason. She is setting the example and controlling the dialogue (Chavez, 1999). For those clients who do not respond to verbal attempts to defuse the situation, the next step for the human services worker is to give assurance that violent behavior by anybody, including both staff and clients, is unacceptable, and then to indicate what the person's choices and consequences will become if the behavior persists (Kinney, 1995, p. 49; Wood & Khuri, 1984, pp. 67–68).

Carol: You can choose to pick up a chair, Jason, but that'll mean a number of things will happen. First, nobody is allowed to hit anybody else here, and that goes for both staff and kids. If it comes to that, we will restrain you, something I'd not like to see happen. Second, if you choose to do that, no one else will get to hear your side of it, and we won't have a chance to work your problem out with Mr. Richardson. Another choice would be to go back to your room and then ask for a drink. If you do that, I will get Mr. Richardson and we'll all sit down and work this through. Would you be willing to do that?

Carol is absolutely truthful with what will happen to the client. At this stage, loss of credibility would be catastrophic (Chavez, 1999). Clients should be confronted with their inappropriate behavior, but in a caring, supportive, and problem-solving way that is not tinged with sarcasm or challenge. If the situation is deteriorating so rapidly that the worker no longer feels that communication can be maintained, it may be fruitful to have someone else enter the scene whom the client will perceive as a neutral party (Lakeside Hospital, 1988). This tactic is risky and involves a judgment call on the worker's part. Allowing clients to be rewarded for acting out by getting other people to come to the scene may reinforce inappropriate behavior and lead clients to believe that they and not the institution control the situation. Carol uses a combination of confrontation and empathy. She also provides options for Jason and sets limits as to what will be tolerated (Newhill, 2003, p. 158).

Jason: It ain't just Richardson. This whole place sucks. They won't let me do nothin'. And you don't understand either. Chaplain Gentry's the only guy who I can really talk to.

Carol: I understand that you're really disappointed and mad that you couldn't get a drink. I also know you're pretty angry at me and everybody else right now, and about the last thing you want to do is go peacefully back to your room. I know that you and Chaplain Gentry are pretty close. Would you be willing to go to your room and wait quietly while I get him?

If the client does not choose this option, then the worker will have to move the client to a safe place, which will be a time-out room. A show of force may be necessary to send a clear message: "If you can't handle yourself, we will."

Carol: Jason, I want you to go down to observation for 15 minutes and think this out. (*speaking to technicians*) Bob and Jerry, will you see that Jason gets to observation? In 15 minutes I'll be down to see if you're ready to talk this through.

Stage 3: Appeasement. Stages 3 and 4 are probably most appropriate in emergency situations in which the worker has little basis to judge the client's aggressiveness and violence and is unable to obtain immediate assistance. Appeasement is not applicable in a number of settings under ordinary circumstances, and if Jason had reached the point of being removed to involuntary time-out, appeasement or deflection of feelings (Stage 4) would be highly inappropriate and run counter to good therapeutic practice.

However, generally it is better in all situations to err on the side of humility than to project a "tough guy" image, regardless of the client's verbal barbs, threats, and exhortations. This recommendation does not mean that the human services worker should become a doormat to be walked all over by the client. It does mean that by operating in an empathic mode we can see just how frightening and alarming the situation is to the client. The reason threats are made is mostly because clients are scared, frustrated, and at a loss as to what to do over situations they can't control (Newhill, 2003, p. 175). Any attempts by the workers to counter threat with threat in an emergency situation are likely to confirm the client's suspicions that bad things are going to happen.

Appeasement can be attempted if the client's demands are simple and reasonable, even if those demands are made in a bellicose manner. Early on it is better to grant demands and to defer until later worry about what "lessons" need to be taught (Piercy, 1984, p. 148). This approach may be difficult for some human services workers to accept, because it is based on the idea that there is no winner or loser in a potentially violent confrontation between an agitated client and the institution (Moran, 1984, p. 234). In Jason's case, when he feels that his use of anger to make his point is ignored, that makes him more aggressive and his anger moves up to hostility and threat.

Jason: (*barges into the human services worker's office, fists clenched, and starts shouting in an agitated, high-pitched voice*) Listen, big shot! I wanted to mail this letter to my girl. She doesn't know what's happened to me, and that jerk Richardson won't give me a stamp. I could bust all yer heads!

Carol: (*in a calm, collected voice*) He's going by the rules, but I understand your being hot under the collar. Please sit down at the table here, and I'll see what can be done about getting a stamp.

The human services worker meets this demand because it is easily done and does not seriously conflict with institutional rules. She is also alone with an extremely agitated client who may or may not act out. There may be a discussion afterward with the other worker who gave the original order, but there needs to be a clear understanding among all workers that in emergencies, judgment calls may bend the rules a bit or countermand orders of others.

Stage 4: Deflection. Deflection of angry feelings is attempted by shifting to other, less threatening topics. This may be done in a variety of ways. Asking the client to take a physically less threatening position shifts the focus away from agitated motor activity to problem solving (Wood & Khuri, 1984, p. 68).

Carol: (repeating her statement patiently, firmly, and respectfully) Jason, I understand how important it is for you to be able to write to your girlfriend, and how it frustrates you when things don't seem to go your way, but getting in my face won't get you what you want. Please sit down. I'm going for my mid-morning snack. Since you're in a writing mood, if you can write out how to replay this meeting with Mr. Richardson and handle your feelings when you feel like the rules are unfair, then maybe a snack shows up for you too while we talk about and see if we can iron out this problem, and if that happens then maybe a stamp shows up too.

The human services worker literally and figuratively gets the client off his feet and in a less threatening operating mode (Epstein & Carter, 1988). The worker is also quietly but firmly setting limits by asking the client to sit and write. When clients engage in bullying behavior, it is important for the worker not to threaten the person's critical need to get control, but it is equally important to let the client know you will not be intimidated by it (Fauteux, 2010). Because agitated people seldom listen closely to requests for compliance, Carol acknowledges Jason's feeling state and then uses the broken record routine (Canter & Canter, 1982) of repeating her request. The Somers-Flanigans (1997, pp. 69–74) make an eloquent case for using food as a mood altering device. It's a lot more difficult to be angry when you're eating an ice cream bar. She is also employing another behavior management technique: By making a reward contingent on a compliant behavior, Carol is using "Grandma's law" (Becker, 1971), which basically states, "First you eat your spinach, and then you get your ice cream." By using problem-solving techniques, no matter how small the real or imagined injustice is, the human services worker conveys to the client an interest in the client as an individual and not just another name in the institutional computer (Wood & Khuri, 1984, p. 71). Parceling out the problems into workable pieces, the worker removes them from the realm of the enormous and makes them solvable (Weinger, 2001, p. 45). Having the client write down problems also defuses angry feelings and acting out. In many instances,

the client may just be testing limits. Testing limits is a given with a client such as Jason, and the human services worker can be expected to be tested over and over again (Poliks, 1999). To write down clearly and logically what the problem is calls for time and effort, which very few clients will invest if the problem is not important (Epstein & Carter, 1988). Writing down the particulars of the problem is also cathartic for clients, allowing them to gain some emotional distance from it and view the situation in a more objective light (McCown, 1986).

Jason: I can't get nothin' done here. Everything's screwed up. School, home, people, the food, my freedom. It's a concentration camp.

Carol: OK. There seem to be at least three things that are really bugging you right now. Not being able to get a pass yet, the way your dad got angry in family therapy, and your problem with the math assignment yesterday. Together, I can see how it'd become overwhelming. Let's take them one at a time and see what can be done about each. Let me take some notes, so I can keep all this straight. *(Jason goes into a long-winded explanation while Carol listens and takes notes.)*

Until absolutely sure what the problem is, the human services worker should never make promises about what can or cannot be done when attempting to calm an agitated client (Newhill, 2003, p. 210; Wood & Khuri, 1984, p. 71). By allowing Jason to ventilate and by taking notes, Carol affirms that what he has to say is important and plays up rather than down the client's concerns (Chavez, 1999).

Carol: I know that weekend pass is really important. A pass is based on good behavior and your level status. If you feel like you've gotten jerked around, griping about it won't help much. Very specifically, write down why you think you deserve the pass. I'll take it to the staffing this afternoon.

When other, more overt ploys are ineffective, the client may use manipulation and threat to obtain demands.

Jason: If you don't get that pass for me, you ain't much of a counselor, and they'll be real sorry they didn't give it to me.

Carol: When you try and lay that guilt trip on me and make threats about what you'll do if you don't get your way, that's a pretty good indication that the staff's judgment was right and makes it even more difficult to act as your advocate. It's not so much any of the demands that you want, but more like pushing the limits to see how far you can get by manipulating and threatening me.

The response the human services worker makes is one from Adlerian psychotherapy called "avoiding the tar baby" (Dinkmeyer, Pew, & Dinkmeyer, 1979, p. 118). By responding directly to the client, the human services worker does not allow herself to be caught up in the manipulative trap the client lays for her. Although the response is confrontive, it is exceedingly effective with manipulative individuals because it deflects them from their game plan and causes them to consider the consequences of their actions (Wood & Khuri, 1984, p. 71).

When clients become agitated, deflecting anger through physical activity can be helpful. Clients can take out their frustrations through activities that range from pounding on a heavy bag (Vinick, 1986) to tearing up telephone directories (McCown, 1986). At the same time, the human services worker can reinforce the client for acting in more appropriate ways (Jensen & Absher, 1994). Although teaching anger management skills may be more effective in the long run (LeCroy, 1988), appropriate and safe physical exertion to burn up angry feelings is an effective short-term solution.

Jason: (*tearing up the Yellow Pages*) Umphf! I . . . get so mad . . . I . . . Arggh! I . . . wish this phone book was that no-good SOB's face.

Carol: But in fact you haven't torn anybody's face off. You've made a good choice. Much better than when you were going around clobbering people. You don't have to pay any consequences at all for tearing up the phone book. You get it out of your system and get back in control.

Jason: (*continues ventilating, until finally he runs out of energy and lets his arms hang limply at his side*)

Carol: (*continues to reinforce Jason for acting appropriately and within limits*) Look at what you could have done. You could have swung a chair at Mr. Richardson, which would have gotten you into hot water. The very kinds of thing that got you here in the first place. But you didn't do that. What you did was perfectly acceptable and within the limits here.

Stage 5: Time-Out. When clients cannot contend with the emotion of the moment, they are asked to go to a reduced-stimulus environment, to be alone and

think things out. A clear assessment of how agitated the client is needs to be made at this point. Is the client able and willing to leave a high-stimulus situation for a few minutes to rest and think things over? If the client is not overly reactive, then the worker may ask the client to take a minimal time-out in living quarters.

Jason: I don't want to sit, talk, or be reasonable. I want this scumbag place to do something!

Carol: Right now I can see there's no way this is going to get solved. You can go to your room and think things over. Go for 15 minutes. If you can come back and show me you're in control, that's it, no reduction in level, no write-ups, and it's forgotten.

When a clear threat is made, there is still a possibility of reducing the tension by telling the client that threats will not work, but the client has still not done anything wrong so there is still time to work things out (Fauteux, 2010). However, if the client can't calm down and start to work on the problem constructively, then time-out is the next option (Vinick, 1986).

Carol: I've tried to work this through with you, and you clearly don't want to hear it. When you continue to make threats, you're saying to me you're not willing to abide by the rules and are choosing to have rules enforced. I want you to go to the observation room for 30 minutes right now. At the end of that time I'll be around to see you. If you don't feel like talking, you don't have to, but you can go back in the room for another 30 minutes. You can continue to do that until you're willing to talk to me about how you think you've been treated unfairly.

The human services worker states these conditions in a matter-of-fact manner and does not press the issue (Vinick, 1986). If the client is so agitated as to be beyond the grasp of reality and is unwilling to be compliant with the human services worker's request, then the worker needs help to contain the situation.

Stage 6: Show of Force. If the client is unable to proceed to time-out or is otherwise noncompliant or acting out, then a show of force is needed (Piercy, 1984, p. 148). If the client is already agitated enough to warn the human services workers that help may be warranted, the interview should be carried out in an open hallway or large meeting room where the participants are in plain view of other staff members and the client can be restrained easily (Viner, 1982). The show of force indicates that any display of violence or threat of violence will not be tolerated and often helps disorganized clients regain control of themselves (Wood & Khuri, 1984, p. 68). If this stage is reached, the potential for violence is high, and the worker should not attempt to deal with the client alone. Either by paging help through an emergency code or by having assistance readily available, the worker needs to be able to summon enough help to demonstrate that compliance is now required (Lakeside Hospital, 1988).

However, there are times when, through no fault of the worker, potentially violent situations occur when the worker is alone and not immediately able to call for assistance. The following procedures may keep the worker out of harm's way (Chavez, 1999; Epstein & Carter, 1988; Lakeside Hospital, 1988; Moran, 1984, pp. 238–248; Morrison, 1993, pp. 79–100; Thackrey, 1987; Turnbull et al., 1990).

1. *Stay calm and relaxed.* Tensing of muscles and agitated movement only fuel the situation and cause the client to expect that something bad (for the client) is about to happen. Relaxation techniques such as simple deep breathing are extremely helpful, allowing one to stay loose, anticipate client responses, and move quickly.
2. *Practice positive self-talk.* Even in the worst situations, running positive "billboards" through the mind's eye will help keep control of the situation.
3. *Do not stare at the client.* Keep casual eye contact because the eyes of the individual will typically move to where a blow might be struck. Focus on an imaginary spot on the client's upper chest, about where the first button on a shirt would be, occasionally glancing at the eyes and other parts of the individual's body. Keeping focus on the centerline of the client's body will also let the human services worker avoid being faked out by extremity movements.
4. *Stay an arm's length away or more.* Make a judgment about how long the client's arms are, and stay an arm's length and a bit more away. Remember that agitated clients generally have an expanded sense of personal space and feel threatened when that space is entered.
5. *Stay on the client's dominant side.* Know which of the client's hands is dominant and stay close to the client's dominant side. Especially on males, the watch hand typically indicates the client's weak side. If you cannot determine this for sure, stay on the client's right side since most people are right-handed. In an aggressive stance, a person invariably

places the foot of the weak side forward. If the worker keeps to the dominant, or right, side of an assailant, any blow aimed by the assailant is likely to have less power and be a glancing one, because the assailant will have to pivot to get the worker back on his or her left in order to hit the worker more easily. Staying on the right, or dominant, side means the assailant will have to take time to move into a more favorable position and will not be able to use his or her strength as effectively.

6. *Keep arms at sides and hands open.* Folded arms or hands on hips are bad for two reasons. They imply hostility or authority, and they put the worker at a distinct disadvantage because of the time it takes to unfold them and defend oneself.
7. *Assume a defensive posture.* Stand with feet slightly spread, face to face with the client but tending a bit to the client's weak side. Move the dominant leg slightly to the rear with the knee locked ready to pivot and run. Move the other leg slightly forward of the body and bent slightly at the knee. This position will allow the worker the best chance to stay upright, and staying upright is the best safeguard against being hurt.
8. *Avoid cornering.* When the client is placed in an angle formed by two walls or other objects, with the human services worker directly in front of the client, the only way out is through the worker.
9. *Avoid ordering.* When a client is threatening violence, attempting to order or command a client to do something is likely to aggravate the situation further. Staying with the basic empathic listening and responding skills used throughout this book is far more likely to lead to satisfactory results.
10. *Do perceptual checks.* Ask for the client's help. If current verbal responses are merely agitating the situation, ask the client what solutions or techniques might calm things down.
11. *Admit mistakes.* If you've made an error in judgment, admit it and make an apology. If things have gone this far, do not be afraid to lose face.
12. *Do nothing.* If doing something will make matters worse, do nothing. If the client is determined to leave and help is not immediately available, let the client go. *Never* attempt to touch a client under these circumstances without first indicating what you are about to do and getting the client's agreement to do so.
13. *Give validation.* In a sincere and empathic manner, acknowledge that the person has a good reason for feeling that way and let him or her leave.

All human services providers and especially crisis workers should undergo training in simple self-defense and takedown procedures (Blair, 1991; Morrison, 1993, pp. 79–100; Thackrey, 1987; Turnbull et al., 1990). Gately and Stabb (2005) found restraint and defensive training topics least attended to by training programs. Numerous facilities provide such training for little or no charge. Local YMCAs or YWCAs and college continuing education courses may offer such instruction, or the local high school wrestling coach may even be prevailed on. Instruction should be a priority of the institution, and *all* personnel should receive training. The organization should certainly provide self-defense training. If it doesn't, and you have decided to work there, you absolutely need to get training yourself.

Stage 7: Seclusion. Seclusion may be generally differentiated from time-out by its length, its setting, and its involuntary nature. Seclusion is a severe type of limit setting for the client in a safe and secure environment where the client can reorganize thinking, feeling, and behavior (Mattson & Sacks, 1978). When seclusion or physical or chemical restraints are used, federal and state guidelines must be followed. They should be used only when there is imminent danger to the client or others and no safer or more effective alternatives are available (dos Reis et al., 2003). There is a great deal of controversy as to whether seclusion or restraints should be used, given the potential for physical and psychological harm (Glezer & Brendel, 2010; Kumble & McSherry, 2010; Mohr, 2010). However, in some cases there is no other option if self-harm or harm to others is imminent.

There are a number of reasons for seclusion: (1) the client is agitated, hyperactive, verbally threatening, or damaging property; (2) the client is impulsive or intrusive and does not respond to limit setting; (3) the client is making suicidal gestures and is unable or unwilling to make a verbal contract about controlling behavior; or (4) the client must be protected from possible harm by others (Baradell, 1985; Lewis, 1993, p. 105). This intervention still allows the client some control over mobility, thinking, and autonomy. Seclusion may be of greater benefit to clients who are overstimulated by social contact (dos Reis et al., 2003).

Negative emotions such as anger, guilt, confusion, helplessness, and loss of control are typical client responses to seclusion (Outlaw & Lowery, 1992). Given these negative feelings, it is more than likely that the client may not willingly go to seclusion.

In the confrontation with Jason, a response team has been called and is ready to take Jason to seclusion.

Carol: I'd really like you to go on your own down to time-out. It's up to you. You can go on your own right now, or the technicians will take you to seclusion.

Even at this late hour, the worker is still attempting to allow Jason to exercise options and make choices (Baradell, 1985).

Jason: I ain't gonna go nowhere 'ceptin' outta here.

Carol backs away, and the response team moves in. On a predetermined signal by the leader, they quickly take Jason down. One member holds his head, and the other four carry him to seclusion. Once placed in seclusion, the client is oriented to what is going to occur, and a staff member is assigned to monitor the client. Checks are made at 15-, 30-, or 60-minute intervals, depending on the client's mental status. Copies of nursing and general care orders are given to both staff and the client. Seclusion has a low level of sensory input—no radio or television, no visitors—and emphasis is on biological needs. "Low level" does not mean that the client is sensorially deprived; it is important to prevent feelings of abandonment. The client is shown acceptance by the human services worker and reassured that seclusion is necessary and temporary and that the client can return to normal routine when behavior calms down (Baradell, 1985).

Carol: I'm sorry you chose to go to seclusion, Jason. You decided to exercise that option, but when you can agree to not make threats, control your behavior to the point you can talk this through, and make a written contract as to what you will do, you can come back out.

In an acute stage of agitation such as Jason has just experienced, it is no longer appropriate to explore conflicts or feelings (Ruesch, 1973). Carol's communication with the client is brief, direct, concrete, but kind. Given the client's sensory overload, sleep is an excellent therapeutic modality, and the client should be allowed to use it (Baradell, 1985).

One negative footnote is appropriate here: A few clients may use seclusion as a way of achieving notoriety and a macho image (Gutheil, 1978). If such a hidden agenda is suspected, the human services worker should thoroughly discuss this problem with the other residents and obtain their help in being nonresponsive to the client's "tough guy" behavior.

Stage 8: Restraints. Restraints are most often employed in psychiatric facilities and are used in conjunction with a request from the nursing staff and backed by a doctor's order. When a client is placed in restraints, close observation is absolutely necessary. Under no circumstances should clients be restrained without such guidelines and available professional medical staff. If the client is acting out and will not go to seclusion, restraints will have to be used. Restraints might be either physical or chemical. Restraints are controversial, and their use is closely regulated in both a legal and an ethical sense (dos Reis et al., 2003). Restraints are employed when it is evident that the client may be harmful to self or others (Stilling, 1992; Tardiff, 1984a, p. 48). If the client is to be restrained, then adequate staff should be available, consisting of at least one person for each limb and another person who serves as leader, for a total of five members. Written guidelines and constant rehearsal of procedures with observation and critique should be used to keep the team's skills well honed (Tardiff, 1984b).

Seclusion and restraints should *never* be used as a way of controlling clients, making life "easier" for the custodians, or as punishment. These are truly last-resort measures, because their use can cause a host of other problems for the client (Morrison, 1993, p. 105). If at all possible, the crisis worker should not be involved in the episode, because involvement may erect barriers to future therapeutic endeavors.

Stage 9: Sedation. If all else fails, the client needs to be chemically restrained by a doctor's order (dos Reis et al., 2003). The problem now becomes clearly medical, and until the medical staff believes that medication is no longer necessary, there is little the human services worker can do. If sedation is needed with Jason, it does not mean the end of Jason's story. Stage 9 is essentially a complete time-out for both Jason and the staff. For Jason, it will allow the sensory overload he is experiencing to diminish and return to normal limits. It will give the staff members time to reorganize their thoughts on how best to deal with this highly agitated adolescent. When Jason comes out of sedation, the staff will start down the treatment road with him again and will have developed a new plan to deal with this angry young man.

The Violent Geriatric Client

Although medical science has been able to   **LO11**
prolong the lives of Americans, treatment for neuropsychiatric disorders concomitant with increased longevity remains beyond the reach of medical science at present. Accompanying the neuropsychiatric problems of the geriatric client are reduced judgment and increased impulsivity, limited mobility, drug dependency, multiple personal loss, financial problems, and limited social supports, which all potentially contribute to violent behavior (Mentes & Ferrario, 1989; Petrie, 1984, p. 107). Nursing home staff are at high risk for assault by patients, and they need to be trained to be aware of and respond to potential threats of physical assault (Gates, Fitzwater, & Succop, 2005; Hillman et al., 2005; Newhill, 2003, pp. 91–92; Tardiff, 1989).

The case of Cliff demonstrates how the agitated and mildly disoriented elderly client can be stabilized without medication. Reality orientation (Osborn, 1991; Taulbee & Folsom, 1966), reminiscence (Butler, 1963), and remotivation (Garber, 1965) techniques are workable options for the mildly disoriented elderly client. The case of Grace shows how validation therapy (Feil, 1982) may be used with the severely disoriented elderly. These cases illustrate that psychologically infirm elderly clients need not always spend this final stage of their lives in chemically induced compliance.

Mild Disorientation: The Case of Cliff

Cliff Hastings has lived a full and eventful life, but now, at the age of 74, he is a resident of a skilled nursing care facility. He was a strapping man who had worked all over the world on big construction projects until he was 72. He invented many engineering techniques in steam fitting and chilled water cooling systems. He lost his wife to cancer 10 years ago but submerged himself in his work and lived a highly productive life as a widower. He has had excellent relationships with his two children, Jan and Robert. Although they and their families live geographically distant from Cliff, they love their father very much and are very concerned about him.

At age 73, Cliff got up one morning, prepared to go to work, and fell flat on his face with a stroke. Although he recovered to the extent that he was able to shuffle around the house, lung complications set in. He was diagnosed as having emphysema and went on oxygen. Six months later, he was no longer able to take care of himself physically, was starting to have memory lapses, and was moved to Hursthaven Nursing Home by his children. At Hursthaven, he has become progressively more confused about people, places, and times, and when asked to do something has been either rebellious or passively resistant.

A crisis was precipitated when he knocked over an oxygen tank in the middle of the night because the "Arabs were after him" and broke the nose of a male attendant who tried to calm him down as he attempted to struggle out of his bed. Cliff is about to meet Marilyn, a gerontological counselor. She has just been retained by Hursthaven to deal with crisis situations such as Cliff's.

Assessment. Marilyn has thoroughly reviewed Cliff's chart and has discussed his case with the medical and primary care staff. Many of the primary care staff members maintain that Cliff is noncompliant, badly disoriented, and dangerous, and they would like to keep him heavily sedated. Cliff's stroke, his unplanned aggressive outburst, his hostile and uncooperative behavior, his fear of the medical equipment, and his depression, plus the fact that his outburst occurred at night, all support the staff's contention that little but chemical restraint is left for Cliff.

Marilyn decides to conduct her own assessment by interviewing Cliff. She has three purposes in mind: (1) to determine Cliff's degree of disorientation and agitation, (2) to use her therapeutic skills to reduce his disruptive behavior and help him return to a state of equilibrium with as little reliance on medication as possible, and (3) to help Cliff use whatever resources he has to live this final stage of his life as fully as he is able.

Marilyn: Hello, I'm Marilyn. I don't believe I've met you. You seem pretty angry about something.

Cliff: (*suspiciously*) Who the hell are you?

Marilyn: I'm new here, part of the staff, and I'm getting around meeting all the residents. Sorry you're so angry. What can I do to help?

Cliff: I'm Cliff Hastings, and I'm mad as hell. Look at what those SOBs have done to me. I pay $6,000 a month for this place to strap me down. I'll kill the bastards if I get a chance. Can you get me out of here?

Marilyn: (*speaking in a strong but soft and empathic voice, while pulling up a chair and sitting down directly in his line of sight*) No! I can't right now. I guess I'd be mad too if I were strapped in like that. Do you know where you are?

Cliff: I'm in Hell, and these people are all devils.

Marilyn: It may feel like that right now, but this is Hursthaven Nursing Home. Do you know that?

Cliff: Too damn well.

Marilyn: Do you know what day it is?

Cliff: Who cares? They're all the same in here.

Marilyn assesses Cliff's degree of contact with reality by determining how well oriented he is to person, place, and time. Although he does not give specific, concrete responses, his retorts indicate that he is fairly well in touch with reality, given his present agitated state.

Marilyn: I'm sorry you're feeling so angry. Can I get you a drink of water?

Eliciting Trust. Offering clients food or drink tends to defuse the situation and make them more accepting of initiating overtures the worker may tender (Wood & Khuri, 1984, p. 67). Marilyn also sits down by Cliff and meets him at eye level. She places herself on his physical level and in his direct line of sight. Standing over a client who is confused tends to distort the caregiver's image in grotesque ways and may be very threatening (Wolanin & Phillips, 1981, p. 106).

Cliff: (*takes a sip of water from cup Marilyn offers*) Yeah, that's the least somebody around this place could do for the money I pay to be doped up and trussed up like a pig.

Marilyn: How do you feel?

Cliff: How the hell do you think I feel, young lady?

Marilyn: I guess I'd not only feel like a pig all trussed up, but mad as a wildcat in a gunnysack. How did this happen?

Marilyn matches the vernacular of the client and interjects a bit of humor (Tomine, 1986). She is interested in knowing what happened, but her major concern is to continue posing open-ended questions to assess how much in touch with reality Cliff is and to let him know she is interested in and concerned about him. Marilyn manages to gain a working rapport with Cliff and explores last night's incident.

Marilyn: So what happened last night that got you in that fix?

Cliff: The Arab, he was after me. He was gonna strangle me, but nobody believes me. (*points to attendant*) That guy said it was one of the guys that work here at night. Said I busted his nose. Well, it was the Arabs.

Marilyn: Why do you think it was the Arabs?

Reality Orientation. Marilyn is taking a first step in attempting to relieve Cliff's confusion by using reality orientation (Taulbee & Folsom, 1966). Reality orientation focuses on anchoring clients to who they are, where they are, and why they are there. When a client's response or behavior is out of touch with reality, the worker asks the client a *why* question, in an approach contrary to that of most therapeutic interventions (Taulbee, 1978, p. 207). Marilyn does this because she is trying to find out the reason for the behavior. Once she knows that, she can start to reorient Cliff.

Cliff: I spent a lot of time in Arabia, you know. Worked in construction. Put up a lot of refrigeration plants and steam systems. Hard to believe you'd need steam in that hothouse. Sometimes I wish I was back in Arabia. But that doesn't mean any damn Arab terrorist can come in here in the middle of the night and kill me.

Marilyn: (*genuinely interested*) Hey! That sounds pretty exciting. I've hardly been out of the Midwest. I'll bet you've seen some pretty hair-raising things, and I can guess how you might think somebody was an Arab, being in a strange place like this.

Cliff rambles on for quite a while about his experiences there, with Marilyn listening and responding using person-centered techniques of attending, affirming, restating for clarification, reflecting feelings, and asking open-ended questions.

Pacing. Cliff's response about working in Arabia gives Marilyn a clue about the image Cliff saw attacking him in the night. However, she does not try to change his mind about what happened. She keeps pace with Cliff. She lets him tell his story without hurrying or trying to persuade him that he was mistaken last night. Patience is of maximum benefit in gaining the trust she will need if she is to accomplish anything with him (Taulbee, 1978, p. 210).

Reminiscence Therapy. Marilyn's approach in urging Cliff to talk about his past is contradictory to most standard operating procedures and generally accepted counseling techniques. Most therapeutic systems try very hard to keep clients in present time and view trips to the past as counterproductive to changing real-time problems. However, allowing geriatric clients to ruminate about past experiences can be therapeutically effective (Brooker & Duce, 2000; Buchanan et al., 2002; Cully, LaVoie, & Gfeller, 2001; Ebersole, 1978a, p. 145; Hsieh & Wang, 2003; Hyer et al., 2002).

Reminiscence therapy (Butler, 1963; Osborn, 1991; Society of Clinical Psychology, 2012) is a non-threatening experience designed for older adults with mild to moderate depression. The therapy aims to reduce depression, increase life satisfaction, improve self-esteem, and help older adults cope with crises, losses, and life transitions, which allows older clients to reflect on their lives and restore credibility to them (Miller, 1986). Reminiscence therapy has become one of the standard treatments for the depressed elderly and has been successfully used worldwide in both individual and group formats (Ando, 2005; Cappeliez & Watt, 2005; Haber, 2006; Jo & Song, 2015; McKee et al., 2005; Meléndez et al., 2013; Spar & La Rue, 2006; Van Puyenbroeck & Maes, 2006; Wang, 2005). Reminiscence therapy has been adapted to the computer with touch screen technology with the Computer CIRCA-BC Interactive Reminiscence Conversation Aid (CIRCA) program (Purves et al., 2015).

Memory dysfunction and personality disorganization are central to Cliff's current crisis and confusion. Reminiscence helps in personality reorganization and increases self-confidence because it draws on aspects of long-term memory that have been imprinted and can be recalled easily (Singer, Tracz, & Dworkin, 1991). Reminiscence can be therapeutic and healing for the client; it is a simple, enjoyable sharing of anecdotes that allows the worker to form a close affiliation with the client (Ebersole, 1978a, p. 145).

Individuals may use reminiscing to reconcile and put to rest bitter memories, reconstruct and enjoy pleasant memories, reduce boredom, and prepare for death (Cully, LaVoie, & Gfeller, 2001). Further, if reminiscence is used in groups, interpersonal bonds can be increased as clients relate to historical benchmarks, personal achievements, objects, locations, and people. Older clients regain a sense of empowerment as the "experts" on the times they have lived in. Self-esteem is enhanced through recall of past achievements in the face of declining physical capacities (McMahon & Rhudick, 1964, pp. 292–298). "Unfinished business" from the past may be identified and handled (O'Leary & Nieuwstraten, 2001). It also offers the opportunity for physical contact and validation for what the elderly have done with their lives (Baker, 1985) and helps them cope with grief and depression through social interaction and renewed social skills (Hsieh & Wang, 2003; Singer, Tracz, & Dworkin, 1991).

Cliff: Yeah…(*voice trails off*)…I used to be hot stuff… but I'm not so hot now. Hell, half the time I don't even know who, what, or where I am.

Marilyn: (*touches client's arm lightly with her hand*) It sounds like that's pretty scary, having run things most of your life, and now things are out of control.

Cliff: I hate to admit it, but that's right. Now I got to have help getting to the john! How'd you like that? It embarrasses the hell out of me. They treat me like a 2-year-old.

Marilyn: So being embarrassed and not being treated like a man are the worst parts of being here. I wonder what we might do to change that?

Anchoring. Marilyn uses a reflective statement of feeling to integrate Cliff's past with his present. By bringing up past incidents and hooking them to the present, she attempts to reinforce and help Cliff reassert his competence. Marilyn also uses touch to anchor him psychologically to someone in the institution (Wolanin & Phillips, 1981, pp. 105–106). Prior to the assault, a kind but sterile atmosphere had existed for Cliff at Hursthaven.

Like most human beings, Cliff has not responded well to living in an emotional vacuum. Since the attack, the atmosphere between Cliff and the staff has become adversarial in nature. Marilyn needs to change Cliff's view of the staff as being against him and the staff's view that Cliff is to be avoided. Staff members who have hands-on contact with Cliff on a regular basis need to be given training in the approaches Marilyn is using. Staffing and case review are particularly important for coordinating the different staff members who will deal with Cliff in a 24-hour period. All staff members who come in contact with him during the course of the day will introduce themselves, call Cliff by name, state the date, give a short preview of the next few hours' activities, and also explain any procedures, medical or otherwise, that they are carrying out. By consistently orienting the client, the staff takes a first step in treating confusion (Taulbee, 1978, p. 209).

Marilyn also picks up on Cliff's fear of losing control. Being wildly out of control is completely out of character for clients like Cliff, who are frightened at the prospect of losing their minds. Even more fears are generated when elderly clients sense someone is afraid of them or avoiding them because of fear of violence (Lion & Pasternak, 1973). Marilyn

engages in a number of activities in this dialogue. The most important is that she has made a small but significant change in the interactional system that currently exists between Cliff and the staff by representing herself as an empathic, caring spokesperson for the institution and as an advocate for him (Fisch, Weakland, & Segal, 1983). Second, she reflects Cliff's anger, fear, and loss of control. She acknowledges and validates his experiences, but she is not just mouthing platitudes. She knows that the more he lacks current orientation, the more the staff will tend to avoid him. The more he is avoided, the less contact he has with people, and the more out of touch and disoriented he is likely to become (Petrie, 1984, pp. 114–115). The cycle can become deeper and deeper if uninterrupted and may cause even more disorientation and aggressive acts in the future (Miller, 1986).

Distinguishing Between Illusions and Hallucinations

Marilyn understands that what agitated Cliff was probably not a hallucination, as the staff thinks, but more than likely an illusion. While piecing together the tale of the night before, she determines that one of the Sisters of Charity who works at the nursing home made rounds about the time Cliff became agitated. The sister's habit may have made her look like an Arab in the dim light. Thus, what Cliff saw was probably an illusion based in fact, not fiction.

By proposing an explanation of the event, Marilyn allows Cliff to understand that he was not delusional but was misperceiving reality. The two problems are very different, and the difference is of great significance in calming Cliff. Although this conclusion may sound very pat, such happenings are all too common among mildly confused and disoriented clients. Very definite, concrete stimuli often create illusions that disrupt peace of mind for geriatric clients, leaving them to doubt their own perceptions. It is extremely important for the worker to relate such a hypothesis to mildly confused clients such as Cliff who are very much concerned about keeping in touch with reality (Wolanin & Phillips, 1981, p. 107).

Marilyn: (*relates her hypothesis to Cliff*) So I believe that you weren't really crazy last night, but actually saw Sister Lucy making rounds. If you think about it, it makes sense.

Cliff: I don't know. I still really believe there was an Arab in here.

Marilyn: From all you've told me about your experiences there, I can understand that. But I also know that when you're zonked out in a strange place with the medical equipment around and strangers passing to and fro, suddenly waking up and seeing things differently is not uncommon and doesn't mean you're nuts. I'll bet if you think about it, it has happened before. I know it has happened to me. There's a big difference between misunderstanding what you see and seeing something that isn't there.

Sundown Syndrome. Because the event happened in the early evening, the sundown syndrome must be considered. Events that accompany the end of the day in an institution are strange and unsettling to residents who have been used to a regimen of activities based on their own time and the security of their own home. Unmet toilet needs, absence of a snack, staff members' attitudes, different noises, decreased light, effects of sedatives, and presence of fewer personnel all add up to fear and strangeness without the support of another human being. These conditions can lead the client to act out (Blair & New, 1991; Stilling, 1992; Wolanin & Phillips, 1981, p. 107). Given the need to further assure Cliff about the reality of the situation, Marilyn relates the problems that occur with the approach of evening in the institution and makes some suggestions about how things might be changed to make this time less threatening.

Marilyn: If you could make things here a bit more like home, what would they be?

Cliff: Well, I used to put my earphones on and listen to some country music and have a beer before I hit the hay. I don't know much else, just watch TV and stuff. No special furniture or anything. I lived in apartments and hotels most of my life.

Marilyn: I notice that there's not much of you in this room. It looks like a hospital room instead of Cliff's room. You mentioned a lot of items you collected over the years and picture albums of all your travels. Where are they?

Cliff: Oh, my kids just stored them away.

Marilyn: I'd like to see if we couldn't get some of those in here, dress the place up a bit, so when people come by they'd know it was Cliff Hastings, world-class engineer, who lives here.

Security Blankets. Marilyn proposes that articles familiar to Cliff be brought into the room for two reasons. First, creating a familiar environment may go a long way toward creating a basis in reality for the fact that this is now Cliff's home and reconciling him to this stage in his life (Petrie, 1984, p. 116). Second, suddenly awakening in a medical environment with a variety of strange machines and tubes running in and out of one's body is extremely threatening because such foreign objects alter a person's body images and surroundings in a very negative way (Wolanin & Phillips, 1981, p. 106). Having familiar objects immediately visible can help Cliff reorient without becoming agitated in the process. Marilyn will check with administrative staff to see whether Cliff's sound equipment can be brought into his room. She will also check with medical staff to see whether a bottle of beer in the evening will confound his medication. If possible, providing these amenities will further approximate Cliff's routine at home and provide orientation and security (Miller, 1986).

Remotivation. Finally, Marilyn will attempt to involve Cliff in the activities of the institution. It is important to involve clients interpersonally and have them become physically and psychologically active in their environment. For people like Cliff who have been highly active throughout their lives, it is critical to fill idle time in meaningful ways to keep such clients from drifting into depression (Donahue, 1965). This does not mean forcing and cajoling clients into doing something contrary to what interests them. Playing bingo might be fun for many people, but forcing a person to engage in such an activity is inappropriate (Miller, 1986). After listening to Cliff, Marilyn makes a proposal designed to reinvolve him with other humans.

Marilyn: I'd like you to consider a proposition I have to make. Hursthaven has an alliance with St. Peter's Orphanage. None of those kids have anybody to care about them. I have a couple of boys in mind that I think you could do some good with. You've got some great stories that they'd love and probably some wisdom that could be helpful to those guys. They just mainly need a man to talk to, and I wonder if you'd be willing to help out.

Marilyn's agenda is twofold. She is truthful in what she tells Cliff. She also knows that the two boys will have a positive effect on Cliff in turn. Older people seem particularly interested in sharing their experiences with the young (Ebersole, 1978b, p. 241). Cliff's candidness, wisdom, and trove of stories are likely to have a positive effect on two boys who are as anchorless as Cliff. She focuses on Cliff from a strength perspective (Newhill, 2003, pp. 160–161). Rather than focusing on what is wrong with the client, she capitalizes on the client's strong points, positive qualities, and overall potential for controlling his behavior.

Remotivation therapy is a technique used to stimulate and revitalize people who are no longer interested in the present or the future (Dennis, 1978, p. 219). It is based on a combination of reminiscence and reality orientation. Remotivation attempts to persuade the client that he or she is accepted by others as an individual who has unique and important traits that make him distinguishable from everyone else (Garber, 1965). Reminiscing about one's experiences with the concrete world and identifying and asserting one's experiences through interactions with others often lead to strengthening the concept of reality. Being encouraged to describe oneself concretely as a person with roles and specific social functions and speaking accurately about past and present experiences give a person strength (Dennis, 1978, p. 220).

Severe Disorientation: The Case of Grace

The standard regimen for working with geriatric clients has been to attempt to "reality orient" them to the present. Such an approach becomes problematic for moderately confused clients and profoundly so for those who have almost entirely retreated from the reality of the present. Attempts to orient moderately to severely confused, very old clients to person, place, and time are generally futile. For many of these clients, nothing could be less worthwhile, for there is clearly not much in the present worth remembering (Miller, 1986). Seizing on this notion, Naomi Feil developed validation therapy (Feil, 1982; Feil & deKlerk-Rubin, 2012). **Validation therapy** is a successful way of communicating with older adults with dementia. Her thesis is to acknowledge the feelings of the person, no matter how irrational they may seem to be. By dignifying feelings, the worker validates the person. To deny the client's feelings is to deny past existence and thus deny the personhood of the individual.

Feil also believes that validating early memories enables clients to resolve the past and justify their role in old age. Positive outcomes from using the approach are restoring self-worth, reducing stress, justifying life, resolving unfinished conflicts, restoring dignity, and

establishing a better and more secure feeling for the client (Feil, 1982, p. 1). The worker continuously validates the client as a first step in restoring self-worth and affirming that at least one person is interested and concerned enough to listen to what the client's life has been. Anyone overhearing a dialogue between a worker and a client who has severely regressed into an irrational past would probably wonder at first whether the worker had also become senile. For validation therapy to be effective, the worker must have some creative insight into the verbal meanderings and repetitive behaviors of the client (Miller, 1986).

Listen to Marilyn as she attempts to convince an 83-year-old woman to go to dinner. Grace is standing in the hallway refusing to be moved. She is engaging in a rocking motion with her arms and softly humming to herself. Staff's efforts to get her to go to dinner have been fruitless, and she is becoming increasingly agitated and threatening as a number of staff members are attempting to orient her and get her to comply with their requests. Marilyn enters this scene and asks the rest of the staff to leave them.

Grace: There, there! Don't you cry.

Marilyn: I see you're really concerned about your baby.

Grace: Yes, I've been up all night with Ellen. She must have colic, but I can't seem to get her to settle down. I need to get Dr. Heinz, he's our family doctor, but I don't have anyone to drive me to town.

Marilyn: It really worries you that Ellen doesn't seem to be getting any better. You must be awfully tired and hungry!

Grace: Even though Ellen's cranky, she's no bother. She's really a beautiful baby. It's just that her father isn't around much. He works on the railroad, and I could use some help sometimes.

Marilyn: You must love her very much. Maybe we could go down to dinner together, and you could tell me some more about her.

Grace: She's got to have quiet to get to sleep. It's too noisy there.

Marilyn: It's important to you that she gets to sleep. Perhaps we could have dinner served in your room. It'd be quiet there.

Grace: Well, I suppose, if you'd really like to.

In this short exchange, the worker demonstrates two critical components of validation therapy. The client may well have lost the ability to comprehend and reason with any degree of complexity.

By keeping communication short and simple, the worker avoids losing the client in a variety of ideas that may rapidly become overwhelming. The worker also responds directly and continuously to Grace's feelings, validating to her that the symbolic act she is engaging in is highly important (Miller, 1986). Genuine, deep empathic responding is critical to doing validation (Feil, 1999). Although the purpose of validation therapy is not to manipulate or lie to the client (Feil & Altman, 2004), the worker's approach is far better than forcibly taking the client to the dining room, where she will probably be so distraught over having to neglect her baby that she will not eat anyway.

Whether Grace has ever had a baby named Ellen, or whether she is trying to resolve some shortcoming she has long felt in regard to mothering, is of little concern in the present moment. What is of concern is that the worker treat the situation as if it were real and of importance to the client and acknowledge the client's scattered thoughts and feelings in a congruent, empathic manner (Feil & Altman, 2004). Naomi Feil is adamant that validation therapy is not a "therapeutic lie," as some propose, that is meant only to humor those with dementia. Feil proposes that all people with dementia deserve to be treated with dignity and respect, and to listen to them is an excellent way of doing so. She believes it is absolutely normal for the aged to return to the past to attempt to resolve unfinished business before they die. When these emotions are expressed and someone listens with empathy and unconditional positive regard, frustrations are eased.

Validation therapy is not intended to return the client to reality. However, for the human services worker who has to intervene in a crisis situation with the severely disoriented elderly, it does have the potential to calm them down, avoid situations conducive to acting out, and provide an effective therapeutic technique in an area where few have been found (Miller, 1986). Jankowski and Frey (2012) have pointed out that with the "silver tsunami" of elderly coming and the dementia that comes along with them, this neglected therapy needs to be taught to the students who'll be needed to work with this population. Even though Grace appears to be a pathetic, senile, frail, and confused woman who is easily handled by the crisis worker, don't be misled. The very person Grace represents, if thwarted and frustrated, is the reason that assaults against geriatric workers who discount the "old, senile fragile fool" Graces are so high.

Follow-up with Staff Victims

Follow-up after an assault is critical to both the **LO12** person assaulted and the rest of the staff (Kleespies & Ponce, 2009; Kleespies, 2014). Workers may brush off assaults as just part of the business and then find out that the psychological ramifications are far greater than they imagined (Fauteux, 2010). Workers who are victims of violent attacks by clients may have emotional responses that include hypervigilance, startle responses, intrusive thoughts, unresolved anger, and poorer overall mental health and anger control (Lenehan & Turner, 1984, p. 256; Wykes & Whittington, 1998). They may look much like the victims of PTSD (California Occupational Safety and Health Administration, 1998, p. 17; Murray & Snyder, 1991).

Practitioners who experience assault feel disempowered, anxious, depressed, and fearful (Littlechild, 2002). Their job performance suffers as they lose confidence to carry out their work roles, question their competence, feel less caring and attachment to clients, and experience self-blame, guilt, and anger about the incident. Further, they fear for their future safety, fear reporting future episodes that would label them as incompetent, and fear that their fellow employees and managers will not see them as dependable (Flannery et al., 2001; Littlechild, 1995).

Bard and Sangrey (1986) found that workers go through three stages of trauma resolution after a physical assault. First they experience a **disorganization of self** that includes feelings of shock. They may dissociate from the experience as unreal, as if it didn't happen or they viewed it as a video of themselves. They may blame themselves and start having peritraumatic stress disorder symptoms involving sleep disturbances and emotional outbursts. The second stage, **period of struggle**, is characterized by anxiety attacks, intrusive thoughts, hypervigilance, and psychosomatic symptoms, which are characteristic of acute stress disorder. The third stage is **readjustment of self**. If the worker is able to move forward, then the incident is integrated into the self and the worker becomes the wiser for it, comes to see that clients can be dangerous, and takes more precautions. However, if the worker does not integrate the incident, then the possibility of PTSD looms large.

Lanza (1984) found that nurses who had experienced such attacks had negative emotional, cognitive, and behavioral reactions up to a year afterward. It is extremely important to work through the aftermath of violent behavior suffered by staff, for two reasons: first, so that the victim does not become debilitated personally and professionally by the incident, and second, because other members of the staff will perceive that the institution takes such events very seriously and is concerned for their safety as well.

After an attack, staff members initially may ascribe blame to the victim to ease their own fear and trepidation about the possibility that it could happen to them. Under no circumstances should this be allowed to happen. Sympathy and support for the victim are vital. Pity, condescension, or subtle implications about provoking the assault should be avoided. There should be acknowledgment that the attack occurred and crisis intervention should be started immediately. Normalizing the situation is imperative and lets the worker know that others would feel the same way that he or she is feeling.

Psychoeducation should be conducted with workers to familiarize them with some of the psychological reactions they may have and what strategies they may use to alleviate them (Weinger, 2001, pp. 66–67). Institutional support groups for victims of violence should be available (Stortch, 1991), and staff should be prepared to give immediate help with problem solving and decision making, such as determining injuries, providing medical transportation, staying with the victim, providing moral support, and helping with medical, legal, and police reports (Lenehan & Turner, 1984, pp. 255–256). Unit staff should also receive counseling to prevent "a blame the victim attitude" from developing (California Occupational Safety and Health Administration, 1998, p. 17; Occupational Safety and Health Administration, 2015). We enthusiastically agree with the foregoing. As soon as the victim is able, a psychological autopsy should be performed on the incident. A **psychological autopsy** examines in detail the situation that led to the violent episode. (See Chapter 8, Crisis of Lethality, for a complete description of this procedure.) Having the worker and others write a report as soon as they are able may be helpful in allowing workers an emotional outlet and to further understand and conceptualize the incident. *This report should not be seen as a scapegoating or blame-fixing exercise and should be clearly stated as such by the administrative head.*

All staff members who are involved with the client should attend the autopsy. It dissects what the staff and the client did behaviorally before, during, and after the incident. *It is also not about fixing blame, but finding out what caused the incident to happen so that it won't happen again.* Further attention should be given to the environmental setting to determine whether it played a role in instigating the aggressive behavior. Hopefully, the autopsy will provide clues as to the *why's, how's,* and *what's* of the incident, so it does not recur. The victim's opinions should be solicited and should be used as expert testimony. Staff should gather to discuss what happened, work through feelings about the event, and generate options for preventing a recurrence. Reviewing the traumatic experience also enables the victim to deal with feelings of loss of security and control (Lenehan & Turner, 1984, pp. 254–259).

In the past, mental health institutions have left worker recovery from a client assault pretty much to chance, with a "Suck it up; it's part of the job!" approach. That is now patently unacceptable. Some form of debriefing should be conducted simultaneously with the psychological autopsy in helping the assaulted human services worker attain precrisis equilibrium and homeostasis (California Occupational Safety and Health Administration, 1998, p. 17; Fauteux, 2010; Kinney, 1995; Mitchell & Everly, 1995; Spitzer & Burke, 1993; Spitzer & Neely, 1992; Vandenberg, 1992). Debriefing seeks to alleviate the acute stress crisis that workers experience when they are traumatized by an event such as a physical assault on them. Generally, debriefing should occur as soon after the event as is reasonably possible, but it should also take into consideration the worker's ability to go through it. Dr. James Cavanaugh of the Isaac Ray Center for Rush–Presbyterian–St. Luke's, a pioneer in development of debriefing critical incidents such as assaults on staff, cites compelling evidence that immediate posttrauma care can be very effective in helping both individuals and organizations become stabilized after a crisis (Kinney, 1995, p. 188).

Kleespies (2014, pp. 163–170) advocates using the Assaulted Staff Action Program (Flannery, Fulton, Tausch, & DeLoffi, 1991), which is a system-wide, per-help program to assist staff in coping with the traumatic wake of an assault. The Assaulted Staff Action Program (Flannery et al., 1991) is a combination of the foregoing. When an assault occurs, a staff member responds to offer support, basic psychological first aid, and determine whether additional medical or psychological care is necessary. The responding ASAP member queries the victim as to whether he or she feels able to manage his or her feelings and whether he or she is able to return to work. The ASAP member keeps up with how the member is doing for up to 2 weeks postincident. ASAP also offers support groups for assaulted staff members.

Finally, Gately and Stabb's (2005) survey of doctoral-level counseling and clinical psychology students should serve as a bellwether. Students overwhelmingly reported that their training to deal with violent clients was inadequate and their confidence in working with these clients was low. Since it is beginning practitioners who are most likely to be assaulted, it is your authors' considered opinion that to not train human services students to understand and deal with violent clients, given the degree and knowledge we have today of violence in the human services workplace, is unethical and immoral.

To learn more about what an overview of assessing for violent behavior looks like, the Association of Threat Assessment Professionals (ATAP) has published *Risk Assessment Guideline Elements for Violence: Considerations for Assessing the Risk of Future Violent Behavior* (2006), which is available at www.atapworldwide .org, although you'll have to join to get to know all about the business.

SUMMARY

Violence in the human services setting has increased exponentially in the past three decades. Increased abuse of drugs, the closing down of large state mental hospitals, child and adult abuse reporting laws, gang violence, increased adjudication of felons to mental health facilities, and increases in the geriatric population have been major contributors to this phenomenon. The problem pervades all parts of human services, and institutions as well as workers may be culpable in allowing violence against staff to proliferate. Both service providers and their staffs have largely looked the other way, and when violence against staff has occurred, either it has been seen as going with the territory or the victim has been blamed for being incompetent, stupid, and careless.

Human services statistics indicate a strong likelihood that sometime during the worker's career he or she will become a victim of violence. Given that high probability, it would seem mandatory that both workers in the field and students in human services should be educated about the potential for violence and taught defusing and de-escalating skills to be used with potentially violent clients. Techniques ranging from option therapy to validation therapy are intended not only to help the client stabilize but also to prevent the human services worker from being the object of an assault.

Finally, the worker who has been assaulted should be given immediate support from the administration and fellow workers. Critical incident stress debriefing and psychological autopsies should be mandatory after every assault on staff.

Visit CengageBrain.com for a variety of study tools and useful resources such as video examples, case studies, interactive exercises, flashcards, and quizzes.

Legal and Ethical Issues on Crisis of Trauma

15

Stephen A. Zanskas
University of Memphis

Rick A. Meyer
University of Texas, El Paso

Richard K. James
University of Memphis

LEARNING OBJECTIVES

After studying this chapter, you should be able to:

1. Describe the unique legal and ethical issues related to crisis intervention.
2. Differentiate between ethical decision making and law.
3. Differentiate between the concepts of confidentiality, privacy, and privilege in crisis or disaster situations.
4. Differentiate between the concepts of duty to warn and duty to protect.
5. Explain the concepts of duty, negligence, and malpractice in crisis or disaster situations.
6. Identify five ethical principles as a foundation for ethical decision making
7. Explain the benefits and limitations of ethical decision-making models in crisis intervention.
8. Identify the ethical considerations for mental health providers in international disaster response.
9. Describe the limitations in developing evidence-based research in crisis and disaster response.

Introduction

The context of crisis intervention presents an **LO1** intriguing dilemma and challenge for professionals and volunteers attempting to follow ethical codes. On one hand, ethical codes are guidelines that should be honored; yet the conditions under which crisis intervention services are provided can make following ethical codes virtually impossible. As a mental health practitioner responding to a crisis, you might find yourself on a street corner talking to a family after their house has burnt to the ground, or talking openly with survivors in a shelter housing hundreds of people after a natural disaster. A school or another organization might contact you asking for your services, and everyone would then know who you are and why you are there. It would be obvious that anyone talking to you is having problems and in need of help. A crisis might cause someone to be rendered incapable of making decisions, requiring you (as the crisis worker) to make a decision on the survivors' behalf. These examples are just the tip of the iceberg for issues that beg the question of the way ethical codes and crisis intervention services meet. Not to mention that mental health professionals and volunteers responding to these crises are influenced by their own personal biases and values, the client's worldview, as well as administrative directives, ethical, legal, moral, and political contexts of the situation. Suffice it to say that strictly following ethical guidelines in crises is difficult at best.

Of course, some ethical issues are relatively easy to address. Everyone knows that intimate relationships with clients are inappropriate or that it is generally unethical to release clients' records without their permission. In practice, many ethical issues lack clear or definitive answers. In fact, most ethical issues are not black or white. Rather, most ethical dilemmas fall into a grey area in which resolution of the ethical dilemma depends upon the context and situational variables. Ethical guidelines are regularly encroached upon during crisis intervention. In an office setting, providing procedural informed consent is a standard of practice and among the first items of business for mental health professionals initiating a therapeutic relationship. Can you imagine telling people in crisis to calm down and not to say anything until you have obtained their informed consent? Try asking a person in crisis to sign a form stating that they understand the limits of confidentiality. This chapter is intended to help you begin to think about the nature of legal and ethical dilemmas before responding to a crisis or disaster and offer practical approaches for addressing the legal and ethical issues that inevitably arise.

Ethical codes do not specifically address the unique circumstances surrounding the provision of crisis intervention services (Hanson, Kerkholt, & Bush, 2005; Welfel, 2013). In fact, the American Counseling Association, National Association for Social Work, American Association for Marriage and Family Therapy, and American Psychological Association do not even mention the word *crisis* in their ethical codes. These ethical codes as well as others do not speak directly to the ethics of conduct expected in crisis intervention or disaster situations (Thoburn, Bently, Ahmad, & Jones, 2012). Members of these professional organizations are left on their own to make decisions based upon personal reflection regarding their desire to help, their personal values, and the opportunity to be of benefit to others in order to avoid committing ethical transgressions (Tjeltviet & Gottlieb, 2010). Unfortunately, these efforts are not always sufficient. More guidance is needed in order to increase the chances that decisions minimize ethical violations and are in the best interest of people in crisis.

A discussion of all the ethical codes that apply to the wide variety of professionals providing crisis intervention and disaster services is beyond the scope of this chapter. In fact, one profession does not hold a monopoly on providing mental health services. For brevity's sake, we have used the American Counseling Associations' 2014 Code of Ethics as a generic example. Interested readers are referred to the Ethics and Practice Guidelines website of Dr. Kenneth Pope for a comprehensive list of links to the ethical codes for assessment, therapy, counseling, and forensic practice (Pope, 2015).

As a child, some of you may remember looking through a kaleidoscope. The slightest shift dramatically changed the images' shape and color. Even the slightest variation in lighting affects the viewer's picture. Just as with a kaleidoscope, even minor alterations in the behavior of a person may cause meaningful shifts in the way crisis workers must respond to the legal and/or ethical context of a crisis or disaster situation. The nuances of crisis situation matter. A different inflection, a slight change in the tone of one's voice, something mentioned in passing, or the unexpected gesture of a person in crisis might result in a crisis worker suspecting some sort of abuse or possibly suicidal or homicidal ideation. The point is that the chaos and unpredictability encircling crisis intervention

transforms the ethical and legal landscape quickly and substantially. This chapter is not meant to be the final word on practicing ethically and legally for counseling and therapeutic practice. Instead, the chapter is meant to stimulate thought and provide practical guidance for applying ethical codes and legal guidelines when crisis workers are engaged in crisis intervention. The goal is to provide guidelines that can aid the crisis intervention workers' decision-making process when faced with an ethical or legal dilemma.

Following a review of the fundamental ethical principles, legal precedent, and the unique role and environment of the crisis worker, case studies will be used to illustrate the ethical dilemmas crisis workers face on a day-to-day basis. Each case presents examples of the unique ethical and possible legal dilemmas that crisis workers encounter while offering help to people in crisis. A variety of settings are used to help provide the reader with the opportunity to conceptualize the array of issues that crisis workers must consider while providing services. Crisis workers will often be forced to select the best course of action that may infringe on one or more of the ethical principles. This is expected in ethical decision making. One ethical principle is not inherently more important than another. Discerning which ethical principle becomes most important depends on the context and factors involved within a specific crisis or disaster.

As noted in the Chapter 1, crisis and disaster situations present both risks and opportunities for the client and the mental health provider. Conceptually, helping professionals are encouraged to prepare for crisis and disaster intervention before the crisis arises, throughout one's actions during the crises or disaster, and during the period of postcrisis recovery (McAdams & Keener, 2008). It is important to remember that there can be more than one ethical resolution to an ethical dilemma.

Unfortunately, it is not possible to provide a single definitive protocol that can adequately address all of the potential ethical or legal considerations in crisis situations. Rather, the goal of this chapter is to provide guidelines and stimulate thought in order to assist crisis intervention workers' decision-making process when faced with an ethical or legal dilemma.

Ethical and Legal Interface with Crisis Intervention

Members of professional organizations providing crisis intervention services, paid or volunteer, are obligated to follow their respective ethical codes

(Sommers-Flanagan, 2007). These individuals have been trained to respect and obey the ethical guidelines of their professional organization. Yet the unique circumstances enveloping crisis intervention and the vulnerability of clients place a tremendous ethical burden on crisis workers (Call et al., 2012; Sommers-Flanagan, 2007). Crisis workers may find themselves on a crisis response team on a street corner trying to entice someone off the street and out of traffic. As a volunteer, crisis workers may be helping disaster survivors while sitting at a picnic table under a tree offering support to a family who just lost their home. In the "heat of the moment" the primary thought in these situations centers on helping others with little to no thought of ethical codes or liability (Kleinman & Stewart, 2004). Completing forms and informing people of the limits of confidentiality do not seem critical in those situations where confidentiality is compromised and getting informed consent is awkward at best and possibly impossible. Specialized training, both ethical and legal, is needed for anyone involved in this type of service provision (Gheytanchi et al., 2007).

Factors such as the context, perceptions, and emotions influence ethical decision making (Rogerson et al., 2011) and do have a significant impact when services in crisis situations are provided. This type of ethical decision making has been termed by some as "cowboy ethics" [sic] that use nonrational intuitive and emotional methods together with critical and evaluative strategies to sort through ethical dilemmas (Owen, 2004, as cited in Sommers-Flanagan, 2007). While practical and valuable (Knapp et al., 2007), this method can lead to blind spots because of a failure to consider actions, motives, and preferences that compromise the ethical decision-making process (Rogerson et al., 2011). Overcoming the possible ethical and legal land mines inherent in crisis intervention involves systematic efforts to become cognizant of ways to be deliberate in the decision-making process (Call et al., 2012).

Misconceptions Regarding Ethical Decision Making

Although there are many similarities among the various professions' ethical codes, the nature and type of training varies with the professional organization and instructor. Generally speaking, instruction in ethical practice focuses on upholding standards of care by outlining behavioral guidelines to avoid the most common hazards (Welfel, 2013). A range of models are suggested to resolve ethical dilemmas,

recommendations made to formulate preventive strategies, and advice given with respect to developing an appropriate mindset for ethical practice. While indispensable in training, these frameworks can be cumbersome and are not as functional in the field. This section offers a brief discussion of the myths, or misconceptions, of ethical decision making. Crisis intervention brings to awareness these issues because much of the time decisions about ethical dilemmas must be made in the moment of a given situation—not after time for reflection and speculation about what is best.

Decision-Making Models Are Practical. Many ethical decision models have been developed and prescribe rational routes to ethical decisions (Rogerson et al., 2011). Models are wonderful for training, particularly with new professionals. The models allow for reflection and careful dissection of issues. Yet the ability to work through these models in crisis intervention is impractical. Crisis workers cannot say "time-out," let me use this multiple step model to consider all the possible ramifications of this particular ethical issue. Instead, crisis workers must act using their best judgment at the time in that specific situation. For example, a crisis worker has been asked to sit with a family whose mother was brought into the local hospital emergency room. After talking with the family for several hours, a resident physician enters the room and informs the family that their mother has died. Immediately, several members of the family start running through the emergency room pulling back curtains, crying out for their mother. The hospital security guard calls out to the crisis worker for help and starts running after the family members. What should the crisis worker do in this situation? Try to physically restrain the family member? Use a model to sort through possible ethical and legal implications? A decision has to be made in the moment in order to ensure the safety of the family members and other patients.

Time to Consult. Time to consult is often part of models for working through ethical puzzles. Models often recommend consulting with a peer or contacting a professional organization's hotline for help addressing ethical issues. We completely agree with that recommendation, yet the practicality of suggestion can be argued in crisis situations. Crisis workers should consult when time permits, but time does not always permit. A perfect example is the situation described above with the family whose mother died after being transported to the emergency room. An option would be for the crisis worker to call a peer and ask about the best course of action. The crisis worker and peer could discuss aspects of applying various ethical principles, debating which principle is most important in the situation, and possibly develop a list of potential benefits and drawbacks of each action. In this situation, the deliberation process is impractical. The ethical decision needs to be made instantly.

One Correct Answer. Novice human services workers, regardless of their profession, commonly believe that ethical codes give answers. Yet after gaining some experience, these same aspiring professionals find the codes do not provide specific answers. They find that their belief that there is only one correct answer to an ethical dilemma is a misconception. Many factors come into play and must be considered for many ethical impasses (Welfel, 2013). In fact, the majority of ethical decisions involve a wide range of factors. Again the family in the hospital emergency room is a good example. What factors might be considered? Age of the family members, gender, and possibly even size would influence just how the crisis worker should react. The training of the crisis worker also becomes a factor. Has the crisis worker been trained in restraining individuals? Generally speaking, ethical codes are not a set of rules that prescribe actions for every situation (Remley & Herlihy, 2014). Rather, ethical codes are guidelines intended to direct decision-making processes when an ethical dilemma or issues are encountered.

The Role of the Mental Health Professional. As noted in the preface of this text, crisis intervention ". . . at times is more art than science" (pp. xvi, 2017). Effective crisis workers have also been described as possessing life experience, along with the following personal attributes: assertiveness, creativity, persistence, poise, resilience, and the ability to "think on one's feet." Halpern and Tramontin (2007) described the role of the mental health practitioner working with persons experiencing crises is to provide assistance, normalize the experience, support resilience or strength-based responses in clients, and advise on referral for those experiencing intense reactions to crisis or disaster. Hobfoll and associates (2007) identified five evidence-based principles for trauma intervention that also contribute to an understanding of the role of a crisis intervention worker. These principles included promoting:

1. Safety.
2. Calming.
3. Self and collective efficacy.
4. Connectedness.
5. Hope.

These principles suggest that recovery does not occur in isolation, and crisis workers need to consider more than the person standing before them. Adopting an ecological or systems approach can assist mental health practitioners in addressing the multiple ethical domains relevant to crisis intervention (Zanskas, 2010).

The Confluence of Beliefs, Emotion, Morality, and Values. A helping professional's vulnerability to ethical transgressions and their resilience [LO2] to withstand them are dynamic rather than static (Crowley & Gottlieb, 2012; Tjeltviet & Gottlieb, 2010). In other words, individuals interested in crisis intervention need to think about the reasons they are interested in providing these types of services before they actually begin. Here are two practical suggestions to help you evaluate how your own beliefs, background, and values might contribute to ethical violations. It is the authors' opinion that personal reflection, and when possible, consultation are among the two most effective risk management strategies for mental health practitioners engaged in crisis or disaster intervention. These processes are beneficial as they help crisis workers recognize their own biases, critique their own work, and understand how their personal values influence the quality of services they provide.

Many nonrational factors influence ethical thought and behavior, including the context of the situation, perceptions, relationships, emotions, and **heuristics** (Rogerson et al., 2011). Heuristics simply refers to the process that a person uses to learn something. Research suggests that at times one simply needs to listen to one's heart. Quite literally, physical indicators, such as touch and heart rate, have been found to influence moral decision making (Dumasio, 1994; Sherman & Clore, 2009; Zhong & Liljenquist, 2004; Zhong, Stejcek, & Sivanathan, 2010). Gu, Zhong, and Gould (2012) indicate that physiological perception has an important role in moral decision making. Across four experiments, those individuals who perceived a rapid heartbeat were found more likely to volunteer to assist minorities and were found to be less likely to be deceptive (Gu et al., 2012). So take heart! You can make good ethical decisions in the heat of the moment, but be sure to listen to it!

Crisis workers need to be knowledgeable of the ethical codes and the laws impacting their respective profession and roles in a crisis or disaster. The terms *ethics* and *law* are not synonymous. Laws are a society's minimum requirements, created by legislative bodies, and enforced by the government (Wheeler & Bertram, 2012). Ethics refer to the standards of conduct, or guidelines, for members of a profession (Corey, Corey, Corey, & Callanan, 2015). While laws are **mandatory**, requiring compliance, ethical codes are often **aspirational**, or based upon a "higher good" that goes beyond what is simply required. Regardless, both laws and ethical codes are reactive "living" documents developed in response to the actions or behaviors of others. Both ethical codes and laws change based upon the trends in societal values and **precedent**, or what has occurred in the past.

Professionals differ with respect to their reasons for following ethical codes. Those who follow legal and ethical guidelines as a risk management practice in order to prevent lawsuits are practicing mandatory ethics. However, in our experience, the single best method of avoiding lawsuits is to establish a quality relationship with one's clients. In medical settings this would be referred to as "bedside manner." The importance of this concept cannot be emphasized enough. Physicians are routinely required to tell their patients that they have developed a life-threatening illness, or perhaps despite all efforts, that a loved one could not be saved. Particularly in crises, your ability to communicate compassion, empathy, and genuine concern for an individual or a group of people in crisis means more than any other risk management practice.

In real life, ethical codes and legal requirements can conflict. Mental health practitioners confronted with a legal problem are advised to consult an attorney rather than a colleague, as colleagues often lack experience with legal matters (Remley & Herlihy, 2014). Knapp, Gottlieb, Berman, and Handelsman (2007) suggest that when a professional is confronted with a conflict between the law and one's professional code of ethics, they should either follow the law or their ethical values in a manner that reduces the professional's transgression on the other. Simply stated, at times the crisis worker must choose the least egregious (or harmful course) of action from an array of poor choices, whether or not it violates a law or an ethical code. Arguing for a standard that recognizes

community rather than individual objectives during crises or disaster response, Hodge and Courtney (2010) support this perspective, indicating that during emergencies professional standards can be fluid, adjusting to the context of the situation.

Whether counselors are working with a client experiencing a crisis or responding to a disaster, the American Counseling Association provides minimal specific ethical guidance. Crisis and disaster response is not specifically addressed in the 2014 American Counseling Association Counseling Code of Ethics (ACA, 2014). In fact, the word *crises* only appears under Section F.4.b, establishing a supervisor's responsibility to establish and communicate to their supervisees the procedures for contacting the supervisor or alternate on-call supervisors for assistance in handling crises (ACA, 2014, p. 14). Disaster response is not specifically addressed in any section of the ACA's Code of Ethics (ACA, 2014). Rather, the American Counseling Association's ethical code addresses crisis situations as exceptions to the principle of confidentiality (ACA, 2014). Although the final 2016 CACREP Standards indicate that counseling programs need to address the ethical standards of professional credentialing and accrediting bodies (including the counselor's role and responsibilities as a member of an interdisciplinary outreach and emergency response team), they do not address how this training is to be accomplished.

The American Psychological Association's (APA) ethical principles and code of conduct (2002, 2010) essentially address crisis and disaster situations in a manner similar to the ACA (2014). In fact, a review of the APA's ethical principles and code of conduct reveals no reference at all to ethics in a crisis situation. The only reference to disaster is an indication that the typical prohibition on a psychologist's direct solicitation of business does not apply in disaster or community outreach situations (APA, 2010, § 5.06).

Although the final 2016 Council on Accreditation of Counseling and Educationally Related Programs (CACREP) Standards indicate that counseling programs need to address the ethical standards of professional credentialing and accrediting bodies, including the counselor's role and responsibilities as a member of an interdisciplinary outreach and emergency response team, they do not address how this training is to be accomplished.

Confidentiality and Privacy. The level of trust among parties is a central characteristic impacting the effectiveness of the working or **LO3**

therapeutic alliance (Ahn & Wampold, 2001; Bordin, 1979). **Confidentiality** refers to the ethical duty of mental health professionals to protect the private communications of their clients (ACA, 2014, Section B; Wheeler & Bertram, 2012). Clients trust that their communications with mental health providers will be kept in confidence. Confidentiality is based upon a client's right to privacy (Remley & Herlihy, 2010; Wheeler & Bertram, 2012) and considered a primary duty of mental health professionals (Donner, VandeCreek, Gonsiorek, & Fisher, 2008; Wheeler & Bertram, 2012). Section B.2.e of the 2014 ACA Code of Ethics addresses the concept of privacy. **Privacy**, or the client's right to be left alone and to control the timing of the release of personal information (Wheeler & Bertram, 2012) is often difficult at best in a crisis or disaster. The promise of confidentiality between a client and a mental health provider is not absolute. Regardless of the setting, when it is determined that a practitioner must break confidentiality, it is the practitioner's ethical duty to disclose only necessary information.

Privileged Communication. In states where it exists, **privileged communication** is a legal concept that prevents the disclosure of confidential communications between a client and mental health practitioner in a judicial context (Knapp & VandeCreek, 2012; Wheeler & Bertram, 2012). The U.S. Supreme Court established the primacy of privileged communication between psychotherapists and their clients in their decision regarding the Federal Rules of Evidence between a psychotherapist and the client (*Jaffee v. Redmond*, 1996). Often considered the purview of licensed mental health professionals, the 9th Federal Court of Appeals upheld a district court's decision to apply the federal psychotherapist's privileged communication between unlicensed Employee Assistance Program (EAP) counselors and employees (*Oleszko v. State Compensation Insurance Fund*, 2001).

Although it seems that privileged communication is becoming a professional standard, it can be waived in civil commitment proceedings, when a client presents his or her emotional health at issue in a lawsuit, and during malpractice proceedings or licensing board proceedings against a counselor (Wheeler & Bertram, 2012).

Privilege generally belongs to the client, although mental health professionals are responsible for maintaining the client's privilege in legal proceedings. In order for privilege to be exercised a client's

communication must have been made in confidence, the client indicates either through their action or expression that they want the communication to be held in confidence, and the communication generally cannot occur or be heard by a third party.

Section B.2.a of the ACA's ethical code establishes the guidelines regarding "Serious and Foreseeable Harm and Legal Requirements" (ACA, 2014, p. 7). Essentially, this section of the ethical code indicates that a counselor is not compelled to maintain confidentiality when disclosing confidential information is "required to protect clients or others from serious and foreseeable harm and legal requirements demand that confidential information must be revealed" (ACA, 2014, p. 7). Serious and foreseeable harm is related to the case law developments regarding a mental health professional's duty to warn or protect.

Unfortunately, these concepts are not clearly defined and the ambiguity can be of concern for crisis workers. Here are three general criteria to consider when attempting to evaluate whether a situation has met the serious and foreseeable standard. First, a **"serious" threat** is one that an individual has the means to carry out and that is made in earnest. Second, the standard for **"foreseeable"** is basically what the "reasonable" practitioner would expect to occur given similar actions, behaviors, and circumstance. Finally, a **"reasonable" practitioner** would do what the average practitioner with similar education, training, and credentials would do given a similar set of facts and situation.

Duty to Warn, Protect, and Report. Generally, the mental health practitioner's duty to protect the confidential communications of his or her clients ends when the practitioner learns that a third party could be harmed by the practitioner's client (Remley & Herlihy, 2014).

All states have not adopted the duty to warn precedent established by the *Tarasoff* ruling. For example, a statute in the state of Texas allows mental health practitioners to disclose information to law enforcement or medical providers in situations that involve an impending threat of physical injury to a third party (Wheeler & Bertram, 2012). However, a statute *allowing* a practitioner to break confidentiality is not same as *requiring* disclosure following an imminent threat of bodily harm. As a result, the statute does not eliminate a practitioner's ethical dilemma regarding the decision to break a client's confidentiality and without counselor immunity may represent a more complex legal and ethical dilemma.

Legally, the duty to protect originated from the 1976 California Supreme Court ruling in *Tarasoff* v. *Regents of the University of California*. The *Tarasoff* case is the premier example of a therapist, a supervisory staff, and an institution not adequately dealing with a client threat, and it has changed professional thought regarding confidentiality and the duty to warn a potential victim. The *Tarasoff* case resulted when a male client told his therapist on a university campus that he intended to murder a young woman. Although the intended victim was not specifically identified, the therapist figured out who she was but took no steps to warn her of the client's threats. The therapist wrote a letter to the campus police about the client's homicidal ideation, and the client was immediately taken into custody for observation. After evaluation, the client was found rational and, having promised to stay away from the woman, was released.

The therapist's supervisor requested that the police return the letter and directed that all copies of it and subsequent notes related to the incident be destroyed. Two months later the client killed the woman (Thompson, 1983, p. 167). The parents of the woman sued the university, and on appeal to the State Supreme Court of California, the court found for the plaintiff. In this precedent-setting case, the court held that when a psychotherapist ascertains that a threat is neither remote nor idle in its content, the public good demands that disclosure of the threat to a third party outweighs the benefits of preserving confidentiality (Cohen, 1978).

This finding appears to hold true whether it involves phone counseling, a private therapy session, or working with someone in crisis on a street corner. Based on the foregoing case, the following points are paramount in guiding the human services worker's actions where a client makes a clear threat of violent behavior toward another person or the client's self.

1. It is a good practice to convey very clearly what you can and cannot hold in confidence and to apprise the client of this before intervention is started (Wilson, 1981). As ridiculous as it may seem, prior to starting a counseling group at a correctional facility, we always warn the participants that we cannot preserve their anonymity if they threaten themselves or others, reveal plans to escape, or attempt to smuggle contraband into or out of the facility. It is noteworthy that we have had to act on this statement more than once!

2. The foregoing concept is particularly problematic when children are the clients. This topic is covered extensively in the Chapter 13, Crises in Schools. Planning ahead through consultation with supervisors, fellow professionals, the police, attorneys, and others who are expert and have experience with danger and violence will be invaluable to you when you may have to make split-second decisions. Similarly, developing contingency plans for what you would do, how you would do it, and what you might do given a variety of client reactions is exceedingly important in the fast and furious world of crisis intervention (Costa & Altekruse, 1994).

3. If you are unclear about the implications of a client's threats or unsure about what to do, the cardinal rule is to consult with another professional or an immediate supervisor and keep notes of the consultation (Wilson, 1981). Consultation is substantiating protection from legal and ethical problems that may arise, particularly when the threat is not clear. If for some reason another professional is not available, the general rule for determining a clear and present danger is that such a danger is present if a client specifies victim identity ("my husband"), motive ("revenge"), means ("gun"), and plan ("I'll wait for him after work") (Thompson, 1983, p. 83). Danger is also present if the client is unable to understand what he or she is contemplating, is incapable of exercising self-control, and is incapable of collaborating with the worker. Corey, Corey, Corey, and Callanan (2015) believe if at least two of the foregoing elements are present, the therapist has a duty to warn.

4. If the client does concretely state a threat, then you are bound morally, legally, and ethically to take action. It is your duty to warn the victim if you know who it is (Wilson, 1981), unless state statute clearly indicates otherwise. Patiently and emphatically explain your concerns to the client, and attempt to get the client calmed enough to get him or her to a place of safety. Tell the client what you are doing to keep him or her safe and why. The client is also far less likely to perceive the crisis worker as another "enemy" and place the worker on a "hit list" (Thompson, 1983, p. 169). Apprise clients in a supportive and empathic manner of your responsibility to protect them, and invite the clients to participate in the process if possible and surrender any weapons they may have. Inform

those who need to know, such as your supervisor, the institution's attorney, the police, psychiatric hospital, and so on, and the intended victim (Costa & Altekruse, 1994).

Avoid confrontations with acting out clients. Once this occurs, the matter is now one for the police or security. If neither is immediately available, then get another coworker as a support person to help contain and calm the client until help arrives. In a crisis intervention setting, no worker should ever be alone.

5. Threats of legal reprisal by the client should not dissuade the crisis worker from reporting threats against others (Wilson, 1981). There is no legitimacy in threats of reprisal, given the law in most states. However, to be safe, document in writing that you noted potential danger signs, discussed relevant suicidal and violent issues, and were professional and empathic (Costa & Altekruse, 1994). It is also a good bet to obtain professional liability insurance!

Tarasoff has mandated three conditions that are necessary and sufficient for a duty to warn to occur: (1) there must be a special relationship, such as therapist to client; (2) there must be a reasonable prediction of conduct that constitutes a danger; and (3) there must be a foreseeable victim. But what if there is no malice aforethought or history of violence or any other life-threatening issues except that the client has a fatal and communicable disease?

In *Tarasoff,* the Court ruled:

Once a therapist does in fact determine, or under applicable professional standards reasonably should have determined, that a client poses a serious danger of violence to others, he bears a duty to exercise reasonable care to protect the foreseeable victim of that danger. (p. 345)

This duty was narrowed to an identifiable potential victim by the ruling in *McIntosh* v. *Milano* (1979), a subsequent duty to warn case in New Jersey. A Federal Court case, *Lipari* v. *Sears* (1980), extended a psychotherapist's duty to warn and protect both foreseeable known and unknown victims. However, since the nature of this duty varies between states, mental health practitioners interested in disaster response are encouraged to review the respective jurisdictions prior to responding. California case law supported the precedent for the duty to protect those who surround or are in the vicinity of a client's identified victim that could be foreseeably harmed by a client's threat or actual act of violence (*Hedlund* v. *Superior Court*, 1983; *Jablonski* v. *United States*, 1983). More recent California cases, *Ewing* v. *Goldstein* (2004) and *Ewing* v. *Northridge Hospital Medical Center* (2004), expanded the therapist's duty to protect a third party from harm when the knowledge of the threat is relayed by a client's family member rather than the client themselves. Based upon a brief review of the precedential court cases related to mental health practitioners, the nature of the duty to warn or protect varies between states. Mental health practitioners interested in disaster response are encouraged to review the respective jurisdictions' laws prior to responding to a disaster.

School counselors are not exempt from the duty to warn. Although the counselors were exonerated from liability in a student's suicide by following the school's policies, counselors are responsible for notifying their administration that their policies are either unethical or untenable (*Eisel* v. *Board of Education of Montgomery County,* 1991). Similarly, as a result of a student's suicide in the *Armijo* v. *Wagon Mound Public Schools District* (1998) decision, school counselors were found to be responsible for advising their administration when a student was so agitated that the student needed to be placed in the parents' custody rather than expelling or suspending the child (Stone, 2013).

Stone (2013) noted that negligence lawsuits against school counselors have generally been unsuccessful. The American School Counselor Association Ethical Standards (2010) suggest that if a school counselor through informal or formal assessment determines a student is at a low risk for suicide the counselor is responsible for contacting the student's parents. Safety contracts are controversial for school counselors to use with students expressing suicidal ideation (Stone, 2013). One was utilized by a school counselor prior to the hanging death of a student in the case of *Mikell* v. *School Administrative Unit # 33* (2009). The New Hampshire Supreme Court found that the school administration was not liable as the school did not have custodial care of the student and was not guilty of "extreme and outrageous" conduct precipitating the student's death. Essentially, a school counselor's liability ends once they have notified the student's parents and school administrators that a student is at risk and have recommended reasonable preventative actions (Stone, 2013).

Negligence and Liability. Crisis and disaster `LO5` mental health services, as a developing area of practice, have paid minimal attention to the potential legal and ethical dilemmas practitioners may encounter (Abdel-Monem & Bulling, 2005; Call, Pfefferbaum, Jenuwine, & Flynn, 2012; Hodge & Courtney, 2010). However, negligence is a well-defined legal concept. Wheeler and Bertram (2012) defined **negligence** as the unintentional breach of a duty that one person owes another. Negligence involves four elements: first, the practitioner has a duty; second, that duty has been breached, or broken, through an unprofessional act or omission; third, the client sustained an emotional or physical harm as a result of the breach; and the practitioner's act or omission is the **proximate**, or what could reasonably be considered the immediate cause of the client's injury (Abdel-Monem & Bulling, 2005; Corey, Corey, Corey, and Callanan, 2015; Remley & Herlihy, 2010; & Wheeler & Bertram, 2012). Licensed mental health practitioners in crisis or disaster contexts need to recognize that providing counseling-related services can be considered treatment and the basis for ethical and legal culpability (Kleinman & Stewart, 2004).

In cases of negligence, comparisons are made to the community or professional standards for what the reasonable practitioner would do in a similar circumstance. Although reasonableness is generally compared against national or professional standards, mental health professionals also have exposure to local laws (Call et al., 2012; Hobfoll et al., 2007; Hodge & Courtney, 2010; Hodge et al., 2005; Kleinman & Stewart, 2004; Abdel-Monem & Bulling, 2005). Mental health practitioners are vulnerable to civil or state malpractice lawsuits for a variety of reasons, including the use of procedures outside of accepted practice, a lack of competence, the failure to use more beneficial techniques or procedures, failing to explain the potential consequences of treatment, failing to obtain informed consent, or failing to warn or protect the public from a client (Wheeler & Bertram, 2012).

Determining the reasonable course of action during a crisis or disaster has largely been a matter of opinion as our field lacks agreement on empirical or evidence-based practices when responding to a crisis or disaster (Hobfoll et al., 2007). It is further complicated by the unique circumstances encountered during a crisis or disaster, as both prevent hard and fast rules regarding mental health interventions or approaches. Recently, the Substance Abuse and Mental Health Services Administration (SAMHSA) released a Treatment Improvement Protocol for trauma-informed care in behavioral health (SAMHSA, 2014). This comprehensive document provides a guide for behavioral health treatment following trauma, a trauma-informed care program implementation guide for administrators, and an analysis of the literature with abstracts, a bibliography, and resources for the practitioner.

Whether the mental health practitioner is serving as a volunteer or a mental health professional is also an important distinction. Volunteers face many uncertainties, particularly when responding to a disaster. Practitioners considering whether to volunteer during a disaster need to consider whether their own professional liability coverage will be in effect while serving as a volunteer rather than in the course of one's employment, their potential liability for harm to clients, and the potential for compensation for their own harm as a volunteer professional (Abdel-Monem & Bulling, 2005; Hodge & Courtney, 2010; Hodge et al., 2005).

In 1996, PL 104-321, the Emergency Medical Assistance Compact (EMAC), authorized license reciprocity for health care practitioners during declared emergencies in 48 states and territories. The liability protections extended from this act are contingent upon the practitioner working in some manner for a state during a declared emergency (EMAC, 1996; Hodge et al., 2005). Many states have adopted Good Samaritan laws to provide immunity for persons who assist at the emergency site although their coverage and protections vary among states (Abdel-Monem & Bulling, 2005; Hodge et al., 2005). Essentially, protections for volunteers remain a matter of jurisdiction. Despite calls for uniform standards for public health in emergencies, mental health practitioners considering volunteering to serve in disasters are advised to be aware of the potential risks they might incur (Abdel-Monem & Bulling, 2005; Hodge & Courtney, 2010; Hodge et al., 2005).

In response to the 9/11 disaster, Congress authorized the Department of Health and Human Services (DHSS) to develop systems for the advanced registration of volunteers through the Public Health Security and Bioterrorism Response Act of 2002. Hodge, Gable, and Calves (2005) noted the role of a volunteer might be informal, limited in scope, time, place, and position. As a result, the liability exposure of volunteers remains unclear (Abdel-Monem & Bulling, 2005; Hodge et al., 2005). Are you concerned about how providing crisis intervention or disaster services are affected by federal legislation such as HIPAA or FERPA and what kind of trouble you might get into if you divulged information that gave away confidential information? The Health Insurance Portability and Accountability Act of 1996 (HIPAA) covers any entity that transmits any protected health information in electronic form. HIPAA has become a standard of care for mental health practitioners (Wheeler & Bertram, 2012). Although a complete review of HIPAA is beyond the scope of this chapter, it is noteworthy that even HIPAA permits counselors to release information to "prevent or lessen a serious and imminent threat to the health and safety of an individual or the public" (45 C.F.R. § 164.512(j)(1)(i)).

Tragedies in Columbine, Virginia Tech, and Sandy Hook have raised our awareness of the threats of violence in schools. Counselors in schools or universities that receive federal funds are subject to the Family Educational Rights and Privacy Act of 1974 (FERPA). However, counselors in schools or universities acting to protect the health and safety of students or others can release pertinent counseling and educational records (34 C.F.R. § 99.31 (a)(10)). Thus, in an emergency, such as the imminent danger of harm to one's self or others, even a student's personally identifiable information can be released by a mental health professional to law enforcement, public health officials, or trained medical staff (34 C.F.R. § 99.36 (2010)).

Little has been written about the legal and ethical exposure mental health professionals incur while providing services following acute disasters (Call, Pfefferbaum, Jenuwine, & Flynn, 2012). Disasters produce special psychiatric needs with special psychiatric-legal situations (Hodge, Gable, & Calves, 2005; Kleinman & Stewart, 2004). These include practitioner liability, practitioner interaction through the media with the general population, and participation in legal proceedings. Conceptually, Hodge and Courtney (2010) argued that without national standards for practitioner liability protections during catastrophic health emergencies, claims against a practitioner should be evaluated based upon how the practitioner's actions are consistent with the need to protect community health rather than community standards of care.

Providing clinical supervision during crises or disasters can be challenging (Rudick, 2012). Having a strong supervisor–supervisee relationship and the supervisor's knowledge of trauma theory appear to be critical characteristics of effective supervision in crises or disaster situations (Rudick, 2012; Sommer, 2008). However, research suggests that practitioners who are working in crises or disaster contexts believe that both the consistency and/or frequency of supervision they receive is insufficient (Hanson, Hesselbrock, Tworkoski, & Swan, 2002; Rudick, 2012; Sommer & Cox, 2005).

Supervisors bear both direct and vicarious liability for their supervisee. Direct liability refers to a supervisor's gross negligence or failure to provide adequate supervision to their supervisees when it was evident to a reasonable practitioner that it was required (Abdel-Monem & Bulling, 2005; Remley & Herlihy, 2014; Wheeler & Bertram, 2012). In direct liability, it is the supervisor's awareness of a case and their supervisees' actions that are relevant.

Vicarious liability refers to the allocation of responsibility among supervisors and supervisees (Abdel-Monem & Bulling, 2005). Vicarious liability is based upon the old English legal notion of the master and servant relationship (Remley & Herlihy, 2014; Wheeler & Bertram, 2012). In practice, supervisors have the authority to direct the work of their supervisees and, as a result, are responsible for their supervisees' actions (Remley & Herlihy, 2014; Wheeler & Bertram, 2012). The extent of a supervisor's vicarious liability depends upon a number of factors, including whether an employment relationship exists, the extent of control that the supervisor has over a supervisee's actions, and in the case of multiple layers of supervision, which supervisor spends more direct time with the supervisee (Abdel-Monem & Bulling, 2005; Remley & Herlihy, 2014; Wheeler & Bertram, 2012). Regardless of the setting, consultation, either with one's peers, or a supervisor, and reflective practice (considering one's actions and their implications) are essential to sound ethical decision making.

The Five Moral Principles of Ethical Decision Making

Kitchener (1984) identified five moral principles as the foundation for ethical decision making: autonomy, beneficence, fidelity, justice, and nonmaleficence. Veracity was subsequently added to the 2014 ACA COE's Preamble. Theoretically, each of these ethical principles is balanced and considered to be of equal value. However, the crisis or disaster worker's personal values influence the priority each ethical principle is assigned. Crisis workers are confronted with an ethical dilemma when two or more ethical principles conflict. Recognizing one's own "blind spots" and reflecting upon these principles, crisis workers can begin to address the complex ethical dilemmas inherent in crisis and disaster work.

Autonomy. The principle of **autonomy** refers to a client's right to self-determination (ACA, 2014). Ultimately, clients are responsible for their own decisions. Informed consent and confidentiality are fundamental client rights supported by the principle of autonomy. During a crisis or disaster, individuals may feel helpless and often experience the sense that they have lost control over their lives (Bonnano, 2004). Sommers-Flanagan (2007) cautioned mental health practitioners to assume that individuals in a crisis or disaster retain the ability to make their own decisions and resist the temptation to perceive the persons as incapable of choice. During the chaos of a crisis or disaster, the complexity of trying to ensure these most basic client rights can be overwhelming. How does one provide informed consent and ensure confidentiality to clients that decompensate as they stand in line waiting for basic support services?

Beneficence. **Beneficence** refers to working for the good of the client and society (ACA, 2014). Sommers-Flanagan (2007) indicated that when mental health providers apply beneficence as their guiding ethical principle, their assistance must offer more opportunity for good than harm. By definition, the principle of beneficence involves dialectical thought, balancing the good of the presenting client and/or society.

Mental health practitioners in this context need the capacity or experience to be able to empathize with a client in crisis and consider his or her worldview in order to even begin to conceptualize what the client considers beneficial (IASC, 2007). Ethical practitioners also assess their own motives for engaging in humanitarian interventions (Sommers-Flanagan, 2007). Many motives for practitioners engaging in humanitarian work may conflict with the ethical principle of beneficence. The desire to avoid one's own problems, the desire for media exposure, religious witnessing or conversion, rescue fantasies, and Nouwen's 1972 construct of the wounded healer represent dubious beneficent motives (Sommers-Flanagan, 2007).

The principle of beneficence includes the mental health practitioner's competence. Mental health practitioners are responsible for acquiring the necessary skills, knowledge, and capacity to work with clients prior to engaging in crisis or disaster response (Tarvydas & Ng, 2012). However, in the absence of a more skilled professional, a mental health practitioner confronted with a crisis or disaster situation that exceeds his or her level of competence should simply do the best that he or she can until a more competent professional arrives.

Fidelity. The principle of **fidelity** involves keeping one's promises and commitments (ACA, 2014). Although the principle of fidelity in the past included the principle of veracity, the ACA Code of Ethics (2014) indicates veracity involves the mental health professionals' truthful interaction with individuals. As indicated earlier, individuals often feel helpless, a loss of control, or having been violated following a crisis or disaster. Survivors of a crisis or disaster are vulnerable. Without their customary supports and protective factors, survivors are less resilient. This vulnerability leaves survivors open to exploitation, fraud, and incompetent providers (Sommers-Flanagan, 2007; Tarvydas & Ng, 2012). According to Sommers-Flanagan (2007), "A very real test of morality is how we behave when no one is looking" (p. 192).

The integrity and veracity of mental health provider can facilitate a sense of safety, stability, and security (Tarvydas & Ng, 2012). Rather than succumb to the temptation of offering assurances that cannot be fulfilled, Tarvydas and Ng (2012) recommend that mental health practitioners in these contexts emphasize truthfulness in both their actions and words.

Sommers-Flanagan (2007) also noted that the scarcity of resources and the emergent nature of crisis or disaster work often challenge the mental health providers' traditional ethical perspectives. She cites the lack of resources, abbreviated informed consent processes, the difficulty of attempting to maintain confidentiality in open settings, a lack of record keeping, and boundary crossings among the conflicts with traditional ethical practices (Sommers-Flanagan, 2007).

Justice. **Justice** involves fostering fairness, equality, and providing equitable care (ACA, 2014). On the surface, fairness and equality seem to be reasonable expectations. However, in the chaos of a crisis or a disaster, decisions about how resources are distributed and whose needs take priority are less clear. They are often made in a manner that might seem questionable to survivors. Individuals involved in, or following a crisis, might question in disbelief, "Why has this happened to me?" The survivor may perceive life as unfair and question his or her spiritual beliefs. Survivors might also expect that services will be distributed based upon their socioeconomic status. Some believe that services should be prioritized, or restored, consistent with their precrisis or disaster station in life. Among the biggest considerations following a disaster are logistics and distributive justice or triage.

Distributive justice involves a mental health practitioner's ethical judgment about how relief resources should be divided (Reamer, 2015). Triage is fraught with ethical conflict and dilemmas involving autonomy, beneficence, and justice (Repine et al., 2005). During triage, the ethical principle of beneficence, or concern for members of society, outweighs the concern for any individual in response to a crises or disaster. During triage, individual autonomy is considered secondary to the collective good. As noted by Repine and associates (2005), triage does not mean the equitable treatment of all patients.

Repine, Lisagor, and Cohen (2005) suggested applying the dynamics and ethics of health care rationing and military triage to nonmilitary contexts. In a military context, triage describes the prioritization of wounded soldiers and available medical resources. Examples of military triage include prehospitalization, catastrophic, emergency department, intensive care, waiting lists, and battlefield situations. On the battlefield, there are two main scenarios that represent the continuum of medical care: (1) when the number of patients and the severity of their injuries do not exceed the capability to provide care and (2) when the number of patients and the severity of their injuries exceed the capability to provide care.

According to Repine et al. (2005), most crises in the United States have not risen to the level where the number of patients or the severity of injuries exceeds the ability to provide care. However, in the second scenario, patients with the greatest chance of survival and requiring the least resources, time, equipment, and supplies are treated first. Patients are sorted into immediate, delayed, minimal, and expectant service categories based upon their prognosis. This categorization is controversial. Unlike the military, in social work or rehabilitation contexts it is often those with the fewest resources or most severe impairments that are prioritized for service. Although triage involves all of the ethical principles, beneficence, or the concern for all members of society, survival outweighs the concern for any individual's autonomy in response to a crises or disaster. Indeed, Repine et al. (2005) contend that the ethical and practical concerns of triage can only be reviewed from the context of survival.

Nonmaleficence. By the very nature of our role, mental health practitioners working with clients experiencing a crisis or disaster are serving vulnerable populations (Tarvydas & Ng, 2012). The ethical principle of **nonmaleficence** emphasizes avoiding actions that cause harm (ACA, 2014). Harm, however, is defined by the client and can be either unintended or intentional (Cottone & Tarvydas, 2007). Mental health practitioners working with clients in crisis or following a disaster need to strive to understand the client's perspective of both good and harm. Assigning a diagnosis or otherwise labeling a client is generally not the purview of mental health practitioners working with a client who is experiencing an unexpected situational loss or disaster. Employing a psychosocial approach that emphasizes normalization of the experience, client strengths, and attempting to restore a sense of safety may reduce the tendency of mental health practitioners to pathologize a client's experience (Halpern & Tramontin, 2007; Zanskas, 2010).

Competent use of evidence-based interventions for crisis or disaster response represents an example of nonmaleficence (Sommers-Flanagan & Sommers-Flanagan, 2008). For example, The National Center for PTSD (Brymer et al., 2006) published an evidence-based manual regarding *psychological first aid* to facilitate short- and long-term adjustment. However, research support for critical incident stress debriefing (CISD) has been equivocal (Gist & Lubin, 1999; Gist, Lubin, & Redburn, 1999) and is not recommended for survivors of a crisis or disaster (Brymer et al., 2009; Gray & Litz, 2005; James & Gilliland, 2013). Although mental health providers might assume a more authoritative or directive approach during an emergency, they should still respect the autonomy of the people they serve. In order to avoid the marginalization of the survivors' experience, crisis workers are cautioned to avoid the rigid imposition of their own personal beliefs and values (Foa, 2000; Sommers-Flanagan, 2007).

The ability to self-monitor and maintain professional boundaries is another facet of nonmaleficence. Contextually, the typical boundaries of the professional-client relationships become blurred during crises. Vestiges of the professional power differential such as manner of dress, meeting in an office, receptionists, and other traditional boundaries are often absent during a mental health provider's response to crises. Tarvydas and Ng (2012) noted during the extraordinary shared experience of crises or disasters that mental health professionals frequently form intimate social or unprofessional relationships with their peers or those they serve. Perhaps it is a normal human response to sharing extreme events, and mental health practitioners as well as those experiencing crises naturally seek reassurance and support. However, this shared experience is temporary at best and clients are often at the most vulnerable point in their lives. According to Tarvydas and Ng (2012), these intimate social or unprofessional relationships are unethical during the mental health practitioners' period of service.

Benefits of Ethical Decision–Making Models.

Each respective mental health profession along with voluntary organizations and nongovernmental organizations subscribe to their own respective ethical code or standard of conduct. These professional guidelines, although necessary, are not sufficient to address ethical problem solving.

Helping professionals can avoid most ethical violations by simply taking the time to think. Consultation, review of ethical codes, knowledge of jurisdictional laws, and use of ethical decision-making models are methods intended to ensure that helping professionals allow sufficient time to process and consider the implications of a decision and develop a best course of action.

Limitations of Implementing EDMs in the Context of Crisis

The term *crisis* implies a sense of immediacy and urgency. Time, although a premium during a time of crisis, does not preclude pausing to consider the implications of one's actions. A plethora of ethical decision-making models exist (Cottone, 2001; Cottone & Claus, 2000; Garcia, Cartwright, Winston, & Borzuchowska, 2003; Jordan, 2010; Kitchener, 1984; Rest, 1984; Tarvydas & Ng, 2012). Complex, lengthy models of ethical decision making often seem impractical to volunteers or professionals serving others during a crisis or disaster.

Cross-cultural counseling is particularly vulnerable to ethical conflict and dilemmas. The ethical decision-making models, assumptions, assessments, and interventions of individuals engaged in crisis intervention have been developed from one cultural perspective but are often implemented within the worldview of another culture (Pedersen & Marsella, 1982).

Ethical decision-making models and ethical codes are helpful guidelines but are not sufficient to resolve ethical dilemmas. Possessing a fundamental understanding of basic ethical principles and one's own values can aid the crisis worker in ethical decision making. How does one validate one's actions and

decisions? One evidence-based method of triaging individuals following a crisis or disaster is the Triage Assessment Form (TAF).

Discernment and Heuristics

Discernment during an ethical dilemma refers to the crisis worker's ability to perceive or distinguish a course or direction during the ambiguity of chaos. Rest (1984) suggested that helping professionals make an interpretation about the circumstances of the crisis or disaster, decide which moral principles are involved, and select a course of action that is grounded in the selected moral principles. Glaser (2002) suggests that discernment in the ethical decision-making process should also include the community of people relevant to the decision. Kahneman (2011) placed heuristics within a two-system framework for thinking and decision making: intuitive and critical thinking. Whether intuition or critical thinking dominates one's decision-making process during a crisis varies with the interventionist's personal preference for one of the two forms of thought and the context of the situation (Kleespies, 2014).

Kahneman, Slovic, and Tversky (1982) cautioned practitioners to also consider the **affect heuristic**. The affect heuristic suggests that judgments and decision making are primarily based on personal biases, the feelings of either disliking or liking an individual, and circumstance or context (Kahneman et al., 1982). Due to the nature and presence of the affect heuristic, Kahneman and associates advised that practitioners trust no one, including themselves, to validate their intuition. As emphasized throughout this chapter and text, it is helpful for anyone contemplating engaging in crisis intervention to have a deep understanding of themselves, their biases, personal values, and motivations as these are the basis for critiquing one's work and reflective practice.

Kleespies (2014) advocates the use of naturalistic decision-making models (NDMs). These types of models emphasize clinician experience and long-term memory as the tools facilitating the crisis interventionist's ability to "think on one's feet" in order to make decisions while under time pressure and constraints. Situational awareness and the ability to rapidly gather, analyze, and synthesize information are all considered essential abilities to make decisions under stress (Kleespies, 2014). Accrued situational experience and the ability to rapidly conceptualize the context of the current crisis situation are characteristics of an effective crisis interventionist.

Reflective Practice. Cottone and Tarvydas **LO8** (1998) emphasized four attitudes, or themes, necessary for ethical decision making; balance, collaboration, context, and reflection. **Reflective practice** entails thinking about both your reasons for entering crisis and disaster work, as well as your actions during a crisis response, and how that response could be improved. In fact, many of the authors' best counseling sessions have occurred 30 minutes after their session has ended. In our opinion, this mindset is perhaps more important for crisis workers to maintain than any particular ethical decision-making model while intervening in a crisis or disaster situation. The chaotic nature of a crisis or disaster situation seems to demand immediacy. However, it is important to consider the perspectives of those involved and attempt to maintain a sense of balance within the context of the situation. Crises and disasters occur within a context with implications for the counselor–client relationship, other members of the response team, organizations, and society. Emphasizing a process of collaboration with the client, effective crisis interventionists attempt to engage all parties with a stake in the decision-making process. Often overlooked, practitioners engaged in crisis intervention need to recognize that they are themselves involved in the crisis resolution process. Crisis interventionists need to maintain an attitude of reflection, in other words, be aware of their own beliefs, biases, values, and the worldview of those they are attempting to serve in order to facilitate sound decision making.

Self-Care. Codes of ethics and standards of **LO9** conduct often refer to the practitioner's duty to care for oneself. The Green Cross Academy of Traumatology first published their Guidelines or Standards for Self-Care (2005). The Academy's ethical guidelines emphasize respect for the dignity and worth of self, the practitioner's responsibility for self-care, and the recognition that without self-care one cannot adequately carry out his or her duty (Green Cross Academy of Traumatology, 2005; SAMHSA, 2014).

Helping professionals can benefit from reflective practice (Green Cross Academy of Traumatology, 2008; James & Gilliland, 2013; Rudick, 2012; Tarvydas & Ng, 2012). The process of reflection is based in the ethical principles of beneficence, fidelity, and nonmaleficence (Welfel, 2005). In the event that a helping professional has transgressed ethical guidelines in some manner, Welfel (2005) proposed a four-step model of recovery: recognition that an error has occurred, experiencing regret or remorse, evaluation of the possibilities of restitution, and rehabilitation to prevent reoccurrence.

The first step of Welfel's (2005) recovery model involves the recognition that one has made an error. Recognition requires personal ownership of the ethical violation and self-appraisal, reflecting upon the ways one's behavior was unethical. Consultation with a peer or a supervisor can be helpful in this process as he or she is in a position to help the practitioner maintain objectivity and perspective. Change is unlikely to occur unless the practitioner regrets his or her actions and has a sense of remorse. Welfel (2005) differentiates regret and remorse from punishment and shame, noting that remorse motivates counselors to change. Once the practitioner has both recognized that a problem exists and is motivated to change, he or she is in a position to assess whether to address the quality of services provided. This can be done directly to the person or group of people harmed by the practitioner's level of care or indirectly to future clients or the profession. The final phase in Welfel's model involves reflection and the practitioner's developing the skills or strategies necessary to prevent future ethical transgressions.

Ethical codes are created by professionals, people in relationships with other people (Cottone, 2001; Guterman & Rudes, 2008). Thoburn and associates (2012) proposed a nested family systems model of social justice and psychological ethics for addressing international disaster. Their nested model suggests that mental health practitioners conceptualize human rights within a context of economic, procedural, and political processes.

Culture influences ethical approaches to international crises and disasters (Gauthier, 2005; Leach & Harbin, 1997; Thoburn, Bentley, Ahmad, & Jones, 2012). Pettifor (2004) contrasted the professional ethical codes among Eastern and Western cultures. Whereas all Western cultures emphasized the primacy of the individual in ethical decision making, Asian cultures' ethical codes prioritized nation, community, family, and then the individual (Pettifor, 2004). Writing for the International Union of Psychological Science, Gauthier (2005) suggested a universal approach emphasizing the common themes across all ethical codes: respect for the dignity and rights of all people, caring for others, competence, integrity, and professional, scientific, and social responsibility.

Similarly, the 2007 Inter-Agency Standing Committee (IASC) guidelines on mental health and psychosocial support in emergency settings emphasized that ethical decision making is integrated and employs an ecological and systemic approach. In the absence of any psychological code of ethics that specifically addresses international disaster situations, the IASC's (2007) task force recommended the following ethical guidelines as the foundation for mental health practitioners engaged in international mental health and psychosocial support: promote human rights and equity, maximize local participation, do no harm, promote capacity building and the use of indigenous resources, and utilize multiple-layered integrated systems based support systems.

The American Psychological Association (APA) affirmed the Inter-Agency Standing Committee's (IASC's) Guidelines Regarding Mental Health and Psychosocial Support in Emergency Settings (IASC, 2007) for the role of psychologists in international emergencies (APA, 2008). The IASC guidelines (2007) recommend that any prospective international service provider work through an established organization such as the International Red Cross or Red Crescent Societies, UNICEF, or similar organizations operating in the affected country. Unless a mental health provider is affiliated or invited by one of these organizations, or meets the criteria below, the APA suggests that psychologists serve in consulting or training roles and avoid directly responding to an international emergency.

Mental health professionals are discouraged from responding to disaster-affected areas unless they have previously worked in emergency settings, have prior experience outside of their own sociocultural context, have developed basic competence in the interventions identified in the IASC (2007, 2012) guidelines, have an understanding of community psychology or public health principles, have received a written invitation from a nation or established nongovernmental organization to work in the country, are invited to work as part of an organization that is likely to maintain a sustained community presence in the emergency area, and emphasize consultation and capacity building approaches (IASC, 2007, 2012).

Piotrowski (2012) noted an increased emphasis on ethical issues and natural disasters in professional psychological literature during the period 2005–2012. However, the majority of this research is conceptual rather than applied. Research to improve and expand effective disaster response and treatment has inherent obstacles (Jesus & Michael, 2009). Practically, the nature of crises and disasters hampers a researcher's ability to identify adequate information to include in a research proposal submission to an Institutional Review Board (IRB). Insufficient staffing, distribution of overwhelmed resources, the acute needs of vulnerable populations, the dual role of practitioners as researchers, the ability of participants experiencing a disaster or crisis to provide informed consent, and the publics' perception and trust of research into disaster response to treatment are among the primary barriers to evidence-based research following disasters or crises. Jesus and Michael (2009) have suggested the use of probabilistic models and simulation or the application of a minimal-risk waiver already utilized by the U.S. Food and Drug Administration (FDA) disaster research to address these obstacles to research into effective disaster response and treatment.

Case Studies

The following case studies are designed to give you a broad representation of crisis contexts and a broad range of people in those contexts. Certainly these are not all inclusive, but what they are designed to do is to get you thinking about the ethical and legal principles that have laid the foundation for this chapter.

As these cases unfold we are going to examine them from four perspectives: ethical, legal, moral, and political. Few texts on legal and ethical issues in the human services spend much ink or paper speaking of the moral aspects of decision making. Yet each of us has a moral yardstick that we measure our personal behavior by, and more often than not, we are not only measuring our behavior in an ethical sense but in a moral one as well as we are faced with tough decisions regarding people in crisis. Even fewer texts speak to the political ramifications of gut-wrenching decisions that are made, particularly when a crisis is occurring. Over and over, when decisions are made on the best ethical grounds, they may run counter to the political exigencies and realities institutions face. Mental health practitioners can find themselves facing extremely hard choices as pressure is placed on them to do the "right" thing in accord with institutional policy or goals. We think that is something worth thinking about as you work through these cases.

Mental Health Center

Chapter 5, Crisis Case Handling, describes the majority of walk-in mental health clients are experiencing chronic mental illness, sudden interpersonal or environmental problems, or a combination of both types of events. Those precipitated by interpersonal or environmental events are often immediate and unexpected crises. The intense, sudden, and unanticipated nature of these types of events are demanding for both clients and crisis workers and represent among the most challenging ethical and legal situations for crisis workers. In order to facilitate an understanding of the potential issues ahead for crisis workers, the case of Benjamin is presented below.

The Case of Benjamin. Benjamin is a young white male in his late 20s or early 30s who shows up unexpectedly at the Midtown Mental Health Clinic, a store-front crisis center in Memphis, Tennessee. He is crying and looks around as if he is confused. His appearance is disheveled and he has a slight unwashed odor about him. He tells the receptionist that he has been wandering the streets for 3 days sleeping little during that time. Benjamin quietly says he needs to talk to someone as soon as possible. The receptionist makes a call and a crisis worker comes to the front office. The receptionist points to the man whose head is buried in his lap sitting in the waiting room. The crisis worker walks over and says, "Hi, my name is Keith. Let's go back to my office so we can talk."

In the office Benjamin sits in a chair directly across from Keith, the crisis worker. The crisis worker asks Benjamin what brings him in today. As Keith begins to sit down, Benjamin looks up and blurts out that he has been diagnosed with HIV and then buries his head in his lap. He confesses that just before a business trip he and his partner had a fight and discussed breaking up. Benjamin said he thought "everything was over." While on a business trip he got drunk and was intimate with someone else. Benjamin explained that when he returned home from the trip, he and his partner had a long talk and made up. Benjamin is in tears as he talks. Keith assesses Benjamin affectively as an 8 on the TAF with fear being the primary feeling. Benjamin's behavioral reaction is rated as a 6 and immobile because his situation is not immediately dangerous. Keith rates Benjamin's cognitive reaction as a 7 or maybe an 8 with loss being the primary reaction. Benjamin denies being suicidal in spite of the fact that he says the situation is hopeless and that he has lost everything that meant anything to him. He now says he is afraid that his partner is also infected and that his partner will probably break up with him

again. Benjamin repeats over and over again, "I have lost everything and I am going to die."

After talking with Benjamin for 30 minutes, he seems more coherent and significantly calmer. Benjamin says he does not know much about his prognosis but knows he has to find out. He says that he had been having flu-like symptoms and a fever for a month or so and decided to get a checkup; that is when blood tests showed that he was infected with HIV. Keith also found out that Benjamin had contacted his partner right after he found out about his diagnosis and said that he had to leave town for a sudden business trip. As a corporate attorney, these types of unanticipated trips were not uncommon for Benjamin. Since then Benjamin has had no contact with his partner but says that he wants desperately to talk with him. He says he just does not know what to say or how to say it. He starts asking Keith for help in order to know what to say.

Commentary

This case study presents numerous ethical issues, and depending upon the jurisdiction, legal issues. The crisis worker must make decisions to provide the best therapeutic course of action while balancing ethical and legal concerns. In this situation the crisis worker is put into a position in which ethical codes are silent or ambiguous and legal requirements may exist (Knapp et al., 2007).

Ethical Issues. In situations where the ethical guidelines are vague or ambiguous and legal requirements are also unclear, the crisis worker may need to use personal values as a guide as the primary resource in sorting through the ethical dilemmas (Knapp et al., 2007). Stanard and Hazler (1995) would suggest that the core ethical principles that seem most relevant to Benjamin's case are autonomy, beneficence, justice, and nonmaleficence. The crisis worker does not want to do harm and instead wanted to do what is best for Benjamin. The issue of confidentiality is also an issue. Depending on the jurisdiction, a requirement to inform partners of someone who has been diagnosed with HIV, or having unprotected sex when one knows they have a life-threatening disease may also be an issue.

In this case, Benjamin, a young corporate attorney, is attempting to cope with his recent diagnosis of HIV. Other than the person who infected Benjamin, Benjamin's only other sexual contact has been with his unnamed partner. Benjamin has clearly expressed that he wants to tell his partner that he has HIV and that his partner has now also been exposed. He expressed that he is just unsure how to proceed. Benjamin feels he has lost everything as a result of this brief affair following a quarrel with his partner. Now he is concerned that he will lose his health, his own life, and the possibility that his indiscretion will lead to the loss of his significant other.

The ethical standard for breaking confidentiality of clients with contagious life threatening diseases has been that the mental health professional *may* warn others provided the client's diagnosis is known, there is an identifiable third party, and the clients do not themselves intend to tell those that they have been exposed to the life-threatening condition. This evolving standard is similar to Cohen's (1990) opinion that counselors are only obligated to break confidentiality if the diagnosis of a life-threatening condition is known, that the client continues to engage in an unprotected sexual relationship, and the client is unlikely to disclose the condition independently. Indeed, Stanard and Hazler (1995) suggested that as an alternative to breaking the client's confidentiality that crisis workers counsel the client to abstain from sexual relations in the future.

Beneficence can be demonstrated through Keith's offering to be present to support Benjamin and his partner while Benjamin discloses his diagnosis. Another example of Keith demonstrating the ethical principle of doing good would be discussing the importance of safe sex with Benjamin and offering safe sex resources. Benjamin is already suffering. For many mental health professionals, the primary ethical obligation is nonmaleficence, or to take no action that would harm their client. Unless mandated by state law, breaking Benjamin's confidentiality in order to disclose that Benjamin believes he may have exposed his partner to HIV may be more harmful than the other courses of action already discussed. Remember, confidentiality is considered the central characteristic of the services provided by mental health professionals. Confidentiality is a duty to one's client and the decision to break confidentiality should not be taken lightly.

Legal Issues. The duty to protect Benjamin's partner *may* be present if Keith is reasonably certain that Benjamin intends to continue to have unprotected sex with his partner. According to Corey and associates (2015), courts have yet to apply the duty to protect to mental health professionals in cases involving HIV

infection. However, state laws regarding HIV or AIDS vary considerably with respect to confidentiality and its limits for licensed mental health professionals (Corey et al., 2015). Although all states currently have laws requiring the reporting of HIV or AIDS cases to public health officials, they frequently are limited to physicians (Wheeler & Bertram, 2012). Mental health practitioners need to know the laws regarding the duty to warn or protect identifiable third parties exposed to HIV or AIDS by their clients. In some states, a mental health practitioner who does disclose a client's HIV or AIDS status to an unauthorized person is subject to malpractice claims or even criminal charges. If you are uncertain what to do in your state, contact your state's public health department, your attorney, or seek consultation from other professionals more experienced with these issues for legal and ethical guidance (Wheeler & Bertram, 2012).

Moral Issues. In this scenario, Benjamin does have much to lose. Respecting his autonomy, Keith would allow Benjamin to determine when and where to tell his partner that he has been exposed to HIV. Keith could offer to meet jointly with Benjamin and his partner to provide support to both parties when Benjamin decides to disclose his diagnosis. The case presents both health and relationship issues as Benjamin's partner may feel betrayed by Benjamin's affair. Interestingly, considering the nature of human relationships, there is also the possibility that Benjamin contracted HIV from his partner after consummating their relationship and "making up." Benjamin clearly feels guilty and assumes that he contracted HIV as a result of his affair while on his business trip following the argument with his partner. However, the diagnosis was not made until he returned from his business trip and consummated his relationship with his partner. This scenario represents just one potentially severe interpersonal issue crisis workers may confront.

Political Issues. Politically, Keith's actions in this case could result in an increased referral base for his walk-in counseling center. Individuals that are marginalized or stigmatized seek providers that are open and have empathy for their experience. If he demonstrates compassion, empathy, and skill, Keith will receive word of mouth referrals from clients that have similar experiences. On the other hand, HIV+ cases are hot potatoes even in a more enlightened era where open homosexuality has become more socially and politically acceptable. However, as indicated in Chapter 10, Partner Violence, the threat of outing (letting people know a person is homosexual) or "double outing," adding on that they are HIV+, is a very real problem that needs to be handled carefully.

Disaster Center: Potential Sexual Abuse

The following case takes place following a major flood that displaced hundreds of people and families as well as destroying the infrastructure for hundreds of miles. Among the ethical issues involved in this case are confidentiality, dual relationships, and competence. Legal issues that also emerge raise issues related to being a mandated reporter because of possible abuse. The circumstances of this scenario dictate that flexibility is needed in order rationalize stretching guidelines and decisions that need to be made.

The Case of Miranda. The crisis worker, Miranda, is a volunteer and has been on site for 5 days. She is from a neighboring state and volunteered to help offer crisis intervention to survivors. Miranda was assigned to do crisis intervention and live in a shelter alongside the survivors of the flood. Her duties have ranged from helping to serve meals, assisting survivors in completing paperwork, arbitrating conflicts, and providing crisis intervention for survivors as requested. Miranda arrived on site several days before she was introduced as a mental health professional and was assigned to the shelter to help survivors as they cope with the impact of the flood. Miranda added that she is sorry for all the tragedy and everyone's loss. She also announces that she is looking forward to helping however she can.

Miranda spends time each day wandering around the shelter talking with different survivors. Sometimes she sits with survivors on their cots and other times at the tables where everyone eats. She has also trolled the long lines of survivors as they wait to talk with officials about the status of their claims and complete required forms. Miranda used these ad hoc conversations to identify individuals and families that are having difficulties. She invites them to talk more if and when they want. During this time she has become acquainted with several survivors and speaks to them daily. She has become particularly close to one family, the Gonzalezes. The Gonzalezes are a Hispanic family that moved to the region several years ago. Mr. Gonzalez is an engineer and Mrs. Gonzalez is a high school teacher teaching in the bilingual program. They have three children, two girls ages 14 and

12, and a son age 18. Sometimes Miranda sits on the cot and talks to various family members, and at other times they seek her out and she talks with them at a table that is used at meal times. Sometimes she talks with the entire family, and other times with individual family members. Over a few days Miranda has felt caught between talking with the family as well as helping individual family members.

At least once a day Miranda helps out serving meals. On her last day to be on site Miranda is assigned to help with dinner. Many of the survivors know her and take time to ask her questions about something they discussed earlier. A few give her a hug and thanks for helping out or figuring out a way to get something done. Late one afternoon, the 14-year old girl, Heather Gonzalez, stops and asks if she can talk with Miranda after dinner. Miranda says, "Of course, I can come to your cot when dinner is over." Heather shakes her head no, "Not there please, can we meet at the back table over there?" Miranda agrees and continues serving dinner. After dinner is over and the tables are cleaned, Miranda sees Heather waiting at the table with a book. Miranda walks over and sits down and Heather takes a deep breath. Heather says quietly that she needs to talk with someone about something that happened. She looks down and says that tomorrow her family is set to go to another shelter. She pauses and quietly says that something had been happening before the flood. Miranda, attempting to reassure Heather, states, "You know I will listen to whatever you want to say." Heather looks up and hastily says, "Sometimes my brother comes into my room and messes with me." Miranda hears a noise and looks up to see that a couple of the survivors are walking over and are obviously going to sit down. Heather abruptly leaves, but pleads for Miranda not to say anything. Miranda says for her to wait, but Heather says she can't and she was only making it up. Miranda does not see her for the rest of the evening and leaves the next morning at 7 A.M. in order to travel to the airport for the trip back to her home.

Commentary

Ethical Issues. As with any disaster, ethical and legal issues abound. The primary ethical issues in this scenario involve beneficence, fidelity, justice, and nonmaleficence. In the chaos of disaster, crisis workers are often required to make decisions when the facts are unclear or partially known and make judgments with incomplete information. On the surface, it would appear the ethical dilemma is whether or not Miranda should report Heather Gonzalez's disclosure.

However, the ethical dilemmas for Miranda are far more complex. Beneficence, or the ethical principle to "do good," requires that disaster response workers have received adequate training. Miranda's case study does not provide any indication of her qualifications. She should provide the best services that she can until a more qualified provider is available. She is an out-of-state responder to a flood. It is clear that she is present to help. However, it is only after she had been on site for several days that she was labeled a "mental health worker." This announcement alone might compromise the ethical principle of fidelity as Miranda's competence or qualifications to serve in the role of a mental health worker is unknown. Her described role appears to be "to do whatever is necessary," which included serving as a listening ear to those living in the shelter to alleviate the flood survivors' distress. This is not to minimize the importance of Miranda's role. She is serving a purpose and contributing to the overall safety and well-being of the flood survivors. However, fidelity involves the principle of veracity, or truthfulness. Announcing that a crisis worker is a mental health worker implies endorsement of their competence.

The ethical principle of nonmaleficence is also compromised in this setting. Miranda is being housed with the people she has volunteered to serve. Privacy, confidentiality, and privilege are all compromised by the nature of this setting. Miranda's responsibility is to find as private a place possible to speak with the survivors. She makes no attempt to provide verbal informed consent, assent, or describe the limits of confidentiality. Even if privilege would normally be extended between a client and his or her mental health provider, nothing is privileged in an open setting within earshot of a passerby. Immersed in the intensity of the survivor's experience, traditional client–counselor boundaries are set aside. This can contribute to role confusion for both the client and crisis worker. It is difficult to discern whether Heather feels she is confiding in a new friend or disclosing an incident of potential child sexual abuse to a professional. The shared experience of this disaster is only temporary and volitional for Miranda. This is not the case for Heather or her family who are about to be redirected to another relief shelter.

The ethical principle of justice, or in this case distributive justice, underlies all disaster relief situations. As noted earlier in this chapter, disaster services are provided on a triage basis. Triage does not imply that all clients receive equal or similar levels of care. In fact, as discussed in the comments regarding the politics of the situation, Heather's individual needs will likely receive lower priority than the needs of the larger group being served.

Legal Issues. The legal environment for volunteer mental health professionals is complex (Abdel-Monem & Bulling, 2005; Hodge, Gable, & Calves 2005). Many important variables are not clearly addressed in Miranda's case. Has the flood been declared a state of emergency by the state? A declared state of emergency provides higher levels of liability protection to volunteers than the needs of disaster survivors following an undeclared emergency (Abdel-Monem & Bulling, 2005; Hodge, Gable, & Calves, 2005). Among the first considerations is whether Miranda is a licensed mental health professional or an unlicensed disaster mental health volunteer. Miranda, our volunteer disaster mental health provider, is first introduced as a "mental health worker" several days after her arrival at the scene. In our vignette, Miranda's actual qualifications are never provided. We are aware she serves food, does whatever she can to alleviate the survivors' pain and discomfort, and serves as an empathic listening ear whenever one is needed. All of these activities are important in disaster relief and not to be discounted. However, as a reader, we have no way of determining whether Miranda is a qualified licensed mental health provider from another state, or simply a well-intentioned volunteer with good listening skills. However, her role and credentials could be material in determining her legal responsibilities and liability in this case. Waivers of liability depend upon fine distinctions in the role and compensation of the mental health provider. A licensed professional compensated for their disaster relief services through a for-profit organization has greater liability exposure than an unlicensed disaster mental health worker volunteering for a nonprofit agency (Abdel-Monem & Bulling, 2005; Hodge, Gable, & Calves, 2005).

Most states do not prescribe a statutory limitation on reporting child sexual abuse. If the crisis worker is in fact a mandatory reporter, it is not her responsibility to investigate the allegations regarding sexual abuse. Rather, it is simply the responsibility of the mandated reporter to contact the state Child Protective Services (CPS) office and allow them to determine whether or not the case warrants further investigation and follow-up. Reports may be made anonymously and do not require the reporter's name (Lambie, 2005). In many states, provided they made the report in good faith, volunteers working for a nonprofit organization or mandatory reporters are often immune from civil and criminal prosecution due to alleged negligence or malpractice. The actions of an unlicensed disaster mental health worker may however become the liability of his or her supervising licensed mental health worker (Abdel-Monem & Bulling, 2005).

Would our answer differ in the event that Miranda was a licensed professional from another state? As a licensed practitioner, Miranda is likely a mandated reporter. Does Heather's statement, made and then retracted, rise to the level of a reportable incident? Is her expressed concern a priority while the family is in a shelter requiring emergency relief? Heather indicated that her brother comes into her room and "messes with me." What does this really mean? Is her brother simply teasing his younger sister as older brothers often due? Or is it something darker and an expression of sexual misconduct? Is her expressed concern a priority while the family is in a shelter requiring emergency relief? Heather's statement is vague and subject to interpretation. Miranda was unable to get any further clarification of what the phrase "messes with me" before Heather ran off and departed the next morning for home. Without additional information, the legal answer to this question is unclear. However, considering the case from a moral position, Miranda's choice might be more apparent.

Moral Issues. Morally, Miranda feels obligated to help Heather Gonzalez and prevent her from experiencing further abuse. The conversation is interrupted and Miranda was unable to explore Heather's concern as she even denied that it happened. Miranda has stated to Heather that she will "listen to anything" Heather had to say. Demonstrating fidelity, Miranda did listen to Heather and to that extent honored her promise. The case becomes more complicated as both Miranda and Heather are transient. Neither Miranda nor Heather expected to be at the shelter the following day. In fact, Miranda is scheduled to leave for home the next day at 7 A.M., and Heather also is expected to be transferred to another shelter. In reality, it is the very transiency of the situation that may have contributed to Heather's disclosure. The primary moral question for Miranda is what to do with the disclosure Heather made in passing. Morally, Miranda may feel best by making the anonymous report, or passing the information along to her supervisor to address. In

that way Miranda will feel that she took some form of action that might prevent further abuse. However, in our experience, it is likely Miranda will never be provided with a sense of complete closure, and she will always wonder what happened to Heather Gonzalez.

Political Issues. Miranda is serving as a volunteer. She is in a time-limited position serving in an unclear role in an out-of-state shelter. Without individuals like Miranda, disaster relief would not be possible. However, there are many political realities in this situation. Miranda, as an out-of-state volunteer, is not vested with a great deal of power. She is working on the front line of disaster relief following a flood. As important as Heather's allegations might be for Heather, the concerns of an individual will not be prioritized as being as important as providing immediate large-scale disaster relief services to the masses. Politically, the matters of distributive justice, the logistics of providing services to families in emergency shelters, and triage will overshadow Heather Gonzalez's concerns about the past. Perhaps this sounds cynical. Our cynicism is not intended to dissuade crisis workers from doing what they consider ethical or right. Rather, we would encourage crisis workers to follow their heart and do what they consider ethical and/or moral instead of endorsing what we consider the political realities presented in this scenario.

Community College Suicide

Working with suicidal clients is among the most stressful situations crisis workers experience (Corey, Corey, Callanan, & Corey, 2015). Considering the context and nature of crisis intervention, crisis workers must be prepared to avert suicide attempts (Slaby, 1998). Preventing suicide is not always possible, and often the steps involved in attempting to prevent suicide require compromising client confidentiality and disrupting his or her life in order to save that life (Remley & Herilhy, 2010). However, preventative measures require conducting a risk assessment, and, based upon the assessed level of risk, might include the development of a stay-alive contract, involving a client's significant others in prevention planning, increasing the frequency of counseling sessions, working in conjunction with the client to arrange voluntary hospitalization, or initiating involuntary commitment procedures.

Stay-Alive Contracts. Research about the efficacy of stay-alive contracts as a technique for crisis intervention is equivocal. Stay-alive contracts alone are not a substitute for thorough case management and treatment planning (Bongard & Sullivan, 2013, p. 6; Stone, 2013), and there is little research to support their use as effective suicide deterrents (Range et al., 2002). However, Davis and associates (2002) interviewed psychiatric inpatients and found that they viewed them as beneficial to treatment with the exception of multiple attempters who did not. Davis's research shows that stay-alive contracts might be beneficial for first-time attempters, or people who have never attempted but are considering suicide. Further, the Granellos (2007, p. 239) and Jacobs (1999) believe that most clients view contracts as positive, and that they communicate a sense of caring and help build a strong therapeutic relationship. In that regard, stay-alive contracts are merely one technique in a much more comprehensive plan.

In order to illustrate the complexity of ethical decision making while working with suicidal cases, consider the case of Ms. Smathers, a counselor at a local community college, and one of her students named George. The case is rife with ethical, moral, legal, and political choices. Following the case study, Ms. Smather's actions will be highlighted and summarized with our judgment call about the strengths and limitations of her approach.

The Case of Ms. Linda Smathers and George. George is a 19-year-old student attending the metal work program at Tech Community College. He is planning on earning his community college degree this semester and moving to North Dakota to work in an oilfield as a pipeline welder. George's girlfriend since middle school has broken up with him. They had planned on getting married after he graduated. When she broke the news, George stopped going to class and is currently not passing. He shows up despondent at the office of Ms. Linda Smathers, the Tech Community College counselor. After talking with George, Ms. Smathers gives George the Beck Depression Inventory II. The inventory shows George is very depressed. George states that he has been pretty happy throughout his whole life, had a good home life, and saw a bright future with his girlfriend until she dumped him. He now thinks about suicide and in fact has made some plans in regard to it. He states that he has access to welding gas and can either asphyxiate himself or blow himself up by running the hose into his pickup. His real reason for coming to the counselor is to get help in getting his girl back. He tells

the counselor she is his last hope. He expressed that he came to see Ms. Smathers as he has heard other students say she was good at helping them with some of their relationship problems.

Ms. Smathers, the counselor, has a master's degree in student personnel services and has worked in the community college for 3 years. She has indeed helped students out with personal problems along with her job as an academic and financial aid advisor. She has never dealt with someone who is suicidal. When she tells George she really isn't qualified and that he needs to go to a mental health clinic to see a psychologist, he empathically tells her "NO, I am not nuts!" He is broken to pieces because of the breakup. After a lengthy discussion the counselor relents because she believes he will become lethal and says she will see him since he clearly will not seek help for his depression. She has read some literature on stay-alive contracts and for the past 3 years has taken the annually required one-day workshop mandated for all community counselors on suicide intervention. George agrees to a stay-alive contract but only if they can work on "getting his girl back." Ms. Smathers agrees and develops the following contract:

George's Stay-Alive, Do-No-Harm Contract
I will not harm myself or anyone else for the next month while I work on my problems of getting Denise back. I will go to my classes regularly so I can come and talk to Ms. Smathers about my problems. If I drop out of school I can no longer see the college counselor. I will not attempt to kill myself or kill anyone else without talking to Ms. Smathers. If I cannot reach you, that is not an excuse for abrogating the contract. I will call the suicide hotline and talk to them or even the National Suicide Hotline. I will come for weekly counseling sessions to work on my problems and will not carry forward with my plan while doing so.

Date: 8/10/16   Signature: George Rutherford,
                 Student Tech Community College

Date: 8/10/16   Witness: Linda Smathers,
                 Counselor Tech Community College

George sees Ms. Smathers three more times while she attempts to move him forward with his broken relationship. Regardless, he stays adamantly stuck in his despair. Upon coming to school on a Monday morning, Ms. Smathers is called to the president's office and informed that George was found earlier this morning in his pickup with severely burned lungs from inhaling welding gas and that he is on a ventilator in critical condition in the ICU at the local hospital. A note was left thanking Ms. Smathers, but he just couldn't take it anymore since he found out his girlfriend moved to California. The college president has the college's lawyer present throughout his meeting with Ms. Smathers. He informs her that George's parents are coming in later this morning with their lawyer to speak with her about her counseling with George, and the Tech Community College lawyer also wishes to conduct a deposition with Ms. Smathers regarding her counseling sessions with George.

Commentary

Ethical Issues. Ethical principles represent **dialectical thought:** the ability to hold and consider two diametrically opposed thoughts simultaneously. On the surface, it seems Ms. Smathers has attempted to honor the ethical principle of autonomy and beneficence in response to George's crisis. Consistent with this principle and respect for George's autonomy, she agreed to counsel George despite his refusal to seek care from a psychologist. Desiring to "do good" by counseling George despite his refusal to seek more experienced help is acceptable provided the crisis worker steps aside once more experienced service providers are available. Ms. Smather's stay-alive contract did not include a reference to the types of conditions in which George would agree to increase his level of care through seeking providers with experience counseling suicidal clients, and pursuing voluntary, or even involuntary, hospitalization. Her inclusion of the requirement that George continue his classes in order to receive counseling reflects her attempt to have George reengage in his classes. This contingency can be interpreted either as an attempt to facilitate a healthy activity or politically as an administrative attempt to retain a student. Ms. Smathers would be subject to accusations of abandonment as her stay-alive contract did not include a contingency for an alternate service provider in the event George drops out of classes. Her decision to provide care reflects her perception that any form of counseling is less harmful (nonmaleficence) than George not receiving any form of counseling.

Another aspect of the principle of beneficence is competence. Ms. Smathers has 3 years of experience as a community college counselor and a master's degree in student personnel services rather than a clinically focused degree. Her annual training in suicide prevention is useful to identify a potentially suicidal client but it does not qualify her as a suicidologist and is not sufficient to counsel a truly suicidal client.

Her lack of competence to counsel a client in crisis is evident at several levels. She administers the Beck Depression Inventory II that reflects George is "very depressed." This finding, along with George's suicidal ideation, a plan, and means suggest the need for a stepped up plan of care. George provided Ms. Smathers information about protective factors in his life as well as his suicide plan and means. Ms. Smathers failed to thoroughly assess or consider George's suicide risk factors, nor consulted with peers or other providers experienced in working with suicidal clients. As a result, she develops a stay-alive contract to form a bond with George and keep him coming to counseling in the hopes of "cooling him off." Davis and associates' (2002) research shows that for first-time attempters or people who have never attempted stay-alive contracts might be beneficial which George certainly is. However, crisis workers need to be aware that a stay-alive contract is merely one technique in a much more comprehensive plan. Be advised that a stay-alive contract alone won't hold up in court and an in-depth suicide management/treatment plan *must* accompany the contract.

Ms. Smathers engaged in a counseling relationship under the auspices of helping George "get his girl back." Although her desire was to help George, this action reflects violations of the ethical principles of fidelity and veracity as she has made a promise that she cannot possibly keep. When working with a vulnerable person, it is important that crisis workers remain truthful and promise only what is feasible. Clearly, George's goal of getting his girlfriend back differs from Ms. Smather's goal of keeping him engaged in the Tech Community College metal work program and cooling him down. This goal conflict reflects a weakness in the therapeutic alliance formed between George and Ms. Smathers. When it was apparent that George was "stuck" in his goal of getting his girlfriend back, Mrs. Smathers failed to increase the level of care. Ms. Smather's attempt to honor George's confidentiality failed to recognize the *serious and foreseeable danger* inherent in his case. Placing a priority on life over confidentiality, most ethical codes allow crisis workers to break confidentiality in response to a client's serious and foreseeable danger to oneself or others. Similarly, neither the federal laws FERPA nor HIPAA preclude breaking confidentiality to preserve life.

Legal Issues. Although the research regarding their use is equivocal at best, it is not uncommon for school counselors to use stay-alive contracts in educational settings (Stone, 2013). Among the problems with their use is the word *contract,* which implies a legally binding agreement (Stone, 2013). Ms. Smathers arrives at work one morning only to be greeted by the college president and legal counsel. Both the president and the staff attorney are concerned about appearances and liability of Tech Community College rather than Ms. Smathers. In our experience, Ms. Smathers will be expendable as soon as Tech Community College's interests are secured. The Tech Community College attorney requests a deposition and Mrs. Smathers is advised of George's family desire to meet her with their attorney to discuss what transpired during her counseling sessions with George. Crisis workers need to be aware that when approached by attorneys with a request for a deposition or upon receipt of a subpoena, they are no longer engaged in an ethical issue. Simply stated, when an attorney is involved, the case has become a legal issue rather than an ethical matter and the crisis worker needs to retain an attorney experienced with professional negligence.

Moral Issues. Ms. Smathers made a moral judgment based upon her genuine concern for George and belief that she could help him as she has helped other students with their love lives. However, a degree in student personnel services does not make one a relationship expert and that was not truly her goal for George. In our opinion, Ms. Smathers exceeded her level of competence. Although the outcome of her case will depend upon many factors, it is likely that she will be exposed to a malpractice lawsuit. Whether Ms. Smather's desire to help George will outweigh her many variations from recognized standards of practice of ethical and legal guidelines is questionable and likely to be debated in a court of law.

Political Issues. Although the American School Counselor Association's (ASCA) Standards for Ethical Conduct (ASCA, 2010) indicate that school counselors should report the results of risk assessments to parents when they suggest a need for them to act on their child's behalf, George would not be considered a minor in many states. Despite the courts' reluctance to find in favor of parents (Stone & Zirkel, 2012), in our experience, Ms. Smathers will be expendable as soon as Tech Community College's interests are secured. Both the college's president and legal counsel are concerned about the college's appearance, liability, and legal exposure. Ms. Smathers, although beloved

by the students, will likely become the scapegoat for the college. The threat of suicide requires immediate attention. Her use of the stay-alive contract implied that Ms. Smathers, a representative of the college, could ensure George's safety and that he was able remain in classes at Tech Community College. Neither case was true in this scenario.

Crisis Hotline: Potential Elder Abuse

Multiple ethical and possible legal issues surface in the following case involving an elderly person calling a crisis hotline. Crisis hotlines represent a fascinating predicament since many, if not all, publicize that calls are anonymous. However, technological advances with respect to caller ID mean phone calls are no longer anonymous unless great pains are taken to conceal a phone number. This situation puts crisis workers receiving the call between a rock and a hard place since the publicized "informed consent" implies anonymity. Several ethical choice points occur in this case during the interaction between the person calling and crisis worker. Each point involves critical decisions that are made in the moment with the crisis worker's rapidly weighing various pros and cons including potential legal issues around elder abuse while talking with the caller.

The Case of Mrs. Frazier. One weekend evening, shortly after 11:15 P.M., a call comes into the crisis hotline. Answering the call is Nan, a crisis worker with several years of experience. The crisis worker quickly recognizes the caller as an elderly person because of the quality and tone of her voice. The caller identifies herself as Mrs. Frazier. She says that she has not been able to sleep because she and her children had a big argument earlier that tremendously upset her. When asked about the disagreement, Mrs. Frazier explains that she is 82 years old and her children, two boys and a girl, are just trying to get rid of her. She states her children do "mean things" to her and that they "are only after my money." She expresses, "They all just want to put me in a nursing home in order to wither up and die." She says they only come over when they want something, and she thinks that the food they bring is "rotten leftover stuff that isn't fit for anyone to eat." Suspecting elder abuse, Nan asks if Mrs. Frazier's children have ever harmed her in any way. That question is a catalyst for Mrs. Frazer who begins a nonstop monologue extending over 10 minutes in which she describes all the "mean" things her children have done. Mrs. Frazier lists such things as her children making her walk until she feels that she is about to fall over, forcing her to eat awful food, rummaging through her things, and shoving hundreds of pills down her throat that cause her to forget things. Mrs. Frazier adds that she hears them whispering and is sure they are planning things to make her die sooner so they "can get all of my money and my house."

Throughout the phone call, the crisis worker listens intently and encourages Mrs. Frazier to provide more details and expand on the things she is talking about. Mrs. Frazier seems to ignore these requests and continues rambling, occasionally saying she is "just a silly old woman" and does not know why she called. As the conversation continues Mrs. Frazier starts interjecting that it is so nice to have someone to listen. She expressed it would be nice if her children were like the crisis worker. Mrs. Frazier says even though she is just talking on the phone for a few minutes that Nan is a good person that she has a grown to trust. The crisis worker thanks her and says Mrs. Frazier seems like a nice person as well and surely is a good mother. Soon Mrs. Frazier starts talking about her finances and her will. Mrs. Frazier begins insisting that the crisis worker give her some advice about both. She begins to cry saying she wishes her children still loved her. She then says she is so sorry for bothering the crisis worker but needed to talk with someone. Eventually, Mrs. Frazier expresses that she should never have called the hotline since Nan is a stranger but the place she found the number said it was "anonymous" so she thought it would be okay. The crisis worker did not say anything about caller ID and that Mrs. Frazier's phone number appeared on a screen, along with her name, and her location.

Commentary

Ethical Issues.
Mrs. Frazier felt safe calling the crisis hotline as she believed her call was anonymous. The fundamental ethical dilemma for Nan is whether to honor the principle of beneficence, or the potential for doing good, by allowing Mrs. Frazier to believe her call was anonymous, or to honor the principle of veracity and advise Mrs. Frazier that her call was not anonymous. Nan, the hotline worker, in her attempt to be beneficent, did not advise Mrs. Frazier that her call was not truly anonymous. In this case the authors concur with Nan's action. The potential good of allowing Mrs. Frazier to speak freely outweighs the benefit of telling her that her call was not anonymous.

In her conversation with Mrs. Frazier, Nan, an experienced crisis hotline worker, was able to gather information about Mrs. Frazier's allegations regarding her children's mistreatment. Reviewing Mrs. Frazier's complaints regarding her children, it appears that rather than being harmful, her children are involved and merely attempting to care for their aging mother. Regardless, Nan must decide whether to break confidentiality and have someone do a "well-check" on Mrs. Frazier. Unfortunately, this judgment is based upon experience and intuition.

Legal Issues.
Consider the alternative to keeping Mrs. Frazier's confidence. Nan could contact Adult Protective Services as a mandated reporter and provide the details of Mrs. Frazier's call. She can adopt "a better safe than sorry" approach. A widely accepted definition of **elder abuse** is any knowing, intentional, or negligent act by a caregiver or other person that causes harm or serious risk of harm to an older person or failure to meet an elder's basic needs (National Research Council, 2003). Does what Mrs.Frazier says meet this criteria? Although this compromises the principle of fidelity and Mrs. Frazier's belief that she is making an anonymous call, Nan can use the principle of nonmaleficence as justification. Is this truly an example of no harm? Nan knows from experience on the crisis line that the elderly do get mistreated. Wiglesworth and associates (2010) found that about 47% of persons who were cognitively impaired with geriatric maladies were mistreated by a caregiver. Even for those elderly who were not faced with cognitive disabilities, about 11% were found to be mistreated (Acierno et al., 2009), so there is a good deal of evidence to suggest that self-reports should be taken seriously, particularly when many of these elderly people are entirely dependent on the people they are reporting. Adult Protective Services (APS), not Nan, is responsible for deciding whether the report warrants investigation. In the event APS decides that Nan's report warrants investigation, they will make a site visit or "well check." Mrs. Frazier's call reflects that she is having some difficulty living independently. The call does not reflect the extent that family members are involved and attempting to do what they can to help their mother live independently. Would Nan's call to APS jeopardize Mrs. Frazier's independence? That is, would there be a self-fulfilling prophecy and her children would say, "That's it! Off to a nursing home!" Or would that call indeed keep her from being exploited or harmed by less than charitable family members?

Moral Issues. The crisis worker's choice is whether or not to contact, or defer contacting, law enforcement or adult protective services for an on-site evaluation of Mrs. Frazier. Ingram and associates (2008) described over 300,000 crisis calls made to a national hotline over a 5-year period. Approximately half of these callers were first-time callers and reports of loneliness increased with the callers' age. In your opinion, do Mrs. Frazier's complaints rise to the serious and foreseeable harm standard necessary to break confidentiality? Or is she just a lonely old woman who is dissatisfied with her children's attempts to keep her living independently? What would you do if you were in Nan's role as the crisis worker? You have her number. Would you call her back? That will tell her that her anonymity has been compromised.

Political Issues. According to Chapter 6, Telephone and Online Crisis Counseling, telephone and cyber-counseling account for the majority of crisis work conducted throughout the world. In the United States, the majority of telephone hotline workers are volunteers and the agencies that utilize them are often immune from state or federal legislation (Seely, 1997a, 1997b). The rationale is to encourage the provision of a service most consider beneficial. However, as the use of technology increases, more states are regulating professional counselors who provide telephone or cybercounseling.

The current trend is for states to regulate licensed professional counselors and to require them to hold a license in their respective state. Shaw and Shaw (2006) found that online counselors who identified themselves as licensed professionals or as members of a professional association had significantly higher scores (problems) on a 16-item ethical intent checklist than did their unlicensed counterparts. In the future, crisis workers will need to clearly consider their role and whether they are functioning as a volunteer immune from liability by the nature of their role and the agency for which they volunteer or as a licensed professional subject to state regulation.

Schools: A Potential Runaway

Any crises that occur in a school automatically bring into play a host of issues that are generally not present in other settings. First and foremost is the fact that most of the crises that occur in schools will involve minors, and that means that a parent or guardian will likely be involved sooner or later. The mission of schools and all the personnel in them is singular—to advance the child academically and, perhaps, build good citizens in the bargain. To that end, in the United States, the guiding principle of **in loco parentis** (in place of the parent) has held sway since the beginnings of the public school system in this country. The thought is that while the parents are not present, the school has the wisdom to act in their behalf. The problem is that emotional and social issues have come to be recognized as playing an integral a part in that academic progress, and the concept of in loco parentis has expanded to meet those needs. That expansion is not always greeted well by parents who feel the school is trespassing and crossing into what are purely family matters.

The Case of Josh and Lucinda Martinez, School Counselor. Josh Whitmore, a 16-year-old male Caucasian sophomore, comes to the office of Lucinda Martinez, a veteran school counselor at Central High School in El Paso, Texas. Josh seems to be scared. He says, "I can't stand it anymore. I just want to get out." Talking with Josh, Lucinda determines that his parents are constantly badgering him to go out for sports and to do better in school. He reports loud shouting and that his father almost hit him before he left the house. He says his father raised his fist at him and threatened that this is what would happen if he didn't do what his parents said. He says they are not well off financially. His father is a maintenance worker and his mother is a waitress at a local restaurant. Josh's parents think that the only way he will get into college is by getting an athletic or academic scholarship. They are religious conservatives and severely sanction any social engagements for Josh other than church. Lucinda remembers working with Josh's sister, Mary Anne, who expressed experiencing the same concerns about her parents. Mary Anne eventually ran away with her secret boyfriend to Los Angeles. Lucinda recalls that the parents were extremely rigid and very vocal about their expectations for their daughter. When Lucinda attempted to act as Mary Anne's advocate, her parents called the school's principal and told her there was to be no more communications between Lucinda and their daughter. Mary Anne's parents told the principal in no uncertain terms, that other than helping with applications for college, Lucinda was a minion of the devil. After Mary Anne ran away with her boyfriend, her parents filed a complaint with the school board against Lucinda and attempted to get her fired.

Josh says he is seriously thinking about running away. He confesses that he has already bought a bus ticket to L.A. and shows Lucinda the ticket. He plans on going to live with his older sister. The boy says while he likes sports and has good grades, he just cannot live up to his parents' expectations. He says they badger him about how his grades are in school, and incessantly question him: "Do you need help?" "What can they do?" "Are you getting your assignments in on time?" and on and on. They will not let him date girls and constantly put his "bad, slutty sister" up to him as an example of being immoral, lazy, oppositional defiant, and likely "to burn in hell for her sins." Josh complains that his dad is always asking about practice and what the coaches are saying. He always finds fault with Josh's skills as a baseball pitcher and constantly pressures him to do better. Josh feels his dad never says anything positive about his abilities. Josh's dad almost got in a fistfight with the coach over Josh and recently had to be escorted away from practice by the school resource police officer. Josh says he has e-mailed his 19-year-old sister and she is encouraging him to come to Los Angles and live with her and her boyfriend. Josh says that his sister has offered to let him stay with her and finish school. Lucinda eventually extracts a promise from Josh to do nothing for 24 hours while she looks for some options.

After school, while Josh is at baseball practice, Lucinda is in her office and toying with the following options:

1. Report the parents to Children and Family Protective Services for abuse.
2. Do nothing. Don't encourage him but don't discourage him. Let Josh run away to his sister's house where he'll be safe from his parents' harassment, be able to finish high school, and go on with his life.
3. As uncomfortable as it might be, call Josh's parents and inform them of his plan to run away. Rest assured, Lucinda is convinced that Josh's parents will probably complain about that interfering "Mexican" counselor and become even more punitive toward their son.
4. Talk to the baseball coach and see what Josh's chances are of getting a college scholarship. If it is likely he will be able to earn a baseball scholarship, counsel Josh to remain at home and "stick it out."
5. Talk to the principal, who has had many interactions with the Whitmores before, and get her opinion about how to proceed. Lucinda is aware that the school principal is no fan of the family's parenting style.
6. Contact her old professor at UTEP, Dr. Myer, and ask him what to do.

Commentary

Ethical Issues. Lucinda has extracted Josh's promise that he would not take any action for the next 24 hours while she attempts to identify options. The basic ethical principles involved in this scenario include autonomy, beneficence, nonmaleficence, and fidelity. Honoring the ethical principle of autonomy, Lucinda could decide to do nothing and allow Josh to independently decide his course of action without interference. In most states, Josh, a 16-year-old minor, is not considered fully autonomous or capable of making independent decisions. Opting to allow Josh to exercise his autonomy and decide whether or not to run away might become a legal issue in the event he ran away.

Lucinda's dilemma then becomes deciding whether "doing nothing" is in Josh's best interest or whether that exposes Josh from experiencing any potential harm. Josh clearly is uncomfortable with the pressure he receives from his parents. Determining what is in the best interest of another is always a difficult path. At the moment Josh feels running away is in his best interest. Although Lucinda has not spoken with Josh's parents about him, Josh's parents would likely feel that they are only trying to help Josh have a better life than they have experienced (a goal most parents share). They hope to keep him from their own fate, working as a maintenance man or waiter. From his parents' perspective, obtaining a scholarship and attending college represents Josh's only opportunity to have a better life. His parents recognize that based upon their own socioeconomic status, that Josh does not have all of the advantages or opportunities available to children of more affluent families. However, his parents recognize that Josh is intelligent and athletic enough to pitch for the high school baseball team and hope that he will become eligible for a scholarship. Perhaps counseling Josh regarding his parents' perspective and reframing their concern would be beneficial. Knowingly allowing a 16-year-old child to run away because he feels he is being "badgered" to work harder academically and athletically in school is unlikely to be considered a reasonable standard of care for any school counselor. Despite the disagreeable nature of Josh's parents, it is probably less harmful for Lucinda to speak with Josh's parents than it would be for him to run away to Los Angeles. However, the authors would also talk to Josh's baseball coach first in order to get an idea of Josh's future athletic scholarship potential as this might help to defuse the intensity of the conversation with Josh's family. The ethical course of action is not always comfortable. Although we believe that speaking with Josh's parents would be uncomfortable for Lucinda, counseling is not about the counselor. Josh and his needs are paramount. Josh has purchased a bus ticket and his sister has already offered him a place to stay. Time is of the essence and the risk of Josh's running away is too great to not involve informing his parents. The authors' would recommend Lucinda do her "homework" (i.e., speaking with the principal, Josh's coach, and resource development). Lucinda should also contact Josh's parents and arrange an appointment to meet with Josh and his parents at school. Stone (2013) recommended that school counselors should develop a list of resources for crisis or emergency situations. Lucinda should provide the family referral resources in order to strengthen the family system, communication, and parenting skills.

Legal Issues. Consulting a former professor is always a reasonable option. In fact, consultation with a peer, a supervisor, or a mentor regarding a hypothetical situation is always a reasonable course of action. However, Lucinda would not be able to reveal any personally identifiable information regarding Josh or his family without breaking Josh's confidentiality or violating FERPA.

Lucinda is at risk of violating the legal concept of in loco parentis, in other words, making a decision about Josh's stability that only his parents are responsible for determining. Deciding not to act remains an action. Lucinda is not Josh's custodian. She should provide referral resources that are accessible to Josh's parents. Parents have the right to attempt to intervene on behalf of their child (Stone, 2013). Either Josh's parental failure to act or their potential overreaction to the situation might require Lucinda to notify Child Protective Services on Josh's behalf. However, whether Lucinda will need to make that contact will depend upon the outcome of her counseling session and the future actions of all parties.

Moral Issues. Morality is based in part on Lucinda's beliefs regarding what is right or good for Josh,

what constitutes being a caring and effective parent, and Josh's family. She has experienced ethnic and religious bigotry in the past. Lucinda has made moral judgments regarding Josh's family and his parent's motives. This is in part based upon her prior experience with Josh's family and the parents' past actions toward their daughter, Mary Anne. Lucinda at best considers Josh's description of his parents' behavior to reflect an inept and ineffective overbearing and authoritarian parenting style. She also perceives Josh's parents to be bigoted as referenced in her thought that she will be referred to as that interfering "Mexican." These perceived realities, or value judgments, require Lucinda's reflection as they hold the potential to reduce Lucinda's effectiveness in her provision of services to Josh during this crisis.

Political Issues. Lucinda's political considerations include contacting Josh's baseball coach and the principal. Both are potential allies to Lucinda. In our scenario, the principal is described as being well aware of Josh's parents. She does not endorse their past and will likely not endorse their current parenting style. Regardless of her good intentions, contacting Josh's parents will likely incur their wrath and Lucinda would be wise to let her principal know what to expect. It is better that the principal find out what to expect from Lucinda before it occurs than to have Josh's parents angrily contact the principal, blaming Lucinda for their son's plan to run away. Some might be concerned that this compromises Josh's sense of confidentiality. However, the potential good outweighs the harm to Josh.

Involving Josh's coach is also a political decision. Lucinda could inquire about Josh's future potential without disclosing his plans to run away. In the event Josh truly was a talented pitcher and he did run away, the coach would hold Lucinda responsible for not allowing him to also attempt to intervene. She could also ask whether he would be available to speak with Josh's parents if Lucinda believed that it would be beneficial. This largely depends upon the relationship between Josh and his baseball coach. Josh's father is described as being both negative and derogatory. Coaches are often influential father-like figures to student athletes. Although Josh's father clearly has disagreed with the coach's decisions in some games, Josh may have greater respect for his coach's opinions and perspectives regarding his potential than he has for his father's.

SUMMARY AND IMPLICATIONS FOR PRACTICE

Crisis situations, regardless of their size, are rife with legal and ethical dilemmas. Unfortunately, due to their nature there are many opinions but little empirical guidance on the best ethical practice in crisis or disaster contexts. In fact, the majority of the literature is conceptual. Professional ethical codes largely stand silent on how to proceed in an ethical manner when responding to a crisis or disaster. Ethical codes provide guidelines regarding acceptable behavior but usually do not provide specific answers on how best to proceed. As a crisis worker, you are entering the unknown. Crisis workers are routinely called upon to make decisions under time constraints and with incomplete information. How you approach each case is based upon your own unique beliefs, personal values, morals, and the sociopolitical context of the situation. Fortunately, your actions will be judged based upon the standard of what the reasonable person would do in your situation in a similar context.

Research does suggest that applied experience is beneficial in resolving ethical or legal dilemmas. At best a textbook can help stimulate thought and perhaps direct you to consider situations in a novel way. Reading is not a substitute for experience. The case examples have been presented to assist the readers in understanding the authors' thought processes as they attempt to aid a person or group in crisis. What this textbook cannot convey is how quickly each of these different strands of thought is considered by the experienced crisis worker in order to arrive at the best course of action.

The best course of action is not always the most comfortable course for the crisis worker. However, crisis intervention is not about the crisis worker. Crisis work is about the individual or groups of people in crisis. Before entering this type of practice, practitioners are urged to consider their reasons and preparation for choosing crisis intervention. The ethical principles of autonomy, beneficence, fidelity, justice, and nonmaleficence provide a basic structure for evaluating what is occurring in the field. An ethical dilemma exists when two or more principles conflict. Inevitably, the crisis workers' decisions will prioritize certain ethical principles and minimize the value of others. Effective crisis workers recognize that this is simply part of the process and attempt to minimize any harm their client might experience as a result of their decisions or actions.

Visit CengageBrain.com for a variety of study tools and useful resources such as video examples, case studies, interactive exercises, flashcards, and quizzes.

Human Services Workers in Crisis 16

Burnout, Vicarious Traumatization, and Compassion Fatigue

LEARNING OBJECTIVES

After studying this chapter, you should be able to:

1. Understand the dynamics of burnout.
2. Be aware of the myths surrounding burnout.
3. Recognize the host of behavioral, physical, attitudinal, and interpersonal symptoms that indicate burnout.
4. Know the levels of burnout.
5. Know the stages of burnout.
6. Understand the interrelationships and differences among secondary traumatic stress, vicarious traumatization, and compassion fatigue.
7. Understand that compassion satisfaction is a buffer against compassion fatigue and burnout.
8. Understand the role of organizations in perpetuating burnout.
9. Understand and know individual intervention strategies for burnout.
10. Understand both individual and organizational assessment devices for uncovering burnout.
11. Understand culture's influence on burnout.

Respond to the following questions with a yes or no.

1. Have you left parties early because the occasions offered you no opportunity to counsel?
2. Do you continue to counsel even though it interferes with your earning a living?
3. Do you sometimes have the "shakes" in the morning and find that this unpleasantness is relieved by counseling a little?
4. Do you repeat everything you hear? I mean, do you repeat or paraphrase everything you hear?

These questions are part of Adam's (1989) humorous, satirical test of counseling addiction. Yet the questions may not be too far off target when viewed in terms of another severe problem that strikes many professionals in the human services business—burnout—and its handmaidens, compassion fatigue and vicarious traumatization.

So you are a brand new human services worker with a diploma fresh off the presses and ready to go out and cure the world. You are full of vim and vigor and one salty dog! What's with burnout? That's just old dudes that are washed up! Apparently, since the last edition of this book went to press in 2012, 1,475 articles on burnout retrieved from the American Psychological Association (2015) search engine, Psychinfo, felt otherwise. They also seem to be talking about you, young grasshopper! Research indicates that if you are younger and female you are more likely to wind up in the burned out category of human services workers (Baum et al., 2014; de Figueiredo et al., 2014; Star, 2015; Volpe et al., 2014).

If you were a teacher from Ireland (Foley & Murphy, 2015), a Chinese civil servant (Hao et al., 2015), or a Peruvian correctional officer (Clemente et al., 2015), there was some concern you might be burning out.

Indeed, it appears that about every country and occupation in the world is concerned about burnout, and it is far from humorous. Burnout is not just some pop psychology term designed to elicit sympathetic responses from one's coworkers or spouse. It is a complex individual-societal phenomenon that affects the welfare of not only millions of human services workers but also tens of millions of those workers' clients (Farber, 1983, pp. vii, 1). Put in economic terms, billions of dollars are lost each year because of workers in all fields who can no longer function adequately in their jobs. Signs and symptoms of burnout include turnover, absenteeism, lowered productivity, and psychological problems (Golembiewski, Munzenrider, &

Stevenson, 1986; Leiter & Maslach, 2005, pp. 3–9). Yet if burnout has been discussed in all occupations, why should it be endemic to the helping professions?

Helping Professionals: Prime Candidates

The bulk of writing and research that has been done on burnout has come from the helping professions because of its poorer job satisfaction and higher turnover and burnout compared to other occupations (Coates & Howe, 2014). The very nature of the job is to be intensely involved with people, and generally these are people who are not at the highest levels of self-actualized behavior (Maslach, 1982b, pp. 32–33). Burnout tends to afflict people who enter their professions highly motivated and idealistic and who expect their work to give their life a sense of meaning (Pines & Aronson, 1988, p. 11). When many of the clients get worse instead of better despite all of the workers' skill and effort, burnout becomes a high probability for these idealistic people.

Compounding the harsh realities of historically low success rates, the human services business is becoming more difficult. Human services workers are likely to intervene with people with severe psychological and physical traumatic problems connected with sexual and physical assault, murder, Alzheimer's disease, and AIDS. Because of managed care and restricted budgets, human services workers are expected to handle larger caseloads in shorter time periods. These traumatic problems call for tremendous amounts of the worker's energy, resilience, and hardiness. Day in and day out, the severity of these problems and their duration can wear down the optimism and motivation of any worker (McRaith, 1991).

AIDS counselors are an outstanding example of prime candidates for burnout. They must deal with concerns about safe working practices, fear of infection, intensity of counselor/client/significant other relationships over long periods of physical decline to death, the broad range of services needed, transcrisis events involving a variety of issues, increasing numbers of clients, lack of support by other organizations, and shunning by many health care providers (Miller, 1995; Oktay, 1992).

The foregoing problems are at the core of the helping professions, making them not just some of the most challenging but also some of the most stress-prone occupations. Thus, human services professionals must be able to tolerate a variety of complex problems that are generally couched in ambiguity, deal with conflict from both clients and institutions, and somehow meet a myriad of demands from the ecological framework in which they operate (Paine, 1982, p. 21).

For the crisis worker, this is true many times over. Crisis center work settings are notorious for long and erratic hours, low pay, poorly functioning clients, immediate deadlines, a lack of control over when clients will arrive or phone, few second chances, repeat callers with chronic problems, hostile and emotionally "raw" clients, and interagency red tape. These are only a few of the stressors that assault crisis workers, making them prime candidates for burnout (Distler, 1990). Because the crisis worker is exposed to a high incidence of trauma for extended periods of time, phrases such as "compassion fatigue" (Figley, 1995, 2002), "traumatic" or "event" countertransference (Dahlenberg, 2000, pp. 12–13), "vicarious traumatization" (McCann & Pearlman, 1990; Pearlman & Mac Ian, 1995; Pearlman & Saakvitne, 1995a, 1995b; Saakvitne, 2002), and "traumatoid states" (Thomas & Wilson, 2004) have found their way into the literature to describe what happens when workers are faced over and over with unspeakable trauma.

However, a question arises about whether burnout and its newer derivatives are really dynamically identifiable. There is a lively ongoing discussion in the professional literature at this writing as to whether burnout is an identifiable, stand-alone malady or is really just clinical depression dressed up in work clothes and struggling through a workday (Bianchi & Laurent, 2015; Bianchi et al., 2015; Chiu et al., 2015). Indeed, Hafkenscheid (2005) proposes that the term *vicarious traumatization* is no more than a fancy term made up to excuse therapeutic failure. Paine (1982, p. 11) and Maslach (1982b, p. 29) report that critics propose that burnout is "part of the job," so if a human services professional "can't stand the heat then he or she ought to get out of the kitchen" because there "always has been stress on this job and always will be." Such cursory dismissal of burnout does not consider the major personal, social, and organizational costs that accrue when job stress turns into crisis (Paine, 1982, p. 11). Burnout is connected to loss of job productivity, impairment of inter- and intrapersonal relationships, and a variety of health problems (Golembiewski et al., 1992; Golembiewski & Munzenrider, 1993; Golembiewski, Munzenrider, & Stevenson, 1986). Indeed, there is ominous research accumulating that indicates people who manifest burnout have significant changes in body chemistry that are biomarkers for cardiovascular disease (Grossi et al., 2005; Melamed et al., 2006; Toker et al., 2005). Burnout is not just part of the territory; it has major ramifications for both individuals and institutions (Maslach, 1982b, p. 39). It is a very real problem, with chronic occupational stress as the primary cause (Paine, 1982, p. 16; Tubesing & Tubesing, 1982, p. 156).

Dynamics of Burnout

A historical definition of burnout places it **LO1** as a child of the 1970s. The term comes from the psychiatric concept of patients who were "burned out" physically, emotionally, spiritually, interpersonally, and behaviorally to the point of exhaustion (Paine, 1982, p. 16). It was first coined as a workplace term by Herbert Freudenberger to describe young, idealistic volunteers who were working with him in alternative health care settings and who started to look and act worse than many of their clients (Freudenberger, 1974, 1975). Yet defining burnout adequately is not simple.

A very broad definition depicts **burnout** as an internal psychological experience involving feelings, attitudes, motives, and expectations (Maslach, 1982b, p. 29). Being burned out means that the total psychic energy of the person has been consumed in trying to fuel the fires of existence. This energy crisis occurs because the psychic demand exceeds the supply (Tubesing & Tubesing, 1982, p. 156). It is experienced as a state of physical, mental, and emotional exhaustion caused by long-term involvement in emotionally demanding situations. It is accompanied by an array of symptoms including physical depletion, feelings of helplessness and hopelessness, disillusionment, negative self-concept, and negative attitudes toward work, people, and life itself. It represents a breaking point beyond which the ability to cope with the environment is severely hampered (Pines & Aronson, 1988, pp. 9–10) and the inability to work effectively (Stamm, 2010).

Put in plain language, burnout is lost energy. You are exhausted. A good night's sleep is out of the question and sleep aids (including alcohol) don't help much. Aborted attempts to get away don't help and you come back feeling worse than ever. Work is demanding beyond reason and exceeds the best you are able to do. Burnout is also lost enthusiasm. As Rhett Butler said to Scarlett O'Hara in *Gone with the Wind*,

"Frankly my dear, I just don't give a damn!" Passion has been replaced by cynicism. You despise your bosses and the clients, and aren't overly thrilled with your coworkers either. All the zeal, energy, creativity, expertise, and enthusiasm you brought to the job are long gone. Going the extra mile has turned into wondering whether you can go the few yards to the break room. Finally, your confidence has gone out the window. The less effective you become, the more your self-worth shrinks. Why keep going (Leiter & Maslach, 2005, p. 2)? Indeed you are now a candidate for the long shopping list of maladies you'll soon see that come out of this thing called *burnout*!

Burnout is not generally perceived as a crisis event because its onset is slow and insidious. There is no one point or incident that is readily identifiable as the instigating trauma. Rather, it is a slow and steady erosion of the spirit and energy as a result of the daily struggles and chronic stress typical of everyday life and work (Pines & Aronson, 1988, p. 11). Because of the difficulty in identifying burnout, it becomes much easier to chalk it up as a character deficit. A crisis appears only when people are so defeated and exhausted by the environment that they take extraordinary means to find relief, such as quitting a job or occupational field, developing a serious psychosomatic disease, becoming a substance abuser, or attempting suicide. What is even more problematic is that recovery from burnout is not always linear and tends toward chaos and crisis as the individual tries to come to grips with core issues of vocation, personality, and relationships (Kesler, 1990). As a result, the precipitating crisis of job burnout may move toward a more global, existential crisis wherein the person is in a state of crisis over living.

Occupationally, burnout occurs when past and present problems from the job continuously pile up. Leiter and Maslach (2005, pp. 14–19) propose that there are six major sources of burnout: **workload**, when the work is too complex, too much, too urgent, or just too awful; **control** issues from being micromanaged or having ineffective leaders or teams; lack of **reward** in the form of compensation, recognition, or pleasure; an **absence of community** that provides social support; lack of **fairness**, with little justice and lots of arbitrary and secretive decision making and favoritism; and **discordant values** that indicate you and the organization are severely at odds regarding your belief in the validity and worth of the organization and the organization's belief about your validity and worth. The foregoing problems may vary in degree and kind, but the result is a continuous and grinding interface between the person and the work environment (Pines & Aronson, 1988, pp. 43–44; Riggar, 1985, p. xvi). From the worker's standpoint, no short- or long-term relief is forthcoming.

The body's nonspecific response to any demand is stress. Humans need some stress for optimal performance. However, there comes a point of maximal return for each person. That point is a function of genetic, biological, behavioral, and acquired physiological factors. Beyond that point, stress is harmful (Selye, 1974). Environmental events may either "cause" the activation of the stress response or, more often, set the stage for it through cognitive-affective processing (Everly, 1989, p. 45). The stress response itself involves enervation of neurological, neuroendocrine, and endocrine systems either singularly or in tandem with one another, which in turn activates various physiological mechanisms directed toward numerous target organs (p. 47). In Selye's (1956) **general adaptation syndrome (GAS)**, overstimulation and excessive wear of target organs lead to stress-related dysfunction and disease. If the stressor is persistent and there is a chronic drain on adaptive energy, eventual exhaustion of the target organ will occur. The end result physiologically may be as dramatic as a heart attack or as common as a headache. Indeed, where GAS is found burnout may not be far behind, and it has been linked to a wide range of both physical and mental illnesses (Maslach et al., 2001).

Stress occurs when there is a substantial imbalance (perceived or real) between environmental demands and the individual's response capability. Burnout occurs when the stress becomes unmediated and the person has no support systems or other buffers to ease the unrelenting pressure (Farber, 1983, p. 14). The outcome is a person affected in every dimension of life by unlimited combinations of symptoms. Such a description very adequately meets the crisis conditions of being in a state of disequilibrium and paralysis.

Cornerstones of Burnout

Let us now look at two human services professionals who are experientially and professionally different, but by almost any definition are in the process of burning out.

Mr. Templeton. Mr. Templeton has worked as a school counselor at Central Junior High School for 2 years. In that time he has instituted some sweeping changes in a guidance program that was, before he came, notorious for running attendance checks and not much more. Mr. Templeton's counseling approach changed all that. Formerly, the last place that students would have gone for help with personal problems would have been the counseling office. By getting out and explaining what his job was all about to students, faculty, parent groups, civic organizations, and anybody else who would listen, and indeed making good on his promises, Mr. Templeton has turned the guidance office into something akin to a land office during the California gold rush. His principal would now fight a circular saw to keep Mr. Templeton around.

What the principal does not know is that Mr. Templeton has fantasies about sending the entire ninth grade to an Outward Bound camp in the Sahara Desert. He has not had a new idea about how to improve the counseling program in 6 months and is wondering if maybe that stockbroker's job that he so capriciously turned down last year was not such a bad idea after all. As he considers all this, he wistfully looks at his wristwatch, then at the ninth grader sitting across from him, and wonders whether she is in his office because of grade problems or a problem at home. She has been talking for 30 minutes, and he cannot remember two sentences she has said.

Josh. Josh is a social worker at an outpatient clinic for a community mental health center. He has worked there for 5 years. His patient load resembles something on the order of bus traffic to Mecca. He has just received a memorandum from the director further increasing his caseload by 20%, along with a rather curt directive to move on some of those old cases and get them off the clinic rolls. Josh is sitting in his friendly local tavern quietly getting drunk and wondering how he is going to put 20 people out on the street with no support. He is also mulling over what response he will make to his wife, who just this morning asked for a separation. Among the complaints she voiced, his job was prominent: the lousy pay for somebody with a master's degree, the long hours with no compensatory time, the emergencies in the middle of the night, and particularly forgetting he is the father of their two children and a husband to her. Josh stares across the bar and orders another drink. While waiting for his order, he swallows an antacid tablet for the dull, burning pain slowly working its way outward from the pit of his stomach.

What do these two human services professionals have in common? They are alike in that they are empathic, sensitive, humane, idealistic, and people oriented and have been highly committed and dedicated to their profession. However, like most other human services workers prone to burnout, they also tend to be overly anxious, obsessional, enthusiastic, a bit neurotic, extraverted, conscientious, and susceptible to identifying with their clients (Farber, 1983, p. 4; Piedmont, 1993). For both of them, one or more of the following foundation blocks of burnout have been laid (Borritz et al., 2005; Farber, 1983, p. 6; Hamois, 2015; Lee & Ashforth, 1993; Olivares-Faundez et al., 2014; Powell, 1994; Rupert, 2015).

1. *Role ambiguity.* They lack clarity concerning rights, responsibilities, methods, goals, status, and accountability to themselves or their institutions.
2. *Role conflict.* Demands placed on them are incompatible, inappropriate, and inconsistent with values and ethics.
3. *Role overload.* The quantity and quality of demands placed on them have become too great.
4. *Inconsequentiality.* They have a feeling that no matter how hard they work, the outcome means little in terms of recognition, accomplishment, appreciation, or success.
5. *Isolation.* They have little social support either in the institution or outside of it.
6. *Autonomy.* Their ability to make decisions as to what they will do and how they will deal with their clients is co-opted by the bureaucracy of their place of employment.

These foundation stones are not thrown down haphazardly. They are built up slowly but surely over time through a variety of dynamics.

Research on Burnout Dynamics

The following points have been supported to varying degrees by research on burnout (Baird & Jenkins, 2003; Bianchi et al., 2014; Borritz et al., 2005; Carroll & White, 1982; Decker, Bailey, & Westergaard, 2002; Golembiewski & Munzenrider, 1993; Golembiewski, Munzenrider, & Stevenson, 1986; Golembiewski et al., 1992; Grossi et al., 2005; Grouse, 1984; Hoeksma et al., 1993; Koeske, Kirk, & Koeske, 1993; Lee & Ashforth, 1993; Linley, Joseph, & Loumidis, 2005; Lyndall & Bicknell, 2001; Oerlamans & Bakker, 2014; Maslach, 1982a; Mather et al., 2014; Melamed et al., 2006; Piedmont, 1993; Pines & Aronson, 1988; Powell, 1994; Rupert et al., 2015; Salston & Figley, 2003; Toker et al., 2005).

1. All stressors are cumulative and can help lead to burnout.

2. Burnout is psychobiological.
3. Environmental factors other than work can be contributors.
4. A lack of effective interpersonal relationships contributes to burnout.
5. Signs of burnout will occur, but recognition of them depends on the observer's astuteness.
6. Symptoms sometimes appear quickly, but most usually occur over time.
7. Burnout is process oriented rather than event oriented.
8. Burnout varies in severity from mild energy loss to death.
9. Burnout also varies in duration.
10. Burnout and resulting crisis can occur more than once.
11. Awareness varies from complete denial to full consciousness of the problem.
12. Burnout is infectious in that it puts additional stress on other workers.
13. Burnout is greatest for beginning and long-term workers and least for midduration workers.
14. Those who are single experience the most burnout, whereas those with families experience the least. However, stressors that enter family life can exacerbate burnout.
15. Restorative and preventive measures have to be individually tailored because of the idiosyncratic nature of burnout.
16. Burnout has progressive phases that can be identified by the varying degrees of depersonalization, personal accomplishment (or lack thereof), and emotional exhaustion the individual exhibits.
17. Burnout is not a disease, and the medical model is not an appropriate analytical model.
18. Burnout should not be confused with malingering.
19. Progressive deterioration in physical and mental health occurs as burnout increases.
20. Job autonomy, sense of coherence, and social support buffers are critical to preventing, containing, and reducing burnout.
21. Making time for leisure and using it wisely are as important as any job variable.
22. Burnout can lead to personal and professional growth as well as to despair and trauma.
23. More education, training specific to trauma work, supervision, and institutional support are all related to lower burnout rates.
24. A personal history of trauma is a contributing factor.

Myths That Engender Burnout

Candidates for burnout believe a number of myths about themselves and how they must operate in their environment (Everly, 1989; Friedman & Rosenman, 1974; Kesler, 1990; Maslach, 1982a; Pines & Aronson, 1988; Rodesch, 1994). They tend to distort the reality of the situation in typical type A personality patterns (Friedman & Rosenman, 1974), generating a variety of irrational statements about themselves and their work. These statements are modeled after Albert Ellis's (Patterson, 1980, pp. 68–70) unhealthy thoughts people say to themselves about their predicaments.

1. "My job is my life." This means long hours, no leisure time, and difficulty delegating authority. Anxiety, defensiveness, anger, and frustration are the result when things do not go perfectly.
2. "I must be totally competent, knowledgeable, and able to help everyone." Unrealistic expectations of performance, a need to prove oneself, lack of confidence, and overriding guilt occur when one is not perfect.
3. "To accomplish my job and maintain my own sense of self-worth, I must be liked and approved of by everyone with whom I work." Such workers cannot assert themselves, set limits, say no, disagree with others, or give negative feedback. Therefore, they get manipulated by others in the work setting—including by clients. Self-doubt, passive hostility, insecurity, and subsequent depression are the reward.
4. "Other people are hardheaded and difficult to deal with, do not understand the real value of my work, and should be more supportive." Stereotyping and generalizing about specific problems and people occur, and lack of creativity, wasted energy, and decreased motivation result. The person has a defeatist attitude and a passive acceptance of the status quo.
5. "Any negative feedback indicates there is something wrong with what I do." The person cannot evaluate his or her work realistically and make constructive changes. There is a great deal of anger with critics, which may manifest itself in either passive or aggressive hostility, depending on the person toward whom the anger is directed. Frustration and immobilization are the outcomes.
6. "Because of past blunders and failures by others, things will not work the way they must." Old programs are not carried to fruition, nor are new ones

created. Stagnation and decay in the work setting are the result.
7. "Things have to work out the way I want." The person's behavior is thus characterized by working extra hours and checking up on staff members' work, an inability to compromise or delegate, over attention to detail, repetition of tasks, impatience with others, and an authoritarian style.
8. "I must be omniscient and infallible." The person can never be wrong. The very act of doing therapy with humans in all their infinite ways of behaving means fallibility for the worker, particularly when the client is in crisis.

These dynamics lead to a wide array of symptoms.

Symptoms of Burnout

Burnout is a multidimensional phenomenon, consisting of behavioral, physical, interpersonal, and attitudinal components. Table 16.1 is a ready reference. While the list is lengthy, it is undoubtedly not all-encompassing. Certainly not all human services workers in crisis manifest all the symptoms listed. Yet for the watchful observer, many will become noticeable, particularly if one looks back in time and notes any pronounced changes in the worker.

Levels of Burnout

Burnout can be categorized as occurring at one of three levels: *trait*, *state*, and *activity* (Forney, Wallace-Schutzman, & Wiggers, 1982). At a trait level, it is all-pervasive, encompassing every facet of the worker's life. The worker is completely nonfunctional in regard to person, place, and time. The trait level of burnout is extremely serious and calls for immediate intervention in the worker's life. At a state level, burnout may be periodic or situational. A classic example is what occurs during the period of full moon at a crisis line center. At such times it seems as if every crisis-prone person in town takes a signal from a lunar clock to go berserk. Although problematic, such crisis situations are relieved when the moon wanes, and the crisis line worker returns to some semblance of normalcy. However, over the long term, such state events contribute mightily to anticipatory anxiety, which if not dealt with can precipitate total burnout.

Finally, burnout may be activity based. Any activity that is performed over and over at an intense level, as in encounter group counseling of substance abusers or serving as a chaplain to the grief stricken in a trauma center, will invariably wear the armor off the most

TABLE 16.1 Symptoms of Burnout

Behavioral	Physical	Interpersonal	Attitudinal
Reduced quantity or efficiency of work	Chronic fatigue and exhaustion	Withdrawal from family	Depression
Use and abuse of alcohol and illicit drugs	Lower resistance	Compulsion to do all and be all at home	Feeling of emptiness, meaninglessness
Increase in absenteeism	Maladies occurring at organ weak points: ulcers, migraines, gastrointestinal upset, facial tics, etc.	No mature interactions—keeping hidden agendas	Ranging from omnipotence to incompetence
Increase in risk taking	Colds and viral infections	Keeping everyone subservient	Cynicism
Increase in medication	Poor coordination	Feeling drawn to people who are less secure	Paranoia
Clock watching	Insomnia, nightmares, and excessive sleeping	Reduction of significant others to status of clients	Compulsiveness and obsessiveness
Complaining	Muscular tension	Breaking up of long-lasting relationships	Callousness
Changing or quitting the job	Addiction to alcohol and/or drugs	Becoming therapeutically minded and overreacting to comments of friends	Guilt
Inability to cope with minor problems	Increased use of tobacco and caffeine	No separation of professional and social life	Boredom
Lack of creativity	Over- or undereating	Allowing clients to abuse privacy of home by calls or visits at any time	Helplessness and/or hopelessness Suicidal/homicidal ideation
Loss of enjoyment	Hyperactivity	No opportunity for or enjoyment in just being oneself	Terrifying and paralyzing feelings and thoughts
Loss of control	Sudden weight gain or loss	Loneliness, trust issues	Stereotyping
Tardiness	Flare-ups in preexisting medical conditions: high blood pressure, ulcers, asthma, diabetes, etc.	Loss of authenticity	Depersonalizing
Dread of work	Injury from high-risk behavior	Loss of ability to relate to friends, family, or clients	Pessimism
Vacillation between extremes of overinvolvement and detachment	Missed menstrual cycle	Avoidance of close interpersonal contact	Air of righteousness
Mechanistic responding	Increased premenstrual tension	Switch from open and accepting to closed and denying	Grandiosity
Accident proneness	Injury from accident	Inability to cope with minor interpersonal problems	Sick humor, particularly aimed at clients
Change in or cessation of religious affiliation	Rapid heartbeat	Isolation from or overbonding with staff	Distrust of management, supervisors, and peers
Errors in setting therapeutic boundaries	Breathing difficulties	Increased expression of anger and mistrust	Hypercritical attitude toward institution and coworkers
Errors in judgment and strategy in and outside therapy	Anxiety and panic attacks	Increased vigilance and safety issues for self and loved ones	

TABLE 16.1	*(continued)*		
Behavioral	**Physical**	**Interpersonal**	**Attitudinal**
PTSD-like symptoms of intrusive thoughts, numbing of affect, sleep disturbance, nightmares, and hypervigilance	Dizziness	Overprotection as a parent	Entrapment in job and relations
Regression	Impaired immune system	Decreased interest in intimacy or sex	Free-floating feelings of inadequacy, inferiority, incompetence, and survivor guilt
Impatient and irritable			Self-criticism and perfectionism
Withdrawn			Rapid mood swings
Losing things			Loss of faith, meaning, purpose
Suicide attempts			Change in religious beliefs
Homicide attempts			Sense of grounding, inner balance lost
			Increased sense of vulnerability to world at large

emotionally bulletproof crisis worker. A simple way of decreasing chances of burnout when the stressor is activity based is to change the routine. However, such change is not always easily accomplished or even recognized as needed.

Stages of Burnout

Another way of characterizing the road to burnout is by stages. Edelwich and Brodsky (1982, pp. 135–136) delineated four stages through which the typical candidate for burnout goes.

Stage 1: Enthusiasm. The worker enters the job with high hopes and unrealistic expectations. If such idealism is not tempered by orientation and training programs that define what the worker can reasonably expect to accomplish, such a rose-colored view of human services work will inevitably lead to the stage of stagnation.

Stage 2: Stagnation. Stagnation occurs when the worker starts to feel that personal, financial, and career needs are not being met. Awareness may come from seeing people perceived as less able moving up the career ladder faster, pressures from home to meet increased financial obligations, and lack of personal intrinsic reinforcement for doing the job well. Astute management policy will head off stagnation by providing a variety of incentives that clearly say to the worker, "You're doing a good job here, and we appreciate it." If intrinsic and extrinsic reinforcement does not occur, the worker will move into the next stage, frustration.

Stage 3: Frustration. Frustration clearly indicates that the worker is in trouble. The worker starts questioning the effectiveness, value, and impact of his or her efforts in the face of ever-mounting obstacles. Because the effects of burnout are highly contagious in the organizational setting, one person's frustration is likely to have a domino effect on others. One appropriate way of meeting frustration is to confront the problem head on by arranging workshops or support groups to increase awareness of the burnout syndrome, and generate problem solving as a group to bring about changes within both the institution and the individual. Catching the problem at this stage may well lead back to a more tempered stage of enthusiasm. If the problem is not resolved, then the final stage, apathy, is reached.

Stage 4: Apathy. Apathy is burnout. It is a chronic indifference to the situation and defies most efforts at intervention. Apathy is truly a crisis stage: The person is in a state of disequilibrium and immobility. Further compounding this stage are denial and little objective understanding of what is occurring. At this point psychotherapy is almost mandatory for reversal to take place.

Worker–Client Relationships

As crisis intervention has spread to more and more areas of psychological trauma, interest in what happens to the workers who deal with these clients has led to the concept of **secondary traumatic stress disorder (STSD)**. STSD is a consequence for health care professionals who are frequently exposed to the stress and trauma of others in the course of treating them (Hensel et al., 2015) or what McCann and Pearlman (1990) call **vicarious traumatization (VT)**. **Compassion fatigue (CF)** is manifested in the continuous negative aspects of care provision for tough cases and customers in a demanding work environment that generally revolve around some type of trauma (Stamm, 2010). These terms are often used interchangeably to describe what is going on when the crisis worker–client relationship becomes pathological. These are the very real, concrete negative effects that occur when human services workers have prolonged exposure to traumatized clients who are in crisis.

Research does indicate that health services workers experience more negative effects from crisis work than other types of health services workers (Arvay & Uhlemann, 1996; Blanchard & Jones, 1997; Charney & Pearlman, 1998; Johnson & Hunter, 1997; Smart et al., 2014). The potential for STSD is even more pronounced in crisis workers who work with long-term disasters. Wee and Myers (2002) conducted a study of mental health workers who did long-term follow-up in the Murrah Federal Building bombing in Oklahoma City, and found that about half of the respondents reported being more stressed than doing normal mental health work and being at high risk for both compassion fatigue and burnout. Why is this so?

It is so because trauma work and crisis intervention are so potentially addictive and at the same time so potentially destructive! Much like the "rush" that police officers, paramedics, and other emergency workers experience from being in the middle of traumatic events, crisis workers feel the "adrenaline high" of successful crisis intervention, and this can become highly addictive. As an example, psychologists who worked the aftermath of 9/11 in New York City reported more positive than negative feelings regarding their work (Eidelson, D'Alessio, & Eidelson, 2003). Yet the constant exposure to the "highs" that come with dealing with traumatic events also means that the crisis worker is exposed to a constant barrage of some of the most graphic and horrible physical and psychological ramifications that nature or humankind can visit on people. Two psychological concepts are hallmarks of dealing with crisis clients and, if not understood and dealt with, have the potential to infect the crisis worker and lead to burnout. Those two concepts are

countertransference and secondary traumatic stress or vicarious traumatization/compassion fatigue.

Countertransference

Whenever therapy becomes intense, as in crisis work, the potential for countertransference rises dramatically. **Countertransference** is the attributing to the client, by the crisis worker, of traits and behaviors of past and present significant others or events in the crisis worker's own life. Countertransference responses may be positive or negative, spoken or unspoken, conscious or unconscious. They may include physical, psychological, social, gender, racial, moral, spiritual, cultural, or ecological factors that have impacted the worker through past experiences and are manifested in the "here and now" of therapy by the client. At times, emotional aspects of the client may agitate feelings, thoughts, and behaviors that are deeply buried within the worker's own personality.

When confronted with their own shortcomings, fears, faults, prejudices, and stereotypes as mirrored by the client, human services workers may begin behaving in inappropriate ways. Workers may act in ways designed to meet their own needs and not the clients'. The result is that clients are made to fit neatly into the workers' preconceived patterns for the way things "ought to be," and not necessarily in reference to the client but how they "ought to be" for the crisis worker (Freudenberger, 1977).

The general axiom of psychoanalytic therapy is that countertransference needs to be guarded against, and the therapist's refusal to recognize it and deal with it can, at the least, inhibit the therapist's effectiveness, and at the most, be destructive to the relationship (Dahlenberg, 2000, pp. 1–6). If the phenomenon of countertransference is not recognized and dealt with in positive ways, the human services worker ends up feeling guilty about having negative feelings toward the client and is not even sure why those feelings are occurring. Such feelings are antithetical to what the worker has been taught and believes and can significantly compound the occupational stresses that lead to burnout.

However, Pearlman and Saakvitne (1995a, pp. 22–24) propose that if crisis workers are to deal successfully and understand the pain of their clients in deeply empathic ways, then countertransference is inevitable and necessary. Particularly emotion-laden issues such as physical and sexual abuse of children, terminal illnesses, and chronic suicidal ideation are prime examples of content that may be exceedingly stressful to the worker because of strong feelings and experiences the worker may have about the problem (Dahlenberg, 2000; Fox & Cooper, 1998; Pearlman & Saakvitne, 1995a). The pluses and minuses of countertransference as it applies to trauma appear to balance precariously on a very thin psychological high wire. Main's (2008) study of sexual offender treatment providers found that while they manifested disruptions in cognitions, emotions, and behaviors consistent with those that characterize compassion fatigue and vicarious traumatization, they also possessed many of the components for **compassion satisfaction** (the positive feelings and intrinsic rewards one feels from helping others who have experienced a traumatic event) (Stamm, 2010) and reported that their child sexual abuse histories were an advantage in the treatment of sex offenders. As such, one of the critical components to handling countertransference effectively would appear to be close and competent supervision.

Secondary Traumatic Stress/Vicarious Traumatization/Compassion Fatigue

STS/VT and CF are different from the phenomenon of countertransference. As these terms have evolved, they have taken on somewhat different, more discrete meanings. **Secondary traumatic stress/vicarious traumatization** is the transformation that occurs when an individual begins to change in a manner that mimics a client's trauma-related symptoms. It is a constructivist model in which the individual's experience and worldview are changed as a direct result of secondary exposure to trauma through crisis work (Pearlman & Mac Ian, 1995). As an example, in a study conducted by Alexander and associates (1989), researchers who were deeply involved in reading and reviewing rape cases and not actually talking to the victims started to manifest victim pathology. The bottom line is that all of these terms apply to a worker who has been affected by long-term, intense involvement of some type with very traumatized clients.

STS/VT and CF occur as a result of an accumulation of experiences across therapies and clients and are felt far beyond the transference–countertransference issues of a specific client–therapist relationship. Whereas countertransference is temporary, STS/VT and CF have the potential to permanently change the psychological constructs of workers who engage in intense and long-term trauma and are an inevitable occupational hazard of trauma work (Saakvitne & Pearlman, 1996, p. 31). In summary, a worker who

has a full-blown case of STS/VT doesn't look and act very much different than the PTSD clients they are treating.

The end result of VT and CF is their generalizing effects on countertransference issues. As VT is multiplied and generalized over clients, countertransference reactions become stronger through the human services worker acting them out against the client or submerging them even deeper from awareness (Saakvitne & Pearlman, 1996, p. 48). For human services workers in general, and crisis workers in particular, VT/STS and CF are major mediating factors that lead to burnout. In fact, Cieslak and associates (2014) conducted a meta-analysis that examined the relationship between STS/VT and burnout and found a substantial overlap between the two particularly if measured in the framework of compassion fatigue.

Worker Vulnerability. Maslach (1982b, pp. 36–37) states that the only human services workers who burn out are the ones who are on fire. For such workers, Saakvitne and Pearlman (1996, pp. 26, 49) and Figley (1995) believe that the deep empathy needed to deal with the heart-wrenching situations that often accompany crises makes workers vulnerable to intense and overwhelming feelings and profound disruptions in their beliefs, and assaults the very core of their hope and idealism. Over time, such assaults lead to compassion fatigue (Figley, 1995), wherein the crisis workers' energy is literally wrung out by the incidence and amplitude of dealing with the horrific problems that trauma clients face.

Between a very real dedicatory ethic and at times an insatiable need to assist everyone with any type of problem, the idealistic human services worker sees his or her job as a calling. In an imperfect world, such an idealistic outlook can lead to over involvement and identification with the client—often to the worker's detriment (Koeske & Kelly, 1995). As the human services worker becomes more deeply enmeshed in the helping relationship, the worker's strong need to be accepted and liked makes it harder and harder to say no to the client's demands. At this point, the worker has started to take on responsibility for the client.

The worker's over involvement with the client may be manifested in a variety of ways. Some of the many indicators that the worker is not paying attention to his or her own needs, or frankly to the client's, include extending the session beyond its usual time limit, taking and responding to phone calls at home at all hours of the night, experiencing hurt feelings over client failures, attempting dramatic cures on impossible cases, becoming panic stricken when well-laid plans go awry, refusing to withdraw from the case when it is clearly beyond the worker's purview, becoming angry, sarcastic, or bored with clients, changing the subject and avoiding the topic, providing pat answers, discounting the client's problems and minimizing distress, not believing clients, fearing what the client will say, silencing client trauma talk, wishing or suggesting the client would "just get over it," feeling numb or avoidant, not being able to pay attention, being constantly reminded of one's own personal trauma events, hoping the client won't show up, becoming frustrated over lack of progress, and losing one's sense of humor over the human dilemma (Baranowsky, 2002; Dahlenberg, 2000; Van Auken, 1979). The foregoing are all indicators that unresolved countertransference and vicarious trauma/compassion fatigue issues are flourishing.

Under these circumstances, the worker comes to see the helping relationship as a chore, and the client may regress and act out as a way of announcing the client's awareness of the worker's apathetic attitude. As this psychological vortex continues to swirl and the worker becomes even more overwrought and discouraged, the client is likely to terminate the therapeutic relationship (Dahlenberg, 2000; Watkins, 1983). Such negative reinforcement does little to mollify the worker's already bruised ego and may lead to a further downward spiral into burnout. Whether exposure to these occupational hazards has negative or positive outcomes depends a great deal on how both the individual worker and the human services institution deal with them in proactive ways (Dahlenberg, 2000; Deiter & Pearlman, 1998; Figley, 1995; Pearlman & Saakvitne, 1995a; Saakvitne & Pearlman, 1996).

Compassion Satisfaction

Stamm (2005) describes compassion satisfac- **LO7** tion as simply the pleasure you derive from being able to do your work well. The reason compassion satisfaction as a construct has gained notoriety is that it appears to be an extremely effective buffer against burnout. Human services workers who are satisfied with the effect they have on clients consistently show low levels of vicarious traumatization and burnout (Conrad & Keller-Guenther, 2006; Eastwood, 2007; Killian, 2008; LaFauci Schutt, 2009; Lawson & Myers, 2011; Ling et al., 2014; Ringenbach, 2009; Sullivan, 2004). Therefore, it would seem reasonable that

organizations do everything in their power to tell their workers that they are doing a good job and further to get direct feedback from clients that they are satisfied with the care they have been given and the concern they have been shown by the crisis worker.

The Culpability of Organizations

Much of the responsibility for burnout rests **LO8** with the employing agency and its inability to either recognize or do anything about organizational problems that lead to burnout (de Figueiredo et al., 2014; Everly, 1989, pp. 295–297; Kulkami et al., 2013; Pines & Aronson, 1988, pp. 97–111; Shinn & Mørch, 1983, p. 238). Savicki and Cooley (1987) compared degree of burnout with work environment and found that those workers who scored highest on burnout indexes felt that they had little impact on procedural and policy issues, lacked autonomy within the guidelines of the job structure, were unclear about agency objectives, had a high intensity of work assignments over extended periods of time, were highly restricted in how they could deal with clients, and felt generally unappreciated by their coworkers or supervisors. One example is handling client verbal and physical aggression as a major mediating factor in burnout (Gascon et al., 2013; Hensel et al., 2012; Yung, 2013; Ho et al., 2013). Although personal safety is a major concern, when workers feel their safety concerns are not responded to by management then threat level goes up (Evans & Petter, 2012) along with the potential for burnout with it.

Above all, the organization's inability to clearly define job roles and functions causes role conflict and role ambiguity, and these are two of the best predictors of the workplace's contribution to burnout (Barber & Iwai, 1996). These findings should not be construed as representing "gripes" of the respondents. Numerous other studies (Burke & Greenglass, 1995; de Figueiredo et al., 2014; Duquette et al., 1994; Jayaratne, Vinokur-Kaplan, & Chess, 1995; Lee & Ashforth, 1993) have substantiated findings that agencies that do not take pains to communicate clearly with and support their staff have high burnout rates.

One of the critical support mechanisms for crisis workers is easy access to consultation, support, and supervision (de Figueiredo et al., 2014; Handran, 2014; Ling et al., 2014; Salloum et al., 2015). Crisis intervention should never be done in isolation, and the case example presented in this chapter is an excellent example of why that is so. Yet, as Pearlman and Saakvitne (1995a, p. 359) report, unsupervised trauma therapy seems all too common. Pearlman and Mac Ian (1995) found that less than two-thirds of trauma therapists they interviewed reported getting any kind of supervision, although more than 80% of those who did receive supervision and consultation found it helpful.

In contrast, those agencies that do allow input into the mission of the organization, are flexible in providing instrumental and emotional support to workers, generate support groups, provide consultation, have job clarity, promote managers with social leadership styles, retain realistic expectations for the progress of their clients, and furnish supervision to help workers solve problems associated with the high stress of their jobs report workers with lower indexes of burnout (Everly, 1989, pp. 299–309; Kahn, 2005; Melchior et al., 1997; Pines & Aronson, 1988, pp. 107–111; Savicki & Cooley, 1987).

Self-Recognition of Burnout

Whatever the degree of burnout, human services workers and their organizations have a notorious blind spot. What they can detect in others and change by therapeutic intervention, they are generally unaware of in themselves. Furthermore, they have extreme difficulty maintaining both the personal and professional objectivity to self-diagnose burnout or muster the discipline and devote the energy to integrate effective intervention strategies into their own lives (Spicuzza & Devoe, 1982).

When they finally are confronted with the fact that something is terribly wrong in their professional lives, their initial maladaptive response is likely to be "What's wrong with me?" rather than "What can I do to change the situation?" Their typical operating mode is not to change the situation but rather to increase the amount of effort and consequently increase the original problem (Pines & Aronson, 1988, pp. 5–9).

Before delving into intervention, your authors want to be very clear that they agree with Watkins (1983) that no one—and we would go a step further and state that *absolutely* no one—who practices in the human services professions is immune to burnout. Furthermore, it has been our experience that human services workers who, like some of you who are reading this passage, think "It'll never happen to me" are invariably the kinds of fellow professionals we end up treating; or, in the absence of treatment, become those who can no longer stand to ply the trade and quit; or, at the extreme, become substance abusers or suicidal or homicidal. In these circumstances, the outcomes range from bad to worse: bad for the profession and worse for you, the professional.

Intervention Strategies

While there is a great deal of literature on LO9 self-care and balancing other life experiences against work as a buffer against burnout (Ling et al., 2014; Oerlemans & Bakker, 2014), there have been few protocol and hard data studies to identify specific treatments that work with those who are experiencing STS and are burned out (Bercier & Maynard, 2015).

Practitioners on the road to burnout typically are perfectionistic workaholics (Falco et al., 2014) who push relentlessly toward emotional exhaustion, becoming more inefficient and unhappy as they do so. Note the "aholic" component because our experience is that burning up professionals are much the same as alcoholics in their vehement denial that things are going badly awry until a severe crisis of their own is created such that it finally gets their attention. Thus, when we consider individual crisis intervention with an impaired fellow professional, emphasis in applying the crisis task model in this book will usually focus on the directive end of the continuum because of the depth of the crisis and an "I know more than you do, and I'm not nuts" fellow worker. The crisis interventionist who helps a burned-out human services worker typically must proceed in a very directive manner while confronting the client's irrational beliefs, proposing definite alternatives, and getting the client to commit to specific action steps that will get the person out of the state of immobility. Put in simple terms, fellow human services workers are some of the most stubborn and denial-prone clients there are when they have reached the later stages of burnout.

Intervention for the human services worker suffering from burnout may best be considered in three distinct dimensions: intervention through training, intervention with the organization, and intervention with the individual. Triage assessment of the level of burnout is important in determining the type of intervention to be used. At a trait level, individual therapeutic intervention will clearly be warranted. At a state or activity level, training or organizational intervention may be sufficient. When the organization itself becomes a client, triage assessment would clearly include the administering of both burnout and work-setting instruments to all members of the organization and following up that administration with individual interviews.

Assessment

Three types of instruments are important in **LO10** determining burnout and compassion fatigue.

Burnout. The first type has to do with determining the degree of burnout in the individual. The most widely used instrument is the Maslach Burnout Inventory–Human Services Survey (MBI-HSS; Maslach & Jackson, 1981a), which is a valid cross-occupational and cross-cultural (Bakker, Demerouti, & Schaufeli, 2002; Gorter et al., 1999) instrument that measures three symptom patterns associated with burnout. The Emotional Exhaustion scale assesses feelings of being emotionally worn out by work. The Personal Accomplishment scale measures feelings of competence and achievement with work. The Depersonalization scale measures unfeeling and impersonal responses toward clients. The scales can also be combined to produce a total frequency and intensity score for burnout. A variation of the scale for professional burnout in general (MBI-GS; Maslach, Jackson, & Leiter, 1996) measures exhaustion, cynicism, and reduced personal efficiency, three components that parallel the original MBI-HSS. There is also a Maslach Burnout Inventory for educators (MBI-ES; Maslach, Jackson, & Leiter, 1996), which uses the foregoing components to measure degree of burnout in educators.

Golembiewski, Munzenrider, and Stevenson (1986) used the Maslach Burnout Inventory's three domains to develop a progressive phase model of burnout. In their model, depersonalization is seen as the least potent and initial burnout phase. It must occur prior to any substantial reduction in feelings of personal accomplishment, which they see as a secondary response and more potent level of burnout. Emotional exhaustion, the third and most potent indicator of burnout (Lee & Ashforth, 1996; Wright & Bonett, 1997), would follow heightening of the prior two stages.

Lee and associates (2007) have developed the Counselor Burnout Inventory. This instrument measures five burnout dimensions: Exhaustion, Incompetence, Negative Work Environment, Devaluing Client, and Deterioration of Personal Life. This instrument attempts to integrate both personal and organizational components of potential burnout factors and

determine how much workplace factors contribute to overall burnout. They have attempted to determine what particular patterns of these scales best classify levels of burnout and pattern clusters (Lee et al., 2010). Their research, which sampled counselors who worked in a variety of settings, identified three sets of counselor profiles. A cluster they called "Well-Adjusted Counselors" (WACs) had low scores and flat profiles across all the scales. WACs also reported high job satisfaction, good self-esteem, and decent pay. Their MBI scores correlated with their CBI profiles, with low scores on Emotional Exhaustion and Depersonalization and high scores on Personal Accomplishment.

Lee and his associates (2010) found a second cluster they called "Disconnected Counselors" (DCs), who had medium-level scores on Exhaustion, Negative Work Environment, and Deterioration in Personal Life with high Incompetence and Devaluing Client scores. DCs' scores on the MBI paralleled their CBI scores, with a very high Depersonalization score, low Personal Accomplishment, and midrange Emotional Exhaustion scores. They reported low job satisfaction, poor self-esteem, and low pay.

A third cluster, which the researcher named "Persevering Counselors" (PCs), was characterized by high Exhaustion, Negative Work Environment, and Deterioration in Personal Life, but low scores on the Incompetence and Devaluing Client scales. Of the three groups, the PCs scored far higher on the MBI Emotional Exhaustion scale, in the midrange on Depersonalization, and high on sense of Personal Accomplishment. They reported the most counseling experience, highest positive self-esteem, and highest pay of the three groups, even though they reported the most dissatisfaction with their jobs. The PC cluster is interesting in that they are still performing well, but all the indicators are there for burnout. As such, it would appear that this instrument could identify not only workers who were functioning well as opposed to those who were burning or burned out, but those who were moving in that direction.

Compassion Fatigue and Compassion Satisfaction. Newer tests that specifically target different facets of secondary stress include the Compassion Fatigue Self-Test (Figley, 1995). From Wee and Myers's (2003) preliminary work with this test, it appears that satisfaction with doing crisis intervention work is indeed a counterbalance to compassion fatigue. What they found was that although approximately half the workers sampled had high compassion fatigue scores, almost 90% had high satisfaction scores and low burnout scores. The belief is that compassion satisfaction can act as a protective buffer against compassion fatigue and burnout (Collins & Long, 2003).

The Professional Quality of Life Scale (ProQOL; Stamm, 2002, 2005, 2010) measures compassion satisfaction, compassion fatigue, and burnout. It is a test for workers in the human services field but is particularly designed for first responders such as police, EMTs, firefighters, and ER personnel. The Compassion Satisfaction and Fatigue Test is of particular interest because it factors in the worker's satisfaction and therapeutic fatigue with clients. Certainly not all crisis workers manifest STSD; many workers are resilient, hardy, and continuously involved in crisis work over long terms with no ill effects. Stamm (2002) hypothesizes that it is because their satisfaction with doing the job counterweights and compensates for the heavy fatigue factors they experience. Therefore, this test gives scores for compassion satisfaction (CS), compassion fatigue (CF), and burnout (BO). Research indicates that indeed compassion satisfaction is an ameliorating factor in both compassion fatigue and burnout.

Work Environment. The third type of instrument measures the work setting. Typical of this type of assessment device is the Work Environment Scale (Moos, 1981), which measures 10 different dimensions of an organizational component named "social climate." These dimensions are job commitment, support from coworkers, management support, independence in decision making, efficient and planful approaches to tasks, performance pressure, role clarity, degree of control by management, variety and change in job, and physical comfort. Taken together, these various instruments provide a way of examining the degree of burnout in relation to environmental factors within the organization, yield a fairly comprehensive picture of how burned out the worker is, and indicate the degree of intervention necessary (Savicki & Cooley, 1987).

Intervention Through Training

Early in a human services worker's training, and on an ongoing basis when in practice, emphasis needs to be placed on correcting worker attitudes that lead to over involvement (Koeske & Kelly, 1995). Although Saakvitne and Pearlman (1996, pp. 25–26) argue that the deep empathy needed for trauma work inevitably

begets countertransference and the possibility of vicarious traumatization, at least a part of training should focus on increasing therapeutic detachment and moderating idealism (Warnath & Shelton, 1976). A delicate balance exists between providing empathy and manifesting sympathy for a client. To that end, trauma-informed worker development training has been found to be a strong predictor against burnout (Handran, 2014; Salloum et al., 2015).

Beginning human services practitioners need to have their rose-colored glasses gently removed, so they can see that their good intentions are doing neither themselves nor their clients much good (Pines & Aronson, 1988, p. 194). Most particularly, students need to examine their limited insight into their own unresolved issues and conflicts and how those interact with those of their clients, particularly when they are dealing with the often horrific material that is a hallmark of crisis intervention and trauma work (Dahlenberg, 2000; Pearlman & Saakvitne, 1995a, pp. 359–380; Watkins, 1983).

Not all students in the human services field are psychologically equipped to go into crisis work. Although this work is absolutely some of the most gratifying and reinforcing there is in the human services field, it is also some of the most gut-wrenching and heartbreaking. Students who are not exposed to realistic field experiences and good supervision may go blindly into one of the most stressful occupational fields known.

Intervention with the Organization

Much of the literature shows burnout to be situation based (Barber & Iwai, 1996; Kesler, 1990; Melchior et al., 1997; Schaufeli, 2006). Thus, the organization can also be considered as client. When an organization is in danger of burnout, all those who work in the organization should be involved in restructuring working conditions. Indeed, one of the major criticisms of burnout intervention has been the lack of change in the total system (Carroll & White, 1982, p. 56). What makes the major difference in obtaining peak performance from workers as opposed to having them burn out is whether the work environment is supportive or stressful (Pines & Aronson, 1988, p. 48).

Lack of positive reinforcement by the institution is not at all uncommon and fits neatly into an aversive management policy: "There is no such thing as burnout, only staff who don't work and have malicious motives toward the organization." As staff become increasingly burned out, they tend to fulfill management's negative predictions about them (Carroll & White, 1982, pp. 53–54). Although much is mentioned in the burnout literature about eradicating the negative aspects of the work environment, research indicates that a lack of positive features is significantly correlated with burnout independent of the presence of negative work features (Pines & Aronson, 1988, p. 48).

Human services organizations are notorious for having to live continuously on the edge of financial exigency. Lack of physical, human, and financial resources militates against comprehensive service provision and long-term planning. Organizations that face crises such as funding and human resource cutbacks often cope with problems by unwittingly adopting crisis characteristics and operating in a state of disequilibrium and immobility. Just letting the crisis "run its course" is no more appropriate for organizations than for individuals in crisis (Devine, 1984).

Therefore, from an ecological standpoint, the organization needs to move away from piecemeal interventions and apply techniques that have general inputs to the total organization rather than just inputs focused on individuals (Paine, 1982, p. 25). Ideally, interventions should be multifaceted and take into consideration both individual and environmental issues in a balanced and sensitive fashion (Carroll & White, 1982, p. 53). As a start, the administration can take the time to articulate clearly the organization's mission. Cherniss and Krantz (1983) found that organizations that have a clear ideology of purpose have reduced burnout in staff because they minimize ambiguity and doubt about what kind of action is to be taken. Time should be devoted both to establishing positive coworker and supervisory relationships and to reducing the rules, regulations, and paperwork that line staff face as they attempt to provide service to their clients (Savicki & Cooley, 1987). Improved job design, flexible hours, continuous supervision and training, intrinsic and extrinsic reinforcement, and emotional support are a few of many changes that will go a long way toward reducing burnout (Shinn & Mørch, 1983, p. 238).

Most attempts to deal with the organization by people who are burned out are typified by passively hostile actions that include physical, emotional, and mental withdrawal from problems the organization faces (Pines & Aronson, 1988, pp. 91–93). However, effective organizational change rarely is generated solely by the administration or by the individual. Both parties must decide that stopping burnout in its tracks is a good thing to do. To effect change in the organization, each individual must recognize that there is an institutional problem and be responsible for doing something about it. Likewise, administrators and boards of directors must be constantly vigilant and not deny these kinds of problems exist in the organization. Beginning to take responsibility for effecting change in a difficult situation is therapeutic in and of itself simply because it reduces the debilitating effects of the feeling of helplessness.

Yet workers who believe that everything about an organization is wrong and should be changed are the most likely to be burnouts, and administrators and boards of directors who believe the same about their workers are likely to go out of business. Some aspects of the bureaucracy cannot be changed short of destroying it. Thus workers need to develop the ability to distinguish between those aspects of the organization that can be changed and those that cannot (Pines & Aronson, 1988, p. 29).

Burnout-Proofing an Agency. Probably one of the very best organizations at preventing burnout your authors are aware of is the Exchange Club–Carl Perkins Center for the Prevention of Child Abuse in Jackson, Tennessee, which is used as an example of an exemplary child abuse treatment program in Chapter 9, Sexual Assault. One of the reasons for Carl Perkins Center's excellence is that its directors attempt, to the best of their ability, to burnout-proof the agency and the people in it. As described by East, James, and Keim (2001), they use several strategies to prevent burnout, STS/VT, and CF that are recommended by many of the researchers in this chapter. They are:

1. Nobody works more than a 40-hour week. Although emergencies may arise, workers will immediately take comp time off after the emergency has passed. Nobody works through lunch. Lunch is downtime and is expected to be taken.

2. The center takes quality time to promote inservice education as a way of continuously updating staff on the most effective and innovative practices available in the field. Quarterly inservices combine staff development, organizational issues, and fun events on skill building.

3. Supervision is continuous and supportive. The supervisor-to-worker ratio is 1:6. Each worker has a weekly session with a supervisor. The role of the supervisor is to listen, provide empathic support, consult, and plan cases.

4. The center expedites logistical problems. Work areas are clean, well lit, with cheerfully decorated offices and meeting rooms. Therapy rooms have brightly colored carpets and colorful children's murals on the walls. There is a well-stocked resource center with videos, instructional programs, reference books, and a complete, full-sized, Kids on the Block puppet set. There is adequate office and clerical help for all workers, so they do not drown in paperwork. Supplies are adequate and readily available.

5. Case staffings are carefully constructed in a comprehensive manner with team inputs. A clear treatment plan is laid out. There is little confusion about what mission goals are. There is a definite feeling of "we" between the administration and the staff. All supervisors have worked their way up through the organization, so they are acutely aware of the problems and issues staff face.

6. There is a clear delineation between work and home. Home and family are an overriding priority, and the directors of the center are adamant that families come first and work comes second.

7. Faith-based renewal and spiritual growth are encouraged. As one worker stated, "I can't do this alone. I have to give it over to God." This approach is encouraged without regard to denomination. Prayer is a powerful tool for these people, and they use it. There is a saying in war that there are few atheists in foxholes. A parallel can be made to the trauma and crisis business. Finding a sacrosanct spiritual center that one can believe in and retreat to is paramount, given the often heinous nature of crisis work (Collins, 2005; Kennedy, 2006). Because Jackson, Tennessee, is in the "Bible Belt" you may suppose that the staff's deep reliance on faith is a southern cultural artifact. You would be wrong. A good deal of research (Harrison & Westwood, 2009; Lawson & Myers, 2011; Reese, 2009; Simpson, 2006) demonstrates that spirituality is a key component in keeping the nastiness in this chapter out of your life. Short of proselytizing, your authors believe that anybody in this business needs to find some spiritual rock to anchor them. Go to a church, synagogue, mosque. Hug a cypress tree if you are green. Meditate, read theology, worship the Great Spirit, Buddha, God, but get a spiritual foundation in your life. You'll need it if you do this work.

8. Debriefing is used continuously. Whenever a tragedy occurs, such as a child's death or other traumatic event, workers are debriefed, and it is done as expeditiously as possible.

9. The center does not work on an assembly-line basis with repetitious, day-in-day-out work assignments that grind staff down. Workers are expected to schedule variety into their days.

10. The center provides technical support. All of the staff have offices, computers, cell phones, VCRs, and other equipment necessary for optimal performance.

11. The center is well maintained. It is a pleasant place to work with bright colors, nice furniture, individual spacious offices, and conference and therapy rooms that are well lit with good AV and IT facilities and equipment.

12. Workers use a team approach. No one is above getting her or his hands "dirty," and everyone pitches in when something needs to be done. It is not frowned upon to ask for assistance. The center does not deify go-it-alone, heroic martyrs.

13. Safety is the most important product of the center, for both its clients and staff. Clear-cut safety procedures are constantly taught and reinforced to ensure the workers' well-being both at the center and during home visits.

14. The workload is "doable." Over the years, the center has lightened workers' caseloads. As the total number of caseloads rises, more workers are hired. The center has been able to increase staff because its administration is very adept at convincing its constituency that it is doing a great job and should be given the financial support to continue to do so. The administration works very closely with its board and continuously educates it regarding the financial and staffing needs of the center.

15. The center does an excellent job of networking. It serves a large geographic area and therefore has established relationships with other social services agencies (such as schools, police departments, and state welfare agencies) in outlying counties. The center also goes out of its way to provide support for other agencies within its service area. This not only increases the center's credibility with the agencies and institutions, but it also allows for reciprocal perquisites: center employees can utilize office space and the support of staff in other agencies when the employees are far away from their home office.

16. The administration is very thorough in its hiring selection. Candidates are carefully screened to determine how well they will fit into the overall scheme of things.

17. Staff are positively reinforced both intrinsically and extrinsically on a consistent basis. Workers are told they are doing a good job in specific behavioral terms, and they are told often. After a particularly horrific incident in which three sexually abused children all died in a house fire at a foster home, the associate director went to the field office and picked up the workers who had been engaged nonstop in dealing with this tragedy. She piled them into her van and, without a word, took them to a local spa, where they spent the day getting makeovers, massages, aromatherapy, yoga lessons, and a nice lunch. While a day trip to a spa can in no way assuage the grief and stress these workers felt, it does say very clearly, "We care about you!" and that message comes across loud and clear to all of the staff.

The Carl Perkins Center sees its workers as its most important asset and understands the perils of the kind of work it does. The outcomes are proof positive that a proactive program to prevent burnout works. The attrition rate is extremely low. Because this is a fairly young and rapidly expanding agency, many of the workers are young. Research indicates (Meyers & Cornille, 2002) that the demographics and job role of this group would cause them to be at high risk for burnout or STSD. They are not!

The following tests were administered to the Carl Perkins staff: the Los Angeles Symptom Checklist (LASC; King et al., 1995) to measure PTSD symptoms, the Impact of Events Scale (IES; Horowitz, Wilner, & Alvarez, 1979) to measure subjective perceptions of stress experienced by human services workers as a result of working with their clients, and the Maslach Burnout Inventory (MBI; Maslach & Jackson, 1981a) to measure burnout. While the IES indicated that traumatic events have had a high impact on workers, the LASC and MBI scores were very low, indicating that these workers do not have PTSD symptoms and they are not burned out. Particularly noteworthy were their extremely high "personal accomplishment" scores on the MBI (East, James, & Keim, 2001).

In conclusion, the administrative staff at Carl Perkins understand the effects that vicarious traumatization, compassion fatigue, and burnout can have on their organization and set aside time and resources to deal with it. In providing support to staff, the Carl Perkins Center follows very closely the six points proposed by Pines (1983), listed and described in the next section. It would thus appear that even in one of the most stressful of all types of crisis agencies—one that

works with traumatized children (Meyers & Cornille, 2002)—the institution can stop burnout dead in its tracks if it has the will to do so.

Social Support Systems. Social support systems act as buffers for the individual and help maintain psychological and physical well-being over time (Ling et al., 2014; Oerlemans & Bakker, 2014; Pines, 1983, p. 157). They are just as critical to avoiding burnout, whether at home or in the workplace (Distler, 1990; Greenglass, Fiksenbaum, & Burke, 1996; Halbesleben, 2006; Kesler, 1990; Pines & Aronson, 1988; Sullivan, 2004). Family systems are major sources of support (Killian, 2008; Lawson & Myers, 2011; Sullivan, 2004) and can help insulate workers against burnout (Bakker, Demerouti, & Schaufeli, 2005; Halbesleben, 2006; Maslach & Jackson, 1981b). However, it is impossible for one's spouse, partner, family, or friends to fulfill all the support tasks a crisis worker who engages specifically in trauma work will need (Pines, 1983, p. 172). Clearly, the worker needs to have functioning support systems at the job site (Handran, 2014; Li et al., 2014). How, then, might this occur if it does not happen spontaneously?

In that regard, Golembiewski, Munzenrider, and Stevenson (1986) propose that both instrumental support to achieve an end, such as material assistance, and expressive support to provide a sense of belonging and caring are needed in the workplace (p. 52). They found that employee concern and commitment to the job, peer friendliness and support for one another, and management's support and encouragement of employees all characterized low-burnout groups (p. 189).

Social support systems have six basic functions: listening, technical support, technical challenge, emotional support, emotional challenge, and sharing social reality (Pines, 1983).

1. *Listening.* Periodically, all workers need someone to listen actively to them in an empathic manner without giving advice or making judgments (p. 158).
2. *Technical support.* When confronted with complex client problems, all workers need someone who can affirm confidence in their endeavors. Such a person must have the expertise to understand the complexities of the job and be able to give the worker honest feedback (p. 158).
3. *Technical challenge.* If workers are not intellectually challenged, they will stagnate. Intellectual contact

with significant others stretches the worker in a positive way. Such challenges can come only from people who do not intend to humiliate or gain an advantage and who have professional expertise equivalent to that of the worker (p. 158).

4. *Emotional support.* Workers need someone to be on their side in difficult situations, even if the significant others do not necessarily agree totally with the workers. Professional expertise is not necessary for this function (pp. 158–159).

5. *Emotional challenge.* It is comforting for workers to believe that they have explored all avenues in attempting to resolve their problems. Support persons serve a valuable function when they question such assumptions and confront the worker's excuses. This function should be used sparingly; otherwise it may be construed as nagging (p. 159).

6. *Sharing social reality.* When workers become unsure of the reliability of their own perceptions about the reality of the situation, they need external validation. This function is especially important when workers feel that they are losing the ability to evaluate what is happening with their clients and with the organization (p. 159).

Support Groups. Within the organizational structure, time should be set aside for formal, structured support groups. Structurally, a support group resembles a problem-solving discussion group. The goal of such a group is to build a sense of competence and help workers feel that they can deal with the stresses they encounter in their work situation. A support group is a safe place for workers to disagree and challenge feelings of helplessness.

The group serves as a cathartic agent for releasing pent-up emotions related to the job. Once catharsis occurs, members can realistically examine feelings associated with job stressors. By providing feedback, the support group validates for members that they are not alone in their feelings and reassures them that they are not abnormal in their response to the situation (Sculley, 1983, pp. 188–191).

To do this effectively, a support group not only needs the support of the administration but also must have a consultant/facilitator who is sensitive to the issues involved and can walk a tightwire between allowing the group to vent feelings and keeping the group in a problem-solving model. The buffering effect of a third party consultant/facilitator can help reduce conflict stressors (Giebels & Janssen, 2005). The consultant/facilitator also needs to be in a position

to provide the administration with information from the group that will allow for effective organizational change without becoming a "snitch" in the process (Sculley, 1983, pp. 193–194).

Finally, for those members suffering from vicarious traumatization, compassion fatigue, and the later stages of burnout, referring them for personal counseling should be done with the understanding that these outcomes are indeed occupational hazards no different from carpal tunnel syndrome for keyboard operators or arthritis for concrete finishers. In that regard, organizations must be careful not to secondarily victimize such people as being of weak character or lacking in the "right stuff."

The Individual and the Organization. Vocationally, there are four major maladaptive responses to the onset of burnout. As the level of burnout increases, so does escape avoidance behavior (Thornton, 1992). Workers may attempt horizontal job mobility. They continuously look for the "right" boss or organization when it is the job they are in that is causing their unhappiness.

Others tire of the constant interaction with clients and decide to move vertically up the job ladder into administrative positions. What they fail to realize is that their cynical and jaundiced view of the system will not be left behind but will be carried with them into a whole new set of stresses. It is an understatement to say that these people do not make very good bosses.

There are also people who become what Pines and Aronson (1988, p. 18) call "deadwood." These people have long ago decided that their best bet is to not "rock the boat" so they can make it to retirement. If you have ever read the comic strip *Dilbert*, Wally best represents these individuals. When asked to do something, they politely indicate they are too busy, or agree with every idea put forth but venture none of their own, or contribute only what is minimally necessary to escape notice or censure, or turn the tables and cast incompetence on others to cover up their own failings.

Finally, some people quit their job and the vocation, and in some instances this may be the wisest choice of all.

At this stage of frustration, choices may seem to be limited to job change or job stagnation, but the individual does have other options. First, clearly defining one's role within the organization is a high priority (Kesler, 1990). The worker should conduct a job analysis and determine which tasks are necessary, which are self-imposed, and which contribute to role overload (Pines & Aronson, 1988, p. 109). Through assertive negotiation with the administration, the worker needs to define a reasonable work level and commensurate financial or other rewards for the work performed. Clients should be clearly apprised of the limits of service in regard to time as well as the amount and kind of service to be provided. Although service to clients needs to be a high priority, other tasks should be clearly prioritized. If chores that do not have a high priority cannot be delegated, then serious consideration should be given to dropping them (Leiter & Maslach, 2005).

Finally, if it is apparent that the organization is so entrenched and regressive that little change in policies and programs can be effected, it is probably time to look for greener occupational pastures. It would behoove a worker who is in the frustration stage to consider what a near-future job change entails and start planning for it before reaching the apathy stage. Knowing company severance policies and state unemployment benefits, updating a resume, saving money, and commencing a job search are examples of prudent measures workers may take before they are so mentally, physically, and emotionally exhausted that there is little energy left for a major shift in one's life.

Self-Care

As we have said, burnout is a two-way street with both individual and organizational culpability. There are literally volumes of research that find self-care as *the* critical ingredient for the crisis worker (Alkema, Linton, & Davies, 2008; Eastwood, 2007; Harrison & Westwood, 2009; Killian, 2008; Lawson, 2009; Lawson & Myers, 2011; Ling et al., 2014; Morkides, 2009; Oerlemans & Bakker, 2014; Rupert et al., 2015; Ringenbach, 2009; Thomas, 2007). We have already spoken to the significance of support systems and spirituality. What follows sounds a lot like what your mother lectured you on: eating right, sleeping right, getting exercise, taking care of your general hygiene, and after all of those things are done, not forgetting to have fun! One of the toughest parts of this business is doing that.

In William Glasser's reality therapy/control theory (1985), one of the central axes on which his theory revolves is engaging in positive addicting behaviors, and central to those positive addicting behaviors is having fun. The whole notion of Glasser's theory is that when you engage in these positive addicting behaviors your personal world grows much larger, and so does your social world as you interact with it.

Nobody can make you get out of your rut, and it is extremely easy to stay in it, as in the case of one of your authors who right now has been word processing 12 days in a row on this $!%#@$%#! book and not getting his workouts in and feeling very guilty and even physically edgy about missing his positive addiction. The word *recreate* makes a lot more sense when you break it down into *re-create*. So meditate, play rugby, work up your fantasy football team, make a quilt, run a marathon, shoot some pool, play bridge or poker, kill all the video game aliens, go fishing, see a ballgame, weed your flower garden—any of those will do as long as you are having fun, enjoying it, and it has absolutely nothing to do with anything in this book. Hey! You cannot use that as an excuse to your professor that you needed to go recreate and didn't finish this chapter so flunked the exam because you were afraid of burning out!

Private Practitioners and Burnout

The occupational dream of many of our students is to start their own private practice. They fantasize that they could do the kind of therapy they wanted with the clients they selected, be rid of overbearing supervisors and be their own boss, not be bothered with bureaucratic hassles and avalanches of paperwork, set their own hours, and make lots of money! Yet the private practitioner has the potential for even greater problems.

Generally, private practitioners are type A personalities who tend to invest a great deal of time in the job as a means of finding a sense of fulfillment and identity. Competition and achievement serve as guiding values that correlate highly with the need to be seen as worthy and capable (Everly, 1989, p. 105; Pines & Aronson, 1988, pp. 6–9). In a word, they are "driven" workaholics (Falco et al., 2014).

Although the aloneness that pervades a private practice is not the same as the isolation that agency workers sometimes impose on themselves when placed in high-stress situations, it can be more complete. Fenced off from other professionals by ethical and ecological boundaries, the private practitioner has few others with whom to discuss client problems. More important, there are few other individuals with whom they can discuss their own personal problems.

Private practice is clearly a business. As such, it promotes the continuing fear that there will be no clients or that there will never be enough no matter how successfully the business is going (Mitchell, 1977, pp. 145–146). Every client termination raises questions: "Will there be someone to take her place?" "Will he pass the word along that I did him some good?" The private practitioner who is moving toward crisis invariably answers these questions negatively and redoubles his or her efforts to increase client loads and effect cures.

Starting and maintaining a private practice also call for maintaining a public presence. Whether such a presence involves making speeches to the Rotary Club on stress and the businessperson, consulting with the oncology staff on death and dying at the local hospital, or giving a workshop on discipline for Parents Without Partners, the continuous pressure of needing to be seen as active, abreast of current developments, and visible is part of a sales program that must constantly be maintained and upgraded.

Although the private practitioner is his or her own boss, being an independent businessperson also means being completely responsible for maintaining the practice. Long hours and difficult work periods are the rule rather than the exception. Because most clients work regular hours, private practitioners devote many evenings and weekends to their work. Usually there is no one to pick up caseloads, so vacations or even short respites are few and far between. Certainly not all private practitioners suffer from burnout. However, when burnout does occur with human services workers who are in private practice, it is accelerated by the foregoing problems and issues.

Intervention with the Individual: A Case Study

Direct action, in which the worker tries to master the environmental stressors, and palliative action, in which the worker tries to reduce disturbances when unable to manage the environment, are the two positive ways to cope with stress (Pines & Aronson, 1988, p. 144). Direct action is applied externally to the situational stressor in the environment, whereas palliative action is applied internally to one's cognitions and emotions about the stressor. Social support groups, workshops, assertiveness training, flextime, taking time off, salary increase, and role shifts are all examples of direct action. Meditation, relaxation techniques, biofeedback, physical exercise with no ego involvement, adopting positive cognitions, engaging in leisure-time pursuits, adopting better eating

habits, reducing addictive substance intake, and adding more humor and joy to one's life are all palliative "decompensation activities" that allow the worker to put stressors aside (Hoeksma et al., 1993; Melamed, Meir, & Samson, 1995; Oerlemans & Bakker, 2014; Pines & Aronson, 1988, p. 152; Rupert et al., 2015; Saakvitne & Pearlman, 1996, pp. 78–87; Stark, 1994).

Whereas workers who are at the frustration stage may well be helped by being involved in self-initiated directive and palliative actions, those at the more serious stage of apathy will not be (Edelwich & Brodsky, 1982, p. 137). In such cases, individual counseling is more appropriate (Baron & Cohen, 1982). Kesler (1990) proposed using Arnold Lazarus's (1976) BASIC ID (behavior, affect, sensation, imagery, cognition, interpersonal relationships, and drugs/biology) paradigm as a treatment approach to burnout. To this formulation Kesler adds an *S* for setting. Given the interactive effects of burnout across multiple facets of the individual, the BASIC IDS approach seems valid for attacking burnout in a comprehensive way.

The following case illustrates the crisis worker using combinations of direct and palliative actions in an abbreviated BASIC IDS approach. It should be clearly understood that neither symptoms nor intervention procedures are all-inclusive. For example, Tubesing and Tubesing (1982, p. 161) listed 36 possible intervention strategies that cover physical, intellectual, social, emotional, spiritual, and environmental components of burnout, and those are not comprehensive by any means. If the client is identified as having more compassion fatigue or vicarious traumatization, a more specific program that focuses on STSD symptoms may be used, such as the Accelerated Recovery Program (ARP; Gentry, Baranowsky, & Dunning, 2002). The case presented is that of a professional with a doctorate and many years of experience, but neophytes should understand that Dr. Jane Lee is genotypical of any human services worker. Her case clearly points out that no worker is immune to burnout, no matter how much experience or expertise that worker may have.

The Client. Dr. Jane Lee is a striking, raven-haired, 43-year-old woman with aquiline features, a low, melodious voice, aquamarine eyes that twinkle, and a smile that could serve as a toothpaste commercial. She is extremely witty and incisive of intellect, is widely read, and can talk as easily with truck drivers as she can with lawyers. At any social function people gravitate toward her. She seems to have been born with the natural empathy and easy familiarity that many people consciously work their whole lives for, yet never quite attain. Divorced for 10 years, Jane has raised her only son while carrying on an exceedingly successful professional life.

Jane has a thriving practice in marriage and family therapy. She has a heavy client load and is clearing approximately $150,000 a year. She is seen by her peers as extremely capable, and her clients speak highly of her. Jane has been in private practice for 8 years. Prior to entering private practice she worked in a community mental health facility. She was so skillful at therapy there that she rose to the directorship of the clinical program.

Jane graduated from a major university with a doctorate in counseling psychology and completed her internship in a VA hospital. She then successfully completed an American Association of Marriage and Family Therapists internship at a private clinic. She has written and published many articles on therapy for anorexics and the families of individuals suffering from catastrophic illnesses. She has also given many inservice programs and presentations at national human services conferences.

By any criteria imaginable, Jane appears to be a highly competent, successful therapist and an exceptionally endowed woman overall. Her ability and demeanor have made her a role model that many in her community aspire to emulate. As Jane sits down with the crisis worker, she is seriously considering drinking a good deal of wine, closing her garage door, climbing into her new Lexus, turning on the ignition, and killing herself.

Jane: I came here today because of what you said to me the other night when we were having a drink. You pretty much have me pegged. I'm burned out even more than what you think, more than what I like to admit. Today I had a decision to make, whether to kill myself or come here. I came here, but I'm not sure it's the right decision. If I killed myself, it seems like it would just be over and done with. I've taken care of everything concerning Bobby, my son. He's practically through with college, and even though we're very close, I really think it'd be better for him if I were gone.

He wouldn't have to put up with my lousy behavior, and believe me, it's lousy right now. There's enough insurance to get him finished up in school, and he could sell the house. He's the only one that really matters besides my clients, and right now I'm not

doing worth a damn with them. I'm probably hurting more than I help, and I'm just not up to it anymore. So much pain and so damn little I can do about it. The only thing I can think about now when I go into a cancer ward is how bad the patients smell. Whoever said "You don't have to smell them. All you gotta do is help them!" sure wasn't in this end of the business. I'm also starting to behave like those screwed-up anorexics I work with too. It's starting to seem pretty reasonable to me that they aren't eating. Why the hell should they? Why the hell should *I*? Just sort of fade away and look thin while you're doing it. At least I'd make a great-looking corpse. Anyway, the main reason I came over today was to see if you'd be willing to take my clients. I've thought this over, and you've got what it takes. I think you could help them, and if you agree, I'll start talking to them about coming over to your practice.

CW: What you just said scares the living hell out of me. There's a part of me that wants to run right out of here, because what you're saying is really hitting home with the way I feel at times. There's another part of me that wants to tie you up in log chains until you come to your senses. Finally, there's another part of me that cares for you so much that I'm angry that you've let yourself get into this predicament. Most of all, though, I'm glad I made that reflection the other night and that it finally sank in. I've seen you going downhill for quite a while now. My guess is that you didn't even know it was happening or just laid another piece of armor plate over yourself and said something like "I've got to gut this through" or some of that other irrational garbage I hear you unload on yourself. First of all, I won't even consider what you said about the clients until we agree on one thing, and that is you don't do any harm to yourself until we talk this through. So I want an agreement both as your therapist and as your friend that we shake on that before anything else happens. I won't take no for an answer. If that's not acceptable, we'll negotiate it. No matter what, we're now in this together.

Ethical Issues. The crisis worker is in a difficult position as the client's friend, fellow professional, and now as a therapist dealing with another human being in crisis. When a human services professional who is a colleague becomes impaired, it is the ethical duty of the fellow professional to do something to prevent harm to clients (Harrison & Westwood, 2009;

Thomas & Levitt, 2010), and there is research that impaired therapists can hurt clients (Lawson et al., 2007). The overall principle of nonmaleficence (do no harm) comes into play. It is simpler if impairment is due to drugs or alcohol abuse that can be readily observed, or if the professional works in a setting where other professionals can observe the behavior, but it becomes much more difficult when the professional is in private practice or the impairment is burnout, which cannot be smelled or seen in slurred speech or unsteady walking.

Oftentimes close friends and colleagues of burned-out professionals are the first to notice the impairment. Clearly, there are many personal and social dilemmas about "snitching" out one's colleague. The question then becomes: Should colleagues report the impaired professional to the state licensing board or attempt to intervene and help the person by themselves? It is a slippery slope and, as with many ethics questions, there is no clear answer.

Although there are ethical issues in treating a friend and a colleague, when a client is in crisis and lethality is involved, the primary concern is keeping the client safe and returning the individual to a state of equilibrium. Depending on what comes of this crisis intervention, if Jane can regain her psychological equilibrium and manage her own self-care, the crisis worker may do nothing more. If Jane doesn't, the worker is ethically bound to notify a licensing board although that might well spell the end of the friendship (Thomas & Levitt, 2010).

The nuances of this ethical dilemma can be argued after the fact, but right now the crisis worker needs to act. Particularly in small towns where there are essentially no other professionals with the necessary expertise to provide immediate assistance, the appropriate ethical response would be to provide the best level of care as quickly as possible. In that regard, it is most likely that the crisis worker will have some personal or professional relationship with the client.

Because the crisis worker knows the client, she feels free to make some initial owning statements that let the client know exactly how she feels about the situation without becoming sympathetic in the bargain, which she could easily do because she has felt much the same way at prior times in her professional life (countertransference). The crisis worker also makes an initial assessment of the lethality level of the client. Her reflective statement to the client a few evenings earlier was not idle conversation. The crisis worker has seen a slow but steady change coming over Jane in the last 3 months, and as she thinks about it she sees that it was coming a good while before that. Jane has been keeping a stiff upper lip, but there have been indicators that all has not been well lately. She has been rather cynical about clients, as evidenced by her comment about how they smell. She has been suffering a variety of physical maladies that have ranged from unending colds to some severe gastrointestinal problems ominous enough to indicate that surgery might be needed in the near future.

As the crisis worker continues to assess the situation, she further realizes that Jane has truncated relationships with most of her acquaintances and has done this lately with the crisis worker on at least two occasions. Their relationship had been characterized by an easy rivalry, good comradeship, and just generally a lot of good times together without ever engaging in one-upmanship. Lately, though, the crisis worker has had the feeling that Jane has treated her more as a client than as a friend and has attributed some deeper psychological meaning to even the most innocent conversation.

Assessment. Behaviorally, Jane is in serious trouble. Her performance of daily tasks has become seriously compromised. Her uncharacteristic behavior coupled with her suicidal thoughts places her at a triage level of 7 to 8 on behavior. The only positive behavior she is currently exhibiting is seeking out her colleague. Even though she says she is doing that only to transfer clients, dynamically she is making a clear call for help.

The rather detached, mechanistic way that Jane has reported all this and her blank, hollow look are completely at odds with Jane's usual sparkle, which has been absent the past few months. Performing a quick synthesis of all this background knowledge, what Jane is saying, and the depressed way she is looking and behaving, the crisis worker makes the assessment that Jane is not kidding about killing herself and that the threat must be taken seriously. The crisis worker immediately goes into a suicide prevention mode and institutes a verbal contract with Jane not to kill herself. Even though Jane is a practicing therapist, she is no different from any other client in this regard.

Besides the threat of suicide, a triage assessment of Jane by a worker unfamiliar with burnout might cursorily dismiss her problem as typical whining about one's work. However, the difficult clients she deals with, the amount of time that she has done so, the isolation she has imposed on herself, and the absence of social support systems in her work and at home all lead to a hypothesis of vicarious trauma/compassion fatigue that is rippling out into every component of her life (Figley, 2002, p. 7). Research clearly indicates that the more traumatic clients are and the more often they are seen, the more likely it is that the therapist will experience compassion fatigue, vicarious traumatization, and burnout (Simpson, 2006). In short, Jane is fitting many of the behavioral, attitudinal, emotional, and interpersonal descriptors mentioned earlier in this chapter regarding symptoms of burnout.

Triage assessment for affect is 7 to 8. Although her outward demeanor is calm and collected, her affective responses are uncharacteristically angry and hostile for someone in the helping professions. Jane is using considerable effort to control her feelings. Coupled with the emotional exhaustion that is the most salient factor of burnout, she is close to being acutely depressed. This should come as no surprise, because depression and burnout often go hand in hand (Lawson, 2009; McKnight & Glass, 1995).

Cognitively, Jane is operating at a triage level of 6 to 7. Although Jane is thinking in a linear manner, her logic is twisted, and her belief system is severely compromised by obsessional self-doubt. She is manifesting a great deal of Ellis's (1973) "musturbatory" thinking and demonstrating another hallmark of burnout: a severe decline in her belief in her personal competence, along with depersonalization of her clients. Her complaints go beyond her job and indicate problems with social relationships, physical health, personal integrity, professional identity, belief system, and her total environment. Jane's total triage assessment scale score of 20 to 23 places her in the low to moderate marked impairment range. She is currently functioning between the frustration and apathy stage of burnout and is at a trait level where burnout has become pervasive across her environments. Without intervention, she is likely to move quickly into severe and lethal impairment.

Jane has done one thing right. She has gone to a significant other and is using that trusted other to self-disclose in a very intimate way some of her most troubled feelings (Maslach, 1976; Watkins, 1983). Because Jane's problems have spread out across her environment, the crisis worker will do exploratory counseling across BASIC IDS (Lazarus, 1976) components with the idea that no component of Jane's life is immune to the burnout currently assailing her.

Jane: All right, I can agree to a no-suicide contract. I know that's part of the procedure. Hell, I guess I knew you'd do that when I came in here. Maybe

I'm only kidding myself about all this anyway, just a bit of the blues, feeling sorry for myself, and all that crap.

CW: I'm glad you came here, for whatever reason, and I'm also glad you agree to our contract even though you know it's part of the program. I also don't believe that about having the blues, either. I think it's much more than that. I believe right now you're hurting quite a bit. But first I'd like to hear what you think and feel is going on in your life right now.

Intervention. While the crisis worker is acknowledging her regard for Jane, she is also doing quite a bit more. First, she has decided to take a pretty directive stance with Jane for the time being. The worker balances between making emotional challenges to the client and listening closely and accurately to Jane's problems. She also knows Jane is extremely astute at the business they are engaged in, as evidenced by her comment about the contract. She is not going to let Jane play the game ahead of her. Her analysis is that Jane is out of control right now. The crisis worker is therefore going to take control of the situation and will not sit back in a passive mode.

Jane: I don't know. I've dealt with all kinds of problems in my life, and right now there's nothing I can really put my finger on. In comparison to what is going on now, I can tell you that going through the divorce with Jeff, taking off on my own to finish up the doctorate, fighting my way up the ladder in the agency, and then finally making a decision to go out on my own while raising Bobby make what's happening to me now seem like peanuts.

CW: Right! Those were really tough times, and you went through those like Superwoman. But that was then, and we're right here, right now, and from the looks of it you don't much feel like you're Superwoman, and what's happening in your life surely isn't peanuts, or we wouldn't be having this talk right now. So what do you feel like right now?

The crisis worker acknowledges how tough the client has been, but will not let her get stuck in the past. The crisis worker wants to find out what is happening right now. What is more important about this now than it was a year ago? Furthermore, the crisis worker will not let the client discount the problem. It is interesting that if Jane were the counselor here, she would probably ferret out what she has just done—retreating into the past—in a second. The difference is that Jane has really become a client, and she is as blind to the way she talks, thinks, and behaves as any other client. Jane's being a therapist gives her no edge in dealing with her own problems. In fact, her own expertise may militate heavily against her (Kesler, 1990).

Jane: All I can tell you is I'm washed out. Like I get dates and appointments all mixed up. Last week topped that all off. I saw 44 clients last week. I think I got about a dozen appointments mixed up. My appointment book was really screwed up. It was a madhouse, and some of the people got agitated. Nothing like that ever happened before.

CW: Never?

Jane: Well, to a far lesser extent. I've been strung out before, but I could always get it straightened out.

CW: How?

Jane: About every 3 months things would start to get out of hand. I'd just sit back and say, "Janie, old girl, you've got to get out of here for a while." I'd just hop in the car and take off for a weekend in Chicago. Check into a hotel, take in a show, eat some really special meals, and use about half the hotel's hot water washing the clients off of me. Seems like that would clear the cobwebs out of my head.

CW: When was the last time you did that?

Jane: (*wistfully*) About 9 months ago.

CW: Why so long?

Jane: Well, I bought that new office and went in and remodeled the whole thing. I cut the contractor a deal. If I could work on it too, he'd reduce the price.

CW: So being the omnipotent individual you are, you threw out at least one thing that keeps you on an even keel. In fact, rather than getting away from the office, you've been spending almost all your time there. Let's see, we've got a couple of characters running around inside of Jane—Dr. Jane, healer to the world, and Jane the carpenter. Wonder who else is inside there?

The crisis worker is looking for a link between the past and the present. If Jane had some coping mechanisms in the past, what were they? She is specifically looking for coping mechanisms in the past that can be linked to the present and what is happening in the present to keep those coping mechanisms from

being put into place. She is also beginning to build a character repertoire with Jane in the hope that Jane can start to see all the various aspects of herself that are now motivating her to do some of the things she does (Butts, 1996). To set the stage for the client's regaining control of her life, the crisis worker proposes a positive character in Jane.

CW: I also heard a character that I'd call Janice, a person who knows when her stress bucket is full and is practical and smart enough to get away from the crap that goes on at that office. Where have you stuck her?

Jane: Back up on the shelf with Janie?

CW: Who's Janie?

Jane: She's the gal who's a little crazy, who can joke with her clients and get up in the middle of the night and go out and start seeding her lawn and sing Chuck Berry songs while she's doing it. (*embarrassed*) There's just no time for them right now. It's not just the new office, but I also needed another car, and since Bobby has changed schools there were a lot of added expenses in that. So I really needed to devote my time to building my caseload up. If I can get through the next 2 years, I can breathe easier.

CW: Well, I'm sure glad to hear you're planning on being around for the next 2 years, anyway. But that's not the question now, is it, because right now it sounds to me as if you're wrung out. You don't have any more energy to give, and you've set up on the wall a couple of people who are pretty important in recharging your batteries. Do you see how important they are and what it's cost you to do that?

The crisis worker is not yet making direct suggestions as to what Jane needs to do; however, she is hoping to raise Jane's consciousness to the fact that she has unconsciously changed her operating method. The crisis worker attempts to get her to recognize this by describing what these very positive characters have done for her. By doing so, the crisis worker is attempting to reintroduce some very healthy defense mechanisms that have previously helped Jane cope well with the stressful life she leads. Three major pathways that keep Jane in equilibrium are currently missing from her life: resiliency, self-management and self-care, and connection with others (Gentry, Baranowsky, & Dunning, 2002). The crisis worker will attempt to reintegrate those into Jane's life.

Jane: I guess so, but I don't know how to get out of it.

CW: What will happen if you don't work on the office this next weekend?

Jane: The new plumbing isn't in. Clients wouldn't be able to use the bathroom. I'd also feel guilty for not working on it.

CW: (*laughing*) Well, the first part of that problem is pretty easily handled. Call the Porta-Potty people. I can imagine a sign that says, "The crap stops here," hanging from the door as clients walk in. (*Jane starts to smile and giggle for the first time since walking in the door.*) The other part of that is, who's the character laying a guilt trip on you? Tell me some more about her.

The crisis worker takes a little bit of a well-gauged risk here by injecting some humor into the situation (Moran, 2002). She does this because humor has been important in Jane's life, is helpful to her in coping, and turns her away from some of the cynicism she feels toward her clients and starts to allow her to laugh at herself a little. The ability to laugh at one's own foibles and some of the bizarre and ridiculously funny things that happen in our clients' lives cannot be overemphasized (Pines & Aronson, 1988, p. 154). Van Auken (1979) extols the judicious use of humor even in the most pathetic of situations. Getting a smile or a laugh from clients is a direct intrusion into the depressive thought processes and behaviors in which they are mired.

The crisis worker also starts to hammer a bit on Jane's guilt. Generally the crisis worker sees guilt as a pretty useless emotion, consumptive of energy that could be used in other, more positive ways. Guilt is invariably an emotion of the past, and whatever was done can never again be retrieved. It is one thing to learn from one's past mistakes and quite another to carry past, unfinished business into the present, particularly when one is feeling guilty about not measuring up.

Jane: That's Mother Superior. I get all kinds of lectures from her. (*bitterly*) She's just like Sister Angeline at St. Mary's, where I went to school. "Say your Hail Mary's and Our Father's. Get your homework done. God doesn't like a shirker. Watch how you dress." Jesus, I hated that!

CW: You hate it, but it sure sounds like you're living it. Small wonder you're feeling so lousy.

The crisis worker starts hooking up feelings with thoughts and actions. The response the crisis worker gets indicates that the burnout has spread out into the client's family life.

Jane: You know, I think that's maybe why Bobby and I are having problems right now. I really sound and act like a Mother Superior to him. My Lord! He's 21 years old, and I've started treating him like he was a 6-year-old. He's about like some of those clients I have to lead around by the nose.

CW: Did you hear what you just said? "He's about like some of those clients I lead around." First of all, I didn't know that was the business you were in. Sounds like Jane the handywoman. Fix 'em up the way you do your office. Second, I wonder how many people outside the office you've decided to fix up and look out for. I have to tell you that's one of the kinds of feelings I've had around you lately.

With this information, the client gives the crisis worker a chance to plunge into some core issues that have definable behavioral outcomes. By stating how she deals with Bobby, Jane is manifesting another of the typical signs of burnout: trying to treat significant others in her life as if they were in the therapeutic situation (Van Auken, 1979). Her relationship with Bobby is extremely important because one way of decreasing burnout is to have a satisfying family life, especially with one's children (Forney, Wallace-Schutzman, & Wiggers, 1982). Worse yet is that she has become autocratic in the therapeutic situation, so it is not surprising that a major component of her life that has been highly reinforcing to her is no longer so and, in fact, has taken on some very negative connotations.

The crisis worker lays that squarely on her. She is mixing up her characters and has replaced Dr. Jane with Jane the handywoman. This state of events is not so surprising since both characters are working in the same office. Jane needs a break in her day-to-day activities and needs to get away from the office to do it (Forney, Wallace-Schutzman, & Wiggers, 1982).

Finally, the crisis worker relates and owns her own experience of having been treated the same way by Jane. She tries to make Jane aware that, like rings on a pond, the ripple effect from her burnout goes far beyond her immediate line of sight (Kesler, 1990).

CW: Indeed, I wonder about your relationships other than those with Bobby, myself, and your clients. Anyone else you're trying to control right now?

Jane: (*frostily*) If you mean men, absolutely no. When I get home at night, I'm so bushed all I want to do is fall asleep, but then all those clients go tumbling around in my head, and I start thinking about car payments, mortgage payments, how to straighten things out with Bobby, and I wind up getting about 2 or 3 hours of sleep a night.

CW: So right now you're so exhausted that you'd just rather be alone.

Jane: That's right, but I feel like I ought to be out mingling with people. I'm so damned isolated anyway.

CW: OK! I can understand that, and I'd agree with you, but let's look at right now. Seems as if you really need some time to just curl up in the fetal position, turn the electric blanket up to nine, and get your batteries recharged. Could you just go home and go to bed, put the answering service on until Monday, and not get up for the whole weekend?

Jane: I suppose.

CW: No supposes. If you don't want to do that, we'll look at something else. But right now you look like *The Grapes of Wrath* and just seem to really need to rest before you think about doing anything else. Are you willing to call the contractor up and tell him you won't be there Saturday and Sunday without feeling guilty about it?

Jane: I could use the rest. All right! I'll give it this weekend.

CW: Fine. But there's one more thing. If you really get to feeling blue, plug the phone in and call me at home. I also want a report next week, so what time do you want to come in?

Jane: Sounds like I'm a client.

CW: Sounds like you're right. *(laughs)*

The crisis worker is basically assisting Jane to make a simple commitment to do one thing—get some rest. A critical component in treating burnout is revitalization (Tubesing & Tubesing, 1982, p. 160). Jane is physically fatigued, and the first order of business is to get her physical batteries recharged. A number of other options are available at this juncture, but the crisis worker follows Tubesing and Strosahl's (1976) advice to let the client make the choice of what treatment is appropriate. Keying on the client's own words about needing sleep, the crisis worker follows up and gains commitment to a specific behavior that the client will engage in over the short term. This is not a dramatic first step, but considering the least dramatic steps first is probably the way to go (Van Auken, 1979). The most important objective of this initial encounter is finding some short-term intervention techniques the client is able and willing to use (Freudenberger & Robbins, 1979).

A particular behavior the crisis worker touches on is the use of the telephone. Private practitioners are notorious for taking phone calls from clients at all hours of the night and on weekends. Van Auken (1979) urges human services workers not to let clients run—or, for that matter, ruin—their personal lives. The crisis worker makes sure that Jane follows this dictum, even though the crisis worker herself doesn't practice what she preaches, which leads one to wonder whom the crisis worker may soon need to be talking to about burnout. Finally, the worker provides emotional support, but once Jane is able to ventilate her feelings, the worker moves into a problem-solving mode.

The Next Week

Jane: I'll have to admit I do feel better. Couldn't sleep at all Friday night, but I got 10 hours in Saturday. I can't believe it! I woke up, and I was all curled up in the fetal position. The clients looked somewhat better this week. I can't say it was wonderful, but at least I wasn't an ogre to them. I guess what bothers me most about that is that I've lost all my creativity.

CW: OK! Let's talk about that a bit. You haven't been paying very much attention to the right side of your brain, so what do you expect? What could you do creatively that isn't client involved that'd get the right side of your head going again?

Jane: I've got a couple of articles I've been putting off—how about that?

CW: Got anything to do with clients?

Jane: Yes.

CW: Is that going to help you out?

Jane: I don't guess so, the same old stuff, only I'm writing about it.

CW: What else, then?

Forney, Wallace-Schutzman, and Wiggers (1982) propose that a variety of professional activities may be an excellent coping mechanism; nevertheless, the crisis worker confronts Jane about this suggested alternative. The crisis worker is fairly sure that the client's stress bucket is full to the brim professionally. Jane needs to become less, not more, involved in her professional life.

Jane: Well, there is something else. I bought this sailboat for Bobby and me. The Coast Guard Auxiliary is putting on a sailing class. It would sure surprise Bobby if the next time he came home I could handle that Y-Flyer.

CW: Is that something you want to do? Would like to do it, not need to do it?

Jane: Yes!

CW: And not pile it on top of everything else. Really reserve some time for yourself to enjoy it.

Jane: You sure drive a hard bargain, but I can do it.

This is a wedge in the behavioral repertoire of the client that the crisis worker has been looking to find. Writer after writer in the burnout literature has promoted the use of leisure, particularly physical exercise, as a way of breaking up the dogmatic, work-brittle behavior of just going through the motions that often characterize the burned-out human services worker (Hoeksma et al., 1993; Melamed, Meir, & Samson, 1995; Oerlemans & Bakker, 2014; Savicki & Cooley, 1982).

By proposing for the client a combination of leisure, physical exercise, and quality time with her son, the crisis worker has neatly integrated a number of positive interventions. The crisis worker is moving methodically around Myers, Sweeney, and Witmer's Wellness Wheel (Myers, Sweeney, & Witmer, 2000; Myers & Sweeney, 2005), which has at its center spiritual self-direction, and which Dr. Jane is now mostly without. Specific spokes that radiate out from that wheel that the worker is attempting to put back in place in the client's life are nutrition, exercise, self-care, stress management, a sense of control, realistic beliefs, a sense of humor, renewed creativity, and awareness and coping across her entire ecosystem. With that many spokes missing, it is no surprise that Dr. Jane's psychological vehicle has about lost its spiritual axle as it careens down a crisis cliff that has become a burnout landslide of behavioral, physical, interpersonal, and attitudinal problems.

The crisis worker now takes on the main issue of the client's private practice.

CW: Fine. Let's talk about your practice for a while.

Jane: You know as well as I do about that. Sure, I've got a great caseload now. But who knows, it might dry up next week, and then where would I be?

CW: Has it ever dried up? Even in the last recession?

Jane: No, it hasn't, but I keep expecting the worst.

CW: You've been in private practice 8 years now, right? Has it ever been such that you didn't have enough clients to keep the wolves away from your door?

Jane: No. I guess there's something else. I feel a little foolish saying this, but it's almost like if I don't live up to my reputation and take on those really tough cases, I start feeling like I'm not the queen of the mountain. I mean, in the past I've been real proud of that, but now I don't seem to feel anything but that there's an albatross around my neck.

CW: Sounds like Superwoman again. I frankly admire you for dealing with those terminals' families, and you're right! Not many could do that. But if there's no intrinsic payoff, why are you fooling yourself into thinking you can heal the whole world? See the trap you've put yourself into?

Jane: Well, no! I guess I don't.

CW: OK! I want to try something. Maybe you've used it on some of your clients before. It's a game of "Who Told You?" I want you to move over to my chair and ask that empty chair, which will represent Jane, some questions. I'm going to stand aside and process as we go along, but it'll mostly be up to you. I want you to use all your insight as a therapist and really bore in and go to work on Jane's fictional goals, those crazy things she tells herself that have no counterpart in reality.

Jane as CW: (*shifts chairs and gets a glitter in her eyes*) OK, toots! Who told you you had to be Superwoman?

CW: Now shift back.

Jane: Nobody, really, I've just got a lot of responsibilities.

Jane as CW: Responsibilities, my foot! You've been going up that success ladder so fast you've scorched the rungs. Always got to show them. Be number one. My God! You little twerp. You're 43 years old, and you still think you're back on the VA ward. Got to show them you're better than any man. Volunteer for the worst cases. Scared to death you won't succeed. And when you did, you were scared you wouldn't succeed the second time. Who told you that?

Jane: Nobody! It was reality. I had to be better than the men there.

Jane as CW: That was 20 years ago, nerd! The only men you deal with now are your clients. And that's another thing. Is that why you're so afraid of going out with any other man? And don't give me that stuff about getting burned again. You know why that divorce happened, and it sure doesn't have anything to do with having good social relationships now.

Jane: It's just that with the financial obligations for Bobby, I really don't have the time.

Jane as CW: (*really angry and shouting*) I won't have that! How long will you be responsible for him? He's 21 years old. Who supported you when you were 21? I'll tell you who. You did! You just use that as an excuse. Just like you use all those clients as an excuse. You don't fool me, you little martyr. Oh, sure! You get those strokes. (*dripping sarcasm*) Just like Annette here said, "I really admire you, Jane." You go around fooling everybody, but worst of all you fool yourself. Look at you. Sitting here the pathetic little wretch. You don't fool me. You're not little Miss Goody Two-Shoes. Behind all that depression is a really angry, bitter bitch who's always going around being everybody's servant. So just who told you you had to be that?

Jane: (*Breaks and sobs. The CW goes to Jane, gathers her into her arms, and hugs her for dear life. Five minutes elapse.*) Good Lord! I didn't realize that was all in there. I really got on a roll.

CW: Neither did I, but I figured if anybody could get it out, you could. What have you got out of that?

Jane: Besides spilling my guts, which I haven't done in 25 years, I see now how I got into this. I really set myself up.

CW: What do you want to do?

Jane: Well, I'm not going to kill myself, literally or figuratively. I've got some living to do, and although I'm not going to quit the practice, there sure are going to be some limits put on it.

The "Who Told You?" technique is a combination of Adlerian, rational-emotive behavior, and Gestalt therapy that is extremely powerful. Given a person with the kind of insight Jane has, it often has dramatic results in pointing out the way clients delude themselves. By using Jane as her own therapist, the crisis worker provides no one for the client to rationalize to, attack, manipulate, or otherwise attempt to fool but herself. For a person with Jane's abilities and insight, that seldom happens for very long. Underneath most depression lies anger. If that anger can be mobilized, then the client has taken a major step toward getting back into control of the situation. By putting Jane in a position to view her behavior from outside herself and also giving her a stimulus to attack her irrational ideas by the "Who Told You?" technique, the crisis worker provides an arena in which Jane can combat the apathy she is experiencing.

Such a dramatic shift to being mobile is uncommon among the general populace, and Jane's case is a condensed version of what may generally happen. The crisis worker often must provide the stimulus statements that are the core of clients' irrational ideas because of clients' poor cognition of their own negative self-talk. However, in dealing with highly trained professionals, it is not uncommon for such rapid shifts to occur.

Given the initial stimulus, they may pick up on the technique and provide their own dialogue with little or no help from the crisis worker. When emotional catharsis occurs, the crisis worker then takes a nondirective stance and serves as little more than a sounding board as their fellow professionals put reasonable parameters back into their lives. At that point, human services workers as clients tend to be able to make good decisions quickly about the behavioral, emotional, and cognitive aspects of their lives.

Indeed, if burnout syndrome is successfully overcome, it is not unreasonable to expect that human services workers will come back to their profession with hardier personalities, stronger commitments to self and profession, better self-temperance, a greater sense of meaningfulness, and increased vigor toward their environment (Kobasa, 1979). Furthermore, new coping styles that include greater self-awareness, increased self-insight, and a more direct approach to problem solving are likely to result for those who successfully navigate these treacherous waters (Cooley & Keesey, 1981). Finally, it is our own observation that human services professionals who have successfully conquered burnout respond not only to their work but also to their daily living with calmer and wiser choices, behaviors, and work style.

Summary. In this vignette the crisis worker uses the BASIC IDS model to deal with multiple, overlapping issues in the client's life (Kesler, 1990). Jane's workload affects her relationship with her family and friends. Her role as mother affects her image of herself. Her image of herself affects her beliefs about her abilities as therapist and mother and finally affects her coping behaviors across the board. The crisis worker links all of these dimensions into a unified whole because each modality interacts with other modalities and should not be treated in isolation (Cormier & Cormier, 1985, p. 153). Jane's sailing expeditions not only will provide her with fun, relaxation, and togetherness with her son, but also are as necessary to her therapeutic functioning as her doctoral training. Achieving balance among the various parts of her life and compartmentalizing them to the extent that they do not start to run into or over one another allow Dr. Jane Lee to be fully functioning in all of them and at the same time limit the stresses inherent in each (Pines & Aronson, 1988, p. 152). Oerlemans and Bakker (2014) have conducted a one-day-at-a-time plan that focused on physical vigor and cognitive liveliness through low-effort social and physical activities and got positive results on burnout reduction indicators. In other words, don't take your work home with you and follow Glasser's theory (1985) and have some fun!

Webb (2007) has listed the following points that can help crisis workers who deal with traumatized children stave off vicarious traumatization, compassion fatigue, and ultimately burnout.

1. Pursue training and professional activities that promote learning. Keeping up in this business is important not only for the knowledge gained and skills learned but for meeting other professionals and continuing to build a professional support system.

2. Work with a variety of clients and limit exposure to trauma in general. It is tempting to specialize in trauma work. Many crisis workers take pride in doing work not everyone can do. It is also an adrenal rush and addictive. However, the old saying "Pride goeth before a fall" is true here. Varied client issues are not only a good way to keep the worker on his or her game but also provide relief from the constant grit and grind of trauma work. One of your authors startled a student he was doing some career counseling with after having worked with five suicidal/homicidal students in a row. His statement, "Thanks for coming in, you're the first normal student I've met today," probably made her wonder just exactly who was enrolling in the university.

3. Create boundaries between work and home, and maintain a personal identity. One of your authors is married to a middle school counselor. Do we talk about our work? Yes! Do we talk about it all the time? Absolutely not! We leave most of it at the door. "It'll be there tomorrow" are words to live by.

4. Find professional friends who understand the stress of this business. You can't have too many professional friends and colleagues. One of your authors makes regular dates to watch baseball games with a psychologist who works at a VA hospital. We talk about psychology, but we also discuss theology and politics, watch baseball, eat peanuts, and sing "Take Me Out to the Ballgame" during the seventh inning stretch.

5. Spend time with people who have not been victimized to maintain a balanced perspective that not all people have pathology. That's why it is important to get into a church, civic organization, fitness center, bridge club, model train club, or benevolent organization where there are just "regular" folks engaged in just "regular" activities.

6. Confront intrusive images and work through them. After reading this chapter, you should understand full well that if you start having pop-ups in your mind of the bad stuff you deal with or have nightmares about the stuff, don't punch it back as part of the job. Go get help.

7. Engage in activities that promote a sense of efficacy and empowerment. You may not decide to run for U.S. Senator, but getting involved in a community action program or government committee is an excellent way of feeling empowered and helping promote causes that give you a sense of self-esteem.

8. Engage in your own psychotherapy. While we do not advocate becoming your own "shrink," what is meant by this point is knowing yourself. If you saw Crazy walking down the other side of the street, would you run over and go lay a body wrap on it? Knowing yourself as to your psychological strengths and weak points is critical in this work. Practicing **mindfulness** techniques by increasing awareness and acceptance of feeling and body states and gently letting go allows one to preempt stress as it starts to arise and ameliorate when it's present. Research (Decker et al., 2015; Felton et al., 2015; Thieleman & Cacciatore, 2014; Thompson et al., 2014) has shown that practicing mindfulness has positive effects on decreasing CF and increasing CS.

9. Get supervision from somebody who knows his or her business about trauma work. Your bartender, hairdresser, minister, golfing buddies, or book club members are fine to talk with, but they are "regular" folks up in point 5. You do need somebody who knows this business and how to effectively supervise you as you do it.

Epilogue: Cross-Cultural Comparisons

This chapter is not just for human services **LO11** workers in the United States. If you are reading this book in Germany, Scotland, Australia, Poland,

Austria, Canada, Denmark, China, Korea, Israel, Japan, or some other country, this chapter is also for you. Victor Savicki (2002) conducted a landmark study of child care workers, culture, work environment, and burnout across the United States, Australia, a number of European countries, and Israel and compared them on Maslach Burnout Inventory subscales (Maslach & Jackson, 1981a). What Savicki found when he compared 13 different cultures was that all of you out there don't do well and tend to burn out when there are heavy workloads, unsupportive middle-level managers, an atmosphere in which new ideas and practices are restricted, and inefficiently organized work. Conversely, when the work environment offers encouragement for new ideas, a team of coworkers lends support, and managers set the stage for positive feelings of goal attainment, low burnout scores are the result (Savicki, 2002, pp. 80–87).

However, when culture is factored in, Maslach's three components of burnout change dramatically. For example, Danish and both French Canadian and English Canadian workers have low emotional exhaustion, low depersonalization, and high sense of personal accomplishment scores. Child care workers in what was formerly West Germany have high burnout profiles with a low sense of personal accomplishment and high emotional exhaustion and depersonalization scores. Interestingly, in what was formerly East Germany respondents had very little sense of personal accomplishment, yet they were not emotionally exhausted nor did they feel much depersonalization. Clearly, even though those are both German populations, the political cultural artifacts left over from what was formerly a communist country seem to play a role in how child care workers operate and what their culture expects from them, in contrast to the democracy of the former West Germany. Now compare the German scores to those of the Israelis, who had very low depersonalization, very high sense

of personal accomplishment, but were at the median on emotional exhaustion. Then look at the United States, whose workers scored extremely high in sense of personal accomplishment, but unhappily also had high emotional exhaustion and high depersonalization scores (Savicki, 2002, pp. 78–79).

Both general environmental work measures and individual cultural conformity measures showed significant relationships to the burnout subscales (Savicki, 2002, pp. 88–89). For example, the concept of **power distance** means the amount of control that bosses feel they have over workers and vice versa. High power distances mean that bosses believe they can dictate the behavior of their subordinates. It should come as no surprise that high power distances lead to burn out. Likewise, the **uncertainty avoidance principle** is the degree to which cultures establish rules, procedures, and rituals to compensate for uncertainty and chaos (Savicki, 2002, pp. 38–41). Again it should be no surprise that those cultures with high uncertainty avoidance and many rules to guide the bureaucracy tend to have high burnout scores.

The implications of Savicki's (2002) work would seem to be that not only are the individual worker and the work setting complicit in whether burnout potential is high or low, but also that the overall culture may be a factor as well. If that is true, changing the cultural factor is a tall order indeed! Savicki's (2002) study examines countries whose cultures are generally seen to be more individualist as opposed to collectivist, although arguments could certainly be made for a more collectivist Gestalt in what used to be East Germany and other former Soviet bloc countries of Eastern Europe. It would be interesting to see how child care workers from Middle Eastern, African, and Asian cultures that tend to operate more on the collectivist end of the cultural continuum would fare on the Burnout Inventory. Much like avian flu, burnout circles the globe, and you can catch it pretty much anywhere.

SUMMARY

Burnout is not simply a sympathy-eliciting term to use when one has had a hard day at the office. It is a very real malady that strikes people and can have extremely severe consequences. It is prevalent in the human services professions because of the kinds of clients, environments, working conditions, and

resultant stresses that are operational there. Because of the intense and stressful nature of crisis intervention, a major contributor to burnout is constant exposure to clients who have had horrific experiences.

Prolonged exposure can induce what is variously called *vicarious traumatization*, *compassion fatigue*, or *secondary traumatization* in the crisis worker. No one particular individual is more prone to experience burnout than another. However, by their very nature, most human services workers tend to be highly committed to their profession, and such commitment is a necessary precursor to burnout. Private practitioners may experience burnout even more severely than their counterparts in organizations because of their professional isolation. All human services workers, public or private, tend to be unable to identify the problem when it is their own. No one is immune to its effects.

Burnout moves through stages of enthusiasm, stagnation, frustration, and apathy. In its end stage, burnout is a crisis situation. The crisis takes many forms. It can be manifested behaviorally, physically, interpersonally, and attitudinally. It pervades the professional's life and can have effects on clients, coworkers, family, friends, and the organization itself.

Recognition of the beginning symptoms of burnout can alleviate its personal and organizational ramifications. Raising consciousness levels in regard to the dynamics of burnout in training programs and conducting on-the-job workshops are important ways of halting and ameliorating its effects. Support groups within the organization that provide instrumental and emotional resources to victims are important. In the past, burnout has been regarded as a malady that resides only within the individual. That view is archaic. Burnout should also be viewed in a systems perspective and as an organizational and cultural problem. At its end stage, burnout is a crisis situation that calls for immediate, direct, and reality-oriented therapeutic intervention. Given corrective remediation, victims of burnout can return to the job and again become productive.

Visit CengageBrain.com for a variety of study tools and useful resources such as video examples, case studies, interactive exercises, flashcards, and quizzes.

No Man's Land
Facing Disaster

The last part of this book is aptly named "No Man's Land" because it deals with the large-scale crisis and megacrisis that result when disaster strikes. The chaos that greets survivors and first responders of large-scale crises or mega-disasters is very much like the desolate, wrecked landscape that lies between two battle lines in trench warfare. What has been called the "fog of war" holds true here.

The final chapter of this book is divided into two parts. The first part deals with how the system operates in response to a disaster. A large-scale disaster can never be taken out of the context of its systemic impact. The second part deals with the people who go into that no man's land and the survivors who are there to greet them. It is our belief that a lot of you who aspire to a career in this field will be going into wrecked landscapes like this.

Disaster Response

17

A Brief History of Disaster Mental Health Provision

When the first edition of this book was pub- **LO1** lished in 1988, it didn't have a chapter on disaster response. The simple reason was that we would have been hard pressed to fill up three pages of print on theory, research, or practice with regard to the provision of mental health services after a large-scale disaster. Although the federal government has been involved in disaster relief since the 19th century, until recently it has paid very little attention to the psychological aftershocks of a disaster. It wasn't until 1974, as part of a major overhaul of disaster policy, that the Disaster Relief Act was passed. In that bill was section 413, which authorized the National Institute of Mental Health (NIMH) to supply counseling services to victims of disasters and also provided funds to train professionals in the provision of mental health services to disaster victims. Since 1985 there has been close to a 400% increase in global natural disasters and on average over 1,000,000 people are killed a year by disaster and 216 million become victims (Center for Research on the Epidemiology of Disasters, 2014).

We believe that the notion that people would need mental health assistance after a disaster has roots similar to those of the crisis movement itself. It appears that at least four distinct variables fell into place prior to 2000 to make this happen. First was the birth of community mental health, authorized by the Community Mental Health Act of 1963, which put mental health workers in places like Rapid City, South Dakota, Wilkes-Barre, Pennsylvania, and Logan County, West Virginia. These were "hometown" folks, not bureaucrats in

some far away capital city, and they would give voice to the mental misery survivors were suffering after a large-scale natural disaster.

Second was the classification of PTSD as a personality disorder in the DSM-III in 1980. That medical classification acknowledged and legitimized the concept of people suffering enduring mental problems after direct exposure to a life-threatening event. That diagnosis can admirably fit survivors of disasters.

Third was the American Red Cross's decision in the early 1990s to establish a mental health certification program after hurricane Hugo and the Loma Prieta earthquake in 1989. Indeed, the American Red Cross separated out disaster mental health from its disaster nursing mainly because of its workers' breaking down from prolonged field placements in

LEARNING OBJECTIVES

After studying this chapter, you should be able to:

1. Understand the history and development of disaster mental health relief in the United States.
2. Understand the status of disaster mental health in the world.
3. Know the part ecosystems play in crisis intervention.
4. Know what national crisis response teams are and what they do.
5. Know what a disaster mental health plan entails.
6. Know what crisis workers do in a disaster.
7. Know how multiculturally competent crisis workers operate in a disaster.
8. Understand how the crisis worker handles spiritualism and religion in disasters.
9. Know the principles and techniques of debriefing.

the back-to-back disasters of hurricane Hugo and the Loma Prieta earthquake (Morris, 2011).

Fourth was the women's movement during the 1960s and 1970s, which brought increased awareness of how often trauma strikes families and what its aftershocks do to a family whose entire belongings have been swept, blown, or burned away. When combined, these variables would play a major role in moving the concept of disaster mental health from an idle backwater into a tsunami of disaster mental health assistance in 2011. Given that movement, you are now going to read a whole lot more in this eighth edition than the few pages we might have scraped together in the first edition back in 1987.

If you harken back to Chapter 1, where we talked about the coalescing of grassroots movements into a large voice that attracts attention from the media, and soon after that legislatures, you will begin to understand why specific places like Rapid City, South Dakota, Wilkes-Barre, Pennsylvania, and Logan County, West Virginia, became important players in the birthing of disaster mental health. All three of these places suffered terrible flooding in 1972, and Logan County became particularly notorious because of a mining company's failure to maintain the Buffalo Creek dam, which ruptured. The resulting flood waters at Buffalo Creek killed 125 people and wrecked or badly damaged 1,500 homes. To make matters worse, God or Mother Nature didn't cause the disaster but the coal company did, so there was someone to focus attention on that could have prevented the disaster.

Local mental health providers were overwhelmed by survivors needing psychological assistance in all three places, and both state and federal officials were slow to react in providing help. This issue caught the eyes and ears of reporters, and a great deal of publicity was garnered in support of providing mental health assistance to disaster survivors. So legislators who were already attuned to the notion that victims would need psychological help thought it made good common sense (and particularly good reelection sense) to include mental health funding in the 1974 bill.

There was little research to back up the notion that a lot of people would need psychotherapy after a disaster, but that made little difference given the publicity these three floods received. The few mental health workers that were on scene and their cries for help made good subjects for interviews. One of the best examples of how well disaster mental health assistance could be played in the media was the San Fernando Child Guidance clinic that decided to get

into the trauma game after an earthquake struck the San Fernando Valley in California in 1971. The clinic announced that they were offering counseling services for children who had been in the quake area. Over the next few weeks they counseled more than 500 children in the quake area and got the attention of the national media, which generated headlines like "Quake proofing kids." Dr. Stephen Howard, director of clinical services, got nationwide attention when he declared in an interview with the *New York Times* that the American Red Cross's attitude of "keeping a stiff upper lip" wouldn't work and that survivors needed to "talk about their issues" (Morris, 2011).

Return now to Rapid City, South Dakota. The local government's small number of overwhelmed mental health professionals and the federal government's lack of interest in the survivors' plight prompted a call for help from a steering committee the local mayor organized that reached all the way to the Denver, Colorado, office of the National Institute of Mental Health. The NIMH finally responded by sending psychiatric help to the beleaguered city. The problems of adequate mental health provision that were uncovered at Rapid City motivated U.S. senators from the state to become very active in funding these provisions for the Disaster Recovery Act.

In Wilkes-Barre a model program developed by local community mental health providers and the National Institute of Mental Health served as a blueprint for the creation of disaster mental health programs. Called Operation Outreach, one component of this program was the training of outreach workers to go out and meet survivors as they tried to reassemble their lives and provide basic mental health services. Their initial attempts to provide those services were not accepted kindly by the survivors until the workers started giving them assistance in getting the basic necessities of living back in their lives. Then the survivors started to take them into their confidence. Please note that this is a hard lesson to learn for zealous mental health practitioners who volunteer to go to a disaster. Like the workers at Wilkes-Barre, and Dr. Holly Branthoover whom you will get to meet later in the chapter, it is about moving boxes, procuring lice kits, and having your underarm deodorant fail before you ever get to the counseling stage.

Finally, rescue workers in the Buffalo Creek dam failure in Logan County noticed many of the symptoms in survivors that would later be formalized into PTSD criteria. The resulting lawsuit against the mining company whose failed dam had caused the

Buffalo Creek disaster brought a number of famous mental health experts into the courtroom. One of them was Robert Lofton, a psychiatrist from Yale, who had done extensive study on Vietnam veterans and would later lay the foundation blocks for what would become PTSD from his work with them. He recognized some of the same pathology in the flood survivors and testified that everybody in Buffalo Creek was affected (Morris, 2011).

A group of people from all three of these disasters were gathered by the medical advisor to the Office of Emergency Preparedness (then the leader in disaster mitigation). There was general agreement that there was not a large outbreak of mental illness, but it was acknowledged that the emotional security of a large number of individuals had been compromised (Morris, 2011). Thus was born the Disaster Relief Act of 1974. This act then evolved into the Stafford Disaster Relief and Emergency Assistance Act of 1986, whose section 416 provided for enhanced mental health services to disaster survivors.

To really understand why mental health generally did not get front row status for a long time, you need to understand that the U.S. government's historical approach to disasters was piecemeal and spread over a variety of agencies. It wasn't until 1978 that the Federal Emergency Management Agency (FEMA) was authorized. It absorbed a variety of agencies that ranged from insurance to weather prediction to civil defense to dam and building safety to counterterrorism. It essentially became a catchall for everything that might create some kind of disaster in the United States. After 9/11, FEMA itself was absorbed into the Department of Homeland Security, becoming the Department of Emergency Preparedness and Response Directorate, which pretty much put FEMA in the back seat politically, financially, and prioritywise. After the debacle of hurricane Katrina, FEMA once again regained stand-alone status as a department. So it is not just mental health that has been given short shrift, but the overall coordination of natural and human-made disasters in the United States. So why has all this now changed?

Since 1974 there has been a huge change in that now psychological services and the people who provide them are seen as an integral part of disaster intervention by the federal government (Dodgen & Meed, 2010). The trauma business meandered along in the 1990s, but school shootings such as the Columbine and Sandy Hook public schools, the Virginia Tech massacre, and the Colorado movie shooting focused attention on

disaster in suburbia, the carnage of 9/11 put trauma back up in lights on the national marquee, and the horrific foul-ups by FEMA during hurricane Katrina sealed the notion that mental health would be an important part of any disaster in the 20th century in the United States.

In the aftermath of Katrina, the government poured $52 million for mental health support into Project Recovery in Mississippi, Project Rebound in Alabama, and Louisiana Spirit in Louisiana. That sum of money was second only to the $132 million that went in to mental health services after 9/11 (Morris, 2011).

The emerging concern is how very large intervention systems interact with one another to deal with large-scale crises and megacrises that may arise at the national, state, or community level and directly or indirectly affect neighborhoods, families, and ultimately the individual. Part of the problem is that crisis response systems have not been upgraded along with the times. Remember from Chapter 1 that large disaster relief systems in the United States that are designed to physically aid communities after catastrophes are about 100 years old (Echterling & Wylie, 1999). The field of individual crisis intervention as it is applied in a scientific and systematic manner is about 60 years old (Lindemann, 1944). Systematic and comprehensive intervention by the U.S. government is about 30 years old (Federal Emergency Management Agency, n.d.). The addition of psychological crisis intervention systems and their incorporation into those large macrosystems are about 35 years old—if we are very generous in our time estimation.

While there has been a great deal of research since 9/11 on what kinds of mental health intervention and techniques work on individuals (Watson, Brymer, & Bonanno, 2011), there has been very little research in large-scale **ergonomics**. Cognitive and organizational ergonomics is the rather exotic scientific discipline concerned with understanding the interactions among humans and other elements of a system. It is the profession that applies theory, principles, data, and methods to product design in order to optimize human well-being and overall system performance—which also applies to coordinating, collaborating, and allocating resources after a disaster.

While system interfaces with individuals and ergonomics are pretty cerebral and exotic and not likely to be the topic of discussion over coffee at Starbucks or beer at a sports bar, understanding how those systems work, what effects they have in the fight against terrorism and in large-scale natural disasters, and the mental health issues that go with them is critically important. In a compelling article on this subject, Nickerson (2011) points out that his literature search turned up very little on how ergonomics could help deal with the effects of terrorism when they occur. That research is compelling because, over and over, communication between human beings operating in different systems becomes problematic. Former members of the 9/11 Commission, meeting on the 10th anniversary of that act of terrorism, stated that there were still problems of communication among first responders (Callahan, 2011).

Further, there is little research on how these large systems work—or, in fact, whether they do work—in a palliative psychological manner with various subsystems or individuals (Dziegielewski & Powers, 2005; Litz & Gibson, 2006). Finally, even less is known about what effects vicarious traumatization has on large systems, or indeed what we should do about the effects that instantaneous real-time electronic media can have on various subsystems and the individual (Ursano & Friedman, 2006). How well systems communicate with one another and understanding the effects of rapid changes in technological, geophysical, and societal forces on prevention, intervention, and postvention are key issues in the mitigation of a disaster (Aten et al., 2011; Stokols et al., 2009).

To the contrary, research into evidence-based post-trauma practices for individuals has exploded since 9/11 in the quest to find the best way to help people with mental health issues postdisaster (Watson, Brymer, & Bonanno, 2011). The acronym PTSD was known to few people in the first edition of this book in 1988—even our students! Now PTSD has become a household abbreviation for somebody who is traumatized. Professional organizations have ramped up their focus on trauma. Division 56, Trauma Psychology, has been formed by the American Psychological Association and is one of its fastest growing divisions. The Council on Accreditation of Counseling and Related Educational Programs (CACREP), the accrediting body for counselors, has mandated crisis intervention as part of a required curriculum, as has the National Association of School Psychologists. Government, government-subsidized agencies, and professional organizations have published psychoeducational materials that range from mental health reactions after a disaster (National Center for PTSD, 2014) and providing schools with memorial guides to 9/11 (American School Counselor Association, 2011). Two centers for dissemination of information and research, the National Center for PTSD and the National Child Traumatic Stress Network have come into existence in the last 10 years as a direct or indirect consequence of 9/11, Katrina, and Columbine High School.

Where the World Is

The United States is not alone in its changed **LO2** attitudes toward mental health provision after a natural disaster. Australia has been one of the leaders in the area because of the many natural disasters it has faced. Beverly Raphael, a professor of psychiatry in Australia, has been in the forefront of disaster research and practice with her landmark books *The Anatomy of Bereavement* (1984), *When Disaster Strikes* (1986), and *Disaster Mental Health Response Handbook* (2000), and dozens of research articles, chapters, and edited books on trauma and disaster.

Europe has established the European Network for Traumatic Stress (TENTS, 2011) in response to a need for consensus on what evidence-based outcomes work. TENTS has been funded by the European Union and has built Europe-wide networks of expertise in the psychosocial management of victims of natural and other disasters. It provides services, expertise, and support to areas of the Union that lack resources and availability of trained personnel (TENTS, n.d.).

Internationally, the United Nations' Inter-Agency Standing Committee (IASC, 2007) has published *IASC Guidelines on Mental Health and Psychosocial Input Support in Emergency Situations*. Those guidelines are being used by countries as small and remote as Nepal to put into operation their disaster responses (Jordans et al., 2010).

International Terrorism and Human–Made Disasters

The ecological, contextual model of crisis intervention, based on ecosystem theory that has emerged on the international scene, is characterized by continuously accelerating events in dynamically changing cultures and environments (Conyne et al., 2003; James, Cogdal, & Gilliland, 2003; James & Gilliland, 2003, pp. 341–342; Myer & Moore, 2006; Norris et al., 2006). Foremost among these events in the United States has been the September 11, 2001, hijackings and terrorist attacks and destruction of the World Trade Center towers in New York City, the attack on the Pentagon, and the crashed airliner in Pennsylvania. These tragedies caused untold grief, loss of property, loss of life, economic damage, and a change in the attitudes of most Americans regarding safety and security (Bass & Yep, 2002; Pyszczynski, Solomon, & Greenberg, 2002). The actions following 9/11 also set in motion other unprecedented events, such as the passage of the Homeland Security Act by the U.S. Congress and the invasions of Afghanistan and Iraq, and placed security in the United States at wartime levels. Practically every American had the feeling of having been individually attacked (Brainerd, 2002) and that we were, indeed, at war.

Add to 9/11 other terrifying events—the bombing of the Murrah Federal Building in Oklahoma City, the attacks on students in high schools from Littleton, Colorado, to Springfield, Oregon, to college students at Virginia Tech University and Northern Illinois University—and there is good reason for most Americans to think the United States is no longer a sanctuary but a battleground. Across the world, events such as the taking of hostages by Chechens and their resulting deaths in a rescue attempt in a Moscow theater and a southern Russian school, Palestinian suicide bombings in the streets of Israel, Muslim radicals' bombing of a nightclub and hotel in Bali and Jakarta and trains in Madrid, the Charlie Hebdo magazine attack in Paris, the assassination of armed services recruiters in Chattoonga, Tennessee, drug gang wars in Mexico that approach total war, embassies and nightclubs blown up in Africa and Asia by al Qaida, and the postwar chaos in Iraq and Afghanistan all send clear messages that the world is an unsafe place and that terror may strike unannounced anywhere and at any time. As a result, the hypervigilance of being constantly on guard, the economic loss because of these attacks, and the social and financial expenses of guarding against them cause a variety of previously unknown stressors to appear that impact and crosscut entire nations, cultures, and ecosystems.

Disaster in the form of terrorism has its own special brand of traumatic wake for survivors and has the potential to have metastasizing effects across large systems (Huddy & Feldman, 2011; Morgan, Wisneski, & Skitka, 2011; Ursano & Friedman, 2006). This is true because of the unpredictability of the when, where, and to whom it will happen. Further, the seeming randomness creates fear and anxiety because there is no assurance it will not happen again, and where is anybody's guess. The use of insidious means such as poison gas, germ warfare, or nuclear arms causes horror and incredulity at their seemingly immoral use in the business of mass murder. Information is often inaccurate or highly controlled by the government, which creates uncertainty and anxiety. Increased, constant hypervigilance creates constant and heightened anxiety, which causes both immediate and long-term physical health problems.

Media coverage enhances the horror of gruesome death and injuries. Constant viewing of scenes of death and destruction increases trauma risk. Further compounding the trauma is the aftermath of the terrorist attack with ruinous financial loss and frustration and anxiety at the government's inability to act or bring the perpetrators to justice—particularly when they are outside the country's borders. Finally, there is the added difficulty of finding victim services and mental health professionals who have the know-how to deal with the unique issues that terrorist victims bring with them (Dziegielewski & Sumner, 2005; Myers & Wee, 2005, pp. 247-248). Pastel and Ritchie (2006) aptly call these weapons of mass *disruption* because of the profound psychological ripple effects they cause.

The Israelis are no strangers to terror. Practically all Israeli children carry cell phones so that they can immediately contact their parents and let them know they are safe after bombing or rocket attacks. It is somewhat chilling that one of the favorite children's costumes during the Israeli Purim holiday (somewhat equivalent to Halloween in the United States) among ultraorthodox Jews was a replica of the "Zaka" uniform. Zaka is an ultraorthodox volunteer organization dedicated to ensuring proper burial according to Jewish rituals. In the immediate aftermath of a terrorist attack, they search for body parts to bring as much of the body as possible to burial (Galai-Gat, 2004). After Galai-Gat delivered the paper just cited at the Annual Convening of Crisis Intervention Personnel, she related how amazed she was that people could come and go so freely from the downtown Chicago hotel where the convention was being held. Thus in a changing world, the question arises, "As go the Israelis, shall the rest of the world go also, and does our mental health system go with it?"

Terrorism brings unique challenges to mental health professionals when weapons of mass destruction are used. The ratio of physical dead and wounded to psychologically afflicted is astounding. Obhu and associates (1997) found that in the Tokyo subway gas attack 11 people died but up to 9,000 people sought medical care because they *thought* they had been gassed. There is also the potential for organic mental disorders along with standard stress reactions given the type of weapon used. Medical isolation and quarantine can create additional stress in individuals who may not be able to receive support from their social systems and in fact may be seen as lepers to be avoided (Flynn, 1998).

The worldview of individuals subjected to terrorist-generated disasters may be very different from others'. There is a good deal of evidence to indicate that these individuals experience PTSD, panic and anxiety disorders, and depression at a far greater and more intense rate than others who are subject to "natural" disasters (U.S. Department of Justice, 2000). While there has been progress, with the counseling field becoming more trauma aware (Shallcross, 2011) and the Red Cross making concerted efforts to provide crisis intervention training to wider segments of first responders, there is as yet little unified training for the sheer number of mental health providers needed in *any* large-scale disaster or megadisaster. This issue is even more pressing with the lack of expertise to deal specifically with terrorist acts (Myers & Wee, 2005, p. 251; Roberts, 2005).

Lastly, the mental health infrastructure itself may be destroyed or disabled by human-made or natural disasters or simply be overwhelmed by the staggering volume of people it will be expected to service. In her pictorial representation of early interventions with survivors of terrorist attacks, Galai-Gat (2004) showed a Gary Larson cartoon of a crisis center going over a waterfall while on fire—a good analogy for the worldwide state of crisis intervention and what kinds of chaos ecosystemic crises can bring to local agencies, as witnessed by New Orleans mental health facilities attempting to get back into operation after being completely shut down by hurricane Katrina (Shraberg, 2006).

New Directions and New Visions

Crisis intervention is no longer just a one-on- **LO3** one proposition. We would like to introduce you to what we and some others (Cook, 2012; Collins & Collins, 2005; Gist & Lubin, 1999; Kilmer et al., 2010; Myer & Moore, 2006; Stokols et al., 2009) believe will characterize more and more of what crisis intervention will become in the 21st century—ecosystemic crisis intervention in the wake of a large-scale crisis or megadisaster (James, Cogdal, & Gilliland, 2003). An ecosystemic crisis is one that reaches out and pervades at a minimum the community and perhaps whole regions or nations. It may be immediate and horrific, like 9/11, with a relatively small loss of life, but have

immense ramifications and spread shockwaves around the world. It may slowly and surely spread out across whole continents and have the potential for a tremendous loss of life, such as the African Ebola epidemic or bird flu. It may be human-made, occur dramatically, and then have long-lasting environmental effects that span thousands of years and destroy the social and governing infrastructure of an entire region, such as the Chernobyl nuclear power plant explosion and contamination (Bromet, 1995). It may be malevolent terrorism, creating widespread fear and anger, such as 9/11. It may be a smorgasbord of natural disasters such as the tsunami that struck Japan or hurricane Katrina that drastically altered the landscape and the lives of those in the surrounding area.

In varying degrees, an ecosystemic crisis does all of the foregoing. An ecosystemic crisis not only creates victims who directly experience the traumatic event in widespread numbers, but also creates potential victims because of their vicarious experiencing of the event—even though they may be some geographical or psychological distance from the event itself (Chung et al., 2003; North, 2004; Shallcross, 2011).

This is particularly problematic because often insurance or other mental health care providers do not recognize these groups of survivors as being in need of assistance (Galai-Gat, 2004). Therefore, the definition of an ecosystemic crisis used in this chapter is somewhat different from the definition of crisis as it applies to individuals that is used in the rest of the book. An **ecosystemic crisis** is any disruptive or destructive event that occurs at a rate and magnitude beyond the ability of the normal social process to control it. Unless dedicated resources are brought to ease the crisis, the integrity of the social fabric is generally degraded in the course of the event such that it becomes very difficult if not impossible to sustain the way of life as it was before the crisis occurred (Ren, 2000).

Although a number of theorists and researchers have examined wide-scale disasters and the collective experiences of the populations who experience them (Freedy & Hobfoll, 1995; Gist & Lubin, 1989; Hobfoll, 1988; Hobfoll & deVries, 1995; Kaplan, 1996), most of the literature focuses on a dissection of the individual's psychological responses (Kaniasty & Norris, 1999). Kaniasty and Norris (1999) propose that the individual's psychological response to disaster cannot be understood without considering the collective response that interacts with the political, cultural, environmental, and social realities of the ecosystem as it operated prior to and after the disaster.

Alternatively, on a very pragmatic and mundane level, the Federal Emergency Management Agency (FEMA) and its various departments spend a great deal of time and energy on providing education, information, and direct service in regard to operational responses to disasters of all kinds (Federal Emergency Management Agency, n.d.). However, what FEMA—or anyone, for that matter—doesn't do is determine how this all goes together, and as you will see in a short while, that had ominous implications when hurricane Katrina came ashore. What one also does not find is a way of making sense out of how crisis intervention strategies interface with the community-wide stressors people experience after a disaster and the various agencies that respond to help them.

Although the impact of community-wide and national traumatic events go back historically at least as far as Pompeii being buried by volcanic explosion nearly 2,000 years ago or the Black Plague killing millions of Europeans in the Middle Ages, the knowledge of those catastrophes and their resulting impact were slow to be felt because news of the disaster traveled only by word of mouth. Likewise, help could come only as fast as responders could spread the word and bring together resources that might arrive in horse-drawn carts or be carried on one's back. Often help was simply unavailable, as there was no known way to mitigate the spread of disease.

Communities were isolated, and when a natural or human-made disaster struck, it was typically felt only at the local level. Further, at the local level, the constituents were essentially of the same race, tribe, or clan, or other social identity and commonly held the same cultural, moral, and religious values. In short, until the 20th century, if Haiti suffered an earthquake, it was known and dealt with by the local community and perhaps the regional ruler. The prevailing philosophy was that people took care of themselves because they were the only ones affected by the traumatic event. In fact, if "strangers" had come to offer help, they probably would have been viewed with distrust and suspicion, given the insular cultural values of the time. The best that could be done proactively was to build cities that wouldn't be washed away by flood or blown away by winds, or to quarantine cities infected with disease. Historically, then, most crisis responses were by passive, preventive means that were meant to minimize the damage before it occurred. Little could be done after the fact to minimize the deaths, economic loss, or societal disintegration.

It should also be understood that there is a rather spirited debate today in world health circles as to whether there is in the Third World any need for a Western world mental health disaster mitigation plan as opposed to the need to obtain basic necessities for survival. PTSD is seen as a Western cultural artifact contrived to justify and propagate the medical mental health model (Summerfield, 2005). To the contrary, others do not see PTSD as a cultural artifact, but indeed a phenomenon that is cross-cultural in nature, and that to deny it would be a terrible professional error and subvert the prevention of suffering (deVries, 1998; Dyregrov et al., 2002).

With the advent of the industrial and information ages, active crisis intervention came to mean that a whole society could be rapidly mobilized and coordinated to reshape the total dynamics of a crisis by using the machines and the command/control/communications/intelligence systems that have evolved in the last two centuries (Ren, 2000). With the condensing of geographic and communication distances, a fundamental but essential trend is that a crisis can no longer be contained within an enclave. The interventionist must necessarily function within and become an integral part of an ecological system that is continually and often richly interwoven with environmental components in the immediate neighborhood, town, district, borough, city, county, parish, canton, state, province, country, continent, hemisphere, and ultimately the world.

This fundamental trend is a melding of systemic crisis intervention strategies that interact in the total environmental and multicultural context of a pluralistic and dynamically changing world. Yet this view is clearly not shared by everyone and may be seen by some as a pretext to impose Western medical practices on the rest of the world. Thus, in the early edition of the Sphere Project world health working paper on disaster response ("Humanitarian Charter," 1998), mental health was not even covered. Indeed the term **psychosocial** (having mental distress as a result of social upheaval) has been coined to take away the stigma that a person is mentally ill (Van Ommeren, Saxena, & Saraceno, 2005). Note what the International Inter-Agency Standing Committee Mental Health and *Psychosocial* Support calls itself to make it more palatable to some parts of the international community (IASC, 2007). Indeed, most survivors of a catastrophe may only need social support, and "psychosocial support" is a lot more psychologically palatable than the designator of being "mentally ill."

You should thus understand that what is being proposed in this chapter is not universally loved and admired, or even thought to be necessary or right by a number of people.

To that end, this chapter deals with an emerging *ecosystemic* view of what crisis intervention is becoming as it operates in large systems and deals with metastasizing crises, large-scale crises, and megacrises. **Metastasizing crises** are those that start small but, if not contained both physically and psychologically, can quickly turn into large-scale crises (James, 2006). **Large-scale crises** are those that at a minimum affect whole communities or regions either directly or vicariously. **Megacrises** are defined as those that affect entire countries or the world, either directly or vicariously.

System Overview

The ecological, contextual crisis intervention approach that is described in this chapter reaches far beyond the relational interactions between and among the various members of the crisis client's family, or individuals in the client's workplace and immediate surroundings. Essentially, it is a dynamic, sociocultural, and multicultural view of all ecological influences that impinge upon the individual. It consists of five environmental systems, ranging from the fine-grained inputs of direct communications with social agents (individuals capable of interacting directly with crisis clients) to the broad-based inputs of local community agencies as well as the widespread influences of national imperatives and attitudes and ideologies of the cultures within which these systems operate (Santrock, 1999, pp. 42–44). Cook (2012, p. 5) defines the term **ecosystem** as "The total sum of the interactive influences operating within an individual's life in varying degrees of proximity ranging from his or her biologically determined characteristics to the broader socio cultural context which structures human interactions." The approach is continually changing, emerging, evolving, and developing to accommodate the ecological and multicultural contexts within which it exists. It represents a paradigmatic shift: a newly emerging ecosystem that encompasses an interdependency among and within people at all different levels of the total environment. This is not some static amorphous entity. It is very much alive, and as one part is impacted, other parts react.

This ecosystemic view of crisis intervention is adapted from Uri Bronfenbrenner's (1986, 1995;

Bronfenbrenner & Morris, 1998; Santrock, 1999, pp. 41–46) ecosystemic theory of human development, and our own (James, Cogdal, & Gilliland, 2003; James & Gilliland, 2003, pp. 336–337, 341–342) and other psychotheorists' views (Cook, 2012; Conyne & Cook, 2003; Conyne et al., 2003; Klotz, 2003) of ecosystems as they apply to psychotherapy in general and crisis in particular (Collins & Collins, 2005; Norris et al., 2006; Vernberg, 1999). In crisis intervention terms, not only is the individual in crisis affected but also the client's total environment becomes the context that must be considered by crisis workers (Myer & Moore, 2006). Bronfenbrenner (1986, 1995) identified the five environmental components as the microsystem, mesosystem, exosystem, macrosystem, and chronosystem. (See Figure 17.1.)

Microsystem

The **microsystem** is the setting in which the person in crisis lives. The microsystem setting's contexts may include the individual's family, friends, coworkers, peers, school, neighborhood, and usual haunts. It is within the microsystem that the individual in crisis experiences the most direct social interactions and communications with others. In the microsystem setting, whatever difficulties individuals experience tend to spill over into the family constellation and compound the difficulties caused by the disaster (Green & Solomon, 1995). In the traumatic wake of a disaster, many previous relationships, alliances, partnerships, bonds, and compacts in the microsystem, which were held together in the immediate aftermath as a means of mutual survival, crumble under the weight of compound stresses (Smith & Belgrave, 1995).

The crisis worker adhering to the ecological, contextual, multicultural approach views the person in crisis not as a passive recipient of experiences in those microsystemic settings but as an individual who actively participates in the construction of the settings (Santrock, 1999, p. 42). Reciprocally, the settings have a positive or negative effect on the individual and family and may ameliorate or exacerbate the crisis depending on the person's proximity, relationship to, and perception and meaning of the event (Myer & Moore, 2006).

Mesosystem

In Bronfenbrenner's (1995) developmental system, the mesosystem serves as the communications channel, pathway, or interactive mechanism between components in the microsystem and the exosystem.

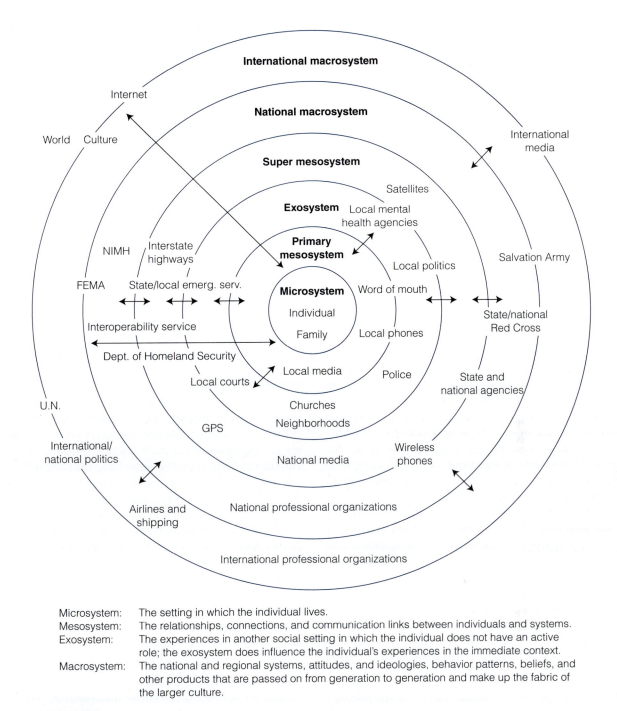

Microsystem: The setting in which the individual lives.
Mesosystem: The relationships, connections, and communication links between individuals and systems.
Exosystem: The experiences in another social setting in which the individual does not have an active
               role; the exosystem does influence the individual's experiences in the immediate context.
Macrosystem: The national and regional systems, attitudes, and ideologies, behavior patterns, beliefs, and
               other products that are passed on from generation to generation and make up the fabric of
               the larger culture.

FIGURE 17.1   Adaptation of Bronfenbrenner's Ecosystemic Model for Crisis

The mesosystem is essentially the total communications network that allows all individuals and groups within each ecological system to exchange information. It includes every form of communication—from word of mouth to the most sophisticated electronic technology—and is far more than cell phones and television news announcements. In terms of crisis and crisis intervention, the mesosystem and its function as the command-and-control structure of the total system are critical.

The crisis mesosystem is interspersed not only between the microsystem and exosystem (primary mesosystem) but between the exosystem and the macrosystem as well (super mesosystem). Both the primary and super mesosystems play critical roles in resolving ecosytemic crises. These two systems are extremely fluid and may expand very rapidly during a crisis. Think of a lava lamp where, as the oil heats up there are rapid and nonsymmetrical movements of the colored oil. This analogy carries over to a rapidly heating and expanding crisis. (Whether this expansion alleviates or exacerbates the crisis depends a great deal on how and what is communicated by whom and under what circumstances.) One of the major failures in the aftermath of hurricane Katrina was the breakdown of this system at both the primary and super levels. It should be understood that disaster mental health systems are complex mesosystems (networks of other systems) in and of themselves, and what makes them even more complex is that they will be imposed on to host micro- and exo-mental health systems that have their own agendas, vary in preparedness for a disaster, and may well suffer severe disruption themselves due to the disaster (Norris et al., 2006).

Local emergency management agencies (LEMAs) expend a great deal of time and effort conducting tabletop and on-scene exercises to determine the most effective way of handling a crisis, dealing with logistics, and field-testing communication links (Freeman, 2003; Lane, 2003). These systems directly link crisis interventionists with emergency management agencies. Human services workers trained by NOVA, FEMA, the American Red Cross, and state and local mental health agencies are on call for emergencies, and when a disaster of a magnitude greater than what the local authorities can handle is encountered, these crisis teams are called up and go into action. In the United States, calling up the National Guard is a fair analogy to what happens when a call goes out for crisis workers. Hurricane Katrina is an excellent example of the need for both.

Primary Mesosystem. Communication in the primary crisis mesosystem means having translators to speak to victims whose native tongue is not the national language. It means having ham radio operators and trained weather spotters with two-way radios and crisis response teams and search-and-rescue teams with walkie-talkies to communicate with one another in wrecked buildings or in a blown-down forest. It means establishing clear links from emergency management agencies to media outlets. It means creating integrated communication networks between emergency management agencies and a wide variety of supportive agencies that range from law enforcement and fire departments to heavy equipment operators and mental health professionals.

A primary **mesosystem** is everything from sign language for a deaf person to the most sophisticated wireless computer satellite uplinks to state and federal emergency management agencies (EMAs) (Freeman, 2003; Lane, 2003). It maintains connections and communications within and among workplaces, schools, churches, families, peer groups, and local social, medical, and governmental services (Bronfenbrenner, 1995; Freeman, 2003; James & Gilliland, 2003, pp. 341–342; Lane, 2003; Santrock, 1999; Stewart-Sickening & Mutai, 2012).

For crisis intervention agencies, fast, effective, clear communication is at the center of everything they do. Communication redundancy is critical because if one system fails, another can be substituted. For example, during an electrical storm, the emergency management director of Nassau County, Florida (Jacksonville area), was in her car and attempting to communicate with a member of her staff about storm damage. But she quickly found that communication was impossible because of electrical interference. Despite all of the sophisticated equipment that the county EMA had, the only thing that worked was leaving messages on each other's voice mail (Freeman, 2003). It is not accidental that Jerry Lane, the former emergency manager of the city of Sycamore, Illinois, is a licensed advanced-class amateur radio operator (Lane, 2003). One of the more aggravating problems of hurricane Katrina was that various local agencies used different radio frequencies and could not communicate with one another, nor could they communicate with the super mesosystem. Thus a recurring theme throughout disaster intervention is that communication is vital to the ability to respond in a disaster (Rebman, Carrico, & English, 2008).

Super Mesosystem. Interlinking the macrosystem with all interior systems is the **super mesosystem**. The super mesosystem that connects the exosystem and the macrosystem serves many of the same coordinating functions, but on a national level. The super mesosystem is composed of information systems that range from the postal service, to national commercial radio and television corporations, to the Internet and its websites, e-mail, instant messaging, and chat rooms, to satellite communication and global positioning systems. Federal agencies such as FEMA, and its parent, the Bureau of Homeland Security, are linked with other governmental agencies such as the Bureau of Justice and private agencies such as the Red Cross and National Organization of Victims Assistance, National Oceanic and Atmospheric Administration weather satellites, the U.S. Weather Service storm prediction centers, supercomputers at national agencies that model and predict disaster scenarios and relief efforts, and the National Emergency Broadcast systems for the public.

National agency and federal department interlinks and downlinks to state EMAs and agencies are all part of the super mesosystem for crisis intervention that operates in the United States. It has major command-and-control centers that can be linked to state communication and control centers, which in turn are linked to local emergency operations centers. These national organizations and agencies have complete mobile command, control, and communications centers that can be rapidly moved on tractor trailers by highway, rail, or ship, or flown into any disaster site. This system was so devastated during hurricane Katrina that the base of operations for repairing the levees and pumping systems in New Orleans was situated in the U.S. Army Corps of Engineers office in Memphis, Tennessee, more than 400 miles up the Mississippi River!

Therefore, the mesosystem is of primary concern to crisis interventionists and the crisis intervention process because it coordinates and drives the dynamic linkages among all components (people, groups, contextual connections, ecological resources). The crisis interventionist—in the role of consultant, collaborator, coordinator, and communicator—is a key resource person operating within the mesosystem.

The advent of smartphones with multiple applications has enhanced the potential of both the primary and super mesosystems in a variety of ways that were unimaginable as little as 5 years ago. Aten and associates (2011) have detailed a number of applications made possible by this new technology:

1. Texting takes far less bandwidth than talking. When other phone systems are plugged up, text messages are likely to get through. Many universities now have text warning systems that can get to any student who has a cell phone on.
2. Smartphone users with weather and news apps can access outside information when they might not otherwise have access to current conditions that affect the crisis.
3. Social networking sites such as MySpace, Facebook, Twitter, Flickr, and LinkedIn allow people to stay in synchronous contact with other net users. Clearly these sites can be used for organizing activities of large groups of people, as witnessed by the recent revolutions in Egypt and Libya which used these devices to organize large demonstrations and avoid police dragnets. These sites would seem to have the same applicability in organizing people during disasters.
4. Global positioning systems (GPS) have proliferated both as hardwired applications in automobiles and trucks and in portable systems such as smartphones. These have tremendous applicability in a disaster for directing traffic, giving directions, providing alternate routes, and locating people who don't know where they are. Onstar is a satellite communication, GPS, and emergency notification communications system hardwired into new General Motors (GM) vehicles. GM has teamed with the American Red Cross to provide information on shelters, medical services, safe routes, food sources, and other services. Aten and associates (2011) reported that Onstar's usage rate went up 30% during hurricane Gustave, which is a pretty good indication of how much its subscribers relied on it during what they considered to be an emergency ("GM's Onstar," 2008).
5. When super mesosystems use systems like Onstar, a great many people can access these systems in a hurry, and they don't need an electrical transmission line to do it. The Centers for Disease Control have picked up on this technology and made podcasts that provide "what to do and what to know" information about disease epidemics, safety tips, and other health-related information that can be used by people in disaster areas with no electricity who might otherwise be cut off from critical health information (CDC, n.d.).

The point of all this new technology is that for many people in the primary mesosystem, using it daily is standard practice. Thus super mesosystems like those operated by the federal government or international charitable organizations can use it not only with their own workers when standard communication links are down, but also with a large number of primary system users who are not mystified by the technology and can then spread the information by word of mouth. If these new devices and systems are put to use wisely, they may do much to push the communication problems that have plagued relief efforts into the dustbin of history.

Exosystem

The **exosystem** exposes the crisis client or clients to experiences in a wider social setting than those encountered in the microsystem context (Bronfenbrenner, 1986, 1995). The exosystem reaches much farther out into the community and may even include state or regional entities. Legal and social welfare services, local mass media, and all governmental agencies and programs that are in a position to impact the individual and to assist persons, families, or groups who are in crisis are part of the exosystem. Crisis workers who live in other parts of the state or province may be called in to help. Typically, in the United States, each local EMA has backup personnel who are in place or on standby support if a crisis arises that temporarily exceeds local capacity to handle the situation.

How effective the exosystem and macrosystem are in providing services depends in large part on how well information passes back and forth through the primary and super mesosystems and how well resources are allocated, delivered, and used based on that information. The FEMA on-site, one-stop-shopping for all related disaster assistance to individuals is an excellent super mesosystem example of direct communication between victims in the microsystem and national providers in the macrosystem.

Macrosystem

The **macrosystem** includes the national government and all its agencies, and national charitable, religious, service, professional, and benevolent organizations. It encompasses the national rail, air, marine, and highway transportation modalities, and food, fuel, and energy transmission systems. The macrosystem encompasses the total culture in which people live (Bronfenbrenner, 1995). Total culture refers to the behavior patterns, traditions, beliefs, mores, historical artifacts, legal constructs, and all other traits and pursuits that are endemic to a group of people and that are passed on from generation to generation (Santrock, 1999, p. 44). The macrosystem has importance in crisis intervention for two reasons. First and foremost, when a disaster exceeds the normal coping capacity of the disaster impact area, the macrosystem is most likely the place from which help and resources will flow. Second, if the crisis is of a national magnitude such as 9/11, it will be important to do a triage assessment of the national psyche to determine what if any intervention needs to occur with the entire ecosystem.

Disasters do not have to be large in geographic scope or have large numbers of fatalities to be considered macrosystemic. The killing rampage of Seung-hui Cho at Virginia Tech in April 2007 was an isolated incident. Although 32 people were killed, that number

pales in comparison to the number of dead on 9/11 in 2001 or the almost daily casualty rate in the Afghan War or the weekly death tolls on U.S. highways. By all objective measures, the Virginia Tech killings were a small disaster. Yet the fact that the tragedy occurred on a quiet college campus, in a place where one's children are supposed to be safe, upset the nation's sense of control much as the Columbine High School and Sandy Hook shootings did. The Virginia Tech tragedy quickly turned into a metastasizing crisis that carried far beyond Blacksburg, Virginia. While landline telephone connections jammed up, text messaging, which takes far less bandwidth, did not. Facebook and other social networks were relaying news of the tragedy as it took place and identified danger zones the students needed to stay out of and get away from (Aten et al., 2011).

Most particularly, parents who had sent their children off to college became very concerned about their children's health and well-being, no matter what university or college they attended and no matter what part of the country it was in. Those parents immediately began sending a deluge of phones calls, letters, and e-mails to universities across the country (a national macrosystem), demanding to know what safety measures were in place to protect their children from psychotic gunmen and other potential predators.

Perhaps even more important, the constituency of the universities, students and professors, are highly capable of communicating across the super mesosystem via e-mail, blogs, cell phones, and text messages. That rapidly expanding super mesosystem put the information, conjecture, hypotheses, and rumors about the massacre at Virginia Tech out into the international macrosystem within hours of the shootings. As an example, the dark, violent, and macabre plays that Seung-hui Cho is alleged to have written as a student at Virginia Tech were published in the blogosphere 24 hours after the shootings occurred.

Chronosystem

The Individual. The **chronosystem** is identified by Bronfenbrenner (1995) as the patterning of environmental events and transactions over the life span as well as the social and historical circumstances that influence the individual, family, peers, coworkers, and others. The essence of the chronosystem is the dynamic influence that time has on events, and time, with its movement, is an absolutely critical variable in regard to disasters. The crisis chronosystem starts with the birth of the traumatic event and not the birth of the person. Although the crisis chronosystem starts with the event, if possible the crisis interventionist needs to backtrack over the personal developmental chronosystem of the individual to determine what, if any, precursors may have contributed to the incident's impact and what antecedent events may cause it to be exacerbated.

In crisis intervention, understanding the part the chronosystem plays in exacerbating or ameliorating the crisis is particularly important. There are two types of disaster trauma—individual and collective (Erikson, 1976). **Individual trauma** hammers the individual psyche and breaks through the person's defense so forcefully and suddenly that reaction is impossible. **Collective trauma** does the same thing, only it does it across the microsystem (the community) to the extent that the social bonds that connect people are torn apart and the community is rent asunder. The chronosystem is important for both individual and collective traumatic responses and can be marked in phases that are generally linear and progressive in nature (see Figure 17.2). Following are brief descriptions of those phases.

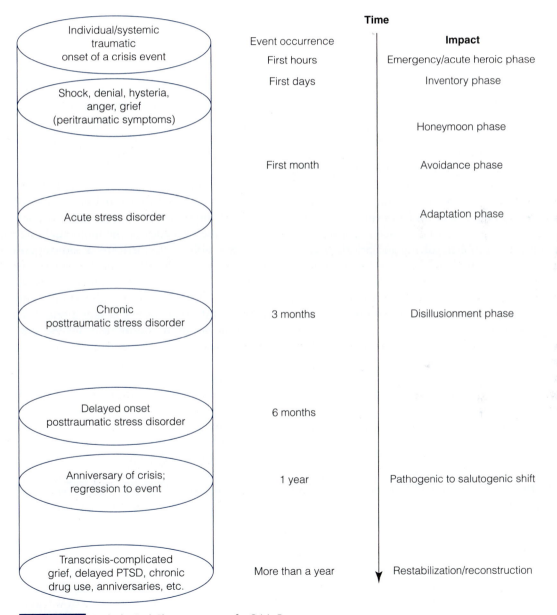

FIGURE 17.2 Pathological Chronosystem of a Crisis Event

Impact phase. The first few minutes and hours during and immediately after the crisis are critically important. While fear and shock are common, most people behave adaptively and take action to protect themselves and their loved ones. Time may become disoriented and slowed down, with disbelief and denial at what has happened. However, while a good deal of collective chaos may ensue, people react mainly in proactive ways (Myers & Wee, 2005, p. 20). Maslow's hierarchy of needs comes into operation, particularly when the crisis is a disaster that leaves people without food, shelter, or clothing. As the crisis plays out in the traumatic wake of the next few days, the resolution of problems ranging from having a roof over one's head to communicating or being physically reunited with one's family becomes critical.

Emergency/acute heroic/rescue phase. Immediately after impact, people spring into action to save others and to save property and regain control of the situation and environment. During this heroic or rescue stage (Myers & Wee, 2005, pp. 20–21; NIMH, 2002; Pennebaker & Harber, 1993) individuals are generally highly energized physically and emotionally, have great morale, cognitively perseverate on the event, and gain relief by talking about their anxieties surrounding the crisis and their responses to it. While individuals are highly energized, problem solving and priority setting are often compromised by the sheer magnitude of the disaster, which many times translates into lots of activity and low efficiency. Seeking or finding out that family members are safe and can be reunited is critical.

Inventory/recovery phase. At some point between the impact and the heroic stage an inventory and initial attempts at recovery phase occur. People conduct an appraisal of the situation and start to plan what they are going to do (NIMH, 2002). They engage in information seeking in regard to finding loved ones, determining whether they are safe or injured, and finding out how well their homes and places of employment have fared (Myers & Wee, 2005, p. 21). Typically there is frustration with the inability to find loved ones or anger at authorities for not letting the survivors back into their neighborhoods to find out about their homes.

Honeymoon phase. There is a collective "we are in this together" attitude. This may last anywhere from 1 week to up to 3 months postimpact. The community pulls together. There is optimism about recovery, and

the belief that there will be full restitution of financial loss is high. There is a great deal of media coverage and high-level political attention. Public outpouring in the form of physical and financial donations give the community a sense of hope for rebuilding, and there is a strong sense of having shared a horrific experience but having prevailed over the worst of it (Farberow & Frederick, 1978).

At any time from 2 weeks to 2 years, depending on the severity and scope of the event, individuals will experience reintegration and return to a pre-event level of functioning or better, or they may not.

Avoidance phase. As individuals work their way through the next few weeks, the kinds of physical and psychological support systems that are provided affect whether acute stress disorder will arise and whether it will eventually turn into posttraumatic stress disorder. As time passes, an avoidance phase generally emerges (Pennebaker & Harber, 1993). People stop talking about the event, but the images and thoughts about it continue to dominate cognitive functioning.

Adaptation phase. Whether the pathology of the event continues and the individual enters the adaptation phase (Pennebaker & Harber, 1993) depends a great deal on the resiliency of the individual and the crisis worker's ability to institute a **salutogenic model** (Antonovsky, 1980, 1991) that emphasizes health and wellness over sickness and pathology. The salutogenic concept affirms what we historically know about people and crisis. Stress is ever present, and severe stress is going to occur, but people are resilient, recover, and can thrive and grow from it. If people can come to grips with the financial, emotional, and environmental problems they will invariably face, and come to see that no matter what they do things will never quite be the same as they were before but they can move forward, they will have adapted and move on. However, for many adaptation will be difficult because of the disillusionment that sets in.

Disillusionment phase. Disillusionment may begin several days or weeks after impact and may last for years, depending on how individuals adjust to their new environment. Disillusionment occurs because the media and politicians go home, bureaucratic red tape slows recovery, insurance money doesn't pay out as much as expected, and multiple other problems arise that say that recovery will be slow if at all. Fatigue finally sets in, and the individual is emotionally and physically exhausted from extended psychological and physical stress. A variety of public health problems may arise from poor living and sanitary conditions, environmental pathogens, and communicable diseases. Stress-related health symptoms, ranging from high blood pressure to exacerbation of preexisting health problems, may occur. Disaster relief workers ironically refer to this period as the **second disaster**. Psychological problems may range from PTSD to panic and anxiety disorders to depression and suicidal ideation (Myers & Wee, 2005, pp. 23).

Anniversary phase. As time moves forward into the next year, the anniversary of the occurrence may become significant (Cohen et al., 2006). After a year or more has passed since the incident, a transcrisis state may be reached, depending on whether the individual has resolved the trauma or not. For some victims, the need to talk about and seek help validating their experience will go on and on, much to the dismay of others. This continuing need for catharsis and rumination about the crisis may be met with disapproval and outright anger by others in the victim's support system who seek to distance themselves from it (Smith & Belgrave, 1995). The result is often a perception by the victim of secondary victimization.

Pathogenic to salutogenic shift. Around the time of the first anniversary of the traumatic event, a benchmark is usually reached. If individuals have put the traumatic event into past context, mourned their losses, and started to rebuild their lives, then they have made a **salutogenic shift** in their lives (a shift that is healthful, wholesome, promoting psychological growth) (Antonovsky, 1980). They have met the challenge the traumatic event posed for them and are able to move on with their lives. In contrast, if individuals have remained mired in the traumatic event long past the acute stage, then they may be said to have made a **pathogenic** (diseased, unwholesome, psychologically debilitating) **shift** that may become residual and chronic, bringing on a host of physical and psychological maladies. A continuing and contentious issue in the field of trauma therapy is how individuals attain and retain a salutogenic state and if they do or do not need assistance in doing so (Stuhmiller & Dunning, 2000). Antonovsky (1991) has demonstrated that the stronger a person's sense of coherence (the extent to which the stress is deemed manageable, coherent, and meaningful), the more likely he or she is able to cope with life's stressors.

If that model is adopted, then much of the role and function of the crisis worker ceases to exist, because in a salutogenic model stress is universal, humans have adapted to it, and they do not necessarily crumble under traumatic stress (Stuhmiller & Dunning, 2000).

Restabilization/reconstruction phase. As time passes, decisions have to be made as to whether to rebuild one's life in the same environment or move on to a different place. Rebuilding is not just putting a new house up after an earthquake. It is also about rebuilding and restabilizing one's emotional and social self. Even though there are setbacks, with denied loans, divorce papers, homes that are a total loss, friendships that have been lost, or friends who have died in the disaster, somehow over the months and perhaps years, stabilization and new constructs replace the old.

Therefore, as time moves forward, the survivor needs to engage in a process that is much like Schneider's (1984) transformational model of grief. Monitoring and following up on this transformational process to the client's final acceptance and putting the disaster in perspective may require tracking the client for a year or more. Richard Tedeschi and Lawrence Calhoun have been hard at work on the concept of posttraumatic growth (Calhoun & Tedeschi, 2008; Taku et al., 2015; Tedeschi & Calhoun, 2009, 2010, 2012; Triplett et al., 2012). These two researchers have developed different inventories—Post Traumatic Growth Inventory (Taku et al., 2008), Post Traumatic Growth Inventory for Children (Kilmer et al., 2009), Short Form of the Traumatic Growth Inventory (Cann et al., 2010), and The Event Related Rumination Inventory (Cann et al., 2011)—to assess people's ability to discover new possibilities such as better ways of relating to others, new personal strengths, positive spiritual changes, and stronger appreciation of life in the wake of a crisis (DeAngelis, 2011). One might say they are putting the empirical test to the Chinese Kanja characters indicating both crisis and opportunity.

The Society. When we move from the individual to the society at large (the micro-, exo-, or macrosystem), the chronosystem also plays an important part in what is going to happen systemically. In the immediate hours and days of the aftermath of the crisis, all of the resources, agencies, and personnel needed to bring control and equilibrium back to the community are brought to bear, and time becomes acutely important. During this heroic stage

(Raphael, 2000), the system responds with unselfishness, self-sacrifice, and heroism in its attempts to rescue people and provide shelter and emergency assistance. Indeed, if there is forewarning, such as the landfall of a hurricane, timelines will extend backward to precede the occurrence.

As an example, the Nassau County Florida Emergency Management Department has a nine-stage sequence that extends from an awareness stage, which starts 72 hours before the hurricane's projected landfall, to a reconstruction stage, which may be continuous and ongoing for weeks or months after the hurricane is over (Nassau County Emergency Management Department, n.d.). During the immediate aftermath, a psychological honeymoon stage (Raphael, 2000) occurs in which there is a great deal of attention by the media, massive intervention by disaster relief agencies, and the notion that things will be set right and services quickly restored. There is an overall "We're all in the same boat, and everybody is equal" attitude.

After all of the emergency crews have finished getting power and phone lines back on, the wonderful outside assistance and resource support have gone home, and the media have moved on to the next disaster, the long-term degrading effects of the disaster are still there and consuming additional resources. When physical facilities—such as churches, schools, parks, and community centers—are gone, activities and interpersonal contacts that were taken for granted may be lost. State and federal bureaucracies and insurance companies seem to have miles and miles of red tape and may deny requests for compensation and support for reconstruction of basic infrastructure. Both for individuals and communities, this phase has often been called the "second disaster" (Myers & Wee, 2005, p. 29).

Losing access to community gathering places has symbolic, social, spiritual, and psychological meaning and may have long-term toxic effects on the community. Rebuilding these structures and reestablishing social links that were severely fractured take a great deal of time and effort (Kaniasty & Norris, 1999). At this point, a disillusionment stage may emerge (Raphael, 2000). There is a sense of frustration, hopelessness, and abandonment that things will never be the same. Widespread posttraumatic stress and depressive symptoms are likely to appear if continuous and long-term mental health assistance is not available. Thus, a very real question arises as to the "when" of provision of services. It is not nearly as

glamorous 6 months after a disaster strikes to appear on the scene "ready to help," but it may be as critically important to provide mental health services in the long term as it is in the short term.

Community resilience has become a key component in federal emergency plans. Whether a community rebirths or dies after a disaster has a lot to do with how well it plans for disaster by building community resilience through both individual preparedness and establishing a supportive context within that community (Plough et al., 2013). That supportive context particularly speaks to providing social justice for vulnerable populations that typically experience short shrift in the provision of goods and services in the aftermath of a disaster (Baker & Cormier, 2015; DeAngelis, 2014; Royiscar, 2013; Roysicar et al., 2013).

The chronosystem, then, represents the development of events in individuals' lives and larger social systems over time, and crisis interventionists need to be aware of how important time and timing are in responding to crises. The phrases "Time changes everything" and "Time is of the essence" appear to capture the flavor of the chronosystem (James & Gilliland, 2003, p. 342).

Defining Principles of a Crisis Intervention Ecosystem

Coming to grips with complex ecosystem service delivery issues is daunting, to say the least. However, Conyne and Cook (2003) and Norris and her associates (2006) have generated the following principles for doing so.

1. *Systems must be interdisciplinary.* No single discipline or "ology" has a corner on this market. Emergency management agencies and crisis intervention systems must rely on a broad spectrum of people, ranging from sanitation workers and electrical linemen to civil and logistical engineers to medical emergency staff and communication workers to law enforcement and fire and rescue personnel to sociologists and psychologists to bankers and economists to ministers and social workers. Further, all of the people in these skills, crafts, trades, and professions must work in an integrated manner. The competent crisis worker integrates seamlessly into this smorgasbord of "ologies"; the pretentiousness sometimes associated with a college degree and the egotism of a particular profession have no place in an ecosystemic

crisis. Ecosytemic crisis intervention is the most egalitarian of all mental health endeavors, and layperson volunteers may be just as effective as psychiatrists. Anyone with an inflated ego will soon be humbled in a large crisis.

2. *The system must be multitheoretical.* If we look at only the psychological component of wide-scale crises, no single psychological theory is presently adequate to deal with the complex swirl of human dynamics that comes out of a crisis. It should be stated absolutely and unequivocally that nobody has a theoretical corner on this market. That includes proselytizers for any of the "alphabet" techniques such as CISD, EMDR, TFT or, alternatively, those who would rail against them. It especially includes the authors of this book! When dealing with large-scale crises or megacrises, psychological theory must at the very least harmonize with logistics, medical, communications, economic, and political theory. To further complicate matters, it is not just which psychological theories and techniques are used, but also when and how those services are delivered.

3. *Individuals are part of the ecosystem.* Like it or not, unless we can somehow find a place in the desert or mountains to become hermits, we are part of the total ecosystem of the world. Our biological makeup, interpersonal relationships, physical environment, and sociological context are all becoming more tightly interwoven into the total ecosystem of the world.

4. *Multiple contexts must be considered.* Micro-, meso-, exo-, and macrosystems are all components of the total ecological system that impact the individual when a megacrisis occurs. To deny that these systems are vectors and forces that impinge on the individual is to have a very parochial view of what this business is about and is to be doomed to fail.

5. *Time is of the essence.* If we believe any of the PTSD research about the deleterious effects the passage of time has on the individual if nothing is done to alleviate the possible effects of the trauma, we need to understand that what occurs in the chronosystem is critical. The availability of adequate physical and psychological resources to deal with a crisis in a timely manner is paramount.

6. *Meaning is important.* What sense we make of the crisis from a broad systemic view is as important as what sense we make of it individually and has much to do with how quickly and effectively it is resolved for both individuals and society.

7. *Parsimonious interventions are needed.* Concordance and coordination within various systems are needed if large amounts of precious time and energy are not to be wasted. At the federal level, sufficient funding and information resources must be generated and disseminated. At the state level, preparedness plans should address multiple levels of the response across relevant jurisdictions, which includes clear plans on how the state agencies will communicate with the public and providers. Optimal utilization of resources is critical, and collaborative relationships and understanding between agencies need to be formed in advance. Intervention in large-scale crises is extremely expensive in terms of person power and material resources. One of the major balancing acts of local EMAs is to have just enough resources available to bring maximum effort to bear at just the right time to experience maximum effect.

8. *The process is cooperative, collaborative, and consultative.* Just as no single discipline holds sway in a large-scale crisis or megacrisis, cooperation, collaboration, and consultation within, among, and between systems and individuals are paramount. The provision of mental health services is important, but so are getting communication and power systems back on and determining where there is available shelter and whether buildings are safe.

9. *There is a full range of targeted interventions aimed at individuals, institutions, communities, on up to the national level, depending on how widespread the crisis is, and they are ongoing in response to longer-term needs.* Each involved system component, from the individual to the nation, needs to be triaged. Based on that assessment, target-specific interventions need to be made. How things will wind up after a disaster is not just determined in the days after it, but in the months after it. The infrastructure and community as client is as important long range as are individuals.

10. *The service characteristics of credibility, acceptability, accessibility, proactivity, continuance, and confidentiality should be adopted as "cast in stone" goals for service delivery in disaster-stricken areas.* Norris and her associates (2006) found adherence to these characteristics to be one of the most impressive of her findings of the 9/11 response in New York City. Meeting this gold standard of service delivery most likely means that the whole disaster mesosystem is integrated with host systems and running well. To do that effectively requires a

variety of organizations and individuals who operate with a high level of cooperation to make that system work.

Overarching all of the foregoing points are planning, more planning, practicing, critiquing, evaluating, and yet more planning. The necessity for vertical and horizontal links in the ecosystem of disaster planning cannot be overemphasized. The result of not having such links became clearly evident after hurricane Katrina. One of the critical components to planning is making sure that disaster mental health planning and activities do not take a backseat to security and safety concerns; people who can make clear decisions must be in place and have the authority to make those decisions (Flynn, 2003). That issue became abundantly clear in the aftermath of Katrina, with local and state leaders bickering about plans that should have been carved in stone long before the hurricane made landfall (Flynn, 2003; Gheytanchi et al., 2007).

National Crisis Response Teams

Perhaps the most important outreach approach **LO4** has been taken by national agencies in on-site delivery of mental health services at major disasters and the coordination of these services with other relief efforts. Because of past criticism of how both charitable and federal agencies have handled major disasters, those agencies have done a great deal of work to better coordinate their efforts in providing comprehensive disaster relief that cuts across the survivors' total environment (Bass & Yep, 2002; Pyszczynski, Solomon, & Greenberg, 2002; Smith, 2002). Mental health support does little good when people don't have a roof over their heads because it has been blown away in a hurricane. However, it also does little good for survivors to obtain housing but be so traumatized and depressed from the disaster that they cannot begin to regain control over their lives. From plane crashes to university campus shootings, to floods, to post office shootings, to forest fires, to train wrecks, to building bombings, to earthquakes, to school shootings, and to 9/11, some of the most potent and appropriate examples of the ecological nature of crisis intervention have occurred in the United States in the last 10 years, as has a large mobilization, training, and response effort to provide emergency mental health services to victims and survivors of any type of imaginable disaster.

An enormous number of mental health workers from throughout the country, working under the auspices of the American Red Cross, NOVA, FEMA, and state and local EMAs, and supported by the major

professional mental health organizations in the United States, have contributed monumental services to the thousands of clients affected by those disasters (Bass & Yep, 2002; Gladding, 2002; Hayes, 2002; Juhnke, 2002; McCarthy, 2002; Modrak, 1992; Morrissey, 1995; Pyszczynski, Solomon, & Greenberg, 2002; Riethmayer, 2002a, 2002b; Smith, 2002; Sullivan, 2002; Underwood & Clark, 2002). Among the comments of hundreds, perhaps thousands, of mental health workers over dozens of major crises, the following is perhaps both descriptive and representative:

> In that capacity, I was an escort who walked with families from the front of the building to the back and talked with them about what they were feeling, what they had felt, or what they anticipated doing in regard to the emotions that would be coming. I also accompanied families to Ground Zero so they could see for themselves the horror and finality of the event. The view from the site helped many individuals begin the process of grieving in depth, as they realized in a stark and striking way that those they had loved and cherished in so many ways were indeed dead and would not be coming back to be with them. (Gladding, 2002, p. 7)

Development of Crisis Response Teams (CRTs). The Oklahoma City federal building bombing, the shootings at Columbine High School and Sandy Hook Elementary School, and the 9/11 attacks struck a nerve in the United States. The massive amounts of media coverage of those traumatic experiences and the disaster relief that followed in their wake brought graphic attention to how disasters are handled, including the work of immediate follow-up rapid response teams. These teams did not just spring up full grown at the time of those disasters. Rather, throughout the late 1980s and 1990s, rapid response teams were developed to handle numerous tragedies and disasters, including hurricanes (Shelby & Tredinnick, 1995), serial murders (Wakelee-Lynch, 1990), plane crashes (Modrak, 1992; Shafer, 1989a), bank robberies and hijackings (Brom & Kleber, 1989), campus shootings (Guerra, 1999; Guerra & Schmitt, 1999; Sleek, 1998), and train explosions and post office shootings (National Organization for Victim Assistance, n.d.).

National Organization for Victim Assistance (NOVA) CRTs. The rapid crisis response team movement received impetus and support on a national level with the establishment of the National Crisis Response Project by the National Organization for Victim Assistance (NOVA) in the late 1980s (Young, 1991). Originally established to help victims of crime, NOVA, a private, not-for-profit organization, has branched out to offer help to victims of all kinds of disasters through the National Crisis Response Project. It has state and local affiliates throughout the United States. The project set up national crisis response teams (NCRTs) to assist communities following community-wide crises or disasters. One of the first major organized national responses of an NCRT for the specific purpose of providing mental health assistance was on August 20, 1986, when an Edmond, Oklahoma, postal worker shot and killed 14 coworkers and himself.

The main objective of an NCRT in dealing with a local community disaster is to form local crisis response teams that are in a position to deal with the community's grief reactions, stress effects, and posttraumatic stress disorder resulting from the disaster. According to Young (1991), the "project is based on the premise that disasters can cause individual and community-wide crisis reactions and that immediate intervention can provide communities with tools that are useful in mitigating long-term distress" (pp. 83–84).

NCRTs are dispatched at the request of leaders in the affected community. "When a disaster occurs, NOVA is placed in contact with the community in one of two ways: either the community calls NOVA, or NOVA, on hearing of the tragedy, calls the community and offers assistance" (Young, 1991, p. 95). Three types of disaster service are available: (1) providing written material giving details on how to deal with the aftermath of disaster; (2) providing telephone consultation to leading caregivers in the area affected; and (3) sending in a trained team of volunteer crisis workers to assist the community.

The Red Cross. The American Red Cross, like its Red Cross and Red Crescent counterparts around the world, is tasked with dealing with all kinds of disasters. Founded by Clara Barton, the American Red Cross has been in business for about 120 years. It is a private organization that has close ties with local, state, and federal governments. It helped the federal government start the Federal Emergency Management Agency. It is a major contributor to crisis intervention in the wake of large-scale disasters and megadisasters through its training of mental health professionals as members of rapid response teams (Red Cross, 2015). Professional organizations in counseling, psychology, and social work are closely linked with and provide candidates for its mental health training program.

Federal Emergency Management Agency (FEMA) and the National Institute of Mental Health (NIMH). FEMA was born in 1979 as the result of complaints about federal agencies' slowness, bureaucratic red tape, inefficiency, ineptitude, and duplication of effort in responding to a disaster. Several different agencies were merged into FEMA, and it is now housed in the Department of Homeland Security. FEMA has numerous responsibilities. Among them are education about all kinds of disaster preparedness and coordination between federal, state, and local emergency management agencies in regard to preparedness, training, and disaster mitigation. It provides disaster assistance that ranges from debris removal and rescue efforts to disaster loans for rebuilding and on-site mental health crisis response teams. Its Emergency Management Institute at Emmitsburg, Maryland, is a virtual university of emergency preparedness courses. Courses range from training community emergency response teams (CERTS), made up of ordinary local citizen volunteers who provide support to first responders to aid in rescue efforts, to colloquiums with state mental health service providers on the latest techniques for providing mental health services after a large-scale disaster (Federal Emergency Management Agency, 2015).

Sometimes more than one agency of the federal government coordinates the work of crisis response teams. Several instances of events during modern times that triggered such a coordinated effort were the earthquakes in both the Los Angeles and San Francisco areas; hurricanes Hugo, Andrew, Floyd, and Katrina that brought devastation and flooding to large parts of the southeastern United States; the nuclear accident at Three Mile Island; and the Love Canal contamination. The response teams were sent in by the National Institute of Mental Health (NIMH) and sponsored and funded by FEMA. In all such national disasters, FEMA and NIMH provide the widely affected areas with instruction, consultation, and expertise in developing local and regional support systems to cope with the enormous aftermath of these disasters (Shafer, 1989b).

Professional Organizations. Professional organizations, such as the American Psychiatric Association, the American Psychological Association, the American

Counseling Association, and the National Association of Social Workers, provide volunteers for the Red Cross and NOVA CRTs. These organizations also provide a variety of publications for both professionals and laypersons that can be obtained on their websites or ordered from them. Their conferences and conventions provide formats for discussion and dissemination of the theory and practice of crisis intervention.

The American School Counseling Association and the National Association of School Psychologists are involved in providing crisis intervention services to schoolchildren and adolescents in the face of a large-scale disaster. As an example, on April 19, 1995, immediately after the Oklahoma City federal building bombing, an American Counseling Association team of Oklahoma school counselors and an art teacher wrote and illustrated *The Terrible, Scary Explosion*. This book, modeled after one written for children after hurricane Hugo in South Carolina, was in the hands of Oklahoma City schoolchildren by April 25, with local school counselors serving as facilitators. The purpose of the book was to help children of all ages process the whole incident and provide a tool to help adults help children (Morrissey, 1995).

The National Association of School Psychologists has national emergency assistance teams (NEATs), which are tied in with NOVA. The mission of NEAT is to develop policies and procedures, disseminate information, provide consultation, and facilitate the training of school-based crisis teams in response to significant emergencies affecting children and adolescents. These NEAT teams go to the scene of school disasters and provide support for local agencies. They are composed of nationally certified school psychologists who have expertise in crisis prevention, intervention, and postvention. The intention of the NEAT team is to help save lives, reduce trauma and injury, facilitate the psychological well-being of students and staff, and allow schools to return to regular activities as soon as possible (Zenere, 1998).

Constructing an Outreach Team. Depending on the nature of the crisis and the ecological setting, outreach teams generally have a diverse occupational range: from psychiatric nurses, paramedics, emergency workers, and psychiatrists to social workers, volunteers, rehabilitation counselors, police officers, and psychologists. These outreach teams are characterized by their multidisciplinary team approach, strong social and community networks, user participation in policy and service delivery, and egalitarianism in

the workplace (Gulati & Guest, 1990). Alise Bartley, a private practice licensed professional counselor, describes her experience as a volunteer worker following hurricane Katrina. Based in Gulfport, Mississippi, she slept in a large Navy Seabee storage facility with 600 other volunteers. She slept two feet from a retired nurse on one side and a Vietnam veteran on the other, both of whom she had just met for the first time in her life (Kennedy, 2007).

Integrative-collaborative teams have a distinctive operational setup and are characteristic of many geographical areas where financial and human resources are not sufficient to form freestanding, specialized crisis units. They are not an ad hoc group collected after a crisis, but rather are trained prior to the crisis. Each member has different skills that, combined, allow the team to respond to a variety of crisis situations. They operate much as a volunteer fire department does. Members typically have primary jobs in other settings, but when a crisis call comes in on a hotline, they immediately leave their regular job, form a crisis team, and go to the crisis site. They are identifiable within the community as the crisis response team and are a cost-efficient and effective way to provide generic crisis intervention (Silver & Goldstein, 1992).

Vertically and Horizontally Integrated Local Emergency Management Systems

Overarching all local agencies involved in crisis after a disaster are the local emergency management agencies. They are the offspring of the old Civil Defense system of the cold war. The examples that follow refer to Florida, where each local agency is directly linked to one of seven regional areas, and Illinois, where there are eight regions linked to the state emergency management agency. In turn, the state agency is linked to FEMA (Freeman, 2003; Lane, 2003).

Role of Local EMA Directors. Jerry Lane and Nancy Freeman are two public servants whose lives have been anything but simple. They both have run local emergency management agencies.

Jerry was executive director for the Dekalb County, Illinois, Community Mental Health Board and director of the Sycamore, Illinois, Emergency Management Agency. Sycamore is a small town in northern Illinois, located in rolling farmland about 60 miles west of Chicago. It is not famous or notorious for much of anything. However, it does have grain elevator and agricultural chemical warehouse fires, tornadoes, straight-line windstorms, blizzards, and flooding.

But does it really need an emergency management system and a local manager? Listen to Greg Brown, former director of EMT services in White County, Illinois, and chemical mixing and applications supervisor for Brown Feed and Chemical in Carmi, Illinois. "If you want to talk about the potential for terrorism or accidental disaster, talk about what we have in this warehouse. We easily have enough agricultural chemicals, if used with malice or handled incorrectly, to kill everybody in this town twice over and have some left to spare. You'd better have somebody around who knows what to do with them, and that would apply to about every town in the country that has an agricultural base" (G. Brown, personal communication, December 15, 2004).

For Jerry Lane, living in a small town that may need his skills is the greatest reward of the job. His agency's problems were those of most beginning crisis agencies: inadequate funding, little respect, and a whole lot of politics. Many emergency management jobs were filled by patronage seekers, which may satisfy the needs of a political party but will probably leave a lot to be desired when the crisis starts—as evidenced at the national level with hurricane Katrina. Listen to the comment of a county commissioner in White County, Illinois, about the volunteer EMT program that was asking for an increase in funds from the county board: "Why, they could train a monkey to do that job! Why do they need to be paid any more?" We certainly hope that commissioner doesn't have a heart attack "way out there on Possum Road" because we doubt whether a chimpanzee could make the drive in an ambulance and keep him alive long enough until a life flight arrived, piloted by—we would guess—a baboon.

Although you may consider the commissioner's comment outrageous and patently stupid, this is not an atypical response to any new upstart agency that deals in crisis. Until it becomes politically necessary, little government funding is forthcoming to support crisis intervention programs. Certainly 9/11 and hurricane Katrina put a new perspective on the need for local emergency management agencies and competent people to run them.

Nancy Freeman is a retired deputy director of the Nassau County, Florida, Emergency Management Agency. Nassau County is next to Jacksonville, Florida. Nancy got into the emergency management business doing research analysis for hazard mitigation while she was a graduate assistant at the University of North Florida. While doing research for various counties in north Florida, she learned enough about the business of emergency management that she applied for a job with one of the counties and got it! Besides being adjacent to a large urban population—with all of its potential hazards for disaster—Nassau County is situated on the shore of the Atlantic Ocean, with all of the hurricane risks attendant to that locale. To add a little more to the hazardous, potential-for-disaster mix, the county also has military facilities with nuclear capabilities. Suffice it to say that the Nassau County EMA is very, very interested in hurricanes and their potential effects under a variety of conditions.

Nancy's world is defined by the term *networking* and, as is true for most emergency managers, it is a double-edged sword. On the one hand, Nancy sees networking with a variety of very committed professionals as one of the most rewarding parts of her job. On the other hand, when egos, turf guarding, and politics get involved, it can be one of her major headaches.

These managers are a new breed of technocrat that is being placed in charge of coordinating a welter of activities, agencies, and logistical problems in regard to managing every conceivable emergency you might imagine and then some. If you'd like a job like this, you had better be good with acronyms and know what they stand for. Want to be able to do a HHVA (hospital hazard vulnerability analysis) or get a RACES (radio amateur civil emergency system) up and running? Curious to know what the difference between cold, warm, and hot zones are, or whether you need a Level A protection suit when you venture into one of them? Does that sound like an interesting job? Think you'd like to do that?

Background and Training. What are the qualifications? you may ask. What university do I need to attend to major in that "stuff"? The answer to that question now is, "About any place in the world!" Specifically in regard to mental health crisis intervention, the University of South Dakota had established the first doctoral program with a specialty track in clinical/disaster psychology. Now, if you go to www.chds.us/?partners/institutions, which is the website for the Center for Homeland Defense and Security (2015), you will find 477 programs that range across associate, bachelor's, master's, doctorate, and certification programs in just about any type of emergency management program with any type of focus you can imagine. You should understand that the content of these degrees varies quite a bit because as of yet there is no clear consensus on what all that "stuff" should be.

If you sought to earn an interdisciplinary bachelor's degree with a major in emergency management from Western Carolina University, for example, your courses could range from International Terrorism to Crisis Communications to the Politics of Budgeting (Western Carolina University Emergency Management Institute, 2015).

However, as Nancy Freeman (2003) says, "My bachelor's degree and graduate work is in the humanities, with an emphasis in interior design, history, and historical preservation, and you wouldn't think that would be anything like what you'd need for this job, but I learned about architecture in that program, and I can read a building plan and know what 'load bearings under initial impact' means, and that is critically important when we are designing evacuation and safety plans. I also know how to do research and that is critically important in this job."

Jerry Lane holds a master's degree in community mental health. Jerry sort of wandered into this business by being an amateur radio operator and weather spotter. As Jerry says, "I'm kind of a rare breed. Most emergency managers don't have a mental health background. They tend to be retired military and have a pretty good handle on how to handle logistics problems, which is indeed important in this job" (Lane, 2003).

Both of these directors have taken many courses through the Federal Emergency Management Association's Emergency Management Institute, which has a campus in Emmitsburg, Maryland, and various correspondence and Internet courses. Besides critical incident stress debriefing and PTSD training, you might also be required to take Preparedness Planning in a Nuclear Crisis, Mortuary Services in Emergency Management, Hazardous Materials Basic Awareness, and Executive Analysis of Fire Service Organization and Emergency Management. If you are getting the idea that you had better be a Jack or Jill of all trades and a master of many, you are right!

There is a national certification process and an international association of emergency managers. In Florida, emergency managers must be certified through a combination of course work, training, and work experience. They must also take 150 hours of education courses every 4 years to retain their certification. There is continuous ongoing training in management tools resources, new technology, and communications. There are two annual conferences managers are expected to attend, one of which covers general emergency preparedness. Lots of training exercises are developed at the national and state levels and then are brought down to the local level to be used in training exercises (Freeman, 2003). Still interested in this job?

What Do Emergency Managers Do? Certainly, disasters don't happen every day. Does that mean that emergency managers sit around playing pinochle, drinking coffee, eating doughnuts, pitching horseshoes, and polishing the fire engine, waiting for something to happen? Local EMAs are in the business of preparing for, preventing, intervening in, and mitigating the effects of any and all kinds of disasters. To do that takes a great deal of planning and coordinating. Direct your attention to the matrix of city and county agencies and the support functions they engage in as primary or secondary supports in a disaster (see Figure 17.3). While you might think of roads, bridges, potable water, and sewage disposal as being critical, the last thing you might think of would be animal issues. But if you had severe flooding after a hurricane, animals—both alive and dead—would be a very real problem.

Planning for Disasters. There are two types of disasters, those that have prior warning time and those that do not. As a result, local EMAs have various disaster plans that are implemented in stages. Although there might be very little warning in the case of a tornado or a chemical spill from a derailed train, hurricanes and forest fires generally do have lead time for preparation. Nassau County has a very complex and lengthy hurricane plan that is divided into 10 stages. A brief description of those stages follows to give you an idea of just how involved this business is (Nassau County Emergency Management Department, 2003). For each stage, a particular action is noted and the responsible section is designated to implement it. Those sections are emergency operation center (EOC) command, planning, logistics, operations, administration, recovery task force, and elected policy makers.

Awareness stage. 72–60 hours Estimated Land Fall (ELF) of hurricane. Activate emergency command center. Establish liaison with the National Weather Service, state department of emergency management, surrounding counties, media, utility services, law enforcement, and fire agencies. Conduct vulnerability analysis. Activate alert phone system. Prepare primary evacuation routes. Notify all gas and diesel wholesalers

Agencies (P = Primary, S = Support)	ESF 1 Transportation	ESF 2 Communication	ESF 3 Public Works	ESF 4 Fire Fighting/Emerg. Medic	ESF 5 Information & Planning	ESF 6 Mass Care	ESF 7 Resource Support	ESF 8 Health and Medical	ESF 9 Search & Rescue	ESF 10 Hazardous Materials	ESF 11 Food & Water	ESF 12 Energy	ESF 13 Military Support	ESF 14 Public Information	ESF 15 Volunteers & Donations	ESF 16 Law Enforcement	ESF 17 Animal Issues
All local media														S			
Amateur Radio Emerg. Serv.		S			S									S			
Acme County Medical Center				S	S			S						S			
Goodwill Industries Center														S	S		
Midville City Public Works Dept.	S		S		S		S						S	S			
Midville City Fire Department		S		S	S				S	S				S			
Midville City Police Department		S			S									S		S	
Midville City Planning Department					S									S			
Civil Air Patrol	S				S									S			
Contracted Medical Examiner								S						S			
State Dept. of Law Enforcement													P	S			
State Highway Patrol													S			P	
State National Guard Forces													S	S			
State Power and Light Dept.												S		S			
State Public Utilities Dept.												P		S			
Animal emergency care centers														S			S
Home Health Care Agencies								P						S			
Regional Electrical Authority		S					S					S		S			
Medical Supply Companies										S				S			
Acme County Building Dept.		S			S		S							S			
Acme County Cattleman's Assoc.														S			S
Acme County Clerk of Court							S							S			
Acme County Coordinator														S			
Acme County Council on Aging	S				S		S	S						S			
Acme County Emergency Mgmt.			S	P	S	S	S	S		S	S	S		P	S		S
Acme County Engineering Services			S	S	S									S			
Acme County Extension Agency						S	S				S			S	P		S
Acme County Facilities Maintenance		S			S		S							S			
Acme County Fire/Rescue		S		P	S		S		P	P				S			
Acme County Geog. Info. Systems					S		S							S			
Acme County Health Dept.						S	S	P						S			
Acme County Humane Society														S			P
Acme County Jail							S							S			
Acme County Library System														S			
Acme County Planning Dept.					S		S							S			
Acme County Risk Management							P				P			S			
Acme County Road & Bridge Dept.	S		P		S		S						S	S			
Acme County School Board	P				S	P	S	S						S			
Acme County Sheriff's Office	S	P		S	S		S	S	S	S	S			S		P	S
Acme County Solid Waste Dept.			S		S		S							S			
Acme County Veterinary Society														S			S
Acme County Volunteer Center							S							S	S		
Regional American Red Cross						P		S				S		S	S		
State Parks & Recreational Services													S	S			
Private businesses											S			S			
Salvation Army						S					S			S	S		
Mental health centers								S						S			
Volunteer organizations												S		S			

FIGURE 17.3 Midville City/Acme County Emergency Support Function Matrix

SOURCE: Adapted from Nassau County, Florida, Emergency Management Department (Freeman, 2003).

to restock retail outlets within 12–24 hours. Test EOC communications equipment.

Standby stage. 60–48 hours ELF. Activate emergency broadcast system. Notify amateur radio group to go on standby. Use local media and National Weather Service bulletins to advise boat owners, home owners, drawbridge operators, and motel and hotel managers, and detail causeway and bridge closings and evacuation routes. Coordinate establishment of emergency worker shelters. Secure EMS ambulances, transport vehicles, oil spill trailers, and heavy equipment.

Decision stage. 48–45 ELF. Activate traffic control plan and emergency transport plan. Declare state of emergency and activate county emergency plan. Recommend/order evacuation. Designate nonessential businesses to close. Coordinate decision-making actions and link all municipalities, law enforcement agencies, fire districts, utility companies, hospitals, and medical care facilities with State Division of Emergency Management and the National Hurricane Center.

Preparation stage. 45–36 ELF. Begin implementing evacuation plan for "at risk" populations such as mobile homes, people with special needs, tourists, campers, people without transportation, and low-lying areas. Activate all EOC communication systems. Announce public closings. Implement 24-hour operation of fleet management garage and fueling resources. Activate emergency transportation plan. Prepare shelters for opening.

Evacuation stage. 36–4 ELF. Issue evacuation orders. Identify areas at risk. Announce shelter openings and transportation pickup points. Request National Weather Service to broadcast information on road closures. Activate/coordinate shutdown of electric power services. Maintain communications with public shelters, emergency worker family shelters, special care centers, emergency transportation, area hospitals, animal emergency care facilities, power, water, sewage, utilities, fire districts, law enforcement, and public works. Begin preplanning poststorm activities.

Storm/emergency stage. Monitor storm/emergency characteristics. Continue preplanning poststorm activities. Continue communications with other agencies.

Immediate emergency stage. Commence local emergency response activities. Determine long-term human

service needs, including mental health care counseling. Determine information and referral services. Assess temporary housing needs. Distribute resources: food, water, clothing, and cleanup kits. Activate recovery task force and review damage reports. Recommend implementation of appropriate moratoriums and adoption of emergency resolutions and ordinances. Determine if curfew is needed. Activate Damage Assessment Teams. Monitor public health conditions.

Evaluation stage. Determine if primary threat still exists. Conduct/coordinate initial impact assessment effort. Reaffirm and/or reestablish communications with all shelters, hospitals, towns, state emergency operations, law enforcement, public works, fire districts, and surrounding counties. Enact emergency resolutions. Determine initial mutual aid requirements and request assistance from state EOC. Discuss emergency ordinances to be enacted. Issue news media releases. Establish times for briefings/planning meetings. Report accidents to date and update status. Assess damage to areas with existing or potential hazardous materials. Summarize current operational activities underway. Discuss current strategy. Review human resource needs. Determine additional resources needed. Implement rest and rotation policies for emergency workers. Assess logistics of transportation routes opened, distribution sites, feeding procedures, and available sleeping facilities.

Reconstruction stage. Perform long-term activities or projects focused on improving or strengthening community's economy. Complete restoration of services. Dispose of debris and allocate resources to cleanup chores. Focus on community recovery planning, building and construction issues, and environmental/ecological issues. Continue/complete human services delivery assistance of information and referral, resource distribution, health care delivery, mental health care counseling, and transportation assistance. Complete activities for presidential disaster declaration. Perform hazard mitigation projects to reduce community's susceptibility and vulnerability to hurricanes. Repair, replace, modify, or relocate public facilities in hazard-prone areas.

Restoration stage. Perform assessment of community needs and economic damage. Address the following restoration issues: economic and job base assessment, community recovery planning, building and construction issues, public information and citizen outreach, and environmental issues and ecological concerns. Provide health care delivery for both pre- and postdisaster needs, including home health-care management and case referral. Put mental health care counseling into operation. Determine victims' counseling needs by triage assessment. Determine training needs for mental health professions on disaster-related issues. Place mental health professions/CISD team members on community assessment teams. Determine where counseling services will operate. Determine transportation needs to public feeding sites, shelters, and disaster service sites. Reestablish and implement public transportation service. Chore service needs assessment for cleanup. Determine needs and coordinate with volunteer groups for debris cleanup, interior home cleanup, window repair, etc. Coordinate with FEMA to set up Disaster Field Office and Disaster Application Centers. Assist in establishing temporary housing sites. Establish a federal public assistance office to coordinate all disaster relief efforts to clients. Participate in interagency hazard mitigation team and hazard mitigation survey activities. Complete after-evacuation report and county incident report. Critique the management of the storm emergency.

Throughout the unfolding stages of the disaster, constant needs assessment should occur. A community mental health needs assessment formula (Flynn, 2003, p. 23) that constantly updates the dead, hospitalized, nonhospitalized injured, homes destroyed, homes with major and minor damage, unemployed due to job loss, and other losses will give a good indication of the potential numbers of people in need of crisis counseling services. The same community-wide assessment should continuously occur in regard to mental health (Katz, 2011). Nancy Freeman was asked when she would know that the crisis is over. She stated, tongue in cheek, that she'd know because no one had called and everyone had found his or her dog and Aunt Nellie. In reality, the immediate crisis is considered passed when everyone's safety is assured from any effects of the disaster, public works are back in operation, and services are returning to normal. That's when the EOC can get a doughnut and some sleep!

The foregoing plan for hurricanes can be adapted to any kind of disaster, whether natural or human-made. While timelines may be very compressed or in some instances operations may start at the emergency stage, the format is replicable with just about any kind of community-wide crisis. Although local EMAs have very little preparation time for other types of disasters, they do not stand idly by waiting for something to happen. Continuous interagency tabletop exercises give them practice in responding to a variety of potential disasters. Assessment of particularly vital and vulnerable public sites, ranging from water treatment plants to nursing homes, is made to determine what needs and weak points there may be. Jerry Lane spends a fair amount of time working with individual agencies to develop their own internal disaster plans to fit with the overall one that the local EMA has.

Mental Health Components of Local EMAs

Any local mental health clinic should have **LO5** a prototype disaster response plan (Lane, 2003). While each community will have variations due to its own particular regional and state systems of mental health delivery, geographic locale, and population differences, they should generally follow along with what Hartsough (1982) has outlined for mental health agencies' typical response to a disaster.

The following points are abstracted from Hartsough (1982) and Lane (2003). First of all, the centers must have a plan that assumes that they may be victims themselves and have breakdowns in communications; loss of or inability to find staff; loss of equipment, supplies, and records; inability of staff to cope with loss; and problems recognizing their functional limits. The mental health center must be prepared to provide services in two situations—a localized but traumatic event and a large-scale disaster. A localized event can be responded to without affecting operations to any great degree. A disaster will most likely disrupt operations to some degree, while drastically increasing the demand for services. A clear chain of command with redundancy features is mandatory. There should be an assessment of population groups in the area with regard to high-risk groups such as children, non-English-speaking, elderly, and low socioeconomic groups. Interagency cooperative agreements should be made. A specific mental health liaison person should be named to the local EOC.

Predisaster training encompasses development of outreach programs that target "normal people acting normally in an abnormal situation." Training specifically targets practitioners who have not had formal training in outreach or who historically perform poorly when they have to rely on their formal training. Consideration should be given to sending local clinicians to Red Cross training. Drills and tabletop exercises should be developed and conducted in coordination with the local EOC.

Personnel. Volunteers who would function as reserve crisis counselors should be recruited and trained in crisis intervention skills. Specified workers should be selected for multidisciplinary crisis response teams. A chief of operations should be nominated and will be the individual actually running the disaster response. There should also be an emergency preparedness coordinator who will be responsible for planning and preparation prior to a disaster and will function as a consultant to the chief of operations during an actual emergency. This person will be the liaison to the local EOC.

An outside clinical consultant should be retained to assess the physical and mental condition of the staff. A command-and-control and communications center should be established and staffed by a team leader and other staff necessary for it to function effectively. A historian should keep an ongoing journal of activities that occur as a result of the disaster. The decisions, events, problems, and information should include details, names and addresses, times, and issues that can later be used for debriefings, psychological autopsies, system improvements, grant requests, or reimbursement.

A personnel liaison will assist the chief of operations in assessing, making, and tracking staff and volunteer assignments. A media/information liaison will provide information to the media and local government, develop press releases, and distribute general information regarding service delivery. Staff may be made available to the local EOC to provide psychological support.

Transdisaster (0–14 Days). The mental health unit needs to initiate immediate mental health services when the disaster occurs; restore services to clients served during normal times; act as the disaster mental health advisor to the local government; provide outreach programs and coordinate resources for the delivery of disaster mental health services from the Red Cross, NOVA, FEMA, and other religious and philanthropic organizations; coordinate the responses of any contractors for services with particular emphasis on evacuation of residential facilities; target specific areas, such as evacuation centers, emergency relief centers, and FEMA "one-stop" service centers; provide support services for disaster workers; and assist with mental health emergencies in hospitals with victims requiring medical or psychiatric care.

Postdisaster (15–365 Days). Evaluate and assess the need for postdisaster services; implement prepared immediate services grant and prepare regular services grant if a presidential disaster is declared; establish linkages with American Red Cross mental health workers to hand off clients requiring longer-term care; monitor for long-term psychological effects; educate the public regarding disaster-related psychological phenomena; evaluate program response, both short and long term; perform psychological autopsy on total crisis response and debrief workers.

In the foregoing sections of this chapter you have read about the overall composition of disaster planning and infrastructure. In an ideal world, even in a world of disasters, all of this runs smoothly. While 9/11 certainly had its share of chaos and confusion (Halpern & Tramontin, 2007, pp. 171–197; Kaul & Welzant, 2005; Norris et al., 2006), order came out of that maelstrom fairly quickly, and everybody thought they had learned a lot of lessons. Then along came hurricane Katrina and everything got turned upside down.

What Happened with Katrina?

In any disaster there is invariably an attempt to fix blame. If blame can be fixed, then people may start to believe that the impossible, out-of-control, insane, unbelievable, chaotic, and unfathomable event can be contained, made sense of as to the reasons it occurred, and a sense of control regained as to what went wrong and how it can be made right the next time. In that sense hurricane Katrina is no different from multitudes of other natural disasters that have hit other countries. Indeed, in comparison to typhoons and earthquakes that have plagued Asia and the Middle East, it is a relatively small event, and certainly so in regard to loss of life. Yet the recriminations from hurricane Katrina are unending and rub raw nerves from the standpoints of socioeconomic, racial, political, and even interstate rivalries. While it is expected, rightly or wrongly, that there will be disasters in countries like Bangladesh, it "cannot happen" in the United States. We pride ourselves on controlling our destiny through science and industry, up to and including controlling nature. After Katrina, apparently not!

This is not an exposition about who's to blame or what's to blame. The emerging facts suggest that there is plenty of blame to pass around and share. However, what Anahita Gheytanchi and her associates (2007) have compiled is worth reporting as a way of looking at how the various systems within a disaster ecosystem operate, or in the case of hurricane Katrina . . . don't! Gheytanchi and her associates report 12 key failures of response.

1. *Lack of efficient communication.* The sine qua non of disaster mitigation is communication. Both within and between the primary and super mesosystems, communication failed. At least four separate command structures were operating in Katrina's aftermath: two command structures in FEMA and two military command structures. That's at least two too many and resulted in crossed communications, duplicated or incomplete efforts, and generally clouded decision making.

2. *Poor coordination plans.* Coordination is about moving assets to where they are most needed. The inability to coordinate relief efforts ranged from not utilizing one of the finest hospital ships in the world, the U.S.S. *Bataan,* which sat idly offshore, to an inability of FEMA to find buses and drivers and move people out of the Superdome, to hundreds of trucks filled with ice sitting idly in Memphis freight yards with no place to go, to thousands of house trailers sitting in Arkansas when they were desperately needed in Mississippi and Louisiana.

3. *Ambiguous authority relationships.* The Department of Homeland Security remained on a "pull" basis, which means that the state had to request federal assets, rather than a "push" basis, which means that assets would be immediately made available to the state. The National Response Plan Catastrophic Incident Annex (NPR-CIA) should have been invoked prior to landfall, but in fact was never invoked. The prevarication and waffling by Louisiana state and local governments on instituting mandatory evacuation because of the cost, even though they were getting intense pressure from federal authorities to do so, caused severe problems that culminated in the Superdome fiasco.

4. *Who's in charge?* Factious political fights plagued relief efforts. The shifting of blame from the mayor of New Orleans to the governor of Louisiana to the president of the United States settled nothing. Lessons from previous hurricanes about coordination among federal, state, and local governments have not been learned or at least not been put into practice. Laws that govern the use of the armed forces in the continental United States also severely hamstring efforts to quickly deploy military personnel and need to be changed.

5. *Counterterrorism versus all-hazards response.* Money, staff, and other assets have been drained out of FEMA and moved to Homeland Security efforts to combat terrorism. A natural disaster the size of hurricane Katrina dwarfs any terrorist attack up to a nuclear detonation or release of the plague. Yet Homeland Security funded disaster preparedness for terrorism as opposed to natural disaster at a 7-to-1 ratio pre-Katrina.

6. *Ambiguous training standards and lack of preparation.* Across the board, training and experience with disasters were lacking. While the aforementioned FEMA training to become a certified LEMA manager sounds good, the reality is that the training requirements to become an emergency manager and become certified were cumbersome and difficult to complete. Standards for accreditation of response agencies were also vague and not tied to any performance-based evidence.

7. *Where is the "learning" in lessons learned?* A multiagency hurricane exercise that very closely resembled Katrina was completed prior to the storm. Outcomes closely paralleled what actually happened. Yet failure of local and state governments to follow up and take advantage of the exercise doomed it to collect dust on the shelf. This is not the first instance of failure to heed learning from the past. Putting into practice all of the procedures necessary to stave off a disaster like Katrina is difficult, costly, and time consuming; it demands expertise and interagency cooperation at the local level and vertical integration with state and federal agencies. Tackling the logistical and tactical problems involved in implementing those procedures takes a backseat when the danger is not imminent.

8. *Performance assessment was not integrated into the process.* In an evidence-based world, continuous performance assessment should be built into disaster relief efforts, but that is not the case. Performance evaluation is especially lacking in mental health provision. An assessment device that provides benchmarks and rubrics to gauge how relief is proceeding and how well it is going is sorely needed so that best practices models may be generated. There was discussion about that after 9/11, but it still hadn't happened 7 years later. To this day there still is no clear way of systematically evaluating the services rendered (Watson, Brymer, & Bonanno, 2011).

9. *The geography of poverty.* Are race and socioeconomic status response factors? While race became a factor because the majority of the poor in New Orleans were black, the fact is that disaster plans as they are currently formulated put the poor, the elderly, the sick, and other disenfranchised

individuals who are not financially or physically able to evacuate, relocate, or rebuild at extreme risk without regard to race, creed, color, national origin, religion, sexual preference, or any other distinctive human quality.

10. *Rumor and chaos.* Urban legend and rumor, the bane of any disaster, ran rampant in New Orleans. No clearly designated official spokesperson appeared, giving clear, unconflicted, factual messages that could be believed. Exaggeration by elected officials of armed violence was given airtime by the media, and these rumors then turned into "facts" and took on a life of their own. At its best rumor served to warn people and put them on their guard. At its worst it turned into a self-fulfilling prophecy that slowed rescue efforts. Concrete, factual, up-to-the-minute information by an official spokesperson with both face and content validity was essentially absent. Above all else, an ironclad rule in any disaster is that one highly valid, knowledgeable spokesperson gives facts out in a timely manner and dispels rumors as they arise.

11. *Personal and community preparedness.* There was clearly a sharp divide between what happened in Louisiana and Mississippi in regard to recovery efforts. Both states suffered an equal amount of catastrophic devastation along their coast. However, for whatever reasons, and there are many variables to be examined, Mississippi was more resilient. Whether the majority of its people had better resources and support systems is a different question from whether they were prepared. However, that question needs to be examined carefully, for both physical and psychological differences and perhaps even cultural differences that were demonstrated and heavily influenced long-term outcomes in the two states.

12. *Disaster mental health and the role of mental health professionals.* What actually works for reducing mental health problems in people afflicted with a disaster like Katrina is still not clear, and a great deal of research needs to be done to find out what evidence-based practices do work. Critical incident stress debriefing (CISD), which has been used and most certainly abused as a panacea, appears not to be the ultimate answer. Further, attributions that label survivors as suffering from a mental illness don't work very well either. The preferred operating mode now is the use of psychological first aid and social support (Watson, Brymer, & Bonanno, 2011). Self-efficacy models that foster self-reliance, coping, and problem-solving skills, focus on individual needs, seek to extinguish PTSD at early onset, and concentrate on functional recovery rather than looking for pathology seem to hold promise (Ruzek, 2006).

Psychological First Aid and Psychosocial Support as Applied to Disaster Survivors

As detailed in Chapter 1, the National Institute of Mental Health (2002) defines psychological first aid (PFA) as establishing safety of the client, reducing stress-related symptoms, providing rest and physical recuperation, and linking clients to critical resources and social support systems. Psychological first aid has now been adapted and modified from its initial use by Raphael (1977) into a first-order, evidence-based approach to working with survivors of mass disasters (Brymer et al., 2006; Hobfoll et al., 2007). It may be taught to paraprofessionals and nonprofessionals. For example, it is one of the training modules (CERT, 2011) that volunteer CERT workers get as part of their search and rescue work training.

Psychological first aid as it is applied in a disaster is designed to reduce distress, generate short- and long-term adaptive functioning, and link survivors with additional services (Watson, Brymer, & Bonanno, 2011). *The Field Operations Guide for Psychological First Aid* developed by the National Child Traumatic Stress Network and the National Center for PTSD (NCTSN/NCPTSD, 2006) is considered state-of-the art in that regard (Webber, Mascari, & Runte, 2010). Delivery of PFA includes a number of core actions (NCTSN/NCPTSD, 2006): make initial respectful contact by a warm engaging presence; gather and provide information in regard to supports needed to deal with immediate physical and safety concerns; provide and direct people in regard to practical assistance needed; provide for their safety and comfort both from a physical and psychological standpoint by linking them with social services; teach them basic coping skills if requested; and get information and help that will connect them to social supports, such as reuniting them with family and other social groups with which they are involved.

The job of CFA workers is not to attempt to engage in therapy or elicit details of the tragedy; rather, it is to reduce acute psychological distress by their supportive and compassionate presence through basic active listening and responding skills (Everly & Flynn, 2005). Initiating contact involves the notion of "just being there" or "compassionate loitering" (Webber, Mascari, & Runte, 2010), which emphasizes careful observation, a nonintrusive presence, and caring, respectful contact. One example is the crisis workers who were available in the dining halls of Virginia Tech residence facilities and classrooms immediately after the shootings there. Volunteers had handouts on normal reactions to tragedies, self-care tips about trauma, and resource lists. Workers were instructed to engage and support students who seemed to be struggling by a respectful, nonintrusive introduction as a way to offer their support. They wore purple armbands to identify their presence. They reported that students initially would not speak to them, but as time went by and students started coming to terms with their grief, they would stop by and thank them for being there (Lawson, Bodenhorn, & Welfare, 2010).

Even doing the foregoing may not be necessary as most people are pretty resilient after a disaster (Hobfoll et al., 2007). As indicated in Chapter 2, Culturally Effective Helping in Crisis, insistence on participating in "psychotherapy" may be met with anger and extreme resistance. In support of the concept of voluntary participation, Bonanno, Westphal, and Mancini (2011) found that a one-size-fits-all intervention might hold no advantage over, and could even undermine, the self-efficacy and resiliency of survivors. For many others, PFA may be both necessary and sufficient. Finally, for some few others, PFA may be necessary but not sufficient.

When More Than PFA Is Needed

It was first thought that severity of exposure to the event and severity of postevent stress and adversity would be the greatest factors indicating the need for more in-depth intervention for serious and chronic psychological problems (Norris, 2006). However, since 9/11 it is clear that degree of exposure or proximity to the attacks does not explain all of the persons presenting with severe psychological problems after a disaster. An individual waving an American flag for hours and hours over an interstate highway 1,000 miles from the impact sites, and refusing to come down for safety, is one example among literally thousands of individuals across the country who "lost it" after 9/11 and needed something more than PFA. In other words, vicarious traumatization through exposure to merely seeing or hearing about disaster events could instigate maladaptive psychological responding. As a consequence, Watson, Brymer, and Bonanno (2011) have compiled a laundry list from their own

and a number of other researchers that total 22 risk factors for adults and 13 for children. We believe it doesn't make a lot of sense to try to go through that list and winnow out significant variables. What we do believe in is knowing how to use the Triage Assessment Form in this book. People scoring 20 or more are going to need something more than PFA for sure; they are going to need someone to monitor them closely until they regain some precrisis equilibrium and most likely should not be turned loose on their own. People in the high 20s, who are potentially lethal to themselves or others either by intended commission of unsafe acts or unintended omissions of activities needed to keep them safe, should not be turned loose. People in the high teens will most likely profit from PFA *and* a good deal of on-site psychosocial support so that they don't escalate into the 20s. People in the low teens are probably ideal candidates for PFA. Anybody in the single digits on the TAF probably needs to counsel us!

The Current State of Affairs

The problem with this latter approach, however, is twofold. First, it assumes that a large enough number of practitioners have the necessary crisis intervention skills to do this. If mental health practitioners are not available, then paraprofessionals or laypersons like those who operate in Community Emergency Response Teams (CERTs) and are taught psychological first aid as part of their training may be initial providers of psychological support. That may be stretching it a bit. With all due respect to CERT volunteers, we spend a lot of time teaching these "first aid" techniques to graduate students. They are not easy to implement, particularly when faced with a person in crisis, and we wonder if the estimated learning time of 1 hour and 15 minutes (including video) will be sufficient (CERT, 2011).

You will soon hear from a licensed professional counselor who was deployed in Louisiana post-Katrina. This counselor has extensive training and practice in crisis intervention. She is still the exception rather than the rule. Given her background and training, she struggled and reevaluated her therapeutic worldview as she went through her tour of duty. Her story is not much different from that of many others who were there with her. While the American Red Cross crisis counseling training program has trained thousands of practitioners, that resource was clearly not enough for hurricane Katrina. The Red Cross and government agencies were forced to suspend their standards and bring in any licensed counselor, psychologist, social worker, psychiatric nurse, or psychiatrist they could get their hands on.

FEMA's crisis counseling assistance and training program (CCA-TP) is available to state mental health authorities once an area has been declared a disaster area by the president. That is a lot like closing the barn door after the horse has escaped. Way too many things are happening to stop and say, "OK, we now have a large, metastasizing disaster on our hands; let's do some training!" This training occurred in Memphis approximately a month after Katrina. To say it was mostly useless is being kind. We believe that training should come prior to any catastrophic event and follow-up refresher courses should go with it. After a congressional inquiry into this program's problems in south Florida, a critical review of it was instigated and a number of worthwhile recommendations were made to tighten it and beef it up—particularly in regard to coordination activities (Department of Homeland Security, 2008). None of those recommendations, however, made clear whether a municipality can actually get training prior to a disaster.

Young and his associates (Young, 2006; Young et al., 2006) have developed a comprehensive predisaster training program that holds much promise. It has a conceptual framework that differentiates natural and human-caused disaster and examines effects on both individuals and communities. It has both practitioner and administrative training components and specific modules on high-risk client populations and interfaces with other organizations. This fine program is time consuming, most likely expensive, and requires trainers who have expertise in both disaster mental health practice and administration. Those are difficult commodities to find.

Consistent and comprehensive training for mental health providers in crisis intervention as they matriculate through professional training programs has been piecemeal at best (Coke-Weatherly, 2005), as clearly described by Roberts (2005). That appears to be changing to some extent. The Council for Accreditation of Counseling and Related Educational Programs and the National Association of School Psychologists both require the teaching of crisis intervention in their accrediting criteria. While that may now be seen as necessary, it remains to be seen whether what is taught will be sufficient. Other professional accreditation agencies appear to make the provision of crisis intervention training voluntary.

Most certainly, Katrina was a megacrisis that had metastasizing effects far beyond its geographic landfall and a physical scope that had never before been experienced, with disenfranchised people shipped all over the United States. The terrorist attack on 9/11 probably had the widest range of vicarious psychological effects ever experienced in the United States, with the possible exception of the Japanese attack on Pearl Harbor. A number of national committees issuing from both 9/11 and Katrina have made numerous recommendations in regard to the provision of crisis services to individuals following these human-made and natural disasters. These recommendations have been summarized by Watson, Brymer, and Bonanno (2011) in their article on postdisaster psychological intervention since 9/11.

1. Be proactive ahead of time with pragmatic, flexible plans that match appropriate services to each phase of the recovery period.
2. Promote a sense of safety, connectedness, calm, hope, and efficacy.
3. Participate in groups with stakeholders to coordinate and learn from others, minimize duplication, and mend gaps in service.
4. Be culturally sensitive and consider human rights.
5. Be willing to undergo evaluation and open to scrutiny of practices.
6. Stay up to date on evidence-based practices.
7. Maximize participation by local populations and find and use local resources and capabilities.
8. Integrate activities and programs into larger systems to reduce stand-alone services, reach more people, and be more sustainable over time and space.
9. Use a stepped approach that focuses early efforts on practical help and pragmatic support, with psychological first aid for a generally resilient population.
10. Use triage assessment and focused care for those with specialized needs who require increased levels of intervention.
11. Provide technological assistance, consultation, and training to local providers.
12. Conduct needs assessment of the community with ongoing monitoring of services and program evaluation.
13. Support community-based cultural rituals, memorial services, and spiritual healing practices.

Priscilla Dass-Brailsford's book *Crisis and Disaster Counseling: Lessons Learned From Hurricane Katrina and Other Disasters* (2010) examines many of these recommendations, and the lack of their in-depth implementation. The book places particular emphasis on cultural variables (Boyd, Quevillon, & Engdahl, 2010; Boyd-Franklin, 2010; Dass-Brailsford, 2010) that affected mitigation efforts post-Katrina. How the worker interacts in the first few minutes and hours of contact will most likely determine how effective intervention is and can profoundly affect the recovery course of survivors (Miller, 2010). You should understand that this is why we included a chapter on multiculturalism in this book—not just to be politically correct, but because this is one of the most important variables in disaster crisis intervention.

You should also understand that, as yet, we believe the foregoing 13 principles are neither well known nor practiced regularly by a sufficient number of folks in this business to handle a megadisaster or a pandemic. That is particularly true of pandemics, in which the needs will be exponentially greater than in local megadisasters like Katrina (Webber & Mascari, 2010).

Crisis intervention is not the major occupational definition of most of the people who are called to a mass disaster, nor are you going to find it named in the Dictionary of Occupational Titles. Until that happens, there are likely to be, both on an individual and systemic basis, problems from people attempting to ply this trade who don't know what they are doing or, worse yet, think they do but don't. Frankly, the mere fact that you are reading this book most likely makes you more knowledgeable about crisis intervention than a lot of other professionals who hold Ph.D.s in the helping services fields. The recent birth of Division 56 (Trauma Psychology) of the American Psychological Association and the requirements of counseling and school psychology accrediting agencies for the provision of crisis intervention are a start, along with the American Red Cross's view to expand its psychological intervention curriculum and conduct outreach to more constituencies. Evidence-based treatment practices are starting to be published, but the real-time chaos of disasters makes it hard to do much other than do ex post facto studies. We agree with Silverman, Allen, and Ortiz (2010) that with all due respect to PFA, which appears to have replaced CISD as the treatment de jour, we would like to see a whole lot more outcome studies on its effectiveness, particularly in regard to whom it is applied to, by what kinds of people, and under what kinds of conditions. Please forgive us for being flinty-eyed about panaceas, but 40 years in this business have seen a lot of cure-alls come and go.

The People of Disasters: Responders and Survivors

Crisis Workers at the Disaster

Crisis workers have a wide range of duties after a disaster. **LO6** Foremost is simply being available for survivors to talk with, listening to their experiences, empathizing, and processing with them as they attempt to make sense of it. These activities fall mostly within provision of psychosocial support services and psychological first aid. Workers may help survivors locate significant others, help relatives with identification of victims, or help make arrangements for the deceased. They may provide information on the affective, behavioral, cognitive, interpersonal, and physiological responses to traumatic events (Friedman, Ritchie, & Watson, 2006).

Crisis workers may help relatives through the grieving process, promote social support systems for survivors, and devise a plan of action to mobilize the survivors' resources. They may make appropriate referrals and provide follow-up services. They may also provide debriefing to other emergency service workers (Walker, 1990), prepare food, find clothing, wash dishes, move rubble, help people find lost puppies, talk about how a family who has just lost everything is going to get their 17-year-old into the private college they had planned sending her to but now have no money to do so, administer first aid, help people figure out insurance and FEMA claim procedures, help determine what to do with a grandmother whose nursing home is now full of black mold, conflict-resolve angry feelings between tired, hot, smelly inhabitants of a disaster shelter, and do a thousand other things that lend physical and psychological support—all while dining on military MREs, contracting head lice, going without a bath for a *very* long time, getting bitten by fire ants, and seeing a dermatologist for an unknown skin condition after their tour of duty. Following are some reflections by Dr. Holly Branthoover (personal communication, October 18, 2006) on her experience post-Katrina.

Thoughts of a Mental Health Worker on Katrina One Year Later

Dr. Holly Branthoover, Licensed Professional Counselor and Associate Professor of Counseling, Indiana University of Pennsylvania

I was recruited by the National Board for Certified Counselors via e-mail on Sunday, September 4, 2005, to respond to hurricane Katrina for the Red Cross. I filled out the application packet immediately, faxed it back, and expected to hear from them in a few weeks. The Red Cross contacted me 2 days later, on Tuesday, September 6, asking, "When can you leave?" I garnered permission from the university, prepared coverage for my classes, and flew out on Saturday, September 10. Preparation for the trip included a Red Cross phone orientation and faxed material providing me instructions.

I flew into Baton Rouge, Louisiana, and completed my "in processing" with the Red Cross. I slept in a staff shelter in Baton Rouge that evening and received my assignment the next morning. I was assigned as a part of a team of three mental health workers—a team leader who was a licensed clinical social worker and another team member who was also a licensed professional counselor. We drove to Covington, Louisiana, to the regional Red Cross headquarters for the eastern region of Louisiana. At Covington, we were given our field assignment—to live and work with evacuees at Pearl River High School in Pearl River, Louisiana (275 residents), and to also service three other shelters: Riverside Elementary (25 residents), 6th Ward Elementary (36 residents), and Abita Springs Middle School (35 residents). We also added 5th Ward Elementary (50 residents) when we got to the field.

I stayed in Louisiana for 2 weeks, leaving on Saturday, September 24. However, my departure was very stressful as hurricane Rita arrived on Friday, September 23, closing the Baton Rouge airport and necessitating a drive to Jackson, Mississippi, to catch a flight. Here are some of the points I feel are important if you decide to do disaster mental health work:

In addition to my initial mental health team of three, we received another mental health team member and heavily utilized some local mental health people who had volunteered. The local people were very important in that they were a potential constant in people's lives, whereas we could only be available for a short time. So we had them handle people or families that were potentially staying in the area. It worked very well. I believe this use of local resources is paramount to a successful operation on this scale.

Another thing that I feel very strongly about after my experience is that roving teams may work for medical personnel, but they do not work for mental health. You must join the system. My team lived in the shelter. We ate from the ERV [emergency response vehicle]. We showered (or didn't, in some cases) in the same showers as the residents. Although we certainly

did not share their experience of loss, we did share their experience of the frustration of living in a shelter, and I believe it helped them develop a rapport with us that facilitated assistance.

When we first got to Pearl River High School, we were assigned a counseling room in which to see people. How many people came to that room? Not one! People in crisis do not present for counseling; they are not looking for self-actualization. We had to be out there, in the shelter, sitting with them, talking to them, listening to their stories. As previously mentioned, our team was covering several other shelters, not just Pearl River High School. Our team leader made a wise decision that we needed to provide a constant presence there, as well, so the same people traveled to the same shelters on a daily basis.

One of the things that crisis textbooks talk about is that crisis responders should have the quality of flexibility—I never realized the importance of this until my experience in Louisiana. I had no idea where I was going when I boarded the plane to Louisiana. I had to call a phone number when I landed to get more information. Talk about an adventure! After I reached my assignment in Pearl River, communication was terrible. Even 2 weeks after the storm, cell phone service, landline phone service, TV, Internet, electricity, and so on were all unreliable or nonexistent. Information was carried by courier in some instances, and by the time a directive reached us, it could be wrong or changed.

Misinformation was rampant. We spent some time on rumor control. We actually traveled by car to sites that we "heard" were providing services—like water, cleaning kits, food, blue roofs (tarpaulins to cover damaged roofs), and so on. We tried to confirm what information was factual and pass that to our residents. Who would want to use the last of their gas to drive to a site for assistance and find there is no assistance available? We also acted as a liaison with FEMA representatives in the area, getting accurate information and facilitating services. Much of our time was spent in linking clients to assistance—more social work than counseling.

Medical services are also a part of what the Red Cross provides during a disaster. The mental health staff worked closely to assist the medical staff. Some people were in crisis because of their injuries (e.g., a woman with a severe vaginal infection from being in the floodwater who thought she was dying). Some were in crisis because they could not get their medication (everything from life-sustaining medication to methadone). We detoxed half a dozen people from their methadone in the shelter. Lack of medication was a big issue. Since we, as a team, had a car, we tried to barter and borrow supplies and medication when we came into contact with staff at other locations or on trips to regional headquarters. Things like hand sanitizer and lice kits were quite a commodity.

Working with the children in the shelters was another important activity that we engaged in. One of the members of my team was the head of a day care center in New York, so she was very invested in setting up children's programs. Again, we did very little counseling here. Our team member set up children's activities three times per day at Pearl River. Activities included arts and crafts, games, movies, and the like. This served two positive purposes, providing structure to the children's day (the shelter is a boring place) and giving parents a break. We had to put boundaries on the parent break because some took advantage. For example, we had to make a rule that parents could not leave the shelter while children's activities were going on (so they could be available if there was a problem). Although it varied by developmental level, children began to express their feelings about the hurricane and their current life situation via the artwork and games.

When we first arrived, and periodically throughout, we worked with disaster relief services staff a great deal. Staff were stressed and burned out. At some of the smaller shelters, we were the only professional mental health service providers that the disaster relief staff had seen since the hurricane. At one shelter, several medically needy residents had died, and staff needed to talk about and process this experience. They were angry at the lack of supplies and communication—so much food was available that it was sometimes thrown away, but there was a great lack of medical supplies. At times, staff members got into arguments, and we would mediate. Sometimes, staff was just stressed and needed to talk. Our team leader consulted often with the shelter manager, assisting in administrative decisions about shelter services. I believe this was a strength of our shelter manager—getting mental health input on shelter operation. In one instance, I was asked to talk with a staff member who had violated Red Cross policy and was going to be relieved of her duties and sent home early.

In the shelter, we had National Guard protection for only the first 2 days. From then on, we had 24-hour protection from local law enforcement—parish sheriffs, with at least two on duty at all times. We worked closely with the sheriffs—assisting with resident arguments, and so on. There were two cocaine arrests at the shelter, with those residents being taken to jail. We had two domestic violence incidents—we worked with security to come up with a safety plan for all residents (this meant moving the two offending husbands to a different shelter). I spoke personally with a least two people who were suicidal, and we worked with security to observe them since there were no inpatient mental health facilities available.

Another incident that was particularly scary happened two nights before I left. When hurricane Rita was coming, a mandatory evacuation of New Orleans resulted in our shelter numbers swelling to close to 500 people. Many were Hispanic workers from construction crews who spoke little or no English. A local person and a worker got into a fight in the cafeteria, and a gun was pulled. Although security directly dealt with the gun issue, we assisted with crowd control and calming everyone down afterward—including staff!

Some of my philosophies of crisis intervention were challenged as a result of this experience. The goal of crisis intervention is to return clients to their precrisis state of functioning. In this case, the majority of the clients in the shelter had a precrisis state of functioning that was dysfunctional! By 2 weeks poststorm, most of the residents left in shelters were people who had little before the storm in the way of resources—both personal and financial. People with family support systems or money were already gone. The majority of our residents had supported themselves via public assistance or SSI disability. Many were involved with community mental health, child protective services, and the legal system. Several were inmates from the county jail who had been released as the storm approached. Drug abuse, child abuse, and domestic violence were prevalent. Given the demographics, it was hard to tell when crisis intervention should end! I also found it important to help people problem-solve within the context of their culture. One man felt trapped about making a decision to go back to work. He did not want to leave his wife alone at the shelter, as he felt it was his duty to protect her. His wife had been called back to work, too. However, he did not want her working while he was not (who would watch their stuff?), and his duty as a man was to provide. I had to work within these values—not my own.

My last two thoughts are related to actually being a part of a team response. Just because you are "mental health" doesn't mean that you are not part of the entire shelter team. Pitch in! I did kitchen work, carried and moved things, and cleaned. Each night, after residents went to bed (curfew at 10 P.M.), the whole shelter was disinfected. I helped with this every night. Working alongside someone can give a great opportunity for them to share their feelings or vent. It also allowed us to be part of the staff—not separate. This said, I do not minimize the benefit of doing mental health things for staff. The second week I was there, a local pizza place opened. The mental health team organized a pizza party for staff for after residents went to bed. It turned out to be a great stress reliever.

Last, all of the things I have talked about are occurring while you are living the experience of a disaster and trying to help people at the same time. I slept on a cot, showered only once the first week, and tried to avoid getting lice (which I did, luckily, because the thought alone freaked me out!). In our travels, we saw the horrific devastation in Slidell, Louisiana, which borders Pearl River and was where the eye of the hurricane passed through. We also traveled, on our day off, into New Orleans, again witnessing the loss and devastation of the storm. During our trip to the city, we got free pizzas from Dominos (they were passing them out) and water. We drove around the city to different National Guard troops, firemen, and EMS companies, passing out pizza and water, and spent time just talking to them—something they were grateful for when they found out we were "mental health." It was scary to be in a city that looked like a ghost town, patrolled by military personnel with M16s. We got to see the Superdome and the Convention Center. I believe it was important to have this R&R even though we were still, in a way, doing our mental health job. There were several times in the 2 weeks when I got really stressed out (like when I asked for lice kits at headquarters and was told we couldn't have lice at our shelter—because they hadn't gotten a report of it!). So it is important to find a way to take care of yourself—phone calls home, camaraderie with other staff, watching a DVD (after the power is back on!), and so on. You can't help others if you are a stressed-out, burned-out mess!

Source: Used with permission from Dr. Holly Branthoover, Associate Professor of Counseling, Indiana University of Pennsylvania

Now switch to Memphis, Tennessee, 450 miles away.

Lessons I Learned from Katrina

Dr. Richard James, Licensed Professional Counselor, Psychologist, National Board Certified School Counselor, Department of Counseling, Educational Psychology and Research, University of Memphis

When Katrina hit the Gulf Coast, little did mental health providers in Memphis, Tennessee, realize that they also would be in the eye of the hurricane. As the magnitude of the disaster started to become clearer and the flow of evacuees moved away from the coast, one thing became very clear in a hurry. We were not prepared for the onslaught of people with wide-ranging mental and medical problems that were about to descend on us. Compounding the problems those medically and mentally fragile people brought into our community were 13,000 homeless individuals who were essentially living out of their cars or motels for the first 2 weeks post-Katrina. As it became clearer that these people were not going back home immediately, a variety of crisis situations arose.

Three anecdotes will give you a pretty good idea of how ill prepared the city of Memphis and Shelby County, Tennessee, were to deal with a major disaster as far as provision of mental health service was concerned. This is probably more ominous when considering that the scene of the actual disaster was more than 400 miles away from us.

On September 3, 2006, I was helping my daughter and her fiancé load my truck with gasoline, lantern and cooking fuel, lanterns, cooking equipment, firearms, meals ready to eat, sleeping bags, and other supplies as they prepared to go back to see what was left of their home in Long Beach, Mississippi, after hurricane Katrina sent a 5-foot wall of water through it. At 10:00 A.M. I received a phone call from a harried Shelby County Red Cross director of medical services who had located me by word of mouth and was told I might be able to help since "I knew everything about crisis intervention." He asked if I could provide assistance to the crew of the *American Queen* sternwheeler passenger liner that was docked in Memphis with a crew of 250 very agitated individuals. The boat and crew all shipped out of New Orleans, and they had no word of their families or homes because they had been on the Mississippi River since Katrina hit. The problem was that no one could find this 400-foot-long boat—in Memphis, not even the police. Finally, the riverboat was located at 5 P.M. I got another counselor and headed for the boat. Now the problem was that the boat was set to sail at 6 P.M., passengers were filing on board, and dinner was being served, so no one could come to talk to us. That was the start of what came to be a deluge that we were ill prepared to handle and caused us to reevaluate every facet of our disaster preparedness and mental health provision system in Memphis.

The bishop of the Memphis Catholic diocese had witnessed Katrina firsthand from a hotel room as he saw his car go floating away in Bay St. Louis, Mississippi. He immediately flung open the doors of all the Catholic schools in Memphis and welcomed any and all families from the coast to enroll their children tuition free in the Memphis Catholic school system. Many of these children came from very poor families with extreme deficits in their educational backgrounds. A lot of these kids were the toughest of the tough to teach and found their way into new Catholic inner-city Jubilee schools, which operate on very tight budgets with little support staff. Since I was "the guy who knew all about crisis" and was also a school counselor educator, I was asked to put a workshop together for the private schools in Memphis on dealing with traumatized children. On September 10, together with Dr. Jo Epstein, a National Certified School Counselor and an elementary school counselor with the city of Memphis, I delivered a workshop at the University of Memphis that was attended by 31 counselors and teachers from 19 private schools. After we finished delivering a 3-hour workshop on trauma and what they might expect to see in their school buildings, I looked out over the room and saw that many of those faces looked like deer caught in the headlights of an oncoming truck! I immediately knew that I would need help in dealing not only with evacuees but also with teachers and counselors, who would be suffering from secondary traumatization from attempting to deal with those children. For the next 6 months, these teachers and counselors met with me for supervision as they valiantly attempted to deal with these high-risk children and stave off compassion fatigue and burnout.

It quickly became apparent that we didn't have enough mental health professionals to deal with the people coming into our city with a host of medical and mental issues. We also did not have anyone in charge of handling these people. The coordinator of the local crime victims' assistance center, a licensed clinical social worker, and another LCSW at one of the local mental health clinics stepped into the breach and started to make order out of what was rapidly turning into a classic example of chaos theory at work (see Chapter 1, Approaching Crisis Intervention). Picture your author sitting in a reception center talking with a methadone maintenance heroin addict from New Orleans.

Addict: Hey, man, they won't give me any methadone, say I got to have a prescription. If I don't get some methadone pretty damn quick, I'll go rob a liquor store and get the real deal!

By the middle of September we had approximately 13,000 expatriates from New Orleans and the Gulf Coast in our city. All thoughts about licensing and certifying mental health workers for disaster work went right out the window with Katrina. The faculty at our university mobilized 200 students in the counseling, school psychology, and social work departments, and with faculty supervisors they started working in the shelters. These students and faculty served up to 2 months in this capacity until some semblance of order could be restored.

The bottom line was that we too were not prepared for this megadisaster. The outcome of this disaster was the establishment of a planning committee for the Greater Memphis Area Emergency Preparedness for Mental Health. That committee's composition ranges from mental health personnel from hospitals, community agencies, and human services provision organizations to religious leaders, school system personnel, city and county officials, the police, fire, and EMT departments, charitable organizations, homeland security, medical facilities, and universities. This is certainly a work in progress. Will we be better prepared than we were for Katrina? That's a good question! Wherever you are in this country, or any other country for that matter, you might ask yourself the same question. The ripple effects of a disaster this large flow far out from the epicenter. Disasters that affect such a great number of people need all of the professions mentioned above if successful crisis intervention is going to occur, as you will soon see.

Case Study of the Benefield Family

Now meet the Benefield family, who are about to experience the crisis of their lives. The Benefields typify, in an encapsulated way, how the ecosystemic crisis intervention model *should* (note the emphasis on "should") operate when a large-scale disaster afflicts a family.

Tuesday, April 21, 14:00 Hours Military Time (2:00 P.M. CDT)

An F-4 tornado has hit Midville, Tennessee, a town with a population of approximately 40,000 in the south-central United States. The storm cut across the town and left a path of destruction about one-quarter to one-half mile wide for a distance of more than 5 miles. It effectively cut a path through the industrial park, damaging numerous buildings but particularly wreaking havoc on the automotive plant, which employed more than 1,000 people. The plant is close to a total loss. The storm continued through several residential areas and a housing development, hop-scotched, and then hit the main elementary school of Midville and reduced it to rubble. All 600 students were inside the building at the time, under cover in the hallways.

The water plant received a direct hit from the storm and can no longer keep water pressure up or produce potable drinking water. The power grid has been disrupted by downed power lines and wrecked substations, and the city is currently without power. Both cellular and landline telephone systems are inoperable because of downed towers and lines. The local hospital has received minor damage but is still in operation. Local fire, police, and emergency services have emerged largely unscathed and are close to fully operational. There has been a significant loss of life in addition to injuries that appear to be in the hundreds.

Now meet the Benefield family: Travis Benefield, age 33, a machinist at the local automobile plant; Sara Lee Benefield, age 32, a dental assistant; Jason Benefield, age 13, an eighth-grader at Midville Middle School; Lou Ann Benefield, age 11, a sixth-grader at Midville Middle School; Shawn Benefield, age 6, a first-grader at Midville Elementary School; and Loretta Benefield, age 54, the mother of Travis.

April 21, 14:15 Hours Military Time (2:15 P.M., 15 minutes after the tornado)

Travis Benefield is emerging from the rubble of the automobile plant. He has no major injuries, just minor cuts and bruises from falling and flying debris. While frantically helping dig others out, he is also attempting to reach his wife on his cell phone, but that is not working. Sara Lee Benefield is currently upside down in her van in a water-filled ditch. She is there because she heard the tornado siren and, instead of taking cover in the dentist's office where she worked, became hysterical and was on her way to school to pick up her children. She is semiconscious, bleeding, and clearly in need of rescue and medical assistance.

Jason Benefield is currently looking for his sister, Lou Ann, in the melee that is now Midville Middle School. No one was hurt in either the middle school or the high school, and neither school was significantly damaged. Everyone in both the middle and high schools had been protected in the hallways; however, chaos now reigns as teachers attempt to control

panic-stricken students who heard the tornado go over and can now see the destructive path it has made. Lou Ann is likewise attempting to find her brother Jason. She is also hysterical because she has seen that the tornado essentially destroyed the elementary school that her brother Shawn attends. Shawn is currently missing, probably buried somewhere under the rubble of the elementary school. Loretta, the grandmother who resides with the family, is currently lying in a field, dead from a broken neck and back, about one-quarter mile from where the family lived in a manufactured home that has been blown away and no longer exists.

April 21, 14:25 Hours, Emergency Command Center

LEM director, Thaddeus Washington: (*on short-wave radio to all ham operators and state police emergency and state emergency broadcast systems*) It appears we have had a major tornado disaster here involving most of Midville. We currently have no power or cellular or landline telephone communication. It appears that there is a large path of destruction throughout the city, and there is also a very high casualty rate as we had less than 15 minutes' warning time. We have ruptured gas lines and water lines and have no ability to pump water. We have at least two fires. We are requesting immediate assistance from the region IV and state emergency management network. We are making a damage assessment now. Instructions will follow in about 30 minutes.

As the reports from police cars and ham radio operators start to come into the center, the director has to make several quick decisions about the magnitude of the disaster. From the initial reports he decides to alert the regional and state emergency management coordinators. He also needs a better assessment of what is going on in the community. He therefore asks for a state police helicopter and instructs his emergency preparedness manager to get airborne and conduct an assessment.

April 21, 14:35 Hours, Midville Middle School, School Crisis Response Team Meeting in Cafeteria

Linda Gidcome, Assistant Superintendent, Crisis Response Coordinator: It appears that we have a major crisis involving not only the elementary school but the whole town. The police are over at the elementary school, but we have many children trapped in there. Undoubtedly there are casualties in that building. Jackson Little, the elementary school counselor and our crisis intervention coordinator, is not yet accounted for. Until he is found, Jim Constansis, the high school vocational coordinator, is his backup and in charge of intervention. We also have some other missing people, so, Jim, I want you to get backups for them. I am going to turn the meeting over to Jim.

Jim Constansis, Crisis Intervention Coordinator: We also have to deal with our children here and in the high school to be sure they are safe. We need to get everybody back in their rooms and run the roll. Right now we don't have any good information about where "safe" is. As such, we are going to hold all middle and secondary school students in their respective buildings. It appears that right now there is no way into the school from outside due to debris on the roads. I want to get backups for all the missing members of the team. Our first priority is to run the rolls and see who is missing. So we need to take the TO GO boxes' primary hard copy and send three teams (Red, Blue, Green) over to the elementary school, while the Orange Team stays here and the Purple Team stays at the high school to start receiving kids. We will bring K through third grades here and fourth and fifth grades to the high school. Red has K and 1, Blue has 2 and 3, and Green has 4 and 5. They are going to need medical assistance over there, so I want the Orange Team to pull all of our available medical supplies out of the sports facility storage and set up a dispensary in the cafeteria.

Luda Sarapokin, our school nurse, will be running that. We're going to get on the radio and let OEC know what our condition is just as soon as the building engineer can get the generator hooked up to it and running. All of you pick up your two-way radios. Things are going to get pretty hectic, so remember your radio manners and protocol. We have done this in an exercise; the only difference was that the middle school was the target. We can do this. Let's go to work!

The Incident Command System has been in place for 2 years in the Midville School District. It has a clear incident command system (Thomae, 2002) that has been activated on the tornado's departure. Its first and primary job is to account for all the children. Any parents who could somehow manage to get to the school would be taken to a waiting area before any children would be released. The parents have been informed of this plan and know what to expect and what to do.

April 21, 15:05 Hours, above Midville in a helicopter

Saria Wickeramasaka, Emergency Preparedness Coordinator: (in a state police helicopter above Midville, on the radio speaking to the LEM director) The Packard engine plant is completely ruined; the total building is involved. I can see human movement, but there are undoubtedly people trapped in the plant. I do not see any evidence of fire. We will need heavy equipment including cranes and hoists. We will need EMTs and rescue equipment and units. The Hi Power petroleum bulk plant got hit and there is leakage from their storage tanks. It appears both gasoline and fuel oil are being discharged, although the berms seem to be containing the fuel at present. We will need a containment and cleanup crew there along with fire equipment and spillage trucks. I see no evidence of fire. The elementary school has received a direct hit. The middle of the building has sustained a great deal of damage and the east wing has collapsed. I can see movement, and it appears the school CRTs are working at the elementary school. There are undoubtedly many casualties.

The roads to the school are currently impassable. We will need heavy equipment including teams with chain saws to get in there. I would recommend this as our first priority. We do have two house fires, one on Appleton at Branch and one on Sycamore past Hoover. The one on Sycamore is in danger of involving an apartment complex. It should be fought immediately. The street is blocked from the north, but trucks can come in from the east side and through the apartment complex.

The waterworks is a total loss with the pumping station and filter house completely wrecked. You can probably assume that the available water supply is what is currently in the two north and south standpipes, which appear to have sustained no damage. The sanitary works is operational. The path of the tornado is pretty steady from southwest to northeast approximately one-quarter to one-half mile wide running from state highway 37 to just south of I-69 for a stretch of about 5 miles. There are some skips, but it has pretty much gone through Midville from the industrial park on the southwest side of town through the west side of town. Before it went back up in the air, it got the mobile home park on Breezemore Road. There are mobile homes blown apart and on top of one another. I can see human movement here also, but there are going to be lots of casualties here as well.

I estimate about 200 homes destroyed or heavily damaged and 600 more with some damage. We need to notify Midville Central and St. Andrew's hospitals that they need to go to Code Red [highest emergency status]. We are going to need Tennessee Valley Power to do the same, as it appears we have a complete power outage across the city. Midville Power and Light will not be able to handle this outage alone.

As this assessment comes into the emergency operations center (EOC), information is relayed through the regional EOC coordinator and transmitted to the state EOC. As the magnitude of the disaster unfolds, the governor is notified and mobilizes National Guard units. Word goes out to FEMA, the Red Cross, and the Salvation Army, and these groups begin mobilizing human resources to go to Midville. Within 1 hour and 10 minutes, a massive mobilization effort is underway. Food, drinking water, medicine, medical supplies, emergency medical personnel in the form of EMTs and fire departments, rescue teams, and heavy equipment all move toward Midville.

As Lane (2003) indicates, if roads are impassable and it is possible, someone with the EOC needs to get airborne and conduct a visual assessment of the extent of the damage and relay information to the center about what and who are going to be needed where and under how high a priority.

April 21, 15:21 Hours, Command Center

As the LEMA director sends out mobilization orders, a number of workers you will soon meet swing into action. In these first few hours and days they will be administering what is generally construed to be psychological first aid as they attempt to gain control over the chaotic scenes and traumatized individuals who are survivors of the disaster. As they enter the setting, they will be sensitive to the culture and diversity of the populations they are servicing. They will also be aware of and looking for at-risk populations. They are, first and foremost, interested in the immediate physical safety of survivors. To that end, they will attempt to provide a sense of predictability, control, comfort, and safety to survivors by providing straightforward and easily understood information about disaster response activities and services. They will attempt to protect survivors from additional traumatic experiences and trauma reminders while they go about their work. Major tasks will be reuniting

children with their caregivers, stabilizing emotionally overwhelmed survivors, and providing support for acutely bereaved persons (National Center for PTSD, n.d.a.).

To accomplish the foregoing tasks, the workers will engage in a great deal of information gathering in regard to current needs and concerns about the following:

1. Nature and severity of experiences during the disaster
2. Death of a family member or close friend
3. Concerns about immediate postdisaster circumstances and ongoing threat
4. Separations from or concern about the safety of loved ones
5. Physical illness and need for medications
6. Losses incurred as a result of the disaster (home, school, pets, personal property, etc.)
7. Extreme feelings of guilt or shame
8. Thoughts about causing harm to self or others
9. Lack of adequate supportive social network
10. Prior alcohol or drug use
11. Prior exposure to trauma or loss
12. Prior psychological problems (National Center for PTSD, n.d.a.)

When the workers have the foregoing information, they will identify and clarify the most immediate needs of the survivor, discuss an action plan with the person, and then act to address the identified needs. Integral to this process is providing information on traumatic stress and coping mechanisms to help alleviate the stress and linking the individual with the disaster relief services they will need (National Center for PTSD, n.d.c.). Follow these crisis workers now as they put the foregoing points into action.

April 21, 15:51 Hours, Midville Elementary School

Jack Tankersly, School CRT Blue Team member at Midville Elementary: (*helping a dazed boy with some cuts and blood on him out of the rubble of the east hallway of Midville Elementary School*) I'm Mr. Tankersly from the middle school. How are you doing?

Shawn: Iah guess Ah'm OK, Iah dunno. . . . Whaaat happened?

Jack: There was a tornado, but you are going to be all right. If you can walk OK, we are going to take you to the middle school and get you checked out. Can you do that?

Shawn: Yeah, I guess. I jest got some little cuts on my arms. There's some other kids hurt bad back in the hallway, though. Jamie's eyes were shut and he wasn't talkin' even when I shook him. He was hurt real bad, maybe even dead or somethin'.

Jack: Yes, I know, and we will get them out. So don't worry about that. Right now let's focus on you. Can you give me your name and tell me who your teacher is?

Shawn: Shawn Benefield. Ah'm in Mrs. Cruz's first-grade class.

Jack: (*checks over the two-way radio with the documentation leader on the student in the central elementary To Go box*) Good. You have a brother and a sister in the middle school, Jason and Lou Ann, right?

Shawn: Yes.

Jack: I am going to have someone take you up to the middle school and get those cuts cleaned up and check you out. I'll let them know you are coming, so your sister and brother will know you are OK.

One of the critical components in any disaster in a school is keeping track of and accounting for children. Nowhere is the concept of the school as in loco parentis (in place of the parent) more important. Portable, centralized, and redundant To Go boxes (Thomae, 2002) are critical to such an endeavor; they hold classroom lists, student names, addresses, telephone numbers, medical issues, release forms, and parent and guardian names. Moving a school full of injured, confused, and terrified students is an undertaking that must be done carefully and precisely so that no student is lost or unaccounted for. While there is a school Critical Incident Stress Management Team to deal with students' psychological concerns, it is separate and distinct from the incident command system and will not come into operation until the physical safety of the students is assured. Particularly important staff members on this team are bus drivers, secretaries, and custodians who have knowledge of children and building facilities that educators do not (Allen & Sheen, 2005). Reuniting missing children with parents is a critical component and one of the highest priorities in any disaster (National Center for PTSD, n.d.a.). As an example, one of the Herculean efforts accomplished by the National Center for Missing and Exploited Children after hurricane Katrina was reuniting all 5,192 children reported missing with their families (Missing Children, 2006).

April 21, 15:30 Hours, EOC Command Center

Thaddeus Washington: (*addressing command center staff*) We have a Class One disaster. We are going to be overwhelmed with dead, wounded, and people needing shelter, food, water, clothing, and mental health assistance. We are setting a shelter up at the National Guard Armory. We are going to set up a morgue at the Seabrook Packing Plant. The high school and the middle school are going to be reception and clearing centers, so we can get people sorted out and families reunited.

We may have to turn them into shelters too. As soon as we get that done, we will probably set up for the Red Cross and FEMA teams here at the Civic Center. Our first priority is to get the kids out of the elementary school. Preliminary reports indicate that there are a number trapped in the building.

We need to get the roads opened so we can get heavy equipment in there. The EMAs from Sawyer, Plainfield, and Cumberland are sending fire and rescue units. The state EOC has been notified and informed the governor, who is going to call for a presidential disaster order. We need to get the road opened, so get all of Howell Paving and Construction and the State Highway department equipment on the road and heading in that direction, and get three of our CERT teams to help them clear trees, so let them know we have to have chain saws. Saria landed and says we will need at least one and possibly two tracked cranes.

Our second priority will be the Packard plant. I want Cassius Mendoza, the construction superintendent for Norton Metal Frame Buildings, to go out there and tell us what we need. We also need to get people out there to help organize them—although Joel Pickard, the plant superintendent, and I have gone over their emergency plan and they seem to be functioning pretty well given the way the whole thing came down. Get the rest of the CERT teams spread out along the line from state route 37 up to I-69. Be sure we get one team up to the mobile home park on Breezemore. We need to get the water system back on line. It appears most of our staff at the waterworks, including Joe Mulvidge, the chief engineer, and Hack Townsend, the superintendent, have been injured. I have asked staff from the Sawyer water system to come and give us an assessment. Until further notice we will ration water and put a boil order out because we are bound to lose pressure on the system. I have a feeling that this is going to be really bad. I hope our practices have paid off. Dr. Benjamin, we are going to need to get your mental health team assembled. I am afraid there is going to be work for them. OK, everybody, you know your jobs, let's go to work!

April 21, 15:35 Hours

Dr. Yolanda Benjamin, Executive Director of Hatchie County Mental Health Center and mental health liaison to the Midville EOC: (*speaking to Ester Carey, her secretary, at the mental health center on an emergency band radio*) How many staff have we got that are at the center? OK, good! They know what to do. We are going to need counselors at the National Guard Armory and out at Seabrook Packing. We are also going to need to send counselors out to both hospitals to work with the chaplains out there. As soon as they open the road to the schools, I'll go out there and see what kind of assistance they need there. There are going to be Red Cross counselors coming in, but right now we are it.

Both Washington and Benjamin are going to have to balance between being responders and coordinators. For the present, they are in the responding business, but as more outside assistance arrives, their job will change to consulting and coordination with the external support systems that are going to flood into the area (Lane, 2003). It is critically important that integration of mental health services with other disaster responders occurs and that it is recognized as a critical component to overall relief efforts, as exemplified by Mr. Washington and his immediate referral to Dr. Benjamin and her mental health teams (Ørner et al., 2006).

April 21, 17:12 Hours

Juanita Sanchez, leader of Community Emergency Response Team (CERT) 10: (*Looking for survivors, she clambers down a steep ravine into a muddy creek bottom where Sara Lee Benefield's SUV is upside down. Sara is barely conscious and keeps rambling incoherently about needing to get her kids.*) (*speaking into her two-way radio*) Jake, notify the medical OEC that CERT 10 has a woman pinned in her car at the bottom of Rutledge Creek at the Brunner Street Bridge. We are going to need medical assistance, a wrecker, and an extraction team. (*speaking to Sara Lee*) Can you hear me? I want you to talk to me. OK? We are getting help here for you. Can you tell me your

name? Mine is Juanita. I am on a CERT team. I found you down here where the tornado blew you and your car. We are going to get you out of here.

Sara Lee: I . . . need mah children . . . Shawn and . . . I cain't remember . . . (*eyes roll back*)

Juanita: OK, I understand that is what you need to do. Now you stay with me. Stay awake! We will help you with that. Do you hurt anywhere?

Sara Lee: (*slow, measured, and staggered speech in a low voice*) Mah . . . legs . . . are . . . numb and mah chest hurts. Iah cain't move. Iah need to git mah kids. Where . . . are . . . mah . . . kids? Iah need . . . some . . . hep!

Juanita: There are people at the school right now taking care of all of the kids. Good! Great! You are talking to me! Stay awake! (*radios information back to the team*) I am not going to leave you. My name is Juanita Sanchez. Can you say my name?

Sara Lee: Juanita . . . Juanita Ramras.

Juanita: Close enough! (*Starts to conduct a head-to-toe basic medical assessment. Covers Sara and keeps her talking to postpone shock and unconsciousness.*)

CERT volunteer teams are common everyday citizens who have undergone FEMA training as a rapid and immediate reaction force to help save lives. The FEMA training teaches volunteers skills needed to assist before, during, and after a disaster, such as fire suppression, diagnosing and dealing with the three major killers of injured—airway obstruction, bleeding, and shock—first aid, light search-and-rescue operations, disaster psychology and team organization, and disaster simulation exercises (Federal Emergency Management Agency, 2015). Juanita is a volunteer who has gone through CERT training. Her occupation is a bookkeeper at a local auto dealership.

April 21, 18:23 Hours

Allie Tran Nyguen, CERT Team 4 member: (*in a field 300 yards northeast of the Breezemore Mobile Home Park, speaking into his two-way radio*) I have a female, approximately age 50, who is unresponsive and who has no pulse, lying about 150 yards north of Breezemore Road. We need to get her ID'ed. She has no identification on her. Can we get her transported? We will need a four-wheel drive.

Carl Hanratty, Team 4 leader: I'll send Sheila, Jon, and Jerry over there with the 4 × 6 ATV. EOC is setting up a morgue at the Seabrook Packing Plant. We'll get her out of the field and then they can pick her up.

Write down her description and the details of where she was found and we'll attach that to her bag.

April 21, 19:02 Hours, Midville Civic Center

Travis Benefield: (at the Civic Center, stunned, irate, and half-hysterical, speaking rapidly and loudly to Kate McClain, mental health counselor) I NEED SUM BY-GOD HEP HERE AND RITE NOW! I cain't git to mah house. Iah heared that everything in the Breezemore Park has done blowed away. Mah momma was at our home there sleepin'. I don't know where mah wife is, there weren't no one at the dentist's office 'cause it was all beat up from the twister. Iah heared that everybody at the elementary school done got kilt, and Iah got kids there, but they won't let me near there neither. Iah walked and hitched a ride into here 'cause Iah ain't got no vehicle 'cause part of the Packard plant is on top of it. And Iah cain't find mah dad-burned tools nowheres.

Kate: (de-escalating Travis) I see how upset you are. I am Kate McClain. I do not know your name.

Travis: Ah'm Travis Benefield. Iah work out to the Packard plant and mah wife's Sara Lee and she works at Doc Collard's office. She's his dental assistant, and Iah got three kids out to the schools—Shawn, Lee Ann, and Jason, and then there's mah momma, Loretta, and Iah been out at the Packard plant pullin' folks outta there, and there's a lotta people bad hurt, and Iah lost all mah durn tools, and Jim Houston, the other millsetter, is dead under a stamping machine, and . . . I'm ahm ABOUT TO GO NUTS AND AH NEED SOME DAD GUM HEP! *(rapid, panting breathing, eyes rapidly moving back and forth, fists clinched pounding hand in fist, rapid, random pacing verging on hysteria)*

Kate: (Gently interrupting his continuous, escalating, out-of-control verbiage, she starts with enough command in her voice to get Travis's attention, then rapidly diminishes her voice level.) TRAVIS! T-R-A-V-I-S. IF I AM TO HELP YOU, I NEED YOUR FULL ATTENTION. *(Travis gives a startled look, but slows down and attends to the worker.)* Thank you, Travis. I want you to take a deep breath and just listen to me for a moment. Good. Just take a deep breath. Again, I understand all the confusion. It is a mess, but we will get it straightened out. I hear how concerned you are about all your family and how terrifying that is not knowing anything. I need you to get grounded here so I can be of the most help. To do that I need for you to have your

wits about you. OK! So humor me here a moment. Tell me where you are right now, tell me what time it is on that clock behind me, and tell me what they're doing over there in the corner?

Travis: Ah, well, we'uns are here into the com-mun-it-ee center and it's ah well . . . I think that thar clock has done stopped. Them ladies is settin' up what looks like some sammiches 'n' sodas 'n' water and what-not.

Kate: Excellent. I just wanted to get your feet planted back on the ground here so we can make some headway. OK?

Travis: (rather sheepishly) Yes'um, I do indeed have my wits about me now. I do apologize for my unseemly behavior thar.

Kate: Thank you. You have every right to be upset. That is normal. But we will get this squared away. I am a counselor here, and I am going to help you. Right now I need you to help me, though. How about let's go over here and sit down and let me get Jodell Brown over here. She is one of the coordinators, and we will see what we can start to find out, and get you reunited with your family. I bet you haven't had anything to eat or drink since the tornado hit. I need you to be calm and collected, so we can get the information we need, so do you suppose you could sit here and maybe eat a sandwich and have a soda and tell me and Jodell what we need to know to help you?

Travis: Well, OK. Ah'm jest so scared, though. It were purely awful out there to the plant, and Iah cain't find out nuthin'. Iah done pulled people out of there as much as Iah could until they done got there with the heavy equipment, then Iah didn't want to leave but Iah had to find out about mah family.

Kate: So you did what you could out there. It is certainly understandable that you want to find out about your family and get them together. Not knowing is really the worst part, but here is Jodell, and she is going to get the information she needs from you, and then we will be able to tell you something. And that's really what you want to know, isn't it? Let me go get you a sandwich and a soda and just tell Jodell.

In the preliminary stage of a crisis, mental health counselors need to understand that they can best help by providing very practical support (Ørner et al., 2006). A central information area will be a trip into Bedlam with people attempting to reunite with families. Getting order and direction is a first priority. This is not a time to attempt to do "counseling." Help is what is needed, and the mental health crisis worker can best do that by calming and defusing people who are very distraught, angry, grief stricken, and in shock.

Kate is helpful in de-escalating and defusing a very distraught individual who has been severely traumatized and is now terrified that his family has fared even worse. She uses two standard techniques with excitable and distraught clients. First is **entrainment** (literally synchronization of the organism [Travis]to an external rhythm [hers] here slowing Travis down by use of verbal calming techniques) and then **grounding** (a reality orientation technique that helps keep someone in the present and helps reorient a person to the here-and-now and in reality) (Webber, Mascari, & Runte, 2010). She raises her voice in a command level manner, but not quite as loud as the client's; she then tails off her decibel level and speaks more slowly. This tactic catches the client's attention, but then hopefully models for him to tone down and slow down. She uses simple calming techniques of introducing herself and asking for his name. She then asks him to take a deep breath to slow him down. She does a quick reality orientation that refocuses him into his present environment. She then offers him food and drink and a place to sit. All of these are basic calming and grounding techniques that are simple but effective. Her negative interrogative question is generally a very bad counseling technique because it implies agreement, but in this case Kate specifically uses it to get agreement and further stabilize and get Travis under control.

April 21, 19:22 Hours, Civic Center Reception and Clearing Area

Jodell Brown, clearing coordinator: (*Kate McClain, mental health crisis worker, is also present.*) Mr. Benefield, here is what I have. All of your children are safe. Shawn had some minor cuts and bruises, but he has received medical attention for those and is fine. They are all at the middle school. They are getting supper served to them. We will relay to them that you are safe also. Your wife is in the hospital. She was pinned in her car, but they got her out. She had to have one leg operated on because it was fractured. She has two fractured ribs, but she is OK and in stable condition. She already knows the children are safe, and we are now relaying to her that you are safe. From what we now know, I am sorry to tell you that there are no homes left standing in Breezemore Park. There were many people who were killed and there were many injured out there, and presently it is off limits as they sort through

the debris looking for survivors. We have no one identified as Loretta Benefield at any hospital. As of now we are listing her as missing. We will have transportation here to take you to the children. If you do not have any friends' or relatives' home you can go to, then we can take you to the National Guard Armory for tonight. There will be a FEMA field office set up tomorrow, and there will be all of the major insurance carriers here in mobile disaster units by tomorrow morning. As soon as we have any word about your mother, we will let you know. Now Kate will go with you and get you out to the children. Do you have any questions for me?

Travis: (*Dazed, taking in all of that information, hesitates and thinks. The crisis worker waits patiently.*) Well, no, I don't rightly guess. I guess mah sister over to Crowley could take we'uns in, but I don't know how to git word to her. I guess fer tonight we'uns just best go to the Armory. Ah'm sick to death about not knowing about momma. But I do thank you for findin' out all the rest. I 'preciate it most kindly, ma'am.

Jodell: You are welcome, Mr. Benefield. If you will give me her phone number and address, we will try to get in touch with her. Just so I can be sure that you have gotten all that, could you sort of summarize it so I'm sure that I haven't left anything out or have been unclear?

The crisis worker very carefully and specifically goes through the items she needs to cover. She then asks Travis to recapitulate what she has said so that they all have a clear understanding of what has been covered and what is going to happen. Kate will see that Travis and his children are reunited and will hand him off to another crisis worker at the shelter. This is basic psychological first aid that is designed to slow things down, get some control back in the situation, provide support and reassurance, and improve short-term functioning (Halpern & Tramontin, 2007, pp. 203–218).

April 22, 08:35 Hours, National Guard Armory Disaster Shelter

Ollie Naifeh, MSW, Red Cross disaster counselor from Memphis: Mr. Benefield, hello, I am Oliver Naifeh, a Red Cross counselor from Memphis. You can call me Ollie. I just got your name as one of my people. How did your night go?

Travis: Well, not real well, sir. Iah didn't sleep much, but the kids did. Iah'd like to git over to see

Sara Lee. And Iah'd shore like to find out about momma.

Ollie: We have contacted your sister, and she is on her way over here now. The whole city has been declared a disaster area, so it is going to take her some time to get here. I do not have any good news to tell you about your mother, Travis. She was not among the survivors. I am sorry to tell you that a woman answering the description you gave us was found in a field about 300 yards from your home, and she was deceased when she was found. She is at a temporary morgue. This is a terrible task, but we need you to go down there and see if the person is your mother. There will be another counselor there. His name is Jeffrey Chung. He knows you are coming, and he will be there to help you if indeed it is your mother. I will stay with you until your sister comes, and we will talk about what you will need to do about housing and insurance and any other assistance you may need. There will be counselors at the FEMA One Stop to help you with any questions you may have or assistance you may need.

April 22, 09:42 Hours, Seabrook Packing Plant Temporary Morgue

Travis Benefield and Jeffrey Chung, Licensed Professional Counselor from Hatchie County Community Mental Health Center and grief specialist, look on as a medical assistant gently unzips a body bag.

Travis: (*recoils in shock, then gently touches his mother's cheek*) Oh Lordy, momma! You have done gotten yourself kilt dead. I told you and done told you to go to the shelter if'n a twister was comin', but you didn't never pay no mind to me. Oh, dear God! Mah momma is dead! (*starts sobbing*)

Jeffrey: (*nods to the attendant and gently turns Travis away*) I am terribly sorry for your loss. Come on, let's go outside and sit down and talk.

Travis: (*crying*) Did she . . . do you . . . know . . . ah . . . suffer much?

Jeffrey: The field report said she was dead when they found her, and the autopsy shows she died of a broken neck, so I would say no. (*The counselor waits patiently while Travis weeps.*)

Travis: (*head in his hands*) Iah jest . . . it is jest too much. Iah don't know . . . cain't think. Too much.

Jeffrey: (*Uses STOP technique. Slowly and easily puts his hand on Travis's shoulder and gently guides him out of* *morgue and over to a chair, where he sits down with him. After a while of letting Travis sob quietly, he begins speaking very gently and slowly while making eye contact.*) It is overwhelming, and that's why I am here. I would be happy to get the paperwork together and move your mother to a funeral home if you would like. Or we can keep her here for a while and give you some time to decide what kind of arrangements you would like to make. Oliver Naifeh is your counselor, so he will work with me. Given all you have gone through, it is understandable that you feel overwhelmed. Anyone would. It is a common response to an awful, abnormal situation. You may feel guilty about not doing enough to get your mom to go to a shelter, but that was her choice. (*sits patiently and gently touches Travis's forearm while he silently sobs*) Do you have a minister or anybody else I could call?

Travis: Oh . . . OK. If'n you could do that. Our family has always done gone to Kittinger's Funeral Home. Iah guess you could call them up. Iah hadn't even thought about church. We'uns go to the First Baptist Church. Pretty near every Sunday. Reverend Dehl is the minister, but Iah 'spect he is right busy about now. I guess he'd like to know 'bout Loretta 'cause she sang in the choir and was a pretty staunch member. If'n you could take care of it, Ah'd 'preciate it most greatly. Seems like Iah cain't take care of mah family what's alive right now hardly a'tall, let 'lone what's done and gone.

The morgue counselor does three things. First he implements the STOP technique, which for a morgue counselor is standard operating procedure given the further trauma people will experience when they identify loved ones. **STOP** is an acronym for Sit, Think, Observe, Plan (Webber, Mascari, & Runte, 2010). The counselor slowly moves the client away from his mother and guides him over to a chair where they sit down. He gauges that it will be okay to put his hand on Travis's shoulder given what he has observed about the cultural norms of the area in times of grief. He observes that indeed Travis will need basic assistance and starts to plan out what he will need to help him with. Being in charge of a morgue at a disaster site takes a great deal of compassion and sensitivity, and the STOP system is a sort of default way of slowing things down and gently moving the bereaved in helping them get mobilized.

Second, he offers to provide very specific help with details concerning Travis's mother's death. Jeffrey's triage rating of Travis is in the low 20s. He sees a person who is cognitively overwhelmed and behaviorally and emotionally exhausted, has narrowly escaped death as has the rest of his family, and now has to identify his mother's body. As a result, Jeffrey needs to gently but firmly provide support and direction. How access to the dead is provided to loved ones and the interaction that occurs while this is happening are often critical to the survivors' ability to integrate the traumatic event and avoid further psychological injury (Shalev et al., 1998).

Finally, the worker suggests help from his church. Faith-based organizations play huge roles in disaster relief (Phillips & Jenkins, 2010). The worker is fairly sure that, given the culture of the area, Travis's church and minister can and will provide a great deal of support to him. Thus, he asks if he can contact his church.

The morgue counselor is further aware of the stages of survivor grief (see Chapter 12, Personal Loss: Bereavement and Grief) and empathically responds to Travis's shock, sadness, anxiety, and guilt without judging Travis's ability to "handle" all of it. Further, Jeffrey does not judge what Travis has or has not done, nor does he offer meaningless platitudes about Travis's losses. The scenario is played out over and over with other families in the immediate aftermath of a disaster. Local crisis workers work closely with Red Cross, NOVA, and FEMA crisis workers to provide an integrated, efficient, and seamless operation. While these crisis workers will provide immediate mental health assistance, it will be most often in terms of support. This support provides for both the family's survival needs and emotional needs.

April 24, 11:00 Hours, Hatchie County Mental Health Center

Sara Lee Benefield: Well, we'uns are in a fine fix right now. We are both out of work and livin' with Travis's sister, and we still have funeral arrangements to make fer Loretta. It's like we don't know where to start. We did have some home insurance, but Iah don't think it will be near enough. There isn't a thing left of our home, so we'uns have to start all over again. About what we've got is the clothes on our backs and $437.12 in the bank. Travis hasn't even got his tools, which he cain't seem to quit worryin' about all along with the other stuff.

Ollie Naifeh, social worker: OK, I am going to drive you over to the Civic Center, and we will go to the Disaster Recovery Center. I am going to introduce you to some people I know in the Red Cross and the Salvation Army. They can help with immediate assistance for food and shelter and maybe even tools. We can go to the FEMA One Stop and see about getting you a home loan to get you back on your feet and a roof over your heads. They will send an inspector out there really quickly and get the ball rolling, and they will work with your insurance company. They will also work with you on what is called disaster unemployment compensation. It is not quite your paycheck, but it will help out a good bit. Jeffrey has gotten your mother taken care of, and we can talk about funeral arrangements for your mother, Travis. I am guessing that money may be a problem?

Travis: Well no, momma had one of them universal burial policies, although I don't have no idea where it is, and she had about $5,000 put back. Reverend Dehl said he would be proud to preach momma's funeral as soon as we let him know, and there was Wednesday night services, and everybody done gave us their condolences and said what a fine person Loretta was and not to worry over much, that they would help take care of things.

The crisis counselor does very little mental health counseling at this juncture. He is far more concerned with just getting the basic survival needs of this family met (Ruzek, 2006). There will be time enough for the other later on. As soon as external crisis workers help the community regain control after the immediate aftershock of the crisis, they will leave and turn their clients back over to the local mental health unit.

April 25, 18:00 Hours, High School Gymnasium

Eva Jane Walters, Superintendent, Midville Public School District: (*speaking to about 500 parents*) Thank you for being here under the tough circumstances you are facing. I know many of you have lost your homes or have your home heavily damaged. I know this because I have been sleeping with many of you at the National Guard Armory as my own home is heavily damaged. We are now 4 days post-tornado. It is Friday. It is time to get your children back to learning. I also know we are going to have school Monday morning, and that includes all the elementary school students. We have been working this week to make those arrangements happen. At the end of my talk there will be a number of teachers in the cafeteria with homerooms, children's names, and new attendance centers for them. St. Benedict's Catholic Church and Midville First Baptist have graciously opened their doors to us, and we are going to hold classes there. That will be in walking or carpooling distance, and we will have buses at the shelters for those children still housed there. Some of your children will have different teachers because their teachers are dead or injured. We are going to have school counselors trained in crisis intervention from Saline, Wahatchie, and Forked Deer counties' schools here working with our counselors, school psychologists, and school social workers from the Tennessee River Special Education District will be here as well, and teachers to deal with any emotional issues children have. We are composing a series of classroom guidance meetings, which should go a long way towards helping us identify and work through problems that children are having. We are going to work very closely with you in this regard, and we want you to work very closely with us. We know this community does not lack for courage and mental toughness, and we know you and your children are tough minded and resilient, but there is toughness and there is smartness and we want to be smart about taking care of your children's academic, social, and emotional needs because we know if those other needs are taken care of we get better academic results, and in the end that is what we are about, the best academic success we can get. Midville schools have long been outstanding and part of the glue that holds this city together and gives it pride. We are not stepping back from that one inch, but to do that we are going to need all of the cooperation this community can bring to bear on getting these schools up and running. If you have any questions, I will be happy to take them now or talk with you or individually later on.

I also want to say something about our loss, not only of a building but of teachers and students who made it into the viable academic community it was and will be again. We are now planning with the PTA a commemorative memorial service in the Civic Center that will take place before school is out at the end of May. We understand that many of you are dealing with your own personal grief and loss right now and we want to give you time to work through that. We want to be supportive of you in any way we can because we know it is important to you and your children. The Hatchie Mental Health Center and grief counselors will be available if you

or your children have need of them. You can call the Hatchie clinic or call us at the high school counselor's number. All the calls will be kept confidential. Thank you for coming. If you have questions now, there are teachers who will bring you a microphone so everybody can hear. I have the rest of the schools' administrative staff here, so if I don't have the answer one of them probably will. When we are done here, we'll exit towards the cafeteria where you can pick up your child's school, room, and teacher assignment. We will have e-mail as power becomes available again but are not sure when that will happen. So we've resurrected some old mimeograph machines and you grandparents will recognize the purple bulletins. Welcome back to the 1950s, but we'll get information to you, rest assured. This is not going to be easy, but with your help we will get the Golden Eagles back up and running.

The superintendent does five things that are critical when a school suffers a calamitous event. First, the "whole child" is the focus. Academic, social, and emotional components are all targeted. Second, she is intent on moving the school and the community as quickly as possible back to day-to-day living and a sense of "normalcy." Third, she seeks to develop a strong sense of community with the families whose children attend the school. Fourth, she has the school function as a valid and reliable source of information by telling parents specifically what is happening and keeping a communication line open to them so that they know there is a centralized and trusted source of information that they can go to when the rumor mill gets going (Kilmer, Gil-Rivas, & MacDonald, 2010).

The superintendent also does something else that is critical in the face of a disaster in which children's lives are lost. Students' ability to work through the grieving process is in part a social phenomenon that is anchored in their peer group when friends are lost (Worden, 2002). Therefore, school needs to get started again to serve as the place where they come together to grieve friends' loss. Providing not only counselors to deal with adjustment problems but grief counselors who can work with the whole family to help them come to terms with their loss is not an easy sale at times. However, providing the common ground of the school as a brokerage for such deeply personal issues can go a good way toward easing the stigma of having to seek help with one's loss. Even if parents have not lost a relative, many people will have lost houses, places of employment, or social gathering places such as churches, clubs, and organizations that play integral parts in their lives, fracturing both their micro- and to a large extent their exosystem supports. We are fully aware that a school system should not get into the funeral business (see Chapter 13, Crises in Schools). However, when faced with a large-magnitude disaster that affects the whole community, the school system certainly needs to provide a process for students to grieve and move on. It also needs to take part in memorial exercises that are inclusive of all students and parents as a way of acknowledging the loss, allowing expression of feelings, and effecting reengagement with school (Kerr, 2009, pp. 130–132). You may wonder why we included this piece about schools here and not in the school chapter. It is important to understand how critical a school is in the fabric of a community and its recovery in disaster (Kilmer, Gil-Rivas, & MacDonald, 2010). To not have one example of the part the school plays in disaster mitigation is to leave out a critical part indeed of the exosystem of a community.

April 30, 16:00 Hours, Hatchie County Mental Health Center

Kate McClain, licensed professional mental health counselor: How are things going? I spoke with Ollie before he left, and he said things were moving along. How do you feel about that?

Sara Lee: Well, we have done got the loan approved, and the insurance company has been real good about things. We have got us temporary housing assistance and have a place over in Crowley. The kids want to stay here with their friends, so we'uns are gonna bring them over here every day. Mah dentist office is gonna open up next week. But we don't know when or if the Packard plant will reopen, so Travis is gonna be on unemployment.

Travis: Maybe y'all could talk to Shawn some. He is wakin' up at night screamin'. Iah don't think he is near over the school fallin' in and his best friend gittin' kilt. It was tough buryin' momma, but we got that done, and the church really hept.

Sara Lee: And maybe you could talk to Travis here too about him feelin' so durn guilty about leaving the plant to come look fer us. And Iah don't suppose it would hurt for me to talk some too, seein' as how I feel so stupid about runnin' off like a chicken with mah head cut off and makin' things even worse, durn fool that Iah am.

Kate: OK, I will be glad to do that. I think you are making progress and showing me that you have some strong fiber, that you are moving forward rapidly to getting things back to some kind of normalcy. Maybe your minister has told you, but there is going to be a community-wide meeting put on by NOVA. It's called "Y'all come" for all those who were in the tornado or affected by it, kind of a community memorial, talking, and bonding service. That might be something you would want to go to. That really sort of helps when people come together to talk about their experiences. I would also like our psychologist to give you some tests that will tell us how much this is affecting you. Those will help me better plan what we might want to do. Some of what you are experiencing is quite common. We just don't want it to turn into PTSD. (*Explains the difference between ASD and PTSD and what they are all about. She puts a positive view on the disorders by explaining that while most people start out with these symptoms, they tend to go away, particularly when people are proactive about doings things like what she is proposing to the Benefields.*) We are having some small support groups meet, and you are welcome to join them immediately.

I will also contact Shawn's school counselor, Janet Beverly from the middle school, who is filling in there since Mr. Little is still in the hospital, and see if we can set up something for Shawn. We have worked pretty closely together. We might want to have you all in as a family. I know she is starting some family groups there for people whose kids are having some problems. I also want to tell you that I really respect your observations and request for help about your children. That tells me you are truly caring parents. That is going to be really important in the days and months ahead.

The counselor does some psychoeducation with the Benefields in regard to ASD and PTSD. While there is limited evidence about the benefits of psychoeducation, particularly self-help materials in regard to trauma, Wessely and associates (2008) recommend that any psychoeducation should promote resilience and adaptability rather than pathology. Therefore, the counselor commonizes and attempts to allay fears that this means they are losing their minds rather than having a naturally occurring response to what they have been through. For many people, the psychological symptoms of hypervigilance, startle responses, nightmares, and the like, are as scary or more so than what they have just been through. While the education does not make the symptoms disappear immediately, it is calming to know they are common occurrences and that these survivors are not losing their minds.

The counselor also seeks to get them involved in a group. It is one of the best ways to share experience, bond with other survivors, and start back on the road to recovery. Finally, the counselor reinforces the mother for thinking about her children and husband. It is extremely important that caregivers provide a supportive, understanding environment in which children may manifest symptoms, can process thoughts and feelings without fear of recrimination, and otherwise attempt to integrate the trauma into their lives and come to terms with it (Gil-Rivas et al., 2010). Many times caregivers' ability to support their children will be compromised by their own trauma-related issues (Gil-Rivas et al., 2007).

May 8, 09:00 Hours, Midville Baptist Church (Temporary Site for Midville Elementary School)

Janet Beverly, elementary school counselor: Shawn, I wonder how you are getting along?

Shawn: Yes, ma'am. All right, I guess.

Janet: I looked at some of your drawings you made when we had the classroom meeting about the tornado. (*shows him one of his drawings*) I wonder if you could tell me about this?

Shawn: Yes, ma'am. That's me and that there's Jamie and that's Leotis. They were mah best friends. Jamie was right next to me in the hall when the tornado hit, but he's dead now. Ah'm red 'cause I thought I was all bloody, but it was really his blood. Leotis was with Mrs. Cruz. He and her both got kilt, and Iah don't know why. Ma says it was God's will, but Iah jest don't rightly know. Iah don't think much of God if he done let this happen, to tell the truth. Ma wouldn't like me sayin' that, but Iah reckon that's how Iah feel. Iah don't sleep too good at night neither, and Iah shore don't like storms. Sometimes Iah think Iah hear Jamie and Leotis. We used to play a lot together, soldiers and stuff down by Brunner's Creek. Iah miss them somethin' terrible.

Janet: I wonder if you might like to come to a group I am starting, Shawn. It is for a bunch of kids who have friends who died or got hurt or lost other things, who just plain feel sad and maybe a little lonely right now.

Shawn: Yes, ma'am. Iah guess that'd be OK. Iah sure wish Jamie and Leotis could come. Iah miss mah grandma too. She used to have cookies made when Iah'd git home.

As indicated throughout this book, when children are involved with traumatic events, as Stacy Overstreet, a Tulane University school psychology student who worked with post-Katrina students in the New Orleans school, stated, "There are two vital keys to recovery: social support and putting experiences in context" (Dingfelder, 2006). This is exactly what the school counselor is doing with Shawn when she uses expressive arts and group counseling to help him start to come to terms with his traumatic experiences, put them in his past, and grow from them (Malchiodi, Steele, & Kuban, 2008, p. 299). Groups are powerful ways to bring children together to share commonality of experience, own feelings that range from scared to angry to guilty, decrease isolation, enhance coping and adaptation, seek commonalities, build cohesion and trust, and help members cope with those bad feelings (Nisivoccia & Lynn, 2007). There is not a lot of outcome evidence on postdisaster groups for children, but at least two studies indicate that they do help to reduce posttrauma stress symptoms (Chemtob, Nakashima, & Hamada, 2002; Salloum & Overstreet, 2008).

A child with traumatic grief can get "stuck" on the traumatic aspects of the death, which then interferes with the normal grieving process (DeAngelis, 2011). The fact that Shawn was covered with the blood of his close friend and lay there with his friends' bodies admirably fits such criteria. Chapter 7, Posttraumatic Stress Disorder, describes how, by using trauma-focused cognitive-behavioral therapy in creating a trauma narrative using a combination of stress management, play therapy, and cognitive behavior techniques to monitor and control emotional dysregulation, children can move through both their grief and the posttrauma stress symptoms that often accompany it (Cohen, Mannarino, & Deblinger, 2006).

Indeed, if intervention is used as indicated in Chapter 13, Crises in Schools, the school can become a postdisaster anchor for children (Clark et al., 2006; Munsey, 2006). The CD-ROM *Transcending Trauma After a Disaster: A Guide for Schools* (Clark et al., 2006) provides an excellent example of how a school district can mobilize its resources after a disaster to help normalize and bring a modicum of control into an anything-but-normal situation.

May 15, 16:00 Hours, Hatchie County Mental Health Center

Kate McClain, licensed professional mental health counselor: (*meeting with Sara Lee and Travis*) I have talked with Janet Beverly, the school counselor. She is recommending that Shawn go into one of her counseling groups. Her report and what the psychologists report is that he has had a pretty rough time and is suffering from what we call acute stress disorder. (*reiterates what ASD is and why it is important for it to be dealt with before it becomes PTSD*) I am also going to recommend that you all come to the clinic as a family. I think it will be helpful for all the kids to talk about some of this stuff and see that, even though you have suffered some severe losses, your family is still together.

Sara Lee: I 'spect you're right. I don't suppose Travis will own up to it, but he's not the same, and neither am I. Shawn isn't the only one havin' nightmares. I jump near outta mah skin every time there's a thunderstorm. Travis and I have never had a hard word with one another, but the other night we done had a huge fight over nuthin'. It was jest nuthin'. (*Tears start to well up in her eyes.*) It was awful. It was in front of his sister's family and the kids. (*starts to cry*) He went and apologized, and so did I, but that is not like us a t'all. I don't know what we're becomin', and it scares me half to death.

Travis: (*puts his arm comfortingly around his wife*) Iah 'spect you're right, honey. Iah still cain't git them durn tools off mah mind, and that is plumb ridiculous. Iah got a whole new set, though. The church has really hept out and all, but it jest seems like things keep tumblin' through mah mind, and Iah cain't git no peace with them. That's why Iah got mad 'cause Sara Lee kept tellin' me to git over it, that we had other things to think about. And Iah got mad. Iah don't like it much neither.

Kate: I want to assure you that those are perfectly normal responses to an abnormal situation. But that doesn't make them any easier to bear. I would really like you to go to the NOVA "Y'all come" meeting. The ministerial association is going to put on some stuff along with it. I think you will find it helpful to hear and share some of the things you have gone through. You are strong folks, but everyone could use a little help and support, and I think this would be good.

The counselor is very interested in how her client family is dealing with the traumatic wake of the disaster. She coordinates her efforts with the school counselor and the clinic psychologist. The NOVA meeting and the church provide community support, but there are specific individual mental health issues that assail this family that need to be worked on so that the family does not fracture (Myers & Wee, 2005, p. 33). While most people are resilient in a disaster and will recover, it is critically important to intervene when there are indicators things are not going well (Ruzek, 2006). This emergency mental health is set up on a family assistance center model (Halpern & Tramontin, 2007, pp. 190–191; Leskin et al., 2006), in which one person acts as a broker and communicator to deal with the many social, psychological, and financial issues that will assail them. Getting all the family into therapy is a positive move because no one then feels the stigma of being the identified "sick" person when everybody else is doing well.

May 22, 16:00 Hours, Hatchie County Mental Health Center

Travis: Well, we went to that "Y'all come" meeting, and I would say it was hepful. Sort o' gives you a sense of pride 'n' hope, I guess. Kinda like we'uns are all in this together. They had a pretty good community church memorial service and all afterwards. Eighty-three dead and over 600 hurt. Lord A'mighty!

Sara Lee: Iah'd agree. But what Iah really liked was our first family meeting. Iah talked to the kids afterwards. Lee Ann and Jason both didn't want to come, but they both said afterwards they wouldn't mind coming again, which means they really did like it. Iah jest feel a little more peaceful somehow. Like we'uns are on the right track.

Travis: Iah guess it is like gittin' back in control. Ain't felt like that much.

Kate: I am glad to hear that. We will take this slow and easy. We have plenty of time. We will work on this as long as you feel the need to.

The counselor seeks to reinforce the Benefields for their courage and willingness to commit to some pretty arduous mental health work in addition to all the other challenges they face. She reemphasizes that there is no rush to working through their problems. Kate is now working on what is called *second phase* crisis intervention in the crisis chronosystem. The immediate crisis is over. Basic physiological needs have been met. At this point, the crisis worker is more concerned about possible long-term effects on the whole family; therefore, she is treating the family system as a client. She seeks to coordinate her efforts with other human services workers both from an individual perspective, as in the case of Shawn, and a wider community perspective, such as helping support the NOVA and the community church program. The more social support that can be generated, the more likely the victims are to use it to help with the distress (Yates, Axsom, & Tiedeman, 1999).

April 25 (1 year and 4 days after the tornado), 16:00 Hours, Hatchie County Mental Health Center

Sara Lee: Iah guess we'uns are ready to say good-bye, Kate. We'uns really 'preciate what you have done fer us. We'uns couldn't have done this a t'all without you. We all went to the big memorial service last week out to the Civic Center. It'll always be part of our lives, but it's behind us now, and we kin go on. Shawn is really doing well. He is off antidepressants and has a couple of new friends. We'uns couldn't go back to Breezemore. Jest too many bad memories, but we done got a lot out south o' town and put our new manufactured home on it, and there are some new kids out there Shawn met at Southside Elementary. None of us are having any nightmares either, although Iah still don't like thunderstorms, and we have a tornado shelter by our home now.

Travis: Iah guess Ah'd agree. Iah shore do appreciate what y'all have done fer us. It was tough, but Iah think we'uns are better fer it as a family. We're a whole lot tighter than before. Iah don't even think about mah tools no more, and even though Iah got mah head shrunk it feels better. (*laughs*) Durndest thing about them tools. We got momma buried beside paw out to Big Prairie Cemetery. Got her a nice stone, too. Pink marble. She always liked pink. She's at peace . . . and I guess fer that matter, so am Iah—as fer as one could be, given the circumstances. We are about ready to reopen the engine works, and Iah been workin' gittin' the machines all set up.

Kate: I am glad to have worked with you. I agree. I think we are ready to get divorced. (*Everybody laughs.*) I expect I will see you around town, so I look forward to seeing you out and about. I also want to tell you I really respect you for what you have done. I have learned from you, probably as much as you have learned from me, and I appreciate you coming into and touching my life. It makes me feel even more sure that this is the business I was meant to do.

Sara Lee: Well Iah think the good Lord put you in the right job. Thanks and good-bye.

Travis: Amen to that. (*Both hug Kate and go out the door and on with their lives.*)

Over the long haul, most people, even when they suffer comprehensive and horrific loss like the Benefields, are resilient and equal to the task of moving on with their lives (Gist, Lubin, & Redburn, 1999). What the crisis counselor provides is not so much therapy as information and programs that help families like the Benefields normalize an abnormal situation and address their material resource losses (Farberow & Frederick, 1978). The crisis worker also takes precautionary steps to monitor this family very closely for a while. While people sometimes do develop delayed PTSD, the vast majority are amazingly resilient and do not (Drabek, 1986).

The major role that the crisis worker initially plays is one of victim advocate by facilitating the return of basic services to survivors (Salzer & Bickman, 1999). The crisis worker then shifts from problem-focused to more emotion-focused coping (Lazarus & Folkman, 1984) and seeks to help the family move forward and reframe the crisis and distance themselves from it through preventive and support therapy (Chemtob, 2000).

Often the lack of use of mental health services by families like the Benefields is not happenstance (Norris & Alegria, 2006). There are many reasons, some good and some bad, why mental health services are underused after a disaster (Yates, Axsom, & Tiedeman, 1999). Some individuals see the use of such services and facilities as a sign of mental illness and therefore a major character flaw that would label them as "nut" cases. To avoid being perceived as outcasts by peers, these individuals may be very loath to use mental health services (Bethel & Oates, 2007). If such services are poor, uncoordinated, culturally insensitive, and intrusive, they indeed may do more harm than good. In this instance, good mesosystem coordination and communication among a number of local and national agencies in the micro-, exo-, and macrosystems worked to provide nonintrusive help and support. The sensitivity, caring, support, and unconditional positive regard of a variety of different helping professionals working in close coordination—including social workers, psychologists, licensed professional counselors, school counselors, and "just plain folks"—helped make the Benefield family's experience with mental health services a positive one.

The anniversary of the disaster is a benchmark for positive resolution, and like most people, the Benefields are resilient and capable of moving forward with a little help. The tornado has left an indelible imprint on their lives that will never go away, but like the Chinese symbols that start every chapter in this book, they have found opportunity in the crisis and have come out of it stronger than they were before.

Multiculturalism at Work. While the Benefields represent the stereotype of a white, Anglo-Saxon, fundamentalist Christian, blue-collar family in the south-central United States, you might gather from the surnames of some of the people who came to their assistance or who worked on the overall disaster that they represented a rainbow coalition of Americans of all races, ethnicity, and cultural backgrounds. That was not done to be politically correct. The fact of the matter is that even in rural west Tennessee, we are becoming a melting pot of races, ethnicity, and divergent cultural backgrounds. As such, a multicultural perspective is critical to any crisis intervention—and, indeed, people with just such divergent surnames work on crisis teams with which we are involved.

A Top Down–Bottoms Up Cultural Approach. This crisis team operates on Wei Chen Hwang's (2012) psychotherapy adaptation and modification framework (PAMF) and formative method for adapting psychotherapy (FMAP). While Hwang generated these approaches with Chinese Americans in mind, we believe these approaches have universal transferability to any culturally different environment crisis workers enter. The PAMF has a top-down three-tiered approach of domains, principles, and rationales. Domains are general areas that practitioners should consider when modifying therapeutic approaches to client. Principles involve more specified recommendations of adapting therapy for specific groups. Rationales are corresponding explanations for why these adaptations may be effective when used with the target population. This paradigm serves two critical purposes when applied to the real world of crisis intervention with people whose culture is very different from our own. PAMF seeks to build evidence-based therapies (EBTs) and manualized treatments that can be used universally and to help practitioners shift from the abstract notion of "multicultural sim" into being concretely multicultural competent in real time under crisis conditions.

The FMAP is a community-based bottom up approach that consists of five phases: generating knowledge and collaborating with stakeholders, integrating generated information with theory and empirical and clinical knowledge, reviewing the initial culturally adapted clinical intervention with stake holder and revising the culturally adapted intervention, then testing it and finalizing it. The FMAP was developed to generate ideas for culturally adapted EBTs while the PAMF was designed to improve the cultural competency of clinicians (Hwang, 2012). It appears that Goodman and associates (2014) successfully used an approach that closely resembles Hwang's FAMP model in their work with Haitian communities in Florida after the 2010 Haiti earthquake. During peer supervision sessions, they used content information on the community's culture, strengths, and sociopolitical issues to conceptualize the community's needs and informed their outreach process. Their success appears to be in stark contrast to a number of international programs that offered help after the 2004 Indian Ocean tsunami which was not well received in the Indian state of Aceh because sensitivity to and building intervention strategies with the local culture didn't happen (Fananay & Fanany, 2013).

As these two concepts are integrated, they can be used to build EBTs that are custom made to different cultural groups whether they be Chinese Americans in San Francisco or Southern Caucasians in Appalachia. We would propose that using this protocol is critical in crisis intervention and should be operationalized in real time in conjoint dialogues between leaders in the local population and crisis team leaders in the daily debriefings that occur in the context of a large-scale disaster. This approach fits admirably into contextual/ecological models of crisis intervention (Cook, 2012; Myer & Moore, 2006).

A Final Word on Multiculturalism. The worker should also understand that his or her own cultural biases have an even higher potential for surfacing when faced with oppositionally defiant clients who may not think, talk, act, look, or even smell like the worker. For example, more than one of the editors of this book has queried the author when reading the dialogues of the Benefield family.

Editors have questioned words such as *we'uns* (which literally means "we ones") and *fer* (meaning "far" or "for") because they were unsure themselves of the meaning and were equally unsure that you, the reader, would understand what was being said. Those words were intentionally used in the dialogues to test readers' responses to the deep southern rural dialect of Travis Benefield and his family. If you were put off by that dialect, found it hard to understand, and knew it was not proper English, then you might be put off by Travis as an "ignorant redneck" as well. Despite all your good works and good intentions, you might then unintentionally treat him with less respect than you would a person who talked like a 6 o'clock network news broadcaster. As a result, do you suppose Travis's reaction to you would be different than it was to the social workers, licensed professional counselors, and other crisis workers who were culturally sensitive to him and treated him respectfully despite his language? Cultural sensitivity is displayed when the worker translates into primary language that the client can understand (Myers & Wee, 2005, p. 62), whether that be Spanish, Urdu, or English with a deep southern accent.

Although you might think that Travis's obsessive concern about his tools is somewhat bizarre, in fact it has a deep cultural basis. Bethel and Oates (2007) have found that an Appalachian male like Travis, the patriarchal head of his family, is expected to be a good "hunter" who provides for and takes care of his family by supplying them with food, shelter, and clothing. The loss of his tools strikes at the very heart of who Travis is and how his culture defines him as an independent, hardworking, self-reliant provider for his family. In Travis's world, a blue-collar job in which a man can be skillful with tools may be more valued than a white-collar job. It is no accident that Travis persists in brooding on the loss of his tools, for those tools are in fact symbolic of his very identity as a man. The wise and culturally sensitive crisis worker will understand that the loss of his tools is as critical to Travis as the loss of his house, and that worker will be empathic and supportive, placing a high priority on helping Travis get his "durn" tools replaced.

Spiritualism/Religion. Aten and associates **LO8** (2015) report a great deal of research on the central role of religious institutions and prayer in recovery from a disaster and maintain one of the most critical components for the recovery of a community is through the religious organizations that support it. The deep roots that the Benefield family have in their religion and spiritual values should also be understood as a significant part of their life and culture. Religion and spirituality help buffer individuals from the negative and emotional and physical consequences that happen after a disaster. Ai and associates (2005) found that their stronger faith, hope, and spirituality staved off the depression and anxiety that was related to exposure of those who experienced 9/11. Conversely, Cook and associates (2013) found that lack of religious faith exacerbated poor physical and mental health following a disaster. Given that support is one of the most critical components to moving through any crisis, to not use and honor their religion and spiritual values to help salve the wounds of their losses would be a grave mistake indeed (Bethel & Oates, 2007; Stambor, 2005). Graham (2014) proposes that provision of pastoral care is a critical part of a community's recovery after a disaster and occurs in three parts: sharing the anguish with God, examining the causes from a spiritual perspective, and reinvesting in hope and rebirth. Graham also maintains that organized religion plays a critical part in the political aftermath of a disaster in process of ensuring solace and safety along with guidance and influence in helping rebuild the community and its sense of coherence and meaning.

In that regard, any crisis worker who enters a disaster area would be well advised to follow Aten and associates' (2015) general guidelines for how to handle spiritual issues in a crisis aftermath.

1. If you don't feel comfortable discussing religious issues, say so and refer the person to another worker.
2. Do not argue with or try to persuade a person that your spiritual beliefs are better.
3. Let people tell you what their beliefs are. Don't assume anything.
4. Help people use their spiritual beliefs to cope.
5. Assure individuals that it is normal to ask questions about God and/or their beliefs.
6. If they are angry with God, let them cathart.
7. Do affirm the injustice and wrongness of what has happened.
8. Encourage people to use the spiritual writings in their religion to find answers, solace, and peace.

Focus on the Worker
Debriefing Models   **LO9**

"Debriefing is an intervention designed to assist workers and survivors in dealing with intense thoughts, feelings, and reactions that occur after a traumatic event, and to decrease their impact and facilitate the recovery of normal people having normal reactions to abnormal events" (Myers & Wee, 2005, p. 173). Probably no emergent technique in crisis intervention has created more controversy than **debriefing** procedures. The attacks on debriefing psychotherapy (Gist & Lubin, 1999) have been some of the most vituperative we have seen in 50 years in the field of counseling, and while there are several different models of debriefing (Armstrong, O'Callahan, & Marmar, 1991; McWhirter & Linzer, 1994; Myers & Zunin, 1994), these attacks have been especially virulent in regard to Mitchell and Everly's (1995a) critical incident stress debriefing (CISD) model and their lack of hard research evidence to demonstrate its effectiveness (Gist, Lubin, & Redburn, 1999). Further, like most wishful searches for a panacea in dealing with an intractable problem, debriefing has been hailed as a potent vaccination against PTSD. However, research indicates it is not (Bisson & Deahl, 1994; Bisson, Jenkins, & Bannister, 1997; Deahl, 1999; Hobbs et al., 1996; Kenardy et al., 1996; Lee, Slade, & Lygo, 1996; Raphael, Meldrum, & McFarland, 1995). It has come to the point that psychological debriefing cannot be endorsed for use with survivors (Brymer et al., 2009; Gray & Litz, 2005).

In fact, Mitchell and Everly have not been able to provide scientific evidence that CISD does much of anything beneficial for workers or victims (Gist, Woodall, & Magenheimer, 1999), and at least one study found it to be harmful (Avery & Orner, 1998a, 1998b). Further, caustic rebukes have rained down on CISD as a get-rich-quick scheme for "quack" therapists and a "get out of jail free" (or almost free) card for businesses and insurance companies who can claim it is an effective vaccination against PTSD and therefore do not have to pay for much more expensive rehabilitation procedures to employees who come down with PTSD symptoms (Gist, Woodall, & Magenheimer, 1999; Raphael, 1999). CISD has also been roundly criticized for mandating that all workers who were victims of the crisis obtain CISD, even though it may be personally or culturally inappropriate (Silove, 1999; Weisaeth, 1999). Finally, there is a serious ethical question as to the blanket use of CISD for all kinds of populations for all kinds of trauma under all kinds of conditions (Raphael, 1999). At the National Institute of Mental Health consensus conference, the following recommendation was approved:

> Early intervention in the form of a single one-on-one recital of events and expression of emotions evoked by a traumatic event (as advocated in some forms of psychological debriefing) does not consistently reduce risks of later developing PTSD or related adjustment difficulties. Some survivors (e.g., those with high arousal) may be put at heightened risk of adverse outcomes as a result of such early interventions. (National Institute of Mental Health, 2002, p. 8)

On the other side of the debate, adherents absolutely believe in its effectiveness, and there are studies to support that (Chemtob, 2000; Jacobs, Horne-Moyer, Jones, 2004; MacDonald, 2003; Pender & Prichard, 2008, 2009; Robinson, Sigman, & Wilson, 1997; Wagner, 2005). Many of its adherents tend to be frontline workers. Their responses to those who would vilify CISD are that it does work—if the procedure is used correctly and if the people who do it are trained to use it the way Mitchell and Everly (1999) propose (Freeman, 2003; Lane, 2003; Montano & Dowdall-Thomae, 2003). One of the major issues has been its profligate use for *anybody for any kind of traumatic event.* Mitchell and Everly (1999) never intended it to be that. It was intended to be applied directly to emergency service workers, firefighters, and police officers to help them quickly integrate feelings and thoughts so that the experiences would lose their potential to become disturbing. Part of why it has been so successful (and so abused and misapplied) is that at face value it *should* work, survivors appreciate that someone cares enough about them to listen, and talking bad stuff out is a good way to get rid of it (Halpern & Tramontin, 2007, pp. 265–266).

Sharing experiences is one way of bonding through an adverse experience. If you don't believe that, get invited to an American Legion bar and talk to some ex-marines, or spend some time with police officers at "choir practice" after a tough drug bust where shots were fired. Debriefing objectives of ventilation of feelings, reordering and reorganization of cognitions, normalization of experience, increased group support, verbal reconstruction and integration, and screening for traumatic stress referral would seem to be laudable goals for postintervention with any disaster worker (Halpern & Tramontin, 2007, pp. 267–268; Myers & Wee, 2005, pp. 172–174).

Your authors tend to be in guarded agreement with the use of CISD for specific populations of first responders. We have seen this technique work in powerful ways with some very cynical and tough police field commanders who were very much in need of debriefing a multitude of traumatic events and the stress and pent-up emotions that went with them (Addy & James, 2002). It is also worth noting that when we do role-play CISD shooting scenarios with our students

(Dr. James is certified as a CISD-trained debriefer), they almost universally agree that they thought the debriefing was helpful. Having presented the foregoing arguments for and against, the fact stands that different types of debriefing strategies still predominate in the field of trauma work. For that reason alone, the following description of debriefing emergency workers is presented.

Debriefing Emergency Workers

Critical Incident Stress Debriefing (CISD). CISD was developed by Jeffrey Mitchell, a firefighter and paramedic in Baltimore County, Maryland, as a result of his own responses to the traumatic incidents he continuously witnessed. Originally designed to deal only with firefighters and EMTs who were first responders to fires, accidents, and other events where they saw and dealt with horrific sights, sounds, and smells, CISD is now used with a variety of people who have suffered trauma (Morrissey, 1994). CISD teams are typically composed of two members who must hold a minimum of a master's degree in the mental health professions and who have undergone training and received certification in CISD. Debriefing is designed to mitigate the psychological impact of a traumatic event, restore homeostasis and equilibrium, prevent PTSD from developing, and identify people who will need professional mental health follow-up (Mitchell & Everly, 1995a, p. 270).

Informal Defusing. Informal defusing is a first-order intervention following traumatic incidents and is typically performed by CISD-trained on-site personnel. The goal of defusing is to lessen the impact of a traumatic event and accelerate the normal recovery process by providing a brief, time-limited format to air feelings and thoughts of the event (Myers & Wee, 2005, p. 167). This three-stage intervention is a shortened version of a full-scale debriefing and usually takes about 1 hour. First, team members introduce themselves and then explain the process and delineate expectations. Second, the traumatic experience is explored via participants' disclosure of facts, cognitive and emotional reactions, and finally symptoms of distress related to the traumatic event. Third, participants receive information to normalize the dissonant cognitions of the event and educate them with regard to stress, stress management, and trauma (Mitchell & Everly, 1995a, p. 275).

Formal Debriefing. The formal debriefing process has seven stages and typically takes place within 24 hours to 7 days after a traumatic event. It is generally 2 to 3 hours long. It is a combination of psychological and educational elements formatted in a structured group setting, and it involves personnel who have been directly affected by a traumatic event such as police officers, firefighters, EMTs, and ER staff. It is not intended for use with the general public (Pender & Prichard, 2008). Debriefing helps make the transition from processing facts about the event to emotional responses to the event and, finally, back to cognitive information about reactions and coping with traumatic experiences. It is not psychotherapy, but rather a controlled meeting that allows participants to discuss their emotions and thoughts about the event in a nonthreatening environment (Mitchell & Everly, 1995b).

The seven stages are described as follows:

1. *Introduction.* The introduction is crucial to setting the tone of the debriefing. Besides introducing team members and explaining the process and guidelines for the CISD, the introduction also seeks to lower resistance and motivate the participants by discussing sensitive issues such as confidentiality (Mitchell & Everly, 1995a, p. 271).
2. *Fact finding.* Facts are discussed first because they are easiest to deal with and are typical of what may be discussed with emergency workers after a traumatic event. The leaders typically start by making statements such as "We only have a sketch of what happened. We'd like you to fill us in on what happened. So we can get an overall picture, we'd like everyone—no matter what part you played—to give us your perspective on it. If you don't feel ready to do that, that's OK too. Just shake your head, and we'll move past you. We need to know who you are, what your involvement was, and what happened from your point of view." Order doesn't matter; the episode will sort itself through the facilitative ability of the CISD leaders (Mitchell & Everly, 1995a, p. 272).
3. *Thoughts.* The CISD leaders ask the participants for their initial or most poignant thoughts about what happened. Moving from facts to thoughts starts to personalize the event and allows emotions to surface. As participants voice their thoughts, the leaders should elicit those emotions that come naturally with their thinking about the situation and that allow for movement into the

next phase, reaction (Mitchell & Everly, 1995a, p. 272).

4. *Reaction.* This phase is the most emotionally powerful for participants. Questions that elicit responses are variations on a theme of "What about the situation was most bothersome to you? If you could change one part of it, what would it be?" Leaders will act more as passive facilitators at this point, as participants spontaneously speak to their affective responses to the event (Mitchell & Everly, 1995a, pp. 272–273).

5. *Symptoms.* The symptom phase is used to shift the group back to more cognitive material. The discussion deals with what went on both during and after the event. The leaders ask the group to describe their experience in terms of affective, behavioral, cognitive, or physical experiences they had. To get the group going, the leaders may give examples such as "My whole body was shaking for 5 minutes after the firing quit; I was under control, but I kept thinking I can't stand another minute of this; I wanted to say something, but my tongue was tied; I'm scared to death, but I know I have to go back into that building so my feet move me there somehow" (Mitchell & Everly, 1995a, p. 273).

6. *Teaching.* Leaders may point out that what the participants have talked about fits precisely into the symptoms of acute stress. The leaders let the participants know that these are normal, typical reactions, that they are not losing their minds or are otherwise somehow not equal to the task. The participants are instructed in how to recognize and understand symptoms that might not have surfaced yet. Participants are also given information in stress management techniques. This phase moves the participants even farther away from the emotional content they have worked through in the reaction phase (Mitchell & Everly, 1995a, p. 274).

7. *Reentry.* The reentry phase is a final opportunity to summarize and bring closure to all the issues that have been discussed. The CISD team's job at this time is to answer questions, provide reassurance, reflect on any agendas they believe have not been brought out, dispense handouts, and provide referral sources for extended psychological work (Mitchell & Everly, 1995a, p. 274).

In summary, the CISD derives its effectiveness from early intervention, the opportunity to experience catharsis in safety, the opportunity to verbalize the trauma, a definite behavioral structure, group

and peer support, and a provision for follow-up if needed (Mitchell & Everly, 1995b, p. 41).

Debriefing Crisis Workers

Whether one buys the CISD model or not, it seems abundantly clear that *some* kind of debriefing process is indispensable in assisting crisis workers themselves to regain a state of emotional, cognitive, and behavioral equilibrium following their intensive intervention work in the aftermath of a chaotic crisis. The detailed procedures that follow are provided because it is essential for crisis workers to know how to debrief disaster workers as well as to understand the value of being debriefed themselves. The techniques and perspectives offered here may even enable the crisis worker to debrief the debriefers.

The Need for Debriefing. Throughout this book crisis intervention is often depicted as complex and chaotic. Natural disaster, mechanical, or human-caused large-scale accidents, mass murders resulting from terrorism, or death and destruction from floods and tornadoes all create the confused and chaotic disorder that, much like a battle, are so disorienting that, for crisis workers, there are no scripts and little time for reflection, planning, or rehearsal. It is not surprising that crisis workers themselves tend to suffer psychological problems from the same trauma they are trying to alleviate in others. What the crisis worker sees, hears, smells, and touches may also rattle long-buried skeletons in the worker's own emotional closet. This phenomenon is known as vicarious traumatization (Saakvitne & Pearlman, 1996) or compassion fatigue (Figley, 2002), wherein the worker unwittingly absorbs and internalizes the very trauma that the client manifests (see Chapter 16, Human Services Workers in Crisis, for more on this phenomenon).

CERT team members are all citizens with different occupations. They are not therapists and they do not receive supervision. Corey-Souza (2007) conducted a study of 96 members of the Florida Crisis Responses team on measures of compassion fatigue and compassion satisfaction. She found a strong negative correlation between compassion fatigue and compassion satisfaction, and that burnout is one of the strongest predictors of compassion fatigue. So put yourself in the place of Jeffrey Chung, the Midville morgue counselor, or any of the CERT team members who found Loretta Benefield. Do you think you would be up for some kind of psychological debriefing? Finally, compounding it all, mental health crisis workers may be called on to debrief other emergency personnel who have been up to their arms in blood, gore, wreckage, and a panoply of human tragedy. It is important, then, that crisis workers themselves go through debriefing and that certain precautions are taken to arm them against the multiple stressors they will face when doing disaster work (Armstrong, O'Callahan, & Marmar, 1991). As an example, Leffler and Dembert (1998) conducted a study of U.S. Navy divers involved in the recovery of wreckage and passenger remains from TWA Flight 800, which crashed en route to Paris in 120 feet of water off the coast of Long Island, New York. They reported that divers who were exposed to human remains, especially those of children, found that experience to be far more stressful than the safety hazards they encountered.

First responders to the twin towers of the World Trade Center manifest all of the themes of what Robert Lifton (1983) calls the psychology of survival—psychic numbing, guilt over having not done enough or living when others did not, paranoia over attempts to provide psychological help, vivid death imprints, and futile and abortive attempts to make sense out of what they saw, heard, smelled, and touched (Henry, 2004). If this sounds to you suspiciously like PTSD or the vicarious traumatization you read about in Chapter 16 on burnout, you are correct. Compound this with Henry (2004) and Addy and James's (2002) research, which found that responders such as police officers tend to be very wary of "head shrinkers." If you are an EMT, firefighter, or police officer, just to admit you may have some kind of mental problem puts you at risk because your partners may fear that your inability to function under pressure may harm them (Henry, 2005). So what is to be done? Above all else is self-care (Merlino, 2011), which means knowing you are not a super crisis worker, nor is anyone else, and having enough sense to look out for yourself and your team both physically and psychologically.

Precautions. First of all, crisis work of this kind is done in teams. Whether at the scene with a number of specialists or in an after-action debriefing, workers do not act in isolation. Using the buddy system allows workers to rotate with difficult clients, ventilate to one another, check out perceptions, watch each other for signs of fatigue, and give each other a break (Hayes, Goodwin, & Miars, 1990; Mitchell & Everly, 1995b; SAMHSA, 2003; Talbot, Manton, & Dunn, 1995, p. 286; Walker, 1990).

Second, crisis workers in a disaster need to take time off to sleep and decompress. An 8-hour shift under disaster conditions is a long time (Hayes, Goodwin, & Miars, 1990). Crisis workers need to be rotated out of high-stress jobs, such as body identification and survivor notification, on a regular basis and be given less stressful duties (Walker, 1990). They also need time off between crises to rest and recuperate physically and psychologically (Talbot, Manton, & Dunn, 1995, p. 293). The U.S. Department of Mental Health proposes a maximum of 12-hour shifts followed by 12 hours off. They also propose that work rotations should change from high-stress to lower-stress functions (SAMHSA, 2003).

Third, as trite as it sounds, it is important to have plenty of water and nutritious food at the scene (SAMHSA, 2003). One of your authors has been in a crisis negotiation situation in which he and two police officers were unable to get food or water. The salvaged contents of the lunchbox of one of the officer's children that had been left in the backseat of her squad car was a lifesaver after we had been there from 5 P.M. until 3 A.M. without food and with very little water!

Fourth, have a clear chain of command with clear role and function statements. Nothing is worse or potentially more lethal than going into a disaster without a clear understanding of what one is going to do and to whom one is going to report. Correlative to the foregoing is having adequate and timely supervision to process what one is doing (SAMHSA, 2003).

Fifth, on-site crisis workers should not debrief one another (Spitzer & Neely, 1992; Talbot, Manton, & Dunn, 1995, p. 286). Another team of crisis workers who have not been at the scene should be brought in to lead debriefing. In this manner, the leaders cannot be construed as engaging in recriminations, second-guessing, or accusations about who did or didn't do what.

Sixth, the debriefing should be held away from the crisis scene if possible (Talbot, Manton, & Dunn, 1995, p. 286). Moving away from the scene physically allows the crisis workers to move away psychologically.

Seventh, the organizational context within which the group operates should be taken into consideration because it too plays a part in how the group is affected (Talbot, Manton, & Dunn, 1995, p. 286). The way the organization—and this includes even charitable organizations such as the Red Cross—runs its disaster relief program is critically important to how the individual handles stress at the disaster site.

Eighth, the crisis workers need to be in excellent physical and mental health themselves. From both a physical and mental standpoint, they will be stretched to the limit. Diving into the wake of a traumatic event is no place for someone who is out of shape either physically or mentally (Walker, 1990). But even if a crisis worker is in excellent physical and psychological condition, no one is immune from the cumulative and acute onset of stress (see Chapter 16, Human Services Workers in Crisis).

Although overuse of the procedure and policies requiring mandatory CISD attendance can create passive participation and even negative resentment, it would seem that a standing operational order for all emergency workers and crisis workers should be some kind of regular debriefing (not necessarily the CISD model). There are a variety of models that focus on different aspects of the event, such as positive reframing (Charlton & Thompson, 1996), group processing (Dyregrov, 1997), intensive follow-up after the debriefing (Solomon, 1995), multiple stressor debriefing (Armstrong, O'Callahan, & Marmar, 1991), dynamic understanding of the event (Talbot, Manton, & Dunn, 1995), and disaster debriefing (Myers & Zunin, 1994).

While there are concerns that traditional CISD may sabotage personal integrity in favor of victim status by emphasizing pathology over resiliency and trauma over strength, Echterling, McKee, and Presbury (2000) believe that linking people in crisis, hearing one another's crisis stories, normalizing reactions, and facilitating the group's coping are positive outcomes that are critical to resolution. Your authors absolutely agree. Debriefing should be the natural and final act of the emergency and crisis workers' job and should be no less expected than that of a fighter pilot after a combat mission.

Dynamics of Debriefing. The debriefers of crisis workers are dealing with a matrix of issues: the crisis event and its victims, the response to that event by the crisis workers, the individual crisis worker's personal and professional response to the survivors, the dynamics of the group as it goes through the debriefing process, and developing a collective plan for handling the next crisis (Echterling, McKee, & Presbury, 2000; Silove, 1999; Talbot, Manton, & Dunn, 1995, p. 286).

From a professional standpoint, each crisis worker needs to understand and evaluate the usefulness of his or her interventions, explore alternatives, and plan future courses of action. Focusing on survivor aspects rather than victimization is important in refocusing

the individual on perseverance, creativity, and sensitivity, which often fade into the background in the face of the pain, anguish, and helplessness that the worker feels (Echterling, McKee, & Presbury, 2000). Individual crisis workers also need to look at how they operate as members of the group. Group dynamics and cohesiveness impart a powerful influence on each worker, so the group as client may need to be examined. Such dynamics may, in fact, parallel the dynamics of the victim group and are referred to as **parallel processing** (Talbot, Manton, & Dunn, 1995, p. 291).

On a personal basis, the debriefers need to explore with workers their own personal issues that may intrude into their crisis intervention work. Particularly, parallel processing and countertransference issues need to be examined. As opposed to the CISD approach of Mitchell and Everly (1995b), which does not delve into the personal dynamics of emergency workers, Talbot, Manton, and Dunn (1995) believe that psychological understanding and integration are exceedingly important to crisis workers, because this is the stuff they are made of and how they operate. The personal history of the individuals in the group and of the group itself may also be of importance. Past baggage of the group, or the individual workers' issues with the group, may carry over into the present, and everyone needs to acknowledge that baggage and be helped to set it down and leave it.

Confidentiality. A continuing issue in debriefings centers on ethical concerns about acts of commission or omission, issues of responsibility or integrity, and even larger questions concerning life-and-death decisions (Walker, 1990). In that regard, all debriefings of emergency workers or mental health workers should be absolutely confidential, and that fact should be stated and enforced from the beginning (Mitchell & Everly, 1995a).

Understanding. One of the main tasks of the debriefer is to make psychological sense of what is going on and to help the crisis workers absorb that knowledge. Thus debriefers should be well grounded in group dynamics, group functioning, and group counseling skills. They need to be able to compliment workers on their respective strengths—accentuating the positive rather than the multitude of negatives that can easily pervade a crisis (Echterling, McKee, & Presbury, 2000).

The debriefer needs to summarize, and allow people to verbalize, what they have learned from the crisis and the debriefing, in order to minimize workers' vulnerability to the phenomenon of vicarious traumatization (Saakvitne & Pearlman, 1996). Crisis workers need to have a sense of mastery over what they have done as well as to feel positive about themselves as they take leave of the traumatic event and the debriefing (Echterling, McKee, & Presbury, 2000; Silove, 1999; Talbot, Manton, & Dunn, 1995, p. 296).

Qualifications to be an excellent debriefer do not come from one weekend workshop such as one of your authors went through. An excellent debriefer, according to Jordan (2002), will have experience not only in crisis intervention but in trauma counseling as well. Jordan proposes that anyone who does trauma supervision needs to have not only an excellent understanding of what trauma is about, but also an understanding of oneself as he or she operates in a traumatic situation both with people who are suffering from trauma and with those who are intervening with the traumatized. Knowing how secondary traumatization affects first responders and mental health workers is critical. Also knowing what to do about secondary traumatization and how to convince hardheaded veteran first responders and mental health workers are the zenith of this business, and not many achieve those heights.

In summary, the combined processes that Mitchell and Everly (1995a), Echterling, McKee, and Presbury (2000), and Talbot, Manton, and Dunn (1995) describe derive their effectiveness from:

1. An early intervention before the trauma is concretized and becomes a disease reservoir.
2. An opportunity for catharsis by ventilating emotions in safe surroundings with a structured environment and a knowledgeable and trusted facilitator.
3. An opportunity to verbalize the traumatic event and the parts played by reconstructing it, making sense of it, and integrating it into awareness.
4. The provision of structure through the debriefing procedure of a definite beginning and a definite end that provides a clear, linear sequence of events that leads to closure, as opposed to the chaos so recently encountered.
5. The dispelling of myths that one must be able to "handle" all things and that emotions are liabilities.
6. Peer support from others who belong to the same "club."
7. Provision of follow-up if the traumatic stress and the symptoms are not expunged.
8. Education about the effects of stress and the concept that it is a naturally occurring process and not a "weakness."
9. Dynamic understanding of both past and present motivators and causative factors that actuate specific responses in each individual.
10. Reframing and emphasizing the positive outcomes and strengths demonstrated by the worker.
11. The knowledge that such debriefings allow individuals not only to survive job stress but to do their jobs better.

However, when debriefings don't work and crisis moves beyond acute stress disorder into PTSD territory, then we revert back to the heavy duty prolonged exposure and cognitive-behavioral therapies you read about in Chapter 7, Posttraumatic Stress Disorder (Olden et al., 2015).

Final Thoughts

It has now been 27 years since we wrote the first edition of this book. Burl Gilliland, coauthor of the book, has been dead for 14 years, so these final thoughts will be those of your other coauthor, Richard "Dick" James. Claire Verduin, our editor at Brooks/Cole at the time of the first edition in 1988, remarked with some humor and some cynicism that it would probably be a nice onetime edition that would wind up gathering dust on library bookshelves, and that would be it. At that time there were three or four books on crisis and very little research or theory that made it into professional journals. Burl Gilliland started a crisis class at the University of Memphis back in 1975 with little more than pamphlets, mimeographed handouts, and guest speakers from various grassroots organization that were doing crisis work of different kinds. Crisis intervention was a psychological backwater that had few adherents and even fewer practitioners. Almost none of the material that appears in this closing chapter was in existence at that time. In fact, most of the material in the entire book was not! That should give you an idea about how much this field has grown in that short time.

I was on a panel of Brooks/Cole authors at the 2007 American Counseling Association convention in Detroit. That panel met with students to discuss careers in the field of human services. I started out in my professional life as a junior high school counselor 40 years ago, and I am now the coordinator of the counselor education doctoral program at the University of Memphis. Those have both been great experiences, but they pale in comparison to the field of crisis intervention. I got into the crisis business through sheer dumb luck and the inability to say no to a request to start the Crisis Intervention Team program with the Memphis Police Department that has since become world renowned. That has been the best career decision I ever made. There is now little question in my mind that crisis intervention is in the mainstream of psychotherapy. That's what I told the students in Detroit. If you want a career that will give you the ride of your life, get into this business!

SUMMARY

This chapter is predicated on emergent trends that encompass the total ecological and cultural environments in which we live and work. It is a multisystemic approach to crisis intervention. The five-dimensional circle and cylinder of systems that impact crisis workers and the individuals and groups who are their clients include the microsystem, mesosystem, exosystem, macrosystem, and chronosystem. These five systems, based on the Bronfenbrenner model, make up the arena in which crisis workers intervene in situations that may include individuals, families, groups, and organizations in a variety of crises at the local level as well as in widely dispersed geographical areas and cultural settings.

The rise of the Federal Emergency Management Agency (FEMA) and the various state and local emergency management agencies has given a great deal of impetus to the integration of emergency services and the crisis intervention that goes along with them. The case study of the Benefield family as a model of integrated crisis intervention services is the ideal and demonstrates how these various systems interface and act on individuals in the microsystem. Given hurricane Katrina's traumatic wake, it appears that ideal state of service has not yet been reached.

Crisis workers and first responders to disasters and other traumatic events themselves need a format to air their thoughts and feelings, to ventilate and decompress from the horrific work they engage in. In response to this need, defusing and debriefing strategies have been developed. Chief among them has been critical incident stress debriefing (CISD). CISD in particular has come under sharp criticism as being not helpful and in some cases harmful to go through. However, adherents just as vehemently state that it is absolutely necessary to keep them sane. From that standpoint, it appears that some model of debriefing for crisis workers is imperative. However, at the start of the 21st century one thing is abundantly clear: Crisis intervention is a growth industry, and it is here to stay.

Visit CengageBrain.com for a variety of study tools and useful resources such as video examples, case studies, interactive exercises, flashcards, and quizzes.

References

A

Aarts, P. G., & Op den Velde, W. (1996). Prior traumatization and the process of aging. In B. A. van der Kolk, A. C. McFarlane, & L. Weisaeth (Eds.), *Traumatic stress* (pp. 359–377). New York: Guilford Press.

Abbas, M., & Hoyt, W. T. (2014, August). *Virtual reality exposure treatment to PTSD: A meta-analysis.* Paper presented at the 122nd American Psychological Association, Washington, DC.

Abbey, A., McAuslan, P., & Ross, L. T. (1998). Sexual assault perpetration by college men: The role of alcohol, misperception of sexual intent, and sexual beliefs and experiences. *Journal of Social and Clinical Psychology, 17,* 167–195.

Abdel-Monem, T., & Bulling, D. (2005). Liability of professional and volunteer mental health practitioners in the wake of disasters: A framework for further considerations. *Behavioral Sciences and the Law, 23,* 573–590.

Abei, E., & Kruger, M. L. (2009). The widowhood effect: A comparison of Jews and Catholics. *Omega: Journal of Death and Dying, 59*(4), 325–337.

Abel, N. J., & O'Brien, J. M. (2015). *Treating addictions with EMDR therapy and the stages of change.* New York: Springer.

Abramson, L. Y., Alloy, L. B., Hogan, M. E., Whitehouse, W. G., Gibb, B. E., Hankin, B. L., et al. (2000). The hopelessness theory of suicidality. In T. Joiner & M. D. Rudd (Eds.), *Suicide science: Expanding the boundaries* (pp. 18–32). Boston: Kluwer Academic.

Achenbach, T. M. (1991). *Manual for the Child Behavior Checklist/4-18 and 1991 Profile.* Burlington, VT: University of Vermont, Department of Psychiatry.

Acierno, R., Herndadez-Tejada, M., Muzzy, E., & Steve, K. (2009). *Prevalence and correlates of emotional, physical, sexual, and financial abuse and potential neglect in the United States: The National Elder Mistreatment Study* (NCJ Publication No. 2226455). Washington, DC: U.S. Department of Justice.

Ackerman, P. T., Newton, J. E. O., McPherson, W. B., Jones, J. G., & Dykman, R. A. (1998). Prevalence of posttraumatic stress disorder and other psychiatric diagnoses in three groups of abused children (sexual, physical, and both). *Child Abuse and Neglect, 22*(8), 759–774.

Adams, C. (2013). *Millions went to war in Iraq and Afghanistan.* Retrieved from mcclatchydc.cm/2013/03/14/185880/

Adams, D., & McCormick, A. (1982). Men unlearning violence: A group approach based on the collective model. In M. Roy (Ed.), *The abusive partner* (pp. 170–197). New York: Van Nostrand Reinhold.

Adams, K. B. (2006). The transition to caregiving: The experience of family members embarking on the dementia caregiving career. *Journal of Gerontological Social Work, 47*(3/4), 3–29.

Adams, K. O. (1989). Have you been counseling too hard and too long? *School Counselor, 36,* 165–166.

Adams, W., Owens, C., & Small, K. (2010, July). Effects of federal legislation on the commercial exploitation of children. *Juvenile Justice Bulletin.* Washington, DC: Office of Justice Programs. Retrieved from https://www.ncjrs.gov/pdffiles1/ojjdp/228631.pdf

Addy, C., & James, R. K. (2002, April). *Lieutenants in the crosshairs: Alternative approaches in the treatment of crisis and trauma in field command level staff.* Paper presented at the 25th Annual Convening of Crisis Intervention Personnel, Chicago.

Addy, C., & James, R. K. (2005, May). *Finding the best CIT practices across the country.* Paper presented at the First Annual National Conference on Crisis Intervention Team Convention, Columbus, Ohio.

Adler, A. B., Bliese, P. D., & Castro, C. A. (2011). *Deployment psychology: Evidence-based strategies promote mental health in the military.* Washington, DC: American Psychological Association.

Adler, N. L. (1997). *International dimensions of organizational behavior.* Cincinnati, OH: South-Western.

Adlington, J. (2009). *Online therapy: Reading between the lines.* London: MX Publishing.

Adúriz, M., Bluthgen, C., & Knopfler, C. (2011). Helping child flood victims using EMDR intervention in Argentina: Treatment outcome and gender differences. *International Perspective in Psychology, Research, Practice, Consultation, 1*(S), 58–67.

Agency for Healthcare Research and Quality. (2010). Domestic violence on the decline but young women are at highest risk. *Research activities no. 360.* Washington, DC: U.S. Department of Health and Human Services.

Aguilar, R. J., & Nightingale, N. N. (1994). The impact of specific battering experiences on the self-esteem of abused women. *Journal of Family Violence, 9,* 35–45.

Aguilera, D. C. (1998). *Crisis intervention: Theory and methodology* (8th ed.). St. Louis, MO: Mosby.

Aguilera, D. C., & Messick, J. M. (1982). *Crisis intervention: Theory and methodology* (4th ed.). St. Louis, MO: C. V. Mosby.

Aguileria, D. C. (1997). *Crisis intervention: Theory and methodology* (8th ed.). St. Louis, MO: Mosby.

Aguirre, R. T., McCoy, M. K., & Roan, M. (2013). Development guidelines from a study of suicide prevention mobile applications. *Journal of Technology in Human Services, 31*(3), 269–293.

Ahmedani, B. K., Simon, F., Stewart, C., Beck, A., Waltzfelder, B., Rossom, R., . . .Solberg, L. (2014). Health care contacts in the year before suicide death. *Journal of General Internal Medicine, 29*(6), 870–877.

Ahn, H., & Wampold, B. (2001). Where oh where are the specific ingredients? A meta-analysis of component studies in counseling and psychotherapy. *Journal of Counseling Psychology, 48*(3), 251–257.

Ahrens, C. E., Rios-Mandel, L. C., Isas, L., & Lopez, A. D. (2010). Talking about interpersonal violence: Cultural influence of Latinas' identification and disclosure of sexual assault and partner violence. *Psychological Trauma: Theory, Research, Practice, and Policy, 2*(4), 273–283.

Ai, A., Cascio, T., Santangelo, L. K., & Evans-Campbell, T. (2005). Hope, meaning and growth following the September 11, 2001 terrorist attacks. *Journal of Interpersonal Violence, 20,* 523–548.

Al, C. M. W., Stams, G. J. J. M., van der Laan, P. H., & Asscher, J. J. (2011). The role of crisis in family crisis intervention: Do crisis experience and crisis change matter. *Children and Youth Services Review, 33,* 991–998.

Alaggia, R., & Millington, G. (2008). Male child abuse: A phenomenology of betrayal. *Clinical Social Work Journal, 36*(3), 265–275.

Aldarondo, E., & Castro-Fernandez, M. (2011). Risk and protective factors for domestic violence perpetration. In J. W. White, M. Koss, & A. E. Kazdin (Eds.), *Violence against women and children: Vol.1. Mapping the terrain* (pp. 221–242). Washington, DC: American Psychological Association.

Alexander, J. G., de Chesnay, M., Marshall, E., & Campbell, A. R. (1989). Parallel reactions in rape victims and rape researchers. *Violence and Victims, 4*(1), 57–62.

Alexy, E., Burgess, A., Baker, T., & Smoyak, S. (2005). Perceptions of cyberstalking among college students. *Brief Treatment and Crisis Intervention, 5*(3), 279–289.

Alink, L., Euser, S., Bakermans-Kranenburg, M., & van IJzendoorn, M. (2014). A challenging job: Physical and sexual violence towards group workers in youth residential care. *Child and Youth Forum, 43*(2), 243–250.

Alkema, K., Linton, J. M., & Davies, R. (2008). A study of the relationship between self-care, compassion satisfaction, compassion fatigue, and burnout among hospice professionals. *Journal of Social Work in End-of-Life and Palliative Care, 4*(2), 101–119.

Allan, J., & Berry, P. (1987). Sandplay. *Elementary School Guidance and Counseling, 21,* 300–306.

Allen, B., Wilson, K. L., & Armstrong, N. E. (2014). Changing clinician's beliefs about treatment for children experiencing trauma: The impact of intensive training in an evidence-based, trauma-focused treatment. *Psychological Trauma: Theory, Research, Practice, and Policy, 6*(4), 384–389.

Allen, C. M. (1991). *Women and men who sexually abuse children: A comparative analysis.* Orwell, VT: Safer Society Press.

Allen, J. G. (2001). *Interpersonal trauma and serious mental disorder.* Chicester, UK: Wiley.

Allen, M., & Sheen, D. (2005). *School-based crisis intervention: Preparing all personnel to assist.* New York: Guilford Press.

Allen, M., Burt, K., Rashid, E., Carter, D., Orsi, R., & Durkan, L. (2002). School counselors' preparation for and participation in crisis intervention. *Professional School Counseling, 6*(2), 96–103.

Allen, R. S., Haley, E., Roff, L. L., Schmid, B., & Bergman, E. J. (2006). Responding to the needs of caregivers near the end of life: Enhancing benefits and minimizing burdens. In J. L. Werrh & D. Blevins (Eds.), *Psychosocial issues near the end of life: A resource for professional care providers* (pp. 183–201). Washington, DC: American Psychological Association.

Allen, S. (1996, November). *The rural school counselor.* Paper presented at the Tennessee Counseling Association Convention, Memphis, TN.

Allumbaugh, D. L., & Hoyt, W. T. (1999). Effectiveness of grief therapy: A meta-analysis. *Journal of Counseling Psychology, 46*(3), 370–388.

Almvik, R., Woods, P., & Rasmussen, K. (2007). Assessing risk for imminent violence in the elderly: The Brøset Violence Checklist. *International Journal of Geriatric Psychiatry, 22*(9), 862–867.

Altmaier, E., & Prieto, L. (2012). Through a glass darkly: Meaning making, spiritual transformation and posttraumatic growth. *Counseling Psychology Quarterly, 4,* 345.

Altmaier, E. M. (2011). Best practices in counseling grief and loss: Finding benefit from trauma. *Journal of Mental Health Counseling, 33*(1), 33–42.

Alvarez, T. (1999). APA and MTV launch youth anti-violence initiate. *Practitioner Focus,* May–June 1999. Washington, DC: American Psychological Association, Public Relations and Communications Practice Directorate.

Amano, T., & Toichi, M. (2014). Effectiveness of on-the-spot-EMDR method for the treatment of behavioral symptoms in patients with severe dementia. *Journal of EMDR Practice and Research, 8*(2), 50–65.

American Association of Suicidology. (1991). *Postvention guidelines for the schools.* Denver, CO: Author.

American Association of Suicidology. (1997). *Youth suicide fact sheet* (revised). Washington, DC: Author.

American Association of Suicidology. (1998, Fall). *News Link, 24*(3), 126–128.

American Association of Suicidology. (n.d.). *Understanding and helping the suicidal person: Be aware of the warning signs.* Retrieved from www.suicidiology.org/web/web/guest/stats-and-tools /warning signs

American Counseling Association. (2014). *ACA code of ethics.* Alexandria, VA: Author.

American Psychiatric Association. (1974). *Clinical aspects of the violent individual.* Washington, DC: American Psychiatric Association Press.

American Psychiatric Association. (1980). *Diagnostic and statistical manual of mental disorders* (3rd ed.). Washington, DC: Author.

American Psychiatric Association. (2000). Diagnostic and statistical manual of mental disorders (4th ed., Text Revision). Arlington, VA: Author

American Psychiatric Association. (2013). *Diagnostic and statistical manual of mental disorders* (5th ed.). Washington, DC: Author.

American Psychological Association. (2000). *Division 12, section VII report on education and training in behavioral emergencies.* Retrieved February 20, 2003, from www.apa.org/divisions /div12/sections/div12/sections/ section7/tfreport.html

American Psychological Association. (2002). Ethical principles of psychologists and code of conduct. *American Psychologist, 57,* 1060–1073.

American Psychological Association. (2008). *APA statement on the role of psychologists in international emergencies.* Washington, DC: Author. Retrieved from http://www.apa.org/international /resources/info/emergency-statement.aspx

American Psychological Association. (2010). *Ethical principles of psychologists and code of conduct including 2010 amendments.* Washington, DC: Author. Retrieved from http://www.apa .org/ethics/code/American School Counselor Association. (2010). *Ethical standards for school counselors.* Retrieved from http://www.schoolcounselor.org/asca/media/asca/Resource %20Center/Legal%20and%20Ethical%20Issues/Sample%20 Documents/EthicalStandards2010.pdf

American Psychological Association. (2015). *Burnout.* PsychInfo search. Retrieved from www.psychnet.apa.org/index.cfm? fa=search.searchResults

American School Counselor Association. (2011). *9/11 memorial teaching guide.* Retrieved from www.schooolcounselor.org /content.asp?contentid=645

Americans with Disabilities Act. (1990). PL 110-325.

Amichai-Hamburger, M. Y., Klomek, A. B., Friedman, D., Zuckerman, O., & Shani-Sherman, T. (2014, December). The future of online therapy. *Computers in Human Behavior,* Vol. 41, Vol. 41, 288–294.

Ammar, A., & Burdin, S. (1991, April). *Psychoactive medication: An introduction and overview.* Paper presented at the Fifteenth Annual Convening of Crisis Intervention Personnel, Chicago.

Anderson, C. A. (2001). Heat and violence. *Current Directions in Psychological Science, 10*(1), 33–38.

Anderson, C. A., Shibuya, A., Ihori, N., Swing, E., Bushman, B., Sakamoto, A., et al. (2010). Violent video game effects on aggression, empathy, and prosocial behavior in Eastern and Western countries: A meta-analytic review. *Psychological Bulletin, 136*(2), 151–173.

Anderson, K., Danis, F., & Havig, K. (2011). Adult daughters of battered women: Recovery and posttraumatic growth following childhood adversity. *Families in Society, 92*(2), 154–160.

Anderson, M. A., Kaufman, J., & Simon, T. R. (2001). School-associated violent deaths in the United States, 1994–1999. *Journal of the American Medical Association, 286*, 2695–2702.

Ando, M. (2005). A case study of usefulness of cognitive therapy based on reminiscence method for cancer patient. *Japanese Journal of Health Psychology, 18*(2), 53–64.

Annis, L. V., McClaren, H. A., & Baker, C. A. (1984). Who kills us? In J. T. Turner (Ed.), *Violence in the medical care setting: A survival guide* (pp. 19–31). Rockville, MD: Aspen Systems.

Ansbacher, H. L., & Ansbacher, R. R. (1956). *The individual psychology of Alfred Adler.* New York: Greenberg.

Anthony, K., & Nagel, D. M. (2010). *Therapy online: A practical guide.* London: Sage.

Antonovsky, A. (1980). *Health, stress, and coping.* San Francisco: Jossey-Bass.

Antonovsky, A. (1991). The structural sources of salutogenic strengths. In C. Cooper & R. Payne (Eds.), *Personality and stress: Individual differences in the stress process* (pp. 67–104). London: John Wiley & Sons.

Antunes-Alves, S., & Comeau, T. (2014). A clinician's guide to the neurobiology underlying the presentation and treatment of PTSD and subsequent growth. *Archives of Psychiatry and Psychotherapy, 16*(3), 9–17.

Aosyed, A. C., Long, P., & Voller, E. K. (2011). Sexual revictimization and adjustment in college men. *Psychology of Men and Masculinity, 12*(3), 285–296.

Apuzzo, M. (2007, April 19). Gunman's goodbye manifesto of murder. *Memphis Commercial Appeal,* pp. 1A, 4A.

Arai, M. (2004). Japan. In K. Malley-Morrison (Ed.), *International perspective on family violence and abuse: A cognitive-ecological approach* (pp. 282–299). New York: Erlbaum.

Archambeau, O. G., Frueh, B. C., Deliramich, A. N., Elhai, J. D., Grubaaugh, A. N., Herma, S., & Kim, B. S. (2010). Interpersonal violence and mental health outcomes among Asian American and Native Hawaiian/Other Pacific Islander college students. *Psychological Trauma: Theory, Research, Practice, and Policy, 2*(4), 273–283.

Archibald, H. C., Long, D. M., Miller, C., & Tuddenham, R. D. (1962). Gross stress reaction in combat—A 15-year follow-up. *American Journal of Psychiatry, 119,* 317–322.

Armijo v. Wagon Mound Public Schools, 159 F.3d 1253 (10th Cir. 1998).

Armistead-Jehle, P., Johnston, S. L., Wade, N. G., & Ecklund, C. J. (2011). Posttraumatic stress in U.S. Marines: The role of unit cohesion and combat exposure. *Journal of Counseling and Development, 89*(1), 81–88.

Armitage, D., Rice, D., James, R., & Groenendyk, P. (2007, July). *Triage for psychological disorders.* Paper presented at the Association of College and University Housing Officers Convention, Seattle, WA.

Armstrong, D., & Shakespeare-Finch, J. (2011). Relationship to the bereaved and perceptions of severity of trauma differentiate elements of posttraumatic growth. *Omega: Journal of Death and Dying, 63*(2), 125–140.

Armstrong, K., O'Callahan, W., & Marmar, C. (1991). Debriefing Red Cross disaster personnel: The multiple stressor debriefing model. *Journal of Traumatic Stress, 4,* 581–593.

Armsworth, M. W., & Holaday, M. (1993). The effects of psychological trauma on children and adolescents. *Journal of Counseling and Development, 72*(1), 49–56.

Arnold, D., Calhoun, L. G., Tedeschi, R., & Cann, A. (2005). Vicarious posttraumatic growth in psychotherapy. *Journal of Humanistic Psychology, 45*(2), 239–263.

Aron, L., Honberg, R., Duckworth, K., Kimball, A., Edgar, E., Carolla, B., et al. (2009). *Grading the states: A report on America's health care system for adults with serious mental illness.* Arlington, VA: National Alliance for Mental Illness.

Aronin, L., & Ransdell, J. (1994). *A handbook for crisis intervention.* Reseda, CA: Los Angeles Unified School District.

Arredondo, P. (1999). Multicultural counseling competencies as tools to address oppression and racism. *Journal of Counseling and Development, 77*(1), 102–108.

Arredondo, P., & Arciniega, G. M. (2001). Strategies and techniques for counselor training based on the multicultural counseling competencies. *Journal of Multicultural Counseling and Development, 24,* 42–78.

Arredondo, P., & Glauner, T. (1992). *Personal dimensions of an identity model.* Boston: Empowerment Workshops.

Artieda-Urrutia, P., Parra Uribe, I., Garcia-Pares, G., Palao, D., de Leon, J., & Blasco-Fontecilla, H. (2014). Management of suicidal behaviour: Is the world upside down? *Australian and New Zealand Journal of Psychiatry, 48*(5), 399–401.

Arvay, M. J., & Uhlemann, M. R. (1996). Counselor stress in the field of trauma: A preliminary study. *Canadian Journal of Counselling, 30*(3), 193–210.

Asberg, M., & Forslund, K. (2000). Neurobiological aspects of suicidal behavior. *International Review of Psychiatry, 12*(1), 62–74.

Asberg, M., Eriksson, B., Martensson, B., & Traaskman-Bendz, L. (1986). Therapeutic effects of serotonin uptake inhibitors in depression. *Comprehensive Psychiatry, 42,* 70–75.

Association of Threat Assessment Professionals. (2006). *Risk assessment guideline elements for violence (RAGE-V): Considerations for assessing the risk of future violent behavior.* Sacramento, CA: Author.

Astin, M. C., Lawrence, K. J., & Foy, D. W. (1993). Posttraumatic stress disorder among battered women: Risk and resiliency factors. *Violence and Victims, 8,* 17–28.

Astin, M. C., Ogland-Hand, S. M., Coleman, E. M., & Foy, D. W. (1995). Posttraumatic stress disorder and childhood abuse in battered women: Comparisons with maritally distressed women. *Journal of Consulting and Clinical Psychology, 63,* 308–312.

Astor, R. (1999). Unknown places and times. *American Educational Research Journal, 36,* 3–42.

Astroem, S., Bucht, G., Eisemann, M., Norberg, A., & Saveman, B. (2002). Incidence of violence towards staff caring for the elderly. *Scandinavian Journal of Caring Services, 16*(1), 66–72.

Astur, R. S., Germain, S., Tolin, D., Ford, J., Russell, D., & Stevens, S. (2006). Hippocampus function predicts severity of posttraumatic stress disorder. *Cyber Psychology and Behavior, 9*(2), 234–240.

Aten, J. D., Leavell, K., Gonzalez, R., Luke, T., Defee, J., & Harrison, K. (2011). Everyday technologies for extraordinary circumstances: Possibilities for enhancing disaster communication. *Psychological Trauma, Theory, Research, and Practice, 3*(1), 16–20.

Aten, J. D., O'Grady, K., Milsten, G., Boan, D., Smigelsky, M., Schruba, A., & Weaver, I. (2015). Providing spiritual and emotional care in response to a disaster. In D. F. Walker, C. A. Courtois, & J. D. Aten (Eds.), *Spiritually oriented psychotherapy for trauma* (pp. 189–210). Washington, DC: American Psychological Association.

Atkinson, D., Bui, U., & Mori, S. (2001). Multiculturally sensitive empirically supported treatments: An oxymoron? In J. G. Ponterotto, J. M. Casas, L. A. Suzuki, & C. M. Alexander (Eds.), *Handbook of multicultural counseling* (2nd ed., pp. 542–574). Thousand Oaks, CA: Sage.

Atkinson, D., Morten, G., & Sue, D. W. (1998). *Counseling American minorities*. Boston: McGraw-Hill.

Atkinson, R. M., Sparr, L. F., & Sheff, A. G. (1984). Diagnosis of posttraumatic stress disorder in Vietnam veterans: Preliminary findings. *American Journal of Psychiatry, 141,* 694–696.

Attig, T. (2000). *The heart of grief: Death and the search for lasting love.* New York: Oxford University Press.

Augsburger, D. W. (1992). *Conflict mediation across cultures.* Louisville, KY: Westminster/John Knox Press.

Austin, S. (2003). Multiple lessons from multiple suicides. *ASCA School Counselor, 41*(2), 22–27.

Australian Center for Posttraumatic Mental Health. (2007). *Australian guidelines for the treatment of adults with acute stress disorder and posttraumatic stress disorder.* Carlton, Australia: Australian Centre for Posttraumatic Mental Health.

Avery, A., & Orner, R. (1998a, Summer). First report of psychological debriefing abandoned—The end of an era? *Traumatic Stress Points, 12*(3), 1112.

Avery, A., & Orner, R. (1998b, July). More on debriefing: Report of psychological debriefing abandoned—The end of an era? *Australian Traumatic Stress Points,* pp. 4–6.

Avis, J. M. (1992). Where are all the family therapists? Abuse and violence within families and family therapy's response. *Journal of Marital and Family Therapy, 18,* 225–232.

Ayalon, O. (1983). Coping with terrorism. In D. Meichenbaum & M. Jaremko (Eds.), *Stress reduction and prevention (pp. 293–340).* New York: Plenum Press.

Aymer, S. R. (2008). Beyond power and control: Clinical interventions with men engaged in partner abuse. *Clinical Social Work Journal, 36*(4), 323–332.

Azar, B. (2010). Virtual violence. *Monitor on Psychology, 41*(11), 36–39.

B

Babcock, J. C., Green, C. E., & Robie, C. (2004). Does batterers' treatment work? A meta-analytic review of domestic violence treatment. *Clinical Psychology Review, 23,* 1023–1053.

Babcock, J. C., Jacobson, N. S., Gottman, J. M., & Waltz, J. (1993). Power and violence: The relationship between communication patterns, power discrepancies, and domestic violence. *Journal of Counseling and Clinical Psychology, 61,* 40–50.

Bach y Rita, G., Lion, J. R., & Climent, C. E. (1971). Episodic dyscontrol: A study of 630 violent patients. *American Journal of Psychiatry, 128,* 1473–1478.

Baechler, J. (1979). *Suicides.* New York: Basic Books.

Bagge, C., Nickell, A., Stepp, S., Durrett, C., Jackson, K., & Trull, T. J. (2004). Borderline personality disorder features predict negative outcomes 2 years later. *Journal of Abnormal Psychology, 113*(2), 279–288.

Bahora, M., Hanafi, S., Chien, V. H., & Compton, M. T. (2008). Preliminary evidence of effects of crisis intervention team training on self-efficacy and social distance. *Administration and Policy in Mental Health and Mental Health Services Research, 35*(3), 159–167.

Bailey, C. R., Cordell, E., Sobin, S. M., & Neumeister, A. (2013). Recent progress in understanding the pathophysiology of post-traumatic stress disorder: Implications for targeted pharmacological treatment. *CNS Drugs, 27*(3), 221–232.

Bailey, K. A. (2001). Legal implications of profiling students for violence. *Psychology in the Schools, 38,* 141–155.

Bailey, K. A., West, R., & Anderson, C. A. (2011). The association between chronic exposure to video game violence and affective picture processing: An ERP study. *Cognitive, Affective, and Behavioral Neuroscience, 11*(2), 259–276.

Bain, S. F. (2011). Itinerant counseling services for rural communities: A win/win opportunity. *Journal of Rural Community Psychology, 13*(1). Retrieved from http://www.marschall.edu/jrcp/current.htlm

Baird, B. N., Bossett, S. B., & Smith, B. J. (1994). A new technique for handling sexually abusive calls to telephone crisis lines. *Community Mental Health Journal, 30,* 55–60.

Baird, S., & Jenkins, S. R. (2003). Vicarious traumatization, secondary traumatic stress, and burnout in sexual assault and domestic violence agency staff. *Violence and Victims, 18*(1), 71–86.

Baker, D. A. (1995, June). *Talking with young people who have experienced sexual abuse.* Paper presented at the American School Counselor Association Conference and Exposition, New Orleans.

Baker, D. G., Risbrough, V. B., & Schork, N. J. (2008). Posttraumatic stress disorder: Genetic and environmental risk factors. In B. J. Lukey & V. Tepe (Eds.), *Biobehavioral resilience to stress* (pp. 177–218). Boca Raton, FL: CRC Press, Taylor & Francis Group.

Baker, L. R., & Cormier, L. A. (2015). *Disaster and vulnerable populations: Evidence-based practice for the helping professions.* New York: Springer.

Baker, N. J. (1985). Reminiscing in group therapy for self-worth. *Journal of Gerontological Nursing, 11,* 21–24.

Bakker, A. B., Demerouti, E., & Schaufeli, W. B. (2002). Validation of the Maslach Burnout Inventory—General survey: An Internet study. *Anxiety, Stress and Coping: An International Journal, 15*(3), 245–260.

Bakker, A. B., Demerouti, E., & Schaufeli, W. B. (2005). The crossover of burnout and work engagement among working couples. *Human Relations, 58*(5), 661–689.

Balk, D. E. (1990, August). *The many faces of bereavement on the college campus.* Paper presented at the annual meeting of the American Psychological Association, Boston.

Balk, D. E. (2009). Adolescent development: The back story to adolescent encounters with death and bereavement. In D. E. Balk & C. A. Corr (Eds.), *Adolescent encounters with death, bereavement, and coping* (pp. 3–20). New York: Springer.

Balk, D. E., & Corr, C. A. (2001). Bereavement during adolescence: A review of research. In M. S. Stroebe, R. O. Hansson, H. Schut, & W. Stroebe (Eds.), *Handbook of bereavement research: Consequences, coping and care* (pp. 199–218). Washington, DC: American Psychological Association.

Balk, D. E., Zaengle, D., & Corr, C. A. (2011). Strengthening grief support for adolescents coping with a peer's death. *School Psychology International, 32*(2), 144–162.

Balson, P., & Dempster, C. (1980). Treatment of war neurosis from Vietnam. *Comprehensive Psychiatry, 21,* 167–176.

Baradell, J. G. (1985, February). Humanistic care of the patient in seclusion. *Journal of Psychosocial Nursing and Mental Health Services, 23,* 9–14.

Baranowsky, A. B. (2002). The silencing response in clinical practice: On the road to dialogue. In C. R. Figley (Ed.), *Treating compassion fatigue* (pp. 155–170). New York: Brunner/Routledge.

Barber, C., & Iwai, M. (1996). Role conflict and role ambiguity as predictors of burnout among staff caring for elderly dementia patients. *Journal of Gerontological Social Work, 26*(1–2), 101–116.

Barber, C. Azael, D., Hemenway, D. (2013). A truly National Violent Death Reporting System. *Injury Prevention* 19(4), 225–226.

Barber, S. J., & Wright, E. M. (2010). Predictors of completion in a batterer treatment program: The effects of referral source supervision. *Criminal Justice and Behavior, 37*(8), 847–859.

Bard, M., & Sangrey, D. (1986). *The crime victim's book* (2nd ed.). New York: Brunner/Mazel.

Barnes, P. G. (1998). "It's just a quarrel": Some states offer no domestic violence protection to gays. *ABA Journal, 84,* 24–26.

Barnes, V. A., Davis, H. M., & Treiber, F. A. (2007). Perceived stress, heart rate, and blood pressure among adolescents with family members deployed in Operation Iraqi Freedom. *Military Medicine, 172,* 40–43.

Barnett, E. R., Pittman, C. R., Ragan, C., & Salus, M. K. (1980). *Family violence: Intervention strategies* (DHHS Publication No. OHD 580-30258). Washington, DC: U.S. Government Printing Office.

Barnett, J. E., & Scheetz, K. (2003). Technological advances and telehealth: Ethics, law, and the practice of psychotherapy. *Psychotherapy: Theory, Research, Practice, Training, 40*(1–2), 86–93.

Barnett, O. W., & Hamberger, L. K. (1992). The assessment of maritally violent men on the California Personality Inventory. *Violence and Victims, 7,* 15–28.

Baron, A., Jr., & Cohen, R. B. (1982). Helping telephone counselors cope with burnout: A consciousness-raising workshop. *Personnel and Guidance Journal, 60,* 508–510.

Baron, L., & Straus, M. A. (1989). *Four theories of rape in American society.* New Haven, CT: Yale University Press.

Barret, K. E., Riggar, T. F., & Flowers, C. R. (1997). Violence in the workplace. Preparing for the age of rage. *Journal of Rehabilitation Administration, 21*(3), 171–188.

Barrick, A. L., Rader, J., Hoeffer, B., Sloane, P. D., & Biddle, S. (2008). General guidelines for bathing persons with dementia. In A. L. Barrick, J. Rader, J. B. Hoeffer, P. D. Sloane, & S. Biddle (Eds.), *Bathing without a battle: Person-directed care of individuals with dementia* (2nd ed., pp. 17–21). New York: Springer.

Bartholomew, K. (1999, August). *Violence in male same-sex relationships: Prevalence, incidence, and injury.* Paper presented at the 107th Annual Convention of the American Psychological Association, Symposium on Outing Same-Sex Partner Abuse—Defining the Issues, Boston.

Barton, A. M. (1969). *Communities in disaster.* Garden City, NY: Doubleday.

Bass, D. D., & Yep, R. (Eds.). (2002). *Terrorism, trauma, and tragedies: A counselor's guide to preparing and responding.* Alexandria, VA: American Counseling Association.

Bass, E., & Davis, L. (1992). *The courage to heal: A guide for women survivors of child sexual abuse.* New York: Harper.

Bass, E., & Thornton, L. (Eds). (1983). *I never told anyone: Writings by women survivors of child sex abuse.* New York: Harper & Row.

Bassilios, B., Harris, M., Middleton, A., Gunn, J., & Pirkis, J. (2015). Characteristics of people who use telephone counseling: Findings from secondary analysis of a population-based study. *Administration and Policy in Mental Health and Mental Health Services Research, 42*(5), 621–632.

Bateman, A., & Fonagy, P. (2006). *Mentalization-based treatment for borderline personality disorder.* New York: Oxford University Press.

Battaglia, T., Finley, E., & Liebschutz, J. (2003). Survivors of intimate partner violence speak out: Trust in the patient-provider relationship. *Journal of General Internal Medicine, 18,* 617–623.

Battle, A. O., Battle, M. V., & Tolley, E. A. (1993). Potential for suicide and aggression in delinquents at juvenile court in a southern city. *Suicide and Life Threatening Behavior, 23*(3), 230–243.

Battle, C. L., Shea, M., Johnson, D. M., Yen, S., Zlotnik, C., Zanarini, M. C., et al. (2004). Childhood maltreatment associated with adult personality disorders: Findings from the collaborative longitudinal personality disorders study. *Journal of Personality Disorders, 18,* 193–211.

Baty, S. (2013). Healing the invisible wound: Examining spirituality in the posttraumatic growth of sexual trauma survivors. *Dissertation Abstracts International: Section B the Sciences and Engineering, 73*(11-B(E)), 415.

Baum, N., Rahav, G., & Sharon, M. (2014). Heightened susceptibility to secondary traumatization: A meta-analysis of gender differences. *American Journal of Orthopsychiatry, 84*(2), 111–122.

Bauman, S. (2011). *Cyberbullying: What counselors need to know.* Alexandria, VA: American Counseling Association.

Baumeister, R. F. (1990). *Escaping the self: Alcoholism, spirituality, masochism and flights from the burden of selfhood.* New York: Basic Books.

Beamish, P. M. (2005). Introduction to the special section—severe and persistent mental illness on college campuses: Consideration for service provision. *Journal of College Counseling, 8*(2), 138–139.

Beane, A. L. (1999). *Bully-free classroom.* Minneapolis, MN: Free Spirit Press.

Beck, A., & Freeman, A. (1990). *Cognitive therapy of personality disorders.* New York: Guilford Press.

Beck, A. T. (1976). *Cognitive therapy and the emotional disorders.* New York: International Universities Press.

Beck, A. T., & Steer, R. A. (1987). *BDI, Beck Depression Inventory: Manual.* San Antonio, TX: Psychological Corporation.

Beck, A. T., Shaw, A. J., Rush, B. F., & Emery, G. (1979). *Cognitive theory of depression.* New York: Guilford Press.

Beck, A. T., Weissman, A., Lester, D., & Trexler, L. (1974). The measurement of pessimism: The Hopelessness Scale. *Journal of Consulting and Clinical Psychology, 42,* 861–865.

Beck, J. C. (1988). The therapist's legal duty when the patient may be violent. *Psychiatric Clinics of North America, 11,* 665–679.

Becker, S., & Tinkler, J. (2015). "Me getting plastered and her provoking my eyes." Young people's attribution of blame for sexual aggression in public drinking places. *Feminist Criminology, 10*(3), 235–238.

Becker, W. C. (1971). *Parents are teachers.* Champaign, IL: Research Press.

Becvar, D. S. (2001). *In the presence of grief.* New York: Guilford Press.

Bedikian, S. (2008). The death of mourning: From Victorian crepe to the little black dress. *Omega: Journal of Death and Dying, 57*(1), 35–52.

Beebe, L., Smith, K., & Phillips, C. (2014). A comparison of telephone and texting interventions for persons with schizophrenia spectrum disorders. *Issue in Mental Health Nursing, 35*(5), 323–329.

Beech, A. R., Ward, T., & Fisher, D. (2006). The identification of sexual and violent motivations in men who assault women: Implication for treatment. *Journal of Interpersonal Violence, 21*(12), 1635–1653.

Belak, A. G., & Busse, D. (1993). Legal issues. In P. E. Blumenreich & S. Lewis (Eds.), *Managing the violent patient: A clinician's guide* (pp. 137–149). New York: Brunner-Mazel.

Belkin, G. S. (1984). *Introduction to counseling* (2nd ed.). Dubuque, IA: William C. Brown.

Bell, C. C., Richardson, J., & Blount, M. (2006). Suicide prevention. In J. R. Lutzker (Ed.), *Preventing violence: Research and evidence based strategies* (pp. 217–238). Washington, DC: American Psychological Assocation.

Belling, S., Bozzatello, P., De Grandi, E., & Bogetto, F. (2014). Interpersonal psychotherapy: A model of intervention for borderline personality disorder. *Rivista di Psichiatria, 49*(4), 158–163.

Bemak, F., & Keys, S. (2000). *Violent and aggressive youth: Intervention and prevention strategies for changing times.* Thousand Oaks, CA: Sage.

Bender, K., Brown, S., Thompson, S., Ferguson, K., & Langenderfer, L. (2015). Multiple victimizations before and after leaving home associated with PTSD, depression, and substance abuse disorder among homeless youth. *Child Maltreatment, 20*(2), *115–124.*

Bender, M. G. (1986). Young adult chronic patients: Visibility and style of interaction in treatment. *Hospital and Community Psychiatry, 37,* 265–268.

Bender, T. W., Gordon, K. H., Bresin, K., & Joiner, T. E. (2011). Impulsivity and suicidality: The mediating role of painful experience. *Journal of Affective Disorders, 129*(1–3), 301–307.

Benedict, H. (1985). *Recovery: How to survive sexual assault—for women, men, teenagers, their friends and families.* Garden City, NY: Doubleday.

Bengelsdorf, H., Church, J. O., & Kaye, R. A. (1993). The cost effectiveness of crisis intervention: Admission diversion savings can offset the high cost of service. *Journal of Nervous Mental Disorders, 181,* 757–762.

Benjamin, L., & Walz, G. R. (1983). *Violence in the family: Child and spouse abuse* (Report No. EDN00001). Washington, DC: National Institute of Education (ERIC Document Reproduction Service No. ED 226-309).

Bennell, C., Jones, J., & Taylor, A. (2011). Determining the authenticity of suicide notes: Can training improve judgment? *Criminal Justice and Behavior, 38*(7), 669–689.

Bennett, L. W., & Vincent, N. V. (2001). Standards for batterer programs: A formative evaluation of the Illinois protocol. *Journal of Aggression, Maltreatment, and Trauma, 5,* 181–197.

Bennett, N., & O'Donohue, W. (2014). The construct of grooming in child sexual abuse: Conceptual and measurement issues. *Journal of Child Sexual Abuse: Research, Treatment, and Program Innovations for Victims, Survivors, and Offenders, 23*(8), 957–976.

Bennett, Y. (2015). The "It's no secret" bra drive: An example of a collaborative practice. *Journal of Forensic Nursing, 11*(1), 59–61.

Benson, H. (1976). *The relaxation response.* New York: Avon.

Bent-Goodley, T. B., Rice, J., Williams, O., & Pope, M. (2011). Treatment for perpetrators of domestic violence. In M. P. Koss, J. White, & A. Kazdin (Eds.), *Violence against women and children: Vol. 2. Navigating solutions* (pp. 199–213). Washington, DC: American Psychological Association.

Benton, S. A., Robertson, J. M., Tseng, W., Newton, F., & Benton, S. L. (2003). Changes in counseling center client problems across 13 years. *Professional Psychology: Research and Practice, 34*(1), 66–72.

Bercier, M., & Maynard, B. (2015). Interventions for secondary traumatic stress with mental health workers: A systematic review. *Research on Social Work Practice, 25*(1), 81–89.

Bergman, L. (1992). Dating violence among high school students. *Social Work, 37,* 17–21.

Bergman, U. (2012). *Neurobiological foundations for EMDR practice.* New York: Springer.

Berk, M. S., Henriques, G. R., Warman, D. M., Brown, G. K., & Beck, A. T. (2004). A cognitive therapy intervention for suicide attempters: An overview of the treatment and case example. *Cognitive and Behavior Practice, 11*(3), 265–277.

Berk, R. A., Newton, P. J., & Berk, S. (1986). What a difference a day makes: An empirical study of the impact of shelters for battered women. *Journal of Marriage and the Family, 48,* 481–490.

Berkowitz, L., McCauley, J., Schuurman, D., & Jordan, J. R. (2011). Organizational postvention after suicide death. In J. R. Jordan & J. L. McIntosh (Eds.), *Grief after suicide: Understanding the consequences and caring for the survivors* (pp. 157–168). New York: Routledge/Taylor & Francis Group.

Berman, A. L., & Jobes, D. A. (1991). *Adolescent suicide: Assessment and intervention.* Washington, DC: American Psychological Association.

Berman, A. L., & Jobes, D. A. (1994). Treatment of the suicidal adolescent [Special Issue: Suicide assessment and intervention]. *Death Studies, 18,* 375–389.

Berman, A. L., Jobes, D. A., & Silverman, M. M. (Eds.). (2006*). Adolescent suicide: Assessment and intervention* (2nd ed.). Washington, DC: American Psychological Association.

Bernal, G., & Rodriguez, D. (2012). Cultural adaption in context: Psychotherapy as a historical account of adaptions. In G. Bernal & D. Rodriguez (Eds.), *Cultural adaptions: Tools for evidence-based practice with diverse populations* (pp. 3–22). Washington, DC: American Psychological Association.

Bernardy, N. C., & Friedman, M. J. (2015). Antidepressant strategies for managing PTSD. In N. C. Bernardy & M. J. Friedman (Eds.), *A practical guide to treatment: Pharmacological and psychotherapeutic approaches* (pp. 55–70). Washington, DC: American Psychological Association.

Bernardy, N. C., Souter, T., & Friedman, M. J. (2015). The use of anxiolytics in the management of PTSD. In N. C. Bernardy & M. J. Friedman (Eds.), *A practical guide to treatment: Pharmacological and psychotherapeutic approaches* (pp. 71–88). Washington, DC: American Psychological Association.

Bernecker, S. L., Levy, K. N., & Ellison, W. D. (2014). A meta-analysis of the relation between patient adult attachment style and the working alliance. *Psychotherapy Research, 24*(1), 12–24.

Bernstein, A. (1986). The treatment of noncompliance in patients with posttraumatic stress disorder. *Psychosomatic Medicine, 27,* 37–40.

Bernstein, J. R. (1997*). When the bough breaks: Forever after the death of a son or daughter.* Kansas City, MO: Andrews & McKeel.

Berrouiquet, S., Gravey, M., Le Galudec, M., Alavi, Z., & Walter, M. (2014). Post-acute crisis text messaging outreach for suicide prevention: A pilot study. *Psychiatry Research, 217*(3) 154–157.

Besharov, D. J. (1990). *Recognizing child abuse: A guide for the concerned.* New York: Free Press.

Best, P., Foye, U., Taylor, B., Hazlett, D., & Manktelow, R. (2013). Online interactive suicide support services: Quality and accessibility. *Mental Health Review Journal, 18*(4), 226–239.

Bethel, B., & Oates, J. A. (2007, March). *The untold story of the Beverly Hillbillies.* Paper presented at the Thirty-first Convening of Crisis Intervention Personnel and the Contact USA Conference, Chicago.

Betz, G., & Thorngren, J. M. (2006). Ambiguous loss and the family grieving process. *Family Journal, 14*(4), 359–365.

Bianchi, R., & Laurent, E. (2015). Emotional information processing in depression and burnout: An eye tracking study. *European Archives of Psychiatry and Clinical Neuroscience, 265*(1), 27–34.

Bianchi, R., Schoenfield, I., & Laurent, E. (2015). Burnout-depression overlap. *Clinical Psychology Review, 36,* 28–41.

Bianchi, R., Truchot, D., Laurent, E., Brisson, R., & Schonfeld, S. (2014). Is burnout solely job related? A critical comment. *Scandinavian Journal of Psychology, 55*(4), 357–361.

Bierens de Haan, B. (1998). Le débriefing émotionnel collectif des intervenants humanitaires: L'expérience du CICR. *Schweizer Archiv für Neurologie und Psychiatrie, 149*(5), 218–228.

Bigot, T., & Ferrand, I. (1998). Individualologie de la prise d'otage: Etude auprès de 29 individuelles. *Annales Médico Psychologiques, 156*(1), 22–27.

Bingham, R. (2010). My life is a balance between . . . In J. G. Ponterotto, J. M. Casas, L. A. Suzuki, & C. M. Alexander (Eds.), *Handbook of multicultural counseling* (3rd ed., pp. 19–25). Thousand Oaks, CA: Sage.

Bishop, J. B. (2006). College and university counseling centers: Questions in search of answers. *Journal of College Counseling, 9*(1), 6–19.

Bishop, S., Lau, M., Shapiro, S., Carlson, L., Anderson, N., Caromdy, J., . . . Devis, G. (2004). Mindfulness: A proposed operational definition. *Clinical Psychology: Science and Practice, 11,* 230–241.

Bisson, J., & Andrews, M. (2009). Psychological treatment in posttraumatic stress disorder (PTSD). *Cochran Data Base of Systematic Reviews, 2007*(3), 1–48.

Bisson, J., Ehlers, A., Matthews, R., Pilling, S., Richards, D., & Turner, S. (2007). Psychological treatments for post-traumatic stress disorder: Systematic review and meta-analysis. *British Journal of Psychiatry, 190,* 97–104.

Bisson, J. I., & Deahl, M. P. (1994). Psychological debriefing and prevention post-traumatic stress—More research is needed. *British Journal of Psychiatry, 165,* 717–720.

Bisson, J. I., Jenkins, J. A., & Bannister, C. (1997). Randomized controlled trial of psychological debriefing for victims of acute burn trauma. *British Journal of Psychiatry, 171,* 78–81.

Black, B., Chido, L., Preble, K., Weisz, A., Yoon, J., Delaney-Black, V., . . . Lewandowski, L. (2015). Violence exposure and teen dating violence among African-American youth. *Journal of Interpersonal Violence, 30*(12), 2174–2195.

Black, M., Baslie, K., Breiding, M., Smith, S., Walters, M., Merrick, M., . . .Stevens, M. (2011). *The National Intimate Partner and Sexual Violence Survey: 2010 summary report*. Centers for Disease Control and Prevention, National Center for Injury Prevention and Control. Retrieved from http://www.cdc.gov/ViolencePrevention/pdf/NISVS_Report2010-aPDF

Blair, D. T. (1991). Assaultive behavior: Does provocation begin in the front office? *Journal of Psychosocial Nursing and Mental Health Services, 29,* 21–24.

Blair, D. T., & New, S. A. (1991). Assaultive behavior: Know the risks. *Journal of Psychosocial Nursing and Mental Health Services, 29,* 25–29.

Blake, D. D., Weathers, F., Nagy, L. M., Kaloupek, D. G., Klauminzer, G., & Charney, D. S. (1990). A clinician rating scale for assessing current and lifetime PTSD: The CAPS-1. *Behavior Therapist, 13,* 187–188.

Blancett, J. (2008). *A reliability and validity study of the Triage Assessment System for Students in Learning Environments*. University of Memphis, Memphis, TN.

Blanchard, E. A., & Jones, M. (1997). Care of clinicians doing trauma work. In M. Harris & C. L. Landis (Eds.), *Sexual abuse in the lives of women diagnosed with serious mental illness: New direction in therapeutic interventions* (Vol. 2, pp. 303–319). New Delhi: Harwood Academic.

Blauvelt, P. D. (1998). *Blauvelt . . . on making our schools safe* (2nd rev. ed.). College Park, MD: National Alliance for Safe Schools.

Blix, I., Skogbrott, B., Hanse, M., & Heir, T. (2015). Posttraumatic growth and centrality of event: A longitudinal study in the aftermath of the 2011 Oslo bombing. *Psychological Trauma: Theory, Research, Practice, and Policy, 7*(1),18–23.

Bloch, D. A., Silber, E., & Perry, S. E. (1956). Some factors in the emotional reaction of children to disaster. *American Journal of Psychiatry, 113,* 416–422.

Blocher, D. H. (2000). *Counseling: A developmental approach* (4th ed.). New York: John Wiley & Sons.

Bloom, B. L. (1984). *Community mental health: A general introduction* (2nd ed.). Pacific Grove, CA: Brooks/Cole.

Blore, D. (2014). EMDR for mining and related trauma. In M.Luber (Ed.), *Implementing EMDR early mental health interventions for man-made and natural disasters: Models, scripted protocols, and summary sheet* (pp. 451–466). New York: Springer.

Blount, R. W., Silverman, I. J., Sellers, C. S., & Seese, R. A. (1994). Alcohol and drug use among abused women who kill, abused women who don't, and their abusers. *Journal of Drug Issues, 24,* 165–177.

Blumenreich, P. E. (1993a). Assessment. In P. E. Blumenreich & S. Lewis (Eds.), *Managing the violent patient: A clinician's guide* (pp. 35–40). New York: Brunner/Mazel.

Blumenreich, P. E. (1993b). Etiology. In P. E. Blumenreich & S. Lewis (Eds.), *Managing the violent patient: A clinician's guide* (pp. 21–33). New York: Brunner/Mazel.

Blumenthal, S., & Kupfer, D. (1986). Generalizable treatment strategies for suicidal behavior. *Annals of the New York Academy of Sciences, 487,* 327–340.

Bodnarchuk, M., Kropp, R., Ogloff, J., Hart, S., & Dutton, D. (1995). *Predicting cessation of intimate assaultiveness after group treatment* (No. 4887-10-91-106). Ottawa: Health Canada, Family Violence Prevention Division.

Boelen, P. A., & Prigerson, H. G. (2007). The influence of symptoms of prolonged grief disorder, depression, and anxiety on quality of life among bereaved adults: A prospective study. *European Archives of Psychiatry and Clinical Neuroscience, 257*(8), 442–452.

Boelen, P. A., & Prigerson, H. G. (2012). Commentary on the inclusion of persistent complex bereavement-related disorder in DSM-5. *Death Studies, 36,* 771–794.

Boelen, P. A., de Keijser, J., & Smid, G. (2015). Cognitive-behavioral variables mediate the impact of violent loss on post-loss psychopathology. *Psychological Trauma, Theory, Research, Practice, and Policy, 7*(4), 382–390.

Boelen, P. A., van de Schoot, R., van den Hout, M. A., de Keijser, J., & van den Bout, J. (2010). Prolonged grief disorder, depression, and posttraumatic stress disorder are distinguishable syndromes. *Journal of Affective Disorders, 125*(1–3), 374–378.

Boes, M., & McDermott, V. (2002). Helping battered women: A health care perspective. In A. R. Roberts (Ed.), *Handbook of domestic violence: Intervention strategies* (pp. 255–277). New York: Oxford University Press.

Bograd, M. (1992). Values in conflict: Challenges to family therapists' thinking. *Journal of Marital and Family Therapy, 18,* 245–256.

Bograd, M. (2005). Strengthening domestic violence theories: Intersections of race, class, sexual orientation, and gender. In N. Sololoff & C. Pratt (Eds.), *Domestic violence at the margins: Reading on race, class, gender, and culture* (pp. 25–38). New Brunswick, NJ: Rutgers University Press.

Bologna, M. J., Waterman, C. K., & Dawson, L. J. (1987). *Violence in gay male and lesbian relationships: Implications for practitioners and policy makers*. Paper presented at the Third National Conference for Family Violence Researchers, Durham, NH.

Bonanno, G. A., Papa, A., Lalande, K., Zhang, N., & Noll, J. G. (2005). Grief processing and deliberate grief avoidance: A prospective comparison of bereaved spouses and parents in the United States and the People's Republic of China. *Journal of Consulting and Clinical Psychology, 73*(1), 86–98.

Bonanno, G. A., Westphal, M., & Mancini, A. D. (2011). Resilience to loss and potential trauma. *Annual Review of Clinical Psychology, 7,* 511–535.

Bondu, R., & Scheithauer, H. (2015). Leaking and death threats by students: A study in German schools. *School Psychology International, 35*(6), 592–608.

Bonfine, N., Ritter, C., & Munetz, M. R. (2014). Police officer perceptions of the impact of crisis intervention team (CIT) programs. *International Journal of Law and Psychiatry, 37*(4), 341–350.

Bongar, B., & Sullivan, G. (2013). *The suicidal patient: Clinical and legal standards of care.* Washington, DC: American Psychological Association.

Bonnano, G. A. (2004). Loss, trauma, and human resilience. *American Psychologist, 59,* 20–28.

Bonnefil, M., & Jacobson, G. F. (1979). Family crisis intervention. *Clinical Social Work Journal, 7,* 200–213.

Bonner, R. (2001). Moving suicide risk assessment into the next millennium: Lessons from our past. In D. Lester (Ed.), *Suicide prevention: Resources for the millennium* (pp. 83–102). Philadelphia: Brunner-Routledge.

Boon, H., Ruiter, R. A., James, S., van den Borne, B., Williams, E., & Reddy, P. (2010). Correlates of grief among older adults caring for children and grandchildren as a consequence of HIV and AIDS in South Africa. *Journal of Aging and Health, 22*(1), 48–67.

Bordin, E. (1979). The generalizability of the psychoanalytic concept of the working alliance. *Psychotherapy: Theory, Research and Practice, 16,* 252–260.

Bordow, J. (1982). *The ultimate loss: Coping with the death of a child.* New York: Beaufort Books.

Bornstein, R. F. (2006). The complex relationship between dependency and domestic violence: Converging psychological and social forces. *American Psychologist, 61*(6), 595–606.

Borritz, M., Bültmann, U., Rugulies, R., Christensen, K., Viladsen, E., & Kristensen, T. S. (2005). Psychosocial work characteristics as predictors for burnout: Findings from 3-year follow up of the PUMA study. *Journal of Occupational and Environmental Medicine, 47*(10), 1015–1025.

Borschmann, R., & Moran, P. (2011). Crisis management in borderline personality disorder. *International Journal of Social Psychiatry, 57*(1), 18–20.

Borschmann, R., Barret, B., Hellier, J., Byford, S., Henderson, C., et al. (2013). Joint crisis plans for people with borderline personality disorder: Feasibility and outcomes in a randomized controlled trial. *The British Journal of Psychiatry, 202*(5), 357–364.

Borum, R. (2000). Improving high risk encounters between people with mental illness and the police. *Journal of the American Academy of Law and Psychiatry, 28,* 332–337.

Borum, R., Lodewijks, H., Bartel, P., & Forth, A. (2010). Structured Assessment of Violence Risk in Youth (SAVRY). In R. Oyyo & K. Douglas (Eds.), *Handbook of violence risk assessment* (pp. 63–80). New York: Routledge.

Boschen, M. J. (2009). Mobile telephones and psychotherapy: Capability and applicability. *Behavior Therapist, 32*(8), 168–175.

Bosquet, M. (2004). How research informs clinical work with traumatized young children. In J. D. Osofsky (Ed.), *Young children and trauma: Intervention and treatment* (pp. 301–325). New York: Guilford Press.

Boss, P. (2002). *Family stress management: A contextual approach* (2nd ed.). Thousand Oaks: Sage.

Boss, P. (2006). *Loss, trauma, and resilience: Therapeutic work with ambiguous loss.* New York: W. W. Norton.

Bosworth, K., Espelage, D., Dubay, T., Dahlberg, L., & Daytner, G. (1996). Using multi-media to teach conflict-resolution skills to young adolescents. *American Journal of Preventive Medicine, 12*(Supp. 5), 65–74.

Bottoms, B. L., Nielsen, M., Murray, R., & Filipas, H. (2003). Religion-based related child psychical abuse: Characteristics of psychological outcomes. In J. L. Mullings, J. W. Marquart, & D. J. Hartley (Eds.), *The victimization of children: Emerging issues* (pp. 87–114). Binghamton, NY: Haworth Trauma and Maltreatment Press.

Bottoms, D. (Speaker). (1999, September). *The role of the Exchange Club–Carl Perkins Child Advocacy Center in treating child sexual abuse* (Cassette Recording #7411-99). Memphis, TN: Department of Counseling, Educational Psychology and Research, University of Memphis.

Bovin, M. J., Ratchford, E., & Marx, B. P. (2014). Perittraumatic dissociation and tonic immobility: Clinical findings. In U. F. Lanius, S. Paulsen, & F. Corrigan (Eds.), *Neurobiology and treatment of traumatic dissociation: Toward an embodied self* (pp. 51–67). New York: Springer.

Bowen, E. L. (2009). *Domestic violence treatment for abusive women: A treatment manual.* New York: Taylor/Routledge.

Bower, G. H. (1981). Mood and memory. *American Psychologist, 36,* 129–148.

Bower, S. A., & Bower, G. H. (1976). *Asserting yourself: A practical guide for positive change.* Reading, MA: Addison-Wesley.

Bowlby, J. (1969). *Attachment and loss: Vol. 1. Attachment.* London: Hogarth/New York: Basic Books.

Bowlby, J. (1973). *Attachment and loss: Vol. 2. Separation, anxiety, and anger.* London: Hogarth/New York: Basic Books.

Bowlby, J. (1980). *Attachment and loss: Vol. 3. Loss, sadness, and depression.* London: Hogarth/New York: Basic Books.

Bowlby, J. (1982). *Attachment and loss: Vol. 1. Attachment* (2nd ed.). New York: Basic Books.

Bowlby, J. (1988). *A secure base: Parent–child attachment and healthy human development.* New York: Basic Books.

Bowman, R. P. (1987). Approaches for counseling children through music. *Elementary School Guidance and Counseling, 21,* 284–291.

Boyd, B., Quevillon, R. P., & Engdahl, R. M. (2010). Working with rural and diverse communities after disasters. In P. Dass-Braillsford (Ed.), *Crisis and disaster counseling: Lessons learned from hurricane Katrina and other disasters* (pp. 149–163). Thousand Oaks, CA: Sage.

Boyd, T. (2000, April 7). Date-rape drug: GBH means socializing in a new way—even with friends. *Pensacola News Journal,* pp. B1, B3.

Boyd-Franklin, N. (2010). Families affected by hurricane Katrina and other disasters: Learning from the experiences of African-American survivors. In P. Dass-Braillsford (Ed.), *Crisis and disaster counseling: Lessons learned from hurricane Katrina and other disasters* (pp. 67–82). Thousand Oaks, CA: Sage.

Bradley, R. G., Green, J., Russ, E., Dutra, L., & Westen, D. (2005). A multidimensional analysis of psychotherapy for PTSD. *American Journal of Psychiatry, 162,* 214–227.

Bradley v. State of Mississippi, 1 Miss. 156 (1824).

Brainerd, A. M. (2002). Tragic events and the effects on all of us. In D. D. Bass & R. Yep (Eds.), *Terrorism, trauma, and tragedies: A counselor's guide to preparing and responding* (pp. 111–112). Alexandria, VA: American Counseling Association.

Brammer, L. M. (1985). *The helping relationship: Process and skills* (3rd ed.). Upper Saddle River, NJ: Prentice Hall.

Brammer, L. M., Abrego, P., & Shostrom, E. (1993). *Therapeutic counseling and psychotherapy* (6th ed.). Upper Saddle River, NJ: Prentice Hall.

Brand, A. G. (1987). Writing as counseling. *Elementary School Guidance and Counseling, 21,* 266–275.

Brandsma, L. L. (2003, January). Letters: Much ado about multiculturalism, part 4. *Counseling Today, 45,* 31.

Brandt, M. R. (2014). War, trauma and technologies of the self: The making of virtual reality exposure therapy. *Dissertation Abstracts International Section A: Humanities and Social Sciences, 74*(10-A(E)), 1231.

Brasseur, J. W. (1994, October). The battered woman: Identification and intervention. *Clinical Reviews, 4,* 45–74.

Braun, M. J., & Berg, D. H. (1994). Meaning reconstruction in the experience of parental bereavement. *Death Studies, 18,* 105–129.

Braverman, M. (1999). *Preventing workplace violence: A guide to employers and practitioners.* Thousand Oaks, CA: Sage.

Breiding, M., Chen, J., & Black, M. (2014). *Intimate partner violence in the United States 2010.* Centers for Disease Control and Prevention, National Center for Injury Prevention and Control. Retrieved from http://www.cdc.gov/ViolencePrevention/pdf/cdc_Report2013_v17_single_s.pdf

Breiding, M. J. (2015). Prevalence and characteristics of sexual violence, stalking, and intimate partner violence. National Intimate Partner and Sexual Violence Survey, United States 2011. *American Journal of Public Health, 105*(4), e11–e12.

Bremner, J. D. (1998). Traumatic memories lost and found: Can memories of abuse be found in the brain? In L. M. Williams & V. L. Banyard (Eds.), *Trauma and memory* (pp. 217–227). Thousand Oaks, CA: Sage.

Bremner, J.D., Krystal, J. H. Southwick, S.M. & Charney, D. S.(1995). Functional neuroanatomical correlates of the effects of stress on memory. Journal of Traumatic Stress, 8, 527–550.

Bremner, J. D., Randall, P. K., Scott, T. M., Bronen, R. A., Seibyl, J. P., Southwick, S. M., et al. (1997). Magnetic resonance imaging based measurement of hippocampal volume in posttraumatic stress disorder related to childhood physical and sexual abuse: A preliminary report. *Biological Psychiatry, 41*(1), 23–32.

Brende, J. O., & Parson, E. R. (1985). *Vietnam veterans: The road to recovery.* New York: Plenum Press.

Brenner, L. A., Vanderploeg, R. D., & Terro, H. (2009). Assessment and diagnosis of mild traumatic brain injury, posttraumatic stress disorder, and other polytrauma conditions: Burden of adversity hypothesis. *Rehabilitation Psychology, 54,* 239–246.

Brent, D., & Brown, C. (2015). Effectiveness of school-based suicide prevention programmes. *The Lancet, 385*(9977), 1489–1491.

Brent, D., McMakin,F., Kennard, B., Goldstein, T., Mayes, T., & Douaihy, A. (2013). *Journal of the American Academy of Child and Adolescent Psychiatry, 52*(12), 1260–1271.

Breuer, J., & Freud, S. (1955). Studies on hysteria. In J. Strachey (Ed. & Trans.), *The standard edition of the complete psychological works of Sigmund Freud* (Vol. 2, pp. 1–10). London: Hogarth Press. (Original work published 1895)

Breux, C., & Ryujin, D. H. (1999). Use of mental health services by ethnically diverse groups within the United States. *Clinical Psychologist, 52,* 4–15.

Brewi, B. (Speaker). (1986). *Crisis intervention with the Vietnam veteran* (Cassette recording No. 9). Memphis, TN: Department of Counseling and Personnel Services, Memphis State University.

Brewin, C. (2003). *Posttraumatic stress disorder: Myth or malady.* New Haven, CT: Yale University Press.

Brewin, C. (2005). Risk factor effect sizes in PTSD: What this means for intervention. *Journal of Trauma and Dissociation, 6*(2), 123–130.

Brewington, J. O., Nassar-McMillan, S., Flowers, C. P., & Furr, S. R. (2004). A preliminary investigation of factors associated with job loss grief. *Career Development Quarterly, 53*(1), 78–83.

Brewster, M. P. (2002). Domestic violence theories, research, and practice implications. In A. R. Roberts (Ed.), *Handbook of domestic violence: Intervention strategies* (pp. 23–48). New York: Oxford University Press.

Briere, J. (1995). *Trauma Symptom Inventory.* Odessa, FL: Psychological Assessment Resources.

Briere, J. (1996). *Trauma Checklist for Children.* Odessa, FL: Psychological Assessment Resources.

Briere, J. (2005). *Trauma Checklist for Young Children.* Odessa, FL: Psychological Assessment Resources.

Briere, J., & Conte, J. (1993). Self-reported amnesia for abuse in adults molested as children. *Journal of Traumatic Stress, 6,* 21–31.

Briere, J., & Runtz, M. (1987). Post sexual abuse trauma: Data and implications for clinical practice. *Journal of Interpersonal Violence, 2,* 367–379.

Briere, J., & Runtz, M. (1988). Symptomatology associated with childhood sexual victimization in a nonclinical adult sample. *Child Abuse and Neglect, 12,* 51–59.

Briere, J., & Runtz, M. (1993). Childhood sexual abuse: Long-term sequelae and implications for psychological assessment. *Journal of Interpersonal Violence, 8,* 312–330.

Briere, J., & Scott, C. (2006). *Principles of trauma therapy: A guide to symptoms, evaluation, and treatment.* Thousand Oaks, CA: Sage.

Brittain, D. E., & Merriam, K. (1988). Groups for significant others of survivors of child sexual abuse: A report of methods and findings. *Journal of Interpersonal Violence, 3,* 90–101.

Britton, P. C., Bossarte, R. M., Thompson, C., Kemp, J., & Conner, K. R. (2013). Influence on call outcomes among veteran caller to the National Veterans Crisis Line. *Suicide and Life-Threatening Behavior, 43*(5), 494–502.

Britton, P. J. (2001). Guidelines for counseling clients with HIV spectrum disorders. In E. R. Welfel & R. E. Ingersoll (Eds.), *The mental health desk reference* (pp. 60–66). New York: John Wiley & Sons.

Brock, S. E., Nickerson, A. B., Reeves, M. A., Savage, T. A., & Woitaszewski, S. A. (2011). Development, evaluation, and future directions of the PREPaRE school crisis prevention and intervention training curriculum. *Journal of School Violence, 10,* 34–52.

Brock, S. E., Sandoval, J., & Hart, S. (2006). Suicidal ideation and behaviors. In G. Bear & K. Minke (Eds.), *Children's needs III: Development, prevention and intervention* (pp. 225–238). Washington, DC: National Association of School Psychologists.

Brock, S. E., Sandoval, J., & Lewis, S. (1996). *Preparing for crisis in the schools.* Brandon, VT: Clinical Psychology.

Brockian, N. R. (2002). *New hope for people with borderline personality disorder: Your friendly, authoritative guide to the latest in traditional and complementary solutions.* Roseville, CA: Prima Publishing.

Brockopp, G. W. (1973a). The covert cry for help. In D. Lester & G. W. Brockopp (Eds.), *Crisis intervention and counseling by telephone* (pp. 193–198). Springfield, IL: Charles C Thomas.

Brockopp, G. W. (1973b). The nuisance caller. In D. Lester & G. W. Brockopp (Eds.), *Crisis intervention and counseling by telephone* (pp. 206–210). Springfield, IL: Charles C Thomas.

Brockopp, G. W. (2002a). The therapeutic management of the chronic caller. In D. Lester & G. W. Brockopp (Eds.), *Crisis intervention and counseling by telephone* (2nd ed., pp. 159–164). Springfield, IL: Charles C Thomas.

Brockopp, G. W. (2002b). Working with the silent caller. In D. Lester & G. W. Brockopp (Eds.), *Crisis intervention and counseling by telephone* (2nd ed., pp. 182–186). Springfield, IL: Charles C Thomas.

Brockopp, G. W., & Lester, D. (2002). The chronic caller. In D. Lester & G. W. Brockopp (Eds.), *Crisis intervention and counseling by telephone* (2nd ed., pp. 154–167). Springfield, IL: Charles C Thomas.

Brom, D., & Kleber, R. J. (1989). Prevention of posttraumatic stress disorders. *Journal of Traumatic Stress, 2,* 335–351.

Brom, D., Kleber, R. J., & Defares, P. B. (1989). Brief psychotherapy for posttraumatic stress disorders. *Journal of Consulting and Clinical Psychology, 57*, 607–612.

Bromet, E. J. (1995). Methodological issues in designing research on community-wide disasters with special reference to Chernobyl. In S. E. Hobfoll & M. W. de Vries (Eds.), *Extreme stress and communities: Impact and intervention* (pp. 307–324). Dordrecht, Netherlands: Kluwer.

Bronfenbrenner, U. (1986). Ecology of the family as a context for human development: Research perspectives. *Developmental Psychology, 22*, 723–742.

Bronfenbrenner, U. (1995). Developmental ecology through space and time: A future perspective. In P. Moen, G. H. Elder, Jr., & K. Luscher (Eds.), *Examining lives in context: Perspectives on the ecology of human development* (pp. 619–647). Washington, DC: American Psychological Association.

Bronfenbrenner, U., & Morris, P. A. (1998). The ecology of developmental processes. In W. Damon & R. M. Lerner (Eds.), *Handbook of child psychology* (5th ed., Vol. 1, pp. 993–1028). New York: John Wiley & Sons.

Brooker, D., & Duce, L. (2000). Well-being and activity in dementia: A comparison of group reminiscence therapy, structured goal-directed group activity and unstructured time. *Aging and Mental Health, 4*(4), 354–358.

Brooks, J. D., & Martinez, C. (1999). Animals as neglected members of the family in studies of death and dying. In B. De Vries (Ed.), *End of life issues: Interdisciplinary and multidimensional perspectives* (pp. 167–179). New York: Springer.

Brown, A., Marquis, A., & Guiffrida, D. (2013). Mindfulness-based interventions in counseling. *Journal of Counseling and Development, 91*(1), 96–104

Brown, D. (2009). Assessment of attachment and abuse history, and adult attachment style. In C. A. Courtois & J. D. Ford (Eds.), *Treating complex traumatic stress disorders* (pp. 124–144). New York: Guilford Press.

Brown, E. B. (1988). *Sunrise tomorrow: Coping with a child's death.* Grand Rapids, MI: Baker Bookhouse.

Brown, E. B. (1999). *Loss, change and grief: An educational perspective.* London: David Fulton.

Brown, E. J., & Bobrow, A. L. (2004). School entry after a community-wide trauma: Challenges and lessons learned from September 11, 2001. *Clinical Child and Family Psychology Review, 7*(4), 211–221.

Brown, G. K., Wenzel, A., & Rudd, M. D. (2011) Cognitive therapy for suicidal patients. In K. Michel & D. A. Jobes (Eds.), *Building a therapeutic alliance with the suicidal patient* (pp. 273–292). Washington, DC: American Psychological Association.

Brown, J., James, K., & Taylor, A. (2010). Caught in the rejection abuse cycle: Are we really treating perpetrators of domestic abuse effectively? *Journal of Family Therapy, 32*(3), 280–307.

Brown, L. (2008). *Cultural competence in trauma therapy.* Washington, DC: American Psychological Association.

Brown, L. (2009). *Cultural competence in trauma therapy: Beyond the flashback.* Washington, DC: American Psychological Association.

Brown, R. (2012, October 10). New Orleans limits hurricane themed excursions. *New York Times.* Retrieved from http://www.nytimes.com/2012/10/12/us/new-orleaqns-limits-hurricane-excursion

Brown, R., Bute, S., & Ford, P. (1986). *Social workers at risk: Management of violence.* London: Macmillan.

Brown, S., & Manning, W. (2009). Family boundary ambiguity and the measurement of family structure. *Demography, 46*, 85–102.

Browne, A. (1997). Violence in marriage: Until death do us part? In A. P. Cardarelli (Ed.), *Violence between intimate partners: Patterns, causes, and effects* (pp. 48–69). Needham Heights, MA: Allyn & Bacon.

Browne, A., & Finkelhor, D. (2000). Impact of child sexual abuse. In A. C. Donnelly & K. Oates (Eds.), *Classic papers in child abuse* (pp. 217–238). Thousand Oaks, CA: Sage.

Browne, K., & Herbert, M. (1997). *Preventing family violence.* Chichester, England: John Wiley & Sons.

Brownmiller, S. (1975). *Against our will: Men, women, and rape.* New York: Simon & Schuster.

Bruce, M. L., & Kim, K. M. (1992). Differences in the effects of divorce on major depression in men and women. *American Journal of Psychiatry, 149*, 914–917.

Brummert-Lennings, H., & Warburton, W. A. (2011). The effect of auditory versus visual violent media exposure on aggressive behavior. *Journal of Experimental Social Psychology, 47*(4), 794–799.

Bryan, C. J., & Rudd, M. D. (2006). Advances in the assessment of suicide risk. *Journal of Clinical Psychology, 62*, 185–200.

Bryant, R., & Harvery, A. (2000). *Acute stress disorder: A handbook of theory, assessment and treatment.* Washington, DC: American Psychological Association.

Bryant, R., Moulds, M., Guthrie, R., Dang, S., & Nixon, R. (2003). Imaginal exposure alone and imaginal exposure with cognitive restructuring in treatment of posttraumatic stress disorder. *Journal of Consulting and Clinical Psychology, 71*(4), 706–712.

Bryant, R. A., & Harvey, A. G. (2000). Telephone crisis intervention skills: A simulated caller paradigm. *Crisis, 21*(2), 90–94.

Bryant-Davis, T. (2010). Cultural consideration of trauma: Physical mental and social correlates of intimate partner violence exposure. *Psychological Trauma: Theory, Research, Practice, and Policy, 2*(4), 263–266.

Brymer, M., Jacobs, A., Layne, C., Pynoos, R., Ruzek, J., Steinberg, A., Vernberg, E., & Watson, P. (2006). National Child Traumatic Stress Network and National Center for PTSD. *Psychological First Aid: Field Operations Guide* (2nd ed.). Retrieved from www.nctsn.org and www.ncptsd.va.gov

Brymer, M. J., Steinberg, A. M., Vernberg, E. M., Laynes, C. M., Watson, P. J., Jacobs, S. A., et al. (2009). Acute interventions for children and adolescents. In E. Foa, T. Keane, M. Friedman, & J. Cohen (Eds.), *Effective treatments for PTSD* (2nd ed., pp. 106–116). New York: Oxford University Press.

Buchanan, D., Moorhouse, A., Cabaico, L., Krock, M., Campbell, H., & Spevakow, D. (2002). A critical review and synthesis of literature on reminiscing with older adults. *Canadian Journal of Nursing Research/Revue, 34*(3), 123–139.

Buchbinder, E., & Eisikovits, Z. (2003). Battered women's entrapment in shame: A phenomenological study. *American Journal of Orthopsychiatry, 73*(4), 355–366.

Buckley, T., McKinley, S., Tofler, G., & Bartrop, R. (2010). Cardiovascular risk in early bereavement: A literature review and proposed mechanisms. *International Journal of Nursing Studies, 47*(2), 229–238.

Bucolo, D. (2011). Violent video game exposure and physical aggression in adolescence: Test of the general aggression model. *Dissertation Abstracts International: Section B, The Sciences and Engineering,* 5180.

Buhr, G. T., Kuchibhatla, M., & Clipp, E. C. (2006). Caregivers' reasons for nursing home placement: Clues for improving discussions with families prior to the transition. *The Gerontologist, 46*, 52–61.

Burcky, W., Reuterman, N., & Kopsky, S. (1988). Dating violence among high school students. *School Counselor, 35*, 353–358.

Bureau of Justice Statistics. (2003). U.S. Department of Justice. *Crime characteristics 2002*. Washington, DC: U.S. Department of Justice.

Burgess, A. W., & Holmstrom, L. L. (1985). Rape trauma syndrome and post-traumatic stress response. In A. W. Burgess (Ed.), *Rape and sexual assault: A research handbook* (pp. 56–60). New York: Garland.

Burgess, N., Christensen, H., Leach, L., Farrer, L., & Griffiths, K. (2008). Mental health profile of callers to a telephone counseling service. *Journal of Telemedicine and Telecare, 14*(1), 42–47.

Burgess-Watson, I. P., Hoffman, L., & Wilson, G. V. (1988). The neuropsychiatry of post-traumatic stress disorder. *British Journal of Psychiatry, 152*, 164–173.

Burke, R. J., & Greenglass, E. R. (1995). A longitudinal examination of the Cherniss model of psychological burnout. *Social Science and Medicine, 40*, 1357–1363.

Burnham, B. (2011). Schoolwide bully prevention. *ASCA School Counselor, 48*(6), 13–17.

Burnham, J., Wright, V., & Houser, R. (2010, July). *Reduce cyberbullying with virtual world scenarios*. American School Counselor Conference, Boston.

Burrow-Sanchez, J. J., Call, M. E., Zheng, R., & Drew, C. (2011). How school counselors can prevent online victimization. *Journal of Counseling and Development, 89*(1), 3–10.

Burry, C. L. (2002). Working with potentially violent clients in their homes: What child welfare professionals need to know. *Clinical Supervisor, 21*(1), 145–153.

Burt, M. R. (1998). Rape myths. In M. E. Odem & J. Clay-Warner (Eds.), *Confronting rape and sexual assault* (pp. 93–108). Wilmington, DE: Scholarly Resources.

Butler, C. S., & Lagoni, L. S. (1996). Children and pet loss. In C. A. Corr & D. M. Corr (Eds.), *Handbook of childhood death and bereavement* (pp. 179–200). New York: Springer.

Butler, R. (1963). The life review: An interpretation of reminiscence in the aged. *Psychiatry, 26*, 65–76.

Butryn, T. M. (2003). Wrestling with manhood: Boys, bullying, and battering. *Sport Psychologist, 17*(4), 487–489.

Buttell, F., & Hamel, J. (2014, July). *Goodness of fit of the Duluth Model for LGBT and ethnic minority batterers: Is there any evidence?* International Family Violence and Child Victimization Research Conference, Portsmouth, NH.

Butts, S. (Speaker). (1996). *Therapeutic techniques, marriage and family therapy* (Cassette Recording No. 7640-96). Memphis, TN: Department of Counseling, Educational Psychology and Research, University of Memphis.

Butz, M. R. (1995, October). Chaos theory, philosophically old, scientifically new. *Counseling and Values, 39*, 84–98.

Butz, M. R. (1997). *Chaos and complexity: Implications for psychological theory and practice*. Washington, DC: Taylor & Francis.

Buydens, S. L., Wilensky, M., & Hensley, B. J. (2014). Effects of the EMDR protocol for recent traumatic events on acute stress disorder: A case series. *Journal of EMDR Practice and Research, 8*(1), 2–12.

C

Cable, D. G. (1996). Grief counseling for survivors of traumatic loss. In K. J. Doka (Ed.), *Living with grief after sudden loss: Suicide, homicide, accident, heart attack, stroke* (pp. 117–126). Washington, DC: Hospice Foundation of America.

Cain, A., & Fast, I. (1966). Children's disturbed reactions to parent suicide. *American Journal of Orthopsychiatry, 36*, 17–32

Calam, R., Cox, A., Glasgow, D., Jimmieson, P., & Larsen, S. G. (2000). Assessment and therapy with children: Can computers help? *Clinical Child Psychology and Psychiatry, 5*(3), 329–343.

Calhoun, L. G., & Tedeschi, R. G. (1998). *Posttraumatic growth: Future directions*. Mahwah, NJ: Erlbaum.

Calhoun, L. G., & Tedeschi, R. G. (2001). Posttraumatic growth: The positive lessons of loss. In R. A. Neimeyer (Ed.), *Meaning reconstruction and the experience of loss* (pp. 157–172). Washington, DC: American Psychological Association.

California Department of Education. (2002). *Safe Schools: A planning guide for action*. Sacramento, CA: Author.

California Occupational Safety and Health Administration. (1998). *Guidelines of security and safety of health care and community service workers*. Sacramento, CA: Author.

California State Auditor. (2006). *Batterer intervention program: County probation departments could improve compliance with state law, but progress in batterer accountability also depends on the courts*. Sacramento, CA: Author.

Call, J. A., Pfefferbaum, B., Jenuwine, M. J., & Flynn, B. W. (2012). Practical legal and ethical considerations for the provision of acute disaster mental health services. *Psychiatry, 75*, 305–322.

Callahan, C. J. (2001). Protecting and counseling gay and lesbian students. *Journal of Humanistic Counseling, Education and Development, 40*(1), 5–10.

Callahan, J. (1998). Crisis theory and crisis intervention in emergencies. In P. M. Kleespies (Ed.), *Emergencies in mental health: Evaluation and management* (pp. 22–40). New York: Guilford Press.

Callahan, J. (2009). Emergency intervention and crisis intervention. In P. M. Kleespies (Ed.), *Behavioral emergencies: An evidence-based resource for evaluating and managing risk of suicide, violence, and victimization* (pp. 13–32). Washington, DC: American Psychological Association.

Callahan, R. (2011, September 16). Sept. 11 panelists still see threats. *Memphis Commercial Appeal*, A3.

Callanan, V. J., & Davis, M. S. (2009). A comparison of suicide note writers with suicides who did not leave notes. *Suicide and Life-Threatening Behavior, 39*(5), 558–568.

Camelley, K. B., Wortman, C. B., Bolger, N., & Burke, D. T. (2006). The time course of grief reactions to spousal loss: Evidence from a national probability sample. *Journal of Personality and Social Psychology, 91*(3), 476–492.

Cameron, C. (1994). Women survivors confronting their abusers: Issues, decisions, and outcomes. *Journal of Child Sexual Abuse, 3*(1), 7–35.

Campbell, C. L., McCoy, S., Burg, M. A., & Hoffman, N. (2014). Enhancing home health care staff safety through reducing client aggression and violence in noninstitutional care settings: A systematic review. *Home Health Care Management and Practice, 26*(1), 3–10.

Campbell, F. R. (2011). Baton Rouge Crisis Intervention Center's LOSS Team Active Postvention Model approach. In J. R. Jordan & J. L. McIntosh (Eds.), *Grief after suicide: Understanding the consequences and caring for the survivors* (pp. 327–332). New York: Routledge/Taylor & Francis Group.

Campbell, J. C. (1989). A test of two explanatory models of women's responses to battering. *Nursing Research, 38*, 18–24.

Campbell, R., Patterson, D., & Lichty, L. F. (2005). The effectiveness of sexual assault nurse examiner (SANE) programs: A review of psychological, medical, legal, and community outcomes. *Trauma, Violence, and Abuse, 6*(4), 313–329.

Cann, A., Calhoun, L., Tedeschi, R., Triplett, K., Vishnevsky, T., & Lindstrom, C. (2011). Assessing posttraumatic cognitive processes: The Event-Related Rumination Inventory. *Anxiety, Stress, and Coping: An International Journal, 24*(2), 137–156.

Cann, A., Calhoun, L., Tedeschi, R. Taku, K., Vishnevsky, T., Triplett, K., et al. (2010). A short form of the Posttraumatic Growth Inventory. *Anxiety, Stress, and Coping: An International Journal, 23*(2), 127–137.

Canter, L., & Canter, E. (1982). *Assertive discipline for parents.* Santa Monica, CA: Canter Associates.

Cantor, C. H. (2000). Suicide in the western world. In K. Hawton & K. Van Heeringen (Eds.), *The international handbook of suicide and attempted suicide* (pp. 9–28). Chichester, England: John Wiley & Sons.

Caplan, G. (1961). *An approach to community mental health.* New York: Grune & Stratton.

Caplan, G. (1964). *Principles of preventive psychiatry.* New York: Basic Books.

Cappeliez, P., & Watt, L. (2005). L'integrazione della retrospettiva di vita e della terapia cognitiva della depressione con le persone anziane. *Piscioterpaia Cognitiva e Comportamentale, 11*(2), 151–164.

Capps, M. (1982, April). *The co-optive and repressive state versus the battered women's movement.* Paper presented at annual meeting of Southern Sociological Society, Memphis, TN.

Capuzzi, D. (2002). Legal and ethical challenges in counseling suicidal students. *Professional School Counselor, 6*(1), 36–45.

Capuzzi, D. (2009). *Suicide prevention in the schools: Guidelines for middle and high school settings.* Alexandria, VA: American Counseling Association.

Capuzzi, D., & Gross, D. R. (Eds.). (1995). *Counseling and psychotherapy: Theories and interventions.* Upper Saddle River, NJ: Prentice Hall.

Carden, A. D. (1994). Wife abuse and the wife abuser: Review and recommendations. *Counseling Psychologist, 22,* 539–582.

Carey, L. (Ed.). (2006). *Expressive and creative methods for trauma survivors.* London: Kingsley.

Carkhuff, R. R. (1987). *The art of helping* (6th ed.). Amherst, MA: Human Resource Development Press.

Carkhuff, R. R., & Berenson, B. G. (1977). *Beyond counseling and therapy* (2nd ed.). New York: Holt, Rinehart & Winston.

Carney, J. (2008). Perceptions of bullying and associated trauma in adolescence. *Professional School Counseling, 11*(3), 179–187.

Carney, J., Hazler, R., Higgins, J., & Danser, S. (1999, April). *Peer-on-peer violence.* Poster session at the American Counseling Association World Conference, San Diego.

Carrado, M., George, M., Loxam, E., Jones, L., & Templar, D. (1996). Aggression in British heterosexual relationships: A descriptive analysis. *Aggressive Behavior, 22,* 401–415.

Carroll, J. F. X., & White, W. L. (1982). Theory building: Integrating individual and environmental factors within an ecological framework. In W. S. Paine (Ed.), *Job stress and burnout* (pp. 41–60). Newbury Park, CA: Sage.

Carroll, J. S., Olson, C. D., & Buckmiller, N. (2007). Family boundary ambiguity: A 30-year review of theory, research, and measurement. *Family Relations, 56,* 2120–2130.

Carter, S. R. (1987). Use of puppets to treat traumatic grief. *Elementary School Guidance and Counseling, 21,* 210–215.

Caserta, M., Lund, D., Utz, R., & de Vries, B. (2009). Stress-related growth among the recently bereaved. *Aging and Mental Health, 13*(3), 463–476.

Casey, G. W. (2011). Comprehensive soldier fitness: A vision for psychological resilience in the U.S. Army. *American Psychologist, 66*(1), 1–3.

Cass, A., & Mallicoat, S. (2015). College student perceptions of victim action: Will targets of stalking report to police? *American Journal of Criminal Justice, 40*(2), 250–269.

Cassinerio, C., & Lane-Garon, P. (2006). Changing school climate one mediator at a time: Year-one analysis of a school-based mediation program. *Conflict Resolution Quarterly, 23*(4), 447–460.

Castelnuovo, G., Gaggioli, A., Mantovani, F., & Riva, G. (2003). New and old tools in psychotherapy: The use of technology for the integration of traditional clinical treatments. *Psychotherapy: Theory, Research, Practice, Training, 40*(1/2), 33–44.

Castro, W., Sanchez, M., Gonzalez, C., Bethencourt, J., de la Fuente Portero, J., & Marco, R. (2014). Cognitive behavioral treatment and anti-depressants combined with virtual reality exposure for patients with chronic agoraphobia. *International Journal of Clinical and Health Psychology, 14*(1), 9–17.

Cattanach, A. (2008). Working creatively with children and their families after trauma: The storied life. In C. A. Malchiodi (Ed.), *Creative interventions with traumatized children* (pp. 211–225). New York: Guilford Press.

Cautela, J. R. (1976). The present status of covert modeling. *Journal of Behavior Therapy and Experimental Psychiatry, 6,* 323–326.

Cavanaugh, M. M., & Gelles, R. J. (2005). The utility of male domestic violence offender typologies: New directions for research, policy, and practice. *Journal of Interpersonal Violence, 20*(2), 155–165.

Cavezza, C., & McEwan, T. (2014). Cyberstalking versus off-line stalking in a forensic sample. *Psychology, Crime, and Law, 20*(10), 955–970.

Cawood, J. S., & Corcoran, M. H. (2009). *Violence assessment and intervention: The practitioner's handbook* (2nd ed.). Boca Raton, FL: CRC Press/Taylor & Francis.

Center for Homeland Defense and Security. (2015). *Colleges and universities offering homeland security programs.* Retrieved from www.chds.us/?partners/institutions

Center for Research on the Epidemiology of Disasters. (2014). *Executive summary.* Retrieved from www.disaster.ir/files/ADSR_2013.pdf

Centers for Disease Control (CDC). (n.d.). *Podcasts at CDC.* Retrieved September 16, 2011, from www.2c.cdc.gov/podcasts

Centers for Disease Control. (2001). *Surveillance of homicides among intimate partners—United States, 1981–1998.* Atlanta, GA: Author.

Centers for Disease Control. (2002). *Adolescent health survey.* Atlanta, GA: U.S. Department of Health and Human Services, Public Health Service.

Centers for Disease Control and Prevention. (2008). *Suicide and self-inflicted injury.* Retrieved from www.cdc.gov/nchs/fastats/suicide.html

Centers for Disease Control and Prevention. (2015a). *Suicide prevention.* Atlanta, GA: U.S. Department of Health and Human Services, Public Health Service. Retrieved from http://www.cdc.gov/injury/wisqars/pdf/leading_causes_of_death_by_age_group_2013-a.pdf

Centers for Disease Control and Prevention. (2015b). *Suicide prevention: Youth suicide.* Atlanta, GA: U.S. Department of Health and Human Services, Public Health Service. Retrieved from http://www.cdc.gov/ViolencePrevention/pub/youth_suicide.html

CERT. (2011). *Community Emergency Response Team training manual module 7: Psychological first aid.* Retrieved from www.citizencorps.gov/cert/training_mat.shtm.#CERTIG_IG_unit7_Jan2011-3.doc

Chalk, R., & King, P. A. (Eds.). (1998). *Violence in families: Assessing prevention and treatment programs.* Washington, DC: National Academy Press.

Chamberlain, L. (1993, August). *Strange attractors in patterns of family interactions.* Paper presented at the Annual Convention of the American Psychological Association, Toronto.

Chamberlain, L. (1994, August). *Is there a chaotician in the house? Chaos and family therapy.* Paper presented at the Annual Convention of the American Psychological Association, Los Angeles.

Chamberlin, J. (2006). Cyberbullies increasingly target peers online. *Monitor on Psychology, 37*(9), 17.

Chandra, A., Burns, R. M., Tanielian, T., Jaycox, L. H., & Scott, M. M. (2008). *Understanding the impact of deployment on children and families: Findings from a pilot study of Operation Purple Camp participants* (Working paper). Santa Monica, CA: Rand Corporation.

Chang, J. C., Decker, M. R., Moracco, K. E., Martin, S. L., Petersen, R., & Frasier, P. (2005). Asking about intimate partner violence: Advice from female survivors to healthcare providers. *Patient Education and Counseling, 59*, 141–147.

Chapman, L. (2014). *Neurobiologically informed trauma therapy with children and adolescents: Understanding mechanisms of change.* New York: W. W. Norton.

Chapman, L., Morabito, D., Ladakakos, C., Schreier, H., & Knudson, M. (2001). The effectiveness of art therapy interventions in reducing posttraumatic stress disorder (PTSD) symptoms in pediatric trauma patients. *Art Therapy, 18*(2), 100–104.

Charach, A., Pepler, D., & Zeigler, S. (1995). Bullying at school—A Canadian perspective: A survey of problems and suggestions for intervention. *Education Canada, 35*(1), 12–18.

Chard, K. M., & Gilman, R. (2014). Cognitive processing therapy with adolescents. In R. M. Reece, R. F. Hanson, & J. Sargents (Eds.), *Treatment of child abuse: Common ground for mental health, medical and legal practitioners* (2nd ed., pp. 148–153). Baltimore, MD: Johns Hopkins University Press.

Charles-Edwards, D. (2009). Introduction to the special section on death, loss, and work. *Death Studies, 33*(5), 399–401.

Charlton, P. F. C., & Thompson, J. A. (1996). Ways of coping with psychological distress after trauma. *British Journal of Psychology, 35*, 517–530.

Charney, A. M., & Pearlman, L. A. (1998). The ecstasy and the agony: The impact of disaster and trauma work on the self of the clinician. In P. M. Kleespies (Ed.), *Emergencies in mental health practice: Evaluation and management* (pp. 418–435). New York: Guilford Press.

Chatham, P. M. (1989). *Treatment of the borderline personality.* Northvale, NJ: Aronson.

Chavez, L. (1999). *Workplace violence awareness for managers and supervisors.* Internet course. Retrieved May 3, 2003, from members.aol.com/hrtrainer/defuse.html

Chemtob, C., Nakashima, J., & Carlson, J. (2002). Brief treatment for elementary school children with disaster -related posttraumatic stress disorder: A field study. *Journal of Clinical Psychology, 58*(1), 99–112.

Chemtob, C. M. (2000). Delayed debriefing after a disaster. In B. Raphael & J. P. Wilson (Eds.), *Psychological debriefing: Theory, practice, and evidence* (pp. 227–240). New York: Cambridge University Press.

Chemtob, C. M. (2000). Delayed debriefing after a disaster. In B. Raphael & J. P. Wilson (Eds.), *Psychological debriefing: Theory, practice, and evidence* (pp. 227–240). New York: Cambridge University Press.

Chemtob, C. M., Nakashima, J. P., & Hamada, R. S. (2002). Psychosocial intervention for postdisaster trauma symptoms in elementary school children: A controlled community field study. *Archives of Pediatric and Adolescent Medicine, 156*, 211–216.

Chen, H., Bersani, C., Myers, S. C., & Denton, R. (1989). Evaluating the effectiveness of a court sponsored abuser treatment program. *Journal of Family Violence, 4*, 309–322.

Chen, J., Dunne, M., & Wang, X. (2003). Childhood sexual abuse: An investigation among 239 male high school students. *Chinese Mental Health Journal, 17*(5), 345–347.

Chen, S. O., & Mak, W. S. (2008). Seeking professional help: Etiology beliefs about mental health illness across cultures. *Journal of Counseling Psychology, 55*(4), 442–450.

Cheng, A. T., & Lee, C. (2000). Suicide in Asia and the Far East. In K. Hawton & K. Van Heeringen (Eds.), *The international handbook of suicide and attempted suicide* (pp. 29–48). Chichester, England: John Wiley & Sons.

Chermack, S. T., Fuller, B., & Blow, F. (2000). Predictors of expressed partner and non-partner violence among patients in substance abuse treatment. *Drug and Alcohol Dependence, 58*(1–2), 43–54.

Cherniss, C., & Krantz, D. L. (1983). The ideological community as an antidote to burnout in the human services. In B. A. Farber (Ed.), *Stress and burnout in the human service professions* (pp. 198–212). New York: Pergamon Press.

Chiang, W. (2012). The effects of the telephone crisis service helpers' interventions on non-suicidal, suicidal, acute suicidal callers in Taiwan: An efficacy study. *Dissertation Abstracts International: Section B: The Sciences and Engineering, 72*(11-B), 7107.

Chiles, J. A., & Strosahl, K. D. (1995). *The suicidal patient: Principles of assessment, treatment, and case management.* Washington, DC: American Psychiatric Press.

Chiu, L., Stewart, K., Woo, C., & Yatham, L., & Lam, R. (2015). The relationship between burnout and depressive symptoms in patients with depressive disorders. *Journal of Affective Disorders, 172*(1), 361–366.

Cho, J., Kang, D. R., Moon, K., Suh, M., Kyoung, H., Kim., C., . . . Jung, S. (2013). Age and gender differences in medical care utilization prior to suicide. *Journal of Affective Disorders, 146*(2), 181–188.

Choudhary, E., Coben, J., & Bossarte, R. M. (2010). Adverse health outcomes, perpetrator characteristics, and sexual violence victimization among U.S. adult males. *Journal of Interpersonal Violence, 25*(8), 1523–1541.

Christensen, D. R., Landes, R. D., Jackson, L., Marsch, L. A., Mancino, M., Chopra, M., & Bickel, W. K. (2014). Adding an Internet-delivered treatment to an efficacious treatment package for opioid dependence. *Journal of Consulting and Clinical Psychology, 82*(6), 964–972.

Christogiorgos, S., Vassilopoulou, V., Florou, A., Xydou, V., Douvou, M., & Vgenopoulou, S. (2010). Telephone counseling with adolescents and counter-transference phenomena: Particularities and challenges. *British Journal of Guidance and Counseling, 38*(3), 313–325.

Chu, J. (1999). Trauma and suicide. In D. G. Jacobs (Ed.), *The Harvard Medical School guide to suicide assessment and intervention* (pp. 332–354). San Francisco: Jossey-Bass.

Chung, M. C., Easthope, Y., Farmer, S., Werrett, J., & Chung, C. (2003). Psychological sequelae: Post-traumatic stress reactions and personality factors among community residents as secondary victims. *Scandinavian Journal of Caring Science, 17*(3), 265–270.

Cicila, L., Georgia, E. J., & Doss, B. D. (2014). Incorporating Internet-based interventions into couple therapy: Available resources and recommended uses. *Australian and New Zealand Journal of Family Therapy, 35*(4), 414–430.

Cienfuegos, A. J., & Monelli, O. (1983). The testimony of political repression as a therapeutic instrument. *American Journal of Orthopsychiatry, 53*, 43–51.

Cieslak, R., Shoji, K., Douglas, A., Melville, E., Luszczynska, A., & Benight, C. (2014). A meta-analysis of the relationship between job burnout and secondary traumatic stress among workers with indirect exposure to trauma. *Psychological Services, 11*(1), 75–86.

CIT International. (2014, October). *Report presented to the general assembly.* CIT International Conference, Monterey, CA.

Clark, J., Hayes, R. L., Hayes, L., Millner, V. S., Sharpe, T., & Waltman, R. (2006). *Transcending trauma after a disaster: A guide for schools* [CD]. Mobile: University of South Alabama and Mobile County Public School System.

Clark, S. C., & McKiernan, W. (1981). Contacts with a Canadian "street level" drug and crisis centre, 1975–1978. *Bulletin on Narcotics, 33,* 23–31.

Classen, C., Pearson, J., Khodyakov, D., Satow, P., Gebbia, R., Berman, A., . . . Insel, T. (2014). Reducing the burden of suicide in the U.S.: The aspirational research goals of the National Action Alliance for Suicide Prevention Research Prioritization Task Force. *American Journal of Preventive Medicine, 47*(3), 309–314.

Clay, R. C. (2010). Treating traumatized children. *Monitor on Psychology, 41*(7), 36–39.

Clemente, M., Reiq-Botella, A., & Coloma, R. (2015). The occupational health of correctional officers in Peru: The impact of length of work experience. *The Prison Journal, 95*(2), 244–263.

Cloitre, M., & Rosenberg, A. (2006). Sexual revictimization: Risk factors and prevention. In V. M. Follette & J. Ruzek (Eds.), *Cognitive behavior therapies for trauma* (pp. 321–361). New York: Guilford Press.

Cloitre, M., Stovall-McClough, K. C., Miranda, R., & Chembtrob, C. M. (2004). Therapeutic alliance, negative mood regulation, and treatment outcome in child abuse–related posttraumatic stress disorder. *Journal of Consulting and Clinical Psychology, 72*(3), 411–416.

Coates, D., & Howe, D. (2014, October). *The design and development of staff well being initiatives: Staff stressors, burnout and emotional exhaustion at children and young people's mental health in Australia.* Sidney, Australia: Administration and Policy in Mental Health Services Research.

Cochran, M., & Niego, S. (2002). Parenting and social networks. In M. H. Bornstein (Ed.), *Handbook of parenting: Vol. 4, Social conditions and applied parenting* (2nd ed., pp. 393–418). Mahwah, NJ: Erlbaum.

Cochran, S. (2014). Basic plays. In Memphis Police Department, *Crisis intervention team training manual* (pp. 45–48). Memphis, TN: Memphis Police Department.

Cogdal, P. A., & James, R. K. (1991, August). *Combinatorial technique to treatment of adult incest survivors.* Paper presented at the American Psychological Association convention, San Francisco.

Cohen, A. (2002). Gestalt therapy and post-traumatic stress disorder: The potential and its (lack of) fulfillment. *Gestalt! 6*(1), 21–28.

Cohen, A. (2003). Gestalt therapy and post traumatic stress disorder: The irony and the challenge. *Gestalt Review, 7*(1), 42–55.

Cohen, A. B. (2009). Many forms of culture. *American Psychologist, 64,* 194–204.

Cohen, D. (2003). Homicide-suicide in older persons: How you can help prevent a tragedy. *Violence and Injury Prevention Program: Homicide/Suicide Prevention and Intervention Resources.* Retrieved November 15, 2003, from http//:www.fmhi.usf.edu/amh/homicide-suicide/art _hs_inolder.html

Cohen, E. (1990). Confidentiality, counseling clients who have AIDS: Ethical foundations of a modern rule. *Journal of Counseling and Development, 66,* 282–286.

Cohen, J., Mannarino, J. A., & Deblinger, E. (2006). *Treating trauma and traumatic grief in children and adolescents.* New York: Guilford Press.

Cohen, J. A., & Mannarino, A. P. (2011). Supporting children with traumatic grief: What educators need to know. *School Psychology International, 32*(2), 117–131.

Cohen, J. A., Mannarino, A. P., & Deblinger, E. (2006). *Treating trauma and traumatic grief in children and adolescents.* New York: Guilford Press.

Cohen, J. A., Mannarino, A. P., & Knudsen, K. (2004). Treating childhood traumatic grief: A pilot study. *Journal of the American Academy of Child and Adolescent Psychiatry, 43,* 1225–1233.

Cohen, J. A., Mannarino, A. P., Greenberg, T., Padlo, S., & Shipley, C. (2002). Childhood trauma and grief: Concepts and controversies. *Trauma, Violence, and Abuse, 3,* 307–327.

Cohen, P., Kasen, S., Chen, H., Gordon, K., Berenson, K., Brook, J., et al. (2006). Current affairs and the public psyche: American anxiety in the post 9/11 world. *Social Psychiatry and Psychiatric Epidemiology, 41*(4), 251–260.

Cohen, P. A., Kulik, J. A., & Kulik, C. C. (1982). Educational outcomes of tutoring. A meta-analysis of findings. *American Educational Research Journal, 19,* 237–248.

Cohen, R. N. (1978). Tarasoff v. Regents of the University of California. The duty to warn: Common law and statutory problems for California psychotherapists. *California Western Law Review, 14,* 153–182.

Cohen, S. (2004). Social relationships and health. *American Psychologist, 59,* 676–684.

Coke-Weatherly, A. (2005). *An analysis of where and how crisis intervention is taught and learned.* Unpublished doctoral dissertation, University of Memphis, Memphis, Tennessee.

Cokley, K. (2007). Critical issues in the measurement of ethnic and racial identity: A referendum on the state of the field. *Journal of Counseling Psychology, 54*(3), 224–234.

Cole, J., Logan, T., & Shannon, L. (2005). Intimate sexual victimization among women with protective orders: Types and associations of physical and mental health problems. *Violence and Victims, 11*(7), 695–715.

Cole, T. B. (2006). Rape at US colleges often fueled by alcohol. *Journal of the American Medical Association, 296*(5), 504–505.

Coleman, F. (1997). Stalking behavior and the cycle of domestic violence. *Journal of Interpersonal Violence, 12,* 420–432.

Colgrove, M., Bloomfield, H. H., & McWilliams, P. (1991). *How to survive the loss of a love.* Los Angeles: Prelude Press.

Collier, C. (1999). *School violence: Facts, causes and recommendations.* Poster session at the American Counseling Association World Conference, San Diego.

Collins, B. G., & Collins, T. M. (2005). *Crisis and trauma: Developmental-ecological intervention.* Lahaska, PA: Lahaska Press.

Collins, S., & Long, A. (2003). Working with the psychological effects of trauma: Consequences for mental health care workers. *Journal of Psychiatric and Mental Health Nursing, 10*(4), 417–424.

Collins, W. L. (2005). Embracing spirituality as an element of professional self-care. *Social Work and Christianity, 32*(3), 263–274.

Collins, W. L., & Doolittle, A. (2006). Personal reflections of funeral rituals and spirituality in a Kentucky African American family. *Death Studies, 30*(10), 957–969.

Coloroso, B. (2003). *The bully, the bullied, and the bystander.* New York: Harper Collins.

Colucci, E. (2013). Culture, culture meanings and suicide. In E. Colucci & D. Lester, (Eds.), *Suicide and culture: Understanding the context* (pp. 25–46). Cambridge MA: Hogrefe.

Comans, T., Visser, V., & Scuffham, P. (2013). Cost effectiveness of a community-based crisis intervention program for people bereaved by suicide. *Crisis: The Journal of Crisis Intervention and Suicide Prevention, 34*(6), 390–397

Como, G., & Bouschard, S. (2015). An innovative positive psychology VR application for victims of sexual violence: A qualitative study. In P. Cipresso & S. Serino (Eds.), *Virtual reality: Technologies, medical applications and challenges: Psychology research progress* (pp. 229–267). Hauppage, NY: Nova Science Publishers.

Compassionate Friends (2015). *Chapter locator*. Retrieved from http://www.compassionatefriends.org/Find_Support/Chapters/Chapter_Locator.aspx

Compassionate Friends. (2007). *Compassionate Friends credo*. Retrieved from https://www.compassionatefriends.org/about_us.aspx

Compton, M. T., Bahore, M., Watson, A. C., & Oliva, J. R. (2008). A comprehensive review of extant research on CIT programs. *American Academy of Psychiatry and the Law, 36*, 47–55.

Compton, M. T., Bakeman, R., Broussard, B., Hankerson- Dyson, D., Husbands, L., Krishan, . . . Watson, A. (2014a). The police based crisis intervention team (CIT) model: I. Effects on officers' knowledge, attitudes, and skills. *Psychiatric Services, 65*(4), 517–522.

Compton, M. T., Bakeman, R., Broussard, B., Hankerson-Dyson, D., Husbands, L., Krishan, S, . . . Watson, A. (2014b). The police based crisis intervention team (CIT) model: II. Effects on level of force and resolution, referral and arrest. *Psychiatric Services, 65*(4), 523–529.

Compton, M. T., Esterberg, M. L., McGee, R., Kotwicki, R. J., & Oliva, J. R. (2006). Crisis Intervention Team training: Changes in knowledge, attitudes, and stigma related to schizophrenia. *Psychiatric Services, 57*(8), 1199–1202.

Confer, J. C., Easton, J. A., Fleischman, D. S., Goetz, C. D., Lewis, D., Perrilloux, C., & Buss, D. M. (2010). Evolutionary psychology: Controversies, questions, prospects, and limitations. *American Psychologist, 65*(2), 110–126.

Congress, E. P. (1996). Family crisis: Life cycle and bolts from the blue: Assessment and treatment. In A. R. Roberts (Ed.), *Crisis management and brief treatment: Theory, technique, and practice* (pp. 142–159). Chicago: Nelson-Hall Publisher.

Congress, E. P. (2000). Crisis intervention with culturally diverse families. In A. E. Roberts (Ed.), *Crisis intervention handbook: Assessment, treatment and research*. New York: Oxford University Press, pp. 430–449.

Conoley, J. C., & Goldstein, A. P. (Eds.). (2004). *School violence intervention: A practical handbook* (2nd ed.). New York: Guilford Press.

Conrad, D., & Kellar-Guenther, Y. (2006). Compassion fatigue, burnout, and compassion satisfaction among Colorado child protection workers. *Child Abuse and Neglect, 30*(10), 1071–1080.

Conroy, K. (1982). Long-term treatment issues with battered women. In J. P. Flanzer & B. Star (Eds.), *The many faces of violence* (pp. 53–75). Springfield, IL: Charles C Thomas.

Conte, C. (2005). *Examination of the reliability and validity of the Triage Assessment Survey: Organizations*. Duquesne University, Pittsburgh, PA.

Conte, J. R., & Schuerman, J. R. (1988). Research with child victims. In G. E. Wyatt & G. J. Powell (Eds.), *Lasting effects of child sexual abuse* (pp. 157–170). Newbury Park, CA: Sage.

Conwell, Y., & Heisel, M. J. (2006). The elderly. In R. I. Simon & R. E. Hales, (Eds.), *The American Psychiatric Publishing textbook of suicide assessment and management* (1st ed., pp. 57–76). Arlington, VA, US: American Psychiatric Publishing.

Conyne, R. K., & Cook, E. P. (2003, March). *Understanding persons within environment: An introduction to ecological counseling*. Program and paper presented at the annual meeting of the American Counseling Association, Anaheim, CA.

Conyne, R. K., Cook, E. P., Wilson, R. F., Tang, M., O'Connell, W. P., McWhirter, B. T., et al. (2003, March). *Ecological counseling: An approach for the 21st century*. Program and paper presented at the annual meeting of the American Counseling Association, Anaheim, CA.

Cook, E. P. (2012). Introduction. In E. P. Cook (Ed.), *Understanding people in context: The ecological perspective in counseling* (pp. 3–11). Alexandria, VA: American Counseling Association.

Cook, P. F., McCabe, M., Emiliozzi, S., & Pointer, L. (2009). Telephone nurse counseling improves HIV medication adherence: An effectiveness study. *JANAC: Journal of the Association of Nurses in AIDS care, 20*(4), 316–325.

Cook, P. F., McCabe, M., Emiliozzi, S., & Pointer, L. (2009). Telephone nurse counseling improves HIV medication adherence: An effectiveness study. *Journal of the Association of Nurses in AIDS Care, 20*(4), 316–325.

Cook, S., Pinazzola, J., Ford, J. D., Lanktreee, C., Blaustein, M., & Cloitre, M. (2005). Complex trauma in children and adolescents. *Psychiatric Annals, 35*, 390–398.

Cook, S. W., Aten, J. D., Moore, M., Hook, J. N., & Davis, D. E. (2013). Resource loss, religiousness, health, and posttraumatic growth following Hurricane Katrina. *Mental Health, Religion and Culture, 16*, 352–366.

Cooley, E. J., & Keesey, J. C. (1981). Relationship between life change and illness in coping versus sensitive persons. *Psychological Reports, 48*, 711–714.

Copeland, N. J. (2000). Brain mechanisms and neurotransmitters. In D. Nutt, H Davidson, J. Zohar (Eds.), *Post traumatic stress disorder: Diagnosis, management and treatment* (pp. 69–100). London: Martin Dunitz.

Corder, B. F., Ball, B. C., Haizlip, T. M., Rollins, R., & Beaumont, R. (1976). Adolescent paracide: A comparison with other adolescent murder. *American Journal of Psychiatry, 133*(8), 957–961.

Corey, G., Corey, M. S., Corey, C., & Callanan, P. (2015). *Issues and ethics in the helping* professions (9th ed.). Stamford, CT: Brooks/Cole, Cengage.

Corey-Souza, P. (2007). Compassion fatigue in members of the Florida Crisis Response Team: A consequence of caring. *Dissertation Abstracts International: Section B. The Sciences and Engineering, 2695.*

Cormier, L. S., & Hackney, H. (1987). *The professional counselor: A process guide to helping*. Upper Saddle River, NJ: Prentice Hall.

Cormier, W. H., & Cormier, L. S. (1985). *Interviewing strategies for helpers: Fundamental skills and cognitive behavioral interventions* (2nd ed.). Pacific Grove, CA: Brooks/Cole.

Cormier, W. H., & Cormier, L. S. (1991). *Interviewing strategies for helpers: Fundamental skills and cognitive behavioral interventions* (3rd ed.). Pacific Grove, CA: Brooks/Cole.

Corneil, W., Beaton, R., Murphy, S., Johnson, C., & Pike, K. (1999). Exposure to traumatic incidents and prevalence of posttraumatic stress symptomatology in urban firefighters in two countries. *Journal of Occupational Health Psychology, 4*(2), 131–141.

Cornille, T. A., & Boroto, D. R. (1992). The family distress model: A conceptual and clinical application of Reiss strong bonds finding. *Contemporary Family Therapy, 14*, 181–198.

Cornille, T. A., Meyer, A. S., Mullis, A. K., Mullis, R. L., & Boroto, D. (2008). The family outreach model: Tolls for engaging and working with families in distress. *Journal of Family Social Work, 11*, 185–201.

Corr, C. A., & Corr, D. M. (1996). *Handbook of childhood death and bereavement*. New York: Springer.

Corvo, K. M., Dutton, S., & Chen, W. (2009). Do Duluth model interventions with perpetrators of domestic violence violate mental health professional ethics? *Ethics and Behavior, 19*(4), 323–340.

Costa, L., & Altekruse, M. (1994). Duty-to-warn guidelines for mental health counselors. *Journal of Counseling and Development, 72,* 346–350.

Costa, L., & Holliday, D. (1994). Helping children cope with the death of a parent. *Elementary School Guidance and Counseling, 28,* 206–213.

Costin, L. B., Karger, H. J., & Stoesz, D. (1996). *The politics of child abuse in America.* New York: Oxford University Press.

Cottone, R. R. (2001). A social-constructivist model of ethical decision making in counseling. *Journal of Counseling and Development, 79*(1), 39–45.

Cottone, R. R., & Claus, R. E. (2000). Ethical decision making models: A review of the literature. *Journal of Counseling and Development, 78,* 275–283.

Cottone, R. R., & Tarvydas, V. M. (1998). *Ethical and professional issues in counseling.* Upper Saddle River, NJ: Pearson/Merrill Prentice-Hall.

Cottone, R. R., & Tarvydas, V. M. (2007). *Counseling ethics and decision making* (3rd ed.). Upper Saddle River, NJ: Pearson/Merrill Prentice-Hall.

Counce, C., & Sommer, L. (2003, June). *Gentle guidance eases grief.* Paper presented at the American School Counselor Conference, St. Louis, MO.

Council for Accreditation of Counseling & Related Educational Programs. (2009). *CACREP 2009 standards and procedures manual.* Retrieved from http://www.cacrep.org/template/page

Courtois, C. A. (1988). *Healing the incest wound: Adult survivors in therapy.* New York: W. W. Norton.

Courtois, C. A. (1991, August 16). *The self-destructive person and the suicidal bind.* Paper presented at the 99th Annual Convention of the American Psychological Association, San Francisco.

Courtois, C. A. (1999). *Recollections of sexual abuse: Treatment principles and guidelines.* New York: W. W. Norton.

Courtois, C. A. (2001). Implications of the memory controversy for clinical practice: An overview of treatment recommendations and guidelines. *Journal of Child Sexual Abuse, 9*(3/4), 183–210.

Courtois, C. A. (2015). First, do no harm: Ethics of attending to spiritual issues in trauma treatment. In D. F. Walker, C. A. Courtois, & J. Aten (Eds.), *Spiritually oriented psychotherapy for trauma* (pp. 55–76). Washington, DC: American Psychological Association.

Courtois, C. A., & Ford, J. D. (2009). *Treating complex traumatic stress disorder.* New York: Guilford Press.

Courtois, C. A., & Gold, S. N. (2009). The need for inclusion of psychological trauma in the professional curriculum: A call to action. *Psychological Trauma: Theory, Research, Practice, and Policy, 1,* 3–25.

Courtois, C. A., Ford, J. D., & Cloitre, M. (2009). Best practices in psychotherapy for adults. In C. A. Courtois & J. D. Ford (Eds.), *Treating complex traumatic stress disorders: An evidence-based guide* (pp. 82–103). New York: Guilford Press.

Cowan, D. S. (2010). Death of a friend during childhood. In C. A. Corr & D. E. Balk (Eds.), *Children's encounters with death, bereavement, and coping* (pp. 219–236). New York: Springer.

Cowan, P. A., & Cowan, C. P. (2012). Normative family transitions, couple relationships, and healthy child development. In S. J. Price, C. A. Price, & P. C. McKenry (Eds.), *Families and change: Coping with stressful events and transitions* (pp. 428–451). Los Angeles: Sage.

Craft, S. M., Serovich, J. M., McKenry, P. C., & Lim, J. (2008). Stress, attachment style, and partner violence among same sex couples. *Journal of GLBT Family Issues, 4*(1), 57–73.

Cramer, S. H., Keitel, M. A., & Zevon, M. A. (1990). Spouses of cancer patients: A review of the literature. *Journal of Counseling and Development, 69,* 163–166.

Crase, D. (1994). Important consumer issues surrounding death. *Thanatos, 19*(1), 22–26.

Crenshaw, D. A., & Lee, J. (2010). The disenfranchised grief of children. In N. B. Webb (Ed.), *Helping bereaved children: A handbook for practitioners* (3rd ed., pp. 91–108). New York: Guilford Press.

Crews, W. (1998). *Memphis Police Department procedures manual for school police officers.* Memphis, TN.

Crisis textline. (2015). Retrieved from www.crisistextline.org/get-help-now

Crosswhite, J., Rice, D., & Asay, S. (2014). Texting among United States young adults: An exploratory study on texting and its use within families. *The Social Science Journal, 51*(1), 70–78.

Crothers, L. M., & Levinson, E. M. (2004). Assessment of bullying. *Journal of Counseling and Development, 82*(4), 496–503.

Crow, G. A. (1977). *Crisis intervention: A social interaction approach.* New York: Association Press.

Crow, T. J., & Johnstone, E. C. (1987). Schizophrenia: Nature of the disease process and its biological correlates. *Handbook of physiology* (Vol. 5). Bethesda, MD: American Physiological Society.

Crowley, J. D., & Gottlieb, M. C. (2012). Objects in the mirror are closer than they appear: A primary prevention model for ethical decision making. *Professional Psychology: Research and Practice, 43,* 65–72.

Cruz, J. M. (2003). "Why doesn't he just leave?" Gay male domestic violence and the reasons victims stay. *Journal of Men's Studies, 11*(3), 309–323.

Cryder, C. H., Kilmer, R. P., Tedeschi, R. G., & Calhoun, L. G. (2006). An exploratory study of posttraumatic growth in children following a natural disaster. *American Journal of Orthopsychiatry, 76*(1), 65–69.

Cukrowicz, K. C., Wingate, L. R., Driscoll, K. A., & Joiner, T. E. (2004). A standard of care for the assessment of suicide risk and associated treatment: The Florida State University Psychology Clinic as an example. *Journal of Contemporary Psychotherapy, 34,* 87–100.

Culliford, L. (2002). Spirituality and clinical care. *British Medical Journal, 325,* 1413–1435.

Cully, J., LaVoie, D., & Gfeller, J. D. (2001). Reminiscence, personality, and psychological functioning in older adults. *Gerontologist, 41*(1), 89–95.

Cummock, V. (1996). Journey of a young widow. In K. J. Doka (Ed.), *Living with grief after sudden loss: Suicide, homicide, accident, heart attack, stroke* (pp. 1–10). Washington, DC: Hospice Foundation of America.

Cunningham, N. J., & Davis, B. (1999, April). *A study of middle school bullying using a framework for violence prevention.* Poster session at the American Counseling Association World Conference, San Diego.

Curran, D. K. (1987). *Adolescent suicidal behavior.* New York: Hemisphere.

Curran, L. A. (2013). *101 trauma-informed interventions: Activities, exercises and assignments to move the client and therapy forward.* Eau Claire, WI: Pesi Publishng and Media.

Currier, J. M., Holland, J. M., & Neimeyer, R. A. (2007). The effectiveness of bereavement interventions with children: A meta-analytic review of controlled outcome research. *Journal of Clinical Child and Adolescent Psychology, 36*(2), 253–259.

Currier, J. M., Neimeyer, R. A., & Berman, J. S. (2008). The effectiveness of psychotherapeutic interventions for bereaved persons: A comprehensive quantitative review. *Psychological Bulletin, 134*(5), 648–661.

Cutler, D. L., Yeager, K. R., & Nunley, W. (2013). Crisis intervention and support. In K. R. Yeager, D. L. Cutler, D. Svendsen, & G. M. Sills (Eds.), *Modern community mental health: An interdisciplinary approach* (pp. 243–255). New York: Oxford University Press.

Cypress, S., & Green, R. (2002). Preventing fatal shooting attacks in schools. *Global Visions for Counseling Professionals, 6*(1), 43–49.

D

Dagastino, A. (1984). *Crisis intervention series: Helping abused women in abuse centers and shelters* (Cassette Recording No. 4-1). Memphis, TN: Memphis State University Department of Counseling and Personnel Services.

Daggett, L. M. (2002). Living with loss: Middle-aged men face spousal bereavement. *Qualitative Health Research, 12*(5), 625–639.

Dahlenberg, C. J. (2000). *Countertransference and the treatment of trauma*. Washington, DC: American Psychological Association.

Daigneault, I., Hébert, M., McDuff, P., Michaud, F.,Vezina-Gagnon, P., Henry, A., & Porter-Vignola, E. (2015). Effectiveness of a sexual assault awareness and prevention workshop for youth: A 3-month follow-up pragmatic cluster randomization study. *Canadian Journal of Human Sexuality, 24*(1), 19–30.

Dalgin, R., Maline, S., & Driscoll, P. (2011). Sustaining recovery through the night: Impact of a peer-run warmline . *Psychiatric Rehabilitation Journal, 35*(1),65–68.

Dallos, R., & Vetere, A. (2009). *Systemic therapy and attachment narrative: Applications in a range of clinical settings*. New York: Routledge/Taylor & Francis Group.

Damasio, A. R. (1994). *Descartes' error: Emotion, reason, and the human brain*. New York: Grosset/Putnam.

Dang, S. (1990). When the patient is out of control. *RN, 59*, 57–58.

Daniels, J. K., Lamke, J., Gaebler, M., Walter, H., & Scheel, M. (2013). White matter integrity and its relationship to PTSD and childhood trauma: A systematic review and meta-analysis. *Depression and Anxiety, 30*(3), 207–216.

Danish, S. J. (1977). Human development and human services: A marriage proposal. In I. Iscoe, B. L. Bloom, & C. C. Speilberger (Eds.), *Community psychology in transition* (pp. 44–77). New York: Halstead.

Dardis, C., Murphy, M., Bill, A., & Gidycz, C. (2015, June 15). An investigation of the tenets of social norms theory as they relate to sexually aggressive attitudes and sexual assault perpetration: A comparison of men and their friends. *Psychology of Violence, 5*(4), 20–32.

Darves-Bornoz, J. M., Lepine, J. P., Choquet, M., Berger, C., Degiovanni, A., & Gaillard, P. (1998). Predictive factors of chronic post-traumatic stress disorder in rape individuals. *European Psychiatry, 13*, 281–287.

Dass-Brailsford, P. (2008). After the storm: Recognition, recovery and reconstruction. *Professional Psychology Research and Practice, 39*(1), 24–30.

Dass-Brailsford, P. (Ed.). (2010). *Crisis and disaster counseling: Lessons learned from hurricane Katrina and other disasters*. Thousand Oaks, CA: Sage.

Davidson, J. R., & van der Kolk, B. A. (1996). The psychopharmacological treatment of posttraumatic stress disorder. In B. A. van der Kolk, A. C. McFarlane, & L. Weisaeth (Eds.), *Traumatic stress* (pp. 510–524). New York: Guilford Press.

Davis, D. L. (2004). *Your angry child: A guide for parents*. Binghamton, NY: Haworth Press.

Davis, H. T., & Salasin, S. E. (1975). The utilization of evaluation. In E. L. Struening & M. Guttentag (Eds.), *Handbook of evaluation research* (Vol. 1, pp. 621–666). Beverly Hills, CA: Sage.

Davis, J. L., Combs-Lane, A. M., & Jackson, T. L. (2002). Risky behaviors associated with interpersonal victimization: Comparison based on type, number and characteristics of assault incidents. *Journal of Interpersonal Violence, 17*(6), 611–629.

Davis, J. L., De Arellano, M., Falsetti, S. A., & Resnick, H. S. (2003). Treatment of nightmares related to post-traumatic stress disorder in an adolescent rape individual. *Clinical Case Studies, 2*(4), 283–294.

Davis, M. (2002). Male sexual assault victims: A selective review of the literature and implications for support services. *Aggression and Violent Behavior, 7*(3), 203–214.

Davis, S., & Davis, L. (2003). *Schools where everyone belongs: Practical strategies for reducing bullying*. Wayne, ME: Stop Bullying Now.

Davis, S. E., Williams, I. S., & Hays, L. W. (2002). Psychiatric inpatients' perceptions of written no-suicide agreements: An exploratory study. *Suicide and Life Threatening Behavior, 32*, 51–66.

Davis, S. E., Willians, I. S., & Hays, L. W. (2002) . Psychiatric inpatients' perceptions of written no-suicide agreements: An exploratory study. *Suicide and Life Threatening Behavior, 32*, 51–66.

Day, R. (2009). Counseling victims of intimate partner violence: Listening to the voices of clients—excerpts from a qualitative study. *Trauma Psychology Newsletter, 4*(3), 5–6.

Day, S. X., & Schneider, P. L. (2002). Psychotherapy using distance technology: A comparison of face-to-face, video, and audio treatment. *Journal of Counseling Psychology, 49*(4), 499–503.

Day-Vines, N., Day-Hairston, B. O., Carruthers, W. L., Wall, J. A., & Lupton-Smith, H. (1996). Conflict resolution: The value of diversity in the recruitment, selection, and training of peer mediators. *School Counselor, 43*, 393–410.

Day-Vines, N. L., Wood, S. M., Grothaus, T., Craigen, L., Holman, A., Dotson-Blake, K., & Douglass, M. J. (2007). Broaching the subject of race, ethnicity, and culture during the counseling process. *Journal of Counseling and Development, 85*, 401–409.

Deahl, M. (1999). Debriefing and body recovery: War grave soldiers. In B. Raphael & J. P. Wilson (Eds.), *Psychological debriefing: Theory, practice, and evidence* (pp. 108–117). New York: Cambridge University Press.

DeAngeis, T. (2014). What every psychologist should know about disaster. *Monitor on Psychology, 45*(7), 62–65.

DeAngelis, T. (2007). A new diagnosis for childhood trauma. *Monitor on Psychology, 38*(3), 32–33.

DeAngelis, T. (2009). Can Second Life therapy help with autism? *Monitor on Psychology, 40*(9), 40.

DeAngelis, T. (2011). Helping kids cope in an uncertain world. *Monitor on Psychology, 42*(8), 67–70.

De Arellano, M. A., Lyman, D., Jobes-Shields, L., George, P., Doougherty, R., . . . Delphin-Rittmon, M. (2014). Trauma-focused cognitive behavioral therapy for children and adolescents: Assessing the evidence. *Psychiatric Services, 65*(5), 591–602.

Deblinger, E., McLeer, S. V., Atkins, M. S., & Ralphe, D. (1989). Posttraumatic stress in sexually abused, physically abused, and nonabused children. *Child Abuse and Neglect, 13*, 403–408.

Deblinger, E., Thakkar-Kolar, R., & Ryan, E. (2006). Trauma in childhood. In V. M. Follette & J. I. Ruzek (Eds.), *Cognitive behavior therapies for trauma* (pp. 405–431). New York: Guilford Press.

deBont, P. A., van Minnen, A., & deJongh, A. (2013). Treating PTSD in patients with psychosis: A within group controlled feasibility study examining the efficacy and safety of evidence-based PE and EMDR protocols. *Behavior Therapy, 44*(4), 717–730.

Decker, J. T., Bailey, T. L., & Westergaard, N. (2002). Burnout among child care workers. *Residential Treatment for Children and Youth, 19*(4), 61–77.

Decker, J. T., Constantine, J. L., Ong, J., & Stiney-Ziskind, C. (2015). Mindfulness, compassion fatigue and compassion satisfaction among social work interns. *Social Work and Christianity, 42*(1), 28–42

Deering, R., & Mellor, D. (2011). An exploratory qualitative study of self-reported impact of female-perpetrated childhood sexual abuse. *Journal of Child Sexual Abuse: Research, Treatment and Program Innovations for Victims, Survivors, and Offenders, 20*(1), 58–76.

de Figueiredo, S., Yetwin, A., Shere, S., Radzik, M., & Iverson, E. (2014). A cross-disciplinary comparison of perceptions of compassion fatigue and satisfaction among service providers of highly traumatized children and adolescents. *Traumatology, 20*(4), 286–295.

Deiter, P. J., & Pearlman, L. A. (1998). Responding to self-injurious behavior. In P. M. Kleespies (Ed.), *Emergencies in mental health practice: Evaluation and management* (pp. 235–257). New York: Guilford Press.

Deitz, M., Williams, S., Rife, S., & Cantrell, P. (2015). Examining cultural, social and self-related aspects of stigma in relation to sexual assault and trauma symptoms. *Violence Against Women, 21*(5), 598–615.

Dejong, S. (2014). *Blogs and tweets, texting and friending: Social media and online professionalism in health care*. San Diego, CA: Elsevier Academic Press.

Dejong, S., & Gorrindo, T. (2014). To text or not to text: Applying clinical and professionalism principles to decisions about text messaging with patients. *Journal of the American Academy of Child and Adolescent Psychiatry, 53*(7), 713–715.

De Leo, D., Draper, B., Snowdon, J., & Kolves, K. (2013). Contacts with health professionals before suicide: Missed opportunities for prevention? *Comprehensive Psychiatry, 54*(7), 1117–1123.

Deleon, P. H., Crimmins, D. B., & Wolf, A. W. (2003). Afterword: The 21st century has arrived. *Psychotherapy: Research, Training, and Practice, 40*(1/2), 164–169.

Demaris, A. (1989). Attrition in batterers' counseling: The role of social and demographic factors. *Social Service Review, 63*, 142–154.

DeMause, L. (1974). *The history of childhood*. New York: Psychohistory Press.

De Moss, C. (2003, April). *Forgiveness—What's the secret?* Twenty-Seventh Convening of Crisis Intervention Personnel, Chicago.

Dennis, H. (1978). Remotivation therapy groups. In I. M. Burnside (Ed.), *Working with the elderly: Group process and techniques* (pp. 219–235). North Scituate, MA: Duxbury Press.

Department of Homeland Security. (2008). *FEMA's crisis counseling assistance and training program: State of Florida Project Hope*. Retrieved from www.dhs.gov/xoig/assets/mgmtrptsl/OIG_08-96_Sep08.pdf.

Department of Veterans Affairs & Department of Defense. (2010). *VA/DoD clinical practice guideline for management of post-traumatic stress*. Retrieved from http://www.healthquality.vagov/guideliens/MH/ptsd/cpg.PTSD -FULL-201011612.pdf

Derkx, H., Rethans, J., Maiburg, B., Winkens, R., Muitiens, A., & van Rooii, H. (2009). Quality of communication during telephone triage at Dutch after-hours centres. *Patient Education and Counseling, 74*(2), 174–178.

Dershimer, R. A. (1990). *Counseling the bereaved*. New York: Pergamon Press.

de Shazer, S. (1985). *Keys to solutions in brief therapy*. New York: W. W. Norton.

de Shazer, S. (1994). *Words were originally magic*. New York: W. W. Norton.

De Silva, S., Parker, A., Purcell, R., Callahan, P., Liu, P., & Hetrick, S. (2013). Mapping the evidence of prevention and intervention studies for suicidal and self-harming behaviors in young people. *The Journal of Crisis Intervention and Suicide Prevention, 34*(4), 223–232.

Devine, I. (1984). Organizational crisis and individual response: New trends for human service professionals (Special issue: Education and training in Canadian human services). *Canadian Journal of Community Mental Health, 3*, 63–72.

Devoe, E. R., Bannon, W., Klein, T., & Miranda-Julian, C. (2011). Young children in the aftermath of the World Trade Center attack. *Psychological Theory, Trauma, Research, Practice, and Policy, 3*(1), 1–7.

Devoe, E. R., Klein, T. P., Bannon, W. Jr., & Miranda-Julian, C. (2011). Young children in the aftermath of the World Trade Center attacks. *Psychological Trauma, Theory, Research, Practice, and Policy, 3*, 1–7.

deVries, F. (1998). To make a drama out of trauma is fully justified. *Lancet, 351*, 1579–1580.

deVries, M. (1996). Trauma in cultural perspective. In B. A. van der Kolk, A. C. McFarlane, & L. Weisaeth (Eds.), *Traumatic stress* (pp. 398–413). New York: Guilford Press.

Dewey, L., Allwood, N., Fava, J., Arias, E., Pinizzotto, A., & Schlesinger, L. (2013). Suicide by cop: Clinical risks and subtypes. *Archives of Suicide Research, 17*(4), 448–461.

DeWolfe, D. J. (2000). *Training manual for mental health and human service workers in major disasters* (2nd ed.). DHHS Publication No. ADM 90-538. Retrieved January 15, 2002, from http://www.mentalhealth.org/publications/allpubs;ADM90-538/index.htm

Dickens, M. (1985). *Miracles of courage: How families meet the challenge of a child's critical illness*. New York: Dodd, Mead.

Dickson, A., O'Brien, G., Ward, R., Allan, D., & O'Carroll, R. (2010). The impact of assuming the primary caregiver role following traumatic spinal cord injury: An interpretative phenomenological analysis of the spouse's experience. *Psychology and Health, 25*(9), 1101–1120.

Diehle, J., Opmeer, B., Boer, F., Mannarino, A., & Lindauer, R. (2015). Trauma focused cognitive behavior therapy or eye movement desensitization and reprocessing: What works in children with posttraumatic stress symptoms? A randomized controlled trial. *European Child and Adolescent Psychiatry, 24*(2), 227–236.

Diemer, J., Muhlberger, A., Pauli, P., & Zwanzger, P. (2014). Virtual reality exposure in anxiety disorders: Impact on psychophysiological reactivity. *The World Journal of Biological Psychiatry, 15*(6), 427–442.

Dierkhising, C. B., Ko, S. J., Woods-Jaeger, B., & Pynoos, R. (2013). Trauma histories among justice-involved youth: Findings from the National Child Traumatic Stress Network. *European Journal of Psycho-Traumatology, 4*, 1–10.

Dillenburger, K., & McKerr, L. (2009). "40 years is an awful long time": Parents caring for adult sons and daughters with disabilities. *Behavior and Social Issues, 18*, 155–174.

Dines, G. (1992). Pornography and the media: Cultural representations of violence against women. *Family Violence and Sexual Assault Bulletin, 8*, 17–20.

Dingfelder, S. (2013). Predicting and preventing violence. *Monitor on Psychology, 44*(3), 68.

Dingfelder, S. F. (2006). New needs in New Orleans schools. *Monitor on Psychology, 37*(6), 28–29.

Dinkmeyer, D. C., Pew, W. L., & Dinkmeyer, D. C., Jr. (1979). *Adlerian counseling and psychotherapy.* Pacific Grove, CA: Brooks/Cole.

Distler, B. J. (1990). *Reducing the potential for burnout.* Paper presented at the Fourteenth Annual Convening of Crisis Intervention Personnel, Chicago.

Dobash, R. E., & Dobash, R. P. (1979). *Violence against wives.* New York: Free Press.

Dobash, R. E., & Dobash, R. P. (1992). *Women, violence, and change.* London: Routledge.

Dodgen, D., & Meed, J. (2010). The federal government in disaster mental health response: An ever-evolving role. In P. Dass-Brailsford (Ed.), *Crisis and disaster counseling: Lessons learned from hurricane Katrina and other disasters* (pp. 181–195). Thousand Oaks, CA: Sage.

Dogutas, C. (2008). Reactive vs. proactive strategies: The effectiveness of school resource officers to prevent violence in schools. *Section A: Humanities and Social Sciences, 68*(10-A), 4470.

Doka, K. J. (1989). *Disenfranchised grief: Recognizing hidden sorrow.* Lexington, MA: D. C. Heath.

Doka, K. J. (1994). Disenfranchised grief. In L. A. DeSpelder & A. L. Strickland (Eds.), *The path ahead* (pp. 271–275). San Francisco: Mayfield.

Doka, K. J., & Davidson, J. D. (Eds.). (1998). *Living with grief: Who we are, how we grieve.* Washington, DC: Hospice Foundation of America.

Dollard, J., Doob, L. W., Miller, N. E., Mower, O. H., & Sears, R. R. (1939). *Frustration and aggression.* New Haven, CT: Yale University Press.

Doms, R. W. (1984). Personal distress devices for health care personnel. In J. T. Turner (Ed.), *Violence in the medical care setting: A survival guide* (pp. 225–229). Rockville, MD: Aspen Systems.

Donahue, H. H. (1965). Expanding the program. *Hospital and Community Psychiatry, 17,* 117–118.

Donahue, M. (2010). Investigating the grief process related to job loss. *Dissertation Abstracts International: Section B. The Sciences and Engineering,* 7850.

Donaldson, M. A., & Gardner, R., Jr. (1985). Diagnosis and treatment of traumatic stress among women after childhood incest. In C. R. Figley (Ed.), *Trauma and its wake: The study of posttrauma stress disorder* (pp. 356–377). New York: Brunner/Mazel.

Donat, P. L. N., & D'Emilio, J. (1998). A feminist redefinition of rape and sexual assault: Historical foundations and change. In M. E. Odem & J. Clay-Warner (Eds.), *Confronting rape and sexual assault* (pp. 35–49). Wilmington, DE: Scholarly Resources.

Donnelly, C. (2003). Pharmacologic treatment approaches for children and adolescents with posttraumatic stress disorder. *Child and Adolescent Psychiatric Clinics of North America, 12*(2), 251–269.

Donner, M. B., VandeCreek, L., Gonsiorek, J. C., & Fisher, C. B. (2008). Balancing confidentiality: Protecting privacy and protecting the public. *Professional Psychology: Research and Practice, 39*(3), 369–376.

Doran, G., & Hansen, N. D. (2006). Constructions of Mexican American family grief after the death of a child: An exploratory study. *Cultural Diversity and Ethnic Minority Psychology, 12*(2), 199–211.

Dorn, F. J. (Ed.). (1986). *The social influence process in counseling and psychotherapy.* Springfield, IL: Charles C Thomas.

Dorn, M., & Dorn, C. (2005). *Innocent targets when terrorism comes to school.* Macon, GA: Safe Haven International.

Dorrmann, W. (2005). Pros and cons of contracts with patients in acute suicidal crises. *Verhaltenstherapie, 15*(1), 39–46.

Dorstyn, D. S., Mathias, J. L., & Denson, L. A. (2011). Psychosocial outcomes of telephone-based counseling for adults with an acquired physical disability: A meta-analysis. *Rehabilitation Psychology, 56*(1), 1–14.

dos Reis, S., Barnett, S. R., Love, L. C., Riddle, M. A., & Maryland Youth Practice Improvement Committee. (2003). A guide for managing acute aggression among youths. *Psychiatric Services, 54*(10), 1357–1363.

Doughty, E. A. (2009). Investigating adaptive grieving styles: A Delphi study. *Death Studies, 33*(5), 462–480.

Douglas, D. (1991). Intervention with male toddlers who have witnessed parental violence. *Journal of Contemporary Human Services, 72,* 515–523.

Douglas, K. S., Nicholls, T. L., & Brink, J. (2009). Reducing the risk of violence among people with serious mental illness: A critical analysis of treatment approaches. In P. M. Kleespies (Ed.), *Behavioral emergencies: An evidence-based resource for evaluating and managing risk of suicide, violence, and victimization.* (pp. 351–376). Washington, DC: American Psychological Association.

Douglas, K. S., Ogloff, J. R., & Hart, S. D. (2003). Evaluation of a model of violence risk assessment among forensic psychiatric patients. *Psychiatric Services, 54*(10), 1372–1379.

Douglas, K. S., Webster, C., Hart, S., Eaves, D., & Ogloff, J. (2001). *HCR-20 violence risk assessment companion guide.* Burnaby, Canada: Simon Fraiser University Mental Health, Law, and Policy Institute.

Douglas, M. A., & Perrin, A. (1987, July). *Recidivism and accuracy of self-reported violence and arrest.* Paper presented at the Third National Conference for Family Violence Researchers, University of New Hampshire, Durham.

Dowling, M. J., & Rickwood, D. J. (2014). Experience of counsellors providing online chat counselling to young people. *Australian Journal of Guidance and Counselling, 24*(2), 183–196.

Drabek, T. E. (1986). *Human systems response to disaster: An inventory of sociological findings.* New York: Springer.

Drapeau, M., & Perry, J. C. (2004). Interpersonal conflicts in borderline personality disorder: An exploratory study using the CCRT-LU. *Swiss Journal of Psychology, 63*(1), 53–57.

Dreisbach, V. (2003). Post-traumatic stress disorder in fire and rescue personnel. *Journal of American Academy of Psychiatry and Law, 31*(1), 120–123.

Drescher, K., & Foy, D. W. (2010). When horror and loss intersect: Traumatic experience and traumatic bereavement. *Pastoral Psychology, 59*(2), 147–158.

Dressing, H., Kuehner, C., & Gass, P. (2006). The epidemiology and characteristics of stalking. *Current Opinion in Psychiatry, 19*(4), 395–399.

Drieschner, K., & Lange, A. (1999). A review of cognitive factors in the etiology of rape: Theories, empirical studies, and implications. *Clinical Psychology Review, 19*(1), 57–77.

Drucker, K. (2001). Why can't she control herself? A case study. In J. Murphy (Ed.), *Art therapy with young survivors of sexual abuse: Lost for words* (pp. 101–125). New York: Brunner-Routledge.

Dryden, W. (1984). *Rational emotive therapy: Fundamentals and innovations.* London: Croom Helm.

Dryden, W., & Neenan, W. M. (2004). *Counselling individuals: A rational emotive behavioural handbook* (4th ed.). London: John Wiley & Sons.

Duberstein, P., & Witte, T. (2009). Suicide risk in personality disorders: An argument for a public health perspective. In P. M. Kleespies (Ed.), *Behavioral emergencies: An evidence-based resource for evaluating and managing risk of suicide, violence, and victimization* (pp. 257–286). Washington, DC: American Psychological Association.

Dubin, W. R. (1981). Evaluating and managing the violent patient. *Annals of Emergency Medicine, 10*, 481–484.

Dublin, L. I. (1969). Suicide prevention. In E. S. Shneidman (Ed.), *On the nature of suicide*. San Francisco: Jossey-Bass, 43–67.

Ducharme, F., Couture, M., & Lamontange, J. (2012). Decision-making process of family caregivers regarding placement of a cognitively impaired elderly relative. *Home Health Care Services Quarterly, 31*, 197–218.

Duggan, D. (2007). Children and young people affected by AIDS. In S. Books (Ed.), *Invisible children in the society and its schools* (3rd ed., pp. 235–261). Mahwah, NJ: Erlbaum.

Duncan, A., Delisle, D., & Esquith, D. (2013). *Guide for preparing high quality school emergency plans*. Washington, DC: U.S. Department of Education.

Duncan, J. W., & Duncan, G. M. (1971). Murder in the family: A study of some homicidal adolescents. *American Journal of Psychiatry, 127*(11), 74–78.

Duncan, K. A. (2004). *Healing from the trauma of childhood sexual abuse: The journey for women*. Westport, CT: Praeger.

Dunn, P. C., Vail-Smith, K., & Knight, S. M. (1999). What date/acquaintance rape victims tell others: A study of college student recipients of disclosure. *Journal of American College Health, 47*, 213–219.

Duquette, A., Kerouac, S., Sandhu, B. K., & Beaudet, L. (1994). Factors related to nursing burnout: A review of empirical knowledge. *Issues in Mental Health Nursing, 15*, 337–358.

DuRant, R. H., Treiber, F., Getts, A., McCloud, K., Linder, C. W., & Woods, E. R. (1996). Comparison of two violence prevention curricula for middle school adolescents. *Journal of Adolescent Health, 19*, 111–117.

Durivage, A. (1989). Assaultive behavior: Before it happens. *Canadian Journal of Psychiatry, 34*, 393–397.

Durkheim, E. (1951). *Suicide*. New York: Free Press. (Original work published 1897).

Dutro, K. R. (1994, April). *A dynamic, structural model of grief*. Paper presented at the Eighteenth Annual Convening of Crisis Intervention Personnel, Chicago.

Dutton, D. G. (1985). An ecologically nested theory of male violence towards intimates. *International Journal of Women's Studies, 8*, 404–413.

Dutton, D. G. (1994). The origin and structure of the abusive personality. *Journal of Personality Disorders, 8*(3), 181–191.

Dutton, D. G. (1995). *The domestic assault of women*. Vancouver: University of British Columbia Press.

Dutton, D. G. (2007). *The abusive personality: Violence and control in intimate relationships* (2nd ed.). New York: Guilford Press.

Dutton, D. G., & Corvo, K. (2006). Transforming flawed social policy: A call to revive psychology and science in domestic violence research and practice. *Aggression and Violent Behavior, 11*(5), 457–483.

Dutton, D. G., & Corvo, K. (2007). The Duluth model: A data-impervious paradigm and a failed strategy. *Aggression and Violent Behavior, 12*(6), 658–667.

Dutton, D. G., & Starzomski, A. (1993). Borderline personality organization in perpetrators of psychological and physical abuse. *Violence and Victims, 8*(4), 327–338.

Dutton, D. G., & Starzomski, A. (1994). Psychological differences between court-referred and self-referred wife assaulters. *Criminal Justice and Behavior: An International Journal, 21*(2), 203–222.

Dwyer, K., Osher, D., & Warger, C. (1998). *Early warning, timely response: A guide to safe schools*. Washington, DC: U.S. Department of Education.

Dyckman, J. (2011). Exposing the gloss in Seligman and Fowler's (2011) straw-man arguments. *American Psychologist, 66*, 644–645.

Dyer, W. O., Murrell, D. S., & Wright, D. (1984). Training for hospital security: An alternative to training negligence suits. In J. T. Turner (Ed.), *Violence in the medical care setting: A survival guide* (pp. 1–18). Rockville, MD: Aspen Systems.

Dykeman, C. (1999, June). *Preventing school-based violence: Practical steps for school counselors*. Paper presented at the American School Counselor Association Convention, Phoenix, AZ.

Dyregrov, A. (1997). The process in psychological debriefings. *Journal of Traumatic Stress, 10*, 589–605.

Dyregrov, A., Gupta, L., Gjestad, R., & Raundalen, M. (2002). Is the culture always right? *Traumatology, 8*, 1–10.

Dyregrov, K., & Dyregrov, A. (2008). *Effective grief and bereavement support: Friends, colleagues, schools, and support professionals*. Philadelphia: Jessica Kingsley.

Dziegielewski, S. F., & Powers, G. T. (2005). Designs and procedures for evaluating crisis intervention. In A. R. Roberts (Ed.), *Crisis intervention handbook* (3rd ed., pp. 742–773). New York: Oxford University Press.

Dziegielewski, S. F., & Sumner, K. (2005). An examination of the U.S. response to bioterrorism: Handling the threat and aftermath through crisis intervention. In A. R. Roberts (Ed.), *Crisis intervention handbook* (3rd ed., pp. 262–290). New York: Oxford University Press.

D'Andrea, M., & Daniels, D. (2005, Spring). Sport psychology: A multidimensional-multicultural competency model. *ESPNews, 19*(1), 9.

D'Andrea, M., & Heckman, E. F. (2008). A 40-year review of multicultural counseling outcome research: Outlining a future research agenda for the multicultural counseling movement. *Journal of Counseling and Development, 86*, 356–363.

E

Eakin, E. G., Lawler, S., Vanderlanotte, C., & Owen, N. (2007). Telephone interventions for physical activity and dietary behavior change: A systemic review. *American Journal of Preventive Medicine, 32*(5), 419–434.

East, P., & Hokoda, A. (2015). Risk and protective factors for sexual dating violence victimization: A longitudinal, prospective study of Latino and African-American adolescents. *Journal of Youth and Adolescence, 44*(5), 1288–1300.

East, T. W., James, R. K., & Keim, J. (2001, April). *The best little vicarious trauma prevention program in Tennessee*. Paper presented at the Twenty-Fifth Annual Convening of Crisis Intervention Personnel, Chicago.

Easton, S., Saltzman, L., & Willis, D. (2014). "Would you tell under circumstances like that?" Barriers to disclosure of child sexual abuse for men. *Psychology of Men and Masculinity, 15*(4), 460–469.

Eastwood, C. D. (2007). Compassion fatigue risk and self-care practices among residential treatment center childcare workers. *Dissertation Abstract International: Section B. The Sciences and Engineering, 67*(10), 2645.

Ebersole, P. P. (1978a). A theoretical approach to the use of reminiscence. In I. M. Burnside (Ed.), *Working with the elderly: Group process and techniques* (pp. 139–154). North Scituate, MA: Duxbury Press.

Ebersole, P. P. (1978b). Establishing reminiscence groups. In I. M. Burnside (Ed.), *Working with the elderly: Group process and techniques* (pp. 236–254). North Scituate, MA: Duxbury Press.

Echterling, L. G., & Stewart, A. (2008). Creative crisis intervention techniques with children and families. In C. A. Malchiodi (Ed.), *Creative interventions with traumatized children* (pp. 189–210). New York: Guilford Press.

Echterling, L. G., & Wylie, M. L. (1999). In the public arena: Disaster as a socially constructed problem. In R. Gist & B. Lubin (Eds.), *Response to disaster: Psychosocial, community, and ecological approaches* (pp. 327–352). Philadelphia: Brunner/Mazel.

Echterling, L. G., McKee, E. J., & Presbury, J. (2000, March). *Resolution-focused crisis debriefing for traumatized groups.* Paper presented at the American Counseling Association Conference, Washington, DC.

Eck, J. E., & Spelman, W. (1987). *Problem-solving: Problem oriented policing in Newport News.* Washington, DC: Police Executive Research Forum.

Eckardt, M. H. (2011). The use of the telephone to extend our therapeutic availability. *Journal of the American Academy of Psychoanalysis Dynamic Psychiatry, 39*(1), 151–154.

Eckart, J. (2014). Is texting better than suicide for men. Retrieved at http://www.military.com/spouse/military-life/military-resources/is-texting-better-suicide-intervention-for-men.html

Ectherling, L G., Presbury, J. H., & McKee, J. E. (2005). *Crisis intervention: Promoting resilience and resolution in troubled times.* Upper Saddle River, NJ: Pearson.

Eddy, S. (1998). Risk management with the violent patient. In P. M. Kleespies (Ed.), *Emergencies in mental health practice: Evaluation and management* (pp. 217–231). New York: Guilford Press.

Edelson, M. G., & Joa, D. (2010). Difference in legal outcomes for male and female children who have been sexually abused. *Sexual Abuse: Journal of Research and Treatment, 22*(4), 427–442.

Edelstein, L. (1984). *Maternal bereavement: Coping with the unexpected death of a child.* New York: Praeger.

Edelwich, J., & Brodsky, A. (1982). Training guidelines: Linking the workshop experience to needs on and off the job. In W. S. Paine (Ed.), *Job stress and burnout* (pp. 133–154). Newbury Park, CA: Sage.

Edleson, J. L., & Syers, M. (1990). Relative effectiveness of group treatments for men who batter. *Social Work Research and Abstracts, 26,* 10–17.

Edleson, J. L., & Tolman, R. M. (1992). *Intervention for men who batter.* Newbury Park, CA: Sage.

Edwards, S. M. (1989). *Policing domestic violence: Women, the law, and the state.* London: Sage.

Efrid, D. M. (2013). Address anger management. *ASCA School Counselor, 51*(2), 22–27.

Egan, G. (1975). *The skilled helper: A model for systematic helping and interpersonal relating.* Pacific Grove, CA: Brooks/Cole.

Egan, G. (1982). *The skilled helper: Model, skills, and methods for effective helping* (2nd ed.). Pacific Grove, CA: Brooks/Cole.

Egan, G. (1986). *The skilled helper: A systematic approach to effective helping* (3rd ed.). Pacific Grove, CA: Brooks/Cole.

Egan, G. (1990). *The skilled helper: Model, skills, and methods for effective helping* (4th ed.). Pacific Grove, CA: Brooks/Cole.

Egan, S. J., van Noort, E., Chee, A., Kane, R. T., Hoiles, K. J., Shafan, R., & Wade, T. D. (2014). A randomized controlled trial of face to face versus pure online self-help cognitive behavioural treatment for perfectionism. *Behavior Research and Therapy, 63,* 107–113.

Egendorf, A. (1975). A Vietnam veteran rap group and themes of post-war life. *Journal of Social Issues, 31,* 111–124.

Ehlers, A., Clark, D., Hckman, A., McManus, F., & Fennel, L. (2005). Cognitive therapy for post-traumatic stress disorder: Development and evaluation. *Behavior Research and Therapy, 43*(4), 413–431.

Ehrensaft, M. K., Cohen, P., Brown, J., Smailes, E., Chen, H., & Johnson, J. G. (2003). Intergenerational transmission of partner violence: A twenty-year prospective study. *Journal of Consulting and Clinical Psychology, 71*(4), 741–753.

Ehrensaft, M. K., Moffitt, T. E., & Caspi, A. (2006). Is domestic violence followed by an increased risk of psychiatric disorder among women but not among men? A longitudinal study. *American Journal of Psychiatry, 163*(5), 885–892.

Ehring, T., Welboren, R., Morina, N., Wicherts, J., Freitag, J., & Emmelkamp, P. (2014). Meta-analysis of psychological treatments for posttraumatic stress disorder in adult survivors of childhood abuse. *Clinical Psychology Review, 34*(8), 645–657.

Eidelson, R., Pilisuk, M., & Soldz, S. (2011). The dark side of Comprehensive Soldier Fitness. *American Psychologist, 66,* 643–644.

Eidelson, R. J., & Eidelson, J. I. (2003). Dangerous ideas: Five beliefs that propel groups toward conflict. *American Psychologist, 58,* 182–192.

Eidelson, R. J., D'Alessio, G. R., & Eidelson, J. I. (2003). The impact of September 11 on psychologists. *Professional Psychology: Research and Practice, 34*(2), 144–150.

Eisel v. Board of Education of Montgomery County, 597 A2d 447 (Md. 1991).

Eisler, R. (1987–1995). *The chalice and the blade: Our history, our future.* San Francisco: HarperCollins.

Eisler, R. (1995). *Sacred pleasure: Sex, myth, and the politics of the body.* San Francisco: HarperCollins.

Eke, A., Hilton, N. Z, Harris, G. T., Rice, M. E., & Houghton, R. E. (2011). Intimate partner homicide risk assessment and prospects for prediction. *Journal of Family Violence, 26*(3), 211–216.

El Ghaziri, M., Zhu, S., Lipscomb, J., & Smith, B. (2014). Work schedule and client characteristics associated with workplace violence experience among nurses and midwives in sub-Sahara Africa. *JANAC: Journal of the Association of Nurses in AIDS Care, 25*(Supp. 1), S79–S89.

Elharrar, E., Warhaftig, G., Issier, O., Szainberg, Y., Dikshtein, Y., et al. (2013). Over expression of corticotropin-releasing factor receptor type 2 in the bed nucleus of stria terminalis improves posttraumatic stress disorder-like symptoms in a model of incubation of fear. *Biological Psychiatry, 74*(11), 827–836.

Eliason, G., LaPore, M., & Myer, R. A. (2008). The historical advancement of grief counseling. In A. Tomer, G. Eliason, & T. P. Wong (Eds.), *Existential and spiritual issues in death attitudes* (pp. 417–438). Mahwah, NJ: Erlbaum.

Elklit, A., & Brink, O. (2004). Acute stress disorder as a predictor of post-traumatic stress disorder in physical assault individuals. *Journal of Interpersonal Violence, 19*(6), 709–726.

Elliot, D. M., & Briere, J. (1995). Posttraumatic stress associated with delayed recall of sexual abuse: A general population study. *Journal of Traumatic Stress, 8*(4), 629–647.

Elliot, M. (1994). *Female sexual abuse of children.* New York: Guilford Press.

Elliot, P. (1996). Shattered illusions: Same-sex domestic violence. In C. M. Renzetti (Ed.), *Violence in gay and lesbian domestic relationships* (pp. 1–8). Binghamton, NY: Haworth.

Ellis, A. (1971). *Growth through reason.* Hollywood, CA: Wilshire Books.

Ellis, A. (1973). *Humanistic psychology: The rational-emotive approach.* New York: Julian.

Ellis, A. (1990). *Anger: How to live with it and without it.* New York: Carroll.

Ellis, A., & Abrahms, E. (1978). *Brief psychotherapy in medical and health practice.* New York: Springer.

Ellis, A., & Dryden, W. (1977). *The practice of rational emotive behavior therapy.* New York: Springer

Ellis, A., & Grieger, R. (1977). *Handbook of rational-emotive therapy.* New York: Springer.

Ellis, A., & Harper, R. A. (1975). *A new guide to rational living* (rev. ed.). Hollywood, CA: Wilshire Books.

Ellis, A. E. (1962). *Reason and emotion in psychotherapy.* New York: Lyle Stuart.

Ellis, A. E. (1982). Major systems. *Personnel and Guidance Journal, 61,* 6–7.

Ellis, H. A. (2014). Effects of a Crisis Intervention Team (CIT) training program upon police officers before and after Crisis Intervention Team training. *Archives of Psychiatric Nursing, 28*(1), 10–18.

Elwert, F., & Christakis, N. A. (2006). Widowhood and race. *American Sociological Review, 71*(1), 16–41.

Elwert, F., & Christakis, N. A. (2008). The effect of widowhood on mortality by the causes of death of both spouses. *American Journal of Public Health, 98*(11), 2092–2098.

Embry, D. L., Flannery, D. J., Vazsonyi, A. T., Powell, K. B., & Atha, H. (1996). Peacebuilders: A theoretically driven, school-based model for early violence prevention. *American Journal of Preventive Medicine, 12*(5), 91–100.

Emergency Management Assistance Compact, PL 104-321 (1996).

Engel, R. C., Gallagher, L. B., & Lyle, D. S. (2010). Military deployments and children's academic achievement: Evidence from Department of Defense education activity schools. *Economics of Education Review, 29,* 73–82.

Engle, J. L., & Follette, V. (2012). Acceptance and commitment therapy for trauma related problems. In R. A. McMackin, E. Newman, J. M. Fogler, & T. M. Keane (Eds.), *Trauma therapy in context: The science and craft of evidence-based practice* (pp. 353–372). Washington, DC: American Psychological Association.

Englehardt, C. R., Bartholow, B. D., Kerr, G., & Bushman, B. (2011). This is your brain on violent video games: Neural desensitization to violence predicts increased aggression following violent video game exposure. *Journal of Experimental Social Psychology, 31*(4), 35–47.

Epstein, M., & Carter, L. (1988). *Training manual for Headquarters staff.* Lawrence, KS: Headquarters.

Epstein, M., & Carter, L. (1991). *Headquarters training manual.* Lawrence, KS: Headquarters Crisis Center.

Epstein, R., Fullerton, C., & Ursano, R. (1998). Posttraumatic stress disorder following an air disaster: A prospective study. *American Journal of Psychiatry, 155*(7), 934–938.

Erdur-Baker, O., Aberson, C., Barrow, J., & Draper, M. (2006). Nature and severity of college students' psychological concerns: A comparison of clinical and nonclinical national samples. *Professional Psychology: Research and Practice, 37*(3), 317–323.

Erikson, E. (1963). *Childhood and society* (2nd ed.). New York: Norton.

Erikson, E. (1968). *Identity, youth, and crisis.* New York: Norton.

Erikson, K. T. (1976). *Everything in its path: Destruction of community in the Buffalo Creek flood.* New York: Simon & Schuster.

Erlangsen, A., Nordenstoft, J., Conwell, Y., Waern, M., De Leo, D., Lindner, R., et al. (2011). Key considerations to prevent suicide in older adults: Consensus opinion of an expert panel. *Crisis: The Journal of Crisis Intervention and Suicide Prevention, 32*(2), 106–109.

Erstling, S. (2006). Police and mental health collaborative outreach. *Psychiatric Services, 57*(3), 417–418.

Espelage, D., & Swearer, S. (2003). Research on school bullying and victimization: What have we learned and where do we go from here? *School Psychology Review, 32*(3), 365–384.

Espelage, D., Bosworth, K., & Simon, T. R. (2000). Examining the social context of bullying behaviors in early adolescence. *Journal of Counseling and Development, 78*(3), 326–333.

Eth, S., & Pynoos, R. S. (1985). Developmental perspective on psychic trauma in childhood. In C. R. Figley (Ed.), *Trauma and its wake: The study of post-trauma stress disorder* (pp. 36–52). New York: Brunner/Mazel.

Evans, B. (2003). Hypnosis for post-traumatic stress disorders. *Australian Journal of Clinical and Experimental Hypnosis, 31*(1), 54–73.

Evans, L., McHugh, T., Hopwood, M., & Watt, C. (2003). Chronic posttraumatic stress disorder and family functioning of Vietnam veterans and their partners. *Australian and New Zealand Journal of Psychiatry, 37*(6), 765–772.

Evans, R., & Petter, S. (2012). Identifying mitigating and challenging beliefs in dealing with threatening patients: An analysis of experiences of clinicians working in a psychiatric intensive care unit. *Journal of Psychiatric Intensive Care, 8*(2), 113–119.

Evans, R. L., Smith, K. M., Werkhoven, W. S., Fox, H. R., & Pritzl, D. O. (1986). Cognitive telephone group therapy with physically disabled elderly persons. *Gerontologist, 26,* 8–11.

Evans, W. P., Davidson, L., & Sicafuse, L. (2013). Someone to listen: Increasing youth self-help seeking behavior through a test based crisis line for youth. *Journal of Community Psychology, 41*(4), 471–487.

Everly, G. S., & Flynn, B. W. (2005). Principles and procedures of acute psychological first aid training for personnel without mental health experience. *International Journal of Emergency Mental Health, 8*(2), 93–100.

Everly, G. S., Jr. (1989). *A clinical guide to the treatment of the human stress response.* New York: Plenum.

Everstine, D. S., & Everstine, E. (2006). *Strategic interventions for people in crisis, trauma, and disaster-revised edition.* New York: Routledge.

Everstine, L. (1998). *The anatomy of suicide: Silence of the heart.* Springfield, IL: Charles C Thomas.

Ewing v. Goldstein, 120 Cal. App. 4th 807 (2004).

Ewing v. Northridge Hospital Medical Center, 120 Cal. App. 4th 1289 (2004).

F

Fairbank, J. A., & Keane, T. M. (1982). Flooding for combat-related stress disorders: Assessment of anxiety reduction across traumatic memories. *Behavior Therapy, 13,* 499–510.

Fairbank, J. A., Briggs, E. C., Carmody, K. A., Greeson, J., & Woods, B. A. (2014). Children. In L. A. Zoellner & N. C. Feeny (Eds.), *Facilitating resilience and recovery following trauma* (pp. 91–112). New York: Guilford Press.

Falco, A., Piccirelli, A., Girardi, D., Di Sipio, A., & De Carlo, N. (2014). "The best or nothing" : The mediating role of workaholism in the relationship between perfectionism and burnout. *TMP—Testing, Psychometrics, Methodology in Applied Psychology, 21*(2), 213–232.

Falkenstrom, F., Granstrom, F., & Holmqvist, R. (2013). Therapeutic alliance predicts symptomatic improvement session by session. *Journal of Counseling Psychology, 60*(3), 317–328.

Falkenstrom, F., Granstrom,F., & Holmqvist, R. (2014). Working alliance predicts psychotherapy outcome even while controlling for prior symptom improvement. *Psychotherapy Research, 24*(2), 146–159.

Family Educational Rights and Privacy Act of 1974 (FERPA), 34 C.F.R. § (a)(10) and § 99.36 (2010).

Fanany, R., & Fananay, I. (2013). Post-disaster coping in Aceh: Sociocultrual factors and emotional response. In C. Banwell, S. Uijaszek, & J. Dixon (Eds.), *When culture impacts health: Global lessons for effective health research* (pp. 225–235). San Diego: Elsevier Academic Press.

Farber, B. A. (Ed.). (1983). *Stress and burnout in the human service professions.* New York: Pergamon Press.

Farberow, N. (2001). Helping suicide survivors. In D. Lester (Ed.), *Suicide prevention: Resources for the millennium* (pp. 189–212). Philadelphia: Brunner-Routledge.

Farberow, N. L., & Frederick, C. J. (1978). *Training for human service workers in major disasters.* Rockville, MD: National Institute of Mental Health.

Fareta, G. (1981). A profile of aggression from adolescence to adulthood: An 18-year follow-up of psychiatrically disturbed and violent adolescents. *American Journal of Orthopsychiatry, 51,* 439–453.

Farina, A. (2000). The few gains and many losses for those stigmatized by psychiatric disorder. In J. H. Harvey & E. D. Miller (Eds.), *Loss and trauma: General and close relationship perspectives* (pp. 183–207). Philadelphia: Brunner-Routledge.

Farrell, A. D., & Camou, S. (2006). School-based interventions for youth violence prevention. In J. R. Lutzker (Ed.), *Preventing violence: Research and evidence-based intervention strategies* (pp. 125–146). Washington, DC: American Psychological Association.

Farrell, S. P., Hains, A. A., & Davies, W. H. (1998). Cognitive behavioral interventions for sexually abused children exhibiting PTSD symptomology. *Behavior Therapy, 29,* 241–255.

Farrer, L., Griffiths, K., Christensen, H., Mackinnon, A., & Batterham, P. (2014). Predictors of adherence and outcome in internet based cognitive behavior therapy delivered in a telephone counseling setting. *Cognitive Therapy and Research, 38*(3), 358–367.

Faschingbauer, T., Zisook, S., & DeVaul, R. (1987). The Texas Revised Inventory of Grief. In S. Zisook (Ed.), *Biopsychosocial aspects of bereavement* (pp. 111–124). Washington, DC: American Psychiatric Press.

Fatum, W. R., & Hoyle, J. C. (1996). Is it violence? School violence from the student perspective: Trends and interventions. *School Counselor, 44*(1), 28–34.

Fauteux, K. (2010). De-escalating angry and violent clients. *American Journal of Psychotherapy, 64*(2), 195–213.

Federal Bureau of Investigation. (2002, June). *Workplace violence symposium.* Landover, MD. Retrieved from www.fbi.gov/stats-services/publications/workplace-violence.

Federal Emergency Management Agency. (2015). *Community emergency response team overview.* Retrieved from www.training.fema.gov/community-emergency-response-teams

Federal Emergency Management Agency. (n.d.). *History of FEMA.* Retrieved August 6, 2003, from www.fema.gov.

Feeny, N., Hembree, E., & Zoellner, L. (2003). Myths regarding exposure therapy for PTSD. *Cognitive and Behavioral Practice, 10*(1), 85–90.

Fehrenbach, P., & Monastersky, C. (1988). *A sourcebook on child sexual abuse.* Newbury Park, CA: Sage.

Feigon, E. A., & de Rivera, J. (1998). "Recovered memory" therapy: Profession at a turning point. *Comprehensive Psychiatry, 39,* 338–344.

Feil, N., & deKlerk-Rubin, V. (2012). *The validation breakthrough: Simple communication techniques with people with Alzheimer's and other dementias* (3rd ed.). Baltimore, MD: U.S. Health Professions.

Feil, N. (1982). *Validation: The Feil method.* Cleveland, OH: Edward Feil Productions.

Feil, N. (1999). Current concepts and techniques in validation therapy. In M. Duffy (Ed.), *Handbook of counseling and psychotherapy with older adults* (pp. 590–613). Hoboken, NJ : John Wiley & Sons.

Feil, N., & Altman, R. (2004). Validation theory and the myth of the therapeutic lie. *American Journal of Alzheimer's Disease and Other Dementias, 19*(2), 77–78.

Fein, A. H., Carlisle, C. S., & Issacson, N. S. (2008). School shootings and counselor leadership: Four lessons from the field. *Professional School Counseling, 11*(4), 246–252.

Fein, R. A., Vossekuil, B., Pollack, W. S., Borum, M., Modzeleski, W., & Reddy, M. (2002). *Threat assessment in schools: A guide to managing threatening situations and creating safe school climates.* Washington, DC: U.S. Secret Service and U.S. Department of Education.

Feindler, E. L., & Scalley, M. (1998). Adolescent anger management for violence reduction. In K. C. Stoiber & T. R. Kratochwill (Eds.), *Handbook of group intervention for children and families* (pp. 100–119). Boston: Allyn & Bacon.

Feindler, E. L., & Weisner, S. (2006). Youth anger management treatments for school violence prevention. In S. R. Jimerson & M. Furlong (Eds.), *Handbook of school violence and school safety: From research to practice* (pp. 353–363). Mahwah, NJ: Erlbaum.

Felix, E., Afifi, T., Kia-Keating, M., Brown, L., Afifi, W., & Reyes, G. (2015). Family functioning and posttraumatic growth among parents and youth following wildfire disasters. *American Journal of Orthopsychiatry, 85,* 191–200.

Felmingham, K., Kemp, A., Williams, L., Das, P., Hughes, G. Peduto, A., et al. (2007). Changes in anterior cingulate and amygdala after cognitive behavior therapy of posttraumatic stress disorder. *Psychological Science, 18,* 127–129.

Felthous, A. R. (1987). Liability of treaters for injuries to others: Erosion of three immunities. *Bulletin of the American Academy of Psychiatry and the Law, 15,* 115–125.

Felthous, A. R., & Kellert, S. (1986). Violence against animals and people: Is aggression against living creatures generalized? *Bulletin of the American Academy of Psychiatry and Law, 14*(1), 55–69.

Felton, T., Coates, L., & Christopher, J. (2015). Impact of mindfulness training on counseling students' perceptions of stress. *Mindfulness, 6*(2), 159–169.

Fenelon, D. A. (1990, April). *Recognizing and dealing with the bogus sex caller.* Paper presented at the Fourteenth Annual Convening of Crisis Intervention Personnel, Chicago.

Ferguson, C. J. (2011). Video games and youth violence: A prospective analysis in adolescents. *Journal of Youth and Adolescence, 40*(4), 377–391.

Ferguson, C. J., & Kilburn, J. (2009). The public health risks of media violence: A meta-analytic review. *Journal of Pediatrics, 154*(5), 759–763.

Ferguson, C. J., & Kilburn, J. (2010). Much ado about nothing: The misestimation and overinterpretation of violent video game effects in Eastern and Western nations: Comment on Anderson et al., 2010. *Psychological Bulletin, 136*(2), 174–178.

Ferguson, C. J., Colwell, J., Mlacic, B., Milas, G., & Miklousic, I. (2011). Personality and media influences on violence and depression in a cross-national sample of young adults: Data from Mexican-Americans, English and Croatians. *Computers in Human Behavior, 27*(3), 1195–1200.

Fichtner, C., Podding, B., & deVito, R. (2000). Posttraumatic stress disorder: Pathophysiological aspects and pharmacological approaches to treatment. In K. Palmer (Ed.), *Pharmacotherapy of anxiety disorders* (pp. 61–92). Hong Kong: Adis International Publications.

Fiebert, M., & Gonzalez, D. (1997). Women who initiate assaults: The reasons offered for such behavior. *Psychological Reports, 80,* 583–590.

Figley, C. R. (1985). From individual to survivor: Social responsibility in the wake of catastrophe. In C. R. Figley (Ed.), *Trauma and its wake: The study of post-trauma stress disorder* (pp. 398–416). New York: Brunner/Mazel.

Figley, C. R. (1988). Post-traumatic family therapy. In F. M. Ochberg (Ed.), *Posttraumatic therapy and individuals of violence* (pp. 83–113). New York: Brunner/Mazel.

Figley, C. R. (1989) *Helping traumatized families.* San Francisco: Jossey-Bass.

Figley, C. R. (1996). Traumatic death: Treatment implications. In K. J. Doka (Ed.), *Living with grief after sudden loss: Suicide, homicide, accident, heart attack, stroke* (pp. 91–102). Washington, DC: Hospice Foundation of America.

Figley, C. R. (2002). *Treating compassion fatigue.* New York: Brunner-Routledge.

Figley, C. R. (Ed.). (1978). *Stress disorder among Vietnam veterans.* New York: Brunner/Mazel.

Figley, C. R. (Ed.). (1995). *Compassion fatigue: Coping with secondary traumatic stress disorder in those who treat the traumatized.* New York: Brunner/Mazel.

Figley, C. R. (Ed.). (2002). *Treating compassion fatigue.* New York: Brunner-Routledge.

Figley, C. R. (Speaker). (1990). *Posttraumatic stress disorder: Managing bad memories in individuals and family systems* (National teleconference). Tallahassee: Florida State University, School of Social Work.

Filteau, M., Leblanc, J., & Bouchard, R. (2003). Quetiapine reduces flashbacks in chronic posttraumatic stress disorder. *Canadian Journal of Psychiatry, 48*(4), 282–283.

Fine, R. (1973). Psychoanalysis. In R. J. Corsini (Ed.), *Current psychotherapies* (pp. 1–33). Itasca, IL: F. E. Peacock.

Finkbeiner, A. K. (1998). *After the death of a child: Living with loss through the years.* Baltimore, MD: Johns Hopkins University Press.

Finkelhor, D. (1979). *Sexually victimized children.* New York: Free Press.

Finkelhor, D. (1984). *Child sexual abuse: New theory and research.* New York: Free Press.

Finkelhor, D. (1987). The trauma of child sexual abuse: Two models. *Journal of Interpersonal Violence, 2,* 348–366.

Finkelhor, D., Gelles, R. J., Hotaling, G. T., & Straus, A. A. (Eds.). (1983). *The dark side of families.* Newbury Park, CA: Sage.

Finkelhor, D., Hotaling, G., Lewis, I., & Smith, C. (1990). Sexual abuse in a national survey of adult men and women. Prevalence, characteristics, and risk factors. *Child Abuse and Neglect, 14,* 19–29.

Finkelhor, D., Omrod, R., Turner, H., & Hamby, S. L. (2005). The victimization of children and youth: A comprehensive, national survey. *Child Maltreatment, 10*(1), 5–25.

Finklehor, D., Hammer, H., & Sedlak, A. (2008, August). Sexually assaulted children: National estimates and characteristics. *NISMART,* 1–12. Washington, DC: U.S. Department of Justice.

Finn, P. (2006). School resource officer programs: Finding the funding, reaping the benefits. *Law Enforcement Bulletin, 75*(8), 1–7.

Finn, P., Townsend, M., Shively, M., & Rich, T. (2005). *A guide to developing, maintaining, and succeeding with your school resource officer program: Practices from the field for law enforcement and school administration.* A report submitted to the U.S. Department of Justice Office of Community Oriented Policing Services. Cambridge MA: Abt Associates.

Fisch, R., Weakland, J. H., & Segal, L. (1983). *The tactics of change.* San Francisco: Jossey-Bass.

Fishbain, D. A., Cutler, R. B., Rosomoff, H. L., & SteeleRosomoff, R. (2000). Risk for violent behavior in patients with chronic pain: Evaluation and management in the pain facility setting. *Pain Medicine, 1*(2), 140–155.

Fisher, B. S., Daigle, L., Cullen, F., & Turner, M. (2003). Reporting sexual victimization to the police and others: Results from a national-level study of college women. *Criminal Justice and Behavior, 30*(1), 6–38.

Fisher, C. B., & Fried, A. L. (2003). Internet-mediated psychological services and the American Psychological Association Ethics Code. *Psychotherapy: Theory, Research, Practice, Training, 40*(1/2), 86–93.

Flack, W., Litz, B., Weathers, F., & Beaudreau, S. (2002). Assessment and diagnosis of PTSD in adults: A comprehensive psychological approach. In M. Williams & J. Sommer (Eds.), *Simple and complex post-traumatic stress disorder: Strategies for comprehensive treatment in clinical practice* (pp. 9–22). Binghamton, NY: Haworth Press.

Flake, E. M., Davis, B. E., Johnson, P. L., & Middleton, L. S. (2009). The psychosocial effects of deployment on military children. *Journal of Developmental and Behavioral Pediatrics, 30,* 271–278.

Flannery, R. (2009). *The violent person: Professional risk management strategies for safety and care.* Riverdale, NY: American Mental Health Foundation Books.

Flannery, R., Fulton, P., Tausch, J. M., & DeLoffi, A. (1991). A program to help staff cope with psychological sequelae of assaults by patients. *Hospital and Community Psychiatry, 42,* 935–938.

Flannery, R., Le Vitre, V., Rego, S., & Walker, P. (2011). Characteristics of staff victims of psychiatric patient assaults: 20-year analysis of the Assaulted Staff Action Program. *Psychiatric Quarterly, 82*(1), 11–21.

Flannery, R., Stone, P., Rego, S., & Walker, A. (2001). Characteristics of staff victims of patient assault: Ten year analysis of the Assaulted Staff Action Program (ASAP). *Psychiatric Quarterly, 72,* 237–248.

Flemons, D., & Grainik, L. (2013). *Relational suicide assessment: Risks, resources, and possibilities for safety.* New York: W.W. Norton.

Flett, G., Hewitt, P., & Heisel, M. (2014). The destructiveness of perfectionism revisited: Implications for the assessment of suicide risk and the prevention of suicide. *Review of General Psychology, 18*(3), 156–172.

Flynn, B. W. (1998, April). *Terrorist events using weapons of mass destruction: Confronting the mental health consequences.* Paper presented at the Third Harvard Symposium on Complex Humanitarian Disasters, Disaster Medical Response: Current Challenges and Strategies, Boston.

Flynn, B. W. (2003). *Mental health all-hazards planning guide.* Rockville, MD: National Technical Assistance Center of the National Association of State Mental Health Directors.

Foa, E., Johnson, K., Feeny, N., & Treadwell, K. (2001). The Child PTSD Symptom Scale: A preliminary examination of its psychometric properties. *Journal of Clinical Child Psychology, 30*(3), 376–384.

Foa, E., Zoellner, L., Feeny, N., Hembree, E., & Alvarez-Conrad, J. (2002). Does imaginal exposure exacerbate PTSD symptoms? *Journal of Consulting and Clinical Psychology, 70*(4), 1022–1028.

Foa, E. B. (2000). Psychosocial treatment of post-traumatic stress disorder. *Journal of Clinical Psychiatry, 61*(Supp. 5), 43–51.

Foa, E. B., & Rauch, S. A. (2004). Cognitive changes during prolonged exposure versus prolonged exposure plus cognitive restructuring in female assault survivors with posttraumatic stress disorder. *Journal of Consulting and Clinical Psychology, 72*(5), 879–884.

Foley, C., & Murphy, M. (2015). Burnout in Irish teachers: Investigating the role of individual differences, work environment, and coping factors. *Teaching and Teacher Education, 50,* 46–55.

Follette, V. M., Iverson, K. M., & Ford, J. D. (2009). Contextual behavior trauma therapy. In C. A. Courtois & J. D. Ford (Eds.), *Treating complex traumatic stress disorders: An evidence-based guide* (pp. 264–285). New York: Guilford Press.

Fonagy, P., Luyten, P., & Strathearn, L. (2011). Borderline personality disorder, mentalization, and the neurobiology of attachment. *Infant Mental Health Journal, 32,* 47–69.

Forbes, D., Creamer, M., Bisson, J., Cohen, J., Crow, B. E., Foa, E. B., . . . Ursano, R. J. (2010). In E. B. Foa, T. M. Keane, M. J. Friedman, & J. A. Cohen (Eds.), A guide to the guidelines for the treatment of PTSD and related conditions. *Journal of Traumatic Stress, 232,* 537–552.

Forbes, D., Phelps, A., McHugh, A., Debenham, P., Hopwood, M., & Creamer, M. (2003). Imagery rehearsal in the treatment of posttraumatic nightmares in Australian veterans with chronic combat-related PTSD: 12-month follow-up data. *Journal of Traumatic Stress, 16*(5), 509–513.

Ford, J. D. (2009). Neurobiological and developmental research: Clinical implications. In C. A. Courtois & J. D. Ford (Eds.), *Treating complex traumatic stress disorders: An evidence-based guide* (pp. 31–58). New York: Guilford Press.

Ford, J. D., & Courtois, C. A. (Eds.). (2013*). Treating complex traumatic stress disorders in children and adolescents: Scientific foundations and therapeutic models.* New York: Guilford Press.

Ford, J. D., Hartman, J. K., Hawke, J., & Chapman, J. (2008). Traumatic individualization, posttraumatic stress disorder, suicidal ideation, and substance abuse risk among juvenile justice-involved youths. *Journal of Child and Adolescent Trauma, 1,* 72–92.

Forney, D. S., Wallace-Schutzman, F., & Wiggers, T. T. (1982). Burnout among career development professionals: Preliminary findings and implications. *Personnel and Guidance Journal, 60,* 435–439.

Forster, J. (1994). The psychiatric emergency: Heading off trouble. *Patient Care, 28,* 130.

Forstmeier, S., & Maercker, A. (2007). Comparison of two diagnostic systems for complicated grief. *Journal of Affective Disorders, 99*(1–3), 203–211.

Fosha, D., Paivio, S. C., Gleiser, K., & Ford, J. D. (2009). Experiential and emotion-focused therapy. In C. A. Courtois & J. D. Ford (Eds.), *Treating complex traumatic stress disorders: An evidence-based guide* (pp. 286–310). New York: Guilford Press.

Foshee, V., Dixon, K., Ennett, S., Moracco, K., Bowling, J., Chang, L., & Moss, J. (2015). The process of adapting a universal dating abuse prevention program to adolescents exposed to domestic violence. *Journal of Interpersonal Violence, 30*(2), 2151–2173.

Foulkes, S. H. (1948). *Introduction to group analytic psychotherapy.* London: Heineman.

Fowler, J. W. (1991). Stages in faith consciousness. *New Directions for Child Development, 52,* 27–45.

Fowler, K., & Western, D. (2011). Subtyping perpetrators of intimate partner violence. *Journal of Interpersonal Violence, 26*(4), 607–639.

Fox, B., Perez, N., Cass, E., Baglivio, M., & Epps, N. (2015). Trauma changes everything: Examining the relationship between adverse childhood experiences and serious violent and chronic juvenile offenders. *Child Abuse and Neglect, 46,* 163–174.

Fox, R., & Cooper, M. (1998). The effects of suicide on the private practitioner: A professional and personal perspective. *Clinical Social Work Journal, 26*(2), 143–157.

Frankl, V. (1969). *The will to meaning: Foundations and applications of logotherapy.* New York: World.

Frazier, P. A., Andes, S., Perera, S., Tomich, P., Tennen, H., Park, C., & Tashiro, T. (2009). Traumatic events among undergraduate students: Prevalence and associated symptoms. *Journal of Counseling Psychology, 56*(3), 450–460.

Frazier, P. A., Steward, J., Tashiro, T., & Rosenberger, S. (2001). Responding to survivors of sexual assault. In E. R. Welfel & R. E. Ingersoll (Eds.), *The mental health desk reference* (pp. 252–258). New York: John Wiley & Sons.

Frazier, P. A., Valtinson, G., & Candell, S. (1994). Evaluation of a coeducational interactive rape prevention program. *Journal of Counseling and Development, 73,* 153–158.

Frederick, C. (1980). Effects of natural versus human induced violence upon individuals. *Evaluation and Change* (Special Issue), 71–75.

Freedy, J. R., & Hobfoll, S. E. (Eds.). (1995). *Traumatic stress: From theory to practice.* New York: Plenum Press.

Freeman, L. (1978). *The sorrow and the fury: Overcoming hurt and loss from childhood to old age.* Upper Saddle River, NJ: Prentice Hall.

Freeman, N. (Speaker). (2003, May 28). *Ecological disaster crisis management* (Cassette Recording No. 052803). Fernandina Beach, FL: Nassau County Emergency Management Department.

Freidel, R. O. (2004). *Borderline personality disorder demystified: An essential guide for understanding and living with BPD.* New York: Marlowe & Company.

Freud, S. (1916). Trauer und melancholie. *Gesammelte Werke* (Vol. 10, pp. 427–446). London: Imago.

Freud, S. (1959). Introduction to psychoanalysis and the war neurosis. In J. Strachey (Ed. & Trans.), *The standard edition of the complete psychological works of Sigmund Freud* (Vol. 5). London: Hogarth Press. (Original work published 1919)

Freud, S. (1963). Introductory lectures on psychoanalysis XVII. In J. Strachey (Ed. & Trans.), *The standard edition of the complete psychological works of Sigmund Freud* (Vol. 16). London: Hogarth Press. (Original work published 1917)

Freudenberger, H. J. (1974). Staff burn-out. *Journal of Social Issues, 30,* 159–165.

Freudenberger, H. J. (1975). The staff burnout syndrome in alternative institutions. *Psychotherapy: Theory, Research, and Practice, 12,* 73–82.

Freudenberger, H. J. (1977). Burn-out: Occupational hazard of child care workers. *Child Care Quarterly, 6,* 90–99.

Freudenberger, H. J., & Robbins, A. (1979). The hazards of being a psychoanalyst. *Psychoanalytic Review, 66,* 275–296.

Freyd, J. (1993). Personal perspectives on the delayed memory debate. *Family Violence and Sexual Assault Bulletin, 9*(3), 28–33.

Frick, R., & Bogart, M. L. (1982). Transference and countertransference in group therapy with Vietnam veterans. *Bulletin of the Menninger Clinic, 46,* 429–444.

Friedman, H. S., & Schustack, M. W. (2010). *Personality: Classic theories and modern research* (5th ed.). Boston: Pearson, Allyn & Bacon.

Friedman, M., & Rosenman, R. (1974). *Type A behavior and your heart.* Greenwich, CT: Fawcett.

Friedman, M. J. (2015). The human stress response. In N. C. Bernardy & M. J. Friedman (Eds.), *A practical guide to treatment: Pharmacological and psychotherapeutic approaches* (pp. 9–20). Washington, DC: American Psychological Association.

Friedman, M. J., Ritchie, E. C., & Watson, P. J. (2006). Overview. In E. C. Ritchie, P. J. Watson, & M. J. Friedman (Eds.), *Interventions following mass violence and disasters: Strategies for mental health practice* (pp. 3–15). New York: Guilford Press.

Friedman, R., & James, J. W. (2009, March). The myth of the stages of grieving, death, and grief. *Counseling Today*, 48–52.

Friess, S. (1997). Behind closed doors: Domestic violence. *The Advocate, 7*, 48–52.

Frueh, B. C., Monnier, J., Yim, E., Grubaugh, A. L., Hamner, M. B., & Knapp, R. G. (2007). A randomized trial of telepsychiatry for posttraumatic stress disorder. *Journal of Telemedicine and Telecare, 13*, 142–147.

Fujimura, L. E., Weis, D. M., & Cochran, J. R. (1985). Suicide: Dynamics and implication for counseling. *Journal of Counseling and Development, 63*, 612–615.

Fukkink, R., & Hermanns, J. (2009). Counseling children at a helpline: Chatting or calling. *Journal of Community Psychology, 37*(8), 938–948.

Fulton, L. (2015). Mean girls and rough boys. *ASCA School Counselor, 52*(5), 18–21.

Furst, S. S. (1967). A survey. In S. S. Furst (Ed.), *Psychic trauma* (pp. 23–33). New York: Basic Books.

Furst, S. S. (1978). The stimulus barrier and the pathogenicity of trauma. *International Journal of Psychoanalysis, 59*, 345–352.

Fusick, L., & Bordeau, W. (2004). Counseling at-risk Afro-American youth: An examination of contemporary issues and effective school-based strategies. *Professional School Counseling, 8*(2), 102–115.

G

Gabe, J., & Elston, M. (2009). "We don't have time to take this." Zero tolerance of violence against health care workers in a time of insecurity. D. Denney (Ed.), *Living in dangerous time: Fear, insecurity, risk and social policy* (pp. 131–149). London, GB: Wiley-Blackwell.

Gaggioli, A. (2014). Cybersightings. *Cyberpsychology, Behaviorism and Social Networking, 17*(9), 630–631.

Gaggioli, A., Pllavicini, F., Morganti, L., Serino, S., Scaratti, C., Briguglio, M., Crifaci, G., . . . Riva, G. (2014). Experimental virtual scenarios with real-time monitoring (interreality) for the management of psychological stress. *Journal of Internet Medical Research, 16*(7), 93–111.

Galai-Gat, T. (2004, April). *Early interventions with survivors of terrorist attacks in Jerusalem.* Paper presented at the 28th Annual Convening of Crisis Intervention Personnel and 2nd Collaborative Crisis Centers Conference, Chicago.

Galatzen-Levy, A. (1993). Adolescent violence and the adolescent self. *Adolescent Psychiatry, 19*, 418–441.

Galvin, K. M., Grill, L. H., Arnston, P. H., & Kinahan, K. E. (2012). Beyond the crisis: Communication between parents and children who survived cancer. In F. C. Dickson & L. M. Webb (Eds.), *Communication for families in crisis: Theories, research, and strategies.* (pp. 229–327). New York: Peter Lang.

Ganas, K., Sampson, G., Cozzi, C., & Stewart, T. (1999, April). *Exposing our biases: Dealing with a rape survivor in a nonjudgmental manner.* Paper presented at the Twenty-third Annual Convening of Crisis Intervention Personnel, Chicago.

Ganas, K., Sampson, G., Vermi, S., & Stewart, T. (1998, April). *Non-judgmentalism in rape crisis.* Paper presented at the Twenty-second Annual Convening of Crisis Intervention Personnel, Chicago.

Garber, R. S. (1965). A psychiatrist's view of remotivation. *Mental Hospitals, 16*, 219–221.

Garcia, J. G., Cartwright, B., Winston, S. M., & Borzuchowska, B. (2003). A transcultural integrative model for ethical decision making in counseling. *Journal of Counseling and Development, 81*, 268–277.

Garfield, P. (1984). *Your child's dreams.* New York: Ballantine Books.

Garrity, S. E. (2011). Sexual assault prevention programs for college-aged men: A critical evaluation. *Journal of Forensic Nursing, 7*(1), 40–48.

Gartner, R. B. (2005*). Beyond betrayal: Taking charge of your life after boyhood sexual abuse.* Hoboken, NJ: John Wiley & Sons.

Gascon, S., Leiter, M., Andres, E., Santed, M., Pereira, J., Cunha, M., . . . Garcia-Campayo, J. (2013). The role of aggressions suffered by healthcare workers as predictors of burnout. *Journal of Clinical Nursing, 22*(21–22), 3120–3129.

Gascon, S., Leiter, M., Andres, E., Santed, M., Pereira, J., Cunha, M., . . . Martinez-Jarreta, B. (2013). The role of aggression suffered by health care workers as predictors of burnout. *Journal of Clinical Nursing, 22*(21–22), 3120–2129.

Gately, L. A., & Stabb, S. D. (2005). Psychology students' training in the management of potentially violent clients. *Professional Psychology: Research and Practice, 36*(6), 681–687.

Gates, D., Fitzwater, E., & Succop, P. (2005). Reducing assaults against nursing home caregivers. *Nursing Research, 54*(2), 119–127.

Gauthier, J. (2005). Toward a universal declaration of ethical principles for psychologists: A progress report. In M. J. S. D. Wedding (Ed.), *Psychology: International Union of Psychological Science (IUPsyS) global resource* (pp. 2–5). Hove, UK: Psychology Press.

Gebhard, P. H. (1997). Memorandum on the incidence of homosexuals in the United States. Bloomington: Indiana University, Center for Sex Research.

Geffner, R. A., & Rosenbaum, A. (2002). Domestic violence offenders: Treatment and intervention standards. *Journal of Aggression, Maltreatment, and Trauma, 5*(2), 1–9.

Gelles, R. J. (1993). Constraints against family violence: Do they work? *American Behavioral Scientist, 36*, 575–586.

Gelles, R. J., & Cornell, C. P. (1985). *Intimate violence in families.* Newbury Park, CA: Sage.

Gentry, J. E., Baranowsky, A. B., & Dunning, K. (2002). ARP: The accelerated recovery program (ARP) for compassion fatigue. In C. R. Figley (Ed.), *Treating compassion fatigue* (pp. 123–137). New York: Brunner/Routledge.

Gerler, E. R., Jr. (Ed.). (2004). *Handbook of school violence.* New York: Haworth Press.

Ghafoori, B., & Hierholzer, R. W. (2010). Personality patterns among black, white, and Hispanic combat veterans. *Psychological Trauma Research, Theory, Practice, and Policy, 2*(1), 12–18.

Gheytanchi, A., Joseph, L., Gierlach, E., Kimpara, S., Housley, J., Franco, Z., et al. (2007). The dirty dozen: Twelve failures of the hurricane Katrina response and how psychology can help. *American Psychologist, 62*(2), 118–130.

Gibbons, P., Collins, M., & Reid, C. (2011). How useful are indices of personality pathology when assessing domestic violence perpetrators? *Psychological Assessment, 23*(1), 164–173.

Gibson, L. (2015). Acute Stress Disorder. U.S. Department of Veterans Affairs, National Center for PTSD. Retrieved from http://www.ptsd.va.gov/professiona/treatment/early/acute-stress-disorder.asp

Giduck, J. (2005). *Terror at Beslan.* Golden, CO: Archangel Group.

Gidycz, C., Orchowski, L., Probst, D., Edwards, K., Murphy, M., & Tansil, E. (2015). Concurrent administration of sexual assault prevention and risk reduction pogramming: Outcomes for women. *Violence Against Women, 21*(6), 780–800.

Giebels, E., & Janssen, O. (2005). Conflict stress and reduced well-being at work: The buffering effect of third-party help. *European Journal of Work and Organizational Psychology, 14*(2), 137–155.

Giel, R. (1990). Psychosocial process in disaster. *International Journal of Mental Health, 19*, 7–20.

Gil, E., & Johnson, T. C. (1993). *Sexualized children: Assessment and treatment of sexualized children and children who molest.* Rockville, MD: Launch Press.

Gil-Rivas, V., Kilmer, R. P., Hypes, A. W., & Roof, K. A. (2010). The caregiver–child relationship and children's adjustment following hurricane Katrina. In R. P Kilmer, V. Gil-Rivas, R. G. Tedeschi, & L. G. Calhoun (Eds.), *Helping families and communities recover from disaster: Lessons learned from hurricane Katrina and its aftermath* (pp. 55–76). Washington, DC: American Psychological Association.

Gil-Rivas, V., Silver, R. C., Holman, E. A., McIntosh, D., & Poulin, M. (2007). Parental response and adolescent adjustment to the September 11th terrorist attacks. *Journal of Traumatic Stress, 20,* 1063–1068.

Gilbertson, M. W., Shenton, M. E., Ciszewski, A., Kasai, K., Lasko, N. B., Orr, S. P., et al. (2002). Smaller hippocampal volume predicts pathologic vulnerability to psychological trauma. *Neuroscience, 5,* 1242–1247.

Gillespie, D., & Campbell, F. (2011) Effect of stroke on family careers and family relationships. *Nursing Standard, 26,* 39–46.

Gillies, J., & Neimeyer, R. A. (2006). Loss, grief, and the search for significance: Toward a model of meaning reconstruction in bereavement. *Journal of Constructivist Psychology, 19,* 31–65.

Gillig, P. M., Dumaine, M., Stammer, J. W., Hillard, J. R., & Grubb, P. (1990). What do police officers really want from the mental health system? *Hospital and Community Psychiatry, 41,* 663–665.

Gilliland, B. E., & James, R. K. (1998). *Theories and strategies in counseling and psychotherapy* (4th ed.). Boston: Allyn & Bacon.

Gillis, J. R. (1999, August). *Community education and services for same-sex partner abuse.* Paper presented at the 107th Annual Convention of the American Psychological Association, Symposium on Outing Same-Sex Partner Abuse—Defining the Issues, Boston.

Ginnis, K., White, E., Riss, A., & Wharff, E. (2015). Family-based crisis intervention in the emergency department: A new model of care. *Journal of Family studies, 24*(1), 172–179.

Gist, R., & Lubin, B. (Eds.). (1989). *Psychological aspects of disaster.* New York: John Wiley & Sons.

Gist, R., & Lubin, B. (Eds.). (1999). *Response to disaster: Psychosocial, community, and ecological responses.* Philadelphia: Brunner/Mazel.

Giunta, R., & Giunta, C. (2002). *Grief recovery workbook.* Brentwood, TN: Integrity Publishers.

Gladding, S. T. (1987). Poetic expressions: A counseling art in elementary schools. *Elementary School Guidance and Counseling, 21,* 307–311.

Gladding, S. T. (2002). From Pier 94, near Ground Zero, New York City. In D. D. Bass & R. Yep (Eds.), *Terrorism, trauma, and tragedies: A counselor's guide to preparing and responding* (pp. 7–9). Alexandria, VA: American Counseling Association.

Gladding, S. T. (2010). *Family therapy: History, theory and practice* (5th ed.). Upper Saddle River, NJ: Merrill.

Glanzt, K., Rizzo, A., & Graap, K. (2003). Virtual reality for psychotherapy: Current reality and future possiblities. *Psychotherapy: Theory, Research, Practice, Training, 40*(1/2), 55–67.

Glaser, J. W. (2002). The community of concern. An ethical discernment process should include and empower all people relevant to the decision. *Health Progress, 83,* 17–20.

Glasser, N., Eden, K. B., Bloom, T., & Perrin, N. (2010). Computerized aid improves safety decision process for survivors of intimate partner violence. *Journal of Interpersonal Violence, 25*(11), 1947–1964.

Glasser, W. (1965). *Reality therapy.* New York: Harper & Row.

Glasser, W. (1969). *Schools without failure.* New York: Harper & Row.

Glasser, W. (1976). *Positive addiction.* New York: Harper & Row.

Glasser, W. (1985). *Control theory: A new explanation about how we control our lives.* New York: Harper & Row.

Glasser, W. (2000, May 28). Invited address at the Evolution of Psychotherapy Conference, Anaheim, CA. Retrieved August 14, 2002, from www.wglasser.com

Glatt, S. J., Tylee, D. S., Chandler, S. D., Pazol, J., Nievergeit, C. M., et al. (2013). Blood-based gene-expression predictors of PTD risk and resilience among deployed marines: A pilot study. *American Journal of Medical Genetics Part B: Neuropsychiatric Genetics, 162*(4), 313–326.

Glazer, H. R. (2010). Filial play therapy for grieving preschool children. In C. E. Schaefer (Ed.), *Play therapy for preschool children* (pp. 89–105). Washington, DC: American Psychological Association.

Glazer, H. R., Clark, M. D., Thomas, R., & Haxton, H. (2010). Parenting after the death of a spouse. *American Journal of Hospice and Palliative Medicine, 27*(8), 532–536.

Gleick, J. (2008). *Chaos: Making a new science.* New York: Penguin Books.

Glenn, C. (2014). A bridge over troubled waters: Spirituality and resilience with emerging adult childhood trauma survivors. *Journal of Spirituality in Mental Health, 16*(1), 37–50.

Glezer, A., & Brendel, R. W. (2010). Beyond emergencies: The use of physical restraints in medical and psychiatric settings. *Harvard Review of Psychiatry, 18*(6), 353–358.

GM's Onstar, American Red Cross partner to provide emergency services in crisis situations (2008, September). *Domain B.* Retrieved from http://domain-b.com.

Golan, N. (1978). *Treatment in crisis situations.* New York: Free Press.

Golan, N. (1987). In A. Minahan (Ed.), Crisis intervention. *Encyclopedia of Social Work, 18,* 360–372. Washington, DC: National Association of Social Workers.

Gold, S. N. (2009). Contextual therapy. In C. A. Courtois & J. D. Ford (Eds.), *Treating complex traumatic stress disorders: An evidence-based guide* (pp. 227–242). New York: Guilford Press.

Goldenberg, H., & Goldenberg, I. (2013). *Family therapy: An overview* (8th ed.). Belmont, CA: Brooks/Cole, Cengage.

Goldney, R. D. (2000). Prediction of suicide and attempted suicide. In K. Hawton & K. Van Heeringen (Eds.), *The international handbook of suicide and attempted suicide* (pp. 85–595). Chichester, England: John Wiley & Sons.

Goldney, R. D. (2005). Suicide prevention: A pragmatic review of recent studies. *Crisis: The Journal of Crisis Intervention and Suicide Prevention, 26*(3), 128–140.

Goldstein, A. P. (1991). *Delinquent gangs: A psychological perspective.* Champaign, IL: Research Press.

Goldstein, A. P., & Kodluboy, D. W. (1998). *Gangs in schools: Signs, symbols, and solutions.* Champaign, IL: Research Press.

Golec, J. A. (1983). A contextual approach to the social psychological study of disaster recovery. *International Journal of Mass Emergencies and Disasters, 1,* 255–276.

Golembiewski, R. T., & Munzenrider, R. F. (1993). Health-related covariants of phases of burnout: A replication. *Organization Development Journal, 11,* 1–12.

Golembiewski, R. T., Munzenrider, R. F., & Stevenson, J. G. (1986). *Stress in organizations: Toward a phase model of burnout.* New York: Praeger.

Golembiewski, R. T., Munzenrider, R. F., Scherb, K., & Billingsley, W. (1992). Burnout and "psychiatric" cases: Early evidence of an association. *Anxiety, Stress and Coping: An International Journal, 5,* 69–78.

Golomb, M. R., Warden, S. J., Fess, E., Rabin, B., Yonkman, J., & Shirley, B. (2011). Maintained hand function and forearm bone health 14 months after an in-home virtual reality videogame and tele-rehabilitation intervention in an adolescent with hemiplegic cerebral palsy. *Journal of Child Neurology, 26*(3), 389–393.

Goncalves, R., Pedrozo, A. L., Coutinho, E., Figueria, I., & Ventura, P. (2012). Efficacy of virtual reality exposure therapy in the treatment of PTSD: A systematic review. *PLoS ONE, 7*(12), e48469.

Gondolf, E. (1984). *Men who batter: Why they abuse women and how they stop their abuse.* Indiana, PA: Domestic Violence Study Center, Indiana University of Pennsylvania.

Gondolf, E. (1985). Fighting for control: A clinical assessment of men who batter. *Social Casework, 65,* 48–54.

Gondolf, E. (2007). Theoretical and research support for the Duluth model: A reply to Dutton and Corvo. *Aggression and Violent Behavior, 12*(6), 644–657.

Gondolf, E., & Fisher, E. R. (1988). *Battered women as survivors: An alternative to treating learned helplessness.* Lexington, MA: Lexington Books.

Gonzales, R., Ang, A., Murphy, D., Glik, D., & Anglin, D. (2014). Substance abuse recovery outcomes among a cohort of youth participating in a mobile-based texting aftercare pilot program. *Journal of Substance Abuse Treatment, 47*(1), 20–26.

Gonzalez, A. (2013). How do social workers in the ICU perceive their role in providing end-of-life care? What factors impede or help them in carrying out this role in end-of-life care and is social work education a contributing component? Unpublished dissertation, University of Pennsylvania.

Goodman, L. A., & Epstein, D. (2011). The justice system response to domestic violence. In J. W. White, M. Koss, & A. E. Kazdin (Eds.), *Violence against women and children: Vol.1. Mapping the terrain* (pp. 215–235). Washington, DC: American Psychological Association.

Goodman, R. D., Calderon, A. M., &Tate, K. A. (2014). Liberation focused community outreach: A qualitative exploration of peer group supervision during disaster response. *Journal of Community Psychology, 42*(2), 228–236.

Goodwin, J. (1982). *Sexual abuse: Incest victims and their families.* Boston: John Wright.

Goodwin, J. (1988). Post-traumatic symptoms in abused children. *Journal of Traumatic Stress, 1,* 475–488.

Gordon, N. S., Farberow, N. L., & Maida, C. A. (1999). *Children and disaster.* Philadelphia: Brunner/Mazel.

Gorter, R., Albrecht, G., Hoostraten, J., & Eijkman, M. (1999). Factor validity of the Maslach Burnout Inventory—Dutch version (MBI-NL) among dentists. *Journal of Organizational Behavior, 20*(2), 209–217.

Gottfredson, D. C., Gottfredson, G. D., & Skroban, S. (1998). Can prevention work where it is needed most? *Evaluation Review, 22*(3), 315–340.

Gottman, J. M., Gottman, J. S., & Atkins, C. L. (2011). The Comprehensive Soldier Fitness program: Family skills component. *American Psychologist, 66*(1), 52–57.

Gould, M., & Shaffer, D. (1986). The impact of suicide in television movies: Evidence of imitation. *New England Journal of Medicine, 315,* 690–693.

Gould, M. S., Kalafat, J., Harris-Munfakh, J., & Kleinman, M. (2007). An evaluation of crisis hotline outcomes part 2: Suicidal callers. *Suicide and Life-Threatening Behavior, 37*(3), 338–352.

Gradus, J. L., Suvak, M. K., Wisco, B., Marx, B. P., & Resick, P. A. (2013). Treatment of posttraumatic stress disorder reduces suicidal ideation. *Depression and Anxiety, 30*(10), 1046–1053.

Graham, L. K. (2014). Political dimensions of pastoral care in community disaster responses. *Pastoral Psychology, 63*(4), 471–488.

Granello, D. H., & Granello, P. F. (2007). *Suicide: An essential guide for helping professionals and educators.* Boston: Pearson/Allyn & Bacon.

Grassi, L., Peron, L., Mafangoni, C., Zanchi, P., & Vanni, A. (2001). Characteristics of violent behavior in acute psychiatric inpatients: A 5-year Italian study. *Acta Psychiatrica Scandinavica, 104*(4), 273–279.

Gray, M. J., & Litz, B. T. (2005). Behavioral interventions for recent trauma: Empirically informed practice guidelines. *Behavior Modification, 29,* 189–215.

Gray, R. E. (1988). The role of the school counselor with bereaved teenagers: With and without peer support groups. *School Counselor, 35,* 185–192.

Grayson, P. A., & Meilman, M. W. (Eds.). (2006). *College mental health practice.* New York: Routledge.

Greason, P. (2015). Mindfulness meditation. In T. Robert & V. Kelly (Eds.), *Critical incidents in integrating spirituality into counseling* (pp. 247–254). Alexandria, VA: American Counseling Association.

Green, B. L., & Solomon, S. D. (1995). The mental health impact of natural and technological disasters. In J. R. Freedy & S. E. Hobfoll (Eds.), *Traumatic stress: From theory to practice* (pp. 163–180). New York: Plenum Press.

Green, J. W. (2008). *Beyond the good death: The anthropology of modern dying.* Philadelphia: University of Pennsylvania Press.

Green, M. A., & Berlin, M. A. (1987). Five psychosocial variables related to the existence of post-traumatic stress disorder symptoms. *Journal of Clinical Psychology, 43,* 643–649.

Green Cross Academy of Traumatology. (2005). *Standards of self-care guidelines.* Retrieved from http://www.greencross.org/

Greene, D. B. (1994). Childhood suicide and myths surrounding it. *Social Work, 39,* 230–233.

Greenfield, L., Rand, M., & Craven, D. (1998). *Violence by intimates: Analysis of data on crime by current and former spouses, boyfriends, and girlfriends.* Washington, DC: U.S. Department of Justice.

Greenfield, T. K., McNeil, D. E., & Binder, R. L. (1989). Violent behavior and length of psychiatric hospitalization. *Hospital and Community Psychiatry, 40,* 809–814.

Greenglass, E., Fiksenbaum, L., & Burke, R. (1996). Components of social support, buffering effects and burnout: Implications for psychological functioning. *Anxiety, Stress, and Coping, 9*(3), 185–197.

Greenspan, M. (2003). *Healing through the dark emotions: The wisdom of grief, fear, and despair.* Boston: Shambhala.

Greenstone, J. L., & Leviton, S. C. (1993). *Elements of crisis intervention.* Pacific Grove, CA: Brooks/Cole.

Greenstone, J. L., & Leviton, S. C. (2011). *Elements of crisis intervention: Crises and how to respond to them* (3rd ed.). Belmont, CA: Brooks/Cole.

Greenwald, B. (1985a). *In-Touch Hotline training materials: Coping.* Chicago: University of Illinois at Chicago Circle Campus, Counseling Center.

Greenwald, B. (1985b). *In-Touch Hotline training materials: The disturbed caller.* Chicago: University of Illinois at Chicago Circle Campus, Counseling Center.

Gressard, C. F. (1986). Self-help groups for Vietnam veterans experiencing post-traumatic stress disorder. *Journal for Specialists in Group Work, 11,* 74–79.

Griffing, S., Ragin, D., Morrison, S., Sage, R., Madry, L., & Primm, B. (2005). Reasons for returning to abusive relationships: Effects of prior victimization. *Journal of Family Violence, 20*(5), 341–348.

Griffith, J. L. (2010). *Religion that heals, religion that harms: A guide for clinical practice* New York: Guilford Press.

Griffith, T. (2003). Assisting with the "big hurts, little tears" of the youngest grievers: Working with three-, four-, and five-year-olds who have experienced loss and grief because of death. *Illness, Crisis, and Loss, 11*(3), 217–225.

Grills, C. (2004). African-centered psychology: Basic principles. In T. Parham (Ed.), *Counseling persons of African descent: Raising the bar of practitioner competence* (pp. 32–56). Thousand Oaks, CA: Sage.

Grinker, R. R., & Spiegel, J. P. (1945). *Men under stress.* Philadelphia: Blakiston.

Grollman, E. A. (1996). Spiritual support after a sudden loss. In K. J. Doka (Ed.), *Living with grief after sudden loss: Suicide, homicide, accident, heart attack, stroke* (pp. 185–188). Washington, DC: Hospice Foundation of America.

Gross, S., & Anthony, K. (Eds.). (2003). *Technology in counseling and psychotherapy: A practitioner's guide.* New York: Palgrave Macmillan.

Grossi, G., Perski, A., Ekstedt, M., Johansson, T., Lindstrom, M., & Holm, K. (2005). The morning salivary cortisol response in burnout. *Journal of Psychosomatic Research, 59*(2), 103–111.

Grossman, D. (1995). *On killing: The psychological cost of learning to kill in war and society.* Boston: Little, Brown.

Groth, N., & Birnbaum, H. J. (1979). *Men who rape: The psychology of the offender.* New York: Plenum Press.

Grouse, A. S. (1984). The effects of organizational stress on inpatient psychiatric medication patterns. *American Journal of Psychiatry, 141*, 878–881.

Grunsted, V. L., Cisneros, M. X., & Belen, D. V. (1991, April). *Working with the disturbed hotline caller.* Paper presented at the Fifteenth Annual Convening of Crisis Intervention Personnel, Chicago.

Grusznski, R. J., & Carrillo, T. P. (1988). Who completes batterers' treatment groups? An empirical investigation. *Journal of Family Violence, 3*(2), 141–150.

Gu, J., Zhong, C. B., & Page-Gould, E. (2012). Listen to your heart: When false somatic feedback shapes moral behavior. *Journal of Experimental Psychology: General, 142*, 307–312.

Gudas, L. (1990, August). *Children's reactions to bereavement: A developmental perspective.* Paper presented at the annual meeting of the American Psychological Association, Boston.

Gueritault-Chalvin, V., Kalichman, S. C., Demi, A., & Peterson, J. L. (2000). Work-related stress and occupational burnout in AIDS caregivers: Test of a coping model with nurses providing AIDS care. *AIDS Care, 12*(2), 149–161.

Guerra, P. (1999, May). Counselors help victims of school shooting. *Counseling Today, 41*, 12–14.

Guerra, P., & Schmitt, S. M. (1999, June). Reactions to Littleton shooting. *Counseling Today, 41*, 26–27.

Guerriero-Austrom, M. G., & Fleming, S. J. (1990, August). *Effects of sibling death on adolescents' physical and emotional well-being: A longitudinal study.* Paper presented at the annual meeting of the American Psychological Association, Boston.

Guida, A. (2001). Depression . . . or just the blues? *ASCA School Counselor, 39*(5), 10–13.

Gulati, P., & Guest, G. (1990). The community centered model: A garden-variety approach or a radical transformation of community practice? *Social Work, 35*, 63–68.

Gumaer, J. (1984). *Counseling and therapy for children.* New York: Free Press.

Gunn, J., & Lester, D. (2013). Using goggle searches on the internet to monitor suicidal behavior. *Journal of Affective Disorders, 148*(2–3), 411–412.

Gurvitz, T. V., Shenton, M. E., & Pittman, R. K. (1995). *Reduced hippocampal volume on magnetic resonance imagining in chronic post-traumatic stress disorder.* Paper presented at the International Society for Traumatic Stress Studies, Miami.

Guterman, J. T., & Rudes, J. (2008). Social constructionism and ethics: Implications for counseling. *Counseling and Values, 52*, 136–144.

Guterman, N. B., Jayaratme, S., & Bargal, D. (1996). Workplace violence and victimization experienced by social workers: A cross-national study of Americans and Israelis. In G. R. VandenBos & E. Q. Bulatao (Eds.), *Violence on the job: Identifying risks and developing solutions* (pp. 175–188). Washington, DC: American Psychological Association.

Gutermman, J. T. (2013). *Mastering the art of solution focused counseling* (2nd ed.). Alexandria, VA: American Counseling Association.

Gutheil, T. G. (1978). Observation on the theoretical basis for seclusion of the psychiatric inpatient. *American Journal of Psychiatry, 135*, 325–328.

Guthrie, E., Kapur, N., Mackway-Jones, K., Chew-Graham, C., Moorey, J., Mendel, E., et al. (2001). Randomized controlled trial of brief psychological intervention after deliberate self-poisoning. *British Medical Journal, 323*, 135–138.

Gutner, C. A., Casement, M. D., Gilbert, K. S., & Resick, P. A. (2013). Change in sleep symptoms across Cognitive Processing Therapy and Prolonged Exposure: A longitudinal perspective. *Behaviour Research and Therapy, 51*(12), 817–822.

Guy, J. D., Brown, C. K., & Poelstra, P. L. (1990). Who gets attacked? A national survey of patient violence directed at psychologists in clinical practice. *Professional Psychology: Research and Practice, 21*, 493–495.

H

Haber, D. (2006). Life review: Implementation, theory, research, and therapy. *International Journal of Aging and Human Development, 63*(2), 153–171.

Hacker, K., Suglia, S., Fried, L., Rappaport, N., & Cabral, H. (2006). Developmental differences in risk factors for suicide attempts between ninth and eleventh graders. *Suicide and Life-Threatening Behavior, 36*(2), 154–166.

Haen, C. (2008). Vanquishing monsters: Drama therapy for treating childhood trauma in the group setting. In C. A. Malchiodi (Ed.), *Creative interventions with traumatized children* (pp. 225–246). New York: Guilford Press.

Hafkenscheid, A. (2005). Event countertransference and vicarious traumatization: Theoretically valid and clinically useful concepts? *European Journal of Psychotherapy, Counseling and Health, 7*(3), 159–168.

Hage, S. M. (2006). Profiles of women survivors: The development of agency in abusive relationships. *Journal of Counseling and Development, 84*(1), 83–93.

Hague, G., & Sardinha, L. (2010). Violence against women: Devastating legacy and transforming services. *Psychiatry, Psychology and Law, 17*(4), 503–522.

Haines, J., Williams, C., & Lester, D. (2011). The characteristics of those who do and do not leave suicide notes: Is the method of residuals valid? *Omega: Journal of Death and Dying, 63*(1), 79–94.

Haj-Yahia, M. M. (2003). Beliefs about wife beating among Arab men from Israel: The influence of their patriarchal ideology. *Journal of Family Violence, 18*(4), 193–206.

Halbesleben, J. R. (2006). Sources of social support and burnout: Meta-analytic test of the Conservation of Resources model. *Journal of Applied Psychology, 91*(5), 1134–1145.

Halbsgut, J. L. (2011). Masculine gender role norms: Understanding the conformity of domestic violence perpetrators.

Dissertation Abstracts International: Section B. The Sciences and Engineering, 7087.

Haley, J. (1973). *Uncommon therapy.* New York: Norton.

Haley, J. (1976). *Problem-solving therapy.* New York: McGraw-Hill.

Haley, W. E., Allen, R. S., Reynolds, S., Chen, H., Burton, A., & Gallagher-Thompson, D. (2002). Family issues in end-of-life decision making and end-of-life care. *American Behavioral Scientist, 46,* 284–298.

Haley, W. E., Bergman, E. J., Roth, D. L., McVie, T., Gaugler, J., & Mittleman, M. S. (2008). Long-term effects of bereavement and caregiver intervention on dementia caregiver depressive symptoms. *Gerontologist, 48*(6), 732–740.

Hall, E. (1976). *Beyond culture.* Garden City, NY: Anchor Press/Doubleday.

Halpern, J., & Tramontin, M. (2007). *Disaster mental health: Theory and practice.* Belmont, CA: Brooks/Cole.

Hamberger, L. K. (1994). The battered woman: Identification and intervention. *The Female Patient, 19,* 29–30, 32–33.

Hamberger, L. K., & Hastings, J. E. (1986, August). *Skills training for treatment of spouse abusers: An outcome study.* Paper presented at the meeting of the American Psychological Association, Washington, DC.

Hamby, S. L. (1998). Partner violence: Prevention and intervention. In J. L. Jasinski & L. M. Williams (Eds.), *Partner violence: A comprehensive review of 20 years of research* (pp. 210–258). Newbury Park, CA: Sage.

Hamel, J., (2014, July). *Evidenced-based practice for domestic violence: Politics and practicalities.* International Family Violence and Child Victimization Research Conference, Portsmouth, NH.

Hamilton, B., & Coates, J. (1993). Perceived helpfulness and use of professional services by abused women. *Journal of Family Violence, 8,* 313–321.

Hamilton, J., & Workman, R. (1998). Persistence of combat-related posttraumatic stress symptoms for 75 years. *Journal of Traumatic Stress, 11*(4), 763–768.

Hammond, L. C., & Gantt, L. (1998). Using art in counseling: Ethical considerations. *Journal of Counseling and Development, 76,* 271–275.

Hamois, D. A. (2015). The impact of coping strategies on work stress, burnout, and job satisfaction in school counselors. *Dissertation Abstracts International: Section B. The Sciences and Engineering, 75*(8-B(E)).

Hampton, R. L., Vandergriff-Avery, M., & Kim, J. (1999). Understanding the origins and incidence of spousal violence in North America. In T. P. Gullotta & S. J. McElhaney (Eds.), *Violence in homes and communities: Prevention, intervention and treatment* (pp. 39–70). Thousand Oaks, CA: Sage.

Hamstra, B. (1986). Neurobiological substrates of violence: An overview for forensic clinicians. *Journal of Psychiatry and Law, 14,* 349–374.

Handford, H. A., Mayes, S. D., Mattison, R. E., Humphrey, F. J., Bahnato, S., Bixler, E. O., & Kales, J. D. (1986). Child and parent reactions to the Three Mile Island nuclear accident. *Journal of the American Academy of Child Psychiatry, 25,* 346–356.

Handran, J. (2014). Trauma-informed organizational culture: The prevention, reduction, and treatment of compassion fatigue. *Dissertation Abstracts International: Section A. Humanities and Social Sciences, 74*(10-A(E)).

Hansen, J. C., & Frantz, T. T. (Eds.). (1984). *Death and grief in the family.* Rockville, MD: Aspen Systems.

Hanson, B. (2002). Interventions for batterers: Program approaches, program tensions. In A. R. Roberts (Ed.), *Handbook of domestic violence: Intervention strategies* (pp. 419–450). New York: Oxford University Press.

Hanson, R. O., & Hayslip, B. (2000). Widowhood in later life. In J. H. Harvey & E. D. Miller (Eds.), *Loss and trauma: General and close relationship perspectives* (pp. 345–354). Philadelphia: Brunner-Routledge.

Hanson, S., Kerkholt, T., & Bush, S. (2005). Health care ethics for psychologists: A casebook (pp. 9–37). Washington, DC: American Psychological Association.

Hanson, T. C., Hesselbrock, M., Tworkoski, S. H., & Swan, S. (2002). The prevalence and management of trauma in the public domain: An agency and clinical perspective. *Journal of Behavioral Health Science and Research, 29*(4), 365–380.

Hansson, K., & Cederblad, M. (2004). Sense of coherence as a meta-theory for salutogenic family therapy. *Journal of Family Psychotherapy, 15,* 39–54.

Hansson, R. O., & Stroebe, M. S. (2007). *Bereavement in late life: Coping, adaptation, and developmental influences.* Washington, DC: American Psychological Association.

Hao, S., Hong, W., Xu, H., Zhou, L., & Xie, Z., (2015). Relationship between resilience, stress, and burnout among civil servants in Beijing, China: Mediating and moderating effect analyses. *Personality and Individual Differences, 83,* 65–71.

Hardiman, P., & Simmonds, J. (2013). Spiritual well- being, burnout, and trauma in counsellors and psychotherapists. *Mental Health, Religion, & Culture, 16*(10), 1044–1055.

Hardwick, P. J., & Rowton-Lee, M. A. (1996). Adolescent homicide: Toward assessment of risk. *Journal of Adolescence, 19*(3), 263–276.

Hardy, K. V. (Therapist). (1997). *Family systems therapy* (Videotape No. 0-205-32931-4, T. Labriola, Producer). In J. Carlson & D. Kjos, *Family systems with Hardy: Psychotherapy with the experts.* Boston: Allyn & Bacon.

Hare, R. (1991). *Manual for the Hare Psychopathy Checklist–Revised.* Toronto, Canada: Multi-health Systems.

Harms, P. D., Herian, M. N., Krasikova, D. V., Vanhove, A., & Lester, D. B. (2013). *The Comprehensive Soldier Fitness Program evaluation report #4: Evaluation of resilience training mental and behavioral health outcomes. U.S. Army.* Retrieved at www.ppc.sas .upem.edu/csftechreport4mrt .pdf

Harris, B., & Leather, P. (2012). Levels and consequences of exposure to service user violence: Evidence from a sample of UK social care staff. *British Journal of Social Work, 42*(5), 851–869.

Harris, D. L. (2011). Navigating intimate relationship loss: When the relationship dies but the person is still living. In D. L. Harris (Ed.), *Counting our losses: Reflecting on change, loss, and transition in everyday life* (pp. 65–74). New York: Routledge/Taylor & Francis Group.

Harris, D. L., & Isenor, J. (2011). Loss of employment. In D. L. Harris (Ed.), *Counting our losses: Reflecting on change, loss, and transition in everyday life* (pp. 163–170). New York: Routledge/Taylor & Francis Group.

Harris-Bowlsby, J. (2000). The Internet? Blessing or bane for the counseling profession. In J. W. Bloom & G. R. Walz (Eds.), *Cybercounseling and cyberlearning: Strategies and resources for the millennium.* Alexandria, VA: American Counseling Association 39–50.

Harrison, R. L., & Westwood, M. J. (2009). Preventing vicarious traumatization of mental health therapists: Identifying protective practices. *Psychotherapy: Theory, Research, Practice, Training, 46*(2), 203–219.

Hart, B. (1980, June). Testimony at a hearing before the U.S. Commission on Civil Rights, Harrisburg, PA.

Hart, B. (1986). Lesbian battering: An examination. In K. Loebel (Ed.), *Naming the violence: Speaking out about lesbian battering* (pp. 173–189). Seattle, WA: Seal.

Hart, C. L., Hole, D. J., Lawlor, D. A., Smith, G., & Lever, T. F. (2007). Effect of conjugal bereavement on mortality of the bereaved spouse in participants of the Renfrew/Paisley study. *Journal of Epidemiology and Community Health, 61*(5), 455–460.

Harte, J. M., van Leeuwen, M. E., & Theuws, R., (2013). The nature, extent, and judicial response to aggression and violence directed against care workers in psychiatry. *Tijdschrift vooor Psychiatrie, 55*(5), 325–335.

Hartel, J. A. (1993). The prosecution of assaultive clients. *Perspectives in Psychiatric Care, 29*, 7–14.

Hartsough, D. (1982). Planning for disaster: A new community outreach program for mental health centers. *Journal of Community Psychology, 10*, 255–264.

Harvey, M. R., Tummala-Narra, P., & Hamm, B. (2012). An ecological view of recovery and resilience in trauma survivors: Implications for clinical and community intervention. In R. A. McMackin, E. Newman, J. M. Fogler, & T. M. Keane (Eds.), *Trauma therapy in context: The science and craft of evidence-based practice.* (pp. 99–120). Washington, DC: American Psychological Association.

Harwood, D., & Jacoby, R. (2000). Suicidal behavior in the elderly. In K. Hawton & K. Van Heeringen (Eds.), *The international handbook of suicide.* (pp. 275–292). New York: John Wiley & Sons.

Hassan, M., Gary, F., Killon, C., Lewin, L., & Totten, V. (2015). Patterns of sexual abuse among children: Victims' and perpetrators' characteristics. *Journal of Aggression, Maltreatment, and Trauma, 24*(4), 400–418.

Hastings, J. E., & Hamberger, L. K. (1988). Personality characteristics of spouse abusers: A controlled comparison. *Violence and Victims, 3*, 31–47.

Hathaway, S., & McKinley, J. (1989). *The MMPI-2.* Minneapolis: University of Minnesota Press.

Hattendorf, J., Ottens, A., & Lomax, R. (1999). Type and severity of abuse and posttraumatic stress disorder symptoms reported by women who killed abusive partners. *Violence Against Women, 5*(3), 292–312.

Hatton, C. L., & Valente, S. M. (1984). Bereavement group for parents who suffered a suicidal loss of a child. In C. L. Hatton & S. M. Valente (Eds.), *Suicide assessment and intervention* (2nd ed., pp. 163–173). East Norwalk, CT: Appleton-Century-Crofts.

Hausman, A., Pierce, G., & Briggs, L. (1996). School-based violence prevention education. *Journal of Adolescent Health, 19*(2), 104–110.

Hawkins, R., & Beauvais, C. (1985, August). *Evaluation of group therapy with abusive men: The police record.* Paper presented at the meeting of the American Psychological Association, Los Angeles.

Hawton, K., & Van Heeringen, K. (Eds.). (2000). *International handbook of suicide and attempted suicide.* Chichester, England: John Wiley & Sons.

Hayes, G. (2002). Intervening with school students after terrorist acts. In D. D. Bass & R. Yep (Eds.), *Terrorism, trauma, and tragedies: A counselor's guide to preparing and responding* (pp. 63–65). Alexandria, VA: American Counseling Association.

Hayes, G., Goodwin, T., & Miars, B. (1990). After disaster: A crisis support team at work. *American Journal of Nursing, 2*, 61–64.

Hayes, L. L. (1999, May). Breaking the blue wall of silence: Counseling police officers. *Counseling Today, 41*(11), 1, 6.

Hayes, S. C., Strosahl, K. D., & Wilson, K. G. (1999). *Acceptance and commitment therapy: An experiential approach to behavior change.* New York: Guilford Press.

Haynes, R. A., & Henderson, C. L. (2001). *Essential strategies for school security: A practical guide for teachers and school administrators.* Springfield, IL: Charles C Thomas.

Hays, K. F. (1985). Electra in mourning: Grief work and the adult incest survivor. *Psychotherapy Patient, 2*, 45–58.

Hays, P. A. (2001). *Addressing cultural complexities in practice: A framework for clinicians and counselors.* Washington, DC: American Psychological Association.

Hays, P. A. (2008). *Addressing cultural complexities in practice: Assessment, diagnosis, and therapy* (2nd ed.). Washington, DC: American Psychological Association.

Haywood, C., & Leuthe, J. (1980, September). *Crisis intervention in the 1980s: From networking to social influence.* Paper presented at the annual convention of the American Psychological Association, Montreal.

Hazell, P., & Lewin, T. (1993). An evaluation of postvention following adolescent suicide. *Suicide and Life Threatening Behavior, 23*(2), 101–109.

Hazen, M. (2009). Recognizing and responding to workplace grief. *Organizational Dynamics, 38*(4), 290–296.

Hazler, R. J. (1996). *Breaking the cycle of violence: Interventions for bullying and victimization.* Washington, DC: Accelerated Development.

Healthful Chat. (2015). Retrieved at http://www.healthfulchat.org/mental-health-chat-rooms.html.

Health Insurance Portability and Privacy Act of 1996 (HIPAA), Pub. L. No. 104-191 (1996).

Healy, D. (1987). Rhythm and blues: Neurochemical, neuropharmacological, and neuropsychological implications of a hypothesis of circadian rhythm dysfunction in the affective disorders. *Psychopharmacology, 93*, 271–285.

Healy, M. J., Smith, C., & O'Sullivan, C. (1998). *Batterer intervention: Program approaches and criminal justice strategies* (Report No. NCJ 168638). Washington, DC: U.S. Department of Justice.

Heath, M. A., & Hudnall, G. (2011). Special issue on strengthening school-based support for bereaved students: Editors' introduction. *School Psychology International, 32*(2), 115–117.

Heath, M. A., & Sheen, D. (2005). *School-based crisis intervention: Preparing all personnel to assist.* New York: Guilford Press.

Hedlund v. Superior Court, 34 Cal. 3d 695, 669 P2.d 41 (1983).

Hefferon, K., Grealy, M., & Mutrie, N. (2009). Post-traumatic growth and life threatening physical illness: A systematic review of the qualitative literature. *British Journal of Health Psychology, 14*, 343–378.

Heilbrun, A. B. (1990). The measurement of criminal dangerousness as a personality construct: Further validation of a research index. *Journal of Personality Assessment, 54*, 141–148.

Heilbrun, A. B., & Heilbrun, M. R. (1989). Dangerousness and legal insanity. *Journal of Psychiatry and Law, 17*, 39–53.

Heisel, M. J. (2006). Suicide and its prevention among older adults. *Canadian Journal of Psychiatry, 51*(3), 143–154.

Helfrich, C. A. (Ed.). (2001). *Domestic abuse across the life span: The role of occupational therapy.* Binghamton, NY: Haworth Press.

Hellman, D. S., & Blackman, S. (1966). Enuresis, fire setting, and cruelty to animals: A triad predictive of adult crime. *American Journal of Psychiatry, 122*, 1431–1435.

Hembree, E., Rauch, S., & Foa, E. (2003). Beyond the manual: The insider's guide to prolonged exposure therapy for PTSD. *Cognitive and Behavioral Practice, 10*(1), 22–30.

Henning, K., & Connor-Smith, J. (2011). Why doesn't he leave? Relationship continuity and satisfaction among male domestic offenders. *Journal of Interpersonal Violence, 26*(7), 1366–1387.

Henry, V. E. (2004). *Death work: Police, trauma, and the psychology of survival.* New York: Oxford University Press.

Henry, V. E. (2005). In A. E. Roberts (Ed.), *Crisis intervention handbook* (3rd ed., pp. 171–199). New York: Oxford University Press.

Hensel, J., Lunsky, Y., & Dewa, C. (2012). Exposure to client aggression and burnout among community staff who support adults with intellectual disabilities in Ontario, Canada. *Journal of Intellectual Disability Research, 56*(9), 910–915.

Hensel, J., Ruiz, C., Finney, C., & Dewa, C. (2015). Meta-analysis of risk factors for secondary traumatic stress in therapeutic work with trauma victims. *Journal of Traumatic Stress, 28*(2), 83–91.

Henson, B., Reyns, B., & Fisher, B. (2013). *Fear of online interpersonal victimization measures test.* Shippensburg, PA: Shippensburg University.

Henton, J., Cate, R., Koval, J., Lloyd, S., & Christopher, S. (1983). Romance and violence in dating relationships. *Journal of Family Issues, 4,* 467–482.

Hepp, U., Wittman, L., Schnyder, U., & Michel, K. (2004). Psychological and psychosocial interventions after attempted suicide: An overview of treatment studies. *Crisis: The Journal of Crisis Intervention and Suicide Prevention, 25*(3), 108–117.

Heppner, M. J. (1978). Counseling the battered wife: Myths, facts, and decisions. *Personnel and Guidance Journal, 56,* 522–525.

Heppner, M. J., Good, G. E., Hillenbrand-Gunn, T. L., Hawkins, A. K., Hacquard, L. L., Nichols, R. K., et al. (1995). Examining sex difference in altering attitudes about rape: A test of the elaboration likelihood model. *Journal of Counseling and Development, 73,* 640–647.

Heppner, P., Heppner, M. J., Lee, D., Wang, Y., Park, H., & Wang, L. (2006). Development and validation of a collectivist coping styles inventory. *Journal of Counseling Psychology, 53*(1), 107–125.

Herman, J. (1981). *Father–daughter incest.* Cambridge, MA: Harvard University Press.

Herman, J. L. (1992). *Trauma and recovery: The aftermath of violence—from domestic abuser to political terror.* New York: Basic Books.

Herman, J. L. (1997). *Trauma and recovery.* New York: Basic Books.

Herman, J. L., Perry, C., & van der Kolk, B. A. (1989). Childhood trauma in borderline personality disorder. *American Journal of Psychiatry, 146,* 490–494.

Hermann, C. F. (1963). Some consequences of crisis which limit the viability of organizations. *Administrative Science Quarterly, 8,* 61–81.

Herpertz-Dahlmann, B., Hahn, F., & Hempt, A. (2005). Clinical assessment and therapy of post-traumatic stress disorder in childhood and adolescence: Responsibilities of an outpatient clinic for traumatized children. *Nervenarzt, 76*(5), 546–556.

Herringa, R. J., Phillips, M. L. Fournier, J. C., Kronhaus, D. M., & Germain, A. (2013). Childhood and adult trauma both correlate with dorsal anterior cingulate activation to threat in combat veterans. *Psychological Medicine, 43*(7), 1533–1542.

Hersh, J. B. (1985). Interviewing college students in crisis. *Journal of Counseling and Development, 63,* 286–289. Hersh, S. P. (1996). After heart attack and stroke. In K. J. Doka (Ed.), *Living with grief after sudden loss: Suicide, homicide, accident, heart attack, stroke* (pp. 17–24). Washington, DC: Hospice Foundation of America.

Hertel, R., & Johnson, M. (2013). How the traumatic experiences of students manifest in school settings. In E. Rossen & R. Hull (Eds.), *Supporting and educating traumatized students: A guide for school-based professionals* (pp. 23–35). New York: Oxford University Press.

Hertlein, K. M., Blumer, M., & Mihaloliakos, J. H. (2015). Marriage and family counselors perceived ethical issues related to online therapy. *The Family Journal, 23*(1), 5–12.

Herzog, A., & Resnik, K. (1967). A clinical study of parental response to adolescent death by suicide. In N. Farberow (Ed.), *Proceedings of the 4th International Conference on Suicide Prevention.* (pp. 154–168). Los Angeles: Delmar.

Heyman, R. E., Jouriles, E. N., & O'Leary, K. D. (1995). Alcohol and aggressive personality styles: Potentiator of serious aggression against wives? *Journal of Family Psychology, 9,* 44–57.

Hibberd, R., Elwood, L. S., & Galovski, T. E. (2010). Risk and protective factors for posttraumatic stress disorder, prolonged grief and depression in survivors of the violent death of a loved one. *Journal of Loss and Trauma, 15*(5), 426–447.

Hickman, R. I., & Douglas, S. L. (2010). Impact of chronic critical illness on the psychological outcomes of family members. *AACN Advanced Critical Care, 21,* 80–91.

Hicks, J. F. (2015). Empowering youth victimized by cyber bullying. *Counseling Today, 57*(9). 48–53.

Hien, D., Litt, L. C., Cohen, L. R., Miele, G. M., & Campbell, A. (2009). *Trauma service for women in substance abuse: An integrated approach.* Washington, DC: American Psychological Association.

Hilbert, J. C., & Hilbert, H. C. (1984). Battered women leaving the shelter: Which way do they go? A discriminate function analysis. *Journal of Applied Social Sciences, 8,* 291–297.

Hill, R. (1965). Generic features of families under stress. In H. J. Parad (Ed.), *Crisis intervention: Selected readings* (pp. 32–52). New York: Family Service Association of America.

Hill, R. M., & Pettit, J. W. (2014). Perceived burdensomeness and suicide-related behaviors in clinical samples: Current evidence and future directions. *Journal of Clinical Psychology, 70*(7), 631–643.

Hillenbrand-Gunn, T. L., Heppner, M. J., Mauch, P. A., & Park, H. (2010). Men as allies: The efficacy of a high school rape prevention intervention. *Journal of Counseling and Development, 88*(1),43–51.

Hilliard, R. E. (2008). Music and grief work with children. In C. A. Malchiodi (Ed.), *Creative interventions with traumatized children* (pp. 63–80). New York: Guilford Press.

Hillman, J., Flicker, S., LeGendre, L., & Traczuk, K. (2005). The pervasiveness of patient aggression among elderly residents in long-term care: Implications for intervention and prevention. In J. P. Morgan (Ed.), *Psychology of aggression* (pp. 69–85). New York: Nova Science Publishers.

Hiltz, S. R. (1992). The virtual classroom: Software for collaborative learning. In E. Barrett (Ed.), *Sociomedia: Multimedia, hypermedia, and the social construction of knowledge. Technical communication and information systems* (pp. 347–368). Cambridge, MA: MIT Press.

Himelein, M. J., Vogel, R. E., & Wachowiak, D. G. (1994). Nonconsensual sexual experiences in precollege women: Prevalence and risk factors. *Journal of Counseling and Development, 72,* 411–415.

Hindley, N., & Gordon, H. (2000). The elderly, dementia, aggression and risk management. *International Journal of Geriatric Psychiatry, 15*(3), 254–259.

Hines, D. A., & Douglas, E. M. (2011). Symptoms of posttraumatic stress disorder in men who sustain intimate partner violence: A study of help seeking and community samples. *Psychology of Men and Masculinity, 12*(2), 112–127.

Hinrichsen, G. A., & Clougherty, K. F. (2006). *Interpersonal psychotherapy for depressed older adults.* Washington, DC: American Psychological Association.

Hipple, J. (1985). *Suicide: The preventable tragedy.* Unpublished manuscript, North Texas State University, Denton.

Hipple, J., & Cimbolic, P. (1979). *The counselor and suicidal crisis.* Springfield, IL: Charles C Thomas.

Hirsch, J., & Cukrowicz, K. (2014). Suicide in rural areas: An updated review of the literature. *Journal of Rural Mental Health, 38*(2), 65–78.

Hirschel, J. D., Hutchison, I. W., & Dean, C. W. (1992). The failure of arrest to deter spouse abuse. *Journal of Research in Crime and Delinquency, 29,* 7–33.

Ho, F., Chung, K., Yeung, W., Ng, T., & Cheng, S. (2014). Weekly brief phone support in self-help cognitive behavioral therapy for insomnia disorder: Relevance to adherence and efficacy. *Behaviour Research and Therapy, 63,* 147–156.

Ho, S., Lo, R., & Pau, N. (2013). Roles of intra- and extra-organizational support, coping strategies, and perceived control in combating burnout among health care workers after workplace violence. In B. R. Doolittle (Ed.), *Psychology of burnout: New research, psychology of emotions, motivations and actions* (pp. 85–106). Hauppage, NY: Nova Science Publishers.

Hobbs, M., Mayou, R., Harrison, B., & Worlock, P. (1996). A randomised control of psychological debriefing for victims of road traffic accidents. *British Medical Journal, 313,* 1438–1439.

Hobfoll, S. E. (1988). *The ecology of stress.* New York: John Wiley & Sons.

Hobfoll, S. E., & deVries, M. W. (Eds.). (1995). *Extreme stress and communities: Impact and intervention.* Dordrecht, Netherlands: Kluwer.

Hobfoll, S. E., Watson, P., Bell, C., Bryant, R. A., Brymer, M. J., Friedman, M. J., Friedman, M., Gersons, B. P. R., de Jong, J., Layne, C. M., Maguen, S., Neria, Y., Norwood, A. E., Pynoos, R. S., Reisman, D., Ruzek, J. L., Shalev, A. Y., Solomon, Z., Stenberg, A. M., & Ursano, R. J. (2007). Five essential elements of immediate and mid-term mass trauma intervention: Empirical elements. *Psychiatry, 70,* 283–315.

Hobfoll, S. E., Watson, P. J., Bell, C. C., Bryant, R. A., Brymer, M. J., Friedman, M. J., et al. (2007). Five essential elements for immediate and mid-term crisis in mass trauma intervention: Empirical evidence. *Psychiatry, 70,* 283–315.

Hodge, J. J. G., & Courtney, B. (2010). Assessing the legal standard of care in public health emergencies. *Journal of the American Medical Association, 303,* 361–362.

Hodge, J. J. G., Gable, L. A., & Calves, S. H., (2005). Volunteer health professionals and emergencies: Assessing and transforming the legal environment. *Biosecurity and Bioterrorism: Biodefense Strategy, Practice, and Science, 3,* 216–223.

Hoeksma, J. H., Guy, J. D., Brown, C. K., & Brady, J. L. (1993). The relationship between psychotherapist burnout and satisfaction with leisure activities. *Psychotherapy in Private Practice, 12,* 51–57.

Hoff, I. A., Hallisey, B. J., & Hoff, M. (2009). *People in crisis: Clinical and diversity perspectives.* New York: Routledge, Taylor, & Francis Group.

Hoffman, M. A. (1996). *Counseling clients with HIV disease: Assessment, intervention, and prevention.* New York: Guilford Press.

Hogan, N. S., Greenfield, D. B., & Schmidt, L. A. (2001). Development and validation of the Hogan Grief Reaction Checklist. *Death Studies, 25*(1), 1–32.

Hoge, C. W., Auchterlonie, J. L, & Milliken, C. S. (2006). Mental health problems: Use of mental health services and attrition from military service after returning from deployment to Iraq or Afghanistan. *Journal of the American Medical Association, 295,* 1023–1035.

Holladay, J. (2010, Fall). Cyberbullying. *Teaching Tolerance,* 43–46.

Holland, J. M., & Neimeyer, R. A. (2011). Separation and traumatic distress in prolonged grief: The role of cause of death and relationship to the deceased. *Journal of Psychopathology and Behavioral Assessment, 33*(2), 254–263.

Holmes, J. (2011). Attachment theory and the suicidal patient. In K. Michel & D. A. Jobes (Eds.), *Building a therapeutic alliance with the suicidal patient* (pp. 149–168). Washington, DC: American Psychological Association.

Holmes, R. M., & Holmes, S. T. (2006). *Suicide theory, practice, and investigation.* Thousand Oaks, CA: Sage.

Holmes, R. M., Holmes, A. T., & Unholz, J. (1993). Female pedophilia: A hidden abuse. *Law and Order, 41*(8), 77–79.

Holmes, W. C., & Slap, G. B. (1998). Sexual abuse of boys: Definition, prevalence, correlates, sequelae, and management. *Journal of the American Medical Association, 280,* 1855–1862.

Holt, H., & Beutler, L. E. (2014). Concerns about the dissemination of evidenced-based psychotherapies in the Veterans Affairs health care system. *American Psychologist, 69*(7), 705.

Holt, H., Beutler, L. A., Castonguay, L. G., Silberchutz, G., Forrester, B., Temkin, R. S., . . . Miller, T. W. (2013). A critical examination for the movement towards evidence based mental health in the U.S. Department of Veterans Affairs health care system. *The Clinical Psychologist, 664,* 8–14.

Holtzworth-Munroe, A., & Stuart, G. L. (1994). Typologies of male batterers: Three subtypes and the differences among them. *Psychological Bulletin, 116*(3), 476–497.

Holtzworth-Munroe, A., Meehan, J., Herron, K., & Stuart, G. (1999). A typology of batterers: An initial examination. In X. B. Ariagapa & S. Oskamp (Eds.), *Violence in intimate relationships* (pp. 45–72). Thousand Oaks, CA: Sage.

Holtzworth-Munroe, A., Meehan, J., Herron, K., Rehman, U., & Stuart, G. (2003). Do subtypes of maritally violent men continue to differ over time? *Journal of Consulting and Clinical Psychology, 71*(4), 728–740.

Homeland Security Administration. (2015). School safety. Retrieved from www.dhs.gov/school-safety Hoover, J. H., & Hazler, R. J. (1991). Bullies and victims. *Elementary School Guidance and Counseling, 25,* 212–219.

Home of the Duluth Model. (2011). *What is the Duluth Model? Why it works.* Retrieved from www.theduluthmodel.org

Hooven, C. (2013). Parents-CARE: A suicide prevention program for parents of at-risk youth. *Journal of Child and Adolescent Psychiatric Nursing, 26*(1), 85–95.

Hopkins, O., & King, N. (1994). PTSD in children and adolescents. *Behavior Change, 11,* 110–120.

Hopper, M. J., Johnston, J., & Brinkhoff, J. (1988). Creating a career hotline for rural residents. *Journal of Counseling and Development, 66,* 340–343.

Horn, J. (2002). Law enforcement and trauma. In M. Williams & J. Sommer (Eds.), *Simple and complex post-traumatic stress disorder: Strategies for comprehensive treatment in clinical practice* (pp. 311–323). Binghamton, NY: Haworth Press.

Horne, A. M., Bartolomucci, C. L., & Newman-Carson, D. (2003). *Bully busters: A teacher's manual for helping bullies, victims, and bystanders.* Champaign, IL: Research Press.

Horowitz, L., Bridge, J., Tach, S., Ballard, E., Klima, J., Rosenstein, D., . . . Pao, M. (2012). Ask suicide-screening questions (ASQ): A brief instrument for the pediatric emergency department. *Archives of Pediatrics and Adolescent Medicine, 166*(12), 1170–1176.

Horowitz, L., Snyder, D., Ludi, E., Rosensein, D., Kohn-Godbout, J., Lee, L., . . .Pao, M. (2012). Ask suicide questions to everyone in medical settings: The asQ'em quality improvement project. *Psychosomatics: Journal of Consultation and Liaison Psychiatry, 54*(3), 239–327.

Horowitz, M., Wilner, N., & Alvarez, W. (1979). Impact of Events Scale: A measure of subjective stress. *Psychosomatic Medicine, 41*(3), 209–218.

Horowitz, M. J. (1976). *Stress response syndromes.* New York: Aronson.

Horowitz, M. J. (1986). *Stress response syndromes* (2nd ed.). Northvale, NJ: Jason Aronson.

Horowitz, M. J., & Solomon, G. F. (1975). A prediction of delayed stress response syndromes in Vietnam veterans. *Journal of Social Issues, 31*, 67–80.

Horowitz, M. J., Siegel, B., Holen, A., Bonnanno, G., Milbrath, C., & Stinson, C. H. (1997). Diagnostic criteria for complicated grief disorder. *American Journal of Psychiatry, 154*(7), 904–910.

Horowitz, M. J., Wilner, N., & Alvarez, W. (1979). Impact of Events Scale: A measure of subjective stress. *Psychosomatic Medicine, 41*, 209–218.

Horowitz, M. J., Wilner, N., Kaltreider, N., & Alvarez, W. (1980). Signs and symptoms of post-trauma stress disorders. *Archives of General Psychiatry, 37*, 85–92.

Horton, A. L. (1995). Sex-related hotline calls. In A. R. Roberts (Ed.), *Crisis intervention and time-related cognitive treatment* (pp. 292–312). Thousand Oaks, CA: Sage.

Hotaling, G. T., & Sugarman, D. B. (1986). An analysis of risk markers in husband to wife violence: The current state of knowledge. *Violence and Victims, 1*, 101–124.

Hotaling, G. T., & Sugarman, D. B. (1990). A risk marker analysis of assaulted wives. *Journal of Family Violence, 5*, 1–13.

Howarth, R. A. (2011). Promoting the adjustment of parentally bereaved children. *Journal of Mental Health Counseling, 33*(1), 21–32.

Howe, E., Marini, J., Haymes, E. , & Tenor, T. (2013). Bullying: Best practices for prevention and intervention in schools. In C. Franklin, M. Harris, & P. Allen-Meares (Eds.), *The school source book: A guide for school based professionals* (2nd ed., pp. 473–480). New York: Oxford University Press.

Howell, S. (1999). *The Memphis Rape Crisis Center* (Cassette Recording #6760-99). Memphis, TN: Department of Counseling, Educational Psychology and Research, University of Memphis.

Hsieh, H., & Wang, J. (2003). Effect of reminiscence therapy on depression in older adults: A systematic review. *International Journal of Nursing Studies, 40*(4), 335–345.

Hsiung, R. C. (2002). *E-therapy: Case studies, guiding principles, and the clinical potential of the Internet.* New York: W.W. Norton.

Hsu, M. V. (2010). Continuing bonds expressions in pet bereavement. *Dissertation Abstracts International: Section B. The Sciences and Engineering*, 2049.

Hubbard, J. A., Dodge, K. A., Cillessen, A. H. N., Coie, J. D., & Schwartz, D. (2001). The dyadic nature of social information processing in boys' reactive and proactive aggression. *Journal of Personality and Social Psychology, 80*, 268–280.

Huber, J. T. (1993). Death and AIDS: A review of the medico-legal literature. *Death Studies, 17*, 225–232.

Huddy, L., & Feldman, S. (2011). Americans respond politically to 9/11: Understanding the impact of terrorist attacks and their aftermath. *American Psychologist, 66*(5), 455–467.

Hughes, H. M. (1982). Brief interventions with children in a battered women's shelter: A model preventive program. *Family Relations, 31*, 495–502.

Hughes, R. B. (1988). Grief counseling: Facilitating the healing process. *Journal of Counseling and Development, 67*, 77.

Humanitarian charter and minimum standards in disaster response. (1998). *Sphere Project.* Geneva: World Health Organization.

Hummer, G. A., Wang, Y., Kronenberger, W., Mosier, K., Kalnin, A., Dunn, D., et al. (2010). Short-term violent video game play by adolescents alters prefrontal activity during cognitive inhibition. *Media Psychology, 13*(2), 136–154.

Humphrey, K. M. (2009). *Counseling strategies for loss and grief.* Alexandria, VA: American Counseling Association.

Humphrey, N., & Brooks, A. (2006). An evaluation of a short cognitive-behavioural anger management intervention for pupils at risk of exclusion. *Emotional and Behavioural Difficulties, 11*(1), 5–23.

Humphrey, N. M. (2009). *Counseling strategies for loss and grief.* Alexandria, VA: American Counseling Association.

Hunt, R. D., Osten, C., & Teague, S. (1991). Youth suicide: Teachers should know. . . *Tennessee Teacher, 91*, 16–21, 29.

Hurtig, R., Bulitt, E., & Kates, K. (2011). Samaritans grief support services. In J. R. Jordan & J. L. McIntosh (Eds.), *Grief after suicide: Understanding the consequences and caring for the survivors. Series in death, dying, and bereavement* (pp. 341–348). New York: Routledge/Taylor & Francis Group.

Husky, M., Olfson, M., Nock, H., Swanson, S., Alsemgeest, M., & Ries, K. (2012). Twelve-month suicidal symptoms and use of services among adolescents: Results from the National Comorbidity Survey. *Psychiatric Services, 63*(10), 989–996.

Hutchinson, M., Jackson, D, Haigh, C., & Hayter, M. (2013). Editorial. Five years of scholarship on violence, bullying and aggression towards nurses in the workplace: What have we learned? *Journal of Clinical Nursing, 22*(7–8), 903–905.

Hwang, W. (2012). Integrating top-down bottom-up approaches to culturally adapting psychotherapy application to Chinese Americans. In G. Bernal & M. M. Domenech-Rodriguez (Eds.), *Cultural adaptions: tools for evidence-based practice with diverse populations* (pp. 179–198). Washington, DC: American Psychological Association.

Hyer, L., Sohnle, S., Mehan, D., & Ragan, A. (2002). Use of positive core memories in LTC: A review. *Clinical Gerontologist, 25*(1/2), 51–90.

I

Ibrahim, F. A., & Herr, E. L. (1987). Battered women: A developmental life-career counseling perspective. *Journal of Counseling and Development, 65*, 244–248.

Imber-Black, E. (2012). The value of rituals in family life. In F. Walsh (Ed.), *Normal family processes: Growing diversity and complexity* (4th ed., pp. 483–497). New York: Guilford Press.

Ingram, S., Ringle, J. L., Hallstrom, K., Schill, D. E., Gohr, V. M., & Thompson, R. W. (2008). Coping with crisis across the lifespan: The role of a telephone hotline. *Journal of Child and Family Studies, 17*, 663–674.

Inter-Agency Standing Committee (IASC). (2007). *IASC guidelines on mental health and psychosocial input support in emergency situations.* Geneva, SW: Author.

Inter-Agency Standing Committee (IASC). (2012). Reference Group on Mental Health and Psychosocial Support in Emergency Settings. *IASC Reference Group Mental Health and Psychosocial Support Assessment Guide*, IASC RG MHPSS.

International Federation of Red Cross and Red Crescent Societies. (2014). *Psychsocial support.* Retrieved from http://www.ifrc.org/en/what-we-do/health/psycho -social-support/

International Society for the Study of Trauma and Dissociation. (2015). *Dissociation FAQs.* Retrieved from http://www.isst -dorg./default.asp?contentID=76#diss

Irwin, E. C. (1987). Drama: The play's the thing. *Elementary School Guidance and Counseling, 21*, 276–283.

Isaksson, U., Graneheim, U. H., Ricter, J., Eisenmann, M., & Astrom, S. (2008). Exposure to violence in relation to personality traits, coping abilities and burnout among caregivers in nursing homes: A case-control approach. *Scandinavian Journal of Caring Sciences, 22*(4), 551–559.

Ishimoto, W. (1984). Security management for health care administrators. In J. T. Turner (Ed.), *Violence in the medical care setting: A survival guide* (pp. 209–223). Rockville, MD: Aspen Systems.

Island, D., & Letellier, P. (1991). *Men who beat the men who love them: Battered gay men and domestic violence.* New York: Harrington Park.

Isley, P. J., & Gehrenbeck-Shim, D. (1997). Sexual assault of men in the community. *Journal of Community Psychology, 25,* 159–166.

Issacs, J. S. (2004). Numerical distraction therapy: Initial assessment of a treatment for posttraumatic stress disorder. *Traumatology, 10*(1), 39–54.

Italiano, F. (2001). Listening and learning at North Arlington High School. *Police Chief, 68*(9), 53–55.

Iverson, K. M., King, M. W., Cunningham, K. C., & Resick, P. A. (2015). Rape survivors' trauma-related beliefs before and after cognitive processing therapy: Associations with PTSD and depression symptoms. *Behaviour Research and Therapy, 66,* 49–55.

Ivey, A. E. (1987). Cultural intentionality: The core of effective helping. *Counselor Education and Supervision, 26,* 168–172.

J

Jablonski v. United States, 712 F2.d 391 (9th Cir. 1983).

Jackson, K., & Harding, M. (2010, July). *Advocating for LGBTQ students.* American School Counselor Conference, Boston.

Jacobs, D. G. (Ed.). (1999). *The Harvard Medical School guide to suicide assessment and intervention.* San Francisco: Jossey-Bass.

Jacobs, J. (2010). Suicide prevention on the Golden Gate Bridge. *American Journal of Psychiatry, 167*(4), 473.

Jacobs, J., Horne-Moyer, H. L., & Jones, R. (2004). The effectiveness of critical incident stress debriefing with primary and secondary trauma victims. *International Journal of Emergency Mental Health, 6,* 5–14.

Jacobs, J. A. (1967). Phenomenological study of suicide notes. *Social Problems, 15,* 60–72.

Jaffee v. Redmond, 518 U.S. 1 (1996).

Jahoda, M., Lazarfield, P. F., & Zeisel, H. (1971). *"Marrienthal": The sociography of an unemployed community.* Chicago: Aldine. (Original work published 1933)

Jaime, M., McCauley, H., Tancredi, D., Nettiksimmons, J., Decker, M., Silverman, J., . . . Miller, E. (2015). Athletic coaches as violence prevention advocates. *Journal of Interpersonal Violence, 30*(7), 1090–1111.

James, D. J., & Glaze, L. E. (2006, September 6). Mental health problems of prison and jail inmates. Bureau of Justice Statistics. Retrieved from http://www.bjs.gov/content/pub/pdf/mhppji.pdf

James, R. (2003, April). *Drawing out the trauma.* Paper presented at the Twenty-seventh Convening of Crisis Intervention Personnel, Chicago.

James, R., & Crawford, R. (2002). The estranged, violent, juvenile offender: Profiling, screening, intervention, and legal considerations. *Global Visions for Counseling Professionals, 6*(1), 1–14.

James, R., & Dorner, K. (1999, June). *Profiling, screening, and counseling the estranged juvenile violent offender.* Paper presented at the American School Counselor Association Convention, Phoenix, AZ.

James, R., Kirchberg, T., Nobbman, K., & Skirius, M. (2013, October). *Where and why are your social locations important?* Paper presented at Crisis Intervention Team International convention, Hartford, CT.

James, R., Logan, J., & Davis, S. (2011). Including school resource officers in school-based crisis intervention: Strengthening student support. *School Psychology International, 32*(2), 210–224.

James, R., Myer, R., Skirius, M., & Nobbman, K. (2013, October). *Crisis intervention and diversity: A story of social locations.* Paper presented at American Counselor Education and Supervision conference, Denver, CO.

James, R. K, Davis, S., & Myer, R. A. (2014, October). Why use the TACKLE? Crisis Intervention Team International Convention, Monterey, CA.

James, R. K. (1994). Commentary to "Dial 911: Schizophrenia and the Police Response." In P. Backlar (Ed.), *The family face of schizophrenia* (pp. 182–200). New York: Jeremy Tarcher/Putnam.

James, R. K. (2003, April). *Drawing out the trauma.* Paper presented at the Twenty-seventh Annual Convening of Crisis Intervention Personnel, Chicago.

James, R. K. (2006, May). *Four hundred miles from landfall: Lesson learned from Katrina.* Paper presented at the Thirtieth Annual Convening of Crisis Intervention Personnel and the Contact USA Conference, Chicago.

James, R. K. (2014). Basic verbal practicum techniques. In Memphis Police Department, *Crisis intervention team training manual* (pp. 56–60). Memphis, TN: Memphis Police Department.

James, R. K., & Crews, W. (2009). Systems consultation: Working with a metropolitan police department. In A. M. Dougherty (Ed.), *Psychological consultation and collaboration in schools and community settings: A casebook* (5th ed., pp. 93–114). Belmont, CA: Brooks/Cole.

James, R. K., & Crews, W. (2014). Systems consultation: Working with a metropolitan police department. In A. M. Dougherty (Ed.), *Psychological consultation and collaboration in schools and community settings: A casebook* (6th ed., pp. 93–114). Belmont, CA: Brooks/Cole.

James, R. K., & Gilliland, B. E. (2003). *Theories and strategies in counseling and psychotherapy* (5th ed.). Boston: Allyn & Bacon.

James, R. K., & Gilliland, B. E. (2013). *Crisis intervention strategies* (7th ed.). Belmont, CA: Brooks/Cole.

James, R. K., & Myer, R. (1987). Puppets: The elementary counselor's right or left arm. *Elementary School Guidance and Counseling, 21,* 292–299.

James, R. K., Blancett, J., & Addy, C. (2007, March). *Adapting the TACKLE form to civilian use: The Triage Assessment Severity Checklist for Civilians.* Paper presented at the Thirty-First Convening of Crisis Intervention Personnel and Contact USA, Chicago.

James, R. K., Cogdal, P., & Gilliland, B. E. (2003, April). *An ecological theory of crisis intervention.* Paper presented at the American Counseling Association convention, Kansas City, MO.

James, R. K., Cogdal, P., & Gilliland, B. E. (2003, April). *Crisis intervention in the ecosystem.* Paper presented at the American Counseling Association Convention, Kansas City, MO.

James, R. K., Myer, R., & Moore, H. (2006). *Triage Assessment Checklist for Law Enforcement (TACKLE) manual and CD.* Pittsburgh, PA: Crisis Intervention and Prevention Solutions.

Jankowski, J., & Frey, A. (2012). Students connecting with the elderly: Validation as a tool. *Educational Gerontology, 38*(7), 486–490.

Janosik, E. H. (1984). *Crisis counseling: A contemporary approach.* Monterey, CA: Wadsworth Health Sciences Division.

Janosik, S. M. (2004). Parents' views on the Clery Act and campus safety. *Journal of College Student Development, 45*(1), 43–56.

Jarero, I., & Ureibe, S. (2012). The EMDR protocol for recent critical incidents: Follow-up report of an application in a human massacre situation. *Journal of EMDR Practice and Research, 6*(2), 50–61.

Jarvie, I. (1991). Pornography and/as degradation. *International Journal of Law and Psychiatry, 14,* 13–27.

Jasinski, J. L., & Williams, L. M. (Eds.). (1998). *Partner violence: A comprehensive review of 20 years of research.* Newbury Park, CA: Sage.

Jayaratne, S., Vinokur-Kaplan, D., & Chess, W. A. (1995). The importance of personal control: A comparison of social workers in private practice and public agency settings. *Journal of Applied Social Sciences, 19,* 47–59.

Jeffreys, M. D. (2015). Atypical antipsychotics and anticonvulsants in the treatment of PTSD: Treatment options that include cognitive behavioral therapies. In N. C. Bernardy & M. J. Friedman (Eds.), *A practical guide to treatment: Pharmacological and psychotherapeutic approaches* (pp. 89–98). Washington, DC: American Psychological Association.

Jeffreys, M. D., Reinfeld, C., Nair, P. V., Garcia, H. A., Mata-Galan, E., & Rentz, T. O. (2014). Evaluating treatment of posttraumatic stress disorder with cognitive processing therapy and prolonged exposure therapy in a VHA specialty clinic. *Journal of Anxiety Disorders, 28*(1) 108–114.

Jennicus, M. (2013). Manners on the internet. *Counseling Today, 56*(3), 16–17.

Jennings, K. (2011). Federal action to stop bullying. *ASCA School Counselor, 48*(6), 14–15.

Jensen, D., & Absher, J. (1994, April). *Assaultive behavior, the crisis is over: Preventing another crisis.* Paper presented at the Eighteenth Annual Convening of Crisis Intervention Personnel, Chicago.

Jensen, D., & Absher, J. (1998, April). *Predicting/managing violence in crisis situations: Ensuring provider safety.* Paper presented at the Twenty-Second Annual Convening of Crisis Intervention Personnel, Chicago.

Jensen, T. K., Holt, T., Ormhaug, S., Egeland, K., Granly, L., Hoaas, L. C., . . . Wentzel-Larsen, T. (2014). A randomized effectiveness study of trauma-focused cognitive behavioral therapy with therapy as usual for youth. *Journal of Clinical Child and Adolescent Psychology, 43*(3), 356–369.

Jesus, J. E., & Michael, G. E., (2009). Ethical considerations of research in disaster-stricken populations. *Prehospital and Disaster Medicine, 24,* 109–114.

Jimenez, X. F. (2013). Patients with borderline personality disorder who are chronically suicidal: Therapeutic alliance and therapeutic limits. *American Journal of Psychotherapy, 67*(2), 185–201.

Jimerson, S. R., & Furlong, M. J. (Eds.). (2006). *Handbook of school violence and school safety: From research to practice.* Mahwah, NJ: Erlbaum.

Jimerson, S. R., Brock, S. E., & Pletcher, S. W. (2005). An integrated model of school preparedness and intervention: A shared foundation to facilitate international crisis intervention. *School Psychology International, 26*(3), 275–296.

Jo, H., & Song, E., (2015). The effect of reminiscence therapy on depression, quality of life, ego-integrity, social behavior function, and activities of daily living in elderly patients with mild dementia. *Educational Gerontology, 41*(1), 1–13.

Jobes, D. A. (2006). *Managing suicidal risk: A collaborative approach.* New York: Guilford Press.

Joffrion, L. P., & Douglas, D. (1994). Grief resolution: Facilitating transcendence in the bereaved. *Journal of Psychosocial Nursing and Mental Health Services, 32*(3), 13–19.

Johannes, C. K. (2003, January). Letters: Much ado about multiculturalism, part 4. *Counseling Today, 45,* 31.

Johnson, C. N. E., & Hunter, M. (1997). Vicarious traumatization in counsellors working in the New South Wales Sexual Assault Service: An exploratory study. *Work and Stress, 11*(4), 319–328.

Johnson, D. R. (2000a). Creative therapies. In E. Foa & T. Keane (Eds.), *Effective treatments for PTSD: Practice guidelines from the International Society for Traumatic Stress Studies* (pp. 356–358). New York: Guilford Press.

Johnson, D. R. (2000b). Creative therapies. In E. Foa & T. Keane (Eds.), *Effective treatments for PTSD: Practice guidelines from the International Society for Traumatic Stress Studies* (pp. 302–314). New York: Guilford Press.

Johnson, D. R., Feldman, S. C., & Southwick, S. M. (1994). The concept of the second-generation program in the treatment of PTSD among Vietnam veterans. *Journal of Traumatic Stress, 7,* 217–235.

Johnson, I. M. (1999). School violence: The effectiveness of a school resource officer program in a southern city. *Journal of Criminal Justice, 27*(2), 173–192.

Johnson, K. (2000). *School crisis management: A hands-on guide to training crisis response teams* (2nd ed.). Alameda, CA: Hunter House.

Johnson, M. (1995). Patriarchal terrorism and common couple violence: Two forms of violence against women. *Journal of Marriage and Family, 57,* 283–294.

Johnson, M., & Leone, J. (2005). The differential effects of intimate terrorism and situational couple violence: Findings from the National Violence Against Women Survey. *Journal of Family Issues, 26*(3), 322–349.

Johnson, R. G. (1987). Using computer art in counseling children. *Elementary School Guidance and Counseling, 21,* 262–265.

Johnson, S. M. (1977). *First person singular: Living the good life alone.* Philadelphia: Lippincott.

Joiner, T. E. Jr., Van Orden, K., Witte, T. K., & Rudd, D. M. (2009). *The interpersonal theory of suicide: Guidance for working with suicidal clients.* Washington, DC: American Psychological Association.

Joiner, T. E. Jr., Walker, R. L., Rudd, M. D., & Jobes, D. A. (1999). Scientizing and routinizing the assessment of suicidality in outpatient practice. *Professional Psychology: Research and Practice, 30,* 447–453.

Jones, G., & Stokes, A. (2009). *Online counseling: A handbook for practitioners.* London: Palgrave Macmillan.

Jones, J. (1984). *Counseling in correctional settings* (Cassette Recording No. 25-6611). Memphis, TN: Memphis State University, Department of Counseling and Personnel Services.

Jones, M. K. (1985, June). Patient violence: Report of 200 incidents. *Journal of Psychosocial Nursing and Mental Health, 23,* 12–17.

Jones Farrelly, M., & Robles-Fernandez, R. (2011, April). *Counseling skills and issues in gay straight alliance advisement and LGBTQ youth.* Paper presented at the American Counseling Association Conference, New Orleans, LA.

Jordan, J. R., & McIntosh, J. L. (Eds.). (2011). *Grief after suicide: Understanding the consequences and caring for the survivors. Series in death, dying and bereavement.* New York: Routledge,Taylor & Francis Group.

Jordan, K. (2002). Providing crisis counseling to New Yorkers after the terrorist attack on the World Trade Center. *The Family Journal, 10*(2), 139–144.

Jordan, K. (2010). An ethical decision making model for crisis counselors. *Vistas.* Retrieved from http://counselingoutfitters .com/vistas/vistas10/Article_89.pdf

Jordans, M., Upadhaya, N., Tol, W., Shrestha, P., Doucet, J., Gurung, R., et al. (2010). Introducing the IASC mental health and psychosocial support guidelines in emergencies in Nepal: A process description. *Intervention, 8*(1), 52–63.

Joszkowski, K., & Wiersma, J. (2015). Does drinking alcohol prior to sexual activity influence college students' consent? *International Journal of Sexual Health, 27*(2), 156–174.

Jouriles, E. M., & Norwood, W. D. (1995). Physical aggression toward boys and girls in families characterized by the battering of women. *Journal of Family Psychology, 9,* 69–78.

Jovanovic, A., Aleksandric, B. V., Dunjic, D., & Todorovic, V. (2004). Family hardiness and social support as predictors of post-traumatic stress disorder. *Psychiatry and Law, 11*(2), 263–268.

Juhnke, G. A. (2002). Intervening with school students after terrorist attacks. In D. D. Bass & R. Yep (Eds.), *Terrorism, trauma, and tragedies: A counselor's guide to preparing and responding* (pp. 55–58). Alexandria, VA: American Counseling Association.

Jurgersen, T. S., Dailey, S., Uhernik, J., & Smith, C. M. (2013). All trauma is not the same. *Counseling Today, 55*(9), 47–50.

K

Kabat-Zinn, J. (2013). *Full catastrophe living: Using the wisdom of your body and mind to face stress, pain and illness.* New York: Batam Books, Random House.

Kaehler, L. A., & Freyd, J. F. (2009). Borderline personality characteristics: A betrayal approach. *Psychological Trauma: Theory, Research, Practice, and Policy, 1*(4), 261–268.

Kagan, R., & Schlosberg, S. (1989). Families in perpetual crisis. New York: W. W. Norton.

Kahn, W. A. (2005). *Holding fast: The struggle to create resilient caregiving organizations.* Philadelphia: Brunner/Routledge.

Kahneman, D. (2011). *Thinking fast and slow.* New York: Farrar, Strauss, and Giroux.

Kahneman, D., Slovic, P., & Tversky, A. (Eds.). (1982). *Judgment under uncertainty: Heuristics and biases.* New York: Cambridge University Press. doi: 10.1017/CBO9780511809477

Kalafat, J. (1990). Adolescent suicide and the implications for school response programs. *School Counselor, 37,* 359–369.

Kalafat, J. (2003). School approaches to youth suicide prevention. *American Behavioral Scientist, 46*(9), 1211–1223.

Kalayjian, A., & Dominque, E. (Eds.). (2010). *Mass trauma and emotional healing around the world: Rituals and practice for resilience and meaning-making: Vol. 1. Natural disasters.* Santa Barbara, CA: Praeger/ABC-CLIO.

Kalayjian, A., & Dominque, E. (Eds.). (2010). *Mass trauma and emotional healing around the world: Rituals and practice for resilience and meaning-making: Vol. 2. Human-made disasters.* Santa Barbara, CA: Praeger/ABC-CLIO.

Kalichman, S. C. (1995.) *Understanding AIDS: A guide for mental health professionals.* Washington, DC: American Psychological Association.

Kandt, V. E. (1994). Adolescent bereavement: Turning a fragile time into acceptance and peace. *School Counselor, 41,* 203–211.

Kanel, K. (1999). *A guide to crisis intervention.* Pacific Grove, CA: Brooks-Cole.

Kanel, K. (2011). *A guide to crisis intervention* (4th ed.). Belmont, CA: Brooks/Cole.

Kaniasty, K., & Norris, F. (1995). In search of altruistic community: Patterns of social support mobilization following Hurricane Hugo. *American Journal of Community Psychology, 20,* 211–241.

Kaniasty, K., & Norris, F. (1997). Social support dynamics in adjustment to disaster. In S. Duck (Ed.), *Handbook of personal relationships* (2nd ed., pp. 596–619). London: Wiley.

Kaniasty, K., & Norris, F. (1999). The experience of disaster: Individuals and communities sharing trauma. In R. Gist & B. Lubin (Eds.), *Response to disaster: Psychosocial, community, and ecological approaches* (pp. 25–62). Philadelphia: Brunner/Mazel.

Kaniasty, K., Norris, F., & Murrell, S. A. (1990). Received and perceived social support following natural disaster. *Journal of Applied Social Psychology, 20,* 85–114.

Kanuha, V. K. (2005). Compounding the triple jeopardy: Battering in lesbian of color relationships. In N. Sololoff & C. Pratt (Eds.), *Domestic violence at the margins: Readings on race, class, gender, and culture* (pp. 71–82). New Brunswick, NJ: Rutgers University Press.

Kaplan, C. P., & Gallagher-Thompson, D. (1995). Treatment of clinical depression in caregivers of spouses with dementia. *Journal of Cognitive Psychotherapy, 9,* 35–44.

Kaplan, H. B. (1996). *Psychosocial stress: Perspectives on structure, theory, life course and methods.* San Diego: Academic Press.

Kardiner, A. (1941). *The traumatic neurosis of war.* New York: Hoeber.

Kariane, H. M., Fisher, B. F., & Cullen, F. T. (2005, December). *Sexual assault on campus: What colleges and universities are doing about it.* National Institute of Justice. Retrieved from www.ncjrs.gov/pdffiles1/nij/205521.pdf

Karkazis, J. L., & Lazaneo, S. L. (2000). Unyielding custody disputes: Tempering loss and courting disaster. In J. H. Harvey & E. D. Miller (Eds.), *Loss and trauma* (pp. 375–385). Philadelphia: Brunner/Mazel.

Karl, A., Malta, L. S., & Maercker, A. (2006). Meta-analytic review of event-related potential studies in post-traumatic stress disorder. *Biological Psychology, 71*(2), 123–147.

Karpman, S. (1968). Fairy tales and script drama analysis. *Transactional Analysis Bulletin, 26*(7), 39–43.

Kasick, D. P., & Bowling, C. D. (2013). Crisis intervention teams: A boundary spanning collaboration between the law enforcement and mental health communities. In K. R. Yeager, D. L. Cutler, D. E. Svendsen, & G. M. Sills (Eds), *Modern community mental health: An interdisciplinary approach* (pp. 304–315). New York: Oxford University Press.

Kass, A., Trockel, M., Safer, D. L., Sinton, M. M., Cunning, D., Risk, M. T., . . . Taylor, C. (2014). Internet-based preventive intervention for reducing eating disorder risk: A randomized controlled trial comparing guided with unguided help. *Behaviour Research and Therapy, 63,* 90–98.

Kassing, R. L., & Prietio, L. (2003). The rape myth and blame-based beliefs of counselors-in-training toward male victims of rape. *Journal of Counseling and Development, 81*(4), 455–461.

Kasturirangan, A., & Williams, E. N. (2003). Counseling Latina battered women: A qualitative study of the Latina perspective. *Journal of Multicultural Counseling and Development, 31*(3), 162–178.

Kato, P. M., & Mann, T. (1999). A synthesis of psychological interventions for the bereaved. *Clinical Psychology Review, 19*(3), 275–296.

Katz, C., Bolton, S., Katz, L., Isaak, C., Tilston-Jones, T., & Sareen, J. (2013). Swampy Cree Suicide Prevention Team. *Depression and Anxiety, 30*(10), 1030–1045.

Katz, C. L. (2011). Needs assessment. In F. J. Stoddard, A. Pandya, & C. Katz (Eds.), *Disaster psychiatry: Readiness, evaluation, and treatment* (pp. 49–68). Arlington, VA: American Psychiatric Publishing.

Kaufman, B., & Wohl, A. (1992). *Casualties of childhood: A developmental perspective on sexual abuse using projective drawings.* New York: Brunner/Mazel.

Kaufman, P., Chen, X., & Choy, S. P. (2002). *Indicators of school crime and safety: 2001* (NCES 2002.113/NCJ-190075). Washington, DC: U.S. Departments of Justice and Education.

Kaufman Kantor, G., & Jasinski, J. L. (1998). Dynamics and risk factors in partner violence. In J. L. Jasinski & L. M. Williams (Eds.), *Partner violence: A comprehensive view of twenty years of research* (pp. 1–44). Newbury Park, CA: Sage.

Kaukinen, C., Buchanan, L., & Gover, A. (2015). Child abuse and the experience of violence in college dating relationships: Examining the moderating effect of gender and race. *Journal of Family Violence, 40*(3), 120–128.

Kaul, R. E., & Welzant, V. (2005). Disaster mental health: A discussion of best practices applied after the Pentagon attack.

In A. R. Roberts (Ed.), *Crisis intervention handbook* (3rd ed., pp. 200–220). New York: Oxford University Press.

Kaut, K. P. (2006). End-of-life assessment within a holistic bio-psycho-social-spiritual framework. In J. L. Werth & D. Blevins (Eds.), *Psychosocial issues near the end of life: A resource for professional care providers* (pp. 111–135). Washington, DC: American Psychological Association.

Kay, W. J., Neiburg, H. A., Kutscher, A. H., Grey, R. M., & Fudin, C. E. (Eds.). (1984). *Pet loss and human bereavement.* Ames: Iowa State University Press.

Kazdin, A. E. (1975). Covert modeling, imagery assessment, and assertive behavior. *Journal of Consulting and Clinical Psychology, 43*, 716–724.

Kazdin, A. E. (2008). Trauma in children: How can we communicate what we know? *Monitor on Psychology, 39*(9), 5.

Keane, T. M. (1976). *State dependent retention and its relationship to psychopathology.* Unpublished manuscript, State University of New York at Binghamton.

Keane, T. M., & Kaloupek, D. G. (1982). Imaginal flooding in the treatment of a posttraumatic stress disorder. *Journal of Consulting and Clinical Psychology, 50*, 138–140.

Keane, T. M., Caddell, J., & Taylor, K. (1988). Mississippi Scale for Combat-Related Posttraumatic Stress Disorder: Three studies in reliability and validity. *Journal of Consulting and Clinical Psychology, 56*, 85–90.

Keane, T. M., Fairbank, J. A., Caddell, J. M., & Zimmering, R. T. (1989). Implosive (flooding) therapy reduces symptoms of PTSD in Vietnam veterans. *Behavior Therapy, 20*, 245–260.

Keane, T. M., Fairbank, J. A., Caddell, J. M., Zimmering, R. T., & Bender, M. E. (1985). A behavioral approach to assessing and treating posttrauma stress disorder in Vietnam veterans. In C. R. Figley (Ed.), *Trauma and its wake: The study of post-traumatic stress disorder* (pp. 257–294). New York: Brunner/Mazel.

Keane, T. M., Malloy, P. F., & Fairbank, J. A. (1984). Empirical development of an MMPI subscale for the assessment of combat-related posttraumatic stress disorder. *Journal of Consulting and Clinical Psychology, 52*, 888–891.

Keene, J. R., & Prokos, A. H. (2008). Widowhood and the end of spousal caregiving: Relief or wear and tear? *Ageing and Society, 28*(4), 551–570.

Kelly, B., & Torres, A. (2006). Campus safety: Perceptions and experiences of women students. *Journal of College Student Development, 47*(1), 20–36.

Kenardy, J., Webster, R., Lewin, T., Carr, V., & Carter, G. (1996). Stress debriefing and patterns of recovery following natural disaster. *Journal of Traumatic Stress, 9*, 37–49.

Kendall-Tackett, K. (2008). Chronic pain in adult survivors of childhood abuse. *Trauma Psychology Newsletter, 3*(3), 20–24.

Kendrick, J. M. (1991). Crisis intervention in child abuse: A family treatment approach. In A. R. Roberts (Ed.), *Contemporary perspectives on crisis intervention* (pp. 34–52). Upper Saddle River, NJ: Prentice Hall.

Kennedy, A. (2006, November). Know when to say "no" and let go. *Counseling Today, 1*, 22–23.

Kennedy, A. (2007, July). Responding to the call. *Counseling Today.*

Kerkhof, J. F. (2000). Attempted suicide: Patterns and trends. In K. Hawton & K. van Heeringen (Eds.), *The international handbook of suicide and attempted suicide* (pp. 49–64). Chichester, England: John Wiley & Sons.

Kerr, M. M. (2009). *School crisis prevention and intervention.* Upper Saddle River, NJ: Pearson.

Kersting, A., & Kroker, K. (2010). Prolonged grief as a distinct disorder, specifically affecting female health. *Archives of Women's Mental Health, 13*(1), 27–28.

Kersting, A., Brahler, E., Glaesmer, H., & Wagner, B. (2011). Prevalence of complicated grief in a representative population-based sample. *Journal of Affective Disorders, 131*(13), 339–343.

Kesler, K. D. (1990). Burnout: A multimodal approach to assessment and resolution. *Elementary School Guidance and Counseling, 24*, 303–311.

Kessler, B. L., & Bieschke, K. J. (1999). A retrospective analysis of shame, dissociation, and adult victimization in survivors of childhood sexual abuse. *Journal of Counseling Psychology, 46*, 335–341.

Kessler, R. C., Berglund, P., Demler, O., Jin, R., Merikangas, K. R., & Walters, E. E. (2005). Life time prevalence and age-of-onset distributions of DSM-IV disorders in the National Comorbidity Survey Replication. *Archives of General Psychiatry, 62*, 593–602

Kessler, R. C., Sonnega, A., Bromer, E., Hughes, M., & Nelson, C. B. (1995). Posttraumatic stress disorder in the National Comorbidity Survey. *Archives of General Psychiatry, 52*, 1048–1060.

Khosravan, S., Salehi, S., Ahmadi, F., Sharif, F., & Zamani, A. (2010). Experiences of widows with children: A qualitative study about spousal death in Iran. *Nursing and Health Sciences, 12*(2), 205–211.

Kids on the Block. (1995). *Keeping up with the kids.* Columbia, MD: Author.

Kilijanek, T., & Drabek, T. E. (1979). Assessing long-term impacts of a natural disaster: A focus on the elderly. *Gerontologist, 19*, 555–566.

Killian, K. D. (2008). Helping till it hurts? A multi-method study of compassion fatigue, burnout, and self-care in clinicians working with trauma survivors. *Traumatology, 14*(2), 32–44.

Kilmer, R. P, & Gil-Rivas, V. (2010). Responding to the needs of children and families after a disaster: Linkages between unmet needs and caregiver functioning. *American Journal of Orthopsychiatry, 80*, 135–142.

Kilmer, R. P., Gil-Rivas, V., & MacDonald, J. (2010). Implications of major disaster for educators, administrators, and school-based mental health professionals: Needs, actions, and the example of Mayfair Elementary. In R. P. Kilmer, V. Gil-Rivas, R. G. Tedeschi, & L. G. Calhoun (Eds.), *Helping families and communities recover from disaster: Lessons learned from hurricane Katrina and its aftermath* (pp. 167–191). Washington, DC: American Psychological Association.

Kilmer, R. P., Gil-Rivas, V., Tedeschi, R. G., & Calhoun, L. G. (Eds.). (2010). *Helping families and communities recover from disaster: Lessons learned from hurricane Katrina and its aftermath.* Washington, DC: American Psychological Association.

Kilmer, R. P., Gil-Rivas, V., Tedeschi, R. G., Cann, A., Calhoun, L., Buchanan, T., & Taku, K. (2009). Use of the revised Posttraumatic Growth Inventory for Children. *Journal of Traumatic Stress, 22*(3), 248–253.

Kim, B. S. K., Liang, C. T. H., & Li, L. C. (2003). Counselor ethnicity, counselor nonverbal behavior, and session outcome with Asian American clients: Initial findings. *Journal of Counseling and Development, 81*(2), 202–207.

Kim, H. S., Sherman, D. K., & Taylor, S. E. (2008). Culture and social support. *American Psychologist, 63*(6), 518–526.

King, C. A., Foster, C., & Rogalski, K. (2013). *Teen suicide risk: A practitioner guide to screening, assessment , and management.* New York: Guilford Press.

King, C. A., Kramer, A., Preuss, L., Kerr, D., Weisse, L., & Venkataraman, S. (2006). Youth-nominated support team for suicidal adolescents (Version 1): A randomized controlled test. *Journal of Consulting and Clinical Psychology, 74*(1), 199–206.

King, D., O'Reiley, A., Thompson, C., Conwell, Y., He, H., & Kemp, J. (2014). Age-related concerns of male veteran callers to a suicide crisis line. *Archives of Suicide Research, 18*(4), 445–452.

King, K. A. (2000). Preventing adolescent suicide: Do high school counselors know the risk factors? *Professional School Counseling, 3,* 255–263.

King, L. A., King, D. W., Leskin, G., & Foy, D. W. (1995). The Los Angeles Symptom Checklist: A self-report measure of post-traumatic stress disorder. *Assessment, 2*(1), 1–17.

King, N., Heyne, D., Tonge, B. Mullen, P., Myerson, N., & Rollings, S. (2003). Sexually abused children suffering from post-traumatic stress disorder: Assessment and treatment strategies. *Cognitive Behaviour Therapy, 32*(1), 2–12.

Kingsbury, S. J. (1988). Hypnosis in the treatment of posttraumatic stress disorder: An isomorphic intervention. *American Journal of Clinical Hypnosis, 31,* 81–90.

Kinney, J. A. (1995). *Violence at work.* Upper Saddle River, NJ: Prentice Hall.

Kinzie, J., & Goetz, R. (1996). A century of controversy surrounding posttraumatic stress-spectrum syndromes: The impact of DSM-III and DSM-IV. *Journal of Traumatic Stress, 9,* 159–179.

Kirchberg, T. (2014). Initiating contact. In *Memphis Police Department Crisis Intervention Team training manual* (pp. 23–25). Memphis, TN: Memphis Police Department.

Kirchberg, T. M., James, R. K., Dupont, R., & Cochran, S. (2014, October). Something old, something new, something borrowed for the blue. Paper presented at the annual Crisis Intervention Team International convention, Hartford, CT.

Kirk, A. (1989). The prediction of violent behavior during short-term civil commitment. *Bulletin of the American Academy of Psychiatry and the Law, 17,* 345–353.

Kirk, W. (1993). *Adolescent suicide: A school-based approach to assessment and intervention.* Champaign, IL: Research Press.

Kiselica, M. S. (1998). Preparing Anglos for the challenges and joys of multiculturalism. *Counseling Psychologist, 26,* 5–21.

Kisely, S., Campbell, L. A., Peddle, S., Hare, S., Pyche, M., Spicer, D., & Moore, M. (2010). A controlled before-and-after evaluation of a mobile crisis partnership between mental health and police services in Nova Scotia. *Canadian Journal of Psychiatry, 55*(10), 662–668.

Kisiel, C., Ferenbach, T., Liang, L., Stolbach, B., McClelland, G., Griffin, G., . . . Spinazzola, J. (2014). Examining child sexual abuse in relation to complex patterns of trauma exposure: Findings for the national Child Traumatic Stress Network. *Psychological Trauma: Theory, Research, Practice, and Policy, 6*(Supp. 1), S28–S39.

Kitchener, K. S. (1984). Intuition, critical evaluation and ethical principles: The foundation for ethical decisions in counseling psychology. *The Counseling Psychologist, 12*(3), 43–55.

Kitzman, K. M., & Gaylord, N. K. (2001). Divorce counseling. In E. R. Welfel & R. E. Ingersoll (Eds.), *The mental health desk reference* (pp. 32–37). New York: John Wiley & Sons.

Kivlighan, Jr., D. M., Mamarosh, C. L., & Hilsenroth, M. J. (2014). Client and therapist therapeutic alliance, session evaluation, and client reliable change: A moderated actor-partner interdependence model. *Journal of Counseling Psychology, 61*(1), 15–23.

Klass, D. (1995). Spiritual aspect of the resolution of grief. In H. Wass & R. A. Neimeyer (Eds.), *Dying: Facing the facts* (pp. 243–268). Washington, DC: Taylor & Francis.

Klassen, D., & O'Connor, W. A. (1988). A prospective study of predictors of violence in adult male mental health admissions. *Law and Human Behavior, 12,* 143–158.

Klavir, O., Genud-Gabai, R., & Paz, R. (2012). Low- frequency stimulation depresses the primate anterior-cingulate-cortex and prevents spontaneous recovery of aversive memories. *The Journal of Neuroscience, 32*(25), 8589–8597.

Kleespies, P. M. (2009). *Behavioral emergencies: An evidence-based resource for evaluating and managing risk of suicide, violence, and victimization.* Washington, DC: American Psychological Association.

Kleespies, P. M. (2014). *Decision making in behavioral emergencies.* Washington, DC: American Psychological Association.

Kleespies, P. M., & Ponce, A. N. (2009). The stress and emotional impact of clinical work with the patient at risk. In P. Kleespies (Ed.), *Behavioral emergencies: An evidence-based resource for evaluating and managing risk of suicide, violence and victimization* (pp. 431–448). Washington, DC: American Psychological Association.

Kleespies, P. M., & Richmond, J. S. (2009). Evaluating behavioral emergencies. In P. M. Kleespies (Ed.), *Behavioral emergencies: An evidence-based resource for evaluating and managing risk of suicide, violence, and victimization* (pp. 33–58). Washington, DC: American Psychological Association.

Kleespies, P. M., Hough, S., & Romeo, A. M. (2009). Suicide risk in people with medical and terminal illness. In P. M. Kleespies (Ed.), *Behavioral emergencies: An evidence-based resource for evaluating and managing risk of suicide, violence, and victimization* (pp. 103–122). Washington, DC: American Psychological Association.

Kleinman, S. B., & Stewart, L. (2004). Psychiatric-legal considerations in providing mental health assistance to disaster survivors. *Psychiatric Clinics of North America, 27,* 559–570.

Kliman, A. S. (1978). *Crisis: Psychological first aid for recovery and growth.* New York: Holt, Rinehart & Winston.

Klotz, J. M. (2003). Welcome to ecological counseling.org. Retrieved April 21, 2003, from www.ecologicalcounseling.org

Knapp, S., & VandeCreek, L. (2012). *Practical ethics for psychologists: A positive approach.* Washington, DC: American Psychological Association.

Knapp, S., Gottlieb, M., Berman, J., & Handelsman, M. M. (2007). When law and ethics collide: What should professional psychologists do? *Professional Psychology: Research and Practice, 38*(1), 54–59.

Knauer, S. (2000). *No ordinary life: Parenting the sexually abused child and adolescent.* Springfield, IL: Charles C Thomas.

Knight, R. A. (1999). Validation of a typology for rapists. *Journal of Interpersonal Violence, 14*(3), 303–330.

Knipe, J. (2015). *EMDR toolbox: Theory and treatment of complex PTSD and dissociation.* New York: Springer.

Knopp, F. H., & Lackey, L. B. (1987). *Female sexual abusers: A summary of data from 44 treatment providers.* Orwell, VT: Safer Society Press.

Knowles, R., Sasser, D. D., & Besty Garrison, M. E. (2010). Family resilience and resiliency following Hurricane Katrina. In R. P. Kilmer, V. Gil-Rivas, R. G. Tedeschi, & L. G. Calhoun (Eds.), *Helping families and communities recover from disaster* (pp. 97–116). Washington, DC: American Psychological Association.

Knox, K., & Roberts, A. R. (2005). Crisis intervention with stalking victims. In A. R. Roberts (Ed.), *Crisis intervention handbook* (3rd ed., pp. 483–498). New York: Oxford University Press.

Knudson, M. (1991, April). *Chronic and abusive callers: Appropriate responses and interventions.* Paper presented at the Fifteenth Annual Convening of Crisis Intervention Personnel, Chicago.

Kobasa, S. (1979). Stressful life events, personality, and health: An inquiry into hardiness. *Journal of Personality and Social Psychology, 37,* 1–11.

Kocmur, M., & Zavasnik, A. (1993). Problems with borderline patients in a crisis intervention unit: A case history. *Crisis, 14,* 71–75, 89.

Koeske, G. F., & Kelly, T. (1995). The impact of over involvement on burnout and job satisfaction. *American Journal of Orthopsychiatry, 65,* 282–292.

Koeske, G. F., Kirk, S. A., & Koeske, R. D. (1993). Coping with job stress: Which strategies work best? *Journal of Occupational and Organizational Psychology, 66,* 319–335.

Kolb, L. C., & Mutalipassi, L. R. (1982). The conditioned emotional response: A subclass of the chronic and delayed stress disorder. *Psychiatric Annals, 12,* 969–987.

Kolski, T. D., Jongsma Jr., A. E., & Myer, R. A. (2012). *The crisis counseling and trauma event treatment planner, with DSM-V updates.* Hoboken, NJ: John Wiley & Sons.

Komar, A. A. (1994). Adolescent school crises: Structures, issues, and techniques for postventions. *International Journal of Adolescence and Youth, 5*(1/2), 35–46.

Konigsberg, R. D. (2011). *The truth about grief: The myth of its five stages and the new science of loss.* New York: Simon & Schuster.

Koocher, G. (1975). Why isn't the gerbil moving? Discussing death in the classroom. *Children Today, 4,* 18–36.

Koritsas, S., Coles, J., & Boyle, M. (2010). Workplace violence towards social workers: The Australian experience. *British Journal of Social Work, 40*(10), 257–271.

Kornblum, R. (2002). *Disarming the playground: Violence prevention through movement and prosocial skills.* Oklahoma City: Woods and Barnes.

Koss, M. P. (1998). Hidden rape: Sexual aggression and victimization in a national sample of students in higher education. In M. E. Odem & J. Clay-Warner (Eds.), *Confronting rape and sexual assault* (pp. 51–70). Wilmington, DE: Scholarly Resources.

Koss, M. P., & Achilles, M. (2008). *Restorative justice responses to sexual assault.* Harrisburg, PA: VAWnet, a project of the National Resource Center on Domestic Violence /Pennsylvania Coalition Against Domestic Violence. Retrieved from www.vawnet.org

Kottak, C. (2006). *Mirror for Humanity.* New York: McGraw-Hill.

Koverola, C., & Panchanadeswaran, S. (2004). Domestic violence interventions with women of color: The intersection of victimization and cultural diversity. In K. Kendall-Tackett (Ed.), *Health consequences of abuse in the family: A clinical guide for evidence-based practice. Application and practice in health psychology* (pp. 45–61). Washington, DC: American Psychological Association.

Kraft, S. G. (2003). Sudden unexpected deaths create unique challenges when counseling children. *Counseling Today, 46*(1), 12.

Krahe, B., & Moller, I. (2011). Links between self-reported media violence exposure and teacher ratings of aggression and prosocial behavior among German adolescents. *Journal of Adolescence, 34*(2), 279–287.

Krahe, B., Moller, I., Huesmann, L., Kirwil, L., Felber, J., & Berger, A. (2011). Desensitization to media violence: Links with habitual media violence exposure, aggressive cognitions, and aggressive behavior. *Journal of Personality and Social Psychology, 100*(4), 630–646.

Kramer, B. J., Kavanaugh, M., Trentham-Dietz, A., Walsh, M., & Yonker, J. A. (2010). Complicated grief symptoms in caregiver of persons with lung cancer: The role of family conflict, intrapsychic strains, and hospice utilization. *Omega: Journal of Death and Dying, 62*(3), 210–220.

Kramer, T., Lindy, J., Green, B., & Grace, M. (1994). The comorbidity of post-traumatic stress disorder and suicidality in Vietnam veterans. *Suicide and Life Threatening Behavior, 24,* 58–67.

Krebs, C. P., Lindquist, C. H., Warner, T. D., Fisher, B. S., & Martin, S. L. (2007, October). The campus sexual assault study final report xiii, 55. National Criminal Justice Reference Service. Retrieved from www.ncjrs.gov/pdffiles1/nij/grants/221153.pdf

Kreidler, M., Briscoe, L., & Beech, R. (2002). Pharmacology for post-traumatic stress disorder related to childhood sexual abuse: A literature review. *Perspectives in Psychiatric Care, 38*(4), 135–145.

Kreisman, J. J., & Straus, H. (2004). *Sometimes I act crazy: Living with borderline personality disorder.* Hoboken, NJ: John Wiley & Sons.

Kreisman, J. J., & Straus, H. (2010). I hate you—Don't leave me: Understanding the borderline personality (rev. ed.). New York: Perigee/Penguin Group.

Kriner, L., & Waldron, B. (1988). Group counseling: A treatment modality for batterers. *Journal of Specialists in Group Work, 13,* 110–116.

Kroger, C., Roepke. S., & Kliem, S. (2014). Reasons for premature termination of dialectical behavior therapy for inpatients with borderline personality disorder. *Behavior Research and Therapy, 60*(1), 46–52.

Kroll, J. (2003). Posttraumatic symptoms and the complexity of response to trauma. *Journal of the American Medical Association, 290*(5), 667–670.

Krueger, J. I. (2011). Shock without awe. *American Psychologist, 66,* 642–643.

Kuhn, J. (2008). Countertransference reactions in psychotherapy group work with HIV positive children. *Psycho-analytic Psychotherapy in South Africa, 16*(1), 33–60.

Kuhn, J. A., Charleanea, M., & Chavez, E. L. (1998). Correlates of sexual assault in Mexican-American and White non-Hispanic adolescent males. *Violence and Victims, 13*(1), 11–20.

Kuhn, T. S. (1962). *The structure of scientific revolutions.* Chicago: University of Chicago Press.

Kukla, R. A., Schlenger, W. E., Fairbank, J. A., Hough, R. L., Jordan, B. K., & Marmar, C. R. (1990). *Trauma and the Vietnam War generation: Report of findings from the National Vietnam Veterans' Readjustment Study.* New York: Brunner/Mazel.

Kulkami, S., Bell, H., Hartman, J., & Herman-Smith, R. (2013). Exploring individual and organizational factors contributing to compassion satisfaction, secondary traumatic tress, and burnout in domestic violence service providers. *Journal of the Society for Social Work Research, 4*(2), 114–130.

Kumble, S., & McSherry, B. (2010). Seclusion and restraint: Rethinking regulation from a human rights perspective. *Psychiatry, Psychology and Law, 17*(4), 551–561.

Kurdek, L. (1994). Areas of conflict for gay, lesbian, and heterosexual couples: What couples argue about influences relationship satisfaction. *Journal of Marriage and the Family, 56,* 923–934.

Kurlowicz, L. H. (1990). Violence in the emergency department. *American Journal of Nursing, 90,* 35–40.

Kushner, H. S. (1983). *When bad things happen to good people.* New York: Avon.

Kvarstein, E. H., Pedersen, G., Umes, Ø. Hummelem , B., Wilberg, T., & Karterud, S. (2015). Changing from a traditional psychodynamic treatment programme to mentalization-based treatment for patients with borderline personality disorder. *Psychology and Psychotherapy: Theory, Research and Practice, 88*(1), 71–86.

Kübler-Ross, E. (1969). *On death and dying.* New York: Macmillan.

Kübler-Ross, E. (1975). *Death: The final stage of growth.* Upper Saddle River, NJ: Prentice Hall.

Kübler-Ross, E. (1983). *On children and death.* New York: Macmillan.

Kübler-Ross, E. (1987). *AIDS: The ultimate challenge.* New York: Macmillan.

Kübler-Ross, E., & Kessler, D. (2005). *On grief and grieving: Finding the meaning of grief through the five stages of loss.* New York: Scribner.

L

Lachkar, J. (2011). *How to talk to a borderline.* New York: Routledge & Taylor.

LaCoursiere, R. B., Bodfrey, K. E., & Ruby, L. M. (1980). Traumatic neurosis in the etiology of alcoholism: Vietnam and other trauma. *American Journal of Psychiatry, 137,* 966–968.

LaFauci Schutt, J. M. (2009). Personal and environmental predictors of posttraumatic stress in emergency management professionals. *Dissertation Abstracts International: Section A. Humanities and Social Sciences, 69*(1), 483.

Lagoni, L., Butler, C., & Hetts, S. (1994). *The human–animal bond and grief.* Philadelphia: Saunders.

Lakeside Hospital. (1988). *Verbal techniques for deescalating violent behavior.* Memphis, TN: Author.

Lalor, K., & McElvaney, R. (2010). Child sexual abuse, links to later sexual exploitation/high-risk sexual behavior, and prevention/treatment programs. *Trauma, Violence, and Abuse, 11*(4), 159–177.

Lam, J., McNeil, D. E., & Binder, R. L. (2000). The relationship between patients' gender and violence leading to staff injuries. *Psychiatric Services, 51*(9), 1167–1170.

Lamb, C. W. (1973). Telephone therapy: Some common errors and fallacies. In D. Lester & G. W. Brockopp (Eds.), *Crisis intervention and counseling by telephone* (pp. 105–110). Springfield, IL: Charles C Thomas.

Lamb, C. W. (2002). Telephone therapy: Some common errors and fallacies. In D. Lester (Ed.), *Crisis intervention and counseling by telephone* (2nd ed., pp. 83–87). Springfield, IL: Charles C Thomas.

Lamb, H. R., Weinberger, L. E., & DeCuir, W. J. (2002). The police and mental health. *Psychiatric Services, 53*(10), 1266–1271.

Lamb, H. R., Weinberger, L. E., & Gross, B. H. (2004). Mentally ill persons in the criminal justice system: Some perspectives. *Psychiatric Quarterly, 75*(2), 107–126.

Lambie, G. W. (2005). Child abuse and neglect: A practical guide for professional school counselors. *Professional School Counseling, 8*(3), 249–258.

Lamoureaux, B., Jackson, A., Palmieri, P., & Hobfoll, S. (2012). Child sexual abuse and adulthood-interpersonal outcomes: Examining pathways for intervention. *Psychological Trauma: Theory, Research, Practice and Policy, 4*(6), 605–613.

Lancman, S., Mangia, E., & Muramoto, M., (2013). Impact of conflict and violence on workers in a hospital emergency room. *Journal of Prevention, Assessment, and Rehabilitation, 45*(4), 519–527.

Lanctot, N., & Guay, S., (2014). The aftermath of workplace violence among healthcare workers: A systematic literature review of the consequences. *Aggression and Violent Behavior, 19*(5), 492–501.

Landreth, G. L. (1987). Play therapy: Facilitative use of child's play in elementary school counseling. *Elementary School Guidance and Counseling, 21,* 253–261.

Lane, J. (2003). *Ecological crisis management* (Cassette Recording No. 082803). Memphis, TN: University of Memphis.

Lang, A. J., Stein, M., Kennedy, C., & Foy, D. W. (2004). Adult psychopathology and intimate partner violence among survivors of childhood maltreatment. *Journal of Interpersonal Violence, 19*(10), 1102–1118.

Langer, N. (2011). Who did you *used* to be? Loss for older adults. In D. L. Harris (Ed.), *Counting our losses: Reflecting on change,* loss, and transition in everyday life (pp. 215–221). New York: Routledge/Taylor & Francis Group.

Langhinrichsen-Roling, J., Neidig, P., & Thorn, G. (1995). Violent marriages: Gender difference in levels of current violence and past abuse. *Journal of Family Violence, 10*(2), 159–176.

Langley, R., & Levy, R. C. (1977). *Wife beating: The silent crisis.* New York: Dutton.

Langman, P. (2009). *Why kids kill: Inside the minds of school shooters.* New York: Palgrave MacMillan.

Lanius, R., Frewen, P., Nazarov, A., & McKinnnon, M. C. (2014). A social-cognitive-neuroscience approach to PTSD: Clinical and research perspectives. In U. F. Lanius, S. L. Paulsen, & F. M. Corrigan (Eds.), *Neurobiology and treatment of traumatic dissociation: Towards an embodied self* (pp. 69–80). New York: Springer.

Lanius, R. A., Bluhm, R., & Frewen, P. A. (2013). Childhood trauma, brain connectivity and the self. In J. Ford & C. A. Courtois (Eds.), *Treating complex stress disorders in children and adolescents: Scientific foundations and therapeutic models* (pp. 24–38). New York: Guilford Press.

Lanza, M. L. (1984). A follow-up study of nurses' reactions to physical assault. *Hospital and Community Psychiatry, 35,* 492–494.

Lanza, M. L. (1985, June). How nurses react to patient assault. *Journal of Psychosocial Nursing and Mental Health, 23,* 6–11.

Lapierre, C. B., Schwegler, A. F., & LaBauve, B. J. (2007). Posttraumatic stress and depression symptoms in soldiers returning from combat operations in Iraq and Afghanistan. *Journal of Traumatic Stress, 20,* 933–943.

Lapierre, S., Erlanger, A., Waern, M., De Leo, D., Oyama, H., Scocco, P., et al. (2011). A systematic review of elderly suicide prevention programs. *Crisis: The Journal of Crisis Intervention and Suicide Prevention, 32*(2), 88–98.

Laporte, L., Jiang, D., Pepler, D., & Chamberland, C. (2011). The relationship between adolescents' experience of family violence and dating. *Youth and Society, 43*(1), 3–27.

Larson, D. G. (1993). *The helper's journey: Working with people facing grief, loss, and life-threatening illness.* Champaign, IL: Research Press.

Larson, J. (1994). Violence prevention in the schools: A review of selected programs and procedures. *School Psychology Review, 23*(2), 151–164.

Lating, J. M., & Everly, G. S. (1995). Psychophysiological assessment of PTSD. In G. S. Everly, Jr., & J. M. Lating (Eds.), *Psychotraumatology* (pp. 129–146). New York: Plenum Press.

Laub, B., & Bar-Sade, E. (2014). The Imma EMDR Group Protocol. In M. Luber (Ed.), *Implementing EMDR early mental health interventions for man-made and natural disasters: Models, scripted protocols and summary sheets* (pp. 267–273). New York: Springer.

Laufer, R., Yager, T., & Grey-Wouters, E. (1981). Postwar trauma: Social and psychological problems of Vietnam veterans in the aftermath of the Vietnam War. In A. Egendorf, C. Kadushin, & R. S. Laufer (Eds.), *Legacies of Vietnam* (Vol. 1) (pp. 154–176). Washington, DC: U.S. Government Printing Office.

Laux, J. (2003). A primer on suicidology: Implications for counselors. *Journal of Counseling and Development, 80,* 380–383.

Lawlor-Savage, L., & Prentice, J. L. (2014). Digital cognitive behavior therapy (CBT) in Canada: Ethical considerations. *Canadian Psychology, 55*(4), 231–239,

Lawrence, K. A., Allen, J., & Chanen, A. (2011). A study of maladaptive schema and borderline personality disorder in young people. *Cognitive Therapy and Research, 35*(1), 30–39.

Lawson, D. M. (2003). Incidence, explanations, and treatment of partner violence. *Journal of Counseling and Development, 81*(1), 19–32.

Lawson, D. M. (2013). *Family violence: Explanations and evidence based practice*. Alexandria, VA: American Counseling Association.

Lawson, G., & Myers, J. E. (2011). Wellness, professional quality of life, and career-sustaining behaviors: What keeps us well? *Journal of Counseling and Development, 89*(2), 163–171.

Lawson, G., Bodenhorn, N., Welfare, L. (2010). Virginia Tech: A campus and a community respond. In J. Webber & J. B. Mascari (Eds.), *Terrorism, trauma, and tragedies: A counselor's guide to preparing and responding* (3rd ed., pp. 73–76). Alexandria, VA: American Counseling Association Foundation.

Lawson, G., Venart, E., Hazler, R. J., & Kottler, J. A. (2007). Toward a culture of counselor wellness. *Journal of Humanistic Counseling, Education, and Development, 46*, 5–19.

Lawson, S. K. (2009). Hospice social workers: The incidence of compassion fatigue. *Dissertation Abstracts International: Section A. Humanities and Social Sciences, 69*(8), 4505.

Lazarus, A. (1977). *In the mind's eye: The powers of imagery for personal enrichment*. New York: Guilford Press.

Lazarus, A. (1989). *The practice of multimodal therapy*. Baltimore: Johns Hopkins University Press.

Lazarus, A. A. (1976). *Multimodal behavior therapy*. New York: Springer.

Lazarus, R. S., & Folkman, S. (1984). *Stress, appraisal, and coping*. New York: Springer-Verlag.

Leach, M. M., & Harbin, J. J. (1997). Psychological ethics codes: A comparison of twenty-four countries. *International Journal of Psychology, 32*, 181–192.

Leadbetter, D. (1993). Trends in assault on social work staff: The experience of one Scottish department. *British Journal of Social Work, 23*, 613–628.

Leahy, M. J. (1993). A comparison of depression in women bereaved of a spouse, child, or parent. *Omega: Journal of Death and Dying, 26*(3), 207–215.

Lear, M. W. (1972, January 30). Q: If you rape a woman and steal her TV, what can they get you for in New York? A: Stealing her TV. *New York Times Magazine*, pp. 10–11.

Leavitt, F. (2000). Surviving the roots of trauma: Prevalence of silent signs of sex abuse in patients who recover memories of childhood sex abuse as adults. *Journal of Personality Assessment, 74*(2), 311–323.

Lebow, J., & Stroud, C. B. (2012). Assessment of effective couple and family functioning. In S. J. Price, C. A. Price, & P. C. McKenry (Eds.), *Families and change: Coping with stressful events and transitions* (pp. 501–528). Los Angeles: Sage.

Lechner, S., & Weaver, K. (2009). Lessons learned about benefit finding among individuals with cancer or HIV/AIDS. In C. L. Park, S. C. Lechner, M. H. Antoni, & A. L. Stanton (Eds.), *Medical illness and positive life change: Can crisis lead to a personal transformation?* (pp. 107–124). Washington, DC: American Psychological Association.

LeCroy, C. W. (1988). Anger management or anger expression: Which is most effective? *Residential Treatment for Children and Youth, 5*, 29–39.

Lee, C., & Cuijpers, P. (2013). A meta-analysis of eye movements in processing emotional memories. *Journal of Behavior Therapy and Experimental Psychiatry, 44*(2), 231–239.

Lee, C., Slade, P., & Lygo, V. (1996). The influence of psychological debriefing on emotional adaption in women following early miscarriage: A preliminary study. *British Journal of Medical Psychology, 69*, 37–49.

Lee, C., Taylor, G., & Drummond, P. (2006). The active ingredient of EMDR: Is it traditional exposure or dual focus of attention? *Clinical Psychology and Psychotherapy, 13*(2), 97–107.

Lee, M. Y. (2002). Asian battered women: Assessment and treatment. In A. R. Roberts (Ed.), *Handbook of domestic violence: Intervention strategies* (pp. 472–482). New York: Oxford University Press.

Lee, R. T., & Ashforth, B. E. (1993). A longitudinal study of burnout among supervisors and managers: Comparisons between the Leiter and Maslach and Golembiewski models. *Organizational Behavior and Human Decision Processes, 54*, 369–398.

Lee, R. T., & Ashforth, B. E. (1996). A meta-analytic examination of the correlates of the three dimensions of job burnout. *Journal of Applied Psychology, 81*(2), 123–133.

Lee, S. M, Cho, S. H., Kissinger, D., & Ogle, N. (2010). A typology of burnout in professional counselors. *Journal of Counseling and Development, 88*(2), 131–138.

Lee, S. M., Baker, C. R., Cho, S. H., Heckathorn, D. E., Holland, M. W., & Newgent, R. A. (2007). Development and initial psychometrics of the Counselor Burnout Inventory. *Measurement and Evaluation in Counseling and Development, 40*(2), 142–154.

Leenaars, A. A. (1994). Crisis intervention with highly lethal suicidal people. In A. A. Leenaars, J. T. Maltsberger, & R. A. Neimeyer (Eds.), *Treatment of suicidal people* (pp. 45–61). Washington, DC: Taylor & Francis.

Leenaars, A. A. (1996). Suicide: A multidimensional malaise. *Suicide and Life-Threatening Behavior, 26*(3), 221–236.

Leenaars, A. A. (2004). *Psychotherapy and suicidal people: A person-centered approach*. Chichester, England: John Wiley & Sons.

Leffert, M. (2003). Analysis and psychotherapy by telephone: Twenty years of clinical experience. *Journal of the American Psychoanalytic Association, 51*, 101–130.

Leffler, C. T., & Dembert, M. L. (1998). Posttraumatic stress symptoms among U.S. Navy divers recovering TWA Flight 800. *Journal of Nervous and Mental Disease, 186*, 574–577.

Lehmann, P., & Rabenstein, S. (2002). Children exposed to domestic violence: The role of impact, assessment, and treatment. In A. R. Roberts (Ed.), *Handbook of domestic violence: Intervention strategies* (pp. 343–364). New York: Oxford University Press.

Lehmann, P., & Simmons, C. (Eds.). (2009). *Strengths-based batterer intervention: A new paradigm in ending family violence*. New York: Springer.

Leichsenring, F., Leibing, E., Kruse, J., New, A., & Leweke, F. (2011). Borderline personality disorder. *Lancet, 377*, 74–84.

Leiter, M. P., & Maslach, C. (2005). *Banishing burnout: Six strategies for improving your relationship with work*. San Francisco: Jossey-Bass.

Leitner, L. A. (1974). Crisis counseling may save a life. *Journal of Rehabilitation, 40*, 19–20.

Lempp, R. C. (1990). To the diagnostic of "incomprehensible" offenses of adolescents and juveniles. *Acta Paedopsychiatrica, 53*, 173–175.

Lenehan, G. P., & Turner, J. T. (1984). Treatment of staff victims of violence. In J. T. Turner (Ed.), *Violence in the medical care setting: A survival guide* (pp. 251–260). Rockville, MD: Aspen Systems.

Lenihan, G. O., & Kirk, W. (1999, April). *Rural community level crisis intervention*. Paper presented at the Twenty-Third Annual Convening of Crisis Intervention Personnel, Chicago.

Lenz, S., Bruijn, B., Serman, N., & Bailey, L. (2014). Effectiveness of cognitive processing therapy for treating posttraumatic stress disorder. *Journal of Mental Health Counseling, 36*(4), 360–376.

Leo, J. (2010, Fall). Let the hot air out of bullies! *Teaching Tolerance,* 12.

Leonard, B. E. (2005). The biochemistry of suicide. *Journal of Crisis Intervention and Suicide Prevention, 26*(4), 153–156.

Lerner, M. J. (2000). The human cost of organizational downsizing: The irrational effects of the justice motive on managers, dismissed workers, and survivors. In J. H. Harvey & E. D. Miller (Eds.), *Loss and trauma: General and close relationship perspectives* (pp. 208–224). Philadelphia: Brunner-Routledge.

Leskin, G. A., Huleatt, W., Jerrmann, J., Ladue, L., & Gusman, F. (2006). Rapid development of family assistance centers: Lessons learned following the September 11 terrorist attacks. In E. C. Ritchie, P. J. Watson, & M. J. Friedman (Eds.), *Interventions following mass violence and disasters: Strategies for mental health practice* (pp. 257–277). New York: Guilford Press.

Lester, D. (1988). *The biochemical basis of suicide.* Springfield, IL: Charles C Thomas.

Lester, D. (1995). The concentration of neurotransmitter metabolites in the cerebrospinal fluid of suicidal individuals. *Pharmacopsychiatry, 28,* 45–50.

Lester, D. (1997). *Making sense of suicide.* Philadelphia: Charles Press.

Lester, D. (2000). Decades of suicide research: Where from and where to? In T. Joiner & M. D. Rudd (Eds.), *Suicide science: Expanding the boundaries* (pp. 9–16). Boston: Kluwer Academic.

Lester, D. (2001). The epidemiology of suicide. In D. Lester (Ed.), *Suicide prevention: Resources for the millennium* (pp. 3–16). Philadelphia: Brunner-Routledge.

Lester, D. (2002). When things go wrong. In D. Lester & G. W. Brockopp (Eds.), *Crisis intervention and counseling by telephone* (2nd ed., pp. 167–170). Springfield, IL: Charles C Thomas.

Lester, D. (2004). Denial in suicide survivors. *Journal of Crisis Intervention and Suicide Prevention, 25*(2), 78–79.

Lester, D. (2005). Blood types and national suicide rates. *Journal of Crisis Intervention and Suicide Prevention, 25*(3), 237–238.

Lester, D. (Ed.). (2001). *Suicide prevention: Resources for the millennium.* Philadelphia: Brunner-Routledge.

Lester, D., & Brockopp, G. W. (Eds.). (1973). *Crisis intervention and counseling by telephone.* Springfield, IL: Charles C Thomas.

Lester, D., & Gunn, J. F. (2011). National anthems and suicide rates. *Psychological Reports, 108*(1), 43–44.

Lester, P. B., Harms, O. D., Herian, M. N., Krasikova, D. V., & Beal, S. J. (2011). *The Comprehensive Soldier Fitness evaluation report #3: Longitudinal analysis of the impact of master resilience training on self-reported resilience and psychological health data, U.S. Army.* Retrieved at www.ppc.sas.upenn.edu/csftechreport3mrt.pdf

Lester, P. B., McBride, S., & Cornum, R. L. (2013). Comprehensive soldier fitness: Underscoring the facts, dismantling the fiction. In R. R. Sinclair & T. W. Britt (Eds.), *Building psychological resilience in military personnel: Theory and practice* (pp. 193–220). Washington, D.C.: American Psychological Association.

Leventhal, B. L., & Lundy, S. E. (1999). *Same-sex violence: Strategies for change.* Thousand Oaks, CA: Sage.

Levinson, D. (1989). *Family violence in cross-cultural perspective.* Newbury Park, CA: Sage.

Levinson, D. J. (1986). A concept of adult development. *American Psychologist, 41*(1), 3–133.

Levinson, D. J., & Levinson, J. D. (1996). *The seasons of a woman's life.* New York: Knopf.

Levinson, J. D. (1986). A conception of adult development. *American Psychologist, 41*(1), 3–13.

Levis, D. O. (1992). From abuse to violence: Psychophysiological consequences of maltreatment. *Journal of American Academy Child and Adolescent Psychiatry, 142*(10), 1161–1166.

Lew, M. (2004). *Victims no longer: The classic guide for men recovering from sexual child abuse.* New York: HarperCollins.

Lewellyn, A. (1985). *Counseling emotionally disturbed high school students: The Mattoon, Illinois, TLC program* (Cassette Recording No. 12-6611). Memphis, TN: Memphis State University, Department of Counseling and Personnel Services.

Lewis, M. D. (2005). Self-organizing individual differences in brain development. *Developmental Review, 25,* 27–43.

Lewis, S. (1993). Restraint and seclusion. In P. E. Blumenreich & S. Lewis (Eds.), *Managing the violent patient: A clinician's guide* (pp. 101–109). New York: Brunner-Mazel.

Li, A., Early, S., Mahrer, N., Klaristenfeld, J., & Gold, J. (2014). Group cohesion and organizational commitment: Protective factors for nurse residents' job satisfaction, compassion fatigue, compassion satisfaction and burnout. *Journal of Professional Nursing, 30*(1), 89–99.

Li, J., Theng, Y., & Foo, S. (2014). Game-based digital interventions for depression therapy: A systematic review and meta-analysis. *Cyberpsychology, Behavior, and Social Networking, 17*(8), 519–527.

Lie, G. Y., & Gentlewarrier, S. (1991). Intimate violence in lesbian relationships: Discussion of survey findings and practice implication. *Journal of Social Service Research, 15*(1/2), 41–59.

Liese, B. S. (1994). Brief therapy, crisis intervention, and the cognitive therapy of substance abuse. *Crisis Intervention, 1,* 11–29.

Lifton, R. J. (1973). *Home from the war: Vietnam veterans—neither individuals nor executioners.* New York: Simon & Schuster.

Lifton, R. J. (1974). "Death imprints" on youth in Vietnam. *Journal of Clinical Child Psychology, 3,* 47–49.

Lifton, R. J. (1975). The postwar war. *Journal of Social Issues, 31,* 181–195.

Lifton, R. J. (1983). *The broken connection: On death and the continuity of life.* New York: Basic Books.

Ligon, J. (2000). Mobile crisis units: Frontline community mental health services. In A. R. Roberts (Ed.), *Contemporary perspectives on crisis intervention and prevention* (pp. 357–372). Upper Saddle River, NJ: Prentice Hall.

Linaker, O. M., & Busch-Iversen, H. (1995). Predictors of imminent violence in psychiatric inpatients. *Acta Psychiatrica Scandinavica, 92*(4), 250–254.

Lindemann, E. (1944). Symptomatology and management of acute grief. *American Journal of Psychiatry, 101,* 141–148.

Lindemann, E. (1956). The meaning of crisis in individual and family. *Teachers College Record, 57,* 310.

Lindsay, J., & Brady, D. (2002). "Nurturing fragile relationships": Early reflections on working with victims of domestic violence on the National Probation Service's Duluth Pathfinder research programme. *Issues in Forensic Psychology, 3,* 59–71.

Lindsay, M., & Lester, D. (2004). *Suicide-by-cop: Committing suicide by provoking police to shoot you.* Amityville, NY: Baywood Publishing.

Lindstrom, C. M., Cann, A., Calhoun, L. G., & Tedeschi, R. G. (2013). The relationship of core belief challenge, rumination, disclosure, and sociocultural elements to posttraumatic growth. *Psychological Trauma: Theory, Research, Practice, and Policy, 5*(1), 50–55.

Lindy, J. D. (1996). Psychoanalytic psychotherapy of posttraumatic stress disorder: The nature of the therapeutic relationship. In B. A. van der Kolk, A. C. McFarlane, & L. Weisaeth (Eds.), *Traumatic stress* (pp. 525–536). New York: Guilford Press.

Lindy, J. D. (2012). Listening to what the trauma patient teaches us: A 35-year perspective. In R. A. McMackin, E. Newman, J. M. Fogler, & T. M. Keane (Eds.), *Trauma therapy in context: The science and craft of evidence-based practice* (pp. 15–28). Washington, DC: American Psychological Association.

Linehan, M. M. (1997). Validation and psychotherapy. In A. Bohart & L. Greenberg (Eds.), *Empathy reconsideration: New directions in psychotherapy* (pp. 353–392). Washington, DC: American Psychological Association.

Linehan, M. M., & Schmidt, H. (1995). The dialectics of effective treatment of borderline personality disorder. In L. Kraneer & W. O'Donohue (Eds.), *Theories of behavior therapy: Exploring behavior change* (pp. 553–584). Washington, DC: American Psychological Association.

Linehan, M. M., Comtois, K. A., Murray, A. M., Brown, M. Z., Gallop, R. J., Heard, H. L., et al. (2006). Two-year randomized controlled trial and follow-up of dialectical behavior therapy vs. therapy by experts for suicidal behaviors and borderline personality disorder. *Archives of General Psychiatry, 63*(7), 757–766.

Linehan, M. M., Goodstein, J. L., Nielsen, S. L., & Chiles, J. A. (1983). Reasons for staying alive when you are thinking of killing yourself: The Reasons for Living Inventory. *Journal of Consulting and Clinical Psychology, 51*(2), 276–286.

Linehand, M. (1993). *Dialectical behavior therapy for borderline personality disorder*. New York: Guilford Press.

Ling, J., Hunter, S., & Maple, M. (2014). Navigating the challenges of trauma counseling: How counsellors thrive and sustain their engagement. *Australian Social Work, 67*(2), 297–310.

Ling, R., Bertel, T., & Sundsøy, P. (2012). The socio-demographics of texting: An analysis of traffic data. *New Media and Society, 14*(2), 281–298.

Linley, A., Joseph, S., & Loumidis, K. (2005). Trauma work, sense of coherence and positive and negative changes in therapists. *Psychotherapy and Psychosomatics, 74*(3), 185–188.

Lion, J. R., & Pasternak, S. A. (1973). Countertransference reactions to violent patients. *American Journal of Psychiatry, 130,* 207–210.

Lipari v. Sears, Roebuck, and Co., Fed Suppl. 1980, July 17; 497: 185–97.

Lippy, E., & Kelzenber, B. (2012). Sympathetic system modulation to treat post-traumatic stress disorder: A review of clinical evidence and neurobiology. *Journal of Affective Disorders, 142*(1–3),1–5.

Lipsey, M. W. (1992). Juvenile delinquency treatment: A meta-analytic inquiry into the variability of effects. In T. D. Cook (Ed.), *Meta-analysis for explanation* (pp. 67–89). Beverly Hills, CA: Sage.

Lisek, D., & Miller, P. M. (2002). Repeat rape after multiple offending among undetected rapists. *Violence and Victims, 14,* 241–260.

Lisek, D., & Roth, S. (1988). Motivational factors in nonincarcerated sexually aggressive men. *Journal of Personality and Social Psychology, 55,* 795–802.

Lisek, D., Gardinier, L., Nicksa, S., & Cole, A. (2010). False allegations of sexual assault: An analysis of ten years of reported cases. *Violence Against Women, 16*(2), 1318–1334.

Littlechild, B. (1995). Violence against social workers. *Journal of Interpersonal Violence, 10,* 123–131.

Littlechild, B. (2002). The effects of client violence on child protection networks. *Trauma, Violence, and Abuse, 3,* 144–158.

Litz, B. T., & Gibson, L. E. (2006). Conducting research on mental health interventions. In E. C. Ritchie, P. J. Watson, & M. J. Friedman (Eds.), *Interventions following mass violence and disasters: Strategies for mental health practice* (pp. 387–404). New York: Guilford Press.

Livingston, M. (2011). A longitudinal analysis of alcohol outlet density and domestic violence. *Addiction, 106*(5), 919–925.

Lockhart, L. L., White, B. W., Causby, V., & Isaac, A. (1994). Letting out the secret: Violence in lesbian relationships. *Journal of Interpersonal Violence, 9*(4), 469–492.

Loeber, R. (1990). Development and risk factors of juvenile antisocial behavior and delinquency. *Clinical Psychology Review, 10,* 1–41.

Loeber, R., Farrington, D. P., Rumsey, C. A., & Allen-Hagen, B. (1998, May). Serious and violent juvenile offenders. *Juvenile Justice Bulletin.* Washington, DC: U.S. Department of Justice.

Logan, J., Myer, R., & James, R. May (2006). *How to TACKLE an excessive force complaint.* Paper presented at the Second Annual Crisis Intervention Team Conference, Orlando, FL.

Logie, R. (2014). EMDR: More than just a therapy for PTSD. *The Psychologist, 27*(7), 512–516.

Lohr, J. M., Montgomery, R. W., Lilienfeld, S. O., & Tolin, D. F. (1999). Pseudoscience and the commercial promotion of trauma treatments. In R. Gist & B. Lubin (Eds.), *Response to disaster: Psychosocial, community and ecological approaches* (pp. 291–321). Philadelphia: Brunner/Mazel.

Loinaz, I., (2014). Typologies, risk and recidivism in partner-violent men with the B-SAFER: A pilot study. *Psychology, Crime, and Law, 20*(2), 183–198.

Longdon, C. (1994). A survivor and therapist's viewpoint. In M. Elliot (Ed.), *Female sexual abuse of children* (pp. 47–56). New York: Guilford Press.

Lopata, H. Z. (1996). *Current widowhood: Myths and realities.* Thousand Oaks, CA: Sage.

Lopes de Lara, C., Dumais, A., Rouleau, G., Lesage, A., Dumont, M., Chawky, N., et al. (2006). STin2 variant and family history of suicide as significant predictors of suicide completion in major depression. *Biological Psychiatry, 59*(2), 114–120.

Lopez, A., (2015). An investigation of the use of Internet based resources in support of the therapeutic alliance. *Clinical Social Work Journal, 43*(2), 189–200.

Lord, J. H. (1996). America's number one killer: Vehicle crashes. In K. J. Doka (Ed.), *Living with grief after sudden loss: Suicide, homicide, accident, heart attack, stroke* (pp. 25–41). Washington, DC: Hospice Foundation of America.

Lorenz, E. N. (1993). *The essence of chaos.* Seattle: University of Washington Press.

Loumeau-May, L. V. (2008). Grieving in the public eye: Art therapy with children who lost parents in the World Trade Center attacks. In C. A. Malchiodi (Ed.), *Creative interventions with traumatized children* (pp. 112–131). New York: Guilford Press.

Louvre, C. (2002). Helping students grieve a friend's death. *School Counselor, 39*(5), 10–11.

Louvre, C. (2008). Weaving the community tapestry. *School Counselor, 45*(5), 28–31.

Lovell, D., Allen, D., Johnson, C., & Jemelka, R. (2001). Evaluating the effectiveness of residential treatment for prisoners with mental illness. *Criminal Justice and Behavior, 28,* 83–104.

Lovre, C. (2013). Student threat assessment. *ASCA School Counselor, 51*(2), 17–21.

Lu, S., Gao, W., Wei, Z., Wei, W., Liao, M., Ding, Y., Zhang, Z., & Li., L. (2013). Reduced cingulate gyrus volume associated with enhanced cortisol awakening response in young healthy adults reporting childhood trauma. *PLos ONE, 8*(7), e69350.

Lubell, K. M., & Vetter, J. B. (2006). Suicide and youth violence prevention: The promise of an integrated approach. *Aggression and Violent Behavior, 11*(2), 167–175.

Lublin, N. (2012). Texting that saves lives. Retrieved from www.ted.com/talks/nancy_lubin_textng_that_saves_lives.

Luckett, J. B., & Slaikeu, K. A. (1990). Crisis intervention by police. In K. A. Slaikeu (Ed.), *Crisis intervention: A handbook for practice and research* (2nd ed., pp. 227–242). Boston: Allyn & Bacon.

Luna, J. T., & Hoffman, R. M. (1999, June). *The counselor as catalyst: Forming partnerships for school violence reduction.* Paper presented at the American School Counselor Convention, Phoenix, AZ.

Lundberg-Love, P. K., Marmion, S., Ford, K., & Geffner, R. (1992). The long-term consequences of childhood incestuous victimization upon adult women's psychological symptomatology. *Journal of Child Sexual Abuse, 1*(1), 81–102.

Lupton-Smith, H., Carruthers, W. L., Flythe, R., Goette, E., & Modest, K. H. (1996). Conflict resolution as peer mediation:

Programs for elementary, middle, and high school students. *School Counselor, 43,* 375–391.

Lutz, B. J., Young, M. E., Cox, K. J., Martz, C., & Creasy, K. R. (2011). The crisis of stroke: Experiences of patients and their family caregivers. *Top Stroke Rehabilitation, 18,* 1–16.

Lyndall, D., & Bicknell, J. (2001). Trauma and the therapist: The experience of therapists working with the perpetrators of sexual abuse. *Australasian Journal of Disaster and Trauma Studies, 5*(1), 1–12.

Lyons, J. A., & Keane, T. M. (1989). Implosive therapy for the treatment of combat-related PTSD. *Journal of Traumatic Stress, 2,* 137–152.

M

MacDonald, C. M. (2003). Evaluation of stress debriefing interventions with military populations. *Military Medicine, 168,* 961–967.

MacDonald, G., & Sirotich, F. (2001). Reporting client violence. *Social Work, 46,* 107–114.

Mack, D. A., Shannon, C., Quick, J. D., & Quick, J. C. (1988). Stress and the preventative management of workplace violence. In R. W. Griffin & A. O'Leary-Kelly (Eds.), Dysfunctional behavior in organizations: Violent and deviant behavior. *Monographs in organizational behavior and industrial relations, 23,* Parts A and B (pp. 119–141). Stamford, CT: Jai Press.

Maclean, G. (1977). Psychic trauma and traumatic neurosis: Play therapy with a four-year-old boy. *Canadian Psychiatric Association Journal, 22,* 71–76.

MacPherson, M. (1984). *Long time passing: Vietnam and the haunted generation.* New York: Doubleday.

Madden, D. J., Lion, J. R., & Penna, M. W. (1976). Assaults on psychiatrists by patients. *American Journal of Psychiatry, 133,* 422–425.

Maheu, M. M. (2001). Practicing psychotherapy on the Internet: Risk management challenges and opportunities. *Register Report, 27,* 23–28.

Maheu, M. M. (2003). The online clinical practice management model. *Psychotherapy: Theory, Research, Practice, Training, 40*(1/2), 20–32.

Main, B. (2008). The effects of treating sex offenders on treatment providers who have a history of child sexual abuse. *Dissertation Abstracts International: Section B. The Sciences and Engineering, 68*(12), 1960.

Main, M. (1996). Introduction to the special section on attachment and psychopathology: Overview of the field of attachment. *Journal of Consulting and Clinical Psychology, 64*(2), 237–243.

Main, M. (2000). Attachment theory. In A. Kazdin (Ed.), *Encyclopedia of psychology* (Vol. 1, pp. 289–293). Washington, DC: American Psychological Association.

Makepeace, J. (1983). Life-events stress and courtship violence. *Family Relations, 32,* 101–109.

Malchiodi, C., Steele, W., & Kuban, C. (2008). Resilience and posttraumatic growth in traumatized children. In C. Malchiodi (Ed.), *Creative interventions with traumatized children* (pp. 285–301). New York: Guilford Press.

Malchiodi, C. A. (2008). *Creative interventions with traumatized children.* New York: Guilford Press.

Malchiodi, C. A., & Ginns-Gruenberg, D. (2008). Trauma, loss, and bibliotherapy: The healing power of stories. In C. A. Malchiodi (Ed.), *Creative interventions with traumatized children* (pp. 167–188). New York: Guilford Press.

Male Survivor. (2011). *Male sexual victimization and myths.* Retrieved from www.malesurvivor.org/myths.html

Malizia, A., & Nutt, D. (2000). Human brain imagining and post-traumatic stress disorder. In D. Nutt, J. Davidson, & J. Zohar (Eds.), *Post-traumatic stress disorder: Diagnosis, management, and treatment* (pp. 41–52). London: Martin Dunitz.

Malkinson, R. (2007). *Cognitive grief therapy: Constructing a rational meaning to life following loss.* New York: W. W. Norton.

Mallen, M. J., Day, S. X., & Green, M. A. (2003). Online versus face-to-face conversations: An examination of relational and discourse variables. *Psychotherapy: Theory, Research, Practice, Training, 40*(1/2), 155–163.

Malley, P. B., Kush, F., & Bogo, R. J. (1994). School-based adolescent suicide prevention and intervention programs. *School Counselor, 42,* 130–136.

Malloy, P. F., Fairbank, J. A., & Keane, T. M. (1983). Validation of a multimodal assessment of posttraumatic stress disorders in Vietnam veterans. *Journal of Consulting and Clinical Psychology, 51,* 488–494.

Malmquist, C. P. (2006). Combined murder-suicide. In R. I. Simon & R. E. Hales (Eds.), *The American Psychiatric Publishing textbook of suicide assessment and management* (pp. 495–509). Washington, DC: American Psychiatric Publishing.

Malone, P. (2011). The impact of peer death on adolescent girls: An efficacy study of the adolescent grief and loss group. *Dissertation Abstracts International: Section A. Humanities and Social Sciences,* 4568.

Mandatory Treatment of Mental Health Patients. (2007). Virginia Codes 37.2-817.1 through 37.2-817.3.

Manly, J., Kim, J., Rogosch, F., & Cicchetti, D. (2001). Dimensions of child maltreatment and children's adjustment: Contributions of developmental timing and subtype. *Development and Psychopathology, 13,* 759–782.

Maples, M. F., Packman, J., Abney, P., Daughtery, R., Casey, J., & Pirtle, L. (2005). Suicide by teenagers in middle school: A postvention team approach. *Journal of Counseling and Development, 83*(4), 397–405.

Maran, D.,Varetto, A., Zedda, M., & Munai, J. (2014). Stalking victimization among Italian university students. *Gender and Behavior, 12*(1), 6070–6079.

Marcus, A. C., Garrett, K. M., Cella, D., Wenzel, L., Brady, M., & Fairclough, D. (2010). Can telephone counseling post-treatment improve psychosocial outcomes among early stage breast cancer survivors? *PsychoOncology,19*(9), 923–932.

Margolies, L., & Leeder, E. (1995). Violence at the door: Treatment of lesbian batterers. *Violence Against Women, 1*(2), 129–157.

Marlasca, M. (2014). Tracking violence against health care workers in Spain. *The Lancet, 384*(9947), 955.

Marmar, C. R., Neylan, T. C., & Schoenfeld, F. (2002). New directions in the pharmacotherapy of posttraumatic stress disorder. *Psychiatric Quarterly, 73*(4), 2159–2170.

Marmar, C. R., Weiss, D. S., Schlenger, W. E., Fairbank, J. A., Jordan, K., Kulka, R. A., et al. (1991). Peritraumatic dissociation and posttraumatic stress in male Vietnam theater veterans. *American Journal of Psychiatry, 151,* 902–907.

Marohn, R., Locke, E., Rosenthal, R., & Curtis, G. (1982). Juvenile delinquents and violent deaths. *Adolescent Psychiatry, 10,* 147–170.

Marohn, R. C. (1982). Adolescent violence: Causes and treatment. *Journal of the American Academy of Child Psychiatry, 21,* 354–360.

Marrujo, B., & Kreger, M. (1996). Definition of roles in abusive relationships. *Journal of Gay and Lesbian Social Services, 4*(1), 22–32.

Marsac, M., Winston, F. K., Kohser, K. L., March, S., Kenardy, J., & Kassam-Adams, N. (2015). Systematic, theoretically grounded development and feasibility testing of an innovative, preventive web-based game for children exposed to acute trauma. *Clinical Practice in Pediatric Psychology, 3*(1), 12–124.

Marsella, A. J., Friedman, M. J., Gerrity, E. T., & Scurfield, R. M. (1996). *Ethnocultural aspects of posttraumatic stress disorder: Issues, research, and clinical applications.* Washington, DC: American Psychological Association.

Marshall, R. D., Bryant, R. A., Amsel, L., Suh, E. J., Cook, J. M., & Neria, Y. (2007). The psychology of ongoing threat: Relative risk appraisal, the September 11 attacks and terrorism related fears. *American Psychologist, 62*(4), 304–316.

Martin, E. S. (2008). Medical art and play therapy. In C. A. Malchiodi (Ed.), *Creative interventions with traumatized children* (pp. 112–131). New York: Guilford Press.

Martin, L., Francisco, E., Nichol, C., & Schweiger, J. L. (1991). A hospital-wide approach to crisis control: One inner-city hospital's experience. *Journal of Emergency Nursing, 17,* 395–401.

Martin, T., & Doka, K. (2000). *Men don't cry . . . Women do: Transcending gender stereotypes of grief.* Philadelphia: Brunner/Mazel.

Martin-Baro´, I. (1996). *Writings for a liberation psychology.* Cambridge, MA: Harvard University Press.

Marx, B. P., & Gutner, C. A. (2015). Post traumatic stress disorder: Patient interview, clinical assessment, and diagnosis. In N. C. Bernardy & M. J. Friedman (Eds.), *A practical guide to treatment: Pharmacological and psychotherapeutic approaches* (pp. 35–51). Washington, DC: American Psychological Association.

Maschi, T., Baer, J., Morrissey, M., & Moreno, C. (2013). The aftermath of childhood trauma on late life mental and physical health: A review of the literature. *Traumatology, 19*(1), 49–64.

Masi, D., & Freedman, M. (2001). The use of telephone and online technology in assessment, counseling, and therapy. *Employee Assistance Quarterly, 16*(3), 49–63.

Masino, T., & Norman, S. (2105). Challenging presentations in PTSD. Post traumatic stress disorder: Patient interview, clinical assessment, and diagnosis. In N. C. Bernardy & M. J. Friedman (Eds.), *A practical guide to treatment: Pharmacological and psychotherapeutic approaches* (pp. 163–178). Washington, DC: American Psychological Association.

Maslach, C. (1976). Burned-out. *Human Behavior, 5,* 16–22.

Maslach, C. (1982a). *Burnout: The cost of caring.* Upper Saddle River, NJ: Prentice Hall.

Maslach, C. (1982b). Understanding burnout: Definitional issues in analyzing a complex phenomenon. In W. S. Paine (Ed.), *Job stress and burnout* (pp. 29–40). Newbury Park, CA: Sage.

Maslach, C., & Jackson, S. E. (1981). *The Maslach Burnout Inventory.* Palo Alto, CA: Consulting Psychologists Press.

Maslach, C., & Jackson, S. E. (1981a). The measurement of experienced burnout. *Journal of Occupational Behavior, 2,* 99–113.

Maslach, C., Jackson, S. E., & Leiter, M. P. (1996). *Maslach Burnout Inventory—GS manual.* Palo Alto, CA: Consulting Psychologist's Press.

Maslach, C., Schaufeli, W., & Leiter, M. (2001). Job burnout. *Annual Review of Psychology, 52,* 397–422.

Massachusetts Coalition of Battered Women Service Groups. (1981). *For shelter and beyond: An educational manual for working with women who are battered.* Boston: Red Sun Press.

Mather, L., Blom, V., & Svedberg, P. (2014). Stressful and traumatic life events are associated with burnout: A cross-sectional twin study. *International Journal of Behavioral Medicine, 21*(6), 899–907.

Matsakis, A. (2003). *The rape recovery handbook: Step-by-step help for survivors of sexual assault.* Oakland, CA: New Harbinger.

Matter, D., & Matter, R. (1982). Developmental sequences in children's understanding of death with implications for counselors. *Elementary School Guidance and Counseling, 17,* 112–118.

Matthews, C., & Lease, S. H. (1999, August). *Lesbian, gay, and bisexual family.* Paper presented at the 107th Annual Convention of the American Psychological Association, Symposium on Research and Practice with Lesbian, Gay and Bisexual Clients, Boston.

Matthews, M. D. (2009). *Self-report knowledge of posttraumatic stress disorder and posttraumatic growth among West Point cadets.* Unpublished raw data, United States Military Academy, West Point, NY.

Matthews, R., Matthews, J., & Speltz, K. (1989). *Female sexual offenders: An exploratory study.* Orwell, VT: Safer Society Press.

Mattson, M. R., & Sacks, M. H. (1978). Seclusion: Uses and implications. *American Journal of Psychiatry, 135,* 1210–1212.

Maurer, C. M., & Sheets, T. E. (Eds.). (1999). *Encyclopedia of associations* (34th ed.) (Vol. I, Parts 1–3). Farmington Hills, MI: Gale Research.

Maziak, W., & Asfar, T. (2003). Physical abuse in low-income women in Aleppo, Syria. *Health Care for Women International, 24*(4), 313–326.

Mazza, J., & Reynolds, W. M. (1998). A longitudinal investigation of depression, hopelessness, social support, and major and minor life events and their relation to suicidal ideation in adolescents. *Journal of Suicide and Life-Threatening Behavior, 28,* 358–374.

McAdams, C. R., & Keener, H. J. (2008). Preparation, action, recovery: A conceptual framework for counselor preparation and response in client crisis. *Journal of Counseling and Development, 86,* 388–398.

McAdams, C. R., & Schmidt, C. (2007). How to help a bully: Recommendation for counseling the proactive aggressor. *Professional School Counseling, 11*(2), 121–127.

McCabe, M. P., & Wauchope, M. (2005). Behavioral characteristics of men accused of rape: Evidence for different types of rapists. *Archives of Sexual Behavior, 34*(2), 241–253.

McCann, I. L., & Pearlman, L. A. (1990). Vicarious traumatization: A framework for understanding the psychological effects of working with victims. *Journal of Traumatic Stress, 3*(1), 131–149.

McCann, R. A., Armstrong, C. M., Skopp, N. A., Edwards-Stewart, A., Smolenski, D. J., June, J. D., . . .Reger, G. (2014). Virtual reality exposure therapy for the treatment of anxiety disorder: An evaluation of research quality. *Journal of Anxiety Disorders, 28*(6), 625–631.

McCart, M. R., Fitzgerald, M. M., Acierno, R. E., Resnick, H. S., & Kilpatick, D. G. (2009). Evaluation and acute intervention with victims of violence. In P. Kleespies (Ed.), *Behavioral emergencies: An evidence-based resource for evaluating and managing risk of suicide, violence, and victimization* (pp. 167–188). Washington, DC: American Psychological Association.

McCarthy, J. J. (2002). How a school district crisis response team can help. In D. D. Bass & R. Yep (Eds.), *Terrorism, trauma, and tragedies: A counselor's guide to preparing and responding* (pp. 53–54). Alexandria, VA: American Counseling Association.

McCarthy, M. C., Clarke, N., Ting, C., Conroy, R., Anderson, V., & Heath, J. (2010). Prevalence and predictors of parental grief and depression after the death of a child from cancer. *Journal of Palliative Medicine, 13*(11), 1321–1326.

McCarty, L. (1986). Mother-child incest: Characteristics of the offender. *Child Welfare, 65,* 457–558.

McCaskie, M., Ward, S., & Rasor, L. (1990, April). *Short-term crisis counseling and the regular caller.* Paper presented at the

Fourteenth Annual Convening of Crisis Intervention Personnel, Chicago.

McCauley, M., Schwartz-Kenney, B. M., Epstein, M. A., & Tucker, E. J. (2001). United States. In B. M. Schwartz-Kenney, M. McCauley, & M. A. Epstein (Eds.), *Child abuse: A global view* (pp. 241–255). Westport, CT: Greenwood Press.

McCollum, E., Stith, S., & Thomsen, C. (2012). Solution-focused brief therapy in conjoint couples treatment of intimate partner violence. In C. Franklin, T. Tepper, W. Gingerich, & E. McCollum (Eds.), *Solution-focused brief therapy: A handbook of evidence-based practice* (pp. 183–195). New York: Oxford University Press.

McCollum, S. (2010, Fall). Country outposts. *Teaching Tolerance, 33*–35.

McCown, C. (1986). *Counseling in an adolescent psychiatric treatment facility* (Cassette Recording No. 7). Memphis, TN: Memphis State University, Department of Counseling and Personnel Services.

McCown, D. E., & Davies, B. (1995). Patterns of grief in young children following the death of a sibling. *Death Studies, 19,* 41–53.

McCubbin, H., Joy, C., Cauble, E., Comeau, J., Patterson, J., & Needle, R. (1980). Family stress and coping: A decade review. *Journal of Marriage and Family, 43,* 855–872.

McCubbon, H. I., & Patterson, J. M. (1983). The family stress process: The Double ABCX model of adjustment and adaptation. *Marriage and Family Review, 6,* 7–37.

McCutcheon, K. A., & Fleming, S. J. (2001–2002). Grief resulting from euthanasia and natural death of companion animals. *Omega: Journal of Death and Dying, 44*(2), 169–188.

McDonald, H. Z., Franz, M. R., & Vasterling, J. J. (2012). Assessment and treatment of neuropsychological deficits in posttraumatic stress disorder. In R. A. McMackin, E. Newman, J. M. Fogler, & T. M. Keane (Eds.), *Trauma therapy in context: The science and craft of evidence-based practice* (pp. 331–352). Washington, DC: American Psychological Association.

McDonald, R., Jouriles, E., Ramisetty-Mikler, S., Caetano, R., & Green, C. E. (2006). Estimating the number of American children living in partner-violent families. *Journal of Family Psychology, 20*(1), 137–142.

McFarlane, A. C., & de Girolamo, G. (1996). The nature of traumatic stressors and the epidemiology of posttraumatic reactions. In B. A. van der Kolk, A. C. McFarlane, & L. Weisaeth (Eds.), *Traumatic stress* (pp. 129–148). New York: Guilford Press.

McFarlane, A. C., & Yehuda, R. (1996). Resiliency, vulnerability, and the course of posttraumatic reactions. In B. A. van der Kolk, A. C. McFarlane, & L. Weisaeth (Eds.), *Traumatic stress* (pp. 155–181). New York: Guilford Press.

McGlone, G. J. (2003). The pedophile and the pious: Towards a new understanding of sexually offending and nonoffending Roman Catholic priests. In J. L. Mullings, J. W. Marquart, & D. J. Hartley (Eds.), *The victimization of children: Emerging issues* (pp. 115–132). Binghamton, NY: Haworth Trauma and Maltreatment Press.

McGlothin, J. M. (2008). *Developing clinical skills in suicide assessment, prevention, and treatment.* Alexandria, VA: American Counseling Association.

McGoldrick, M., & Ashton, D. (2010). Culture: A challenge to concepts of normality. In S. J. Price, C. A. Price, & P. C. McKenry (Eds.), *Families and change: Coping with stressful events and transitions* (pp. 249–272). Los Angeles: Sage.

McGoldrick, M., & Shisbusawa, T. (2010). The family life cycle. In S. J. Price, C. A. Price, & P. C. McKenry (Eds.), *Families and change: Coping with stressful events and transitions* (pp. 375–398). Los Angeles: Sage.

McGuire, T. M., Lee, C., & Drummond, P. (2014). Potential of eye movement desensitization and reprocessing therapy in the treatment of post-traumatic stress disorder. *Psychology Research and Behavior Management, 7,* 273–283.

McHenry, S. S. (1994). When the therapist needs therapy: Characterological countertransference issues and failures in the treatment of the borderline personality disorder. *Psychotherapy, 31,* 557–570.

McIntosh v. Milano, 403 A.2d 500, 168 N.J. Super. 466 (1979).

McKee, K. J., Wilson, F., Chung, M., Hinchliff, S., Goudie, F., & Elford, H. (2005). Reminiscence, regrets and activity in older people in residential care: Associations with psychological health. *British Journal of Clinical Psychology, 44*(4), 543–561.

McKenna, S. (1999, September 28). *Stages of grieving.* Retrieved May 13, 2003, from www.thirdage.com/features/family/alone/sb01.html

McKeon, B., McEwan, T., & Luebbers, S. (2015). It's not really stalking if you know the person: Measuring community attitudes that normalize, justify, and minimize stalking. *Psychiatry, Psychology, and Law, 22*(2), 291–306.

McKnight, D. J., & Glass, D. C. (1995). Perceptions of control, burnout, and depressive symptomatology: A replication and extension. *Journal of Consulting and Clinical Psychology, 63,* 490–494.

McLay, R. N., Graap, K., Spira, J., Perlman, K., Johnson, S., Rothbaum, B., . . . Rizzo, J. M. (2012). Development and testing of virtual reality exposure therapy for post-traumatic stress disorder inactive service members who served in Iraq and Afghanistan. *Military Medicine, 177*(6), 635–642.

McLean, L. M., & Gallop, R. (2003). Implications of childhood sexual abuse for adult borderline personality disorder and complex posttraumatic stress disorder. *American Journal of Psychiatry, 160*(2), 369–371.

McLean, P., & Taylor, S. (1994). Family therapy for suicidal people. In A. A. Leenaars, J. T. Maltsberger, & R. A. Neimeyer (Eds.), *Treatment of suicidal people* (pp. 75–87). Washington, DC: Taylor & Francis.

McLeer, S., & Anwar, R. (1989). A study of women presenting in an emergency medical department. *American Journal of Public Health, 79*(1), 65–66.

McLeer, S. V., Deblinger, E., Henry, D., & Orvaschel, H. (1992). Sexually abused children at high risk for post-traumatic stress disorder. *Journal of the American Academy of Child and Adolescent Psychiatry, 31*(5), 875–978.

McLeer, S. V., Dixon, J. F., Henry, D., Ruggiero, K., Escovitz, K., Niedda, T., & Scholle, R. (1998). Psychopathology in non-clinically referred sexually abused children. *Journal of the American Academy of Child and Adolescent Psychiatry, 37,* 1326–1333.

McLendon, D., & Petr, C. G. (2005). Family-direct structural therapy. *Journal of Marital and Family Therapy, 31,* 327–339.

McLeod, A. L., Hays, D. G., & Chang, C. Y. (2010). Female intimate partner violence survivors' experiences with accessing resources. *Journal of Counseling and Development, 88*(3), 303–310.

McMahon, A., & Rhudick, P. (1964). Reminiscing: Adaptational significance in the aged. *Archives of General Psychiatry, 10,* 292–298.

McMahon, M., Neville-Sorvilles, J., & Schubert, L. (1999). Undoing harm to children: The Duluth Family Visitation Center. In M. F. Shepard & E. L. Pence (Eds.), *Coordinating community responses to domestic violence: Lessons from Duluth and beyond* (pp. 151–167). Thousand Oaks, CA: Sage.

McNeil, D. (2009). Assessment and management of acute risk of violence in adult patients. In P. M. Kleespies (Ed.), *Behavioral emergencies: An evidence-based resource for evaluating and managing risk of suicide, violence, and victimization* (pp. 125–146). Washington, DC: American Psychological Association.

McNeil, D., & Binder, R. L. (1994). The relationship between acute psychiatric symptoms, diagnosis, and short-term risk of violence. *Hospital and Community Psychiatry, 45,* 133–137.

McNeil, D. E., Binder, M. R., & Greenfield, T. L. (1988). Predictors of violence in civilly committed acute psychiatric patients. *American Journal of Psychiatry, 8,* 965–970.

McNeil, D. E., Gregory, A. L., Lam, J. L. M., Binder, R. L., & Sullivan, G. R. (2003). Utility of decision support tools for assessing acute risk of violence. *Journal of Consulting and Clinical Psychology, 71,* 945–953.

McNeil, D. E., Hatcher, C., Zeiner, H., Wolfe, H. L., & Myers, R. S. (1991). Characteristics of persons referred by police to the psychiatric emergency room. *Hospital and Community Psychiatry, 42,* 425–427.

McRaith, C. F. (1991, April). *Coping with society's secret: Social support, job stress, and burnout among therapists treating victims of sexual abuse.* Paper presented at the Fifteenth Annual Convening of Crisis Intervention Personnel, Chicago.

McWhirter, E. H., & Linzer, M. (1994). The provision of critical incident services by EAPs: A case study. *Journal of Mental Health Counseling, 16,* 403–414.

McWhirter, J. J., McWhirter, B. T., McWhirter, E. H., & McWhirter, R. J. (2013). *At risk youth: A comprehensive for counselors, teachers, psychologists, and human-service professionals.* Belmont, CA: Brooks/Cole Cengage.

Meadows, E. A., & Foa, E. B. (1999). Cognitive behavioral treatment for traumatized adults. In P. A. Saigh & J. D. Bremner (Eds.), *Posttraumatic stress disorder: A comprehensive text.* Boston: Allyn & Bacon.

Meagher, D. K. (2009). *Zach and his dog: A story of bonding, love, and loss for children and adults to share together.* Bloomington, IN: Authorhouse.

Mederos, F. (1999). Batterer intervention programs: The past and future prospects. In M. F. Shepard & E. L. Pence (Eds.), *Coordinating community response to domestic violence: Lessons from Duluth and beyond* (pp. 127–150). Thousand Oaks, CA: Sage.

Meehl, P. (1954). *Clinical versus statistical prediction: A theoretical analysis and review of the evidence.* Minneapolis: University of Minnesota Press.

Mehrabian, A. (1971). Nonverbal betrayal of feeling. *Journal of Experimental Research in Personality, 5,* 64–73.

Meichembaum, D. (1985). *Stress inoculation training.* Elmsford, NY: Pergamon Press.

Meichenbaum, D. (1985, May). Cognitive behavior modification: Perspectives, techniques, and applications. Two-day workshop, St. Louis, MO, presented by Evaluation Research Associates (Syracuse, NY).

Meichenbaum, D. H. (1977). *Cognitive behavior modification: An integrative approach.* New York: Plenum.

Melamed, S., Meir, E. I., & Samson, A. (1995). The benefits of personality–leisure congruence: Evidence and implications. *Journal of Leisure Research, 27,* 25–40.

Melamed, S., Shirom, A., Toker, S., Berliner, S., & Shapira, I. (2006). Burnout and risk of cardiovascular disease: Evidence, possible causal paths, and promising research directions. *Psychological Bulletin, 132*(3), 327–353.

Melchior, M., van der Berg, A., Halfens, R., & Abu-Saad, H. (1997). Burnout and the work environment of nurses in psychiatric long-stay care settings. *Social Psychiatry and Psychiatric Epidemiology, 32*(3), 158–164.

Melhem, N., Day, N., Shear, M., Day, R., Reynolds, C., & Brent, D. (2004). Predictors of complicated grief among adolescents exposed to a peer's suicide. *Journal of Loss and Trauma, 9*(10), 21–34.

Melhem, N. M., Porta, G., Walker Payne, M., & Brent, D. (2013). Identifying prolonged grief reactions in children: Dimensional and diagnostic approaches. *Journal of the American Academy of Child and Adolescent Psychiatry, 52,* 599–607.

Meloy, J. T., & O'Toole, M. E. (2011). The concepts of leakage in threat assessment. *Behavioral Sciences and the Law, 29*(4), 513–527.

Melton, B. (2001). Seeing the unseen. *ASCA School Counselor, 39,* 21–25.

Meléndez, Moral, J. C., Charco-Ruiz, L., Mayordomo-Rodriguez, T., & Sales-Galan, A. (2013). Effects of a reminiscence program among institutionalized elderly adults. *Psicothema, 25*(3), 319–323.

Memphis Police Department. (2010). *Crisis intervention training manual.* Memphis, TN: Author.

Memphis Police Department. (2011). *Crisis Intervention Team training manual* (5th rev. ed.). Memphis, TN: Author.

Memphis Vietnam Veterans Center. (1985). *The nonveteran helper* (Pamphlet). Memphis, TN: Author.

Mental Health Advisory Team V. (2008, February 14). *Mental Health Advisory Team (MHAT) V Operation Iraqi Freedom 06-08* (Report chartered by the Office of the Surgeon Multi-National Force-Iraq and the Office of the Surgeon General United States Army Medical Command). Retrieved from http://www.armymedicine.army.mil/reports/mhat/mhat-v/Redacted1-MHATVOIF-4-FEB-2008Report.pdf

Mentes, J., & Ferrrario, J. (1989). Calming aggressive reactions: A prevention program. *Journal of Gerontological Nursing, 15,* 22–27.

Meris, D. (2001). Responding to the mental health and grief concerns of homeless HIV-infected gay men. *Journal of Gay and Lesbian Social Services: Issue in Practice, Policy, and Research, 13*(4), 103–112.

Merlino, J. P. (2011). Rescuing ourselves: Self-care in the disaster response community. In F. J. Stoddard, A. Pandya, & C. Katz (Eds.), *Disaster psychiatry: Readiness, evaluation, and treatment* (pp. 35–48). Arlington, VA: American Psychiatric Publishing.

Merrick, M. V., Allen, B. M., & Crase, S. J. (1994). Variables associated with positive treatment outcomes for children surviving sexual abuse. *Journal of Child Sexual Abuse, 3*(2), 67–87.

Mester, R., Birger, M., & Margolin, J. (2006). Stalking. *Israel Journal of Psychiatry and Related Sciences, 43*(2), 102–111.

Metha, A., Cohen, R., & Chan, L. S. (2009). Palliative care: A need for family systems approach. *Palliative and Supportive Care, 7,* 235–243.

Meyers, T. W., & Cornille, T. A. (2002). The trauma of working with traumatized children. In C. R. Figley (Ed.), *Treating compassion fatigue* (pp. 39–55). New York: Brunner/Routledge.

Mezey, G., & King, M. (1998). The effects of sexual assault on men: A survey of twenty-two victims. In M. E. Odem & J. Clay-Warner (Eds.), *Confronting rape and sexual assault* (pp. 83–92). Wilmington, DE: Scholarly Resources.

Michaels, K. (2009, November). Recession depression: Coping and survival techniques. *Counseling Today,* 48–50.

Michel, K. (2011). General aspects of therapeutic alliance. In K. Michel & D. A. Jobes (Eds.), *Building a therapeutic alliance with the suicidal patient* (pp. 13–28). Washington, DC: American Psychological Association.

Michel, K., & Jobes, D. A. (Eds.). (2011). *Building a therapeutic alliance with the suicidal patient.* Washington, DC: American Psychological Association.

Michenbaum, D. (2005). Thirty-five years of working with suicidal patients: Lessons learned. *Canadian Psychology, 46*(2), 64–72.

Middleton, A. M., Gunn, J., Bassilios, B., & Pirkis, J. (2014). Systematic review of research into frequent callers to crisis helplines. *Journal of Telemedicine and Telecare, 20*(2), 89–98.

Middleton, W., Raphael, B., Burnett, P., & Martinek, N. (1998). A longitudinal study comparing bereavement phenomena in recently bereaved spouses, adult children and parents. *Australian and New Zealand Journal of Psychiatry, 32*, 235–241.

Mikell v. School Administrative Unit #33, 972 A.2d 1050 (N.H. 2009).

Miller, D. (1990). Diagnosis and treatment of acute psychological problems related to HIV infection and disease. In D. G. Ostrow (Ed.), *Behavioral aspects of AIDS* (pp. 187–206). New York: Plenum Press.

Miller, D. (1995). Stress and burnout among health care staff working with people affected by HIV. *British Journal of Guidance and Counselling, 23*, 19–31.

Miller, E., McCaw, B., Humphreys, B., & Mitchell, C. (2015). Integrating intimate partner violence assessment and intervention into healthcare in the United States: A systems approach. *Journal of Women's Health, 24*(1), 92–99.

Miller, G. (1983). *SASSI: Substance Abuse Subtle Screening Inventory.* Bloomington, IN: SASSI Institute.

Miller, G. (2015). Healing and trauma: Response. In T. E. Robert & V. A. Kelly, *Critical incidents in integrating spirituality into counseling* (pp. 111–114). Alexandria, VA: American Counseling Association.

Miller, J., Martin, I., & Schamess, G. (2003). *School violence and children in crisis: Community and school interventions for social workers and counselors.* Denver, CO: Love Publishing.

Miller, L. (2006a). *Practical police psychology: Stress management and crisis intervention for law enforcement.* Springfield, IL: Charles C Thomas.

Miller, L. (2006b). Suicide by cop: Causes, reactions, and practical intervention strategies. *International Journal of Emergency Mental Health, 8*(3), 165–174.

Miller, L. (2010). On-scene crisis intervention: Psychological guidelines and communication strategies for first responders. *International Journal of Emergency Mental Health, 12*(1), 11–19.

Miller, M. (1986). *Counseling geriatric clients* (Cassette Recording No. 14). Memphis, TN: Memphis State University, Department of Counseling and Personnel Services.

Miller, M. W., Wolf, E. J., Martin, E., Kaloupek, D. G., & Keane, T. M. (2008). Structural equation modeling of associations among combat exposure, PTSD symptom factors, and global assessment of functioning. *Journal of Rehabilitation Research and Development, 45*, 359–370.

Miller, S. (Ed.). (2010). Discussing the Duluth curriculum: Creating a process of change for men who batter. *Violence Against Women, 16*(9), 1007–1021.

Miller, T. R., Cohen, M., & Wiersema, B. (1996). *Victim of costs and consequences: A new look* (NCJ 155282). U.S. Department of Justice, Office of Justice Programs, National Institute of Justice. Retrieved from https://www.ncjrs.gov/pdffiles/victcost.pdf

Miller-Perrin, C. L. (2001). Child maltreatment: Treatment of child and adolescent victims. In E. R. Welfel & R. E. Ingersoll (Eds.), *The mental health desk reference* (pp. 169–177). New York: John Wiley & Sons.

Millon, T. (1987). *Manual for the Millon Clinical Multiaxial Inventory* (2nd ed.). Minneapolis, MN: National Computer Systems.

Mills, C. S., & Granoff, B. J. (1992). Date and acquaintance rape among a sample of college students. *Social Work, 37*(6), 504–509.

Minuchin, S. (1974). *Families and family therapy.* Cambridge, MA: Harvard University Press.

Mishara, B. L., Houle, J., & Lavoie, B. (2005). Comparison of the effects of four suicide prevention programs for family and friends of high-risk suicidal men who do not seek help themselves. *Suicide and Life-Threatening Behavior, 35*(3), 329–342.

Mishara, L. B. L., Chagnon, F., Daigle, M., Balan, B., Raymond, S., & Marcous, I. (2005). *A silent monitoring of telephone help provided over the Hopeline network and its short-term effects.* Montreal: Center for Research and Intervention on Suicide and Euthanasia.

Missing Children. (2006). Missing Children: Getting home after disaster strikes. *Challenge, 14*(1), 1–2.

Missouri School Counselor Association. (2002). *Crisis manual.* Hamilton, MO: Author.

Misurell, J., Springer, C., Acosta, L., Liotta, L., & Kranzier, A. (2014). Game-based cognitive-behavioral therapy individual model (GB-CBT-IM) for child sexual abuse: A preliminary outcome study. *Psychological Trauma: Theory, Research, Practice, and Policy, 6*(3), 250–258.

Mitchell, A. M., & Wesner, S. (2011). A bereavement crisis debriefing intervention for survivors after a suicide. In J. R. Jordan & J. L. McIntosh (Eds.), *Grief after suicide: Understanding the consequences and caring for the survivors* (pp. 397–402). New York: Routledge/Taylor & Francis Group.

Mitchell, A. M., Kim, Y., Prigerson, H. G., & Mortimer-Stephens, M. (2004). Complicated grief in survivors of suicide. *Crisis, 25*, 12–18.

Mitchell, J. (1983). When disaster strikes: The critical incident stress debriefing process. *Journal of Emergency Medical Services, 8*, 36–39.

Mitchell, J. M., & Morse, J. (1998). *From victims to survivors: Reclaimed voices of women sexually abused in childhood by females.* Washington, DC: Accelerated Development.

Mitchell, J. T., & Everly, G. S., Jr. (1995). *Advanced critical incidents stress debriefing.* Ellicott City, MD: International Critical Incidents Stress Foundation.

Mitchell, J. T., & Everly, G. S., Jr. (1995). Critical incidents stress debriefing (CISD) and the prevention of work-related traumatic stress among high risk occupational groups. In G. S. Everly, Jr., & J. T. Lating (Eds.), *Psychotraumatology* (pp. 267–280). New York: Plenum Press.

Mitchell, J. T., & Everly, G. S., Jr. (1995). *Critical incidents stress debriefing: The basic course workbook.* Ellicott City, MD: International Critical Incidents Stress Foundation.

Mitchell, J. T., & Everly, G. S., Jr. (1999). Critical incident stress management and critical incident stress debriefings: Evolutions, effects, and outcomes. In B. Raphael & J. P. Wilson (Eds.), *Psychological debriefing: Theory, practice, and evidence* (pp. 71–90). New York: Cambridge University Press.

Mitchell, M. D. (1977). Consultant burnout. In J. W. Pfeiffer & J. E. Jones (Eds.), *1977 annual handbook for group facilitators* (pp. 143–146). La Jolla, CA: University Associates.

Moberg, T., Stenbacka, M., Josson, J., Nordstrom, P., Asberg, M., & Jokinen, J. (2014). Risk factors for adult interpersonal violence in suicide attempters. *BMC Psychiatry, 14*, article 195.

Modrak, R. (1992, January). Mass shootings and airplane crashes: Counselors respond to the changing face of community crisis. *Guidepost, 34*, 4.

Moeller, T. P., Bachmann, G. A., & Moeller, J. R. (1993). The combined effects of physical, sexual, and emotional abuse during childhood: Long-term health consequences for women. *Child Abuse and Neglect, 17*(5), 623–640.

Mohl, A. (2010). Sexual abuse of the child: A treatment model for the incestuous family. *Journal of Psychohistory, 38*(2), 168–181.

Mohr, D. C., Vella, L., Hart, S., Heckman, T., & Simon, G. (2008). The effect of telephone-administered psychotherapy on symptoms of depression and attrition: A meta-analysis. *Clinical Psychology: Science and Practice, 15*(3), 243–253.

Mohr, W. K. (2010). Restraints and the code of ethics: An uneasy fit. *Archives of Psychiatric Nursing, 24*(1), 3–14.

Monahan, J. (1981). *The clinical prediction of violent behavior.* Rockville, MD: National Institute of Mental Health.

Monahan, J. (1984). The prediction of violent behavior: Toward a second generation of theory and policy. *American Journal of Psychiatry, 141,* 10–15.

Monahan, J. (1988). Risk assessment of violence among the mentally disordered: Generating useful knowledge. *International Journal of Law and Psychiatry, 11,* 249–257.

Monahan, J., Steadmam, H. J., Silver, E., Applebaum, P. S., Robbins, P. C., & Mulvey, E. P. (2001). *Rethinking risk assessment: The McArthur Study of mental disorder and violence.* New York: Oxford University Press.

Monk, G., Drewery, W., & Winslade, J. (2005). Using narrative ideas in group work: A new perspective. *Counseling and Human Development, 38*(1), 1–13.

Monk, G., Winslade, J., Crocket, K., & Epston, D. (Eds.). (1997). *Narrative therapy in practice: The archeology of hope.* San Francisco: Jossey-Bass.

Monk-Turner, E., & Light, D. (2010). Male sexual assault and rape: Who seeks counseling? *Sexual Abuse: Journal of Research and Treatment, 22*(3), 255–265.

Monson, C. M., & Shnaider, P. (2014). *Treating PTSD with cognitive-behavioral therapies: Interventions that work.* Washington, DC: American Psychological Association.

Montano, R., & Dowdall-Thomae, C. (2003, June). *Are you ready for the crisis?* Paper presented at the American School Counselor Association Convention, St. Louis, MO.

Montano, R., & Dowdall-Thomae, C. (2003, June). *Are you ready for the crisis?* Paper presented at the American School Counselor Association Convention, St. Louis, MO.

Moon, K. (2014). Texting between client and therapist: An ethical dilemma on an effective tool? *Dissertation Abstracts International: Section B: The Sciences and Engineering, 74*(11B(E)), 3024.

Moore, B. A., & Jongsma, A. E. (2009). *The veterans and active duty military psychotherapy treatment planner.* Hoboken, NJ: John Wiley & Sons.

Moore, M. M., & Freeman, S. J. (1995). Counseling survivors of suicide: Implications for group postvention. *Journal for Specialists in Group Work, 20*(1), 40–47.

Mooren, T., & Stöfsel, M. (2015). *Diagnosing and treating complex PTSD.* New York: Routledge/Taylor &Francis Group.

Moos, R. H. (1981). *Work Environment Scale manual.* Palo Alto, CA: Consulting Psychologists Press.

Moran, C. C. (2002). Humor as a moderator of compassion fatigue. In C. R. Figley (Ed.), *Treating compassion fatigue* (pp. 139–154). Philadelphia: Brunner/Routledge.

Moran, J. F. (1984). Teaching the management of violent behavior to nursing staff: A health care model. In J. T. Turner (Ed.), *Violence in the medical care setting: A survival guide* (pp. 231–250). Rockville, MD: Aspen Systems.

Morgan, G. S., Wisneski, D. C., & Skitka, L. J. (2011). The expulsion from Disneyland: The social psychological impact of 9/11. *American Psychologist, 66*(5), 447–454.

Morgan, J. D., & Laungani, L. (Eds.). (2002). *Death and bereavement around the world* (Vol. 1). Amityville, NY: Baywood.

Morgan, J. D., & Laungani, L. (Eds.). (2003). *Death and bereavement around the world* (Vol. 2). Amityville, NY: Baywood.

Morgan, J. D., & Laungani, L. (Eds.). (2004a). *Death and bereavement around the world* (Vol. 3). Amityville, NY: Baywood.

Morgan, J. D., & Laungani, L. (Eds.). (2004b). *Death and bereavement around the world* (Vol. 4). Amityville, NY: Baywood.

Morgan, J. D., Laungani, L., & Palmer, S. (Eds.). (2009). *Death and bereavement around the world* (Vol. 5). Amityville, NY: Baywood.

Morgan, L., Scourfield, J., Williams, D., Jasper, A., & Lewis, G. (2003). The Aberfan disaster: 33-year follow-up of survivors. *British Journal of Psychiatry, 182*(6), 532–536.

Morgan, M. C. (2009). The impact of traumatic brain injury in the survivor's partner or spouse: Implications for treatment. *Dissertation Abstracts International: Section B. The Sciences and Engineering,* 3180.

Morgan, S. M. (1982). *Conjugal terrorism: A psychological and community treatment model of wife abuse.* Palo Alto, CA: R & E Research Associates.

Moritz, S., Voigt, M. K., Kother, U., Leighton, L., Kiahili, B., Babur, Z., Jungclaussen, D., & Grzella, K. (2014). Can virtual reality reduce reality distortion? Impact of performance feedback on symptom change in schizophrenia patients. *Journal of Behavior Therapy and Experimental Psychiatry, 45*(2), 267–271.

Morkides, C. (2009, May). From burning bright to simply burned out. *Counseling Today,* 11–13.

Morris, A. J. (2011). Psychic aftershocks: Crisis counseling and disaster relief policy. *History of Psychology, 14*(3), 264–286.

Morrison, J. M. (1993). Physical techniques. In P. E. Blumenreich & S. Lewis (Eds.), *Managing the violent patient: A clinician's guide* (pp. 79–100). New York: Brunner-Mazel.

Morrissey, M. (1994, June). ACA, Red Cross to work together to help disaster victims. *Guidepost, 36,* 1, 6.

Morrissey, M. (1995, June). Members write children's book to help youngsters cope with Oklahoma City tragedy. *Counseling Today, 37*(12), 20.

Morrow, S. L. (2000). First do no harm: Therapist issues in psychotherapy with lesbian, gay, and bisexual clients. In R. M. Perez, K. A. DeBord, & K. A. Bieschke (Eds.), *Handbook of counseling and psychotherapy with lesbian, gay, and bisexual clients* (pp. 137–156). Washington, DC: American Psychological Association.

Morse, B. (1995). Beyond the Conflict Tactics Scale: Assessing gender difference in partner violence. *Violence and Victims, 10*(4), 251–272.

Morse, G. A. (2000). On being homeless and mentally ill: A multitude of losses and the possibility of recovery. In J. H. Harvey & E. D. Miller (Eds.), *Loss and trauma: General and close relationship perspectives* (pp. 249–262). Philadelphia: Brunner-Routledge.

Mott, J. M., Galovski, T. E., Walsh, R. M., & Elwood, L. S. (2015). Change in trauma narrative and perceived recall ability over a course of cognitive processing therapy for PTSD. *Traumatology, 21*(1), 47–54.

Mowbray, C. T. (1988). Post-traumatic therapy for children who are victims of violence. In F. M. Ochberg (Ed.), *Post-traumatic therapy and individuals of violence* (pp. 196–212). New York: Brunner/Mazel.

Moyer, C. (2012). Cyberchondria: The one diagnosis most patients miss. *AMED News.Com.* Retrieved from http://www.amednews.com/article/20120130 /health/301309952/1/

Moylan, C., Lindhorst, T., & Tajima, E. (2015). Sexual assault response teams (SARTS): Mapping a research agenda that incorporates an organizational perspective. *Violence Against Women, 21*(4), 516–534.

Mphande-Finn, J., & Sommers-Flanagan, J. (2007). The experience of HIV/AIDS among rural women in the Northwestern United States: A qualitative analysis. *Journal of Community Psychology, 35*(1), 3–11.

Mulvey, E. P., & Cauffman, E. (2001). The inherent limits of predicting school violence. *American Psychologist, 56*(10), 797–802.

Mulvey, E. P., & Lidz, C. W. (1984). Clinical considerations on the prediction of dangerous mental patients. *Clinical Psychology Review, 4*, 379–401.

Munoz, M., Joaquin, C., Noval, D., Moringo, A., & Garcia de la Concha, J. A. (2000). Factores predictores de agresividad en esquizofrenicos hospitalizados. *Actas Espanolas de Psiquiatria, 28*(3), 151–155.

Munsey, C. (2006). Schools: A post-Katrina anchor for children. *Monitor on Psychology, 37*(9), 46–47.

Munsey, C. (2008). Stay safe in practice. *Monitor on Psychology, 39*(4), 37–39.

Munsey, C. (2009). Women and war. *Monitor on Psychology, 40*(8), 34–35.

Munsey, C. (2010). More students with serious psychological issues are showing up at campus counseling centers. *Monitor on Psychology, 41*(4), 10–11.

Munsey, C. (2011). APA is front and center at White House bullying conference. *Monitor on Psychology, 42*(5), 18–19.

Munsey, C. (2012). Anti-bullying efforts ramp up. *Monitor on Psychology, 43*(2), 55–57.

Murdach, A. D. (1993). Working with potentially assaultive clients. *Health and Social Work, 18*, 307–312.

Murdaugh, C., Hunt, S., Sowell, R., & Santana, I. (2004). Domestic violence in Hispanics in the Southeastern United States: A survey and needs analysis. *Journal of Family Violence, 19*(2), 107–115.

Muro, J. J., & Kottman, T. (1995). *Guidance and counseling in the elementary and middle schools.* Dubuque, IA: William C. Brown.

Murray, C. I., Toth, K., Larsen, B. L., & Moulton, S. (2010). Death, dying, and grief in families. In S. J. Price, C. A. Price, & P. C. McKenry (Eds.), *Families and change: Coping with stressful events and transitions* (pp. 73–96). Los Angeles: Sage.

Murray, G., & Snyder, J. C. (1991). When staff are assaulted. *Journal of Psychosocial Nursing, 29*, 24–29.

Myer, R. A. (1999, April). *Crisis intervention using the Internet.* Paper presented at the Twenty-third Annual Convening of Crisis Intervention Personnel, Chicago.

Myer, R. A. (2001). *Assessment for crisis intervention: A triage assessment model.* Belmont, CA: Thomson Brooks/Cole.

Myer, R. A. (2014). *A reliability study of the modified TAF using an earthquake disaster scenario.* Ankara, Turkey: Attilian University.

Myer, R. A. (2014). *Practical guide to disaster counseling.* Pacific Grove, CA: Cengage.

Myer, R. A. (2015). Triage Assessment Form for Family Therapy (TAFFT). In R. K. James & B. E. Gilliland (Eds.), *Crisis intervention strategies* (8th ed.). Belmont, CA: Brooks-Cole/Cengage.

Myer, R. A., & James, R. K. (2005). *Crisis intervention workbook and CD-ROM.* Belmont, CA: Thomson Brooks/Cole.

Myer, R. A., & Moore, H. (2006). Crisis in context theory: An ecological model. *Journal of Counseling and Development, 84*, 139–147.

Myer, R. A., James, R. K., & Moulton, P. (2011). *This is not a fire drill: Crisis intervention and prevention on college campuses.* Hoboken, NJ: John Wiley & Sons.

Myer, R. A., Lewis, J. S., & James, R. K. (2013). The introduction of a task model for crisis intervention. *Journal of Mental Health Counseling, 35*(2), 95–107.

Myer, R. A., Moore, H., & Hughes, T. (2003). September 11th survivors and the refugee model. *Journal of Mental Health Counseling, 25*, 245–258.

Myer, R. A., Moulton, P., Cogdal, P. C., Rice, N. D., James, R. K., & Allen, S. (2007). *Triage Assessment System Training Manual: Higher education: Instructor's manual.* Pittsburgh, PA: CIPS-Solutions Inc.

Myer, R. A., Rice, D., Moulton, P., Cogdal, P., Allen, S., & James, R. (2007). *Triage Assessment System for Students in Learning Environments (TASSLE) manual and CD.* Pittsburgh, PA: Crisis Intervention and Prevention Solutions.

Myer, R. A., Williams, R. C., Haley, M., Brownfield, J., Austin, K., & Pribozie, N. (2014). Crisis intervention with families: Assessing changes in family characteristics. *The Family Journal, 22*, 179–185.

Myer, R. A., Williams, R. C., Ottens, A. J., & Schmidt, A. E. (1992). A three-dimensional model for triage. *Journal of Mental Health Counseling, 14*, 137–148.

Myers, D., & Wee, D. F. (2005). *Disaster mental health services.* New York: Brunner-Routledge.

Myers, D., & Zunin, L. (1994). Debriefing and grief: Easing the pain. *Today's Supervisor, 6*(12), 14–15.

Myers, J. E., & Sweeney, T. J. (Eds.). (2005). *Counseling for wellness.* Alexandria, VA: American Counseling Association.

Myers, J. E., Sweeney, T. J., & Witmer, J. E. (2000). The wheel of wellness counseling for wellness: A holistic model for treatment planning. *Journal of Counseling and Development, 78*(3), 251–266.

Myers, M. F. (1986). Men sexually assaulted as adults and sexually molested as boys. *Archives of Sexual Behavior, 18*, 203–215.

Myers, W. C., & Mutch, P. J. (1992). Language disorders in disruptive behavior-disordered homicidal youth. *Journal of Forensic Sciences, 37*(3), 919–992.

Mørkved, N., Hartmann, K., Aarsheim, L. M., Holen, D., Milde, A. M., Bomyea, J., & Thorp, S. R. (2014). A comparison of narrative exposure therapy and prolonged exposure therapy for PTSD. *Clinical Psychology Review, 34*(6), 453–467.

N

Nadel, B. (2004). *Security: Handbook for architectural planning and design.* New York: McGraw-Hill.

Nader, K. O. (1997). Assessing traumatic experiences in children. In J. P. Wilson & T. M. Keane (Eds.), *Assessing psychological trauma and PTSD* (pp. 291–348). New York: Guilford Press.

Nader, K. O., Kreigler, J. A., Blake, D. D., & Pynoos, R. S. (1994). *Clinician Administered PTSD Scale, Child and Adolescent Version (CAPS-C).* White River Junction, VT: National Center for PTSD.

Nagel, D. M., & Anthony, K. (2011). Ethical framework for the use of technology in disaster mental health. Online Therapy Institute. Retrieved from www.onlinetherapyinstitute.com/disaster-mental-health/

Najavits, L. M. (2012). Posttraumatic Stress Disorder and substance abuse disorder comorbidity treatment: Principles and practices in real-world settings. In R. A. McMackin, E. Newman, J. M. Fogler, & T. M. Keane (Eds.), *Trauma therapy in context: The science and craft of evidence-based practice* (pp. 271–292). Washington, DC: American Psychological Association.

Nassau County Emergency Management Department. (2003). *Storm time and event schedule.* Fernandina Beach, FL: Author.

Nathan, P., & Ward, T. (2001). Females who sexually abuse children: Assessment and treatment issues. *Psychiatry, Psychology, and Law, 8*(1), 44–55.

National Action Alliance for Suicide Prevention (NAASP). (2014). *Research prioritization task force.* Retrieved from http://actionallianceforsuicideprevention.org/task-force/research-prioritization

National Alliance on Mental Illness. (2011). Crisis Intervention Team resource center. Retrieved from http://www.nami.org/Template.cfm?Section=CIT2

National Association of School Psychologists. (2010). *NASP Professional Standards (2010)*. Retrieved from http://www.nasponline.org/standards/2010standards.aspx

National Association of School Resource Officers. (2011). *NASRO training*. Retrieved from www.nasro.org/mc/page.do?sitePageId=114191&orgId=naasrp

National Center for Education Statistics. (2004). *Indicators of school crime and safety: 2004*. Retrieved from http://nces.ed.gov/pubsearch/pubsinfo.asp?pubid=2005002

National Center for Education Statistics. (2005a). *Indicators of school crime and safety: 2005*. Retrieved from http://nces.ed.gov/pubs2006/2006001.pdf

National Center for Education Statistics. (2005b). *Public elementary and secondary students, staff, schools, and school districts: School year 2002–03*. Retrieved from http://nces.ed.gov/pubsearch/pubsinfo.asp?pubid=2005314

National Center for Education Statistics. (2010). *Indicators of school crime and safety: 2010*. Retrieved from http://nces.ed.gov/programs/crimeindicators/crimeindicators2010/key.asp

National Center for Health Statistics. (2012). *First marriages in the United States: Data from the 2006–2010 national survey of family growth*. Retrieved from www.cdc.gov/nchs/fdata/nhsr049.pdf

National Center for PTSD. (2011, July). *PTSD in children and teens*. U.S. Department of Veterans Affairs. Retrieved from http://www.ptsd.va.gov/public/pages/ptsd-children-adolecents.asp

National Center for PTSD. (2014a). *Mental health effects following disaster: Risk and resilience factors*. Retrieved from www.ptsd.va.gov/professional/treatment/early/mental-health-following-disasters.asp

National Center for PTSD. (2014b). *Findings from the National Vietnam Veterans' Readjustment Study*. Retrieved from http://www.ptsd.va.gov/professional/research-bio/research/vietnam-vets-study.asp

National Center for PTSD. (2014c). *Mental health effects of serving in Afghanistan and Iraq*. Retrieved from http://www.ptsd.va.gov/public/PTSD-overview/reintegration/overview-mental-health-effects.asp

National Child Traumatic Stress Network and National Center for PTSD (NCTSN/NCPTSD). (2006). *Psychological first aid: Field operations guide* (2nd ed.). Retrieved from www.nctsn.org/sites.default/files/pfa/english/1-psyfirstaid_complete_manual.pdf

National Domestic Violence Hotline. (2015). *We're here to listen*. Retrieved from www.hotline.org

National Incident Management System. (2011). *About the National Incident Management System*. Retrieved from www.fema.gov/emergency/nims/AboutNIMS.shtm

National Institute for Health and Care Excellence. (2005). *Clinical guideline 26: Posttraumatic stress disorder (PTSD): The management of PTSD in adults and children in primary and secondary care*. London, UK: National Collaborating Centre for Mental Health.

National Institute for Occupational Safety and Health. (1992, October). *Epidemiology of workplace violence*. Atlanta, GA: Centers for Disease Control.

National Institute of Justice. (1998). *Crime in the schools: A problem-solving approach*. Summary of a Presentation by Dennis Kenney, Police Executive Research Forum. Washington, DC: Author.

National Institute of Justice and Centers for Disease Control. (1998). *National violence against women survey*. Washington, DC: United States Bureau of Justice.

National Institute of Mental Health. (2002). *Mental health and mass violence: Evidence-based early psychological intervention for victims/survivors of mass violence* (NIH Publication No. 02-5138). Washington, DC: U.S. Government Printing Office.

National Institute of Mental Health. (2003). *U.S. suicide rates by age, gender, and racial group*. Bethesda, MD: National Institutes of Health.

National Institute of Mental Health. (2011). *Suicide in the U.S.: Statistics and prevention*. Retrieved from www.nimh.nih.gov/health/publicaitons/suicide-in-the-us-statistics-and-prevention/index.shmtl

National Institutes of Health (1994). *NIH guidelines for the inclusion of women and minorities as subjects in clinical research*. Retrieved from http://grants.nih.gov/grants/funding/women_min/women_min.htm

National Organization for Victim Assistance. (1997). *Community crisis response team training manual* (2nd ed.). Washington, DC: Author.

National Organization for Victim Assistance. (2015). *Crisis response team training*. Retrieved from http://www.trynova.org/help-crisis-victims/crisis-training/

National Organization for Victim Assistance. (n.d.). *NOVA's mission, purposes, accomplishments, and organizational structure*. Retrieved from www.trynova.org/about-us/overview

National Research Council. (2003). *Elder mistreatment: Abuse, neglect, and exploitation in aging America: Panel to review risk and prevalence of elder abuse and neglect*. Washington, DC: National Academies Press.

National Runaway Safeline. (2015). National Runaway Safeline: Keeping America's runaway, homeless, and at-risk youth safe and off the streets. Retrieved from www.1800runaway.org

National School Safety Center. (1998). *Checklist of characteristics of youth who have caused school-associated violent deaths*. Westlake Village, CA: Author.

National Sexual Violence Resource Center. (2011). Child sexual abuse prevention: Overview. Retrieved from http://www.nsvrc.org/sites/defaultfiles/Publications_NSVRC_Overview_Child-sexual abuse-prevention_0.pdf

National Sexual Violence Resource Center. (2015). *Statistics about sexual violence*. Retrieved from http://www.nsvrc.org/sites/default/files/publications_nsvrc_factsheet_media-packet_statistics-about-sexual-violence_0.pdf

National Suicide Prevention Lifeline. (2011). Retrieved from www.suicidepreventionlifeline.org

Naz, I., Suri, S., & Parveen, S. (2012, October). *Spirituality, self-efficacy and burnout: A study of health professionals*. Paper presented at 2nd Indian Psychological Science Congress, Chandigarh, India.

Neimeyer, R. A. (2000). Searching for the meaning of meaning: Grief therapy and the process of reconstruction. *Death Studies, 24,* 541–558.

Neimeyer, R. A. (2010a). Reconstructing the continuing bond: A constructivist approach to grief therapy. In J. D. Raskin, S. K. Bridges, & R. Neimeyer (Eds.), *Studies in meaning 4: Constructivist perspective on theory, practice, and social justice* (pp. 65–91). New York: Pace University Press.

Neimeyer, R. A. (2010b). Reconstructing life out of loss: Reorganizing the continuing bond. In M. Kerman (Ed.), *Clinical pearls of wisdom: Twenty-one leading therapists offer their key insights* (pp. 104–117). New York: W. W. Norton.

Neimeyer, R. A. (Ed.). (2001). *Meaning reconstruction and the experience of loss*. Washington, DC: American Psychological Association.

Neimeyer, R. A., & Kosminsky, P. (2014). Bereavement. In L. Grossman & S. Walfish (Eds.), *Translating psychological research into practice* (pp. 132–139). New York: Springer.

Neimeyer, R. A., & Levitt, H. M. (2000). What's narrative got to do with it? Construction and coherence in accounts of loss. In J. H. Harvey & E. D. Miller (Eds.), *Loss and trauma: General and close relationship perspectives* (pp. 401–413). Philadelphia: Brunner-Routledge.

Neimeyer, R. A., & Mahoney, M. J. (Eds.). (1995). *Constructivism in psychotherapy*. Washington, DC: American Psychological Association.

Neimeyer, R. A., & Pfeiffer, A. M. (1994). The ten most common errors of suicide interventionists. In A. A. Leenaars, J. T. Maltsberger, & R. A. Neimeyer (Eds.), *Treatment of suicidal people* (pp. 207–219). Washington, DC: Taylor & Francis.

Neimeyer, R. A., Holland, J. M., Currier, J. M., & Mehta, T. (2007). Meaning reconstruction in later life: Toward a cognitive-constructivist approach to grief therapy. In D. Gallagher-Thompson, A. M. Steffen, & L. W. Thompson (Eds.), *Handbook of behavioral and cognitive therapies with older adults* (pp. 264–277). New York: Springer.

Nelson, E. R., & Slaikeu, K. A. (1990). Crisis intervention in schools. In K. A. Slaikeu (Ed.), *Crisis intervention: A handbook for research and practice* (2nd ed., pp. 329–347). Boston: Allyn & Bacon.

Nelson, R. E., & Galas, J. (1994). *The power to prevent suicide: A guide to helping teens*. Minneapolis, MN: Free Spirit.

Nelson, R. J. (2013). Is virtual reality exposure therapy effective for service members and veterans experiencing PTSD? *Traumatology, 19*(3), 171–178.

Nelson, W. M., Finch, A., & Ghee, A. (2006). Anger management with children and adolescents: Cognitive-behavior therapy. In P. C. Kendall (Ed.), *Child and adolescent therapy: Cognitive-behavioral procedures* (3rd ed., pp. 114–165). New York: Guilford Press.

Neubauer, F., Deblinger, E., & Sieger, K. (2007). Trauma-focused cognitive-behavioral therapy for child sexual abuse and exposure to domestic violence: Case of Mary, age 6. In N. B. Webb (Ed.), *Play therapy with children in crisis: Individual, group, and family treatment* (3rd ed., pp. 107–132). New York: Guilford Press.

Newcomb, M. D., Munoz, D. T., & Carmona, J. V. (2009). Child sexual abuse consequences in community samples of Latino and European American adolescents. *Child Abuse and Neglect, 33*(8), 533–544.

Newgass, S., & Schonfeld, D. J. (2005). School crisis intervention, crisis prevention, and crisis response. In A. R. Roberts (Ed.), *Crisis intervention handbook* (pp. 499–518). New York: Oxford University Press.

Newhill, C. E. (2003). *Client violence in social work practice: Prevention, intervention, and research*. New York: Guilford Press.

Newman, C. F. (1994). Understanding client resistance: Methods for enhancing motivation to change. *Cognitive and Behavioral Practice, 1,* 47–69.

Newman, C. J. (1976). Children of disaster: Clinical observations at Buffalo Creek. *American Journal of Psychiatry, 133,* 306–312.

Newman, D. A., Horne, A. M., & Bartolomucci, C. L. (2000). *Bully busters: A teacher's manual for helping bullies, victims, and bystanders, grades 6–8*. Champaign, IL: Research Press.

Newman, E., Kaloupkek, D. G., & Keane, T. M. (1996). Assessment of posttraumatic stress disorder in clinical and research settings. In B. A. van der Kolk, A. C. McFarlane, & L. Weisaeth (Eds.), *Traumatic stress* (pp. 242–273). New York: Guilford Press.

Newman, K. S. (1993). *Declining fortunes: The withering of the American dream*. New York: Basic Books.

NFL lifeline. (2012). Retrieved from www.NFLlifeline.org /about/

Ng, A. T. (2006). Mobile crisis teams. In P. M. Gillette & H. L. McQuistion (Eds.), *Clinical guide to the treatment of the mentally ill homeless person* (pp.73–82). Arlington, VA: American Psychiatric Publishing.

Nicholson, E. L., Bryant, R. A., & Felmingham, K. L. (2013). Interaction of noradrenaline and cortisol predicts negative intrusive memoire sin posttraumatic stress disorder. *Neurobiology of Learning and Memory, 1,* 23–34.

Nickelson, D. W. (1998). Telehealth and the evolving health care system: Strategic opportunities for professional psychology. *Professional Psychology: Research and Practice, 29,* 527–535.

Nickerson, R. S. (2011). Roles of human factors and ergonomics in meeting the challenge of terrorism. *American Psychologist, 66*(6), 555–566.

Nicoletti, J., & Spooner, K. (1996). Violence in the workplace: Response and intervention strategies. In G. R. VandenBos & E. Q. Bulatao (Eds.), *Violence on the job: Identifying risks and developing solutions* (pp. 267–282). Washington, DC: American Psychological Association.

Nieburg, H. A., & Fischer, A. (1982). *Pet loss: A thoughtful guide for adults and children*. New York: Harper & Row.

Niles, B. L., Klun-Gillis, J., Ryngala, D. J., Silberbogen, A. K., & Paysnick, E. J. (2012). Comparing mindfulness and psycho-education treatments for combat-related PTSD using a telehealth approach. *Psychological Trauma: Theory, Research, Practice and Trauma, 4*(5), 538–547.

Niolon, P., Vivolo-Kantor, A., Latzman, N., Valle, L., Kuoh, H., Burton, T., . . .Tharp, A. (2015). Prevalence of teen dating violence and co-occurring risk factors among middle school youth in high-risk urban communities. *Journal of Adolescent Health, 56*(Supp. 2), S5–S13.

Nisbett, R. E. (1993). Violence and U.S. regional culture. *American Psychologist, 48,* 441–449.

Nishith, P., Nixon, R., & Resick, P. A. (2005). Resolution of trauma-related guilt following treatment of PTSD in female rape victims: A result of cognitive processing therapy targeting comorbid depression. *Journal of Affective Disorders, 86*(22/23), 259–265.

Nisivoccia, D., & Lynn, M. (2007). Helping forgotten victims: Using activity groups with children who witness violence. In N. B. Webb (Ed.), *Play therapy with children in crisis: Individual, group, and family treatment* (pp. 294–321). New York: Guilford Press.

Niv, S. (2013). Clinical efficacy and potential mechanisms of neurofeedback. *Personality and Individual Differences, 54*(6), 676–686.

Nkomo, N., Freeman, M., & Skinner, D. (2009). Experiences of children heading households in the wake of the human immunodeficiency virus/acquired immune deficiency syndrome (HIV/AIDS) epidemic in South Africa. *Vulnerable Children and Youth Studies, 4*(3), 255–263.

Nobbman, K., Skirius, M., & James, R. (2014, April). *Social locations*. Paper presented at the F. E. Woodall Spring Conference, Delta State University, Greenville, MS.

Nock, M. K., & Marzuk, P. M. (2000). Suicide and violence. In K. Hawton & K. Van Heeringen (Eds.), *The international handbook of suicide and attempted suicide* (pp. 437–456). New York: John Wiley & Sons.

Noll, J. G., Horowitz, L., Bonanno, G., Trickett, P., & Putnam, F. (2003). Revictimization and self-harm in females who experienced childhood sexual abuse: Results from a prospective study. *Journal of Interpersonal Violence, 18*(12), 1452–1471.

Noonan, J. H., & Vavra, M. C. (2007). *Crime in schools and colleges: A study of offenders and arrestees reported via national incident-based reporting system data*. Retrieved from http://www.fbi.gov /about-us/cjis/ucr/nibrs/crime-in-schools-and-colleges-pdf

Noonan, P. (2007, April 21–22). Cold standard. *Wall Street Journal,* p. 16.

Nord, D. (1997). *Multiple AIDS-related loss: A handbook for understanding and surviving a perpetual fall*. Washington, DC: Taylor & Francis.

Nordstrom, L., Hedman, E., Etienne, J., Bodin, J., Kadowski, A., Erikson, S., . . . Carlbring, P. (2014). Effectiveness and cost effectiveness of individually tailored internet-delivered cognitive behavior therapy for anxiety disorders in a primary population. *Behaviour Research and Therapy, 59*(1), 1–11.

Norris, F., Friedman, M., Watson, P., Byrne, C., Diaz, E., & Kaniasty, K. (2002). 60,000 disaster individuals speak: Part I. An empirical review of the literature, 1981–2001. *Psychiatry: Interpersonal and Biological Process, 65*(3), 207–243.

Norris, F. H. (2006). Disaster research methods: Past progress and future directions. *Journal of Traumatic Stress, 19*(2), 173–184.

Norris, F. H., & Alegria, M. (2006). Promoting disaster recovery in ethnic-minority individuals and communities. In E. C. Ritchie, P. J. Watson, & M. J. Friedman (Eds.), *Interventions following mass violence and disasters* (pp. 319–342). New York: Guilford Press.

Norris, F. H., Hamblen, J., Watson, P., Ruxek, J., Gibson, L., Pfefferbaum, B., et al. (2006). Toward understanding and creating systems of postdisaster care. In E. C. Ritchie, P. J. Watson, & M. J. Friedman (Eds.), *Interventions following mass violence and disasters: Strategies for mental health practice* (pp. 343–364). New York: Guilford Press.

Norris, J., & Cubbins, L. A. (1992). Dating, drinking, and rape. *Psychology of Women Quarterly, 16*, 179–191.

Norris-Shortle, C., Young, P. A., & Williams, M. A. (1993). Understanding death and grief for children three and younger. *Social Work, 38*, 736–741.

North, C. S. (2004). Approaching disaster mental health research after the 9/11 World Trade Center terrorist attacks. *Psychiatric Clinics of North America, 27*(3), 589–602.

Notman, M., & Nadelson, C. (1976). The rape individual: Psychodynamic considerations. *American Journal of Psychiatry, 133*, 408–412.

Nouwen, H. J. M. (1972). *The wounded healer: Ministry in contemporary society.* New York: Doubleday.

Novotney, A. (2014). Blogging for mental health. *Monitor on Psychology, 45*(6), 44–45.

Number of "cyberchondriacs"—U.S. adults who go online for health information—increases to estimated 117 million. (2005). *Healthcare News, 5*(8). Retrieved from www.harrisinteractive .com/news/newsletters/healthnews/HI_HealthCareNews 2005Vol5_Iss08.pdf

Nurius, P. S. (1984). Stress: A pervasive dilemma in psychiatric emergency care. *Comprehensive Psychiatry, 25*, 345–354.

O

Oates, R. K., O'Toole, B. I., Lynch, D. L., Stern, A., & Cooney, G. (1994). Stability and change in outcomes for sexually abused children. *Journal of the American Academy of Child and Adolescent Psychiatry, 33*, 945–953.

Oatley, A. (1994). Domestic violence doesn't discriminate on the basis of sexual orientation. *Suncoast News,* pp. 19–21.

Ober, C., Peeters, L., Archer, R., & Kelly, K. (2000). Debriefing in different cultural frameworks: Responding to acute trauma in Australian Aboriginal contexts. In B. Raphael & J. P. Wilson (Eds.), *Psychological debriefing: Theory, practice, and evidence* (pp. 241–253). New York: Cambridge University Press.

Obhu, S., Yamashina, A., Takasu, N., Yamaguchi, T., Murai, T., Naknbao, K., et al. (1997). Sarin poisoning on the Tokyo subway. *Southern Medical Journal, 90*, 587–593.

Occupational Safety and Health Administration. (2003). *Guidelines for preventing workplace violence for healthcare and social service workers.* OSHA 3148. Washington, DC: U.S. Department of Labor.

Occupational Safety and Health Administration. (2015). *Guidelines for preventing workplace violence for healthcare and social service workers.* OSHA 3148. Washington, DC: U.S. Department of Labor.

Ochberg, F. M. (1988). *Post-traumatic therapy and victims of violence.* New York: Brunner/Mazel.

Oerlemans, W., & Bakker, A. (2014). Burnout and daily recovery: A day reconstruction study. *Journal of Occupational Health Psychology, 19*(3), 302–314.

Office for Victims of Crime. (2002). *Strengthening anti-stalking statutes* (NCJ Publication No. 189192). Washington, DC: U.S. Department of Justice.

Ogloff, J. R., & Daffern, M. (2006). The Dynamic Appraisal of Situational Aggression: An instrument to assess risk for imminent aggression in psychiatric inpatients. *Behavioral Sciences and the Law, 24*, 799–813.

Oktay, J. S. (1992). Burnout in hospital social workers who work with AIDS patients. *Social Work, 37*, 432–437.

Okun, B., & Nowinski, J. (2011). *Saying goodbye: How families can find renewal through loss.* New York: Berkley Books/Penguin Group.

Okun, L. (1986). *Woman abuse: Facts replacing myths.* Albany: State University of New York Press.

Olden, M., Mello, B., Cukor, J., Wyka, K., Jayasinghe, N., & Difede, J. (2015). Implementation of evidence-based assessment, treatment , and research programs following the World Trade Center disaster on September 11, 2001. In M. Safir, J. Wallach, & A. Rizzo (Eds.), *Future directions in post-traumatic stress disorder: Prevention, diagnosis, and treatmen* (pp. 367–387). New York: Springer.

Oleszko v. State Compensation Insurance Fund, 99-15207 (9th Circuit Court of Appeals 2001).

Olivares-Faundez,V., Gil-Monte, P., Mena, L., Jelvez -Wilke, C., & Figueiredo-Ferraz, H. (2014). Relationships between burnout and role ambiguity, role conflict and employees absenteeism among health workers. *Terapia Psicologicaa, 32*(2), 111–120.

Olson, D. H. (2000). Circumplex model of marital and family system, *Journal of Family Therapy, 22*, 144–167.

Olson, L., Anctil, C., Fullerton, L., Brillman, J., Arbuckle, J., & Sklar, D. (1996). Increasing emergency room physician recognition of domestic violence. *Annals of Emergency Medicine, 27*(6), 741–746.

Oras, R., de Ezpeleta, S., & Ahmad, A. (2004). Treatment of traumatized refugee children with Eye Movement Desensitization and Reprocessing in a psychodynamic model. *Nordic Journal of Psychiatry, 58*(3), 199–203.

Organista, K. C., & Munoz, R. F. (1996). Cognitive behavior therapy with Latinos. *Cognitive Behavioral Practice, 3*(2), 255–270.

Oropeza, B. A., Clark, F., Fitzgibbon, M., & Baron, A. (1991). Managing mental health crises of foreign college students. *Journal of Counseling and Development, 69*, 280–283.

Osborn, C. L. (1991). Reminiscence: When the past eases the present. *Journal of Gerontological Nursing, 15*, 6–11.

Osofsky, J. D. (1995). The effects of exposure to violence on young children. *American Psychologist, 50*(9), 781–788.

Osofsky, J. D., Osofsky, H. J., Kronenberg, M., & Hansel, T. C. (2010). The aftermath of Hurricane Katrina: Mental health considerations and lessons learned. In R. P. Kilmer, V. Gil-Rivas, R. G. Tedeschi, & L. G. Calhoun (Eds.), *Helping families and communities recover from disaster: Lessons learned from Hurricane Katrina and its aftermath* (pp. 241–263). Washington, DC: American Psychological Association.

Osterweis, M., Solomon, F., & Green, M. (Eds.). (1984). *Bereavement: Reactions, consequences, and care.* Washington, DC: National Academy Press.

Ostrow, D. G. (Ed.). (1990). *Behavioral aspects of AIDS.* New York: Plenum Medical.

Ott, C. H. (2003). The impact of complicated grief on mental and physical health at various points in the bereavement process. *Death Studies, 27*(3), 249–272.

Ott, C. H., Sanders, S., & Kelber, S. T. (2007). Grief and personal growth experience of spouses and adult-child caregivers of individuals with Alzheimer's disease and related dementias. *Gerontologist, 47*(6), 798–809.

Ouimette, P., & Read, J. P. (2014). *Trauma and substance abuse: Causes, consequences, and treatment of comorbid disorders.* Washington, DC: American Psychological Association.

Ouimette, P., Read, J., & Brown, P. J. (2005). Consistency of retrospective reports of DSM-IV Criterion A traumatic stressors among substance use disorder patients. *Journal of Traumatic Stress, 18*(1), 43–51.

Outlaw, F. H., & Lowery, B. J. (1992). Seclusion: The nursing challenge. *Journal of Psychosocial Nursing, 30*, 13–17.

Owen, J., Leach, M. M., Wampold, B., & Rodolfa, E. (2011). Client and therapist variability in clients' perceptions of their therapists' multicultural competencies. *Journal of Counseling Psychology, 58*(1), 1–9.

Owen, J. P. (2004). *Cowboy ethics: What Wall Street can learn from the code of the west.* Ketchum, ID: Stoeckleinm.

Owens, K. A., Haddock, G., & Berry, K. (2013). The role of the therapeutic alliance in the regulation of emotion in psychosis: An attachment perspective. *Clinical Psychology and Psychotherapy, 20*(6), 523–530.

Oyserman, D., Coon, H. M., & Kemmelmeier, M. (2002). Rethinking individualism and collectivism: Evaluation of theoretical assumptions and meta-analyses. *Psychological Bulletin, 128*, 3–72.

O'Connor, M., Nickerson, A., Aderka, I., & Bryant, R. (2015). The temporal relationship between change in symptoms of prolonged grief and posttraumatic stress following old age spousal bereavement. *Depression and Anxiety, 32*(5), 335–340.

O'Keefe, M. (1998). Posttraumatic stress disorder among incarcerated battered women: A comparison of battered women who kill their abusers and those incarcerated for other offenses. *Journal of Traumatic Stress, 11*(1), 71–85.

O'Leary, E., & Nieuwstraten, I. M. (2001). The exploration of memories in Gestalt reminiscence therapy. *Counseling Psychology Quarterly, 14*(2), 165–180.

O'Leary, P. J. (2009). Men who were sexually abused in childhood: Coping strategies and comparison in psychological functioning. *Child Abuse and Neglect, 33*(7), 471–479.

O'Reilly, J. T., Hagan, P., & de la Cruz, P. (2001). *Environmental and workplace safety: A guide for university, hospital, and school management.* New York: John Wiley & Sons.

O'Rinn, S., Lishak, V., Muller, R., & Classen, C.(2013). A preliminary examination of perceptions of betrayal and its association with memory disturbance among survivors of childhood sexual abuse. *Psychological Trauma: Theory, Research, Practice, and Policy, 5*(4), 343–349.

O'Toole, M. E. (2003). *The school shooter: A threat assessment perspective.* Quantico, VA: Federal Bureau of Investigation.

P

Padach, K. M. (1984). Long-term telephone counseling. In F. W. Kaslow (Ed.), *Counseling with psychotherapists* (pp. 173–190). New York: Haworth Press.

Page, J. M., Daniels, J., & Craig, S. (2015). *Violence in schools.* Chaim, Switzerland: Springer International Publishing.

Page, R. M. (1997). Helping adolescents avoid date rape: The role of secondary education. *High School Journal, 80*, 75–80.

Pagelow, M. D. (1981). *Woman battering: Victims and their experiences.* Newbury Park, CA: Sage.

Pagelow, M. D. (1992). Adult victims of domestic violence: Battered women. *Journal of Interpersonal Violence, 7*, 87–120.

Paine, W. S. (1982). Overview of burnout stress syndromes and the 1980's. In W. S. Paine (Ed.), *Job stress and burnout* (pp. 11–25). Newbury Park, CA: Sage.

Palfrey, J., & Gasser, U. (2009). *Born digital: Understanding the first generation of digital natives.* New York: Basic Books.

Palmstierna, T., & Wistedt, B. (1990). Risk factors for aggressive behaviour are of limited value in predicting the violent behaviour of acute involuntarily admitted patients. *Acta Psychiatrica Scandinavica, 81*, 152–155.

Parcesepe, A., Martin, S., Pollock, M., & Garcia-Moreno, C. (2015). The effectiveness of mental health interventions for adult female survivors of sexual assault: A systematic review. *Aggression and Violent Behavior, 14*(4), 220–245.

Pargament, K. I. (2007). *Spiritually integrated psychotherapy: Understanding and addressing the sacred.* New York: Guilford Press.

Pargament, K. I., & Sweeney, P. J. (2011). Building spiritual fitness in the Army. *American Psychologist, 66*(1), 58–64.

Parikh, S., V., & Huniewicz, P. (2015). E-health: An overview of uses on the Internet, social media, apps, and websites for mood disorders. *Current Opinion in Psychiatry, 28*(1), 13–17.

Paris, J. (2008). *Treatment of borderline personality disorder: A guide to evidence-based practice.* New York: Guilford Press.

Park, C., Park, S., Gwak, A. Sohn, B., Lee, J., Jung, H., Choi, S., . . . Choi, J. (2015). The effect of repeated exposure to virtual gambling cues on the urge to gamble. *Addictive Behaviors,41*(1), 61–64.

Parker, B., McFarlane, J., Soeken, K., Torres, T., & Campbell, D. (1993). Physical and emotional abuse in pregnancy: A comparison of adult and teenage women. *Nursing Research, 42*, 173–177.

Parker, C., Barnett, D., Everly, G., & Links, J. (2006). Establishing evidence-informed core intervention competencies in Psychological First Aid for public health personnel. *International Journal of Emergency Mental Health, 8*(2), 83–92.

Parker, J. G., & Gottman, H. J. M. (1989). Social and emotional development in a relational context. In T. J. Berndt & G. W. Ladd (Eds.), *Peer relationships in child development* (pp. 95–131). New York: John Wiley & Sons.

Parkes, C., & Prigerson, H. A. (2010). *Bereavement: Studies of grief in adult life* (4th ed.). New York: Routledge/Taylor-Francis Group.

Pascual-Leone, A., Bierman, R., Arnold, R., & Stasiak, E. (2011). Emotion-focused therapy for incarcerated offenders of intimate partner violence: A three year outcome using a new whole sample match. *Psychotherapy Research, 21*(3), 3312–3347.

Pastel, B. H., & Ritchie, E. C. (2006). Mitigation of psychological weapons of mass destruction. In E. C. Ritchie, P. J. Watson, & M. J. Friedman (Eds.), *Interventions following mass violence and disasters: Strategies for mental health practice* (pp. 300–318). New York: Guilford Press.

Paterson, J. (2010). Bullies with byte. *Counseling Today, 53*(12), 44–47.

Paterson, J. (2011). Young and depressed. *Counseling Today, 54*(1), 32–35.

Path, Ä. M. (2002). *Surviving stalking.* Cambridge, UK: Cambridge University Press.

Patros, P. G., & Shamoo, T. K. (1989). *Depression and suicide in children and adolescents: Prevention, intervention, and postvention.* Boston: Allyn & Bacon.

Patterson, C. H. (1980). *Theories of counseling and psychotherapy* (3rd ed.). New York: Harper & Row.

Patterson, J. (2002). Integrating family resilience and family stress theory. *Journal of Marriage and Family, 64,* 349–360.

Patterson, W. M., Dohn, H. H., Bird, J., & Patterson, G. A. (1983). Evaluation of suicidal patients: The SAD PERSON scale. *Psychosomatics, 24*(4), 343–349.

Paunovic, N. (2002). Prolonged exposure counterconditioning (PEC) as a treatment for chronic posttraumatic stress disorder and major depression in an adult survivor of repeated child sexual and physical abuse. *Clinical Case Studies, 1*(2), 148–169.

Paunovic, N. (2003). Prolonged exposure counterconditioning as a treatment for chronic posttraumatic stress disorder. *Journal of Anxiety Disorders, 17*(5), 479–499.

Paunovic, N., & Ost, L. (2001). Cognitive-behavior therapy vs. exposure therapy in the treatment of PTSD in refugees. *Behavior Research and Therapy, 39*(10), 1183–1197.

Pauwels, S. M. (2003, April). *The scarlet R: Profile of a victim.* Paper presented at the Twenty-seventh Annual Convening of Crisis Intervention Personnel, Chicago.

Paymar, M. (2015). *Violent no more: Helping men end domestic abuse* (3rd ed.). Nashville, TN: Hunter House/Turner Publishing.

Pazar, J. (2005). *A reliability study of the triage assessment scale.* Unpublished doctoral dissertation, University of Memphis.

Pearlman, L. A., & Mac Ian, P. S. (1995). Vicarious traumatization: An empirical study of the effects of trauma work on trauma therapists. *Professional Psychology, 26*(6), 558–565.

Pearlman, L. A., & Saakvitne, K. W. (1995a). *Trauma and the therapist.* New York: Norton.

Pearlman, L. A., & Saakvitne, K. W. (1995b). Treating therapists with vicarious traumatization and secondary traumatic stress disorders. In C. R. Figley (Ed.), *Compassion fatigue: Coping with secondary traumatic stress disorder in those who treat the traumatized* (pp. 150–177). New York: Brunner-Mazel.

Pearlman, M. Y., Schwalbe, K. D., & Cloitre, M. (2010). *Grief in childhood: Fundamentals of treatment in clinical practice.* Washington, DC: American Psychological Association.

Pearson, Q. M. (1994). Treatment techniques for adult female survivors of childhood sexual abuse. *Journal of Counseling and Development, 73,* 32–37.

Pearsons, L. (1965). *The use of written communications in psychotherapy.* Springfield, IL: Charles C Thomas.

Pedersen, P. (1987). Ten frequent assumptions of cultural bias in counseling. *Journal of Multicultural Counseling and Development, 15,* 16–24.

Pedersen, P. (1998). *Multiculturalism as a fourth force.* New York: Brunner/Mazel.

Pedersen, P. B., & Marsella, A. J. (1982). The ethical crisis for cross-cultural counseling and therapy. *Professional Psychology, 13,* 492–500.

Peled, E. (1997). The battered women's movement response to children: A critical analysis. *Violence Against Women, 3*(4), 424–446.

Pence, E. L., & McDonnell, C. (2000). Developing policies and protocols in Duluth, Minnesota. In J. Hanmer & C. Itzin (Eds.), *Home truths about domestic violence: Feminist influences on policy and practice: A reader* (pp. 249–268). New York: Routledge.

Pence, E. L., & Paymar, M. (1993). *Education groups for men who batter: The Duluth model.* New York: Springer.

Pence, E. L., & Shepard, M. F. (1999). An introduction: Developing a coordinated community response. In M. F. Shepard & E. L. Pence (Eds.), *Coordinating community response to domestic violence: Lessons from Duluth and beyond* (pp. 3–24). Thousand Oaks, CA: Sage.

Pender, D. A., & Prichard, K. K. (2008). Group process research and emergence of therapeutic factors in Critical Incident Stress Debriefing. *International Journal of Emergency Mental Health, 10,* 39–48.

Pender, D. A., & Prichard, K. K. (2009). AGSW best practices guidelines as a research tool: A comprehensive examination of critical incident stress debriefing. *Journal of Specialists in Group Work, 34*(2), 175–192.

Pengpid, S., & Peltzer, K. (2014) Sexual assault and other type of intimate partner violence in women with protection orders in Vhembe district, South Africa. *Violence and Victims, 29*(5), 857–871.

Pennebaker, J. W., & Harber, K. D. (1993). A social stage model of collective coping: The Loma Prieta earthquake and the Persian Gulf War. *Journal of Social Issues, 49,* 125–146.

Perilla, J., Norris, F., & Lavizzo, E. (2002). Ethnicity, culture, and disaster response: Identifying and explaining ethnic differences in PTSD six months after Hurricane Andrew. *Journal of Social and Clinical Psychology, 21,* 28–45.

Perkins, H. W., & Berkowitz, A. D. (1986). Perceiving the community norms of alcohol use among students: Some research implications for campus alcohol education programming. *International Journal of Addictions, 21,* 961–976.

Perkonigg, A., Kessler, A. C., Storz, S., & Wittchen, H. (2000). Traumatic events and post-traumatic stress disorder in the community: Prevalence, risk factors and comorbidity. *Acta Psychiatrica Scandinavica, 101,* 46–59.

Perrin, S., Van Hasselt, V., Basilio, I., & Hersen, M. (1996). Assessing the effects of violence on women in battering relationships with the Keane MMPI-PTSD Scale. *Journal of Traumatic Stress, 9*(4), 805–816.

Peterman, L. M., & Dixon, C. G. (2003). Domestic violence between same-sex partners: Implications for counseling. *Journal of Counseling and Development, 81*(1), 40–47.

Petersen, J. V. (2008). The role of the Chandler Police Department resource officers as law-related educational leaders. *Dissertation Abstracts International, 69*(6-A), 2078.

Petersen, S. (1999, April). *School crisis planning.* Workshop at the American Counseling Association World Conference, San Diego.

Petersen, S., & Straub, R. L. (1992). *School crisis survival guide: Management techniques and materials for counselors and administrators.* West Nyack, NY: Center for Applied Research in Education.

Peterson, B., & Schoeller, B. (1991, April). *Identifying and responding to problem and repeat callers.* Paper presented at the Fifteenth Annual Convening of Crisis Intervention Personnel, Chicago.

Peterson, C., Park, N., & Castro, C. A. (2011). Assessment for the U.S. Army Comprehensive Soldier Fitness program: The Global Assessment Tool. *American Psychologist, 66*(1), 10–18.

Peterson, G. W., Hennon, C. B., & Knox, T. (2010). Conceptualizing parental stress with family stress theory. In S. J. Price, C. A. Price, & P. C. McKenry (Eds.), *Families and change: Coping with stressful events and transitions* (pp. 25–50). Los Angeles: Sage.

Peterson, L. W., & Hardin, M. E. (1997). *Children in distress: A guide for screening children's art.* New York: W. W. Norton.

Peterson, L. W., & Zamboni, S. (1998). Quantitative art techniques to evaluate child trauma: A case review. *Clinical Pediatrics, 37*(1), 45–49.

Petrie, W. M. (1984). Violence: The geriatric patient. In J. T. Turner (Ed.), *Violence in the medical care setting: A survival guide* (pp. 107–122). Rockville, MD: Aspen Systems.

Petrik, D., Lagace, D. C., & Eisch, A. J. (2012). The neurogenesis hypothesis of affective and anxiety disorders: Are we mistaking the scaffolding for the building? *Neuropharmacology, 62*(1), 21–34.

Pettifor, J. L. (2004). Professional ethics across national boundaries. *European Psychologist, 9,* 264–272. doi:10.1027/1016-9040.9.4.264

Pew Research Center. (2011). Texting is nearly universal among young cell phone owners. Retrieved from www.pewresearch .org

Pfeffer, C. R. (2006). Suicide and suicidality. In M. K. Dulcan & J. M. Wiener (Eds.), *Essentials of child and adolescent psychiatry* (pp. 621–632). Washington, DC: American Psychiatric Publishing.

Pfefferbaum, B. (1997). Posttraumatic stress disorder in children: A review of the past 10 years. *Journal of the American Academy of Child and Adolescent Psychiatry, 36,* 1503–1511.

Phillips, B., & Jenkins, P. (2010). The roles of faith-based organizations after Hurricane Katrina. In R. P. Kilmer, V. Gil-Rivas, R. G. Tedeschi, & L. G. Calhoun (Eds.), *Helping families and communities recover for disaster* (pp. 215–238), Washington, DC: American Psychological Association.

Phipps, A., Byrne, M., & Deane, F. (2007). Can volunteer counselors help prevent psychological trauma? A preliminary communication on volunteers' skill using the "Orienting Approach" to trauma counseling. *Stress and Health: Journal of the International Society of the Investigation of Stress, 23*(1), 15–21.

Phipps, S. (2011). Positive psychology and war: An oxymoron. *American Psychologist, 66,* 641–642.

Piedmont, R. L. (1993). A longitudinal analysis of burnout in the health care setting: The role of personal dispositions. *Journal of Personality Assessment, 61,* 457–473.

Pierce, G. R., Sarason, B. R., & Sarason, I. G. (Eds.). (1996). *Handbook of social support and the family.* New York: Plenum Press.

Piercy, D. (1984). Violence: The drug and alcohol patient. In J. T. Turner (Ed.), *Violence in the medical care setting: A survival guide* (pp. 123–152). Rockville, MD: Aspen Systems.

Pietrzak, R. H., Huang, Y., Corsi-Travali, S., Zheng, M., Lin, S., et al. (2014). Cannabinois type 1 receptor availability in the amygdala mediates threat processing in trauma survivors. *Neuropsychochochopharmacology, 39*(11), 2519–2528.

Pifalo, T. (2002). Pulling out the thorns: Art therapy with sexually abused children and adolescents. *Art Therapy, 19*(1), 12–22.

Pine, V. R. (1996). Social psychological aspects of disaster death. In K. J. Doka (Ed.), *Living with grief after sudden loss: Suicide, homicide, accident, heart attack, stroke* (pp. 103–116). Washington, DC: Hospice Foundation of America.

Pines, A. (1983). On burnout and the buffering effects of social support. In B. A. Farber (Ed.), *Stress and burnout in the human service professions* (pp. 155–173). New York: Pergamon Press.

Pines, A., & Aronson, E. (1988). *Career burnout: Causes and cures.* New York: Free Press.

Piotrowski, C. (2012). Research areas of emphasis in professional psychology: Past and current trends. *Journal of Instructional Psychology, 39,* 131–135.

Piper, W. E., Ogrodniczuk, J. S., Joyce, S. S., & Weideman, R. (2011). Risk factors for complicated grief. In W. E. Piper, J. S. Ogrodniczuk, S. S. Joyce, & R. Weideman (Eds.), *Short-term group therapies for complicated grief: Two research-based models* (pp. 193–202). Washington, DC: American Psychological Association.

Pisarick, G. (1981, September). The violent patient. *Nursing,* pp. 63–65.

Pitcher, G. D., & Poland, S. (1992). *Crisis intervention in the schools.* New York: Guilford Press.

Pittman, F. S. (1987). *Turning points: Treating families in transition and crisis.* New York: W. W. Norton.

Pivar, I., & Field, N. P. (2004). Unresolved grief in combat veterans with PTSD. *Journal of Anxiety Disorders, 18*(6), 745–755.

Pizarro, J., Silver, R. C., & Prause, J. (2006). Physical and mental health costs of traumatic war experiences among Civil War veterans. *Archives of General Psychiatry, 63*(2), 193–200.

Pizzetti, P., & Manfredini, M. (2008). "The shock of widowhood": Evidence from an Italian population (Parma 1989–2000). *Social Indictors Research, 85*(3), 499–513.

Pizzey, E. (1974). *Scream quietly or the neighbors will hear.* London: Penguin Books.

Planchon, L. A., Templer, D. I., Stokes, S., & Keller, J. (2002). Death of a companion cat or dog and human bereavement. *Society and Animals, 10*(3), 327.

Pleck, E. (1987). *The making of societal policy against family violence from colonial times to the present.* New York: Oxford University Press.

Pledge, D. S. (2003). *When something feels wrong: A survival guide about abuse.* Minneapolis, MN: Free Spirit.

Pledge, D. S., Lapan, R., Heppner, P., Kivlighan, D., & Roehlke, H. (1998). Stability and severity of presenting problems at a university counseling center: A 6-year analysis. *Professional Psychology: Research and Practice, 29*(4), 386–389.

Plough, A., Fielding, J., Chandra, A., Williams, M., Eisenman, D., Wells, K., . . . Magana, A. (2013). Building community disaster resilience: Perspectives form a large urban county department of public health. *American Journal of Public Health, 103*(7), 1190–1197.

Plutchik, R., & van Praag, H. M. (1990). Psychosocial correlates of suicide and violence risk. In H. M. van Praag, R. Plutchik, & A. Apter (Eds.), *Violence and suicidality: Perspectives in clinical and psychobiological research* (pp. 76–88). New York: Brunner/ Mazel.

Poijula, S., Dyregrov, A., Wahleberg, K., & Jokelainen, J. (2001). Reactions to adolescent suicide and crisis intervention in three secondary schools. *International Journal of Emergency Mental Health, 3*(2), 97–106.

Poland, S. (1994). The role of school crisis intervention team to prevent and reduce school violence and trauma. *School Psychology Review, 239*(2), 175–189.

Poland, S. (1999). *School crisis and youth violence: Lessons learned.* Houston, TX: Cypress-Fairbanks Independent School District, Department of Psychological Services.

Poland, S. (2004). School crisis teams. In J. Conoley & A. P. Goldstein (Eds.), *School violence intervention: A practical handbook* (2nd ed., pp. 131–163). New York: Guilford Press.

Poland, S., & McCormick, J. S. (1999). *Coping with crisis: Lessons learned.* Longmont, CO: Sophris West.

Poliks, O. (1999, April). *The noble victim: Survival, self-care and spirituality.* Paper presented at the Twenty-Third Annual Convening of Crisis Intervention Personnel, Chicago.

Polster, E., & Polster, M. (1973). *Gestalt therapy integrated.* New York: Brunner/Mazel.

Polusny, M. A., Ries, B. J., Meis, L. A., DeGarmo, D., McCormick-Deaton, D., Thuras, C. M., & Paul Erbes, C. R. (2011). Effects of parents' experiential avoidance and PTSD on adolescent disaster-related posttraumatic stress symptomatology. *Journal of Family Psychology, 25,* 220–229.

Ponterotto, J. G., & Mallinckrodt, B. (2007). Introduction to the special section on racial and ethnic identity in counseling psychology: Conceptual and methodological challenges and proposed solutions. *Journal of Counseling Psychology, 54*(3), 219–233.

Ponterotto, J. G., & Pedersen, P. (1993). *Preventing prejudice: A guide for counselors and educators.* Newbury Park, CA: Sage.

Pope, K. S. (2015, July 30). *Ethical standards and practice guidelines for assessment, therapy, counseling, and forensic practice.* Retrieved from http://kspope.com/ethcodes/index.php

Pope, R. (Speaker). (1991). *Crisis counseling of the walk-in* (Videotape Recording No. 6611-91B). Memphis, TN: Memphis State University, Department of Counseling and Personnel Services.

Pope, R. (Speaker). (1991). *Crisis counseling of the walk-in* (Videotape Recording No. 6611-91B). Memphis, TN: Memphis State University, Department of Counseling and Personnel Services.

Postrel, V. (1998). *The future and its enemies: The growing conflict over creativity, enterprise, and progress.* New York: Free Press.

Potter, L. B. (2001). Moving suicide risk assessment into the next millennium: Lessons from our past. In D. Lester (Ed.), *Suicide prevention: Resources for the millennium* (pp. 67–82). Philadelphia: Brunner-Routledge.

Powell, W. E. (1994). The relationship between feelings of alienation and burnout in social work. *Families in Society, 75,* 229–235.

Powers, R., & Griffith, J. (1987). *Understanding life-style: The psychoclarity process.* Chicago: American Institute of Adlerian Studies.

Poynter, T. L. (1989). An evaluation of a group programme for male perpetrators of domestic violence. *Australian Journal of Sex, Marriage, and Family, 10,* 133–142.

Preziosa, A., Grassi, A., Gaggioli, A., & Riva, G. (2009). Therapeutic applications of the mobile phone. *British Journal of Guidance and Counselling, 37*(3), 313–325.

Price, B., & Rosenbaum, A. (2007, July). *A national survey of perpetrator intervention programs.* Paper presented at the International Family Violence and Child Victimization Research Conference, Portsmouth, NH.

Price, J. L. (2011). Findings from the National Vietnam Veterans' Readjustment Study. United States Department of Veterans Affairs. Retrieved from www.ptsd.va.gov/professional/pages/Vietnam-vets-study.asp

Price, M. (2007). TV violence harms children, APA member testifies to Congress. *Monitor on Psychology, 38*(8), 16.

Price, M. (2010). Suicide among preadolescents. *Monitor on Psychology, 41*(9), 52–53.

Price, R. H., Friedland, D. S., & Vinokur, A. D. (1998). Job loss: Hard times and eroded identity. In J. H. Harvey (Ed.), *Perspective on loss: A sourcebook* (pp. 303–316). Philadelphia: Brunner/Mazel.

Price, S. J., Price, C. A., & McKenry, P. C. (2010). Families coping with change. In S. J. Price, C. A. Price, & P. C. McKenry (Eds.), *Families and change: Coping with stressful events and transitions* (pp. 1–24). Los Angeles: Sage.

Pridmore, S., & Walter, G. (2013). Suicide prediction and prevention. *Australasian Psychiatry, 21*(4), 410–411.

Prigerson, H. G., & Jacobs, S. (2001). Traumatic grief as a distinct disorder: A rationale, consensus criteria, and a preliminary empirical test. In M. S. Stroebe, R. O. Hansson, & H. Schut (Eds.), *Handbook of bereavement research and practice: Consequences, coping, and caring* (pp. 613–641). Washington, DC: American Psychological Association.

Prigerson, H. G., Maciewjewski, P. K., Reynolds, C. F., Bierhals, A. J., Newsom, J. T., Fasiczka, A., et al. (1995). Inventory of Complicated Grief: A scale to measure maladaptive symptoms of loss. *Psychiatry Research, 59*(1/2), 65–79

Prigerson, H. G., Vanderwerker, L. C., & Maciejewski, P. K. (2008). A case for inclusion of prolonged grief disorder in DSM-V. In M. S. Stroebe, R. O. Hansson, H. Schut, & W. Stroebe (Eds.), *Handbook of bereavement research and practice: Advances in theory and intervention* (pp. 165–186). Washington, DC: American Psychological Association.

Prochaska, J. O., DiClemente, C. C., & Norcross, J. C. (1992). In search of how people change: Applications to addictive behaviors. *American Psychologist, 47,* 1102–1114.

Professional School Counseling. (2012). Standards for anti-bullying. *15*(3), 98.

Progoff, I. (1975). *At a journal workshop.* New York: Dialogue House Library.

Prothrow-Stith, D. (1987). *Violence prevention curriculum for adolescents.* Newton, MA: Education Development Center

Public Broadcasting Service. (2002). Faith and doubt at ground zero. [VHS Tape]. Retrieved from http://www.pbs.org/wgbh/pages/frontline/programs/

Purves, B. A., Phinney, A., Hulko, W., Puurveen, G., & Astell, A. (2015). Developing CIRCA-BC and exploring the role of the computer as a third participant in conversation. *American Journal of Alzheimer's Disease and Other Dementias, 30*(1), 101–107.

Pynoos, R. S., & Eth, S. (1986). Witness to violence: The child interview. *Journal of the American Academy of Child Psychiatry, 25*(3), 306–319.

Pynoos, R. S., & Nader, K. (1988). Psychological first aid and treatment approach to children exposed to community violence: Research implications. *Journal of Traumatic Stress, 1,* 445–473.

Pynoos, R. S., Steinberg, A. M., & Goenjian, A. (1996). Traumatic stress in childhood and adolescence: Recent developments and current controversies. In B. A. van der Kolk, A. C. McFarlane, & L. Weisaeth (Eds.), *Traumatic stress* (pp. 331–358). New York: Guilford Press.

Pynoos, R. S., Steinberg, A. M., Layne, C. M., Liang, L., Vivrette, R. L., Briggs, E.,. . . Fairbank, J. (2014). Modeling constellations of trauma exposure in the National Child Traumatic Stress Network Core Data Set. *Psychological Trauma: Theory, Research, Practice, and Policy, 6* (Supp. 1), S9–S17. Special Section.

Pyszczynski, T., Solomon, S., & Greenberg, J. (2003). *In the wake of 9/11: The psychology of terror.* Washington, DC: American Psychological Association.

Ørner, J. R. J., Kent, A., Pfefferbaun, B., Raphael, B., & Watson, P. (2006). The context of providing immediate postevent intervention. In E. C. Ritchie, P. J. Watson, & M. J. Friedman (Eds.), *Interventions following mass violence and disasters: Strategies for mental health practice* (pp. 121–133). New York: Guilford Press.

Q

Quero, S., Pererz-Ara, M., Breton-Lopez, J., Garcia- Palacios, A., Banos, R., & Botella, C. (2014). Acceptability of virtual reality interoceptive exposure for the treatment of panic disorder and agoraphobia. *British Journal of Guidance and Counselling, 42*(2), 123–137.

R

Rach-Beisel, J. M., Scott, J., & Dixon, L. (1999). Co-occurring severe mental illness and substance use disorders: A review of recent research. *Psychiatric Services, 50,* 1427–1434.

Rada, R. T. (1981). The violent patient: Rapid assessment and management. *Psychosomatics, 22,* 101–109.

Ragusea, A. S., & VandeCreek, L. (2003). Suggestions for the ethical practice of online psychotherapy. *Psychotherapy: Theory, Research, Practice, Training, 40*(1/2), 94–102.

Rainone, G. A., Schmeidler, J., Frank, B., & Smith, R. (2006). Violent behavior, substance use, and other delinquent behaviors among middle and high school students. *Youth Violence and Juvenile Justice, 4*(3), 247–265.

Raison, C. L., & Miller, A. H. (2003). When not enough is too much: The role of insufficient glucocorticoid signaling in the pathophysiology of stress-related disorders. *American Journal of Psychiatry, 169*, 1554–1565.

Ram, V., Webb-Murphy, J., McLay, R. N., Baird, A. R., Nebeker, B. J., . . . Johnson, S. (2014, August). *Interim analysis of head-to-head comparison of virtual reality exposure treatment for PTSD.* Paper presented at American Psychological Association 122nd Conference, Washington, DC.

Ramsey, J. L., & Blieszner, R. (2000). Transcending a lifetime of losses: The importance of spirituality in old age. In J. H. Harvey & E. D. Miller (Eds.), *Loss and trauma: General and close relationship perspectives* (pp. 225–236). Philadelphia: Brunner-Routledge.

Ramshaw, E. J. (2010). The personalization of postmodern postmortem rituals. *Pastoral Psychology, 59*(2), 171–178.

Randle, A. A., & Graham, C. A. (2011). A review of the evidence on the effects of intimate partner violence on men. *Psychology of Men and Masculinity, 12*(2), 97–111.

Rando, E. T. (1984). *Parental loss of a child.* Champaign, IL: Research Press.

Rando, T. A. (1984). *Grief, dying, and death: Clinical interventions for caregivers.* Champaign, IL: Research Press.

Rando, T. A. (1993). *Treatment of complicated mourning.* Champaign, IL: Research Press.

Rando, T. A. (1996). Complications in mourning traumatic death. In K. J. Doka (Ed.), *Living with grief after sudden loss: Suicide, homicide, accident, heart attack, stroke* (pp. 139–160). Washington, DC: Hospice Foundation of America.

Rando, T. A. (Ed.). (1986). *Parental loss of a child.* Champaign, IL: Research Press.

Range, L. M. (2005). No-suicide contracts. In R. I. Yufit & D. Lester (Eds.), *Assessment, treatment, and prevention of suicidal behavior* (pp. 181–203). New York: John Wiley & Sons.

Range, L. M., Campbell, C., Kovac, S. H., Marion-Jones, M., Aldridge, H., Kogos, S., & Crump, Y. (2002). No-suicide contracts: An overview and recommendations. *Death Studies, 26*, 51–74.

Raphael, B. (1977). Preventive intervention with the recently bereaved. *Archives of General Psychiatry, 34*, 1450–1454.

Raphael, B. (1984). *The anatomy of bereavement.* New York: Basic Books.

Raphael, B. (1986). *When disaster strikes: How individuals and communities cope with catastrophe.* New York: Basic Books.

Raphael, B. (1999). Conclusion: Debriefing—Science, belief, and wisdom. In B. Raphael & J. P. Wilson (Eds.), *Psychological debriefing: Theory, practice, and evidence* (pp. 351–359). New York: Cambridge University Press.

Raphael, B. (2000). *Disaster mental health response handbook: An educational resource for mental health professionals involved in disaster management.* New South Wales, Australia: New South Wales Institute of Psychiatry.

Raphael, B., & Dobson, M. (2000). Bereavement. In J. H. Harvey & E. D. Miller (Eds.), *Loss and trauma: General and close relationship perspectives* (pp. 45–61). Philadelphia: Brunner-Routledge.

Raphael, B., & Minkov, C. (1999). Abnormal grief. *Current Opinion in Psychiatry, 12*, 99–102.

Raphael, B., & Wilson, J. (2000). *Psychological debriefing: Theory, practice, and evidence.* Cambridge UK: Cambridge University Press.

Raphael, B., Meldrum, L., & McFarland, A. C. (1995). Does debriefing after psychological trauma work? *British Medical Journal, 310*, 1479–1480.

Rapoport, L. (1967). Crisis-oriented short-term case work. *Social Services Review, 41*, 31–44.

Raskin, N. J., & Rogers, C. R. (1995). Person-centered therapy. In R. J. Corsini & D. Wedding (Eds.), *Current psychotherapies* (5th ed.). Itasca, IL: F. E. Peacock, pp. 130–165.

Ratnarajah, D., & Schofield, M. J. (2008). Survivors' narrative of the impact of parental suicide. *Suicidal and Life-Threatening Behavior, 38*, 618–630.

Ratts, M., Ayers, L., & Bright, M. (2009). Sticks and stones. *ASCA School Counselor, 47*(1), 20–25.

Ratts, M. J., & Pedersen, P. B. (2014). *Counseling for multiculturalism and social justice: Integration, theory and practice* (4th ed.). Alexandria, VA: American Counseling Association.

Read, J., Bollinger, A., & Sharansky, E. (2003). Assessment of comorbid substance abuse disorder and posttraumatic stress disorder. In P. Ouimette & P. Brown (Eds.), *Trauma and substance abuse: Causes, consequences, and treatment of comorbid disorders* (pp. 111–125). Washington, DC: American Psychological Association.

Reamer, F. G. (2015). Eye on ethics: The challenge of distributive justice, *Social Work Today*. Retrieved from http://www.socialworktoday.com/news/eoe_011515.shtml

Rebmann, T., Carrico, R., & English, J. F. (2008). Lessons public health professionals learned from past disasters. *Public Health Nursing, 25*, 344–352.

Red Cross. (2015). *What we do.* Retrieved from www.redcross.org/what-we-do

Reddy, M., Borum, R., Berglund, J., Vossekuil, B., Fen, R., & Modzeleski, W. (2001). Evaluating risk for targeted violence in schools: Comparing risk assessment, threat assessment, and other approaches. *Psychology in the Schools, 38*, 157–173.

Redmon, L. M. (1996). Sudden violent death. In K. J. Doka (Ed.), *Living with grief after sudden loss: Suicide, homicide, accident, heart attack, stroke* (pp. 53–72). Washington, DC: Hospice Foundation of America.

Reese, M. T. (2009). Compassion fatigue and spirituality with emergency health care providers. *Dissertation Abstracts International: Section B. The Sciences and Engineering, 69*(12), 7843.

Reese, R. J., Conoley, C. W., & Brossart, D. F. (2002). Effectiveness of telephone counseling: Field-based investigation. *Journal of Counseling Psychology, 49*(2), 233–242.

Reese, R. J., Conoley, C. W., & Brossart, D. F. (2006). The attractiveness of telephone counseling: An empirical investigation of client perceptions. *Journal of Counseling & Development, 84*(1), 54–60.

Reeves, N. C. (2011). Death acceptance through ritual. *Death Studies, 35*(5), 408–419.

Regehr, C., Cadell, S., & Jansen, K. (1999). Perceptions of control and long-term recovery from rape. *American Journal of Orthopsychiatry, 69*, 110–115.

Reger, G., Holloway, K., Candy, C., Rothbaum, B., Difede, J., Rizzo, A., & Gahm, G. (2011). Effectiveness of virtual reality exposure therapy for active duty soldiers in a military mental health clinic. *Journal of Traumatic Stress, 24*(1), 93–96.

Reger, G. M., Rizzo, A. A., & Gahm, D. A. (2015). Initial development and dissemination of virtual reality exposure therapy for combat-related PTSD. In M. P. Safir, H. S. Wallach, & A. Rizzo (Eds.), *Future directions in post-traumatic stress disorder: Prevention, diagnosis and treatment* (pp. 289–302). New York: Springer.

Reich, W., Shayka, J. J., & Taibleson, C. (1991). *Diagnostic Interview for Children and Adolescents (DICA).* St. Louis, MO: Washington University.

Reichle, B., Schneider, A., & Montada, L. (1998). How do observers of victimization preserve their belief in a just world cognitively or actionally? Findings from a longitudinal study. In

L. Montanda & J. Lerner (Eds.), *Responses to victimizations and belief in a just world* (pp. 55–87). New York: Plenum Press.

Reinecke, A., Thilo, K., Filippini, N., Croft, A., & Hamer, C. (2014). Predicting rapid response to cognitive-behavioural treatment for panic disorder: The role of hippocampus, insula, and dorsolateral prefrontal cortex. *Behaviour Research and Therapy, 62,* 120–128.

Reis, C., & Cornell, D. (2008). An evaluation of suicide gatekeeper training for school counselors and teachers. *Professional School Counseling, 11*(6), 386–394.

Reitmeyer, R. (2000). Dog gone? From cats to snakes, counselors help heal human hearts following a pet loss. *Counseling Today, 42*(9), 1, 26–27.

Reivich, K. J., Seligman, M. P., & McBride, S. (2011). Master resilience training in the U.S. Army. *American Psychologist, 66*(1), 25–34.

Remboldt, C. (1994). *Violence in schools: The enabling factor.* Minneapolis, MN: Johnson Institute.

Remer, R., & Ferguson, R. A. (1995). Becoming a secondary survivor of sexual assault. *Journal of Counseling and Development, 73,* 407–413.

Remley, T. P., & Herlihy, B. P. (2010). Ethical, legal and professional issues in counseling (3rd ed.). Upper Saddle River, NJ: Merrill/Prentice Hall.

Remley, T. P., & Herlihy, B. P. (2014). Ethical, legal and professional issues in counseling (4th ed.). Upper Saddle River, NJ: Merrill/Prentice Hall.

Ren, C. H. (2000). Understanding and managing the dynamics of linked crisis events. *Disaster Prevention and Management, 9*(1), 12–17.

Renzetti, C. (1992). *Violent betrayal: Partner abuse in lesbian relationships.* Newbury Park, CA: Sage.

Renzetti, C. (1996). The poverty of services for battered lesbians. In C. M. Renzetti & C. H. Miley (Eds.), *Violence in gay and lesbian domestic partnerships* (pp. 61–68). Binghamton, NY: Haworth Press.

Repine, T. B., Lisagor, P., & Cohen, D. J. (2005). The dynamics and ethics of triage: Rationing care in hard times. *Military Medicine, 170,* 505–509.

Resick, P. A., & Schnicke, M. K. (1993). *Cognitive processing therapy for rape victims: A treatment manual.* Thousand Oaks, CA: Sage.

Resick, P. A., Monson, C. M., & Chard, K. M. (2008). *Cognitive processing therapy: Veterans/Military version.* Washington, DC: Department of Veterans Affairs.

Resick, P. A., Monson, C. M., & Gutner, C. (2007). Psychological treatments for PTSD. In N. J. Friedman, T. M. Keane, & P. A. Resick (Eds.), *Handbook of PTSD: Science and practice* (pp. 330–358). New York: Guilford Press.

Resnik, H. (1969). Psychological resynthesis: A clinical approach to the survivors of a death by suicide. In E. Shneidman & M. Ortega (Eds.), *Aspects of depression* (pp. 124–148). Boston: Little, Brown.

Rest, J. R. (1984). Research on moral development: Implications for training psychologists. *The Counseling Psychologist, 12*(3), 19–29.

Rew, L. (1989). Long-term effects of childhood sexual exploitation. *Issues in Mental Health Nursing, 10,* 229–244.

Reyes, G., Elhai, J. D., & Ford, J. D. (Eds.). (2008). *The encyclopedia of psychological trauma.* Hoboken, NJ: John Wiley & Sons.

Rhee, W. K., Merbaum, M., Strube, M. J., & Self, S. (2005). Efficacy of brief telephone psychotherapy with callers to a suicide hotline. *Suicide and Life-Threatening Behavior, 35*(3), 317–328.

Ribeiro, J. D., Bodell, L. P., Hames, J. L., Hagan, C. R., & Joiner, T. (2013). An empirically based approach to the assessment and management of suicidal behavior. *Journal of Psychotherapy Integration, 23*(3), 207–221.

Rice, M., & Harris, G. (1995). Violent recidivism: Assessing predictive validity. *Journal of Consulting and Clinical Psychology, 63,* 737–748.

Richards, P. S., Hardman, R. K., Lea, T., & Berrett, M. E. (2015). Religious and spiritual assessment of trauma survivors. In D. F. Walker, C. A. Courtois, & J. Aten (Eds.), *Spiritually oriented psychotherapy for trauma.* (pp. 77–102). Washington, DC: American Psychological Association.

Richman, J. (1994). Psychotherapy with older suicidal adults. In A. A. Leenaars, J. T. Maltsberger, & R. A. Neimeyer (Eds.), *Treatment of suicidal people* (pp. 101–113). Washington, DC: Taylor & Francis.

Ricks, J. L., Vaughan, C., & Dziegielewski, S. F. (2002). Domestic violence among lesbian couples. In A. R. Roberts (Ed.), *Handbook of domestic violence: Intervention strategies* (pp. 451–463). New York: Oxford University Press.

Ridley, C. R. (1995). *Overcoming unintentional racism in counseling and therapy: A practitioner's guide to intentional intervention.* Newbury Park, CA: Sage.

Ridley, C. R., & Shaw-Ridley, M. (2011). Multicultural counseling competencies: An analysis of research on clients' perceptions: Comments on Owens, Leach, Wampold, and Rodolfa. *Journal of Counseling Psychology, 58*(1), 16–21.

Riethmayer, J. (2002a). Dealing with the impact of trauma. In D. D. Bass & R. Yep (Eds.), *Terrorism, trauma, and tragedies: A counselor's guide to preparing and responding* (pp. 107–109). Alexandria, VA: American Counseling Association.

Riethmayer, J. (2002b). Explaining terrorism to children. In D. D. Bass & R. Yep (Eds.), *Terrorism, trauma, and tragedies: A counselor's guide to preparing and responding* (pp. 27–31). Alexandria, VA: American Counseling Association.

Riggar, T. F. (1985). *Stress burnout: An annotated bibliography.* Carbondale: Southern Illinois University Press.

Ringenbach, R. (2009). A comparison between counselors who practice meditation and those who do not on compassion fatigue, compassion satisfaction, burnout, and self-compassion. *Dissertation Abstracts International: Section B. The Science and Engineering, 69*(6), 3820.

Riordan, R. J., & Allen, L. (1989). Grief counseling: A funeral home–based model. *Journal of Counseling and Development, 67,* 424–425.

Ristock, J. L. (1999, August). *Exploring dynamics in abusive lesbian relationships.* Paper presented at the 107th Annual Convention of the American Psychological Association, Symposium on Outing Same-Sex Partner Abuse, Boston.

Ritter, C., Teller, J., Marcussen, K., Munetz, M., & Teasdale, B. (2011). Crisis Intervention Team officer dispatch, assessment, and disposition: Interactions with individuals with severe illness. *International Journal of Law and Psychiatry, 34*(1), 30–38.

Riva, G. (2003). Virtual environments in clinical psychology. *Psychotherapy: Theory, Research, Practice, Training, 40*(1/2), 68–76.

Rizvi, S. L. (2011). The therapeutic relationship in dialectical behavior therapy for suicidal individuals. In K. Michel & D. A. Jobes (Eds.), *Building a therapeutic alliance with the suicidal patient* (pp. 255–274). Washington, DC: American Psychological Association.

Rizzo, A., Difede, J., Rothbaum, B., Buckwater, J., Daughtry, J., & Reger, G. M. (2015). Update an expansion of the virtual Iraq/Afghanistan PTSD exposure therapy system. In M. P. Safir, H. S. Wallach, & A. Rizzo (Eds.), *Future directions in post-traumatic stress disorder: Prevention, diagnosis and treatment* (pp. 303–328). New York: Springer.

Robbins, S., & Bell, M. (2008). *Second life for dummies.* Indianapolis, IN: Wiley.

Robers, S., Zhang, J., Truman, J., & Snyder, T. D. (2010, November). *Indicators of school crime and safety: 2010.* U.S. Department of Education & U.S. Department of Justice. Retrieved from bjs.ojp.usdoj.gov/content/pub/pdf/iscs10.pdf

Robert, T. E., & Kelly, V. A. (2015). *Critical incidents in integrating spirituality into counseling.* Alexandria,VA: American Counseling Association.

Roberts, A. R. (1991). Crisis intervention units and centers in the United States. In A. R. Roberts (Ed.), *Contemporary perspectives on crisis intervention and prevention* (pp. 18–31). Upper Saddle River, NJ: Prentice Hall.

Roberts, A. R. (2002). Myths, facts, and realities regarding battered women and their children: An overview. In A. R. Roberts (Ed.), *Handbook of domestic violence: Intervention strategies* (pp. 3–22). New York: Oxford University Press.

Roberts, A. R. (2005). *Crisis intervention handbook: Assessment, treatment, and research* (3rd ed.). New York: Oxford University Press.

Roberts, A. R. (Ed.). (1991). *Contemporary perspectives on crisis intervention and prevention.* Upper Saddle River, NJ: Prentice Hall.

Roberts, A. R. (Ed.). (2005). *Crisis intervention handbook* (3rd ed.). New York: Oxford University Press.

Roberts, A. R., & Kurst-Swanger, K. (2002). Police responses to battered women: Past, present, and future. In A. R. Roberts (Ed.), *Handbook of domestic violence: Intervention strategies* (pp. 101–126). New York: Oxford University Press.

Roberts, A. R., & Roberts, B. S. (2002). A comprehensive model for crisis intervention with battered women and their children. In A. R. Roberts (Ed.), *Handbook of domestic violence: Intervention strategies* (pp. 365–395). New York: Oxford University Press.

Roberts, A. R., & Roberts, B. S. (2005). A comprehensive model for crisis intervention with battered women and their children. In A. R. Roberts (Ed.), *Crisis intervention handbook* (3rd ed., pp. 441–482). New York: Oxford University Press.

Robertson, H, (2013). Common crises. *ASCA School Counselor, 50*(4), 40–45

Robinson, G. E. (2003). International perspectives on violence against women: Introduction. *Archives of Women's Mental Health, 6*(3), 155–156.

Robinson, H. M., Sigman, M. R., & Wilson, J. P. (1997). Duty-related stressors and PTSD symptoms in suburban police officers. *Psychological Reports, 81*, 835–845.

Rodesch, C. K. (1994, April). *Keeping the counselor sane.* Paper presented at the Eighteenth Annual Convening of Crisis Intervention Personnel, Chicago.

Rodriguez, D., & Bernal, G. (2012). Frameworks, models, and guidelines for cultural adaption. In G. Bernal & D. Rodriguez (Eds.), *Cultural adaptions: Tools for evidence-based practice with diverse populations* (pp. 23–44). Washington, DC: American Psychological Association.

Rofman, E. S., Askinazi, C., & Fant, E. (1980). The prediction of dangerous behavior in emergency civil commitment. *American Journal of Psychiatry, 137*, 1061–1064.

Rogers, C. R. (1961). *On becoming a person.* Boston: Houghton Mifflin.

Rogers, C. R. (1969). *Freedom to learn: A view of what education might become.* Columbus, OH: Merrill.

Rogers, C. R. (1977). *Carl Rogers on personal power: Inner strength and its revolutionary impact.* New York: Delacorte.

Rogers, J. R. (2001a). Suicide risk assessment. In E. R. Welfel & R. E. Ingersoll (Eds.), *The mental health desk reference* (pp. 259–263). New York: John Wiley & Sons.

Rogers, J. R. (2001b). Theoretical grounding: The "missing link" in suicide research. *Journal of Counseling and Development, 79*, 16–25.

Rogers, J. R., Bromley, J. L., Christopher, J., & Lester, D. (2007). Content analysis of suicide notes as a test for the motivational component of the existentialist- constructivist model of suicide. *Journal of Counseling and Development, 85*, 182–188.

Rogerson, M. D., Gottlieb, M. C., Handelsman, M. M., Knapp, S., & Younggren, J. (2011). Nonrational processes in ethical decision making. *American Psychologist, 66*, 614–623.

Rohland, B. M., Saleh, S. S., Rohrer, J. E., & Romitti, P. A. (2000). Acceptability of telepsychiatry to a rural population. *Psychiatric Services, 51*(5), 672–674.

Rolland, J. S. (2012). Mastering family challenges in serious illness and disability. In F. Walsh (Ed.), *Normal family processes: Growing diversity and complexity* (4th ed., pp. 452–482). New York: Guildford Press.

Romanoff, B. (1993). When a child dies: Special consideration for providing mental health counseling for bereaved parents. *Journal of Mental Health Counseling, 15*, 384–393.

Romig, C. A., & Gruenke, C. (1991). The use of metaphor to overcome inmate resistance to mental health counseling. *Journal of Counseling and Development, 69*(4), 414–418.

Ronan, G. F., Dreer, L., Maurelli, K., Wollerman-Ronan, D., & Gerhart, J. (2014). *Practitioner's guide to empirically supported measures of anger, aggression, and violence: ABCT clinical assessment series.* New York: Springer.

Rose, R. D. (2014). Self-guided multimedia stress management and resilience training. *The Journal of Positive Psychology, 9*(6), 489–493.

Rosenbaum, A., & Kunkel, T. S. (2009). Group interventions for intimate partner violence. In K. D. O'Leary & E. Woodin (Eds.), *Psychology and physical aggression in couples: Causes and interventions* (pp. 191–210). Washington, DC: American Psychological Association.

Rosenberg, S. (2004). Inoculation effect in prevention of increased verbal aggression in schools. *Psychological Reports, 95*(2), 1219–1226.

Rosenblatt, P. C. (2010). Shame and death in cultural context. In J. Kauffman (Ed.), *The shame of death, grief, and trauma* (pp. 113–137). New York: Routledge/Taylor & Francis Group.

Rosencrans, B. (1997). *The last secret: Daughters sexually abused by mothers.* Brandon, VT: Safer Society Press.

Rosenfeld, B. (1992). Court-ordered treatment of spousal abuse. *Clinical Psychology Review, 12*(2), 205–226.

Rosenfeld, L. B., Caye, J. S., Ayalon, O., & Lahad, M. (2005). *When their world falls apart: Helping families and children manage the effects of disasters.* Washington, DC: National Association of Social Workers Press.

Rosenheck, R., & Fontana, A. (1998). Warrior fathers and warrior sons: Intergenerational aspects of trauma. In Y. Danieli (Ed.), *International handbook of multigenerational legacies of trauma* (pp. 225–242). New York: Plenum Press.

Rosner, R., & Powell, S. (2006). Posttraumatic growth after war. In L. G. Calhoun & R. G. Tedeschi (Eds.), *Handbook of posttraumatic growth after war* (pp. 197–213). Mahwah, NJ: Erlbaum.

Rosner, R., Kruse, J., & Hagl, M. (2010). A meta-analysis of interventions for bereaved children and adolescents. *Death Studies, 34*(2), 99–136.

Ross, E. B. (1999, April). *After suicide: A ray of hope.* Paper presented at the Twenty-Third Annual Convening of Crisis Intervention Personnel, Chicago.

Ross, M., & Glesson, C. (1991). Bias in social work intervention with battered women. *Journal of Social Services Research, 14*, 79–105.

Roth, L. (2000, April). *Preventing school violence through community organization*. Proceedings of the Twenty-Fourth Annual Convening of Crisis Intervention Personnel, Chicago.

Rothschild, B. (2000). *The body remembers: The psychophysiology of trauma and trauma treatment*. New York: Norton.

Rothschild, B. (2010). *8 Keys to safe recovery*. New York: Norton.

Rouse, B. A. (1998). *Substance abuse and mental health statistics source book*. Washington, DC: U.S. Government Printing Office.

Rowan, E. L. (2006). *Understanding child sexual abuse*. Jackson: University of Mississippi Press.

Rowe, L., Jouriles, E., & McDonald, R. (2015). Reduced sexual victimization among adolescent girls: A randomized controlled pilot trial of My Voice, My Choices. *Behavior Therapy, 46*(3), 315–327.

Rowett, C. (1986). *Violence in social work*. Cambridge, MA: Institute of Criminology.

Roy, A., Nielsen, D., Rylander, G., & Sarchiapone, M. (2000). The genetics of suicidal behavior. In K. Hawton & K. Van Heeringen (Eds.), *The international handbook of suicide and attempted suicide* (pp. 209–222). Chichester, England: John Wiley & Sons.

Roysircar, G. (2013). Disaster counseling: A Haitian family case post January 12, 2010 earthquake. In S. Poyrazli & C. E. Thompson (Eds.), *International case studies in mental health* (pp. 155–180). Thousand Oaks, CA: Sage.

Roysircar, G., Podkova, M., & Pignatiello, V. (2013). Crisis intervention, social class, and counseling: Macrolevel disaster effects. In W. Ming Liu (Ed.), *The Oxford handbook of social class in counseling*, Oxford Library of Psychology (pp. 144–163). New York: Oxford University Press,

Ruane, M. E. (2007, April 22). Cho's bizarre behavior alarmed suite mate. *Memphis Commercial Appeal*, pp. 1A, 5A.

Ruben, I., Wolkon, G., & Yamamoto, J. (1980). Physical attacks on psychiatric residents by patients. *Journal of Nervous and Mental Disease, 168*, 243–245.

Rubin, L. J. (1996). Childhood sexual abuse: Whose memories are faulty? *Counseling Psychologist, 24*, 140–143.

Rubin, R. (1999, June). *Crisis intervention*. Paper presented at the American School Counselor Association Convention, Phoenix, AZ.

Rubin, S. (1999). The two-track model of bereavement: Overview, retrospect and prospect. *Death Studies, 23*(8), 681–714.

Rubin, S., & Yasien-Esmael, H. (2004). Loss and bereavement among Israel's Muslims: Acceptance of God's will, grief, and the relationship of the deceased. *Omega: Journal of Death and Dying, 49*(2), 149–162.

Rudd, M. D. (2004a). Cognitive therapy for suicidality: An integrative, comprehensive, and practical approach to conceptualization. *Journal of Contemporary Psychotherapy, 34*, 59–72.

Rudd, M. D. (2004b). University counseling centers: Looking more and more like community clinics. *Professional Psychology: Research and Practice, 35*(3), 316–317.

Rudd, M. D., Joiner, T. E., Jr., & Rajab, M. H. (2001). *Treating suicidal behavior: An effective, time-limited approach*. New York: Guilford Press.

Rudick, C. D. (2012). Therapist self care: Being a healing counselor rather than a wounded healer. In L. Lopez Levers (Ed.), *Trauma counseling: Theories and interventions* (pp. 554–568). New York: Springer.

Ruesch, J. (1973). *Therapeutic communication*. New York: W. W. Norton.

Ruiz, N. J., & Lipford-Sanders, J. A. (1999, October). Online counseling: Further considerations. *Counseling Today, 42*(4), 12, 33.

Rupert, P. A., Miller, A. O., & Dorociak, K. E. (2015). Preventing burnout: What does the research tell us? *Professional Psychology Research and Practice, 46*(3), 168–174.

Rural Assistance Center. (2011). *Health professional shortage area: Mental health*. Retrieved March 20, 2011, from http://www.raconlineorg/info_guides/mental_health /#bib

Russell, B., & Uhlemann, M. R. (1994). Women surviving an abusive relationship: Grief and the process of change. *Journal of Counseling and Development, 72*, 362–367.

Russell, S. T., Ryan, C., Toomey, R. B., Diaz, R. B., & Sanchez, J. (2011). Lesbian, gay, bisexual, and transgender adolescent school victimization: Implications for young adult health and adjustment. *Journal of School Health, 81*(5), 223–230.

Ruzek, J. I. (2006). Models of early intervention following mass violence and other trauma. In E. C. Ritchie, P. J. Watson, & M. J. Friedman (Eds.), *Interventions following mass violence and disasters: Strategies for mental health practice* (pp. 16–36). New York: Guilford Press.

Ryan, E. P., Hart, V., Messick, D., Jeffrey, A., & Burnette, M. (2004). A prospective study of assault against staff by youths in a state psychiatric hospital. *Psychiatric Services, 55*(6), 665–670.

Rynearson, E. K. (2010). The clergy, the clinician, and the narrative of violent death. *Pastoral Psychology, 59*(2), 179–189.

S

Saakvitne, K. W. (2002). Shared trauma: The therapist's increased vulnerability. *Psychoanalytic Dialogues, 12*(3), 443–449.

Saakvitne, K. W., & Pearlman, L. A. (1996). *Transforming the pain: A workbook on vicarious traumatization*. New York: W. W. Norton.

Sabella, R. A. (2010, July). *Cyberbullying*. Paper presented at the American School Counselor Conference, Boston.

Sadowski, P. M., & Loesch, L. C. (1993). Using children's drawings to detect potential child sexual abuse. *Elementary School Guidance and Counseling, 28*, 115–123.

Sage, R., & Dietz, W. (1994). Television viewing and violence in children: The pediatrician's agent for change. *Paediatrics, 94*(4), 600–607.

Saigh, P. A. (1987). In vitro flooding of childhood posttraumatic stress disorders: A systematic replication. *Professional School Psychology, 2*, 135–146.

Salloum, A., & Overstreet, S. (2008). Evaluation of individual and group grief and trauma interventions of children post disaster. *Journal of Clinical Child and Adolescent Psychology, 37*, 495–507.

Salloum, A., Kondraf, D., Johnco, C., & Olson, K. (2015). The role of self-care on compassion satisfaction, burnout, and secondary trauma, among child welfare workers. *Children and Youth Services Review, 49*, 54–61.

Salston, M. D., & Figley, C. R. (2003). Secondary traumatic stress effects of working with survivors of criminal victimization. *Journal of Traumatic Stress, 16*(2), 167–174.

Salter, A. C. (1988). *Treating child sex offenders and victims: A practical guide*. Newbury Park, CA: Sage.

Salter, A. C. (1995). *Transforming trauma: A guide to understanding and treating adult survivors of child sexual abuse*. Newbury Park, CA: Sage.

Salter, M. (2013). *Organised sexual abuse*. New York: Routledge.

Salzer, M. S., & Bickman, L. (1999). The short- and long-term psychological impact of disasters: Implications for mental health interventions and policy. In R. Gist & B. Lubin (Eds.), *Response to disaster: Psychological, community and ecological approaches* (pp. 63–82). New York: Brunner/Mazel.

SAMHSA. (2014). SAMHSA's suicide prevention efforts. Retrieved from http://www.samsha.gov/suicide-prevention/samshas -efforts

Samide, L. L., & Stockton, R. (2002). Letting go of grief: Bereavement groups for children in the school setting. *Journal of Specialists in Group Work, 27*(2), 192–204.

Sanday, P. R. (1998). The socio-cultural context of rape: A cross-cultural study. In M. E. Odem & J. Clay-Warner (Eds.), *Confronting rape and sexual assault* (pp. 93–108). Wilmington, DE: Scholarly Resources.

Sandberg, D. N., Crabbs, S. K., & Crabbs, M. A. (1988). Legal issues in child abuse: Questions and answers for counselors. *Elementary School Guidance and Counseling, 22*, 268–274.

Sanders, B., & Moore, D. L. (1999). Childhood maltreatment and date rape. *Journal of Interpersonal Violence, 14*, 115–124.

Sanders, C. M., Mauger, P. A., & Strong, P. N. (1985). *A manual for the Grief Experience Inventory.* Palo Alto, CA: Consulting Psychologists Press.

Sanderson, C. (2013). *Counseling skills for working with trauma: Healing from child sexual abuse, sexual violence, and domestic abuse.* London, UK: Jessica Kingsley Publishers.

Sandhu, D. S. (2000, June). *Psycho-cultural profiles of violent students: Implications for counseling and therapy.* Paper presented at the American School Counselor Association Convention, Cherry Hill, NJ.

Sandler, I. N., Ayers, T. S., Wolchik, S. A., Tein, J. Y., Kwok, O. M., Haine, R., et al. (2003). The Family Bereavement Program: Efficacy evaluation of a theory-based prevention program for parentally bereaved children and adolescents. *Journal of Consulting and Clinical Psychology, 71*(3), 587–600.

Sansone, R. A., Chu, J., & Wiederman, M. (2011). Sexual behavior and borderline personality disorder among female psychiatric inpatients. *International Journal of Psychiatry in Clinical Practice, 15*(1), 69–73.

Santa Ana, E. J., Saladin, M. E., Back, S., Waldrop, A., Spratt, E., McRae, A., et al. (2006). PTSD and the HPA axis: Difference in response to the cold pressor task among individuals with child vs. adult trauma. *Psychoneuroendocrinology, 31*(4), 501–509.

Santiago, G. B. (2002). Latina battered women: Barriers to service delivery and cultural considerations. In A. R. Roberts (Ed.), *Handbook of domestic violence: Intervention strategies* (pp. 464–471). New York: Oxford University Press.

Santrock, J. W. (1999). *Life-span development* (7th ed.). Boston: McGraw-Hill.

Sarri, S. (2005). *A bolt from the blue: Coping with disaster and acute trauma.* London: Jessica Kingsley.

Sartin, R. M. (2005). Characteristics associated with domestic violence perpetration: An examination of factors related to response and the utility of a batterer typology. *Dissertation Abstracts International: Section B. The Sciences and Engineering,* 4303.

Sass, S., Berenbaum, H., & Abrams, E. (2013). Discomfort with emotion moderates distress reduction in a brief mindfulness intervention. *International Journal of Behavioral Consultation and Therapy, 7*(4), 24–27.

Sassetti, M. R. (1993). Domestic violence. *Primary Care, 20,* 289–303.

Saufler, C. (2010, July). *Bringing the brain to bullying prevention.* Paper presented at the American School Counselor Conference, Boston.

Saunders, D. G. (1992). A typology of men who batter: Three types derived from cluster analysis. *American Journal of Orthopsychiatry, 62*, 264–275.

Saunders, D. G., & Hanusa, D. (1986). Cognitive behavioral treatment of men who batter: The short-term effects of group therapy. *Journal of Family Violence, 1*, 357–372.

Saunders, M. (2010, Summer). CIT statistics. *The Team News.* CIT International. Retrieved March 20, 2011, from http://www .citinternational.org/news-letters/139-citintnewsletters.html

Savicki, V. (2002). *Burnout across thirteen cultures: Stress and coping in child and youth care workers.* Westport, CT: Praeger.

Savicki, V. (2002). *Burnout across thirteen cultures: Stress and coping in child and youth care workers.* Westport, CT: Prager.

Savicki, V., & Cooley, E. J. (1982). Implications of burnout research and theory for counselor education. *Personnel and Guidance Journal, 60*, 415–419.

Savicki, V., & Cooley, E. J. (1987). The relationship of work environment and client contact to burnout in mental health professionals. *Journal of Counseling and Development, 65*, 249–252.

Sawyer, R. G., Pinciaro, P. J., & Jessell, J. K. (1998). Effects of coercion and verbal consent on university students' perception of date rape. *American Journal of Health Behavior, 22*, 46–53.

Saxe, G. N., Ellis, B. H., & Kaplow, J. B. (2007). *Collaborative treatment of traumatized children and teens: The trauma systems therapy approach.* New York: Guilford Press.

Saylor, C. F., Cowart, B. L., Lipovsky, J. A., Jackson, C., & Finch, A. (2003). Media exposure to September 11: Elementary school students' experiences and posttraumatic symptoms. *American Behavioral Scientist, 46*(12), 1622–1642.

Saywitz, K., & Dorado, J. (2013). Interviewing children about sexual abuse. In G. Koocher, J. Norcross, & B. Greene (Eds.), *Psychologists' desk reference* (3rd ed., pp. 425–432). New York: Oxford University Press.

Scaer, R. (2014). *The body bears the burden: Trauma, dissociation, and disease* (3rd ed.). New York: Routledge/Taylor & Francis Group.

Scales, K., & Winter, B. (1991, April). *Anger management for spouse abusers: The interpersonal transaction group.* Paper presented at Crisis Convening XV, Chicago.

Scarce, M. (1997). Same-sex rape of male college students. *Journal of College Health, 45*(5), 171–173.

Schaefer, C. E., & Reid, S. E. (Eds.). (2001). *Game play* (2nd ed.). New York: John Wiley & Sons.

Schaefer-Schiumo, K., & Ginsberg, A. (2003). The effectiveness of the warning signs program in high school youth about violence prevention: A study with urban high school students. *Professional School Counseling, 7*(1), 1–8.

Schaufeli, W. B. (2006). The balance of give and take: Toward a social exchange model of burnout. *Revue Internationale de Psychologie Sociale, 19*(1), 87–131.

Schechter, S. (1982). *Women and male violence.* Boston: South End Press.

Schetky, D. H. (1990). A review of the literature on the long-term effects of childhood sexual abuse. In R. P. Kluft (Ed.), *Incest-related syndromes of adult psychopathology* (pp. 35–54). Washington, DC: American Psychiatric Press.

Schlesinger, L. B. (2006). Celebrity stalking, homicide, and suicide: A psychological autopsy. *International Journal of Offender Therapy and Comparative Criminology, 50*(1), 39–46.

Schliebner, C. T., & Peregoy, J. J. (1994). Unemployment effects on the family and the child: Interventions for counselors. *Journal of Counseling and Development, 72*, 368–372.

Schlosser, L. Z., Foley, P. F., Stein, E. P., & Holmwood, J. R. (2010). Why does counseling psychology exclude religion? A content analysis and methodological critique. In J. G. Ponterotto, J. M. Casas, L. A. Suzuki, & C. M. Alexander (Eds.), *Handbook of multicultural counseling* (3rd ed., pp. 453–466). Thousand Oaks, CA: Sage.

Schmidt, C. K., & Welsh, A. C. (2010). College adjustment and subjective well-being when coping with family member's illness. *Journal of Counseling and Development, 88,* 397–406.

Schneider, J. (1984). *Stress, loss, and grief: Understanding their origins and growth potential.* Baltimore, MD: University Park Press.

Schoenberg, B. M. (Ed.). (1980). *Bereavement counseling: A multidisciplinary handbook.* Westport, CT: Greenwood Press.

Schonfeld, D. J. (1989). Crisis intervention for bereavement support: A model of intervention in the children's school. *Clinical Pediatrics, 28,* 27–33.

School Safety Advisory Council. (2015, July). *National School Safety Conference.* Retrieved from www.schoolsafety.org

School Violence Resource Center. (2003). *Weapons and schools: II. Fact sheet.* Fayetteville: University of Arkansas System.

Schore, A. N. (2013). Relation trauma, brain development, and dissociation. In J. Ford & C. A. Courtois (Eds.), *Treating complex stress disorders in children and adolescents: Scientific foundations and therapeutic models* (pp. 3–23). New York: Guilford Press.

Schreier, H., Ladakakos, C., Morabito, D., Chapman, L., & Knudson, M. (2005). Posttraumatic stress symptoms in children after mild to moderate pediatric trauma: A longitudinal examination of symptom prevalence, correlates, and parent–child symptom reporting. *Journal of Trauma-Injury Infection and Critical Care, 58*(2), 352–363.

Schrumpf, F., Crawford, D. K., & Bodine, R. J. (1997). *Peer mediation: Conflict resolution in schools: Student manual* (rev. ed.). Champaign, IL: Research Press.

Schumacher, J. A., Fals-Stewart, W., & Leonard, K. K. (2003). Domestic violence treatment referrals for men seeking alcohol treatment. *Journal of Substance Abuse Treatment, 24*(3), 279–283.

Schutte, N. S., Bouleige, L., Fix, J. L., & Malouff, J. M. (1986). Returning to partner after leaving a crisis shelter: A decision faced by battered women. *Journal of Social Behavior and Personality, 1,* 295–298.

Schutte, N. S., Malouff, J. M., & Doyle, J. S. (1988). The relationship between characteristics of the victim, persuasive techniques of the batterer, and returning to a battering relationship. *Journal of Social Psychology, 128,* 605–610.

Schuurman, D. L., & DeCristofaro, J. (2007). After a parent's death: Group, family, and individual therapy to help children. In N. B. Webb (Ed.), *Play therapy with children in crisis* (pp. 173–196). New York: Guilford Press.

Schwartz, A. J. (2006). Are college students more disturbed today? Stability in the acuity and qualitative character of psychopathology of college counseling center clients: 1992–1993 through 2001–2002. *Journal of American College Health, 54*(6), 327–337.

Schwartz, M. D., & Leggett, M. S. (1999). Bad dates or emotional trauma? The aftermath of campus sexual assault. *Violence Against Women, 5,* 251–271.

Schwartz, M. D., & Mattley, C. (1993). The battered woman scale and gender identities. *Journal of Family Violence, 8,* 277–287.

Schwartz-Kenney, B. M., McCauley, M., & Epstein, M. A. (Eds.). (2001). *Child abuse: A global view.* Westport, CT: Greenwood Press.

Schwiebert, V. L., Myers, J. E., & Dice, C. (2000). Ethical guidelines for counselors working with older adults. *Journal of Counseling and Development, 78,* 123–129.

Scott, A., Gavin, J., Sleath, E., & Sheridan, L. (2014). The attribution of responsibility in cases of stalking. *Psychology, Crime, and Law, 20*(7), 705–721.

Scruggs, T. E., Mastropieri, M. A., & Richter, L. (1985). Peer tutoring with behaviorally disordered students: Social and academic benefits. *Behavioral Disorders, 10,* 283–294.

Sculley, R. (1983). The work-setting support group: A means of preventing burnout. In B. A. Farber (Ed.), *Stress and burnout in the human service professions* (pp. 198–212). New York: Pergamon Press.

Scully, D., & Marolla, J. (1998). "Riding the bull at Gilley's": Convicted rapists describe the rewards of rape. In M. E. Odem & J. Clay-Warner (Eds.), *Confronting rape and sexual assault* (pp. 109–128). Wilmington, DE: Scholarly Resources.

Scurfield, R. M. (1985). Post-trauma stress assessment and treatment: Overview and formulations. In C. R. Figley (Ed.), *Trauma and its wake: The study of posttrauma stress disorder* (pp. 219–256). New York: Brunner/Mazel.

Seely, M. F. (1997a). The discrete role of the hotline. *Crisis, 18*(2), 53–54.

Seely, M. F. (1997b). The role of hotlines in the prevention of suicide. In R. M. Maris & M. M. Silverman (Eds.), *Review of suicidology* (pp. 251–279). New York: Guilford Press.

Segal, D. L., Chatman, C., Bogaards, J. A., & Becker, L. A. (2001). One-year follow-up of an emotional expression intervention for bereaved older adults. *Journal of Mental Health and Aging, 7*(4), 465–472.

Selye, H. (1956). *The stress of life.* New York: McGraw-Hill.

Selye, H. (1974). *Stress without distress.* Philadelphia: Lippincott.

Selye, H. (1976). *The stress of life.* New York: McGraw-Hill.

Senn, C., Eliasziw, M., Barata, P., Thurston, W., Newby-Clark, I., Rastke, L., & Hobden, K. (2015). Efficacy of a sexual assault resistance program for university women. *The New England Journal of Medicine, 372*(24), 2326–2335.

Sestir, M. A., & Bartholow, B. (2010). Violent and nonviolent video games produce opposing effects on aggressive and prosocial outcomes. *Journal of Experimental Social Psychology, 46*(6), 934–942.

Sethi, S., & Bhargava, S. C. (2003). Child and adolescent survivors of suicide. *Crises, 24,* 4–6.

Seto, M. C. (2013). *Internet sex offenders.* Washington, DC: American Psychological Association.

Sev'er, A. (1997). *A cross-cultural exploration of wife abuse.* Lewiston, NY: Edwin Mellen Press.

Sexton-Radek, K. (Ed.). (2004). *Violence in schools: Issues, consequences, and expressions.* Westport, CT: Praeger.

Sgroi, S. M. (1982). *Handbook of clinical intervention in child sexual abuse.* Lexington, MA: Lexington Books.

Sgroi, S. M., Porter, F. S., & Blick, L. C. (1982). Validation of child sexual abuse. In S. M. Sgroi (Ed.), *Handbook of clinical intervention in child sexual abuse* (pp. 39–79). Lexington, MA: Lexington Books.

Shafer, C. (1989a, September). Counselors offer crisis intervention at Iowa crash site. *Guidepost,* pp. 1, 3, 6.

Shafer, C. (1989b, December). Recent disasters trigger NIMH response. *Guidepost,* pp. 1, 5.

Shaffer, D. (1988). The epidemiology of teen suicide: An examination of risk factors. *Journal of Clinical Psychiatry, 49,* 36–41.

Shaffer, D., Garland, A., Gould, M., Fisher, P., & Tratuman, P. (1988). Preventing teen suicide: A critical review. *Journal of the American Academy of Child and Adolescent Psychiatry, 27,* 675–687.

Shaffer, D., Vieland, V., & Garland, A. (1990). Adolescent suicide attempters: Response to suicide prevention programs. *Journal of the American Medical Association, 264,* 3151–3155.

Shah, A. K., Fineberg, N. A., & James, D. V. (1991). Violence among psychiatric in-patients. *Acta Psychiatrica Scandinavica, 84,* 305–309.

Shalev, A., Sahar, T., Freedman, S., Peri, T., Lick, N., Brandes, D., et al. (1998). A prospective study of heart rate response following trauma and the subsequent development of posttraumatic stress disorder. *Archives of General Psychiatry, 55,* 553–559.

Shalev, A. Y. (1996). Stress versus traumatic stress: From acute homeostatic reactions to chronic psychopathology. In B. A. van der Kolk, A. C. McFarlane, & L. Weisaeth (Eds.), *Traumatic stress* (pp. 77–101). New York: Guilford Press.

Shallcross, L. (2009, September). Rewriting the "rules" of grief. *Counseling Today,* 28–31.

Shallcross, L. (2010). Treating trauma. *Counseling Today, 52*(10), 26–35.

Shallcross, L. (2011). A day that changed the nation and a profession. *Counseling Today, 54*(3), 36–40.

Shallcross, L. (2013). Bully pulpit. *Counseling Today, 55*(8), 30–38.

Shandley, K., & Moore, S. (2008). Evaluation of Gambler's Helpline: A consumer perspective. *International Gambling Studies, 8*(3), 315–330.

Shanhinfar, A., Vishnevsky, T., Kilmaer, R. P., & Gil-Rivas, V. (2010). Service needs of children and families affected by Hurricane Katrina. In R. P. Kilmer, V. Gil-Rivas, R. G. Tedeschi, & L. G. Calhoun (Eds.), *Helping families and communities recover from disaster* (pp. 143–166). Washington, DC: American Psychological Association.

Shapiro, B. L., & Chwarz, J. C. (1997). Date rape: Its relationship to trauma symptoms and sexual self-esteem. *Journal of Interpersonal Violence, 12,* 407–419.

Shapiro, E., & Laub, B. (2014). The recent traumatic episode protocol (R-TEP): An integrative protocol for early EMDR intervention (EEI). In M. Luber (Ed.), *Implementing EMDR early mental health interventions for man-made and natural disaster: Models, scripted protocols, and summary sheets* (pp. 193–207). New York: Springer.

Shapiro, F. (1989a). Efficacy of the eye movement desensitization procedure in the treatment of traumatic memories. *Journal of Traumatic Stress, 2,* 199–223.

Shapiro, F. (1989b). Eye movement desensitization: A new treatment for posttraumatic stress disorder. *Journal of Behavior Therapy and Experimental Psychiatry, 20,* 211–217.

Shapiro, F. (1991). Eye movement desensitization and reprocessing procedure: From EMD to EMD/R—A new treatment model for anxiety and related traumata. *Behavior Therapist, 14,* 128, 133–135.

Shapiro, F. (1995). *Eye movement desensitization and reprocessing: Basic principles, protocols, and procedures.* New York: Guilford Press.

Shapiro, F. (2014, Spring). EMDR therapy: Brief overview of trauma research, clinical practice, and proposed neurobiological mechanisms. *Trauma Psychology Newsletter,*5–8.

Shapiro, F., & Maxfield, L. (2002). Eye movement desensitization and reprocessing (EMDR): Information processing in the treatment of trauma. *Journal of Clinical Psychology, 58*(8), 933–946.

Sharp, S. R., & McCallum, R. (2005). A rational emotive behavior approach to improve anger management and reduce office referrals in middle school children: A formative investigation and evaluation. *Journal of Applied School Psychology, 21*(1), 39–66.

Sharpiro, F., & Laliotis, D. (2015). EMDR therapy for trauma-related disorder. In U. Schnyder & M. Cloitre (Eds.), *Evidence based treatments for trauma-related psychological disorders: A practical guide for clinicians* (pp. 205–228). Cham, Switzerland: Springer International Publishing.

Shaver, P. R., & Fraley, R. C. (2008). Attachment, loss, and grief: Bowlby's views and current controversies. In J. Cassidy & P. Shaver (Eds.), *Handbook of attachment: Theory, research, and clinical applications* (2nd ed., pp. 48–77). New York: Guilford Press.

Shaw, H. E., & Shaw, S. F. (2006). Critical ethical issues in online counseling: Assessing current practices with an ethical intent checklist. *Journal of Counseling and Development, 84,* 41–53.

Shea, S. (2002). *The practical art of suicide assessment: A guide for mental health professionals and substance abuse counselors.* Hoboken, NJ: John Wiley & Sons.

Shear, K., & Frank, E. (2006). Treatment of complicated grief: Integrating cognitive-behavioral methods with other treatment approaches. In V. M. Follette & J. I. Ruzek (Eds.), *Cognitive-behavioral therapies for trauma* (2nd ed., pp. 290–320). New York: Guilford Press.

Shear, M. K., & Mulhare, E. (2008). Complicated grief. *Psychiatric Annals, 38*(10), 662–670.

Shear, M. K., Simon, N., Wall, M., Zisook, S., Neimeyer, R., Duan, N.,…Reynolds, C. (2011). Complicated grief and related bereavement issues for DSM-5. *Depression and Anxiety, 28*(2), 103–117.

Shectman, Z., Hiradin, A., & Zina, S. (2003). The impact of culture on group behavior: A comparison of three ethnic groups. *Journal of Counseling and Development, 81*(2), 208–216.

Sheehan, P. L. (1994). Treating intimacy issues of traumatized people. In M. B. Williams & J. F. Sommers, Jr. (Eds.), *Handbook of post-traumatic therapy* (pp. 94–105). Westport, CT: Greenwood Press.

Shelby, J. S., & Tredinnick, M. G. (1995). Crisis intervention with survivors of natural disaster: Lessons from Hurricane Andrew. *Journal of Counseling and Development, 73,* 491–497.

Shelby, R. D. (1995). *People with HIV and those who help them: Challenges, integration, intervention.* Binghamton, NY: Hayworth Press.

Shepard, M. F. (1999). Advocacy for battered women: Implications for a coordinated community response. In M. F. Shepard & E. L. Pence (Eds.), *Coordinating community responses to domestic violence: Lessons from Duluth and beyond* (pp. 115–126). Thousand Oaks, CA: Sage.

Sherman, G. D., & Clore, G. L. (2009). The color of sin: White and black are perceptual symbols of moral purity and pollution. *Psychological Science, 20,* 1019–1025. doi: 10.1111/j.1467-9280.2009.02403x

Sherman, L. W., & Berk, R. A. (1984). The specific deterrent effects of arrest for domestic assaults. *American Sociological Review, 49,* 1261–1272.

Sherman, L. W., Gottfredson, D., MacKenzie, D., Eck, J., Reuter, P., & Bushway, S. (1997). *Preventing crime: What works, what doesn't, what's promising* (Report to the United States Congress). Baltimore: University of Maryland, Department of Criminology and Criminal Justice, Office of Justice Program.

Shinn, M., & Mørch, H. (1983). A tripartite model of coping with burnout. In B. A. Farber (Ed.), *Stress and burnout in the human service professions* (pp. 227–239). New York: Pergamon Press.

Shneidman, E. (2001*). Comprehending suicide: Landmarks in 20th century suicidology.* Washington, DC: American Psychological Association.

Shneidman, E. S. (1971). Prevention, intervention, and postvention of suicide. *Annals of Internal Medicine, 75,* 453–458.

Shneidman, E. S. (1973). Suicide notes reconsidered. *Psychiatry, 36,* 379–394.

Shneidman, E. S. (1975). Postvention: The care of the bereaved. In R. O. Pasnau (Ed.), *Consultation in liaison psychiatry* (pp. 245–256). New York: Grune & Stratton.

Shneidman, E. S. (1980). *Voices of death.* New York: Harper & Row.

Shneidman, E. S. (1985). *Definition of suicide.* New York: Wiley.

Shneidman, E. S. (1987). A psychological approach to suicide. In G. R. Vandenbos & B. K. Bryant (Eds.), *Cataclysms, crises and catastrophes: Psychology in action* (pp. 147–183). Washington, DC: American Psychological Association.

Shneidman, E. S. (1993). Suicide as psychache. *Journal of Nervous and Mental Disease, 181,* 147–149.

Shneidman, E. S. (1999a). A formal definition with explication. In A. A. Leenaars (Ed.), *Lives and deaths: Selections from the works of E. S. Shneidman* (pp. 154–163). Philadelphia: Brunner/Mazel.

Shneidman, E. S. (1999b). How to prevent suicide. In A. A. Leenaars (Ed.), *Lives and deaths: Selections from the works of E. S. Shneidman* (pp. 154–163). Philadelphia: Brunner/Mazel.

Shneidman, E. S. (1999c). Self-destruction: Suicide notes and tragic lives. In A. A. Leenaars (Ed.), *Lives and deaths: Selections from the works of E. S. Shneidman* (pp. 277–303). Philadelphia: Brunner/Mazel.

Shneidman, E. S. (1999d). The psychological autopsy. In A. A. Leenaars (Ed.), *Lives and deaths: Selections from the works of E. S. Shneidman* (pp. 387–414). Philadelphia: Brunner/Mazel.

Shneidman, E. S. (1999e). The Psychological Pain Assessment Scale. In A. A. Leenaars (Ed.), *Lives and deaths: Selections from the works of E. S. Shneidman* (pp. 41–46). Philadelphia: Brunner/Mazel.

Shneidman, E. S. (2001). *Comprehending suicide: Landmarks in 20th century suicidology.* Washington, DC: American Psychological Association.

Shneidman, E. S., & Farberow, N. L. (1961). Statistical comparisons between committed and attempted suicides. In N. L. Farberow and E. S. Shneidman (Eds.), *The cry for help* (pp. 44–59). New York: McGraw-Hill.

Shneidman, E. S., Farberow, N. L., & Litman, R. E. (1976). *The psychology of suicide.* New York: Aronson.

Shore, J. H., Tatum, E. L., & Vollmer, W. M. (1986). Evaluation of mental health effects of disaster: Mount St. Helen's eruption. *American Journal of Public Health, 76*(3), 76–86.

Shorey, R., Brasfield, H., Zapor, H., Febres, J., & Stuart, G. (2015, July). The relation between alcohol use and psychological, physical, and sexual dating violence perpetration among male college students. *Violence Against Women, 21*(7), NP1.

Shorey, R., Comelius, T., & Strauss, C. (2015). Stalking in college student dating relationships: A descriptive investigation. *Journal of Family Violence, 40*(30), 1–2.

Shraberg, M. (2006, May). *Disaster planning for a crisis center.* Paper presented at the Thirtieth Convening of Crisis Intervention Personnel/Contact USA Conference, Chicago.

Shupe, A., Stacey, W. A., & Hazlewood, L. R. (1987). *Violent men, violent couples.* Lexington, MA: Lexington Books.

Siegel, D. J. (1995). Memory, trauma, and psychotherapy: A cognitive science view. *Journal of Psychotherapy Practice and Research, 4,* 93–122.

Sikkema, K. J., Kochman, A., DiFranceiso, W., Kelly, J., & Hoffman, R. G. (2003). AIDS-related grief and coping with loss among HIV-positive men and women. *Journal of Behavioral Medicine, 26*(2), 165–181.

Silbert, M. (1988). Compounding factors in the rape of street prostitutes. In A. W. Burgess (Ed.), *Rape and sexual assault* (Vol. II, pp. 75–90). New York: Garland.

Silove, D. (1998). Is PTSD an overlearnt survival response? An evolutionary learning hypothesis. *Psychiatry, 61,* 181–190.

Silove, D. (1999). A conceptual framework for mass trauma: Implications for adaptation, intervention, and debriefing. In B. Raphael & J. P. Wilson (Eds.), *Psychological debriefing: Theory, practice, and evidence* (pp. 337–350). New York: Cambridge University Press.

Silver, T., & Goldstein, H. (1992). A collaborative model of a county intervention team: The Lake County experience. *Community Mental Health Journal, 28,* 249–253.

Silverman, P. R. (1986). The perils of borrowing: Role of the professional in mutual self-help groups. *Journal of Specialists in Group Work, 11,* 68–73.

Silverman, P. R. (2000). *Never too young to know: Death in children's lives.* New York: Oxford University Press.

Silverman, W. K., Allen, A., & Ortiz, C. D. (2010). Lessons learned from hurricane Katrina and other devastating hurricanes: Steps necessary for preparedness, response, and intervention. In R. P. Ryan, V. Gil-Rivas, R. G. Tedeschi, & L. G. Calhoun (Eds.), *Helping families and communities recover from disaster: Lessons learned from hurricane Katrina and its aftermath* (pp. 289–311). Washington, DC: American Psychological Association.

Simmons, J. (2000, October). FBI release study aimed at identifying dangerous students. *Counseling Today, 43*(4), 1, 22.

Simon, N. M., Wall, M. M., Keshaviah, A., Dryman, M. T., LeBlanc, N. J., & Shear, M. K. (2011). Informing the symptom profile of complicated grief. *Depression and Anxiety, 28*(2), 118–126.

Simon, R. I., & Hales, R. E. (Eds.). (2012). *The American Psychiatric Publishing textbook of suicide assessment and management* (2nd ed.). Arlington, VA: American Psychiatric Publishing.

Simonds, J. F., & Kashani, J. (1980). Specific drug use and violence in delinquent boys. *American Journal of Drug and Alcohol Abuse, 7,* 305–322.

Simpson, L. R. (2006). Level of spirituality as a predictor of the occurrence of compassion fatigue among counseling professionals in Mississippi. *Dissertation Abstracts International: Section A. Humanities and Social Sciences, 66*(6), 3223.

Singer, V. I., Tracz, S. M., & Dworkin, S. H. (1991). Reminiscence group therapy: A treatment modality for older adults. *Journal for Specialists in Group Work, 16,* 167–171.

Singh, J. P., Grann, M., & Fazel, S. (2011). A comparative study of violence risk assessment tools: A systematic review and meta regression analysis of 68 studies involving 25,980 participants. *Clinical Psychology Review, 31,* 499–513.

Sitterle, K. A., & Gurwitch, R. H. (1999). The terrorist bombing in Oklahoma City. In E. S. Zinner & M. B. Williams (Eds.), *When community weeps: Case studies in group survivorship* (pp. 161–189). Philadelphia: Brunner/Mazel.

Skeem, J., & Bibeau, L. (2008). How does violence potential relate to crisis intervention team responses in emergencies? *Psychiatric Services, 59*(2), 201–204.

Skelton, K., Ressler, K. J., Norrholm, S. D., Jovanovic, T., & Bradley-Davino, B. (2012). PTSD and gene variants: New pathways and new thinking. *Neuropharmacology, 62*(2), 628–637.

Slaby, A. E. (1998). Outpatient management of suicidal patients. In B. Bongar, A. Bergman, R. Maris, M. Silverman, E. Harris, & W. Packman (Eds.), *Risk management in suicidal patients* (pp. 34–64). New York: Guilford Press.

Slagel, L. (2009). *Examination of the reliability and validity of the Triage Assessment Survey: Families.* Duquesne University, Pittsburgh, PA.

Slaikeu, K. A. (1990). *Crisis intervention: A handbook for practice and research* (2nd ed.). Boston: Allyn & Bacon.

Slaikeu, K. A., & Leff-Simon, S. I. (1990). Crisis intervention by telephone. In K. A. Slaikeu (Ed.), *Crisis intervention: A handbook for practice and research* (2nd ed., pp. 319–328). Boston: Allyn & Bacon.

Slattery, J. M., & Park, C. L. (2015). Spirituality and meaning making: Implications for therapy with trauma survivors. In D. F. Walker, C. A. Courtois, & J. D. Aten (Eds.), *Spiritually oriented psychotherapy for trauma* (pp. 127–146). Washington, DC: American Psychological Association.

Sleek, S. (1998, August). Experts scrambling on school shootings: School violence in rural areas could worsen. *APA Monitor, 29,* 1, 35–36.

Sloan, J. H. (1988). Handgun regulations, crime, assaults, and homicide. *New England Journal of Medicine, 319,* 1256–1262.

Sloore, H. (1988). Use of the MMPI in the prediction of dangerous behavior. *Acta Psychiatrica Belgica, 88,* 42–51.

Slovenko, R. (2006). Violent attacks in psychiatric and other hospitals. *Journal of Psychiatry and Law, 34*(2), 249–268.

Smart, D., English, A., James, J., Wilson, M., Darantha, K., Childers, B., & Magera, C. (2014). Compassion fatigue and satisfaction: A cross-sectional survey among US health care workers. *Nursing and Health Sciences, 16*(1), 3–10.

Smith, D. C., Larson, J., & Nuckles, D. (2006). A critical analysis of school-based anger management programs for youth. In S. R. Jimerson & M. Furlong (Eds.), *Handbook of school violence and school safety: From research to practice* (pp. 365–382). Mahwah, NJ: Erlbaum.

Smith, H. B. (2002). The American Red Cross: How to be a part of the solution, rather than a part of the problem. In D. D. Bass & R. Yep (Eds.), *Terrorism, trauma, and tragedies: A counselor's guide to preparing and responding* (pp. 37–38). Alexandria, VA: American Counseling Association.

Smith, K. J., & Belgrave, L. L. (1995). The reconstruction of everyday life: Experiencing hurricane Andrew. *Journal of Contemporary Ethnography, 24,* 244–269.

Smith, N. D. (2003). Competing models for reduction of physical spouse abuse in the United States Marine Corps: Which model of treatment is most effective for reducing recidivism in the Marine Corps? *Dissertation Abstracts International: Section B. The Sciences and Engineering,* 4387.

Smith, P. H., White, J. W., & Holland, L. J. (2003). A longitudinal perspective on dating violence among adolescent and college-age women. *American Journal of Public Health, 93*(7), 1104–1109.

Smith, S. (2009, September). Why does it hurt so much? Grieving the loss of a pet. *Your Mind Your Body.* American Psychological Association. Retrieved from www.yourmindy ourbody.org /about-2

Smith, S. (2013). Could Comprehensive Soldier Fitness have iatrogenic consequences? A commentary. *The Journal of Behavioral Health Sciences and Research, 40*(2), 242–246.

Smith, S. G., & Cook, S. L. (2004). Are reports of posttraumatic growth positively biased? *Journal of Traumatic Stress, 17*(4), 353–358.

Smith, T. C., Ryan, M. A., Wingard, D. L., Slymen, D. J., Sallis, J. F., & Kritz-Silverstein, D. (2008). New onset and persistent symptoms of post-traumatic stress disorder self reported after deployment and combat exposures: Prospect population based US military cohort study. *British Medical Journal, 336,* 366–371.

Snider, L., Hoffman, Y., Littrell, M., Fry, M. W., & Thornburgh, M. (2010). Supporting children after Hurricane Katrina: Reflections on psychosocial principles in practice. In R. P. Kilmer, V. Gil-Rivas, R. G. Tedeschi, & L. G. Calhoun (Eds.), *Helping families and communities recover from disaster* (pp. 25–51). Washington, DC: American Psychological Association.

Snyder, J. A. (1994). How we do it: Emergency department protocols for domestic violence. *Journal of Emergency Nursing, 20,* 64–68.

Snyder, L. A., Chen, P., & Vacha-Haase, T. (2007). The underreporting gap in aggressive incidents from geriatric patients against certified nursing assistants. *Violence and Victims, 22*(3), 367–379.

Society of Clinical Psychology. (2012). *Reminiscence/life review therapy for depression.* Washington, DC: American Psychological Association.

Sofka, C. J. (2004). What kind of funeral? Identifying and resolving family conflicts. *Generations, 28,* 21–25.

Softas-Nall, B. C., & Francis, P. C. (1998). A solution- focused approach to a family with a suicidal member. *Family Journal: Counseling and Therapy for Couples and Families, 6,* 227–230.

Sokolski, K., Denson, T., Lee, R., & Reist, C. (2003). Quetiapine for treatment of refractory symptoms of combat-related post-traumatic stress disorder. *Military Medicine, 168*(6), 486–489.

Solomon, R. M. (1995). Critical incidents stress management in law enforcement. In G. S. Everly (Ed.), *Innovations in disaster and trauma psychology: Applications in emergency services and disaster response* (pp. 123–157). Baltimore, MD: Chevron.

Solomon, Z. (1986). The effect of combat-related stress disorder on the family. *Psychiatry, 51,* 323–329.

Solomon, Z., Neria, Y., & Ram, A. (1998). Mental health professionals' responses to loss and trauma of holocaust survivors. In J. H. Harvey (Ed.), *Perspective on loss: A sourcebook* (pp. 221–231). Philadelphia: Brunner/Mazel.

Somers-Flanigan, J., & Somers-Flanigan, R. (1997). *Tough kids, cool counseling: User friendly approaches with challenging youth.* Alexandria, VA: American Counseling Association.

Sommer, C. A. (2008). Vicarious traumatization, trauma-sensitive supervision, and counselor preparation. *Counselor Education and Supervision, 48,* 61–71.

Sommer, C. A., & Cox, J. A. (2005). Elements of supervision in sexual violence counselors' narratives: A qualitative analysis. *Counselor Education and Supervision, 45,* 119–134.

Sommers-Flanagan, J., & Sommers-Flanagan, R. S. (1997). *Tough kids, cool counseling: User-friendly approaches with challenging youth.* Alexandria, VA: American Counseling Association.

Sommers-Flanagan, R. (2007). Ethical considerations in crisis and humanitarian interventions. *Ethics and Behavior, 17,* 187–202.

Sommers-Flanagan, R., & Sommers-Flanagan, J. (2008). Advanced ethical considerations in the use of evidenced-based practices. In G. R. Walz, J. Bleuer, & R. K. Yep (Eds.). *Compelling counseling interventions: celebrating VISTA's fifth anniversary.* (pp. 259–269). Alexandria, VA: American Counseling Association.

Sommers-Flanagan, R., Sommers-Flanagan, J., & Lynch, K. (2001). Counseling interventions with suicidal clients. In E. R. Welfel & R. E. Ingersoll (Eds.), *The mental health desk reference* (pp. 264–270). New York: John Wiley & Sons.

Sonkin, D. J., & Dutton, D. (2003). Treating assaultive men from an attachment perspective. *Journal of Aggression, Maltreatment, and Trauma, 7*(1/2), 105–133.

Sonkin, D. J., Martin, D., & Walker, L. E. (1985). *The male batterer: A treatment approach.* New York: Springer.

Soriano, M., Soriano, F., & Jimenez, E. (1994). School violence among culturally diverse populations: Sociocultural and institutional considerations. *School Psychology Review, 23*(2), 216–235.

Southwick, S., & Watson, P. (2015). The emerging scientific and clinical literature on resilience and psychological first aid. Post traumatic stress disorder: Patient interview, clinical assessment, and diagnosis. In N. C. Bernardy and M. J. Friedman (Eds.), *A practical guide to treatment: Pharmacological and psychotherapeutic approaches* (pp. 21–34). Washington, DC: American Psychological Association.

Spangaro, J. M., Zwi, A. B., & Poulos, R. (2011). "Persist. Persist.": A qualitative study of women's decisions to disclose and their perceptions of the impact of routine screening for intimate partner violence. *Psychology of Violence, 1*(2), 150–162.

Spanno, T. K. (1990, April). *Eclipse of the self: The grief of the battered women.* Paper presented at Crisis Convening XIV, Chicago.

Spar, J., & La Rue, A. (2006). *Clinical manual of geriatric psychiatry.* Washington, DC: American Psychiatric Publishing.

Speigel, J. (2003). *Sexual abuse of males: The SAM model of theory and practice.* New York: Brunner-Routledge.

Spence, J. T., & Helmreich, R. (1972). The attitude toward women scale: An objective instrument to measure attitudes towards the rights and roles of women in contemporary society. *JSAS, Catalog of Selected Documents in Psychology, 2*(66), 1–51.

Spicuzza, F. J., & Devoe, M. W. (1982). Burnout in the helping professions: Mutual aid as self-help. *Personnel and Guidance Journal, 61,* 95–98.

Spiegel, D. (1981). Vietnam grief work under hypnosis. *American Journal of Clinical Hypnosis, 24,* 33–40.

Spiegel, D. (1989). Hypnosis in the treatment of victims of sexual abuse. *Psychiatric Clinics of North America, 12,* 295–305.

Spielberg, S. (Director). (1989). *Always* [Motion picture]. Los Angeles: United Artists.

Spittal, M. J., Fedyszyn, I., Middleton, A., Bassilios, B., Gunn, J, Woodward, A., & Pirkis, J. (2015). Frequent callers to crisis helplines: Who are they and why do they call? *Australian and New Zealand Journal of Psychiatry, 49*(1), 54–64.

Spitzer, W. H., & Neely, M. K. (1992). Critical incident stress: The role of hospital-based social work in developing a statewide intervention system for first-responders delivering emergency services. *Social Work in Health Care, 18,* 39–58.

Spitzer, W. J., & Burke, L. (1993). A critical-incident stress debriefing program for hospital-based health care personnel. *Health and Social Work, 18*(2), 149–156.

Spitzer, W. J., & Neely, K. (1992). The role of hospital-based social work in developing a statewide intervention system for first responders delivering emergency services. *Social Work in Health Care, 18,* 39–58.

Sroufe, L., Egeland, B., Carlson, E., & Collins, W. (2005). *The development of the person: The Minnesota study of risk and adaptation from birth to adulthood.* New York: Guilford Press.

Stack, S. (2001). Sociological research into suicide. In D. Lester (Ed.), *Suicide prevention: Resources for the millennium* (pp. 17–30). Philadelphia: Brunner-Routledge.

Stalker, C. A., & Davies, F. (1995). Attachment organization and adaptation in sexually abused women. *Canadian Journal of Psychiatry, 40,* 234–240.

Stambor, Z. (2005). Responders must consider victim's culture, experts say. *Monitor on Psychology, 36*(11), 28.

Stamm, B. H. (2002). Measuring compassion satisfaction as well as fatigue: Developmental history of the Compassion Satisfaction and Fatigue Test. In C. R. Figley (Ed.), *Treating compassion fatigue* (pp. 107–119). New York: Brunner/Routledge.

Stamm, B. H. (2005). *The ProQOL manual.* Towson, NY: Sidran Press.

Stamm, B. H. (2010). *The concise ProQOL manual* (2nd ed.). Pocotello, ID: ProQOl.org. Retrieved from http://proqol.org/uploads /ProQOL_Concise_2ndEd_12-2010.pdf

Stampfl, T. G., & Lewis, D. J. (1967). Essentials of implosive therapy: A learning-theory-based psychodynamic behavioral therapy. *Journal of Abnormal Psychology, 72,* 496–503.

Stanard, R., & Hazler, R. (1995). Legal and ethical implications of HIV and duty-to-warn for counselors: Does *Tarasoff* apply? *Journal of Counseling and Development, 73,* 397–400.

Stanley, B., & Brown, G. (2012). Safety planing intervention: A brief intervention to mitigate suicide risk. *Cognitive and Behavioral Practice, 19,* 256–264.

Stanley, J. (1999, August). *Exploration of partner violence in male same-sex relationships.* Paper presented at the 107th Annual Convention of the American Psychological Association, Symposium on Outing Same-Sex Partner Abuse, Defining the Issues, Boston.

Stanley, J., Bartholomew, K., Taylor, T., Oram, D., & Landolt, M. (2006). Intimate violence in male same-sex relationships. *Journal of Family Violence, 21*(1), 31–41.

Star, K. L. (2015). The relationship between self-care practices, burnout, compassion fatigue, and compassion satisfaction among professional counselors and counselors-in-training. *Dissertation Abstracts International: Section A. Humanities and Social Sciences, 75*(8-A(E)).

Stark, E. (1994). Stress! It's all relative . . . and relatively easy to manage. In R. Yarian (Ed.), *Health 94/95* (15th ed., pp. 62–65). Guilford, CT: Dushkin.

Stark, E., & Flitcraft, A. (1987). Violence among intimates: An epidemiological review. In V. B. Van Hasselt, R. L. Morrison, A. S. Bellack, & M. Hersen (Eds.), *Handbook of family violence.* New York: Plenum.

Stark, E., & Flitcraft, A. (1988). Personal power and institutional victimization: Treating the dual trauma of women battering. In F. M. Ochberg (Ed.), *Posttrauma therapy and victims of violence* (pp. 115–151). New York: Brunner/Mazel.

State of North Carolina v. *Oliver,* 70 N. C. 60, 61–62 (1874).

Steadman, H. J., Osher, F. C., Robbins, P. C., Case, B., & Samuels, S. (2009). Prevalence of serious mental illness among jail inmates. *Psychiatric Services, 60,* 761–765.

Steele, W., & Malchiodi, C. A. (2008). Interventions for parents of traumatized children. In C. A. Malchiodi (Ed.), *Creative interventions with traumatized children* (pp. 264–281). New York: Guilford Press.

Steele, W., & Raider, M. (2001). *Structured sensory intervention for traumatized children, adolescents, and parents: Strategies to alleviate trauma.* Lewiston, NY: Mellen Press.

Steenkamp, M. M., & Litz, B. T. (2014). One-size-fits-all approach to PTSD in the VA not supported by the evidence. *American Psychologist, 69*(7), 706.

Steenkamp, M. M., Nash, W. P., & Litz, B. T. (2013). Post-traumatic stress disorder: Review of the Comprehensive Soldier Fitness Program. *American Journal of Preventive Medicine, 44*(5), 507–512.

Steger, M. F., & Park, C. L. (2012). The creation of meaning following trauma: Meaning making and trajectories of distress and recovery. In R. A. McMackin, E. Newman, J. M. Fogler, & T. M. Keane (Eds.), *Trauma therapy in context: The science and craft of evidence-based practice* (pp. 171–191). Washington, DC: American Psychological Association.

Stein, M. B., Hannah, C., Koverola, C., Yehuda, R., Torchia, M., & McClarty, B. (1994, December). *Neuroanatomical and neuroendocrine correlates in adulthood of severe sexual abuse in childhood.* Paper presented at the 33rd Annual Meeting of the American College of Neuropsychopharmacology, San Juan, Puerto Rico.

Steinberg, A. M., Brymer, M., Decker, K., & Pynoos, R. S. (2004). The UCLA PTSD Reaction Index. *Current Psychiatry Reports, 6,* 96–100.

Steinberg, A. M., Brymer, M. J., Kim, S., Briggs, E. C., Ippen, C., Ostrowski, S., . . . Pynoos, R. S. (2013). Psychometric properties of the UCLA PTSD Reaction Index: Part I. *Journal of Traumatic Stress, 26*(1), 1–9.

Steinberg, A. M., Pynoos, R. S., Biggs, E. C., Gerrity, E. T., Layne, C. M., Vivrette, R. L., Beyerlein, B., & Fairbank, J. A. (2014). The National Child Traumatic Stress Network Core Data Set: Emerging findings, future directions, and implications for theory, research, practice, and policy, *Psychological Trauma: Theory, Research, Practice, and Policy, 6*(1), 50–57.

Stephen Ministries, Saint Louis. (2011). *Transforming lives and equipping the saints for ministry since 1975*. Retrieved from stephenministries.org

Stephens, R. D. (1997). National trends in school violence: Statistics and prevention strategies. In A. P. Goldstein & J. C. Conoley (Eds.), *School violence prevention: A practical handbook* (pp. 72–90). New York: Guilford Press.

Stern, A. (1938). Psychoanalytic investigation of and therapy in the borderline group of neuroses. *Psychoanalytic Quarterly, 7*, 467–489.

Stets, J. E., & Straus, M. A. (1990). Gender differences in reporting of marital violence and its medical and psychological consequences. In M. A. Straus & R. J. Gelles (Eds.), *Physical violence in American families: Risk factors and adaptations to violence in 8,145 families* (pp. 151–165). New Brunswick, NJ: Transaction.

Stevens, D. (2014). Online and on-the-couch virtuality: The real, the imagined, and the perverse. *Journal of the American Psychoanalytic Association, 62*(6), 1105–1116.

Stevenson, J. (1999). The treatment of long-term sequelae of child abuse. *Journal of Child Psychology and Psychiatry and Allied Disciplines, 40*(1), 89–111.

Steveson, S. (1991). Heading off violence with verbal de-escalation. *Journal of Psychosocial Nursing, 29*, 7–10.

Stewart, C., & MacNeil, G. (2005). Crisis intervention with chronic school violence and volatile situations. In A. R. Roberts (Ed.), *Crisis intervention handbook* (3rd ed., pp. 519–540). New York: Oxford University Press.

Stewart, H. (2012). Regression post-Ferenczi. In J. Szekacs-Weisz & T. Keve (Eds.), *Ferenczi and his world: Rekindling the spirit of the Budapest school*. The history of psychoanalysis series. London, England: Karnac Books.

Stewart-Sicking, J. A., & Mutai, W. W. (2012). Working with faith based communities in ecological counseling. In E. P. Cook (Ed.), *Understanding people in context: The ecological perspective in counseling.* (pp. 259–278). Alexandria, VA: American Counseling Association.

Stige, S., Traeen, B., & Rosenvinge, J. (2013). The process leading to help seeking following childhood trauma. *Qualitative Health Research, 23*(10), 1295–1306.

Stilling, L. (1992). The pros and cons of physical restraints and behavior controls. *Journal of Psychosocial Nursing, 30*, 18–20.

Stillion, J. M., & McDowell, E. E. (1996). *Suicide across the life span: Premature exits* (2nd ed.). Washington, DC: Taylor & Francis.

Stith, S., McCollum, E., & Rosen, K. (2011). *Couples therapy for domestic violence: Finding safe solutions*. Washington, DC: American Psychological Association.

Stith, S., Rosen, K., McCollum, E., & Thomsen, C. (2004). Treating intimate partner violence within intact couple relationships: Outcomes of multi-couple versus individual couple therapy. *Journal of Marital and Family Therapy, 30*(3), 305–318.

Stoff, D. M., & Mann, J. J. (Eds.). (1997). *Annals of the New York Academy of Sciences: Vol. 836. The neurobiology of suicide: From the bench to the clinic*. New York: New York Academy of Sciences.

Stokols, D., Misra, S., Runnerstrom, J. M., & Hipp, J. A. (2009). Psychology in an age of ecological crisis: From personal angst to collective action. *American Psychologist, 64*(3), 181–193.

Stone, C. (2013). Suicide contracts assessments, and parental/guardian notification: Err on the side of caution. *American School Counselor Association School Counselor, 51*(2), 6–8.

Stone, C. (2015). Cyber bullying: Disruptive conduct or free speech? *ASCA School Counselor, 60*(5), 6–9.

Stone, C., & Zirkel, P. A. (2012). Student suicide: Legal and ethical implications. *American School Counselor Association School Counselor 49*(5), 24–30.

Stone, G. (1999). *Suicide and attempted suicide: Methods and consequences*. New York: Carroll & Graf.

Stoop, D., & Arterburn, S. (1991). *The angry man: "Why does he act that way?"* Dallas, TX: Word Publishing.

Stortch, D. D. (1991). Starting an in-hospital support group for victims of violence in the psychiatric hospital. *Psychiatric Hospital, 22*, 5–9.

Stosny, S. (1995). *Treating attachment abuse: A compassion approach*. New York: Springer.

Stover, C., Meadows, A., & Kaufman, J. (2009). Interventions for intimate partner violence: Review and implications for evidence-based practice. *Professional Psychology: Research and Practice, 40*(3), 223–233.

Straus, M. A. (1979). Measuring intra-family conflict and violence: The C.T. Scale. *Journal of Marriage and Family, 41*, 75–88.

Straus, M. A., & Gelles, R. J. (1986). Societal change and change in family violence from 1975 to 1985 as revealed by two national surveys. *Journal of Marriage and Family, 48*, 465–479.

Straus, M. A., & Gelles, R. J. (Eds.). (1990). *Physical violence in American families: Risk factors and adaptations to violence in 8,145 families*. New Brunswick, NJ: Transaction.

Straus, M. A., Gelles, R. J., & Steinmetz, S. (1980). *Behind closed doors: Violence in the American family*. Garden City, NY: Anchor/Doubleday.

Strawhun, J., Adams, N., & Huss, M. (2013). The assessment of cyberstalking: An expanded examination including social networking, attachment, jealousy, and anger in relation to violence and abuse. *Violence and Victims, 28*(4), 715–730.

Strawn, J. R., & Geracioti, T. D., Jr. (2008). Noradrenergic dysfunction and the psychopharmacology of posttraumatic stress disorder. *Depression and Anxiety, 25*, 260–271.

Stroebe, M., Schut, H., & Stroebe, W. (2005). Attachment in coping with bereavement: A theoretical integration. *Review of General Psychology, 9*, 48–66.

Stroebe, M. S., Hansson, R. O., Schut, H., & Stroebe, W. (Eds.). (2008). *Handbook of bereavement research and practice: Advances in theory and intervention*. Washington, DC: American Psychological Association.

Stroebe, W., & Schut, H. (1999). The dual process model of coping with bereavement: Rationale and description. *Death Studies, 23*, 197–224.

Stroebe, W., & Schut, H. (2001). Making meaning in the dual process model of coping with bereavement. In R. A. Neimeyer (Ed.), *Meaning reconstruction and the experience of loss* (pp. 55–69). Washington, DC: American Psychological Association.

Stuart, G., Meehan, J., Moore, T., Morean, M., Hellmuth, J., & Follansbee, K. (2006). Examining a conceptual framework of intimate partner violence in men and women arrested for domestic violence. *Journal of Studies on Alcohol, 67*(1), 102–112.

Stubenbort, K. M., Donnelly, G. R., & Cohen, J. (2001). Cognitive-behavioral group therapy for bereaved adults and children following an air disaster. *Group Dynamics: Theory, Research, and Practice, 5*, 261–176.

Stuhlmiller, C., & Dunning, C. (2000). Challenging the mainstream: From a pathogenic to salutogenic models of post-trauma interventions. In J. M. Violanti, D. Paton, & C. Dunning (Eds.), *Posttraumatic stress intervention: Challenges, issues and perspectives* (pp. 10–42). Springfield, IL: Charles C Thomas.

Stuhmiller, C., & Dunning, C. (2000). Concerns about debriefing: Challenging the mainstream. In B. Raphael & J. P. Wilson (Eds.), *Psychological debriefing: Theory, practice, and evidence* (pp. 305–320). New York: Cambridge University Press.

Su, Y., & Chen, S. (2015). Emerging posttraumatic growth: A prospective study with pre- and posttrauma psychological predictors. *Psychological Trauma: Theory, Research, Practice, and Policy, 7*(2), 103–111.

Suar, D., & Khuntia, R. (2004). Caste, education, family and stress disorders in Orissa Supercyclone. *Psychology and Developing Societies, 16*(1), 77–91.

Substance Abuse and Mental Health Services Administration (SAMHSA). (2003). *Tips for emergency and disaster response workers stress prevention and management approaches for rescue workers in the aftermath of terrorist acts.* Retrieved from http://search.usa.gov/search/docs?affiliate=samhsa-store&dc=1415&query=Tips%20%20for%20emergency%20and%20disaster%20%20response%20%20workers

Substance Abuse and Mental Health Services Administration. (2014). *Trauma-informed care in behavioral health services.* Treatment Improvement Protocol (TIP) Series 57. HHS Publication No. (SMA) 13-4801. Rockville, MD: Substance Abuse and Mental Health Services Administration.

Sue, D. W. (1977). Community mental health services to minority groups: Some optimism, some pessimism. *American Psychologist, 32*(6), 616–624.

Sue, D. W. (1992, Winter). The challenge of multiculturalism: The road less traveled. *American Counselor, 1,* 5–14.

Sue, D. W. (1999a, August). *Multicultural competencies in the profession of psychology.* Symposium address delivered at the 107th Annual Convention of the American Psychological Association, Boston.

Sue, D. W. (1999b, August). *Surviving monoculturalism and racism: A personal journey.* Division 45 Presidential Address delivered at the 107th Annual Convention of the American Psychological Association, Boston.

Sue, D. W., & Sue, D. (2013). *Counseling the culturally diverse: Theory and practice* (6th ed.). New York: Wiley.

Sue, D. W., Arredondo, P., & McDavis, R. J. (1992). Multicultural counseling competencies and standards: A call to the profession. *Journal of Counseling and Development, 70,* 477–486.

Suglia, S. F., Staudenmayer, J., Cohen, S., Enlow, M., Rice-Edwards, J., & Wright, R. (2010). Cumulative stress and cortisol disruption among Black and Hispanic pregnant women in an urban cohort. *Psychological Trauma: Theory, Research, Practice, and Policy, 2*(4), 326–334.

Suler, J. (2004). The online disinhibition effect. *Cyberpsychology and Behavior, 7*(3), 321–326.

Sullivan, C., & Cottone, R. R. (2010). Emergent characteristics of effective cross-cultural research: A review of the literature. *Journal of Counseling and Development, 88*(3), 357–362.

Sullivan, C. M., Campbell, R., Angelique, H., Eby, K. K., & Davidson, W. S. (1994). An advocacy intervention program for women with abusive partners: Six-month follow-up. *American Journal of Community Psychology, 22,* 101–120.

Sullivan, G. R., & Bongar, B. (2006). Psychological testing in suicide risk management. In R. I. Simon and R. E. Hales (Eds.), *The American Psychiatric Publishing textbook of suicide assessment and management* (pp. 177–196). Washington, DC: American Psychiatric Publishing.

Sullivan, G. R., & Bongar, B. (2009). Assessing suicide risk in the adult patient. In P. M. Kleespies (Ed.), *Behavioral emergencies: An evidence-based resource for evaluating and managing risk of suicide, violence, and victimization* (pp. 59–78). Washington, DC: American Psychological Association.

Sullivan, J. (2002). How should HR and managers react in the aftermath of terrorism events? In D. D. Bass & R. Yep (Eds.), *Terrorism, trauma, and tragedies: A counselor's guide to preparing and responding* (pp. 67–68). Alexandria, VA: American Counseling Association.

Sullivan, K. (2011). *The anti-bullying handbook.* Thousand Oaks, CA: Sage.

Sullivan, L. (2004). Staff development and secondary traumatic stress among AIDS staff. *Dissertation Abstracts International: Section A. Humanities and Social Sciences, 64*(4), 2365.

Sullivan, L. A., & Robinson, S. L. (1994, April). *An evaluation of a preschool child abuse and neglect prevention program: The Kids on the Block go to preschool.* Research report from the University of Alabama at Birmingham, presented at the Conference on Human Development, Birmingham, AL.

Summerfield, D. (1999). A critique of seven assumptions behind psychological trauma programmes in war- affected areas. *Social Science and Medicine, 48,* 1449–1462.

Summerfield, D. (2005). What exactly is emergency or disaster "mental health"? *Bulletin of the World Health Organization, 83*(1), 76.

Suniti Bhat, C., Chang, S. H., & Linscott, J. A. (2010). Bullying as a media literacy issue. *New Horizons in Education, 58*(3), 44–57.

Sussman, L., & Bordwell, S. (1981). *The rapist file: Interviews with convicted rapists.* New York: Chelsea House.

Sutano, J., Phang, C., Tan, C., & Lu, X. (2011). Dr. Jekyll vis-a-vis Mr. Hyde: Personality variation between virtual and real worlds. *Information and Management, 48*(1), 19–26.

Sutherland, S. (1993). Movement therapy: Healing mind and body. *Treating Abuse Today, 3,* 21–24.

Swihart, J., Silliman, B., & McNeil, J. (1992). Death of a student: Implications for secondary school counselors. *School Counselor, 40,* 55–58.

Swirsky, J. M., Carfagno, L., Milligan, F., & Raiff, B. (2014, August). *Systematic review of studies utilizing serious games, 2014.* Paper presented at the American Psychological Association convention, Washington, DC.

T

Tabachnick, J. (2013). Why prevention? Why now? *International Journal of Behavioral Consultation and Therapy, 8* (3–4), 55–61.

Taku, K., Cann, A., Calhoun, L. G., & Tedeschi, R. G. (2008). The factor structure of the Posttraumatic Growth Inventory: A comparison of five models using confirmatory factor analysis. *Journal of Traumatic Stress, 21*(2), 158–164.

Taku, K., Cann, A., Tedeschi, R. R., & Calhoun, L. G. (2015). Core beliefs shaken by an earthquake correlate with posttraumatic growth. *Psychological Trauma: Theory, Research, Practice, and Policy, 7*(2), 145–156.

Talbot, A., Manton, M., & Dunn, P. J. (1995). Debriefing the debriefers: An intervention strategy to assist psychologists after a crisis. In G. S. Everly, Jr., & J. M. Lating (Eds.), *Psychotraumatology* (pp. 281–298). New York: Plenum Press.

Tarasoff v. *Regents of the University of California,* 529 P.2d 553, 118 Cal. Rptr. 129 (1974) vacated, 17 Cal. 3d 425, 551 P2.d 334, 131 Cal. Rptr.14 (1976).

Tardiff, K. (1984a). Violence: The psychiatric patient. In J. T. Turner (Ed.), *Violence in the medical care setting: A survival guide* (pp. 33–55). Rockville, MD: Aspen Systems.

Tardiff, K. (1984b). *The psychiatric uses of seclusion and restraint.* Washington, DC: American Psychiatric Association Press.

Tardiff, K. (1989). *Assessment and management of violent patients.* Washington, DC: American Psychiatric Association Press.

Tardiff, K. (2003). Violence. In R. E. Hales, S. C. Yudofsky, & J. A. Talbot (Eds.), *Textbook of clinical psychiatry* (4th ed., pp. 1489–1509). Washington, DC: American Psychiatric Press.

Tarrier, N., & Humphreys, A. L. (2003). PTSD and the social support of the interpersonal environment: The development of social cognitive behavior therapy. *Journal of Cognitive Psychotherapy, 17*(2), 187–198.

Tarvydas, V., & Ng, H. K. Y., (2012). Ethical perspectives on trauma work. In L. Lopez Levers (Ed.), Trauma counseling: Theories and interventions. New York: Springer.

Tarvydas, V. M. (2012). Ethics and ethical decision making. In R. Maki & V. M. Tarvydas (Eds.), *The professional practice of rehabilitation counseling* (pp. 339–370). New York: Springer.

Taulbee, L. R. (1978). Reality orientation: A therapeutic group activity for elderly persons. In I. M. Burnside (Ed.), *Working with the elderly: Group process and techniques* (pp. 206–218). North Scituate, MA: Duxbury Press.

Taulbee, L. R., & Folsom, J. C. (1966). Reality orientation for geriatric patients. *Hospital and Community Psychiatry, 17*, 133–135.

Taylor, D. H., Kuchibhatia, M., Østbye, T., Plassman, B. L., & Clipp, E. C. (2008). The effect of spousal caregiving and bereavement on depressive symptoms. *Aging and Mental Health, 12*(1), 100–107.

Taylor, F. (2003). Tiagabine for posttraumatic stress disorder: A case series of 7 women. *Journal of Clinical Psychiatry, 64*(12), 1421–1425.

Taylor, R. J., Chatters, L. M., & Levin, J. S. (2004). *Religion in the lives of African Americans: Social, psychological, and health perspectives.* Thousand Oaks, CA: Sage.

Taylor, S. (2003). Outcome predictors for three PTSD treatments: Exposure therapy, EMDR, and relaxation training. *Journal of Cognitive Psychotherapy, 17*(2), 149–161.

Taylor, S. E. (2007). Social support. In H. S. Friedman & R. C. Silver (Eds.), *Foundations of health psychology* (pp. 145–171). New York: Oxford University Press.

Tedeschi, R. G., & Calhoun, L. G. (2009). The clinician as expert companion. In C. L. Park, S. C. Lechhner, M. Antoni, & A. Stanton (Eds.), *Medical illness and positive life change: Can crisis lead to personal transformation?* (pp. 215–235). Washington, DC: American Psychological Association.

Tedeschi, R. G., & Calhoun, L. G. (1995). *Trauma and transformation: Growing in the aftermath of suffering.* Thousand Oaks, CA: Sage.

Tedeschi, R. G., & Calhoun, L. G. (2003). Routes to posttraumatic growth through cognitive processing. In D. Paton, J. M. Volanti, & L. M. Smith (Eds.), *Promoting capabilities to manage posttraumatic stress: Perspective on resilience* (pp. 12–26). Springfield, IL: Charles C Thomas.

Tedeschi, R. G., & Calhoun, L. G. (2004). Posttraumatic growth: Conceptual foundations and empirical evidence. *Psychological Inquiry, 15*(1), 1–18.

Tedeschi, R. G., & Calhoun, L. G. (2006). Time of change? The spiritual challenges of bereavement and loss. *Omega: Journal of Death and Dying, 53*(1/2), 105–116.

Tedeschi, R. G., & Calhoun, L. G. (2009). The clinician as expert companion. In C. L. Park, S. C. Lechner, M. H. Antoni, & A. Stanton (Eds.), *Medical illness and positive life change: Can crisis lead to personal transformation?* (pp. 215–235). Washington, DC: American Psychological Association.

Tedeschi, R. G., & Calhoun, L. G. (2010). A surprise attack, a surprise result: Posttraumatic growth through expert companionship. In G. W. Burns (Ed.), *Happiness, healing, enhancement: Your case book collection of applying positive psychology in therapy* (pp. 226–236). Hoboken, NJ: John Wiley & Sons.

Tedeschi, R. G., & Calhoun, L. G. (2012). Pathways to personal transformation: Theoretical and empirical developments. In P. T. Wong (Ed.), *The human quest for meaning : Theories, research, and applications* (2nd ed., pp. 559–572). Personality and *clinical psychology series.* New York: Routledge/Taylor & Francis Group.

Tedeschi, R. G., & McNally, R. J. (2011). Can we facilitate posttraumatic growth in combat veterans? *American Psychologist, 66*(1), 19–24.

Tedeschi, R. G., Park, C. L., & Calhoun, L. G. (Eds.). (1998). *Posttraumatic growth: Positive changes in the aftermath of crisis.* Mahwah, NJ: Erlbaum.

Teller, J. L., Munetz, M. R., Gil, K. M., & Ritter, C. (2006). Crisis intervention team training for police officers responding to mental disturbance calls. *Psychiatric Services, 57*(2), 232–237.

TENTS. (2011). *TENTS–TP: The European Network for Traumatic Stress—Training and Practice.* Retrieved from www.estss.org /uploads/2011/07/146TENTS-TP_TTT_Trainers_manual _draft_1-18th_Jan.pdf

ter Kuile, H., & Ehring, T. (2014). Predictors of change in religiosity after trauma: Religiosity and posttraumatic stress disorder. *Psychological Trauma, Theory, Research, Practice, and Policy, 6*(4), 353–360

Terr, L. C. (1979). Children of Chowchilla: Study of psychic trauma. *Psychoanalytic Study of the Child, 34*, 547–623.

Terr, L. C. (1981). "Forbidden games": Posttraumatic child's play. *Journal of the American Academy of Child Psychiatry, 22*, 221–230.

Terr, L. C. (1983). Chowchilla revisited: The effects of psychic trauma four years after a school-bus kidnapping. *American Journal of Psychiatry, 140*, 1543–1550.

Terr, L. C. (1995). Childhood traumas: An outline and overview. In G. S. Everly, Jr., & J. M. Lating (Eds.), *Psychotraumatology* (pp. 301–320). New York: Plenum Press.

Tesarz, J., Leisner, S., Gerhardt, A., Janke, S., Seidler, G., Eich, W., & Hartmann, M. (2014). Effect of eye movement desensitization and reprocessing (EMDR) treatment in chronic pain patients: A systematic review. *Pain Medicine, 15*(2), 247–263.

Thackrey, M. (1987). *Therapeutics for aggression.* New York: Human Sciences Press.

The gang threat. (2009, February 6). Federal Bureau of Investigation. Retrieved from www.fbi.gov/news/stories/2009/february /ngta_020609

Theuninck, A. C., Lake, N., & Gibson, S. (2010). HIV-related posttraumatic stress disorder: Investigating the traumatic stress. *AIDS patient care and STDS, 24*(8), 458–491.

Thielman, K., & Cacciatore, J. (2014). Witness to suffering: Mindfulness and compassion fatigue among traumatic bereavement volunteers and professionals. *Social Work, 59*(1), 34–41.

Thoburn, J. W., Bentley, J. A., Ahmad, Z. S., & Jones, K. C. (2012). International disaster psychology ethics: A social justice model imbedded in a systems paradigm. *Traumatology, 18*(4), 79–85. doi: 10.177/1534765612444880

Thomae, C. (2002). *The incident command system and standard operating procedures for a school crisis team.* Tucson: Arizona School Counselor Association.

Thomas, A. M., & Levitt, D. (2010, August). Self-care: An ethical obligation and preventive tool. *Counseling Today*, 44–46.

Thomas, B. J. (2007). The relationship between affect balance, self-care behavior, and secondary traumatic stress reactions. *Dissertation Abstracts International: Section B. The Sciences and Engineering, 67*(8), 4145.

Thomas, C., Kitchen, D., & Smith, A. (2005). The management of aggression care plans: Implementation and efficacy in a forensic learning disability service. *British Journal of Forensic Science, 7*(2), 3–9.

Thomas, R. B., & Wilson, J. P. (2004). Issues and controversies in the understanding and diagnosis of compassion fatigue, vicarious traumatization and secondary traumatic stress disorder. *International Journal of Emergency Mental Health, 6*(2), 81–92.

Thompson, A. (1983). *Ethical concerns in psychotherapy and their legal ramification.* Lanham, MD: University Press of America.

Thompson, B. E. (2014). Sketching out the story. B. E. Thompson & R. A. Neimeyer (Eds.), *Grief and the expressive arts: Practices for creating meaning. Series in death, dying, and bereavement* (pp. 139–145). New York: Routledge/Taylor & Francis Group.

Thompson, C. (2014). Police add texting to crisis negotiation. Retrieved from http://cnsnews.com/news/article/police-add-texting-crisis-negotiation-arsenal

Thompson, C. E., & Neville, H. A. (1999). Racism, mental health, and mental health practice. *Counseling Psychologist, 27,* 155–223.

Thompson, C. L., & Rudolph, L. B. (1992). *Counseling children.* Pacific Grove, CA: Brooks/Cole.

Thompson, I., Amatea, E., & Thompson, E. (2014). Personal and contextual predictors of mental health counselors' compassion fatigue and burnout. *Journal of Mental Health Counseling, 36*(1), 58–77.

Thompson, M., Kaslow, N., Kingree, J., Puett, R., Thompson, N., & Meadows, L. (1999). Partner abuse in posttraumatic stress disorder as risk factors for suicide attempts in a sample of low-income, inner-city women. *Journal of Traumatic Stress, 12*(1), 59–72.

Thompson, R. A. (2004). *Crisis intervention and crisis management: Strategies that work in schools and communities.* New York: Brunner-Rutledge.

Thompson, R. S., Bonomi, A., Anderson, M., Reid, R., Dimer, J., Carrell, D., et al. (2006). Intimate partner violence: Prevalence, types, and chronicity in adult women. *American Journal of Preventive Medicine, 30*(6), 447–457.

Thorne, F. C. (1973). Eclectic psychotherapy. In R. Corsini (Ed.), *Current psychotherapies* (pp. 445–486). Itasca, IL: F. E. Peacock.

Thorne, F. C. (Ed.). (1968). *Psychological case handling: Vol. 1. Establishing the conditions necessary for counseling and psychotherapy.* Brandon, VT: Clinical Psychology Publishing.

Thornhill, R., & Palmer, C. T. (2000). *A natural history of rape: Biological bases of sexual coercion.* Cambridge, MA: MIT Press.

Thornton, P. T. (1992). The relation of coping, appraisal, and burnout in mental health workers. *Journal of Psychology, 126,* 261–271.

Threat assessment team formation. (2008). Virginia Code 23-31 9.2:3C.

Threat of violence. (2008). Virginia Code 23-31 92:10.

Tilden, V. P., & Shepard, P. (1987). Increasing the rate of identification of battered women in an emergency department: Use of a nursing protocol. *Research in Nursing and Health, 10,* 209–215.

Tilden, V. P., Schmidt, T. A., Limandri, B. J., Chiodo, G. T., Garland, M. J., & Loveless, P. A. (1994). Factors that influence clinicians' assessment and management of family violence. *American Journal of Public Health, 84*(4), 628–633.

Tillman, K., & Rust, J. (2011). Kids supporting kids. *ASCA School Counselor, 49*(1), 18–23.

Tinnin, L., Bills, L., & Gantt, L. (2002). Short-term treatment of simple and complex PTSD. In M. Williams & J. Sommer (Eds.), *Simple and complex post-traumatic stress disorder: Strategies for comprehensive treatment in clinical practice* (pp. 99–118). Binghamton, NY: Haworth Press.

Tjaden, L., & Thoennes, N. (2000). *Full report of the prevalence, incidence and consequences of violence against women* (NCJ 183781). National Institute of Justice, Office of Justice Programs.

Tjaden, P., & Thoennes, N. (1998a). Battering in America: Findings from the National Violence Against Women Survey. *Research*

in brief (pp. 606–666). Washington, DC: National Institute of Justice, U.S. Department of Justice.

Tjaden, P., & Thoennes, N. (1998b). *Stalking in America: Findings from the National Violence Against Women Survey* (NCJ Report #169592). Washington, DC: National Institute of Justice, and Centers for Disease Control and Prevention.

Tjaden, P., & Thoennes, N. (2000). *Extent, nature, and consequences of intimate partner violence.* Washington, DC: National Institute of Justice, and Centers for Disease Control and Prevention.

Tjeltveit, A. C., & Gottlieb, M. C. (2010). Avoiding the road to ethical disaster: Overcoming vulnerabilities and developing resilience. *Psychotherapy Theory, Research, Practice, Training, 47,* 98–110.

Tjersland, O. A., Mossige, S., Gulbrandsen, W., Jensen, T. K., & Reichelt, S. (2006). Helping families when child sexual abuse is suspected but not proven. *Child and Family Social Work, 11,* 297–306.

Toker, S., Shirom, A., Shapira, I., Berliner, S., & Melamed, S. (2005). The association between burnout, depression, anxiety, and inflammation biomarkers: C-reactive protein and fibrinogen in men and women. *Journal of Occupational Health Psychology, 10*(4), 344–362.

Tollefson, D., & Phillips, I. (2015). A mind-body bridging treatment program for domestic violence offenders: Program overview and evaluation results. *Journal of Family Violence, 40*(3), 212–220

Tolmach, J. (1985). "There ain't nobody on my side." A new day treatment program for black urban youth. *Journal of Clinical Child Psychology, 14,* 214–219.

Tolman, R. M., & Bennett, L. W. (1990). A review of quantitative research on men who batter. *Journal of Interpersonal Violence, 5,* 87–118.

Tomine, S. (1986). Private practice in gerontological counseling. *Journal of Counseling and Development, 68,* 406–409.

Tomko, J. R. (2012). Neurobiological effects of trauma and psychopharmacology. In L. Lopez-Levers (Ed.), *Trauma counseling: Theory and interventions* (pp. 59–76). New York: Springer.

Tomko, R.L., Trull, T., Wood, P., & Sher, K. (2014) Characteristics of borderline personality disorder in a community sample: Comorbidity, treatment utilization and general functioning. *Journal of Personality Disorders, 28* ((5), 734–750.

Tomlinson-Clarke, S. (2013). Multicultural counseling competencies: Extending multicultural training paradigms toward globalization. Retrieved from http://www.counseling.org/knowledge-center/vistas/by-subject2/vistas-multicultural-issues/docs/default-source/vistas/multicultural-counseling-competencies

Tomoko, I., Asukai, K., Toshilo, I., Inamoto, E., & Kageyama, T. (2002). Mental health effects of child sexual victimization in Japan. *Journal of Mental Health, 48,* 23–28.

Toro-Alfonso, J., & Rodriguez-Madera, S. (2004). Domestic violence in Puerto Rican gay male couples. *Journal of Interpersonal Violence, 19,* 639–654.

Tortella-Feliu, M., Botella, C., Llabres, J., Breton-Lopez, J., del Amo, A., Banos, R., & Gelabert, J. (2011). Virtual reality versus computer-aided exposure treatments for fear of flying. *Behavior Modification, 35*(1), 3–30.

Townsend, E., Hawton, K., Altman, D. G., Arensman, E., Gunnell, D., Hazell, P., et al. (2001). The efficacy of problem-solving treatments after deliberate self-harm: Meta-analysis of randomized controlled trials with respect to depression, hopelessness, and improvement in problems. *Psychological Medicine, 31,* 978–988.

Treatment Advocacy Center. (2014). The treatment of persons with mental illness in prisons and jails. *Research from the Treatment Advocacy Center.* Arlington, VA: Author. Retrieved from http://www.tacrepports.org /treatment-behind-bars

Tremblay, G. (2013, August). *The maze of gender identity and sexual orientation of sexually abused young men.* Paper presented at the 121st American Psychological Association Convention, Honolulu, HI.

Trimble, J. E. (2007). Prolegomena for the connotation of construct use in the measurement of ethnic and racial identity. *Journal of Counseling Psychology, 54,* 247–258.

Trimble, M. R. (1985). Post-traumatic stress disorder: History of a concept. In C. R. Figley (Ed.), *Trauma and its wake: The study of post-trauma stress disorder* (pp. 5–14). New York: Brunner/Mazel.

Triplett, K., Tedeschi, R., Cann, A., Calhoun, L., & Reeve, C. (2012). Posttraumatic growth, meaning in life, and life satisfaction in response to trauma. *Psychological Trauma: Theory, Research, Practice, and Policy, 4(4),* 400–410.

Tripod, S., & Pettus-Davis, C. (2013). Histories of childhood victimization and subsequent mental health problems, substance abuse, and sexual victimization for a sample of incarcerated women in the U.S. *International Journal of Law and Psychiatry, 36*(1), 30–40.

Trotter, S. (2003, June). *Handling a crisis at school.* Paper presented at the American School Counselor Association Conference, St. Louis, MO.

Ttofi, M., & Farrington, D. (2011). Effectiveness of school based programs to prevent bullying. *Journal of Experimental Criminology, 7*(1), 27–56.

Tuber, S., Boesch, K., Gorkin, J., & Terry, M. (2014). Chronic early trauma as a childhood syndrome and its relationship to play. In C. Malchiodi & D. A. Crenshaw (Eds.), *Creative arts and play therapy or attachment problems: Creative arts and play therapy* (pp. 215–226). New York: Guilford Press.

Tubesing, D. A., & Strosahl, S. G. (1976). *Wholistic health centers: Survey research report.* Hinsdale, IL: Society for Wholistic Medicine.

Tubesing, N. L., & Tubesing, D. A. (1982). The treatment of choice: Selecting stress skills to suit the individual and the situation. In W. S. Paine (Ed.), *Job stress and burnout* (pp. 155–172). Newbury Park, CA: Sage.

Tucker, P., Pfefferbaum, B., Nixon, S., & Foy, D. (1999). Trauma and recovery among adults highly exposed to a community disaster. *Psychiatric Annals, 29*(2), 78–83.

Tuerk, P. W., Yoder, M., Ruggiero, K. J., Gros, D. F., & Acierno, R. (2010). A pilot study of prolonged exposure therapy for post-traumatic stress disorder delivered via telehealth technology. *Journal of Traumatic Stress, 23,* 116–123.

Tufnell, G. (2005). Eye movement desensitization and reprocessing in the treatment of pre-adolescent children with post-traumatic symptoms. *Clinical Child Psychology and Psychiatry, 10*(4), 587–600.

Tull, M. (2013). *Suicide hotline just for veterans.* U.S. Department of Veterans Affairs. Retrieved from www.ptsdabout.com/od /ptsdandthemilitary/qt/hotline.htm?utm_term=veterans hotline_content

Tunick, R. A., Gavin, J. A., DeMaso, D. R., & Meyer, E. C. (2013). Pediatric psychology critical care consultation: An emerging subspecialty. *Clinical Practice in Pediatric Psychology, 1*(1), 42–54.

Turnbull, J., Aitken, I., Black, L., & Patterson, B. (1990, June). Turn it around: Short-term management for aggression and anger. *Journal of Psychosocial Nursing and Mental Health Services, 28,* 7–13.

Turner, J. (Ed.). (1984). *Violence in the medical care setting: A survival guide.* Rockville, MD: Aspen Systems.

Turner, S. F., & Shapiro, C. H. (1986). Battered women: Mourning the death of a relationship. *Social Work, 31,* 372–376.

Turner, S. W., McFarlane, A. C., & van der Kolk, B. A. (1996). The therapeutic environment and new explorations in the treatment of posttraumatic stress disorder. In B. A. van der Kolk, A. C. McFarlane, & L. Weisaeth (Eds.), *Traumatic stress* (pp. 537–558). New York: Guilford Press.

Turner, W. A., & Casey, L. M. (2014). Outcomes associated with virtual reality in psychological interventions: Where are we now? *Clinical Psychology Review, 34*(8), 634–644.

Turns, D. M. (1993). Institutional response to violent incidents. In P. E. Blumenreich & S. Lewis (Eds.), *Managing the violent patient: A clinician's guide* (pp. 131–135). New York: Brunner-Mazel.

Turns, D. M., & Blumenreich, P. E. (1993). Epidemiology. In P. E. Blumenreich & S. Lewis (Eds.), *Managing the violent patient: A clinician's guide* (pp. 5–20). New York: Brunner-Mazel.

Tuttle, A. (1991). *Advantages and strategies of telephone crisis counseling* (audiotape). Memphis, TN: The Crisis Center.

Tutty, L. M., & Rothery, M. A. (2002). Beyond shelters: Support groups and community-based advocacy for abused women. In A. R. Roberts (Ed.), *Handbook of domestic violence: Intervention strategies* (pp. 396–418). New York: Oxford University Press.

Tutty, L. M., Bidgood, B. A., & Rothery, M. A. (1993). Support groups for battered women: Research on their efficacy. *Journal of Family Violence, 8,* 325–343.

Twomey, C., O'Reilly, G., Byrne, M., Bury, M., White, A., Kissane, S., McMahon, A., & Clancy, N. (2014). A randomized control trial of the computerized CBT programme, moodGYM, for public mental health service users waiting for intervention. *British Journal of Clinical Psychology, 53*(4), 433–450.

Tyrka, A. R., Burgers, D. E., Philip, N. S., Price, L. H., & Carpenter, L. (2013). The neurobiological correlates of childhood adversity and implications for treatment. *Acta Psychiatria Scandinavica, 128*(6), 434–447.

U

U.S. Department of Education (2015). *Anti-bully tool kit.* Retrieved from www.ed.gov/blog/tag/bullying/

U.S. Department of Education. (2003). *Practical information on crisis planning: A guide for schools and communities.* Retrieved from www 2.ed.gov/admins/lead/safety/emergencyplan/crisisplanning .pdf

U.S. Department of Education. (2011, April 4). *Dear colleague letter: Sexual violence background, summary, and fast facts.* Retrieved from www.ed.gov/about/offices/list/ocr/docs/dcl-factsheet-201104 .html

U.S. Department of Education. (2013). *Guide for developing high quality school emergency operations plans.* Retrieved from www.rems .ed.gov/docs/rems_k-12_guide_5508pdf

U.S. Department of Health and Human Services. (1997). *Study findings: Study of national incidence and prevalence of child abuse and neglect: 1988.* Bethesda, MD: U.S. Government Printing Office.

U.S. Department of Health and Human Services. (2003). *Developing cultural competence in disaster mental health programs: Guiding principles and recommendations.* DHHS Pub. No. SMA 3828. Rockville, MD: Center for Mental Health Services, Substance Abuse and Mental Health Services Administration.

U.S. Department of Health and Human Services. (2003). *Suicide in the United States.* Atlanta, GA: Centers for Disease Control and Prevention, National Center for Injury Prevention and Control.

U.S. Department of Health and Human Services. (2015). *Stop bullying.* Retrieved from www.stopbullying.gov

U.S. Department of Justice, Bureau of Justice Statistics. (1998). *Data from the National Crime Victimization Survey, 1992–1996.* Washington, DC: Author.

U.S. Department of Justice, Bureau of Justice Statistics. (2001). *Data from the National Crime Victimization Survey, 1993–1999.* Washington, DC: Author.

U.S. Department of Justice. (1998). *National violence against women survey.* Washington, DC: Author.

U.S. Department of Justice. (2000). *Response to terrorism victims: Oklahoma City and beyond.* Washington, DC: Author.

U.S. Department of Justice. (2000, May). Children as victims: 1999 National Report Series. *Juvenile Justice Bulletin.* Washington, DC: Author.

U.S. Department of Justice. (2003). *National crime victimization survey—2002.* Washington, DC: Author.

U.S. Department of Labor, Bureau of Labor Statistics. (2001). *Survey of occupational injuries and illnesses, 2000.* Washington, DC: Author.

U.S. Department of Labor, Bureau of Labor Statistics. (2002). *Census of fatal occupational injuries and illnesses, 2000.* Washington, DC: Author.

U.S. Department of Veterans Affairs. (2011). *Psychological first aid: Field operations guide.* Retrieved January 11, 2011, from http://ptsd.va.gov/prfessional/manuals/psych -first-aid.asp

U.S. Department of Veterans Affairs. (2014). Veterans crisis line. Retrieved from http://veteranscrisisline.net/

U.S. Office of Juvenile Justice and Delinquency Prevention. (1995). *A comprehensive response to America's youth gang problem.* Washington, DC: Author.

Ulibarri, M., Strathdee, S., Lozada, R., Maigs-Rodriquez, C., Amaro, H., O'Campo, P., & Pattterson, T. L. (2010). Intimate partner violence among female sex workers in two Mexico-U.S. border cities: Partner characteristics and HIV risk behaviors as correlates of abuse. *Psychological Trauma: Theory, Research, Practice, and Policy, 2*(4), 318–325.

Ullman, S. E. (1996a). Correlates and consequences of adult sexual assault disclosure. *Journal of Interpersonal Violence, 11,* 554–571.

Ullman, S. E. (1996b). Social reactions, coping strategies, and self-blame attributions in adjustment to sexual assault. *Psychology of Women Quarterly, 20,* 505–526.

Ullman, S. E., & Brecklin, L. R. (2002). Sexual assault history and suicidal behavior in a national sample of women. *Suicide and Life Threatening Behavior, 32*(2), 117–130.

Ullman, S. E., & Brecklin, L. R. (2003). Sexual assault history and health-related outcomes in a national sample of women. *Psychology of Women Quarterly, 27*(1), 46–57.

Ullman, S. E., & Siegel, J. M. (1994). Predictors of exposure to traumatic events and posttraumatic stress sequelae. *Journal of Community Psychology, 22,* 328–338.

Ullman, S. E., Karabatsos, G., & Koss, M. P. (1999). Alcohol and sexual assault in a national sample of college women. *Journal of Interpersonal Violence, 14,* 603–625.

Underwood, M. M., & Clark, C. (2002). Using metaphor to help children cope with trauma: An example from September 11th. In D. D. Bass & R. Yep (Eds.), *Terrorism, trauma, and tragedies: A counselor's guide to preparing and responding* (pp. 33–36). Alexandria, VA: American Counseling Association.

Urhausen, M. T. (2015). Eye movement desensitization and reprocessing and art therapy with traumatized children. In C. A. Malchiodi (Ed.), *Creative interventions with traumatized children* (2nd ed., pp. 45–74). New York: Guilford Press.

Ursano, R., Fullerton, C., Vance, K., & Kao, T. (1999). Posttraumatic stress disorder and identification in disaster workers. *American Journal of Psychiatry, 156*(3), 353–359.

Ursano, R. J., & Friedman, M. J. (2006). Mental health and behavioral interventions for victims of disasters and mass violence: Systems, caring, planning and needs. In E. C. Ritchie, P. J. Watson, & M. J. Friedman (Eds.), *Interventions following mass violence and disasters: Strategies for mental health practice* (pp. 405–414). New York: Guilford Press.

V

Vaaler, A. E., Morken, G., & Linaker, O. (2005). Effects of different interior decorations in the seclusion area of a psychiatric acute ward. *Nordic Journal of Psychiatry, 59*(1), 19–24.

Vahtera, J., Kivimäki, M., Väänägen, A., Linna, A., Pentti, J., Helenius, H., et al. (2006). Sex differences in health effects of family death or illness: Are women more vulnerable than men? *Psychosomatic Medicine, 68*(2), 283–291.

Vaiva, G., Ducrocq, F., Meyer, P., Mathieu, D., Philippe, A., Libersa, C., & Goudemand, M. (2006). Effect of telephone contact on further suicide attempts in patients discharged from an emergency department: Randomised controlled study. *British Medical Journal, 332*(7552), 1241–1245.

Van Auken, S. (1979). Youth counselor burnout. *Personnel and Guidance Journal, 58,* 143–144.

van Ballegoojien,W., Cuijpers, P., van Straten, A., Karvotaki, E., Andersson, G., Smit, J., & Riper, H. (2014). Adherence to internet-based and face-to-face cognitive behavioural therapy for depression: A meta-analysis. *PLos ONE, 9*(7), e100674.

Van Bruggen, M. L., Runtz, M., & Kadlec, H. (2006). Sexual revictimization: The role of self-esteem and dysfunctional sexual behaviors. *Child Maltreatment, 11*(2), 131–145.

Van Brunt, B. (2015). *Harm to other: The assessment and treatment of dangerousness.* Alexandria, VA: American Counseling Association.

Vancleave, J. A. (2008). School resource officers: What high school teachers consider to be the most important tasks. *Dissertations Abstracts International: Section A. Humanities and Social Sciences, 69*(1-A), 389.

Vandenberg, N. (1992). Using critical incidents and debriefing to mediate organizational crisis, change, and loss. *Employee Assistance Quarterly, 8,* 35–55.

van den Brink, R. H., Hooijschuur, A., van Os, T. W., Savenije, W., & Wiersma, D. (2010). Routine violence risk assessment in community forensic mental health care. *Behavioral Sciences and the Law, 28*(3), 396–410.

van den Eynde, J., & Veno, A. (1999). Coping with disastrous events: An empowerment model for community healing. In R. Gist & B. Lubin (Eds.), *Response to disaster: Psychosocial, community and ecological approaches* (pp. 167–192). Philadelphia: Brunner/Mazel.

Van der Heijden, I., & Swartz, S. (2010). Bereavement, silence, and culture within a peer-led HIV/AIDS-prevention strategy for vulnerable children in South Africa. *African Journal of AIDS Research, 9*(1), 41–50.

van der Kolk, B. (2005). Developmental trauma disorder in childhood. *Psychiatric Annals, 35*(5), 401–408.

van der Kolk, B. A. (1996a). The body keeps the score: Approaches to the psychobiology of posttraumatic stress disorder. In B. A. van der Kolk, A. C. McFarlane, & L. Weisaeth (Eds.), *Traumatic stress* (pp. 214–241). New York: Guilford Press.

van der Kolk, B. A. (1996b). Trauma and memory. In B. A. van der Kolk, A. C. McFarlane, & L. Weisaeth (Eds.), *Traumatic stress* (pp. 279–297). New York: Guilford Press.

van der Kolk, B. A., & McFarlane, A. C. (1996). The black hole of trauma. In B. A. van der Kolk, A. C. McFarlane, & L. Weisaeth

(Eds.), *Trauma stress: The effects of overwhelming experience on the mind, body, and society* (pp. 3–23). New York: Guilford Press.

van der Kolk, B. A., Dreyfuss, D., Michaels, M., Shera, D., Berkowitz, B., Fisler, R., et al. (1994). Fluoxetine in posttraumatic stress disorder. *Journal of Clinical Psychiatry, 55*(12), 517–522.

van der Kolk, B. A., McFarlane, A. C., & van der Hart, O. (1996). A general approach to treatment of posttraumatic stress disorder. In B. A. van der Kolk, A. C. McFarlane, & L. Weisaeth (Eds.), *Traumatic stress* (pp. 417–440). New York: Guilford Press.

van der Kolk, B. A., van der Hart, O., & Burbridge, J. (2002). In M. Williams & J. Sommer (Eds.), *Simple and complex posttraumatic stress disorder: Strategies for comprehensive treatment in clinical practice* (pp. 23–45). Binghamton, NY: Haworth Press.

van der Kolk, B. A., Weisaeth, L., & van der Hart, O. (1996). History of trauma in psychiatry. In B. A. van der Kolk, A. C. McFarlane, & L. Weisaeth (Eds.), *Traumatic stress* (pp. 47–74). New York: Guilford Press.

Van Deusen, S., & Courtois, C.A. (2015). Spirituality, religion, and complex trauma. In D. F. Walker, C.A. Courtois, & J. Aten (Eds.), *Spiritually oriented psychotherapy for trauma* (pp. 29–54). Washington, DC: American Psychological Association.

Van Dyk, A. C. (2007). Occupational stress experienced by caregivers working in the HIV/AIDS field in South Africa. *African Journal of AIDS Research, 6*(1), 49–66.

Van Ommeren, M., Saxena, S., & Saraceno, S. (2005). Mental and social health during and after acute emergencies: Emerging consensus? *Bulletin of the World Health Organization, 83*(1), 71–75.

Van Orden, K. A., Witte, T. K., Cukrowicz, K. C., Braithwaite, S. R., Selby, E., & Joiner, T. E. (2010). The interpersonal theory of suicide. *Psychological Review, 117,* 575–600.

Van Orden, K. A., Witte, T. K., Gordon, K. H., Bender, T. W., & Joiner, T. E. (2008). Suicidal desire and the capability for suicide: Tests of the interpersonal psychological theory of suicidal behavior among adults. *Journal of Consulting and Clinical Psychology, 76,* 72–83.

van Praag, H. (2001). Suicide and aggression: Are they biologically two sides of the same coin? In D. Lester (Ed.), *Suicide prevention: Resources for the millennium* (pp. 45–66). Philadelphia: Brunner-Routledge.

Van Praagh, J. (2000). *Healing grief: Reclaiming life after any loss.* New York: Random House.

Van Puyenbroeck, J., & Maes, B. (2006). Program development of reminiscence group work for ageing people with intellectual disabilities. *Journal of Intellectual and Developmental Disability, 31*(3), 139–147.

Varelas, N., & Foley, L. A. (1998). Blacks' and Whites' perceptions of interracial and intraracial date rape. *Journal of Social Psychology, 138,* 392–400.

Vasterling, J. J., & Brewin, C. R. (Eds.). (2005). *Neuropsychology of PTSD: Biological, cognitive, and clinical perspectives.* New York: Guilford Press.

Vermette, H. S., Pinals, D. A., & Applebaum, P. S. (2005). Mental health training for law enforcement professionals. *Journal of the American Academy of Psychiatry and the Law, 33*(1), 42–46.

Vermetten, E., & Bremner, J. (2002). Circuits and systems in stress: II. Applications to neurobiology and treatment in posttraumatic stress disorder. *Depression and Anxiety, 16*(1), 14–38.

Vermetten, E., & Lanius, R. A. (2012). Biological and clinical framework for post traumatic stress disorder. In T. E. Schlaepfer and C. B. Nemeroff (Eds.), *Neurobiology of psychiatric disorders: Handbook of clinical neurology, 3rd series* (pp. 291–342). Amsterdam, Netherlands: Elsevier Science Publishers.

Vermetten, E., Vythilingam, M., Southwick, S. M., Charney, D. S., & Bremmer, J. D. (2003). Long-term treatment with paroxetin increases verbal declarative memory and hippocampal volume in posttraumatic stress disorder. *Biological Psychiatry, 54,* 693–702.

Vernberg, E. M. (1999). Children's responses to disaster: Family and systems approaches. In R. Gist & B. Lubin (Eds.), *Response to disaster: Psychosocial, community and ecological approaches* (pp. 193–210). Philadelphia: Brunner/Mazel.

Vickers, M. H. (2009). Journeys into grief: Exploring redundancy for a new understanding of workplace grief. *Journal of Loss and Trauma, 14*(5), 401–419.

Viner, J. (1982). Toward more skillful handling of acutely psychotic patients: Part I. Evaluation. *Emergency Room Report, 3,* 125–130.

Vinick, B. (1986). *Counseling in a state mental hospital* (Cassette Recording No. 13). Memphis, TN: Memphis State University, Department of Counseling and Personnel Services.

Vinturella, L., & James, R. K. (1987). Sand play: A therapeutic medium with children. *Elementary School Guidance and Counseling, 21,* 229–238.

Violanti, J. M. (2000). Scripting trauma: The impact of pathogenic intervention. In J. M. Violanti, D. Paton, & C. Dunning (Eds.), *Posttraumatic stress intervention: Challenges, issues and perspectives* (pp. 153–165). Springfield, IL: Charles C Thomas.

Vitaro, F., & Brendgen, M. (2005). Proactive and reactive aggression: A developmental perspective. In R. E. Tremblay, W. W. Hartup, & J. Archer (Eds.), *Developmental origins of aggression* (pp. 178–201). New York: Guilford Press.

Vitaro, F., Brendgen, M., & Tremblay, R. E. (2002). Reactively and proactively aggressive children: Antecedent and subsequent characteristics. *Journal of Child Psychology and Psychiatry, 43,* 495–505.

Vladutiu, C. J., Martin, S. L., & Macy, R. J. (2011). College- or university-based sexual assault prevention programs: A review of program outcomes, characteristics, and recommendations. *Trauma, Violence, and Abuse, 12*(2), 67–86.

Voelkel, E., Pukay-Martin, N. D., Walter, K., & Chard, K. (2015). Effectiveness of cognitive processing therapy for male and female veterans with and without military exual trauma. *Journal of Traumatic Stress, 28*(3), 174–182.

Volpe, U., Luciano, M., Palumbo, C., Sampogna, G., Del Vecchio, V., & Fiorillo, A. (2014). Risk of burnout among early career mental health professionals. *Journal of Psychiatric and Mental Health Nursing, 21*(9), 774–781.

Vossekuil, B., Fein, R. A., Reddy, M., Borum, R., & Modzelski, W. (2002). *The final report and findings on the safe school initiative: Implications for the prevention of school attacks in the United States.* Washington, DC: U.S. Secret Service and U.S. Department of Education.

Vossekuil, B., Reddy, M., Fein, R., Borum, R., & Modzeleski, W. (2000). *U.S. Safe School Initiative: An interim report on the prevention of targeted violence in schools.* Washington, DC: U.S. Secret Service, National Threat Assessment Center.

W

Wachen, J., Jimenez, S., Smith, K., & Resick, P. A. (2014). Long-term functional outcomes of women receiving cognitive processing therapy and prolonged exposure. *Psychological Trauma: Theory, Research, Practice, and Policy, 6*(Supp. 1), S58–S65

Wachter, C. A. (2007, March). *Crisis in the schools: Crisis, crisis intervention training, and school counselor burnout.* Paper presented at the American Counseling Association Convention, Detroit.

Wagner, B. (1997). Family risk factors for child and adolescent suicidal behavior. *Psychological Bulletin, 121,* 246–298.

Wagner, S. L. (2005). Emergency response service personnel and the critical incident stress debriefing debate. *International Journal of Emergency Mental Health, 7,* 33–41.

Wakefield, J. C., Schmitz, M. F., & Baer, J. C. (2011). Did narrowing the major depression bereavement exclusion from DSM-III-R to DSM-IV increase validity? Evidence from a national comorbidity study. *Journal of Nervous and Mental Disease, 199*(2), 66–73.

Wakelee-Lynch, J. (1990, October). Florida crisis elicits aid from college officials and counselors. *Guidepost,* pp. 1, 3.

Waldron, J., Wilson, L., Patriquin, M., & Scarpa, A. (2015). Sexual victimization history, depression, and task physiology as predictors of sexual revictimization: Results from a 6-month prospective pilot study. *Journal of Interpersonal Violence, 30*(40), 622–639.

Walker, D., Neighbors, C., Mbilinyi, L., O'Rouke, A., Zegree, J., et al. (2010). Evaluating the impact of intimate partner violence on the perpetrator: The Perceived Consequences of Domestic Violence Questionnaire. *Journal of Interpersonal Violence, 25*(9), 1684–1698.

Walker, D. F., Courtois, C. A., & Aten, J. (Eds.). (2015). *Spiritually oriented psychotherapy for trauma.* Washington, DC: American Psychological Association.

Walker, D. F., Courtois, C. A., & Aten, J. D. (2015). Basics of working on spiritual matters with traumatized individuals. In D. F. Walker, C. A. Courtois, & J. D. Aten (Eds.), *Spiritually oriented psychotherapy for trauma* (pp. 15–28). Washington, DC: American Psychological Association.

Walker, D. F., Gorusch, L., & Tan, S. Y. (2004). Therapists' integration of religion and spirituality in counseling: A meta-analysis. *Counseling and Values, 49,* 69–80.

Walker, D. F., McGregor, K. L., Quagliana, F., Stephens, R. L., & Knodel, K. (2015). Understanding and responding to changes in spirituality and religion after traumatic events. In D. F. Walker, C. A. Courtois, & J. Aten (Eds.), *Spiritually oriented psychotherapy for trauma* (pp. 147–168). Washington, DC: American Psychological Association.

Walker, G. (1990). Crisis-care in critical incident debriefing. *Death Studies, 14,* 121–133.

Walker, J. I. (1983). Comparison of "rap" groups with traditional group therapy in the treatment of Vietnam combat veterans. *Group, 7,* 48–57.

Walker, L. E. (1979). How battering happens and how to stop it. In D. Moore (Ed.), *Battered women* (pp. 59–78). Newbury Park, CA: Sage.

Walker, L. E. (1984). *The battered woman syndrome.* New York: Springer.

Walker, L. E. (1989). *Terrifying love: Why battered women kill and how society responds.* New York: Harper & Row.

Walker, L. E. (2000). *The battered woman syndrome* (2nd ed.). New York: Springer.

Walker, Z., & Seifert, R. (1994). Violent incidents in a psychiatric intensive care unit. *British Journal of Psychiatry, 164,* 826–828.

Waller, R., Mahmood, T., Gandi, R., Delves, S., Humphrys, N., & Smith, D. (2005). Student mental health: How can psychiatrists better support the work of university medical centre and university counseling services? *British Journal of Guidance and Counseling, 33*(1), 117–128.

Wallerstein, J. S., & Kelly, J. B. (1975). The effects of parental divorce: Experiences of the preschool child. *Journal of the American Academy of Child Psychiatry, 14,* 600–616.

Walsh, F. (2009). Integrating spirituality and family therapy: Wellsprings for health, healing, and resilience. In F. Walsh (Ed.),

Spiritual resources in family therapy (2nd ed., pp. 31–61). New York: Guilford Press.

Walsh, F. (2009). Spiritual resources in family adaptation to death and loss. In F. Walsh (Ed.), *Spiritual resources in family therapy* (2nd ed., pp. 81–102). New York: Guilford Press.

Walsh, F. (2012a). Clinical views of family normality, health, and dysfunction: From a deficits to a strength perspective. In F. Walsh (Ed.), *Normal family processes: Growing diversity and complexity* (4th ed., pp. 28–54). New York: Guildford Press.

Walsh, F. (2012b). Family resiliency: Strengths forged through adversity. In F. Walsh (Ed.), *Normal family processes: Growing diversity and complexity* (4th ed., pp. 399–428). New York: Guildford Press.

Walsh, K., King, M., Jones, L., Tookman, A., & Blizard, R. (2002). Spiritual beliefs may affect outcome of bereavement: Prospective study. *British Medical Journal, 324*(7353), 1551.

Walsh, K., Latzman, N., & Latzman, R. (2014). Pathway from child sexual and physical abuse to risky sex among emerging adults: The role of trauma-related intrusions and alcohol problems. *Journal of Adolescent Health, 54*(4), 442–448.

Walter, J. L., & Peller, J. E. (1992). *Becoming solution-focused in brief therapy.* New York: Routledge Taylor & Francis.

Walters, M. L. (2011). Straighten up and act like a lady: A qualitative study of lesbian survivors of intimate partner violence. *Journal of Gay and Lesbian Social Services, 23*(2), 250–270.

Walz, G. R., Bluer, J. C., & Yep, R. K. (Eds.). (2009). *Compelling counseling interventions: Celebrating VISTAS' 50th anniversary* (pp. 259–269). Ann Arbor, MI: Counseling Outfitters.

Wang, J. (2005). The effects of reminiscence on depressive symptoms and mood status of older institutionalized adults in Taiwan. *International Journal of Geriatric Psychiatry, 20*(1), 57–62.

Wark, V. (1982). A look at the work of the telephone counseling center. *Personnel and Guidance Journal, 61,* 110–112.

Wark, V. (1984). *The sex caller and the telephone counseling center.* Springfield, IL: Charles C Thomas.

Warnath, C. F., & Shelton, J. L. (1976). The ultimate disappointment: The burned out counselor. *Personnel and Guidance Journal, 55,* 172–175.

Warren, J. I., South, S., Burnette, M., Rogers, A., Friend, R., Bale, R., et al. (2005). Understanding the risk factors for violence and criminality in women: The concurrent validity of the PCL-R and the HCR-20. *International Journal of Law and Psychiatry, 28*(3), 269–289.

Wasserman, D., Hoven, D., Wasserman, C., Wall, M., Eisenberg, R., Hadlaczky, G., . . . Carli, V. (2015). School-based suicide prevention programmes: The SEYLE cluster-randomized controlled trial. *The Lancet, 3285*(9977), 1536–1544.

Waters, J., & Finn, E. (1995). Handling crisis effectively on the telephone. In A. R. Roberts (Ed.), *Crisis intervention and time-limited cognitive treatment* (pp. 251–289). Thousand Oaks, CA: Sage.

Watkins, C. E. (1983). Burnout in counseling practice: Some potential professional and personal hazards of becoming a counselor. *Personnel and Guidance Journal, 61,* 304–308.

Watson, A. C., & Fulambarker, A. J. (2012). The crisis intervention team model of police response to mental health crises: A primer for mental health practitioners. *Best Practices in Mental Health: An International Journal, 8*(2), 71–81.

Watson, A. C., Ottai, V. C., Morabito, M., Draine, J., Kerr, A. N., & Angell, B. (2010). Outcomes of police contacts with persons with mental illness: The impact of CIT. *Administration and Policy in Mental Health and Mental Health Services Research, 37*(4), 302–317.

Watson, P. J., Brymer, M. J., & Bonanno, G. (2011). Postdisaster psychological intervention since 9/11. *American Psychologist, 66*(6), 482–494.

Watson, R. J., McDonald, J., & Pearce, D. (2006). An exploration of calls to Lifeline Australia: Social support or urgent suicide intervention? *British Journal of Guidance and Counselling, 34*(4), 471–482.

Wattendorf, G. E. (2002). School threat decision demonstrates support for early action. *Police Chief, 69*(3), 11–12.

Watters, D. (1997). A study of the reliability of the Triage Severity Scale. (Doctoral dissertation, University of Memphis.) *Dissertation Abstracts International, 58-08A*, 3028.

Weaver, T. L. (1998). Method variance and sensitivity of screening for traumatic stressors. *Journal of Traumatic Stress, 11*(1), 181–185.

Webb, C. Hayes, A., Grasso, D., Laurenceau, P., & Deblinger, E. (2014). Trauma -focused cognitive behavioral therapy for youth Effectiveness in a community setting. Psychological Trauma : Theory ,Research, Practice ,and Policy, 6 (5), 555–562.

Webb, L. M., & Dickson, F. C. (2012). Effective family communication for coping with crises. In F. C. Dickson & L. M. Webb (Eds.), *Communication for families in crisis: Theory, research, strategies* (pp. 1–26). New York: Peter Lang.

Webb, N. (Ed.). (2007). Play therapy with children in crisis. New York: Guilford Press.

Webb, N. B. (2005). The impact of traumatic stress and loss on children and families. In C. B. Webb (Ed.), *Mass trauma and violence: Helping families and children cope* (pp. 3–22). New York: Guilford Press.

Webb, N. B. (2007a). *Play therapy with children in crisis: Individual, group, and family treatment* (3rd ed.). New York: Guilford Press.

Webb, N. B. (2007b). Sudden death of a parent in a terrorist attack: Crisis intervention conjoint therapy with a preschool boy and his mother. In N. B. Webb (Ed.), *Play therapy with children in crisis: Individual, group, and family treatment* (pp. 389–407). New York: Guilford Press.

Webb, N. B. (2011). Play therapy for bereaved children: Adapting strategies to community, school, and home settings. *School Psychology International, 32*(2), 132–143.

Webb, N. B. (Ed.). (2007). *Play therapy with children in crisis: Individual, group, and family treatment* (3rd ed.). New York: Guilford Press.

Webb, S. B., & Griffiths, F. (1998–1999). *Young people at risk of suicide: Part A. School facilitators' handbook; Part B. Supplementary resources.* Auckland, New Zealand: College of Education, Massey University.

Webb, S. B., & Griffiths, F. (1998–1999). *Young people at risk of suicide: Part A. School facilitators' handbook; Part B. Supplementary resources.* Palmerston North, New Zealand: College of Education, Massey University.

Webber, J., & Mascari, J. B. (Eds.). (2010). *Terrorism, trauma, and tragedies: A counselor's guide to preparing and responding* (3rd ed.). Alexandria, VA: American Counseling Association Foundation.

Webber, J., Bass, D., & Yep, R. (Eds.). (2005). *Terrorism, trauma, and tragedies: A counselor's guide to preparing and responding.* Alexandria, VA: American Counseling Association.

Webber, J., Mascari, J. B., & Runte, J. (2010). Psychological first aid: A new paradigm for disaster mental health. In J. Webber & J. B. Mascari (Eds.), *Terror, trauma, and tragedies: A counselor's guide to preparing and responding* (3rd ed., pp. 201–205). Alexandria, VA: American Counseling Association Foundation.

Webber, R., & Moors, R. (2015). Engaging in cyberspace: Seeking help for sexual assault. *Child and Family Social Work, 20*(1), 40–49.

Weber, J. G. (2011). *Individual and family stress and crises.* Los Angeles: Sage.

Webersinn, A. L., Hollinger, C. L., & Delamatre, J. E. (1991). Breaking the cycle of violence: An examination of factors relevant to treatment follow-through. *Psychological Reports, 68,* 231–239.

Websdale, N., & Johnson, B. (2005). Reducing woman battering: The role of structural approaches. In N. Sololoff & C. Pratt (Eds.), *Domestic violence at the margins: Readings on race, class, gender, and culture* (pp. 389–415). New Brunswick, NJ: Rutgers University Press.

Webster, C. D., Douglas, K. S., Eaves, D., & Hart S. D. (1997). *HCR-20: Assessing risk of violence.* Burnaby, BC: Simon Fraser University.

Webster, C. D., Haqu, Q., & Hucker, S. J. (2014). *Violence risk assessment and management: Advances through structured professional judgment and sequential redirections* (2nd ed.). Hoboken, NJ: Wiley-Blackwell.

Webster, D. W., & Wilson, M. (1994). Gun violence, angry youth and the pediatrician's role in primary prevention. *Paediatrics, 94*(4), 617–622.

Wee, D. F., & Myers, D. (2002). Stress response of mental health workers following disaster: The Oklahoma City bombing. In C. R. Figley (Ed.), *Treating compassion fatigue* (pp. 57–83). New York: Brunner/Routledge.

Wee, D. F., & Myers, D. (2003). Compassion satisfaction, compassion fatigue, and critical incidents stress management. *International Journal of Emergency Mental Health, 5*(1), 33–37.

Weinberg, H. (2014). *The paradox of internet groups: Alone in the presence of virtual others.* London, England: Kamac Books.

Weincourt, R. (1985). Never to be alone: Existential therapy for battered women. *Journal of Psychosocial Nursing, 23,* 24–29.

Weiner, M., & Mehrabian, A. (1968). *Language within language.* New York: Appleton-Century-Croft.

Weinger, S. (2001). *Security risk: Preventing client violence against social workers.* Washington, DC: National Association of Social Workers Press.

Weinrach, S. G. (2003, January). Letters: Much ado about multiculturalism, part 4. *Counseling Today, 45,* 31.

Weinrach, S. G., & Thomas, K. R. (1998). Diversity-sensitive counseling today: A postmodern clash of values. *Journal of Counseling and Development, 76,* 115–122.

Weinreb, M., & Groves, B. M. (2007). Child exposure to parental violence: Case of Amanda, age 4. In Nancy Webb (Ed.), *Play therapy with children in crisis: Individual, group, and family treatment* (3rd ed., pp. 73–90). New York: Guilford Press.

Weinstock, R., Read, S., Leong, G. B., & Silvia, J. (2008). The elderly. In R. I. Simon & K. Tardiff (Eds.), *Textbook of violence assessment and management* (pp. 381–406). Arlington, VA: American Psychiatric Publishing.

Weisaeth, L. (2000). Briefing and debriefing: Group psychological interventions in acute stressor situations. In B. Raphael & J. P. Wilson (Eds.), *Psychological debriefing: Theory, practice, and evidence* (pp. 43–57). New York: Cambridge University Press.

Weisman, A. D. (1990–1991). Bereavement and companion animals. *Omega: Journal of Death and Dying, 22,* 241–248.

Weiss, D. S., & Marmar, C. R. (1997). The impact of event scale-revised. In J. P. Wilson & T. M. Keane (Eds.), *Assessing psychological trauma and PTSD: A practitioner's handbook* (pp. 399–411). New York: Guilford Press.

Weiss, K. G. (2010). Too ashamed to report: Deconstructing the shame of sexual victimization. *Feminist Criminology, 5*(3), 145–163.

Weiss, R. S. (1998). Issues in the study of loss and grief. In J. H. Harvery (Ed.), *Perspectives on loss: A sourcebook* (pp. 343–353). Philadelphia: Brunner/Mazel.

Weitzman, S. (2000). *Not to people like us*. New York: Basic Books.

Welfel, E. R. (2005). Accepting fallibility: A model for personal responsibility for nonegregious ethics infractions. *Counseling and values, 49*, 120–131.

Welfel, E. R. (2013). *Ethics in counseling and psychotherapy* (5th ed.). Pacific Grove, CA: Brooks-Cole, Cengage.

Welsh, J. A., & Domitrovich, C. (2006). Safe schools, healthy students initiative in rural Pennsylvania. In S. R. Jimerson & M. Furlong (Eds.), *Handbook of school violence and school safety: From research to practice* (pp. 511–524). Mahwah, NJ: Erlbaum.

Wenzel, A., Brown, G. K., & Beck, A. T. (2009). *Cognitive therapy for suicidal patients: Scientific and clinical applications*. Washington, DC: American Psychological Association.

Werner, P. D., Rose, T. L., Murdach, A. D., & Yesavage, J. A. (1989). Social workers' decision making about the violent client. *Social Work Research and Abstracts, 25*, 17–20.

Wessely, S. C., Bryant, R. A., Greenberg, N., Earnshaw, N., Shapley, J., & Hacker-Huges, J. (2008). Does psychoeducation help prevent post traumatic psychological distress? *Psychiatry, 71*(2), 287–302.

West, C. M. (1998). Leaving a second closet: Outing partner violence in same-sex couples. In J. L. Jasinski & L. M. Williams (Eds.), *Partner violence: A comprehensive review of 20 years of research* (pp. 163–183). Newbury Park, CA: Sage.

West, C. M., Kaufman Kantor, G., & Jasinski, J. L. (1998). Sociodemographic predictors and cultural barriers to help-seeking behavior by Latina and Anglo-American battered women. *Violence and Victims, 13*(4), 361–375.

West, D. J. (1966). *Murder followed by suicide*. Cambridge, MA: Harvard University Press.

Westefeld, J. S., Range, L. M., Rogers, J. R., Maples, M. R., Bromley, J. L., & Alcorn, J. (2000). Suicide: An overview. *Counseling Psychologist, 28*, 445–510.

Western Carolina University Emergency Management Institute. (2015). *Emergency and disaster management program*. Retrieved from http://www.wcu.edu/academics/departments-schools-colleges/cas/casdepts/crimcj/edm/

Whaley, A. L., & Davis, K. E. (2007). Cultural competence and evidence-based practice in mental health services. *American Psychologist, 62*(6), 563–574.

Whealin, J. A., DeCarvalho, L. T., & Vega, E. M. (2008). *Clinician's guide to treating stress after war: Education and coping interventions for veterans*. Hoboken, NJ: John Wiley & Sons.

Wheeler, A. M., & Bertram, B. (2012). *The Counselor and the Law: A Guide to Legal and Ethical Practice* (6th ed.). Alexandria, VA: American Counseling Association.

Wheeler, I. (2001). Parental bereavement: The crisis of meaning. *Death Studies, 25*(1), 51–66.

Wheeler, J. R., & Berliner, L. (1988). Treating the effects of sexual abuse on children. In G. E. Wyatt & G. J. Powell (Eds.), *Lasting effects of child sexual abuse* (pp. 227–247). Newbury Park, CA: Sage.

Wheeler, K. (2014). Inadequate treatment and research for PTSD at the VA. *American Psychologist, 69*(7), 706.

White, A. C. (1989). Post-traumatic stress. *British Journal of Psychiatry, 154*, 886–887.

White, B. D., Martin C, S., Walk, R., Pollice, L., Weissfeld, L., Hong, S., Landefeld, C. S., & Arnold, R. M. (2012). Nurse-led intervention to improve surrogate decision making for patients with advance critical illness. *American Journal of Critical Care, 21*, 396–409.

White, G. F., Katz, J., & Scarborough, K. E. (1992). The impact of professional football games on violent assaults on women. *Violence and Victims, 7*, 157–171.

White, J., & Allers, C. T. (1994). Play therapy with abused children: A review of the literature. *Journal of Counseling and Development, 72*, 390–394.

White, M. (1989). *Selected papers*. Adelaide, Australia: Dulwich Centre.

White, M. (2005). *An outline of narrative therapy*. Retrieved from www.massey.ac.nz

Whittle, H., Hamilton-Giachritsis, C., Beech, A., & Collins, G. (2013). A review of young people's vulnerabilities to online grooming. *Aggression and Violent Behavior, 18*(1), 135–146.

Wiederhold, A. M. (2014). Cyberbullying and LGBTQ youth: A deadly combination. *Cyberpsychology, Behavior, and Social Networking, 17*(9), 569–570.

Wiederhold, B. K., & Wiederhold, M. D. (2005) *Virtual reality therapy for anxiety disorders: Advances in evaluation and treatment*. Washington, DC: American Psychological Association.

Wiehe, V. R. (1998). *Understanding family violence*. Thousand Oaks, CA: Sage.

Wigderson, S., & Katz, J. (2015). Feminine ideology and sexual assault: Are more traditional college women at greater risk? *Violence Against Women, 21*(5), 616–631.

Wiglesworth, A., Mosqueda, L., Mulnard, R., Liao, S., Gibbs, L., & Fitzgerald, W. (2010). Screening for abuse and neglect of people with dementia. *Journal of the American Geriatric Society, 58*, 493–500.

Wilkinson, C. B. (1983). Aftermath of a disaster: The collapse of the Hyatt Regency steel skywalk. *American Journal of Psychiatry, 140*, 1134–1139.

Willard, N. (2007). *Cyberbullying and cyberthreats: Responding to the challenge of online social aggression, threats, and distress*. Champaign, IL: Research Press.

Williams, B. (2003). The worldview dimensions of individualism and collectivism: Implications for counseling. *Journal of Counseling and Development, 81*(3), 370–372.

Williams, C. C. (1983). The mental foxhole: The Vietnam veteran's search for meaning. *American Journal of Orthopsychiatry, 53*, 4–17.

Williams, J., & Koocher, J. P. (1999). Medical crisis counseling on a pediatric intensive care unit: Case examples and clinical utility. *Journal of Clinical Psychology in Medical Settings, 6*, 249–258.

Williams, J. E., & Holmes, K. A. (1981). *The assault: Rape and public attitudes*. Westport, CT: Greenwood Press.

Williams, L. M. (1995). Recovered memories of abuse in women with documented child sexual victimization histories. *Journal of Traumatic Stress, 8*(4), 649–673.

Williams, M. (1997). *Cry of pain: Understanding suicide and self-harm*. London: Penguin Books.

Williams, M., Teasdale, J., Segal, Z., & Kabat-Zinn, J. (2007). *The mindful way through depression*. New York: Guilford Press.

Williams, M. B. (2004). How schools respond to traumatic events: Debriefing intervention and beyond. In N. B. Webb (Ed.), *Mass trauma and violence: Helping families and children cope* (pp.120–141). New York: Guilford Press.

Williams, M. B. (2006). How schools respond to traumatic events: Debriefing interventions and beyond. *Journal of Aggression, Maltreatment and Trauma, 12*(1), 57–81.

Williams, R. J., & Stafford, W. B. (1991). Silent casualties: Partners, families, and spouses of persons with AIDS. *Journal of Counseling and Development, 69*, 423–427.

Williams, R. L., & Long, J. D. (1979). *Toward a self-managed life style* (2nd ed.). Boston: Houghton Mifflin.

Williams, R. L., & Long, J. D. (1983). *Toward a self-managed life style* (3rd ed.). Boston: Houghton Mifflin.

Williams, T., & Douds, J. (2002). The unique contributions of telephone therapy. In D. Lester & G. W. Brockopp (Eds.), *Crisis intervention and counseling by telephone* (2nd ed., pp. 57–63). Springfield, IL: Charles C Thomas.

Wilson, G., & Lester, D. (2002). Crisis intervention by e-mail. In D. Lester & G. W. Brockopp (Eds.), *Crisis intervention and counseling by telephone* (2nd ed., pp. 212–219). Springfield, IL: Charles C Thomas.

Wilson, J. P. (1980). Conflict, stress, and growth: Effects of the war on psychosocial development. In C. R. Figley & S. Leventman (Eds.), *Strangers at home*. New York: Praeger.

Wilson, J. P., Friedman, M. J., & Lindy, J. D. (2001). *Treating psychological trauma and PTSD*. New York: Guilford Press.

Wilson, J. P., Smith, W. K., & Johnson, S. (1985). A comparative analysis of PTSD among various survivor groups. In C. R. Figley (Ed.), *Trauma and its wake: The study of post-trauma stress disorder* (pp. 142–172). New York: Brunner/Mazel.

Wilson, L. (1981). Thoughts on *Tarasoff*. *Clinical Psychologist, 34*, 37.

Windmeyer, S. (2009). Helping LGBTQ & ally students find the right college fit. *ASCA School Counselor, 47*(1), 24.

Winslade, M. J., & Monk, F. (1999). *Narrative counseling in schools: Powerful and brief*. Thousand Oaks, CA: Corwin Press.

Winter, B. (1991). *The Family Trouble Center anger management program* (Videocassette recording #6781-A-91). Memphis, TN: Memphis State University, Department of Counseling and Personnel Services.

Winter, B., & Battle, L. (2007, March). *Rolling sessions: Squad car therapy*. Paper presented at Thirty-first Annual Convening of Crisis Intervention Personnel and CONTACT USA Conference, Chicago.

Wintersteen, M. B., & Diamond, G. S. (2013). Youth suicide prevention in primary care: A model program and its impact on psychiatric emergency referrals. *Clinical Practice in Pediatric Psychology, 1*(3), 295–305.

Wirth, J. L. (1999). Introduction to the issue of rational suicide. In J. L. Wirth (Ed.), *Contemporary perspectives on rational suicide* (pp. 1–12). Philadelphia: Brunner/Mazel.

Wirth-Cauchon, J. (2001). *Women and borderline personality disorder*. New Brunswick, NJ: Rutgers University Press.

Witko, T., Martinez, R., & Milda, R. (2006). Understanding domestic violence within the urban Indian community. In T. Witko (Ed.), *Mental health care for urban Indians: Clinical insights from native practitioners* (pp. 104–114). Washington, DC: American Psychological Association.

Wolak, J., & Finkelhor, D. (1998). Children exposed to partner violence. In J. L. Jasinski & L. M. Williams (Eds.), *Partner violence: A comprehensive review of 20 years of research* (pp. 73–112). Newbury Park, CA: Sage.

Wolanin, M. O., & Phillips, L. R. (1981). *Confusion: Prevention and care*. St. Louis, MO: Mosby.

Wolf, A. W. (2003). Introduction to the special issue. *Psychotherapy: Theory, Research, Practice, Training, 40*(1/2), 3–7.

Wolfe, V. V., Gentile, C., & Wolfe, D. A. (1989). The impact of sexual abuse on children: A PTSD formulation. *Behavior Therapy, 20*, 215–228.

Wolpe, J. (1958). *Psychotherapy by reciprocal inhibition*. Stanford, CA: Stanford University Press.

Wolpe, J. (1982). *The practice of behavior therapy*. New York: Pergamon Press.

Won, H., Myung, W., Song, G., Lee, W., Kin, J., Carroll, B., & Kim, D. (2013). Predicting national suicide numbers with social media data. *PLoS ONE, 8*(4), e61809.

Wong, S., Gordon, A., & Gu, D. (2007). Assessment and treatment of violence-prone forensic clients: An integrated approach. *British Journal of Psychiatry, 190*(49), 66–74.

Wood, A. D., & McHugh, M. C. (1994). Woman battering: The response of the clergy. *Pastoral Psychology, 42*, 185–196.

Wood, K., Chase, E., & Aggleton, P. (2006). "Telling the truth is the best thing": Teenage orphans' experiences of parental AIDS-related illness and bereavement in Zimbabwe. *Social Sciences and Medicine, 63*(7), 1923–1933.

Wood, K. A., & Khuri, R. (1984). Violence: The emergency room patient. In J. T. Turner (Ed.), *Violence in the medical care setting: A survival guide* (pp. 57–84). Rockville, MD: Aspen Systems.

Worden, J. W. (1991). *Grief counseling and grief therapy: A handbook for the mental health practitioner* (2nd ed.). New York: Springer.

Worden, J. W. (1996). *Children and grief: When a parent dies*. New York: Guilford Press.

Worden, J. W. (2002). *Grief counseling and grief therapy: A handbook for the mental health practitioner* (3rd ed.). New York: Springer.

World Health Organization. (2011). *Mental health: Country reports and charts available*. Retrieved from www.who.int/mental_health/prevention/suicide/country_reports/en/index.html

Worthington, R. L., & Dillon, F. R. (2011). Deconstructing multicultural counseling competencies research: Comment on Owen, Leach, Wampold, and Rodolfa. *Journal of Counseling Psychology, 58*(1), 10–15.

Worthington, R. L., Sott-McNett, A. M., & Moreno, M. V. (2007). Multicultural counseling competencies research: A 20-year content analysis. *Journal of Counseling Psychology, 54*, 35–361.

Wortman, C. B., & Lehman, D. R. (1985). Reactions to victims of life crises: Support attempts that fail. In I. G. Sarason & B. R. Sarason (Eds.), *Social support: Theory, research and application* (pp. 463–489). Dordrecht: Martinus Nijhodff.

Wright, T., & Bonett, D. (1997). The contribution of burnout to work performance. *Journal of Organizational Behavior, 18*(5), 491–499.

Wuang, Y., Chiang, C., Su, C., & Wang, C. (2011). Effectiveness of virtual reality using Wii gaming technology in children with Down syndrome. *Research in Developmental Disabilities, 32*(1), 312–321.

Wubbolding, R. E. (2003, January). Letters: Much ado about multiculturalism, part 3. *Counseling Today, 45*, 30–31.

Wykes, T., & Whittington, R. (1998). Prevalence and predictors of early traumatic stress reactions in assaulted psychiatric nurses. *Journal of Forensic Psychiatry, 9*(3), 643–658.

Wylie, M. S. (2004, September–October). Mindsight. *Psychotherapy Networker*, 29–39.

Y

Yalom, I. D. (1980). *Existential psychotherapy*. New York: Basic Books.

Yates, K., Kunz, M., Czobar, P., Rabinowitz, S., Lindenmayer, J. P., & Volavka, J. (2005). A cognitive, behaviorally based program for patients with persistent mental illness and a history of aggression, crime, or both: Structure and correlates of completers of the program. *Journal of the American Academy of Psychiatry and the Law, 33*, 214–222.

Yates, S., Axsom, S., & Tiedeman, K. (1999). The help-seeking process for distress after disasters. In R. Gist & B. Lubin (Eds.), *Response to disaster: Psychosocial, community, and ecological approaches* (pp. 133–166). Philadelphia: Brunner/Mazel.

Yeater, E., Austin, J., Green, M., & Smith, J. E. (2011). Coping mediates the relations between posttraumatic stress disorder (PTSD) symptoms and alcohol use in homeless, ethnically diverse women: A preliminary study. *Psychological Trauma: Theory, Research, Practice, and Policy, 2*(4), 307–310.

Yehuda, R. (2006). Advances in the understanding neuroendocrine alterations in PTSD and their therapeutic implications. *Annals of the New York Academy of Sciences, 1071*, 137–166.

Yehuda, R., & LeDoux, J. (2007). Response variation following trauma: A translational neuroscience approach to understanding PTSD. *Neuron, 56,* 19–32.

Yeomans, F. (1993). When a therapist overindulges a demanding borderline patient. *Hospital and Community Psychiatry, 44,* 334–336.

Yesavage, J. A., & Zarcone, V. (1983). History of drug abuse and dangerous behavior in inpatient schizophrenics. *Journal of Clinical Psychiatry, 44,* 259–261.

Yin, C. W., Sien, N. Y., Ying, L. A., Chung, S., & Leng, D. T. (2014). Virtual reality for upper extremity rehabilitation in early stroke: A pilot randomized control trial. *Clinical Rehabilitation, 28*(11), 1107–1114.

Yorgason, J. B. (2010). Illness and family stress. (2010). In S. J. Price, C. A. Price, & P. C. McKenry (Eds.), *Families and change: Coping with stressful events and transitions* (pp. 97–118). Los Angeles: Sage.

Yoshimura, S., Okamoto, Y., Onoda, K., Matsunaga, M., Okada, G., Kunisato, Y., . . . Yamawaka, S. (2014). Cognitive behavioral therapy for depression changes medial prefrontal and ventral anterior cingulate cortex activity associated with self-referential processing. *Social Cognitive and Affective Neuroscience, 9*(4), 487–493.

Yoshioka, M., Gilbert, L., El-Bassel, N., & Baig-Amin, M. (2003). Social support and disclosure of abuse: Comparing South Asian, African American, and Hispanic battered women. *Journal of Family Violence, 18*(3), 171–180.

Young, B. H. (2006). The immediate response to disaster: Guideline for adult psychological first aid. In E. C. Ritchie, P. J. Watson, & M. J. Friedman (Eds.), *Intervention following mass violence and disaster: Strategies for mental health practice* (pp. 134–155). New York: Guilford Press.

Young, B. H., Ruzek, J. I., Wong, M., Salzer, M. S., & Naturale, A. J. (2006). Disaster mental health training: Guidelines, considerations, and recommendations. In E. C. Ritichie, P. J. Watson, & M. J. Friedman (Eds.), *Interventions following mass violence and disasters: Strategies for mental health practice* (pp. 54–79). New York: Guilford Press.

Young, L. (1964). *Wednesday's children.* New York: McGraw-Hill.

Young, M. A. (1991). Crisis intervention and the aftermath of disaster. In A. R. Roberts (Ed.), *Contemporary perspectives on crisis intervention* (pp. 83–103). Upper Saddle River, NJ: Prentice Hall.

Young, M. E. (2015). Response to family sexual abuse. In T. Robert & V. Kelly (Eds.), *Critical incidents in integrating spirituality into counseling* (pp. 247–254). Alexandria, VA: American Counseling Association.

Yule, W. (1998). PTSD in children. In T. W. Miller (Ed.), *Children of trauma: Stressful life events and their effects on children and adolescents* (pp. 219–244). Madison, CT: International Universities Press.

Yung, M. (2013). Predictors of burnout and intentions to leave among staff that care for violence prone, court-dependent and emotionally disturbed youth in residential treatment facilities. *Dissertation Abstracts International: Section B. The Sciences and Engineering, 74*(2-B(E))

Z

Zagar, R., Arbit, J., Sylvies, R., Busch, K., & Hughes, J. (1990). Homicidal adolescent: A replication. *Psychological Reports, 67,* 1235–1242.

Zalaquett, C., Carrion, I., & Exum, H. (2010). Providing disaster services to culturally diverse survivors. In J. Webber & J. B. Mascari (Eds.), *Terrorism, trauma and tragedies: A counselor's guide to preparing and responding* (3rd ed., pp. 19–24). Alexandria, VA: American Counseling Association Foundation.

Zalaquett, C. P., Fuerth, K. M., Stein, C., Ivey, A. E., & Ivey, M. B. (2008). Reframing the DSM-IV-R from a multicultural/social justice perspective. *Journal of Counseling and Development, 86*(3), 364–371.

Zanarini, M., Frankenburg, F., Dubo, E., Sickel, A., Trikha, A., & Levin, A. (1998). Axis I comorbidity of borderline personality disorder. *American Journal of Psychiatry, 155*(12), 1733–1739.

Zanarini, M. C. (2000). Childhood experiences associated with the development of borderline personality disorder. *Psychiatric Clinics of North America, 23,* 89–101.

Zanipatin, J., Welch, S., Yi, J., & Bardina, P. (2005). Immigrant women and domestic violence. In K. Barrett & W. George (Eds.), *Race, culture, psychology, and law* (pp. 375–389). Thousand Oaks, CA: Sage.

Zanskas, S. A. (2010). Systemic response to post-conflict rehabilitation. In E. Martz (Ed.)., *Trauma rehabilitation after war and conflict: Community and individual perspectives* (pp. 111–132). New York: Springer.

Zarzaur, M. (2005, May). *Using a portable sandtray for crisis intervention.* Paper presented at the Twenty-ninth Annual Convening of Crisis Intervention Personnel, Chicago.

Zdziarski, E. L., Dunkel, N. W., & Rollo, J. M. (2007). *Campus crisis management: A comprehensive guide to planning, prevention, response and recovery.* San Francisco: John Wiley & Sons.

Zeigler-Hill, V., & Abraham, J. (2006). Borderline personality features: Instability of self-esteem and affect. *Journal of Social and Clinical Psychology, 25*(6), 668–687.

Zenere, F. (1998, Fall). NASP/NEAT community crisis response. *Newsletter of the Florida Association of School Psychologists.*

Zenere, F. J., & Lazarus, P. J. (1997). The decline of youth suicidal behavior in an urban, multicultural public school system following the introduction of a suicide prevention and intervention program. *Suicide and Life-Threatening Behavior, 27*(4), 387–403.

Zetumer, S., Young, I., Sher, K., Skritskaya, N., Lebowitz, B., Simon, N.,. . . Zisook, S. (2015). The impact of losing a child on the clinical presentation of complicated grief. *Journal of Affective Disorders. 170,* 15–21.

Zhang, B., El-Jawahri, A., & Prigerson, H. (2006). Update on bereavement research: Evidence-based guidelines for the diagnosis and treatment of complicated bereavement. *Journal of Palliative Medicine, 9,* 1188–1202.

Zhao, L., & Jiang, G. (2010). Exposure to violent games: A research about aggression in middle school students. *Chinese Journal of Clinical Psychology, 18*(6), 765–768.

Zhao,Y., Qiu, W., & Xie, N. (2012). Social networking, social gaming, texting. In D. G. Singer & J. L. Singer (Eds.), *Handbook of children and the media* (2nd ed., pp. 97–112). Thousand Oaks, CA: Sage.

Zhong, C. B., & Liljenquist, K. A. (2006). Washing away your sins: Threatened morality and physical cleansing. *Science, 313,* 1451–1452.

Zhong, C. B., Strejcek, B., & Sivanathan, N. (2010). A clean self can render harsh moral judgment. *Journal of Experimental Psychology, 46,* 859–862.

Zhou, X., Wu, X., Fu, F., & An, Y. (2015). Core challenge and rumination as predictors of PTSD and PTG among adolescent survivors of the Wenchuan Earthquake. *Psychological Trauma: Theory, Research, Practice, and Policy, 7*(4), 391–397.

Zilberstein, K. (2014). Neurocognitive considerations in the treatment of attachment and complex trauma in children. *Clinical and Child Psychology and Psychiatry, 19*(3), 336–354.

Zimberhoff, A. K., & Brown, L. S. (2006). "Only the goyim beat their wives, right?" *Psychology of Women Quarterly, 30*, 422–424.

Zimmerman, J. L., & Dickerson, V. C. (1996). *If problems talked: Narrative therapy in action.* New York: Guilford Press.

Zinner, E. S., & Williams, M. B. (1999). *When a community weeps: Case studies in group survivorship.* Philadelphia: Brunner/Mazel.

Zins, J. E., Travis, L., Brown, M., & Knighton, A. (1994). Schools and the prevention of interpersonal violence: Mobilizing and coordinating community resources. *Special Services in the Schools, 8*(2), 1–19.

Zlotnick, C., Warshaw, M., Shea, M., Allsworth, J., Pearlstein, T., & Keller, M. (1999). Chronicity in posttraumatic stress disorder (PTSD) and predictors of course of comorbid PTSD in patients with anxiety disorders. *Journal of Traumatic Stress, 12*(1), 89–100.

Zlotnik, D. (2014). Predictors of revictimization following child sexual abuse: A meta-analytic review. *Dissertation Abstracts International: Section B: The Sciences and Engineering, 74*(12-B(E)), 515.

Zold, A. C., & Schilt, S. C. (1984). Violence: The child and the adolescent patient. In J. T. Turner (Ed.), *Violence in the medical care setting: A survival guide* (pp. 85–106). Rockville, MD: Aspen Systems.

Zullino, D., Krenz, S., & Besson, J. (2003). AMPA blockage may be the mechanism underlying the efficacy of topiramate in PTSD. *Journal of Clinical Psychiatry, 64*(2), 219–220.

Glossary

absence of community One major source of burnout; needed for social support.

abuse Indicates that physical violence is only one weapon in an armory of coercive weapons; abuse denotes the unequal power relationship within which the assault occurs and further suggests that a presumption of trust has been violated.

acceptance Being open and aware of unpleasant emotions, thoughts, and experiences and just letting them be without making attempts to alter their frequency or form. Acceptance also means that the crisis worker feels an unconditional positive regard for the client.

acquire suicidal capability A person's successive approximation toward suicide by engaging in increasingly lethal self-injurious activities that lessen the fear of actually killing oneself.

acute stress disorder (ASD) Symptoms mimic those of PTSD but are time limited, usually dissipating within 1 month. The symptoms continue for a minimum of 2 days and a maximum of 4 weeks and occur within 1 month of the traumatic event; then those time frames will meet the criteria of ASD.

ADDRESSING model The acronym encompasses Age, acquired and Developmental Disabilities, Religion, Ethnicity, Social class, Sexual orientation, Indigenous heritage, National origin, and Gender.

affect dysregulation Alterations in impulse control, attention and consciousness, self-perception, perception of perpetrators, relationships to significant others, and systems of meaning.

affect heuristic Suggests that judgments and crisis workers' decision-making processes are primarily based on personal biases, the feelings of either disliking or liking an individual, and circumstance or context.

alexithymia A condition that develops in many survivors of childhood sexual abuse, which is the inability to recognize and label feelings.

altruistic suicide Related to perceived or real social solidarity, such as the traditional Japanese *hara-kiri* or, to put it in a current context, the suicide attacks by members of Middle Eastern extremist groups.

ambiguous loss This loss is of two types. The first is when a person is physically absent but psychologically present, as in the case of a missing person. The second is when a person is physically present but psychologically absent, as in the case of dementia or schizophrenia.

anger One of four categories of rapists (mad at women).

animated guilt Enables the individual to start taking responsibility for past actions and start to experience new degrees of personal liberation.

anomic suicide Arises from a perceived or real breakdown in the norms of society, such as the financial and economic ruin of the Great Depression.

aspirational A quality of ethical codes, based upon a "higher good" that goes beyond what is simply required.

assaultive behavior Can include not only harmful acts against a person but also both verbal and behavioral threats to significant others, pets, or property.

assertion statements Owning statements that clearly and specifically ask for a specific action from the client.

assisted suicide Suicide when someone else provides the means (lethal agent), but the person who is dying administers it.

autonomic hyperarousal Affective, behavioral, and cognitive responses that occur when stimuli that may be associated with the original trauma, but present no threat, such as smells, clothing, settings, etc., cause a reaction in the individual as if the original threat were now present and imminent.

autonomic/intrusive rumination The initial intrusion of unwanted thoughts that assails an individual after the trauma.

autonomy Principle refers to a client's right to self-determination.

balance of power Refers to the ability of the person to influence and get others to do what he or she wants.

basic crisis theory Focuses on helping people in crisis recognize and correct temporary affective, behavioral, and cognitive distortions brought on by traumatic events.

battered wife syndrome A history of abuse with PTSD-like symptoms due to battering.

battering Indicates any form of physical violence perpetrated by one person on another and typically includes a life-threatening history of injuries and psychosocial problems that entrap a person in a relationship.

battering relationship Where one or both parties in a relationship use physical violence against each other.

behavioral emergency Occurs when a crisis escalates to the point that the situation requires immediate intervention to avoid injury or death to oneself or others or the person is in imminent risk of serious injury or death by another.

behavioral telehealth The use of telecommunication and information technology to provide access to behavioral health assessment, intervention, consultation, supervision, education, and information across distance.

beneficence Principle that refers to working for the good of the client and society; involves dialectical thought, balancing the good of the presenting client and/or society.

bereavement   A period of sorrow following the death of a significant other and a common life transition rather than a clinical disorder.

body scanning   The individual monitors physical sensations throughout the body and gently allows himself or herself to feel, experience, and accept the physical sensations that emanate from various body parts.

bonadaptation   Successful adaptation in restoring balance to the family; considered to be good, useful, and healthy.

brief therapy theory   Typically attempts to remediate more or less ongoing emotional problems.

broaching   Refers to the crisis worker's consistent display of openness to invite the client to explore issues of diversity and a recognition that race, ethnicity, or some universal trait may be contributing to the crisis.

burnout   Total mental, physical, and emotional exhaustion caused by long-term involvement in emotionally demanding psychotherapy.

catharsis   Means simply letting clients talk, cry, swear, berate, rant, rave, mourn, or do anything else that allows them to ventilate feelings and thoughts; it may be one of the most therapeutic strategies the crisis worker can employ.

chronic callers/regular callers   Callers who for various reasons are constant callers to crisis lines and because of this can tie up lines. Therefore, these callers are identified and time limits are usually set for them.

chronic suicide   A person who engages in repeated acts of suicidal behavior, eventually leading to suicide. Also characterized by people who engage in suicidal behavior to cope with and to achieve control over the psychic pain, hopelessness, and emptiness they feel.

chronosystem   The patterning of environmental events and transactions over the life span as well as the social and historical circumstances that influence the individual, family, peers, coworkers, and others.

closed-ended questions   Seek specific, concrete information from the client; they are designed to elicit specific behavioral data and yes or no responses.

collective trauma   One type of disaster trauma that affects the microsystem (the community) to the extent that the social bonds that connect people are torn apart and the community is rent asunder.

collectivism   Based on the assumption that groups bind and mutually obligate individuals, that the personal is simply a component of the larger social group or context and subordinate to it.

combat fatigue   The advent of modern warfare in World Wars I and II generated this term to explain the condition of traumatized soldiers who had no apparent physical wounds.

comorbidity   The presence of two diagnosable disorders such as major depression and substance abuse.

compassion fatigue (CF)   Manifested in the continuous negative aspects of care provision for tough cases and customers in a demanding work environment that generally revolve around some type of trauma.

compassion satisfaction   The positive feelings and intrinsic rewards one feels from helping others who have experienced a traumatic event.

compeers   Are trained volunteers working out of mental health agencies who act as support and socializing agents for clients who do not have friends or relatives to assist and encourage them.

compensation neurosis   Invalidism suffered and compensated by insurers as a result of accidents.

complex PTSD   Disorders of extreme stress not otherwise specified (DESNOS); refers to a broad range of symptoms resulting from exposure to a prolonged or repeated severely traumatizing event.

complicated grief or prolonged grief   These are interchangeable terms, although the latter term now seems to be prevalent. Persons suffering from complicated or prolonged grief are preoccupied with the deceased and may have recurrent, intrusive images or thoughts of the death. Common symptoms include shock, disbelief, and anger about the death, loneliness and isolation, a feeling that a part of the self has died along with the deceased, and a feeling that the future holds little worth.

confidentiality   Refers to the ethical duty of mental health professionals to protect the private communications of their clients.

conjugal or intimate terrorism   Describes a tactic akin to brainwashing and political terrorism, whereby violence or the threat of violence is used to break the victim's resistance and bend her to the will of the terrorist (batterer).

conjugal violence   Where one or both parties in a relationship use physical violence against each other.

conjunctive faith   Wherein an individual can hold two differing beliefs and can deal with the paradoxes and polarities of those beliefs.

contagion suicide   In a school the stimulus of one suicide or suicide attempt may cause a cluster of suicide attempts that occur a short time after the first attempt occurs.

contextual model   Model of family stress that builds on the ABCX model and recognizes that families are unique and that events, the same or similar, will be experienced in distinctive ways.

control   One major source of burnout; control issues from being micromanaged or having ineffective leaders or teams.

coping mechanisms   Actions, behaviors, or environmental resources the client might use to help get through the present crisis.

core listening skills   Empathy, genuineness, and acceptance or positive regard.

countertransference   The attributing to clients of the therapist's own problems; often manifesting persons or significant events in the therapist's personal history from the client's issues.

creating awareness The crisis worker attempts to bring to conscious awareness warded off, denied, shunted, and repressed feelings, thoughts, and behaviors that freeze clients' ability to act in response to the crisis.

crisis (for an individual) The perception or experiencing of an event or situation as an intolerable difficulty that exceeds the person's current resources and coping mechanisms.

Crisis Intervention Team Developed specifically to train patrol officers to deal with the mentally ill and emotionally disturbed.

crisis management Refers to the act of planning a response to recurring suicidal behavior in *collaboration* with the client.

crisis therapy Second-order intervention that seeks to resolve the crisis and is generally provided by trained, licensed human services professionals.

cubic model Combines psychache, perturbation (how disturbed one is and degree of pain), and press (stress increased due to more negative factors piling up); when all three are combined, they create the critical mass necessary to activate a suicide.

cultural adaptation Adapting theories and techniques of counseling and psychotherapy to interface with nonwestern cultures.

culture The beliefs, laws, customs, religious practices, and other artifacts that are passed down through generations that define a group of people.

cyberbullying Using technology to harass, humiliate, or threaten someone.

cyberchondria The use of the Internet to research any and all symptoms of a rare disease, illness, or condition; persons manifest a state of medical anxiety and believe they have the disease.

cyberstalking A type of cyberbullying; the electronic version of pursuing a person who is not interested in the personal attention he or she is receiving, but receiving it anyway.

cyberthreats A type of cyberbullying; clearly meant to evoke fear and imply that danger is imminent.

death One of the four corner posts of existence.

death accepting A dominant belief within a culture that death is unavoidable and life is essentially transitory and usually involves movement in some manner to another plane of existence.

death defying A dominant cultural belief that through the miracle of modern medicine death can be defeated or at least postponed.

death denying A dominant belief within a culture that death is seen as defeat. The United States is generally seen as a death denying and defying culture to the point that the word itself is obscene.

debriefing Historically evolved from World War II debriefing of pilots after a combat mission to ascertain combat problems and how to correct them. Adopted by emergency management services such as police and fire departments after responding to traumatic calls.

Its purpose has evolved in crisis intervention to relieve stress caused by the traumatic event. Its effectiveness, particularly through the CISD model, has been called into question.

decision support tools Understanding and knowing the observable risk factors for violence; these risk factors have been assessed to have high reliability and predictive ability in regard to violence risk.

deconstructing To analyze and break down into specific components that underlie assumptions or ideologies as a way of making sense of and moving forward from a loss.

defusion Focuses on decreasing the perceived literality (it is absolutely true and fact) of the avoidance language that debilitates and keeps sufferers of PTSD stuck in maladaptive value systems; the notion is that clients can be taught to detach from being fused with any idea (including the really bad ones that go with PTSD) by practicing acceptance and mindfulness when negative self and world attributions surface, and by continuous practice can come to believe that these are "just thoughts" that don't control one's behavior.

deliberate rumination A process that issues out of a reflective state when a thorough re-examination of the traumatic event causes the individual to reframe his or her view of life and in fact grow from the experience.

denigration A type of cyberbullying; sending or posting defaming information about someone.

depersonalization As if the person is watching herself from a grandstand or seeing herself as in a movie such that it can't really be happening to her.

derealization As if this is unreal and can't be happening, or the images become distorted and blurred and are hard to sort out and make sense of them.

developmental crises Situations and events that occur during the life cycle of families that changes the families' structural integrity.

dialectical thought The ability to hold and consider two diametrically opposed thoughts simultaneously.

differential vulnerability The degree to which people from different cultural backgrounds are vulnerable to and react to traumatic events.

directive intervention Providing specific information and guidance clients need to make decisions, setting limits on behaviors that range from inappropriate to lethal, and apprising them of consequences of their affective, cognitive, and behavioral responses to the crisis based on the interventionist's expert clinical judgment and the self-same lack thereof in the client.

discernment Refers to judgment during an ethical dilemma; the crisis worker's ability to perceive or distinguish a course or direction during the ambiguity of chaos.

discordant values One major source of burnout; these indicate the worker and the organization are severely at odds regarding the worker's belief in the validity and worth of the organization and the organization's belief about the worker's validity and worth.

disenfranchised grief Occurs when a person has experienced a deep and meaningful attachment, experienced loss, and cannot openly acknowledge or grieve the loss or have it validated by others.

disequilibrium Lack or destruction of emotional stability, balance, or poise in the organism.

disinhibition effect A phenomenon in e-therapy; means that people tend to open up earlier with more distressing issues than they would normally do in a face-to-face therapy session.

disorganization of self The first stage of trauma resolution that workers go through after a physical assault that includes feelings of shock. They may also dissociate from the experience as unreal, as if it didn't happen or they viewed it as a video of themselves. They may blame themselves and start having peritraumatic stress disorder symptoms involving sleep disturbances and emotional outbursts.

dissociation Division of the personality into one component that attempts to function in the everyday world and another that regresses and is fixed in the trauma.

dissociative symptoms Include memory loss, a sense of detachment from the world, belief that things and people are unreal, a blurred sense of identity, and a general disconnect from reality.

dissonant response When a person's typical mode of grieving becomes compromised due to external pressures to adapt to a loss that does not fit the individual's grieving style and severe psychological conflict is the result.

distributive justice Involves a mental health practitioner's ethical judgment about how relief resources should be divided.

diversity Refers to dimensions of personal identity and individual differences.

domestic violence Subsumes any act of assault by a social partner or relative, regardless of marital status.

dysphoric/borderline batterer Has a history of parental rejection and child abuse, delinquent acts, poor communication and social skills, violence-as-a-solution ideation, extreme fears of abandonment, and low remorse.

ecosystem In crisis intervention the total system has interactive effects both on subsystems and individuals within those systems. The mesosystem (communication) and how effectively it operates is a key to understanding ecosystemic crisis intervention.

ecosystemic crisis Any disruptive or destructive event that occurs at a rate and magnitude beyond the ability of the normal social process to control it and is pervasive throughout a large system.

egoistic suicide Related to one's lack of integration or identification with a group.

elder abuse Any knowing, intentional, or negligent act by a caregiver or other person that causes harm or serious risk of harm to an older person or failure to meet an elder's basic needs.

eliciting trust A keystone that communicates that clients have the ability to get through tough times, recover, and grow; it is not cheerleading, but it is gentle encouragement and trust that the client can engage the grief and not avoid it.

emic A cultural view that looks beyond physical features, race, and ethnicity to all of the social locations that make the individual distinct from others.

emotional dysregulated defense systems When a person's normal ability to control emotions is overwhelmed by the traumatic event and subsequently he or she is unable to control his or her emotions. Even small trigger events may cause emotions to spiral out of control.

empathic presence Involves listening, silence, and support through accepting and encouraging the expression of feelings, allowing pain to be expressed, and responding in a noncritical, nonjudgmental manner in allowing the grief-stricken to tell their story.

empathy Means that the crisis worker accurately senses the inner feelings and meanings the client is experiencing and directly communicates to the client that the worker understands how it feels to be the client.

enticement Used by child molesters and may include deceit, trickery, rewards, flattery, or the use of adult authority to tell the child in a matter-of-fact way that the child is expected to participate.

entrainment A specific therapeutic technique that seeks to slow down the individual—whose thoughts, feelings, and acting may be spiraling out of control—through slow, measured responses and the use of calming techniques by the interventionist.

entrapment Used by child molesters to manipulate the child into feeling obligated to participate through traps, blackmail, and so forth.

environment location Refers to the physical and contextual setting in which the crisis occurs. At times changing the environment as opposed to changing the individual may de-escalate the crisis.

equilibrium A state of mental or emotional stability, balance, or poise in the organism.

ergonomics Profession that applies theory, principles, data, and methods to product design in order to optimize human well-being and overall system performance, which also applies to coordinating, collaborating, and allocating resources after a disaster.

etic The traits and factors that are common to all persons within a particular ethnic or racial group.

European Network of Traumatic Stress Network that develops evidence-based responses to large-scale disasters and provides assistance to those parts of the European Union that suffer from a lack of psychological resources.

euthanasia It is the practice of intentionally ending a life in order to relieve pain and suffering.

existential isolation One of the four corner posts of existence; means that each of us enters existence alone and leaves it alone.

exosystem The experiences in another social setting in which the individual does not have an active role; does influence the individual's experiences in the immediate context.

expansion   When people in crisis are so locked into the crisis that they cannot see the bigger picture, and are paralyzed affectively, cognitively, and behaviorally, the crisis worker seeks to broaden their tunnel view of the crisis and thus start focusing on other aspects of the crisis.

expressive   Kinds of crime in which individuals pose a serious threat to themselves or others because of their own anger, fear, vulnerability, depression, or lack of emotional control.

expressive act of homicide   Designed to reduce psychological pain.

externalization   A therapeutic technique used to make a problem distinct and separate from the individual personality such that it is no longer seen as enmeshed in the personality but is now seen as an object or problem in and of itself.

face validity   Outward appearance of having substantial worth and content. In a person, he or she may "look like" he or she knows what he or she is doing whether he or she actually does.

facilitator role   By performing various physical activities and functions that help a person deal with a loss such as helping make organ donor rights or providing information about lawyers who handle wills.

failed belongingness   Means that the person has no attachments or value to any other member of society.

fairness   One major source of burnout; lack of, with little justice and lots of arbitrary and secretive decision making and favoritism.

family communication model   Depicts an approach for families to cope with and prevail during crises using internal and external verbal interactions; the model makes the assumption that the root of family crises is communication.

family crisis   A crisis occurs when perceptions or experiencing of an event comes to bear on the family as a whole, testing the family's structural integrity, because the usual repertoire of problem-solving skills and communication styles are not adequate or have been exhausted. Unless relief is obtained the crisis jeopardizes family homeostasis and has the potential to strip family resilience.

family distress model (FDM)   The purpose for the model is to identify families' patterns of coping in order to develop interventions designed to support attempts at managing the situation; FDM states that when in distress, families use strategies that are different from their daily predictable patterns.

family only batterer   Characteristics include high dependency, impulsivity, poor communication skills, and family-of-origin violence.

family outreach model (FOM)   The family distress model was broadened by the formation of FOM that added a practical intervention component. FOM goes beyond traditional family intervention models based on conceptualizations of pathology that must be diagnosed or dysfunctional families that require expert assessment.

family transcrisis   Unresolved feelings, behaviors, and cognitions of a crises that lie dormant until situations or events occur that reactivate these reactions although not directly related to the current circumstances.

fatalistic suicide   Occurs when a person sees no way out of an intolerable or oppressive situation, such as being confined in a concentration camp.

fidelity   Principle involves keeping one's promises and commitments.

flaming   A type of cyberbullying; refers to angry offensive language.

focus   When people are so scattered in their thinking and behaving that they are paralyzed from taking action affectively, cognitively, and behaviorally, the crisis worker seeks to narrow their view and pick one component of the crisis to work on.

focused view   Looks at multicultural counseling in relation to visible and racial ethnic minorities. Based on physical features and defined racial groupings.

foreseeable   Basically what the "reasonable" practitioner would expect to occur given similar actions, behaviors, and circumstance.

freedom   One of the four corner posts of existence; the absence of external structure, which means that each person is responsible for making choices, taking actions, and enjoying or suffering the consequences of those decisions.

friction location   Stimuli that trigger and escalate the crisis situation, whether they are intrapersonal, interpersonal, or systemic. Finding friction locations and easing them is critical to de-escalating and defusing a crisis.

gender inequality   Refers to the economic, political, and legal status of women in comparison to men.

general adaptation syndrome (GAS)   Overstimulation and excessive wear of target organs lead to stress-related dysfunction and disease.

generally violent/antisocial batterer   Has all the characteristics of family only, disphoric/ borderline, and low-level antisocial batterers, but to a much more profound degree.

gentle conversation   Allows for memory sharing, telling and retelling stories, and owning statements from the worker such as "I am sorry. I don't have words to begin to touch the feelings you must have, but I am here, and I will stay here and listen if you care to talk."

genuineness   Means that the worker is being completely open in the relationship: nothing is hidden, there are no facades, and there are no professional fronts.

goals   May be tangible, intangible, unspoken, or expressed; they motivate families in their desire to attain or achieve something.

grief   A psychic state or condition of mental anguish or emotional suffering and a result or anticipation of the bereavement.

grooming   Seduction phase wherein molesters successively approximate a child to accept that the sexual abuse is okay, appropriate, educational, acceptable, and even a duty.

grounding A reality orientation technique that helps keep someone in the present and helps reorient a person to the here-and-now and in reality.

guidance When the clients don't have the knowledge or resources available to make good decisions, the crisis worker provides information, referral, and direction in regard to clients' obtaining assistance from specific external resources and support systems.

harassment A type of cyberbullying; the technology version of discriminatory or hostile behavior toward someone based on gender, race, religion, disability, or sexual orientation.

helplessness Feminists see this pejorative term as casting women in a victim role with few resources or little empowerment.

hesitation wounds One of multiple, usually superficial and parallel incisions that are self-inflicted in places where major vessels are near the skin surface, in an attempted suicide. Based on the notion that people are hesitant to kill themselves, so they inflict wounds that are superficial in nature.

heuristics Refers to the process that a person uses to learn something.

hypervigilance Being on constant guard for threats when there is no immediate threat.

hysterical neurosis Concept formulated by Sigmund Freud to describe trauma cases of young Victorian women with whom he was working.

"I understand" An owning statement that clearly conveys to the client that you do understand that what is happening right now is causing the client distress.

immobility A state of physical being in which the person is not immediately capable of autonomously changing or coping in response to different moods, feelings, emotions, needs, conditions, influences; inability to adapt to the immediate physical and social world.

impact stage Occurs during the sexual assault and for approximately 2 weeks following it. During this time a kaleidoscope of emotions, thoughts, and behaviors may occur, or conversely the client may be in a state of shock and dissociation, with both physical pain associated with the sexual assault and dissociation, somatic reactions, hypervigilance, nightmares, and startle responses that are symptomatic of the acute stress disorder that often follows.

in loco parentis In place of the parent.

indirect and noncommissioned behavioral emergencies Indirect behavioral emergencies occur when people make bad decisions and wind up placing themselves in potentially lethal situations. Indirect and noncommissioned behavioral emergencies are crises that happen with no directed purpose or intentionality to do something harmful to oneself or others.

indirect suicide Suicide wherein suicidal persons may not have the courage to kill themselves, or they seek to publicize their deaths through the media by "going out in a blaze of glory."

individual trauma One type of disaster trauma that hammers the individual psyche and breaks through the person's defense so forcefully and suddenly that reaction is impossible.

individualism A worldview that centralizes the personal—personal goals, personal uniqueness, and personal control—and peripheralizes the social group or social context within which the individual operates.

individuative/reflective faith Where one is able to reflect critically on one's story and values and disregard personal myths about self, God, and one's relationship with the world.

inescapable One of the three I's and a major cause of perturbation: I can't get away from this pain no matter what I do.

instrumental acts of homicide Occur for some financial or other concrete gain.

instrumental crimes Crimes such as theft, robbery, and assault.

interminable One of the three I's and a major cause of perturbation: "If I don't do something about this now, it'll go on forever." The person sees no relief in the future for the psychic pain he or she is suffering.

International Federation of Red Cross and Red Crescent Societies Helps individuals and communities heal the psychological wounds and rebuild social structures after an emergency or a critical event. Its mission is to change people into active survivors rather than passive victims.

intimate partner violence (IPV) The politically correct term to further amplify the cross-sectional aspects of battering and encompasses all types of couples.

intolerable One of the three I's and a major cause of perturbation: I've gone beyond what any human could endure.

intrusive rumination Unbidden terrifying thoughts entering the person's mind about the trauma.

justice Ethical principle that involves fostering fairness, equality, and providing equitable care.

large-scale crises Those crises that at a minimum affect whole communities or regions either directly or vicariously.

learned helplessness Means that battered women choose behavioral responses that have the highest predictability of causing them the least harm in the known situation, or what is called survivor hypothesis, wherein women become very active and resourceful in protecting themselves and their children.

legitimization of violence The support the culture gives to violence, as portrayed in the mass media (such as television programming), laws permitting corporal punishment in schools, violent sports, military exploits, and video games.

loss A universal human phenomenon, but people respond to it with varying degrees of grief and mourning. Any loss is some form of death. Death of a loved one, death of a relationship through the breakup of a marriage or a friendship, leaving a job, putting down a pet, repossession of a home, geographic moving away from friends and family, even the loss of precious keepsakes can constitute a loss that becomes a crisis. All losses produce some degree of grieving.

loss orientation   One component of the dual process model that focuses on the affective, behavioral, and cognitive reactions that are typically experienced when a severe loss occurs.

low-level antisocial batterer   Has antisocial behavior and moderate levels of domestic and general violence.

macrosystem   Includes the national government and all its agencies, and national charitable, religious, service, professional, and benevolent organizations; encompasses the national rail, air, marine, and highway transportation modalities, and food, fuel, and energy transmission systems. It involves the total culture including beliefs, mores, legal constructs, and all the other artifacts, traits, and pursuits that define a group of people in the environment in which they live.

making contact/predispositioning   A task with families in crises that involves placing yourself in a position of being helpful.

maladaptation   Lack of balance in the family; considered to be negative, ineffective, and unhealthy.

mandatory   A quality of laws; they require compliance.

masquerading   A type of cyberbullying; using someone else's identity to send messages that are rude and inappropriate.

meaning making   The attempt to restore the original global meaning system and not let it be driven by the one traumatic event that changed it; calls for reviewing and reframing the traumatic event in such a way that an acceptable appraisal of the event can be made.

meaninglessness   One of the four corner posts of existence; our attempt to make sense out of a universe that is beyond knowing.

megacrises   Those crises that affect entire countries or the world, either directly or vicariously.

mentalization   The process by which individuals interpret the actions of oneself and others as meaningful representations about what is going on both within themselves and between themselves and others. It is hypothesized that persons with borderline personality disorder have failed to develop this ability and thus cross intra- and interpersonal boundaries most people would not. The object of mentalization treatment is that borderline personality disorder clients increase mentalization capacity which should improve affect regulation and interpersonal relationships and give them better behavior control.

mesosystem   The relationships, connections, and communication links between individuals and systems; everything from sign language for a deaf person to the most sophisticated wireless computer satellite uplinks to state and federal emergency management agencies.

metastasizing crises   Those crises that start small but, if not contained both physically and psychologically, can quickly turn into large-scale crises.

microsystem   The setting in which the person in crisis lives; the microsystem setting's contexts may include the individual's family, friends, coworkers, peers, school, neighborhood, and usual haunts.

mindfulness   The art of being nonjudgmentally aware of body sensations, feeling, and thoughts as they move in and out of consciousness in the present moment.

mobility   A state of physical being in which the person can autonomously change or cope in response to different moods, feelings, emotions, needs, conditions, influences; being flexible or adaptable to the physical and social world.

mobilization   The crisis worker gets the client moving behaviorally to take action on the crisis.

mourning   A social or cultural state or condition expressing grief or feeling because of bereavement; a communal rather than an individual reaction to loss, generally prescribed by cultural protocol and the time frame in which it occurs.

multiculturalism   Refers to race, ethnicity, and culture and has focused on four racial-ethnic minority groups (Asian, Black/African, Latino/Hispanic, and Native American).

mustrabatory behavior   A term coined by Albert Ellis in rational-emotive behavior therapy that indicates a continuous belief that things "must be right, just, or perfect" or one's life or situation becomes intolerable.

mythical literal   Faith development model stage; a one-dimensional view of God as an entity that doles out rewards and punishment based on how rigorously one practices one's faith and follows its commandments (typical of children 8–12).

narrative therapy exposure   Through the use of either speaking or writing about the traumatic event, the trauma survivors reexpose themselves to the traumatic event. The purpose is to come to terms with the feared event by completely uncovering it, examining it as a now past event.

negligence   The unintentional breach of a duty that one person owes another.

netiquette   Civil and appropriate rules of discourse when operating on the net, particularly in synchronous time with other netizens.

netizens   People who spend a great deal of time in online communities; they operate in what is generally called Web 2.0, which is a way of using the web to develop cultural communities and social networking sites.

networking   Having and using personal contacts within a variety of agencies that directly affect crisis workers' ability to serve clients effectively and efficiently.

neurasathenia   Diagnosis as early as the American Civil War as a state of mental and physical exhaustion; also termed *"soldier's heart"* because of the belief that nerves at the base of the heart were somehow affected by combat.

nonmaleficence   Ethical principle emphasizes avoiding actions that cause harm.

nostalgia A 19th-century military term coined by physicians for combat soldiers with extreme homesickness.

off-time developmental crises Occur when transitions are out of sequence, not happening in the expected order, and are particularly troublesome as they can be extremely disruptive to families' resilience and capacity to cope; examples include the untimely death of a parent, unplanned pregnancies, forced retirement, disability due to chronic illness, and so on.

open-ended questions Usually start with *what* or *how* or ask for more clarification or details; they encourage clients to respond with full statements and at deeper levels of meaning.

order What the crisis worker provides by methodically helping clients classify and categorize problems so as to prioritize and sequentially attack the crisis in a logical and linear manner.

outing or trickery A type of cyberbullying; a way of getting people to reveal personal information that might then be used against them.

owning Means communicating possession: "That's mine."

parallel processing In a large-scale crisis when crisis workers as a group start to mimic (countertransfer) their own thoughts, feelings, and actions such that they start to resemble the crisis clients with whom they are working.

parasuicide Engaging in activities that are deliberately self-harming but where there is no result in death. It is a strong indicator for a future suicide attempt.

passive suicide A variety of actions (or inactions) that tend to be self-destructive, but not actively, which are considered to depict suicidal intent. Instances of these actions include failing to feed oneself or to participate in basic self-care. Commonly seen in the elderly particularly after the passing of a spouse; they see their purpose in life as done, they become depressed, and they give up or fail to thrive.

pathogenic shift Individuals have remained mired in the traumatic event long past the acute stage, a shift that may become residual and chronic, bringing on a host of physical and psychological maladies.

perceived burdensomeness The concept is the basic premise of the interpersonal theory of suicidal behavior. It is the perception that one is a burden on loved ones. The theory posits that perceived burdensomeness involves perceptions that the self is so incompetent as to be a liability for others.

period of struggle The second stage of trauma resolution that workers go through after a physical assault, characterized by anxiety attacks, intrusive thoughts, hypervigilance, and psychosomatic symptoms, which are characteristic of acute stress disorder.

peritraumatic Symptoms that mimic those of PTSD such as hypervigilance and startle response that occur immediately after a traumatic event is experienced, but disappear within 2 days.

persistent complex bereavement disorder Terminology formulated by DSM-5 work groups to begin to develop criteria for the concept of complicated or prolonged grief to classify it as a mental disorder.

perturbation How disturbed one is and degree of psychic pain one is suffering.

pornography Reduces women to sex objects, promotes male dominance, and encourages or condones sexual violence against women.

positive and constructive thinking patterns (of the client) Ways of reframing that might substantially alter the client's view of the problem and lessen the client's level of stress and anxiety.

positive traumatic growth Comes out of any personal transformation that occurs as a result of trauma, or the ability to not just survive a traumatic incident, but grow from it.

posttraumatic stress disorder (PTSD) A diagnosable personality disorder that occurs after experiencing or witnessing a traumatic event. It has specific affective, behavioral, and cognitive criteria that must be met according to the American Psychiatric Association DSM-5 before a diagnosis of PTSD may be given.

power distance Means the amount of control that bosses feel they have over workers and vice versa.

power exploitative One of four categories of rapists (show they have power over women).

power reassurance One of four categories of rapists (continuously feel that they are powerful over women).

precedent What has occurred in the past.

predispositioning One important aspect of listening; the worker makes initial owning statements that express exactly what he or she is going to do. Also means getting ready to do something. It is usually the first step in a crisis model: placing oneself, or something, in a position to be of use in some future occurrence.

press Stress increased due to more negative life factors piling up and increasing pressure to end life by suicide.

primary loss Death of a friend, child, parent, or spouse.

primary prevention Stopping a problem before it starts.

privacy The client's right to be left alone and to control the timing of the release of personal information.

privileged communication A legal concept that prevents the disclosure of confidential communications between a client and mental health practitioner in a judicial context.

procedural rules Set the basis for family structure and provide consistency; when followed, they result in families maintaining a state of equilibrium. They determine internal and external interactions of family members as well as set the standard for topics for conversation.

protection What the crisis worker provides by safeguarding clients from engaging in harmful, destructive, detrimental, and unsafe feelings, behaviors, and thoughts that may be psychologically or physically injurious or lethal to themselves or others.

providing available space Has to do with what contemporary research and practice in the field of loss keep harping about—that is, helping the client find support, doing things clients can't do for themselves right now (pumping gas), but letting them tell us what they can and can't do so they have at least a modicum of control in their lives.

proximate   What could reasonably be considered the immediate cause of the client's injury.

psychache   Refers to the hurt, anguish, soreness, and aching pain of the psyche or mind.

psychoeducation   Providing information to victims and survivors about what is happening and probably is going to happen to them psychologically in the aftermath of a traumatic event.

psychological anchor   Therapist who will act as advocate, support, and contact person for client.

psychological autopsy   Examines in detail the situation that led to a violent episode.

psychological first aid   First-order intervention that seeks to address the immediate crisis situation and provide immediate relief, possibly to a wide range of individuals.

psychosocial   Having mental distress as a result of social upheaval.

railway spine   A term used to describe the psychological symptoms of survivors of 19th-century train wrecks. It was thought that somehow these symptoms were related to injured spines.

rape   An unwanted act of oral, vaginal, or anal penetration committed though the use of force, threat of force, or when incapacitated.

readjustment of self   The third stage of trauma resolution that workers go through after a physical assault. If the worker is able to move forward, then the incident is integrated into the self and the worker becomes the wiser for it, comes to see that clients can be dangerous, and takes more precautions. However, if the worker does not integrate the incident, then the possibility of PTSD looms large.

reasonable practitioner   The "reasonable" practitioner would do what the average practitioner with similar education, training, and credentials would do given a similar set of facts and situation.

reestablishing control   An essential, recurring task as families search, sometimes desperately, for ways to regain stable, predictable functioning.

reflective practice   Entails a crisis worker thinking about both his or her reasons for entering crisis and disaster work, as well as his or her actions during a crisis response, and how that response could be improved.

relational markers   Shorten the psychological distance between the client and the worker through the use of such words as "this," "these," "we," "our," "here," and "now" as opposed to "that," "those," "mine," "there," and "then."

remotivation therapy   A technique used to stimulate and revitalize people who are no longer interested in the present or the future.

renewal   The third phase of crisis intervention. The crisis worker helps the family reformulate itself in a context of growth and movement beyond the suicide.

resiliency model   Represents a current focus of family crisis intervention and views families not as damaged, but rather challenged by adversities; concentrates on the potential for recovery and restoration functioning rather than pathologizing families' reactions while experiencing adversity.

RESPECTFUL model   The acronym encompasses Religious/spiritual, Economic class, Sexual identity, Psychological development, Ethnic/racial identity, Chronological age, Trauma and threats to well-being, Family, Unique physical issues, and Language and location of residence.

restatement   Restating what the client is saying in the crisis worker's own words.

restitutive play   Attempting to reenact the trauma through play and somehow resolve it.

restoration orientation   Occurs when grievers start to come to grips with the consequences of the loss and begin to form new roles and identities, develop new relationships, make life changes, and engage in new activities that distract their grief.

resuscitation   The first phase of crisis intervention. Within 24 hours, the crisis worker makes a supportive visit to assist the survivors of suicide in dealing with their initial shock, grief, anger, and most likely self-recrimination, guilt, and blame.

resynthesis   The second phase of crisis intervention. The crisis worker helps the survivors of suicide learn new ways of coping with their loss and prevents the development of pathological family responding.

reward   One major source of burnout; lack thereof, in the form of compensation, recognition, or pleasure.

risk-needs-responsivity (RNR) model   A procedure taken from the corrections field. The risk component proposes that high-risk individuals get more targeted, specific, and tailored therapeutic inputs before they go critical. The needs component focuses on the dynamic risk factors that when changed reduce recidivism. RNR usually incorporates cognitive-behavioral therapy, social skills training, anger management, and behavioral techniques that apply role rehearsal, modeling, and shaping to prosocial behavior.

ritualistic rules   Rules around rituals are ever present in families' lives and create meaning as they remember special times in their lives, such as kissing a partner as one leaves for work, tucking in children at bedtime, and celebrations at birthdays, anniversaries, and holidays.

role   A practical function taken on by someone within the family.

rules   Govern families' day-to-day behaviors and are negotiated in the formation of families; they fall into two categories, procedural and ritualistic.

sadistic   One of four categories of rapists (take joy in hurting women).

safety   Refers to the physical and psychological safety of families and the crisis intervention worker.

SAFETY model   An acronym that is derived from social locations/trauma theory that is specifically applied to crisis intervention.

salutogenic model   Emphasizes health and wellness over sickness and pathology.

salutogenic shift   Individuals have put the traumatic event into past context, mourned their losses, and started to rebuild their lives, a shift that is healthful, wholesome, and promoting psychological growth.

second disaster   After the initial disaster impact and intervention occurs, the residual effects and traumatic wake of the disaster have not dissipated for many survivors. However, when little follow-up occurs over the long term, it may be said to be a second disaster.

secondary intervention   Minimizing the harmful effects that have already occurred by follow-up therapy after the initial crisis has occurred and been stabilized.

secondary loss   A consequence of a primary loss. For example, death of a spouse (primary loss) may cause loss of status, social contacts, financial security, and sexual intimacy, which are secondary losses.

secondary traumatic stress disorder (STSD)   A consequence for health care professionals who are frequently exposed to the stress and trauma of others in the course of treating them; also called *vicarious traumatization (VT)*.

secondary traumatic stress/vicarious traumatization (STS/VT)   The transformation that occurs when an individual begins to change in a manner that mimics a client's trauma-related symptoms; it is a constructivist model in which the individual's experience and worldview are changed as a direct result of secondary exposure to trauma though crisis work.

serious threat   One that an individual has the means to carry out and that is made in earnest.

sexual assault   Refers to a broader range of sexual criminal offenses such as sexual battery and sexual coercion up to and including rape.

shell shock   The advent of modern warfare in World Wars I and II generated this term to explain the condition of traumatized soldiers who had no apparent physical wounds.

situational supports   People known to the client in the present or past who might care about what happens to the client.

social disorganization   Erodes social control and constraints and undermines freedom of individual behavior and self-determination.

social exclusion   A type of cyberbullying; a means of deliberately excluding someone from a buddy list, chat room, discussion board, or game.

social locations   The individual identifiers that go far beyond, race, sex, and skin tone that make us the specific and unique individuals that reside in a cultural group.

social norms theory   Proposes that male peer aggression and female submission are part of the norm and justification for violent sexual interaction.

solicitation/traveling offenders   Online offenders who will attempt to entice a child to meet with them to have sex or encourage them to run away with them.

somatization   Physical problems, associated pain, and functional limitations.

spiritual crisis   Occurs when a previously held religious or spiritual belief is called into question or completely abandoned.

stalking   Generally defined as repeated harassment, following, and/or threats that are committed with the intent of causing the victim emotional distress, fear of bodily harm, and/or actual bodily harm.

STOP   Acronym for Sit, Think, Observe, Plan.

structured professional judgment   Combining what professional crisis workers' experience tells them as they use verbal and visual assessments along with a reliable paper-and-pencil test—if time is available to make a decision on potential lethality.

suicide by cop (SBC)   Behavior instigated by a perpetrator that causes a lethal response from police.

suicide by legal intervention   Coroner's verdict from suicide by cop.

summary clarification   Ribbon-wraps the dialogue; that is, it packages the preceding dialogue and lets both client and crisis worker know they are on the same wavelength.

sundown syndrome   Client disorientation and states of confusion that may arise during evening hours in geriatric settings and mental hospitals, due to the onset of darkness, change of shift, and decrease in staff.

super mesosystem   Connects the exosystem and the macrosystem and serves many of the same coordinating functions, but on a national level. Composed of information systems that range from the postal service, to national commercial radio and television corporations, to the Internet and its websites, e-mail, instant messaging, and chat rooms, to satellite communication and global positioning systems.

support   The crisis worker either finds or assumes temporary responsibility for providing a support system for the person or families in crisis. This support may be as a resource for information or for providing temporary emotional, behavioral, and cognitive support.

support group   Deals with a variety of transcrisis issues that have to do with members' attempts to reintegrate themselves into a useful, functioning role in society.

synthetic-conventional   Faith development model stage; conforms to the community's basic cultural standard of moral behavior, normative beliefs, values, and religious practices (typical of 12 years of age to early adulthood).

systemic crisis   When a traumatic event occurs such that people, institutions, communities, and ecologies are overwhelmed and response systems are unable to effectively contain and control the event in regard to both physical and psychological reactions to it, the crisis has become systemic.

temperament location   What the crisis worker and the client bring to a crisis situation based on both past personal and cultural experiences.

terroristic batterer   Such people are extremely aggressive and impulsive, and view violence as appropriate to any provocation inside or outside the home.

transcrisis points   Occur frequently in transcrisis states within the therapeutic intervention. These points are generally marked by the client's coming to grips with new developmental stages or other dimensions of the problem. Transcrisis points do not occur in regular, predictable, linear progression.

transcrisis state A continuous state of low grade crisis which has not been resolved and much like a sinus infection may flare up, given the right conditions, into a full blown crisis.

trauma-focused cognitive-behavioral therapy (TF-CBT) The use of any of a variety of cognitive-behavioral therapy techniques such as flooding, cognitive restructuring, etc., that specifically targets the traumatic event that caused the PTSD.

trauma metaphor The trauma survivor's use of metaphors that have literal meaning and relate specifically to the trauma, such as a Hurricane Katrina survivor saying "I was drowning in a tidal wave of responsibilities."

traumatic grief Generally subsumed under complicated or prolonged grief, with the additional requirement that the person witnessed or was in close proximity to the violent, sudden, unexpected, horrifying death of a loved one.

uncertainty avoidance principle The degree to which cultures feel threatened by uncertainty and ambiguous situations, so rules, procedures, rituals, and laws may be formulated to buffer uncertainties of individual judgment.

uncomplicated bereavement The process that occurs as the bereaved individual works through a variety of tasks to integrate the reality of moving forward in life without the person who died.

universal view Considers not only racial and ethnic minorities, but other minority or special populations as well.

validation therapy A successful way of communicating with older adults with dementia. The worker acknowledges the feelings of the person, no matter how

irrational they may seem to be. By dignifying feelings, the worker validates the person.

values Arising out of families' belief system, they are those things deemed important for morale and drive families' perceptions.

veiled threats Circuitous statements that do not express a direct warning but contain a menacing message beyond the words.

vicarious liability Refers to the allocation of responsibility among supervisors and supervisees; based upon the old English legal notion of the master and servant relationship.

vicarious traumatization (VT) A consequence for health care professionals who are frequently exposed to the stress and trauma of others in the course of treating them; also called *secondary traumatic stress disorder (STSD)*.

virtual reality (VR) A set of computer technologies that when combined provide an interface to a computer-generated world that can involve the user's hearing, vision, olfactory, and tactile sensing.

war neurosis A term coined by Freud to describe psychological symptoms found in World War I soldiers that would later come to be known as PTSD.

wishing and hoping syndrome The victim wishes the situation would change, that her spouse would treat her the way he used to, and hopes the crisis worker can effect a change in her husband.

witness role To observe, listen, and not do anything other than "be with" the client and allow the client to feel "felt."

working alliance A cooperative and trusting working relationship between interventionist and client.

workload One major source of burnout, when the work is too complex, too much, too urgent, or just too awful.

YAVIS clients Young, Attractive, Verbal, Intelligent, and Socially well-connected clients from higher socioeconomic backgrounds.

Index

Note: Page numbers followed by an "f" indicate figures; by a "t" indicate tables.

A